T0224109

Lecture Notes in Computer Science 9450

Commenced Publication in 1973
Founding and Former Series Editors:
Gerhard Goos, Juris Hartmanis, and Jan van Leeuwen

Advanced Research in Computing and Software Science

Subline of Lecture Notes in Computer Science

More information about this series at http://www.springer.com/series/7407

Martin Davis · Ansgar Fehnker
Annabelle McIver · Andrei Voronkov (Eds.)

Logic for Programming, Artificial Intelligence, and Reasoning

20th International Conference, LPAR-20 2015
Suva, Fiji, November 24–28, 2015
Proceedings

 Springer

Editors

Martin Davis
New York University
New York, NY
USA

Ansgar Fehnker
University of the South Pacific
Suva
Fiji

Annabelle McIver
Macquarie University
Sydney, NSW
Australia

Andrei Voronkov
The University of Manchester
Manchester
UK

ISSN 0302-9743   ISSN 1611-3349   (electronic)
Lecture Notes in Computer Science
ISBN 978-3-662-48898-0   ISBN 978-3-662-48899-7   (eBook)
DOI 10.1007/978-3-662-48899-7

Library of Congress Control Number: 2015954999

LNCS Sublibrary: SL1 – Theoretical Computer Science and General Issues

Springer Heidelberg New York Dordrecht London

Printed on acid-free paper

Springer-Verlag GmbH Berlin Heidelberg is part of Springer Science+Business Media
(www.springer.com)

Preface

This volume contains the papers presented at the 20th International Conference on Logic for Programming, Artificial Intelligence and Reasoning (LPAR-20), held during November 24–28, 2015, at the University of the South Pacific, Suva, Fiji.

Following the call for papers, LPAR-20 received 117 abstracts, materializing into 92 submissions. Each submission was reviewed by a panel of 53 Program Committee (PC) members. The PC was assisted by 107 additional reviewers and decided to accept 43 papers. The EasyChair system provided an indispensible platform for all matters related to the reviewing process, production of these proceedings, program and Web page generation, and registration of participants.

Several workshops were collocated with LPAR-20. The first workshop on Models for Formal Analysis of Real Systems (MARS 2015) was organized by Rob van Glabbeek and Peter Hoefner of NICTA and Jan Friso Groote from Eindhoven University of Technology. The First International Workshop on Focusing was organized by Iliano Cervesato of Carnegie Mellon University and Carsten Schuermann of ITU Copenhagen and Demtech. The 11th International Workshop on the Implementation of Logics was organized by Boris Konev of the University of Liverpool, Stephan Schulz of DHBW Stuttgart, and Laurent Simon of the University of Bordeaux. We were fortunate to have Peter Baumgartner of NICTA as workshop chair.

The local conference organization was arranged by Geoff Sutcliffe and Ansgar Fehnker, and together they put together an excellent event.

LPAR-20 is grateful for the generous support of Microsoft Research and University of the South Pacific.

September 2015

Martin Davis
Ansgar Fehnker
Annabelle McIver
Andrei Voronkov

Organization

Program Committee

Cyrille Valentin Artho	AIST, Japan
Franz Baader	Technical University of Dresden, Germany
Christel Baier	Technical University of Dresden, Germany
Peter Baumgartner	National ICT, Australia
Armin Biere	Johannes Kepler University, Austria
Maria Paola Bonacina	Università degli Studi di Verona, Italy
Lei Bu	Nanjing University, China
Franck Cassez	Macquarie University, Australia
Krishnendu Chatterjee	Institute of Science and Technology (IST)
Michael Codish	Ben-Gurion University of the Negev, Israel
Hubert Comon-Lundh	ENS Cachan, France
Martin Davis	Courant Institute of Mathematical Sciences, New York University, USA
Joerg Endrullis	Vrije Universiteit Amsterdam, The Netherlands
Javier Esparza	Technische Universität München, Germany
Ansgar Fehnker	University of the South Pacific, Fiji
Christian Fermüller	TU Wien, Austria
Bernd Fischer	Stellenbosch University, South Africa
Jürgen Giesl	RWTH Aachen, Germany
Rajeev Gore	The Australian National University, Australia
Tim Griffin	University of Cambridge, UK
Kim Guldstrand Larsen	Aalborg University, Denmark
Miki Hermann	LIX, Ecole Polytechnique, France
Dejan Jovanović	SRI International, Singapore
Laura Kovacs	Chalmers University of Technology, Sweden
Dexter Kozen	Cornell University, USA
Temur Kutsia	RISC, Johannes Kepler University Linz, Austria
Rustan Leino	Microsoft Research, USA
Joe Leslie-Hurd	Intel Corporation, USA
Luigi Liquori	Inria, France
Christopher Lynch	Clarkson University, USA
Annabelle McIver	Macquarie University, Australia
Kenneth McMillan	Microsoft Research, USA
Aart Middeldorp	University of Innsbruck, Austria
Marius Minea	Politehnica University of Timisoara, Romania
Matteo Mio	CNRS/ENS-Lyon, France
Joachim Niehren	Inria Lille, France
Prakash Panangaden	McGill University, Canada

Christine Paulin-Mohring	Université Paris-Sud, France
Andreas Podelski	University of Freiburg, Germany
Sanjiva Prasad	Indian Institute of Technology Delhi, India
Revantha Ramanayake	Vienna University of Technology, Austria
Grigore Rosu	University of Illinois at Urbana-Champaign, USA
Michael Rusinowitch	LORIA–Inria Nancy, France
Torsten Schaub	University of Potsdam, Germany
Helmut Seidl	TU München, Germany
Geoff Sutcliffe	University of Miami, USA
Gancho Vachkov	The University of the South Pacific (USP), Fiji
Ron Van Der Meyden	UNSW, Australia
Tomas Vojnar	Brno University of Technology, Czech Republic
Andrei Voronkov	The University of Manchester, UK
Toby Walsh	NICTA and UNSW, Australia

Additional Reviewers

Abreu, Salvador
Baelde, David
Bellin, Gianluigi
Ben-Amram, Amir
Blanchette, Jasmin
Bochman, Alexander
Borchmann, Daniel
Bordenabe, Nicolás E.
Casini, Giovanni
Cerna, David
Cervesato, Iliano
Chaudhuri, Avik
Chaudhuri, Kaustuv
Clouston, Ranald
Courcelle, Bruno
Cruz-Filipe, Luís
Das, Anupam
Davies, Jessica
Delzanno, Giorgio
Dima, Catalin
Downen, Paul
Dutertre, Bruno
Dyckhoff, Roy
Escobar, Santiago
Felgenhauer, Bertram
Fernandez Gil, Oliver
Fichte, Johannes Klaus

Flouris, Giorgos
Frohn, Florian
Fuhs, Carsten
Gay, Simon
Gebler, Daniel
Gebser, Martin
González De Aledo, Pablo
Gorogiannis, Nikos
Graham-Lengrand,
   Stéphane
Grädel, Erich
Guenot, Nicolas
Hagihara, Shigeki
Heizmann, Matthias
Holik, Lukas
Hölldobler, Steffen
Ibsen-Jensen, Rasmus
Kaliszyk, Cezary
Kincaid, Zachary
Kolanski, Rafal
Kotelnikov, Evgenii
Krishnaswami,
   Neelakantan
Kuijer, Louwe B.
Kuprianov, Andrey
Leino, Rustan
Leuschner, Linda

Ludwig, Michel
Luigi, Liquori
Madelaine, Guillaume
Maffezioli, Paolo
Mathieson, Luke
Mayer-Eichberger,
   Valentin
Mayr, Richard
Meyer, Philipp J.
Michalewski, Henryk
Miculan, Marino
Moore, Brandon
Munch-Maccagnoni,
   Guillaume
Myreen, Magnus O.
Napoli, Amedeo
Nigam, Vivek
Obermeier, Philipp
Parigot, Michel
Park, Daejun
Pek, Edgar
Peled, Doron
Peltier, Nicolas
Pientka, Brigitte
Popeea, Corneliu
Preining, Norbert
Qi, Guilin

Ranise, Silvio
Redl, Christoph
Rezk, Tamara
Ricciotti, Wilmer
Sanchez, Cesar
Sangnier, Arnaud
Saurin, Alexis
Schwitter, Rolf
Schäf, Martin
Seidl, Martina
Sickert, Salomon

Simkus, Mantas
Stefanescu, Andrei
Sternagel, Christian
Strassburger, Lutz
Takeuti, Izumi
Talcott, Carolyn
Terui, Kazushige
Thiemann, René
Toninho, Bernardo
Trivedi, Ashutosh
Verma, Rakesh

Vyskocil, Jiri
Wilson, David
Woltzenlogel Paleo,
  Bruno
Wunderlich, Sascha
Yamada, Akihisa
Zarrieß, Benjamin
Zhang, Cheng
Zhang, Yi

Satisfiability: From Quality to Quantities
(Abstract of Invited Talk)

Nikolaj Bjørner

Microsoft Research
nbjorner@microsoft.com

Satisfiability Modulo Theories, SMT, solvers have in the past decade enabled a number of software engineering tools thanks to improved theorem proving technologies, their support for domains that are commonly used in software and a confluence of advances in symbolic analysis methodologies. These methodologies are diverse and range from bug localization, symbolic model checking algorithms, dynamic symbolic execution for uncovering bugs and creating parametric unit tests, certified development using program verification tools, compiler validation, biological modeling, model based design tools, web sanitizers, and runtime analysis. The synergy with application domains has lead to a constant stream of inspiration for improved domain support and algorithmic advances. A simultaneous trend in applications is leading research on SMT solvers into calculating with quantities. We believe this is part of an overall trend of tools for checking and synthesizing quantitative, including probabilistic, properties.

Using Network Verification as a starting point, we describe how the SMT solver Z3 is used at scale in Microsoft Azure to check network access restrictions and router configurations. Z3 is used in a monitoring system, called SecGuru, that continuously checks configurations as they appear on routers. We learned early on that network operators required a tool that could return a set of models in a compact way. This led us to develop a domain specific algorithm, that works well for access control lists. It enumerates models compactly in fractions of a second. A more ambitious effort is to check reachability properties in large data-centers. Again, our experience was that the domain called for special purpose data-structures and symmetry reduction methods that turn analysis of data-centers with hundreds of routers and a million forwarding rules into very small finite state systems that can be analyzed in fractions of a second.

Our experience with Network Verification is not unlike other domains as we are reaching a point where qualitative analysis has shown its use, but a larger elephant is lurking in the room: most systems rely on performance guarantees. Thus, the need for cheking and synthesizing quantitative properties. To support SMT with quantities we have embarked on long term projects on integrating optimization algorithms with Z3 and integrating methods for counting the number of solutions to constraints. In this context we developed a new MaxSAT algorithm that exploits dualities between unsatisfiable cores and correction sets and we illustrate some uses of the emerging quantitative features in Z3.

The work rests on collaboration with a large number of colleagues including Karthick Jayaraman, George Varghese, Nina Narodytska, Nuno Lopes, Andrey Rybalchenko, Leonardo de Moura, Christoph Wintersteiger, Gordon Plotkin.

Contents

Skolemization for Substructural Logics

Petr Cintula[1], Denisa Diaconescu[2,3(✉)], and George Metcalfe[2]

[1] Institute of Computer Science, Czech Academy of Sciences, Prague, Czech Republic
cintula@cs.cas.cz
[2] Mathematical Institute, University of Bern, Bern, Switzerland
{denisa.diaconescu,george.metcalfe}@math.unibe.ch
[3] Faculty of Mathematics and Computer Science,
University of Bucharest, Bucharest, Romania

Abstract. The usual Skolemization procedure, which removes strong quantifiers by introducing new function symbols, is in general unsound for first-order substructural logics defined based on classes of complete residuated lattices. However, it is shown here (following similar ideas of Baaz and Iemhoff for first-order intermediate logics in [1]) that first-order substructural logics with a semantics satisfying certain witnessing conditions admit a "parallel" Skolemization procedure where a strong quantifier is removed by introducing a finite disjunction or conjunction (as appropriate) of formulas with multiple new function symbols. These logics typically lack equivalent prenex forms. Also, semantic consequence does not in general reduce to satisfiability. The Skolemization theorems presented here therefore take various forms, applying to the left or right of the consequence relation, and to all formulas or only prenex formulas.

1 Introduction

Skolemization is an important ingredient of automated reasoning methods in (fragments of) first-order classical logic. Crucially, a sentence $(\forall \bar{x})(\exists y)\varphi(\bar{x}, y)$ is classically satisfiable if and only if $(\forall \bar{x})\varphi(\bar{x}, f(\bar{x}))$ is satisfiable, where f is a function symbol not occurring in φ. The satisfiability of a sentence in prenex form therefore reduces to the satisfiability of a universal sentence; Herbrand's theorem then permits a further reduction to the satisfiability of a set of propositional formulas. For more details on the classical case, we refer the reader to [3].

For first-order non-classical logics, the situation is not so straightforward. Formulas are not always equivalent to prenex formulas and semantic consequence may not reduce to satisfiability, meaning that (non-prenex) sentences should be considered separately as premises and conclusions of consequences. A Skolemization procedure may in such cases be more carefully defined where strong occurrences of quantifiers in subformulas are replaced on the left, and

P. Cintula–Supported by RVO 67985807 and Czech Science Foundation GBP202/12/G061.
D. Diaconescu–Supported by Sciex grant 13.192.
G. Metcalfe–Supported by Swiss National Science Foundation grant 200021_146748.

© Springer-Verlag Berlin Heidelberg 2015
M. Davis et al. (Eds.): LPAR-20 2015, LNCS 9450, pp. 1–15, 2015.
DOI: 10.1007/978-3-662-48899-7_1

weak occurrences on the right. However, satisfiability or, more generally, semantic consequence, may not be preserved. Notably, in first-order intuitionistic logic, formulas such as $\neg\neg(\forall x)P(x) \to (\forall x)\neg\neg P(x)$ do not skolemize (see, e.g., [2,15], also for methods for addressing these problems).

The goal of this paper is to develop Skolemization theorems for first-order substructural logics based on residuated lattices, a family that spans first-order intermediate logics, exponential-free linear logic, relevance logics, fuzzy logics, and logics without contraction (see, e.g., [7,9,11,14,17]). Although these logics are in general undecidable, their (decidable) fragments provide foundations for knowledge representation and reasoning methods such as non-classical logic programming and description logics (see, e.g., [10,12,13,18]). The work reported here aims to avoid duplicated research effort by providing a general approach to the development of automated reasoning methods in the substructural setting. A first step in this direction was taken in [6] which provides Herbrand theorems for these logics. Skolemization was also considered (briefly) in that paper, but unfortunately, the scope of the process was overstated in Theorem 1: the result applies only to first-order substructural logics based on classes of chains (totally ordered structures). An analysis of the failure of this theorem has, however, stimulated the new more general approach described in this paper. Future work will involve combining the various Herbrand and Skolem theorems obtained here and in [6] to develop resolution methods for a wide class of substructural logics.

The key idea of "parallel Skolemization" is to remove strong occurrences of quantifiers on the left of the consequence relation and weak occurrences of quantifiers on the right by introducing disjunctions and conjunctions, respectively, of formulas with multiple new function symbols. In particular, a sentence $(\forall \bar{x})(\exists y)\varphi(\bar{x}, y)$ occurring as the conclusion of a consequence is rewritten for some $n \in \mathbb{N}^+$ as $(\forall \bar{x}) \bigvee_{i=1}^{n} \varphi(\bar{x}, f_i(\bar{x}))$ where each function symbol f_i is new for $i = 1 \ldots n$. Baaz and Iemhoff use this method in [1] to establish "full" Skolemization results for first-order intermediate logics whose Kripke models (with or without the constant domains condition) admit a finite model property. In this paper, we obtain full parallel Skolemization results for first-order substructural logics admitting certain new variants of the witnessed model property introduced by Hájek in [12]. We also obtain complete characterizations of full parallel Skolemization when these logics have a finitary consequence relation. We then turn our attention to first-order substructural logics that only partially satisfy a witnessing property and hence do not admit full parallel Skolemization. We show that under certain weaker conditions, these logics admit parallel Skolemization for prenex sentences occurring on the left or right of the consequence relation.

2   First-Order Substructural Logics

Predicates, interpreted classically as functions from the domain of a structure to the two element Boolean algebra **2**, are interpreted in first-order substructural logics as functions from the domain to algebras with multiple values that may represent, e.g., degrees of truth, belief, or confidence. For convenience, we consider here algebras for the full Lambek calculus with exchange – equivalently, intuitionistic linear logic without exponentials and additive constants – noting that a more general algebraic setting would lead to similar results, but complicate the presentation somewhat.

An FL$_e$-*algebra* is an algebraic structure $\boldsymbol{A} = \langle A, \&, \rightarrow, \wedge, \vee, \overline{0}, \overline{1} \rangle$ such that:

1. $\langle A, \wedge, \vee \rangle$ is a lattice with an order defined by $x \leq y \Leftrightarrow x \wedge y = x$;
2. $\langle A, \&, \overline{1} \rangle$ is a commutative monoid;
3. $\rightarrow$ is the residuum of $\&$, i.e. $x \& y \leq z \Leftrightarrow x \leq y \rightarrow z$ for all $x, y, z \in A$.

$\boldsymbol{A}$ is called *complete* if $\bigvee X$ and $\bigwedge X$ exist in A for all $X \subseteq A$, and an FL$_e$-*chain* if either $x \leq y$ or $y \leq x$ for all $x, y \in A$.

Example 1. Complete FL$_e$-chains $\boldsymbol{A} = \langle [0,1], *, \rightarrow_*, \min, \max, d, e_* \rangle$ based on the real unit interval $[0,1]$ with the usual order have been studied intensively in mathematical fuzzy logic [7,11,14]. In this setting, $*$ is a residuated uninorm: an associative and commutative binary function on $[0,1]$ that is increasing in both arguments and has a unit e_* and residuum $\rightarrow_*$. (d is an arbitrary element in $[0,1]$). Fundamental examples include the Łukasiewicz t-norm $\max(x + y - 1, 0)$, the Gödel t-norm $\min(x, y)$, and the product t-norm $x \cdot y$.

The class $\mathbb{FL}_e$ of FL$_e$-algebras may be defined equationally and hence forms a *variety*: a class of algebras closed under taking homomorphic images, subalgebras, and products. Subvarieties of $\mathbb{FL}_e$ provide algebraic semantics for a broad spectrum of substructural logics, including those defined via extensions of the sequent calculus for FL$_e$. In particular, FL$_{ew}$-algebras for FL$_e$ with weakening are FL$_e$-algebras satisfying $\overline{0} \leq x \leq \overline{1}$, and FL$_{ewc}$-algebras for intuitionistic logic (term-equivalent to Heyting algebras) are FL$_{ew}$-algebras satisfying $x \& x = x$. Further varieties consist of "involutive" FL$_e$-algebras satisfying $(x \rightarrow \overline{0}) \rightarrow \overline{0} = x$ (corresponding to multiple-conclusion sequent calculi) and "semilinear" FL$_e$-algebras satisfying $((x \rightarrow y) \wedge \overline{1}) \vee ((y \rightarrow x) \wedge \overline{1}) = \overline{1}$ (corresponding to hypersequent calculi). In particular, semilinear FL$_e$-algebras, FL$_{ew}$-algebras, and FL$_{ewc}$-algebras provide algebraic semantics for, respectively, uninorm logic, monoidal t-norm logic, and Gödel logic (see [4,5,9,14]).

A *(countable) predicate language* $\mathcal{P}$ is a triple $\langle \mathbf{P}, \mathbf{F}, \mathbf{ar} \rangle$ where $\mathbf{P}$ and $\mathbf{F}$ are non-empty countable sets of predicate and function symbols, respectively, and $\mathbf{ar}$ is a function assigning to each predicate and function symbol $\star$ an *arity* $\mathbf{ar}(\star) = n \in \mathbb{N}$ ($\star$ is called *n-ary*); nullary function symbols are called *object constants* and nullary predicate symbols are called *propositional atoms*. $\mathcal{P}$-*terms* $s, t, \ldots$, and *(atomic) $\mathcal{P}$-formulas* $\varphi, \psi, \chi, \ldots$ are defined as in classical logic using a fixed countably infinite set OV of *object variables* $x, y, \ldots$, quantifiers $\forall$ and $\exists$, binary connectives $\&, \rightarrow, \wedge, \vee$, and logical constants $\overline{0}, \overline{1}$. Also $\neg \varphi$ is defined as $\varphi \rightarrow \overline{0}$ and $\varphi \leftrightarrow \psi$ as $(\varphi \rightarrow \psi) \wedge (\psi \rightarrow \varphi)$.

Bound and free variables, closed terms, sentences, and substitutability are defined in the standard way. Instead of $\xi_1, \ldots, \xi_n$ (where the ξ_i's are terms or formulas and n is arbitrary or fixed by the context) we sometimes write just $\bar{\xi}$. By the notation $\varphi(\bar{z})$ we indicate that *all* free variables of φ occur in the list of distinct object variables $\bar{z}$. If $\varphi(x_1, \ldots, x_n, \bar{z})$ is a formula and all free occurrences of x_i's are replaced in φ by terms t_i, the resulting formula is denoted simply by $\varphi(t_1, \ldots, t_n, \bar{z})$. We write $\chi[\varphi]$ for a formula χ with a distinguished subformula φ and understand $\chi[\psi]$ as the result of replacing φ in χ with the formula ψ. A set of $\mathcal{P}$-formulas is called a $\mathcal{P}$-theory.

Classical notions of structure, evaluation, and truth are generalized relative to a complete FL_e-algebra $\boldsymbol{A}$ as follows: a $\mathcal{P}$-structure $\mathfrak{S} = \langle \boldsymbol{A}, \mathbf{S} \rangle$ consists of a complete FL_e-algebra $\boldsymbol{A}$ and a triple $\mathbf{S} = \langle S, \langle P^{\mathbf{S}} \rangle_{P \in \mathbf{P}}, \langle f^{\mathbf{S}} \rangle_{f \in \mathbf{F}} \rangle$ where S is a non-empty set, $P^{\mathbf{S}}$ is a function $S^n \to A$ for each n-ary predicate symbol $P \in \mathbf{P}$, and $f^{\mathbf{S}} \colon S^n \to S$ is a function for each n-ary function symbol $f \in \mathbf{F}$. An $\mathfrak{S}$-evaluation is a mapping $v \colon OV \to S$. By $v[x \to a]$ we denote the $\mathfrak{S}$-evaluation where $v[x \to a](x) = a$ and $v[x \to a](y) = v(y)$ for each object variable $y \neq x$. Terms and formulas are evaluated in $\mathfrak{S}$ as follows:

$$\|x\|_v^{\mathfrak{S}} = v(x)$$
$$\|f(t_1, \ldots, t_n)\|_v^{\mathfrak{S}} = f^{\mathbf{S}}(\|t_1\|_v^{\mathfrak{S}}, \ldots, \|t_n\|_v^{\mathfrak{S}}) \qquad \text{for } f \in \mathbf{F}$$
$$\|P(t_1, \ldots, t_n)\|_v^{\mathfrak{S}} = P^{\mathbf{S}}(\|t_1\|_v^{\mathfrak{S}}, \ldots, \|t_n\|_v^{\mathfrak{S}}) \qquad \text{for } P \in \mathbf{P}$$
$$\|\varphi \circ \psi\|_v^{\mathfrak{S}} = \|\varphi\|_v^{\mathfrak{S}} \circ^{\boldsymbol{A}} \|\psi\|_v^{\mathfrak{S}} \qquad \text{for } \circ \in \{\&, \to, \wedge, \vee\}$$
$$\|\star\|_v^{\mathfrak{S}} = \star^{\boldsymbol{A}} \qquad \text{for } \star \in \{\bar{0}, \bar{1}\}$$
$$\|(\forall x)\varphi\|_v^{\mathfrak{S}} = \inf\nolimits_{\leq_{\boldsymbol{A}}} \{\|\varphi\|_{v[x \to a]}^{\mathfrak{S}} \mid a \in S\}$$
$$\|(\exists x)\varphi\|_v^{\mathfrak{S}} = \sup\nolimits_{\leq_{\boldsymbol{A}}} \{\|\varphi\|_{v[x \to a]}^{\mathfrak{S}} \mid a \in S\}.$$

A $\mathcal{P}$-structure $\mathfrak{M} = \langle \boldsymbol{A}, \mathbf{M} \rangle$ is a $\mathcal{P}$-model of a $\mathcal{P}$-theory T, written $\mathfrak{M} \models T$, if for each $\varphi \in T$ and $\mathfrak{M}$-evaluation v, $\|\varphi\|_v^{\mathfrak{M}} \geq \bar{1}^{\boldsymbol{A}}$.

Let us now fix an arbitrary class $\mathbb{K}$ of complete FL_e-algebras. A $\mathcal{P}$-formula φ is a semantic consequence of a $\mathcal{P}$-theory T in $\mathbb{K}$, written $T \models_{\mathbb{K}}^{\mathcal{P}} \varphi$, if $\mathfrak{M} \models \varphi$ for each $\boldsymbol{A} \in \mathbb{K}$ and each $\mathcal{P}$-model $\mathfrak{M} = \langle \boldsymbol{A}, \mathbf{M} \rangle$ of T. We omit the prefixes for the class $\mathbb{K}$ or language $\mathcal{P}$ when known from the context.

To simplify notation, for a formula $\varphi(x_1, \ldots, x_n)$ and an $\mathfrak{S}$-evaluation v with $v(x_i) = a_i$, we write $\|\varphi(a_1, \ldots, a_n)\|^{\mathfrak{S}}$ instead of $\|\varphi(x_1, \ldots, x_n)\|_v^{\mathfrak{S}}$. Observe that, as in classical logic, the truth value of a sentence does not depend on an evaluation. Also, $\mathfrak{M} \models \varphi \to \psi$ iff for each evaluation v, $\|\varphi\|_v^{\mathfrak{M}} \leq \|\psi\|_v^{\mathfrak{M}}$, and $\mathfrak{M} \models \varphi \leftrightarrow \psi$ iff for each evaluation v, $\|\varphi\|_v^{\mathfrak{M}} = \|\psi\|_v^{\mathfrak{M}}$.

The next lemma collects together some useful facts for FL_e-algebras.

Lemma 1 ([7,14,16]). *Given formulas φ, ψ, χ, a variable x not free in χ, and a term t substitutable for x in φ:*

1. $\models_{\mathbb{K}} (\forall x)\varphi(x) \to \varphi(t)$
2. $\models_{\mathbb{K}} \varphi(t) \to (\exists x)\varphi(x)$
3. $\models_{\mathbb{K}} (\forall x)(\chi \to \varphi) \leftrightarrow (\chi \to (\forall x)\varphi)$
4. $\models_{\mathbb{K}} (\forall x)(\varphi \to \chi) \leftrightarrow ((\exists x)\varphi \to \chi)$
5. $\{\varphi, \varphi \to \psi\} \models_{\mathbb{K}} \psi$
6. $\{\varphi\} \models_{\mathbb{K}} \varphi \wedge \bar{1}$
7. $\{\varphi\} \models_{\mathbb{K}} (\forall x)\varphi$
8. $\models_{\mathbb{K}} (\exists x)(\chi \to \varphi) \to (\chi \to (\exists x)\varphi)$
9. $\models_{\mathbb{K}} (\exists x)(\varphi \to \chi) \to ((\forall x)\varphi \to \chi)$
10. $\models_{\mathbb{K}} (\chi \& (\exists x)\varphi) \leftrightarrow (\exists x)(\chi \& \varphi)$
11. $\models_{\mathbb{K}} (\exists x)(\varphi \vee \psi) \leftrightarrow ((\exists x)\varphi \vee (\exists x)\psi)$
12. $\models_{\mathbb{K}} (\chi \vee (\forall x)\varphi) \to (\forall x)(\chi \vee \varphi)$
13. $\models_{\mathbb{K}} ((\forall x)\varphi \wedge (\forall x)\psi) \leftrightarrow (\forall x)(\varphi \wedge \psi)$
14. $\models_{\mathbb{K}} (\exists x)(\chi \wedge \varphi) \to (\chi \wedge (\exists x)\varphi)$.

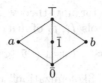

Fig. 1. Example of an FL$_e$-algebra

Moreover, if $\mathbb{K}$ is a class of complete FL$_e$-chains:

15. $\models_{\mathbb{K}} (\forall x)(\chi \vee \varphi) \leftrightarrow \chi \vee (\forall x)\varphi$ 16. $\models_{\mathbb{K}} (\exists x)(\chi \wedge \varphi) \leftrightarrow \chi \wedge (\exists x)\varphi.$

Let us emphasize that some quantifier shifts (8–14) are available for every choice of $\mathbb{K}$, and two more (15–16) if $\mathbb{K}$ consists of FL$_e$-chains, but that, in general, the formulas $(\chi \rightarrow (\exists x)\varphi) \rightarrow (\exists x)(\chi \rightarrow \varphi)$, $((\forall x)\varphi \rightarrow \chi) \rightarrow (\exists x)(\varphi \rightarrow \chi)$, and $(\forall x)(\chi \,\&\, \varphi) \rightarrow (\chi \,\&\, (\forall x)\varphi)$ (where x is not free in χ) are not valid (see, e.g., [7]).

3   Parallel Skolemization

Skolemization fails in many first-order substructural logics. Consider, for example, a language with a binary predicate symbol P and object constants r and s, and a structure $\mathfrak{M} = \langle \boldsymbol{A}, \mathbf{M} \rangle$ of this language where

- $\boldsymbol{A}$ is the FL$_e$-algebra $\langle A, \&, \rightarrow, \wedge, \vee, \bar{0}, \bar{1} \rangle$ depicted in Fig. 1 with

$$x \,\&\, y = \begin{cases} x \wedge y & \text{if } x, y \in \{0, a, b, \top\} \\ x & \text{if } y = \bar{1} \\ y & \text{if } x = \bar{1} \end{cases}$$

and $\rightarrow$ is the residuum of $\&$;
- $M = \{r, s\}$ with $r^{\mathbf{M}} = r$, $s^{\mathbf{M}} = s$, $P^{\mathbf{M}}(s, s) = P^{\mathbf{M}}(r, s) = a$, $P^{\mathbf{M}}(r, r) = \bar{1}$, and $P^{\mathbf{M}}(s, r) = b$.

Then $\mathfrak{M}$ is a model of $(\forall x)(\forall z)(P(x, r) \vee P(z, s))$, but not of $(\exists y)(\forall x)P(x, y)$, since $\|(\exists y)(\forall x)P(x, y)\|^{\mathfrak{M}} = a \not\geq \bar{1}$, so

$$(\forall x)(\forall z)(P(x, r) \vee P(z, s)) \not\models_{\boldsymbol{A}} (\exists y)(\forall x)P(x, y).$$

On the other hand, for any unary function symbol f, we have

$$(\forall x)(\forall z)(P(x, r) \vee P(z, s)) \models_{\boldsymbol{A}} (\exists y)P(f(y), y).$$

Hence "ordinary" Skolemization in this case is not sound. Suppose, however, that we introduce *two* new unary function symbols f_1 and f_2. Then extending the same structure $\mathfrak{M}$ with interpretations $f_1^{\mathbf{M}}(r) = f_1^{\mathbf{M}}(s) = r$ and $f_2^{\mathbf{M}}(r) = f_2^{\mathbf{M}}(s) = s$, we obtain $\|(\exists y)(P(f_1(y), y) \wedge P(f_2(y), y))\|^{\mathfrak{M}} = a \not\geq \bar{1}$ and

$$(\forall x)(\forall z)(P(x, r) \vee P(z, s)) \not\models_{\boldsymbol{A}} (\exists y)(P(f_1(y), y) \wedge P(f_2(y), y)).$$

More generally (see Lemma 4) for any theory $T \cup \{(\exists \bar{y})(\forall x)\varphi(x, \bar{y})\}$ of this language and new function symbols f_1, f_2 of arity $|\bar{y}|$,

$$T \models_{\mathbf{A}} (\exists \bar{y})(\forall x)\varphi(x, \bar{y}) \quad \Leftrightarrow \quad T \models_{\mathbf{A}} (\exists \bar{y})(\varphi(f_1(\bar{y}), \bar{y}) \wedge \varphi(f_2(\bar{y}), \bar{y})).$$

We investigate here this "parallel Skolemization" procedure, introduced by Baaz and Iemhoff in [1] for intermediate logics, in the context of substructural logics.

Let us first recall some useful notions. An occurrence of a subformula ψ in a formula φ is *positive* (*negative*) if, inductively, one of the following holds:

1. φ is ψ;
2. φ is $\varphi_1 \wedge \varphi_2$, $\varphi_2 \wedge \varphi_1$, $\varphi_1 \vee \varphi_2$, $\varphi_2 \vee \varphi_1$, $\varphi_1 \mathbin{\&} \varphi_2$, $\varphi_2 \mathbin{\&} \varphi_1$, $(\forall x)\varphi_1$, $(\exists x)\varphi_1$, or $\varphi_2 \to \varphi_1$, and ψ is positive (negative) in $\varphi_1[\psi]$;
3. φ is $\varphi_1 \to \varphi_2$ and ψ is negative (positive) in $\varphi_1[\psi]$.

The following result is easily established by induction on formula complexity.

Lemma 2. *For $\mathcal{P}$-formulas φ, ψ, χ where ψ has the same free variables as χ:*
(i) *If ψ occurs positively in $\varphi[\psi]$, then $\{\chi \to \psi\} \models_{\mathbb{K}} \varphi[\chi] \to \varphi[\psi]$.*
(ii) *If ψ occurs negatively in $\varphi[\psi]$, then $\{\psi \to \chi\} \models_{\mathbb{K}} \varphi[\chi] \to \varphi[\psi]$.*

An occurrence of a quantified subformula $(Qx)\psi$ in a formula φ is called *strong* if either it is positive and $Q = \forall$, or it is negative and $Q = \exists$, *weak* otherwise.

Fix $n \in \mathbb{N}^+$ and consider a $\mathcal{P}$-sentence φ with a subformula $(Qx)\psi(x, \bar{y})$ and function symbols $f_1, \ldots, f_n \notin \mathcal{P}$ of arity $|\bar{y}|$. Replace this subformula in φ by

$$\bigvee_{i=1}^{n} \psi(f_i(\bar{y}), \bar{y}) \text{ if } Q = \exists \quad \text{and} \quad \bigwedge_{i=1}^{n} \psi(f_i(\bar{y}), \bar{y}) \text{ if } Q = \forall.$$

The replacement strictly decreases the multiset of depths of occurrences of quantifiers according to the standard multiset well-ordering described in [8]. Hence applying this process repeatedly to leftmost *strong* occurrences of quantifiers in an arbitrary $\mathcal{P}$-sentence φ results in a unique (up to renaming of function symbols) $\mathcal{P}'$-sentence $sk_n^r(\varphi)$ for some extension $\mathcal{P}'$ of $\mathcal{P}$ that contains only *weak* occurrences of quantifiers. Similarly, let $sk_n^l(\varphi)$ be the result of applying this process repeatedly to leftmost weak occurrences of quantifiers in φ.

Example 2. Consider a sentence $\varphi = (\forall x)((\exists y)P(x, y) \to (\exists z)Q(x, z))$. Taking $n = 1$, the above process leads to

$$sk_1^l(\varphi) = (\forall x)((\exists y)P(x, y) \to Q(x, g(x))) \quad \text{and} \quad sk_1^r(\varphi) = P(c, d) \to (\exists z)Q(c, z).$$

On the other hand, considering $n = 2$ and applying the procedure to weak occurrences of quantifiers in φ, we produce the formula $sk_2^l(\varphi)$

$$(\forall x)((\exists y)P(x, y) \to (Q(x, g_1(x)) \vee Q(x, g_2(x)))),$$

while applying it to strong occurrences, we obtain first

$$((\exists y)P(c_1, y) \to (\exists z)Q(c_1, z)) \wedge ((\exists y)P(c_2, y) \to (\exists z)Q(c_2, z)),$$

and then a formula $sk_2^r(\varphi)$ of the form

$$((P(c_1, d_1^1) \vee P(c_1, d_2^1)) \to (\exists z)Q(c_1, z)) \wedge ((P(c_2, d_1^2) \vee P(c_2, d_2^2)) \to (\exists z)Q(c_2, z)).$$

Let us fix an arbitrary class of complete FL_e-algebras $\mathbb{K}$. We say that the consequence relation $\models_{\mathbb{K}}$ admits *parallel Skolemization right of degree n*, for a $\mathcal{P}$-sentence φ if for any $\mathcal{P}$-theory T,

$$T \models_{\mathbb{K}} \varphi \quad \Leftrightarrow \quad T \models_{\mathbb{K}} sk_n^r(\varphi).$$

Similarly, we say that $\models_{\mathbb{K}}$ admits *parallel Skolemization left of degree n* for a $\mathcal{P}$-sentence φ if for any $\mathcal{P}$-theory $T \cup \{\psi\}$,

$$T \cup \{\varphi\} \models_{\mathbb{K}} \psi \quad \Leftrightarrow \quad T \cup \{sk_n^l(\varphi)\} \models_{\mathbb{K}} \psi.$$

Note that there exists the following relationship between the left and right forms of parallel Skolemization.

Lemma 3. *If $\models_{\mathbb{K}}$ admits parallel Skolemization left of degree n for all sentences, then $\models_{\mathbb{K}}$ admits parallel Skolemization right of degree n for all sentences.*

Proof. For any $\mathcal{P}$-theory T, $\mathcal{P}$-sentence φ, and propositional atom P not occurring in $T \cup \{\varphi\}$:

$$T \models_{\mathbb{K}} \varphi \quad \Leftrightarrow \quad T \cup \{\varphi \to P\} \models_{\mathbb{K}} P \tag{1}$$
$$\Leftrightarrow \quad T \cup \{sk_n^l(\varphi \to P)\} \models_{\mathbb{K}} P \tag{2}$$
$$\Leftrightarrow \quad T \cup \{sk_n^r(\varphi) \to P\} \models_{\mathbb{K}} P \tag{3}$$
$$\Leftrightarrow \quad T \models_{\mathbb{K}} sk_n^r(\varphi). \tag{4}$$

Equivalences (1) and (4) follow from [6, Corollary 1], (2) follows from the assumption that $\models_{\mathbb{K}}$ admits parallel Skolemization left of degree n for all $\mathcal{P}$-sentences, and (3) follows inductively from the definitions of $sk_n^l(\cdot)$ and $sk_n^r(\cdot)$. □

We are unable to prove the converse direction to this lemma. Suppose, however, that $\models_{\mathbb{K}}$ admits the weaker version of the classical deduction theorem stating that for any $\mathcal{P}$-theory $T \cup \{\psi\}$ and $\mathcal{P}$-sentence φ:

$$T \cup \{\varphi\} \models_{\mathbb{K}} \psi \quad \Leftrightarrow \quad T \models_{\mathbb{K}} (\varphi \wedge \bar{1}) \to \psi.$$

Then if $\models_{\mathbb{K}}$ admits parallel Skolemization right of degree n for all $\mathcal{P}$-sentences, also $\models_{\mathbb{K}}$ admits parallel Skolemization left of degree n for all $\mathcal{P}$-sentences. Just note that for any $\mathcal{P}$-theory $T \cup \{\psi\}$ and $\mathcal{P}$-sentence φ:

$$T \cup \{\varphi\} \models_{\mathbb{K}} \psi \quad \Leftrightarrow \quad T \models_{\mathbb{K}} (\varphi \wedge \bar{1}) \to \psi \tag{1}$$
$$\Leftrightarrow \quad T \models_{\mathbb{K}} sk_n^r((\varphi \wedge \bar{1}) \to \psi) \tag{2}$$
$$\Leftrightarrow \quad T \models_{\mathbb{K}} (sk_n^l(\varphi) \wedge \bar{1}) \to sk_n^r(\psi) \tag{3}$$
$$\Leftrightarrow \quad T \cup \{sk_n^l(\varphi)\} \models_{\mathbb{K}} sk_n^r(\psi) \tag{4}$$
$$\Leftrightarrow \quad T \cup \{sk_n^l(\varphi)\} \models_{\mathbb{K}} \psi. \tag{5}$$

Equivalences (1) and (4) follow from the deduction theorem, (2) and (5) follow from the fact that $\models_{\mathbb{K}}$ admits parallel Skolemization right of degree n for all $\mathcal{P}$-sentences, and (3) follows inductively from the definitions of $sk_n^l(\cdot)$ and $sk_n^r(\cdot)$.

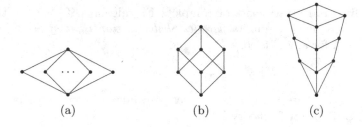

(a)   (b)   (c)

Fig. 2. Examples of 2-compact and 3-compact systems

4   Parallel Skolemization for All Formulas

In this section, we investigate consequence relations $\models_{\mathbb{K}}$ that admit parallel Skolemization of some fixed degree on the left and right for *any* sentence. This is a rather strong property for a consequence relation, but includes all cases where $\models_{\mathbb{K}}$ is equivalent to $\models_{\mathbb{K}'}$ for some finite class $\mathbb{K}'$ of finite algebras, as well as certain non-finite cases.

The crucial requirement for this form of Skolemization is the completeness of $\models_{\mathbb{K}}$ with respect to models based on algebras exhibiting some degree of "compactness". Let L be a lattice and $\mathcal{X} \subseteq \mathfrak{P}(L)$. We say that $\mathcal{X}$ is *n-compact* for some $n \in \mathbb{N}^+$ if for each $A \in \mathcal{X}$,

$$\bigvee A = a_1 \vee \ldots \vee a_n \quad \text{for some } a_1, \ldots, a_n \in A$$
$$\bigwedge A = a_1 \wedge \ldots \wedge a_n \quad \text{for some } a_1, \ldots, a_n \in A.$$

Example 3. It is easily seen that if the lattice L has *height* (the cardinality of a maximal chain in L) smaller than $n + 1$, then any $\mathcal{X} \subseteq \mathfrak{P}(L)$ is n-compact. If L contains no infinite chain and has *width* (the cardinality of a maximal antichain in L) smaller than m, then any $\mathcal{X} \subseteq \mathfrak{P}(L)$ is m-compact. For example, the powerset of a lattice, as depicted in Fig. 2(a), that consists of a (finite or infinite) set of incomparable elements together with a top element and a bottom element, is 2-compact (but not 1-compact). The powerset of the lattice in Fig. 2(b), which may also be generalized by repeating many times the internal elements, is 3-compact (but not 2-compact). On the other hand, the powerset of the lattice in Fig. 2(c) is 2-compact.

It is not necessary for parallel Skolemization that *all* sets of subsets of the algebras in $\mathbb{K}$ be n-compact, only that the set of definable sets of elements in a given $\mathcal{P}$-structure have this property. Let us call a $\mathcal{P}$-structure $\mathfrak{S} = \langle \boldsymbol{A}, \boldsymbol{S} \rangle$ *n-witnessed* if the following system is n-compact:

$$\{\{\|\varphi(b, \bar{a})\|^{\mathfrak{S}} \mid b \in S\} \mid \varphi(x, \bar{y}) \text{ a } \mathcal{P}\text{-formula and } \bar{a} \in S\}.$$

We say that the consequence relation $\models_{\mathbb{K}}$ has *the n-witnessed model property* if for any $\mathcal{P}$-theory $T \cup \{\varphi\}$,

$$T \models_{\mathbb{K}} \varphi \qquad \Leftrightarrow \qquad \text{each } n\text{-witnessed model } \mathfrak{M} \text{ of } T \text{ is a model of } \varphi.$$

Note that this new notion generalizes the (1-)witnessed model property introduced by Hájek in [12] (see also [7]).

Example 4. Suppose that $\mathbb{K}$ is a class of FL_e-algebras whose underlying lattices *either* have height bounded by some fixed $n + 1$, *or* contain no infinite chain and have width bounded by some fixed n (see Example 3). Then $\models_{\mathbb{K}}$ has the n-witnessed model property.

Example 5. Let us emphasize that it is not necessary for parallel Skolemization that all sets of subsets of the algebras in the class $\mathbb{K}$ are n-compact. Suppose, for example, that $\mathbb{K}$ consists of the standard Łukasiewicz algebra on $[0, 1]$. The powerset of $[0, 1]$ is clearly not n-compact for any $n \in \mathbb{N}^+$. However, $\models_{\mathbb{K}}$ has the 1-witnessed model property, as shown by Hájek in [12].

We turn our attention now to the relationship between the n-witnessed model property and parallel Skolemization left and right of degree n. We begin with a crucial lemma which can be seen as "one step" Skolemization on the left.

Lemma 4. *Suppose that $\models_{\mathbb{K}}$ has the n-witnessed model property.*

(a) *For any $\mathcal{P}$-theory $T \cup \{\chi, \psi[(\exists x)\varphi(x, \bar{y})]\}$ where $(\exists x)\varphi(x, \bar{y})$ occurs positively in ψ, for function symbols $f_1, \ldots, f_n \notin \mathcal{P}$ of arity $|\bar{y}|$,*

$$T \cup \{\psi[(\exists x)\varphi(x, \bar{y})]\} \models_{\mathbb{K}} \chi \quad \Leftrightarrow \quad T \cup \{\psi[\bigvee_{i=1}^{n} \varphi(f_i(\bar{y}), \bar{y})]\} \models_{\mathbb{K}} \chi.$$

(b) *For any $\mathcal{P}$-theory $T \cup \{\chi, \psi[(\forall x)\varphi(x, \bar{y})]\}$ where $(\forall x)\varphi(x, \bar{y})$ occurs negatively in ψ, for function symbols $f_1, \ldots, f_n \notin \mathcal{P}$ of arity $|\bar{y}|$,*

$$T \cup \{\psi[(\forall x)\varphi(x, \bar{y})]\} \models_{\mathbb{K}} \chi \quad \Leftrightarrow \quad T \cup \{\psi[\bigwedge_{i=1}^{n} \varphi(f_i(\bar{y}), \bar{y})]\} \models_{\mathbb{K}} \chi.$$

Proof. For the left-to-right directions for both (a) and (b), note that

$$\models_{\mathbb{K}} \bigvee_{i=1}^{n} \varphi(f_i(\bar{y}), \bar{y}) \to (\exists x)\varphi(x, \bar{y}) \quad \text{and} \quad \models_{\mathbb{K}} (\forall x)\varphi(x, \bar{y}) \to \bigwedge_{i=1}^{n} \varphi(f_i(\bar{y}), \bar{y}),$$

and hence, by Lemma 2, for (a) and (b), respectively,

$$\models_{\mathbb{K}} \psi[\bigvee_{i=1}^{n} \varphi(f_i(\bar{y}), \bar{y})] \to \psi[(\exists x)\varphi(x, \bar{y})]$$
$$\text{and} \models_{\mathbb{K}} \psi[\bigwedge_{i=1}^{n} \varphi(f_i(\bar{y}), \bar{y})] \to \psi[(\forall x)\varphi(x, \bar{y})].$$

We prove the right-to-left direction contrapositively just for (a), as (b) is very similar. Suppose that $T \cup \{\psi[(\exists x)\varphi(x, \bar{y})]\} \not\models_{\mathbb{K}} \chi$. So there is an n-witnessed model $\mathfrak{M} = \langle \mathbf{A}, \mathbf{M} \rangle$ of $T \cup \{\psi[(\exists x)\varphi(x, \bar{y})]\}$ such that $\mathfrak{M} \not\models_{\mathbb{K}} \chi$. Because $\mathfrak{M}$ is n-witnessed, for each $\bar{m} \in M$, there are $u_1^{\bar{m}}, \ldots, u_n^{\bar{m}} \in M$ such that

$$\|(\exists x)\varphi(x, \bar{m})\|^{\mathfrak{M}} = \|\varphi(u_1^{\bar{m}}, \bar{m})\|^{\mathfrak{M}} \vee \ldots \vee \|\varphi(u_n^{\bar{m}}, \bar{m})\|^{\mathfrak{M}}.$$

Using the axiom of choice, we define $f_i(\bar{m}) = u_i^{\bar{m}}$ for each $i \in \{1, \ldots, n\}$. Then $\mathfrak{M}$, with these new interpretations, is a model of $T \cup \{\psi[\bigvee_{i=1}^{n} \varphi(f_i(\bar{y}), \bar{y})]\}$ and not χ. $\qquad \square$

Theorem 1. *If $\models_{\mathrm{K}}$ has the n-witnessed model property, then $\models_{\mathrm{K}}$ admits parallel Skolemization left and right of degree n for all sentences. Moreover, the converse implication also holds whenever $\models_{\mathrm{K}}$ is finitary, i.e., for any $\mathcal{P}$-theory $T \cup \{\varphi\}$,*

$$T \models_{\mathrm{K}} \varphi \quad \Leftrightarrow \quad T' \models_{\mathrm{K}} \varphi \ for \ some \ finite T' \subseteq T.$$

Proof. Suppose that $\models_{\mathrm{K}}$ has the n-witnessed model property. Parallel Skolemization left of degree n for all $\mathcal{P}$-sentences follows from Lemma 4 and an induction on the multiset of depths of quantifier occurrences according to the standard multiset well-ordering from [8]. Parallel Skolemization right of degree n for all $\mathcal{P}$-sentences then follows from Lemma 3.

Next we prove the converse: suppose that $\models_{\mathrm{K}}$ is finitary and admits parallel Skolemization left of degree n for all $\mathcal{P}$-sentences. (Note that only Skolemization for certain formulas is needed for the proof). First we establish the following:
Claim. For each $\mathcal{P}$-theory $T \cup \{\varphi\}$ such that $T \not\models_{\mathrm{K}} \varphi$, there exist a language $\mathcal{P}' \supseteq \mathcal{P}$ and a $\mathcal{P}'$-theory $T' \supseteq T$ such that $T' \not\models_{\mathrm{K}} \varphi$ and, for each $\mathcal{P}$-formula $(Qx)\chi(x,\bar{y})$:

$$T' \models_{\mathrm{K}} (\forall \bar{y})((Qx)\chi(x,\bar{y}) \leftrightarrow \bigcirc_{i=1}^{n}\chi(f_i^{\chi}(\bar{y}),\bar{y})),$$

where $\bigcirc = \begin{cases} \bigvee & \text{if } Q = \exists \\ \bigwedge & \text{if } Q = \forall \end{cases}$, and $f_1^{\chi},\dots,f_n^{\chi}$ are function symbols from $\mathcal{P}' \setminus \mathcal{P}$.
Proof of the claim. Let $\varphi_0, \varphi_1, \dots$ be an enumeration of all $\mathcal{P}$-formulas of the form $(\forall x)\chi(x,\bar{y})$ or $(\exists x)\chi(x,\bar{y})$ (recalling that $\mathcal{P}$ is always a countable language). We construct an increasing series of languages $\mathcal{P}_i$ and $\mathcal{P}_i$-theories T_i such that $T_i \not\models_{\mathrm{K}} \varphi$. Let $T_0 = T$ and $\mathcal{P}_0 = \mathcal{P}$. If φ_j has the form $(\forall x)\chi(x,\bar{y})$, then as $\models_{\mathrm{K}}$ admits parallel Skolemization left of degree n for all $\mathcal{P}$-sentences,

$$T_j \models_{\mathrm{K}} \varphi \quad \Leftrightarrow T_j \cup \{(\forall \bar{y})((\forall x)\chi(x,\bar{y}) \to (\forall x)\chi(x,\bar{y}))\} \models_{\mathrm{K}} \varphi$$
$$\Leftrightarrow T_j \cup \{(\forall \bar{y})(\bigwedge_{i=1}^{n} \chi(f_i^{\chi}(\bar{y}),\bar{y}) \to (\forall x)\chi(x,\bar{y}))\} \models_{\mathrm{K}} \varphi.$$

We define $\mathcal{P}_{j+1}$ as the extension of $\mathcal{P}_j$ with the function symbols $f_1^{\chi},\dots,f_n^{\chi}$ and

$$T_{j+1} = T_j \cup \{(\forall \bar{y})(\bigwedge_{i=1}^{n} \chi(f_i^{\chi}(\bar{y}),\bar{y}) \to (\forall x)\chi(x,\bar{y}))\}.$$

The case where φ_j has the form $(\exists x)\chi(x,\bar{y})$ is dealt with similarly. We then let $\mathcal{P}' = \bigcup_{j<\omega} \mathcal{P}_j$ and $T' = \bigcup_{j<\omega} T_j$. Because $\models_{\mathrm{K}}$ is finitary, $T' \not\models_{\mathrm{K}} \varphi$. Moreover, for a formula $(Qx)\chi(x,\bar{y}) = \varphi_j$ for some j and assuming that $Q = \exists$, we have $(\forall \bar{y})((\exists x)\chi(x,\bar{y}) \to \bigvee_{i=1}^{n} \chi(f_i^{\chi}(\bar{y}),\bar{y})) \in T'$ and as the converse implication is always provable the claim follows.

To complete the proof of the theorem, we just iterate the above claim over ω. We obtain a theory $\hat{T}$ whose models are clearly n-witnessed and $\hat{T} \not\models_{\mathrm{K}} \varphi$. $\square$

A natural question to ask at this point is whether the requirement that $\models_{\mathrm{K}}$ be finitary is really necessary to obtain an equivalence in the previous theorem. We do not have an answer. Observe, however, that this requirement could be avoided if we allow Skolemization of infinitely many formulas on the left *simultaneously*.

Theorem 1 and Example 4 establish parallel Skolemization of some finite degree for $\models_{\mathbb{K}}$ for a broad family of classes $\mathbb{K}$ of FL_e-algebras. Also, using Example 5, first-order Łukasiewicz logic based on the standard Łukasiewicz algebra on $[0, 1]$ admits parallel Skolemization of degree 1. However, the consequence relation of this logic is not finitary, so we cannot obtain the 1-witnessed model property directly from the fact that it admits Skolemization left of degree 1.

5 Parallel Skolemization for Prenex Formulas

In the previous section, we proved that consequence relations satisfying a rather strong witnessed model property admit parallel Skolemization to some degree for all formulas. In this section, we investigate the (broader) scope of parallel Skolemization restricted to prenex formulas.

First we show that parallel Skolemization for prenex formulas on the right holds in the presence of a weaker witnessed model property. Let L be a lattice and consider $\mathcal{X} \subseteq \mathfrak{P}(L)$. We say that $\mathcal{X}$ is n-$\wedge$-precompact for some $n \in \mathbb{N}^+$ if for all $A \in \mathcal{X}$ and $b \in L$,

$$\bigwedge A < b \quad \Longrightarrow \quad a_1 \wedge \ldots \wedge a_n < b \text{ for some } a_1, \ldots, a_n \in A.$$

Example 6. The powerset of the (infinite) lattice depicted in Fig. 3(a) is 1-$\wedge$-precompact (but not n-compact for any n), while the powerset of the (infinite) lattice in Fig. 3(b) is 2-$\wedge$-precompact (but neither n-compact for any n, nor 1-$\wedge$-precompact).

We call a $\mathcal{P}$-structure $\mathfrak{S} = \langle A, S \rangle$ n-$\wedge$-*prewitnessed* if the following system is n-$\wedge$-precompact:

$$\{\{\|\varphi(b, \bar{a})\|^{\mathfrak{S}} \mid b \in S\} \mid \varphi(x, \bar{y}) \text{ a } \mathcal{P}\text{-formula and } \bar{a} \in S\}.$$

Then $\models_{\mathbb{K}}$ has the n-$\wedge$-*prewitnessed model property* if for any $\mathcal{P}$-theory $T \cup \{\varphi\}$,

$$T \models_{\mathbb{K}} \varphi \Leftrightarrow \text{ every } n\text{-}\wedge\text{-prewitnessed model } \mathfrak{M} \text{ of } T \text{ is a model of } \varphi.$$

Example 7. If L is a chain, then $\mathfrak{P}(L)$ is 1-$\wedge$-precompact and hence any logic based on chains enjoys the 1-$\wedge$-prewitnessed model property.

We show first that the n-$\wedge$-prewitnessed model property suffices to guarantee "one step" parallel Skolemization of degree n for formulas of a certain form occurring on the right of the consequence relation.

Theorem 2. *If $\models_{\mathbb{K}}$ has the n-$\wedge$-prewitnessed model property, then for any $\mathcal{P}$-theory $T \cup \{\varphi(x, \bar{y}), \psi\}$ and function symbols $f_1, \ldots, f_n \notin \mathcal{P}$ of arity $|\bar{y}|$:*

$$T \models_{\mathbb{K}} (\exists \bar{y})(\forall x)\varphi(x, \bar{y}) \quad \Leftrightarrow \quad T \models_{\mathbb{K}} (\exists \bar{y})(\bigwedge_{i=1}^{n} \varphi(f_i(\bar{y}), \bar{y})).$$

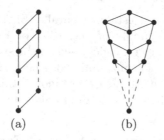

(a)   (b)

Fig. 3. Examples of 1-∧-precompact and 2-∧-precompact systems

Proof. The left-to-right direction follows directly using Lemma 2. We prove the right-to-left direction contrapositively, assuming without loss of generality that T consists of $\mathcal{P}$-sentences. Suppose that $T \not\models_{\mathbb{K}} (\exists \bar{y})(\forall x)\varphi(x, \bar{y})$. Then there is an n-∧-prewitnessed model $\mathfrak{M} = \langle \boldsymbol{A}, \mathbf{M} \rangle$ of T such that $V = \|(\exists \bar{y})(\forall x)\varphi(x, \bar{y})\|^{\mathfrak{M}} \not\geq \bar{1}$, i.e., $V < V \vee \bar{1}$.

Suppose first that $V < V' < V \vee \bar{1}$ for some $V' \in A$. Clearly, for each $\bar{m} \in M$, $\|(\forall x)\varphi(x, \bar{m})\|^{\mathfrak{M}} \leq V < V'$. Since $\mathfrak{M}$ is n-∧-prewitnessed, for each $\bar{m} \in M$, there are $u_1^{\bar{m}}, \dots, u_n^{\bar{m}} \in M$ such that $\|\varphi(u_1^{\bar{m}}, \bar{m})\|^{\mathfrak{M}} \wedge \dots \wedge \|\varphi(u_n^{\bar{m}}, \bar{m})\|^{\mathfrak{M}} < V'$. Now for $i \in \{1, \dots, n\}$, define, using the axiom of choice, $f_i(\bar{m}) = u_i^{\bar{m}}$. But then

$$\|(\exists \bar{y})(\textstyle\bigwedge_{i=1}^{n} \varphi(f_i(\bar{y}), \bar{y}))\|^{\mathfrak{M}} = \bigvee_{\bar{m} \in M} \textstyle\bigwedge_{i=1}^{n} \|\varphi(f_i(\bar{m}), \bar{m})\|^{\mathfrak{M}} \leq V' < V \vee \bar{1}.$$

So $\|(\exists \bar{y})(\bigwedge_{i=1}^{n} \varphi(f_i(\bar{y}), \bar{y}))\|^{\mathfrak{M}} \not\geq \bar{1}$.

Now suppose that no $V' \in A$ satisfies $V < V' < V \vee \bar{1}$. Clearly, for each $\bar{m} \in M$, $\|(\forall x)\varphi(x, \bar{m})\|^{\mathfrak{M}} \leq V < V \vee \bar{1}$. If $\|(\forall x)\varphi(x, \bar{m})\|^{\mathfrak{M}} < V$, then, as $\mathfrak{M}$ is n-∧-prewitnessed, we have $u_1^{\bar{m}}, \dots, u_n^{\bar{m}} \in M$ such that $\|\varphi(u_1^{\bar{m}}, \bar{m})\|^{\mathfrak{M}} \wedge \dots \wedge \|\varphi(u_n^{\bar{m}}, \bar{m})\|^{\mathfrak{M}} < V$. If $\|(\forall x)\varphi(x, \bar{m})\|^{\mathfrak{M}} = V$, then for some $u_1^{\bar{m}}, \dots, u_n^{\bar{m}} \in M$,

$$\|(\forall x)\varphi(x, \bar{m})\|^{\mathfrak{M}} = V \leq \|\varphi(u_1^{\bar{m}}, \bar{m})\|^{\mathfrak{M}} \wedge \dots \wedge \|\varphi(u_n^{\bar{m}}, \bar{m})\|^{\mathfrak{M}} < V \vee \bar{1}.$$

Hence, by assumption, $V = \|\varphi(u_1^{\bar{m}}, \bar{m})\|^{\mathfrak{M}} \wedge \dots \wedge \|\varphi(u_n^{\bar{m}}, \bar{m})\|^{\mathfrak{M}}$. In both cases, for each $i \in \{1, \dots, n\}$, define, using the axiom of choice, $f_i(\bar{m}) = u_i^{\bar{m}}$. But then

$$\|(\exists \bar{y})(\textstyle\bigwedge_{i=1}^{n} \varphi(f_i(\bar{y}), \bar{y}))\|^{\mathfrak{M}} = \bigvee_{\bar{m}} \textstyle\bigwedge_{i=1}^{n} \|\varphi(f_i(\bar{m}), \bar{m})\|^{\mathfrak{M}} \leq V < V \vee \bar{1}.$$

So $\|(\exists \bar{y})(\bigwedge_{i=1}^{n} \varphi(f_i(\bar{y}), \bar{y}))\|^{\mathfrak{M}} \not\geq \bar{1}$. $\qquad\square$

In order to repeat this one step Skolemization process and obtain skolemized formulas for any prenex formula, we require an additional assumption, satisfied in particular whenever all algebras in $\mathbb{K}$ are frames (e.g., chains).

Theorem 3. *Suppose that* $\models_{\mathbb{K}}$ *has the* n-∧-*prewitnessed model property and for all* $\mathcal{P}$-*formulas* φ *and* χ *such that* x *is not free in* χ:

$$\models_{\mathbb{K}} (\chi \wedge (\exists x)\varphi) \to (\exists x)(\chi \wedge \varphi).$$

Then $\models_{\mathbb{K}}$ *admits parallel Skolemization right of degree* n *for prenex sentences.*

Proof. First we define ∧-prenex $\mathcal{P}$-formulas as follows: every quantifier-free $\mathcal{P}$-formula is ∧-prenex, and if φ, ψ are ∧-prenex, then so are $\varphi \wedge \psi$, $(\exists x)\varphi$, and $(\forall x)\varphi$ for any variable x.

Now consider a $\mathcal{P}$-theory T and a ∧-prenex $\mathcal{P}$-sentence χ with a leftmost strong quantifier occurrence $(\forall x)\varphi(x, \bar{y})$. Rewriting variables if necessary and using quantifier shifts, χ is equivalent to a sentence of the form

$$(\exists \bar{y})(\forall x)(\varphi(x, \bar{y}) \wedge \varphi'(\bar{y}))$$

and by Theorem 2,

$$T \models_{\mathbb{K}} (\exists \bar{y})(\forall x)(\varphi(x, \bar{y}) \wedge \varphi'(\bar{y})) \quad \Leftrightarrow \quad T \models_{\mathbb{K}} (\exists \bar{y})(\bigwedge_{i=1}^{n} \varphi(f_i(\bar{y}), \bar{y}) \wedge \varphi'(\bar{y})).$$

But then, shifting the existential quantifiers back to their original positions,

$$T \models_{\mathbb{K}} \chi[(\forall x)\varphi(x, \bar{y})] \quad \Leftrightarrow \quad T \models_{\mathbb{K}} \chi[\bigwedge_{i=1}^{n} \varphi(f_i(\bar{y}), \bar{y})].$$

Note that $\chi[\wedge_{i=1}^{n}\varphi(f_i(\bar{y}), \bar{y})]$ is also a ∧-prenex formula. Hence, the claim follows by an induction on the multiset of depths of quantifier occurrences according to the standard multiset well-ordering from [8].   □

Now we turn our attention to parallel Skolemization for prenex formulas on the *left*, using again a further weaker witnessed model property. Let L be a lattice and consider $\mathcal{X} \subseteq \mathfrak{P}(L)$. We say that an element b in L is *n*-∨-*compact* for some $n \in \mathbb{N}^+$ if for all $A \in \mathcal{X}$,

$$\bigvee A \geq b \quad \Longrightarrow \quad a_1 \vee \ldots \vee a_n \geq b \text{ for some } a_1, \ldots, a_n \in A.$$

We will call a $\mathcal{P}$-structure $\mathfrak{S} = \langle A, S \rangle$ *n*-(∃)-*witnessed* if the element $\bar{1}^{A}$ is *n*-∨-compact in the following system:

$$\{\{\|\varphi(b, \bar{a})\|^{\mathfrak{S}} \mid b \in S\} \mid \varphi(x, \bar{y}) \text{ a } \mathcal{P}\text{-formula and } \bar{a} \in S\}.$$

Then $\models_{\mathbb{K}}$ has *the n*-(∃)-*witnessed model property* if for any $\mathcal{P}$-theory $T \cup \{\varphi\}$,

$$T \models_{\mathbb{K}} \varphi \quad \Leftrightarrow \quad \text{every } n\text{-}(\exists)\text{-witnessed model } \mathfrak{M} \text{ of } T \text{ is a model of } \varphi.$$

Example 8. It is easy to generate examples of FL_e-algebras A whose powerset is not n-compact for any n but where $\bar{1}$ is n-∨-compact: e.g., it would be sufficient to assume that $\bar{1}^{A}$ is the top element in A, that the set $\{a \in A \mid a < \bar{1}^{A}\}$ has a maximal element, and that there is an infinite chain in A. These examples would then naturally yield logics with the n-(∃)-witnessed model property which in general do not have the n-witnessed model property.

The next proposition (which follows directly from [7, Corollary 4.3.10 and Theorem 4.5.5]) presents an important class of logics with the 1-(∃)-witnessed model property given by algebras where, in general, $\bar{1}$ is not 1-∨-compact.

Proposition 1. *Let $\mathbb{K}$ be a class of complete chains that generates a variety in which the class of all chains admits regular completions, i.e., each such chain can be embedded into a complete one by an embedding preserving all (even infinite) existing joins and meets. Then $\models_{\mathbb{K}}$ has the 1-$(\exists)$-witnessed model property.*

Theorem 4. *If $\models_{\mathbb{K}}$ has the n-$(\exists)$-witnessed model property, then for each $\mathcal{P}$-theory $T \cup \{\varphi(x,\bar{y}), \psi\}$ and function symbols $f_1, \ldots, f_n \notin \mathcal{P}$ of arity $|\bar{y}|$,*

$$T \cup \{(\forall \bar{y})(\exists x)\varphi(x,\bar{y})\} \models_{\mathbb{K}} \psi \quad \Leftrightarrow \quad T \cup \{(\forall \bar{y}) \bigvee_{i=1}^{n} \varphi(f_i(\bar{y}),\bar{y})\} \models_{\mathbb{K}} \psi.$$

Proof. The left-to-right direction is easy. For the right-to-left direction, suppose that $T \cup \{(\forall \bar{y})(\exists x)\varphi(x,\bar{y})\} \not\models_{\mathbb{K}} \psi$. By assumption, there is an n-$(\exists)$-witnessed model $\mathfrak{M}$ of $T \cup \{(\forall \bar{y})(\exists x)\varphi(x,\bar{y})\}$ such that $\mathfrak{M} \not\models \psi$. Since for each $\bar{m} \in M$, $\|(\exists x)\varphi(x,\bar{m})\|^{\mathfrak{M}} \geq \bar{1}$, there are $u_1^{\bar{m}}, \ldots, u_n^{\bar{m}} \in M$ such that

$$\|\varphi(u_1^{\bar{m}}, \bar{m})\|^{\mathfrak{M}} \vee \cdots \vee \|\varphi(u_n^{\bar{m}}, \bar{m})\|^{\mathfrak{M}} \geq \bar{1}.$$

But then, using the axiom of choice, we can define functions f_i and expand the model $\mathfrak{M}$ into a model $\mathfrak{M}'$ such that for each $\mathcal{P}$-formula χ and $\bar{m}, \bar{s} \in M$,

$$\|\bigvee_{i=1}^{n} \varphi(f_i(\bar{m}),\bar{m})\|^{\mathfrak{M}'} \geq \bar{1} \quad \text{and} \quad \|\chi(\bar{s})\|^{\mathfrak{M}'} = \|\chi(\bar{s})\|^{\mathfrak{M}}.$$

So $\mathfrak{M}'$ is a model of $T \cup \{(\forall \bar{y}) \bigvee_{i=1}^{n} \varphi(f_i(\bar{y}),\bar{y})\}$ and $\mathfrak{M}' \not\models \psi$. $\qquad \square$

As in the case of Skolemization on the right, this "one step" theorem extends to all prenex formulas, assuming the additional quantifier shift condition, satisfied in particular whenever all algebras in $\mathbb{K}$ are co-frames (e.g., chains).

Theorem 5. *Suppose that $\models_{\mathbb{K}}$ has the n-$(\exists)$-witnessed model property and for all $\mathcal{P}$-formulas φ and χ such that x is not free in χ:*

$$\models_{\mathbb{K}} (\forall x)(\chi \vee \varphi) \to (\chi \vee (\forall x)\varphi)$$

Then $\models_{\mathbb{K}}$ admits parallel Skolemization left of degree n for prenex sentences.

Finally, putting together the results of this section for the special case of first-order substructural logics based on classes of chains, we obtain:

Corollary 1. *Suppose that $\mathbb{K}$ is a class of complete FL_e-chains. Then $\models_{\mathbb{K}}$ admits parallel Skolemization right of degree 1 for all prenex sentences. Moreover, if $\mathbb{K}$ is a class of complete chains that generates a variety in which the class of all chains admits regular completions, then $\models_{\mathbb{K}}$ admits parallel Skolemization left of degree 1 for all prenex sentences.*

It follows in particular from this corollary that any logic axiomatized relative to the first-order version of the logic MTL (the logic of all FL_{ew}-chains, see [5]) by adding axioms from the class P_3 introduced in [4] admits parallel Skolemization left and right of degree 1 for all prenex sentences.

References

1. Baaz, M., Lemhoff, R.: Skolemization in intermediate logics with the finite model property. Submitted
2. Baaz, M., Iemhoff, R.: On Skolemization in constructive theories. J. Symbolic Logic **73**(3), 969–998 (2008)
3. Buss, S. (ed.): Handbook of Proof Theory. Kluwer, Dordrecht (1998)
4. Ciabattoni, A., Galatos, N., Terui, K.: Algebraic proof theory for substructural logics: Cut-elimination and completions. Ann. Pure. Appl. Logic **163**(3), 266–290 (2012)
5. Cintula, P., Hájek, P., Noguera, C. (eds).: Handbook of Mathematical Fuzzy Logic (in 2 volumes), volume 37, 38 of Studies in Logic, Mathematical Logic and Foundations. College Publications, London (2011)
6. Cintula, P., Metcalfe, G.: Herbrand theorems for substructural logics. In: McMillan, K., Middeldorp, A., Voronkov, A. (eds.) LPAR-19 2013. LNCS, vol. 8312, pp. 584–600. Springer, Heidelberg (2013)
7. Cintula, P., Noguera, C.: A general framework for mathematical fuzzy logic. In: Cintula, P., Hájek, P., Noguera, C. (eds.) Handbook of Mathematical Fuzzy Logic. vol. 1, vol. 37 of Studies in Logic, Mathematical Logic and Foundations, pp. 103–207. College Publications, London (2011)
8. Dershowitz, N., Manna, Z.: Proving termination with multiset orderings. Commun. ACM **22**(8), 465–476 (1979)
9. Galatos, N., Jipsen, P., Kowalski, T., Ono, H.: Residuated Lattices: An Algebraic Glimpse at Substructural Logics. Studies in Logic and the Foundations of Mathematics, vol. 151. Elsevier, Amsterdam (2007)
10. García-Cerdaña, À., Armengol, E., Esteva, F.: Fuzzy description logics and t-norm based fuzzy logics. Int. J. Approximate Reasoning **51**(6), 632–655 (2010)
11. Hájek, P.: Metamathematics of Fuzzy Logic. Trends in Logic. Kluwer, Dordrecht (1998)
12. Hájek, P.: Making fuzzy description logic more general. Fuzzy Sets Syst. **154**(1), 1–15 (2005)
13. Meghini, C., Sebastiani, F., Straccia, U.: A model of multimedia information retrieval. J. ACM **48**(5), 909–970 (2001)
14. Metcalfe, G., Olivetti, N., Gabbay, D.M.: Proof Theory for Fuzzy Logics. vol. 36 of Applied Logic Series. Springer, Heidelberg (2008)
15. Minc, G.E.: The Skolem method in intuitionistic calculi. Proc. Steklov Inst. Math. **121**, 73–109 (1974)
16. Ono, H.: Crawley completions of residuated lattices and algebraic completeness of substructural predicate logics. Stud. Logica **100**(1–2), 339–359 (2012)
17. Restall, G.: An Introduction to Substructural Logics. Routledge, New York (2000)
18. Vojtáš, P.: Fuzzy logic programming. Fuzzy Sets Syst. **124**(3), 361–370 (2001)

Reasoning About Embedded Dependencies
Using Inclusion Dependencies

Miika Hannula[(✉)]

Department of Mathematics and Statistics, University of Helsinki,
P.O. Box 68, 00014 Helsinki, Finland
miika.hannula@helsinki.fi

Abstract. The implication problem for the class of embedded dependencies is undecidable. However, this does not imply lackness of a proof procedure as exemplified by the chase algorithm. In this paper we present a complete axiomatization of embedded dependencies that is based on the chase and uses inclusion dependencies and implicit existential quantification in the intermediate steps of deductions.

Keywords: Axiomatization · Chase · Implication problem · Dependence logic · Embedded dependency · Tuple generating dependency · Equality generating dependency · Inclusion dependency

1 Introduction

Embedded dependencies generalize the concept database dependencies within the framework of first-order logic. Their implication is undecidable but however recursively enumerable, thus enabling complete axiomatizations. A standard example of such a proof procedure is the chase that was invented in the late 1970 s [1, 2], and then soon extended to equality and tuple generating dependencies [3]. In this paper we present an axiomatization for the class of embedded dependencies that simulates the chase at the logical level using inclusion dependencies. In particular, completeness of the rules is obtained by constructing deductions in which all the intermediate steps are inclusion dependencies, except for the first and the last step. These inclusion dependencies consist of attributes of which some are new, i.e., such that they are not allowed to appear at any earlier stage of the deduction.

As a background example, consider the combined class of functional and inclusion dependencies. It is well known that the corresponding implication problem is undecidable, lacking hence finite axiomatization [4, 5]. One strategy in such situations has been to search for axiomatizations within a more general class of dependencies, and partly for this reason many different dependency notions were introduced in the 1980 s. For instance, a textbook on dependency theory from 1991 considers more than 80 different dependency classes [6]. In [7] Mitchell proposed another strategy by presenting an axiomatization of functional and inclusion dependencies using a notion of new attributes which should

© Springer-Verlag Berlin Heidelberg 2015
M. Davis et al. (Eds.): LPAR-20 2015, LNCS 9450, pp. 16–30, 2015.
DOI: 10.1007/978-3-662-48899-7_2

be thought of as implicitly existentially quantified. In this paper we take an analogous approach, and present an axiomatization for embedded dependencies where new attributes correspond to new values obtained from an associated chasing sequence. These attributes can be thought of as implicitly existentially quantified in the sense of *team semantics*, that is, a semantic framework that has *teams*, i.e., sets of assignments, as its underlying concept [8]. Team semantics is compositionally applicable to logics that extend first-order logic with various database dependencies [9,10]. In this setting, *inclusion logic*, i.e., first-order logic with additional inclusion dependencies, captures the positive fragment of greatest fixed-point logic and hence all PTIME recognizable classes of finite, ordered models [11–13]. Therefore, inclusion dependencies with new attributes can be thought of as greatest fixed-point logic expressions. This may in part enable succinct intermediate steps in deductions in contrast to axiomatic systems that simulate the chase by composing first-order definable dependencies.

The methods described in this paper generalize the axiomatization of conditional independence and inclusion dependencies presented in [14]. It is also worth noting that extending relations with new attributes reminds of algebraic dependencies, that are, typed embedded dependencies defined in algebraic terms. The complete axiomatization of algebraic dependencies presented in [15] involves also an extension schema that introduces new copies of attributes.

2   Preliminaries

For two sets A and B, we write AB to denote their union, and for two sequences $\boldsymbol{ab}$, we write $\boldsymbol{ab}$ to denote their concatenation. For a sequence $\boldsymbol{a} = (a_1, \ldots, a_n)$ and a mapping f, we write $f(\boldsymbol{a})$ for $(f(a_1), \ldots, f(a_n))$. We denote by id the identity function and by pr_i the function that maps a sequence to its ith projection. For a function f and $A \subseteq \mathrm{Dom}(f)$, we write $f|_A$ for the restriction of f to A, and for a set of mappings F, we write $F|_A$ for $\{f|_A : f \in F\}$.

We start by fixing two countably infinite sets Val and Att, the first denoting possible values of relations and the second attributes. For notational convenience, we will assume that Val = Att. For $R \subseteq$ Att, a *tuple* over R is a mapping $R \to$ Val, and a *relation* over R is a set of tuples over R. We may sometimes write $r[R]$ to denote that r is a relation over R. Values of a relation r over R are denoted by Val(r), i.e., Val$(r) := \{t(A) : t \in r, A \in R\}$. Let f be a *valuation*, i.e., a mapping Val $\to$ Val. Then for a tuple t, we write $f(t) := f \circ t$, and for a relation r, $f(r) := \{f(t) : t \in r\}$. A valuation f *embeds* a relation r (a tuple t) to r' if $f(r) \subseteq r'$ ($f(t) \in r$). Since we are usually interested only valuations of a relation, we say that $f :$ Val$(r) \to$ Val is a *valuation on* r. For a valuation f on r, we say that g is an *extension* of f to another relation r' if g is a valuation on r' such that it agrees with f on values of Val$(r) \cap$ Val(r').

Embedded dependencies (ed's) can be written using first-order logic in the following way.

Definition 1 (Embedded Dependency). *Embedded dependency is a first-order sentence of the form*

$$\forall x_1, \ldots, x_n \big(\phi(x_1, \ldots, x_n) \to \exists z_1 \ldots \exists z_k \psi(y_1, \ldots, y_m) \big)$$

where $\{z_1, \ldots, z_k\} = \{y_1, \ldots, y_m\} \setminus \{x_1, \ldots, x_n\}$ *and*

- ϕ *is a (possibly empty) conjunction of relational atoms using all of the variables* $x_1, \ldots, x_n$;
- ψ *is a conjunction of relational and equality atoms using all of the variables* $z_1, \ldots, z_k$;
- *there are no equality atoms in* ψ *involving existentially quantified variables.*

If at most one relation symbol occurs in an ed, then we say that the ed is *unirelational*, and otherwise it is *multirelational*. An ed is called *typed* if there is an assignment of variables to column positions such that variables in relation atoms occur only in their assigned position, and each equality atom involves a pair of variables assigned to the same position. Otherwise we say that an ed is *untyped*. If ψ contains only one atom, then we say that the ed is *single-head*, and otherwise it is *multi-head*. A single-head ed where ψ is an equality is called an *equality generating dependency* (egd). If ψ is a conjunction of relational atoms, then the ed is called a *tuple generating dependency* (tgd). For notational simplicity, we restrict attention to unirelational ed's. It is easy to se that any ed is equivalent to a set of tgd's and egd's, and hence we restrict attention to ed's that belong to either of these subclasses.

The following alternative tableau presentation for egd's and tgd's are used in this paper.

Definition 2. *Let T and T' be finite relations over R, and $x, y \in \mathsf{Val}(T)$. Then $(T, x = y)$ and (T, T') are an egd and a tgd over R, respectively, with the below satisfaction relation for a relation r over $S \supseteq R$:*

- $r \models (T, x = y) \Leftrightarrow$ *for all valuations f such that $f(T) \subseteq r|_R$, it holds that $f(x) = f(y)$.*
- $r \models (T, T') \Leftrightarrow$ *for all valuations f on T such that $f(T) \subseteq r|_R$, there is an extension g of f to T' such that $g(T') \subseteq r|_R$.*

Sometimes we write $\sigma[R]$ to denote that σ is a dependency over R. If T or T' is a singleton, then we may omit the set braces in the notation, e.g., write (T, t) instead of $(T, \{t\})$.

We also extend valuations to dependencies. For an egd $\sigma = (T, x = y)$ we write $\mathsf{Val}(\sigma) = \mathsf{Val}(T)$, and for a tgd $\tau = (T, T')$ we write $\mathsf{Val}(\sigma) = \mathsf{Val}(T) \cup \mathsf{Val}(T')$. Moreover, if f is a valuation, then $f(\sigma) = (f(T), f(x) = f(y))$ and $f(\tau) = (f(T), f(T'))$.

Example 1. Consider the relation r and the tgd's $\sigma_1 := (\{t, t'\}, \{u\})$ and $\sigma_2 := (\{t, t'\}, \{v, v'\})$ obtained from Fig. 1.[1] We notice that there are two valuations

---

[1] In a tableau presentation of a dependency σ, the distinct values of σ are sometimes denoted by blank cells.

$$r = \begin{array}{c|ccc} & A & B & C \\ \hline s_0 & 0 & 1 & 2 \\ s_1 & 3 & 0 & 1 \\ s_2 & 2 & 3 & 0 \\ s_3 & 1 & 4 & 3 \end{array}$$

$$\sigma_1 = \begin{array}{c|ccc} & A & B & C \\ \hline t & x & y & z \\ t' & & x & y \\ u & z & & x \end{array}$$

$$\sigma_2 = \begin{array}{c|ccc} & A & B & C \\ \hline t & x & y & z \\ t' & & x & y \\ v & z & a & x \\ v' & & & a \end{array}$$

Fig. 1. Relation r and tgd's σ_1, σ_2

on $\{t, t'\}$ that embed $\{t, t'\}$ to r, namely $f := \{(x,0), (y,1), (z,2)\}$ and $g := \{(x,3), (y,0), (z,1)\}$. Then $r \models \sigma_1$ since f and g embed u into r, witnessed by tuples s_2 and s_3, respectively. We also notice that $r \not\models \sigma_2$ since, although $f \cup \{(a,3)\}$ embeds $\{v, v'\}$ into r, no extension of g does the same.

Next we define inclusion dependencies which are examples of possibly untyped tgd's.

Definition 3 (Inclusion Dependency). *Let $A_1, \ldots, A_n$ and $B_1, \ldots, B_n$ be (not necessarily distinct) tuples of attributes. Then $A_1 \ldots A_n \subseteq B_1 \ldots B_n$ is an inclusion dependency (ind) over $R = \{A_i, B_i : i = 1, \ldots, n\}$ with the following semantic rule for a relation r over $S \supseteq R$:*

$$r \models A_1 \ldots A_n \subseteq B_1 \ldots B_n \Leftrightarrow \forall s \in r \exists s' \in r \forall i = 1, \ldots, n : s(A_i) = s'(B_i).$$

The axiomatization presented in the next section involves inclusion dependencies that introduce new attributes. These attributes are here interpreted as existentially quantified in *lax team semantics* sense [9]:

$$r \models \exists A \phi \Leftrightarrow r[f/A] \models \phi \text{ for some } f : r \rightarrow \mathcal{P}(\mathsf{Val}) \setminus \{\emptyset\}, \tag{1}$$

where $r[f/A] := \{t(x/A) : x \in f(A)\}$ and $t(x/A)$ is the mapping that agrees with t everywhere except that it maps A to x. Interestingly, inclusion logic formulae with this concept of existential quantification can be characterized with positive greatest fixed-point logic formulae (see Theorem 15 in [11]).

3   Axiomatization

In this section we present an axiomatization for the class of all embedded dependencies. The axiomatization contains an identity rule and three rules for the chase. We also involve conjunction in the language and therefore incorporate its usual introduction and elimination rules in the definition. Regarding the equalities that appear in the rules, note that both $AB \subseteq AA$ and $AB \subseteq BB$ indicate that the values of A and B coincide in each row. Therefore, we use $A = B$ to denote ind's of either form. For a tgd (an egd) σ, we say that $x \in \mathsf{Val}(\sigma)$ is *distinct* if it appears at most once as a value in σ. Namely,

- for a tgd $\sigma = (T, T')[R]$, x is distinct if for all $t, t' \in T \cup T'$ and $A, B \in R$, if $t(A) = x = t'(B)$, then $t = t'$ and $B = B'$;

- for an egd $\sigma = (T, y = z)[R]$, x is distinct if $x \notin \{y, z\}$ and for all $t, t' \in T$ and $A, B \in R$, if $t(A) = x = t'(B)$, then $t = t'$ and $B = B'$.

Lastly, note that in the following rules we assume that values can appear as attributes and vice versa.

Definition 4. *In addition to the below rules we adopt the usual introduction and elimination rules for conjunction. In the last three rules, we assume that $\boldsymbol{A}$ is a sequence listing the attributes of R.*

EE Equality Exchange:

$$\text{if } A = B \land \sigma, \text{ then } \tau.$$

where σ is an ind and τ is obtained from σ by replacing any number of occurrences of A by B and any number of occurrences of B by A.
CS Chase Start:

$$(T^*, \mathrm{id})[RS] \land \bigwedge_{t \in T} t(\boldsymbol{A}) \subseteq \boldsymbol{A}$$

where $T = T^*|_R$, $S = \mathsf{Val}(T)$ consists of new *attributes, and R consists of distinct values.*
CR Chase Rule:

$$\text{tgd:} \quad \text{if } (T, T')[R] \land \bigwedge_{t \in T} f \circ t(\boldsymbol{A}) \subseteq \boldsymbol{A}, \text{ then } \bigwedge_{t' \in T'} f \circ t'(\boldsymbol{A}) \subseteq \boldsymbol{A},$$

$$\text{egd:} \quad \text{if } (T, x = y)[R] \land \bigwedge_{t \in T} f \circ t(\boldsymbol{A}) \subseteq \boldsymbol{A}, \text{ then } f(x) = f(y),$$

where tgd: f is a valuation that it is 1-1 on $\mathsf{Val}(T') \setminus \mathsf{Val}(T)$, and $f(x)$ is a new attribute for $x \in \mathsf{Val}(T') \setminus \mathsf{Val}(T)$.
CT Chase Termination:

$$\text{tgd:} \quad \text{if } (T^*, \mathrm{id})[RS] \land \bigwedge_{t' \in T'} u \circ t'(\boldsymbol{A}) \subseteq \boldsymbol{A}, \text{ then } (T, T')[R],$$

$$\text{egd:} \quad \text{if } (T^*, \mathrm{id})[RS] \land x = y, \text{ then } (T, x = y)[R],$$

where $T = T^*|_R$, $S = \mathsf{Val}(T)$, and $\mathsf{Val}(T^*|_S)$ consists of distinct values. Moreover, tgd: u is a mapping $\mathsf{Val}(T') \to \mathsf{Att}$ that is the identity on $\mathsf{Val}(T) \cap \mathsf{Val}(T')$, and egd: $x, y \in \mathsf{Val}(T)$.

For a dependency σ over R, we let $\mathsf{Att}(\sigma) := R$, and for a set of dependencies Σ, we let $\mathsf{Att}(\Sigma) := \bigcup_{\sigma \in \Sigma} \mathsf{Att}(\sigma)$.

Definition 5. *A deduction from Σ is a sequence $(\sigma_1, \ldots, \sigma_n)$ such that:*

1. *Each σ_i is either an element of Σ, an instance of [CS], or follows from one or more formulae of $\{\sigma_1, \ldots, \sigma_{i-1}\}$ by one of the rules presented above.*
2. *For each $A \in \mathsf{Att}(\sigma_i)$, if A is new in σ_i, then $A \notin \mathsf{Att}(\Sigma \cup \{\sigma_1, \ldots, \sigma_{i-1}\})$, and otherwise $A \in \mathsf{Att}(\Sigma \cup \{\sigma_1, \ldots, \sigma_{i-1}\})$.*

We say that σ is provable from Σ, written $\Sigma \vdash \sigma$, if there is a deduction $(\sigma_1, \ldots, \sigma_n)$ from Σ with $\sigma = \sigma_n$ and such that no attributes in σ are new in $\sigma_1, \ldots, \sigma_n$.

We will also use the following rules that are derivable from [EE]:

ES **Equality Symmetry:**
$$\text{if } A = B, \text{ then } B = A.$$

ET **Equality Transitivity:**

$$\text{if } A = B \wedge B = C, \text{ then } A = C.$$

One may find the chase rules slightly convoluted at first sight. However, the ideas behind the rules are relatively simple as illustrated in the following examples.

Example 2 (Chase Start). Let $\sigma_0 := (\{t_0, t_1\}, \{u_0\})[RS]$ be as in Fig. 2, for $R := \{A, B, C\}$ and $S := \{x, y, z\}$. Then

$$\sigma_0 = \begin{array}{c|ccc|ccc}
 & A & B & C & x & y & z \\
\hline
t_0 & x & y & z & & & \\
t_1 & & x & y & & & \\
u_0 & & & & x & y & z \\
\end{array}
\qquad
\sigma_1 = \begin{array}{c|ccc}
 & A & B & C \\
\hline
t_0 & x & y & z \\
t_1 & & x & y \\
u_1 & z & & x \\
\end{array}
\qquad
\sigma_2 = \begin{array}{c|ccc}
 & A & B & C \\
\hline
t_0 & x & y & z \\
t_1 & & x & y \\
u_2 & z & & v \\
u_3 & v & & z \\
\end{array}$$

Fig. 2. Dependencies $\sigma_0, \sigma_1, \sigma_2$

$$\tau := \sigma_0 \wedge xyz \subseteq ABC \wedge xy \subseteq BC$$

is an instance of [CS]. Here x, y, z are interpreted either as values or as new attributes. By the latter we intuitively mean that any relation $r[ABC]$ can be extended to some $r'[ABCxyz]$ such that $r' \models \tau$. For instance, one can define $r' := q(r)$ where q is the following SPJR query

$$ABC \bowtie (\pi_{xyz}(\sigma_{xy=BC}(\rho_{xyz/ABC}(ABC) \bowtie ABC)))$$

where σ refers to (S)election, π to (P)rojection, $\bowtie$ to (J)oin, and ρ to (R)ename operator. Then $q(r)$ is a relation over RS such that its restriction to xyz lists all abc for which there exist $s, s' \in r$ such that $s(ABC) = abc$ and $s'(BC) = ab$. Let $\sigma_1 = (\{t_0, t_1\}, \{u_1\})[R]$ be as in Fig. 2. Now,

$$r \models \sigma_1 \Leftrightarrow q(r) \models zx \subseteq AC.$$

Hence proving $\Sigma \models \sigma_1$ reduces to showing that $\Sigma \cup \{\tau\} \models zx \subseteq AC$.

Example 3 (Chase Rule). Assume

$$\sigma_2 \wedge xyz \subseteq ABC \wedge xy \subseteq BC \tag{2}$$

where $\sigma_2 = (\{t_0, t_1\}, \{u_2, u_3\})[R]$ is as in Fig. 2, for $R := \{A, B, C\}$. Then, interpreting f as id, one can derive with one application of [CR]

$$zv \subseteq AC \wedge vz \subseteq AC \tag{3}$$

from (2). Note that in (3) v is interpreted as a *new* attribute, and the idea is that any relation $r[R]$ satisfying (2) and with $v \notin R$ can be extended to a relation $r'[R \cup \{v\}]$ satisfying (3) by introducing suitable values for v.

Example 4 (Chase Termination). Assume

$$\sigma_0 \wedge zx \subseteq AC \tag{4}$$

where $\sigma_0 = (\{t_0, t_1\}, \{u_0\})[RS]$ is as in Fig. 2, for $R := \{A, B, C\}$ and $S := \{x, y, z\}$. Then, letting $u = $ id, one can derive σ_1 as in Fig. 2 from (4) with one application of [CT].

4   Soundness Theorem

In this section we show that the axiomatization presented in the previous section is sound. First note that the next lemma follows from the definitions of egd's, tgd's and ind's.

Lemma 1. *Let σ be a dependency over R, and let r and r' be relations over supersets of R and with $r|_R = r'|_R$. Then $r \models \sigma \Leftrightarrow r' \models \sigma$.*

Then we prove the following lemma which implies soundness of the axioms. For attribute sets R, R' with $R \subseteq R'$ and a relation r over R, we say that a relation r' over R' is an extension of r to R' if $r'|_R = r$. Recall from Eq. 1 that exactly such extensions are used in the existential quantification of lax team semantics.

Lemma 2. *Let r be a relation over $\mathrm{Att}(\Sigma)$ such that $r \models \Sigma$, and let $(\sigma_1, \ldots, \sigma_n)$ be a deduction from Σ. Then there exists an extension r' of r to $\mathrm{Att}(\Sigma \cup \{\sigma_1, \ldots, \sigma_n\})$ such that $r' \models \Sigma \cup \{\sigma_1, \ldots, \sigma_n\}$.*

Proof. We prove the claim by induction on n. We denote by R_n the set $\mathrm{Att}(\Sigma \cup \{\sigma_1, \ldots, \sigma_n\})$. Assuming the claim for $n-1$, we first find an extension r_{n-1} of r to R_{n-1} such that $r_{n-1} \models \Sigma \cup \{\sigma_1, \ldots, \sigma_{n-1}\}$. If σ_n is obtained by an application of a conjunction or some ind rule, then it is easy to see that we may choose $r_n := r_{n-1}$. Hence, it suffices to consider the cases where σ_n is obtained by using one of the chase rules. Due to Lemma 1, it suffices to find an extension r_n of r_{n-1} to R_n such that $r_n \models \sigma_n$. In the following cases, $\boldsymbol{A}$ denotes a sequence listing the attributes of $R \subseteq R_{n-1}$.

Case [CS]. Assume that σ_n is obtained by [CS] and is of the form

$$(T^*, \mathrm{id})[RS] \wedge \bigwedge_{t \in T} t(A) \subseteq A$$

where $T = T^*|_R$, $S = \mathsf{Val}(T)$ consists of *new attributes* and R of *distinct values*. Let $r_n := r_{n-1} \bowtie r$ be an extension of r_{n-1} to $R_n = R_{n-1}S$, where

$$r := \{h : h \text{ is a valuation on } T \text{ such that } h(T) \subseteq r_{n-1}|_R\}.$$

We claim that $r_n \models \sigma_n$. Consider the first conjunct of σ_n, and let h be a valuation on T^* such that $h(T^*) \subseteq r_n|_{RS}$. Then $h|_S$ is is a valuation on T such that $h(T) \subseteq r_n|_R = r_{n-1}|_R$, i.e., $h|_S = t_0|_S$ for some $t_0 \in r_n$. Since R consists of *distinct values* and thus $R \cap \mathrm{Dom}(h) = \emptyset$, we may define h' as an extension of h with $A \mapsto t_0(A)$, for $A \in R$. Then $h'|_{RS} = t_0|_{RS} \in r_n|_{RS}$, and therefore $r_n \models (T^*, \mathrm{id})[RS]$.

Consider then $t(A) \subseteq A$, for $t \in T$, and let $t_0 \in r_n$. By the definition, $t_0|_S = h$ for some valuation h on T such that $h(T) \subseteq r_n|_R$, and hence we obtain that $t_0 \circ t(A) = h \circ t(A) = t_1(A)$ for some $t_1 \in r_n$. Therefore, $r_n \models t(A) \subseteq A$.

Case [CR]. Assume that σ_n is of the form (i) $\bigwedge_{t' \in T'} f \circ t'(A) \subseteq A$ or (ii) $f(x) = f(y)$, and is obtained by [CR] from

(i) $(T, T')[R] \wedge \bigwedge_{t \in T} f \circ t(A) \subseteq A$,
(ii) $(T, x = y)[R] \wedge \bigwedge_{t \in T} f \circ t(A) \subseteq A$,

where in case (ii) f is a valuation on $T \cup T'$ such that it is 1-1 on $S := \mathsf{Val}(T') \setminus \mathsf{Val}(T)$ and $f(x)$ is a *new attribute* for $x \in S$. Let $s \in r_{n-1}$. Since $r_{n-1} \models \bigwedge_{t \in T} f \circ t(A) \subseteq A$, we first obtain that $s \circ f(T) \subseteq r_{n-1}|_R$.

(i) Since $r_{n-1} \models (T, T')[R]$ we find a mapping $g : S \to \mathsf{Val}$ such that $h(T') \subseteq r_{n-1}|_R$, for $h = g \cup (s \circ f)$. Since f is 1-1 on S, we can now define r_n as the relation obtained from r_{n-1} by extending each $s \in r_{n-1}$ with $f(x) \mapsto g(x)$ for $x \in S$. Then for each $s \in r_n$, $s \circ f(T') \subseteq r_n|_R$, and hence we obtain that $r_n \models \bigwedge_{t' \in T'} f \circ t'(A) \subseteq A$.
(ii) It suffices to show that $r_{n-1} \models f(x) = f(y)$. Since $s \circ f(x) = s \circ f(y)$ by $r_{n-1} \models (T, x = y)[R]$, this follows immediately.

Case [CT]. Assume that σ_n is of the form (i) $(T, T')[R]$ or (ii) $(T, x = y)[R]$ and is obtained by [CT] from

(i) $(T^*, \mathrm{id})[RS] \wedge \bigwedge_{t' \in T'} u \circ t'(A) \subseteq A$, where u is a mapping $\mathsf{Val}(T') \to \mathsf{Att}$ that is the identity on $\mathsf{Val}(T) \cap \mathsf{Val}(T')$,
(ii) $(T^*, \mathrm{id})[RS] \wedge x = y$, where $x, y \in \mathsf{Val}(T)$.

Moreover, in both cases $T = T^*|_R$, $S = \mathsf{Val}(T)$, and $\mathsf{Val}(T^*|_S)$ consists of *distinct values*. It suffices to show that $r_{n-1} \models \sigma_n$, so let h be a valuation on T such that $h(T) \subseteq r_{n-1}|_R$. Since $\mathsf{Val}(T^*|_S)$ consists of disctinct values, h can be extended to a valuation h' on T^* such that $h'(T^*) \subseteq r_{n-1}|_{RS}$. Since $r_{n-1} \models (T^*, \mathrm{id})[RS]$, there is an extension h'' of h' to attributes in R such that $h''|_{RS} \in r_{n-1}|_{RS}$. Hence, we obtain that $h|_S \in r_{n-1}|_S$. Let then $s \in r_{n-1}$ be such that it agrees with h on S.

(i) Since $r_{n-1} \models \bigwedge_{t' \in T'} u \circ t'(A) \subseteq A$, we obtain that $s \circ u(T') \subseteq r_{n-1}|_R$. Moreover, we notice that $s \circ u = h$ on $\mathsf{Val}(T) \cap \mathsf{Val}(T')$.

(ii) Since $r_{n-1} \models x = y$, we obtain that $s(x) = s(y)$. Then $h(x) = h(y)$ since $x, y \in S$.

Hence, in both cases we obtain that $r_{n-1} \models \sigma_n$. This concludes the [CT] case and the proof. □

Using the previous lemma, soundness of the rules follows.

Theorem 1. *Let $\Sigma \cup \{\sigma\}$ be a finite set of egd's and tgd's over R. Then $\Sigma \models \sigma$ if $\Sigma \vdash \sigma$.*

Proof. Let r be a relation such that $r \models \Sigma$, and assume that $(\sigma_1, \ldots, \sigma_n)$ is a deduction from Σ where $\sigma = \sigma_n$ contains no attributes that appear as new in $\sigma_1, \ldots, \sigma_n$. If $R' := \mathsf{Att}(\Sigma \cup \{\sigma_1, \ldots, \sigma_n\})$, then by Lemma 2 we find an extension r' of $r|_R$ to R' such that $r' \models \sigma$. Then using Lemma 1 we obtain that $r \models \sigma$. □

5 Chase Revisited

In this section we define the chase for the class of egd's and tgd's. The chase algorithm was generalized to typed egd's and tgd's in [3], and here we present the chase using notation similar to that in [16]. First let us assume, for notational convenience, that there is a total, well-founded order $<$ on the set Val, e.g., $x_1 < x_2 < x_3 < \ldots$ for $\mathsf{Val} = \{x_1, x_2, x_3, \ldots\}$. Let $\Sigma \cup \{\sigma\}$ be a set of egd's and tgd's over R. A *chasing sequence* of σ over Σ is a (possibly infinite) sequence $\sigma_0, \sigma_1, \ldots, \sigma_n, \ldots$ where $\sigma_0 = \sigma$, and σ_{n+1} is obtained from σ_n, with $T := \mathrm{pr}_1(\sigma_n)$, according to either of the following rules.

Let $\tau \in \Sigma$ be of the form $(S, x = y)$, and suppose that there is a valuation f on S such that $f(S) \subseteq T$ but $f(x) \neq f(y)$. Then τ (and f) can be applied to σ_n as follows:

- **egd rule:** Let $\sigma_{n+1} := g(\sigma_n)$ where $g : \mathsf{Val} \to \mathsf{Val}$ is the identity everywhere except that it maps $f(y)$ to $f(x)$ if $f(x) < f(y)$, and $f(x)$ to $f(y)$ if $f(y) < f(x)$.

Let $\tau \in \Sigma$ be of the form (S, S'), and suppose that there is a valuation f on S such that $f(S) \subseteq T$, but there exists no extension f' of f to S' such that $f(S') \subseteq T$. Then τ can be applied to σ_n as follows:

- **tgd rule:** List all $f_1, \ldots, f_n$ that have the above property, and for each f_i choose a *distinct extension* to S', i.e., an extension f_i' to S' such that each variable in $\mathsf{Val}(S') \setminus \mathsf{Val}(S)$ is assigned a distinct new value greater than any value in $\mathsf{Val}(\sigma_0) \cup \ldots \cup \mathsf{Val}(\sigma_n)$. Moreover, no new value is assigned by two f_i', f_j' where $i \neq j$. Then we let $\sigma_{n+1} : (T \cup f_1'(S') \cup \ldots \cup f_m'(S'), \mathrm{pr}_2(\sigma_n))$.

Construction of a chasing sequence is restricted with the following two conditions:

(i) Whenever an egd is applied, it is applied repeatedly until it is no longer applicable.
(ii) No dependency is starved, i.e., each dependency that is applicable infinitely many times is applied infinitely many times.

Let $\overline{(\Sigma, \sigma)} = \sigma_0, \sigma_1, \ldots$ be a chasing sequence of σ over Σ. Due to the possibility of applying egd's, a chasing sequence may not be monotone with respect to $\subseteq$. Hence, depending on whether σ is a tgd or an egd, we define

- egd: $\mathrm{chase}\overline{(\Sigma, \sigma)} := (T^1, x = y)$,
- tgd: $\mathrm{chase}\overline{(\Sigma, \sigma)} := (T^1, T^2)$,

where $T^i := \{u : \exists m \forall n \geq m (u \in \mathrm{pr}_i(\sigma_n))\}$ and $x = y$ is $\mathrm{pr}_2(\sigma_n)$ for $n \in \mathbb{N}$ such that $\mathrm{pr}_2(\sigma_n) = \mathrm{pr}_2(\sigma_m)$ for all $m \geq n$. Note that "newer" values introduced by the tgd rule are always greater than the "older" ones, and values may only be replaced with smaller ones. Hence, no value can change infinitely often, and therefore $\mathrm{chase}\overline{(\Sigma, \sigma)}$ is always well defined and non-empty.

We also associate each chasing sequence with the following descending valuations ρ_n, for $n \geq 0$. We let $\rho_0 = \mathrm{id}$, $\rho_{n+1} = g \circ \rho_n$ if σ_{n+1} is obtained by an application of the egd rule where $\sigma_{n+1} = g(\sigma_n)$, and $\rho_{n+1} = \mathrm{id} \circ \rho_n$ otherwise. We then define $\rho(x) = \lim_{n \to \infty} \rho_n(x)$, i.e., $\rho(x) = \rho_n(x)$ if $n \in \mathbb{N}$ such that $\rho_m(x) = \rho_n(x)$ for all $m \geq n$. Then we obtain that

$$\mathrm{chase}\overline{(\Sigma, \sigma)} = \bigcup_{n=0}^{\infty} \rho(\sigma_n).$$

A dependency τ is *trivial* if

- τ is of the form $(T, x = x)$, or
- τ is of the form (T, T') and there is a valuation f on T' such that f is the identity on $\mathrm{Val}(T) \cap \mathrm{Val}(T')$ and $f(T') \subseteq T$.

It is well-known that the chase algorithm captures unrestricted implication of dependencies. For the proof of the following proposition, see Appendix of the arXiv version of the paper [17].

Proposition 1. *Let $\Sigma \cup \{\sigma\}$ be a set of egd's and tgd's over R. Then the following are equivalent:*

(i) $\Sigma \models \sigma$,
(ii) there is a chasing sequence $\overline{(\Sigma, \sigma)} = \sigma_0, \sigma_1, \ldots$ of σ over Σ such that $\mathrm{chase}\overline{(\Sigma, \sigma)}$ is trivial,
(iii) there is a chasing sequence $\overline{(\Sigma, \sigma)} = \sigma_0, \sigma_1, \ldots$ of σ over Σ such that σ_n is trivial, for some n.

6   Completeness Theorem

In this section we show that the rules presented in Definition 4 are complete for the implication problem of embedded dependencies. Let us first illustrate the use of the axioms in the following simple example.

Example 5. Consider the implication problem $\{\sigma, \sigma'\} \models \tau$ where σ, σ', τ are illustrated in Fig. 3, e.g., $\sigma = (T, t)$ where T consists of the top two rows of σ and t is the bottom row. Note that σ and τ are embedded multivalued dependencies of the form $A \twoheadrightarrow B|C$ and $A \twoheadrightarrow B|CD$, respectively, and σ' is a functional dependency of the form $C \rightarrow D$. It is easy to see that the implication holds, and this can be also verified by a chasing sequence τ_0, τ_1, τ_2 of τ over $\{\sigma, \sigma'\}$ where τ_2 is trivial (Fig. 4). In the chasing sequence, $\tau_0 = \tau$ and τ_1 is the result of applying σ to τ_0. For this, note that there exists two valuations on T that embed T to $\mathrm{pr}_1(\tau_0)$ but has no extension that embeds t into $\mathrm{pr}_1(\tau_0)$. These valuations are the identity and the function f that swaps the values of the top and bottom row of T. Then τ_1 is obtained by adding to $\mathrm{pr}_1(\tau_0)$ $\mathrm{id}^*(t)$ and $f^*(t)$ where id^* and f^* are distinct extensions of id and f to t, e.g., $\mathrm{id}^* = \mathrm{id}$ also on d_2 and f^* maps d_2 to d_3. Also, τ_2 is the result of applying σ' to τ_1 two times, i.e., τ_2 is obtained from τ_1 by replacing d_3 with d_0 and d_2 with d_1. Clearly τ_2 is trivial, and hence we obtain the claim by Proposition 1.

$$\sigma = \begin{array}{|cccc|} A & B & C & D \\ \hline a_0 & b_0 & c_0 & d_0 \\ a_0 & b_1 & c_1 & d_1 \\ \hline a_0 & b_0 & c_1 & d_2 \end{array} \qquad \sigma' = \begin{array}{|cccc|} A & B & C & D \\ \hline a_0 & b_0 & c_0 & d_0 \\ a_1 & b_1 & c_0 & d_1 \\ \hline d_0 & = & d_1 \end{array} \qquad \tau = \begin{array}{|cccc|} A & B & C & D \\ \hline a_0 & b_0 & c_0 & d_0 \\ a_0 & b_1 & c_1 & d_1 \\ \hline a_0 & b_0 & c_1 & d_1 \end{array}$$

Fig. 3. Dependencies σ, σ', τ

This procedure can now be simulated with our axioms as follows. First, with one application of [CS] we derive

$$(T, \mathrm{id})[RS] \wedge a_0 b_0 c_0 d_0 \subseteq ABCD \wedge a_0 b_1 c_1 d_1 \subseteq ABCD$$

where $T = \{t, t'\}$, $R = \{A, B, C, D\}$, and $S = \{a_0, b_0, b_1, c_0, c_1, d_0, d_1\}$ is a set of values that are interpreted as new attributes. Here $t(x)$ and $t'(x)$, for $x \in S$,

$$\tau_0 = \begin{array}{|cccc|} A & B & C & D \\ \hline a_0 & b_0 & c_0 & d_0 \\ a_0 & b_1 & c_1 & d_1 \\ \hline a_0 & b_0 & c_1 & d_1 \end{array} \qquad \tau_1 = \begin{array}{|cccc|} A & B & C & D \\ \hline a_0 & b_0 & c_0 & d_0 \\ a_0 & b_1 & c_1 & d_1 \\ \hline a_0 & b_0 & c_1 & d_2 \\ a_0 & b_1 & c_0 & d_3 \\ \hline a_0 & b_0 & c_1 & d_1 \end{array} \qquad \tau_2 = \begin{array}{|cccc|} A & B & C & D \\ \hline a_0 & b_0 & c_0 & d_0 \\ a_0 & b_1 & c_1 & d_1 \\ \hline a_0 & b_0 & c_1 & d_1 \\ a_0 & b_1 & c_0 & d_0 \\ \hline a_0 & b_0 & c_1 & d_1 \end{array}$$

Fig. 4. Chasing sequence τ_0, τ_1, τ_2

	A	B	C	D	a_0	b_0	b_1	c_0	c_1	d_0	d_1
t	a_0	b_0	c_0	d_0							
t'	a_0	b_1	c_1	d_1							
id					a_0	b_0	b_1	c_0	c_1	d_0	d_1

Fig. 5. $(T, \mathrm{id})[RS]$

and A, B, C, D are interpreted as distinct values. $(T, t)[RS]$ is illustrated in Fig. 5 where all the distinct values are hidden. Now with one application of [CR], letting $f = \mathrm{id}$, we derive $a_0 b_0 c_1 d_2 \subseteq ABCD$ from

$$\sigma \wedge a_0 b_0 c_0 d_0 \subseteq ABCD \wedge a_0 b_1 c_1 d_1 \subseteq ABCD \tag{5}$$

Note that in this step, d_2 is interpreted as a new attribute. Let then f be the valuation that is the identity on a_0, b_0, b_1, d_1, and otherwise maps $a_1 \mapsto a_0$, $c_0 \mapsto c_1$, and $d_0 \mapsto d_2$. We notice that $f(a_0 b_0 c_0 d_0) = a_0 b_0 c_1 d_2$ and $f(a_1 b_1 c_0 d_1) = a_0 b_1 c_1 d_1$. Hence, we may derive with one application of [CR] $f(d_0) = f(d_1)$, i.e., $d_2 = d_1$ from

$$\sigma' \wedge f(a_0 b_0 c_0 d_0) \subseteq ABCD \wedge f(a_1 b_1 c_0 d_1) \subseteq ABCD.$$

Then we apply [EE] and derive $a_0 b_0 c_1 d_1 \subseteq ABCD$ from

$$d_2 = d_1 \wedge a_0 b_0 c_1 d_2 \subseteq ABCD$$

Finally, we may apply [CT] and derive τ from $(T, \mathrm{id})[RS] \wedge a_0 b_0 c_1 d_1 \subseteq ABCD$.

The following lemma shows that the above technique extends to all chasing sequences. The proof is straightforward and hence omitted here (see Appendix of the arXiv version of the paper [17]).

Lemma 3. Let $\overline{(\Sigma, \sigma)} = \sigma_0, \sigma_1, \ldots$ be a chasing sequence of σ over Σ, where $\Sigma \cup \{\sigma\}$ is a finite set of egd's and tgd's over R, let $\boldsymbol{A}$ be a sequence listing the attributes of R, let $T := \mathrm{pr}_1(\sigma)$ and $T_i := \mathrm{pr}_1(\sigma_i)$, and let $n \in \mathbb{N}$. Then there exists a deduction from Σ, with attributes from $R \cup \bigcup_{i \in \mathbb{N}} \mathsf{Val}(T_i)$, listing the following dependencies:

(i) $(T^*, \mathrm{id})[RS]$ where $T^*|_R = T$, $S = \mathsf{Val}(T)$, and $T^*|_S$ consists of distinct values,
(ii) $f(x) = f(y)$, for each application of $(S, x = y)$ and f to σ_m, for $m < n$,
(iii) $t(\boldsymbol{A}) \subseteq \boldsymbol{A}$, for $t \in T_m$ where $m \leq n$.

With the lemma, we can now show completeness.

Theorem 2. Let $\Sigma \cup \{\sigma\}$ be a finite set of egd's and tgd's over R. Then $\Sigma \models \sigma \Leftrightarrow \Sigma \vdash \sigma$.

Proof. Assume that $\Sigma \models \sigma$, and let $\boldsymbol{A}$ be a sequence listing R. Then by Proposition 1 there is a chasing sequence $\overline{(\Sigma, \sigma)} = \sigma_0, \sigma_1, \ldots$ of σ over Σ such that σ_n is trivial for some n. Let $D = (\tau_1, \ldots, \tau_l)$ be a deduction from Σ obtained by Lemma 3, and let $T := \mathrm{pr}_1(\sigma)$ and $T_i := \mathrm{pr}_1(\sigma_i)$.

Assume first that σ is an egd of the form $(T, x = y)$. Then σ_n is $(T_n, z = z)$ where $z = \rho_n(x) = \rho_n(y)$. Now, either $\rho_{i+1}(x)$ is $\rho_i(x)$, or the equality $\rho_{i+1}(x) = \rho_i(x)$ (or its reverse) is listed in D by item (ii). Hence, using repeatedly [ES,ET] we may further on derive $z = x$. Since $z = y$ is derivable analogously, we therefore obtain $x = y$ by [ES,ET]. Then with one application of [CT], we derive $(T, x = y)$ from $(T^*, \mathrm{id})[RS] \wedge x = y$ where $T^*|_R = T$. Note that the $(T^*, \mathrm{id})[RS]$ of the correct form is listed in D by item (i) of Lemma 3.

Assume then that σ is a tgd of the form (T, T'), and let $T_i' := \mathrm{pr}_2(\sigma_i)$. Then σ_n is (T_n, T_n'), and there is a valuation f on T_n' such that f is the identity on $\mathsf{Val}(T_n) \cap \mathsf{Val}(T_n')$ and $f(T_n') \subseteq T_n$. Let $t' \in T'$. Then $\rho_n \circ t' \in T_n'$ and by item (iii) of Lemma 3 we obtain that $f \circ \rho_n \circ t'(\boldsymbol{A}) \subseteq \boldsymbol{A}$ is listed in D. For $A \in R$, we have then two cases :

- If $t'(A) \in \mathsf{Val}(T') \cap \mathsf{Val}(T)$, then we first notice that $f \circ \rho_n \circ t'(A)$ is $\rho_n \circ t'(A)$ since $\rho_n \circ t'(A) \in \mathsf{Val}(T_n') \cap \mathsf{Val}(T_n)$. Also we notice that the equality $\rho_n \circ t'(A) = t'(A)$ can be derived analogously to the egd case.
- If $t'(A) \in \mathsf{Val}(T') \setminus \mathsf{Val}(T)$, then $f \circ \rho_n \circ t'(A) = f \circ t'(A)$ since by the definition of the chase ρ_n is the identity on $\mathsf{Val}(T') \setminus \mathsf{Val}(T)$.

Now, letting f^* be the mapping $\mathsf{Val}(T') \to \mathsf{Att}$ which is the identity on $\mathsf{Val}(T') \cap \mathsf{Val}(T)$ and agrees with f on $\mathsf{Val}(T') \setminus \mathsf{Val}(T)$, we can by the previous reasoning and using repeatedly [EE] derive $f^* \circ t'(\boldsymbol{A}) \subseteq \boldsymbol{A}$ from $f \circ \rho_n \circ t'(\boldsymbol{A}) \subseteq \boldsymbol{A}$. Finally, we can then with one application of [CT] derive (T, T') from

$$(T^*, \mathrm{id})[RS] \wedge \bigwedge_{t' \in T'} f^* \circ t'(\boldsymbol{A}) \subseteq \boldsymbol{A}.$$

$\square$

7   Typed Dependencies

Consider then the class of typed embedded dependencies. In this setting [CS] and [CT] can be replaced with rules that involve only embedded join dependencies (ejd's) and inclusion dependencies. We define ejd's over tuples of attributes as follows.

Definition 6. *Let* $\boldsymbol{A}_1, \ldots, \boldsymbol{A}_n$ *be tuples of attributes listing* $R_1, \ldots, R_n$, *respectively, and let* $R := \bigcup_{i=1}^n R_i$. *Then* $\bowtie (\boldsymbol{A}_i)_{i=1}^n$ *is an* embedded join dependency *with the semantic rule*

- $r \models \bowtie (\boldsymbol{A}_i)_{i=1}^n$ *if and only if* $r|_R = r|_{R_1} \bowtie \ldots \bowtie r|_{R_n}$.

The two alternative rules for the chase are now the following. We call a relation typed if none of its values appears in two distinct columns.

CS* Chase Start*:

$$\bigwedge_{t\in T} A \subseteq t(A) \wedge \bowtie (t(A))_{t\in T} \wedge \bigwedge_{t\in T} t(A) \subseteq A$$

where T is a typed relation and $\mathsf{Val}(T)$ is a set of *new attributes*.

CT* Chase Termination*:

$$tgd : \text{if } \bigwedge_{t\in T} A \subseteq t(A) \wedge \bowtie (t(A))_{t\in T} \wedge \bigwedge_{t'\in T'} u \circ t'(A) \subseteq A, \text{ then } (T,T')[R],$$

$$egd : \text{if } \bigwedge_{t\in T} A \subseteq t(A) \wedge \bowtie (t(A))_{t\in T} \wedge x = y, \text{ then } (T, x = y)[R],$$

where tgd: u is a mapping $\mathsf{Val}(T') \to \mathsf{Att}$ that is the identity on $\mathsf{Val}(T') \cap \mathsf{Val}(T')$, and egd: $x, y \in \mathsf{Val}(T)$.

The first rule is sound for typed dependencies since, for arbitrary r with $\mathsf{Dom}(r) \cap \mathsf{Val}(T) = \emptyset$, an instance of [CS*] is satisfied by $r \bowtie q(r)$ where q is the SPJR query

$$\rho_{t_1(A)/A} A \bowtie \ldots \bowtie \rho_{t_n(A)/A} A,$$

where ρ is the rename operator and $T = \{t_1, \ldots, t_n\}$. However, a counter example for soundness can be easily constructed for untyped dependencies. If T and r are the relations illustrated in Fig. 6, then no extension r' of r to $\mathsf{Val}(T)$ satisfies $\bigwedge_{t\in T} t(AB) \subseteq AB$.

$$T = \begin{array}{c|cc} & A & B \\ \hline t & x & y \\ t' & y & x \end{array} \qquad r = \begin{array}{c|cc} & A & B \\ \hline s & 0 & 1 \end{array}$$

Fig. 6. Relations T and r

Soundness of [CT*] is obtained analogously to that of [CT]. Also, completeness is obtained by deriving exactly in the same way as in the general case, $\bigwedge_{t'\in T'} u \circ t'(A) \subseteq A$ (in the tgd case) or $x = y$ (in the egd case) from $\bigwedge_{t\in T} t(A) \subseteq A$. Let us then write $\Sigma \vdash^* \sigma$ if σ is deduced from Σ in the sense of Definition 5 and using rules [EE,CS*,CR,CT*] together with elimination and introduction of conjunction. Then we obtain the following theorem.

Theorem 3. *Let $\Sigma \cup \{\sigma\}$ be a finite set of typed egd's and tgd's over R. Then $\Sigma \models \sigma \Leftrightarrow \Sigma \vdash^* \sigma$.*

Acknowledgement. The author was supported by grant 264917 of the Academy of Finland.

References

1. Aho, A.V., Beeri, C., Ullman, J.D.: The theory of joins in relational databases. ACM Trans. Database Syst. **4**(3), 297–314 (1979)
2. Maier, D., Mendelzon, A.O., Sagiv, Y.: Testing implications of data dependencies. ACM Trans. Database Syst. **4**, 455–469 (1979)
3. Beeri, C., Vardi, M.Y.: A proof procedure for data dependencies. J. ACM **31**(4), 718–741 (1984)
4. Chandra, A.K., Vardi, M.Y.: The implication problem for functional and inclusion dependencies is undecidable. SIAM J. Comput. **14**(3), 671–677 (1985)
5. Mitchell, J.C.: The implication problem for functional and inclusion dependencies. Inf. Control **56**(3), 154–173 (1983)
6. Thalheim, B.: Dependencies in Relational Databases. Teubner-Texte zur Mathematik. Springer, New York (1991)
7. Mitchell, J.C.: Inference rules for functional and inclusion dependencies. In: Fagin, R., Bernstein, P.A. (eds.) (PODS), pp. 58–69. ACM (1983)
8. Hodges, W.: Compositional semantics for a language of imperfect information. J. Interest Group Pure Appl. Logics **5**(4), 539–563 (1997)
9. Galliani, P.: Inclusion and exclusion dependencies in team semantics: On some logics of imperfect information. Ann. Pure Appl. Log. **163**(1), 68–84 (2012)
10. Väänänen, J.: Dependence Logic. Cambridge University Press, Cambridge (2007)
11. Galliani, P., Hella, L.: Inclusion Logic and Fixed Point Logic. In: Rocca, S.R.D. (ed.) Computer Science Logic 2013 (CSL 2013). Leibniz International Proceedings in Informatics (LIPIcs), vol. 23, pp. 281–295. Dagstuhl, Germany, Schloss Dagstuhl-Leibniz-Zentrum fuer Informatik (2013)
12. Immerman, N.: Relational queries computable in polynomial time. Inf. Control **68**(1), 86–104 (1986)
13. Vardi, M.Y.: The complexity of relational query languages. In: Proceedings of the Fourteenth Annual ACM Symposium on Theory of Computing, pp. 137–146. ACM (1982)
14. Hannula, M., Kontinen, J.: A finite axiomatization of conditional independence and inclusion dependencies. In: Beierle, C., Meghini, C. (eds.) FoIKS 2014. LNCS, vol. 8367, pp. 211–229. Springer, Heidelberg (2014)
15. Yannakakis, M., Papadimitriou, C.H.: Algebraic dependencies. J. Comput. Syst. Sci. **25**(1), 2–41 (1982)
16. Abiteboul, S., Hull, R., Vianu, V.: Foundations of Databases. Addison Wesley, Reading (1995)
17. Hannula, M.: Reasoning about embedded dependencies using inclusion dependencies. CoRR abs/1507.00655 (2015)

Cobra: A Tool for Solving General Deductive Games

Miroslav Klimoš and Antonín Kučera$^{(\boxtimes)}$

Faculty of Informatics, Masaryk University, Brno, Czech Republic
klimos@mail.muni.cz, kucera@fi.muni.cz

Abstract. We propose a general framework for modelling and solving *deductive games*, where one player selects a secret code and the other player strives to discover this code using a minimal number of allowed experiments that reveal some partial information about the code. The framework is implemented in a software tool COBRA, and its functionality is demonstrated by producing new results about existing deductive games.

1 Introduction

Deductive games (also known as *codebreaking games*) are played by two players, the *codemaker* and the *codebreaker*, where the codemaker selects a secret code from a given finite set, and the codebreaker strives to reveal the code through a series of *experiments* whose outcomes give some partial information about the code. A codebreaker's *strategy* is a recipe how to assemble the next experiment depending on the outcomes of the previous experiments so that the code is eventually discovered. The efficiency of a given strategy is measured either by the maximal number of experiments required to discover the code in the worst case, or by the expected number of experiments required to discover the code assuming the uniform probability distribution over the secret codes. Although various special types of deductive games have been deeply analyzed at both theoretical and experimental level (see below), to the best of authors' knowledge there is *no* software tool which inputs a description of a deductive game (written in a suitable high-level language) and then computes optimal strategies automatically. In this paper, we present a software tool COBRA (COde-BReaking game Analyser [1]) which achieves this functionality. Despite its versatility, COBRA can fully analyze non-trivial deductive games where the number of admissible experiments is very large (10^{64} or even more). Note that one cannot even *enumerate* all of these experiments in reasonable time, and COBRA implements advanced methods for identifying and bypassing families of experiments that are equivalent to already considered ones (up to some symmetry) without considering them explicitly. This is perhaps the most advanced part of COBRA's design which is based on nontrivial concepts and observations (see Sect. 2). Using COBRA, we were able to produce results about some standard deductive games that were not known before (see Sect. 3).

A. Kučera— Supported by the Czech Science Foundation, grant No. 15-17564S.

M. Davis et al. (Eds.): LPAR-20 2015, LNCS 9450, pp. 31–47, 2015.
DOI: 10.1007/978-3-662-48899-7_3

Existing Works. Simple examples of well-studied deductive games include various board games and puzzles such as *Mastermind* and the *counterfeit coin problem (CCP)*, which are also used as running examples in this paper. In Mastermind, the codemaker chooses a secret sequence of n code pegs of c colors (repetitions allowed). The codebreaker tries to reveal the code by making guesses (experiments) which are evaluated by a certain number of black and white markers. A black marker is received for each code peg from the guess which is correct in both color and position. A white marker indicates the existence of a correct color code peg placed in the wrong position. For the classical variant with four pegs and six colors, Knuth [17] demonstrated a strategy that requires five guesses in the worst case and 4.478 guesses on average. Later, Irving [14], Neuwirth [20], and Koyama and Lai [19] presented strategies which improve the expected number of guesses to 4.369, 4.364, and 4.34, respectively (the bound 4.34 is already optimal). More recently, strategies for Mastermind were constructed semi-automatically by using evolutionary algorithms [2], simulated annealing [4], genetic algorithms (see, e.g., [3] and the references therein), or clustering techniques [7].

In the basic variant of the *counterfeit coin problem (CCP)*, one is given N coins, all identical in appearance, and all identical in weight except for one, which is either heavier or lighter than the remaining $N - 1$ coins. The goal is to devise a procedure to identify the counterfeit coin using a minimal number of weighings with a balance. This basic variant was considered by Dyson [8] who proved that CCP can be solved with w weighings (experiments) iff $3 \leq N \leq (3^w - 3)/2$. There are numerous modifications and generalizations of the basic variant (higher number of counterfeit coins, additional regular coins, multi-pan balance scale, parallel weighing, etc.) which are harder to analyze and in some cases only partial results exist. We refer to [13] for an overview.

Deductive games can also model certain types of attacks in modern security systems based on *information leakage*, where an unauthorized attacker reveals a part of secret information in some unexpected way. For example, in ATM networks, hardware security modules (HSMs) are used to perform sensitive cryptographic operations such as checking a PIN entered by a customer. These HSMs are controlled by a strictly defined API to enforce security. *API-level attacks* are sequences of unanticipated API calls aiming to determine the PIN value; after each call, a piece of information about the PIN value is leaked, and the whole sequence collects enough data to reconstruct the PIN. One such attack, described in [6,21], can be modeled as a deductive game similar to Mastermind. Clearly, the problem of synthesizing an optimal codebreaker's strategy is highly interesting in this context.

Other examples of deductive games include *string matching games*, where the secret code is a sequence of letters and the codebreaker repeatedly tries to guess the string. Each guess is evaluated by revealing the total number of matching letters. This game was studied already by Erdös and Rényi [10] who gave some asymptotic results about the worst-case number of guesses. Recently, this game found an application in genetics for selecting a subset of genotyped individuals for phenotyping [11,12].

Due to space constraints, some proofs and tables describing the outcomes of experimental results achieved by COBRA are omitted. These can be found in [16].

2   Cobra: The Underlying Principles

Given a finite or countable set A, the set of all propositional formulae over A is denoted by FORM(A). Apart of standard Boolean connectives, we also use the operator EXACTLY$_i$, where $i \in \mathbb{N}$, such that EXACTLY$_i(\varphi_1, \ldots, \varphi_m)$ is true iff exactly i of the formulae $\varphi_1, \ldots, \varphi_m$ are true. For technical convenience, we assume that *all* Boolean connectives used in formulae of FORM(A) are commutative. That is, we allow for $\neg, \wedge, \vee,$ EXACTLY$_i, \ldots$, but we forbid implication which must be expressed using the allowed operators. For a given formula $\varphi \in$ FORM(A), we use $Val(\varphi)$ to denote the set of all valuations of A satisfying φ. We write $\varphi \approx \psi$ and $\varphi \equiv \psi$ to denote that φ and ψ are semantically and syntactically equivalent, respectively, and we extend this notation also to sets of formulae. Hence, if Φ, Ψ are sets of formulae, then $\Phi \approx \Psi$ and $\Phi \equiv \Psi$ means that the two sets are the same up to the respective equivalence. The syntactic equivalence $\equiv$ is considered modulo basic identities such as commutativity or associativity.

Our formal model of deductive games is based on propositional logic. Informally, a deductive game is given by

- a finite set X of propositional variables and a propositional formula φ_0 over X such that every secret code c can be represented by a unique valuation v_c of X, and for every valuation v of X we have that $v(\varphi_0) = true$ iff $v = v_c$ for some secret code c;
- a finite set of allowed experiments T.

To model CCP with N coins, we put $X = \{x_1, \ldots, x_N, y\}$, and we represent a secret code c where the i-th coin is heavier by a valuation v_c where $v_c(x_i) = true$, $v_c(x_j) = false$ for all $j \neq i$, and $v_c(y) = true$ (i.e., y is set to *true* iff the different coin is heavier). The formula φ_0 says that precisely one of the variables $x_1, \ldots, x_N$ is set to *true*. In Mastermind with n pegs and m colors, the set X contains variables $x_{i,j}$ for all $1 \leq i \leq n$ and $1 \leq j \leq m$; the variable $x_{i,j}$ is set to *true* iff the i-th peg has color j. The formula φ_0 says that each peg has precisely one color.

Typically, the number of possible experiments is large but many of them differ only in the concrete choice of participating objects. For example, in CCP with 6 coins there are essentially three types of experiments (we can weight either $1+1$, $2+2$, or $3+3$ coins) which are instantiated by a concrete selection of coins. In Mastermind, we perform essentially only one type of experiment (a guess) which is instantiated by a concrete tuple of colors. In general, we use a finite set Σ of *parameters* to represent the objects (such as coins and colors) participating in experiments. A *parameterized experiment* $t \in T$ is a triple (k, P, Φ) where k is the number of parameters, $P \subseteq \Sigma^k$ is the set of admissible instances, and Φ are possible outcomes given as *abstract propositional formulae* (see below).

Definition 1. *A deductive game* is a tuple $\mathcal{G} = (X, \varphi_0, \Sigma, F, T)$, *where* X *is a finite set of (propositional) variables,* $\varphi_0 \in \text{FORM}(X)$ *is a satisfiable initial constraint,* Σ *is a finite set of* parameters, *and*

- $F \subseteq X^\Sigma$ *is a set of* attributes *such that for all* $f, f' \in F$ *where* $f \neq f'$ *we have that the images of* f *and* f' *are disjoint,*
- T *is a finite set of* parameterized experiments *of the form* (k, P, Φ) *where* $k \in \mathbb{N}$ *is the number of parameters,* $P \subseteq \Sigma^k$ *is a set of* instances, *and* Φ *is a finite subset of* $\text{FORM}(X \cup \{f(\$j) \mid f \in F, 1 \leq j \leq k\})$. *The elements of* Φ *are called* outcomes.

The intuition behind X, φ_0, and Σ is explained above. Each attribute $f \in F$ corresponds to some "property" that every object $a \in \Sigma$ either does or does not satisfy, and $f(a)$ is the propositional variable of X which encodes the f-property of a. In CCP with N coins, the objects are the coins (i.e., $\Sigma = \{coin_i \mid 1 \leq i \leq N\}$), and for each coin we need to encode the property of "being different". So, there is just one attribute d which maps $coin_i$ to x_i for all $1 \leq i \leq N$. In Mastermind with n pegs and m colors, each object (color) has the property of "being the color of peg i", where $i \in \{1, \ldots, n\}$. Hence, there are n attributes $peg_1, \ldots, peg_n$ where $peg_i(color_j) = x_{i,j}$.

Now consider a parameterized experiment $t = (k, P, \Phi)$. An *instance* of t is a k-tuple $\boldsymbol{p} \in P \subseteq \Sigma^k$ of parameters. For every instance $\boldsymbol{p} \in P$ and every outcome $\psi \in \Phi$, we define the $\boldsymbol{p}$-*instance of* ψ as the formula $\psi(\boldsymbol{p}) \in \text{FORM}(X)$ obtained from ψ by substituting each atom $f(\$j)$ with the variable $f(\boldsymbol{p}_j)$. Hence, $f(\$j)$ denotes the variable which encodes the f-attribute of $\boldsymbol{p}_j$. In the rest of this paper, we typically use φ, ψ to range over outcomes, and ξ, χ to range over their instances. We also use E to denote the set of all *experiment instances* (or just *experiments*) defined by $E = \{(t, \boldsymbol{p}) \mid t \in T, \boldsymbol{p} \text{ is an instance of } t\}$. Further, for every experiment $e = (t, \boldsymbol{p})$, we use $\Phi(e)$ to denote the set of $\boldsymbol{p}$-instances of all outcomes of t. An *evaluated experiment* is a pair (e, ξ), where $\xi \in \Phi(e)$. The set of all evaluated experiments is denoted by Ω.

Example 2. CCP with four coins can be modeled as a game $\mathcal{G} = (X, \varphi_0, \Sigma, F, T)$ where $X = \{x_1, x_2, x_3, x_4, y\}$, $\varphi_0 = \text{EXACTLY}_1(x_1, x_2, x_3, x_4)$, $\Sigma = \{coin_1, coin_2, coin_3, coin_4\}$, $F = \{d\}$ where $d(coin_i) = x_i$ for every $1 \leq i \leq 4$, and $T = \{t_1, t_2\}$ where $t_1 = (2, \Sigma^{\langle 2 \rangle}, \{\varphi_<, \varphi_=, \varphi_>\})$, $t_2 = (4, \Sigma^{\langle 4 \rangle}, \{\psi_<, \psi_=, \psi_>\})$, and

$$\varphi_< = (d(\$1) \wedge \neg y) \vee (d(\$2) \wedge y)$$
$$\varphi_= = \neg d(\$1) \wedge \neg d(\$2)$$
$$\varphi_> = (d(\$1) \wedge y) \vee (d(\$2) \wedge \neg y)$$
$$\psi_< = ((d(\$1) \vee d(\$2)) \wedge \neg y) \vee ((d(\$3) \vee d(\$4)) \wedge y)$$
$$\psi_= = \neg d(\$1) \wedge \neg d(\$2) \wedge \neg d(\$3) \wedge \neg d(\$4)$$
$$\psi_> = ((d(\$1) \vee d(\$2)) \wedge y) \vee ((d(\$3) \vee d(\$4)) \wedge \neg y)$$

Here, $\Sigma^{\langle k \rangle} \subseteq \Sigma^k$ consists of all $w \in \Sigma^k$ such that every letter of Σ appears at most once in w. Note that t_1 and t_2 correspond to weighings of $1 + 1$ and $2 + 2$ coins, respectively. The formulae $\varphi_<$, $\varphi_=$, and $\varphi_>$ encode the three possible outcomes of weighing $1 + 1$ coins. In particular, $\varphi_<$ describes the outcome when the left pan is lighter; then we learn that either the first coin is different and lighter, or the second coin is different and heavier. If we put $\boldsymbol{p} = (coin_4, coin_3)$, then $\varphi_<(\boldsymbol{p})$ is the formula $(x_4 \wedge \neg y) \vee (x_3 \wedge y)$.

For the rest of this section, we fix a deductive game $\mathcal{G} = (X, \varphi_0, \Sigma, F, T)$. We assume that $\mathcal{G}$ is *well-formed*, i.e., for every valuation of $Val(\varphi_0)$, each experiment produces exactly one valid outcome (deductive games that correctly encode meaningful problems are well-formed, so this condition is not restrictive). Intuitively, the game $\mathcal{G}$ is played as follows:

1. The codemaker selects a secret code $v \in Val(\varphi_0)$.
2. The codebreaker selects the next experiment $e \in E$.
3. The codemaker evaluates e for v and returns the resulting evaluated experiment (e, ξ).
4. If the codemaker has enough information to determine v, the play ends. Otherwise, it continues with Step 2.

We assume that the only information available to the codebreaker is the history of evaluated experiments played so far. Hence, a *strategy* is a (total) function $\sigma : \Omega^* \to E$ which specifies the next experiment for a given finite history of evaluated experiments.

Every strategy σ determines the associated *decision tree*, denoted by $Tree_\sigma$, where the internal nodes are labeled by experiments, the leaves are labeled by valuations of $Val(\varphi_0)$, and the edges are labeled by evaluated experiments. For every node u of $Tree_\sigma$, let $\lambda_u^\sigma = (e_1, \xi_1), \ldots, (e_n, \xi_n)$ be the unique sequence of evaluated experiments that label the edges of the unique finite path from the root of $Tree_\sigma$ to u (note that if u is the root, then $\lambda_u^\sigma = \varepsilon$). We also use Ψ_u^σ to denote the formula $\varphi_0 \wedge \xi_1 \wedge \cdots \wedge \xi_n$. The structure of $Tree_\sigma$ is completely determined by the following conditions:

- Every node u of $Tree_\sigma$ is either an internal node labeled by $\sigma(\lambda_u^\sigma)$, or a leaf labeled by the only valuation of $Val(\Psi_u^\sigma)$, depending on whether $|Val(\Psi_u^\sigma)| > 1$ or not, respectively.
- Every internal node u of $Tree_\sigma$ labeled by e has a unique successor u_ξ for each $\xi \in \Phi(e)$ such that the formula $\Psi_u^\sigma \wedge \xi$ is still satisfiable. The edge from u to u_ξ is labeled by (e, ξ).

Note that different nodes/edges may have the same labels, and $Tree_\sigma$ may contain infinite paths in general.

Example 3. Consider the game $\mathcal{G}$ of Example 2. A decision tree for a simple strategy σ is shown in Fig. 1 (we write just i instead of $coin_i$, and we use i, ℓ (or i, h) to denote the valuation of $Val(\varphi_0)$ which sets x_i to *true* and y to *false* (or to *true*, respectively)). Note that σ discovers the secret code by performing at most three experiments. Also note that some internal nodes have only two successors, because the third outcome is impossible.

Since $\mathcal{G}$ is well-formed, every strategy σ and every $v \in Val(\varphi_0)$ determine a unique (finite or infinite) path $u_1, u_2, u_3, \ldots$ initiated in the root of $Tree_\sigma$,

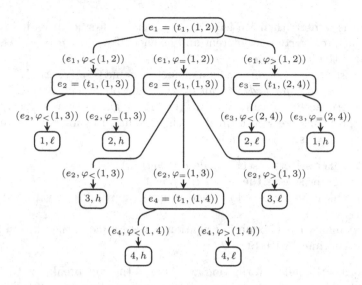

Fig. 1. A decision tree for a simple strategy.

which intuitively correspond to a *play* of $\mathcal{G}$ where the codemaker selects the secret code v. We use $\lambda_v^\sigma = (e_1, \xi_1), (e_2, \xi_2), (e_3, \xi_3), \ldots$ to denote the associated sequence of evaluated experiments, i.e., (e_i, ξ_i) is the label of (u_i, u_{i+1}). The length of λ_v^σ is denoted by $\#\lambda_v^\sigma$. Further, for every $k \leq \#\lambda_v^\sigma$, we use $\Psi_v^\sigma[k]$ to denote the formula $\Psi_{u_k}^\sigma$ which represents the knowledge accumulated after evaluating the first k experiments.

Now we can define the *worst/average case complexity of* σ, denoted by $\mathcal{C}_{worst}(\sigma)$ and $\mathcal{C}_{avg}(\sigma)$, in the following way:

$$\mathcal{C}_{worst}(\sigma) = \max\{\#\lambda_v^\sigma \mid v \in Val(\varphi_0)\} \qquad \mathcal{C}_{avg}(\sigma) = \frac{\sum_{v \in Val(\varphi_0)} \#\lambda_v^\sigma}{|Val(\varphi_0)|}$$

Note that the worst/average case complexity of σ is finite iff *every* $v \in Val(\varphi_0)$ is discovered by σ after a finite number of experiments. We say that $\mathcal{G}$ is *solvable* iff there exists a strategy σ with a finite worst/average case complexity. Further, we say that a strategy σ is *worst case optimal* iff for every strategy σ' we have that $\mathcal{C}_{worst}(\sigma) \leq \mathcal{C}_{worst}(\sigma')$. Similarly, σ is *average case optimal* iff $\mathcal{C}_{avg}(\sigma) \leq \mathcal{C}_{avg}(\sigma')$ for every strategy σ'.

In general, a codebreaker's strategy may depend not only on the outcomes of previously evaluated experiments, but also on their order. Now we show that the codebreaker can select the next experiment *only* according to the semantics of the knowledge accumulated so far.

Definition 4. *A strategy σ is knowledge-based if for all $v_1, v_2 \in Val(\varphi_0)$ and $k_1, k_2 \in \mathbb{N}$ such that $\Psi_{v_1}^\sigma[k_1] \approx \Psi_{v_2}^\sigma[k_2]$ we have that $\sigma(\lambda_{v_1}^\sigma(1), \ldots, \lambda_{v_1}^\sigma(k_1)) = \sigma(\lambda_{v_2}^\sigma(1), \ldots, \lambda_{v_2}^\sigma(k_2))$.*

The next theorem says that knowledge-based strategies are equally powerful as general strategies.

Theorem 5. *Let $\mathcal{G}$ be a well-formed deductive game. For every strategy σ there exists a knowledge-based strategy τ such that for every $v \in Val(\varphi_0)$ we have that $\#\lambda_v^\tau \leq \#\lambda_v^\sigma$.*

In the proof of Theorem 5, we show that the only reason why σ might *not* be knowledge-based is that σ schedules completely useless experiments which can be safely omitted. Thus, we transform σ into τ.

Since the codebreaker may safely determine the next experiment just by considering the currently accumulated knowledge, we can imagine that he somehow "ranks" the outcomes of available experiments and then chooses the most promising one. More precisely, let $\textsc{Know} \subseteq \textsc{Form}(X)$ be the set of all formulae representing an accumulated knowledge, i.e., $\textsc{Know}$ consists of all $\Psi_v^\sigma[k]$ where σ is a strategy, $v \in Val(\varphi_0)$, and $k \in \mathbb{N}$. For every $\varphi \in \textsc{Know}$ and every experiment $e \in E$, we define the set

$$Updates[\varphi, e] = \{\varphi \wedge \xi \mid \xi \in \Phi(e)\}$$

which represents possible "updates" in the accumulated knowledge that can be obtained by performing e. Further, let $r : 2^{\textsc{Know}} \to \mathbb{R}$ be a *ranking function*, and $\preceq$ (some) total ordering over the set E of all experiments.

Definition 6. *A ranking strategy determined by r and $\preceq$ is a function $\tau[r, \preceq] :$ $\textsc{Know} \to E$ such that $\tau[r, \preceq](\varphi)$ is the least element of $\{e \in E \mid r(Updates[\varphi, e]) = Min\}$ w.r.t. $\preceq$, where $Min = \min\{r(Updates[\varphi, e']) \mid e' \in E\}$.*

Note that every ranking strategy can be understood as a "general" strategy, and hence all notions introduced for general strategies (such as the decision tree) make sense also for ranking strategies. Further, for every knowledge-based strategy τ there is an "equivalent" ranking strategy $\tau[r, \preceq]$ where, for all $\varphi \in \textsc{Know}$ and $e \in E$, the value of $r(Updates[\varphi, e])$ is either 0 or 1, depending on whether $Updates[\varphi, e]$ is equal to $Updates[\varphi, \tau(\varphi)]$ or not, respectively. The ordering $\preceq$ can be chosen arbitrarily. One can easily show that for every $v \in Val(\varphi_0)$ we have that $\#\lambda_v^\tau = \#\lambda_v^{\tau[r, \preceq]}$. So, ranking strategies are equally powerful as knowledge-based strategies and hence also general strategies by Theorem 5. In particular, there exist worst/average case optimal ranking strategies, but it is not clear what kind of ranking functions they need to employ. Since optimal strategy synthesis is computationally costly, one may also *fix* some r and $\preceq$, synthesize $\tau[r, \preceq]$, and evaluate its worst/average case complexity. Thus, by experimenting with different r and $\preceq$, one may obtain various strategies that solve the game, and then choose the most efficient one.

Now we introduce several distinguished ranking functions (all of them are implemented in $\textsc{Cobra}$). They generalize concepts previously used for solving Mastermind, and there are also two new rankings based on the number of fixed variables. The associated ranking strategies always use the lexicographical ordering over E determined by some fixed linear orderings over the sets T and Σ.

- **max-models**$(\Psi) = \max_{\psi \in \Psi} |Val(\psi)|$. The associated ranking strategy minimizes the worst-case number of remaining secret codes. For Mastermind, this was suggested by Knuth [17].
- **exp-models**$(\Psi) = \frac{\sum_{\psi \in \Psi} |Val(\psi)|^2}{\sum_{\psi \in \Psi} |Val(\psi)|}$. The associated ranking strategy minimizes the expected number of remaining secret codes. For Mastermind, this was suggested by Irwing [14].
- **ent-models**$(\Psi) = \sum_{\psi \in \Psi} \frac{|Val(\psi)|}{N} \cdot \log(\frac{|Val(\psi)|}{N})$, where $N = \sum_{\psi \in \Psi} |Val(\psi)|$. The associated ranking strategy minimizes the entropy of the numbers of remaining secret codes. For Mastermind, this was suggested by Neuwirth [20].
- **parts**$(\Psi) = -|\{\psi \in \Psi \mid \psi\, is\, satisfiable\}|$. The associated ranking strategy minimizes the number of satisfiable outcomes. For Mastermind, this was suggested by Kooi [18].

We say that a variable $x \in X$ is *fixed* in a formula $\varphi \in \text{FORM}(X)$ if x is set to the same value by all valuations satisfying φ (i.e., for all $v, v' \in Val(\varphi)$ we have that $v(x) = v'(x)$). The set of all variables that are fixed in φ is denoted by $Fix(\varphi)$. We consider two ranking functions based on the number of fixed variables.

- **min-fixed**$(\Psi) = -\min_{\psi \in \Psi} |Fix(\psi)|$. The associated ranking function maximizes the number of fixed variables.
- **exp-fixed**$(\Psi) = -\frac{\sum_{\psi \in \Psi} |Val(\psi)| \cdot |Fix(\psi)|}{\sum_{\psi \in \Psi} |Val(\psi)|}$. The associated ranking function maximizes the expected number of fixed variables.

Intuitively, a "good" ranking function should satisfy two requirements:

- The associateted ranking strategy should have a low worst/average case complexity. Ideally, this strategy should be optimal.
- The ranking function should be easy to evaluate for a given experiment e. This is crucial for automatic strategy synthesis.

Obviously, there is a conflict in these two requirement. For example, the **max-models** ranking often produces a rather efficient strategy, but the number of satisfying valuations of a given propositional formula is hard to compute. On the other hand, **min-fixed** ranking produces a good ranking strategy only in some cases (e.g., for CCP and its variants), but it is relatively easy to compute with modern SAT solvers even for large formulae.

Example 7. Consider again the game $\mathcal{G}$ of Example 2 formalizing CCP with four coins. Further, consider the experiments

- $e_1 = (t_1, (coin_1, coin_2))$,
- $e_2 = (t_2, (coin_1, coin_2, coin_3, coin_4))$

for the first step (i.e., when the current accumulated knowledge is just φ_0). In e_1, we weight $coin_1$ against $coin_2$. The number of satisfying assignments is 2 for the outcomes $\varphi_<$ and $\varphi_>$, and 4 for the outcome $\varphi_=$. For the outcomes $\varphi_<$ and $\varphi_>$, we know that the counterfeit coin is *not* among $coin_3$ and $coin_4$, and for the $\varphi_=$

Table 1. A table summarizing the outcomes of ranking functions.

	max-models	exp-models	ent-models	parts	min-fixed	exp-fixed
e_1	4	3	-1.04	-3	-2	-2
e_2	4	4	-0.69	-2	0	0

outcome, we know it is not among $coin_1$ and $coin_2$. Hence, every outcome fixes 2 variables. Similarly, we can evaluate e_2 and the other ranking functions. The results are summarized in Table 1. Observe that all of the considered ranking strategies would prefer e_1 to e_2 in the first step, possibly except for the **max-models** ranking strategy where the choice depends on the chosen liner ordering over T and Σ (it t_1 is smaller that t_2, this strategy also prefers e_1).

Although computing $\tau[r, \preceq]$ for given r and $\preceq$ appears computationally easier than synthesizing an optimal strategy, we still need to (repeatedly) compute the least element of $\{e \in E \mid r(Updates[\varphi, e]) = Min\}$ w.r.t. $\preceq$, where $Min = \min\{r(Updates[\varphi, e']) \mid e' \in E\}$, which is not achievable by enumerating all experiments. For example, in CCP with 60 coins, there are more than 10^{63} ways of instantiating the parameterized experiment t formalizing the weighing of $20+20$ coins. However, observe that if t is performed in the first step, i.e., when the accumulated knowledge is just φ_0, then *all* instances of t are "equivalent" in the sense that the knowledge learned by these instances is the same up to a permutation of coins. Hence, it suffices to consider only *one* instance of t and disregard the others. COBRA implements an algorithm which can efficiently recognize and exploit such symmetries. Now we briefly explain the main ideas behind this algorithm.

A *permutation* of X is a bijection $\pi : X \to X$. We use $\text{PERM}(X)$ to denote the set of all permutations of X. Given a formula $\varphi \in \text{FORM}(X)$ and a permutation $\pi \in \text{PERM}(X)$, we use $\pi(\varphi)$ to denote the formula obtained from φ by simultaneously substituting every occurrence of every $x \in X$ with $\pi(x)$. For a given $\Phi \subseteq \text{FORM}(X)$, we use $\pi(\Phi)$ to denote the set $\{\pi(\varphi) \mid \varphi \in \Phi\}$.

Definition 8. *Let $e, e' \in E$ and $\pi \in \text{PERM}(X)$. We say that e' is π-symmetrical to e if $\pi(\Phi(e)) \approx \Phi(e')$. A symmetry group of $\mathcal{G}$, denoted by Π, consist of all $\pi \in \text{PERM}(X)$ such that for every $e \in E$ there is a π-symmetrical $e' \in E$.*

We say that $e, e' \in E$ are equivalent *w.r.t. a given $\varphi \in \text{KNOW}$, written $e \sim_\varphi e'$, if there is $\pi \in \Pi$ such that $\{\varphi \wedge \psi \mid \psi \in \Phi(e)\} \approx \{\pi(\varphi \wedge \varrho) \mid \varrho \in \Phi(e')\}$.*

Note that Π is indeed a group, i.e., Π contains the identity and if $\pi \in \Pi$, then the inverse π^{-1} of π also belongs to Π.

Example 9. Consider the game of Example 2. Then $\Pi = \{\pi \in \text{PERM}(X) \mid \pi(y) = y\}$. Hence, for all $\boldsymbol{p}, \boldsymbol{q} \in \Sigma^{\langle 4 \rangle}$ we have that $(t_2, \boldsymbol{p}) \sim_{\varphi_0} (t_2, \boldsymbol{q})$, and the partition $E/\sim_{\varphi_0}$ has only two equivalence classes corresponding to t_1 and t_2. For $\varphi = \varphi_0 \wedge \neg(x_1 \vee x_2)$, we have that $(t_1(coin_4, coin_3)) \sim_\varphi (t_2, (coin_3, coin_1, coin_2, coin_4))$.

The core of COBRA are the algorithms for synthesizing worst/average case optimal strategies, and for analyzing the efficiency of $\tau[r, \preceq]$. For a current accumulated knowledge $\varphi \in$ KNOW, these algorithms need to consider at least one experiment for each equivalence class of $E/\sim_\varphi$. This is achieved by invoking a function EXPERIMENTS(φ) parameterized by φ which computes a set of experiments $S_\varphi \subseteq E$ such that for every $e \in E$ there is at least one $e' \in S_\varphi$ where $e \sim_\varphi e'$. A naive approach to constructing S_φ is to initialize $\hat{S}_\varphi := \emptyset$ and then process every $t = (k, P, \Phi) \in T$ as follows: for every $p \in \Sigma^k$, we check whether $p \in P$ and $(t, p) \not\sim_\varphi e$ for all $e \in \hat{S}_\varphi$; if this test is positive, we put $\hat{S}_\varphi := \hat{S}_\varphi \cup \{(t, p)\}$, and continue with the next p. When we are done with all $t \in T$, we set $S_\varphi := \hat{S}_\varphi$. Obviously, this trivial algorithm is inefficient for at least two reasons.

1. The size of Σ^k can be very large (think again of CCP with 60 coins), and it may not be possible to go over all $p \in \Sigma^k$.
2. The problem of checking $\sim_\varphi$ is computationally hard.

Now we indicate how COBRA overcomes these issues. Intuitively, the first issue is tackled by optimizing the trivial backtracking algorithm which would normally generate all elements of Σ^k lexicographically using some total ordering $\preceq$ over Σ. We improve the functionality of this algorithm as follows: when the backtracking algorithm is done with generating all k-tuples starting with a given prefix $ua \in \Sigma^m$, where $m \in \{1, \ldots, k\}$, and aims to generate all k-tuples starting with ub, we first check whether ub is *dominated* by ua w.r.t. φ and t. The dominance by ua guarantees that all of the experiments that would be obtained by using the k-tuples starting with ub are equivalent to some of the already generated ones. Hence, if ub is dominated by ua w.r.t. φ and t, we continue immediately with the $\preceq$-successor c of b, i.e., we do *not* examine the k-tuples starting with ub at all (note that uc is again checked for dominance by ua). This can lead to drastic improvements in the total number of generated instances which can be *much* smaller than $|\Sigma|^k$. The set of all experiments generated in the first phase is denoted by S_φ^1.

The second issue is tackled by designing an algorithm which tries to decide $\sim_\varphi$ for a given pair of experiments e_1, e_2 by first removing the *fixed variables* in φ and the outcomes of e_1, e_2 using a SAT solver, and then constructing two labeled graphs B_{φ, e_1} and B_{φ, e_1} which are checked for isomorphism (here COBRA relies on existing software tools for checking graph isomorphism). If the graphs are isomorphic, we have that $e_1 \sim_\varphi e_2$, and we can safely remove e_1 or e_2 from S_φ^1. When the experiments are ordered by some $\preceq$, we prefer to remove the larger one. Thus, we produce the set S_φ. Now we explain both phases in greater detail.

Let $t = (k, P, \Phi)$ be a parameterized experiment, and let $i, j \in \{1, \ldots, k\}$ be two positions. We say that i, j are *closely dependent* if $i = j$ or there exists an attribute $f \in F$ such that both $f(\$i)$ and $f(\$j)$ occur in the formulae of Φ. Further, we say that i, j are *dependent* if they are related by the transitive closure of close dependence relation. Note that the set $\{1, \ldots, k\}$ can be partitioned into disjoint subsets of mutually dependent indexes. Further, for every $i \in \{1, \ldots, k\}$

we define the set F_i consisting of all $f \in F$ such that $f(\$j)$ occurs in some formula of Φ where $j \in \{1, \ldots, k\}$ and i, j are dependent.

As an example, consider the parameterized experiment t_2 in the game of Example 2. Then all indexes are mutually dependent and $F_i = \{d\}$ for every $i \in \{1, 2, 3, 4\}$. In Mastermind with n pegs and m colors, there is only one parameterized experiment $t = (n, \{color_1, \ldots, color_m\}^n, \Phi)$, and all indexes are again mutually dependent. We have that $F_i = \{peg_1, \ldots, peg_n\}$ for all $i \in \{1, \ldots, n\}$.

We say that $r \in \Sigma^i$, where $1 \leq i \leq k$, is t-feasible if there is $s \in \Sigma^{k-i}$ such that $rs \in P$. Further, for all $p \in \Sigma^k$, $m \in \{1, \ldots, k\}$, and $a, b \in \Sigma$, we denote by $p[m, a \leftrightarrow b]$ the element of Σ^k obtained from p by simultaneously substituting every occurrence of a with b and every occurrence of b with a at all positions j where m and j are dependent.

Definition 10. *Let* $\varphi \in$ KNOW, $t = (k, P, \Phi) \in T$, *and let* $ua \in \Sigma^m$ *be a* t-*feasible tuple, where* $1 \leq m < k$. *We say that* $ub \in \Sigma^m$ *is dominated by* ua *w.r.t.* φ *and* t *if the following conditions are satisfied:*

- *for every* v *where* $p = ubv \in P$ *we have that* $p[m, a \leftrightarrow b] \in P$ *and* $p[m, a \leftrightarrow b] \preceq p$;
- *for every* $f \in F_m$, *the variables* $f(a)$ *and* $f(b)$ *do not occur in the formulae of* Φ;
- *the permutation* π, *defined by* $\pi(f(a)) = f(b)$, $\pi(f(b)) = f(a)$ *for all* $f \in F_m$, *and* $\pi(y) = y$ *for the other variables, is a symmetry of* φ, *i.e.,* $\varphi \equiv \pi(\varphi)$.

Theorem 11. *Let* $\varphi \in$ KNOW, $t = (k, P, \Phi) \in T$, *and let* $ua \in \Sigma^m$ *be a* t-*feasible tuple, where* $1 \leq m < k$. *If* ub *is dominated by* ua *w.r.t.* φ *and* t, *then for every* $v \in \Sigma^{k-m}$ *such that* $p = ubv \in P$ *we have that* $p[m, a \leftrightarrow b] \in P$ *and* $(t, p) \sim_\varphi (t, p[m, a \leftrightarrow b])$.

Proof. Let $q = p[m, a \leftrightarrow b]$, and let π be the permutation introduced in Definition 10. We show that $\{\varphi \wedge \psi \mid \psi \in \Phi((t, p))\} \equiv \{\pi(\varphi \wedge \varrho) \mid \varrho \in \Phi((t, q))\}$. Since $\varphi \equiv \pi(\varphi)$, it suffices to prove that $\Psi(p) \equiv \pi(\Psi(q))$ for all $\Psi \in \Phi$. Let us fix some $\Psi \in \Phi$. Observe that the formulae $\Psi(p)$ and $\pi(\Psi(q))$ are the same except that all $f(\$i)$ are evaluated either to $f(p_i)$ or to $\pi(f(q_i))$, respectively. Let us examine possible cases.

- If $a \neq p_i \neq b$, then $p_i = q_i$ and $\pi(f(q_i)) = \pi(f(p_i)) = f(p_i)$ by Definition 10.
- If i and m are independent, then again $p_i = q_i$ and $\pi(f(q_i)) = \pi(f(p_i)) = f(p_i)$ by Definition 10 (note that $f \notin F_m$).
- If i, m are dependent and $p_i = a$, then $\pi(f(p_i)) = \pi(f(a)) = f(b) = f(q_i)$ because $f \in F_i$. The case when i, m are dependent and $p_i = b$ is symmetric. $\square$

Theorem 11 fully justifies the correctness of the improved backtracking algorithm discussed above in the sense that the resulting set S^1_φ indeed contains at least one representative for each equivalence class of $E/\sim_\varphi$.

Now we describe the second phase, when we try to identify and remove some equivalent experiments in S^1_φ. The method works only under the condition that for every $t = (k, P, \Phi) \in T$ we have that P is closed under all permutations of Σ (note that this condition is satisfied when $P = \Sigma^k$ or $P = \Sigma^{\langle k \rangle}$). Possible generalizations are left for future work. The method starts by constructing a labeled *base graph* $B = (V, E, L)$ of $\mathcal{G}$, where the set of vertices V is $X \cup F$ (we assume $X \cap F = \emptyset$) and the edges of E are determined as follows:

- $(f, x) \in E$, where $f \in F$ and $x \in X$, if there is $a \in \Sigma$ such that $f(a) = x$;
- $(x, y) \in E$, where $x, y \in X$, if there are $a \in \Sigma$, $f, g \in F$, $t \in T$, some outcome ψ of T, such that $f(a) = x$, $g(a) = y$, and both $f(\$i)$ and $g(\$i)$ appear in ψ for some $i \in \{1, \ldots, k\}$.

The labeling $L : V \to X \cup F \cup \{var\}$, where $var \notin X \cup F$, assigns var to every variable $x \in X$ such that x does not appear in any outcome of any parameterized experiment of T. For the other vertices $v \in V$, we have that $L(v) = v$. The base graph B represents a subset of Π in the following sense:

Theorem 12. *Let π be an automorphism of B. Then π restricted to X belongs to Π.*

Now, let $\varphi \in \text{FORM}_X$ be a formula representing the accumulated knowledge, and let $e_1 = (t_1, \boldsymbol{p})$ and $e_2 = (t_2, \boldsymbol{q})$ be experiments. We show how to construct two labeled graphs B_{φ,e_1} and B_{φ,e_2} such that the existence of an isomorphism between B_{φ,e_1} and B_{φ,e_2} implies $e_1 \sim_\varphi e_2$.

For every formula $\psi \in \text{FORM}_X$, let $Stree(\psi)$ be the syntax tree of ψ, where every inner node is labeled by the associated Boolean operator, the leaves are labeled by the associated variables of X, and the root is a fresh vertex $root(\psi)$ with only one successor which corresponds to the topmost operator of ψ (the label of $root(\psi)$ is irrelevant for now). Recall that we only allow for commutative operators, so the ordering of successors of a given inner node of $Stree(\psi)$ is not significant. Each such $Stree(\psi)$ can be *attached* to any graph B' which subsumes B by taking the disjoint union of the vertices of B' and the inner vertices of $Stree(\psi)$, and identifying all leaves of $Stree(\psi)$ labeled by $x \in X$ with the unique node x of B'. All edges and labels are preserved.

The graph B_{φ,e_1} is obtained by subsequently attaching the formulae $Stree(\overline{\varphi})$, $Stree(\overline{\psi_1(\boldsymbol{p})}), \ldots, Stree(\overline{\psi_n(\boldsymbol{p})})$ to the base graph of B, where $\psi_1, \ldots, \psi_n$ are the outcomes of t_1, and for every $\psi \in \text{FORM}(X)$, the formula $\overline{\psi}$ is obtained from ψ by removing its *fixed variables* (see above) using a SAT solver. The root of $Stree(\overline{\varphi})$ is labeled by acc, and the roots of $Stree(\overline{\psi_1(\boldsymbol{p})}), \ldots, Stree(\overline{\psi_n(\boldsymbol{p})})$ are labeled by out. The graph B_{φ,e_2} is constructed in the same way, again using the labels acc and out.

Theorem 13. *If B_{φ,e_1}, B_{φ,e_2} are isomorphic, then $e_1 \sim_\varphi e_2$.*

The procedure $\text{EXPERIMENTS}(\varphi)$ is used to compute decision trees for ranking strategies and optimal worst/average case strategies in the following way. Let $\tau[r, \preceq]$ be a ranking strategy such that for all $e_1, e_2 \in E$ and $\varphi \in \text{KNOW}$ we have that $e_1 \sim_\varphi e_2$ implies $r(e_1) = r(e_2)$. Note that all ranking functions introduced in this section satisfy this property. The decision tree $Tree_{\tau[r,\preceq]}$ is computed top-down. When we need to determine the label of a given node u where the associated accumulated knowledge is Ψ_u, we first check whether $|Val(\Psi_u)| = 1$ using a SAT solver. If it is the case, we label u with the only valuation of $Val(\Psi_u)$. Otherwise, we need to compute the experiment $\tau[r, \preceq](\Psi_u)$. It follows

```
1  Function OPTIMAL(φ, upper)
2  |   if |Val(φ)| = 1 then return ⟨v, 0⟩ where v ∈ Val(φ)
3  |   if φ is cached then return  the cached result
4  |   [W] if ⌈log_Out(|Val(φ)|)⌉ > upper then return ⟨err, ∞⟩
5  |   S_φ := EXPERIMENTS(φ)
6  |   best := upper;  e_φ := some element of S_φ
7  |   for e ∈ S_φ do
8  |   |   val := 0
9  |   |   for ψ ∈ Φ(e) do
10 |   |   |   if SAT(φ ∧ ψ) then
11 |   |   |   |   ⟨e_ψ, C_ψ⟩ := OPTIMAL(φ ∧ ψ, best − 1)
12 |   |   |   |   [W] val := max(val, 1 + C_ψ)
13 |   |   |   |   [A] val := val + |Val(φ ∧ ψ)| · (1 + C_ψ)
14 |   |   [A] val := val / |Val(φ)|
15 |   |   if val ≤ best then best := val; e_φ := e
16 |   Cache the result ⟨e_φ, best⟩ for φ
17 |   return ⟨e_φ, best⟩
```

Fig. 2. Computing optimal strategies.

immediately that $\tau[r, \preceq](\Psi_u)$ is contained in $S_{\Psi_u} :=$ EXPERIMENTS(Ψ_u). Hence, we label u with the least element of $\{e \in S_{\Psi_u} \mid Updates[\Psi_u, e] = Min\}$ w.r.t. $\preceq$, where $Min = \min\{Updates[\Psi_u, e'] \mid e' \in S_{\Psi_u}\}$. This element is computed with the help of a SAT solver.

The way of computing a decision tree for an optimal worst/average case strategy is more involved. Let WOPT$_G$ and AOPT$_G$ be the sets of all knowledge-based strategies which are worst case optimal and average case optimal, respectively. First, observe that if $\tau \in$ WOPT$_G$ and $\tau(\varphi) = e$ for some $\varphi \in$ KNOW, then for every $e' \in E$ where $e \sim_\varphi e'$ there is $\tau' \in$ WOPT$_G$ such that $\tau'(\varphi) = e'$. Hence, we can safely restrict the range of $\tau(\varphi)$ to EXPERIMENTS(φ). Further, if $\tau(\varphi) = e$ and $\varphi' \equiv \pi(\varphi)$ for some $\pi \in \Pi$, we can safely put $\tau(\varphi') = \pi(e)$. The same properties hold also for the strategies of AOPT$_G$.

A recursive function for computing a worst/average case optimal strategy is shown in Fig. 2. The function is parameterized by $\varphi \in$ KNOW and an upper bound on the worst/average number of experiments performed by an optimal strategy for the initial knowledge φ. The function returns a pair $\langle e_\varphi, C_\varphi \rangle$ where e_φ is the experiment selected for φ and C_φ is the worst/average number of experiments that are needed to solve the game for the initial knowledge φ. Hence, the algorithm is invoked by OPTIMAL(φ_0, ∞). Note that the algorithm caches the computed results and when it encounters that φ is π-symmetric to some previously processed formula, it uses the cached results immediately (line 3). The lines executed only when constructing the worst (or average) case optimal strategy are prefixed by $[W]$ (or $[A]$, respectively). At line 4, the constant Out is equal to $\max_{(k,P,\Phi) \in T} |\Phi(t)|$. Obviously, we need at least $\lceil \log_{Out}(|Val(\varphi)|) \rceil$ experiments to distinguish among the remaining $|Val(\varphi)|$ alternatives.

3   Cobra: The Tool and Experimental Results

COBRA [1] is a command-line tool envoked as follows:

```
cobra [-m <mode>] [-s <sat solver>] [other options] <file>
```

The <file> contains a deductive game description (the syntax implements Definition 1). The <mode> can be either overview, analysis, optimal-worst, or optimal-average. The overview mode serves for basic consistency checks (in particular, the *well-formed* condition is verified, see Sect. 2). The analysis mode allows to analyze the worst/average case complexity of ranking strategies for several ranking functions. Currently, COBRA supports max-models, exp-models, ent-models, part, min-fixed, and exp-fixed ranking functions, where the first four functions minimize the worst-case number of remaining secret codes, the expected number of remaining secret codes, the entropy of the numbers of remaining secret codes, and the number of satisfiable outcomes, respectively, and the last two functions maximize the (expected) number of fixed variables. Finally, the optimal-worst and optimal-average are the modes where COBRA computes the worst and the average case optimal strategies, respectively. The optional -s switch allows to specify the SAT solver used by COBRA for evaluating the supported ranking functions (currently available options are MINISAT [9] and PICOSAT [5]). COBRA also uses the tool BLISS [15] for checking graph isomorphism to determine equivalent experiments. The source code, installation instructions, examples, and a more detailed specification of COBRA's functionality are available freely at GitHub [1].

In the rest of this section we briefly describe some experimental results achieved with COBRA. In the first part, we demonstrate the efficiency of the algorithm for eliminating symmetric experiments discussed at the end of Sect. 2. In the second part, we show that COBRA is powerful enough to produce new results about existing deductive games and their variants.

The functionality of EXPERIMENTS(φ) can be well demonstrated on CCP and Mastermind. Consider CCP with 26, 39, and 50 coins. Table 2 (top) shows the *average* size of S_φ^1 and S_φ when computing the i-th experiment in the decision tree for the max-models ranking strategy. The total number of experiments for 26, 39 and 50 coins is larger than 10^{26}, 10^{46}, and 10^{64}, respectively. Observe that for 26 and 39 coins, only four experiments are needed to reveal the counterfeit coin, and hence the last row is empty. Note that in the first round, *all* equivalent experiments are discovered already in the first phase, i.e., when computing S_1. These experiments correspond to the number of coins that can be weighted (e.g., for 50 coins we can weight $1+1, \dots, 25+25$ coins, which gives 25 experiments). In the second round, when we run EXPERIMENTS(φ) for three different formulae $\varphi \in$ KNOW, the average size of S_φ^1 is already larger, and the second phase (eliminating equivalent experiments) further reduces the average size of the resulting S_φ.

A similar table for Mastermind is shown in Table 2 (bottom). Here we consider three variants with 3/8, 4/6, and 5/3 pegs/colors. The table shows the average size of S_φ when computing the i-th experiment in the decision trees

Table 2. The size of S_φ^1 and S_φ for selected deductive games.

Exp.No.	CCP 26 ($\approx 10^{26}$ exp.)		CCP 39 ($\approx 10^{46}$ exp.)		CCP 50 ($\approx 10^{64}$ exp.)	
	Phase 1	Phase 2	Phase 1	Phase 2	Phase 1	Phase 2
hline 1	13.0	13.0	19.0	19.0	25.0	25.0
2	4,365.0	861.7	26,638.7	3,318.0	83,625.0	8,591.0
3	603.0	36.4	2,263.0	88.1	5,733.4	172.2
4	76.3	4.2	214.7	7.2	405.1	10.4
5	-	-	-	-	153.2	4.1

	MM 3x8 (512 exp.)				MM 4x6 (1296 exp.)				MM 5x3 (243 exp.)			
	max-models		parts		max-models		parts		max-models		parts	
Exp.No.	Phase 1	Phase 2	Phase 1	Phase 2	Phase 1	Phase 2	Phase 1	Phase 2	Phase 1	Phase 2	Phase 1	Phase 2
1	5.00	3.00	5.00	3.00	15.00	5.00	15.00	5.00	41.00	5.00	41.00	5.00
2	70.13	17.38	70.13	17.38	144.82	34.91	337.23	106.62	243.00	59.25	243.00	59.25
3	144.50	72.31	147.29	87.83	587.54	243.40	819.49	580.03	243.00	121.45	243.00	186.90
4	134.25	71.54	155.14	87.98	791.30	344.02	819.68	417.02	-	-	-	-
5	91.36	25.36	100.46	31.97	-	-	334.33	95.83	-	-	-	-

Table 3. The average/worst case complexity of selected deductive games.

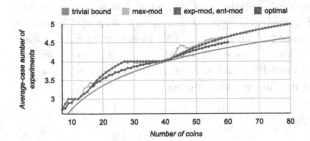

Average-case			
Size	MM	MM+col	MM+pos
2x8	3.67187	3.64062	2
3x6	3.19444	3.18981	3
4x4	2.78516	2.74609	2.78516
Worst-case			
Size	MM	MM+col	MM+pos
2x8	5	5	2
3x6	4	4	3
4x4	3	3	3

for `max-models` and `parts` ranking strategies. Note that for Mastermind, the reduction is more efficient for more colors and less pegs, and that the values for the two ranking strategies significantly differ, which means that they divide the solution space in a rather different way.

Now we present examples of results obtained by running our tool that, to the best of our knowledge, have not yet been published in the existing literature about deductive games. Our first example concerns CCP. While the worst case complexity of CCP is fully understood [8], we are not aware of any results about the *average* case complexity of CPP. Using COBRA, we were able to compute the *average-case optimal strategy* for up to 60 coins. Further, we can compare the average-case complexity of an optimal strategy with the average-case complexities of various ranking strategies, which can be synthesized for even higher number of coins (more than 80). The results are summarized in the graph of Table 3 (left). The precise values shown in the plot can be found in [16].

As the last example, we consider two variants of Mastermind: MM+col, where we can also ask for all pegs colored by a given color, and MM+pos, where we can also ask for the color of a given peg. These extensions are inspired by the API-level attacks mentioned in Sect. 1. Using COBRA, we can compute the optimal worst/average case complexity for 2/8, 3/6, and 4/4 pegs/colors. The results are summarized in Table 3 (right). When comparing these results to "classical" results about Mastermind, the following subtle difference in game rules must be taken into account: Plays of "our" deductive games terminate as soon as we obtain enough information to reveal the secret code. The "classical" Mastermind terminates when the secret code is "played", which may require an extra experiment even if the code is already known. Our numbers are valid for the first setup.

4   Conclusions

The results produced by COBRA witness that non-trivial deductive games can be solved by a generic tool. The main advantage of COBRA is its *versatility*; small changes in the structure of the secret code and/or experiments can easily be reflected in the input description, which greatly simplifies the analysis of new versions of security protocols, new forms of attacks, etc. The challenge is to push the frontiers of fully automatic analysis of deductive games even further. Obviously, there are many ways of improving the functionality of COBRA by elaborating the concepts presented in this paper. The interface to SAT solvers can also be tuned, there is a lot of space for parallelism, etc. One may also try alternative approaches to modeling and solving deductive games based on constraint solving or artificial intelligence techniques.

References

1. COBRA, the COde-BReaking game Analyzer (2014). https://github.com/myreg/cobra
2. Bento, L., Pereira, L., Rosa, A.: Mastermind by evolutionary algorithms. In: Proceedings of the International Symposium on Applied Computing, pp. 307–311. ACM (1999)
3. Berghman, L., Goossens, D., Leus, R.: Efficient solutions for mastermind using genetic algorithms. Comput. Oper. Res. **36**(6), 1880–1885 (2009)
4. Bernier, J., Herraiz, C., Merelo, J., Olmeda, S., Prieto, A.: Solving mastermind using GAs and simulated annealing: a case of dynamic constraint optimization. In: Voigt, H.-M., Ebeling, W., Rechenberg, I., Schwefel, H.-P. (eds.) PPSN IV. LNCS, vol. 1141, pp. 554–563. Springer, Heidelberg (1996)
5. Biere, A.: PicoSAT essentials. J. Satisfiability Boolean Model. Comput. **4**(2–4), 75–97 (2008)
6. Bond, M., Zieliński, P.: Decimalisation table attacks for PIN cracking. Technical report UCAM-CL-TR-560 arXiv:1407.3926, University of Cambridge (2003)
7. Chen, S.T., Lin, S.S., Huang, L.T., Hsu, S.H.: Strategy optimization for deductive games. Eur. J. Oper. Res. **183**, 757–766 (2007)
8. Dyson, F.: The problem of the pennies. Math. Gaz. **30**, 231–234 (1946)
9. Eén, N., Sörensson, N.: An extensible SAT-solver. In: Giunchiglia, E., Tacchella, A. (eds.) SAT 2003. LNCS, vol. 2919, pp. 502–518. Springer, Heidelberg (2004)
10. Erdös, P., Rényi, A.: On two problems of information theory. Magyar Tud. Akad. Mat. Kutató Int. Közl **8**, 229–243 (1963)

11. Gagneur, J., Elze, M., Tresch, A.: Selective phenotyping, entropy reduction, and the Mastermind game. BMC Bioinform. **12**(406), 1–10 (2011)
12. Goodrich, M.: The Mastermind attack on genomic data. In: Proceedings of 30th IEEE Symposium on Security and Privacy, pp. 204–218. IEEE (2009)
13. Guy, R., Nowakowski, R.: Coin-weighting problems. Am. Math. Mon. **102**(2), 164–167 (1995)
14. Irving, R.: Towards an optimum mastermind strategy. J. Recreational Math. **11**(2), 81–87 (1978–1979)
15. Junttila, T., Kaski, P.: Engineering an efficient canonical labeling tool for large and sparse graphs. In: Proceedings of the Ninth Workshop on Algorithm Engineering and Experiments (ALENEX 2007), pp. 135–149. SIAM (2007)
16. Klimoš, M., Kučera, A.: Strategy synthesis for general deductive games based on SAT solving. CoRR abs/1407.3926 (2015)
17. Knuth, D.: The computer as mastermind. J. Recreational Math. **9**(1), 1–6 (1976)
18. Kooi, B.: Yet another mastermind strategy. ICGA J. **28**(1), 13–20 (2005)
19. Koyama, K., Lai, T.: An optimal mastermind strategy. J. Recreational Math. **25**(4), 251–256 (1993)
20. Neuwirth, E.: Some strategies for mastermind. Zeitschrift für Oper. Res. **26**, 257–278 (1982)
21. Steel, G.: Formal analysis of PIN block attacks. Theor. Comput. Sci. **367**(1–2), 257–270 (2006)

On Anti-subsumptive Knowledge Enforcement

Éric Grégoire[✉] and Jean-Marie Lagniez

CRIL, Université d'Artois - CNRS, Rue Jean Souvraz SP18, 62307 Lens, France
{gregoire,lagniez}@cril.fr

Abstract. The anti-subsumptive enforcement of a clause δ in a set of clauses Δ consists in extracting one cardinality-maximal satisfiable subset Δ' of $\Delta \cup \{\delta\}$ that contains δ but that does not strictly subsume δ. In this paper, the computational issues of this problem are investigated in the Boolean framework. Especially, the minimal change policy that requires a minimal number of clauses to be dropped from Δ can lead to an exponential computational blow-up. Indeed, a direct and natural approach to anti-subsumptive enforcement requires the computation of all inclusion-maximal subsets of $\Delta \cup \{\delta\}$ that, at the same time, contain δ and are satisfiable with $\neg\delta_j$ where δ_j is some strict sub-clause of δ. On the contrary, we propose a method that avoids the computation of this possibly exponential number of subsets of clauses. Interestingly, it requires only one single call to a Partial-Max-SAT procedure and appears tractable in many realistic situations, even for very large Δ. Moreover, the approach is easily extended to take into account a preference pre-ordering between formulas and lay the foundations for the practical enumeration of all optimal solutions to the problem of making δ subsumption-free in Δ under a minimal change policy.

Keywords: Preemption · Subsumption · Belief change · Partial-Max-SAT · Boolean logic

1 Introduction

Preemption is a reasoning paradigm that enforces the derivability of some given knowledge[1] δ and blocks the inference of some other given information. The study of preemption has been ubiquitous in Artificial Intelligence for decades: early seminal works that had to cope with this issue can be traced back for example in rule-based expert systems [1], reasoning with inheritance hierarchies [2] and non-monotonic reasoning dealing with exceptions [3,4]. In this paper, we are concerned with preemption in the clausal Boolean framework when the blocked formulas are all the strict sub-clauses of a given clause δ that is intended to prevail. Note that any sub-clause of δ subsumes -and thus entails- δ: this form of preemption mechanism thus blocks the inference of clauses that are logically strictly stronger than δ. It is a required mechanism when δ is encoding

---

[1] In this paper, no distinction is made between *belief, knowledge* and *information.*

© Springer-Verlag Berlin Heidelberg 2015
M. Davis et al. (Eds.): LPAR-20 2015, LNCS 9450, pp. 48–62, 2015.
DOI: 10.1007/978-3-662-48899-7_4

some contents that is considered accurate whereas its strict sub-clauses are not. Indeed, through additional disjuncts, δ can express some more detailed, precise or specific information that must prevail.

For example [5], assume that a set of clauses Δ contains some information about John's current location, namely *John is at home or in his office*. Now assume that a new piece of information δ comes in and must prevail: δ translates that a third possible location for John must also be taken into account with a same level of confidence, for example $\delta = John$ *is at home or in his office or in his car*. Clearly, this new piece of information does not logically contradict the previous one. Furthermore, δ is a logical consequence of Δ. However, in this specific situation, we do not want δ to be merely inserted within Δ since the resulting set of formulas would still allow *John is at home or in his office* to be deduced. Actually, we need to trim $\Delta \cup \{\delta\}$ to yield a set Δ' that entails δ and that does not allow any strict sub-clause of δ to be deduced, like for example *John is at home* and *John is at home or in his car*.

As another example, assume that δ is the clause *not(accepted) or not(in-time) or published* encoding the rule *If the paper is accepted and the final version is sent in time then it will be included in the proceedings*. Clearly, we might want this rule to prevail over the sub-clause δ' of δ that is encoding *If the paper is accepted then it will be included in the proceedings*, at least when sending the final version in time is assumed to be a necessary condition for the paper to be included in the proceedings.

From now on, δ is a non-tautologous and satisfiable clause and Δ is a set of clauses which is not necessarily satisfiable but is made of clauses that are individually satisfiable and non-tautologous.

In the paper, the enforcement of subsumption-free δ in Δ follows a minimal change policy and is defined as the extraction of *one* maximum-cardinality subset Δ' of $\Delta \cup \{\delta\}$ such that δ is derivable from Δ' whereas no strict sub-clause δ' of δ is derivable from Δ'. Equivalently, the last condition amounts to ensuring that δ is a prime implicate of Δ'.

Note that Δ' might not be unique: in this study, we concentrate on extracting *one* such Δ', with no specific preference on which set to select when several of them exist. However, we will comment on extending this study to the extraction of one preferred Δ' and to the enumeration of all Δ' later in the paper.

In the Boolean framework, when δ is an incoming piece of information and when Δ is satisfiable, the anti-subsumptive enforcement of δ departs from usual belief revision paradigms [6,7] in the fundamental following way: when δ is not contradictory with Δ, the anti-subsumptive enforcement of δ in Δ yields a set Δ' that is not necessarily (the deductive closure of) $\Delta \cup \{\delta\}$ since Δ' cannot allow any strict sub-clause of δ to be inferred. On the contrary, according to belief revision techniques, the result should be (the deductive closure of) $\Delta \cup \{\delta\}$ since this set is non-contradictory.

Quite surprisingly, the logical properties of anti-subsumptive enforcement of clauses have only been investigated recently [5]. Rationality postulates have been discussed in [8] and the extension of this paradigm to non-monotonic frameworks has been proposed in two different directions [9,10].

The focus in this paper is on addressing the practical computational challenges in the extraction of one Δ' and on investigating the scalability issue by considering very large Δ. As the number of clauses from $\Delta \cup \{\delta\}$ to be dropped in order to yield Δ' must be minimal, we will see that a direct approach to this problem requires the computation, for every longest strict sub-clause δ' of δ, of all the inclusion-maximal subsets (in short $\mathrm{MSS}_\subseteq$) of $\Delta \cup \{\delta\}$ that are satisfiable with the negation of δ'. As the number of $\mathrm{MSS}_\subseteq$ can be exponential in the number of clauses of $\Delta \cup \{\delta\}$, this approach is clearly intractable in the worst-case. Accordingly, we propose an approach that avoids the computation of all these $\mathrm{MSS}_\subseteq$ and yields Δ' by extracting in a direct way one cardinality-maximal (in short $\mathrm{MSS}_\#$) of $\Delta \cup \{\delta\}$ that is satisfiable with the negation of any of the aforementioned δ'. The approach is experimentally tested on very large Δ. It is easily extended to take into account a preference pre-ordering between clauses and lays down the foundations for the practical enumeration of all optimal solutions to the problem of making δ subsumption-free in Δ under a minimal change policy.

The paper is organized as follows. The preliminaries present basic logical concepts, including subsumption and implicates, as well as maximal satisfiable subsets and Partial-Max-SAT. The problem at hand is defined formally in Sect. 3. In Sect. 4, a natural -but highly intractable- approach is presented. Our approach is then introduced step by step in Sect. 5. Computational complexity issues are addressed in Sect. 6 and our experimental study is presented in Sect. 7. In the conclusion, extensions of the approach are sketched as paths for further studies.

2   Preliminaries

2.1   Logical Framework

We use standard clausal Boolean logic. Let $\mathcal{L}$ be a language of formulas over a finite alphabet of Boolean variables, also called *atoms*. Atoms are denoted by $a, b, c, \ldots \wedge, \vee, \neg, \rightarrow$ and $\equiv$ represent the standard conjunctive, disjunctive, negation, material implication and equivalence connectives, respectively. A *literal* is an atom or a negated atom. Formulas are built in the usual way from atoms, connectives and parentheses; they are denoted by $\alpha, \beta, \gamma, \ldots$ Sets of formulas are denoted by $\Delta, \Gamma, \ldots$ An *interpretation* is a truth assignment function that assigns values from $\{true, false\}$ to every Boolean variable, and thus, following usual compositional rules, to all formulas of $\mathcal{L}$. A formula δ is *consistent* (also called *satisfiable*) when there exists at least one interpretation that satisfies δ, i.e., that makes δ become *true*: such an interpretation is called a *model* of δ. $\models$ denotes deduction, i.e., $\Delta \models \delta$ denotes that δ is a logical consequence of Δ, namely that δ is satisfied in all models of Δ. $\models \alpha$ means that α is tautologous (i.e., *true* in all interpretations) and $\models \neg\alpha$ that α is a contradiction. A set of formulas Δ is consistent iff $\Delta \not\models \bot$, where $\bot$ stands for a contradiction. Without loss of generality, formulas can be represented in Conjunctive Normal Form (CNF), equivalent with respect to satisfiability. A CNF is a conjunction of clauses, where a *clause* is a disjunction of literals. We always assume that any clause contains at most one occurrence of a given literal. The empty clause denotes $\bot$ and is thus unsatisfiable; on the contrary, an empty set of clauses is satisfiable. A *unit clause* is a clause made of a single literal. For convenience, a clause can be identified with the set of its literals. The cardinality or size of a clause α refers to the set-theoretic representation of α and is denoted $card(\alpha)$: a maximal strict sub-clause of α is a strict sub-clause of α of maximal cardinality according to this representation. Deduction in clausal Boolean logic is co-NP-complete. Indeed, $\Delta \models \alpha$ iff $\Delta \cup \{\neg\alpha\}$ is unsatisfiable and checking whether a finite set of Boolean clauses is satisfiable is NP-complete.

The form of preemption paradigm that is addressed in this study is deep-rooted in the concepts of *subsumption* and *prime implicates*, which are well-studied in Boolean logic. In the following definitions, we assume that Δ is a satisfiable non-tautologous CNF, that α, β and δ are satisfiable non-tautologous clauses and that $\Delta \cup \{\delta\}$ is satisfiable.

Definition 1. α strictly subsumes β iff $\alpha \models \beta$ but $\beta \not\models \alpha$.

Definition 2. Δ strictly subsumes β iff $\Delta \models \alpha$ for some α such that α strictly subsumes β.

By abuse of words, we will write "subsume" in place of "strictly subsume".

When α and β are under their set-theoretical representation, α subsumes β iff α is a strict subset of β. When β is made of $n > 1$ literals, β is not subsumed by Δ iff none of the n maximal-inclusion strict sub-clauses of β can be deduced from Δ. Indeed, making sure that none of these latter sub-clauses is derivable in Δ is sufficient to ensure that no smaller strict sub-clause of δ is derivable in Δ.

Definition 3. *A prime implicate of Δ is any clause δ such that*

1. $\Delta \models \delta$, and
2. $\models (\delta' \equiv \delta)$ for every clause δ' such that $\Delta \models \delta'$ and $\delta' \models \delta$.

Prime implicates have already been investigated in belief change mainly because they provide a compact and syntax-independent representation of a belief base that is complete (see [11, 12]) and because useful computational tasks (like satisfiability checking and deduction) are polynomial tasks in this setting [13]. In the worst case, computing the set of prime implicates of Δ containing a clause β is however not in polynomial total time unless P=NP (it is in polynomial total time when for example the clause is positive or Δ is Horn) [14].

2.2   Forms of Maximal Satisfiable Subsets, Partial-Max-SAT

We make use of both the concepts of inclusion-maximal and cardinality-maximal satisfiable subsets of clauses, which have widespread roles in A.I. The condition that Δ is satisfiable is now dropped.

Definition 4. Φ is an inclusion-Maximal Satisfiable Subset of Δ, in short, Φ is an $\mathrm{MSS}_{\subseteq}(\Delta)$, iff Φ is satisfiable and $\forall \alpha \in \Delta \setminus \Phi$, $\Phi \cup \{\alpha\}$ is unsatisfiable.

Definition 5. Φ *is a cardinality-Maximal Satisfiable Subset of* Δ, *in short,* Φ *is an* $\mathrm{MSS}_{\#}(\Delta)$, *iff* Φ *is an* $\mathrm{MSS}_{\subseteq}(\Delta)$ *and* $\nexists\ \Phi'$ *s.t.* Φ' *is an* $\mathrm{MSS}_{\subseteq}(\Delta)$ *and* $\mathit{card}(\Phi)$ $< \mathit{card}(\Phi')$.

A Co-MSS of Δ is the set-theoretic complement in Δ of the corresponding MSS. For convenience, we write (Co-)MSS instead of (Co-)$\mathrm{MSS}_{\subseteq}$ and (Co-)$\mathrm{MSS}_{\#}$ and omit their argument when the context does not make this ambiguous or when no such distinction is necessary.

Definition 6. Ψ *is a Minimal Correction Subset (MCS or Co-MSS) of* Δ *iff* $\Psi = \Delta \setminus \Phi$ *where* Φ *is an MSS of* Δ.

Accordingly, Δ can always be partitioned into a pair made of one $\mathrm{MSS}_{\subseteq}$ and one Co-$\mathrm{MSS}_{\subseteq}$. Unless P=NP, extracting one such partition is intractable in the worst case since it belongs to the $\mathrm{FP}^{NP}[\mathrm{wit,log}]$ class: namely, the set of function problems that can be computed in polynomial time by executing a logarithmic number of calls to an NP oracle that returns a witness for the positive outcome [15]. Techniques to compute one such partition that prove very often efficient are described in [16,17]. Note that in the worst case the number of MSSes is exponential in the number of clauses in Δ: it is in $O(2^{n/2})$ where n is the number of clauses in Δ.

$\mathrm{MSS}_{\subseteq}$ and Co-$\mathrm{MSS}_{\subseteq}$ share strong relationships with MUSes, which are the inclusion-minimal unsatisfiable subsets of a set of clauses. Especially, Co-$\mathrm{MSS}_{\subseteq}$ can be computed as hitting sets on all MUSes.

Definition 7. $\Gamma \subseteq \Delta$ *is a Minimal Unsatisfiable Subset (in sort, MUS) of* Δ *iff* Γ *is unsatisfiable and* $\forall \alpha \in \Gamma$, $\Gamma \setminus \{\alpha\}$ *is satisfiable.*

The instance of the Max-SAT problem w.r.t. Δ consists in delivering the cardinality of any $\mathrm{MSS}_{\#}(\Delta)$. In the following, we consider the variant of Max-SAT that does not only deliver this cardinality but also one such $\mathrm{MSS}_{\#}(\Delta)$. Actually, we make use of the following variant definition of Partial-Max-SAT.

Definition 8. *Let* Σ_S *and* Σ_H *be two sets of clauses. Partial-Max-SAT(Σ_S, Σ_H) computes one cardinality-maximal subset of* Σ_S *that is satisfiable with* Σ_H. Σ_S *and* Σ_H *are called the sets of soft and hard constraints, respectively.*

By convention and for convenience in this paper, we assume that when Σ_H is unsatisfiable, Partial-Max-SAT yields the empty set, which is satisfiable. This variant of (Partial-)Max-SAT belongs to the Opt-P class of intractable problems [18], i.e., the class of functions computable by taking the maximum of the output values over all accepting paths of an NP machine.

3   Anti-subsumptive Enforcement: Definition

Recall that Δ is a (non-necessarily satisfiable) set of clauses, each of them being non-tautologous and satisfiable, and that δ is a satisfiable non-tautologous clause. Let Δ' be a set of clauses.

Definition 9. Δ' *is one anti-subsumptive enforcement of δ iff*

1. $\Delta' \subseteq (\Delta \cup \{\delta\})$, and
2. $\Delta' \models \delta$, and
3. Δ' is satisfiable, and
4. $\nexists \delta'$ such that $\delta' \subset \delta$ and $\Delta' \models \delta'$, and
5. $\nexists \Delta''$ obeying conditions 1. to 4. such that $card(\Delta'') > card(\Delta')$.

We say that δ prevails in Δ'.

Notice that conditions 2 and 4 entail that δ is a prime implicate of Δ'. It is also easy to see that δ belongs to Δ' and that there always exists at least one anti-subsumptive enforcement Δ' of δ in Δ: however, the unicity of Δ' is not guaranteed in the general case. Notice also that in condition 4, the $\delta' = \emptyset$ case is already handled by condition 3.

Although Δ' might not be one $MSS_\#(\Delta\cup\{\delta\})$, by abuse of notation we write that Δ' is one $MSS_\#$ of $(\Delta\cup\{\delta\})$ where δ prevails, denoted $MSS_\#(\Delta\cup\{\delta\}_{Prevail})$. In [8], this definition is refined by taking into account additional possibly desired properties for Δ'. Note that this definition involves some syntactic flavor as Δ' is defined as a subset of $\Delta \cup \{\delta\}$ vs. a subset of the deductive closure of $(\Delta \cup \{\delta\})$. An alternative definition based on the deductive closure of $(\Delta \cup \{\delta\})$ would require computational treatments and concepts that are additional to the ones described in this paper.

Note that the anti-subsumptive enforcement of δ encompasses the handling of inconsistent information within $\Delta \cup \{\delta\}$. Indeed, it yields one satisfiable set of clauses that contains δ. To some extent, this policy towards contradictory information is a form of credulous attitude that opts for δ since it yields one kind of maximal satisfiable subset of clauses containing δ among several possible ones, and discards every subset of clauses that does not contain δ.

4   Direct Approach

A simple situation is when δ is a unit clause. In this case, by definition, Partial-Max-SAT$(\Delta \cup \{\delta\}, \delta)$ yields one anti-subsumptive enforcement of δ in Δ. Let us now consider the case where δ is not a unit clause. Let δ' be any strict non-empty[2] sub-clause of δ. By Definition 8, Partial-Max-SAT$(\Delta \cup \{\delta\}, \{\neg\delta'\})$ extracts one satisfiable subset of $\Delta\cup\{\delta\}$ that does not entail δ' such that this set is cardinality-maximal. Let us note $\Delta_{\delta'}$ and $\Gamma_{\delta'}$ this extracted set and the complement of $\Delta_{\delta'}$ in $(\Delta \cup \{\delta\})$, i.e., $(\Delta \cup \{\delta\}) \setminus \Delta_{\delta'}$, respectively. Clearly, computing one such $\Gamma_{\delta'}$ for every strict sub-clause (or for every maximal strict sub-clause) δ' of δ and set-theoretic unioning the elements of these sets to form a set noted Γ would not ensure that $\Delta' = (\Delta\cup\{\delta\})\setminus\Gamma$ is always one $MSS_\#(\Delta\cup\{\delta\}_{Prevail})$. Indeed, although $card(\Gamma_{\delta'})$ is the minimal number of clauses to be rejected to guarantee

---

[2] From now on, we only consider non-empty sub-clauses δ' of δ and omit the "non-empty" term. Indeed, considering the empty clause δ' is not useful since Δ' must be satisfiable and thus never entails the empty clause.

that $(\Delta \cup \{\delta\}) \setminus \Gamma_{\delta'}$ does not entail δ', there might exist several such sets $\Gamma_{\delta'}$ and $card(\Gamma)$ might be minimal for only some of them. Moreover, not computing all $\Gamma_{\delta'}$ can lead to a wrong result.

Example 1. Assume $\Delta = \{a \vee \neg b, b\}$ and $\delta = a \vee \neg b$. Clearly, there is only one $MSS_{\#}$ of $\Delta \cup \{\delta\}$ where δ prevails, namely $\{a \vee \neg b\}$. Indeed, $\delta = a \vee \neg b$ has two maximal strict sub-clauses, namely a and $\neg b$. For $\delta' = a$, there are two possible $\Gamma_{\delta'}$, namely $\Gamma_a^1 = \{a \vee \neg b\}$ and $\Gamma_a^2 = \{b\}$. Assume that we extract Γ_a^1, only. There is a unique $\Gamma_{\delta'}$ for $\delta' = \neg b$, which is $\Gamma_{\neg b}^1 = \emptyset$ as Δ does not entail $\neg b$. $(\Delta \cup \{\delta\}) \setminus (\Gamma_a^2 \cup \Gamma_{\neg b}^1)$ yields $\{b\}$, which is not intended result $\{a \vee \neg b\}$.

Actually, a correct direct approach requires for each δ' the computation of all $\Gamma_{\delta'}$. Then, a selection of one $\Gamma_{\delta'}$ per δ' needs to be computed in such a way that the total number of different clauses to be dropped is minimal. Not surprisingly, this so-called direct approach proves intractable in the worst case since for each δ' the number of $\Delta_{\delta'}$ can be exponential in the number of clauses in $\Delta \cup \{\delta\}$. As our experimentations illustrate, it is often intractable even in simple situations, too.

5   Transformational Approach

By itself Partial-Max-SAT does not provide a solution to our problem when δ is not a unit clause. Indeed, we need to block the inference of any maximal strict sub-clause of δ while we allow the derivation of δ. Partial-Max-SAT$(\Delta \cup \{\delta\}, \bigcup_{\delta'} \neg \delta')$ would expel δ from the solution since $\{\delta\} \cup \bigcup_{\delta'} \neg \delta'$ is unsatisfiable.

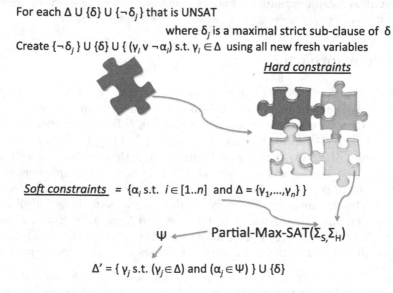

Fig. 1. Transformation into one instance of Partial-Max-SAT.

```
input :
Δ = {α₁, α₂, ..., αₙ}: a set of n non-tautologous Boolean clauses where each
individual clause is satisfiable;
   δ = {ℓ₁, ℓ₂, ..., ℓₘ}: a satisfiable non-tautologous clause represented through a
set of m literals;
output:
Δ': one anti-subsumptive enforcement of δ in Δ.
1  if δ is not a unit clause then
      /* Σ_S will be a set of soft clauses                              */
2     Σ_S ← {εᵢ s.t. i ∈ [1..n]}  /* every εᵢ is a fresh new atom      */
      /* Σ_H will be a set of hard clauses                             */
3     Σ_H ← ∅;
4     Ω ← {αᵢ ∨ ¬εᵢ s.t. αᵢ ∈ Δ};
5     foreach ℓⱼ ∈ δ do
6        δⱼ ← δ \ {ℓⱼ};
         /* δⱼ is a maximal strict sub-clause of δ                     */
7        if Δ ∪ {¬δⱼ} ∪ {δ} is unsatisfiable then
            /* Φⱼ is related to the sub-problem of blocking the
               inference of δⱼ                                          */
8           Φⱼ ← Ω ∪ {¬δⱼ} ∪ {δ};
9           Rename all atoms in Φⱼ (except the εᵢ) with fresh new atoms;
10          Σ_H ← Σ_H ∪ Φⱼ;
11       end
12    end
13    Ψ ← Partial-Max-SAT(Σ_S, Σ_H);
14    Δ' ← {αᵢ s.t. αᵢ ∈ Δ and εᵢ ∈ Ψ} ∪ {δ};
15 else
16    Δ' ← Partial-Max-SAT(Δ ∪ {δ}, {δ})
17 end
18 return Δ';
```

Algorithm 1. Extraction of one anti-assumptive enforcement of δ in Δ.

As a simple example, consider $\delta = a \vee b$, δ has two maximal strict sub-clauses: namely, a and b. $\{a \vee b, \neg a, \neg b\}$ is unsatisfiable. Unfortunately, we cannot simply compute Partial-Max-SAT$(\Delta \setminus \{\delta\}, \bigcup_{\delta'} \neg \delta')$ and then insert δ in the solution since this latter insertion can reinstate strict subsets of δ [5], meaning that the introduction of δ can lead strict sub-clauses of δ to become derivable.

To avoid the so-called *reinstatement* problem, the formal approach to pre-emption from [5,8] requires a multiple contraction [19] of Δ by $\delta \to \delta'$, considering all δ', to be achieved before δ is inserted. However, translated into satisfiability terms, the multiple contraction of Δ by $\delta \to \delta'$ is equivalent to the extraction of maximal subsets that are satisfiable at the same time with δ and $\bigcup_{\delta'} \neg \delta'$: Partial-Max-SAT remains thus inappropriate so far.

To break this deadlock and benefit from the practical efficiency of SAT technology, in particular of Partial-Max-SAT solvers, we transform the enforcement problem into an equivalent one that is solved by means of one single call to

Partial-Max-SAT. The idea is to create a specific sub-problem for each maximal strict sub-clause of δ' of δ that is entailed by $\Delta \cup \{\delta\}$ and merge the sub-problems in an appropriate way so that one call to a Partial-Max-SAT solver delivers the result. Such a transformation is best described using Fig. 1. Let us explain it intuitively.

First, an arbitrary ranking between the n clauses from Δ is selected and used throughout. The set of soft constraints Σ_S is a set of n new atoms α_i that are representing the n clauses from Δ. Note that Δ might already contain δ. Partial-Max-SAT will try to satisfy all these unit clauses, while satisfying at the same time a set of hard constraints Σ_H. Whenever one α_i is not satisfied in the solution to Partial-Max-SAT, this means that the corresponding i^{th} clause in Δ must be dropped from Δ to yield Δ' (which is finally augmented with $\{\delta\}$). This will occur when it appears that α must be falsified in order for a clause in Σ_H to be satisfiable. Σ_H is made of the set-theoretic union of several subsets of clauses and is built in such a way that it is always satisfiable. Each such subset of clauses represents one given sub-problem: namely, for one given maximal strict sub-clause of δ_i of δ, when $\Delta \cup \{\neg \delta_i\} \cup \{\delta\}$ is unsatisfiable, satisfy as many clauses as possible. This sub-problem is created and made independent from the other sub-problems (that are related to other δ_j's) by rewriting $\Delta \cup \{\neg \delta_i\} \cup \{\delta\}$ with all new variables. Now, the "glue" between the sub-problems and the soft constraints is made through the following use of additional $\neg \alpha_i$ disjuncts. Within each sub-problem, each ith clause coming from Δ is augmented with an additional disjunct $\neg \alpha_i$. In this way, each sub-problem is satisfiable but this might require some $\neg \alpha_i$'s to be *true*, which entails that the corresponding unit clauses α_i's from the soft clauses are falsified in any solution to Partial-Max-SAT.

Algorithm 1 depicts the pseudo-code for the transformational approach.

Theorem 1. *Let Δ be a possibly unsatisfiable set of non-tautologous clauses where each clause is satisfiable. Let δ be a satisfiable non-tautologous clause. Let Δ' be the output of Algorithm 1. We have that Δ' is one anti-subsumptive enforcement of δ in Δ.*

6   Computational Complexity Issues

Let n be the number of clauses in Δ and k be the number of literals in δ.

The direct approach is exponential since the number of MSSes of Δ is $O(2^{n/2})$ in the worst case. As mentioned earlier, the extraction of one MSS is itself intractable in the worst case since this task belongs to the $\text{FP}^{NP}[\text{wit,log}]$ class; notice that the cardinality of each of the sets of clauses in which MSSes are extracted is $n + k$ since we augment the n clauses of Δ with δ and with the $k - 1$ unit literals corresponding to $\neg \delta_j$. In practice, several approaches have been proposed to enumerate all MSSes of an unsatisfiable set of Boolean clauses when the number of MSSes remains low (see e.g., [17] for a survey). However, an explicit enumeration of MSSes is often out of reach: for example, when a set of clauses contains m MUSes of size s with empty intersections, there are s^m MSSes. Hence, we expect the direct approach to be out of reach, very often.

Unless P = NP, the transformational approach is intractable in the worst case, too: it belongs to the Opt-P class, due to the call to our variant of Partial-Max-SAT. Fortunately, many large-size instances are solved by SAT and Partial-Max-SAT solvers [20] and we rely on this in proposing the transformational approach. Now, clearly the size of the sets of hard and soft constraints can be effective limiting parameters. In the call to Partial-Max-SAT, the cardinality of the set of soft constraints is n and the worst-case cardinality of the set of hard clauses is $k(n+k)$. When δ is intended to represent a rule, it seems natural to expect k to remain low, as k expresses the number of literals in the rule that must prevail. The actual cardinality of the set of hard clauses is $k'(n+k)$ where $k' \leq k$ is the number of maximal strict sub-clauses of δ that are actually entailed by $\Delta \cup \{\delta\}$. Note also that k' can be actually replaced by a lower number when a pre-processing step expels from Δ all strict sub-clauses of δ that are explicitly present in Δ: accordingly, the corresponding maximal strict sub-clauses might not require the creation of sub-problems for preventing them from being inferable. In the same vein, when δ is explicitly present in Δ, there is no need to create a soft constraint corresponding to δ since δ must belong to any solution Δ': in such a case, n need thus be decremented by 1 in all the above results.

7   Experimental Illustration

Even when SAT checking is performed quickly, the direct approach thus suffers from a combinatorial blow-up threat due a potential exponential number of $MSS_{\subseteq}$. Illustrating through experimentations how this exponential number can actually occur is not much informative by itself: indeed, it is easy to build instances such that δ and/or the negation of strict sub-clauses of δ conflict with Δ in s totally different minimal ways, leading to a number of $MSS_{\subseteq}$ that increases exponentially with s. Nevertheless it might be interesting to illustrate the actual numbers of $MSS_{\subseteq}$ that the direct approach manages to extract as a necessary part of its global task on some realistic instances. But the more interesting question to be investigated from an experimental side is the extent to which Partial-Max-SAT solvers can handle the cardinality increase of the sets of constraints due to the kind of replication, for each maximal strict sub-clause of δ, of the problem of blocking the derivability of one such sub-clause. Obviously, the most informative cases would occur when the direct approach fails due to a combinatorial blow-up of the number of $MSS_{\subseteq}$.

In order to conduct such an illustration, we have made extensive experimentations, using a wide range of usual benchmarks Δ from the planning area as a case study (actually, 248 of them). They represent the domain knowledge, the initial and goal states and some time-horizon for a given planning problem. They include a wide range of such problems with varying horizon lengths, like for example, "*Blocks_right_x*" for the usual blocks-world problem with x blocks; "*Bomb_bx_by*" involves neutralizing bx bombs in by locations. "*Coins_px*" is about px coins that must be tossed for heads and tails such that they reach a same state. "*Comm_px*" is an IPC5 problem about communication signals with several stages, packets, and actions. "*Empty-room_dx_dy*" is about navigating inside a room of size dx and containing dy objects. "*Safe_n*" is about opening a safe that has n possible combinations. "*sort_num_s_x*" is about proposing circuits of compare-and-swap gates to sort x Boolean variables. Finally, "*uts_kx*" is about a network routing for mobile ad-hoc networks where a broadcast from an unknown node must reach all other nodes; the topology of the network is partially known and each node has a fixed number kx of connected neighbors. They were translated into CNF from their initial PDDL 1.2 (Planing Domain Definition Language) and STRIPS format, using H. Palacios' translator, available from http://www.plg.inf.uc3m.es/~hpalacio/.

For each instance, all this information formed a satisfiable Δ. Note that considering an unsatisfiable Δ could have resulted in an increased number of $\mathrm{MSS}_\subseteq$ since the related minimal proofs of unsatisfiability on which they are built would not necessarily contain δ and/or some of the negation of strict subclauses of δ. The size of the instances (namely, of Δ) ranged from 44 to 45087 clauses, and from 22 to 6744 variables (with 4320 clauses and 1155 variables, on average).

Then, for each Δ, we have randomly generated one δ using variables occurring in Δ in such a way that the following conditions were met.

1. $\Delta \cup \{\delta\}$ is satisfiable. In this way, we focused on the pure issue of blocking subsumption itself, not augmented with the problem of recovering from unsatisfiability when $\Delta \cup \{\delta\}$ is unsatisfiable. As already indicated, if unsatisfiable Δ had been selected then the number of $\mathrm{MSS}_\subseteq$ could have been even larger.

2. $k = card(\delta) \in \{5, 7, 10\}$ as we consider these values as realistic for representing some information that must not be subsumed in the planning problem: for example, a clause representing a planning decision rule that should not be subsumed and that involves various detailed pre-conditions, like "if these $k - 1$ preconditions are *true* then do this" where, additionally, we want to make sure that the action is in no way done when some of the preconditions are not met.

3. The number of maximal strict sub-clauses of δ_j of δ that are entailed by $\Delta \cup \{\delta\}$ is $k' \geq (k \ div \ 2)$.

Accordingly, we considered 744 instances since for each of the 248 initial instances, we considered 3 values for $card(\delta)$. We generated δ randomly from the variables occurring in Δ to express some possible information that should preempt any of its strict sub-clauses. As a random generation might lead to very specific non-representative instances, we have mitigated this risk as follows. 3 different random generations of δ satisfying the above conditions were actually made for each of the 744 instances and we recorded the average results for the experimentations on the three corresponding $\Delta \cup \{\delta\}$. However, when time-out or memory-overflow was reached for at least one of the 3 runs for any of the 744 instances, we have recorded this time-out or memory-overflow as the "average"

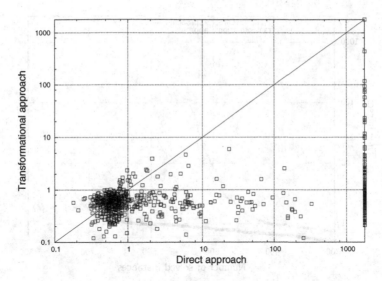

Fig. 2. Time to solve: direct vs. transformational approaches.

value as result for corresponding instance, being thus in that way over-pessimistic on the actual performance of the methods.

All experimentations have been conducted on Intel Xeon E5-2643 (3.30 GHz) processors with 8 Gb RAM on Linux CentOS. For the $MSS_\subseteq$ extractions, we used the CMP method from [16]. CAMUS [21] http://sun.iwu.edu/~mliffito/camus/ was used to enumerate all $MSS_\subseteq$ and Co-$MSS_\subseteq$. MSUNCORE [22] http://logos.ucd.ie/wiki/doku.php?id=msuncore and MINISAT [23] http://minisat.se/ were selected as Partial-Max-SAT and SAT solvers, respectively. Time out was set to 1800 s for each single anti-subsumptive enforcement.

All data and detailed results for each instance are available at http://www.cril.fr/anti-subsumptive.

Algorithm 1 solved 735 instances on a total of 744; each solved instance, except 10 of them, required less than 10 s and 607 less than one second. The approach was thus most often able to cope with the increase of size of the set of constraints: the cardinality of the set of hard constraints was (k div 2) times the size of the initial instance, were $k \in \{5, 7, 10\}$. As we assume that $k = 10$ is a maximum size for a clause that is expected to represent either a pure disjunctive information where each strict sub-clause cannot be derived, or a rule that must not be subsumed, these results are strong points for the viability of the approach. The 10 instances that were solved in more than 10 s and the 9 unsolved ones belonged to the same planning problem, namely "*blocks_right_x*", they were not among the largest instances but appeared harder than the other ones with respect to our problem.

The direct approach solved 514 instances, only. The maximal number of $MSS_\subseteq$ computed for an instance was 601 261 (but the direct approach failed to solve the related problem (namely, *ring2-r6-p-t3*, which is about closing a series of windows in several connected rooms forming a ring) whereas the transformational approach solved it in less than 0.5 s).

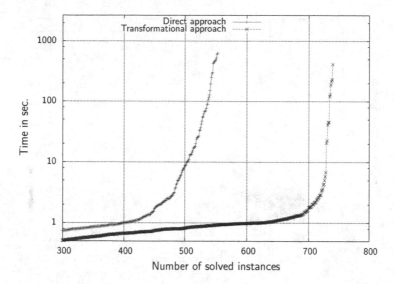

Fig. 3. Cumulated number of solved instances: direct vs. transformational approaches.

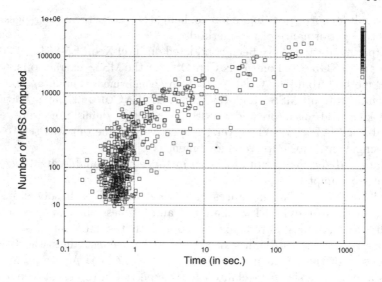

Fig. 4. Number of $MSS_{\subseteq}$ computed by the direct approach.

The cactus plots using logarithmic scales given in Fig. 2 depict the time-efficiency of both approaches: the results do not come as a surprise: the transformational approach proved more efficient, most often. Figure 3 show the cumulated number of solved instances according to the time spent. The cactus plots in Fig. 4 show that the number of $MSS_{\subseteq}$ and their handling was manageable for many instances in our benchmarks. But the upper right corner shows the numerous instances where combinatorial blow-up made the task out of scope for the direct approach. Obviously enough, in the general case, we cannot predict the number of $MSS_\subseteq$ that need to be extracted for one given δ, without computing them.

The number of clauses to be dropped in $\Delta \cup \{\delta\}$ by the transformational approach in order to yield Δ' ranged from 1 to 9, with an average of 3.65.

The full results for each instance are available in table form at http://www. cril.fr/anti-subsumptive. These experimental results thus illustrate the actual viability of the transformational approach, which should be preferred over the direct one.

8 Conclusion and Perspectives

Although it is a very natural and ubiquitous reasoning paradigm, the anti-subsumptive enforcement of knowledge has received little attention in the A.I. research and automated reasoning areas. In this study, we have proposed a method to compute one solution in the Boolean framework that is optimal in terms of the minimization of the number of clauses to be discarded. Interestingly, it proves more effective than a direct approach that requires inclusion-maximal satisfiable subsets to be extracted. Let us conclude this paper by introducing several promising directions according to which it is possible to push the envelope and extend the scope of the transformational approach. Firstly, the approach remains appropriate when one needs to deliver one cardinality-maximal satisfiable subset that obeys a preference pre-ordering between clauses, should this pre-order translate various credibility, uncertainty or preference levels amongst the information. Weighted Max-SAT should be used instead of Partial-Max-SAT and the weights of clauses should reflect the pre-ordering. In the transformation, the soft clauses become clauses with the lowest possible weight whereas δ and the unit clauses that encode the negation of the largest sub-clauses δ_j of δ receive the highest ranking. Secondly, the transformational approach could easily accommodate the anti-subsumptive enforcement of a CNF formula. Indeed, this amounts to making sure that the formula can be deduced whereas no strict non-empty sub-clause of any clause in the formula can be deduced. Finally, the extraction of one enforcement Δ' to is the first step towards computing all such enforcements. Hence, Partial-Max-SAT could be iterated and already extracted enforcements could be marked to avoid duplicate extractions. Techniques described in [16,17] can prove useful to that end. Obviously enough, the complete enumeration cannot always be achieved since the number of possible Δ' is exponential in the worst case.

References

1. Buchanan, B.G., Shortliffe, E.H. (eds.): Rule-Based Expert Systems: The MYCIN Experiments of the Stanford Heuristic Programming Project. Addison-Wesley, Reading (1984)
2. Touretzky, D.S.: The Mathematics of Inheritance Systems. Morgan Kaufmann, Los Altos (1986)

3. Sombe, L. (collective work): Reasoning Under Incomplete Information in Artificial Intelligence: A Comparison of Formalisms Using a Simple Example. Wiley, New York (1990)
4. Ginsberg, D.L.: Readings in Nonmonotonic Authors. Morgan Kaufmann, Los Altos (1988)
5. Besnard, P., Grégoire, É., Ramon, S.: Enforcing logically weaker knowledge in classical logic. In: Xiong, H., Lee, W.B. (eds.) KSEM 2011. LNCS, vol. 7091, pp. 44–55. Springer, Heidelberg (2011)
6. Alchourrón, C., Gärdenfors, P., Makinson, D.: On the logic of theory change: partial meet contraction and revision functions. J. Symbolic Logic **50**(2), 510–530 (1985)
7. Fermé, E.L., Hansson, S.O.: AGM 25 years - twenty-five years of research in belief change. J. Philos. Logic **40**(2), 295–331 (2011)
8. Besnard, P., Grégoire, É., Ramon, S.: Preemption operators. In: Proceedings of the 20th European Conference on Artificial Intelligence (ECAI 2012), pp. 893–894 (2012)
9. Besnard, P., Grégoire, É., Ramon, S.: Overriding subsuming rules. Int. J. Approximate Reasoning **54**(4), 452–466 (2013)
10. Grégoire, É.: Knowledge preemption and defeasible rules. In: Buchmann, R., Kifor, C.V., Yu, J. (eds.) KSEM 2014. LNCS, vol. 8793, pp. 13–24. Springer, Heidelberg (2014)
11. Zhuang, Z.Q., Pagnucco, M., Meyer, T.: Implementing iterated belief change via prime implicates. In: Orgun, M.A., Thornton, J. (eds.) AI 2007. LNCS (LNAI), vol. 4830, pp. 507–518. Springer, Heidelberg (2007)
12. Bienvenu, M., Herzig, A., Qi, G.: Prime implicate-based belief revision operators. In: 20th European Conference on Artificial Intelligence (ECAI 2012), pp. 741–742 (2008)
13. Darwiche, A., Marquis, P.: A knowledge compilation map. J. Artif. Intell. Res. (JAIR) **17**, 229–264 (2002)
14. Eiter, T., Makino, K.: Generating all abductive explanations for queries on propositional horn theories. In: Baaz, M., Makowsky, J.A. (eds.) CSL 2003. LNCS, vol. 2803, pp. 197–211. Springer, Heidelberg (2003)
15. Marques-Silva, J., Janota, M.: On the query complexity of selecting few minimal sets. Electron. Colloquium Comput. Complex. (ECCC) **21**, 31 (2014)
16. Grégoire, É., Lagniez, J.M., Mazure, B.: An experimentally efficient method for (MSS, CoMSS) partitioning. In: Proceedings of the 28th Conference on Artificial Intelligence (AAAI 2014) (2014)
17. Marques-Silva, J., Heras, F., Janota, M., Previti, A., Belov, A.: On computing minimal correction subsets. In: Proceedings of the 23rd International Joint Conference on Artificial Intelligence (IJCAI 2013) (2013)
18. Papadimitriou, C.H., Yannakakis, M.: Optimization, approximation, and complexity classes. J. Comput. Syst. Sci. **43**(3), 425–440 (1991)
19. Fuhrmann, A., Hansson, S.O.: A survey of multiple contractions. J. Logic Lang. Inf. **3**(1), 39–76 (1994)
20. Ninth Max-SAT Evaluation (2014). http://www.maxsat.udl.cat/14/index.html
21. Liffiton, M., Sakallah, K.: Algorithms for computing minimal unsatisfiable subsets of constraints. J. Autom. Reasoning **40**(1), 1–33 (2008)
22. Morgado, A., Heras, F., Marques-Silva, J.: Improvements to core-guided binary search for MaxSAT. In: Cimatti, A., Sebastiani, R. (eds.) SAT 2012. LNCS, vol. 7317, pp. 284–297. Springer, Heidelberg (2012)
23. Eén, N., Sörensson, N.: An extensible SAT-solver. In: Giunchiglia, E., Tacchella, A. (eds.) SAT 2003. LNCS, vol. 2919, pp. 502–518. Springer, Heidelberg (2004)

Value Sensitivity and Observable Abstract Values for Information Flow Control

Luciano Bello[1]([✉]), Daniel Hedin[1,2], and Andrei Sabelfeld[1]

[1] Chalmers University of Technology, Gothenburg, Sweden
bello@chalmers.se
[2] Mälardalen University, Västerås, Sweden

Abstract. Much progress has recently been made on information flow control, enabling the enforcement of increasingly rich policies for increasingly expressive programming languages. This has resulted in tools for mainstream programming languages as JavaScript, Java, Caml, and Ada that enforce versatile security policies. However, a roadblock on the way to wider adoption of these tools has been their limited permissiveness (high number of false positives). Flow-, context-, and object-sensitive techniques have been suggested to improve the precision of static information flow control and dynamic monitors have been explored to leverage the knowledge about the current run for precision.

This paper explores *value sensitivity* to boost the permissiveness of information flow control. We show that both dynamic and hybrid information flow mechanisms benefit from value sensitivity. Further, we introduce the concept of *observable abstract values* to generalize and leverage the power of value sensitivity to richer programming languages. We demonstrate the usefulness of the approach by comparing it to known disciplines for dealing with information flow in dynamic and hybrid settings.

1 Introduction

Much progress has recently been made on information flow control, enabling the enforcement of increasingly rich policies for increasingly expressive programming languages. This has resulted in tools for mainstream programming languages as FlowFox [16] and JSFlow [20] for JavaScript, Jif [26], Paragon [9] and JOANA [17] for Java, FlowCaml [30] for Caml, LIO [31] for Haskell, and SPARK Examiner [5] for Ada that enforce versatile security policies. However, a roadblock on the way to wider adoption of these tools has been their limited permissiveness i.e. secure programs are falsely rejected due to over-approximations. Flow-, context-, and object-sensitive techniques [17] have been suggested to improve the precision of static information flow control, and dynamic and hybrid monitors [19,20,22,27,32] have been explored to leverage the knowledge about the current run for precision. Dynamic and hybrid techniques are particularly promising for highly dynamic languages such as JavaScript. With dynamic languages as longterm goal, we focus on fundamental principles for sound yet permissive dynamic information flow control with possible static enhancements.

© Springer-Verlag Berlin Heidelberg 2015
M. Davis et al. (Eds.): LPAR-20 2015, LNCS 9450, pp. 63–78, 2015.
DOI: 10.1007/978-3-662-48899-7_5

In dynamic information flow control, each value is associated with a runtime *security label* representing the *security classification* of the value. These labels are propagated during computation to track the flow of information through the program. There are two basic kinds of flows: *explicit* and *implicit* [14]. The former is induced by *data flow*, e.g., when a value is copied from one location to another, while the latter is induced by *control flow*. The following example of implicit flow leaks the boolean value of h into l with no explicit flow involved: `l = false;if (h) l = true;`

Dynamic information flow control typically enforces *termination-insensitive non-interference* (TINI) [33]. Under a two-level classification into *public* and *secret* values, TINI demands that values labeled public are independent of values labeled secret in *terminating runs* of a program. Note that this demand includes the label itself, which has the effect of constraining how security labels are allowed to change during computation. This is a fundamental restriction: freely allowing labels to change allows circumventing the enforcement [27].

A common approach to securing label change is the *no secret upgrade (NSU)* restriction that forbids labels from changing under *secret control*, i.e., when the control flow is depending on secrets [2]. In the above example, NSU would stop the execution when h is `true`. This enforces TINI because in all *terminating* runs the l is untouched and hence independent of h.

Unfortunately, his limitation of *pure dynamic* information flow control often turns out to be too restrictive in practice [20], and various ways of lifting the restriction have been proposed [3,8]. They aim to enhance the dynamic analysis with information that allows the label of *write target* to be changed before entering secret control, thus decoupling the label change from secret influence. For instance, a *hybrid* approach [19,22,27,32] is to apply a static analysis on the bodies of *elevated contexts*, e.g., secret conditionals, to find all potential write targets and upgrade them before the body is executed.

This paper investigates an alternative approach that improves both pure and hybrid dynamic information flow control as well as other approaches relying on upgrading labels before elevated contexts. The approach increases the *precision* of the labeling, hence reducing the number of elevated contexts. In a pure dynamic analysis this has the effect of reducing the number of points in the program where execution is stopped with a security error, while in a hybrid approach this reduces the number of places the static analysis invoked further improving the precision by not unnecessarily upgrading write targets.

Resting on a simple core, the approach is surprisingly powerful. We call the mechanism *value sensitive*, since it considers the previous target *value* of a monitored side-effect and, if that value remains *unchanged* by the update, the security label is left untouched. Consider the program in Listing 1.1. It is safe to allow execution to continue even when h is `true` by effectively ignoring the update of l in the body of the conditional. This still satisfies TINI because all runs of the program leaves l untouched and independent of h.

Listing 1.1.

```
l = false;
if (h) {l = false;}
```

The generalization of the idea boosts permissiveness when applied to other notions of values, e.g. the type of a variable, as exemplified on the right. In a dynamically typed language the value

```
t = 2^L ;
t = 1^H ;
l = typeof(t);
```

of t changes from a public to a secret value, but the (dynamic) type of t remains unchanged. By value of t changes from a public to a secret value, but the (dynamic) type of t remains unchanged. By tracking the type of t independently of its value (for example as $\langle value^\sigma, type^{\sigma'} \rangle$), it is possible to leverage value sensitivity and allow the security label of the type to remain public. Thus, l is tagged L, which is safe and more precise than under traditional monitoring.

Similarly, if we consider a language with records, the following snippet illustrates that the field existence of a property can be observable independently. In a language with observable existence (in this case through the primitive in) a monitor might gain precision by labeling this feature independently of the value. The label does not need to be updated when the property assignment is run, since the existence of the property remains the same.

```
o = { p: 2^L };
o['p'] = 1^H ;
l ='p' in o;
```

The type and the existence are two examples of properties of runtime values that can be independently observed and change less often than the values. We refer to such properties as *Observable Abstract Values* (OAV). Value sensitivity can be applied to any OAVs. The synergy between these two concepts has the power to improve existing purely dynamic and hybrid information flow monitors, as well as improving existing techniques to handle advanced data types as dynamic objects. The main contributions of this paper are

- the introduction of the concept of *value sensitivity* in the setting of *observable abstract values*, realized by systematic use of *lifted maps*,
- showing how the notion of value sensitivity naturally entails the notion of *existence* and *structure* labels, frequently used in the analysis of *dynamic objects* in addition to improving the precision of previous techniques while significantly simplifying the semantics and correctness proofs.
- the application of value sensitivity to develop a novel approach to *hybrid* information flow control, where not only the underlying *dynamic* analysis but also the *static* counterpart is improved by value sensitivity.

We believe that systematic application of value sensitivity on identified observable abstract values can serve as a method when designing dynamic and hybrid information flow control mechanism for new languages and language constructs. The full version [1] of the paper contains the full details and proofs.

2   The Core Language $\mathcal{L}$

We illustrate the power of the approach on a number of specialized languages formulated as extensions to a small while language $\mathcal{L}$, defined as follows.

$$e ::= l \mid e \oplus e \mid x \mid x = e \quad s ::= \texttt{if}(e)\{s\}\{s\} \mid \texttt{while}(e)\{s\} \mid s;s \mid \texttt{skip} \mid e$$

The expressions consist of literal values l, binary operators abstractly represented by $\oplus$, variables and variable assignments. The statements are built up by conditional branches, while loops, sequencing and skip, with expressions lifted into the category of statements.

$$S : string \rightarrow LabeledValue \quad v:: = bool \mid integer \mid string \mid \mathbf{undef}$$

$$\dot{v} \in LabeledValue:: = v^{\sigma} \quad C:: = \langle S, \dot{v} \rangle \mid S \quad pc, \sigma, \omega \in Label$$

The semantics of the core language is a standard dynamic monitor. The primitive values are booleans, integers, strings and the distinguished **undef** value returned when reading a variable that has not been initialized. The values are labeled with security labels drawn from a lattice of security labels, *Label*. Let $\perp \in Label$ denote the least element. Unless indicated otherwise, in the examples, a two-point lattice $L \sqsubseteq H$ is used, representing *low* for public information and *high* for secret. The label operator $\sqcup$ notates the least-upper-bound in the lattice.

$$\text{ASSIGN} \frac{\langle S_1, e \rangle \rightarrow_{pc} \langle S_2, \dot{v} \rangle \quad S_2[x \xleftarrow{\text{undef}^{\perp}} \dot{v}]\downarrow_{pc} S_3}{\langle S_1, x = e \rangle \rightarrow_{pc} \langle S_3, \dot{v} \rangle}$$

$$\text{IF} \frac{\langle S_1, e \rangle \rightarrow_{pc} \langle S_2, v^{\sigma} \rangle \quad \langle S_2, s_v \rangle \rightarrow_{pc \sqcup \sigma} S_3}{\langle S_1, \mathbf{if}\,(e)\,\{s_{\text{true}}\}\{s_{\text{false}}\}\rangle \rightarrow_{pc} S_3} \qquad \text{VAR} \frac{S_{\text{undef}^{\perp}}(x) = \dot{v}}{\langle S, x \rangle \rightarrow_{pc} \langle S, \dot{v} \rangle}$$

Fig. 1. Partial $\mathcal{L}$ semantics

The semantics is a big-step semantics of the form $\langle S, s \rangle \rightarrow_{pc} C$ read as: the statement s executing under the label of the program counter pc and initial state S results in the configuration C. The states are *partial maps* from variable names to labeled values and the configurations are either states or pairs of states and values.

The main elements of the semantic are described in Fig. 1, with the remaining rules in the [1] for space reasons. The selected rules illustrate the interplay between conditionals, the pc and assignment. The IF rule elevates the pc to the label of the guard and evaluates the branch taken under the elevated pc. The VAR rule and the ASSIGN rule, for variable look up and side effects, use operations on the *lifted partial map*, $S_{\text{undef}^{\perp}}$, to read and write to variables respectively. In the latter case, this is where the pc constrains the side effects.

Lifted partial maps provide a generic way to safely interact with partial maps with labeled codomains. For example, as shown in Fig. 1, a lifted partial map is used to interact with the variable environment. In general, lifted partial maps are very versatile and in Sect. 3 will be used to model a variety of aspects.

A lifted partial map is a partial map with a default value. For a partial map $\mathcal{M} : X \rightarrow Y$, the map $\mathcal{M}_{\Delta} : X \rightarrow Y \cup \Delta$ is the lifted map with default value Δ, where $\mathcal{M}_{\Delta}(x) = \begin{cases} \mathcal{M}(x) & x \in dom(\mathcal{M}) \\ \Delta & \text{otherwise} \end{cases}$ This defines the reading operation.

For writing, $\mathcal{M}[x\xleftarrow{\Delta}\dot{v}] \downarrow_{pc} \mathcal{M}'$ denotes that x is safely updated with the value $\dot{v}$ in the partial map $\mathcal{M}$, resulting in the new partial map $\mathcal{M}'$. Formally, the MUPDATE rule governs this side-effect as follows:

To update the element x of a lifted partial map with a labeled value $\dot{v}$, the current value of x needs

$$\text{MUPDATE} \ \frac{\mathcal{M}_\Delta(x) = w^\omega \quad pc \sqsubseteq \omega}{\mathcal{M}[x\xleftarrow{\Delta}\dot{v}]\downarrow_{pc} \mathcal{M}[x \mapsto \dot{v}^{pc}]}$$

to be fetched. To block implicit leaks, the label of this value, ω, has to be above the level of the context, pc. In terms of the variable environment above, if a variable holds a low value, it cannot be updated in a high context. If the update is allowed, the label of the new value is lifted to the pc ($\dot{v}^{pc}$) before being stored in x. This implements the standard NSU restriction.

However, there is a situation where this restriction can be relaxed: when the variable to update already holds the value to write, i.e., when the side-effect is not observable. In this case, the update can be safely ignored rather than causing a security error, even if the target of the side-effect is not above the level of the context.

The MUPDATE-VS rule extends the permissiveness of the monitor in cases where $pc \not\sqsubseteq: \omega$, like in Listing 1.1. Intuitively, the assignment statement

$$\text{MUPDATE-VS} \ \frac{\mathcal{M}_\Delta(x) = w^\omega \quad pc \not\sqsubseteq \omega \quad w = v}{\mathcal{M}[x\xleftarrow{\Delta}\dot{v}]\downarrow_{pc} \mathcal{M}}$$

does not break the NSU invariant and it is safe to allow it. We call an enforcement that takes the previous value of the write target into account *value-sensitive*.

Note that, in the semantics, security errors are not explicitly modeled - rather they are manifested as the failure of the semantics to progress. In a semantics with only the MUPDATE rule, any update that does not satisfy the demands will cause execution to stop. The addition of MUPDATE-VS however allows the special case, where the value does not change, to progress.

3 Observable Abstract Values

The notion of value sensitivity naturally scales from values to other properties of the semantics. Any property that can act as mutable state, i.e., that can be read and written, is a potential candidate. In the case where the property changes less frequently than the value, such a modeling may increase the precision. In particular, assuming that the property is modeled with a security label of its own, the NSU label check can be omitted when an idempotent operation, with respect to the property, is performed. We refer to such properties as *Observable Abstract Values* (OAV). Consider the following examples of OAVs:

- **Dynamic Types.** It is common that the value held by a variable is secret, while its type is not. In addition, values of variables change more frequently than types which means that most updates of variables do not change the type.
- **Property Existence.** The existence of properties in records or objects can be observed independently of their value. Changing a value in a property does not affect its existence.

– **List or Array Length.** Related to property existence, the length of a list or array is independent of the values. Mutating the list or the array without adding or deleting values does not affect the length.
– **Graph/Tree Structure.** More generally, not only the number of nodes in a data structure, but any observable structural characteristic can be modeled as OAVs, such as tree height.
– **Security Labels.** Sometimes [9, 10] the labels on the values are observable. Since they change less often than the value themselves, they can be modeled as OAVs.

Different OAVs are not necessarily independent. In the same way an OAV is an abstraction of a value, it is possible to find OAVs that are natural abstractions of other OAVs. Such partial order is of interest both from an implementation and proof perspective. For space reasons we refer the reader to the full version [1] of the paper for more information.

The rest of this section explains the first two examples above as extensions of the core language $\mathcal{L}$. The extension with dynamic types $\mathcal{L}_t$ is detailed in Sect. 3.1, and the extension with records modeling existence and structure $\mathcal{L}_r$ is detailed in Sect. 3.2. The two latter extensions illustrate that the approach subsumes and improves previous handling of records [18].

3.1   Dynamic Types $\mathcal{L}_t$

Independent labeling of OAVs allows for increased precision when combined with value sensitivity. To illustrate this point, consider the example in Listing 1.2 where the types are independently observable from the values themselves, via the primitive

Listing 1.2.

```
t = ⟨1^H, int^L⟩;
if (h) {t = 2;} else {t = 3;}
l = typeof(t);
```

`typeof()`. Assuming that the value of t is initially secret while the type is not, the example in the listing illustrates how the value of t is made dependent on h while the type remains independent.

The precision gain is significant for, e.g., JavaScript. A common defensive programming pattern for JavaScript library code is to probe for the presence of needed functionality in order to fail gracefully in case

Listing 1.3.

```
if (typeof document.cookie
    !==''undefined'') { ... }
```

it is absent. Consider, for instance, a library that interacts with `document.cookie`. Even if all browsers support this particular property, it is dangerous for a library to assume that it is present, since the library might be loaded in, e.g., a sandbox that removes parts of the API. For this reason it is very common for libraries to employ the defensive pattern shown in Listing 1.3, where the dots represent the entire library code. While the value of `document.cookie` is secret its presence is not. If no distinction between the type of a value and its actual value is made this would cause the entire library to execute under secret control.

To illustrate this scenario, we extend $\mathcal{L}$ with dynamic types and a `typeof()` operation that given an expression returns a string representing the type of the expression:

$$e:: = (\cdots \text{as in } \mathcal{L}) \mid \texttt{typeof}(e) \quad s:: = (\cdots \text{as in } \mathcal{L})$$

The semantics is changed to accommodate dynamically typed values. In particular typed values are pairs of a security labeled value, and a security labeled dynamic type. Additionally, the state $\mathcal{S}$ is extended to a tuple holding the value context $\mathcal{V}$ and the type context $\mathcal{T}$.

$$\mathcal{V} : string \rightarrow LabeledValue \quad \mathcal{T} : string \rightarrow LabeledType$$

$$TypedValue:: = \langle \hat{v}, \hat{t} \rangle \quad t \in Type:: = bool \mid int \mid str \mid undef \quad \mathcal{S} \in State:: = \langle \mathcal{V}, \mathcal{T} \rangle$$

A consequence of the extension with dynamic types is that the semantic rules must be changed to operate on typed values. Figure 2 contains the most interesting rules - the remaining rules can be found in the full version of this paper [1].

$$\text{ASSIGN}_t \frac{\langle \mathcal{S}_1, e \rangle \rightarrow_{pc} \langle \langle \mathcal{V}_2, \mathcal{T}_2 \rangle, \langle \hat{v}, \hat{t} \rangle \rangle \quad \mathcal{V}_2[x \xleftarrow{\texttt{undef}^{\perp}} \hat{v}] \downarrow_{pc} \mathcal{V}_3 \quad \mathcal{T}_2[x \xleftarrow{undef^{\perp}} \hat{t}] \downarrow_{pc} \mathcal{T}_3}{\langle \mathcal{S}_1, x = e \rangle \rightarrow_{pc} \langle \langle \mathcal{V}_3, \mathcal{T}_3 \rangle, \langle \hat{v}, \hat{t} \rangle \rangle}$$

$$\text{TYPEOF} \frac{\langle \mathcal{S}_1, e \rangle \rightarrow_{pc} \langle \mathcal{S}_2, \langle \hat{v}, \hat{t} \rangle \rangle}{\langle \mathcal{S}_1, \texttt{typeof}(e) \rangle \rightarrow_{pc} \langle \mathcal{S}_2, \langle string(\hat{t}), str^{\perp} \rangle \rangle}$$

$$\text{VAR}_t \frac{\mathcal{V}_{\texttt{undef}^{\perp}}(x) = \hat{v} \quad \mathcal{T}_{undef^{\perp}}(x) = \hat{t}}{\langle \langle \mathcal{V}, \mathcal{T} \rangle, x \rangle \rightarrow_{pc} \langle \langle \mathcal{V}, \mathcal{T} \rangle, \langle \hat{v}, \hat{t} \rangle \rangle}$$

Fig. 2. Partial $\mathcal{L}_t$ semantics

The `typeof()` operator (TYPEOF) returns a string representation of the type of the given expression. The string inherits the security label of the type of the expression, whereas the type of the result is always str and hence labeled $\perp$.

Further, the rules for variable assignment (ASSIGN$_t$) and variable look-up (VAR$_t$) require special attention. Notice that, for both maps $\mathcal{V}$ and $\mathcal{T}$, the default lookup value is undefined: $\texttt{undef}^{\perp}$ and $undef^{\perp}$ respectively. These maps are independently updated through ASSIGN$_t$, which calls MUPDATE and MUPDATE-VS accordingly. Variable look up is the reverse process: the type and value are fetched independently from their respective maps.

If we return to the example in Listing 1.2, the value of t is updated but not its type. Therefore, under a value-sensitive discipline, the execution is safe and 1 will be assigned to $\langle \text{``}int\text{''}^L, str^L \rangle$ at the end of the execution.

Distinguishing between the type of a value and its actual value in combination with value sensitivity is an important increase in precision for practical analyses.

It allows the execution of the example of wild JavaScript from Listing 1.3, since `typeof document.cookie` returns $\langle \text{"}str\text{"}^{\perp}, str^{\perp}\rangle$, which makes the result of the guarding expression public.

3.2   Records and Observable Property Existence $\mathcal{L}_r$

Previous work on information flow control for complex languages has used the idea of tracking the existence of elements in structures like objects with an independent existence label [18,24,28]. In this section, we show that the notion of OAVs and the use of lifted partial maps are able to naturally express previous models while significantly simplifying the rules. Further, systematic application of those concepts allows us to improve previous models — in particular for property deletion.

Treating the property existence separately increases the permissiveness of the monitor. Consider, for instance, the example in Listing 1.4. After execution, the value of property x depends on h but not its existence. Since the existence changes less often

```
o = {x:1};
if (h) {o['x'] = 0;}
l = 'x' in o;
```

and is observable via the operator `in`, it can be seen as an OAV (of the record).

In order to reason about existence as an OAV, we create $\mathcal{L}_r$ by extending $\mathcal{L}$ with record literals, property projection, property update and an `in` operator that makes it possible to check if a property is present in a record.

$$e ::= (\cdots \text{as in } \mathcal{L}) \mid \{\overline{e : e}\} \mid x[e] \mid x[e] = e \mid e \text{ in } x \qquad s ::= (\cdots \mathcal{L})$$

The records are implemented as tuples of maps $\langle \mathcal{V}, \mathcal{E}\rangle_{\varsigma}$ decorated with a *structure security label* ς.

$$\mathcal{V} : string \rightarrow LabeledValue \quad \mathcal{E} : string \rightarrow LabeledBool$$

$$\mathcal{S} : string \rightarrow LabeledValue \quad v ::= r \mid (\cdots \text{as in } \mathcal{L}) \quad r ::= \langle \mathcal{V}, \mathcal{E}\rangle_{\varsigma}$$

The first map, $\mathcal{V}$, stores the labeled values of the properties of the record, and the second map $\mathcal{E}$ stores the presence (existence) of the properties as a labeled boolean. As in previous work, the interpretation is that present properties carry their own existence label while inexistent properties are modeled by the structure label. As we will see below, the structure label is tightly connected to (the label of) the default value of $\mathcal{V}$ and $\mathcal{E}$. For clarity of exposition we let the records be values rather than entities on a heap.

The semantics of property projection, assignment, and existence query are detailed in Fig. 3. Property update (RECASSIGN) allows for the update of a property in a record stored in a variable and the projection rule (PROJ) reads a property by querying only the map $\mathcal{V}$. There are a number of interesting

$$\text{RecAssign} \frac{\langle S_1, e_1 \rangle \rightarrow_{pc} \langle S_2, f^{\sigma_f} \rangle \quad \langle S_2, e_2 \rangle \rightarrow_{pc} \langle S_3, \dot{v} \rangle}{S_3(x) = \langle V_1, \mathcal{E}_1 \rangle_\varsigma^{\sigma_x} \quad \sigma = pc \sqcup \sigma_f} \frac{V_1[f \xleftarrow{\text{undef}^\varsigma} \dot{v}] \downarrow_\sigma V_2 \quad \mathcal{E}_1[f \xleftarrow{\text{false}^\varsigma} \text{true}^\perp] \downarrow_\sigma \mathcal{E}_2}{\langle S_1, x[e_1] = e_2 \rangle \rightarrow_{pc} \langle S_3[x \rightarrow \langle V_2, \mathcal{E}_2 \rangle_\varsigma^{\sigma_x}], \dot{v} \rangle}$$

$$\text{Proj} \frac{\langle S_1, e \rangle \rightarrow_{pc} \langle S_2, f^{\sigma_f} \rangle \quad S_2(x) = \langle V, \mathcal{E} \rangle_\varsigma^{\sigma_x}}{V_{\text{undef}^\varsigma}(f) = \dot{v} \quad \sigma = \sigma_x \sqcup \sigma_f}{\langle S_1, x[e] \rangle \rightarrow_{pc} \langle S_2, \dot{v}^\sigma \rangle}$$

$$\text{In} \frac{\langle S_1, e \rangle \rightarrow_{pc} \langle S_2, f^{\sigma_f} \rangle \quad S_2(x) = \langle V, \mathcal{E} \rangle_\varsigma^{\sigma_x}}{\mathcal{E}_{\text{false}^\varsigma}(f) = \dot{v} \quad \sigma = \sigma_x \sqcup \sigma_f}{\langle S_1, e \text{ in } x \rangle \rightarrow_{pc} \langle S_2, \dot{v}^\sigma \rangle}$$

Fig. 3. $\mathcal{L}_r$ semantics extension over $\mathcal{L}$

properties of these two rules. For RECASSIGN note the uniform treatment of values and existence and how, in contrast to previous work, this simplifies the semantics to only one rule. Further, note how the structure label is used as the label of the default value in both rules and how this interacts with the rules for lifted partial maps.

Consider Listing 1.5 in a $L \sqsubseteq M \sqsubseteq H$ security lattice to illustrate the logic behind this monitor. In this example, the subindex label in the key of the record denotes the existence label for that property. When the true branch is taken, the assignment o['e']=0 (on line 4) is ignored, since MUPDATE-VS is applied. Although the context is higher than the label of the value and its existence, no label change will occur.

Listing 1.5.

```
0
1  o={ e_L: 0^L,
2    f_L: 1^M, g_H: 2^H}_H;
3  if ( m^M ) {
4    o['e'] = 0;
5    o['h'] = 0;
6    o['f'] = 0;
7    o['g'] = 0;
8  }
```

The second assignment (o['h']=0, on line 5) extends the record. This side effect demands that the structure label of the record is not below M. The demand stems from the MUPDATE rule via the label of the default value and initiated by the update of the existence map from false to true. Since the value changes only MUPDATE is applicable, which places the demand that the label of the previous value (the structure label) is above the label of the control. The new value is tainted with the label of the control, which in this case leads to an existence label of M, resulting in { ..., h_M:0^M}$_H$.

To contrast, consider the next property update (o['f']=0, on line 6), which writes to a previously existing property under M control. In this case no demands will be placed on the structure label, since neither of the maps will trigger use of the default value. The previous existence label is below M, but this does not trigger NSU since the value of the existence does not change, which makes the MUPDATE-VS rule is applicable. This also means that the existence label is untouched and the result after execution is { ..., f_L: 0^M, ...}$_H$.

Finally ($o['g']=0$, on line 7), the previous existence and value labels are both above M, and the MUPDATE rule is applicable. This will have the effect of *lowering* both the existence and value label to then current context in accordance with flow-sensitivity. The result after execution is { ..., g_M: 0^M, ... }$_H$

It is worth noting that the above example can be easily recast to illustrate update using a secret property name, since the pc and the security label of the property name form the security context, σ, of the writes in RECASSIGN.

With respect to reading, the existence label is not taken into account unless reading a non-existent property, in which case the structure of the record is used via the default value. Analogously, the rule IN checks for property existence in a record by performing the same action on the $\mathcal{E}$ map. This illustrates that the lifted maps provide a natural model for existence tracking. The existence map provides all the presence/absence information of a value in a particular property. This generalization, in combination with value sensitivity, both simplifies previous work and increases the precision of the tracking. In particular, as shown in the full version [1] of the paper, this is true when property deletion is considered.

4 Hybrid Monitors $\mathcal{L}_h$

In the quest of more permissive dynamic information flow monitors, *hybrid monitors* have been developed. Some perform static *pre-analyzes*, i.e., before the execution [13,21,25], or code inlining [6,12,23,29]. In other cases, the static analysis is triggered at runtime by the monitor [19,22,27,32]. A value sensitivity criterion can be applied in the static analysis of this second group. This means that fewer potential write targets need to be considered by the static part of these monitors.

Consider, for instance Listing 1.1, where a normal (i.e., value *insensitive*) hybrid monitor would elevate the label of l to the label of h before evaluating the branch. A value-sensitive hybrid analysis, on the other hand, is able to avoid the elevation, since the value of l can be seen not to change in the assignment.

To illustrate how a hybrid value-sensitive monitor might work consider the following hybrid semantics for the core language. Syntactically, $\mathcal{L}_h$ is identical to $\mathcal{L}$ but, similar to [19] and [22], a static analysis is performed when a branching is reached (Fig. 4).

Consider the rule for conditionals (IF$_h$) that applies a static analysis on the body of the conditional in order to update any variables that are potential write targets. In particular, assignments will be statically executed (S-ASSIGN), which elevates the target to the current context using static versions of MUPDATE and MUPDATE-VS. This means that the NSU check of MUPDATE no longer needs to be performed — the static part of the analysis guarantees that all variables are updated before execution. The static update and new dynamic update rules

$$\text{S-IF}\frac{\langle\mathcal{S}_1,e\rangle\Rightarrow_{pc}\langle\mathcal{S}_2,\dot{v}\rangle\quad\langle\mathcal{S}_2,s_{\texttt{true}}\rangle\Rightarrow_{pc}\mathcal{S}_t\quad\langle\mathcal{S}_2,s_{\texttt{false}}\rangle\Rightarrow_{pc}\mathcal{S}_f}{\langle\mathcal{S}_1,\texttt{if}(e)\{s_{\texttt{true}}\}\{s_{\texttt{false}}\}\rangle\Rightarrow_{pc}\mathcal{S}_t\sqcup\mathcal{S}_f}$$

$$\text{S-ASSIGN}\frac{\langle\mathcal{S}_1,e\rangle\Rightarrow_{pc}\langle\mathcal{S}_2,\dot{v}\rangle\quad\mathcal{S}_2[x\xleftarrow{\texttt{undef}^\perp}\dot{v}]\Downarrow_{pc}\mathcal{S}_3}{\langle\mathcal{S}_1,x=e\rangle\Rightarrow_{pc}\langle\mathcal{S}_3,\dot{v}\rangle}$$

$$\text{IF}_h\frac{\langle\mathcal{S}_1,e\rangle\rightarrow_{pc}\langle\mathcal{S}_2,v^\sigma\rangle\quad\langle\mathcal{S}_2,s_{\texttt{true}}\rangle\Rightarrow_{pc\sqcup\sigma}\mathcal{S}_t\quad\langle\mathcal{S}_2,s_{\texttt{false}}\rangle\Rightarrow_{pc\sqcup\sigma}\mathcal{S}_f\quad\langle\mathcal{S}_t\sqcup\mathcal{S}_f,s_v\rangle\rightarrow_{pc\sqcup\sigma}\mathcal{S}_3}{\langle\mathcal{S}_1,\texttt{if}(e)\{s_{\texttt{true}}\}\{s_{\texttt{false}}\}\rangle\rightarrow_{pc}\mathcal{S}_3}$$

Fig. 4. Partial hybrid semantics

are formulated as follows.

$$\text{S-MUPDATE}\frac{\mathcal{M}_\Delta(x)=\dot{w}\quad w\neq v}{\mathcal{M}[x\xleftarrow{\Delta}\dot{v}]\Downarrow_\sigma\mathcal{M}[x\mapsto\dot{w}^\sigma]}\qquad\text{MUPDATE}_h\frac{\mathcal{M}_\Delta(x)=\dot{w}\quad w\neq v}{\mathcal{M}[x\xleftarrow{\Delta}\dot{v}]\Downarrow_{pc}\mathcal{M}[x\mapsto\dot{v}^{pc}]}$$

$$\text{S-MUPDATEVS}\frac{\mathcal{M}_\Delta(x)=\dot{w}\quad w=v}{\mathcal{M}[x\xleftarrow{\Delta}\dot{v}]\Downarrow_\sigma\mathcal{M}}\qquad\text{MUPDATE-VS}_h\frac{\mathcal{M}_\Delta(x)=\dot{w}\quad w=v}{\mathcal{M}[x\xleftarrow{\Delta}\dot{v}]\Downarrow_{pc}\mathcal{M}}$$

The value sensitivity of the static rules is manifested in the S-MUPDATEVS rule. In case the new value is equal to the value of the write target, no label elevation is performed, which increases the permissiveness of the hybrid monitor in the way illustrated in Listing 1.1. Note the similarity between the static and the dynamic rules. In case it can be statically determined that the value does not change we know that MUPDATE-VS$_h$ will be run at execution time and vice versa for MUPDATE$_h$. This allows for the increase in permissiveness while still guaranteeing soundness. Naturally, this development scales to general OAVs under hybrid monitors.

5   Permissiveness

Value-sensitive monitors are strictly more permissive than their value-insensitive counterparts with respect to *termination insensitive non-interference* (TINI). This means that value-sensitive discipline accepts more safe programs without allowing insecure programs to be executed.

For space reasons, the soundness proof can be found in the full version of this paper [1].

In this section we compare the value sensitive languages $\mathcal{L}$, $\mathcal{L}_{rd}$ and $\mathcal{L}_h$ to the value-insensitive counterparts. In particular $\mathcal{L}$ is comparable to the Austin and Flanagan NSU discipline [2], $\mathcal{L}_{rd}$ is compared to the record subset of JSFlow [20] and $\mathcal{L}_h$ is compared to the Le Guernic et al.'s hybrid monitor [22].

5.1   Comparison with Austin and Flanagan's NSU [2]

The comparison with non-sensitive upgrade is relatively straight forward, since $\mathcal{L}$ is essentially the NSU monitor of [2] with one additional value-sensitive rule, MUPDATE-VS.

Let $--\twoheadrightarrow$ denote reductions in the insensitive monitor obtained by removing MUPDATE-VS from $\mathcal{L}$. To show permissiveness we will prove that every reduction $--\twoheadrightarrow$ can be followed by a reduction $\rightarrow$.

Theorem 1 (Value-Sensitive NSU is Strictly more Permissive than Value-Insensitive NSU).

$$\forall s \in \mathcal{L} \cdot \langle S_1, s \rangle --\twoheadrightarrow_{pc} S_2 \Rightarrow \langle S_1, s \rangle \rightarrow_{pc} S_2 \wedge$$
$$\exists s \in \mathcal{L} \cdot \langle S_1, s \rangle \rightarrow_{pc} S_2 \not\twoheadrightarrow \langle S_1, s \rangle --\twoheadrightarrow_{pc} S_2$$

Proof $\Rightarrow$: By contradiction, using that $--\twoheadrightarrow$ is a strict subset of $\rightarrow$. For space reasons the proof can be found in the full version of this paper [1]. $\not\Rightarrow$: The program in Listing 1.1 proves the claim, since it is successfully executed by $\rightarrow$ but not by $--\twoheadrightarrow$.

5.2   Comparison with JSFlow [20]

Hedin et al. [20] present JSFlow, a sound purely-dynamic monitor for JavaScript. JSFlow tracks property existence and object structure for dynamic objects with property addition and deletion. The objects are represented as $\{x \xrightarrow{\epsilon} p^\sigma\}_\varsigma$, i.e., objects are maps from properties, x, to labeled values, p^σ, with properties carrying existence labels, ϵ, and objects structure labels, ς.

Consider the example in Listing 1.6 up to line 3, where the property x is added under secret control. This places the demand that the structure of o is below the pc. In $\mathcal{L}_{rd}$, this demand stems from the MUPDATE rule via the label of the default value and is initiated by the update of the existence map from false to true. For $\mathcal{L}_{rd}$ the resulting object is $\langle \{x \rightarrow 0^H\}, \{x \rightarrow \text{true}^H\} \rangle_H$, while for JSFlow the resulting object would be $\{x \xrightarrow{H} 0^H\}_H$.

Listing 1.6.

```
0   o={}_H
1   if (h^H) {
2     o['x']=0;
3   }
4   delete o['x'];
5   l = 'x' in o;
```

If we proceed with the execution, the deletion on line 5 is under public context, which illustrates the main semantic difference between $\mathcal{L}_{rd}$ and JSFlow. In the former, deletion under public control will have the effect of *lowering* the value and existence labels to the current context, which results in $\langle \{x \rightarrow \text{undef}^L\}, \{x \rightarrow \text{false}^L\} \rangle_H$. In the latter, property absence is not explicitly tracked and deleting a property simply removes it from the map resulting in $\{\}_H$. Therefore, at line 6, $\mathcal{L}_{rd}$ is able to use that the absence of x is independent of secrets, while JSFlow will taint l with H based on the structure level. In this way, $\mathcal{L}_{rd}$ both simplifies the rules of previous work and increases the precision of the tracking.

5.3   Comparison with Le Guernic et al.'s Hybrid Monitor [22]

The hybrid monitor presented by Le Guernic et al. [22] is similar to $\mathcal{L}_h$. In both cases, a static analysis is triggered at the branching point to counter the inherent limitation of purely-dynamic monitors: that they only analyze one trace of the execution.

In the case of Le Guernic et al., the static component of their monitor collects the left-hand side of the assignments in the both sides of branches. Once these variables are gathered their labels are upgraded to the label of the branching guard. Intuitively, the targets of assignments in branch bodies depend on the guard, but as, e.g., Listing 1.1 shows this method is an over-approximation. Such over-approximations lower the precision of the enforcement, and might, in particular, when the monitor tracks OAVs rather than regular values, jeopardize the practicability of the enforcement.

The hybrid monitor $\mathcal{L}_h$ subsumes the monitor by Le Guernic et al. (see [1]). All variable side-effects taken into account by Le Guernic et al. are also considered by the static part of $\mathcal{L}_h$ via the rule for static assignment, S-ASSIGN. More precisely, S-ASSIGN updates the labels of the variables by applying either S-MUPDATE or S-MUPDATEVS depending on the previous value. The case when all variables are upgraded by S-MUPDATE to the level of the guard (σ in the rules of Fig. 4) corresponds to monitor by Le Guernic et al.

6 Related Work

This paper takes a step forward to improve the permissiveness of dynamic and hybrid information flow control. We discuss related work, including work that can be recast or extended in terms of value sensitivity and OAVs.

Permissiveness. Russo and Sabelfeld [27] show that flow-sensitive dynamic information flow control cannot be more permissive than static analyses. This limitation carries over to value-sensitive dynamic information flow analyses.

Austin and Flanagan extend the permissiveness of the NSU enforcement with *permissive upgrades* [3]. In this approach, the variables assigned under high context are tagged as *partially-leaked* and cannot be used for future branching. Bichhawat et al. [7] generalize this approach to a multi-level lattice. Value sensitivity can be applied to permissive upgrades (including the generalization) with benefits for the precision.

Hybrid approaches are a common way to boost the permissiveness of enforcements. There are several approaches to hybrid enforcement: inlining monitors [6,12,23,29], selective tracking [13,25], and the application of a static analysis at branch points [19,22,27,32]. Value sensitivity is particularly suitable for the latter to reduce the number of upgrades and increase precision (cf. Sect. 4).

In Relation to OAVs. Some enforcements track other more abstract properties in addition to standard values. These properties are typically equipped with a dedicated security label, which makes them fit into our notion of OAV.

Buiras et al. [10] extend LIO [31] to handle flow-sensitivity. Their *labelOf* function allows them to observe the label of values. To protect from leaks through observable labels, their monitor implements a *label on the label*, which means that the label itself can be seen as an OAV.

Almeida Matos et al. [24] present a purely dynamic information flow monitor for DOM-like tree structures. By including references and live collections, they get closer to the real DOM specification but are forced to track structural aspects of the tree, like the position of the nodes. Since the attacker can observe changes in the DOM through live collections and, in order to avoid over-approximations, they label several aspects of the node: the node itself, the value stored in it, the position in the forest, and its structure. These aspects are OAVs, since some of the operations only affect a subset of their labels. A value-sensitive version of this monitor might not be trivial given its complexity, but the effort would result in increased precision.

In Relation to Value-Sensitivity. The hybrid JavaScript monitor designed by Just et al. [21] only alters the structure of objects and arrays when properties or elements are inserted or removed. Similarly, Hedin et al. [19,20] track the presence and absence of properties and elements in objects and arrays changing the associated labels on insertions or deletions. Both approaches can be understood in terms of value-sensitivity. Indeed, in this paper we show how to improve the latter by systematic modeling using OAVs in combination with value-sensitivity.

Secure multi-execution [11,15] is naturally value-sensitive. It runs the same program multiple times restricting the input based on its confidentiality level. In this way, the secret input is defaulted in the low execution, thus entirely decoupling the low execution from the secret input. Austin and Flanagan [4] present *faceted values*: values that, depending of the level of the observer, can *return* differently. Faceted values provide an efficient way of simulating the multiple executions of secure multi-execution in a single execution.

7   Conclusion

We have investigated the concept of value sensitivity and introduced the key concept of observable abstract values, which together enable increased permissiveness for information flow control. The identification of observable abstract values opens up opportunities for value-sensitive analysis, in particular in richer languages. The reason for this is that the values of abstract properties typically change less frequently than the values they abstract. In such cases, value-sensitivity allows the security label corresponding to the abstract property to remain unchanged.

We have shown that this approach is applicable to both purely dynamic monitors, where we reduce blocking due to false positives, and to hybrid analysis, where we reduce over-approximation.

Being general and powerful concepts, value sensitivity and observable abstract values have potential to serve as a basis for improving state-of-the-art information flow control systems. Incorporating them into the JSFlow tool [20] is already in the workings.

Acknowledgments. This work was funded by the European Community under the ProSecuToR project and the Swedish research agencies SSF and VR.

References

1. Full version at http://chalmerslbs.bitbucket.org/valsens/fullversion.pdf
2. Austin, T.H., Flanagan, C.: Efficient purely-dynamic information flow analysis. In: Proceedings of ACM PLAS (2009)
3. Austin, T.H., Flanagan, C.: Permissive dynamic information flow analysis. In: PLAS (2010)
4. Austin, T.H., Flanagan, C.: Multiple facets for dynamic information flow. In: PoPL (2012)
5. Barnes, J., Barnes, J.: High Integrity Software: The SPARK Approach to Safety and Security. Addison-Wesley Longman Publishing Co. Inc., Boston (2003)
6. Bello, L., Bonelli, E.: On-the-fly inlining of dynamic dependency monitors for secure information flow. In: Barthe, G., Datta, A., Etalle, S. (eds.) FAST 2011. LNCS, vol. 7140, pp. 55–69. Springer, Heidelberg (2012)
7. Bichhawat, A., Rajani, V., Garg, D., Hammer, C.: Generalizing permissive-upgrade in dynamic information flow analysis. In: PLAS (2014)
8. Birgisson, A., Hedin, D., Sabelfeld, A.: Boosting the permissiveness of dynamic information-flow tracking by testing. In: Foresti, S., Yung, M., Martinelli, F. (eds.) ESORICS 2012. LNCS, vol. 7459, pp. 55–72. Springer, Heidelberg (2012)
9. Broberg, N., van Delft, B., Sands, D.: Paragon for practical programming with information-flow control. In: Shan, C. (ed.) APLAS 2013. LNCS, vol. 8301, pp. 217–232. Springer, Heidelberg (2013)
10. Buiras, P., Stefan, D., Russo, A.: On dynamic flow-sensitive floating-label systems. In: CSF (2014)
11. Capizzi, R., Longo, A., Venkatakrishnan, V.N., Sistla, A.P.: Preventing information leaks through shadow executions. In: ACSAC (2008)
12. Chudnov, A., Naumann, D.A.: Information flow monitor inlining. In: Proceedings of CSF 2010 (2010)
13. Chugh, R., Meister, J.A., Jhala, R., Lerner, S.: Staged information flow for JavaScript. In: PLDI (2009)
14. Denning, D.E., Denning, P.J.: Certification of programs for secure information flow. CACM **20**(7), 504–513 (1977)
15. Devriese, D., Piessens, F.: Non-interference through secure multi-execution. In: SSP (2010)
16. Groef, W.D., Devriese, D., Nikiforakis, N., Piessens, F.: Flowfox: a web browser with flexible and precise information flow control. In: CCS (2012)
17. Hammer, C., Snelting, G.: Flow-sensitive, context-sensitive, and object-sensitive information flow control based on program dependence graphs. JIS **8**(6), 399–422 (2009)
18. Hedin, D., Sabelfeld, A.: Information-flow security for a core of JavaScript. In: Proceedings of IEEE CSF, pp. 3–18, June 2012
19. Hedin, D., Bello, L., Sabelfeld, A.: Value-sensitive hybrid information flow control for a JavaScript-like language. In: CSF (2015)
20. Hedin, D., Birgisson, A., Bello, L., Sabelfeld, A.: JSFlow: tracking information flow in JavaScript and its APIs. In: SAC (2014)
21. Just, S., Cleary, A., Shirley, B., Hammer, C.: Information flow analysis for Javascript. In: Proceedings of ACM PLASTIC, pp. 9–18. ACM, USA (2011). http://doi.acm.org/10.1145/2093328.2093331
22. Le Guernic, G., Banerjee, A., Jensen, T., Schmidt, D.A.: Automata-based confidentiality monitoring. In: Okada, M., Satoh, I. (eds.) ASIAN 2006. LNCS, vol. 4435, pp. 75–89. Springer, Heidelberg (2008)

23. Magazinius, J., Russo, A., Sabelfeld, A.: On-the-fly inlining of dynamic security monitors. Comput. Secur. **31**(7), 827–843 (2012)
24. Almeida-Matos, A., Fragoso Santos, J., Rezk, T.: An information flow monitor for a core of DOM - introducing references and live primitives. In: Maffei, M., Tuosto, E. (eds.) TGC 2014. LNCS, vol. 8902, pp. 1–16. Springer, Heidelberg (2014)
25. Moore, S., Chong, S.: Static analysis for efficient hybrid information-flow control. In: CSF (2011)
26. Myers, A.C., Zheng, L., Zdancewic, S., Chong, S., Nystrom, N.: Jif: Java information flow (2001). http://www.cs.cornell.edu/jif
27. Russo, A., Sabelfeld, A.: Dynamic vs. static flow-sensitive security analysis. In: Proceedings of IEEE CSF, pp. 186–199, July 2010
28. Russo, A., Sabelfeld, A., Chudnov, A.: Tracking information flow in dynamic tree structures. In: Backes, M., Ning, P. (eds.) ESORICS 2009. LNCS, vol. 5789, pp. 86–103. Springer, Heidelberg (2009)
29. Santos, J.F., Rezk, T.: An information flow monitor-inlining compiler for securing a core of JavaScript. In: Cuppens-Boulahia, N., Cuppens, F., Jajodia, S., Abou El Kalam, A., Sans, T. (eds.) SEC 2014. IFIP AICT, vol. 428, pp. 278–292. Springer, Heidelberg (2014)
30. Simonet, V.: The Flow Caml system (2003). http://cristal.inria.fr/simonet/soft/flowcaml
31. Stefan, D., Russo, A., Mitchell, J., Mazières, D.: Flexible dynamic information flow control in haskell. In: 4th Symposium on Haskell (2011)
32. Venkatakrishnan, V.N., Xu, W., DuVarney, D.C., Sekar, R.: Provably correct runtime enforcement of non-interference properties. In: Ning, P., Qing, S., Li, N. (eds.) ICICS 2006. LNCS, vol. 4307, pp. 332–351. Springer, Heidelberg (2006)
33. Volpano, D., Smith, G., Irvine, C.: A sound type system for secure flow analysis. J. Comput. Secur. **4**(3), 167–187 (1996)

SAT-Based Minimization of Deterministic ω-Automata

Souheib Baarir[✉] and Alexandre Duret-Lutz

LRDE, EPITA, Le Kremlin-Bicêtre, France
{sbaarir,adl}@lrde.epita.fr

Abstract. We describe a tool that inputs a deterministic ω-automaton with any acceptance condition, and synthesizes an equivalent ω-automaton with another arbitrary acceptance condition and a given number of states, if such an automaton exists. This tool, that relies on a SAT-based encoding of the problem, can be used to provide minimal ω-automata equivalent to given properties, for different acceptance conditions.

1 Introduction

LTL Synthesis and Probabilistic LTL Model Checking (PMC) are two areas where it is useful to express linear-time temporal properties as deterministic ω-automata. Because it is well known that not all Büchi automata can be made deterministic, these applications use other acceptance conditions such a Rabin or Streett. The model checker PRISM [12], for instance, contains a reimplementation of ltl2dstar [8], a tool that converts non-deterministic Büchi automata (obtained from an LTL formula) into deterministic Rabin or Streett automata, using Safra's construction [14].

In the past few years, there have been a blossoming of tools directly translating LTL formulas into Rabin automata, or generalized variants of Rabin automata [3,5,9–11]. These tools usually give automata smaller than those obtained with ltl2dstar via Safra's construction, and it has been shown that using the generalized Rabin condition can speed PMC up by orders of magnitude [5,9].

The need for interaction between tools producing and consuming ω-automata with various acceptance conditions has led to the introduction of the Hanoi Omega-Automata (HOA) format [4], where the acceptance condition can be specified using an arbitrary Boolean expression of sets that must be visited infinitely often or finitely often. The current implementation of PRISM can perform PMC using deterministic automata having any such arbitrary acceptance condition, and to save memory it is preferable to have automata with as few states as possible, even if this means having a more complex acceptance condition.

In this paper, we present a tool that inputs a deterministic automaton with any acceptance condition, and uses a SAT-based technique to synthetize an equivalent automaton with any given acceptance condition and number of states if such an automaton exists. As a consequence we also have a way to construct

© Springer-Verlag Berlin Heidelberg 2015
M. Davis et al. (Eds.): LPAR-20 2015, LNCS 9450, pp. 79–87, 2015.
DOI: 10.1007/978-3-662-48899-7_6

minimal equivalent deterministic automata for any given acceptance condition. This SAT-based encoding is costly, so it is not suitable for routine simplification of automata; however it is a very useful tool to provide lowerbounds for the size of the deterministic automata that existing LTL translators (or actually, any automaton transformation tool) could produce, so it should help authors of such tools to find cases where there is room for improvement.

The SAT-based encoding we use for this synthesis with any acceptance is an extension of our previous work that was restricted to generalized-Büchi acceptance [2], and that was itself a generalization of the DBAminimizer of [7] for Büchi acceptance.

2   Definitions and Encoding

2.1   Deterministic Transition-Based ω-Automaton

For a set S, S^ω denotes the set of infinite sequences over S. Given such an infinite sequence $\sigma \in S^\omega$, $\mathrm{Inf}(\sigma)$ denotes the subset of elements that occur infinitely often in σ. We use $\mathbb{B} = \{\bot, \top\}$ to denote the set of Boolean constants, and use $[m]$ as a shorthand for $\{1, 2, \ldots, m\}$.

Definition 1 (DTωA). *A (complete) Deterministic Transition-based ω-Automaton (DTωA) is a tuple $\mathcal{A} = \langle Q, \Sigma, \iota, \delta, (F_1, F_2, \ldots, F_m), \mathscr{F} \rangle$ where*

- Q *is a set of states,* $\iota \in Q$ *is the initial state,*
- Σ *is an alphabet,*
- $\delta \subseteq Q \times \Sigma \times Q$ *is a transition relation that is deterministic and complete, i.e., such that* $\forall (s, \ell) \in Q \times \Sigma, |\{d \in Q \mid (s, \ell, d) \in \delta\}| = 1$. *By abuse of notation, we shall also write* $\delta(s)$ *to denote the set* $\{(\ell, d) \in \Sigma \times Q \mid (s, \ell, d) \in \delta\}$.
- $(F_1, F_2, \ldots, F_m)$ *is a tuple of m acceptance sets of transitions $F_i \subseteq \delta$. For convenience, we denote* $\widetilde{F}(t) = \{i \in [m] \mid t \in F_i\}$ *the set of indices of acceptance sets that contain t.*
- $\mathscr{F} : 2^{[m]} \to \mathbb{B}$ *is a Boolean function that tells which combination of acceptance sets should be visited infinitely often along a run for this run to be accepting.*

A run of $\mathcal{A}$ is an infinite sequence of connected transitions $\rho = (q_1, \ell_1, q_2)(q_2, \ell_2, q_3)(q_3, \ell_3, q_4) \ldots \in \delta^\omega$ such that $q_1 = \iota$. This run recognizes the infinite word $\ell_1 \ell_2 \ell_3 \ldots$ and is accepting iff $\mathscr{F}(\bigcup_{t \in \mathrm{Inf}(\rho)} \widetilde{F}(t)) = \top$. The language of $\mathcal{A}$ is the set $\mathscr{L}(\mathcal{A})$ of all infinite words recognized by accepting runs of $\mathcal{A}$.

For brevity, in the rest of this article we simply write *automaton* instead of *complete and deterministic ω-automaton*.

In the HOA format [4], the acceptance function $\mathscr{F}$ is represented by a Boolean expression over primitives of the form $\mathrm{Inf}(i)$ or $\mathrm{Fin}(i)$ meaning respectively that the set F_i has to be visited infinitely often or finitely often. For instance $\mathrm{Fin}(0) \vee \mathrm{Inf}(1)$ is an expression for Streett acceptance with one pair (a run is accepting if it either visits F_0 finitely often, or F_1 infinitely often); in our definition of DTωA, the corresponding $\mathscr{F}$ function would be such that $\mathscr{F}(\{1\}) = \mathscr{F}(\{0,1\}) = \mathscr{F}(\emptyset) = \top$, and $\mathscr{F}(\{0\}) = \bot$.

2.2   Synthesis of Equivalent DTωA

Given an automaton $R = \langle Q_R, \Sigma, \iota_R, \delta_R, (F_1, F_2, \ldots, F_{m'}), \mathscr{F} \rangle$, two integers n and m, and an acceptance function $\mathscr{G} : 2^{[m]} \to \mathbb{B}$, we would like to construct (if it exists) an automaton $C = \langle Q_C, \Sigma, \iota_C, \delta_C, (G_1, G_2, \ldots, G_m), \mathscr{G} \rangle$ with $|Q_C| = n$ states, and such that $\mathscr{L}(R) = \mathscr{L}(C)$. We call R the *reference* automaton, and C, the *candidate* automaton.

Since C and R are complete and deterministic, any word of Σ^ω has a unique run in R and C, and testing $\mathscr{L}(R) = \mathscr{L}(C)$ can be done by ensuring that each word is accepted by R iff it is accepted by C. In practice, this is checked by ensuring that any cycle of the synchronous product $C \otimes R$ corresponds to cycles that are either accepting in both C and R, or rejecting in both. To ensure that property, the SAT-based encoding uses variables to encode the history of acceptance sets visited between two states of the product $C \otimes R$.

SAT Variables. We encode C with two sets of variables:

- The "triplet" variables $\{\langle q_1, \ell, q_2 \rangle \mid (q_1, q_2) \in Q_C^2, \ell \in \Sigma\}$ encode the existence of transitions $(q_1, \ell, q_2) \in \delta_C$ in the candidate automaton.
- The "quadruplet" variables $\{\langle q_1, \ell, i, q_2 \rangle \mid (q_1, q_2) \in Q_C^2, \ell \in \Sigma, i \in [m]\}$ encode the membership of these transitions to each acceptance set G_i of C.

For the product $C \otimes R$, we encode the reachable states, and parts of paths that might eventually be completed to become cycles. We use $SCC_R \subseteq 2^{Q_R}$ to denote the set of non-trivial strongly connected components of R.

- A variable in $\{\langle q, q', q, q', \emptyset, \emptyset \rangle \mid q \in Q_C, q' \in Q_R\}$ encodes the existence of a reachable state (q, q') in $C \otimes R$. The reason we use a sextuplet to encode such a pair is that each (q, q') will serve as a starting point for possible paths.
- A variable in $\{\langle q_1, q_1', q_2, q_2', I, I' \rangle \mid (q_1, q_2) \in Q_C^2, S \in SCC_R, (q_1', q_2') \in S^2, I \subseteq [m], I' \subseteq [m']\}$ denotes that there is a path between (q_1, q_1') and (q_2, q_2') in the product, such that its projection on C visits the acceptance sets G_i for all $i \in I$, and its projection on R visits the acceptance sets F_i for all $i \in I'$. This set of variables is used to implement the cycle equivalence check, so the only q_1' and q_2' that need to be considered should belong to the same non-trivial SCC of R.

SAT Contraints. With the above variables, C can be obtained as a solution of the following SAT problem. First, C should be complete (i.e., δ_C is total):

$$\bigwedge_{q_1 \in Q_C, \ell \in \Sigma} \bigvee_{q_2 \in Q_C} \langle q_1, \ell, q_2 \rangle \tag{1}$$

Then, the initial state of the product must exist. Furthermore, if (q_1, q_1') is a state of the product, $(q_1', \ell, q_2') \in \delta_R$ is a transition in the reference automaton, and $(q_1, \ell, q_2) \in \delta_C$ is a transition in the candidate automaton, then (q_2, q_2') is a state of the product too:

$$\wedge \langle \iota_C, \iota_R, \iota_C, \iota_R, \emptyset, \emptyset \rangle \wedge \bigwedge_{\substack{(q_1, q_2) \in Q_C^2, q_1' \in Q_R, \\ (\ell, q_2') \in \delta_R(q_1')}} \langle q_1, q_1', q_1, q_1', \emptyset, \emptyset \rangle \wedge \langle q_1, \ell, q_2 \rangle \to \langle q_2, q_2', q_2, q_2', \emptyset, \emptyset \rangle \tag{2}$$

Any transition of the product augments an existing path, updating the sets I and I' of indices of acceptance sets visited in each automaton. Unfortunately, we have to consider all possible subsets $J \subseteq [m]$ of acceptances sets to which the candidate transition (q_2, ℓ, q_3) could belong, and emit a different rule for each J.

$$\bigwedge_{\substack{(q_1, q_2, q_3) \in Q_C^3, \\ I \subseteq [m], J \subseteq [m], \\ S \in SCC_R, (q_1', q_2') \in S^2, \\ I' \subseteq [m'], (\ell, q_3') \in \delta_R(q_2')}} \begin{pmatrix} \langle q_1, q_1', q_2, q_2', I, I' \rangle \\ \wedge \langle q_2, \ell, q_3 \rangle \\ \wedge \bigwedge_{i \in J} \langle q_2, \ell, i, q_3 \rangle \\ \wedge \bigwedge_{i \notin J} \neg \langle q_2, \ell, i, q_3 \rangle \end{pmatrix} \rightarrow \langle q_1, q_1', q_3, q_3', I \cup J, \quad (3) \\ I' \cup \widetilde{F}((q_2', \ell, q_3'))\rangle$$

If a path of the product is followed by a transition $(q_2', \ell, q_3') \in \delta_R$ and a transition $(q_2, \ell, q_3) \in \delta_C$ that both close a cycle ($q_3 = q_1 \wedge q_3' = q_1'$), then the cycle formed in the candidate automaton by (q_2, ℓ, q_1) should have the same acceptance (i.e., rejecting or accepting) as the cycle of the reference automaton. In other words, the transition (q_2, ℓ, q_1) belongs to a subset $J \subseteq [m]$ of acceptance sets only if this J satisfies $\mathscr{G}(I \cup J) = \mathscr{F}(I' \cup \widetilde{F}((q_2', \ell, q_1')))$.

$$\bigwedge_{\substack{(q_1, q_2) \in Q_C^2, I \subseteq [m], \\ S \in SCC_R, (q_1', q_2') \in S^2, I' \subseteq [m'], \\ (\ell, q_3') \in \delta_R(q_2'), q_3' = q_1'}} \langle q_1, q_1', q_2, q_2', I, I' \rangle \wedge \langle q_2, \ell, q_1 \rangle \rightarrow \bigvee_{\substack{J \subseteq [m] \\ \mathscr{G}(I \cup J) = \mathscr{F}(I' \cup \widetilde{F}((q_2', \ell, q_1')))}} \left(\bigwedge_{i \in J} \langle q_2, \ell, i, q_1 \rangle \wedge \bigwedge_{i \notin J} \neg \langle q_2, \ell, i, q_1 \rangle \right)$$

$$(4)$$

Optimizations. A first optimization is to use the same symmetry breaking clauses as suggested by [7], to restrict the search space of the SAT solver. Nonetheless, the above encoding requires $O(|Q_R|^2 \times |Q_C|^2 \times 2^{m+m'})$ variables and $O(|Q_R|^2 \times |Q_C|^3 \times 2^{2m+m'} \times |\Sigma|)$ clauses. It is therefore very sensitive to the number of acceptance sets used in the reference and candidate automata. To mitigate this, we implement some additional optimizations:

1. For SCCs that are known to be weak (i.e., all cycles are accepting, or all cycles are rejecting) it is not necessary to remember the history I' of the acceptance sets seen by paths. The sets of variables $\{\langle q_1, q_1', q_2, q_2', I, I' \rangle, \ldots\}$ when q_1' and q_2' belong to a weak SCC can therefore be restricted to only cases where $I' = \emptyset$.
2. In case an SCC S is not weak, it is possible that it does not intersect all the sets $F_1, F_2, \ldots, F_m$. Then the variables $\{\langle q_1, q_1', q_2, q_2', I, I' \rangle, \ldots\}$ can have their history I' restricted to the subset of $[m']$ that actually intersects S.
3. Simplifying histories. Consider a Rabin acceptance condition like $\mathsf{Fin}(0) \wedge \mathsf{Inf}(1)$, where the set F_0 has to be visited finitely often and F_1 has to be visited infinitely often. The histories $I \subseteq [2]$ or $I' \subseteq [2]$ involved in the variables $\{\langle q_1, q_1', q_2, q_2', I, I' \rangle, \ldots\}$ could take any value in $\{\}$, $\{0\}$, $\{1\}$, or $\{0, 1\}$ depending on which sets have been seen along this path. However these variables are only used to detect cycles, and a cycle that contains 0 in its history cannot be prolonged into an accepting cycle: the history $\{0, 1\}$ can

therefore be simplified into $\{0\}$, which is enough to ensure that the cycle will be rejecting. Doing this reduces the number of variables and clauses needed.

4. Equation (4) is not directly expressed as a disjunction. To encode it more efficiently, we use BDDs to express the right-hand side of the implication as an irredundant product of sums: depending on whether $\mathscr{F}(I' \cup \hat{F}((q_2', \ell, q_1'))$ is accepting, we encode the formula $\mathscr{G}$ or its negation as a BDD, assign to true the BDD variables corresponding to the sets listed in I and obtain the resulting product of sums by dualizing the Minato-Morreale algorithm [13].

State-Based Acceptance. This encoding can be tweaked to synthetize automata with state-based acceptance by reducing the quadruplets $\langle q_1, \ell, i, q_2 \rangle$ to pairs $\langle q_1, i \rangle$ in all the above rules.

3 Implementation and Experiments

3.1 Tool Support

The above encoding is implemented in Spot 1.99.4[1], and can be used via the command-line tool autfilt. Tools that produce deterministic ω-automata, such as ltl2dstar [8], ltl3dra [3], and Rabinizer3 [9], have all been recently updated to support the Hanoi Omega-Automata format [4], that autfilt can input.

The following example translates $Gp_0 \lor FGp_1$ using ltl2dstar. The formula is first passed to ltlfilt [6] for conversion into ltl2dstar's input syntax. ltl2dstar outputs its result in dra.hoa: it is a 5-state Rabin automaton with two pairs of acceptance sets.[2]

```
% ltlfilt -f'Gp0 | FGp1' -l | ltl2dstar --output-format=hoa - dra.hoa
% egrep'States:|acc-name:|Acceptance:' dra.hoa
States: 5
acc-name: Rabin 2
Acceptance: 4 (Fin(0) & Inf(1)) | (Fin(2) & Inf(3))
```

Now we can minimize this automaton using our SAT-based approach. We pass the dra.hoa to autfilt --sat-minimize, with additional options to require a complete automaton (-C) with state-based acceptance (-S), in the HOA format (-H). The result has only 3 states.

```
% autfilt -S -C --sat-minimize -H dra.hoa > dra-min.hoa
% egrep'States:|acc-name:|Acceptance:' dra-min.hoa
States: 3
acc-name: Rabin 2
Acceptance: 4 (Fin(0) & Inf(1)) | (Fin(2) & Inf(3))
```

The --sat-minimize option can take additional parameters, for instance to force a particular acceptance condition on the output (the default is the same as for the input). As an example, the following command forces the production of a minimal equivalent automaton with co-Büchi acceptance, which is enough for this formula (and means only one Rabin pair was really necessary).

---

[1] https://spot.lrde.epita.fr/.

[2] In the HOA format [4] the Acceptance: line encodes the $\mathscr{F}$ function of Definition 1, while the acc-name: just supplies a human-readable name when one is known.

Table 1. Sizes of Rabin automata produced by ltl2dstar (L2), ltl3dra (L3), Rabinizer (R3), or our SAT-based minimization procedure **configured to produce deterministic Rabin automata with a single acceptance pair** (min), with either state or transition-based acceptance. The notation "x (y)" denotes an automaton with x states and y acceptances sets. (In Rabin automata, acceptance sets are used as pairs, so y is always even). Timeouts after 1 h are denoted with "t.o". "imp." (for "impossible") indicates that no Rabin automaton with a single pair where found. Finally "n.a." indicates that the formula falls out of the supported LTL fragment of ltl3dra.

	state-based acceptance				tr.-based acc.	
	L2	L3	R3	min	R3	min
$\neg((FGp_0 \vee GFp_1) \wedge (FGp_2 \vee GFp_3))$	9 (4)	9 (4)	9 (8)	t.o.	4 (4)	imp.
$\neg((GFp_1 \wedge GFp_0) \vee (GFp_3 \wedge GFp_2))$	270 (10)	10 (8)	11 (16)	imp.	10 (8)	imp.
$\neg F(G(p_2 \vee (\overline{p_1} \wedge \overline{p_2})) \vee (Xp_1 \, U(p_0 \wedge Xp_1)))$	9 (2)	n.a.	36 (12)	5 (2)	34 (6)	3 (2)
$\neg FG((p_0 \wedge GFp_1 \wedge XXp_1) \, U \, G(XX\overline{p_2} \vee XX(p_0 \wedge p_1)))$	4 (2)	n.a.	16 (4)	2 (2)	16 (2)	1 (2)
$\neg(Fp_0 \wedge (p_1 \vee Gp_2) \wedge (\overline{p_1} \vee F\overline{p_2}))$	9 (6)	8 (6)	15 (16)	8 (2)	13 (8)	8 (2)
$\neg(Fp_0 \wedge GF\overline{p_0})$	4 (4)	3 (4)	4 (8)	3 (2)	2 (4)	2 (2)
$\neg(Fp_0 \wedge GFp_1)$	5 (4)	4 (4)	4 (8)	3 (2)	2 (4)	2 (2)
$\neg(GFp_1 \wedge GFp_0 \wedge GFp_2)$	8 (6)	8 (6)	8 (12)	4 (2)	1 (6)	3 (2)
$\neg(GFp_1 \wedge GFp_0)$	4 (4)	4 (4)	4 (8)	3 (2)	1 (4)	2 (2)
$\neg GFp_0$	2 (2)	2 (2)	2 (4)	2 (2)	1 (2)	1 (2)
$\neg(Xp_0 \, U \, Gp_1)$	7 (2)	n.a.	6 (8)	5 (2)	6 (4)	5 (2)
$(FGp_0 \vee GFp_1) \wedge (FGp_2 \vee GFp_3)$	4385 (14)	18 (8)	19 (16)	imp.	13 (8)	imp.
$F(G(p_2 \vee (\overline{p_1} \wedge \overline{p_2})) \vee (Xp_1 \, U(p_0 \wedge Xp_1)))$	7 (4)	6 (4)	8 (8)	5 (2)	6 (4)	3 (2)
$FG((p_0 \wedge GFp_1 \wedge XXp_1) \, U \, G(XX\overline{p_2} \vee XX(p_0 \wedge p_1)))$	3 (2)	n.a.	7 (4)	2 (2)	6 (2)	1 (2)
$Fp_0 \wedge (p_1 \vee Gp_2) \wedge (\overline{p_1} \vee F\overline{p_2})$	8 (2)	8 (4)	9 (8)	8 (2)	9 (4)	8 (2)
$Fp_0 \wedge GF\overline{p_0}$	3 (2)	3 (2)	3 (4)	3 (2)	3 (2)	2 (2)

```
% autfilt -S -C --sat-minimize='acc="co-Buchi"' -H dra.hoa > dra-min1.hoa
% egrep'States:|acc-name:|Acceptance:' dra-min1.hoa
States: 3
acc-name: co-Buchi
Acceptance: 1 Fin(0)
```

The `colored` option requests that all transitions (or states) belong to exactly one acceptance set. This is useful for instance when requesting parity acceptance:

```
% autfilt -S -C --sat-minimize='acc="parity max even 2",colored' -H \
   dra.hoa >dpa.hoa
% egrep'States:|acc-name:|Acceptance:' dpa.hoa
States: 3
acc-name: parity max even 2
Acceptance: 2 Fin(1) & Inf(0)
```

One section of the web page https://spot.lrde.epita.fr/satmin.html details the usage of `autfilt` with more examples.

3.2 Minimization

To evaluate the usefulness and effectiveness of our tool, we built a benchmark of LTL formulas to convert into deterministic ω-automata by the three translators ltl2dstar 0.5.3, ltl3dra 0.2.2, and Rabinizer 3.1.

Table 2. Size of transition-based generalized Rabin automata produced by `ltl3dra` or `Rabinizer`, and minimized by our procedure **configured to keep the same acceptance condition**. Acceptance conditions are indicated with "Rabin x" meaning Rabin acceptance with x pairs, "gR x" for generalized-Rabin [3,5] with x pairs, or "gcB x" for generalized-co-Büchi with x acceptance sets (one of these x sets has to be seen finitely).

	Rabinizer		ltl3dra	
	orig.	min	orig.	min
$\neg(\overline{p_0}\wedge((G\overline{p_0}\wedge((Fp_0\wedge G\overline{p_1})\vee(G\overline{p_0}\wedge Fp_1)))\vee(Fp_0\wedge(G\overline{p_0}\vee Fp_1))))$	6 (gR 3)	4	6 (gcB 3)	4
$\neg((XFp_0\wedge(p_1\vee XG\overline{p_0}))\vee(XG\overline{p_0}\wedge((\overline{p_1}\wedge XFp_0)\vee(p_1\wedge XG\overline{p_0}))))$	5 (gR 2)	3	5 (gcB 2)	3
$\neg(Fp_0 \wedge (p_1 \vee Gp_2) \wedge (\overline{p_1} \vee F\overline{p_2}))$	8 (gR 4)	8	8 (gcB 3)	8
$\neg(Fp_0 \wedge GFp_1)$	2 (gcB 2)	2	2 (gcB 2)	2
$\neg(p_0 \vee XG(p_1 \wedge F\overline{p_0}))$	4 (gR 2)	4	5 (gcB 2)	4
$\overline{p_0}\wedge((G\overline{p_0}\wedge((Fp_0\wedge G\overline{p_1})\vee(G\overline{p_0}\wedge Fp_1)))\vee(Fp_0\wedge(G\overline{p_0}\vee Fp_1)))$	6 (gR 2)	4	6 (gcB 2)	4
$F(G(p_2 \vee (\overline{p_1} \wedge \overline{p_2})) \vee (Xp_1\, U(p_0 \wedge Xp_1)))$	3 (gR 2)	3	4 (gcB 2)	3
$Fp_0 \wedge (p_1 \vee Gp_2) \wedge (\overline{p_1} \vee F\overline{p_2})$	8 (gR 2)	8	8 (gcB 2)	8
$Gp_0 \wedge XFp_1$	4 (gcB 1)	4	4 (gcB 1)	4
$F\overline{p_0} \wedge Xp_0 \wedge (Gp_1 \vee XF\overline{p_0})$	7 (gR 2)	7	9 (gcB 2)	7
$p_0 \vee XG(p_1 \wedge F\overline{p_0})$	5 (gR 2)	4	4 (gR 3)	4

Table 1, shows the number states of deterministic Rabin automata produced by the translators, as well as the size of the minimal Rabin automata that `autfilt --sat-minimize` could produce using a single acceptance pair. The table distinguishes the use of state-based acceptance or transition-based acceptance. All automata are complete. Because the SAT encoding is exponential in the number of acceptance sets, but polynomial in the size of the automaton, the input automaton supplied to `autfilt --sat-minimize` was chosen among the automata output by the translators as the one with the fewest number of acceptance sets, and in case of equality the fewest number of states. For instance, for $\neg(GFp_1\wedge GFp_0\wedge GFp_2)$ in Table 1, the minimal transition-based automaton of size "3 (2)" was obtained starting from the minimal state-based Rabin automaton of size "4 (2)", not starting from the "1 (6)" automaton produced by `Rabinizer`, as it involves more acceptance sets.

Although this table only shows minimal automata with a single pair, our technique can deal with more pairs (and different acceptance conditions) as well. For instance the formula $(FGp_0 \vee GFp_1) \wedge (FGp_2 \vee GFp_3)$ is translated by `ltl2dstar` into a DRA with 4385 states (and 7 acceptance pairs), by `ltl3dra` into a DRA with 18 states (and 4 pairs) and by `Rabinizer` into a transition-based DRA with 13 states (and 4 pairs). Using `autfilt --sat-minimize` we could reduce it to a transition-based DRA with 2 states and only 3 acceptance pairs, and show that there is no transition-based DRA with 2 states and less acceptance pairs (the problem becomes unsatisfiable).

Finally Table 2 shows minimization examples that use the transition-based generalized Rabin acceptance introduced by `ltl3dra` and `Rabinizer`. Before minimizing the automaton we simplified the acceptance by removing all unused sets, yielding the simpler acceptance conditions displayed in the table.

Complete results and instructions to reproduce this benchmark can be found at https://www.lrde.epita.fr/~adl/lpar15/. In particular, the CSV files include run time information for the SAT solver we used (Glucose 4.0 [1]), and experiments with 2 and 3-pair DRA.

4   Conclusion

We have presented a tool that can read any deterministic ω-automaton and synthetize (if it exists) an equivalent deterministic ω-automaton with a given number of states and arbitrary acceptance condition.

Although the SAT-based encoding is exponential in the number of acceptance sets, our experience is that it is nonetheless usable for automata that have up to 8 acceptance sets. This is enough to cover a large spectrum of temporal properties.

By processing the output of existing translators, we were able to find several cases where smaller automata exist, showing that there is still room for improvement in tools that translate LTL into ω-automata.

As a final remark, we should point that our tool can find a minimal automaton for a user-supplied acceptance condition. It might make sense to specify a more complex acceptance condition in order to obtain a smaller automaton. Could such a better acceptance condition be synthetized automatically?

References

1. Audemard, G., Simon, L.: Predicting learnt clauses quality in modern SAT solvers. In: IJCAI 2009, pp. 399–404, July 2009
2. Baarir, S., Duret-Lutz, A.: Mechanizing the minimization of deterministic generalized Büchi automata. In: Ábrahám, E., Palamidessi, C. (eds.) FORTE 2014. LNCS, vol. 8461, pp. 266–283. Springer, Heidelberg (2014)
3. Babiak, T., Blahoudek, F., Křetínský, M., Strejček, J.: Effective translation of LTL to deterministic Rabin automata: beyond the (F,G)-fragment. In: Van Hung, D., Ogawa, M. (eds.) ATVA 2013. LNCS, vol. 8172, pp. 24–39. Springer, Heidelberg (2013)
4. Babiak, T., Blahoudek, F., Duret-Lutz, A., Klein, J., Křetínský, J., Müller, D., Parker, D., Strejček, J.: The Hanoi omega-automata format. In: Kroening, D., Păsăreanu, C.S. (eds.) CAV 2015. LNCS, vol. 9206, pp. 442–445. Springer, Heidelberg (2015)
5. Chatterjee, K., Gaiser, A., Křetínský, J.: Automata with generalized Rabin pairs for probabilistic model checking and LTL synthesis. In: Sharygina, N., Veith, H. (eds.) CAV 2013. LNCS, vol. 8044, pp. 559–575. Springer, Heidelberg (2013)
6. Duret-Lutz, A.: Manipulating LTL formulas using spot 1.0. In: Van Hung, D., Ogawa, M. (eds.) ATVA 2013. LNCS, vol. 8172, pp. 442–445. Springer, Heidelberg (2013)
7. Ehlers, R.: Minimising deterministic Büchi automata precisely using SAT solving. In: Strichman, O., Szeider, S. (eds.) SAT 2010. LNCS, vol. 6175, pp. 326–332. Springer, Heidelberg (2010)

8. Klein, J., Baier, C.: On-the-fly stuttering in the construction of deterministic ω-automata. In: Holub, J., Žd'árek, J. (eds.) CIAA 2007. LNCS, vol. 4783, pp. 51–61. Springer, Heidelberg (2007)
9. Komárková, Z., Křetínský, J.: Rabinizer 3: safraless translation of LTL to small deterministic automata. In: Cassez, F., Raskin, J.-F. (eds.) ATVA 2014. LNCS, vol. 8837, pp. 235–241. Springer, Heidelberg (2014)
10. Křetínský, J., Esparza, J.: Deterministic automata for the (F,G)-fragment of LTL. In: Madhusudan, P., Seshia, S.A. (eds.) CAV 2012. LNCS, vol. 7358, pp. 7–22. Springer, Heidelberg (2012)
11. Křetínský, J., Garza, R.L.: Small deterministic automata for LTL$_{\backslash GU}$. In: Van Hung, D., Ogawa, M. (eds.) ATVA 2013. LNCS, vol. 8172, pp. 446–450. Springer, Heidelberg (2013)
12. Kwiatkowska, M., Norman, G., Parker, D.: PRISM 4.0: verification of probabilistic real-time systems. In: Gopalakrishnan, G., Qadeer, S. (eds.) CAV 2011. LNCS, vol. 6806, pp. 585–591. Springer, Heidelberg (2011)
13. Minato, S.: Fast generation of irredundant sum-of-products forms from binary decision diagrams. In: SASIMI 1992, pp. 64–73, April 1992
14. Safra, S.: Complexity of automata on infinite objects. Ph.D. thesis, The Weizmann Institute of Science, Rehovot, Israel, March 1989

FEMaLeCoP: Fairly Efficient Machine Learning Connection Prover

Cezary Kaliszyk[1](✉) and Josef Urban[2]

[1] University of Innsbruck, Innsbruck, Austria
cezary.kaliszyk@uibk.ac.at
[2] Czech Technical University in Prague, Prague, Czech Republic
josef.urban@gmail.com

Abstract. FEMaLeCoP is a connection tableau theorem prover based on leanCoP which uses efficient implementation of internal learning-based guidance for extension steps. Despite the fact that exhaustive use of such internal guidance can incur a significant slowdown of the raw inferencing process, FEMaLeCoP trained on related proofs can prove many problems that cannot be solved by leanCoP. In particular on the MPTP2078 benchmark, FEMaLeCoP adds 90 (15.7 %) more problems to the 574 problems that are provable by leanCoP. FEMaLeCoP is thus the first AI/ATP system convincingly demonstrating that guiding the internal inference algorithms of theorem provers by knowledge learned from previous proofs can significantly improve the performance of the provers. This paper describes the system, discusses the technology developed, and evaluates the system.

1 Introduction: Guiding Search by Learned Relevance

Intelligent guidance of the proof search is crucial for automated theorem proving (ATP). While complete ATP calculi such as resolution, superposition, and tableau can in principle find a proof of arbitrary length and complexity, the practical strength of state-of-the-art ATP systems is nowhere near the performance of expert mathematicians in most of mathematical domains.

In particular, experiments over large formal mathematical libraries [2,15] show that current ATP calculi have practically no chance to find a more complicated proof in large-theory mathematics unless they are equipped with *external* axiom-selecting AI methods. Such AI methods are based on various ideas estimating the *relevance* of the axioms to the conjecture based on sufficiently descriptive *features* [9] of the axioms and conjectures. The strongest methods are based on *learning* such relevance from the large libraries of previous related proofs. This is not surprising for two reasons. First, mathematicians also gradually *learn* their problem-solving expertise. Second, the chances of completely

C. Kaliszyk—Supported by the Austrian Science Fund (FWF): P26201.
J. Urban—Supported by NWO grant nr. 612.001.208 and ERC Consolidator grant nr. 649043 *AI4REASON*.

M. Davis et al. (Eds.): LPAR-20 2015, LNCS 9450, pp. 88–96, 2015.
DOI: 10.1007/978-3-662-48899-7_7

manually specifying the most efficient proof-search algorithm for all mathematical domains and problems seem very low.

Despite the ability of the AI/learning methods to focus the proof search towards the most relevant axioms, the power of today's ATPs in most of mathematics is still very limited. The automatically found proofs typically do not go over 20 lines of formal proof-assistant code [8], and are usually easy for trained mathematicians. This limited power is due to fast blow-up of the internal ATP search, which is reminiscent of the blow-up incurred by off-the-shelf ATPs when left to struggle alone with a very large number of axioms.

The success of the axiom-selection AI/learning methods in curbing such search space motivates research in automated learning of smarter guidance of the *internal* search. In the MaLeCoP (Machine Learning Connection Prover) experiment [16] we have shown that in principle it is possible to significantly prune the internal search space of leanCoP (lean Connection Prover) [13] when guiding each extension step by an off-the-shelf machine learner trained on related leanCoP proofs. However, the speed of the guiding machine learner in MaLeCoP was impractically (about 1000 times) slower [16] than the raw leanCoP inferencing process, resulting in MaLeCoP's low real-time performance.

2   Contributions

In this work, we devise much stronger learning-based guidance for connection tableau by developing an AI/ATP system where the learning-based guidance is an optimized and tightly integrated part of the core inferencing algorithm and data structures. This in particular involves (i) developing very fast (*online* in the machine-learning terminology) methods for characterizing the current proof state on which the trained learner gives advice to the inferencing process, (ii) suitable modification and integration of a machine learner whose advising speed is comparable to the core deductive inference mechanisms, (iii) designing mechanisms that suitably combine the learning-based guidance with semantic/deductive pruning methods such as discrimination-tree indexing. The main nontrivial concern is to provide strong proof-state characterization and AI/learning methods for guiding the inference steps, while keeping the speed of such methods sufficiently high.

The rest of the paper is organized as follows. Section 3 briefly summarizes leanCoP, its recent OCaml implementation, and the MaLeCoP prototype, which are the basis for the current system. Then we describe the main techniques developed and used in FEMaLeCoP (Sect. 4). In Sect. 5 we show that the raw inference speed of the resulting AI/ATP system is reasonably high in comparison to unguided leanCoP, and that the system indeed adds 15.7 % more MPTP2078 problems to the 574 problems provable by unguided leanCoP.

3   Background: leanCoP, MaLeCoP and OCAML-leanCoP

leanCoP [13] is an automated theorem prover implementing connected tableau search with iterative deepening, written very economically in Prolog by Otten.

The reduction rule of the connection calculus is applied before the extension rule, and open branches are selected in a depth-first way. Additional inference rules and strategies include *regularity, lemmata,* and *restricted backtracking* (cut) [12]. Given the very compact implementation, leanCoP's performance is surprisingly high, regularly outperforming much larger ATPs such as Metis and even Prover9 in the CASC competition and in particular on problems coming from large formal libraries [10]. Its size/performance ratio makes leanCoP suitable for various experiments and integration with other systems. Two such offsprings of leanCoP relevant here are:

1. Its OCaml implementation (OCaml-leanCoP), which has been linked to the HOL Light LCF-style kernel, resulting in the currently strongest internal automation tactic for interactive theorem provers [10].
2. The MaLeCoP prototype [16], providing the original Prolog-based leanCoP with a communication link to an external learning system (the SNoW system [3]) which is trained on previous leanCoP proofs and guides the choice of the extension steps. A large cache and a number of meta-strategies (e.g., advising only when a large branching factor is encountered) were used to combine the (very) slow external advice with the (much) faster raw inference process. Large speed-ups in terms of the abstract time (number of inferences) were measured, however the system was still too slow to be usable in practice.

4   FEMaLeCoP

4.1   Consistent Clausification, Indexing, and Basic Calculus

The basis of FEMaLeCoP is the OCaml version of leanCoP. As in MaLeCoP, FEMaLeCoP starts by a consistent clausification (with relation to the symbols used) of the FOL problem. This is done by using content-based names for Skolem functions and for the names of the clauses (or rather for the *contrapositives* created from the clauses - see below). For example, formula ?[X]: p(X) thus becomes p('skolem(?[A]:p(A),1)') (involving also variable normalization), and the name of this clause (contrapositive) is just its MD5 hash. Such consistent naming is essential for good recall of similar proof situations and their solutions from the previous problems.

As in leanCoP, the initial clauses and their literals are put into an indexing datastructure – the *lit* matrix. The *lit* matrix keeps all literals L from all input clauses C, remembering the rest of the clause ($C - L$). We call the entries in the *lit* matrix (i.e., the pairs L, $C - L$) *contrapositives*. Contrapositives are the main object of leanCoP's search. The *lit* indexing is used for fast Prolog-style unification of literals during the tableau search. While in leanCoP, the indexing of *lit* is done automatically by Prolog, FEMaLeCoP uses indexing by the toplevel predicate and optional discrimination-tree indexing of the literals.

The core theorem-proving function of leanCoP written in Prolog is shown below, with Cla being the open subgoal and Path being the active path. For simplicity, we omit here the code implementing regularity, lemmata, iterative deepening and restrictive backtracking. The main source of nondeterminism is obviously the tableau extension rule, and this is where we will apply the learning-based guidance.

```
1   %   prove(Cla,Path)
2   prove([Lit|Cla],Path)  :-
3       (-NegLit=Lit;-Lit=NegLit) ->
4       (
5           member(NegL,Path),
6           unify_with_occurs_check(NegL,NegLit)
7       ;   % extension step
8           lit(NegLit,NegL,Cla1,Grnd1),
9           unify_with_occurs_check(NegL,NegLit),
10          prove(Cla1,[Lit|Path])
11      ),
12      prove(Cla,Path).
13  prove([],_,).
```

4.2   Overview of the Learning-Based Guidance

We combine the above basic leanCoP algorithm with a learning-based system that advises the inference process. The interesting choices in such AI setup are *what* exactly should be advised, *how* should the advising algorithm work, and in particular *which features* (properties, characteristics) of the proof state are best for recalling similar past proof states that led (typically after some nontrivial search effort) to successfully solved problems and their solutions are thus more likely to lead to successful proof for the current proof state. All these questions open interesting research topics: for example one could advise selection of high-level problem-solving strategies rather than low-level reasoning steps, and the advising algorithm could be interleaved with a gradual computation of more and more advanced features. While such sophisticated designs will certainly be built in the future, our goal here is to develop good-enough first solutions that will show that learning-based guidance leads to significant improvement of the unguided leanCoP. The summary of the choices that we make is as follows:

What Is Advised: We advise the selection of clause for *every* tableau extension step. This means that each time there are multiple clauses (or rather contrapositives) that unify with the current goal, the advise system is called to estimate the candidates' chances (relevance) for leading to a proof. The candidates are then tried (backtracked over) in the order of their relevance. Advising every extension step in this way is quite extreme and ambitious. It requires that the advising system is comparably fast to the standard inference speed, because we cannot assume that there will always be enough previous proof information to completely avoid mistakes and subsequent backtracking.

How We Advise: We use a fast custom OCaml implementation [8] of the naive Bayes algorithm that learns the association of the features of the proof states (see

below) with the contrapositives that were used for the successful tableau extension steps in previous proofs. During each extension step the advising system
computes the features of the active proof state, and orders the contrapositives by
their estimated relevance for these proof-state features based on the contrapositive's performance on previous similar proof states. The exact computation of
the *relevance* and *feature-based similarity* depends on the machine-learning algorithm used. The implementation details of our advising system and the related
infrastructure are described below 4.3.

Features Used: We characterize the proof state as a weighted vector of symbols
and/or (possibly generalized) terms extracted from all the literals on the active
path. We use frequency-based weighting of such features (the *inverse document
frequency* – IDF scheme [6]) which has turned out to work very well in the
related large-theory axiom-selection task [7], and we additionally experiment
with a simple decay factor (using maximum) for the features depending on the
distance of the path literals from the tip of the path. For example, given decay
factor of 0.8 and a term feature "$1 + 2$" extracted independently from two path
literals $L_1 : 1 + 2 = 3$ and $L_2 : 1 + 2 = 2 + 1$ with L_1 being the active goal and
L_2 being its grandparent on the active path, the (non-IDF) weight of the feature
"$1 + 2$" is $w("1 + 2") = max(0.8^0, 0.8^2) = 1$.

4.3   Learning-Based Advising System and Related Infrastructure

Collecting Training Data: First, the advising system needs to collect the training
data. To achieve this, FEMaLeCoP stores the complete information about the
proof by adding the `prf` argument to the `prove` function and returning and
printing it when a proof is found. `prf` is a list of tuples (examples), each consisting
of the current literal, the path, and the contrapositive used.

Data Indexing: The printed `prf` format is very general and verbose, allowing
experiments with different features and learning algorithms without re-running
the ATP. When extracted from many proofs, the number of printed tuples can
easily go over one million. For the naive-Bayes learning and advising we first turn
this data by a special program (*hasher*) into an efficient datastructures optimized
for the particular choice of features (constants and/or (generalized) subterms –
both are used by default). For the particular choice of features hasher extracts
the proof-state features from each example and maintains a hashtable `cn_pf_no`
keeping for each contrapositive a map of its aggregated (weighted) proof-state
feature frequencies. Additionally the following auxiliary data are maintained for
fast IDF and naive-Bayes processing: `te_num` – the total number of training examples so far, `pf_no` – a hashtable from features to floats storing the (weighted)
sum of occurrences of every feature in all the processed training examples, and
`cn_no` – a hashtable storing the total number of occurrences for each contrapositives in all training examples. This data extraction is fast, taking about 30 s for
10000 FEMaLeCoP proofs. Additionally, this also works incrementally, i.e. when
a new proof is found, this aggregated information can be very quickly updated
by the new training examples.

Problem-Specific Data Preparation: Upon start, FEMaLeCoP reads the problem to solve and the aggregated training data. The first task is to select only the parts of these data that are relevant for the current problem. For this, after the (consistent – Sect. 4.1) clausification the contrapositives and their features are extracted and used for filtering out unnecessary parts of the aggregated training data, resulting in the localized version of the aggregated data structures. The cn_pf_no and cn_no hashtables are then combined with the *lit* indexing (based on the toplevel predicate or using a discrimination tree) of contrapositives. This makes the aggregated previous proof-use information for each contrapositive accessible right when the contrapositive is accessed in the main prove function through the *lit* indexing. This typically allows reasonably fast computation of the naive-Bayes score of the contrapositives that are considered by the *lit* indexing.

An optional problem-specific data-filtering step is to use the k-nearest neighbor (k-NN) algorithm for further restriction of the relevant training data. If this is used, we first find the k solved problems whose conjectures are (in the feature metric) closest to the current conjecture, and extract the training examples only from such problems. Such filtering introduces further parameters to optimize and is not yet used in the Evaluation (Sect. 5).

Efficient Approximate Feature and Relevance Computation: To avoid costly recomputation of the features of the path for each extension step, the prove function passes the proof-state features computed so far as an additional argument, and the feature vector is only updated incrementally when an extension step is to be performed. This means that the features may occasionally be approximate, because the substitutions performed with the literals of the path (line 6 of the simplified leanCoP algorithm in Sect. 4.1) might not be taken into account. This optimization may lose some constant features (e.g., if induced by a unification at a reduce step), however it very significantly speeds up the advising. Given that the features of the current path are f, the relevance of the eligible contrapositives (pre-selected by the *lit* indexing) is then computed according to the following modified naive-Bayes score (used by us for axiom selection in [11]):

$$r(t,s) = \sigma_1 \ln t + \sum_{f \in (\overline{f} \cup \overline{s})} i(f) \ln \frac{\sigma_2 s(f)}{t} + \sigma_3 \sum_{f \in (\overline{f} - \overline{s})} i(f) + \sigma_4 \sum_{f \in (\overline{s} - \overline{f})} i(f) \ln(1 - \frac{s(f)}{t})$$

Here t is the total number of times the contrapositive was used, s is its aggregated feature vector, and i is the vector of IDF weights of all features. The score function is parameterized by the following constants (chosen experimentally): σ_1 – weight of the total number of uses (default = 2), σ_2 – weight of the overlapping features (default = 2), σ_3 – weight of the path-only features (default = −6), σ_4 – weight of the contrapositive-only features (default = −0.05).

5   Evaluation

The system's main evaluation is done on the 2078 related problems coming from the MPTP2078 large-theory benchmark [1] exported from Mizar. This benchmark has two categories: large (chainy) problems containing many redundant axioms, and small (bushy) problems that contain only the axioms used explicitly in the Mizar proofs plus additional "background" formulas encoding the (typically typing) reasoning steps done by Mizar implicitly.

As explained in Sect. 1, in FEMaLeCoP we are interested in the problem of guiding the *internal* ATP search once the right axioms have been (approximately) chosen by one of today's reasonably good (external) AI systems used for axiom selection. This is why we evaluate FEMaLeCoP on the bushy (small) problems rather than on the chainy (large) ones. Because the external axiom-selectors are not perfect, it makes sense to evaluate FEMaLeCoP on problems that still contain some redundant axioms, rather than evaluating it on problems where the set of axioms is minimized in some way (see [1] for some discussion of the minimization techniques and issues). The MPTP2078 bushy problems fit this evaluation scenario quite well, because the "background" formulas included in the problems are typically quite redundant [1].

The results are show in Table 1. Unaided OCaml-leanCoP is first run on all the 2078 bushy problems with a time limit of 60 s.[1] This solves 574 problems. From the proofs of these problems we collect the training data from the successful path decisions and preprocess them as described above. This step is done once for all proofs and takes seconds. In the second round we run FEMaLeCoP with these training data loaded, again with a time limit of 60 s, again attacking all the 2078 problems. While the inference speed drops to about 40 % (for a sample problem: 305098 inferences per second instead of 772208) of the unadvised OCaml-leanCoP, the advised system solves 635 problems, adding 90 (15.7 % more) problems to the original solutions. This is a considerable improvement of the ATP performance. As the union gives 664 solved problems, a portfolio approach might also prove to be effective.

Table 1. OCaml-leanCoP and trained FEMaLeCoP on bushy problems in 60 s.

Prover	Proved (%)
OCaml-leanCoP	574 (27.6 %)
FEMaLeCoP	635 (30.6 %)
Together	664 (32.0 %)

6 Conclusion and Future Work

To the best of our knowledge, FEMaLeCoP is the first ATP system with efficiently integrated internal learning-based guidance that convincingly shows the feasibility and benefits of such exhaustive knowledge re-use when compared to the standard unguided ATP. While the MaLeCoP prototype has provided evidence that large pruning of the ATP search space is possible *in principle* when

---

[1] The hardware used is Intel Xeon E7-4870 2.30 GHz with 256 GB RAM.

using such internal guidance, FEMaLeCoP shows that this is possible *in prac-tice*, adding 15.7 % solutions to unguided OCaml-leanCoP in a fair evaluation scenario.

We believe that this is a rather important step towards producing smart inte-grated AI/ATP systems that do not try to attack each problem in complete iso-lation, but instead re-use the vast problem-solving knowledge accumulated in the formal ITP libraries by human mathematicians and machines. The immediate future work includes similar modification of more complicated state-of-the-art ATP systems based on resolution/superposition, developing better proof-state features, more general learning setups, and combining with external axiom selec-tion. For example, while the current learning is done on the (MD5) names of normalized contrapositives, better transfer of knowledge (and thus recall) will likely be achieved by abstracting away the symbol names, and advising also the resulting abstract clause patterns [4,14]. Integrated machine learning could also be used to reorder subgoals [5]. Similarly, it seems straightforward to modify FEMaLeCoP for learning and advising the choice of higher-level tactics in ITP systems.

References

1. Alama, J., Heskes, T., Kühlwein, D., Tsivtsivadze, E., Urban, J.: Premise selection for mathematics by corpus analysis and kernel methods. J. Autom. Reasoning **52**(2), 191–213 (2014)
2. Blanchette, J.C., Kaliszyk, C., Paulson, L.C., Urban, J.: Hammering towards QED. J. Formalized Reasoning (2015, in press)
3. Carlson, A., Cumby, C., Rosen, J., Roth, D.: The SNoW learning architecture. Technical report UIUCDCS-R-99-2101, UIUC Computer Science (1999)
4. Gauthier, T., Kaliszyk, C.: Matching concepts across HOL libraries. In: Watt, S.M., Davenport, J.H., Sexton, A.P., Sojka, P., Urban, J. (eds.) CICM 2014. LNCS, vol. 8543, pp. 267–281. Springer, Heidelberg (2014)
5. Ibens, O., Letz, R.: Subgoal alternation in model elimination. In: Galmiche, D. (ed.) TABLEAUX 1997. LNCS, vol. 1227, pp. 201–215. Springer, Heidelberg (1997)
6. Jones, K.S.: A statistical interpretation of term specificity and its application in retrieval. J. Documentation **28**, 11–21 (1972)
7. Kaliszyk, C., Urban, J.: Stronger automation for Flyspeck by feature weighting and strategy evolution. In: Blanchette, J.C., Urban, J. (eds.) PxTP 2013. EPiC Series, vol. 14, pp. 87–95. EasyChair (2013)
8. Kaliszyk, C., Urban, J.: MizAR 40 for Mizar 40. J. Autom. Reasoning **55**, 245–256 (2015)
9. Kaliszyk, C., Urban, J., Vyskocil, J.: Efficient semantic features for automated reasoning over large theories. In: Yang, Q., Wooldridge, M. (eds.) IJCAI 2015, pp. 3084–3090. AAAI Press (2015)
10. Kaliszyk, C., Urban, J., Vyskočil, J.: Certified connection tableaux proofs for HOL Light and TPTP. In: Leroy, X., Tiu, A. (eds.) Proceedings of the 4th Conference on Certified Programs and Proofs (CPP 2015), pp. 59–66. ACM (2015)
11. Kühlwein, D., Blanchette, J.C., Kaliszyk, C., Urban, J.: MaSh: machine learning for Sledgehammer. In: Blazy, S., Paulin-Mohring, C., Pichardie, D. (eds.) ITP 2013. LNCS, vol. 7998, pp. 35–50. Springer, Heidelberg (2013)

12. Otten, J.: Restricting backtracking in connection calculi. AI Commun. **23**(2–3), 159–182 (2010)
13. Otten, J., Bibel, W.: leanCoP: lean connection-based theorem proving. J. Symb. Comput. **36**(1–2), 139–161 (2003)
14. Schulz, S.: Learning Search Control Knowledge for Equational Deduction. DISKI, vol. 230. Infix Akademische Verlagsgesellschaft (2000)
15. Urban, J., Hoder, K., Voronkov, A.: Evaluation of automated theorem proving on the Mizar Mathematical Library. In: Fukuda, K., Hoeven, J., Joswig, M., Takayama, N. (eds.) ICMS 2010. LNCS, vol. 6327, pp. 155–166. Springer, Heidelberg (2010)
16. Urban, J., Vyskočil, J., Štěpánek, P.: MaLeCoP: Machine Learning Connection Prover. In: Brünnler, K., Metcalfe, G. (eds.) TABLEAUX 2011. LNCS, vol. 6793, pp. 263–277. Springer, Heidelberg (2011)

Decidability, Introduction Rules and Automata

Gilles Dowek[1]([✉]) and Ying Jiang[2]

[1] Inria, 23 Avenue d'Italie, CS 81321, 75214 Paris Cedex 13, France
gilles.dowek@inria.fr
[2] State Key Laboratory of Computer Science, Institute of Software,
Chinese Academy of Sciences, Beijing 100190, China
jy@ios.ac.cn

Abstract. We present a method to prove the decidability of provability in several well-known inference systems. This method generalizes both cut-elimination and the construction of an automaton recognizing the provable propositions.

1 Introduction

The goal of this paper is to connect two areas of logic: proof theory and automata theory, that deal with similar problems, using a different terminology.

To do so, we first propose to unify the terminology, by extending the notions of *introduction rule*, *automaton*, *cut*, and *cut-elimination* to arbitrary inference systems. An *introduction rule* is defined as any rule whose premises are smaller than its conclusion and an *automaton* as any inference system containing introduction rules only. Provability in an automaton is obviously decidable. A *cut* is defined as any proof ending with a non-introduction rule, whose major premises are proved with a proof ending with introduction rules. We show that a cut-free proof contains introduction rules only. A system is said to have the *cut-elimination property* if every proof can be transformed into a cut-free proof. Such a system is equivalent to an automaton.

Using this unified terminology, we then propose a general *saturation* method to prove the decidability of an inference system, by transforming it into a system that has the cut-elimination property, possibly adding extra rules. The outline of this method is the following. Consider a proof containing a non-introduction rule and focus on the sub-proof ending with this rule

$$\frac{\dfrac{\pi^1}{s^1} \quad \cdots \quad \dfrac{\pi^n}{s^n}}{s} \text{ non-intro}$$

Assume it is possible to recursively eliminate the cuts in the proofs $\pi^1, ..., \pi^n$, that is to transform them into proofs containing introduction rules only, hence ending with an introduction rule. We obtain a proof of the form

© Springer-Verlag Berlin Heidelberg 2015
M. Davis et al. (Eds.): LPAR-20 2015, LNCS 9450, pp. 97–111, 2015.
DOI: 10.1007/978-3-662-48899-7_8

$$\dfrac{\dfrac{\rho_1^1 \quad \rho_{m_1}^1}{s_1^1 \ \ldots \ s_{m_1}^1} \ \text{intro}}{s^1} \quad \cdots \quad \dfrac{\dfrac{\rho_1^n \quad \rho_{m_n}^n}{s_1^n \ \ldots \ s_{m_n}^n} \ \text{intro}}{s^n}}{s} \ \text{non-intro}$$

We may moreover tag each premise s^1, ..., s^n of the non-introduction rule as *major* or *minor*. For instance, each elimination rule of Natural Deduction [14] has one major premise and the cut rule of Sequent Calculus [12] has two. If the major premises are s^1, ..., s^k and *minor* ones $s^{k+1}, ..., s^n$, the proof above can be decomposed as

$$\dfrac{\dfrac{\dfrac{\rho_1^1 \quad \rho_{m_1}^1}{s_1^1 \ \ldots \ s_{m_1}^1} \ \text{intro}}{s^1} \quad \cdots \quad \dfrac{\dfrac{\rho_1^k \quad \rho_{m_k}^k}{s_1^k \ \ldots \ s_{m_k}^k} \ \text{intro}}{s^k} \quad \dfrac{\pi'^{k+1}}{s^{k+1}} \ \ldots \ \dfrac{\pi'^n}{s^n}}{s} \ \text{non-intro}$$

A proof of this form is called a *cut* and it must be reduced to another proof. The definition of the reduction is specific to each system under consideration. In several cases, however, such a cut is reduced to a proof built with the proofs ρ_1^1, ..., $\rho_{m_1}^1$, ..., ρ_1^k, ..., $\rho_{m_k}^k$, π'^{k+1}, ..., π'^n and a derivable rule allowing to deduce the conclusion s from the premises $s_1^1, ..., s_{m_1}^1, ..., s_1^k, ..., s_{m_k}^k, s^{k+1}, ..., s^n$. Adding such derivable rules in order to eliminate cuts is called a *saturation* procedure.

Many cut-elimination proofs, typically the cut-elimination proofs for Sequent Calculus [8], do not proceed by eliminating cuts step by step, but by proving that a non-introduction rule is admissible in the system obtained by dropping this rule, that is, proving that if the premises $s^1, ..., s^n$ of this rule are provable in the restricted system, then so is its conclusion s. Proceeding by induction on the structure of proofs of $s^1, ..., s^n$ leads to consider cases where each major premise s^i has a proof ending with an introduction rule, that is also proofs of the form

$$\dfrac{\dfrac{\dfrac{\rho_1^1 \quad \rho_{m_1}^1}{s_1^1 \ \ldots \ s_{m_1}^1} \ \text{intro}}{s^1} \quad \cdots \quad \dfrac{\dfrac{\rho_1^k \quad \rho_{m_k}^k}{s_1^k \ \ldots \ s_{m_k}^k} \ \text{intro}}{s^k} \quad \dfrac{\pi_{k+1}}{s^{k+1}} \ \ldots \ \dfrac{\pi_n}{s^n}}{s} \ \text{non-intro}$$

In some cases, the saturation method succeeds showing that every proof can be transformed into a proof formed with introduction rules only. Then, the inference system under consideration is equivalent, with respect to provability, to the automaton obtained by dropping all its non-introduction rules. This equivalence obviously ensures the decidability of provability in the inference system. In other cases, in particular when the inference system under consideration is undecidable, the saturation method succeeds only partially: typically some non-introduction rules can be eliminated but not all, or only a subsystem is proved to be equivalent to an automaton.

This saturation method is illustrated with examples coming from both proof theory and automata theory: Finite Domain Logic, Alternating Pushdown Systems, and three fragments of Constructive Predicate Logic, for which several formalizations are related: Natural Deduction, Gentzen style Sequent Calculus, Kleene style Sequent Calculus, and Vorob'ev-Hudelmaier-Dyckhoff-Negri style Sequent Calculus. The complexity of these provability problems, when they are decidable, is not discussed in this paper and is left for future work, for instance in the line of [1, 13].

In the remainder of this paper, the notions of introduction rule, automaton, and cut are defined in Sect. 2. Section 3 discusses the case of Finite State Automata. In Sects. 4 and 5, examples of cut-elimination results are presented. In the examples of Sect. 4, the non-introduction rules can be completely eliminated transforming the inference systems under considerations into automata, while this elimination is only partially successful in the undecidable examples of Sect. 5. The proofs, and some developments, are omitted from this extended abstract. They can be found in the long version of the paper https://who.rocq. inria.fr/Gilles.Dowek/Publi/introlong.pdf.

2   Introduction Rules, Automata, and Cuts

2.1   Introduction Rules and Automata

Consider a set S, whose elements typically are propositions, sequents, etc. Let S^* be the set of finite lists of elements of S.

Definition 1 (Inference rule, Inference system, Proof). *An inference rule is a partial function from S^* to S. If R is an inference rule and $s = R(s_1, ..., s_n)$, we say that the conclusion s is* proved *from the premises $s_1, ..., s_n$ with the rule R and we write*

$$\frac{s_1 \; ... \; s_n}{s} \, R$$

Some rules are equipped with an extra piece of information, tagging each premise $s_1, ..., s_n$ as major *or* minor. *An inference system is a set of inference rules. A proof in an inference system is a finite tree labeled by elements of S such that for each node labeled with s and whose children are labeled with $s_1, ..., s_n$, there exists an inference rule R of the system such that*

$$\frac{s_1 \; ... \; s_n}{s} \, R$$

A proof is a proof of s if its root is labeled by s. An element of S is said to be provable, *if it has a proof.*

Definition 2 (Introduction Rule, Pseudo-automaton). *Consider a set S and a well-founded order $\prec$ on S. A rule R is said to be an* introduction *rule with respect to this order, if whenever*

$$\frac{s_1 \; ... \; s_n}{s} \, R$$

we have $s_1 \prec s, ..., s_n \prec s$. A pseudo-automaton *is an inference system containing introduction rules only.*

Except in the system $\mathcal{D}$ (Sect. 5.4), this order $\prec$ is always that induced by the size of the propositions and sequents. It is left implicit.

Definition 3 (Finitely Branching System, Automaton). *An inference system is said to be* finitely branching, *if for each conclusion s, there is only a finite number of lists of premises $\bar{s}_1, ..., \bar{s}_p$ such that s can be proved from $\bar{s}_i$ with a rule of the system. An* automaton *is a finitely branching pseudo-automaton.*

2.2 Cuts

We define a general notion of cut, that applies to all inference systems considered in this paper. More specific notions of cut will be introduced later for some systems, and the general notion of cut defined here will be emphasized as *general cut* to avoid ambiguity.

Definition 4 (Cut). *A (general) cut is a proof of the form*

$$
\cfrac{\cfrac{\rho_1^1 \quad \rho_{m_1}^1}{\cfrac{s_1^1 \;\; ... \;\; s_{m_1}^1}{s^1} \; \text{intro}} \;\;\; ... \;\;\; \cfrac{\cfrac{\rho_1^k \quad \rho_{m_k}^k}{\cfrac{s_1^k \;\; ... \;\; s_{m_k}^k}{s^k} \; \text{intro}} \quad \cfrac{\pi_{k+1}}{s^{k+1}} \;\; ... \;\; \cfrac{\pi_n}{s^n}}{}}{s} \; \text{non-intro}
$$

where $s^1, ..., s^k$ are the major premises of the non-introduction rule. A proof contains a cut if one of its sub-proofs is a cut. A proof is cut-free *if it contains no cut. An inference system has the* cut-elimination property *if every element that has a proof also has a cut-free proof.*

Lemma 1 (Key Lemma). *A proof is cut-free if and only if it contains introduction rules only.*

Proof. If a proof contains introduction rules only, it is obviously cut-free. We prove the converse by induction over proof structure. Consider a cut-free proof. Let R be the last rule of this proof and $\pi_1, ..., \pi_n$ be the proofs of the premises of this rule. The proof has the form

$$
\cfrac{\cfrac{\pi_1}{s_1} \;\; ... \;\; \cfrac{\pi_n}{s_n}}{s} \; R
$$

By induction hypothesis, the proofs $\pi_1, ..., \pi_n$ contain introduction rules only. As the proof is cut-free, the rule R must be an introduction rule.

Consider a finitely-branching inference system $\mathcal{I}$ and the automaton $\mathcal{A}$ formed with the introduction rules of $\mathcal{I}$. If $\mathcal{I}$ has the cut-elimination property, then every element that has a proof in $\mathcal{I}$ has a cut-free proof, that is a proof formed with introduction rules of $\mathcal{I}$ only, that is a proof in $\mathcal{A}$. Thus, $\mathcal{I}$ and $\mathcal{A}$ are equivalent with respect to provability. Since $\mathcal{A}$ is decidable, so is $\mathcal{I}$.

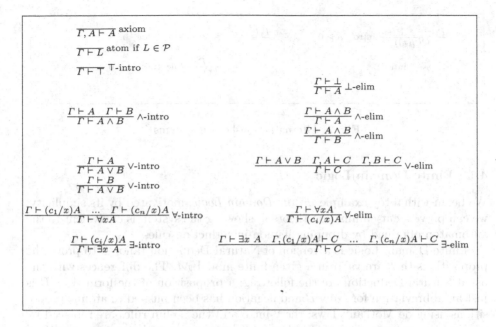

Fig. 1. Finite domain logic

3 Finite State Automata

In this section, we show that the usual notion of finite state automaton is a particular case of the notion of automaton introduced in Definition 3.

Consider a finite state automaton $\mathcal{A}$. We define a language $\mathcal{L}$ in predicate logic containing a constant ε; for each symbol γ of the alphabet of $\mathcal{A}$, a unary function symbol, also written γ; and for each state P of $\mathcal{A}$ a unary predicate symbol, also written P. A closed term in $\mathcal{L}$ has the form $\gamma_1(\gamma_2...(\gamma_n(\varepsilon)))$, where $\gamma_1, ..., \gamma_n$ are function symbols. Such a term is called a *word*, written $w = \gamma_1\gamma_2...\gamma_n$. A closed atomic proposition has the form $P(w)$, where P is a state and w a word. We build an inference system that consists of, for each transition rule $P \xrightarrow{\gamma} Q$ of $\mathcal{A}$, the introduction rule

$$\frac{Q(x)}{P(\gamma(x))}$$

and, for each final state F of $\mathcal{A}$, the introduction rule

$$\overline{F(\varepsilon)}$$

It is routine to check that a word w is recognized by the automaton $\mathcal{A}$ in a state I if and only if the proposition $I(w)$ has a proof in the corresponding system.

4 From Cut-Elimination to Automata

In this section, we present two cut-elimination theorems, that permit to completely eliminate the non-introduction rules and prove, this way, the decidability of Finite Domain Logic and of Alternating Pushdown Systems, respectively.

$$\frac{P_1(x) \ \dots \ P_n(x)}{Q(\gamma(x))} \text{ intro} \quad n \geq 0 \qquad\qquad \frac{P_1(\gamma(x)) \ P_2(x) \ \dots \ P_n(x)}{Q(x)} \text{ elim} \quad n \geq 1$$

$$\frac{}{Q(\varepsilon)} \text{ intro} \qquad\qquad\qquad \frac{P_1(x) \ \dots \ P_n(x)}{Q(x)} \text{ neutral} \quad n \geq 0$$

Fig. 2. Alternating pushdown systems

4.1 Finite Domain Logic

We begin with a toy example, *Finite Domain Logic*, motivated by its simplicity: we can prove a cut-elimination theorem, showing the system is equivalent to the automaton obtained by dropping its non-introduction rules.

Finite Domain Logic is a version of Natural Deduction tailored to prove the propositions that are valid in a given finite model $\mathcal{M}$. The differences with the usual Natural Deduction are the following: a proposition of the form $A \Rightarrow B$ is just an abbreviation for $\neg A \vee B$ and negation has been pushed to atomic propositions using de Morgan's laws; the $\forall$-intro and the $\exists$-elim rules are replaced by enumeration rules, and an *atom* rule is added to prove closed atomic propositions and their negations valid in the underlying model.

If the model $\mathcal{M}$ is formed with a domain $\{a_1, ..., a_n\}$ and relations $R_1, ..., R_m$ over this domain, we consider the language containing constants $c_1, ..., c_n$ for the elements $a_1, ..., a_n$ and predicate symbols $P_1, ..., P_m$ for the relations $R_1, ..., R_m$. The *Finite Domain Logic* of the model $\mathcal{M}$ is defined by the inference system of Fig. 1, where the set $\mathcal{P}$ contains, for each atomic proposition $P_i(c_{j_1}, ..., c_{j_k})$, either the proposition $P_i(c_{j_1}, ..., c_{j_k})$ if $\langle a_{j_1}, ..., a_{j_k} \rangle$ is in R_i, or the proposition $\neg P_i(c_{j_1}, ..., c_{j_k})$, otherwise.

In this system, the introduction rules are those presented in the first column: the axiom rule, the atom rule, and the rules $\top$-intro, $\wedge$-intro, $\vee$-intro, $\forall$-intro, and $\exists$-intro. The non-introduction rules are those presented in the second column. Each rule has one major premise: the leftmost one. A cut is as in Definition 4.

Theorem 1 (Soundness, Completeness, and Cut-elimination). *Let B be a closed proposition, the following are equivalent:*

(1) the proposition B has a proof,
(2) the proposition B is valid in $\mathcal{M}$,
(3) the proposition B has a cut-free proof, that is a proof formed with introduction rules only.

Therefore, provability in Finite Domain Logic is decidable, as the provable propositions are recognized by the automaton obtained by dropping the non-introduction rules. Since the introduction rules preserve context emptiness, the contexts can be ignored and the axiom rule can be dropped. This automaton could also be expressed in a more familiar way with the transition rules

$$L \hookrightarrow \varnothing \text{ if } L \in \mathcal{P} \qquad A \vee B \hookrightarrow \{A\}$$
$$\top \hookrightarrow \varnothing \qquad\qquad A \vee B \hookrightarrow \{B\}$$
$$A \wedge B \hookrightarrow \{A, B\} \qquad \forall x\, A \hookrightarrow \{(c_1/x)A, ..., (c_n/x)A\}$$
$$\exists x\, A \hookrightarrow \{(c_i/x)A\} \text{ for each } c_i$$

4.2 Alternating Pushdown Systems

The second example, *Alternating Pushdown Systems*, is still decidable [2], but a little bit more complex. Indeed these systems, in general, need to be saturated—that is extended with derivable rules—in order to enjoy cut-elimination.

Consider a language $\mathcal{L}$ containing a finite number of unary predicate symbols, a finite number of unary function symbols, and a constant ε. An *Alternating Pushdown System* is an inference system whose rules are like those presented in Fig. 2. The rules in the first column are introduction rules and those in the second column, the elimination and neutral rules, are not. Elimination rules have one major premise, the leftmost one, and all the premises of a neutral rule are major. A cut is as in Definition 4.

Not all Alternating Pushdown Systems enjoy the cut-elimination property. However, every Alternating Pushdown System has an extension with derivable rules that enjoys this property: each time we have a cut of the form

$$\cfrac{\cfrac{\rho_1^1 \quad \rho_{m_1}^1}{s_1^1 \ \cdots \ s_{m_1}^1} \text{intro}}{s^1} \quad \cdots \quad \cfrac{\cfrac{\rho_1^k \quad \rho_{m_k}^k}{s_1^k \ \cdots \ s_{m_k}^k} \text{intro}}{s^k} \quad \cfrac{}{s^{k+1}}\pi_{k+1} \quad \cdots \quad \cfrac{}{s^n}\pi_n \Big/ s \text{ non-intro}$$

we add a derivable rule allowing to deduce directly s from $s_1^1, ..., s_{m_1}^1, ..., s_1^k, ..., s_{m_k}^k, s^{k+1}, ..., s^n$. This leads to the following saturation algorithm [3,9,10].

Definition 5 (Saturation). *Given an Alternating Pushdown System,*

– *if it contains an introduction rule*

$$\frac{P_1(x) \ \cdots \ P_m(x)}{Q_1(\gamma(x))} \text{ intro}$$

and an elimination rule

$$\frac{Q_1(\gamma(x)) \ Q_2(x) \ \cdots \ Q_n(x)}{R(x)} \text{ elim}$$

then we add the neutral rule

$$\frac{P_1(x) \ \cdots \ P_m(x) \ Q_2(x) \ \cdots \ Q_n(x)}{R(x)} \text{ neutral}$$

– *if it contains introduction rules*

$$\frac{P_1^1(x) \ \cdots \ P_{m_1}^1(x)}{Q_1(\gamma(x))} \text{ intro} \qquad \cdots \qquad \frac{P_1^n(x) \ \cdots \ P_{m_n}^n(x)}{Q_n(\gamma(x))} \text{ intro}$$

and a neutral rule

$$\frac{Q_1(x) \quad ... \quad Q_n(x)}{R(x)} \text{ neutral}$$

then we add the introduction rule

$$\frac{P_1^1(x) ... P_{m_1}^1(x) \quad ... \quad P_1^n(x) ... P_{m_n}^n(x)}{R(\gamma(x))} \text{ intro}$$

– *if it contains introduction rules*

$$\overline{Q_1(\varepsilon)} \text{ intro} \qquad ... \qquad \overline{Q_n(\varepsilon)} \text{ intro}$$

and a neutral rule

$$\frac{Q_1(x) \quad ... \quad Q_n(x)}{R(x)} \text{ neutral}$$

then we add the introduction rule

$$\overline{R(\varepsilon)} \text{ intro}$$

As there is only a finite number of possible rules, this procedure terminates.

It is then routine to check that if a closed proposition has a proof in a saturated system, it has a cut-free proof [3], leading to the following result.

Theorem 2 (Decidability). *Provability of a closed proposition in an Alternating Pushdown System is decidable.*

Example 1. Consider the Alternating Pushdown System S

$$\frac{Q(x)}{P(ax)} \text{ i1} \qquad \frac{T(x)}{P(bx)} \text{ i2} \qquad \frac{T(x)}{R(ax)} \text{ i3} \qquad \frac{}{R(bx)} \text{ i4}$$

$$\frac{P(x) \ R(x)}{Q(x)} \text{ n1} \qquad \frac{}{T(x)} \text{ n2} \qquad \frac{P(ax)}{S(x)} \text{ e1}$$

The system S' obtained by saturating the system S contains the rules of the system S and the following rules

$$\frac{Q(x)}{S(x)} \text{ n3} \qquad \frac{}{T(\varepsilon)} \text{ i5} \qquad \frac{}{T(ax)} \text{ i6} \qquad \frac{Q(x) \ T(x)}{Q(ax)} \text{ i7}$$

$$\frac{Q(x) \ T(x)}{S(ax)} \text{ i8} \qquad \frac{}{T(bx)} \text{ i9} \qquad \frac{T(x)}{Q(bx)} \text{ i10} \qquad \frac{T(x)}{S(bx)} \text{ i11}$$

The automaton S'' contain the rules i1, i2, i3, i4, i5, i6, i7, i8, i9, i10, i11.

The proof in the system S

$$\cfrac{\cfrac{\cfrac{\overline{T(\varepsilon)} \text{ n2}}{P(b)} \text{ i2} \quad \cfrac{\overline{R(b)} \text{ i4}}{} }{\cfrac{Q(b)}{P(ab)} \text{ i1}} \text{ n1} \quad \cfrac{\cfrac{\overline{T(b)} \text{ n2}}{R(ab)} \text{ i3}}{} \text{ n1}}{\cfrac{\cfrac{Q(ab)}{P(aab)} \text{ i1}}{S(ab)} \text{ e1}}$$

reduces to the cut-free proof in the system S''

$$\frac{\dfrac{\overline{T(\varepsilon)}\ \text{i5}}{Q(b)}\ \text{i10} \qquad \overline{T(b)}\ \text{i9}}{S(ab)}\ \text{i8}$$

5   Partial Results for Undecidable Systems

In this section, we focus on Constructive Predicate Logic, leaving the case of Classical Predicate Logic for future work. We start with Natural Deduction [14]. As provability in Predicate Logic is undecidable, we cannot expect to transform Natural Deduction into an automaton. But, as we shall see, saturation permits to transform first Natural Deduction into a Gentzen style Sequent Calculus [12], then the latter into a Kleene style Sequent Calculus [12], and then the latter into a Vorob'ev-Hudelmaier-Dyckhoff-Negri style Sequent Calculus [4,6,11,15]. Each time, a larger fragment of Constructive Predicate Logic is proved decidable.

Note that each transformation proceeds in the same way: first, we identify some general cuts. Then, like in the saturation procedure of Sect. 4.2, we add some admissible rules to eliminate these cuts. Finally, we prove a cut-elimination theorem showing that some non-introduction rules can be dropped.

5.1   Natural Deduction

In Natural Deduction (Fig. 3), the introduction rules are those presented in the first column, they are the axiom rule and the rules $\top$-intro, $\wedge$-intro, $\vee$-intro, $\Rightarrow$-intro, $\forall$-intro, and $\exists$-intro. The non-introduction rules are those presented in the second column, each of them has one major premise: the leftmost one.

Natural Deduction has a specific notion of cut: a proof ending with a $\wedge$-elim, $\vee$-elim, $\Rightarrow$-elim, $\forall$-elim, $\exists$-elim rule, whose major premise is proved with a proof ending with a $\wedge$-intro, $\vee$-intro, $\Rightarrow$-intro, $\forall$-intro, $\exists$-intro rule, respectively. The only difference between this specific notion of cut and the general one (Definition 4) is that the general notion has one more form of cut: a proof built with an elimination rule whose major premise is proved with the axiom rule. For instance

$$\frac{\overline{P \wedge Q \vdash P \wedge Q}\ \text{axiom}}{P \wedge Q \vdash P}\ \wedge\text{-elim}$$

So proofs free of specific cuts can still contain general cuts of this form.

Saturating the system, like in Sect. 4.2, to eliminate the specific cuts, would add derivable rules such as

$$\frac{\Gamma \vdash A \qquad \Gamma \vdash B}{\Gamma \vdash A}\ R_\wedge$$

But they are not needed, as they are admissible in cut-free Natural Deduction.

The admissibility of some rules however are based on a substitution of proofs, that may create new cuts on smaller propositions, that need in turn to be eliminated. In other words, the termination of the specific cut-elimination algorithm needs to be proved [14].

$$\frac{}{\Gamma, A \vdash A} \text{ axiom}$$

$$\frac{}{\Gamma \vdash \top} \text{ } \top\text{-intro}$$

$$\frac{\Gamma \vdash \bot}{\Gamma \vdash A} \text{ } \bot\text{-elim}$$

$$\frac{\Gamma \vdash A \quad \Gamma \vdash B}{\Gamma \vdash A \wedge B} \text{ } \wedge\text{-intro}$$

$$\frac{\Gamma \vdash A \wedge B}{\Gamma \vdash A} \text{ } \wedge\text{-elim}$$

$$\frac{\Gamma \vdash A \wedge B}{\Gamma \vdash B} \text{ } \wedge\text{-elim}$$

$$\frac{\Gamma \vdash A}{\Gamma \vdash A \vee B} \text{ } \vee\text{-intro}$$

$$\frac{\Gamma \vdash B}{\Gamma \vdash A \vee B} \text{ } \vee\text{-intro}$$

$$\frac{\Gamma \vdash A \vee B \quad \Gamma, A \vdash C \quad \Gamma, B \vdash C}{\Gamma \vdash C} \text{ } \vee\text{-elim}$$

$$\frac{\Gamma, A \vdash B}{\Gamma \vdash A \Rightarrow B} \text{ } \Rightarrow\text{-intro}$$

$$\frac{\Gamma \vdash A \Rightarrow B \quad \Gamma \vdash A}{\Gamma \vdash B} \text{ } \Rightarrow\text{-elim}$$

$$\frac{\Gamma \vdash A}{\Gamma \vdash \forall x A} \text{ } \forall\text{-intro if } x \text{ not free in } \Gamma$$

$$\frac{\Gamma \vdash \forall x A}{\Gamma \vdash (t/x)A} \text{ } \forall\text{-elim}$$

$$\frac{\Gamma \vdash (t/x)A}{\Gamma \vdash \exists x A} \text{ } \exists\text{-intro}$$

$$\frac{\Gamma \vdash \exists x A \quad \Gamma, A \vdash B}{\Gamma \vdash B} \text{ } \exists\text{-elim if } x \text{ not free in } \Gamma, B$$

Fig. 3. Constructive natural deduction

As general cuts with an axiom rule are not eliminated, this partial cut-elimination theorem is not sufficient to eliminate all elimination rules and to prove the decidability of Constructive Natural Deduction, but it yields a weaker result: a (specific-)cut-free proof ends with introduction rules, as long as the context of the proved sequent contains atomic propositions only. To formalize this result, we introduce a modality [ ] and define a translation that freezes the non atomic left-hand parts of implications, $f(A \Rightarrow B) = [A] \Rightarrow f(B)$, if A is not atomic, and $f(A \Rightarrow B) = A \Rightarrow f(B)$, if A is atomic, $f(A \wedge B) = f(A) \wedge f(B)$, etc., and the converse function u is defined in a trivial way.

Definition 6. *Let $\mathcal{A}$ be the pseudo-automaton formed with the introduction rules of Constructive Natural Deduction, including the axiom rule, plus the introduction rule*

$$\frac{}{\Gamma, [A] \vdash B} \text{ delay}$$

Theorem 3. *Let $\Gamma \vdash A$ be a sequent such that Γ contains atomic propositions only. If $\Gamma \vdash A$ has a (specific-)cut-free proof in Constructive Natural Deduction, then $\Gamma \vdash f(A)$ has a proof in the pseudo-automaton $\mathcal{A}$ and for each leaf $\Delta \vdash B$ proved with the delay rule, the sequent $u(\Delta \vdash B)$ has a proof in Constructive Natural Deduction.*

A first corollary of Theorem 3 is the decidability of the small fragment

$$A = P \mid \top \mid \bot \mid A \wedge A \mid A \vee A \mid P \Rightarrow A \mid \forall x A \mid \exists x A$$

where the left-hand side of an implication is always atomic, that is no connective or quantifier has a negative occurrence. As the pseudo-automaton obtained this way is not finitely branching, we need, as well-known, to introduce meta-variables to prove this decidability result.

A second corollary is that if A is a proposition starting with n connectors or quantifiers different from $\Rightarrow$, then a (specific-)cut-free proof of the sequent $\vdash A$ ends with $n+1$ successive introduction rules. For $n = 0$, we obtain the well-known last rule property of constructive (specific-)cut-free proofsFor a proposition A of the form $\forall x \ (B_1 \lor B_2)$, for instance, we obtain that a (specific-)cut-free proof of $\vdash \forall x \ (B_1 \lor B_2)$ ends with three introduction rules. Thus, it has the form

$$\dfrac{\dfrac{\dfrac{\pi'}{\vdash B_i}\ .}{\vdash B_1 \lor B_2}\ \lor\text{-intro}}{\vdash \forall x \ (B_1 \lor B_2)}\ \forall\text{-intro}$$

and π' itself ends with an introduction rule. As a consequence, if the proposition $\forall x \ (B_1 \lor B_2)$ has a proof, then either the proposition B_1 or the proposition B_2 has a proof, thus the proposition $(\forall x \ B_1) \lor (\forall x \ B_2)$ has a proof. This commutation of the universal quantifier with the disjunction is called a *shocking equality* [7].

5.2   Eliminating Elimination Rules: Gentzen Style Sequent Calculus

To eliminate the general cuts of the form

$$\dfrac{\dfrac{}{A \land B \vdash A \land B}\ \text{axiom}}{A \land B \vdash A}\ \land\text{-elim}$$

we could add an introduction rule of the form

$$\dfrac{}{A \land B \vdash A}\ I$$

But, this saturation procedure would not terminate.

A way to keep the number of rules finite is to add left introduction rules to decompose the complex hypotheses, before they are used by the axiom rule: the left rules of Sequent Calculus. However, this is still not sufficient to eliminate the elimination rules of Constructive Natural Deduction. For instance, the sequent $\forall x(P(x) \land (P(f(x)) \Rightarrow Q)) \vdash Q$ has a proof using elimination rules

$$\dfrac{\dfrac{\dfrac{\dfrac{}{\Gamma \vdash \forall x \ (P(x) \land (P(f(x)) \Rightarrow Q))}\ \text{axiom}}{\Gamma \vdash P(c) \land (P(f(c)) \Rightarrow Q)}\ \forall\text{-elim}}{\Gamma \vdash P(f(c)) \Rightarrow Q}\ \land\text{-elim} \qquad \dfrac{\dfrac{\dfrac{}{\Gamma \vdash \forall x \ (P(x) \land (P(f(x)) \Rightarrow Q))}\ \text{axiom}}{\Gamma \vdash P(f(c)) \land (P(f(f(c))) \Rightarrow Q)}\ \forall\text{-elim}}{\Gamma \vdash P(f(c))}\ \land\text{-elim}}{\Gamma \vdash Q}\ \Rightarrow\text{-elim}$$

where $\Gamma = \forall x \ (P(x) \land (P(f(x)) \Rightarrow Q))$, but none using introduction rules only.

So, we need to add a contraction rule, to use an hypothesis several times

$$\dfrac{\Gamma, A, A \vdash G}{\Gamma, A \vdash G}\ \text{contraction}$$

$$\frac{}{\Gamma, P \vdash P} \text{ axiom } P \text{ atomic} \qquad\qquad \frac{\Gamma, A, A \vdash G}{\Gamma, A \vdash G} \text{ contraction}$$

$$\frac{}{\Gamma \vdash \top} \top\text{-right}$$

$$\frac{}{\Gamma, \bot \vdash G} \bot\text{-left}$$

$$\frac{\Gamma, A, B \vdash G}{\Gamma, A \wedge B \vdash G} \wedge\text{-left}$$

$$\frac{\Gamma \vdash A \quad \Gamma \vdash B}{\Gamma \vdash A \wedge B} \wedge\text{-right}$$

$$\frac{\Gamma, A \vdash G \quad \Gamma, B \vdash G}{\Gamma, A \vee B \vdash G} \vee\text{-left}$$

$$\frac{\Gamma \vdash A}{\Gamma \vdash A \vee B} \vee\text{-right}$$

$$\frac{\Gamma \vdash B}{\Gamma \vdash A \vee B} \vee\text{-right}$$

$$\frac{\Gamma \vdash A \quad \Gamma, B \vdash G}{\Gamma, A \Rightarrow B \vdash G} \Rightarrow\text{-left}$$

$$\frac{\Gamma, A \vdash B}{\Gamma \vdash A \Rightarrow B} \Rightarrow\text{-right}$$

$$\frac{\Gamma, (t/x)A \vdash G}{\Gamma, \forall x A \vdash G} \forall\text{-left}$$

$$\frac{\Gamma \vdash A}{\Gamma \vdash \forall x A} \forall\text{-right if } x \text{ not free in } \Gamma$$

$$\frac{\Gamma, A \vdash G}{\Gamma, \exists x\, A \vdash G} \exists\text{-left if } x \text{ not free in } \Gamma, G$$

$$\frac{\Gamma \vdash (t/x)A}{\Gamma \vdash \exists x\, A} \exists\text{-right}$$

Fig. 4. Gentzen style Sequent Calculus: the system $\mathcal{G}$

To prove that the elimination rules of Natural Deduction can now be eliminated, we prove, using Gentzen's theorem [8], that they are admissible in the system $\mathcal{G}$ (Fig. 4), the Gentzen style Sequent Calculus, obtained by dropping the elimination rules of Constructive Natural Deduction. In this system, all the rules are introduction rules, except the contraction rule. The system $\mathcal{G}$ does not allow to prove the decidability of any larger fragment of Constructive Predicate Logic, but it is the basis of the two systems presented in the Sects. 5.3 and 5.4.

5.3 Eliminating the Contraction Rule: Kleene Style Sequent Calculus

In the system $\mathcal{G}$, the proof

$$\frac{\dfrac{\rho}{\Gamma, \forall x\ A, (t/x)A \vdash B}}{\dfrac{\Gamma, \forall x\ A, \forall x\ A \vdash B}{\Gamma, \forall x\ A \vdash B} \text{ contraction}} \forall\text{-left}$$

is a general cut and we may replace it by the application of the derivable rule

$$\frac{\dfrac{\rho}{\Gamma, \forall x\ A, (t/x)A \vdash B}}{\Gamma, \forall x\ A \vdash B} \text{ contr-}\forall\text{-left}$$

which is a rule *à la* Kleene. The other general cuts yields similar derivable rules. But, as noticed by Kleene, the derivable rules for the contradiction, the

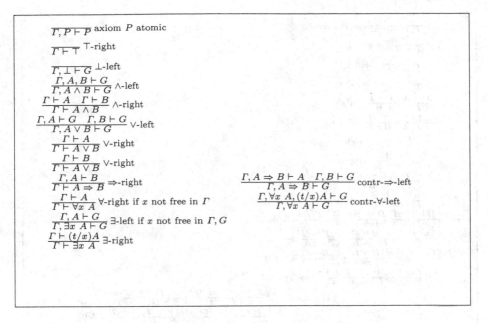

Fig. 5. Kleene style Sequent Calculus: the system $\mathcal{K}$

conjunction, the disjunction and the existential quantifier can be dropped, while that for the implication can be simplified to

$$\frac{\Gamma, A \Rightarrow B \vdash A \quad \Gamma, B \vdash G}{\Gamma, A \Rightarrow B \vdash G} \ \text{contr-}\Rightarrow\text{-left}$$

The rules $\Rightarrow$-left and $\forall$-left of the system $\mathcal{G}$, that are subsumed by the rules contr-$\Rightarrow$-left and contr-$\forall$-left, can be also dropped. There are also other general cuts, where the last rule is a contraction and the rule above is an introduction applied to another proposition, but these cuts can be eliminated without introducing any extra rule. In other words, after applying the contraction rule, we can focus on the contracted proposition [5].

We get this way the system $\mathcal{K}$ (Fig. 5). In this system, all rules are introduction rules, except the rules contr-$\Rightarrow$-left and contr-$\forall$-left. The system $\mathcal{K}$ plus the contraction rule is obviously sound and complete with respect to the system $\mathcal{G}$. To prove that the contraction rule can be eliminated from it, and hence the system $\mathcal{K}$ also is sound and complete with respect to the system $\mathcal{G}$, we prove the admissibility of the contraction rule in the system $\mathcal{K}$—see the long version of the paper for the full proof. The system $\mathcal{K}$ gives the decidability of a larger fragment of Constructive Predicate Logic, where the implication and the universal quantifier have no negative occurrences.

5.4   Eliminating the Contr-$\Rightarrow$-left Rule: Vorob'ev-Hudelmaier-Dyckhoff-Negri Style Sequent Calculus

In order to eliminate the contr-$\Rightarrow$-left rule, we consider the general cuts where a sequent $\Gamma, A \Rightarrow B \vdash G$ is proved with a contr-$\Rightarrow$-left rule whose major premise

$$\frac{}{\Gamma, P \vdash P} \text{ axiom } P \text{ atomic}$$

$$\frac{}{\Gamma \vdash \top} \top\text{-right}$$

$$\frac{}{\Gamma, \bot \vdash G} \bot\text{-left}$$

$$\frac{\Gamma, A, B \vdash G}{\Gamma, A \wedge B \vdash G} \wedge\text{-left}$$

$$\frac{\Gamma \vdash A \quad \Gamma \vdash B}{\Gamma \vdash A \wedge B} \wedge\text{-right}$$

$$\frac{\Gamma, A \vdash G \quad \Gamma, B \vdash G}{\Gamma, A \vee B \vdash G} \vee\text{-left}$$

$$\frac{\Gamma \vdash A}{\Gamma \vdash A \vee B} \vee\text{-right}$$

$$\frac{\Gamma \vdash B}{\Gamma \vdash A \vee B} \vee\text{-right}$$

$$\frac{\Gamma, P, B \vdash G}{\Gamma, P, P \Rightarrow B \vdash G} \Rightarrow\text{-left}_{axiom}$$

$$\frac{\Gamma, B \vdash G}{\Gamma, \top \Rightarrow B \vdash G} \Rightarrow\text{-left}_{\top}$$

$$\frac{\Gamma, C \Rightarrow B \vdash C \quad \Gamma, D \Rightarrow B \vdash D \quad \Gamma, B \vdash G}{\Gamma, (C \wedge D) \Rightarrow B \vdash G} \Rightarrow\text{-left}_{\wedge}$$

$$\frac{\Gamma, C \Rightarrow B, D \Rightarrow B \vdash C \quad \Gamma, B \vdash G}{\Gamma, (C \vee D) \Rightarrow B \vdash G} \Rightarrow\text{-left}_{\vee}$$

$$\frac{\Gamma, C \Rightarrow B, D \Rightarrow B \vdash D \quad \Gamma, B \vdash G}{\Gamma, (C \vee D) \Rightarrow B \vdash G} \Rightarrow\text{-left}_{\vee}$$

$$\frac{\Gamma, D \Rightarrow B, C \vdash D \quad \Gamma, B \vdash G}{\Gamma, (C \Rightarrow D) \Rightarrow B \vdash G} \Rightarrow\text{-left}_{\Rightarrow}$$

$$\frac{\Gamma, (\forall x \ C) \Rightarrow B \vdash C \quad \Gamma, B \vdash G}{\Gamma, (\forall x C) \Rightarrow B \vdash G} \Rightarrow\text{-left}_{\forall} \quad x \text{ not free in } \Gamma, B$$

$$\frac{\Gamma, (\exists x \ C) \Rightarrow B \vdash (t/x)C \quad \Gamma, B \vdash G}{\Gamma, (\exists x \ C) \Rightarrow B \vdash G} \Rightarrow\text{-left}_{\exists}$$

$$\frac{\Gamma, A \vdash B}{\Gamma \vdash A \Rightarrow B} \Rightarrow\text{-right}$$

$$\frac{\Gamma \vdash A}{\Gamma \vdash \forall x A} \forall\text{-right} \quad x \text{ not free in } \Gamma$$

$$\frac{\Gamma, \forall x A, (t/x)A \vdash G}{\Gamma, \forall x A \vdash G} \text{contr-}\forall\text{-left}$$

$$\frac{\Gamma, A \vdash G}{\Gamma, \exists x \ A \vdash G} \exists\text{-left} \quad x \text{ not free in } \Gamma, G$$

$$\frac{\Gamma \vdash (t/x)A}{\Gamma \vdash \exists x \ A} \exists\text{-right}$$

Fig. 6. The system $\mathcal{D}$

$\Gamma, A \Rightarrow B \vdash A$ is proved with an introduction rule, applied to the proposition A. This leads to consider the various cases for A, that is hypotheses of the form $P \Rightarrow B$, $\top \Rightarrow B$, $(C \wedge D) \Rightarrow B$, $(C \vee D) \Rightarrow B$, $(C \Rightarrow D) \Rightarrow B$, $(\forall x \ C) \Rightarrow B$, and $(\exists x \ C) \Rightarrow B$. The case $A = P$, atomic, needs to be considered because the premise $\Gamma, A \Rightarrow B \vdash A$ may be proved with the axiom rule, but the case $\bot \Rightarrow B$ does not, because there is no right rule for the symbol $\bot$. This enumeration of the various shapes of A is the base of the sequent calculi in the style of Vorob'ev, Hudelmaier, Dyckhoff, and Negri [4,6,11,15].

We obtain this way several types of general cuts that can be eliminated by introducing derivable rules. These rules can be simplified leading to the system $\mathcal{D}$ (Fig. 6). The system $\mathcal{D}$ plus the contr-$\Rightarrow$-left rule is obviously sound and complete with respect to the system $\mathcal{K}$. To prove that the contr-$\Rightarrow$-left rule can be eliminated, and hence the system $\mathcal{D}$ also is sound and complete with respect to the system $\mathcal{K}$, we use a method similar to that of [6], and prove the admissibility of the contr-$\Rightarrow$-left rule—see the long version of the paper for the full proof.

This system $\mathcal{D}$ gives the decidability of a larger fragment of Constructive Predicate Logic containing all connectives, shallow universal and existential quantifiers—that is quantifiers that occur under no implication at all—and negative existential quantifiers. This fragment contains the prenex fragment of Constructive Predicate Logic, that itself contains Constructive Propositional Logic.

Acknowledgements. This work is supported by the ANR-NSFC project LOCALI (NSFC 61161130530 and ANR 11 IS02 002 01) and the Chinese National Basic Research Program (973) Grant No. 2014CB340302.

References

1. Basin, D., Ganzinger, H.: Automated complexity analysis based on ordered resolution. J. ACM **48**(1), 70–109 (2001)
2. Bouajjani, A., Esparza, J., Maler, O.: Reachability analysis of pushdown automata: application to model-checking. In: Mazurkiewicz, A.W., Winkowski, J. (eds.) Concurrency Theory. LNCS, vol. 1243, pp. 135–150. Springer, Heidelberg (1997)
3. Dowek, G., Jiang, Y.: Cut-elimination and the decidability of reachability in alternating pushdown systems (2014). arXiv:1410.8470 [cs.LO]
4. Dyckhoff, R.: Contraction-free sequent calculi for intuitionistic logic. J. Symb. Log. **57**(3), 795–807 (1992)
5. Dyckhoff, R., Lengrand, S.: LJQ: a strongly focused calculus for intuitionistic logic. In: Beckmann, A., Berger, U., Löwe, B., Tucker, J.V. (eds.) CiE 2006. LNCS, vol. 3988, pp. 173–185. Springer, Heidelberg (2006)
6. Dyckhoff, R., Negri, S.: Admissibility of structural rules for contraction-free systems of intuitionistic logic. J. Symb. Log. **65**, 1499–1518 (2000)
7. Girard, J.-Y.: Locus solum. Math. Struct. Comput. Sci. **11**, 301–506 (2001)
8. Girard, J.-Y., Lafont, Y., Taylor, P.: Proofs and Types. Cambridge University Press, Cambridge (1989)
9. Frühwirth, T., Shapiro, E., Vardi, M., Yardeni, E.: Logic programs as types for logic programs. In: Logic in Computer Science, pp. 300–309 (1991)
10. Goubault-Larrecq, J.: Deciding H_1 by resolution. Inf. Process. Lett. **95**(3), 401–408 (2005)
11. Hudelmaier, J.: An $O(n \log n)$-space decision procedure for intuitionistic propositional logic. J. Log. Comput. **3**, 63–76 (1993)
12. Kleene, S.C.: Introduction to Metamathematics. North-Holland, Amsterdam (1952)
13. McAllester, D.A.: Automatic recognition of tractability in inference relations. J. ACM **40**(2), 284–303 (1993)
14. Prawitz, D.: Natural Deduction. Almqvist & Wiksell, Stockholm (1965)
15. Vorob'ev, N.N.: A new algorithm for derivability in the constructive propositional calculus. Am. Math. Soc. Transl. **2**(94), 37–71 (1970)

Analyzing Internet Routing Security
Using Model Checking

Adi Sosnovich[1]([✉]), Orna Grumberg[1], and Gabi Nakibly[2]

[1] Computer Science Department, Technion, Haifa, Israel
{sadisos,orna}@cs.technion.ac.il
[2] National Research and Simulation Center, Rafael, Haifa, Israel
gabin@rafael.co.il

Abstract. The goal of this work is to enhance Internet security by applying formal analysis of traffic attraction attacks on the BGP routing protocol. BGP is the sole protocol used throughout the Internet for inter-domain routing, hence its importance. In attraction attacks an attacker sends false routing advertisements to gain attraction of extra traffic in order to increase its revenue from customers, drop, tamper, or snoop on the packets. Such attacks are most common on the inter-domain routing.

We use model checking to perform exhaustive search for attraction attacks on BGP. This requires substantial reductions due to scalability issues of the entire Internet topology. Therefore, we propose static methods to identify and automatically reduce Internet fragments of interest, prior to using model checking.

We developed a method, called BGP-SA, for BGP Security Analysis, which extracts and reduces fragments from the Internet. In order to apply model checking, we model the BGP protocol and also model an attacker with predefined capabilities. Our specifications allow to reveal different types of attraction attacks. Using a model checking tool we identify attacks as well as show that certain attraction scenarios are impossible on the Internet under the modeled attacker capabilities.

1 Introduction

In this work we combine static examination and model checking to examine fragments of the Internet and either identify possible attacks on their routing protocol or prove that specific attacks are not possible.

The Internet is composed of Autonomous Systems (ASes). Each AS is administered by a single entity (such as an Internet service provider, or an enterprise) and it may include dozens to many thousands of networks and routers. Inter-domain routing determines through which ASes packets will traverse. Routing on this level is handled throughout the Internet by a single routing protocol called the *Border Gateway Protocol* [16] (BGP).

It is well known that the Internet is vulnerable to traffic attacks [4,9]. In such attacks malicious Autonomous Systems manipulate BGP routing advertisements in order to attract traffic to, or through, their AS networks. Attracting extra

© Springer-Verlag Berlin Heidelberg 2015
M. Davis et al. (Eds.): LPAR-20 2015, LNCS 9450, pp. 112–129, 2015.
DOI: 10.1007/978-3-662-48899-7_9

traffic enables the AS to increase revenue from customers, drop, tamper, or snoop on the packets. In the recent past, there have been frequent occurrences of traffic attraction attacks on the Internet [12,13,18–21]. Some of those attacks allowed oppressive governments to block their citizens from accessing certain websites. In other attacks the perpetrators eavesdropped or altered the communications of others, while in different attacks spammers sent millions of emails from IP addresses they do not own. In one type of attack scenario the traffic is diverted through the attacker's AS network and then forwarded to its real destination, which allows the attacker to become a "man-in-the-middle" between the source of the traffic and its final destination. Such attacks are called *interception attacks*. In another type of attack scenario, the traffic is not forwarded to its real destination, which allows the attacker to impersonate the real destination or simply block access to it. Such attacks are called *attraction attacks*. In the sequel, when we refer to any attack of these types we call it a *traffic attack*.

Our goal is to provide insights to where and how BGP traffic attacks are possible. Note that BGP is the sole protocol used throughout the Internet for inter-domain routing, hence its importance. We develop a method that exploits model checking to systematically reveal BGP traffic attacks on the Internet, or prove their absence under certain conditions. Our method is based on powerful reductions and abstractions that allow model checking to explore relatively small fragments of the Internet, yet obtain relevant results. Reductions are essential as the Internet nowadays includes roughly 50,000 ASes.

A fragment includes a destination and an attacker AS nodes. The goal of the attacker is to attract traffic sent to the destination while the goal of normal nodes is to direct the traffic to the destination.

In a normal mode of the BGP operation, when no attacker is present, an AS node receives from some of its neighbors their choice of routing path to the destination. When AS A announces a routing update to its neighbor AS B consisting of a target node n and a path π, it means that A announces to B that it is willing to carry packets destined to n from B, and that packets will traverse over the path π. From the announced routing paths, the node chooses its most preferred route (according to business relationship between the entities that administer the ASes, length of path, etc.) and sends it further to some of its neighbors. Its announced path may, in turn, influence the choice of preferred paths of its neighbors. In contrast, an attacker may send its neighbors faulty routing paths whose goal is to convince them and other AS nodes in the Internet to route through the attacker on their way to the destination.

Our static examination investigates the announcements flowing throughout the Internet. The basic idea is that if announcements cannot flow from one part of the Internet to another then nodes in the first part cannot influence the routing decisions of nodes in the second part. Our first reduction is thus based on BGP policies that determine the flow of announcements in the Internet. Given a destination and an attacker, we *statically* identify on the full Internet topology a *self-contained fragment* S that consists of a set of nodes, including the destination and attacker. S is defined so that nodes in S may send announcements inside and outside of S, but nodes outside of S never send announcements to nodes in S. Thus, the routing choices of nodes in S are not influenced by routing choices of the rest of the Internet.

We can now isolate S from the rest of the Internet and apply model checking only to it in order to search for an attack strategy that attracts traffic to the attacker. Since routing decisions in S are made autonomically, an attack strategy found on S will attract the same nodes from S when the full Internet is considered. This result allows to significantly reduce the processing burden on model checking while searching for attacks on the Internet. Similarly, if we show that no attack strategy manages to attract traffic from certain victims in S then the attacker will not manage to attract traffic from those victims in the full Internet as well. Thus, by searching a small fragment we find attacks on the full Internet or show their absence.

The second reduction we suggest is applied within a self-contained fragment S to further reduce it. We *statically* identify nodes in S that for all BGP runs choose the same route to the destination (that does not pass through the attacker), regardless of the attacker's behavior. Such nodes are considered *safe* with respect to the destination and the attacker of S.

The advantage of this reduction is twofold. First, safe nodes can be safely removed from the model, thus easing the burden on model checking. Second, nodes that wish to improve their routing security may decide to route through safe nodes, thus avoiding traffic attacks from this specific attacker. We further elaborate on the latter in Sect. 8.

Our third reduction is based on an abstraction. We can *statically* identify a *routing-preserving* set of nodes that all make the same routing choices. Such a set can be replaced by a single node with similar behavior without changing routing decisions of other nodes in the network.

Note that all three reductions are computed statically by investigating the Internet topology and are therefore easy to compute.

We implemented our method, called BGP-SA, for BGP Security Analysis. We first extracted from the Internet self-contained fragments, which are defined by a destination and an attacker nodes, and applied reductions to them. We chose the attacker and the destination nodes either arbitrarily or in order to reconstruct known recent attacks. In order to apply model checking, we modeled the BGP protocol for each AS node. We also modeled an attacker with predefined capabilities. The BGP model is written in C. We considered several specifications which allow to reveal different types of attacks. We ran IBM's model checking tool ExpliSAT [7] on self-contained, reduced fragments.

We found interception attacks. One of those attacks reconstructs a recent known attack where Syria attracted traffic destined to YouTube [18]. In other cases we showed that some attraction scenarios are impossible under the modeled attacker capabilities. In the latter case, model checking could also reveal additional *safe* nodes.

To summarize, the contributions of this paper are:

- Defining and implementing aggressive *reductions* of the Internet. The resulting (relatively small) self-contained fragments enable an automatic analysis.
- Developing an *automatic analysis* that can reveal possible attacks on the Internet and prove that certain attacks are not possible.
- Identifying *safe nodes* that are not amenable to traffic attacks and can be exploited to reduce vulnerability of other nodes in the Internet.

2   Related Work

There are some past works that use formal methods to analyze convergence properties of BGP. [3] uses a static model of BGP path selection and analyzes configurations of BGP policy. [2] uses static and dynamic models to reason about BGP convergence. [17] analyzes convergence of routing policies with an SMT solver. We use a different modeling to reason about traffic attraction scenarios on the Internet. Our modeling implements runs of the protocol until stabilization, includes an attacker, and is based on the routing policy used by most ASes on the Internet. Our model includes parts of BGP that are most relevant to the analysis of traffic attraction, and is based on the model presented in [9].

Reference [9] discusses the security of BGP and its vulnerability to different attacks. It shows that an attacker may employ non-trivial and non-intuitive attack strategies in order to maximize its gain. This was shown by giving anecdotal evidence (obtained manually) for each attack strategy in specific parts of the Internet. In our work we develop reductions and use model checking to systematically and automatically search for BGP traffic attacks on the Internet.

3   BGP Background

The routers and networks of the Internet are clustered into connected sets. Each such set is called an autonomous system (AS). As of the end of 2014, there are roughly 50,000 autonomous systems on the Internet. An AS is usually administered by a single network operator, such as an ISP (Internet service provider), an enterprise, a university, etc. Each AS has a predefined routing policy determined by the network operator. An autonomous system is assigned a globally unique number, sometimes called an Autonomous System Number (ASN).

Routing of data packets on the Internet works in two levels:

1. Inter-domain routing that determines through which ASes the packets will traverse. This level of routing is handled by a single routing protocol called the Border Gateway Protocol [16] (BGP).
2. Intra-domain routing that determines the path taken by the packets within each AS. This is determined independently in each AS. Each network operator is free to choose any routing protocol to employ within its AS. The most common examples of such routing protocols are OSPF [15], RIP [14], or IS-IS [6].

Note that BGP is the sole protocol used for inter-domain routing. In essence, BGP is the glue that holds the Internet together and which allows to connect between different ASes. The currently used version of BGP is number 4. The protocol's standard is specified by the IETF (Internet Engineering Task Force) standardization body in [16]. The primary function of BGP is to exchange network reachability information between different ASes. Each AS periodically announces to all its neighboring ASes (i.e., the ASes to which it is directly connected) routing updates. A routing update consists of the identity of a target network and a path that consists of a sequence of ASes that starts from the advertising AS and leads to the AS in which the target network resides. Note that BGP advertises routing updates pertaining to networks residing within ASes (not to ASes themselves), while the routing path is at the AS level. When AS A advertises a routing update to its neighbor AS B consisting of a target network n and a path π, it means that A announces to B that it is willing to carry packets destined to n from B, and that packets will traverse over the path π. This routing information will then be propagated by AS B to its neighbors, after prepending itself to π. The propagation of routing information by one AS to all its neighbors is a matter of a policy determined by that AS. We shall elaborate on this in the following.

Every AS stores the routing updates learned from its neighboring ASes in a data structure called Adj-RIBs-In. If several routes were advertised for the same target network by different neighboring ASes, then the AS must choose its most preferable one. Once a route is chosen all packets destined to that target network will be routed via the neighboring AS that announced the chosen route. The chosen routes for all target networks on the Internet are stored in a data structure called Loc-RIB. Choosing the most preferable route is a matter of policy specific to each AS. In this paper we call it a *preference policy*.

As noted above, each AS propagates to its neighbors the routing updates it receives. Only routes within the Loc-RIB may be propagated. Namely, an AS can only propagate a route it has chosen as its most preferable one. Before propagating a route the AS must prepend itself to that route. An AS may choose a subset of its neighbors to which a route is propagated. This is a matter of policy specific to each AS. We call it an *export policy*.

Preference and Export Policies. As noted above, the preference and export policies are a local matter for each AS determined by the network operator. These policies usually abide by business relationships and commercial agreements between the different network operators. While in reality there are many types of business relationships and agreements, the following two relationships are widely believed to capture the majority of the economic relationships [8].

– Customer-provider – in such a relationship the customer pays the provider for connectivity. Usually, the provider AS is larger and better connected than the customer AS. For example, the AS administered by Sprint is a provider of the AS of Xerox corporation. Xerox pays money to Sprint for connecting

Xerox to the rest of the Internet through Sprint. In this paper we denote this kind of relationship with arrow from customer to provider.
- Peer-peer – in such a relationship the two peer ASes agree to transit each other's traffic at no cost. Usually, the two ASes are of comparable size and connectivity. For example, the ASes administered by Sprint and NTT are peers. Each provides the other connectivity to parts of the Internet it may not have access to. In this paper we denote this kind of relationship with an undirected line between the two ASes.

Based on the above business relationships the following is a well-accepted model for the preference and export policies [8].

Preference Policy. This policy is based on the following simple rationale. An AS has an economic incentive to prefer forwarding traffic via customer (that pays him) over a peer (where no money is exchanged) over a provider (that he must pay). Combined with the fact that routing must be loop free and preferably on short routes the following policy is defined:

1. Reject a routing update that contains a route if the AS itself already appears on the announced route.
2. Prefer routes that were announced by a customer over routes announced by a peer over routes announced by a provider.
3. Among the most preferable routes choose the shortest ones, i.e., the ones which traverse the fewest ASes.
4. If there are multiple such paths, choose the one that was announced by the AS with the lowest ASN.

Export Policy. This policy is based on the following simple rationale. An AS is willing to carry traffic to or from other ASes only if it gets paid to do so. Based on this rationale the following policy is defined:

- AS B will announce to AS A a route via AS C if and only if at least one of A and C are customers of B.

To illustrate the above policies consider the topology depicted in Fig. 1. Let us consider the routing of AS 9 to AS 0. There are three possible paths: (9,3,2,1,0), (9,4,5,0), and (9,7,1,0). Due to the above preference policy 9 will favor the first route over the second route which is favored over the third route. This is because the first route is announced by a customer AS (i.e., 3), while the second and third routes are announced by a peer (4) and provider (7) ASes, respectively. Note that the chosen route (9,3,2,1,0) will be propagated to 7 and 4, according to the above export policy.

4   BGP Modeling and Specifications

In this paper we use a BGP standard model acceptable in the literature [9] to facilitate the analysis of traffic attacks using false route advertisements.

The model includes all the relevant parts of the protocol that deal with the dissemination and processing of route advertisements. In particular, the mechanisms of route distribution and route preference are modeled, including malicious routes originated by an attacker.

We assume a single destination, called *Dest*, such that the other ASes want to send traffic to a target network within *Dest*. We can focus on a single destination because routing announcements referring to different destinations flow independently of each other. Namely, the routing to one destination does not influence the routing to another destination. As a result, in our model a routing update does not include the identity of the target network.

Modeling the BGP Network. A BGP network N is a tuple $N = (Nodes, Links, Dest, Attacker)$ where *Nodes* is a set of Autonomous System (AS) nodes in the network graph. *Links* is a set of node pairs with one of the following types: customer-provider or peer-to-peer, representing the business relationships between ASes in the network. *Dest* is an AS from *Nodes* representing a single destination node that contains the target network to which all other nodes build routing paths. *Attacker* is a node from *Nodes* representing an AS that can send false routing advertisements to achieve traffic attraction or interception.

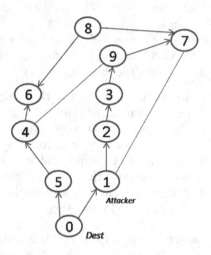

Dest and the *Attacker* are called the *originators* of N. All other nodes are called *regular* nodes.

Fig. 1. BGP network example

Consider the BGP network presented in Fig. 1. *Nodes* = $\{0, 1, \ldots 9\}$, *Links* consists of customer-provider links such as $(1 \rightarrow 2)$ and $(9 \rightarrow 7)$, and also peer-to-peer links such as $(4 - 9)$ and $(1 - 7)$.

A *path* in N is a sequence $\pi = (n_1, \ldots, n_k)$ of nodes in *Nodes*, such that for every $1 \leq i < k$, n_i and n_{i+1} are connected by an edge (of any kind) from *Links*.

Local States and Global Configurations. The *local state* of a regular AS n consists of:

- A message queue $Q(n)$ containing incoming route announcements.
- A Routing Information Base $RIB(n)$ containing a set of possible routes to *Dest*. The most preferred route is denoted *chosen*(n).

A (global) *configuration* of N consists of the local states of all nodes.

Next we define a run of the BGP protocol on network N. A run starts from an *initial* configuration in which all queues and RIBs are empty. Initially *Dest* sends announcements to all its neighbors. The run terminates after all nodes in N terminate their run and their queues are empty. In particular, the originators have already sent out all their announcements. The final configuration of a run is called *stable*.

We often will be interested in referring to export actions along a run. We denote by $export(n, n')$ the action of node n exporting an announcement to its neighbor n'.

4.1 Attack Definitions and Specifications

Attacker Goal. The goal of the attacker in our model is to achieve traffic attraction or interception. We say that a node n is *attracted* by the attacker if in the stable configuration $chosen(n)$ is a path on which the attacker appears. A node n is *intercepted* by the attacker if it is attracted, and in addition the attacker has a routing path to the destination.

Successful Attack. A successful attack is a BGP run such that its final stable configuration satisfies the attacker goal. The attack strategy can be represented by the sequence of actions preformed by the attacker during the attack, where each of its action contains the sent announcement and a set of neighbors to which it was sent.

Normal Outcome. Is the final routing choices of all ASes in N when the attacker acts like a regular AS.

Trivial Attack Strategy. In the trivial strategy the attacker sends a false advertisement to all its neighbors and announces that the target network is located within its own AS.

Specifications. To measure how successful a traffic attraction or interception attack is, we suggest specifications that compare the result of the attack to the normal outcome of the protocol run and to the result of the trivial attack, when applicable. We define specifications of *traffic attraction or interception* from any victim as follows: if the attacker can attract (or intercept) traffic from any victim, while it fails to do so in the normal run and the trivial attack, the attraction (or interception) specification is satisfied. We demonstrate how the specification is implemented in our model on Sect. 6.3.

5 Reductions and Abstractions

The goal of our reductions is to obtain a manageable sized fragment of the large network which is suitable for identifying BGP traffic attacks or show their absence.

5.1   Self-contained Fragments

The extraction of a self-contained fragment is our main reduction that significantly reduces the initial network, such as the full Internet topology. The reduction is based on preserving the flow of announcements in the network during a BGP run. The following is a central notion in our analysis of the flow. It directly follows from the export policy (see Sect. 3). A path $\pi = (n_1, \ldots, n_k)$ in N is *valid* if n_1 is an originating node, no node is repeated on π, and for every $1 < i < k$, at least one of n_{i-1} and n_{i+1} is a customer of n_i. Further, no n_i is an originating node except n_1 and possibly n_k. Examples of valid paths in network N of Fig. 1 are $(0, 5, 4, 6, 8)$ and $(0, 5, 4, 9, 3, 2, 1)$. Note that $(0, 5, 4, 6, 8, 7)$ is not a valid path, since both 6 and 7 are not customers of 8. The following is a key observation about valid paths.

Lemma 1. *If there is no valid path in N with edge from node n to node n' then there is no run in N along which $export(n, n')$ is performed.*

Note, however, that the contrary is not true. There might be an edge (n, n') on a valid path but still no $export(n, n')$ is performed. This is due to the preference policy of nodes.

We say that n *cannot export* to n' if there is no run in which the action $export(n, n')$ is performed.

Let N be a network and let $S \subseteq Nodes$ be a subset of its nodes that includes all originators of N. S is a *self-contained fragment* of N if for every $n \in (Nodes \setminus S)$, n cannot export to any $n' \in S$. This means that nodes outside of S cannot change routing decisions of nodes in S.

The following lemma describes the significance of self-contained fragments.

Lemma 2. *Let N be a network and let S be a self-contained fragment of N. Then, any traffic attack found on S can occur on N as well. Moreover, if we prove that a traffic attack is not possible in S then the corresponding attack is not possible in N as well.*

The lemma implies that instead of searching a huge network N (such as the Internet) we can identify a (relatively small) self-contained fragment, isolate it from the rest of the network, and search for possible attacks on it. Assume an attacker (in S) can attract traffic from a node n' in S. Then since nodes outside of S do not send n' alternative routing options, they cannot "convince" n' to change its routing choice and avoid the route through the attacker. Thus, a traffic attack which is successful in S is also successful in N. Similarly, if a certain node is definitely *not* routing through the attacker in S then the same holds in N as well.

Fragment Importance. Following Lemma 2 , it should be noted that the fragment concept is of great importance for applying significant reductions on BGP networks. The set of announcements that a node within the fragment can receive during any BGP run with an arbitrary attacker on the whole Internet is equal to its counterpart on a similar run that is applied to the fragment only. Therefore, the set of chosen routing paths within the fragment is equal as well, due to the deterministic preference policy of each node. Thus, the task of applying model checking on the whole Internet is reduced to applying it on a self-contained fragment when searching for BGP traffic attacks with our suggested specifications. Additionally, the fragment concept may be useful for other BGP-based formal analyses that require substantial reductions on large networks.

Computing Self-contained Fragments. Given a network $N = (Nodes, Links, Dest, Attacker)$, we describe the computation of a set of nodes which forms a self-contained fragment. The resulting S includes $Dest$ and $Attacker$ and excludes some of N's nodes that cannot export any announcement to S.

Initially, only the set of originators $O = \{Dest, Attacker\}$ and their neighbors are in S. A node c outside of S is inserted to S if c is a neighbor of some $n \in S$, and c is on a valid path from some originator in O to n. The algorithm terminates when for every $c \notin S$ which is a neighbor of some $n \in S$, c is not on a valid path from an originator to n and therefore (by Lemma 1) c cannot export to n.

Example for a Self-contained Fragment Extraction. Consider the 10-nodes-sized network, presented in part A of Fig. 2. In practice the initial network can be much larger. Applying the fragment extraction algorithm results in:

1. Initialization: Insert O and their neighbors. $S = \{22561, 48685, 209, 25934, 6677\}$
2. Add $c = 3257$, due to valid path : $(o = 22561, 209, 3257, n = 6677)$
3. Add $c = 5580$, due to valid path : $(o = 22561, 209, 5580, n = 25934)$

The remaining nodes are not added. For example, 3303 does not appear on any valid path in the original network, and is therefore dropped during the construction of a self-contained fragment. After applying this phase we remain with 7 nodes as presented in part B of Fig. 2.

5.2   Definite Routing Choice

In this reduction we identify nodes that never route via the attacker. If for all runs of BGP on a network N, a node n chooses to route through a specific path π originated by $Dest$ that does not pass through the attacker, then π is the *definite routing choice* of n, denoted $drc(n)$. We consider such nodes as *safe*, since they cannot be attracted by the attacker.

For example, in Fig. 1, $drc(5) = (0)$ and $drc(4) = (5, 0)$. Node 5 is a neighbor of $Dest$ and its link to $Dest$ is more preferred than its other link. Therefore, since the announcement from $Dest$ is guaranteed to be sent to 5, it will always prefer this path regardless of other paths it might get from 4. For a similar reason, and since 5 is guaranteed to export its path to 4, node 4 will always prefer the route

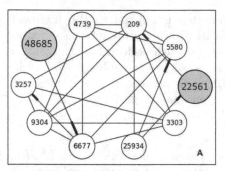 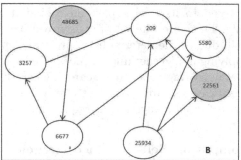

Fig. 2. Fragment Example. The grey node 48685 is the attacker. The yellow node 22561 is the destination. The thick lines in part A represent the arrow direction of the customer-provider links (Color figure online).

via 5. On the other hand, $drc(9)$ is undefined since on different runs its choice of routing may change as a result of the announcements sent by the attacker (which may change from run to run).

$drc(n)$, when defined, is $chosen(n)$ in every run, regardless of the attacker's actions. Consequently, the export actions of n are also determined. We can therefore eliminate such n from our network and initiate a BGP run from a configuration in which the results of its export is already in the queues of the appropriate neighbors. This may significantly reduce the network size to which model checking is applied.

5.3   Routing-Preserving Path

Another source of reduction is the abstraction of routing-preserving paths. A path $\pi = (n_1, \ldots, n_k)$ is *routing-preserving* if for every run r of N, in the final (stable) configuration of r one of the two cases holds: either for all $1 < i \le k$, n_i chooses to route through n_{i-1}, or for all $1 \le i < k$, n_i chooses to route through n_{i+1}.

Intuitively, for every run of the protocol, the nodes on a routing-preserving path all agree on the same route to the destination. As a result, we can replace such a path with a single node (an *abstraction* of the path) without changing the routing of other nodes in the network. The protocol of an abstract node is adjusted such that it exports announcements with lengths that match the number of nodes in the path it represents. An example of a routing-preserving path in Fig. 1 is $(2, 3, 9)$.

6   The BGP-SA Method

Our suggested method, called BGP-SA, for *BGP Security Analysis*, uses reductions and model checking to apply a formal analysis of BGP attraction attacks on a large network topology. We use model checking to perform a systematic

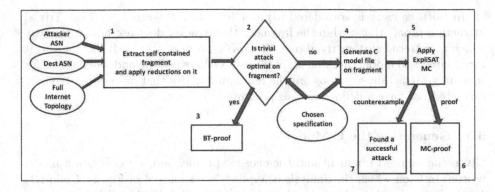

Fig. 3. The BGP-SA method

search for traffic attacks. A systematic search is essential in order to reveal
non-trivial attraction strategies on topologies from the Internet. It has a major
advantage over simple testing techniques that randomly search for attacks. The
model checker we use can perform full verification, thus it can also prove that
no traffic attack is possible under certain conditions.

The BGP-SA method is composed of several stages, as depicted in Fig. 3.
Below we describe them in details.

6.1 Reducing the Network Topology

The input to the BGP-SA method consists
of the full network topology, the chosen
attacker and destination ASN, and the chosen specification. Given this input, we first
extract a self-contained fragment and apply
additional reductions and abstractions. (see
square 1 of Fig. 3). The extraction and reduction algorithms are explained in Sect. 5. The
output is a reduced fragment that contains
the nodes within the extracted fragment S,
without those for which drc is defined. (See
Fig. 4).

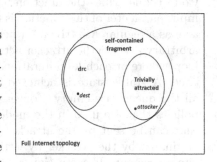

Fig. 4. Partition of node types in
the extracted fragment

6.2 Simulating the Trivial Attack

Here we explain items 2–3 of Fig. 3. Given a reduced fragment, we run a simulation of the trivial attack on it. If the chosen specification is traffic attraction and
if all the nodes in the reduced fragment are trivially attracted, then the attacker
cannot improve its attraction results. If the chosen specification is traffic interception and if the trivial attack satisfies the interception condition additionally
to attracting all nodes in the reduced fragment, then again the attacker cannot
improve its attraction results.

In both cases it is considered a proof (denoted *BT-proof* for Best Trivial attraction proof) that within the fragment the attacker does not have a strategy which is better than the trivial one. When BT-proof is obtained, the analysis is terminated and model checking is not needed. Otherwise, the nodes of interest for searching attraction scenarios are the remaining nodes that are neither trivially attracted nor have a defined *drc*, as presented in Fig. 4.

6.3   Generating the C Model

Given the reduced fragment and the chosen specification, we generate a model written in C on which the analysis is applied (see square 4 of Fig. 3). Code 1.1-1.3 depicts a pseudo-code of the generated code in high level, and below we give more details of it.

- Code 1.1 describes the procedures that implement nodes in our model. *AS_Proc* is the procedure of a regular AS. Its path preference and export policy are as explained in Sect. 3. The attacker has two procedures: *Arbitrary_Attacker_Proc* is the procedure of an attacker that originates arbitrary path announcements and sends them to arbitrary neighbors. *Trivial_Attacker_Proc* is the procedure of an attacker that applies the trivial attack and announces itself as the destination to all its neighbors. *Dest_Proc* is the procedure of *Dest*, in which it announces itself as the destination to all its neighbors.
- Code 1.2 describes the function implementing a BGP run in our model. The input parameter of this function is the type of run: normal – where the attacker acts as a regular AS, trivial – where the attacker applies the trivial attack, or arbitrary - where the attacker acts arbitrarily. The function is composed of a loop, where at each loop iteration each one of the AS procedures is activated once. A stable state is achieved when no message is sent by any AS and all the queues are empty. Convergence is guaranteed [11] due to the routing policies that are used in the model and the finite number of announcements that can be sent by the attacker. We bound the number of announcements originated by the attacker by letting it export to each neighbor at most one announcement. The function returns the routing results at the stable state which include $chosen(n)$ for each node n in the netwrok, where $chosen(n)$ is the preferred route of n.
- Code 1.3 describes the main function in the model and the assertion statement that implements the specification. The main function is composed of three calls to the function BGP_run, with the three types of run: normal, trivial, and arbitrary. The routing results of the three runs are saved. Then, to implement the attraction specification, a boolean flag is set true if there exists some victim that is attracted by the attacker only in the arbitrary run, and not in the normal and trivial runs. The assertion requires that this boolean flag is false. Therefore, if the assertion is violated, the violating run represents a succesful attraction attack. To implement the interception specification, a constraint that the attacker has a routing path to the real destination should be added.

Code 1.1. Node Procedures

```
AS_Proc(){
    check incoming announcement and set chosen path;
    if(chosen path was changed)
        export new chosen path;
}
Arbitrary_Attacker_Proc(){
    Path p = nondeterministic_path();
    Neighbors G = nondeterministic_neighbors();
    foreach(n in G)
        send p to n;
}
Trivial_Attacker_Proc(){
    //attacker pretends to be dest
    Path p = <attacker>;
    send p to all neighbors;
}
Dest_Proc(){
    Path p = <dest>;
    send p to all neighbors ;
}
```

Code 1.2. BGP Run

```
enum RunType {normal, trivial, arbitrary} ;
typedef Map<Node,Path> Routing_Results ;
Topology fragment;

Routing_Results BGP_run(RunType type){
    clear AS states;
    Dest_Proc();
    while(!stable_state()) {
        for(AS in fragment){
            if (AS is attacker and type == trivial)
                Trivial_Attacker_Proc();
            else if(AS is attacker and type == arbitrary)
                Arbitrary_Attacker_Proc();
            else
                AS_Proc();
        }
    }
    return routing results; //chosen paths of all nodes
}
```

Code 1.3. Main Function with Attraction Specification

```
Routing_Results results[3];
int main(){
    results[normal] = BGP_run(normal);
    results[trivial] = BGP_run(trivial);
    results[arbitrary] = BGP_run(arbitrary);
    bool isSomeVictimAttracted = false;
    for(AS in fragment){
        if(AS routes via attacker in arbitrary run and not
            in normal and trivial runs)
            isSomeVictimAttracted = true;
    }
    assert(!isSomeVictimAttracted);
}
```

6.4 Applying Model Checking to the Implemented Model Using ExpliSAT

Here we explain squares 5–7 of Fig. 3. After the C code of the model is generated on the fragment, we apply model checking using ExpliSAT [7]. The model checker systematically scans all possible execution paths of the C program. If it finds a run that violates the assertion, it returns a counterexample that represents a successful attack. If the model checker terminates without any counterexample, it is considered a proof that our attacker cannot perform the specified attack on the fragment. This is denoted as *MC-proof.*

7 Experimental Results

We applied our BGP-SA method on Internet fragments and used IBM's model checking tool ExpliSAT [7] to search for traffic attacks. The model checker can run on multiple cores. The experiments were performed on a 64-cores machine with AMD Opteron(tm) Processor 6376, 125 GB RAM, and 64-bit Linux. The fragments and all model implementations we used in our experiments are available at [1].

ExpliSAT Model Checker. ExpliSAT [7] verifies C programs containing assumptions and assertions. To use ExpliSAT we implement our model in C. Our specifications are negated and added as assertions on stable states. The model

Table 1. Results of BGP-SA application on fragments extracted from the full internet topology

	Fragment size (#nodes)	Reduced size (#nodes)	Trivial attrac- tion (#nodes)	Specification	Result	Time (min)	Dest ASN	Attacker ASN
1	16	11	9	attraction	BT proof	-	31132	16987
2	17	6	4	attraction	BT proof	-	9314	7772
3	22	10	8	attraction	BT proof	-	11669	36291
4	29	9	5	attraction	MC proof	1.5	29117	15137
5	15	13	10	attraction	MC proof	1	12431	18491
6	36	18	7	attraction	MC proof	17	19969	13537
7	69	27	17	attraction	MC proof	340	8296	20091
8	15	13	invalid	interception	counterexample	0.1	12431	18491
9	28	10	invalid	interception	counterexample	0.5	19361	32977
10	80	48	invalid	interception	counterexample	13	9218	43571
11	81	31	invalid	interception	counterexample	9	37177	40473
12	114	30	invalid	interception	counterexample	18	36040	29386
13	71	68	65	interception	N/A	>12h	30894	1290
14	10	-	4	interception	counterexample	0.1	-	-

checker returns a counterexample if there is a violating run, and it can also perform *full verification* and automatically prove that no violating run is possible.

ExpliSAT combines explicit state model checking and SAT-based symbolic model checking. It traverses every feasible execution path of the program, and uses a SAT solver to verify assertions. It performs as many loop iterations as needed, and therefore full verification is possible and no loop bounds are required.

7.1   Results on Internet Fragments

We performed experiments on self-contained fragments extracted from the full Internet topology. The ASes links from the Internet are from [5] and are relevant to October 2014.

Table 1 presents the results of applying our method. The fragments in lines 1–13 are based on randomly chosen destination and attacker from the Internet, with the exception of line 12 which is obtained by choosing the attacker and destination according to a recent attack where Syria attracted traffic destined to Youtube [18]. Line 14 is explained in Sect. 7.2. The first two columns specify the number of nodes in the extracted self-contained fragment and in the reduced fragment. The third column specifies the amount of nodes attracted by the attacker on the trivial attack. The value is invalid if the specification is interception and the trivial attack does not satisfy the interception condition, by which the attacker should have an available routing path to the destination. The specification we used for each instance appears on the fourth column, and is either attraction or interception, which correspond to the specifications defined in Sect. 4.1. Note that in the interception specification, if the trivial attack fails to satisfy the interception condition, we only compare the attraction to the normal outcome. The result column specifies any of the possible results that are described in Sect. 6. The N/A result describes ExpliSAT runs that did not terminate. The last two columns specify the chosen ASN from the Internet of the destination and attacker nodes, from which the fragment was extracted.

The experiments show that the reductions we apply are significant. The simple BGP simulations of the trivial attack allow us to avoid applying model checking on fragments in which the attacker manages to achieve optimal attraction results by the trivial attack.

When we used ExpliSAT with the attraction specification, we got proofs that no better attack strategy exists. It can be explained by the fact that the trivial attack strategy can be considered most efficient in many cases. Consider for instance line 4 on which we got a proof by ExpliSAT. It should be noted that 2 nodes in the fragment are not trivially attracted and do not have definite routing choices, but still there is no attack strategy capable of attracting traffic from them. Thus, these two nodes are also considered *safe*, in addition to the nodes with definite routing choices.

For the interception instances in lines 8–12 the trivial attack failed to achieve the interception goal and ExpliSAT found simple interception attacks. Line 12 was performed on a fragment from a recent attack [18]. The fragment reduction was significant in this case. We found that the trivial attack attracted 12 nodes but did not satisfy the interception condition. The model checker found an attack strategy that achieved interception and attracted 11 nodes. The attacker sent false announcements to 3 of its 4 neighbors in the found interception attack.

7.2   Example Demonstrating Model Checking Advantages

Here we explain line 14 in the table. The network is taken from Fig. 1. The network is a variation of the one presented in [9], where the goal was to show a non-trivial interception attack. We did not apply our reductions on this network topology.

In the normal outcome and trivial attack, the attacker fails to attract traffic from $AS8$. In the attack strategy suggested in [9] the attacker avoids exporting its path to $AS2$, and only exports it to $AS7$. The result is that $AS7$ chooses a shorter path directly via the attacker, and as a result $AS8$ prefers this shorter path. Thus, the attacker manages to apply traffic interception on $AS8$.

Line 14 of Table 1 specifies the experiment we performed on this topology with our BGP model. ExpliSAT automatically found a counterexample with greater attraction. It returned a counterexample in which the attacker exported announcements both to $AS7$ and to $AS2$. The announcement exported to $AS2$ contained $AS9$ on the sent path. Therefore, $AS9$ ignored that announcement, and did not export it to $AS7$. Thus, $AS7$ chose the shorter path via the attacker. Eventually, the attacker managed to achieve attraction from $AS8$, $AS2$, and $AS3$. Note that with the strategy suggested by [9] only $AS8$ is attracted.

An alternative attack that could attract even more nodes to the attacker is to export to $AS2$ an announcement that contains $AS7$ instead of $AS9$ on the sent path. That way it can achieve attraction from $AS9$ as well.

From the above analysis we may conclude that by sending an announcement that creates a loop an attacker can better control on where the propagation of some path should be blocked in order to achieve better attraction results.

It should be noted that some versions of BGP are more secure [10] and may prevent the attacker from sending paths that do not exist in the network. On such versions the attacker cannot apply the loop strategy. Therefore, the loop strategy may have an advantage over the no-export strategy only in the absence of certain BGP security mechanisms.

Note that applying the fragment extraction and reductions would prevent from getting the counterexample. However, by extending the specification and defining that a scenario in which some node is routing via the attacker through a shorter path is also considered a sucessful attack, we were able to find that counterexample on the reduced topology as well. That shorter routing path can potentially attract more nodes from outside the fragment. Given the counterexample, a simulation can be applied on a larger topology. In our case, the counterexample reveals that the routing path of $AS7$ via the attacker can be shortened with respect to its length in the trivial attack, and a simulation of the found attack on the larger topology reveals that $AS8$ is a new attracted node as a result.

8   Conclusion

In this work we propose a method to reveal possible attacks on Internet routing or prove that certain attacks are not possible. We develop substantial reduction techniques that enable to apply model checking in order to formally analyze BGP traffic attacks on the Internet. The use of model checking has a major advantage due to the systematic search, by which it can reveal unexpected or more sophisticated attacks. This is demonstrated in Sect. 7.2, where during an experiment that was done to reconstruct a known attack, the model checker automatically found a different attack strategy that achieved better attraction results than expected.

One obvious implication of our work is a better understanding of the vulnerability of the Internet to traffic attacks. Nonetheless, our suggested method can also be practical and useful for a network operator to increase its resilience to such attacks. In some cases a network operator may fear a traffic attack from potential attacking ASes. For example, telecommunication companies may fear their traffic be attracted by ASes that belong to adversary governments. Such governments can exploit these attacks in order to eavesdrop on traffic of consumers of those telecommunication companies. In such cases, the network operator can use our method in order to discover the identity of the ASes which the attacking AS can not attract traffic from. Once these *safe* ASes are known the network operator may form links to these ASes and prefer routes announced by those ASes, thereby eliminate the chances to be attracted by the attacker.

Acknowledgement. The research was supported by The Prof. A. Pazy Research Foundation.

References

1. http://www.cs.technion.ac.il/~sadisos/bgp/
2. Arye, M., Harrison, R., Wang, R.: The next 10,000 BGP gadgets
3. Arye, M., Harrison, R., Wang, R., Zave, P., Rexford, J.: Toward a lightweight model of BGP safety. In: Proceedings of WRiPE (2011)
4. Ballani, H., Francis, P., Zhang, X.: A study of prefix hijacking and interception in the internet. ACM SIGCOMM Comput. Commun. Rev. **37**, 265–276 (2007)
5. CAIDA. Inferred AS Relationships Dataset (2014). http://data.caida.org/datasets/as-relationships/serial-1/20141001.as-rel.txt.bz2
6. Callon, R.: Use of OSI IS-IS for routing in TCP/IP and dual environments. IETF RFC 1195, December 1990
7. Chockler, H., Pidan, D., Ruah, S.: Improving representative computation in ExpliSAT. In: Bertacco, V., Legay, A. (eds.) HVC 2013. LNCS, vol. 8244, pp. 359–364. Springer, Heidelberg (2013)
8. Gao, L., Rexford, J.: Stable Internet routing without global coordination. IEEE/ACM Trans. Netw. (TON) **9**(6), 681–692 (2001)
9. Goldberg, S., Schapira, M., Hummon, P., Rexford, J.: How secure are secure inter-domain routing protocols? Comput. Netw. **70**, 260–287 (2014)
10. Kent, S., Lynn, C., Mikkelson, J., Seo, K.: Secure border gateway protocol (S-BGP). IEEE J. Sel. Areas Commun. **18**, 103–116 (2000)
11. Lychev, R., Goldberg, S., Schapira, M.: Network-destabilizing attacks. arXiv preprint (2012). arXiv:1203.1681
12. Madory, D.: Sprint, Windstream: Latest ISPs to hijack foreign networks (2014). http://research.dyn.com/2014/09/latest-isps-to-hijack/
13. Madory,D.: The Vast World of Fraudulent Routing (2015). http://research.dyn.com/2015/01/vast-world-of-fraudulent-routing/
14. Malkin, G.: RIP version 2. IETF RFC 2453 (1998)
15. Moy, J.: OSPF version 2. IETF RFC 2328 (1998)
16. Rekhter, Y., Li, T., Hares, S.: A border gateway protocol 4 (BGP-4). IETF RFC 4271 (2006)
17. Ren, Y., Zhou, W., Wang, A., Jia, L., Gurney, A.J.T., Loo, B.T., Rexford, J.: FSR: formal analysis and implementation toolkit for safe inter-domain routing. ACM SIGCOMM Comput. Commun. Rev. **41**, 440–441 (2011)
18. Toonk, A.: BGP hijack incident by Syrian Telecommunications Establishment (2014). http://www.bgpmon.net/bgp-hijack-incident-by-syrian-telecommunications-establishment/
19. Toonk, A.: Hijack event today by Indosat (2014). http://www.bgpmon.net/hijack-event-today-by-indosat/
20. Toonk, A.: The Canadian Bitcoin Hijack (2014). http://www.bgpmon.net/the-canadian-bitcoin-hijack/
21. Vervier, P.A., Thonnard, O., Dacier, M.: Mind your blocks : on the stealthiness of malicious BGP hijacks (2015)

Boolean Formulas for the Static Identification of Injection Attacks in Java

Michael D. Ernst[1], Alberto Lovato[2]([⊠]), Damiano Macedonio[3],
Ciprian Spiridon[3], and Fausto Spoto[2,3]

[1] University of Washington, Seattle, USA
[2] Dipartimento di Informatica, Università di Verona, Verona, Italy
alberto.lovato@univr.it
[3] Julia Srl, Verona, Italy

Abstract. The most dangerous security-related software errors, according to CWE 2011, are those leading to injection attacks — user-provided data that result in undesired database access and updates (*SQL-injections*), dynamic generation of web pages (*cross-site scripting-injections*), redirection to user-specified web pages (*redirect-injections*), execution of OS commands (*command-injections*), class loading of user-specified classes (*reflection-injections*), and many others. This paper describes a flow- and context-sensitive static analysis that automatically identifies if and where injections of tainted data can occur in a program. The analysis models explicit flows of tainted data. Its notion of taintedness applies also to reference (non-primitive) types dynamically allocated in the heap, and is object-sensitive and field-sensitive. The analysis works by translating the program into Boolean formulas that model all possible flows. We implemented it within the Julia analyzer for Java and Android. Julia found injection security vulnerabilities in the Internet banking service and in the customer relationship management of a large Italian bank.

1 Introduction

Dynamic web pages and web services react to user input coming from the network, and this introduces the possibility of an attacker *injecting* special text that induces unsafe, unexpected behaviors of the program. Injection attacks are considered the most dangerous software error [19] and can cause free database access and corruption, forging of web pages, loading of classes, denial-of-service, and arbitrary execution of commands. Most analyses to spot such attacks are dynamic and unsound (see Sect. 3).

This article defines a sound static analysis that identifies if and where a Java bytecode program lets data flow from *tainted* user input (including servlet requests) into critical operations that might give rise to injections. Data flow is a prerequisite to injections, but the user of the analysis must later gage the actual risk of the flow. Namely, analysis approximations might lead to false alarms and proper input validation might make actual flows harmless.

Our analysis works by translating Java bytecode into Boolean formulas that express all possible explicit flows of tainted data. The choice of Java bytecode

© Springer-Verlag Berlin Heidelberg 2015
M. Davis et al. (Eds.): LPAR-20 2015, LNCS 9450, pp. 130–145, 2015.
DOI: 10.1007/978-3-662-48899-7_10

simplifies the semantics and its abstraction (many high-level constructs must not be explicitly considered) and lets us analyze programs whose source code is not available, as is typically the case in industrial contexts that use software developed by third parties, such as banks.

Our contributions are the following:

- an object-sensitive formalization of taintedness for reference types, based on reachability of tainted information in memory;
- a flow-, context- and field-sensitive static analysis for explicit flows of tainted information based on that notion of taintedness, which is able to deal with data dynamically allocated in the heap (not just primitive values);
- its implementation inside the Julia analyzer, through binary decision diagrams, and its experimental evaluation.

Section 6 shows that our analysis can analyze large real Java software. Compared to other tools available on the market, ours is the only one that is sound, yet precise and efficient. Our analysis is limited to explicit flows [25]; as is common in the literature, it does not yet consider implicit flows (arising from conditional tests) nor hidden flows (such as timing channels). In particular, considering implicit flows is relatively simple future work (we could apply our previous work [10], unchanged) but would likely degrade the precision of the analysis of real software.

This article is organized as follows. Section 2 gives an example of injection and clarifies the importance of a new notion of taintedness for values of reference type. Section 3 discusses related work. Section 4 defines a concrete semantics for Java bytecode. Section 5 defines our new object-sensitive notion of taintedness for values of reference type and its use to induce an object- and field-sensitive abstract interpretation of the concrete semantics. Section 6 presents experiments with the implementation of the analysis. Extended definitions and proofs are in a technical report [8].

2   Example

Figure 1 is a Java servlet that suffers from SQL-injection and cross-site scripting-injection attacks. (For brevity, the figure omits exception-handling code.)

A *servlet* (lines 1 and 2) is code that listens to HTTP network connection requests, retrieves its parameters, and runs some code in response to each request. The response (line 2) may be presented as a web page, XML, or JSON. This is a standard way of implementing dynamic web pages and web services. The user of a servlet connects to the web site and provides the parameters through the URL, as in http://my.site.com/myServlet?user=spoto. Code retrieves these through the getParameter method (line 5). Lines 9 and 10 establish a connection to the database of the application, which is assumed to define a table User (line 27) of the users of the service. Line 27 builds an SQL query from the user name provided as parameter. This query is reported to the response (line 15) and executed (line 17). The result is a relational table of all users matching the

```
1   public class MyServlet extends HttpServlet {
2     protected void doGet(HttpServletRequest request, HttpServletResponse response) {
3       response.setContentType("text/html;charset=UTF-8");
4
5       String user = request.getParameter("user"), url = "jdbc:mysql://192.168.2.128:3306/";
6       String dbName = "anvayaV2", driver = "com.mysql.jdbc.Driver";
7       String userName = "root", password = "";
8
9       Class.forName(driver).newInstance();
10      try (Connection conn = DriverManager.getConnection(url + dbName, userName, password);
11           PrintWriter out = response.getWriter()) {
12
13        Statement st = conn.createStatement();
14        String query = wrapQuery(user);
15        out.println("Query : " + query);
16
17        ResultSet res = st.executeQuery(query);
18        out.println("Results:");
19        while (res.next())
20          out.println("\t\t" + res.getString("address"));
21
22        st.executeQuery(wrapQuery("dummy"));
23      }
24    }
25
26    private String wrapQuery(String s) {
27      return "SELECT * FROM User WHERE userId='" + s + "'";
28    }
29  }
```

Fig. 1. A Java servlet that suffers from SQL and cross-site scripting-injections.

given criterion (the **user** parameter might be a specific name or a wildcard that matches more users). This table is then printed to the response (lines 17–20).

The interesting point here is that the user of this servlet is completely free to specify the value of the **user** parameter. In particular, she can provide a string that actually lets line 17 run *any* possible database command, including malicious commands that erase its content or insert new rows. For instance, if the user supplies the string "'; DROP TABLE User; --" as **user**, the resulting concatenation is an SQL command that erases the **User** table from the database. In literature, this is known as an SQL-injection attack and follows from the fact that user (*tainted*) input flows from the **request** *source* into the **executeQuery** *sink* method. There is no SQL-injection at line 22, although it looks very much like line 17, since the query there is not computed from user-provided input.

Another risk exists at lines 15 and 20. There, data is printed to the response object, and is typically interpreted by the client as HTML contents. A malicious user might have provided a **user** parameter that contains arbitrary HTML tags, including tags that will let the client execute scripts (such as Javascript). This might result in evil. For instance, if the user injects a crafted URL such as "http://my.site.com/myServlet?user=<script>malicious</script>", the parameter **user** holds "<script>malicious</script>". At line 15 this code is sent to the user's browser and interpreted as Javascript, running any **malicious** Javascript. In literature, this is known as cross-site scripting-injection and follows from the fact that user (*tainted*) input from the **request** *source* flows into the *sink* output writer of the response object. The same might happen at line 20, where the flow is more complex: in other parts of the application, the user might save her address to the database and store malicious code instead; line 20 will fetch this malicious code and send it to the browser of the client to run it.

Many kinds of injections exist. They arise from information flows from what the user can specify (the parameter of the request, input from console, data on a database) to specific methods, such as `executeQuery` (SQL-injection), `print` (cross-site scripting-injection), reflection methods (that allow one to load any class or execute any method and lead to a reflection-injection), `execute` (that allows one to run any operating system command and leads to a command-injection), etc. This article focuses on the identification of flows of tainted information, not on the exact enumeration of sources and sinks. Our approach can be instantiated from well-known lists of sources and sinks in the literature.

3   Related Work

The identification of possible injections and the inference of information flows are well-studied topics. Nevertheless, no previous sound techniques work on real Java code, even only for explicit flows. Most injection identification techniques are dynamic and/or unsound. Existing static information-flow analyses are not satisfactory for languages with reference types.

Identification of Injections. Data injections are security risks, so there is high industrial and academic interest in their automatic identification. Here, we have space to mention only the most recent works regarding SQL-injection. Almost all techniques aim at the dynamic identification of the injection when it occurs [7,12,14,18,21,28,30,35] or at the generation of test cases of attacks [1,17] or at the specification of good coding practices [29].

By contrast, static analysis has the advantage of finding the vulnerabilities before running the code, and a sound static analysis *proves* that injections *only* occur where it issues a warning. A static analysis is *sound* if it finds all places where an injection might occur (for instance, it must spot line 17 in Fig. 1); it is *precise* if it minimizes the number of false alarms (for instance, it should not issue a warning at line 22 in Fig. 1). Beyond Julia, static analyzers that identify injections in Java are FindBugs (http://findbugs.sourceforge.net), Google's CodePro Analytix (https://developers.google.com/java-dev-tools/codepro), and HP Fortify SCA (on-demand web interface at https://trial.hpfod.com/Login). These tools do not formalize the notion of *taintedness* (as we do in Definition 4). For the example in Fig. 1, Julia is correct and precise: it warns at lines 15, 17, and 20 but not at 22; FindBugs incorrectly warns at line 17 only; Fortify SCA incorrectly warns at lines 15 and 17 only; CodePro Analytix warns at lines 15, 17, 20, and also, imprecisely, at the harmless line 22. Section 6 compares those tools with Julia in more detail. We also cite FlowDroid [2], that however works for Android packages, not on Java bytecode, and TAJ [33], that is part of a commercial product. Neither comes with a soundness proof nor a definition of taintedness for variables of reference type.

Modelling of Information Flow. Many static analyses model explicit and often also implicit information flows [25] in Java-like or Java bytecode programs. There are data/control-flow analyses [5, 15, 20, 26]; type-based analyses [3, 4, 9, 13, 31, 34] and analyses based on abstract interpretation [10]. They are satisfactory for variables of primitive type but impractical for heap-allocated data of reference type, such as strings. Most analyses [4, 5, 9, 13, 15, 20, 26, 34] assume that the language has only primitive types; others [3, 10] are object-insensitive, *i.e.*, for each field f, assume that $a.f$ and $b.f$ are both tainted or both untainted, regardless of the container objects a and b. Even if a user specifies, by hand, which f is tainted (unrealistic for thousands of fields, including those used in the libraries), object-insensitivity leads to a very coarse abstraction that is industrially useless. Consider the `String` class, which holds its contents inside a `private final char[]` value field. If any string's `value` field is tainted, then every string's `value` field must be tainted, and this leads to an alarm at every use of strings in a sensitive context in the program, many of which may be false alarms. The problem applies to any data structure that can carry tainted data, not just strings. Our analysis uses an object-sensitive and *deep* notion of taintedness, that fits for heap-allocated data of reference type. It can be considered as data-flow, formalized through abstract interpretation. This has the advantage of providing its correctness proof in a formal and standard way.

4   Denotational Semantics of Java Bytecode

This section presents a denotational semantics for Java bytecode, which we will use to define an abstraction for taintedness analysis (Sect. 5). The same semantics has been used for nullness analysis [32] and has been proved equivalent [23] to an operational semantics. The only difference is that, in this article, primitive values are decorated with their taintedness.

We assume a Java bytecode program P given as a collection of graphs of *basic blocks* of code, one for each method. Bytecodes that might throw exceptions are linked to a handler starting with a `catch`, possibly followed by bytecodes selecting the right kind of exception. For simplicity, we assume that the only primitive type is `int` and the only reference types are *classes*; we only allow *instance* fields and methods; and method parameters cannot be reassigned inside their body. Our implementation handles full Java bytecode.

Definition 1 (Classes). *The set of* classes $\mathbb{K}$ *is partially ordered w.r.t. the* subclass relation $\leq$. *A type is an element of* $\mathbb{K} \cup \{int\}$. *A class* $\kappa \in \mathbb{K}$ *defines* instance fields $\kappa.f : t$ *(field f of type t defined in κ) and* instance methods $\kappa.m(t_1, \dots, t_n) : t$ *(method m with arguments of type $t_1, \dots, t_n$, returning a value of type t, possibly* `void`*). We consider constructors as methods returning* `void`*. If it does not introduce confusion, we write f and m for fields and methods.*

A *state* provides *values* to program variables. *Tainted* values are computed from servlet/user input; others are *untainted*. Taintedness for reference types (such as string `request` in Fig. 1) will be defined later as a reachability property from the reference (Definition 4); primitive tainted values are explicitly marked in the state.

Definition 2 (State). *A value is an element of* $\mathbb{Z} \cup \boxed{\mathbb{Z}} \cup \mathbb{L} \cup \{null\}$, *where* $\mathbb{Z}$ *are untainted integers,* $\boxed{\mathbb{Z}}$ *are tainted integers, and* $\mathbb{L}$ *is a set of* locations. *A state is a triple* $\langle l \parallel s \parallel \mu \rangle$ *where* l *are the values of the* local variables, s *the values of the* operand stack, *which grows leftwards, and* μ *a memory that binds locations to* objects. *The empty stack is written* ε. *Stack concatenation is* :: *with* $s :: \varepsilon$ *written as just* s. *An object* o *belongs to class* $o.\kappa \in \mathbb{K}$ *(is an* instance of $o.\kappa$) *and maps identifiers (the fields* f *of* $o.\kappa$ *and of its superclasses) into values* $o.f$. *The set of states is* Ξ. *We write* $\Xi_{i,j}$ *when we want to fix the number* i *of local variables and* j *of stack elements. A value* v *has type* t *in a state* $\langle l \parallel s \parallel \mu \rangle$ *if* $v \in \mathbb{Z} \cup \boxed{\mathbb{Z}}$ *and* $t = \textit{int}$, *or* $v = null$ *and* $t \in \mathbb{K}$, *or* $v \in \mathbb{L}$, $t \in \mathbb{K}$ *and* $\mu(v).\kappa \leq t$.

Example 1. Let state $\sigma = \langle [3, null, \boxed{4}, \ell] \parallel \boxed{3} :: \ell'' :: \ell'' \parallel \mu \rangle \in \Xi_{4,3}$, with $\mu = [\ell \mapsto o, \ell' \mapsto o', \ell'' \mapsto o'']$, $o.f = \ell'$, $o.g = 13$, $o'.g = \boxed{17}$ and $o''.g = 10$. Local 0 holds the integer 3 and local 2 holds the integer 4, marked as computed from servlet/user input. The top of the stack holds 3, marked as computed from servlet/user input. The next two stack elements are aliased to ℓ''. Location ℓ is bound to object o, whose field f holds ℓ' and whose field g holds the untainted integer 13. Location ℓ' is bound to o' whose field g holds a tainted integer $\boxed{17}$. Location ℓ'' is bound to o'' whose field g holds the untainted value 10.

The Java Virtual Machine (JVM) allows exceptions. Hence we distinguish *normal* states $\sigma \in \Xi$, arising during the normal execution of a piece of code, from *exceptional* states $\underline{\sigma} \in \Xi$, arising *just after* a bytecode that throws an exception. The latter have only one stack element, *i.e.*, the location of the thrown exception object, also in the presence of nested exception handlers [16]. The semantics of a bytecode is then a *denotation* from an *initial* to a *final* state.

Definition 3 (JVM State and Denotation). *The set of* JVM states *(from now just* states*) with* i *local variables and* j *stack elements is* $\Sigma_{i,j} = \Xi_{i,j} \cup \underline{\Xi}_{i,1}$. *A denotation is a partial map from an* input *or* initial *state to an* output *or* final *state; the set of denotations is* Δ *or* $\Delta_{i_1,j_1 \to i_2,j_2} = \Sigma_{i_1,j_1} \to \Sigma_{i_2,j_2}$ *to fix the number of local variables and stack elements. The sequential composition of* $\delta_1, \delta_2 \in \Delta$ *is* $\delta_1; \delta_2 = \lambda\sigma.\delta_2(\delta_1(\sigma))$, *which is undefined when* $\delta_1(\sigma)$ *or* $\delta_2(\delta_1(\sigma))$ *is undefined.*

In $\delta_1; \delta_2$, the idea is that δ_1 describes the behaviour of an instruction ins_1, δ_2 that of an instruction ins_2 and $\delta_1; \delta_2$ that of the execution of ins_1 and then ins_2.

At each program point, the number i of local variables and j of stack elements and their types are statically known [16], hence we can assume the semantics of the bytecodes undefined for input states of wrong sizes or types. Readers can find the denotations of bytecode instructions in a technical report [8], together with the construction of the concrete fixpoint collecting semantics of Java bytecode, explicitly targeted at abstract interpretation, since it only requires to abstract three concrete operators ;, $\cup$, and *extend* on $\wp(\Delta)$, *i.e.*, on the subsets of Δ and the denotation of each single bytecode distinct from `call`. The operator *extend* plugs a method's denotation at its calling point and implements `call`. The concrete fixpoint computation is in general infinite, but its abstractions converge in a finite number of steps if, as in Sect. 5, the abstract domain has no infinite ascending chain.

5 Taintedness Analysis

This section defines an abstract interpretation [6] of the concrete semantics of Sect. 4, whose abstract domain is made of Boolean formulas whose models are consistent with all possible ways of propagating taintedness in the concrete semantics. The concrete semantics works over $\wp(\Delta)$ and is built from singletons (sets made of a single $\delta \in \Delta$), one for each bytecode, with three operators ;, $\cup$, and *extend*. Hence we define here correct abstractions of those sets and operators.

Our analysis assumes that three other analyses have been performed in advance. (1) $reach(v, v')$ is true if (the location held in) v' is reachable from (the location held in) v. (2) $share(v, v')$ is true if from v and v' one can reach a common location. (3) $updated_M(l_k)$ is true if some call in the program to method M might ever modify an object reachable from local variable l_k. All three analyses are conservative overapproximations of the actual (undecidable) relations. Our implementation computes these predicates as in [11, 22, 27], respectively.

Primitive values are explicitly marked as tainted (Definition 2), while taintedness for references is indirectly defined in terms of reachability of tainted values. Hence, this notion allows $a.f$ and $b.f$ to have distinct taintedness, depending of the taintedness of variables a and b (object-sensitivity).

Definition 4 (Taintedness). *Let $v \in \mathbb{Z} \cup \boxed{\mathbb{Z}} \cup \mathbb{L} \cup \{null\}$ be a value and μ a memory. The property of being* tainted *for v in μ is defined recursively as: $v \in \boxed{\mathbb{Z}}$ or ($v \in \mathbb{L}$ and $o = \mu(v)$ and there is a field f such that $o(f)$ is tainted in μ).*

A first abstraction step selects the variables that, in a state, hold tainted data. It yields a logical model where a variable is true if it holds tainted data.

Definition 5 (Tainted Variables). *Let $\sigma \in \Sigma_{i,j}$. Its* tainted variables *are*

$$tainted(\sigma) = \begin{cases} \{l_k \mid l[k] \text{ is tainted in } \mu,\ 0 \le k < i\} \cup \{s_k \mid v_k \text{ is tainted in } \mu,\ 0 \le k < j\} \\ \quad if\ \sigma = \langle l \,\|\, v_{j-1} :: \cdots :: v_0 \,\|\, \mu \rangle \\ \{l_k \mid l[k] \text{ is tainted in } \mu,\ 0 \le k < i\} \cup \{e\} \\ \quad if\ \sigma = \langle l \,\|\, v_0 \,\|\, \mu \rangle \text{ and } v_0 \text{ is tainted in } \mu \\ \{l_k \mid l[k] \text{ is tainted in } \mu,\ 0 \le k < i\} \\ \quad if\ \sigma = \langle l \,\|\, v_0 \,\|\, \mu \rangle \text{ and } v_0 \text{ is not tainted in } \mu. \end{cases}$$

Example 2. Consider σ from Example 1. We have $tainted(\sigma) = \{l_2, l_3, s_2\}$, since tainted data is reachable from both locations ℓ and ℓ', but not from ℓ''.

To make the analysis flow-sensitive, distinct variables abstract the input (marked with $\check{}$) and output (marked with $\hat{}$) of a denotation. If S is a set of identifiers, then $\check{S} = \{\check{v} \mid v \in S\}$ and $\hat{S} = \{\hat{v} \mid v \in S\}$. The abstract domain contains Boolean formulas that constraint the relative taintedness of local variables and stack elements. For instance, $\check{l}_1 \to \hat{s}_2$ states that if local variable l_1 is tainted in the input of a denotation, then the stack element s_2 is tainted in its output.

$$(const\ v)^\mathsf{T} = U \wedge \neg\breve{e} \wedge \neg\hat{e} \wedge \neg\hat{s}_j \qquad (load\ k\ t)^\mathsf{T} = U \wedge \neg\breve{e} \wedge \neg\hat{e} \wedge (\breve{l}_k \leftrightarrow \hat{s}_j)$$

$$(store\ k\ t)^\mathsf{T} = U \wedge \neg\breve{e} \wedge \neg\hat{e} \wedge (\breve{s}_{j-1} \leftrightarrow \hat{l}_k) \qquad (add)^\mathsf{T} = U \wedge \neg\breve{e} \wedge \neg\hat{e} \wedge (\hat{s}_{j-2} \leftrightarrow (\breve{s}_{j-2} \vee \breve{s}_{j-1}))$$

$$(throw\ \kappa)^\mathsf{T} = U \wedge \neg\breve{e} \wedge \hat{e} \wedge (\hat{s}_0 \to \breve{s}_{j-1}) \qquad (new\ \kappa)^\mathsf{T} = U \wedge \neg\breve{e} \wedge (\neg\hat{e} \to \neg\hat{s}_j) \wedge (\hat{e} \to \neg\hat{s}_0)$$

$$(catch)^\mathsf{T} = U \wedge \breve{e} \wedge \neg\hat{e} \qquad (getfield\ \kappa.f:t)^\mathsf{T} = U \wedge \neg\breve{e} \wedge (\neg\hat{e} \to (\hat{s}_{j-1} \to \breve{s}_{j-1})) \wedge (\hat{e} \to \neg\hat{s}_0)$$

$$(putfield\ \kappa.f:t)^\mathsf{T} = \wedge_{v \in L} R_j(v) \wedge (\neg\hat{e} \to \wedge_{v \in S} R_j(v)) \wedge (\hat{e} \to \neg\hat{s}_0) \wedge \neg\breve{e}.$$

Fig. 2. Bytecode abstraction for taintedness, in a program point with j stack elements. Bytecodes not reported in this figure are abstracted into the default $U \wedge \neg\breve{e} \wedge \neg\hat{e}$.

Definition 6 (Taintedness Abstract Domain $\mathbb{T}$). *Let $i_1, j_1, i_2, j_2 \in \mathbb{N}$. The taintedness abstract domain $\mathbb{T}_{i_1,j_1 \to i_2,j_2}$ is the set of Boolean formulas over $\{\breve{e}, \hat{e}\} \cup \{\breve{l}_k \mid 0 \le k < i_1\} \cup \{\breve{s}_k \mid 0 \le k < j_1\} \cup \{\hat{l}_k \mid 0 \le k < i_2\} \cup \{\hat{s}_k \mid 0 \le k < j_2\}$ (modulo logical equivalence).*

Example 3. $\phi = (\breve{l}_1 \leftrightarrow \hat{l}_1) \wedge (\breve{l}_2 \leftrightarrow \hat{l}_2) \wedge (\breve{l}_3 \leftrightarrow \hat{l}_3) \wedge \neg\breve{e} \wedge \neg\hat{e} \wedge (\breve{s}_0 \leftrightarrow \hat{l}_0) \in \mathbb{T}_{4,1 \to 4,0}$.

The concretization map γ states that a $\phi \in \mathbb{T}$ abstracts those denotations whose behavior, *w.r.t.* the propagation of taintedness, is a model of ϕ.

Proposition 1 (Abstract Interpretation). *$\mathbb{T}_{i_1,j_1 \to i_2,j_2}$ is an abstract interpretation of $\wp(\Delta_{i_1,j_1 \to i_2,j_2})$ with $\gamma : \mathbb{T}_{i_1,j_1 \to i_2,j_2} \to \wp(\Delta_{i_1,j_1 \to i_2,j_2})$ given by*

$$\gamma(\phi) = \left\{ \delta \in \Delta_{i_1,j_1 \to i_2,j_2} \ \middle| \ \begin{array}{l} \text{for all } \sigma \in \Sigma_{i_1,j_1} \text{ s.t. } \delta(\sigma) \text{ is defined} \\ \widecheck{tainted}(\sigma) \cup \widehat{tainted}(\delta(\sigma)) \models \phi \end{array} \right\}.$$

Example 4. Consider ϕ from Example 3 and bytecode `store 0` at a program point with $i = 4$ locals and $j = 1$ stack elements. Its denotation `store 0` $\in \gamma(\phi)$ since that bytecode does not modify locals 1, 2 and 3, hence their taintedness is unchanged $((\breve{l}_1 \leftrightarrow \hat{l}_1) \wedge (\breve{l}_2 \leftrightarrow \hat{l}_2) \wedge (\breve{l}_3 \leftrightarrow \hat{l}_3))$; it only runs if no exception is thrown just before it $(\neg\breve{e})$; it does not throw any exception $(\neg\hat{e})$; and the output local 0 is an alias of the topmost and only element of the input stack $(\breve{s}_0 \leftrightarrow \hat{l}_0)$.

Figure 2 defines correct abstractions for the bytecodes from Sect. 4, but `call`. A formula U (for *unchanged*) is a frame condition for input local variables and stack elements, that are also in the output and with unchanged value: their taintedness is unchanged. For the stack, this is only required when no exception is thrown, since otherwise the only output stack element is the exception.

Definition 7. *Let sets S (of stack elements) and L (of local variables) be the input variables that after all executions of a given bytecode in a given program point (only after the normal executions for S) survive with unchanged value. Then $U = \wedge_{v \in L}(\breve{v} \leftrightarrow \hat{v}) \wedge (\neg\hat{e} \to \wedge_{v \in S}(\breve{v} \leftrightarrow \hat{v}))$.*

Consider Fig. 2. Bytecodes run only if the preceding one does not throw any exception $(\neg\breve{e})$ but `catch` requires an exception to be thrown $(\breve{e})$. Bytecode `const v` pushes an untainted value on the stack: its abstraction says that no variable changes its taintedness (U), the new stack top is untainted $(\neg \hat{s}_j)$ and const v never throws an exception $(\neg \hat{e})$. Most abstractions in Fig. 2 can be explained similarly. The result of add is tainted if and only if at least one operand is tainted $(\hat{s}_{j-2} \leftrightarrow (\check{s}_{j-2} \vee \check{s}_{j-1}))$. For new κ, no variable changes its taintedness (U), if its execution does not throw any exception then the new top of the stack is an untainted new object $(\neg \hat{e} \rightarrow \neg \hat{s}_j)$; otherwise the only stack element is an untainted exception $(\hat{e} \rightarrow \neg \hat{s}_0)$. Bytecode throw κ always throws an exception $(\hat{e})$; if this is tainted, then the top of the initial stack was tainted as well $(\hat{s}_0 \rightarrow \check{s}_{j-1})$. The abstraction of getfield says that if it throws no exception and the value of the field is tainted, then the container of the field was tainted as well $(\neg \hat{e} \rightarrow (\hat{s}_{j-1} \rightarrow \check{s}_{j-1}))$. This follows from the object-sensitivity of our notion of taintedness (Definition 4). Otherwise, the exception is untainted $(\hat{e} \rightarrow \neg \hat{s}_0)$. For putfield, we cannot use U and must consider each variable v to see if it might reach the object whose field is modified $(\check{s}_{j-2})$. If that is not the case, v's taintedness is not affected $(\check{v} \leftrightarrow \hat{v})$; otherwise, if its value is tainted then either it was already tainted before the bytecode or the value written in the field was tainted $((\check{v} \vee \check{s}_{j-1}) \leftarrow \hat{v})$. In this last case, we must use $\leftarrow$ instead of $\leftrightarrow$ since our reachability analysis is a *possible* approximation of actual (undecidable) reachability. This is expressed by formula $R_j(v)$, used in Fig. 2, where $R_j(v) = \check{v} \leftrightarrow \hat{v}$ if $\neg reach(v, s_{j-2})$, and $R_j(v) = (\check{v} \vee \check{s}_{j-1}) \leftarrow \hat{v}$, if $reach(v, s_{j-2})$.

Example 5. According to Fig. 2, the abstraction of store 0 at a program point with $i = 4$ local variables and $j = 1$ stack elements is the formula ϕ of Example 3.

Example 6. Consider a putfield f at a program point p where there are $i = 4$ local variables, $j = 3$ stack elements and the only variable that reaches the receiver s_1 is the underlying stack element s_0. A possible state at p in Example 1. According to Fig. 2, the abstraction of that bytecode at p is $\phi' = (\check{l}_0 \leftrightarrow \hat{l}_0) \wedge (\check{l}_1 \leftrightarrow \hat{l}_1) \wedge (\check{l}_2 \leftrightarrow \hat{l}_2) \wedge (\check{l}_3 \leftrightarrow \hat{l}_3) \wedge (\neg \hat{e} \rightarrow ((\check{s}_0 \vee \check{s}_2) \leftarrow \hat{s}_0)) \wedge (\hat{e} \rightarrow \neg \hat{s}_0) \wedge \neg \check{e} \in \mathbb{T}_{4,3 \rightarrow 4,1}$.

Proposition 2. *The approximations in Fig. 2 are correct w.r.t. the denotations of Sect. 4, i.e., for all bytecode **ins** distinct from* call *we have ins $\in \gamma(\text{ins}^\mathbb{T})$.*

Denotations are composed by ; and their abstractions by $;^\mathbb{T}$. The definition of $\phi_1 ;^\mathbb{T} \phi_2$ matches the output variables of ϕ_1 with the corresponding input variables of ϕ_2. To avoid name clashes, they are renamed apart and then projected away.

Definition 8. *Let $\phi_1, \phi_2 \in \mathbb{T}$. Their abstract sequential composition $\phi_1 ;^\mathbb{T} \phi_2$ is $\exists_{\overline{V}}(\phi_1[\overline{V}/\hat{V}] \wedge \phi_2[\overline{V}/\check{V}])$, where $\overline{V}$ are fresh overlined variables.*

Example 7. Consider the execution of putfield f at program point p and then store 0, as in Example 6. The former is abstracted by ϕ' from Example 6; the latter by ϕ from Example 5. Their sequential composition is $\phi' ;^\mathbb{T} \phi = \exists_{\overline{V}}(\phi'[\overline{V}/\hat{V}] \wedge \phi[\overline{V}/\check{V}]) = \exists_{\overline{V}}([(\check{l}_0 \leftrightarrow \overline{l}_0) \wedge (\check{l}_1 \leftrightarrow \overline{l}_1) \wedge (\check{l}_2 \leftrightarrow \overline{l}_2) \wedge (\check{l}_3 \leftrightarrow \overline{l}_3) \wedge (\neg \overline{e} \rightarrow ((\check{s}_0 \vee \check{s}_2) \leftarrow \overline{s}_0)) \wedge (\overline{e} \rightarrow \neg \overline{s}_0) \wedge \neg \check{e}] \wedge [(\overline{l}_1 \leftrightarrow \hat{l}_1) \wedge (\overline{l}_2 \leftrightarrow \hat{l}_2) \wedge (\overline{l}_3 \leftrightarrow \hat{l}_3) \wedge \neg \overline{e} \wedge \neg \hat{e} \wedge (\overline{s}_0 \leftrightarrow \hat{l}_0)])$ which simplifies into $(\check{l}_1 \leftrightarrow \hat{l}_1) \wedge (\check{l}_2 \leftrightarrow \hat{l}_2) \wedge (\check{l}_3 \leftrightarrow \hat{l}_3) \wedge ((\check{s}_0 \vee \check{s}_2) \leftarrow \hat{l}_0) \wedge \neg \check{e} \wedge \neg \hat{e}$.

The second semantical operator is $\cup$ of two sets, approximated as $\cup^{\mathbb{T}} = \vee$. The third is *extend*, that makes the analysis context-sensitive by plugging the behavior of a method at each distinct calling context. Let ϕ approximate the taintedness behaviour of method $M = \kappa.m(t_1, \ldots, t_n) : t$; ϕ's variables are among $\check{l}_0, \ldots, \check{l}_n$ (the actual arguments including this), $\hat{s}_0$ (if M does not return void), $\hat{l}_0, \hat{l}_1 \ldots$ (the final values of M's local variables), $\check{e}$ and $\hat{e}$. Consider a call M at a program point where the $n+1$ actual arguments are stacked over other b stack elements. The operator plugs ϕ at the calling context: the return value $\hat{s}_0$ (if any) is renamed into $\hat{s}_b$; each formal argument $\check{l}_k$ of the callee is renamed into the actual argument $\check{s}_{k+b}$ of the caller; local variable $\hat{l}_k$ at the end of the callee is temporarily renamed into $\bar{l}_k$. Then a frame condition is built: the set $SA_{b,M,v}$ contains the formal arguments of the caller that might share with variable v of the callee at call-time and might be updated during the call. If this set is empty, then nothing reachable from v is modified during the call and v keeps its taintedness unchanged. This is expressed by the first case of formula $A_{b,M}(v)$. Otherwise, if v is tainted at the end of the call then either it was already tainted at the beginning or at least one of the variables in $SA_{b,M,v}$ has become tainted during the call. The second case of formula $A_{b,M}(v)$ uses the temporary variables to express that condition, to avoid name clashes with the output local variables of the caller. The frame condition for the b lowest stack elements of the caller is valid only if no exception is thrown, since otherwise the stack contains the exception object only. At the end, all temporary variables $\{\bar{l}_0, \ldots, \bar{l}_{i'}\}$ are projected away.

Definition 9. *Let $i, j \in \mathbb{N}$ and $M = \kappa.m(t_1, \ldots, t_n) : t$ with $j = b + n + 1$ and $b \geq 0$. We define $(extend_M^{i,j})^{\mathbb{T}} : \mathbb{T}_{n+1,0 \to i',r} \mapsto \mathbb{T}_{i,j \to i,b+r}$ with $r = 0$ if $t = void$ and $r = 1$ otherwise, as $(extend_M^{i,j})^{\mathbb{T}}(\phi) = \neg \check{e} \wedge \exists_{\{\bar{l}_0, \ldots, \bar{l}_{i'}\}}(\phi[\hat{s}_b/\hat{s}_0][\bar{l}_k/\hat{l}_k \mid 0 \leq k < i'][\check{s}_{k+b}/\check{l}_k \mid 0 \leq k \leq n] \wedge \bigwedge_{0 \leq k < i} A_{b,M}(\bar{l}_k) \wedge (\neg \hat{e} \to \bigwedge_{0 \leq k < b} A_{b,M}(s_k)))$, with $SA_{b,M,v} = \{l_k \mid 0 \leq k \leq n, \neg share(v, s_{b+k})\ or\ \neg updated_M(\bar{l}_k)\}$, $A_{b,M}(v) = \check{v} \leftrightarrow \hat{v}$ if $SA_{b,M,v} = \emptyset$ and $A_{b,M}(v) = ((\check{v} \vee (\bigvee_{w \in SA_{b,M,v}} \bar{w})) \leftarrow \hat{v})$ otherwise.*

Proposition 3. *The operators $;^{\mathbb{T}}$, $extend^{\mathbb{T}}$ and $\cup^{\mathbb{T}}$ are correct.*

Since the number of Boolean formulas over a given finite set of variables is finite (modulo equivalence), the abstract fixpoint is reached in a finite number of iterations. Hence this abstract semantics is a static analysis tool if one specifies the sources of tainted information and the sinks where it should not flow.

Sources. Some formal parameters or return values must be considered as sources of tainted data, that can be freely provided by the external world. Our implementation uses a database of library methods for that, such as the request argument of doGet and doPost methods of servlets and the return value of console and database methods. Moreover, it lets users specify their own sources through annotations. The abstract denotation in Fig. 2 is modified at *receiver_is* (a special bytecode at the beginning of each method) and *return* to force to true those formal arguments and return values that are injected tainted data, respectively.

Sinks. Our implementation has a database of library methods that need untainted parameters (users can add their own through annotations). Hence it knows which `calls` in P need an untainted parameter v (such as `executeQuery` in Fig. 1). But a denotational semantics is an input/output description of the behavior of P's methods and does not say what is passed *at* a `call`. For that, a *magic-sets transformation* [23] of P adds new blocks of code whose denotation gives information at internal program points, as traditional in denotational static analysis. It computes a formula ψ that holds at the `call`. If ψ entails $\neg\hat{v}$ then the `call` receives untainted data for v. Otherwise, the analysis issues a warning.

5.1 Making the Analysis Field-Sensitive

The approximation of getfield f in Fig. 2 specifies that if the value of field f (pushed on the stack) is tainted then the container of f must be tainted as well ($\hat{s}_{j-1} \to \check{s}_{j-1}$). Read the other way round, if the container is untainted then f's value is untainted, otherwise it is conservatively assumed as tainted. This choice is sound and object-sensitive, but field-insensitive: when $\check{s}_{j-1}$ is tainted, both its fields f and g are conservatively assumed as tainted. But if the program never assigns tainted data to f, then f's value can only be untainted, regardless of the taintedness of $\check{s}_{j-1}$. If the analyzer could spot such situations, the resulting analysis would be field-sensitive and hence more precise (fewer false positives).

We apply here a technique pioneered in [32]: it uses a set of fields O (the *oracle*) that might contain tainted data. For getfield f, it uses a better approximation than in Fig. 2: it assumes that f's value is tainted if its container is tainted *and* $f \in O$. The problem is now the computation of O. As in [32], this is done iteratively. The analyzer starts with $O = \emptyset$ and runs the analysis in Sect. 5, but with the new abstraction for getfield f seen in this paragraph. Then it adds to O those fields g such that there is at least one putfield g that stores tainted data. The analysis is repeated with this larger O. At its end, O is further enlarged with other fields g such that there is at least one putfield g that stores tainted data. The process is iterated until no more fields are added to O. As proved in [32], this process converges to a sound overapproximation of O and the last analysis of the iteration is sound. In practice, repeated analyses with larger and larger O are made efficient by caching abstract computations. On average, this process converges in around 5 iterations, also for large programs. By using caching, this only doubles the time of the analysis. Since preliminary analyses are more expensive than information flow analysis, this technique increases the total time by around 25 % on average. (Section 6 shows effects on cost and precision.) This technique is not identical to statically, manually classifying fields as tainted and untainted, as [3,10] do. The classification of the fields is here dynamic, depending on the program under analysis, and completely automatic. Moreover, a field might be in O (and hence be potentially tainted) but the analyzer might still consider its value untainted, because its container is untainted.

Test	Tool	True Positives	False Positives	False Negatives	Analysis Time
CWE89	CodePro Analytix	1332	0	888	20 minutes
	FindBugs	1776	2400	444	2 minutes
	Fortify SCA	700	0	1520	2.5 days
	Julia fs/fi	2220/2220	0/0	0/0	79/65 minutes
WebGoat	CodePro Analytix	26	7	1	1 minute
	FindBugs	22	12	5	20 seconds
	Fortify SCA	23	0	4	164 minutes
	Julia fs/fi	27/27	14/15	0/0	3/2 minutes

Fig. 3. Experiments with the identification of SQL injections.

6 Experiments

We have implemented our analysis inside Julia (http://www.juliasoft.com/julia). Julia represents Boolean formulas via BDDs (binary decision diagrams). We have compared Julia with other tools that identify injections (Sect. 3). For Julia we have compared a field-sensitive analysis with an oracle (Sect. 5.1, *Julia fs*) with a field-insensitive analysis without oracle (*Julia fi*).

Our experiments analyze third-party tests developed to assess the power of a static analyzer to identify injection attacks: WebGoat 6.0.1 (https://www.owasp. org/index.php/Category:OWASP_WebGoat_Project) and 4 tests from the Samate suite (http://samate.nist.gov/ SARD/testsuite.php). The table on the right reports their number of non-blank, non-comment lines of application source code (LoC), without supporting libraries.

Test	LoC
WebGoat	25070
CWE80	68967
CWE81	34317
CWE83	34317
CWE89	748962

Figure 3 reports the evaluation for SQL injections using CWE89 and Web-Goat. It shows that only Julia is sound (no false negatives: if there is an injection, Julia finds it). Julia issued no false positives to CWE89: possibly these tests just propagate information, without side-effects that degrade the precision of Julia (Definition 9; we do not know if and how other tools deal with side-effects). Julia issued 14 false alarms for WebGoat, often where actual information flows from source to sink exist, but constrained in such a way to be unusable to build an SQL-injection attack. Only here the field-insensitive version of Julia is slightly less precise (one false positive more). In general, its cost is around 25 % higher than the field-sensitive version. The conclusion is that field sensitivity is not relevant when object sensitivity is used to distinguish different objects. Analysis time indicates the efficiency, roughly: CodePro Analytix and FindBugs work on the client machine in Eclipse, Fortify SCA on its cloud like Julia, that is controlled from an Eclipse client. Times include all supporting analyses.

We evaluated the same tools for the identification of cross-site scripting injections in CWE80/81/83, and WebGoat. As shown in Fig. 4, Julia is perfectly precise. It missed 11 cross-site scripting attacks in JSP (not in the main Java code of the application), found only by Fortify SCA. If we translate JSP's into Java through Jasper (as a servlet container would do, automatically) and include its

Test	Tool	True Positives	False Positives	False Negatives	Analysis Time
CWE80	CodePro Analytix	180	0	486	9 minutes
	FindBugs	19	0	647	18 seconds
	Fortify SCA	282	0	384	590 minutes
	Julia fs/fi	666/666	0/0	0/0	5/4 minutes
CWE81	CodePro Analytix	0	0	333	10 seconds
	FindBugs	19	0	314	4 seconds
	Fortify SCA	141	0	192	303 minutes
	Julia fs/fi	333/333	0/0	0/0	3/2 minutes
CWE83	CodePro Analytix	90	0	243	5 minutes
	FindBugs	19	0	314	4 seconds
	Fortify SCA	141	0	192	296 minutes
	Julia fs/fi	333/333	0/0	0/0	3/2 minutes
WebGoat	CodePro Analytix	5	0	11	1 minute
	FindBugs	0	0	16	20 seconds
	Fortify SCA	15	21	1	164 minutes
	Julia fs/fi	5/5	0/0	11/11	3/2 minutes

Fig. 4. Experiments with the identification of XSS injections.

bytecode in the analysis, Julia finds the missing 11 attacks. Nevertheless, this process is currently manual and we think fairer to count 11 false negatives.

We have run Julia on real code from our customers. Julia found 6 real SQL-injections in the Internet banking services (575995 LoC) of a large Italian bank, and found 5 more in its customer relation management system (346170 LoC). The analysis never took more than one hour. This shows that Julia is already able to scale to real software and automatically find evidence of security attacks.

7 Conclusion

We have formalized an object-sensitive notion of taintedness that can be applied to reference types. We have built a new, flow-, context- and field-sensitive static taintedness analysis based on this notion, proved it sound, implemented it, and evaluated it. It scales to real code and gives useful results. As far as we know, this is the first object-sensitive taintedness analysis. As usual in static analysis, soundness is jeopardized by the use of reflection or non-standard class loaders. However, soundness is still relevant since it increases the confidence on the results, up to those features. Julia deals instead with the full bytecode generated by Java 8, including the new `invokedynamic`.

The novelty of the approach stems from Definition 4 of a property of reference types as a reachability property, whose relevance goes beyond the case of taintedness analysis. Here, we mean reachability of data from a memory reference, which is not reachability of abstract states through execution paths as in [24]. Definition 4 results in an object-sensitive analysis: the taintedness of an object determines that of its fields; a drawback is that a sound analysis must consider side-effects at `putfield` and `call`. The analysis becomes then field sensitive through an oracle-based approach (Sect. 5.1), already used for nullness analysis [32].

Hence the oracle is a general technique for building sound field-sensitive static analyses.

The extension of this work to implicit and hidden flows would provide a stronger guarantee against injections of tainted information into a set of sinks. The problem is complex: implicit flows in Java are not just due to conditionals but also to exception branches and dynamic resolution of method calls. The risk is that a sound analysis $w.r.t.$ implicit flows would end up being very conservative and imprecise. Declassification might be helpful here, but its meaning for reference types (not just primitive values) must be studied. The extension of this work to the analysis of JSP, that are non-Java code mixed and interacting with Java code, currently not analyzed by Julia (only partially by concurrent tools), would avoid missed alarms, as Sect. 6 shows. It is also important to explain the warnings to the users, with an execution trace where data flows from sources into sinks. Fortify SCA already provides some support in that direction.

Acknowledgments. This material is based upon work supported by the United States Air Force under Contract No. FA8750-12-C-0174.

References

1. Appelt, D., Nguyen, C.D., Briand, L.C., Alshahwan, N.: Automated testing for SQL injection vulnerabilities: an input mutation approach. In: ISSTA, pp. 259–269, San Jose, CA, USA (2014)
2. Arzt, S., Rasthofer, S., Fritz, C., Bodden, E., Bartel, A., Klein, J., Le Traon, Y., Octeau, D., McDaniel, P.: Flowdroid: precise context, flow, field, object-sensitive and lifecycle-aware taint analysis for android apps. In: PLDI, p. 29, Edinburgh, UK, June 2014
3. Barthe, G., Pichardie, D., Rezk, T.: A certified lightweight non-interference java bytecode verifier. Math. Struct. Comput. Sci. **23**(5), 1032–1081 (2013)
4. Barthe, G., Rezk, T., Basu, A.: Security types preserving compilation. Comput. Lang. Syst. Struct. **33**(2), 35–59 (2007)
5. Clark, D., Hankin, C., Hunt, S.: Information flow for ALGOL-like languages. Comput. Lang. **28**(1), 3–28 (2002)
6. Cousot, P., Cousot, R.: Abstract Interpretation: a unified lattice model for static analysis of programs by construction or approximation of fixpoints. In: POPL, pp. 238–252 (1977)
7. Doshi, J.C., Christian, M., Trivedi, B.H.: SQL FILTER – SQL Injection prevention and logging using dynamic network filter. In: Mauri, J.L., Thampi, S.M., Rawat, D.B., Jin, D. (eds.) SSCC 2014. CCIS, vol. 467, pp. 400–406. Springer, Heidelberg (2014)
8. Ernst, M.D., Lovato, A., Macedonio, D., Spiridon, C., Spoto, F.: Boolean Formulas for the Static Identification of Injection Attacks in Java. Technical Report UW-CSE-15-09-03, University of Washington Department of Computer Science and Engineering, Seattle, WA, USA, September 2015
9. Genaim, S., Giacobazzi, R., Mastroeni, I.: Modeling secure information flow with boolean functions. In: Peter Ryan, editor, WITS 2004, April 2004
10. Genaim, S., Spoto, F.: Information flow analysis for java bytecode. In: Cousot, R. (ed.) VMCAI 2005. LNCS, vol. 3385, pp. 346–362. Springer, Heidelberg (2005)

11. Genaim, S., Spoto, F.: Constancy Analysis. In: Huisman, M. (ed.), FTfJP, Paphos, Cyprus, July 2008. Radboud University
12. Jang, Y.-S., Choi, J.-Y.: Detecting SQL injection attacks using query result size. Comput. Secur. **44**, 104–118 (2014)
13. Kobayashi, N., Shirane, K.: Type-based information flow analysis for low-level languages. In: APLAS (2002)
14. Kumar, D.G., Chatterjee, M.: MAC based solution for SQL injection. J. Comput. Virol. Hacking Tech. **11**(1), 1–7 (2015)
15. Laud, P.: Semantics and program analysis of computationally secure information flow. In: Sands, D. (ed.) ESOP 2001. LNCS, vol. 2028, pp. 77–91. Springer, Heidelberg (2001)
16. Lindholm, T., Yellin, F., Bracha, G., Buckley, A.: The Java Virtual Machine Specification, Java SE 7 Edition. Addison-Wesley Professional, 1st edition (2013)
17. Liu, L., Xu, J., Li, M., Yang, J.: A Dynamic SQL injection vulnerability test case generation model based on the multiple phases detection approach. In: COMPSAC, pp. 256–261, Kyoto, Japan (2013)
18. Makiou, A., Begriche, Y., Serhrouchni, A.: Improving web application firewalls to detect advanced SQL injection attacks. In: IAS, pp. 35–40. Okinawa, Japan 2014
19. MITRE/SANS. Top 25 Most Dangerous Software Errors. http://cwe.mitre.org/top25, September 2011
20. Mizuno, M.: A least fixed point approach to inter-procedural information flow control. In: NCSC, pp. 558–570 (1989)
21. Naghmeh, N.M., Sheykhkanloo, M.: Employing neural networks for the detection of SQL injection attack. In: SIN, pp. 318, Glasgow, Scotland, UK (2014)
22. Nikolić, D., Spoto, F.: Reachability analysis of program variables. ACM Trans. Program. Lang. Syst. **35**(4), 14 (2013)
23. Payet, É., Spoto, F.: Magic-sets transformation for the analysis of java bytecode. In: Riis Nielson, H., Filé, G. (eds.) SAS 2007. LNCS, vol. 4634, pp. 452–467. Springer, Heidelberg (2007)
24. Resp, T.W., Horwitz, S., Sagiv, S.: Precise interprocedural dataflow analysis via graph reachability. In: POPL 1995, pp. 49–61. San Francisco, California, USA, January 1995
25. Sabelfeld, A., Myers, A.C.: Language-based information-flow security. IEEE J. Sel. Areas Commun. **21**(1), 5–19 (2003)
26. Sabelfeld, A., Sands, D.: A PER model of secure information flow in sequential programs. High. Order Symbolic Comput. **14**(1), 59–91 (2001)
27. Secci, S., Spoto, F.: Pair-sharing analysis of object-oriented programs. In: Hankin, C., Siveroni, I. (eds.) SAS 2005. LNCS, vol. 3672, pp. 320–335. Springer, Heidelberg (2005)
28. Shahriar, H., Zulkernine, M.: Information-theoretic detection of SQL injection attacks. In: HASE, pp. 40–47. Omaha, NE, USA (2012)
29. Shar, L.K., Tan, K.: H. B. defeating SQL injection. IEEE Comput. **46**(3), 69–77 (2013)
30. Simic, B., Walden, J.: Eliminating SQL injection and cross site scripting using aspect oriented programming. In: Jürjens, J., Livshits, B., Scandariato, R. (eds.) ESSoS 2013. LNCS, vol. 7781, pp. 213–228. Springer, Heidelberg (2013)
31. Skalka, C., Smith, S.: Static enforcement of security with types. In: ICFP, pp. 254–267. ACM press (2000)
32. Spoto, F.: Nullness analysis in boolean form. In: SEFM, pp. 21–30. IEEE, Washington, DC, USA (2008)

33. Tripp, O., Pistoia, M., Fink, S.J., Sridharan, M., Weisman, O.: TAJ: effective taint analysis of web applications. SIGPLAN Not. **44**(6), 87–97 (2009)
34. Volpano, D., Smith, G., Irvine, C.: A sound type system for secure flow analysis. J. Comput. Secur. **4**(2,3), 167–187 (1996)
35. Wu, T.-Y., Pan, J.-S., Chen, C.-M., Lin, C.-W.: Towards SQL injection attacks detection mechanism using parse tree. In: Sun, H., Yang, C.-Y., Lin, C.-W., Pan, J.-S., Snasel, V., Abraham, A. (eds.) Genetic and Evolutionary Computing. AISC, vol. 329, pp. 371–380. Springer, Heidelberg (2015)

An Adequate Compositional Encoding of Bigraph Structure in Linear Logic with Subexponentials

Kaustuv Chaudhuri and Giselle Reis[✉]

Inria & LIX/École Polytechnique, Palaiseau, France
{kaustuv.chaudhuri,giselle.reis}@inria.fr

Abstract. In linear logic, formulas can be split into two sets: classical (those that can be used as many times as necessary) or linear (those that are consumed and no longer available after being used). Subexponentials generalize this notion by allowing the formulas to be split into many sets, each of which can then be specified to be classical or linear. This flexibility increases its expressiveness: we already have adequate encodings of a number of other proof systems, and for computational models such as concurrent constraint programming, in linear logic with subexponentials (SEL). Bigraphs were proposed by Milner in 2001 as a model for ubiquitous computing, subsuming models of computation such as CCS and the π-calculus and capable of modeling connectivity and locality at the same time. In this work we present an encoding of the bigraph structure in SEL, thus giving an indication of the expressive power of this logic, and at the same time providing a framework for reasoning and operating on bigraphs. Our encoding is adequate and therefore the operations of composition and juxtaposition can be performed on the logical level. Moreover, all the proof-theoretical tools of SEL become available for querying and proving properties of bigraph structures.

1 Introduction

Linear logic is excellent at *counting* elements of state since it interprets linear hypotheses as resources that are consumed upon use, and every linear hypothesis must be used in a proof. However, it is not particularly good at reasoning about *relationships* between elements. For example, an office building can have several rooms, with some rooms having a number of cubicles, and some cubicles containing several persons and computers. A precise description of this building must not only inventory all the rooms, cubicles, persons, and computers, but also state which component occurs inside which other components. In ordinary linear logic we can attempt to express the inclusion relation as a separate predicate, say a binary predicate $\texttt{in}(x, y)$ that expresses that the entity with index x is contained in that with index y, but such predicates are nearly impossible to treat linearly as they may be consulted and composed repeatedly. Yet, treating them non-linearly is also problematic: if a person moves from one cubicle to

© Springer-Verlag Berlin Heidelberg 2015
M. Davis et al. (Eds.): LPAR-20 2015, LNCS 9450, pp. 146–161, 2015.
DOI: 10.1007/978-3-662-48899-7_11

another, for example, the old placement needs to be invalidated, but there is no way to "consume" a non-linear resource in linear logic.

Recently, a family of logics called *subexponential logics* (*SEL*) has emerged as a way to capture such intensional relationships between resources [12]. The idea is fairly old [6]: the exponential connectives ! and ? can be split into several different *flavors*, and the linear logic proof system would, *a priori*, make each version of the connectives independent of every other. If we impose a pre-order on them though, we can get a limited form of *promotion* where $?^u A$ entails $?^v A$ assuming the u version of the exponentials are smaller than the v version. In this view, $?^u$ corresponds, roughly, to a *placement* in the *zone u*, while $!^u$ corresponds to *checking* that every resource is placed in a zone larger than u. Subexponential logics are naturally much more expressive than just ordinary linear logic; for instance, even the propositional additive-free fragment is undecidable [5]. Moreover, they can easily express a wide spectrum of other deductive systems at a very high level of *representational adequacy* [4,13,14].

In this paper, we consider the use of *SEL* as a *logical framework* for specifying *bigraphs*, a model of computation proposed by Milner in 2001 [10]. Bigraphs are a very general model, subsuming standard process calculi such as CCS [9] and the π-calculus [8]. Our use of *SEL* for this purpose has two primary goals:

- It gives a good formal indication of the expressive power of *SEL* as a logical framework. If *SEL* can be used for bigraphs, it can probably also be used for any location-aware formalism. A number of such formalisms exist in the literature, such as ambients [3], brane calculi [2], and membrane computing [15].
- It provides an adequate *syntactic* treatment for bigraph structure.[1] By adequate, we mean that any structural operation, such as composition and juxtaposition, can be performed directly on the syntactical representation. Bigraphs certainly have a well developed categorical semantics, but formalizing that semantics can be rather heavyweight. We show straightforward encoding and decoding functions from bigraphs to *SEL* sequents. Such a representation of bigraphs benefits from all the proof-theoretic tools available for querying and proving properties.

In relation to the second goal, another syntactic treatment for bigraphs can be found in [1]. The authors encode a bigraph and its reaction rules in the Concurrent LF (*CLF*) type theory, where both the formation and the reactions of bigraphs are encoded as rewrite rules. The encoding of locations is done by using a (linear) predicate `has_child`, and thus presents the problems previously mentioned. In particular, their use of a multi-set of atoms for encoding a bigraph makes it impossible to query a static structure, or prove its correctness, without damaging the structure itself. The proof that a bigraph is valid in [1] indeed consists of rewriting it to the empty set. Analogously, a containment check cannot be made without consuming the atom(s) encoding the parent relations.

---

[1] We posit that, given the way computer science is evolving, the lack of formal and mechanized reasoning capabilities for any formalisms can be fatal.

In principle, we could use the same approach with rewriting rules to check for the correctness of bigraphs in our encoding, but we have decided to take advantage of the expressiveness of subexponentials by having a more concise and conservative approach. In this work, we will encode bigraphs using fewer predicates than in [1] and in such a way that asking questions about the static structure will not cause any modifications to it. Our bigraph encoding changes only on actual operations, such as juxtaposition and compositions.

Our specific approach is to start with a *sequent calculus* for first-order classical *SEL* (Sect. 2.1). The classical dialect of *SEL* is used simply to keep the proof systems simple; our results extend to the intuitionistic dialect without any complications. The static definition of a bigraph is encoded in *SEL* as follows. The place graph of the bigraph is given in terms of atomic formulas placed in certain subexponential zones, and the *subexponential signature* encodes the parent relationship. The link graph of the bigraph is given in terms of eigenvariable parameters that are shared by every place that has a connection to a hyperedge. Finally, the inner and outer faces of the bigraph are expressed as purely linear formulas that are placed in the *default* zone of the *SEL*. This encoding will be an injection, *i.e.*, it will have a left-inverse that will be able to extract the original bigraph from its sequent encoding. Furthermore, the static structure of the bigraph can be *queried* by trying to derive certain formulas. For example, to check whether a given node occurs inside (perhaps with multiple levels of nesting) a given place is tantamount to deriving a corresponding !-formula.

On top of this static description of a single bigraph, we define bigraph composition by first moving to a *focused* proof system for *SEL*, called *SELF* (Sect. 2.2) [11]. Focusing is a general mechanism for treating certain combinations of inferences in a (well behaved) sequent calulus as *atomic* derived inference rules. Bigraph juxtaposition in our encoding corresponds to a multiplicative composition of the two sequents describing the two bigraphs, and the composition of the bigraphs is given as a small *theory* on these sequents. We then run focused proof search on this sequent, extended with the composition theory, until quiescence, *i.e.*, until no more focused steps are possible. The single unfinished leaf of the proof will then be the representation of the composed bigraph. This gives us the necessary *representational adequacy* theorem (Sect. 3.1).

2   Background

2.1   Subexponential Logic (*SEL*)

Subexponential logic (*SEL*) is a variant of linear logic with a family of exponential connectives—called *subexponentials* (a term coined in [12])—that are indexed and arranged in a pre-order [6,11]. To keep things simple, we will use the classical dialect of *SEL* in this paper. The grammar of *formulas* $(A, B, \dots)$ is as follows:

$$A, B, \ldots ::= \quad a \quad | \quad A \otimes B \quad | \quad 1 \quad | \quad A \oplus B \quad | \quad 0 \quad | \quad \exists x.\, A \quad | \quad !^u A$$
$$| \quad \neg a \quad | \quad A \,\invamp\, B \quad | \quad \bot \quad | \quad A \,\&\, B \quad | \quad \top \quad | \quad \forall x.\, A \quad | \quad ?^u A \tag{1}$$

LITERAL MULTIPLICATIVE ADDITIVE QUANTIFIED SUBEXPONENTIAL

Each column in the grammar is a De Morgan dual pair, and we indicate the dual of A by $(A)^\perp$. The identifiers $a, b, \ldots$ range over *atomic formulas*, which are formulas of the form $\mathsf{p}(t_1, \ldots, t_n)$ where p stands for a predicate symbol and $t_1, \ldots, t_n$ are first-order terms. Each *term* is either a *variable* $(x, y, \ldots)$ or an *application* of the form $\mathsf{f}(s_1, \ldots, s_m)$ where f stands for a *function symbol* and the $s_1, \ldots, s_m$ are terms. Variables, predicates, and function symbols are assumed to be drawn from disjoint infinite sets and arities are fixed. We follow the usual syntactic convention of dropping the parentheses when the arity of a predicate or function symbol is 0. The subexponential connectives $!^u$ and $?^u$ are indexed by *subexponential labels* $(u, w, \ldots)$ that belong to a *subexponential signature*.

$$\frac{}{\vdash \Gamma^{\mathcal{U}}, u{:}\neg a, a} \text{ init} \qquad \frac{\vdash \Gamma^{\mathcal{U}}, \Delta_1, A \quad \vdash \Gamma^{\mathcal{U}}, \Delta_2, B}{\vdash \Gamma^{\mathcal{U}}, \Delta_1, \Delta_2, A \otimes B} \otimes \qquad \frac{}{\vdash \Gamma^{\mathcal{U}}, 1} 1 \qquad \frac{\vdash \Gamma, A_i}{\vdash \Gamma, A_1 \oplus A_2} \oplus_i \qquad \frac{\vdash \Gamma, [t/x]A}{\vdash \Gamma, \exists x.\, A} \exists$$

$$\frac{\vdash \Gamma, A, B}{\vdash \Gamma, A \,\invamp\, B} \invamp \qquad \frac{\vdash \Gamma}{\vdash \Gamma, \bot} \bot \qquad \frac{\vdash \Gamma, A \quad \vdash \Gamma, B}{\vdash \Gamma, A \,\&\, B} \,\& \qquad \frac{}{\vdash \Gamma, \top} \top \qquad \frac{\vdash \Gamma, A}{\vdash \Gamma, \forall x.\, A} \forall \qquad \frac{\vdash \Gamma, u{:}A}{\vdash \Gamma, ?^u A} ?$$

$$\frac{(u \leq \vec{v}) \quad \vdash \vec{v}{:}\vec{A}, C}{\vdash \Gamma^{\mathcal{U}}, \vec{v}{:}\vec{A}, !^u C} ! \qquad \frac{(u \notin \mathcal{U}) \quad \vdash \Gamma, A}{\vdash \Gamma, u{:}A} \text{ derelict} \qquad \frac{(u \in \mathcal{U}) \quad \vdash \Gamma, u{:}A, A}{\vdash \Gamma, u{:}A} \text{ copy}$$

Fig. 1. A cut-free, one-sided, and zoned sequent calculus formulation of *SEL*. In the $\oplus_i$ rules, $i \in \{1, 2\}$. In the $\forall$ rule, x is not free in Γ.

Definition 1. *A* subexponential signature Σ *is a structure* $\langle \Lambda, \mathcal{U}, \leq \rangle$ *where:*

- Λ *is a countable set of* labels;
- $\mathcal{U} \subseteq \Lambda \uplus \{\varepsilon\}$, *called the* unbounded labels;
- $\leq$ *is a pre-order on* $\Lambda \uplus \{\varepsilon\}$—*i.e., it is reflexive and transitive*—*and* $\leq$-*upwardly closed with respect to* $\mathcal{U}$, *i.e., for any* $u, w \in \Lambda \uplus \{\varepsilon\}$, *if* $u \in \mathcal{U}$ *and* $u \leq w$, *then* $w \in \mathcal{U}$; *and*
- ε *is* $\leq$-*minimal, i.e., for every* $u \in \Lambda \uplus \{\varepsilon\}$, $\varepsilon \leq u$.

We say that any label in $\Lambda \uplus \{\varepsilon\} \setminus \mathcal{U}$ *is* bounded.

Intuitively, unbounded labels indicate formulas which can be weakened or contracted, while bound labels indicate linear formulas. We will assume an ambient subexponential signature Σ unless we need to disambiguate particular instances of *SEL*, in which case we will use Σ in subscripts. For instance, the set $\mathcal{U}_\Sigma$ stands for the unbounded labels of Σ.

The true formulas of *SEL* are derived from a *sequent calculus* proof system. There are many variants of such calculi in the literature; here, to keep things simple, we will use a *zoned* formulation where the members of a sequent are *zoned formulas* of the form $u{:}A$ where A is a formula and $u \in \Lambda \uplus \{\varepsilon\}$. When it is unambiguous, we will drop the *default* zone label ε, *i.e.*, write $\varepsilon{:}A$ as just A. A *context* $(\Gamma, \Delta, \dots)$ is a non-empty multiset of zoned formulas, and Γ, Δ and $\Gamma, u{:}A$ stand as usual for the multi-set union of Γ with Δ and $\{u{:}A\}$, respectively.

The inference rules for *SEL* sequents are displayed in Fig. 1. Most of the rules are shared between *SEL* and ordinary linear logic and will not be elaborated upon here; we will therefore explain only the peculiarities of *SEL*.

Definition 2 (Notation). *For $\vec{v} = [v_1, \dots, v_n]$ and $\vec{A} = [A_1, \dots, A_n]$:*

- $\vec{v}{:}\vec{A}$ *stands for the context* $v_1{:}A_1, \dots, v_n{:}A_n$;
- $u \leq \vec{v}$ *means that* $u \leq v_1$, ..., *and* $u \leq v_n$; *and*
- $\vec{v} \in \mathcal{U}$ *stands for* $v_1 \in \mathcal{U}$, ..., *and* $v_n \in \mathcal{U}$.

We write $\Gamma^{\mathcal{U}}$ for a context of the form $\vec{u}{:}\vec{A}$ where $\vec{u} \in \mathcal{U}$.

The rule for !, sometimes called *promotion*, has a side condition that checks that the label of the principal formula is less than the labels of all the other zoned formulas in the context that survive into the premise. This rule cannot be used if there are non-zoned formulas in the context, nor if the labels of some of the bound zoned-formulas are strictly smaller or incomparable with the subexponential label of the principal formula.

Theorem 1. *The following rules are admissible for SEL.*

$$\frac{}{\vdash u{:}(A)^{\perp}, A} \text{ init}^{*}$$

$$\frac{(\forall w{:}C \in \Gamma^{\mathcal{U}} \cup \Delta_1 \cup \{u{:}A\}, v \leq w) \qquad \vdash \Gamma^{\mathcal{U}}, \Delta_1, u{:}A \qquad \vdash \Gamma^{\mathcal{U}}, \Delta_2, v{:}(A)^{\perp}}{\vdash \Gamma^{\mathcal{U}}, \Delta_1, \Delta_2} \text{ cut}$$

Proof (sketch). The init* rule can be shown to be derivable by a straightforward structural induction on A, where reflexivity of $\leq$ is used in the cases for the subexponentials. For cut-admissibility, the standard permutative cut-reduction algorithm works. Transitivity of $\leq$ is used to justify the commutative cut case for !, while upward closure of $\leq$ with respect to $\mathcal{U}$ is used to justify permuting cuts past copy. □

Subexponential logic is considerably more expressive than ordinary linear logic. Even the propositional additive-free fragment can be undecidable with as few as three subexponentials [5]. By choosing the appropriate signature it is possible to encode many proof systems [14] and various models of concurrency in concurrent constraint programming [13] in a natural way. This expressivity is a result of the ability of the ! rule to "check" the emptiness of certain zones in the sequent. Note that this rule can only be applied if all (linear) formulas are in bigger zones, which means that smaller or unrelated zones must be empty. It is natural then to view the zones in a sequent as *locations* where a formula has been stored (by the ? rule).

2.2 Focusing (*SELF*)

In our intended use of *SEL* as a specification logic for bigraphs, we will sometimes need to reason about sequences of inference steps that happen atomically. These *derived* or *synthetic* inference steps will be informed by *focusing*, which is a general technique for determining a normal form for a sequent calculus that eliminates many unnecessary branching points. A focused proof consists of an alternation of two *phases*. The *asynchronous phase* uses[2] the inference rules in the second line of Fig. 1 that are invertible and can therefore always be safely applied. When no such rule is applicable, the proof enters a *synchronized phase* by selecting a formula for *focus*; this formula is decomposed under focus using the rules in the first line of Fig. 1 until no such rule applies, in which case the phase switches back to asynchronous again. To be a bit more explicit, we add a new kind of *focused sequent* of the form $\vdash \Gamma; [A]$ where A is the focused formula.

$$\frac{}{\vdash \Omega^{\mathcal{U}}, u{:}\neg\, a, [a]} \text{[init]} \quad \frac{\vdash \Omega^{\mathcal{U}}, \Omega_1, [B] \quad \vdash \Omega^{\mathcal{U}}, \Omega_2, [C]}{\vdash \Omega^{\mathcal{U}}, \Omega_1, \Omega_2, [B \otimes C]} \text{[\otimes]} \quad \frac{}{\vdash \Omega^{\mathcal{U}}, [1]} \text{[1]} \quad \frac{\vdash \Omega, [A_i]}{\vdash \Omega, [A_1 \oplus A_2]} \text{[}\oplus_i\text{]}$$

$$\frac{\vdash \Omega, [[t/x]A]}{\vdash \Omega, [\exists x.\, A]} \text{[}\exists\text{]} \quad \frac{(u \leq \vec{w}) \quad \vdash \vec{w}{:}\vec{A}, C}{\vdash \Omega^{\mathcal{U}}, \vec{w}{:}\vec{A}, [!^u\, C]} \text{[!]} \quad \frac{\vdash \Omega, N}{\vdash \Omega, [N]} \text{[release]}$$

$$\cdots\cdots\cdots\cdots\cdots\cdots\cdots\cdots\cdots\cdots\cdots\cdots\cdots\cdots\cdots\cdots\cdots\cdots\cdots\cdots\cdots$$

Rules $\mathfrak{N}$, $\perp$, &, $\top$, $\forall$, ? shared with *SEL*

$$\frac{(u \notin \mathcal{U}) \quad \vdash \Omega, [A]}{\vdash \Omega, u{:}A} \text{Idecide} \quad \frac{(u \in \mathcal{U}) \quad \vdash \Omega, u{:}A, [A]}{\vdash \Omega, u{:}A} \text{udecide}$$

Fig. 2. The *SELF* inference system, a focused version of *SEL*. The context Ω is such that if $A \in \Omega$ then A is a positive formula or a negated atom.

The inference rules for the focused version of *SEL*, called *SELF*, are given in Fig. 2. These rules are based on a division of the formulas of *SEL* into *positive formulas* $(P, Q, \dots)$ that come from the first line of (1), and *negative formulas* $(N, M, \dots)$ that come from the second line. We use the convention that Ω stands for a context that consists of zoned formulas where if the zone label is ε then the corresponding formula is positive or a literal. As before $\Omega^{\mathcal{U}}$ stands for a context of the form $\vec{u}{:}\vec{A}$ where $\vec{u} \in \mathcal{U}$. There are two *decision* rules, Idecide and udecide, for focusing on a zoned formula with a bound label and an unbound label respectively. The focus persists through to the immediate subformula in the synchronous phase rules [$\otimes$], [$\oplus_i$], and [$\exists$]. Ultimately, the focused formula becomes negative or a !-formula, in which case focus is released and the asynchronous phase begins, where the inference rules are identical to those of *SEL*. Finally, when no more asynchronous rules are available, a decision rule is used to enter the focused phase again.

Theorem 2 (Soundness and Completeness of *SELF*). *The sequent $\vdash \Gamma$ is derivable in SELF if and only if it is derivable in SEL.*

---

[2] As usual in the view of the sequent calculus as a proof search formalism, we read inference rules from conclusion to premises.

Proof (sketch). Soundness is immediate, since if we interpret ⊢ Ω, [*A*] as ⊢ Ω, *A* then we get a *SEL* proof from a *SELF* proof. For completeness, we can easily adapt any of the existing proofs for related systems, such as [11, chapter 5].   □

3   Bigraphs in *SEL*

Bigraphs were proposed by Milner [10] as a model for ubiquitous computing. It tries to fill in a gap between the current state of computational systems, which involves communications on a global scale and pervasive computing, and the available tools to model and reason about such systems. In bigraphs, *locality* and *connectivity* of agents are treated independently, and they might be equipped with reaction rules (*i.e.*, rewriting) for reconfiguration. It has been shown that bigraphs subsume the calculus of communicating systems (CCS) [9] and π-calculus [8]. Most definitions and examples in this section were taken from [9].

A bigraph is a combination of two graphs (hence the name): a *place graph* and a *link graph*. Both have in common the set of vertices, but the place graph is a set of trees while the link graph is a hypergraph (*i.e.*, one edge can connect any number of nodes). Figure 3 is an example of a bigraph and its components, each representing orthogonally the concepts of locality and connectivity.

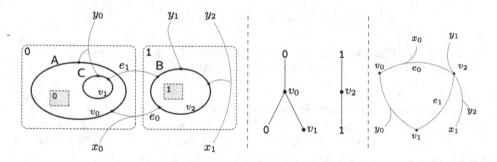

Fig. 3. A bigraph and its place and link graphs.

Each node takes the role of a specific *control* that determines its ports. The controls available for a bigraph are defined in its *signature*, which does not have to be finite or even denumerable.

Definition 3 (Bigraph Signature). *A signature $\mathcal{K}$ is a set of elements called* controls, *each with an* arity *($ar(\mathcal{K})$). The signature also determines which controls are* atomic *and which of the non-atomic controls are* active.

Depending on the system being represented, such signatures can be augmented with, for example, sorts that enforce what kind of controls a non-atomic control can contain, or signs that make sure only ports of opposite polarities are connected. For a discussion on adding sorts to our encoding, see Sect. 4. Given a signature, we can formally define a bigraph.

Definition 4 (Bigraphs). *A bigraph* $\mathcal{B}$ *over the signature* $\mathcal{K}$ *is defined as:*

$$\mathcal{B} = (V, E, ctrl, prnt, link) : \langle m, X \rangle \rightarrow \langle n, Y \rangle.$$

– *V is a set of node names.*
– *E is a set of edge names.*
– *m is the number of sites (i.e., holes which can accommodate other bigraphs).*
– *X is a set of inner names.*
– *n is the number of roots (i.e., which can be accommodated in other bigraphs).*
– *Y is a set of outer names.*
– $ctrl : V \rightarrow \mathcal{K}$ *defines the role of each node.*
– $prnt : m \uplus V \rightarrow n \uplus V$ *defines the parent relation, or the place graph.*
– $link : X \uplus P \rightarrow Y \uplus E$ *defines the connectivity, or the link graph, where*
  $P = \{(v, i) | 1 \leq i \leq ar(ctrl(v))\}$, *i.e.,* (v, i) *is the* i^{th} *port of node* v.

The sets of names V, E, X, *and* Y *must be pairwise disjoint. The terms* m *and* n *are treated notationally as sets of all strictly smaller natural numbers, i.e., the sites are numbered* $0, 1, \ldots, m - 1$, *and likewise for the roots.*

For the bigraph of Fig. 3, we have $\mathcal{K} = \{\mathsf{A} : 2, \mathsf{B} : 4, \mathsf{C} : 2\}$ and:

$$V = \{v_0, v_1, v_2\} \quad E = \{e_0, e_1\} \quad X = \{x_0, x_1\} \quad Y = \{y_0, y_1, y_2\} \quad m = n = 2$$

ctrl	*prnt*	*link*	
$v_0 \mapsto \mathsf{A}$	$0 \mapsto v_0$	$x_0 \mapsto e_0$	$(v_1, 2) \mapsto e_1$
$v_1 \mapsto \mathsf{C}$	$1 \mapsto v_2$	$x_1 \mapsto y_2$	$(v_2, 1) \mapsto y_1$
$v_2 \mapsto \mathsf{B}$	$v_0 \mapsto 0$	$(v_0, 1) \mapsto y_0$	$(v_2, 2) \mapsto y_2$
	$v_1 \mapsto v_0$	$(v_0, 2) \mapsto e_0$	$(v_2, 3) \mapsto e_0$
	$v_2 \mapsto 1$	$(v_1, 1) \mapsto y_0$	$(v_2, 4) \mapsto e_1$

3.1 Encoding Bigraphs

Given a bigraph $\mathcal{B}$, we will show in this section how to encode it using a *SEL* sequent. Intuitively, each *place* is represented by a subexponential index; indices are related according to *prnt* in the place graph. Next, each place which has an assigned control (*i.e.*, the actual *nodes*) will be represented by a predicate, conveniently named `control` and placed in the zone corresponding to its parent. The *links* are encoded by using constants or variables that are shared among the controls if they are linked together. We will use a `typewriter` font to denote constants in our encoding.

Definition 5 (Encoding Function). *Let* $\mathcal{B} = (V, E, ctrl, prnt, link)$: $\langle m, X \rangle \rightarrow \langle n, Y \rangle$ *be a bigraph over a signature* $\mathcal{K}$, *then:*

– *Term and atomic formulas:*
  • `id` *is a unique identifier.*
  • *Each element of* V, E, *and* $\mathcal{K}$ *is a constant.*
  • *Each element of* X *and* Y *is a variable.*
  • `control(K, v, L)` *is an atomic formula, where* L *is a list of size* $ar(\mathsf{K})$.

- $\mathtt{in}(x, l, \mathtt{id})$ and $\mathtt{out}(y, \mathtt{id})$ are atomic formulas, where l is a constant or variable corresponding to an element $e \in E \cup Y$.
- $\mathtt{site}(\mathtt{id})$ and $\mathtt{root}(\mathtt{id})$ are atomic formulas.
- Subexponential signature $\Sigma = \langle \Lambda, \{\infty\}, \leq \rangle$:
  - Each node name is duplicated as a label, i.e., $V \subseteq \Lambda$.
  - $r_0, \ldots, r_{n-1} \in \Lambda \setminus V$ are subexponential variables representing the roots.
  - $\forall (a, b) \in prnt.\ b \leq a \in \Sigma.^3$

The function $E(-)$ maps $\mathcal{B}$ to the SEL_Σ sequent:

$$\vdash_\Sigma \{\mathtt{in}(x, link(x), \mathtt{id}) \mid x \in X\}, \{\mathtt{out}(y, \mathtt{id}) \mid y \in Y\},$$
$$\{r_i\mathtt{:root}(\mathtt{id}) \mid 0 \leq i \leq n - 1\}, \{prnt(i)\mathtt{:site}(\mathtt{id}) \mid 0 \leq i \leq m - 1\},$$
$$\{prnt(\mathtt{v})\mathtt{:control}(ctrl(\mathtt{v}), \mathtt{v}, [link((\mathtt{v}, 1)), \ldots, link((\mathtt{v}, ar(ctrl(\mathtt{v}))))]) \mid \mathtt{v} \in V\}.$$

Note that all x, y and r_i are free in the resulting sequent.

As an example, if $\mathcal{B}$ is the bigraph of Fig. 3, then $E(\mathcal{B})$ is the sequent:

$$\vdash_\Sigma \mathtt{in}(x_0, \mathsf{e}_0, \mathtt{id}), \mathtt{in}(x_1, y_2, \mathtt{id}),$$
$$\mathtt{out}(y_0, \mathtt{id}), \mathtt{out}(y_1, \mathtt{id}), \mathtt{out}(y_2, \mathtt{id}),$$
$$r_0\mathtt{:root}(\mathtt{id}), r_1\mathtt{:root}(\mathtt{id}), \mathsf{v}_0\mathtt{:site}(\mathtt{id}), \mathsf{v}_2\mathtt{:site}(\mathtt{id}),$$
$$r_0\mathtt{:control}(\mathsf{A}, \mathsf{v}_0, [y_0, \mathsf{e}_0]), \mathsf{v}_0\mathtt{:control}(\mathsf{C}, \mathsf{v}_1, [y_0, \mathsf{e}_1]),$$
$$r_1\mathtt{:control}(\mathsf{B}, \mathsf{v}_2, [y_1, y_2, \mathsf{e}_0, \mathsf{e}_1])$$

where $\Sigma = \langle \{r_0, r_1, \mathsf{v}_0, \mathsf{v}_1.\mathsf{v}_2, 0, 1\}, \{\infty\}, \{r_0 \leq \mathsf{v}_0 \leq \mathsf{v}_1; \mathsf{v}_0 \leq 0; r_1 \leq \mathsf{v}_2 \leq 1\} \rangle$.

We will now show that it is possible to define a function that takes a sequent encoding a bigraph and returns the bigraph itself. In order to be a bigraph encoding, a SEL sequent must be of a specific shape and satisfy some conditions which are specified in the definition that follows.

Definition 6 (Decoding Function). Let S be the following SEL sequent:

$$\vdash_\Sigma \{\mathtt{in}(x_i, l_{x_i}, \mathtt{id}) \mid 0 \leq i \leq n_x - 1\}, \{\mathtt{out}(y_i, \mathtt{id}) \mid 0 \leq i \leq n_y - 1\},$$
$$\{r_i\mathtt{:root}(\mathtt{id}) \mid 0 \leq i \leq n - 1\}, \{p_i\mathtt{:site}(\mathtt{id}) \mid 0 \leq i \leq n_v - 1\},$$
$$\{p_i\mathtt{:control}(\mathsf{K}_j, \mathsf{v}_i, L_j) \mid 0 \leq i \leq n_v - 1,\ 0 \leq j \leq n_k - 1\}$$

for integers n, n_x, n_y, n_v and n_k, satisfying the following conditions:

- x_i, y_i and r_i are free variables.
- L_i is a list of variables and constants.
- l_{x_i} is a variable that occurs as the first argument of an $\mathtt{out}$ predicate or a constant that occurs in a L_j for some j.
- p_i is either a variable that occurs as a label for some $\mathtt{root}$, or a constant that occurs as the second argument for some $\mathtt{control}$ predicate different than v_i.

---

[3] If a or b is a natural number $1 \leq i \leq m$ representing a root, than we map it to r_i in the subexponential signature.

- $p_i \leq v_i \in \Sigma$ *for each* p_i *labeling a* `control`(K_j, v_i, L_j).
- $p_i \leq i \in \Sigma$ *for each* p_i *labeling a* `site(id)`.
- *the relation* $\leq$ *in* Σ *defines a tree.*

Then, $D(S)$ *is a bigraph* $(V, E, ctrl, prnt, link) : \langle m, X \rangle \rightarrow \langle n, Y \rangle$ *over a signature* K, *where:*

- K *contains all the* K_j *with* $ar(K_j) = |L_j|$;
- $V = \{v_i | 0 \leq i \leq n_v - 1\}$;
- E *is the set of constants occurring in the lists* L_i;
- $ctrl(v_i) = K_j$ *if* l:`control`$(K_j, v_i, L) \in S$ *(for any* L);
- $prnt$ *is the same as the* $\leq$ *relation in* $\Sigma \setminus \{\varepsilon, \infty\}$;
- $link(x_i) = l_{x_i}$ *if* `in`$(x_i, l_{x_i}, \text{id})$;
- $link((v, i)) = l$ *if* `control`$(\_, v, L) \in S$ *and* $L[i] = l$;
- $X = \{x_i | 0 \leq i \leq n_x - 1\}$;
- $Y = \{y_i | 0 \leq i \leq n_y - 1\}$; *and*
- m *is the number of* `site(id)` *predicates.*

We will now show that D is a left-inverse of E.

Theorem 3 (Representational Adequacy). *Let* $\mathcal{B}$ *be a bigraph,* $S = E(\mathcal{B})$ *and* $\mathcal{B}' = D(S)$. *Then* $\mathcal{B} = \mathcal{B}'$[4].

Proof (sketch). For each element $V, E, prnt, ctrl, link, m, n, X$ and Y of a bigraph, E maps it to a certain element of S and D maps it back.   □

Theorem 4. *The function* D *is surjective, i.e., for every bigraph* $\mathcal{B}$, *there exists a SEL sequent* S *such that* $D(S) = \mathcal{B}$.

Proof. By the totality of E, we know that for every bigraph $\mathcal{B}$, there exists a sequent $S = E(\mathcal{B})$. From Theorem 3, we know that $D(S) = \mathcal{B}$.   □

An encoding of a bigraph in *SEL* will allow us to use the tools available in the logic to reason about it. In particular, we can use the informations about subexponentials to easily deduce when a node v_i is contained in v_j, even if v_j is not v_i's immediate parent.

Theorem 5. *Let* $\mathcal{B}$ *be a bigraph over a signature* K. *Assume that* Σ *is the subexponential signature generated by* $E(\mathcal{B})$. *If the sequent* $\vdash_\Sigma !^{r_j}(A)^\perp \mathbin{\text{⅋}} ?^{r_i} A$ *is provable for an arbitrary* A, *then the node* v_i *is contained in node* v_j *(with an arbitrary number of nestings) in* $\mathcal{B}$.

Proof. While deriving this sequent in *SEL*, the promotion rule generates the side condition $v_j \leq v_i$. Since $\leq$ is transitive, and the parent relation is the kernel of $\leq$, we have $prnt^k(v_i) = v_j$ for some k, so v_i is contained in v_j in $\mathcal{B}$.   □

---

[4] We always consider bigraphs to be equal up to the renaming of elements.

3.2 Juxtaposition

One of the two basic combination mechanisms for bigraphs is juxtaposition, which places two disjoint bigraphs "side-by-side". The formal definition can be found in [10, Definition 2.7]. At a basic level, this is easily achieved in terms of *SEL* sequents as we merely have to take the multiset join of the two encodings of the constituent bigraphs. However, it is not entirely trivial, since the roots and sites need to be renumbered.

Definition 7 (Juxtaposition). *Given* $\Sigma_1 = \langle \Lambda_1, \mathcal{U}_1, \leq_1 \rangle$ *and* $\Sigma_2 = \langle \Lambda_2, \mathcal{U}_2, \leq_2 \rangle$ *with* $\Lambda_1 \cap \Lambda_2 = \{\infty\}$ *that are the subexponential signatures for the encoding of two bigraphs with interfaces* $\langle n_1, X_1 \rangle \rightarrow \langle m_1, Y_1 \rangle$ *and* $\langle n_2, X_2 \rangle \rightarrow \langle m_2, Y_2 \rangle$ *respectively, the signature* $\Sigma_1 \mid \Sigma_2$ *with corresponding substitution on locations* σ *is defined to be the structure* $\langle \Lambda, \mathcal{U}, \leq \rangle$ *where:*

- $\sigma = \{r_{n_1+i}/r_i | 0 \leq i < n_2\}$.[5]
- $\Lambda = \Lambda_1 \cup \Lambda_2\sigma$ *and* $\mathcal{U} = \mathcal{U}_1 \cup \mathcal{U}_2\sigma$.
- $x \leq y$ *iff* $x \leq_1 y$ *or* $x\sigma \leq_2 y\sigma$.

(We use $\mid$ *instead of* $\otimes$ *to indicate juxtaposition to avoid confusion with the SEL connective.)*

Theorem 6 (Adequacy of juxtaposition). *Given disjoint bigraphs* $\mathcal{B}_1$ *and* $\mathcal{B}_2$, *let* $E(\mathcal{B}_1)$ *be* $\vdash_{\Sigma_1} \Gamma_1$ *and* $E(\mathcal{B}_2)$ *be* $\vdash_{\Sigma_2} \Gamma_2$, *such that both encodings use the same identifier* id. *Let* σ *be the substitution for* $\Sigma_1 \mid \Sigma_2$. *Then:* $E(\mathcal{B}_1 \mid \mathcal{B}_2) =\vdash_{\Sigma_1 \mid \Sigma_2} \Gamma_1, (\Gamma_2\sigma)$.

Proof Immediate by inspection.. □

Note that we only need to renumber the roots, since the sites are implicitly numbered in our encoding. This is a consequence of linearity (to distinguish sites) and subexponentials (used to name the immediate parent of every site).

3.3 Composition

The interface of a bigraph, *i.e.*, $\langle m, X \rangle \rightarrow \langle n, Y \rangle$, determines the available links and places for composition with another bigraph. A bigraph $\mathcal{B}_1 : \langle m_1, X_1 \rangle \rightarrow \langle n_1, Y_1 \rangle$ can be composed with a bigraph $\mathcal{B}_2 : \langle m_2, X_2 \rangle \rightarrow \langle n_2, Y_2 \rangle$ if $n_1 = m_2$ and $Y_1 = X_2$. This means that $\mathcal{B}_1$ has n_1 roots that will be placed inside $\mathcal{B}_2$'s m_2 sites, and all $\mathcal{B}_1$'s outer names Y_1 will be connected with $\mathcal{B}_2$'s inner names X_2. This composition is denoted by $\mathcal{B}_2 \circ \mathcal{B}_1$. For a formal definition of bigraph composition, see [10, Definition 2.5]. Such compositions can be adequately captured in our framework by a focused derivation of formulas which will encode the operations of (1) connecting links and (2) placing roots inside sites.

Let $S_1 = E(\mathcal{B}_1)$ be the sequent $\vdash_{\Sigma_1} \Gamma_1$ and $S_2 = E(\mathcal{B}_2)$ be $\vdash_{\Sigma_2} \Gamma_2$ such that the names in S_1 do not clash with those of S_2.[6]. The composition of these into one bigraph will require a common subexponential signature, defined below.

---

[5] t/s denotes the substitution of s by t.

[6] This is always possible due to renaming and α-equivalence.

Definition 8 *Let $\Sigma_1 = \langle \Lambda_1, \mathcal{U}_1, \leq_1 \rangle$ and $\Sigma_2 = \langle \Lambda_2, \mathcal{U}_2, \leq_2 \rangle$ be such that $\Lambda_1 \cap \Lambda_2 = \{\infty\}$. Then, $\Sigma_2 \circ \Sigma_1$ is the signature $\langle \Lambda, \mathcal{U}, \leq \rangle \; \sigma$ such that*

$$\Lambda = \Lambda_1 \cup \Lambda_2, \quad \mathcal{U} = \mathcal{U}_1 \cup \mathcal{U}_2, \quad \leq \, = \leq_1 \cup \leq_2, \quad \sigma = \{\mathtt{v}_i/r_j | v_i \in \Lambda_2 \text{ and } r_j \in \Lambda_1\}.$$

The substitution σ defines a map between sites and roots.[7] In the subexponential signature, this means that the root r_j will be instantiated with the index $\mathtt{v}_i$ at the same time that one of its successors (i.e., a site) is removed, which is equivalent to replacing a numeric successor of v_i by the subtree of r_j.

The composed subexponential signature yields the definition of the formulas encoding the operations of linking and placing. Consider the sequent:

$$\vdash_\Sigma \Gamma_1, \Gamma_2, \infty{:}\exists e. \, (\mathtt{in}(e, e, \mathtt{id2}))^\perp \otimes (\mathtt{out}(e, \mathtt{id1}))^\perp \otimes \perp$$

where all free variables are interpreted as existential variables, *i.e.*, they are unified with terms in applications of the [init] rule. We will henceforth denote this existentially quantified formula in zone ∞ by $\mathtt{CF}(\mathcal{B}_1, \mathcal{B}_2)$. Focusing on $\mathtt{CF}(\mathcal{B}_1, \mathcal{B}_2)$ will result on three premises:

$$P_1 :\vdash_\Sigma \Gamma, (\mathtt{in}(\mathtt{e}, \mathtt{e}, \mathtt{id2}))^\perp \qquad P_2 :\vdash_\Sigma \Gamma', (\mathtt{out}(\mathtt{e}, \mathtt{id1}))^\perp \qquad P_3 :\vdash_\Sigma \Gamma'', \perp$$

In order to prove P_1 and P_2 it must be the case that $\Gamma = \{\mathtt{in}(x, \mathtt{e}, \mathtt{id2})\}$ and $\Gamma' = \{\mathtt{out}(y, \mathtt{id1})\}$. Since these are linear resources, they will not be in Γ''. The unification of the atoms in the initial rule will generate the substitutions $[\mathtt{e}/x]$ and $[\mathtt{e}/y]$, which will be propagated to the formulas in Γ''. While the substitution on x will have no effect (each inner channel occurs only once in the encoded sequent, see Definition 5), the substitution on y will rename an outer channel to a concrete edge which is connected to another component. It will instantiate variables in some `control`'s list of links L, *i.e.*, a `control` in $\mathcal{B}_1$ which was connected to an outer channel y will become connected to a real edge $\mathtt{e}$ in $\mathcal{B}_2$.

The constants `id1` and `id2` guarantee that such channels belong to different bigraphs. Each time a focused derivation is performed on this formula, a connection will be made. All connections will have been made once the formula can no longer be derived.

It is also possible to perform the linking without using free variables and unification by first guessing a linking and then performing proof search to ensure that such a linking exists. Since the bigraphs are composable by assumption, a valid instantiation for the variables always exists. Our search procedure will have to check that all the in links of the outer bigraph have been instantiated in either view of the linking procedure.

The next step is to place $\mathcal{B}_1$'s roots inside $\mathcal{B}_2$'s sites. For this operation, we will need to reason on (and unify) subexponentials. The formula used for placement is constructed according to the sites available in $\mathcal{B}_2$. Let $L = \{l | l{:}\mathtt{site}(\mathtt{id2}) \in \Gamma_2\}$;

---

[7] Note that, by the definition of substitution, the r_j must be pairwise distinct. In contrast, $\mathtt{v}_i$ can be repeated in case a node contains more than one site.

then: $\vdash_\Sigma \Gamma_1, \Gamma_2, \left\{ (?^l \, \texttt{site(id2)})^\perp \otimes (?^l \, \texttt{root(id1)})^\perp \otimes \perp | l \in L \right\}$ is derivable. We will henceforth denote this defined set of formulas as $\texttt{PF}(\mathcal{B}_1, \mathcal{B}_2)$. A focused derivation on each of formulas in $\texttt{PF}(\mathcal{B}_1, \mathcal{B}_2)$ will behave similarly to the case of $\texttt{CF}$: three premises will be generated.

$$P_1 :\vdash_\Sigma \Gamma, l{:}(\texttt{site(id2)})^\perp \qquad P_2 :\vdash_\Sigma \Gamma', l{:}(\texttt{root(id1)})^\perp \qquad P_3 :\vdash_\Sigma \Gamma'', \perp$$

And in order to prove P_1 and P_2 it is necessary that $\Gamma = \{l{:}\texttt{site(id2)}\}$ and $\Gamma' = \{r{:}\texttt{root(id1)}\}$. Since r is a variable, we obtain the substitution $[l/r]$ when proving P_2 which is propagated to Γ''. The variable r represented a root in $\mathcal{B}_1$, while l is the place where a site is located in $\mathcal{B}_2$. Note that Γ'' might have occurrences of r as the label of other formulas, and by replacing it with l, we are in fact changing the location of some formulas. They are moved from the root r in $\mathcal{B}_1$ to a location l in $\mathcal{B}_2$, which is exactly what happens during composition of places. The subexponential signature also needs to be changed accordingly, and this is done by accumulating this substitution in Σ's σ.

Note that, since $\texttt{PF}$ is a linear set, the connection of roots to nodes will only be complete once all formulas in the set are derived. Of course this will be composed of many focused phases.

We can now combine the operations of linking and placement to obtain a sequent whose derivation will result on a premise that encodes the composition of two bigraphs. We will require that such derivation is *exhaustive*, meaning that the formulas in ∞ are focused on until they can no longer be derived and there are no positive formulas in ε.

Theorem 7 (Adequacy of Bigraph Composition). *Let $\mathcal{B}_1$ and $\mathcal{B}_2$ be two bigraphs such that their composition $\mathcal{B}_2 \circ \mathcal{B}_1 = \mathcal{B}$ is well defined. Let $E(\mathcal{B}_1) = \vdash_{\Sigma_1} \Gamma_1$, $E(\mathcal{B}_2) = \vdash_{\Sigma_2} \Gamma_2$ and $\Sigma = \Sigma_2 \circ \Sigma_1$. Then the exhaustive focused derivation of the sequent $\vdash_\Sigma \Gamma_1, \Gamma_2, \texttt{CF}(\mathcal{B}_1, \mathcal{B}_1), \texttt{PF}(\mathcal{B}_1, \mathcal{B}_2)$ will have exactly one open premise $\vdash_\Sigma \Gamma, \infty{:}\Delta$ with $D(\vdash_\Sigma \Gamma) = \mathcal{B}$.*

Proof (sketch). After exhaustive proof search, the failure to derive $\texttt{CF}(\mathcal{B}_1, \mathcal{B}_2)$ and the derivation of all formulas in $\texttt{PF}(\mathcal{B}_1, \mathcal{B}_2)$ means that there are no more $\texttt{in}(x, e, \texttt{id2})$, $\texttt{out}(y, \texttt{id1})$, $\texttt{site(id2)}$ and $\texttt{root(id1)}$ in the sequent. The fact that the bigraphs were compatible for composition in the first place, and the unique identifier in the atoms, guarantees that each of the predicates occurring in the sequent have the same multiplicity (number of inner links and sites of $\mathcal{B}_2$ must be the same as the number of outer links and roots of $\mathcal{B}_1$, respectively). The unifications during the derivations of $\texttt{CF}$'s will ensure that outer links in $\mathcal{B}_1$ are renamed to the proper edges or outer links of $\mathcal{B}_2$. The unifications during the derivations of $\texttt{PF}$'s will ensure that all elements inside of a root in $\mathcal{B}_1$ are correctly placed in the parent of the respective site in $\mathcal{B}_2$. Therefore, decoding the sequent without the ∞-formulas produces a bigraph with the desired structure. $\square$

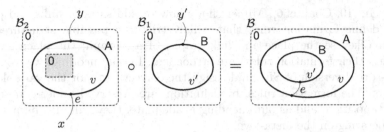

Fig. 4. Bigraph composition

As an example, consider the composition depicted in Fig. 4. The encoding of each operand will be:

$$E(\mathcal{B}_1): \quad \Gamma_1 = \mathtt{out}(y', \mathtt{id1}), r_0':\mathtt{root}(\mathtt{id1}), r_0':\mathtt{control}(\mathtt{B}, \mathtt{v}', [y'])$$
$$\Sigma_1 = (\{r_0', \mathtt{v}', \infty\}, \{\infty\}, \{r_0' \leq_1 \mathtt{v}'\})$$

$$E(\mathcal{B}_2): \quad \Gamma_2 = \mathtt{in}(x, \mathtt{e}, \mathtt{id2}), \mathtt{out}(y, \mathtt{id2}), r_0:\mathtt{root}(\mathtt{id2}),$$
$$\mathtt{v}:\mathtt{site}(\mathtt{id2}), r_0:\mathtt{control}(\mathtt{A}, \mathtt{v}, [y, \mathtt{e}])$$
$$\Sigma_2 = (\{r_0, \mathtt{v}, 0, \infty\}, \{\infty\}, \{r_0 \leq_2 \mathtt{v} \leq_2 0\})$$

The formulas encoding the operation are:

$$\mathtt{CF}(\mathcal{B}_1, \mathcal{B}_2): \quad \infty:\exists e.\, \mathtt{in}(e, e, \mathtt{id2})^{\perp} \otimes \mathtt{out}(e, \mathtt{id1})^{\perp} \otimes \perp$$

$$\mathtt{PF}(\mathcal{B}_1, \mathcal{B}_2): \quad \left\{ \varepsilon:(?^v\, \mathtt{site}(\mathtt{id2}))^{\perp} \otimes (?^v\, \mathtt{root}(\mathtt{id1}))^{\perp} \otimes \perp \right\}$$

The formula CF can only be derived once, indeed there is only one formula of each kind: $\mathtt{in}(x, \mathtt{e}, \mathtt{id2})$ and $\mathtt{out}(y', \mathtt{id1})$. As a result of this derivation, we will obtain the following substitution: $[e/x, y']$. The derivation of the only formula in PF will provide the substitution $\sigma = [\mathtt{v}/r_0']$ for the subexponentials and formula labels. The resulting open sequent will be $\vdash_\Sigma \Gamma$, where:

$$\Gamma = \varepsilon : \mathtt{out}(y, \mathtt{id2})\,,\; r_0 : \mathtt{root}(\mathtt{id2})\,,\; r_0 : \mathtt{control}(\mathtt{A}, \mathtt{v}, [y, \mathtt{e}])\,,\; \mathtt{v} : \mathtt{control}(\mathtt{B}, \mathtt{v}', [\mathtt{e}])$$
$$\Sigma = (\{r_0, \mathtt{v}, 0, \mathtt{v}', \infty\}, \{\infty\}, \{r_0 \leq \mathtt{v} \leq \mathtt{v}'\}).$$

4   Conclusions, Related Work, and Perspectives

Conclusions. Using the expressive power of subexponentials, we have given an adequate encoding of pure bigraphs in *SEL*. We were able to reason about the static structure of bigraphs with only the subexponential signature generated from the encoding. With the full sequent encoding of two bigraphs, we can easily simulate juxtaposition and we can emulate composition using a (focused) derivation in *SELF*.

Sorting. In [10, Chapter 6], Milner shows how to add sorts to links and places, and to define formation rules that will restrict the possible structures of a bigraph. Likewise the place and link graphs of a bigraph, the place and link sorts (and their formation rules) are orthogonal. In our encoding, we would use a multi-sorted version of *SEL* and assign the correct sorts for the variables and constants. The formation rules, by definition, are preserved under composition and juxtaposition, and as our encoding is adequate, they will also be preserved when operating on the meta-level.

Link sorting assigns sorts for each member of the arity of the controls and additionally to the inner and outer edges. The formation rules dictate what sorts of links a hyperedge may have in its extremities. In our encoding, we could transform each control K into a function symbol taking a list of arguments of appropriate type. In this case, the predicates `control(_, K, [`$l_1, \ldots, l_n$`])` become `control(_, K(`$l_1, \ldots, l_n$`))`. Since K is always a constant in the encoding, this change is harmless. As for the inner and outer edges, we simply need to assign the correct types to the x and y variables. Unification will guarantee that the correct type is used on the connections when operating on the encoded bigraphs.

Place sorting assigns sorts for each control K and formation rules determine what sorts can be contained in others. In our encoding, controls are assigned to vertices via the `control` predicate, but the containment relation is modeled by the relation between subexponentials. For this reason, adding sorts to places is a little more tricky then link sorting, but still possible. Sorts now have to be assigned to the v constants, representing nodes and, consistently, to the v subexponentials. Note that we bypass the sorts of controls and deal directly with the nodes (except sites and roots).

Bigraphs with Sharing. The pure bigraphs (with or without sorting) presented so far are sometimes not expressive enough; in particular, the tree-nature of the place graph is often too restrictive. In [16], the place graph was generalized from trees to arbitrary DAGs, allowing it to model an arbitrary Boolean combination of places. For our encoding, supporting DAGs is no harder than trees: our $\leq$ relation simply needs to be generalized to partial orders. This is easy: the meta-theory of *SEL* only requires $\leq$ to be a pre-order, so arbitrary directed graphs (acyclic or not) can be supported. The rest of the encoding remains unchanged.

Directed Bigraphs. A comparatively non-trivial extension is to move from an arbitrary (possibly sorted) hypergraph for the link graph to a directed link graph with link names as nodes [7]. While such a change of perspective does not need a modification of the encoding of bigraphs in this paper, adequacy is a bit more delicate. Specifically, the decoding function D needs to know the exact signature of link names since the encoding represents link names as constants and not as linear resources. If we were to change the encoding to track the link names linearly, then the composition operation will need to be extended with new rules for pairing up the link names.

Perspectives. The most interesting followup to this work would be to develop the necessary reasoning on *SEL* encodings in order to get a bisimulation of bigraph *reactions*. In this way, we would have a full syntactical description of bigraphs with the advantage of having available automated proof theory tools.

Acknowledgment. This work was partially supported by the ERC Advanced Grant *ProofCert*.

References

1. Beauquier, M., Schürmann, C.: A bigraph relational model. In: LFMTP, vol. 71 of EPTCS, pp. 14–28 (2011)
2. Cardelli, L.: Brane calculi. In: Danos, V., Schachter, V. (eds.) CMSB 2004. LNCS (LNBI), vol. 3082, pp. 257–278. Springer, Heidelberg (2005)
3. Cardelli, L., Gordon, A.D.: Mobile ambients. In: Nivat, M. (ed.) FOSSACS 1998. LNCS, vol. 1378, p. 140. Springer, Heidelberg (1998)
4. Chaudhuri, K.: Classical and intuitionistic subexponential logics are equally expressive. In: Dawar, A., Veith, H. (eds.) CSL 2010. LNCS, vol. 6247, pp. 185–199. Springer, Heidelberg (2010)
5. Chaudhuri, K.: Undecidability of multiplicative subexponential logic. In: 3rd LINEARITY, vol. 176 of EPTCS, pp. 1–8, July 2014
6. Danos, V., Joinet, J.-B., Schellinx, H.: The structure of exponentials: Uncovering the dynamics of linear logic proofs. In: Gottlob, G., Leitsch, A., Mundici, D. (eds.) Computational Logic and Proof Theory. LNCS, vol. 713, pp. 159–171. Springer, Heidelberg (1993)
7. Grohmann, D., Miculan, M.: Directed bigraphs. ENTCS **173**, 121–137 (2007)
8. Jensen, O.H., Milner, R.: Bigraphs and mobile processes (revised). Technical Report UCAM-CL-TR-580, University of Cambridge, February 2004
9. Milner, R.: Pure bigraphs: Structure and dynamics. Inf. Comput. **204**(1), 60–122 (2006)
10. Milner, R.: The Space and Motion of Communicating Agents. Cambridge University Press, Cambridge (2009)
11. Nigam, V.: Exploiting non-canonicity in the sequent calculus. Ph.D. thesis, Ecole Polytechnique, September 2009
12. Nigam, V., Miller, D.: Algorithmic specifications in linear logic with subexponentials. In: PPDP, pp. 129–140 (2009)
13. Nigam, V., Olarte, C., Pimentel, E.: On subexponentials, focusing and modalities in concurrent systems. Draft Manuscript submitted for publication (2015)
14. Nigam, V., Pimentel, E., Reis, G.: An extended framework for specifying and reasoning about proof systems. J. of Logic Comput. (2014). doi:10.1093/logcom/exu029, http://logcom.oxfordjournals.org/content/early/2014/06/06/logcom.exu029
15. Păun, G.: Membrane computing. Handbook of Natural Computing, pp. 1355–1377. Springer, Heidelberg (2012)
16. Sevegnani, M., Calder, M.: Bigraphs with sharing. Theor. Comput. Sci. **577**, 43–73 (2015)

Controller Synthesis for MDPs and Frequency LTL\GU

Vojtěch Forejt[1], Jan Krčál[2](✉), and Jan Křetínský[3,4]

[1] Department of Computer Science, University of Oxford, Oxford, UK
forejtv@gmail.com
[2] Department of Computer Science, Saarland University, Saarbrücken, Germany
krcal@cs.uni-saarland.de
[3] IST Austria, Klosterneuburg, Austria
jan.kretinsky@ist.ac.at
[4] Technische Universität München, München, Germany

Abstract. Quantitative extensions of temporal logics have recently attracted significant attention. In this work, we study frequency LTL (fLTL), an extension of LTL which allows to speak about frequencies of events along an execution. Such an extension is particularly useful for probabilistic systems that often cannot fulfil strict qualitative guarantees on the behaviour. It has been recently shown that controller synthesis for Markov decision processes and fLTL is decidable when all the bounds on frequencies are 1. As a step towards a complete quantitative solution, we show that the problem is decidable for the fragment fLTL\GU, where **U** does not occur in the scope of **G** (but still **F** can). Our solution is based on a novel translation of such quantitative formulae into equivalent deterministic automata.

1 Introduction

Markov decision processes (MDP) are a common choice when modelling systems that exhibit (un)controllable and probabilistic behaviour. In controller synthesis of MDPs, the goal is then to steer the system so that it meets certain property. Many properties specifying the desired behaviour, such as "the system is always responsive" can be easily captured by Linear Temporal Logic (LTL). This logic is in its nature qualitative and cannot express *quantitative* linear-time properties such as "a given failure happens only *rarely*". To overcome this limitation, especially apparent for stochastic systems, extensions of LTL with *frequency* operators have been recently studied [7,8].

Such extensions come at a cost, and for example the "frequency until" operator can make the controller-synthesis problem undecidable already for non-stochastic systems [7,8]. It turns out [19,30,31] that a way of providing significant added expressive power while preserving tractability is to extend LTL only by the "frequency globally" formulae $\mathbf{G}^{\geq p}\varphi$. Such a formula is satisfied if the long-run frequency of satisfying φ on an infinite path is at least p. More

© Springer-Verlag Berlin Heidelberg 2015
M. Davis et al. (Eds.): LPAR-20 2015, LNCS 9450, pp. 162–177, 2015.
DOI: 10.1007/978-3-662-48899-7_12

formally, $\mathbf{G}^{\geq p}\varphi$ is true on an infinite path $s_0 s_1 \cdots$ of an MDP if and only if $\frac{1}{n} \cdot |\{i \mid i < n \text{ and } s_i s_{i+1} \cdots \text{ satisfies } \varphi\}|$ is at least p as n tends to infinity. Because the relevant limit might not be defined, we need to consider two distinct operators, $\mathbf{G}^{\geq p}_{\inf}$ and $\mathbf{G}^{\geq p}_{\sup}$, whose definitions use limit inferior and limit superior, respectively. We call the resulting logic *frequency LTL (fLTL)*.

So far, MDP controller synthesis for fLTL has been shown decidable for the fragment containing only the operator $\mathbf{G}^{\geq 1}_{\inf}$ [19]. Our paper makes a significant further step towards the ultimate goal of a model checking procedure for the whole fLTL. We address the general *quantitative* setting with arbitrary frequency bounds p and consider the fragment fLTL\GU, which is obtained from frequency LTL by preventing the $\mathbf{U}$ operator from occurring inside $\mathbf{G}$ or $\mathbf{G}^{\geq p}$ formulas (but still allowing the $\mathbf{F}$ operator to occur anywhere in the formula). The approach we take is completely different from [19] where ad hoc product MDP construction is used, heavily relying on existence of certain types of strategies in the $\mathbf{G}^{\geq 1}_{\inf}$ case. In this paper we provide, to the best of our knowledge, the first translation of a quantitative logic to equivalent *deterministic* automata. This allows us to take the standard automata-theoretic approach to verification [33]: after obtaining the finite automaton, we do not deal with the structure of the formula originally given, and we solve a (reasonably simple) synthesis problem on a product of the single automaton with the MDP.

Relations of various kinds of logics and automata are widely studied (see e.g. [16,29,32]), and our results provide new insights into this area for quantitative logics. Previous work [31] offered only translation of a similar logic to *non-deterministic* "mean-payoff Büchi automata" noting that it is difficult to give an analogous reduction to *deterministic* "mean-payoff Rabin automata". The reason is that the non-determinism is inherently present in the form of guessing whether the subformulas of $\mathbf{G}^{\geq p}$ are satisfied on a suffix. Our construction overcomes this difficulty and offers equivalent deterministic automata. It is a first and highly non-trivial step towards providing a reduction for the complete logic.

Although our algorithm does not allow us to handle the extension of the whole LTL, the considered fragment fLTL\GU contains a large class of formulas and offers significant expressive power. It subsumes the GR(1) fragment of LTL [5], which has found use in synthesis for hardware designs. The $\mathbf{U}$ operator, although not allowed within a scope of a $\mathbf{G}$ operator, can still be used for example to distinguish paths based on their prefixes. As an example synthesis problem expressible in this fragment, consider a cluster of servers where each server plays either a role of a load-balancer or a worker. On startup, each server listens for a message specifying its role. A load-balancer forwards each request and only waits for a confirmation whereas a worker processes the requests itself. A specification for a single server in the cluster can require, for example, that the following formula (with propositions explained above) holds with probability at least 0.95:

$$\Big((l\,\mathbf{U}\,b) \rightarrow \mathbf{G}^{\geq 0.99}\big(\mathbf{r} \rightarrow \mathbf{X}(\mathbf{f} \wedge \mathbf{Fc})\big) \Big) \wedge \Big((l\,\mathbf{U}\,w) \rightarrow \mathbf{G}^{\geq 0.85}\big(\mathbf{r} \rightarrow (\mathbf{Xp} \vee \mathbf{XXp})\big) \Big)$$

Related Work. Frequency LTL was studied in another variant in [7,8] where a *frequency until* operator is introduced in two different LTL-like logics, and undecidability is proved for problems relevant to our setting. The work [7] also yields decidability with restricted nesting of the frequency until operator; as the decidable fragment in [7] does not contain frequency-globally operator, it is not possible to express many useful properties expressible in our logic. A logic that speaks about frequencies on a finite interval was introduced in [30], but the paper provides algorithms only for Markov chains and a bounded fragment of the logic.

Model checking MDPs against LTL objectives relies on the automata-theoretic approach, namely on translating LTL to automata that are to some extent deterministic [15]. This typically involves translating LTL to non-deterministic automata, which are then determinized using e.g. Safra's construction. During the determinization, the original structure of the formula is lost, which prevents us from extending this technique to the frequency setting. However, an alternative technique of translating LTL directly to deterministic automata has been developed [17,25,26], where the logical structure is preserved. In our work, we extend the algorithm for $\text{LTL}_{\setminus \text{GU}}$ partially sketched in [25]. In Sect. 6, we explain why adapting the algorithm for full LTL [17] is difficult. Translation of $\text{LTL}_{\setminus \text{GU}}$ to other kinds of automata has been considered also in [22].

Our technique relies on a solution of a multi-objective mean-payoff problem on MDP [9,13]. Previous results only consider limit inferior rewards, and so we cannot use them as off-the-shelf results, but need to adapt them first to our setting with both inferior and superior limits together with Rabin condition. There are several works that combine mean-payoff objectives with e.g. logics or parity objectives, but in most cases only simple atomic propositions can be used to define the payoff [4,6,11]. The work [3] extends LTL with another form of quantitative operators, allowing accumulated weight constraint expressed using automata, again not allowing quantification over complex formulas. Further, [1] introduces a variant of LTL with a discounted-future operator. Finally, techniques closely related to the ones in this paper are used in [14,18,28].

Our Contributions. To our best knowledge, this paper gives the first decidability result for probabilistic verification against linear-time temporal logics extended by *quantitative* frequency operators with *complex nested subformulas* of the logic. It works in two steps, keeping the same time complexity as for ordinary LTL. In the first step, a $\text{fLTL}_{\setminus \text{GU}}$ formula gets translated to an equivalent *deterministic* generalized Rabin automaton extended with mean-payoff objectives. This step is inspired by previous work [25], but the extension with auxiliary automata for $\mathbf{G}^{\geq p}$ requires a different construction. The second step is the analysis of MDPs against conjunction of limit inferior mean-payoff, limit superior mean-payoff, and generalized Rabin objectives. This result is obtained by adapting and combining several existing involved proof techniques [10,13].

The paper is organised as follows: the main algorithm is given in Sect. 3, relegating details of the two steps above to Sects. 4 and 5. Full proofs are in [20].

2   Preliminaries

We use $\mathbb{N}$ and $\mathbb{Q}$ to denote the sets of non-negative integers and rational numbers. The set of all distributions over a countable set X is denoted by $Dist(X)$. For a predicate P, the *indicator function* $\mathbb{1}_P$ equals 1 if P is true, and 0 if P is false.

Markov Decision Processes (MDPs). An MDP is a tuple $\mathsf{M} = (S, A, Act, \delta, \hat{s})$ where S is a finite set of states, A is a finite set of actions, $Act : S \to 2^A \setminus \{\emptyset\}$ assigns to each state s the set $Act(s)$ of actions enabled in s, $\delta : A \to Dist(S)$ is a probabilistic transition function that given an action a gives a probability distribution over the successor states, and $\hat{s}$ is the initial state. To simplify notation, w.l.o.g. we require that every action is enabled in exactly one state.

Strategies. A strategy in an MDP M is a "recipe" to choose actions. Formally, it is a function $\sigma : (SA)^*S \to Dist(A)$ that given a finite path w, representing the history of a play, gives a probability distribution over the actions enabled in the last state. A strategy σ in M induces a *Markov chain* M^σ which is a tuple $(L, P, \hat{s})$ where the set of *locations* $L = (S \times A)^* \times S$ encodes the history of the play, $\hat{s}$ is an *initial location*, and P is a *probabilistic transition function* that assigns to each location a probability distribution over successor locations defined by $P(h)(h\,a\,s) = \sigma(h)(a) \cdot \delta(a)(s)$. for all $h \in (SA)^*S$, $a \in A$ and $s \in S$.

The probability space of the runs of the Markov chain is denoted by $\mathbb{P}_\mathsf{M}^\sigma$ and defined in the standard way [20,21].

End Components. A tuple (T, B) with $\emptyset \neq T \subseteq S$ and $B \subseteq \bigcup_{t \in T} Act(t)$ is an *end component* of M if (1) for all $a \in B$, whenever $\delta(a)(s') > 0$ then $s' \in T$; and (2) for all $s, t \in T$ there is a path $w = s_1 a_1 \cdots a_{k-1} s_k$ such that $s_1 = s$, $s_k = t$, and all states and actions that appear in w belong to T and B, respectively. An end component (T, B) is a *maximal end component (MEC)* if it is maximal with respect to the componentwise subset ordering. Given an MDP, the set of MECs is denoted by MEC. Finally, an MDP is *strongly connected* if (S, A) is a MEC.

Frequency Linear Temporal Logic (fLTL). The formulae of the logic fLTL are given by the following syntax:

$$\varphi \quad ::= \quad \mathbf{tt} \mid \mathbf{ff} \mid a \mid \neg a \mid \varphi \wedge \varphi \mid \varphi \vee \varphi \mid \mathbf{X}\varphi \mid \mathbf{F}\varphi \mid \mathbf{G}\varphi \mid \varphi\mathbf{U}\varphi \mid \mathbf{G}_{\mathrm{ext}}^{\bowtie p}\varphi$$

over a finite set Ap of atomic propositions, $\bowtie \in \{\geq, >\}$, $p \in [0,1] \cap \mathbb{Q}$, and $\mathrm{ext} \in \{\inf, \sup\}$. A formula that is neither a conjunction, nor a disjunction is called *non-Boolean*. The set of non-Boolean subformulas of φ is denoted by $\mathsf{sf}(\varphi)$.

Words and fLTL Semantics. Let $w \in (2^{Ap})^\omega$ be an infinite word. The ith letter of w is denoted $w[i]$, i.e. $w = w[0]w[1]\cdots$. We write w^{ij} for the finite word $w[i]w[i+1]\cdots w[j]$, and $w^{i\infty}$ or just wi for the suffix $w[i]w[i+1]\cdots$. The semantics of a formula on a word w is defined inductively: for $\mathbf{tt}$, $\mathbf{ff}$, $\wedge$, $\vee$, and for atomic propositions and their negations, the definition is straightforward, for the remaining operators we define:

$$w \models \mathbf{X}\varphi \iff w^1 \models \varphi \qquad\qquad w \models \varphi\mathbf{U}\psi \iff \exists k \in \mathbb{N} : w^k \models \psi \text{ and}$$
$$w \models \mathbf{F}\varphi \iff \exists k \in \mathbb{N} : w^k \models \varphi \qquad\qquad\qquad \forall 0 \leq j < k : w^j \models \varphi$$
$$w \models \mathbf{G}\varphi \iff \forall k \in \mathbb{N} : w^k \models \varphi \quad w \models \mathbf{G}_{\text{ext}}^{\bowtie p}\varphi \iff \text{lr}_{\text{ext}}(\mathbb{1}_{w^0 \models \varphi}\mathbb{1}_{w^1 \models \varphi}\cdots) \bowtie p$$

where we set $\text{lr}_{\text{ext}}(q_1 q_2 \cdots) := \lim \text{ext}_{i \to \infty} \frac{1}{i} \sum_{j=1}^{i} q_i$. By $\mathsf{L}(\varphi)$ we denote the set $\{w \in (2^{Ap})^\omega \mid w \models \varphi\}$ of words satisfying φ.

The $\text{fLTL}_{\backslash \mathbf{GU}}$ fragment of fLTL is defined by disallowing occurrences of $\mathbf{U}$ in $\mathbf{G}$-formulae, i.e. it is given by the following syntax for φ:

$$\varphi :: = a \mid \neg a \mid \varphi \wedge \varphi \mid \varphi \vee \varphi \mid \mathbf{X}\varphi \mid \varphi\mathbf{U}\varphi \mid \mathbf{F}\varphi \mid \mathbf{G}\xi \mid \mathbf{G}_{\text{ext}}^{\bowtie p}\xi$$
$$\xi :: = a \mid \neg a \mid \xi \wedge \xi \mid \xi \vee \xi \mid \mathbf{X}\xi \mid \mathbf{F}\xi \mid \mathbf{G}\xi \mid \mathbf{G}_{\text{ext}}^{\bowtie p}\xi$$

Note that restricting negations to atomic propositions is without loss of generality as all operators are closed under negation, for example $\neg\mathbf{G}_{\text{inf}}^{\geq p}\varphi \equiv \mathbf{G}_{\text{sup}}^{> 1-p}\neg\varphi$ or $\neg\mathbf{G}_{\text{sup}}^{\geq p}\varphi \equiv \mathbf{G}_{\text{inf}}^{\geq 1-p}\neg\varphi$. Furthermore, we could easily allow $\bowtie$ to range also over $\leq$ and $<$ as $\mathbf{G}_{\text{inf}}^{\leq p}\varphi \equiv \mathbf{G}_{\text{sup}}^{\geq 1-p}\neg\varphi$ and $\mathbf{G}_{\text{inf}}^{< p}\varphi \equiv \mathbf{G}_{\text{sup}}^{\geq 1-p}\neg\varphi$.

Automata. Let us fix a finite alphabet Σ. A deterministic *labelled transition system (LTS)* over Σ is a tuple (Q, q_0, δ) where Q is a finite set of states, q_0 is the initial state, and $\delta : Q \times \Sigma \to Q$ is a partial transition function. We denote $\delta(q, a) = q'$ also by $q \xrightarrow{a} q'$. A *run* of the LTS $\mathcal{S}$ over an infinite word w is a sequence of states $\mathcal{S}(w) = q_0 q_1 \cdots$ such that $q_{i+1} = \delta(q_i, w[i])$. For a finite word w of length n, we denote by $\mathcal{S}(w)$ the state q_n in which $\mathcal{S}$ is after reading w.

An *acceptance condition* is a positive boolean formula over formal variables

$$\{Inf(S), Fin(S), MP_{\text{ext}}^{\bowtie p}(r) \mid S \subseteq Q, \text{ext} \in \{\inf, \sup\}, \bowtie \in \{\geq, >\}, p \in \mathbb{Q}, r : Q \to \mathbb{Q}\}.$$

Given a run ρ and an acceptance condition α, we assign truth values as follows:

- $Inf(S)$ is true iff ρ visits (some state of) S infinitely often,
- $Fin(S)$ is true iff ρ visits (all states of) S finitely often,
- $MP_{\text{ext}}^{\bowtie p}(r)$ is true iff $\text{lr}_{\text{ext}}(r(\rho[0])r(\rho[1])\cdots) \bowtie p$.

The run ρ satisfies α if this truth-assignment makes α true. An *automaton* $\mathcal{A}$ is an LTS with an acceptance condition α. The language of $\mathcal{A}$, denoted by $\mathsf{L}(\mathcal{A})$, is the set of all words inducing a run satisfying α. An acceptance condition α is a *Büchi, generalized Büchi,* or *co-Büchi* acceptance condition if it is of the form $Inf(S)$, $\bigwedge_i Inf(S_i)$, or $Fin(S)$, respectively. Further, α is a *generalized Rabin mean-payoff,* or a *generalized Büchi mean-payoff* acceptance condition if it is in disjunctive normal form, or if it is a conjunction not containing any $Fin(S)$, respectively. For each acceptance condition we define a corresponding automaton, e.g. *deterministic generalized Rabin mean-payoff automaton (DGRMA)*.

3   Model-Checking Algorithm

In this section, we state the problem of model checking MDPs against $\text{fLTL}_{\backslash \mathbf{GU}}$ specifications and provide a solution. As a black-box we use two novel routines described in detail in the following two sections. All proofs are in the appendix.

Given an MDP M and a valuation $\nu : S \to 2^{Ap}$ of its states, we say that its run $\omega = s_0 a_0 s_1 a_1 \cdots$ *satisfies* φ, written $\omega \models \varphi$, if $\nu(s_0)\nu(s_1)\cdots \models \varphi$. We use $\mathbb{P}^\sigma[\varphi]$ as a shorthand for the probability of all runs satisfying φ, i.e. $\mathbb{P}^\sigma_M[\{\omega \mid \omega \models \varphi\}]$. This paper is concerned with the following task:

Controller synthesis problem: Given an MDP with a valuation, an fLTL$_{\backslash \mathbf{GU}}$ formula φ and $x \in [0, 1]$, decide whether $\mathbb{P}^\sigma[\varphi] \geq x$ for some strategy σ, and if so, construct such a *witness* strategy.

The following is the main result of the paper.

Theorem 1. *The controller synthesis problem for MDPs and fLTL$_{\backslash \mathbf{GU}}$ is decidable and the witness strategy can be constructed in doubly exponential time.*

In this section, we present an algorithm for Theorem 1. The skeleton of our algorithm is the same as for the standard model-checking algorithm for MDPs against LTL. It proceeds in three steps. Given an MDP M and a formula φ,

1. compute a deterministic automaton $\mathcal{A}$ such that $\mathsf{L}(\mathcal{A}) = \mathsf{L}(\varphi)$,
2. compute the product MDP M $\times$ $\mathcal{A}$,
3. analyse the product MDP M $\times$ $\mathcal{A}$.

In the following, we concretize these three steps to fit our setting.

1. Deterministic Automaton. For ordinary LTL, usually a Rabin automaton or a generalized Rabin automaton is constructed [17,23,24,27]. Since in our setting, along with ω-regular language the specification also includes quantitative constraints over runs, we generate a DGRMA. The next theorem is the first black box, detailed in Sect. 4.

Theorem 2. *For any fLTL$_{\backslash \mathbf{GU}}$ formula, there is a DGRMA $\mathcal{A}$, constructible in doubly exponential time, such that $\mathsf{L}(\mathcal{A}) = \mathsf{L}(\varphi)$, and the acceptance condition is of exponential size.*

2. Product. Computing the synchronous parallel product of the MDP M $= (S, A, Act, \Delta, \hat{s})$ with valuation $\nu : S \to 2^{Ap}$ and the LTS (Q, i, δ) over 2^{Ap} underlying $\mathcal{A}$ is rather straightforward. The product M $\times$ $\mathcal{A}$ is again an MDP $(S \times Q, A \times Q, Act', \Delta', (\hat{s}, \hat{q}))$ where[1] $Act'((s, q)) = Act(s) \times \{q\}$, $\hat{q} = \delta(i, \nu(\hat{s}))$, and $\Delta'((a, q))((s, \bar{q}))$ is equal to $\Delta(a)(s)$ if $\delta(q, \nu(s)) = \bar{q}$, and to 0 otherwise. We lift acceptance conditions Acc of $\mathcal{A}$ to M $\times$ $\mathcal{A}$: a run of M $\times$ $\mathcal{A}$ satisfies Acc if its projection to the component of the automata states satisfies Acc.[2]

3. Product Analysis. The MDP M $\times$ $\mathcal{A}$ is solved with respect to Acc, i.e., a strategy in M $\times$ $\mathcal{A}$ is found that maximizes the probability of satisfying Acc.

---

[1] In order to guarantee that each action is enabled in at most one state, we have a copy of each original action for each state of the automaton.

[2] Technically, the projection should be preceded by i to get a run of the automaton, but the acceptance does not depend on any finite prefix of the sequence of states.

Such a strategy then induces a (history-dependent) strategy on M in a straightforward manner. Observe that for DGRMA, it is sufficient to consider the setting with

$$Acc = \bigvee_{i=1}^{k} (Fin(F_i) \wedge Acc'_i) \tag{1}$$

where Acc'_i is a conjunction of several Inf and MP (in contrast with a Rabin condition used for ordinary LTL where Acc'_i is simply of the form $Inf(I_i)$). Indeed, one can replace each $\bigwedge_j Fin(F_j)$ by $Fin(\bigcup_j F_j)$ to obtain the desired form, since avoiding several sets is equivalent to avoiding their union.

For a condition of the form (1), the solution is obtained as follows:

1. For $i = 1, 2, \ldots, k$:
   (a) Remove the set of states F_i from the MDP.
   (b) Compute the MEC decomposition.
   (c) Mark each MEC C as winning iff ACCEPTINGMEC(C, Acc'_i) returns Yes.
   (d) Let W_i be the componentwise union of winning MECs above.
2. Let W be the componentwise union of all W_i for $1 \leq i \leq k$.
3. Return the maximal probability to reach the set W in the MDP.

The procedure ACCEPTINGMEC(C, Acc'_i) is the second black box used in our algorithm, detailed in Sect. 5. It decides, whether the maximum probability of satisfying Acc'_i in C is 1 (return Yes), or 0 (return No).

Theorem 3. *For a strongly connected MDP M and a generalized Büchi meanpayoff acceptance condition Acc, the maximal probability to satisfy Acc is either 1 or 0, and is the same for all initial states. Moreover, there is a polynomial-time algorithm that computes this probability, and also outputs a witnessing strategy if the probability is 1.*

The procedure is rather complex in our case, as opposed to standard cases such as Rabin condition, where a MEC is accepting for $Acc'_i = Inf(I_i)$ if its states intersect I_i; or a generalized Rabin condition [12], where a MEC is accepting for $Acc'_i = \bigwedge_{j=1}^{\ell_i} Inf(I_{ij})$ if its states intersect with each I_i^j, for $j = 1, 2, \ldots, \ell_i$.

Finishing the Proof of Theorem 1. Note that for MDPs that are not strongly connected, the maximum probability might not be in $\{0, 1\}$. Therefore, the problem is decomposed into a qualitative satisfaction problem in step 1.(c) and a quantitative reachability problem in step 3. Consequently, the proof of correctness is the same as the proofs for LTL via Rabin automata [2] and generalized Rabin automata [12]. The complexity follows from Theorems 2 and 3. Finally, the overall witness strategy first reaches the winning MECs and if they are reached it switches to the witness strategies from Theorem 3.

Remark 1. We remark that by a simple modification of the product construction above and of the proof of Theorem 3, we obtain an algorithm synthesising a strategy achieving a given bound w.r.t. multiple mean-payoff objectives (with a combination of superior and inferior limits) and (generalized) Rabin acceptance condition for *general* (not necessarily strongly connected) MDP.

4   Automata Characterization of fLTL$_{\backslash\mathbf{GU}}$

In this section, we prove Theorem 2. We give an algorithm for translating a given fLTL$_{\backslash\mathbf{GU}}$ formula φ into a deterministic generalized Rabin mean-payoff automaton $\mathcal{A}$ that recognizes words satisfying φ. For the rest of the section, let φ be an fLTL$_{\backslash\mathbf{GU}}$ formula. Further, $\mathbb{F}, \mathbb{G}, \mathbb{G}^{\bowtie}$, and sfs denote the set of $\mathbf{F}$-, $\mathbf{G}$-, $\mathbf{G}_{\text{ext}}^{\bowtie p}$-, and non-Boolean subformulas of φ, respectively.

In order to obtain an automaton for the formula, we first need to give a more operational view on fLTL. To this end, we use expansions of the formulae in a very similar way as they are used, for instance, in tableaux techniques for LTL translation to automata, or for deciding LTL satisfiability. We define a symbolic one-step unfolding (expansion) Unf of a formula inductively by the rules below. Further, for a valuation $\nu \subseteq Ap$, we define the "next step under ν"-operator. This operator (1) substitutes unguarded atomic propositions for their truth values, and (2) peels off the outer $\mathbf{X}$-operator whenever it is present. Formally, we define

$$\text{Unf}(\psi_1 \wedge \psi_2) = \text{Unf}(\psi_1) \wedge \text{Unf}(\psi_2) \qquad (\psi_1 \wedge \psi_2)[\nu] = \psi_1[\nu] \wedge \psi_2[\nu]$$

$$\text{Unf}(\psi_1 \vee \psi_2) = \text{Unf}(\psi_1) \vee \text{Unf}(\psi_2) \qquad (\psi_1 \vee \psi_2)[\nu] = \psi_1[\nu] \vee \psi_2[\nu]$$

$$\text{Unf}(\mathbf{F}\psi_1) = \text{Unf}(\psi_1) \vee \mathbf{XF}\psi_1$$

$$\text{Unf}(\mathbf{G}\psi_1) = \text{Unf}(\psi_1) \wedge \mathbf{XG}\psi_1 \qquad a[\nu] = \begin{cases} \mathbf{tt} & \text{if } a \in \nu \\ \mathbf{ff} & \text{if } a \notin \nu \end{cases}$$

$$\text{Unf}(\psi_1 \mathbf{U}\psi_2) = \text{Unf}(\psi_2) \vee (\text{Unf}(\psi_1) \wedge \mathbf{X}(\psi_1 \mathbf{U}\psi_2))$$

$$\text{Unf}(\mathbf{G}_{\text{ext}}^{\bowtie p}\psi_1) = \mathbf{tt} \wedge \mathbf{XG}_{\text{ext}}^{\bowtie p}\psi_1 \qquad \neg a[\nu] = \begin{cases} \mathbf{ff} & \text{if } a \in \nu \\ \mathbf{tt} & \text{if } a \notin \nu \end{cases}$$

$$\text{Unf}(\psi) = \psi \text{ for any other } \psi$$

$$(\mathbf{X}\psi_1)[\nu] = \psi_1$$

$$\psi[\nu] = \psi \text{ for any other } \psi$$

Note that after unfolding, a formula becomes a positive Boolean combination over literals (atomic propositions and their negations) and $\mathbf{X}$-formulae. The resulting formula is LTL-equivalent to the original formula. The formulae of the form $\mathbf{G}_{\text{ext}}^{\bowtie p}\psi$ have "dummy" unfolding; they are dealt with in a special way later. Combined with unfolding, the "next step"-operator then preserves and reflects satisfaction on the given word:

Lemma 1. *For every word w and fLTL$_{\backslash\mathbf{GU}}$ formula φ, we have $w \models \varphi$ if and only if $w1 \models (\text{Unf}(\varphi))[w[0]]$.*

The construction of $\mathcal{A}$ proceeds in several steps. We first construct a "master" transition system, which monitors the formula and transforms it in each step to always keep exactly the formula that needs to be satisfied at the moment. However, this can only deal with properties whose satisfaction has a finite witness, e.g. $\mathbf{F}a$. Therefore we construct a set of "slave" automata, which check whether "infinitary" properties (with no finite witness), e.g., $\mathbf{FG}a$, hold or not. They pass this information to the master, who decides on acceptance of the word.

4.1 Construction of Master Transition System $\mathcal{M}$

We define a LTS $\mathcal{M} = (Q, \varphi, \delta^{\mathcal{M}})$ over 2^{Ap} by letting Q be the set of positive Boolean functions[3] over sf, by letting φ be the initial state, and by letting the transition function $\delta^{\mathcal{M}}$, for every $\nu \subseteq Ap$ and $\psi \in Q$, contain $\psi \xrightarrow{\nu} (\mathsf{Unf}(\psi))[\nu]$.

The master automaton keeps the property that is still required up to date:

Lemma 2 (Local (Finitary) Correctness of Master LTS). *Let w be a word and $\mathcal{M}(w) = \varphi_0 \varphi_1 \cdots$ the corresponding run. Then for all $n \in \mathbb{N}$, we have $w \models \varphi$ if and only if $wn \models \varphi_n$.*

Example 1. The formula $\varphi = a \wedge \mathbf{X}(b\mathbf{U}a)$ yields a master LTS depicted below.

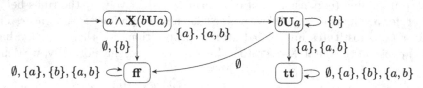

One can observe that for an fLTL formula φ with no $\mathbf{G}$- and $\mathbf{G}_{\mathrm{ext}}^{\bowtie p}$-operators, we have $w \models \varphi$ iff the state $\mathbf{tt}$ is reached while reading w. However, for formulae with $\mathbf{G}$-operators (and thus without finite witnesses in general), this claim no longer holds. To check such behaviour we construct auxiliary "slave" automata.

4.2 Construction of Slave Transition Systems $\mathcal{S}(\xi)$

We define a LTS $\mathcal{S}(\xi) = (Q, \xi, \delta^{\mathcal{S}})$ over 2^{Ap} with the same state space as $\mathcal{M}$ and the initial state $\xi \in Q$. Furthermore, we call a state ψ a *sink*, written $\psi \in \mathsf{Sink}$, iff for all $\nu \subseteq Ap$ we have $\psi[\nu] = \psi$. Finally, the transition relation $\delta^{\mathcal{S}}$, for every $\nu \subseteq Ap$ and $\psi \in Q \setminus \mathsf{Sink}$, contains $\psi \xrightarrow{\nu} \psi[\nu]$.

Example 2. The slave LTS for the formula $\xi = a \vee b \vee \mathbf{X}(b \wedge \mathbf{GF}a)$ has a structure depicted in the following diagram:

Note that we do not unfold any inner $\mathbf{F}$- and $\mathbf{G}$-formulae. Observe that if we start reading w at the ith position and end up in $\mathbf{tt}$, we have $wi \models \xi$. Similarly, if we end up in $\mathbf{ff}$ we have $wi \not\models \xi$. This way we can monitor for which position ξ holds and will be able to determine if it holds, for instance, infinitely often. But what about when we end up in $\mathbf{GF}a$? Intuitively, this state is accepting or rejecting

---

[3] We use Boolean functions, i.e. classes of propositionally equivalent formulae, to obtain a finite state space. To avoid clutter, when referring to such a Boolean function, we use some formula representing the respective equivalence class. The choice of the representing formula is not relevant since, for all operations we use, the propositional equivalence is a congruence, see [20]. Note that, in particular, $\mathbf{tt}, \mathbf{ff} \in Q$.

depending on whether $\textbf{GF}a$ holds or not. Since this cannot be checked in finite time, we delegate this task to yet another slave, now responsible for $\textbf{GF}a$. Thus instead of deciding whether $\textbf{GF}a$ holds, we may use it as an *assumption* in the automaton for ξ and let the automaton for $\textbf{GF}a$ check whether the assumption turns out correct.

Let $\mathcal{Rec} := \mathbb{F} \cup \mathbb{G} \cup \mathbb{G}^{\bowtie}$. This is the set of subformulas that are potentially difficult to check in finite time. Subsets of $\mathcal{Rec}$ can be used as assumptions to prove other assumptions and in the end also the acceptance. Given a set of formulae Ψ and a formula ψ, we say that Ψ *(propositionally) proves* ψ, written $\Psi \vdash \psi$, if ψ can be deduced from formulae in Ψ using only propositional reasoning (for a formal definition see [20]). So, for instance, $\{\textbf{GF}a\} \vdash \textbf{GF}a \vee \textbf{G}b$, but $\textbf{GF}a \not\vdash \textbf{F}a$.

The following is the ideal assumption set we would like our automaton to identify. For a fixed word w, we denote by $\mathcal{R}(w)$ the set

$$\{\textbf{F}\xi \in \mathbb{F} \mid w \models \textbf{GF}\xi\} \cup \{\textbf{G}\xi \in \mathbb{G} \mid w \models \textbf{FG}\xi\} \cup \{\textbf{G}^{\bowtie p}_{\text{ext}}\xi \in \mathbb{G}^{\bowtie} \mid w \models \textbf{G}^{\bowtie p}_{\text{ext}}\xi\}$$

of formulae in $\mathcal{Rec}$ eventually always satisfied on w. The slave LTS is useful for recognizing whether its respective formula ξ holds infinitely often, almost always, or with the given frequency. Intuitively, it reduces this problem for a given formula to the problems for its subformulas in $\mathcal{Rec}$:

Lemma 3 (Correctness of Slave LTS). *Let us fix $\xi \in$ sf and a word w. For any $\mathcal{R} \in \mathcal{Rec}$, we denote by $Sat(\mathcal{R})$ the set $\{i \in \mathbb{N} \mid \exists j \geq i : \mathcal{R} \vdash \mathcal{S}(\xi)(w^{ij})\}$. Then for any $\underline{\mathcal{R}}, \overline{\mathcal{R}} \subseteq \mathcal{Rec}$ such that $\underline{\mathcal{R}} \subseteq \mathcal{R}(w) \subseteq \overline{\mathcal{R}}$, we have*

$$Sat(\underline{\mathcal{R}}) \text{ is infinite} \implies w \models \textbf{GF}\xi \implies Sat(\overline{\mathcal{R}}) \text{ is infinite} \tag{2}$$

$$\mathbb{N} \setminus Sat(\underline{\mathcal{R}}) \text{ is finite} \implies w \models \textbf{FG}\xi \implies \mathbb{N} \setminus Sat(\overline{\mathcal{R}}) \text{ is finite} \tag{3}$$

$$\text{lr}_{\text{ext}}\big((\mathbb{1}_{i \in Sat(\underline{\mathcal{R}})})_{i=0}^{\infty}\big) \bowtie p \implies w \models \textbf{G}^{\bowtie p}_{\text{ext}}\xi \implies \text{lr}_{\text{ext}}\big((\mathbb{1}_{i \in Sat(\overline{\mathcal{R}})})_{i=0}^{\infty}\big) \bowtie p \tag{4}$$

Before we put the slaves together to determine $\mathcal{R}(w)$, we define *slave automata*. In order to express the constraints from Lemma 3 as acceptance conditions, we need to transform the underlying LTS. Intuitively, we replace quantification over various starting positions for runs by a subset construction. This means that in each step we put a *token* to the initial state and move all previously present tokens to their successor states.

Büchi. For a formula $\textbf{F}\xi \in \mathbb{F}$, its slave LTS $\mathcal{S}(\xi) = (Q, \xi, \delta^S)$, and $\mathcal{R} \subseteq \mathcal{Rec}$, we define a Büchi automaton $\mathcal{S}_{\textbf{GF}}(\xi, \mathcal{R}) = (2^Q, \{\xi\}, \delta)$ over 2^{Ap} by setting

$$\Psi \xrightarrow{\nu} \{\delta^S(\psi, \nu) \mid \psi \in \Psi \setminus \text{Sink}\} \cup \{\xi\} \qquad \text{for every } \nu \subseteq Ap$$

and the Büchi acceptance condition $Inf(\{\Psi \subseteq Q \mid \exists \psi \in \Psi \cap \text{Sink} : \mathcal{R} \vdash \psi\})$.

In other words, the automaton accepts if infinitely often a token ends up in an *accepting sink*, i.e., element of Sink that is provable from $\mathcal{R}$. For Example 2, depending on whether we assume $\textbf{GF}a \in \mathcal{R}$ or not, the accepting sinks are $\textbf{tt}$ and $\textbf{GF}a$, or only $\textbf{tt}$, respectively.

Co-Büchi. For a formula $\textbf{G}\xi \in \mathbb{G}$, its slave LTS $\mathcal{S}(\xi) = (Q, \xi, \delta^S)$ and $\mathcal{R} \subseteq \mathcal{Rec}$, we define a co-Büchi automaton $\mathcal{S}_{\textbf{FG}}(\xi, \mathcal{R}) = (2^Q, \{\xi\}, \delta)$ over 2^{Ap} with the same

LTS as above. It differs from the Büchi automaton only by having a co-Büchi acceptance condition $Fin(\{\Psi \subseteq Q \mid \exists \psi \in \Psi \cap \mathsf{Sink} : \mathcal{R} \nvdash \psi\})$.

Mean-payoff. For a formula $\mathbf{G}_{\mathrm{ext}}^{\bowtie p} \xi \in \mathbb{G}^{\bowtie}$, its slave LTS $\mathcal{S}(\xi) = (Q, \xi, \delta^{\mathcal{S}})$, and $\mathcal{R} \subseteq \mathcal{R}ec$ we define a *mean-payoff automaton* $\mathcal{S}_{\mathbf{G}_{\mathrm{ext}}^{\bowtie p}}(\xi, \mathcal{R}) = (|Q|^{Q}, \mathbb{1}_{\xi}, \delta)$ over 2^{Ap} so that for every $\nu \subseteq Ap$, we have $f \xrightarrow{\nu} f'$ where

$$f'(\psi') = \mathbb{1}_{\xi}(\psi') + \sum_{\delta^{\mathcal{S}}(\psi, \nu) = \psi'} f(\psi).$$

Intuitively, we always count the number of tokens in each state. When a step is taken, all tokens moving to a state are summed up and, moreover, one token is added to the initial state. Since the slave LTS is acyclic the number of tokens in each state is bounded.

Finally, the acceptance condition is $MP_{\mathrm{ext}}^{\bowtie p}(r(\mathcal{R}))$ where the function $r(\mathcal{R})$ assigns to every state f the reward:

$$\sum_{\psi \in \mathsf{Sink}, \mathcal{R} \vdash \psi} f(\psi).$$

Each state thus has a reward that is the number of tokens in accepting sinks. Note that each token either causes a reward 1 once per its life-time when it reaches an accepting sink, or never causes any reward in the case when it never reaches any accepting state.

Lemma 4 (Correctness of Slave Automata). *Let* $\xi \in \mathsf{sf}$, w, *and* $\underline{\mathcal{R}}, \overline{\mathcal{R}} \subseteq \mathcal{R}ec$ *be such that* $\underline{\mathcal{R}} \subseteq \mathcal{R}(w) \subseteq \overline{\mathcal{R}}$. *Then*

$$w \in \mathsf{L}(\mathcal{S}_{\mathbf{GF}}(\xi, \underline{\mathcal{R}})) \implies w \models \mathbf{GF}\xi \implies w \in \mathsf{L}(\mathcal{S}_{\mathbf{GF}}(\xi, \overline{\mathcal{R}})) \tag{5}$$

$$w \in \mathsf{L}(\mathcal{S}_{\mathbf{FG}}(\xi, \underline{\mathcal{R}})) \implies w \models \mathbf{FG}\xi \implies w \in \mathsf{L}(\mathcal{S}_{\mathbf{FG}}(\xi, \overline{\mathcal{R}})) \tag{6}$$

$$w \in \mathsf{L}(\mathcal{S}_{\mathbf{G}_{\mathrm{ext}}^{\bowtie p}}(\xi, \underline{\mathcal{R}})) \implies w \models \mathbf{G}_{\mathrm{ext}}^{\bowtie p}\xi \implies w \in \mathsf{L}(\mathcal{S}_{\mathbf{G}_{\mathrm{ext}}^{\bowtie p}}(\xi, \overline{\mathcal{R}})) \tag{7}$$

4.3   Product of Slave Automata

Observe that the LTS of slave automata never depend on the assumptions $\mathcal{R}$. Let $\mathcal{S}_1, \ldots, \mathcal{S}_n$ be the LTS of automata for elements of $\mathcal{R}ec = \{\xi_1, \ldots, \xi_n\}$. Further, given $\mathcal{R} \subseteq \mathcal{R}ec$, let $Acc_i(\mathcal{R})$ be the acceptance condition for the slave automaton for ξ_i with assumptions $\mathcal{R}$.

We define $\mathcal{P}$ to be the LTS product $\mathcal{S}_1 \times \cdots \times \mathcal{S}_n$. The slaves run independently in parallel. For $\mathcal{R} \subseteq \mathcal{R}ec$, we define the acceptance condition for the product[4]

$$Acc(\mathcal{R}) = \bigwedge_{\xi_i \in \mathcal{R}} Acc_i(\mathcal{R})$$

---

[4] An acceptance condition of an automaton is defined to hold on a run of the automata product if it holds on the projection of the run to this automaton. We can still write this as a standard acceptance condition. Indeed, for instance, a Büchi condition for the first automaton given by $F \subseteq Q$ is a Büchi condition on the product given by $\{(q_1, q_2, \ldots, q_n) \mid q_1 \in F, q_2, \ldots, q_n \in Q\}$.

and $\mathcal{P}(\mathcal{R})$ denotes the LTS $\mathcal{P}$ endowed with the acceptance condition $Acc(\mathcal{R})$. Note that $Acc(\mathcal{R})$ checks that $\mathcal{R}$ is satisfied when each slave assumes $\mathcal{R}$.

Lemma 5 (Correctness of Slave Product). *For w and $\mathcal{R} \subseteq Rec$, we have*

(soundness) *whenever $w \in L(\mathcal{P}(\mathcal{R}))$ then $\mathcal{R} \subseteq \mathcal{R}(w)$;*
(completeness) $w \in L(\mathcal{P}(\mathcal{R}(w)))$.

Intuitively, soundness means that whatever set of assumptions we prove with $\mathcal{P}$ it is also satisfied on the word. Note that the first line can be written as

$$w \in L(\mathcal{P}(\mathcal{R})) \implies w \models \bigwedge_{F\xi\in\mathcal{R}} \mathbf{GF}\xi \wedge \bigwedge_{G\xi\in\mathcal{R}} \mathbf{FG}\xi \wedge \bigwedge_{G_{ext}^{\bowtie p}\xi\in\mathcal{R}} \mathbf{G}_{ext}^{\bowtie p}\xi$$

Completeness means that for every word the set of all satisfied assumptions can be proven by the automaton.

4.4 The Final Automaton: Product of Slaves and Master

Finally, we define the generalized Rabin mean-payoff automaton $\mathcal{A}$ to have the LTS $\mathcal{M} \times \mathcal{P}$ and the acceptance condition $\bigvee_{\mathcal{R}\subseteq Rec} Acc_{\mathcal{M}}(\mathcal{R}) \wedge Acc(\mathcal{R})$ where

$$Acc_{\mathcal{M}}(\mathcal{R}) = Fin\left(\left\{ (\psi, (\Psi_\xi)_{\xi\in Rec}) \mid \mathcal{R} \cup \bigcup_{G\xi\in\mathcal{R}} \Psi_\xi[(Rec \setminus \mathcal{R})/\mathbf{ff}] \not\vdash \psi \right\}\right)$$

eventually prohibits states where the current formula of the master ψ is not proved by the assumptions and by all tokens of the slaves for $\mathbf{G}\xi \in \mathcal{R}$. Here $\Psi[X/\mathbf{ff}]$ denotes the set of formulae of Ψ where each element of X in the Boolean combination is replaced by $\mathbf{ff}$. For instance, $\{a\vee Fa\}[\{a\}/\mathbf{ff}] = \mathbf{ff}\vee Fa = Fa$. (For formal definition, see [20].) We illustrate how the information from the slaves in this form helps to decide whether the master formula holds or not.

Example 3. Consider $\varphi = \mathbf{G}(\mathbf{X}a \vee \mathbf{GX}b)$, and its respective master transition system as depicted below:

Assume we enter the second state and stay there forever, e.g., under words $\{a\}^\omega$ or $\{a, b\}^\omega$. How do we show that $\varphi\wedge(a\vee(b\wedge\mathbf{GX}b))$ holds? For the first conjunct, we obviously have $\mathcal{R}\vdash\varphi$ for all $\mathcal{R}$ containing φ. However, the second conjunct is more difficult to prove.

One option is that we have $\mathbf{GX}b \in \mathcal{R}$ and want to prove the second disjunct. To this end, we also need to prove b. We can see that if $\mathbf{GX}b$ holds then in its slave for $\mathbf{X}b$, there is always a token in the state b, which is eventually always guaranteed to hold. This illustrates why we need the tokens of the **G**-slaves for proving the master formula.

The other option is that **GX**b is not in $\mathcal{R}$, and so we need to prove the first disjunct. However, from the slave for **G**(**X**$a \vee$ **GX**b) we eventually always get only the tokens **X**$a \vee$ **GX**b, $a \vee$ **GX**b, and **tt**. None of them can prove $a \vee (b \wedge$ **GX**$b)$. However, since the slave does not rely on the assumption **GX**b, we may safely assume it not to hold here. Therefore, we can substitute **ff** for **GX**b and after the substitution the tokens turn into **X**a, a, and **tt**. The second one is then trivially sufficient to prove the first disjunct.

Proposition 1 (Soundness). *If* $w \in L(\mathcal{A})$, *then* $w \models \varphi$.

The key proof idea is that for the slaves of **G**-formulae in $\mathcal{R}$, all the tokens eventually always hold true. Since also the assumptions hold true so does the conclusion ψ. By Lemma 2, φ holds true, too.

Proposition 2 (Completeness). *If* $w \models \varphi$, *then* $w \in L(\mathcal{A})$.

The key idea is that subformulas generated in the master from **G**-formulae closely correspond to their slaves' tokens. Further, observe that for an **F**-formula χ, its unfolding is a disjunction of χ and other formulae. Therefore, it is sufficient to prove χ, which can be done directly from $\mathcal{R}$. Similarly, for **G**$_{\text{ext}}^{\bowtie p}$-formula χ, its unfolding is just χ and is thus also provable directly from $\mathcal{R}$.

Complexity. Since the number of Boolean functions over a set of size n is 2^{2^n}, the size of each automaton is bounded by $2^{2^{|sf|}}$, i.e., doubly exponential in the length of the formula. Their product is thus still doubly exponential. Finally, the acceptance condition is polynomial for each fixed $\mathcal{R} \subseteq \mathcal{R}ec$. Since the whole condition is a disjunction over all possible values of $\mathcal{R}$, it is exponential in the size of the formula, which finishes the proof of Theorem 2.

5   Verifying Strongly Connected MDPs Against Generalized Büchi Mean-Payoff Automata

Theorem 3 can be obtained from the following proposition.

Proposition 3. *Let* $\mathsf{M} = (S, A, Act, \delta, \hat{s})$ *be a strongly connected MDP, and Acc an acceptance condition over* S *given by:*

$$\bigwedge_{i=1}^{k} Inf(S_i) \quad \wedge \quad \bigwedge_{i=1}^{m} MP_{\text{inf}}^{\bowtie v_i}(r_i) \quad \wedge \quad \bigwedge_{i=1}^{n} MP_{\text{sup}}^{\bowtie u_i}(q_i))$$

The constraints from Fig. 1 have a non-negative solution if and only if there is a strategy σ *and a set of runs* R *of non-zero probability such that Acc holds true on all* $\omega \in R$. *Moreover,* σ *and* R *can be chosen so that* R *has probability 1.*

Intuitively, variables $x_{i,a}$ describe the frequencies of using action a. Equation (9) is Kirchhof's law of flow. Equation (10) says the inferior limits must be satisfied by all flows, while Eq. (11) says the ith limit superior has its own dedicated ith flow. Note that L does not dependent on the initial state $\hat{s}$.

$$\sum_{a \in A} x_{i,a} = 1 \qquad\qquad\qquad \text{for all } 1 \leq i \leq n \qquad (8)$$

$$\sum_{a \in A} x_{i,a} \cdot \delta(a)(s) = \sum_{a \in Act(s)} x_{i,a} \qquad \text{for all } s \in S \text{ and } 1 \leq i \leq n \qquad (9)$$

$$\sum_{s \in S, a \in Act(s)} x_{i,a} \cdot r_j(s) \bowtie v_j \qquad \text{for all } 1 \leq j \leq m \text{ and } 1 \leq i \leq n \qquad (10)$$

$$\sum_{s \in S, a \in Act(s)} x_{i,a} \cdot q_i(s) \bowtie u_i \qquad\qquad \text{for all } 1 \leq i \leq n \qquad (11)$$

Fig. 1. Linear constraints L of Proposition 3

Proof (Sketch). Existing results for multi-objective mean payoff MDPs would only allow to establish the proposition in absence of supremum limits, and so we need to extend and combine results of several works to prove the proposition. In the direction ⇒, [13, Corollary 12] gives a strategy σ_i for every i such that for almost every run $s_0 a_0 s_1 a_1 \ldots$ we have $\mathrm{lr}_{\inf}((\mathbb{1}_{a_t = a})_{t=0}^{\infty}) = x_{i,a}$, and in fact the corresponding limit exists. Hence, for the number $p = \sum_{s \in S, a \in Act(s)} r(s) \cdot x_{i,a}$ the predicates $MP_{\inf}^{\geq p}(r)$ and $MP_{\sup}^{\geq p}(r)$ almost surely holds, for any reward function r. Hence, our constraints ensure that σ_i satisfies $MP_{\inf}^{\bowtie v_j}(r_j)$ for all j, and $MP_{\sup}^{\bowtie u_i}(q_i)$. Moreover, σ_i is guaranteed to visit every state of M infinitely often almost surely. The strategy σ is then constructed to take these strategies $\sigma_i, 1 \leq i \leq n$ in turn and mimic each one of them for longer and longer periods.

For the direction ⇐, we combine the ideas of [9,10,13] and select solutions to $x_{i,a}$ from "frequencies" of actions under the strategy σ.

6 Conclusions

We have given an algorithm for computing the optimal probability of satisfying an fLTL\GU formula in an MDP. The proof relies on a decomposition of the formula into master and slave automata, and on solving a mean-payoff problem in a product MDP. The obvious next step is to extend the algorithm so that it can handle arbitrary formulae of fLTL. This appears to be a major task, since our present construction relies on acyclicity of slave LTS, a property which is not satisfied for unrestricted formulae [17]. Indeed, since $G^{\bowtie p}$-slaves count the number of tokens in each state, this property ensures a bounded number of tokens and thus finiteness of the slave automata.

Acknowledgments. This work is partly supported by the German Research Council (DFG) as part of the Transregional Collaborative Research Center AVACS (SFB/TR 14), by the Czech Science Foundation under grant agreement P202/12/G061, by the EU 7th Framework Programme under grant agreement no. 295261 (MEALS) and 318490 (SENSATION), by the CDZ project 1023 (CAP), by the CAS/SAFEA International Partnership Program for Creative Research Teams, by the EPSRC grant EP/M023656/1, by the People Programme (Marie Curie Actions) of the European Union's Seventh Framework Programme (FP7/2007–2013) REA Grant No 291734, by the Austrian Science Fund (FWF) S11407-N23 (RiSE/SHiNE), and by the ERC Start Grant (279307: Graph Games). Vojtěch Forejt is also affiliated with FI MU, Brno, Czech Republic.

References

1. Almagor, S., Boker, U., Kupferman, O.: Discounting in LTL. In: Ábrahám, E., Havelund, K. (eds.) TACAS 2014 (ETAPS). LNCS, vol. 8413, pp. 424–439. Springer, Heidelberg (2014)
2. Baier, C., Katoen, J.-P.: Principles of Model Checking. MIT Press, Cambridge (2008)
3. Baier, C., Klein, J., Klüppelholz, S., Wunderlich, S.: Weight monitoring with linear temporal logic: complexity and decidability. In: CSL-LICS. ACM (2014)
4. Bloem, R., Chatterjee, K., Henzinger, T.A., Jobstmann, B.: Better quality in synthesis through quantitative objectives. In: Bouajjani, A., Maler, O. (eds.) CAV 2009. LNCS, vol. 5643, pp. 140–156. Springer, Heidelberg (2009)
5. Bloem, R., Jobstmann, B., Piterman, N., Pnueli, A., Sa'ar, Y.: Synthesis of reactive(1) designs. J. Comput. Syst. Sci. **78**(3), 911–938 (2012)
6. Boker, U., Chatterjee, K., Henzinger, T.A., Kupferman, O.: Temporal specifications with accumulative values In: LICS. IEEE (2011)
7. Bollig, B., Decker, N., Leucker, M.: Frequency linear-time temporal logic. In: TASE. IEEE, Beijing, July 2012
8. Bouyer, P., Markey, N., Matteplackel, R.M.: Averaging in LTL. In: Baldan, P., Gorla, D. (eds.) CONCUR 2014. LNCS, vol. 8704, pp. 266–280. Springer, Heidelberg (2014)
9. Brázdil, T., Brožek, V., Chatterjee, K., Forejt, V., Kučera, A.: Markov decision processes with multiple long-run average objectives. LMCS **10**(4), 1–29 (2014)
10. Brázdil, T., Chatterjee, K., Forejt, V., Kučera, A.: Trading performance for stability in Markov decision processes. In: LICS. IEEE (2013)
11. Chatterjee, K., Doyen, L.: Energy and mean-payoff parity markov decision processes. In: Murlak, F., Sankowski, P. (eds.) MFCS 2011. LNCS, vol. 6907, pp. 206–218. Springer, Heidelberg (2011)
12. Chatterjee, K., Gaiser, A., Křetínský, J.: Automata with generalized rabin pairs for probabilistic model checking and LTL synthesis. In: Sharygina, N., Veith, H. (eds.) CAV 2013. LNCS, vol. 8044, pp. 559–575. Springer, Heidelberg (2013)
13. Chatterjee, K., Komárková, Z., Křetínský, J.: Unifying two views on multiple mean-payoff objectives in Markov decision processes. In: LICS (2015)
14. Clemente, L., Raskin, J.-F.: Multidimensional beyond worst-case and almost-sure problems for mean-payoff objectives. In: LICS (2015, To appear)
15. Courcoubetis, C., Yannakakis, M.: The complexity of probabilistic verification. J. ACM **42**(4), 857–907 (1995)
16. Droste, M., Perevoshchikov, V.: Multi-weighted automata and MSO logic. In: Bulatov, A.A., Shur, A.M. (eds.) CSR 2013. LNCS, vol. 7913, pp. 418–430. Springer, Heidelberg (2013)
17. Esparza, J., Křetínský, J.: From LTL to deterministic automata: a safraless compositional approach. In: Biere, A., Bloem, R. (eds.) CAV 2014. LNCS, vol. 8559, pp. 192–208. Springer, Heidelberg (2014)
18. Etessami, K., Kwiatkowska, M., Vardi, M., Yannakakis, M.: Multi-objective model checking of Markov decision processes. LMCS **4**(4), 1–21 (2008)
19. Forejt, V., Krčál, J.: On frequency LTL in probabilistic systems. In: CONCUR, LIPIcs, vol. 42. Schloss Dagstuhl - Leibniz-Zentrum fuer Informatik (2015)
20. Forejt, V., Krčál, J., Křetínský, J.: Controller synthesis for MDPS and frequency LTL$_{\backslash GU}$ (2015). CoRR, abs/1509.04116

21. Kemeny, J., Snell, J., Knapp, A.: Denumerable Markov Chains, 2nd edn. Springer, Heidelberg (1976)
22. Kini, D., Viswanathan, M.: Limit deterministic and probabilistic automata for LTL\GU. In: Baier, C., Tinelli, C. (eds.) TACAS 2015. LNCS, vol. 9035, pp. 628–642. Springer, Heidelberg (2015)
23. Klein, J., Baier, C.: Experiments with deterministic ω-automata for formulas of linear temporal logic. Theor. Comput. Sci. **363**(2), 182–195 (2006)
24. Komárková, Z., Křetínský, J.: Rabinizer 3: Safraless translation of LTL to small deterministic automata. In: Cassez, F., Raskin, J.-F. (eds.) ATVA 2014. LNCS, vol. 8837, pp. 235–241. Springer, Heidelberg (2014)
25. Křetínský, J., Ledesma-Garza, R.: Rabinizer 2: small deterministic automata for LTL\GU. In: ATVA (2013)
26. Křetínský, J., Esparza, J.: Deterministic automata for the (F,G)-fragment of LTL. In: Madhusudan, P., Seshia, S.A. (eds.) CAV 2012. LNCS, vol. 7358, pp. 7–22. Springer, Heidelberg (2012)
27. Kwiatkowska, M., Norman, G., Parker, D.: PRISM 4.0: Verification of probabilistic real-time systems. In: Gopalakrishnan, G., Qadeer, S. (eds.) CAV 2011. LNCS, vol. 6806, pp. 585–591. Springer, Heidelberg (2011)
28. Randour, M., Raskin, J.-F., Sankur, O.: Percentile queries in multi-dimensional Markov decision processes. In: Kroening, D., Păsăreanu, C.S. (eds.) CAV 2015. LNCS, vol. 9206, pp. 123–139. Springer, Heidelberg (2015)
29. Thomas, W.: Languages, Automata, and Logic. Springer, New York (1997)
30. Tomita, T., Hagihara, S., Yonezaki, N.: A probabilistic temporal logic with frequency operators and its model checking. In: INFINITY (2011)
31. Tomita, T., Hiura, S., Hagihara, S., Yonezaki, N.: A temporal logic with mean-payoff constraints. In: Aoki, T., Taguchi, K. (eds.) ICFEM 2012. LNCS, vol. 7635, pp. 249–265. Springer, Heidelberg (2012)
32. Vardi, M.Y.: An automata-theoretic approach to linear temporal logic. In: Moller, F., Birtwistle, G. (eds.) Logics for Concurrency: Structure versus Automata. LNCS, vol. 1043. Springer, Heidelberg (1996)
33. Vardi, M.Y., Wolper, P.: An automata-theoretic approach to automatic program verification (preliminary report). In: LICS. IEEE (1986)

Automated Benchmarking of Incremental SAT and QBF Solvers

Uwe Egly, Florian Lonsing$^{(\boxtimes)}$, and Johannes Oetsch

Institute of Information Systems 184/3, Vienna University of Technology,
Favoritenstraße 9-11, 1040 Vienna, Austria
{uwe,lonsing,oetsch}@kr.tuwien.ac.at

Abstract. Incremental SAT and QBF solving potentially yields improvements when sequences of related formulas are solved. An incremental application is usually tailored towards some specific solver and decomposes a problem into incremental solver calls. This hinders the independent comparison of different solvers, particularly when the application program is not available. As a remedy, we present an approach to automated benchmarking of incremental SAT and QBF solvers. Given a collection of formulas in (Q)DIMACS format generated incrementally by an application program, our approach automatically translates the formulas into instructions to import and solve a formula by an incremental SAT/QBF solver. The result of the translation is a program which replays the incremental solver calls and thus allows to evaluate incremental solvers independently from the application program. We illustrate our approach by different hardware verification problems for SAT and QBF solvers.

1   Introduction

Incremental solving has contributed to the success of SAT technology and potentially yields considerable improvements in applications where sequences of related formulas are solved. The logic of quantified Boolean formulas (QBF) extends propositional logic (SAT) by explicit existential and universal quantification of variables and lends itself for problems within PSPACE. Also for QBFs, incremental solving has been successfully applied in different domains [4,7,12,13].

The development of SAT and QBF solvers has been driven by competitive events like the SAT Competitions, QBF Evaluations (QBFEVAL), or the QBF Galleries. These events regularly result in publicly available benchmarks submitted by the participants which help to push the state of the art in SAT and QBF solving. In the past, the focus was on *non-incremental* SAT solving, and the evaluation of *incremental* solvers does not readily benefit from competitions and available benchmark collections.

Benchmarking incremental solvers requires to solve a sequence of related formulas. To this end, the formulas must be incrementally imported to the solver

---

This work was supported by the Austrian Science Fund (FWF) under grant S11409-N23. An extended version with proofs and detailed experimental results can be found in [8].

M. Davis et al. (Eds.): LPAR-20 2015, LNCS 9450, pp. 178–186, 2015.
DOI: 10.1007/978-3-662-48899-7_13

and solved by means of API calls. The API calls are typically generated by an application program, like a model checker or a formal verification or planning tool, for example, which tackles a problem by encoding it incrementally to a sequence of formulas. In order to compare different incremental solvers on that sequence of formulas, the solvers must be tightly coupled with the application program by linking them as a library. Hence benchmarking of incremental solvers relies on the application program used to generate the sequence of formulas which, however, often is not available. Even if the application program is available, it has to be adapted to support different solvers, where each solver might come with its own API. Further, the same sequence of formulas must be generated multiple times by the application program to compare different solvers.

To remedy this situation, we present an approach to automated benchmarking of incremental SAT and QBF solvers which decouples incremental SAT/QBF solving from incremental generation of formulas using an application program. This is achieved by translating a sequence of related CNFs and QBFs in prenex CNF (PCNF) into API calls of incremental solvers. Such a sequence might be the output of an application program or it was taken from existing benchmark collections. The formulas are then syntactically analyzed and instructions to incrementally import and solve them are generated. For CNFs, the instructions are function calls in the IPASIR API, which has been proposed for the Incremental Library Track of the SAT Race 2015.[1] For PCNFs, the instructions correspond to calls of the API of the QBF solver DepQBF,[2] which generalizes IPASIR and allows to update quantifier prefixes. The result of translating a sequence of formulas to solver API calls is a *standalone benchmarking program* which replays the incremental solver calls. Any incremental SAT/QBF solver supporting the IPASIR API or its QBF extension as implemented in DepQBF can be integrated by simply linking it to the program. This allows to compare different solvers independently from an application.

In some applications, the sequence of formulas depends on the used solver, e.g., if truth assignments are used to guide the process. Even then, our approach allows to compare different incremental solvers on the fixed sequences generated with one particular solver. However, then it is important to note that this comparison is limited to this particular fixed sequence, it would be unfair to conclude something about the performance of the solvers would they have been genuinely used within the application. This problem occurs also in sequences of formulas which are already present in benchmark collections. For experiments in this paper, we only considered applications where the sequences of generated formulas do not depend on intermediate truth assignments.

As our approach is also applicable to already generated formulas that are part of existing benchmark collections, such collections become available to developers of incremental solvers. Furthermore, comparisons between solvers in incremental and non-incremental mode are made possible. In addition, since the input for the benchmarking program describes only the differences between consecutive formulas, we obtain a quite succinct representation of incremental benchmarks.

---

[1] http://baldur.iti.kit.edu/sat-race-2015/.
[2] http://lonsing.github.io/depqbf/.

Our approach to automated benchmarking of incremental SAT and QBF solvers underpins the goal of the Incremental Library Track of the SAT Race 2015. We have generated benchmarks and submitted them to this competition.

2   Background

We consider propositional formulas in CNF and identify a CNF with the set of its clauses. A sequence $\sigma = (F_1, \ldots, F_n)$ of formulas represents the formulas that are incrementally generated and solved by an application program. A QBF $\psi = P.F$ in prenex CNF (PCNF) extends a CNF F by a quantifier prefix P. The prefix $P = Q_1, \ldots, Q_n$ of a QBF is a sequence of pairwise disjoint *quantified sets* Q_i. A quantified set Q is a set of variables with an associated quantifier $quant(Q) \in \{\exists, \forall\}$. We consider only closed PCNFs. For adjacent quantified sets Q_i and Q_{i+1}, $quant(Q_i) \neq quant(Q_{i+1})$. Given a prefix $P = Q_1, \ldots, Q_n$, index i is the *nesting level* of Q_i in P.

Our automated benchmarking approach is based on *solving under assumptions* [5,6] as implemented in modern SAT [1,10,14] and QBF solvers [11–13]. When solving a CNF under assumptions, the clauses are augmented with *selector variables*. Selector variables allow for temporary variable assignments made by the user via the solver API. If the value assigned to a selector variable satisfies the clauses where it occurs, then these clauses are effectively removed from the CNF. This way, the user controls which clauses appear in the CNF in the forthcoming incremental solver run. The IPASIR API proposed for the Incremental Library Track of the SAT Race 2015 consists of a set of functions for adding clauses to a CNF and handling assumptions. A disadvantage of this approach is that the user has to keep track of the used selector variables and assumptions manually.

For incremental QBF solving, additional API functions are needed to remove quantified sets and variables from and add them to a prefix. For QBF solvers, we generate calls in the API of DepQBF which generalizes IPASIR by functions to manipulate quantifier prefixes. Additionally, it allows to remove and add clauses in a stack-based way by push/pop operations where selector variables and assumptions are handled internal to the solver and hence are invisible to the user [11]. For details on the IPASIR and DepQBF interfaces, we refer to the respective webpages mentioned in the introduction.

3   Translating Related Formulas into Incremental Solver Calls

We present the workflow to translate a given sequence $\sigma = (\psi_1, \ldots, \psi_n)$ of related (P)CNFs into a standalone benchmarking program which calls an integrated solver via its API to incrementally solve the formulas from ψ_1 up to ψ_n:

1. First, the formulas in σ are analyzed and the syntactic differences between each ψ_i and ψ_{i+1} are identified. This includes clauses and quantified sets that have to be added or removed to obtain ψ_{i+1} from ψ_i. Also, variables may be

added to or removed from quantified sets. For CNFs, the prefix analysis is omitted.

2. The differences between the formulas identified in the first step are expressed by generic update instructions and are written to a file. A clause set is represented as a stack which can be updated via push and pop operations. The update instructions for quantifier prefixes are adding a quantified set at a nesting level and adding new variables to quantified sets already present in the prefix. Unused variables are deleted from the prefix by the solver.

3. Files that contain generic update instructions are then interpreted by a *benchmarking program* which translates them into calls of the IPASIR API (for CNFs) or QBF solver calls (for PCNFs). For the latter, calls of DepQBF's API are generated.

The benchmarking program is standalone and independent from the application program used to generate σ. It takes the files containing the generic update instructions as the only input. Multiple solvers may be integrated in the benchmarking program by linking them as libraries. Files containing the update instructions can serve as standardised benchmarks for incremental SAT and QBF solvers.

Analyzing CNFs. The algorithm to analyze sequences $\sigma = (F_1, \ldots, F_n)$ of clause sets relies on a stack-based representation of F_i which allows for simple deletion of clauses that have been added most recently. A clause c which appears in some F_i and is removed later at some point to obtain F_j with $i < j \leq n$ is called *volatile in* F_i. A clause which appears in some F_i for the first time and also appears in every F_j with $i < j \leq n$ and hence is never deleted is called *cumulative in* F_i.

The algorithm to analyze sequence σ identifies volatile and cumulative clauses in all clause sets in σ. Cumulative clauses are pushed first on the stack representing the current clause set because they are not removed anymore after they have been added. Volatile clauses are pushed last because they are removed at some point by a pop operation when constructing a later formula in σ. For illustration, consider the following sequence $\sigma = (F_1, \ldots, F_4)$ of clause sets F_i along with their respective sets C_i of cumulative clauses and sets V_i of volatile clauses:

$$F_1 = \{c_1, c_2, v_1\} \qquad C_1 = \{c_1, c_2\} \qquad V_1 = \{v_1\}$$
$$F_2 = \{c_1, c_2, c_3, v_1, v_2\} \qquad C_2 = \{c_3\} \qquad V_2 = \{v_1, v_2\}$$
$$F_3 = \{c_1, c_2, c_3, c_4, v_1, v_3\} \qquad C_3 = \{c_4\} \qquad V_3 = \{v_1, v_3\}$$
$$F_4 = \{c_1, c_2, c_3, c_4, c_5\} \qquad C_4 = \{c_5\} \qquad V_4 = \emptyset$$

After the sets of cumulative and volatile clauses have been identified for each F_i, the clause sets can be incrementally constructed by means of the following operations on the clause stack: adding a set C of clauses permanently to a formula by add(C), pushing a set C of clauses on the stack by push(C), and popping a set of clauses from the stack by pop(). The sequence $\sigma = (F_1, \ldots, F_4)$ from the example above is generated incrementally by executing the following stack operations:

Input : Clause sets $F_1, F_2, \ldots, F_n$ (at least two sets are required)
Output: $C_1, \ldots, C_n$ (sets of cumulative clauses to be added)
                    $V_1, \ldots, V_n$ (sets of volatile clauses to be pushed or popped)

1 $V_1 \longleftarrow F_1 \setminus F_2$; $C_1 \longleftarrow F_1 \setminus V_1$;
2 **for** $i \leftarrow 2$ **to** $n - 1$ **do**
3 | $V_i \longleftarrow F_i \setminus F_{i+1}$;
4 | $C_i \longleftarrow (F_i \setminus F_{i-1}) \setminus V_i$;
5 | **foreach** $c \in V_i \cap F_{i-1}$ **do**
6 | | **for** $j \leftarrow 1$ **to** $i - 1$ **do**
7 | | | **if** $c \in C_j$ **then**
8 | | | | $C_j \longleftarrow C_j \setminus \{c\}$;
9 | | | | **for** $k = j$ **to** $i - 1$ **do**
10 | | | | | $V_k \longleftarrow V_k \cup \{c\}$;
11 | | | | **break** ;

12 $C_n \longleftarrow F_n \setminus F_{n-1}$; $V_n \longleftarrow \emptyset$;

Algorithm 1. Identifying cumulative and volatile clauses.

	add(C_1)	push(V_1)
pop()	add(C_2)	push(V_2)
pop()	add(C_3)	push(V_3)
pop()	add(C_4)	push(V_4)

Note that the above schema of stack operations generalises to *arbitrary* sequences of clause sets, i.e., we need at most one push, one add, and one pop operation in each step, provided that the clauses have been classified as volatile or cumulative before.

The algorithm for identifying cumulative and volatile clauses in a sequence of clause sets appears as Algorithm 1. For SAT solvers supporting the IPASIR API, stack frames for volatile clauses pushed on the clause stack are implemented by selector variables. Our current implementation of the benchmarking program includes **DepQBF** as the only incremental QBF solver which supports push/pop operations natively via its API [11]. Note that the relevant part of the input that potentially limits scalability of Algorithm 1 is the number of variables and clauses in the formulas. The number of formulas is usually relatively low. The operations on clause sets are implemented such that set intersection and difference are in $O(m \cdot log\, m)$, searching an element is in $O(m)$, and adding or deleting elements are in $O(1)$, where m is the maximal number of clauses in any formula.

Analyzing PCNFs. For sequences of QBFs, additionally the differences between quantifier prefixes must be identified. Two quantified sets Q and Q' are *matching* iff $Q \cap Q' \neq \emptyset$. Prefix R is *update-compatible* to prefix S iff all of the following conditions hold: (i) for any quantified set of R, there is at most one matching quantified set in S; (ii) if P is a quantified set of R and Q is a matching quantified set in S, then $quant(P) = quant(Q)$; and (iii) for any two quantified sets P_1 and

Input : Prefix R and S (R has to be update-compatible to S)
Output: Instructions to update R to S

```
1  n ⟵ 0;    m ⟵ 0;
2  foreach quantified set Q in S from left to right do
3  |   if Q has a matching quantified set M in R then
4  |   |   m ⟵ n + nesting level of M in R;
5  |   |   print "Add literals Q \ M to quantified set at nesting level m.";
6  |
7  |   else
8  |   |   n ⟵ n + 1;
9  |   |   m ⟵ m + 1;
10 |   |   print "Add quantified set Q at nesting level m.";
```

Algorithm 2. Generating update instructions for quantifier prefixes.

P_2 in S with matching quantified sets Q_1 and Q_2 in R, respectively, if the nesting level of P_1 is less than the nesting level P_2, then the nesting level of Q_1 is less than the nesting level of Q_2.

The instructions to update quantifier prefixes are adding a quantified set at a given nesting level or adding a variable to a quantified set at a given nesting level. Update compatibility between prefixes R and S guarantees that there is a sequence of instructions to turn R into S after unused variables and empty quantified sets have been deleted by the QBF solver. In particular, Condition (i) guarantees that there is no ambiguity when mapping quantified sets from the prefixes, (ii) expresses that quantifiers cannot change, and (iii) states that quantified sets cannot be swapped. The algorithm to generate update instructions first checks if two quantifier prefixes R and S are update-compatible. If this is the case, then update instructions are computed as illustrated by Algorithm 2.

4   Case Studies

In this section, we showcase our approach using different hardware verification problems for both SAT and QBF solvers. Benchmark problems consist of sequences of formulas that were either generated by a model-checking tool or that were taken from existing benchmark collections where the original application is not available.

SAT: Bounded-Model Checking for Hardware Verification. We consider benchmarks used for the single safety property track of the last Hardware Model Checking Competition (HWMCC 2014)[3]. Based on the CNFs generated by the BMC-based model checker aigbmc[4], we use our tools to generate incremental solver calls and compare different SAT solvers that implement the IPASIR interface. We used the SAT solvers MiniSAT (v.220) [5], PicoSAT (v.961) [2], and

---

[3] http://fmv.jku.at/hwmcc14cav/.
[4] Part of the AIGER package (http://fmv.jku.at/aiger/).

Table 1. Summary of different SAT solvers on hardware verification problems.

	#problems	MiniSAT	PicoSAT	Lingeling	DepQBF
BMC problems unrolled by 50 steps	11	284 / 7	216 / 3	276 / 7	190 / 1
BMC problems unrolled by 100 steps	28	905 / 14	754 / 4	872 / 19	491 / 2

Lingeling (v.ayv) [3] as well as the QBF solver DepQBF (v.4) for the considered problems. All experiments were performed on an AMD Opteron 6238 at 2.6 GHz under 64-bit Linux with a time limit of 3600 s and a memory limit of 7 GB.

Table 1 summarises the results. For each solver and problem class, numbers m / n mean that m formulas in total were solved within the time limit, and n is the number of problems where the maximal number of formulas among all other solvers could be solved. For example, the first line summarises the results for BMC problems that were unrolled by 50 steps. There are 11 problems in this class, thus 550 formulas in total. From these formulas, MiniSAT could solve 284 formulas, and for 7 out of 11 problems, no other solver could solve more formulas than MiniSAT. Not surprisingly, all SAT solvers outperform the QBF solver DepQBF but there are few cases where DepQBF can compete. MiniSAT solves most formulas in total while Lingeling dominates on most benchmarks. More detailed experimental results can be found in [8]. The average time for our analyzing algorithm was 522 s. The number of clauses in the original sequences ranged from 2.3 to 56.3 million with an average of around 19 million clauses. The inputs for the benchmarking program that represent only the update instructions comprise only 1.2 million clauses on average which shows that we obtain a quite compact representation of incremental benchmarks. We have submitted all problems from Table 1 to the Incremental Library Track of the SAT Race 2015.

Table 2. QBF solvers on incomplete design problems.

Benchmark	k	Non-incremental		Incremental		
		QuBE	DepQBF	QuBE (fwd)	QuBE (bwd)	DepQBF
enc04	17	3	3	3	2	1
enc09	17	7	5	7	4	3
enc01	33	31	17	28	24	5
enc03	33	33	16	289	28	27
enc05	33	64	24	61	46	7
enc06	33	29	26	28	24	10
enc07	33	75	16	76	69	5
enc08	33	108	16	110	79	5
enc02	65	271	106	TO	269	175
tlc01	132	26	68	133	130	17
tlc03	132	24	160	8	8	17
tlc04	132	769	2196	1204	27	25
tlc05	152	1330	4201	2057	38	34
tlc02	258	MO	TO	MO	98	1908

QSAT: Partial Design Problems. To illustrate our approach in the context of QBF solving, we consider the problem of *verifying partial designs*, i.e., sequential circuits where parts of the specification are black-boxed. In recent work [12, 13], the question whether a given safety property can be violated regardless of the implementation of a black-box has been translated to QBFs which are solved incrementally by a version of the QBF solver QuBE [9]. Benchmarks are available from QBFLIB,[5] however neither the solver used in [12,13] nor the application program used to generate sequences of QBFs are publicly available. Marin et al. [12] introduced two encoding strategies: forward incremental and backward incremental reasoning. In a nutshell, the quantifier prefix is always extended to the right in the former approach, while it is extended to the left in the latter approach. Both strategies yield the same sequences of formulas up to renaming [12]. We used the publicly available instances from the forward-incremental encoding without preprocessing to evaluate DepQBF. Instances from the backward-incremental approach are not publicly available.

Table 2 shows the comparison between QuBE and DepQBF. Runtimes are in seconds, k is the index of the first satisfiable formula, TO and MO refer to a timeout and memout, respectively. The maximal runtime of Algorithms 1 and 2 was 95 s. Runtimes for QuBE in Table 2 are the ones reported in [12]. There, experiments were carried out on an AMD Opteron 252 processor running at 2.6 GHz with 4 GB of main memory and a timeout of 7200 s. Experiments for DepQBF were performed on a 2.53 GHz Intel Core 2 Duo processor with 4 GB of main memory with OS X 10.9.5 installed. Thus runtimes are not directly comparable because experiments were carried out on different machines, they give, however, a rough picture of how the solvers relate. Like QuBE, DepQBF benefits from the incremental strategy on most instances. The backward-incremental strategy is clearly the dominating strategy for QuBE. A quite eye-catching observation is that forward-incremental solving, while hardly improving the performance of QuBE compared to the non-incremental approach, works quite well for DepQBF.

5   Conclusion

We presented an approach to automated benchmarking of incremental SAT and QBF solvers by translating sequences of formulas into API calls of incremental SAT and QBF solvers executed by a benchmarking program. Several incremental solvers may be tightly integrated into the benchmarking program by linking them as libraries. Thus, we decouple the generation of formulas by an application from the solving process which is particularly relevant when application programs are not available. Additionally, we make sequences of formulas which already exist in public benchmark collections available for benchmarking and testing. We illustrated our approach to automated benchmarking of incremental SAT and QBF solvers on instances from hardware verification problems. To improve the performance of incremental QBF solving on these problems, we want to integrate incremental preprocessing into DepQBF. As shown in [12,13], preprocessing potentially improves the performance of incremental workflows considerably.

---

[5] http://www.qbflib.org.

References

1. Audemard, G., Lagniez, J.-M., Simon, L.: Improving glucose for incremental SAT solving with assumptions: application to MUS extraction. In: Järvisalo, M., Van Gelder, A. (eds.) SAT 2013. LNCS, vol. 7962, pp. 309–317. Springer, Heidelberg (2013)
2. Biere, A.: PicoSAT essentials. JSAT **4**(2–4), 75–97 (2008)
3. Biere, A.: Lingeling essentials, a tutorial on design and implementation aspects of the the SAT solver lingeling. In: Berre, D.L. (ed.) Pragmatics of SAT (POS) Workshop. EPiC Series, vol. 27, p. 88. EasyChair (2014)
4. Bloem, R., Egly, U., Klampfl, P., Könighofer, R., Lonsing, F.: SAT-Based methods for circuit synthesis. In: FMCAD, pp. 31–34. IEEE (2014)
5. Eén, N., Sörensson, N.: An extensible SAT-solver. In: Giunchiglia, E., Tacchella, A. (eds.) SAT 2003. LNCS, vol. 2919, pp. 502–518. Springer, Heidelberg (2004)
6. Eén, N., Sörensson, N.: Temporal induction by incremental SAT solving. Electr. Notes Theor. Comput. Sci. **89**(4), 543–560 (2003)
7. Egly, U., Kronegger, M., Lonsing, F., Pfandler, A.: Conformant planning as a case study of incremental QBF solving. In: Aranda-Corral, G.A., Calmet, J., Martín-Mateos, F.J. (eds.) AISC 2014. LNCS, vol. 8884, pp. 120–131. Springer, Heidelberg (2014)
8. Egly, U., Lonsing, F., Oetsch, J.: Automated benchmarking of incremental SAT and QBF solvers. CoRR abs/1506.08563 (2015). http://arxiv.org/abs/1506.08563, LPAR 2015 proceedings version (short paper) with appendix
9. Giunchiglia, E., Marin, P., Narizzano, M.: QuBE7.0. JSAT **7**(2–3), 83–88 (2010)
10. Lagniez, J.-M., Biere, A.: Factoring out assumptions to speed up MUS extraction. In: Järvisalo, M., Van Gelder, A. (eds.) SAT 2013. LNCS, vol. 7962, pp. 276–292. Springer, Heidelberg (2013)
11. Lonsing, F., Egly, U.: Incremental QBF solving. In: O'Sullivan, B. (ed.) CP 2014. LNCS, vol. 8656, pp. 514–530. Springer, Heidelberg (2014)
12. Marin, P., Miller, C., Lewis, M.D.T., Becker, B.: Verification of partial designs using incremental QBF solving. In: Rosenstiel, W., Thiele, L. (ed.) DATE, pp. 623–628. IEEE (2012)
13. Miller, C., Marin, P., Becker, B.: Verification of partial designs using incremental QBF. AI Commun. **28**(2), 283–307 (2015)
14. Nadel, A., Ryvchin, V., Strichman, O.: Ultimately incremental SAT. In: Sinz, C., Egly, U. (eds.) SAT 2014. LNCS, vol. 8561, pp. 206–218. Springer, Heidelberg (2014)

A Labelled Sequent Calculus for Intuitionistic Public Announcement Logic

Shoshin Nomura[✉], Katsuhiko Sano, and Satoshi Tojo

School of Information Science,
Japan Advanced Institute of Science and Technology, Ishikawa, Japan
{nomura,v-sano,tojo}@jaist.ac.jp

Abstract. Intuitionistic Public Announcement Logic (IntPAL) proposed by Ma et al. (2014) aims at formalizing changes of an agent's knowledge in a constructive manner. IntPAL can be regarded as an intuitionistic generalization of Public Announcement Logic (PAL) whose modal basis is the intuitionistic modal logic IK by Fischer Servi (1984) and Simpson (1994). We also refer to IK for the basis of this paper. Meanwhile, Nomura et al. (2015) provided a cut-free labelled sequent calculus based on the study of Maffezioli et al. (2010). In this paper, we introduce a labelled sequent calculus for IntPAL (we call it **GIntPAL**) as both an intuitionistic variant of **GPAL** and a public announcement extension of Simpson's labelled calculus, and show that all theorems of the Hilbert axiomatization of IntPAL are also derivable in **GIntPAL** with the cut rule. Then we prove the admissibility of the cut rule in **GIntPAL** and also the soundness result for birelational Kripke semantics. Finally, we derive the semantic completeness of **GIntPAL** as a corollary of these theorems.

1 Introduction

Public Announcement Logic (PAL) presented by Plaza [22] is a logic for formally expressing changes of human knowledge, and has been the basis of Dynamic Epistemic Logics. A proof system for PAL has also been provided in terms of Hilbert-style axiomatization in [22], and some other proof systems have been given to it, one of which is a labelled sequent calculus[1] by Maffezioli et at. [15] and its revised version by Balbiani et al. [2] and Nomura et al. [19]. In [19], we provide a cut-free labelled sequent calculus, called **GPAL**.

Epistemic logics including PAL usually employ classical logic as their underlying logic, but we may consider a weaker logic as a basis for expressing different type of knowledge. Intuitionistic modal logic is one of prospects for the purpose; especially, in the context of epistemic logic, knowledge defined in an intuitionistic system can be regarded as knowledge with verification or evidence

---

[1] Labelled sequent calculus (cf. [17]) is one of the most uniform approaches for sequent calculus for modal logic, where each formula has a label corresponding to an element (sometimes called a possible world) of a domain in Kripke semantics for modal logic.

© Springer-Verlag Berlin Heidelberg 2015
M. Davis et al. (Eds.): LPAR-20 2015, LNCS 9450, pp. 187–202, 2015.
DOI: 10.1007/978-3-662-48899-7_14

(cf. [1, 25]). The area of intuitionistic modal logics, since Fitch [9] proposed, have been developed historically by efforts of several logicians (e.g., [5, 8, 20, 23, 24]). Intuitionistic PAL (IntPAL) is both an intuitionistc variant of PAL and a public announcement extension of an intuitionistic modal logic; and on the foundation of the past studies, Ma et al. [14] have recently given a Hilbert-style axiomatization of IntPAL (we called it **HIntPAL**, based on intuitionistic modal logic IK (or IntK) by Fischer Servi [8] and Simpson [24]) which is shown to be semantically complete for birelational Kripke semantics via algebraic semantics.

Meanwhile, it is well-known, since Gentzen [11], that the sequent calculus **LJ** for intuitionistic logic is obtained from the sequent calculus **LK** of classical logic, by restricting the right-hand side of a sequent to at most one formula. It is quite natural to ask if we can obtain an intuitionistic version of **GPAL** by using the same restriction. Therefore, our target of this paper is to construct a labelled sequent calculus (we call it **GIntPAL** and **GIntPAL**$^+$ if it has the cut rule) for **HIntPAL**.

In the recent studies of knowledge representation, several constructive description logics [4, 6, 16] are proposed to investigate possibly incomplete knowledge. Since constructive description logics are technically regarded as intuitionistic multi-modal logics, our Gentzen-style calculus for IntPAL could be applied to a dynamic extension of these constructive description logics which allows an underlying ontology in the semantics to be dynamically changed. It is our expectation that the sequent calculus brings abundant benefits especially for constructive knowledge requiring verification, since such a calculus is usually feasible in computation, compared with a Hilbert-style axiomatizaion.

The outline of the paper is as follows. Section 2 provides the birelational Kripke semantics and the Hilbert-style axiomatization **HIntPAL** for IntPAL. Section 3 introduces our calculus **GIntPAL** (with the cut rule) and shows that all theorems of **HIntPAL** are derivable in **GIntPAL**$^+$ (Theorem 1). Section 4 establishes the cut elimination theorem of **GIntPAL**$^+$ (Theorem 2) and, as a corollary of the theorem, shows that **GIntPAL**$^+$ is consistent. Section 5 tackles the soundness theorem of **GIntPAL**$^+$ (Theorem 3), and it should be noted that its soundness is not straightforward at all by the following two reasons. First, it depends on a non-trivial choice of the notions of validity of a sequent as suggested in [19]. Second, there is another difficulty, pointed out in [24], which is peculiar to intuitionist modal logic. Then the semantic completeness of **GIntPAL** (Corollary 3) is shown through the proven theorems. The last section concludes the paper.

2   Birelational Kripke Semantics and Axiomatization of IntPAL

First of all, we address the syntax of IntPAL. Let Prop $= \{p, q, r, \ldots\}$ be a countably infinite set of propositional variables and G $= \{a, b, c, \ldots\}$ a nonempty finite set of agents. Then the set Form $= \{A, B, C, \ldots\}$ of formulas of IntPAL is inductively defined as follows:

$$A ::= p \mid \bot \mid (A \wedge A) \mid (A \vee A) \mid (A \rightarrow A) \mid \Box_a A \mid \Diamond_a A \mid [A]A \mid \langle A \rangle A,$$

where $p \in \mathsf{Prop}$, $a \in \mathsf{G}$. We define $\neg A := A \rightarrow \bot$, and also define $\top := \bot \rightarrow \bot$. The formula $A \leftrightarrow B$ is an abbreviation of $(A \rightarrow B) \wedge (B \rightarrow A)$. $\Box_a A$ is to read 'agent a knows that A', and $[A]B$ is to read 'after public announcement of A, it holds that B'.

Example 1. Let us consider a propositional variable p to read 'it will rain tomorrow'. Then a formula $\neg(\Box_a p \vee \Box_a \neg p)$ means that a does not know whether it will rain tomorrow or not, and $[\neg p]\Box_a \neg p$ means that after a public announcement (e.g., a weather report) of $\neg p$, a knows that it will not rain tomorrow.

Let us go on to the next subject, the semantics of IntPAL. We mainly follow the birelational Kripke semantics introduced in Ma et al. [14], which is based on intuitionistic version of modal logic K. We call $\mathfrak{F} = \langle W, \leqslant, (R_a)_{a \in \mathsf{G}} \rangle$ an *IntK-frame* if $(W, \leqslant)$ is a nonempty poset (W is also denoted by $\mathcal{D}(\mathfrak{M})$), $(R_a)_{a \in \mathsf{G}}$ is a G-indexed family of binary relations on W^2 such that the following two conditions $(F1)$ and $(F2)$ from Simpson [24, p.50] are satisfied:

$$(F1) : (\geqslant \circ R_a) \subseteq (R_a \circ \geqslant), \quad (F2) : (R_a \circ \leqslant) \subseteq (\leqslant \circ R_a),$$

where $\circ$ is the composition of relations.

Moreover, a pair $\mathfrak{M} = \langle \mathfrak{F}, V \rangle$ is an *IntK-model* if $\mathfrak{F}$ is an IntK-frame and $V : \mathsf{Prop} \rightarrow \mathcal{P}^{\uparrow}(W)$ is a valuation function where

$$\mathcal{P}^{\uparrow}(W) := \{ X \in \mathcal{P}(W) \mid x \in X \text{ and } x \leqslant y \text{ jointly imply } y \in X \text{ for all } x, y \in W \},$$

that is, $\mathcal{P}^{\uparrow}(W)$ is the set of all upward closed sets. Next, let us define the satisfaction relation $\mathfrak{M}, w \Vdash A$. Given an IntK-model $\mathfrak{M}$, a world $w \in \mathcal{D}(\mathfrak{M})$, and a formula $A \in \mathsf{Form}$, we define $\mathfrak{M}, w \Vdash A$ as follows:

$\mathfrak{M}, w \Vdash p$	*iff*	$w \in V(p)$,
$\mathfrak{M}, w \Vdash \bot$		*Never,*
$\mathfrak{M}, w \Vdash A \wedge B$	*iff*	$\mathfrak{M}, w \Vdash A$ and $\mathfrak{M}, w \Vdash B$,
$\mathfrak{M}, w \Vdash A \vee B$	*iff*	$\mathfrak{M}, w \Vdash A$ or $\mathfrak{M}, w \Vdash B$,
$\mathfrak{M}, w \Vdash A \rightarrow B$	*iff*	for all $v \in W : w \leqslant v$ and $\mathfrak{M}, v \Vdash A$ jointly imply $\mathfrak{M}, v \Vdash B$,
$\mathfrak{M}, w \Vdash \Box_a A$	*iff*	for all $v \in W : w(\leqslant \circ R_a)v$ implies $\mathfrak{M}, v \Vdash A$,
$\mathfrak{M}, w \Vdash \Diamond_a A$	*iff*	for some $v \in W : wR_a v$ and $\mathfrak{M}, v \Vdash A$,
$\mathfrak{M}, w \Vdash [A]B$	*iff*	for all $v \in W : w \leqslant v$ and $\mathfrak{M}, v \Vdash A$ jointly imply $\mathfrak{M}^A, v \Vdash B$,
$\mathfrak{M}, w \Vdash \langle A \rangle B$	*iff*	$\mathfrak{M}, w \Vdash A$ and $\mathfrak{M}^A, w \Vdash B$,

where $\mathfrak{M}^A$, in the definition of the announcement operators, is the restricted IntK-model to the truth set of A, defined as $\mathfrak{M}^A = \langle [\![A]\!]_{\mathfrak{M}}, \leqslant^A, (R_a^A)_{a \in \mathsf{G}}, V^A \rangle$ with

---

[2] Epistemic logics are basically based on the modal system S5, but the most primitive modal system K is usually the starting point in the case of constructing a proof system of a modal logic; and we also follow the custom and employ IntK for its semantics.

$$[A]_{\mathfrak{M}} := \{w \in W \mid \mathfrak{M}, w \Vdash A\}$$
$$\leqslant^A \ := \ \leqslant \cap ([A]_{\mathfrak{M}} \times [A]_{\mathfrak{M}})$$
$$R_a^A \ := \ R_a \cap ([A]_{\mathfrak{M}} \times [A]_{\mathfrak{M}})$$
$$V^A(p) := V(p) \cap [A]_{\mathfrak{M}} \qquad (p \in \mathsf{Prop}).$$

We note that the conditions $(F1)$ and $(F2)$ are still satisfied in $\mathfrak{M}^A$. Added to these, the restriction of the composition $(\leqslant \circ R_a)^A$ is defined by $(\leqslant \circ R_a) \cap ([A]_{\mathfrak{M}} \times [A]_{\mathfrak{M}})$.

Definition 1. *A formula A is* valid *in an IntK-model $\mathfrak{M}$ if $\mathfrak{M}, w \Vdash A$ for all $w \in \mathcal{D}(\mathfrak{M})$.*

By the above semantics, the important semantic feature of hereditary may be preserved as follows.[3]

Proposition 1 (Hereditary). *For all IntK-models $\mathfrak{M}$, for all $w, v \in \mathcal{D}(\mathfrak{M})$, if $\mathfrak{M}, w \Vdash A$ and $w \leqslant v$, then $\mathfrak{M}, v \Vdash A$, for any formula A.*

Besides, the following proposition is also significant.

Proposition 2. $(\leqslant \circ R_a)^A = (\leqslant^A \circ R_a^A)$

Proof. We briefly look at the direction of $\subseteq$. Fix any $v, u \in \mathcal{D}(\mathfrak{M})$ such that $v(\leqslant \circ R_a)^A u$. We show $x(\leqslant^A \circ R_a^A)u$. By the above definition, we have $v(\leqslant \circ R_a)u$ and $(v, u) \in [A]_{\mathfrak{M}} \times [A]_{\mathfrak{M}}$, and then there exists some t, such that $v \leqslant t$ and $tR_a u$. Take such t, and by Proposition 1, we get $t \in [A]_{\mathfrak{M}}$. Therefore, we conclude $x(\leqslant^A \circ R_a^A)u$. □

We denote finite lists $(A_1, ..., A_n)$ of formulas by α, β, etc., and do the empty list by ϵ. As an abbreviation, for any list $\alpha = (A_1, A_2, ..., A_n)$ of formulas, we naturally define $\mathfrak{M}^\alpha$ inductively as: $\mathfrak{M}^\alpha := \mathfrak{M}$ (if $\alpha = \epsilon$), and $\mathfrak{M}^\alpha := (\mathfrak{M}^\beta)^{A_n} = \langle W^{\beta, A_n}, (R_a^{\beta, A_n})_{a \in \mathsf{G}}, V^{\beta, A_n} \rangle$ (if $\alpha = \beta, A_n$). We may also denote $(\mathfrak{M}^\beta)^{A_n}$ by $\mathfrak{M}^{\beta, A_n}$ for simplicity. From Proposition 2, the next corollary may be easily shown by induction on the length of α.

Corollary 1. $(\leqslant \circ R_a)^\alpha = (\leqslant^\alpha \circ R_a^\alpha)$

Probably, the reader who is not familiar with IntPAL may not easily see what it is, so the following example might help for understanding the heart of IntPAL.

Example 2. Example 1 can be semantically modeled as follows. Let us consider $\mathsf{G} = \{a\}$ and the following two models such as: $\mathfrak{M} := \langle W, \leqslant, R_a, V \rangle$ where $W := \{w_1, w_2\}, \leqslant := \{(w_1, w_1), (w_2, w_2)\}, R_a := \{w_1, w_2\}^2$ and $V(p) = \{w_1\}$,[4] and,

---

[3] Two conditions, $(F1)$ and $(F2)$, are required to show hereditary (and validity of axioms) in IntK on which **GIntPAL** is based. In fact, one more condition is added to the two in [14] for some specific purpose in their paper. That is $R_a = (\leqslant \circ R_a) \cap (R_a \circ \geqslant)$.

[4] Note that the above IntK frame satisfies the conditions since $(R_a \circ \leqslant) = (\leqslant \circ R_a) = (\geqslant \circ R_a) = (R_a \circ \leqslant) = \{w_1, w_1\}^2$.

$\mathfrak{M}^{\neg p} = \langle \{w_2\}, \{(w_2, w_2)\}, \{(w_2, w_2)\}, V^{\neg p}\rangle$ where $V^{\neg p}(p) = \emptyset$. These models are shown in graphic forms as follows.

In $\mathfrak{M}$, agent a does not know whether p or $\neg p$ (i.e., $\neg(\square_a p \vee \square_a \neg p)$) is valid in $\mathfrak{M}$). But after an announcement of $\neg p$, agent a comes to know $\neg p$ in the restricted model $\mathfrak{M}$ to $\neg p$.

Hilbert-style axiomatization of intuitionistic modal logic IntK consists of axioms of IntK in Table 1 and the rules (MP) and $(Nec\square_a)$ in Table 1. Hilbert-style axiomatization of IntPAL (**HIntPAL**), is defined in Table 1, where the axiom (from $(RA1)$ to $(RA14)$), called *recursion axioms*, and one inference rule $(Nec[.])$ are added to the axiomatization of IntK. Through the axioms and rules, each theorem of **HIntPAL** may be reduced into a theorem of the axiomatization of IntK. And the previous work [14] has shown the completeness theorem of **HIntPAL**.

Fact 1 (Completeness of HIntPAL). *For any formula A, A is valid in all IntK-models iff A is a theorem of* **HIntPAL***.*

Table 1. Hilbert-style axiomatization of IntPAL: **HIntPAL**

Axioms of IntK		Recursion Axioms	
all instantiations of theorems of		$(RA1)$	$[A]\bot \leftrightarrow \neg A$
intuitionistic propositional logic		$(RA2)$	$\langle A\rangle\bot \leftrightarrow \bot$
$(IK1)$	$\square_a(p \to q) \to (\square_a p \to \square_a q)$	$(RA3)$	$[A]p \leftrightarrow (A \to p)$
$(IK2)$	$\Diamond_a(p \vee q) \to (\Diamond_a p \vee \Diamond_a q)$	$(RA4)$	$\langle A\rangle p \leftrightarrow (A \wedge p)$
$(IK3)$	$\neg\Diamond_a\bot$	$(RA5)$	$[A](B \vee C) \leftrightarrow A \to \langle A\rangle B \vee \langle A\rangle C$
$(FS1)$	$\Diamond_a(p \to q) \to (\square_a p \to \Diamond_a q)$	$(RA6)$	$\langle A\rangle(B \vee C) \leftrightarrow (\langle A\rangle B \vee \langle A\rangle C)$
$(FS2)$	$(\Diamond_a p \to \square_a q) \to \square_a(p \to q)$	$(RA7)$	$[A](B \wedge C) \leftrightarrow [A]B \wedge [A]C$
		$(RA8)$	$\langle A\rangle(B \wedge C) \leftrightarrow \langle A\rangle B \wedge \langle A\rangle C$
		$(RA9)$	$[A](B \to C) \leftrightarrow \langle A\rangle B \to \langle A\rangle C$
Inference Rules		$(RA10)$	$\langle A\rangle(B \to C) \leftrightarrow A \wedge (\langle A\rangle B \to \langle A\rangle C)$
(MP)	*From A and $A \to B$, infer B*	$(RA11)$	$[A]\square_a B \leftrightarrow (A \to \square_a[A]B)$
$(Nec\square_a)$	*From A, infer $\square_a A$*	$(RA12)$	$\langle A\rangle\square_a B \leftrightarrow (A \wedge \square_a[A]B)$
$(Nec[.])$	*From A, infer $[B]A$, for any B*	$(RA13)$	$[A]\Diamond_a B \leftrightarrow (A \to \Diamond_a[A]B)$
		$(RA14)$	$\langle A\rangle\Diamond_a B \leftrightarrow (A \wedge \Diamond_a\langle A\rangle B)$

3 Labelled Sequent Calculus for IntPAL

As we have mentioned in the introduction, a labelled sequent calculus for PAL has been provided by Maffezioli et at. [15], and its revised version **GPAL** by Nomura et al. [19]. And **GIntPAL** is basically the same as **GPAL** but the number of labelled expressions in the right-hand side of a sequent is restricted to at most one.

Now we introduce **GIntPAL**. Let $\mathsf{Var} = \{x, y, z, ...\}$ be a countably infinite set of variables. Then, given any $x, y \in \mathsf{Var}$, any list α of formulas and any formula A, we say $x{:}^\alpha A$ is a *labelled formula*, and that, for any agent $a \in \mathsf{G}$, $x\mathsf{R}_a^\alpha y$ is a *relational atom*. Intuitively, the labelled formula $x{:}^\alpha A$ corresponds to '$\mathfrak{M}^\alpha, x \Vdash A$' and is to read 'after a sequence α of public announcements, x still exists (*survives*) in the restricted domain *and* A holds at x', and the relational atom $x\mathsf{R}_a^\alpha y$ is to read 'after a sequence α of public announcements both x and y exist (survive) and there is a accessibility relation of a from x to y'. We also use the term, *labelled expressions* to indicate that they are either labelled formulas or relational atoms and we denote labelled expressions by $\mathfrak{A}, \mathfrak{B}$, etc. A *sequent* $\Gamma \Rightarrow \Delta$ is a pair of finite multi-sets of labelled expressions, where at most one labelled expression can appear in Δ. The set of inference rules of **GIntPAL** is shown in Table 2. Hereinafter, for any sequent $\Gamma \Rightarrow \Delta$, if $\Gamma \Rightarrow \Delta$ is derivable in **GIntPAL**, we write **GIntPAL** $\vdash \Gamma \Rightarrow \Delta$.

Moreover, **GIntPAL**$^+$ is **GIntPAL** with the following rule (*Cut*):

$$\frac{\Gamma \Rightarrow \mathfrak{A} \qquad \mathfrak{A}, \Gamma' \Rightarrow \Delta}{\Gamma, \Gamma' \Rightarrow \Delta} \ (Cut),$$

where $\mathfrak{A}$ in (*Cut*) is called a *cut expression*. And, we use the term *principal expression* of an inference rule of **GIntPAL**$^+$ if a labelled expression is newly introduced on the left uppersequent or the right uppersequent by the rule of **GIntPAL**$^+$.

In this section, we show the set of derivable formulas in **HIntPAL** is equal to the set derivable formulas in **GIntPAL**$^+$. Let us define the length of a labelled expression $\mathfrak{A}$ in advance.

Definition 2. *For any formula A, $\mathsf{len}(A)$ is defined to be the number of the propositional variables and the logical connectives in A.*

$$\mathsf{len}(\alpha) = \begin{cases} 0 & \text{if } \alpha = \epsilon \\ \mathsf{len}(\beta) + \mathsf{len}(A) & \text{if } \alpha = \beta, A, \end{cases} \qquad \mathsf{len}(\mathfrak{A}) = \begin{cases} \mathsf{len}(\alpha) + \mathsf{len}(A) & \text{if } \mathfrak{A} = x{:}^\alpha A \\ \mathsf{len}(\alpha) + 1 & \text{if } \mathfrak{A} = x\mathsf{R}_a^\alpha y. \end{cases}$$

The following lemma is helpful to make our presentation of derivations shorter.

Lemma 1. *For any labelled expression $\mathfrak{A}$ and any finite multi-set of labelled expressions Γ, **GIntPAL** $\vdash \mathfrak{A}, \Gamma \Rightarrow \mathfrak{A}$.*

Next, we define the notion of substitution of variables in labelled expressions.

Table 2. Gentzen-style sequent calculus **GIntPAL**

In what follows in this table, Δ contains at most one labelled expression.

(Initial Sequents)

$$x{:}^\alpha A \Rightarrow x{:}^\alpha A \quad x\mathsf{R}_a^\alpha v \Rightarrow x\mathsf{R}_a^\alpha v$$

$$x{:}^\alpha \bot \Rightarrow$$

(Structural Rules)

$$\frac{\Gamma \Rightarrow \Delta}{\mathfrak{A},\Gamma \Rightarrow \Delta}\ (Lw) \quad \frac{\Gamma \Rightarrow}{\Gamma \Rightarrow \mathfrak{A}}\ (Rw) \quad \frac{\mathfrak{A},\mathfrak{A},\Gamma \Rightarrow \Delta}{\mathfrak{A},\Gamma \Rightarrow \Delta}\ (Lc)$$

(Rules for propositional connectives)

$$\frac{\Gamma \Rightarrow x{:}^\alpha A \quad x{:}^\alpha B,\Gamma \Rightarrow \Delta}{x{:}^\alpha A \to B,\Gamma \Rightarrow \Delta}\ (L\to) \quad \frac{x{:}^\alpha A,\Gamma \Rightarrow x{:}^\alpha B}{\Gamma \Rightarrow x{:}^\alpha A \to B}\ (R\to)$$

$$\frac{x{:}^\alpha A,\Gamma \Rightarrow \Delta}{x{:}^\alpha A \wedge B,\Gamma \Rightarrow \Delta}\ (L\wedge 1) \quad \frac{x{:}^\alpha B,\Gamma \Rightarrow \Delta}{x{:}^\alpha A \wedge B,\Gamma \Rightarrow \Delta}\ (L\wedge 2) \quad \frac{\Gamma \Rightarrow x{:}^\alpha A \quad \Gamma \Rightarrow x{:}^\alpha B}{\Gamma \Rightarrow x{:}^\alpha A \wedge B}\ (R\wedge)$$

$$\frac{x{:}^\alpha A,\Gamma \Rightarrow \Delta \quad x{:}^\alpha B,\Gamma \Rightarrow \Delta}{x{:}^\alpha A \vee B,\Gamma \Rightarrow \Delta}\ (L\vee) \quad \frac{\Gamma \Rightarrow x{:}^\alpha A}{\Gamma \Rightarrow x{:}^\alpha A \vee B}\ (R\vee 1) \quad \frac{\Gamma \Rightarrow x{:}^\alpha B}{\Gamma \Rightarrow x{:}^\alpha A \vee B}\ (R\vee 2)$$

(Rules for knowledge operators)

$$\frac{\Gamma \Rightarrow x\mathsf{R}_a^\alpha y \quad y{:}^\alpha A,\Gamma \Rightarrow \Delta}{x{:}^\alpha \Box_a A,\Gamma \Rightarrow \Delta}\ (L\Box_a) \quad \frac{x\mathsf{R}_a^\alpha y,\Gamma \Rightarrow y{:}^\alpha A}{\Gamma \Rightarrow x{:}^\alpha \Box_a A}\ (R\Box_a)\dagger$$

$$\frac{x\mathsf{R}_a^\alpha y,y{:}^\alpha A,\Gamma \Rightarrow \Delta}{x{:}^\alpha \Diamond_a A,\Gamma \Rightarrow \Delta}\ (L\Diamond_a)\dagger \quad \frac{\Gamma \Rightarrow x\mathsf{R}_a^\alpha y \quad \Gamma \Rightarrow y{:}^\alpha A}{\Gamma \Rightarrow x{:}^\alpha \Diamond_a A}\ (R\Diamond_a)$$

† y does not appear in the lowersequent.

(Rules for IntPAL)

$$\frac{x{:}^\alpha p,\Gamma \Rightarrow \Delta}{x{:}^{\alpha,A} p,\Gamma \Rightarrow \Delta}\ (Lat) \quad \frac{\Gamma \Rightarrow x{:}^\alpha p}{\Gamma \Rightarrow x{:}^{\alpha,A} p}\ (Rat)$$

$$\frac{\Gamma \Rightarrow x{:}^\alpha A \quad x{:}^{\alpha,A} B,\Gamma \Rightarrow \Delta}{x{:}^\alpha [A]B,\Gamma \Rightarrow \Delta}\ (L[.]) \quad \frac{x{:}^\alpha A,\Gamma \Rightarrow x{:}^{\alpha,A} B}{\Gamma \Rightarrow x{:}^\alpha [A]B}\ (R[.])$$

$$\frac{x{:}^\alpha A,\Gamma \Rightarrow \Delta}{x{:}^\alpha \langle A\rangle B,\Gamma \Rightarrow \Delta}\ (L\langle.\rangle 1) \quad \frac{x{:}^{\alpha,A} B,\Gamma \Rightarrow \Delta}{x{:}^\alpha \langle A\rangle B,\Gamma \Rightarrow \Delta}\ (L\langle.\rangle 2) \quad \frac{\Gamma \Rightarrow x{:}^\alpha A \quad \Gamma \Rightarrow x{:}^{\alpha,A} B}{\Gamma \Rightarrow x{:}^\alpha \langle A\rangle B}\ (R\langle.\rangle)$$

$$\frac{x{:}^\alpha A,\Gamma \Rightarrow \Delta}{x\mathsf{R}_a^{\alpha,A} y,\Gamma \Rightarrow \Delta}\ (Lrel_a 1) \quad \frac{y{:}^\alpha A,\Gamma \Rightarrow \Delta}{x\mathsf{R}_a^{\alpha,A} y,\Gamma \Rightarrow \Delta}\ (Lrel_a 2) \quad \frac{x\mathsf{R}_a^\alpha y,\Gamma \Rightarrow \Delta}{x\mathsf{R}_a^{\alpha,A} y,\Gamma \Rightarrow \Delta}\ (Lrel_a 3)$$

$$\frac{\Gamma \Rightarrow x{:}^\alpha A \quad \Gamma \Rightarrow y{:}^\alpha A \quad \Gamma \Rightarrow x\mathsf{R}_a^\alpha y}{\Gamma \Rightarrow x\mathsf{R}_a^{\alpha,A} y}\ (Rrel_a)$$

Definition 3. *Let $\mathfrak{A}$ be any labelled expression. Then the substitution of x for y in $\mathfrak{A}$, denoted by $\mathfrak{A}[x/y]$, is defined by*

$$\begin{aligned} z[x/y] &:= z \quad (\textit{if } y \neq z), & (z{:}^\alpha A)[x/y] &:= (z[x/y]){:}^\alpha A, \\ z[x/y] &:= x \quad (\textit{if } y = z), & (z\mathsf{R}_a^\alpha w)[x/y] &:= (z[x/y])\mathsf{R}_a^\alpha (w[x/y]). \end{aligned}$$

Substitution $[x/y]$ to a multi-set Γ of labelled expressions is defined as

$$\Gamma[x/y] := \{\mathfrak{A}[x/y] \mid \mathfrak{A} \in \Gamma\}.$$

For a preparation of Theorem 1, we show the next lemma.

Lemma 2.

(i) **GIntPAL** $\vdash \Gamma \Rightarrow \Delta$ *implies* **GIntPAL** $\vdash \Gamma[x/y] \Rightarrow \Delta[x/y]$ *for any* $x, y \in$ Var.

(ii) **GIntPAL$^+$** $\vdash \Gamma \Rightarrow \Delta$ *implies* **GIntPAL$^+$** $\vdash \Gamma[x/y] \Rightarrow \Delta[x/y]$ *for any* $x, y \in$ Var.

Proof. By induction on the height of the derivation. We go through almost the same procedure in the proof as in Negri *et al.* [18, p.194]. □

Theorem 1. *For any formula A, if* **HIntPAL** $\vdash A$, *then* **GIntPAL$^+$** $\vdash \Rightarrow x{:}^\epsilon A$ *(for any $x \in$ Var).*

Proof. The proof is carried out by induction on the height of the derivation in **HIntPAL**. Let us take $(FS2)$ and one direction of $(RA14)$ of **HIntPAL** to prove as significant base cases (the derivation height of **HIntPAL** is equal to 0).

The case of (FS2)

$$
\cfrac{
  \cfrac{
    \cfrac{\text{Lemma 1}}{y{:}^\epsilon p, x\mathsf{R}_a^\epsilon y \Rightarrow x\mathsf{R}_a^\epsilon y}
    \quad
    \cfrac{\text{Lemma 1}}{y{:}^\epsilon p, x\mathsf{R}_a^\epsilon y \Rightarrow y{:}^\epsilon p}
  }{y{:}^\epsilon p, x\mathsf{R}_a^\epsilon y \Rightarrow x{:}^\epsilon \Diamond_a p}(R\Diamond_a)
  \quad
  \cfrac{
    \cfrac{
      \cfrac{\text{Initial Seq.}}{x\mathsf{R}_a^\epsilon y \Rightarrow x\mathsf{R}_a^\epsilon y}
      \quad
      \cfrac{\text{Lemma 1}}{y{:}^\epsilon q, x\mathsf{R}_a^\epsilon y \Rightarrow y{:}^\epsilon q}
    }{
      \cfrac{x{:}^\epsilon \Box_a q, x\mathsf{R}_a^\epsilon y \Rightarrow y{:}^\epsilon q}{x{:}^\epsilon \Box_a q, y{:}^\epsilon p, x\mathsf{R}_a^\epsilon y \Rightarrow y{:}^\epsilon q}(Lw)
    }(L\Box_a)
  }{(L\to)}
}{
  \cfrac{
    \cfrac{
      \cfrac{x{:}^\epsilon \Diamond_a p \to \Box_a q, y{:}^\epsilon p, x\mathsf{R}_a^\epsilon y \Rightarrow y{:}^\epsilon q}{x{:}^\epsilon \Diamond_a p \to \Box_a q, x\mathsf{R}_a^\epsilon y \Rightarrow y{:}^\epsilon p \to q}(R\to)
    }{x{:}^\epsilon \Diamond_a p \to \Box_a q \Rightarrow x{:}^\epsilon \Box_a(p \to q)}(R\Box_a)
  }{\Rightarrow x{:}^\epsilon (\Diamond_a p \to \Box_a q) \to \Box_a(p \to q)}(R\to)
}
$$

The case of $(RA14)$**: left to right**

$$
\cfrac{
  \cfrac{
    \cfrac{\text{Initial Seq.}}{x{:}^\epsilon A \Rightarrow x{:}^\epsilon A}
  }{x{:}^\epsilon \langle A \rangle \Diamond_a B \Rightarrow x{:}^\epsilon A}(L\langle\cdot\rangle 1)
  \quad
  \cfrac{
    \cfrac{
      \cfrac{
        \cfrac{
          \cfrac{
            \cfrac{
              \cfrac{\text{Lemma 1}}{y{:}^A B, y{:}^\epsilon A, x\mathsf{R}_a^\epsilon y \Rightarrow x\mathsf{R}_a^\epsilon y}
              \quad
              \cfrac{
                \cfrac{
                  \cfrac{\text{Lemma 1}}{y{:}^A B, y{:}^\epsilon A \Rightarrow y{:}^\epsilon A}
                  \quad
                  \cfrac{\text{Lemma 1}}{y{:}^A B, y{:}^\epsilon A \Rightarrow y{:}^A B}
                }{y{:}^A B, y{:}^\epsilon A \Rightarrow y{:}^\epsilon \langle A \rangle B}(L\langle\cdot\rangle)
              }{y{:}^A B, y{:}^\epsilon A, x\mathsf{R}_a^\epsilon y \Rightarrow y{:}^\epsilon \langle A \rangle B}(Lw)
            }{y{:}^A B, y{:}^\epsilon A, x\mathsf{R}_a^\epsilon y \Rightarrow x{:}^\epsilon \Diamond_a \langle A \rangle B}(R\Diamond_a)
          }{y{:}^A B, y{:}^\epsilon A, x\mathsf{R}_a^A y \Rightarrow x{:}^\epsilon \Diamond_a \langle A \rangle B}(Lrel_a 3)
        }{y{:}^A B, x\mathsf{R}_a^A y, x\mathsf{R}_a^A y \Rightarrow x{:}^\epsilon \Diamond_a \langle A \rangle B}(Lrel_a 2)
      }{y{:}^A B, x\mathsf{R}_a^A y \Rightarrow x{:}^\epsilon \Diamond_a \langle A \rangle B}(Lc)
    }{x{:}^A \Diamond_a B \Rightarrow x{:}^\epsilon \Diamond_a \langle A \rangle B}(L\Diamond_a)
  }{x{:}^\epsilon \langle A \rangle \Diamond_a B \Rightarrow x{:}^\epsilon \Diamond_a \langle A \rangle B}(L\langle\cdot\rangle 2)
}{
  \cfrac{x{:}^\epsilon \langle A \rangle \Diamond_a B \Rightarrow x{:}^\epsilon A \wedge \Diamond_a \langle A \rangle B}{\Rightarrow x{:}^\epsilon \langle A \rangle \Diamond_a B \to A \wedge \Diamond_a \langle A \rangle B}(R\to)
}(R\wedge)
$$

In the inductive step, we show the admissibility of **HIntPAL**'s inference rules, (MP), $(Nec\square_a)$ and $(Nec[.])$, by **GIntPAL**$^+$.

The case of (MP)**:** It is shown with (Cut).

The case of $(Nec\square_a)$**:** It is shown by $(R\square_a)$, (Lw) and Lemma 2.

The case of $(Nec[.])$**:** In the case, we show the admissibility of the following rule:

$$\frac{\Rightarrow x{:}^{\epsilon}A}{\Rightarrow x{:}^{\epsilon}[B]A} \ (Nec[.]).$$

Suppose **GIntPAL** $\vdash \Rightarrow x{:}^{\epsilon}A$. It is obvious that **GIntPAL** $\vdash \Rightarrow x{:}^{\epsilon}A$ implies **GIntPAL** $\vdash \Rightarrow x{:}^{B}A$ since if there is a derivation of $\Rightarrow x{:}^{\epsilon}A$, there can also be a derivation of $\Rightarrow x{:}^{B}A$ where B is added to the most left side of restricting formulas of each labelled expression appeared in the derivation. Therefore, we obtain **GIntPAL** $\vdash \Rightarrow x{:}^{B}A$, and by the application of (Lw) and $(R[.])$, we conclude **GIntPAL** $\vdash \Rightarrow x{:}^{\epsilon}[B]A$. $\qquad \square$

4 Cut Elimination of GIntPAL$^+$

Now, we show the rule (Cut) of **GIntPAL**$^+$ is admissible. For a preparation of the cut elimination theorem, we show the following lemma.

Lemma 3. *If a sequent* $\Gamma \Rightarrow x{:}^{\alpha}\bot$ *can be derivable without using* (Cut)*, then* $\Gamma \Rightarrow$ *can also be derivable without using* (Cut)*.*

Proof. By induction on the height of the derivation. And every case in the inductive step, in which the last applied rule is either (Rw) or one of left rules, can be shown straightforwardly with inductive hypothesis and the same rule as the last rule applied. We only look at the base case.

In the base case, since $\Gamma \Rightarrow x{:}^{\alpha}\bot$ is the initial sequent, Γ must be the singleton $\{x{:}^{\alpha}\bot\}$. Then $x{:}^{\alpha}\bot \Rightarrow$ is also the initial sequent and so derivable. $\square$

Here we prove one of contributions of the paper, the syntactic cut elimination theorem of **GIntPAL**$^+$.

Theorem 2 (Cut elimination of GIntPAL$^+$). *For any sequent* $\Gamma \Rightarrow \Delta$*, if* **GIntPAL**$^+ \vdash \Gamma \Rightarrow \Delta$*, then* **GIntPAL** $\vdash \Gamma \Rightarrow \Delta$*.*

Proof. The proof is carried out in Ono and Komori's method [21] introduced in the reference [12] by Kashima where we employ the following rule $(Ecut)$. We denote the n-copies of the same labelled expression $\mathfrak{A}$ by $\mathfrak{A}^n$, and $(Ecut)$ is defined as follows:

$$\frac{\Gamma \Rightarrow \mathfrak{A}^n \qquad \mathfrak{A}^m, \Gamma' \Rightarrow \Delta}{\Gamma, \Gamma' \Rightarrow \Delta} \ (Ecut)$$

where $0 \leq n \leq 1$ and $m \geq 0$. The theorem is shown by double induction on the height of the derivation and the length of the cut expression $\mathfrak{A}$ of $(Ecut)$. The proof is divided into four cases: (1) at least one of uppersequents of $(Ecut)$ is an initial sequent; (2) the last inference rule of either uppersequents of $(Ecut)$ is a structural rule; (3) the last inference rule of either uppersequents of $(Ecut)$ is a non-structural rule, and the principal expression introduced by the rule is not a cut expression; (4) the last inference rules of two uppersequents of $(Ecut)$ are both non-structural rules, and the principal expressions introduced by the rules used on the uppersequents of $(Ecut)$ are both cut expressions. We look at one of base cases and one of significant subcases of (4) in which principal expressions introduced by non-structural rules are both cut expressions.

A case of (1): The right uppersequent is an initial sequent $x{:}^\alpha \bot \Rightarrow$ **:** In this case, the form of the derivation is like following:

$$\cfrac{\Gamma \Rightarrow x{:}^\alpha\bot \quad \overset{\text{Initial Seq.}}{x{:}^\alpha\bot \Rightarrow}}{\Gamma \Rightarrow} \ (Ecut)$$

From the left uppersequent $\Gamma \Rightarrow x{:}^\alpha\bot$, we get, without $(Ecut)$, the lowersequent $\Gamma \Rightarrow$ by Lemma 3.

A case of (4): principal expressions are $x\mathsf{R}_a^{\alpha,A}y$**:** Let us consider the case where both sides of $\mathfrak{A}$ are $x\mathsf{R}_a^{\alpha,A}y$ and principal expressions. When we obtain the derivation:

$$\cfrac{\cfrac{\overset{\vdots\ \mathcal{D}_1}{\Gamma \Rightarrow x{:}^\alpha A} \quad \overset{\vdots\ \mathcal{D}_2}{\Gamma \Rightarrow y{:}^\alpha A} \quad \overset{\vdots\ \mathcal{D}_3}{\Gamma \Rightarrow x\mathsf{R}_a^\alpha y}}{\Gamma \Rightarrow x\mathsf{R}_a^{\alpha,A}y}\ (Lrel_a) \quad \cfrac{\overset{\vdots\ \mathcal{D}_4}{x{:}^\alpha A, (x\mathsf{R}_a^{\alpha,A}y)^{m-1}, \Gamma' \Rightarrow \Delta}}{(x\mathsf{R}_a^{\alpha,A}y)^m, \Gamma' \Rightarrow \Delta}\ (Lrel_a 1)}{\Gamma, \Gamma' \Rightarrow \Delta}\ (Ecut) \quad ,$$

it is transformed into the following derivation:

$$\cfrac{\cfrac{\overset{\vdots\ \mathcal{D}_1}{\Gamma \Rightarrow x{:}^\alpha A} \quad \cfrac{\overset{\vdots\ \mathcal{D}'_{123}}{\Gamma \Rightarrow x\mathsf{R}_a^{\alpha,A}y} \quad \overset{\vdots\ \mathcal{D}_4}{x{:}^\alpha A, (x\mathsf{R}_a^{\alpha,A}y)^{m-1}, \Gamma' \Rightarrow \Delta}}{x{:}^\alpha A, \Gamma, \Gamma' \Rightarrow \Delta}\ (Ecut)}{\cfrac{\Gamma, \Gamma, \Gamma' \Rightarrow \Delta}{\Gamma, \Gamma' \Rightarrow \Delta}\ (Lc)}\ (Ecut)$$

where the upper application of $(Ecut)$ is possible by the induction hypothesis, since the derivation height of $(Ecut)$ is reduced by comparison with the original derivation. Besides, the lower application of $(Ecut)$ is also allowed by induction hypothesis, since the length of the cut expression is reduced, namely $\mathsf{len}(x{:}^\alpha A) < \mathsf{len}(x\mathsf{R}_a^{\alpha,A}y)$. $\qquad\square$

As a corollary of Theorem 2, the consistency of **GIntPAL**$^+$ is shown.

Corollary 2. *The empty sequent '$\Rightarrow$' cannot be derived in* **GIntPAL**$^+$.

Proof. Suppose for contradiction that **GIntPAL**$^+ \vdash \ \Rightarrow$. By Theorem 2, **GIntPAL** $\vdash \ \Rightarrow$ is obtained. However, there is no inference rule in **GIntPAL** which can derive the empty sequent. A contradiction. $\qquad\square$

5   Soundness of GIntPAL

Now, we switch the subject to the soundness theorem of **GIntPAL**. At first, we define the notion of the satisfaction relation for the labelled expressions, i.e., lift the satisfaction relation for the non-labelled formulas to that of the labelled expressions. Let us say that $f : \mathsf{Var} \to \mathcal{D}(\mathfrak{M})$ is an *assignment*, where we recall that Var is the set of all labells.

Definition 4. *Let $\mathfrak{M}$ be an IntK-model and $f : \mathsf{Var} \to \mathcal{D}(\mathfrak{M})$ an assignment.*

$\mathfrak{M}, f \Vdash x{:}^{\alpha} A$ *iff* $\mathfrak{M}^{\alpha}, f(x) \Vdash A$ *and* $f(x) \in \mathcal{D}(\mathfrak{M}^{\alpha})$
$\mathfrak{M}, f \Vdash x R_a^{\epsilon} y$ *iff* $\langle f(x), f(y) \rangle \in R_a$
$\mathfrak{M}, f \Vdash x R_a^{\alpha, A} y$ *iff* $\langle f(x), f(y) \rangle \in R_a^{\alpha}$ *and* $\mathfrak{M}^{\alpha}, f(x) \Vdash A$ *and* $\mathfrak{M}^{\alpha}, f(y) \Vdash A$

In this definition, we have to be careful of the notion of *surviveness* as suggested in [19]. In brief, $f(x)$ and $f(y)$ above must be defined in $\mathcal{D}(\mathfrak{M}^{\alpha})$ which may be smaller than $\mathcal{D}(\mathfrak{M})$. In the clause $\mathfrak{M}, f \Vdash x{:}^{\alpha} A$, for example, $f(x)$ should survive in the restricted *IntK*-model $\mathfrak{M}^{\alpha}$. Taking into account of the fact, it is essential that we pay attention to the negation of $\mathfrak{M}, f \Vdash x{:}^{\alpha} A$.

Proposition 3. $\mathfrak{M}, f \not\Vdash x{:}^{\alpha} A$ *iff* $f(x) \notin \mathcal{D}(\mathfrak{M}^{\alpha})$ *or* $(f(x) \in \mathcal{D}(\mathfrak{M}^{\alpha})$ *and* $\mathfrak{M}^{\alpha}, f(x) \not\Vdash A)$.

We introduce at first the notion of validity for sequents which is defined in a natural and usual way, called *s-validity*, but the definition will soon turn out to be inappropriate for showing the soundness theorem.

Definition 5 (s-validity). $\Gamma \Rightarrow \Delta$ *is s-validity in* $\mathfrak{M}$ *if for all assignments* $f : \mathsf{Var} \to \mathcal{D}(\mathfrak{M})$ *such that* $\mathfrak{M}, f \Vdash \mathfrak{A}$ *for all* $\mathfrak{A} \in \Gamma$, *there exists* $\mathfrak{B} \in \Delta$ *such that* $\mathfrak{M}, f \Vdash \mathfrak{B}$.

If we follow *s*-validity, then we come to a deadlock on the way to prove the soundness theorem, as we can see the following proposition.

Proposition 4. *There is an IntK-model $\mathfrak{M}$ such that $(R{\to})$ of **GIntPAL** does not preserve s-validity in $\mathfrak{M}$.*

Proof. We use the same models as in Example 2:

where we note that $V^{\neg p}(p) = \emptyset$. Then we consider a particular instance of $(R{\to})$:[5]

$$\frac{x{:}^{\neg p} p \Rightarrow x{:}^{\neg p} \bot}{\Rightarrow x{:}^{\neg p} \neg p} \ (R{\to})$$

---

[5] Note that $\neg p$ is an abbreviation of $p \to \bot$.

We show that the uppersequent is s-valid in $\mathfrak{M}$ but the lowersequent is not s-valid in $\mathfrak{M}$, and so $(R\rightarrow)$ does not preserve s-validity in this case. Note that w_0 does not survive after $\neg p$, i.e., $w_0 \notin \mathcal{D}(\mathfrak{M}^{\neg p}) = \{w_2\}$. We also note that the semantic clause for '$\rightarrow$' at a state w becomes classical when w is a single reflexive point.

First, we show that $x{:}^{\neg p}p \Rightarrow$ is s-valid in $\mathfrak{M}$, i.e., $\mathfrak{M}, f \not\Vdash x{:}^{\neg p}p$ for any assignment $f : \mathsf{Var} \rightarrow \mathcal{D}(\mathfrak{M})$. So, we fix any $f : \mathsf{Var} \rightarrow \mathcal{D}(\mathfrak{M})$. We divide our argument into: $f(x) = w_1$ or $f(x) = w_2$. If $f(x) = w_1$, $f(x)$ does not survive after $\neg p$, and so $\mathfrak{M}, f \not\Vdash x{:}^{\neg p}p$ by Proposition 3. If $f(x) = w_2$, $f(x)$ survives after $\neg p$ but $f(x) \notin V^{\neg p}(p)(= \emptyset)$, which implies $\mathfrak{M}^{\neg p}, f(x) \not\Vdash p$ hence $\mathfrak{M}, f \not\Vdash x{:}^{\neg p}p$ by Proposition 3. Therefore, in either case, the uppersequent is valid.

Second, we show that $\Rightarrow x{:}^{\neg p}\neg p$ is not s-valid in $\mathfrak{M}$, i.e., $\mathfrak{M}, f \not\Vdash x{:}^{\neg p}\neg p$ for some assignment $f : \mathsf{Var} \rightarrow W$. We fix some f such that $f(x) = w_1$. Since $f(x) \notin \mathcal{D}(\mathfrak{M}^{\neg p})$ ($f(x)$ does not survive after $\neg p$), $\mathfrak{M}, f \not\Vdash x{:}^{p}\neg p$ by Proposition 3, as desired. $\square$

Proposition 4 is a counter-example of the soundness theorem with s-validity, and so it forces us to change the definition of validity, A key idea of finding another candidate here is that we read $\Gamma \Rightarrow \Delta$ as 'it is impossible that all of Γ hold and all of Δ fail.' We define the notion of failure for the labelled expressions explicitly by requiring surviveness of states as follows (we read '$\mathfrak{M}, f \Vdash \overline{\mathfrak{A}}$' by 'labelled expression $\mathfrak{A}$ fails under $\mathfrak{M}$ and f').

Definition 6. *Let $\mathfrak{M}$ be an IntK-model and $f : \mathsf{Var} \rightarrow \mathcal{D}(\mathfrak{M})$ an assignment.*

$\mathfrak{M}, f \Vdash \overline{x{:}^{\alpha}A}$ *iff* $\mathfrak{M}^{\alpha}, f(x) \not\Vdash A$ *and* $f(x) \in \mathcal{D}(\mathfrak{M}^{\alpha})$,

$\mathfrak{M}, f \Vdash \overline{x\mathsf{R}_a^{\epsilon}y}$ *iff* $\langle f(x), f(y)\rangle \notin R_a$,

$\mathfrak{M}, f \Vdash \overline{x\mathsf{R}_a^{\alpha,A}y}$ *iff* $\mathfrak{M}, f \Vdash \overline{x\mathsf{R}_a^{\alpha}y}$ *or* $\mathfrak{M}, f \Vdash \overline{x{:}^{\alpha}A}$ *or* $\mathfrak{M}, f \Vdash \overline{y{:}^{\alpha}A}$.

Note that the first item means that $f(x)$ survives at the domain of the restricted model $\mathfrak{M}^{\alpha}$ and A is false at the survived world $f(x)$ in $\mathfrak{M}^{\alpha}$.

Definition 7 (t-validity). $\Gamma \Rightarrow \Delta$ *is t-valid in $\mathfrak{M}$ if there is no assignment* $f : \mathsf{Var} \rightarrow \mathcal{D}(\mathfrak{M})$ *such that $\mathfrak{M}, f \Vdash \mathfrak{A}$ for all $\mathfrak{A} \in \Gamma$, and $\mathfrak{M}, f \Vdash \overline{\mathfrak{B}}$ for all* $\mathfrak{B} \in \Delta$.

Let us denote by $Var(\Gamma \Rightarrow \Delta)$ the set of all labels occurring in $\Gamma \Rightarrow \Delta$. Then, we note that the domain Var of an assignment f in Definition 7 can be restricted to $Var(\Gamma \Rightarrow \Delta)$. The following proposition shows that the clauses for relational atoms and negated form of them characterize what they intend to capture.

Proposition 5. *For any IntK-model $\mathfrak{M}$, assignment f, and $x, y \in \mathsf{Var}$,*

(i) $\mathfrak{M}, f \Vdash x\mathsf{R}_a^{\alpha}y$ *iff* $\langle f(x), f(y)\rangle \in R_a^{\alpha}$,   (ii) $\mathfrak{M}, f \Vdash \overline{x\mathsf{R}_a^{\alpha}y}$ *iff* $\langle f(x), f(y)\rangle \notin R_a^{\alpha}$.

Proof. Both are easily shown by induction of α. Let us consider the case of $\alpha = (\alpha', A)$ in the proof of (ii). We show $\mathfrak{M}, f \not\Vdash x\mathsf{R}_a^{\alpha,A}y$ iff $\langle f(x), f(y)\rangle \in R_a^{\alpha,A}$. $\mathfrak{M}, f \not\Vdash x\mathsf{R}_a^{\alpha}y$ is, by Definition 6 and the induction hypothesis, equivalent to $\langle f(x), f(y)\rangle \in R_a^{\alpha}$ and $\mathfrak{M}^{\alpha}, f(x) \Vdash A$ and $\mathfrak{M}^{\alpha}, f(y) \Vdash A$. That is also equivalent to $\langle f(x), f(y)\rangle \in R_a^{\alpha,A}$. $\square$

In order to establish the soundness of **GIntPAL** for birelational Kripke semantics, we basically employ Simpson's argument [24, p. 153–155] for the soundness of a natural deduction system for IntK with some modifications for the notion of public announcement. Given any sequent $\Gamma \Rightarrow \Delta$, we may extract a directed graph with the help of the relational atoms in Γ as follows.

Definition 8. *The derived graph $Gr(\Gamma \Rightarrow \Delta)$ from a sequent $\Gamma \Rightarrow \Delta$ is a (labelled) directed graph $(L, (E_a)_{a \in \mathsf{G}})$ where L is the set $Var(\Gamma \Rightarrow \Delta)$ of all labels in $\Gamma \Rightarrow \Delta$ and $E_a \subseteq V \times V$ is defined as follows: $xE_a y$ iff $x\mathsf{R}_a^\alpha y \in \Gamma$ for some list α ($a \in \mathsf{G}$).*

Next we recall the notion of tree for a finite directed graph.

Definition 9 (Tree). *Given any finite directed graph $\langle L, (E_a)_{a \in \mathsf{G}} \rangle$, we say that $\langle L, (E_a)_{a \in \mathsf{G}} \rangle$ is a tree if the graph is generated with the root x_0 and, for every node x, there is a unique sequence $(x_1, \ldots, x_m)$ from L such that, for all $0 \le k < m$, there exists an agent $a_k \in \mathsf{G}$ such that $x_k E_{a_k} x_{x+1}$ and $x = x_m$.*

In order to prove the soundness of some rules such as $(R\square_a)$ and $(R[.])$, our attention must be restricted to the sequents whose derived graphs are trees. And, the following lemma (cf. [24, Lemma 8.1.3]) plays a key role in establishing the soundness of the above two rules, where we also note that the restrictions $(F1)$ and $(F2)$ in birelational Kripke semantics are necessary to prove the lemma.

Lemma 4 (Lifting Lemma). *Let $\Gamma \Rightarrow \Delta$ be a sequent such that $Gr(\Gamma \Rightarrow \Delta)$ is a tree, $\mathfrak{M} = (W, \le, (R_a)_{a \in \mathsf{G}}, V)$ an IntK-model, and f an assignment from $Var(\Gamma \Rightarrow \Delta)$ to W such that $\mathfrak{M}, f \Vdash \mathfrak{A}$ for all $\mathfrak{A} \in \Gamma$. Then, for all labels $x \in Var(\Gamma \Rightarrow \Delta)$ and $w \in W$ with $f(x) \le w$, there exists an assignment f' from $Var(\Gamma \Rightarrow \Delta)$ to W such that $f'(x) = w$, $f(z) \le f'(z)$ for all labels $z \in Var(\Gamma \Rightarrow \Delta)$ and $\mathfrak{M}, f' \Vdash \mathfrak{A}$ for all $\mathfrak{A} \in \Gamma$.*

Now, we are ready to prove a stronger form of the soundness theorem of **GIntPAL** with the notion of tree for derived graphs from sequents.

Theorem 3 (Soundness of GIntPAL). *Given any sequent $\Gamma \Rightarrow \Delta$ such that $Gr(\Gamma \Rightarrow \Delta)$ is a finite tree, if $\mathbf{GIntPAL} \vdash \Gamma \Rightarrow \Delta$, then $\Gamma \Rightarrow \Delta$ is t-valid in every IntK-model $\mathfrak{M}$.*

Proof. Suppose $\mathbf{GIntPAL} \vdash \Gamma \Rightarrow \Delta$ such that $Gr(\Gamma \Rightarrow \Delta)$ is a finite tree. Then the proof is carried out by induction on the height of the derivation of $\Gamma \Rightarrow \Delta$ in **GIntPAL**. We confirm the following cases alone.

Base case: we show that $x\mathsf{R}_a^\alpha v \Rightarrow x\mathsf{R}_a^\alpha v$ is t-valid. Suppose for contradiction that $\mathfrak{M}, f \Vdash x\mathsf{R}_a^\alpha v$ and $\mathfrak{M}, f \Vdash \overline{x\mathsf{R}_a^\alpha v}$. By Proposition 5, this is impossible.

The case where the last applied rule is $(R[.])$: In this case, we have a derivation of $x{:}^\alpha A, \Gamma \Rightarrow x{:}^{\alpha, A}B$ in **GIntPAL**, and since $Gr(x{:}^\alpha A, \Gamma \Rightarrow x{:}^{\alpha, A}B) = Gr(\Gamma \Rightarrow x{:}^\alpha[A]B)$, it is trivially a finite tree. Let us denote the graph by $\langle L, (E_a)_{a \in \mathsf{G}} \rangle$. Suppose for contradiction that there is an assignment $f{:}L \to \mathcal{D}(\mathfrak{M})$ such that $\mathfrak{M}, f \Vdash \mathfrak{A}$ for all $\mathfrak{A} \in \Gamma$ and $\mathfrak{M}, f \Vdash \overline{x{:}^\alpha[A]B}$. Fix such

$f:L \to \mathcal{D}(\mathfrak{M})$. Then, it suffices to show that there is an assignment $f':L \to \mathcal{D}(\mathfrak{M})$ such that $\mathfrak{M}, f' \Vdash x:^\alpha A$ and $\mathfrak{M}, f' \Vdash \mathfrak{A}$ for all $\mathfrak{A} \in \Gamma$ and $\mathfrak{M}, f' \Vdash \overline{x:^{\alpha,A}B}$, since this gives us a contradiction with our induction hypothesis to $x:^\alpha A, \Gamma \Rightarrow x:^{\alpha,A}B$. By the supposition, $\mathfrak{M}, f \Vdash \overline{x:^\alpha[A]B}$, which is equivalent to: $f(x) \in \mathcal{D}(\mathfrak{M}^\alpha)$ and there is some $v \in \mathcal{D}(\mathfrak{M}^\alpha)$ such that $f(x) \leqslant^\alpha v$ and $\mathfrak{M}^\alpha, v \Vdash A$ and $\mathfrak{M}^{\alpha,A}, v \nVdash B$. By Lemma 4 and the supposition that $\mathfrak{M}, f \Vdash \mathfrak{A}$ for all $\mathfrak{A} \in \Gamma$, we obtain an assignment $f':L \to \mathcal{D}(\mathfrak{M})$ such that $f'(x) = v$ and $f(z) \leqslant f'(z)$ for all $z \in L$ and $\mathfrak{M}, f' \Vdash \mathfrak{A}$ for all $\mathfrak{A} \in \Gamma$. It also follows that $\mathfrak{M}, f' \Vdash x:^\alpha A$ and $\mathfrak{M}, f' \Vdash \overline{x:^{\alpha,A}B}$, as desired.

The case where the last applied rule is $(R\square_a)$**:** In this case, we have a derivation of $x\mathsf{R}_a^\alpha y, \Gamma \Rightarrow y:^\alpha A$ in **GIntPAL**. Let us denote a tree $Gr(\Gamma \Rightarrow x:^\alpha\square_a A)$ by $\langle L, (E_b)_{b\in\mathsf{G}}\rangle$. Since y is a fresh variable, $Gr(x\mathsf{R}_a^\alpha y, \Gamma \Rightarrow y:^\alpha A) = \langle L \cup \{y\}, E_a \cup \{(x,y)\}, (E_b)_{b\in\mathsf{G}\setminus\{a\}}\rangle$ is still a finite tree. Suppose for contradiction that there is an assignment $f:L \to \mathcal{D}(\mathfrak{M})$ such that $\mathfrak{M}, f \Vdash \mathfrak{A}$ for all $\mathfrak{A} \in \Gamma$ and $\mathfrak{M}, f \Vdash \overline{x:^\alpha\square_a A}$. Fix such assignment $f:L \to \mathcal{D}(\mathfrak{M})$. It suffices to show that there is an assignment $g:L \cup \{y\} \to \mathcal{D}(\mathfrak{M})$ such that $\mathfrak{M}, g \Vdash \mathfrak{A}$ for all $\mathfrak{A} \in \Gamma$ and $\mathfrak{M}, g \Vdash x\mathsf{R}_a^\alpha y$ and $\mathfrak{M}, g \Vdash \overline{y:^\alpha A}$, since this gives us a contradiction with our induction hypothesis to $x\mathsf{R}_a^\alpha y, \Gamma \Rightarrow y:^\alpha A$. Then, by the supposition of $\mathfrak{M}, f \Vdash \overline{x:^\alpha\square_a A}$, we have $f(x) \in \mathcal{D}(\mathfrak{M}^\alpha)$ and there are some $v, u \in \mathcal{D}(\mathfrak{M}^\alpha)$ such that $f(x)\leqslant^\alpha u$, $u R_a^\alpha v$ and $\mathfrak{M}^\alpha, v \nVdash A$. By the supposition that $\mathfrak{M}, f \Vdash \mathfrak{A}$ for all $\mathfrak{A} \in \Gamma$, we apply Lemma 4 to the sequent $\Gamma \Rightarrow x:^\alpha\square_a A$ to find an assignment $f':L \to \mathcal{D}(\mathfrak{M}^\alpha)$ such that $f'(x) = u$, $f(z) \leqslant f'(z)$ for all $z \in L$ and $\mathfrak{M}, f' \Vdash \mathfrak{A}$ for all $\mathfrak{A} \in \Gamma$. Now, f' can be extend to a new assignment $g:L \cup \{y\} \to \mathcal{D}(\mathfrak{M})$ such that g is the same as f' except $g(y) = v$. Then, we obtain $\mathfrak{M}, g \Vdash \mathfrak{A}$ for all $\mathfrak{A} \in \Gamma$, $\mathfrak{M}, g \Vdash x\mathsf{R}_a^\alpha y$ and $\mathfrak{M}, g \Vdash \overline{y:^\alpha A}$, as desired. $\square$

Proposition 6. *If* $\Rightarrow x:^\epsilon A$ *is t-valid in an IntK-model* $\mathfrak{M}$, *then* A *is valid in* $\mathfrak{M}$.

Proof. Suppose that $\Rightarrow x:^\epsilon A$ is *t*-valid. So, it is not the case that there exists some assignment f such that $\mathfrak{M}, f \Vdash \overline{x:^\epsilon A}$. Equivalently, for all assignments f, $\mathfrak{M}, f \nVdash \overline{x:^\epsilon A}$. For any assignment f, $\mathfrak{M}, f \nVdash \overline{x:^\epsilon A}$ is equivalent to $\mathfrak{M}, f(x) \Vdash A$ because $f(x) \in \mathcal{D}(\mathfrak{M})$. So, it follows that $\mathfrak{M}, f(x) \Vdash A$ for all assignments f. Then, it is immediate to see that A is valid in $\mathfrak{M}$, as required. $\square$

Finally, we may establish the completeness theorem as follows.

Corollary 3 (Completeness of GIntPAL). *Given any formula* A *and label* $x \in \mathsf{Var}$, *the following are equivalent:* (i) A *is valid on all IntK-models;* (ii) **HIntPAL** $\vdash A$; (iii) **GIntPAL**$^+$ $\vdash\Rightarrow x:^\epsilon A$; (iv) **GIntPAL** $\vdash\Rightarrow x:^\epsilon A$.

Proof. The direction from (i) to (ii) is established by Fact 1 and the direction from (ii) to (iii) is shown by Theorem 1. Then, the direction from (iii) to (iv) is established by the admissibility of cut, i.e., Theorem 2. Finally, the direction from (iv) to (i) is shown by Theorem 3 and Proposition 6, since $Gr(\Rightarrow x:^\epsilon A)$ is a tree (a single point-tree) and therefore Theorem 3 is applicable, and then Proposition 6 may be applied to its conclusion. $\square$

6   Conclusion

This paper provided a sequent calculus **GIntPAL** for PAL within an intuitionistic framework, and a sequent calculus that is easy to handle may be particularly significant for intuitionistic epistemic logics that regard verification or evidence as important. However, while **GIntPAL** has no frame conditions of an accessibility relation, it should be expanded to satisfy the conditions such as seriality, reflexivity, transitivity and/or symmetricity. It is easily done to impose such conditions to the "modal fragment" of **GIntPAL** by adding an inference rule corresponding to each frame condition (cf, [18, p. 192]); nevertheless, in the case of **GIntPAL** (and also **GPAL**), the situation might gets more involved. For example, seriality might not be preserved under taking public annoucements (i.e., submodels). Although we employ Gentzen's traditional approach, there is another well-known approach for an intuitionistic labelled sequent calculus such as the intuitionistic G3-style system by Dyckhoff et al. [7]. G3-style system is a sequent calculus in which all structural rules including contraction rules are height-preserving admissible (cf, [18]). Since G3-style system has such outstanding features, the possibility of employing it is worth being considered in the future.

Finally, we add two future directions of **GIntPAL**. First, our calculus of this paper for logic of constructive knowledge and its classical variant [19] may be applicable to other intuitionistic and classical Dynamic Epistemic Logics. For example, we may apply our method to construct a calculus for Action model logic [3] (dynamic epistemic logic in a narrow range of the meaning) and its intuitionistic variant. Second, a combined formal treatment of agents and their knowledge naturally leads us to the notion of quantification over agents. Although ordinary epistemic logics and PAL do not have an explicit device for that, Term-modal logic [10] was proposed to deal with the quantification of agents property in the level of object language. We may extend and/or modify our strategy in this paper and [19] to study labelled sequent calculi for Term-modal logic, and its dynamic extension, Dynamic term-modal logic [13]. These are issues to be addressed in the future.[6]

References

1. Artemov, S., Protopopescu, T.: Intuitionistic epistemic logic. Computer Science Technical reports, Paper 401 (2014)
2. Balbiani, P., Demange, V., Galmiche, D.: A sequent calculus with labels for PAL. Presented in Advances in Modal Logic (2014)

[6] We would like to thank the anonymous reviewers for their constructive comments to our manuscript. This work of the first author was supported by Grant-in-Aid for JSPS Fellows, and that of the second author was supported by JSPS KAKENHI Grant-in-Aid for Young Scientists (B) Grant Numbers 15K21025. This work was conducted by JSPS Core-to-Core Program (A. Advanced Research Networks).

3. Baltag, A., Moss, L., Solecki, S.: The logic of public announcements, common knowledge and private suspicions. In: Proceedings of TARK, pp. 43–56. Morgan Kaufmann Publishers, Los Altos (1989)
4. Bozzato, L., Ferrari, M., Fiorentini, C., Fiorino, G.: A decidable constructive description logic. In: Janhunen, T., Niemelä, I. (eds.) JELIA 2010. LNCS, vol. 6341, pp. 51–63. Springer, Heidelberg (2010)
5. Bull, R.A.: A modal extension of intuitionistic logic. Notre Dame J. Formal Logic 6, 142–146 (1965)
6. de Paiva, V., Haeusler, E.H., Rademaker, A.: Constructive description logics hybrid-style. Electron. Notes Theo. Comput. Sci. 273, 21–31 (2011)
7. Dyckhoff, R., Negri, S.: Proof analysis in intermediate logics. Arch. Math. Logic 51, 71–92 (2012)
8. Servi, G.F.: The finite model property for MIPQ and some consequences. Notre Dame J. Formal Logic 19, 687–692 (1978)
9. Fitch, F.B.: Intuitionistic modal logic with quantifiers. Portugaliae Mathematicae 7, 113–118 (1948)
10. Fitting, M., Thalmann, L., Voronkov, A.: Term-modal logic. Studia Logic 69(1), 133–169 (2001)
11. Gentzen, G.: Untersuchungen Über das logische Schließen. I. Mathematische Zeitschrift 39, 176–210 (1934)
12. Kashima, R.: Mathematical Logic. Asakura Publishing Co. Ltd., Osaka (2009). (in Japanese)
13. Kooi, B.: Dynamic term-modal logic. In: A Meeting of the Minds, Proceedings of the Workshop on Logic, Rationality and Interaction, pp. 173–185 (2007)
14. Ma, M., Palmigiano, A., Sadrzadeh, M.: Algebraic semantics and model completeness for intuitionistic public announcement logic. Ann. Pure Appl. Logic 165, 963–995 (2014)
15. Maffezioli, P., Negri, S.: A Gentzen-style analysis of public announcement logic. In: Proceedings of the International Workshop on Logic and Philosophy of Knowledge, Communication and Action, pp. 293–313 (2010)
16. Mendler, M., Scheele, S.: Towards constructive DL for abstraction and refinement. J. Autom. Reason. 44(3), 207–243 (2010)
17. Negri, S., von Plato, J.: Structural Proof Theory. Cambridge University Press, Cambridge (2001)
18. Negri, S., von Plato, J.: Proof Analysis. Cambridge University Press, Cambridge (2011)
19. Nomura, S., Sano, K., Tojo, S.: Revising a sequent calculus for public announcement logic. In: Structural Analysis of Non-classical Logics-The Proceedings of the Second Taiwan Philosophical Logic Colloquium (TPLC-2014) (to appear)
20. Ono, H.: On some intuitionistic modal logics. Publ. RIMS Kyoto Univ. 13, 687–722 (1977)
21. Ono, H., Komori, Y.: Logics without contraction rule. J. Symbolic Logic 50(1), 169–201 (1985)
22. Plaza, J.: Logic of public communications. In: Proceedings of the 4th International Symposium on Methodologies for Intellingent Systems: Poster Session Program, pp. 201–216 (1989)
23. Prior, A.: Time and Modality. Oxford University Press, Oxford (1957)
24. Simpson, A.: The proof theory and semantics of intuitionistic modal logic. Ph.D. thesis of University of Edinburgh (1994)
25. Williamson, T.: On intuitionistic modal epistemic logic. J. Philos. Logic 21(1), 63–89 (1992)

Implicit Computational Complexity
of Subrecursive Definitions and Applications
to Cryptographic Proofs

Patrick Baillot[1], Gilles Barthe[2]($^{(\boxtimes)}$), and Ugo Dal Lago[1,3]

[1] INRIA, UCBL, Université de Lyon, LIP, Lyon, France
[2] IMDEA Software Institute, Madrid, Spain
gilles@barthe.imdea.org
[3] INRIA, Università di Bologna, Bologna, Italy

Abstract. We define a call-by-value variant of Gödel's System T with references, and equip it with a linear dependent type and effect system, called dℓT, that can estimate the complexity of programs, as a function of the size of their inputs. We prove that the type system is intentionally sound, in the sense that it over-approximates the complexity of executing the programs on a variant of the CEK abstract machine. Moreover, we define a sound and complete type inference algorithm which critically exploits the subrecursive nature of dℓT. Finally, we demonstrate the usefulness of dℓT for analyzing the complexity of cryptographic reductions by providing an upper bound for the constructed adversary of the Goldreich-Levin theorem.

1 Introduction

Developing automated analyses that accurately over-approximate the complexity of (stateful) higher-order programs is a challenging task. Sophisticated type systems such as dℓPCF [10,11] *almost* achieve this goal for a (pure) higher-order language with unbounded recursion, using a combination of linear dependent types and constraint solving. However, the type inference algorithm of dℓPCF produces in output a *conditional* bound, in the sense that the bound is only meaningful under the condition that the equational program generated from the original term for computing the bound is terminating. One possible way to achieve automated complexity analysis would be to perform an automated termination analysis of the equational program; however, this approach is impractical, because the type inference algorithm of dℓPCF generates complex equational programs, and unsatisfactory, because one would like to avoid verifying termination of equational programs when the original terms are themselves terminating. Hence, it is natural to consider the following question: *is there a normalizing higher-order language for which one can automatically compute accurate and unconditional complexity bounds?* The first main contribution of this paper is to

---

This work has been partially supported by ANR Project ELICA ANR-14-CE25-0005.

M. Davis et al. (Eds.): LPAR-20 2015, LNCS 9450, pp. 203–218, 2015.
DOI: 10.1007/978-3-662-48899-7_15

answer the question positively for a call-by-value higher-order language with references and primitive recursion in the style of Gödel's system T—a paradigmatic higher-order language with inductive types and higher-order primitive recursion. The second main contribution of the paper is to show that the language is sufficiently expressive to model constructed adversaries from the cryptographic literature. More precisely, we make the following contributions:

- we introduce in Sect. 2 a variant of Gödel's system T with references and define an operational semantics based on a variant of the CEK abstract machine;
- we define in Sect. 3 a type system dℓT which conservatively approximates the cost of executing a program. The key ingredients of our type system are: *linear types*, which we use to ensure that higher-order subexpressions cannot be duplicated; *indexed types*, which we use to keep track of the size of expressions—thus, our use of indexed types is somewhat different from other works on refinement types, which support finer-grained assertions about expressions, e.g. assertions about their values; *indexed effects*, which are used to track the size of references throughout computation;
- we show in Sect. 4 that dℓT is intensionally sound, i.e. correctly overapproximates the complexity of evaluating typable programs;
- we define in Sect. 5 a type inference algorithm and prove its soundness and completeness. Our algorithm critically exploits the constrained form of programs to deliver an equational program that is *provably* terminating. Interestingly, the proof of termination is based on a reducibility argument;
- we demonstrate in Sect. 6 that dℓT can be used to analyze the complexity of the constructed adversary in the Goldreich-Levin theorem, which proves the existence of hardcore predicates. This example is particularly challenging, since it involves computations that are not hereditiraly polytime.

2   Setting

We consider a simply typed λ-calculus with references and higher-order primitive recursion, with a call-by-value evaluation strategy. For the sake of readability, we consider a minimalistic language with natural numbers, booleans, and lists. For the sake of applicability, we allow the set of expressions to be parameterized by a set of function symbols; these functions can be used in cryptographic applications to model random sampling, one-way trapdoor permutations, oracles, *etc.*

The semantics of programs is defined by an abstract machine, which we use to characterize the complexity of programs. We assume that function symbols come equipped with a semantics, and with a cost; thus, the abstract machine and the associated cost of programs are parametrized by the semantics and cost functions. This is formalized through the notion of a *function setting*, which we defined below.

Language. We assume given denumerable sets $\mathbb{V}$ of *variables* and $\mathbb{L}$ of locations, and a set $\mathcal{F}$ of function symbols. *Terms* and *values* are defined mutually recursively:

$$M ::= V \mid x \mid \mathsf{succ}(M) \mid \mathsf{cons}(M, N) \mid \mathsf{let}\ M\ \mathsf{be}\ \langle x, y \rangle\ \mathsf{in}\ N$$

$$\mid M\ N \mid \mathtt{f}(M) \mid \;!r \mid r\mathtt{:=}M;$$

$$V ::= * \mid \mathbf{zero} \mid \mathbf{tt} \mid \mathbf{ff} \mid \mathbf{nil} \mid \mathsf{succ}(V) \mid \mathsf{cons}(V, W) \mid \langle M, N \rangle \mid \lambda x.M$$

$$\mid \mathtt{iter}(V, W) \mid \mathtt{fold}(V, W) \mid \mathtt{if}(V, W) \mid \mathtt{ifz}(V, W) \mid \mathtt{ifn}(V, W);$$

where the last five clauses for values correspond to iterators and selectors (note that the latter have a function type). The constructions $\mathsf{map}(V)$ and $\mathsf{map}_2(V)$ are defined in a standard way, using $\mathtt{fold}(X, Z)$ for suitable X, Z. The following constructions used in the examples are also standard syntactic sugar: if M then V else W, $\lambda\langle x, y \rangle.M$, let $x = M$ in N, as well as $M; N$. The expression $\mathbf{M}$ stands for a sequence of terms.

Linear Type System. We first equip the language with a (non-dependent) linear type system. The sets of base types and types are defined as follows:

$$T ::= \mathsf{unit} \mid \mathbf{B} \mid \mathbf{N} \mid \mathbf{L}(T); \qquad A, B ::= T \mid A \otimes A \mid A \overset{a}{\multimap} A;$$

where a ranges over sets of locations. The types $\mathbf{B}, \mathbf{N}$ and $\mathbf{L}(T)$ stand respectively for booleans, integers, and lists over the type T. If a is the empty set, we write $A \multimap B$ for $A \overset{a}{\multimap} B$. *First-order types* are types in which for any subformula $A \overset{a}{\multimap} B$, A does not contain any $\multimap$ connective. Each function symbol $\mathtt{f}$ is assumed to have an *input type* $T_{\mathtt{f}}$ and an *output type* $S_{\mathtt{f}}$. The set $\mathcal{T}(T)$ of those values which can be given type T can be easily defined by induction on the structure of T.

Variable contexts (resp. *reference contexts*) are denoted as Γ (resp. Θ) and are of the shape $\Gamma = x_1 : A_1, \ldots, x_n : A_n$ (resp. $\Theta = r_1 : A_1, \ldots, r_n : A_n$). A *ground variable context* is a variable context in the form $\{x_1 : T_1, \ldots, x_n : T_n\}$, and is denoted with metavariables like $\ell\Gamma$. *Ground reference contexts* are defined similarly and are denoted with metavariables like $\ell\Theta$.

Typing judgements are of the form $\Gamma; \Theta \vdash M : A; a$. This judgement means that when assigning to free variables types as from Γ and to references types as from Θ, the term M can be given type A, and during its evaluation the set of references that might be read is included in a. The union $\Gamma \uplus \Delta$ of variable contexts is defined only if the variables in common are attributed *the same* base type. Similarly the union $a \uplus b$ of sets of locations (in a judgement) is defined only if the locations in common are attributed the same base type in the reference context Θ of the judgement.

A selection on the typing rules are in Fig. 1. Let us briefly comment on them. When typing a *dereference*, note that r must belong to the set a. In the rule for pairs, if M and N share a variable x, then this variable must have a base type; similarly if they can both read a reference r, then this reference must be

$$\frac{r \in a}{\Gamma; \Theta, r : A \vdash \, !r : A; a} \qquad \frac{\Gamma; \Theta \vdash M : A; a \qquad \Delta; \Theta \vdash N : B; b}{\Gamma \uplus \Delta; \Theta \vdash \langle M, N \rangle : A \otimes B; a \uplus b}$$

$$\frac{\Gamma, x : A; \Theta \vdash M : B; a}{\Gamma; \Theta \vdash \lambda x.M : A \xrightarrow{a} B; b} \qquad \frac{\ell\Gamma; \ell\Theta \vdash W : A; a \qquad \ell\Gamma; \ell\Theta \vdash V : A \xrightarrow{c} A; a}{\ell\Gamma; \ell\Theta \vdash \mathtt{iter}(V, W) : \mathbf{N} \xrightarrow{c} A; b}$$

Fig. 1. Linear typing rules — selection

in a, b and $a \uplus b$, and hence have a base type. The same holds in applications. When reading the rule for abstraction top-down, the set a is "moved" from the judgement to the type $A \xrightarrow{a} B$, and can in this way be used later in the derivation if $\lambda x.M$ is applied to an argument. In rule for $\mathtt{iter}(V, W)$, the variable context $\ell\Gamma$ and the reference context $\ell\Theta$ can only contain base types. Consider the following two examples:

$$M = r\mathbin{:=}\mathbf{zero}; \mathbf{cons}(!r, \mathbf{cons}(!r, \mathbf{nil})); \qquad N = (r\mathbin{:=}\lambda x.x); !r(!r*).$$

Both terms read a reference r twice, but M is typable, while N is not. Indeed, in M the reference r is read twice, but it is of base type $\mathbf{N}$; we can derive:

$$\emptyset; r : \mathbf{N} \vdash M : \mathbf{L}(\mathbf{N}); \{r\}$$

On the contrary, an attempt to type N fails because of the rule for Application and the condition on the sets of locations, since r does not have a base type.

Let us now give another example for computing addition and multiplication on natural numbers, in an imperative style:

$$
\begin{array}{lll}
incr_r & = \lambda x.r\mathbin{:=}\mathbf{succ}(!r) & \text{(increments the content of } r) \\
add_{r,r_1} & = \lambda x.\mathtt{iter}(incr_r, *)!r_1 & \text{(adds the content of } r_1 \text{ to that of } r) \\
mult_{r,r_1,r_2} & = \lambda x.(r\mathbin{:=}0; \mathtt{iter}(add_{r,r_1}, *)!r_2) & \text{(multiplies the contents of } r_1 \text{ and } r_2 \text{ and} \\
& & \text{assigns the result to } r)
\end{array}
$$

The language we have just defined, then, can be seen as an affine variation on Gödel's T with pairs, references, and inductive types, called ℓT.

Function Settings. The behavior of functions is not specified *a priori*, because such functions are meant to model calls to oracles in cryptography. Everything in the following, then, will be parametrized by a so-called *function setting*, which is a pair $(\{\mathbf{S}_f\}_f, \{\mathbf{C}_f\}_f)$, where $\mathbf{S}_f$ is a relation between base type values matching f's input and output types and modeling its (possibly probabilistic) extensional behaviour, while $\mathbf{C}_f$ is a function from $\mathbb{N}$ to $\mathbb{N}$ expressing a bound to the cost of evaluating f on arguments of a given length. In the rest of this paper, we assume that a function setting has been fixed, keeping in mind that type inference can be done independently on a specific function setting, as we will explain in Sect. 5.

Abstract Machine. We consider a variant of Felleisen and Friedman's CEK. As such, our machine will be given as a transition system on configurations, each of them keeping track of both the term being evaluated and the values locations map to. From now on, for the sake of simplicity, we consider natural numbers as the only base type, keeping in mind that all the other base types can be treated similarly. *Closures*, *environments*, and *stacks* are defined as follows, where M denotes a sequence of terms:

$$c ::= (\mathbf{M}, \xi); \qquad \xi ::= \varepsilon \mid \xi \cdot (x \mapsto c); \qquad \pi ::= \varepsilon \mid \delta \cdot \pi;$$

where δ ranges over *stack elements*:

$$\delta ::= \mathtt{lft}(c) \mid \mathtt{rgt}(c) \mid \mathtt{let}(c, x, x) \mid \mathtt{letlft}(c, c, x, x) \mid \mathtt{letrgt}(c, c, x, x)$$
$$\mid \mathtt{fun}(c) \mid \mathtt{arg}(c) \mid \mathtt{succ} \mid \mathtt{sel}(c) \mid \mathtt{iter}(c) \mid \mathtt{ufun}(\mathtt{f}) \mid \mathtt{:=}(r).$$

Machine stores are finite, partial maps of locations to *value closures*, i.e., closures in the form (V, ξ). A machine store $\mathcal{S}$ is said to be *conformant* with a reference context Θ if the value closure $\mathcal{S}(r)$ can be given type A, where $r : A$ is in Θ. *Configurations* are triples in the form $\mathcal{C} = (c, \pi, \mathcal{S})$, where c is a closure, π is a stack and $\mathcal{S}$ is a machine store. Machine transitions are of the form $\mathcal{C} \succ^n \mathcal{D}$, where n is a natural number denoting the cost of the transition. This is always defined to be 1, except for function calls, which are attributed a cost depending on the underlying function setting:

$$((t, \xi), \mathtt{ufun}(\mathtt{f}) \cdot \pi, \mathcal{S}) \succ^{\mathbf{C_f}(|t|)} ((\mathbf{S_f}(t), \xi), \pi, \mathcal{S}).$$

(The other rules are given in [2]). The way we label machine transitions induces a cost model: the amount of time a program takes when executed is precisely the sum of the costs of the transitions the machine performs while evaluating it. This can be proved to be *invariant*, i.e. to correspond to the costs of ordinary models of computation (TMs, RAMs, etc.), modulo a polynomial overhead.

3   Linear Dependent Types

There is nothing in $\ell\mathsf{T}$ types which allows to induce complexity bounds for the programs; in fact, $\ell\mathsf{T}$ can express at least all the primitive recursive functions [9]. This is precisely the role played by linear dependency [10], whose underlying idea consists in decorating simple types with some information about the identity of objects that programs manipulate. This takes the form of so-called index terms, following in spirit Xi's DML [22]. Differently from [10], what indices keep track of here is the *length*, rather than the *value*, of ground-type objects. The fact that higher-order objects cannot be duplicated, on the other hand, greatly simplifies the type system.

Given a set $\mathcal{IV}$ of *index variables*, and a set $\mathcal{IF}$ of *index functions* (each with an arity), *index terms* over $\mathcal{IV}$ and $\mathcal{IF}$ are defined as follows $I ::= a \mid f(I, \ldots, I)$, where $a \in \mathcal{IV}$ and $f \in \mathcal{IF}$. Index functions are interpreted as *total* functions from (n-uples of) positive natural numbers to positive natural numbers, by way of an *equational program* $\mathcal{E}$, which can be specified as, e.g., an orthogonal, terminating, term rewriting system or a primitive recursive Herbrand-Gödel scheme. We often write $\models^{\mathcal{E}} I \leq J$, by which we mean that the semantics $\mathcal{E}$ assigns to I is smaller or equal to the semantics $\mathcal{E}$ assigns to J, this for every value of the index variables occurring in either I or J. We will assume that $\mathcal{IF}$ contains at least 0 (of arity 0), s (for the successor, of arity 1) and $+$, $\cdot$ (addition and multiplication, of arity 2, used with infix notation), with adequate equations in $\mathcal{E}$.

We now define types and effects. *Indexed base types* U, *indexed reference contexts* Θ, *indexed types* D and *indexed effects* α are defined, respectively, as follows:

$$U ::= \text{unit} \mid \mathbf{B} \mid \mathbf{N}^I \mid \mathbf{L}^I(U); \qquad \Theta ::= \{r_1 : D_1, \ldots, r_n : D_n\};$$
$$\alpha ::= \Theta \Rightarrow \Theta; \qquad\qquad\qquad D ::= U \mid D \otimes D \mid D \overset{\alpha}{\multimap} D.$$

where I ranges over index terms. The empty effect $\emptyset \Rightarrow \emptyset$ is denoted as $\mathbf{0}$. Given two effects $\alpha = \Theta \Rightarrow \Xi$ and $\beta = \Xi \Rightarrow \Upsilon$, their *composition* $\alpha; \beta$ is $\Theta \Rightarrow \Upsilon$. An effect $\Theta \Rightarrow \Xi$ is meant to describe how references are modified by terms: if the store is conformant to Θ *before* evaluation, it will be conformant to Ξ *after* evaluation. So in particular an effect $\Theta \Rightarrow \emptyset$ does not provide any information.

If D is an indexed type, $[D]$ is the *type* obtained from D by: (i) forgetting all the index information (ii) replacing on arrows $\overset{\alpha}{\multimap}$ the effect α by the set of locations that appear in it. E.g., if $D = \mathbf{N}^{I_1} \overset{\alpha}{\multimap} \mathbf{N}^{I_2}$ where $\alpha = \{r_1 : D_1, r_2 : D_2\} \Rightarrow \{r_1 : D_4, r_3 : D_3\}$, then $[D] = \mathbf{N} \overset{\{r_1, r_2, r_3\}}{\multimap} \mathbf{N}$.

Given $t \in \mathcal{T}(T)$, we write that $\models^{\mathcal{E}} t \in U$ iff $[U] = T$ and the size of t is bounded by the index terms in U, independently on the values of index variables. Similarly, $\models^{\mathcal{E}} f \in U \multimap V$ stands for $\models^{\mathcal{E}} s \in V$ whenever $\models^{\mathcal{E}} t \in U$ and $(t, s) \in \mathbf{S}_f$. As an example, any lists t whose three elements are natural numbers less or equal to 4 is such that $\models^{\mathcal{E}} t \in \mathbf{L}^7(\mathbf{N}^{4+a})$.

A subtyping relation $\sqsubseteq$ on indexed types and effects is defined in Fig. 2. Note that we have $\vdash^{\mathcal{E}} \mathbf{0} \sqsubseteq \alpha$ iff α is of the shape $\alpha = \Xi_1, \Upsilon, \Xi_2 \Rightarrow \Pi$, where $\vdash^{\mathcal{E}} \Upsilon \sqsubseteq \Pi$. Suppose that r is a reference and that D is an indexed type. Then $\mathcal{ER}(r, D)$

$$\frac{\models^{\mathcal{E}} I \leq J}{\vdash^{\mathcal{E}} \mathbf{N}^I \sqsubseteq \mathbf{N}^J} \qquad \overline{\vdash^{\mathcal{E}} \text{unit} \sqsubseteq \text{unit}} \qquad \frac{\vdash^{\mathcal{E}} D \sqsubseteq E \qquad \vdash^{\mathcal{E}} F \sqsubseteq G}{\vdash^{\mathcal{E}} D \otimes F \sqsubseteq E \otimes G}$$

$$\frac{\vdash^{\mathcal{E}} E \sqsubseteq D \qquad \vdash^{\mathcal{E}} F \sqsubseteq G \qquad \vdash^{\mathcal{E}} \alpha \sqsubseteq \beta}{\vdash^{\mathcal{E}} D \overset{\alpha}{\multimap} F \sqsubseteq E \overset{\beta}{\multimap} G} \qquad \frac{\vdash^{\mathcal{E}} \Upsilon \sqsubseteq \Theta \qquad \vdash^{\mathcal{E}} \Xi \sqsubseteq \Phi \qquad \vdash^{\mathcal{E}} \Pi \sqsubseteq \Lambda}{\vdash^{\mathcal{E}} \Theta \Rightarrow \Xi \sqsubseteq \Upsilon, \Pi, \Psi \Rightarrow \Phi, \Lambda}$$

$$\frac{\vdash^{\mathcal{E}} D_1 \sqsubseteq E_1, \ldots, \vdash^{\mathcal{E}} D_n \sqsubseteq E_n}{\vdash^{\mathcal{E}} \{r_1 : D_1, \ldots, r_n : D_n\} \sqsubseteq \{r_1 : E_1, \ldots, r_n : E_n\}}$$

Fig. 2. Subtyping Rules

$$\frac{\vdash^{\mathcal{E}} D \sqsubseteq E \qquad \vdash^{\mathcal{E}} \mathbf{0} \sqsubseteq \alpha}{\Gamma, x : D \vdash^{\mathcal{E}} x : E; \alpha} \qquad \frac{\models^{\mathcal{E}} t \in U \qquad \vdash^{\mathcal{E}} \mathbf{0} \sqsubseteq \alpha}{\Gamma \vdash^{\mathcal{E}} t : U; \alpha} \qquad \frac{\vdash^{\mathcal{E}} \mathbf{0} \sqsubseteq \alpha}{\Gamma \vdash^{\mathcal{E}} * : \mathsf{unit}; \alpha}$$

$$\frac{\models^{\mathcal{E}} \mathbf{f} \in U \multimap V \qquad \Gamma \vdash^{\mathcal{E}} M : U; \alpha}{\Gamma \vdash^{\mathcal{E}} \mathbf{f}(M) : V; \alpha} \qquad \frac{\Gamma \vdash^{\mathcal{E}} M : D; \alpha \qquad \Delta \vdash^{\mathcal{E}} N : E; \beta}{\Gamma \uplus \Delta \vdash^{\mathcal{E}} \langle M, N \rangle : D \otimes E; \alpha; \beta}$$

$$\frac{\Gamma \vdash^{\mathcal{E}} M : D \otimes E; \alpha \qquad \Delta, x : D, y : E \vdash^{\mathcal{E}} N : F; \beta}{\Gamma \uplus \Delta \vdash^{\mathcal{E}} \mathbf{let}\ M\ \mathbf{be}\ \langle x, y \rangle\ \mathbf{in}\ N : F; \alpha; \beta}$$

$$\frac{\Gamma, x : D \vdash^{\mathcal{E}} M : E; \alpha \qquad \vdash^{\mathcal{E}} \mathbf{0} \sqsubseteq \beta}{\Gamma \vdash^{\mathcal{E}} \lambda x.M : D \overset{\alpha}{\multimap} E; \beta} \qquad \frac{\Gamma \vdash^{\mathcal{E}} M : D \overset{\gamma}{\multimap} E; \alpha \qquad \Delta \vdash^{\mathcal{E}} N : D; \beta}{\Gamma \uplus \Delta \vdash^{\mathcal{E}} MN : E; \alpha; \beta; \gamma}$$

$$\frac{\vdash^{\mathcal{E}} \mathcal{ER}(r, D) \sqsubseteq \alpha}{\Gamma \vdash^{\mathcal{E}} !r : D; \alpha} \qquad \frac{\Gamma \vdash^{\mathcal{E}} M : D; \Theta \Rightarrow \Xi, \{r : E\}}{\Gamma \vdash^{\mathcal{E}} r := M : \mathsf{unit}; \Theta \Rightarrow \Xi, \{r : D\}}$$

Fig. 3. Typing Rules, Part I

is defined to be just $\{r : D\} \Rightarrow \{r : D\}$ if D is an indexed base type, and $\{r : D\} \Rightarrow \emptyset$ otherwise.

Typing contexts and terminology on them are the same as the one we used in the linear type system (Sect. 2) where, of course, *indexed types* plays the role of *types*. A typing judgement has the form $\Gamma \vdash^{\mathcal{E}} M : D; \alpha$. Let us denote $\alpha = \Theta \Rightarrow \Xi$. The intended meaning of the judgement is that if term variables are assigned types in Γ, then M can be typed with D, and if initially the contents of the references are typed as in Θ, then after evaluation of M the contents of the references can be typed as in Ξ. So while the former type system of Sect. 2 only provided information about *which* references might have been read during evaluation, this new system will also provide information about *how* the contents of references might have been modified, more specifically how the size of the contents might have changed.

Now, the typing rules are given in Figs. 3 and 4. A term M is dependently linearly typable if there exists a derivation of a judgement $\Gamma \vdash^{\mathcal{E}} M : D; \alpha$. Before analyzing the type system, let us make a few comments:

- As in the linear type system, all rules treat variables of ground types differently than variables of higher-order types: the former can occur free an arbitrary number of times, while the latter can occur free at most once. Similarly for references. As a consequence, if a term is dependently linearly typable, then it is linearly typable.
- We should also take note of the fact that values can all be typed with the $\mathbf{0}$ effect. This is quite intuitive, since values are meant to be terms which need not be further evaluated.
- The rules typing assignments and location references (two bottom rules in Fig. 3) show how higher-order references are treated. While an assignment simply overwrites the type attributed to the assigned location, a reference is typed with the location effect of the referenced location.

$$\frac{\models^{\mathcal{E}} I+1 \leq J \quad \Gamma \vdash^{\mathcal{E}} M : \mathbf{N}^I; \alpha}{\Gamma \vdash^{\mathcal{E}} \mathtt{succ}(M) : \mathbf{N}^J; \alpha}$$

$$\frac{\ell\Gamma \vdash^{\mathcal{E}} W : D\{a/1\}; \mathbf{0} \qquad \ell\Gamma \vdash^{\mathcal{E}} V : \left(D \xrightarrow{\Xi \Rightarrow \Xi\{a/a+1\}}{\multimap} D\{a/a+1\}\right); \mathbf{0}}{\vdash^{\mathcal{E}} \mathbf{0} \sqsubseteq \alpha \qquad \vdash^{\mathcal{E}} D \sqsubseteq E \qquad \vdash^{\mathcal{E}} E \sqsubseteq E\{a/a+1\} \qquad \vdash^{\mathcal{E}} E\{a/I\} \sqsubseteq F}$$
$$\frac{\vdash^{\mathcal{E}} \Theta \sqsubseteq \Xi\{a/1\} \qquad \vdash^{\mathcal{E}} \Xi \sqsubseteq \Pi \qquad \vdash^{\mathcal{E}} \Pi \sqsubseteq \Pi\{a/a+1\} \qquad \vdash^{\mathcal{E}} \Pi\{a/I\} \sqsubseteq \Phi}{\ell\Gamma \vdash^{\mathcal{E}} \mathtt{iter}(V,W) : \mathbf{N}^I \xrightarrow{\Theta \Rightarrow \Phi}{\multimap} F; \alpha}$$

$$\frac{\ell\Gamma \vdash^{\mathcal{E}} V : D\{a/1\}; \mathbf{0} \qquad \ell\Gamma \vdash^{\mathcal{E}} W : \left(\mathbf{N}^a \xrightarrow{\beta\{a/a+1\}}{\multimap} D\{a/a+1\}\right); \mathbf{0}}{\vdash^{\mathcal{E}} \mathbf{0} \sqsubseteq \alpha \qquad \vdash^{\mathcal{E}} D \sqsubseteq D\{a/a+1\} \qquad \vdash^{\mathcal{E}} D\{a/I\} \sqsubseteq E}$$
$$\frac{\vdash^{\mathcal{E}} \mathbf{0} \sqsubseteq \beta\{a/1\} \qquad \vdash^{\mathcal{E}} \beta \sqsubseteq \beta\{a/a+1\} \qquad \vdash^{\mathcal{E}} \beta\{a/I\} \sqsubseteq \gamma}{\ell\Gamma \vdash^{\mathcal{E}} \mathtt{ifz}(V,W) : \mathbf{N}^I \xrightarrow{\gamma}{\multimap} E; \alpha}$$

Fig. 4. Typing Rules, Part II

As an example, we can derive for the term M of Sect. 2:

$$\vdash^{\mathcal{E}} M : \mathbf{L}^{a+3}(\mathbf{N}^{b+1}); r : \mathbf{N}^c \Rightarrow r : \mathbf{N}^{b+1}$$

As to the terms of Sect. 2 for increment, addition and multiplication, we obtain:

$$\vdash^{\mathcal{E}} incr_r : \mathtt{unit} \xrightarrow{r:\mathbf{N}^a \Rightarrow r:\mathbf{N}^{a+1}}{\multimap} \mathtt{unit}; \mathbf{0}$$

$$\vdash^{\mathcal{E}} add_{r,r_1} : \mathtt{unit} \xrightarrow{r:\mathbf{N}^a, r_1:\mathbf{N}^b \Rightarrow r:\mathbf{N}^{a+b}, r_1:\mathbf{N}^b}{\multimap} \mathtt{unit}; \mathbf{0}$$

$$\vdash^{\mathcal{E}} mult_{r,r_1,r_2} : \mathtt{unit} \xrightarrow{\alpha}{\multimap} \mathtt{unit}; \mathbf{0}$$

where $\alpha = (r : \mathbf{N}^c, r_1 : \mathbf{N}^a, r_2 : \mathbf{N}^b) \Rightarrow (r : \mathbf{N}^{a \cdot b}, r_1 : \mathbf{N}^a, r_2 : \mathbf{N}^b)$.

4   Intensional Soundness

Once a term M has been typed by a derivation π, one can assign a *weight* $\mathbb{W}(\pi)$ to π (and thus indirectly to M) in the form of an index term I. It is meant to estimate the time complexity of M. $\mathbb{W}(\pi)$ is defined by induction on the structure of π; interesting cases are those for iteration and function:

$$\frac{\rho \triangleright \Gamma \vdash^{\mathcal{E}} M : \mathbf{N}^I; \alpha}{\pi \triangleright \Gamma \vdash^{\mathcal{E}} \mathtt{f}(M) : U; \alpha} \qquad \mathbb{W}(\pi) = \mathbb{W}(\rho) + \mathbf{C_f}(I)$$

$$\frac{\rho \triangleright \ell\Gamma \vdash^{\mathcal{E}} W : D\{a/1\}; \mathbf{0}}{\sigma \triangleright \ell\Gamma \vdash^{\mathcal{E}} V : \left(D \xrightarrow{\Xi \Rightarrow \Xi\{a/a+1\}}{\multimap} D\{a/a+1\}\right); \mathbf{0}}{\pi \triangleright \ell\Gamma \vdash^{\mathcal{E}} \mathtt{iter}(V,W) : \mathbf{N}^I \xrightarrow{\Theta \Rightarrow \Phi}{\multimap} F; \alpha} \qquad \mathbb{W}(\pi) = \mathbb{W}(\rho) + \sum_{1 \leq a < I} \mathbb{W}(\sigma) + I$$

It is important to note that the definition of $\mathbb{W}(\pi)$ in the case of $\texttt{iter}(V, W)$ involves a summation, but $\mathbb{W}(\sigma)$ is computed only once and the summation itself is not evaluated. Other cases are defined in the standard way, i.e. the weight of a derivation is the weight of the sum of its subderivations plus 1. The full definition is given in [2].

The weight of a derivation decreases along *machine* transition rules, as defined in Sect. 2. This can be proved by generalizing dℓT to a type system for machine configurations. Following the same ideas, one can also define the weight $\mathbb{W}(\mathcal{S})$ of any conformant store $\mathcal{S}$. By a careful analysis of the reduction rules, one gets Subject Reduction for configurations:

Lemma 1. *If* $\vdash^{\mathcal{E}} (c, \pi) : U; \Theta \Rightarrow \Xi$, *the store* $\mathcal{S}$ *is conformant with* Θ, *and* $(c, \pi, \mathcal{S}) \succ^n (d, \rho, \mathcal{R})$, *then* $\vdash^{\mathcal{E}} (d, \rho) : U; \Upsilon \Rightarrow \Xi$, *the store* $\mathcal{R}$ *is conformant with* Υ, *and* $\mathbb{W}(\pi) + \mathbb{W}(\mathcal{S}) \geq \mathbb{W}(\rho) + \mathbb{W}(\mathcal{R}) + n$.

Proof. One only needs to carefully analyze each of the machine transition rules. Indeed, the way the type system has been extended to configurations and the way the weight of a type derivation has been defined make the task easy. □

As an easy consequence, we obtain intensional soundness.

Theorem 1 (Intensional Soundness). *If* $\pi \triangleright \vdash^{\mathcal{E}} M : U; \Theta \Rightarrow \Xi$, *the store* $\mathcal{S}$ *is conformant with* Θ, *and* $(M, \varepsilon, \mathcal{S}) \succ^n \mathscr{C}$, *then* $n \leq \mathbb{W}(\pi) + \mathbb{W}(\mathcal{S})$.

So this theorem shows that the weight of a dℓT program is indeed a bound on its evaluation time. But how can we type an ℓT program so as to obtain a dℓT type derivation? This is the subject of the next Section.

5   Type Inference

The type inference procedure is defined quite similarly to the one in [11], where the language at hand, called dℓPCF, is more general than the one described here (apart from effects). As a consequence, we will only describe the general scheme of the algorithm, together with the most important cases (noticeably, iteration). For simplification we will also omit the effects, as anyway they don't present specific difficulties ·

A tree whose nodes are labelled by typing judgements, but which is not necessarily built according to our type system is said to be a *pseudo-derivation*. This is to be contrasted with a proper type derivation. Similarly, an incomplete set of rewrite rules which, contrarily to proper equational programs, does not univocally define all the function symbols that occur in them is said to be a *pseudo-program*.

The type inference algorithm TI takes in input a linearly typable term M, together with a finite sequence of index variables $\phi = a_1, \ldots, a_n$, and returns:

- A pseudo-derivation π with conclusion $\Gamma \vdash M : D; \alpha$ where the types in Γ and D match the ones of M.
- A pseudo-program $\mathcal{E}$.

In other words, $\mathtt{TI}(M^A, \phi) = (\pi, \mathcal{E})$. The understanding here is that the undefinded function symbols in $\mathcal{E}$ are those which occur in *negative* positions in the conclusion of π, and the termination of symbols in $\mathcal{E}$ is necessary and sufficient for π to be a correct type derivation (once symbols not defined in $\mathcal{E}$ are properly defined).

The algorithm $\mathtt{TI}$ is recursive, and proceeds by pattern matching on its first argument. Let us just consider the case when the input term is an iteration, i.e. suppose that M is $\mathtt{iter}(V, W)$ and has linear type $\mathbf{N} \multimap A$. For the sake of simplicity, suppose that A is $\mathbf{N} \multimap \mathbf{N}$, and that V and W are closed. The algorithm proceeds by recursively calling itself on V (and ϕ, a, b) and on W (and ϕ, a), obtaining that $\mathtt{TI}(V, \phi, a, b) = (\pi_V, \mathcal{E}_V)$ and $\mathtt{TI}(W, \phi, a) = (\pi_W, \mathcal{E}_W)$, where: $\pi_V \triangleright \vdash V : (\mathbf{N}^{f(\phi,a,b)} \multimap \mathbf{N}^{g(\phi,a,b)}) \multimap (\mathbf{N}^{j(\phi,a,b)} \multimap \mathbf{N}^{h(\phi,a,b)}); \mathbf{0}$ and $\pi_W \triangleright \vdash W : \mathbf{N}^{k(\phi,a)} \multimap \mathbf{N}^{p(\phi,a)}; \mathbf{0}$. Moreover, by construction, $\mathcal{E}_V$ defines f and h (but not g and j), while $\mathcal{E}_W$ defines p (but not k). The algorithm then returns the pseudo-derivation obtained by assembling π_V and π_W by way of the typing rule for $\mathtt{iter}(\cdot)$. About the output equational program, of course we need to return at least the equations in $\mathcal{E}_V \cup \mathcal{E}_W$, but we also need something more, namely the following equations (where q, r are fresh function symbols):

$$k(\phi, 0) = q(\phi); \qquad\qquad k(\phi, a+1) = f(\phi, a, 0);$$
$$g(\phi, a, 0) = p(\phi, a); \qquad\qquad g(\phi, a, b+1) = h(\phi, a+1, b);$$
$$j(\phi, 0, b) = q(\phi); \qquad\qquad j(\phi, a+1, b) = f(\phi, a, b+1);$$
$$r(\phi) = \max_{b \leq s(\phi)} h(\phi, 0, b).$$

The type of M can then be set to be $\mathbf{N}^{s(\phi)} \multimap \mathbf{N}^{q(\phi)} \multimap \mathbf{N}^{r(\phi)}$. Note how the typing rule for $\mathtt{iter}(\cdot)$ can indeed be applied using the type above, by choosing $E = \mathbf{N}^{q(\phi)} \multimap \mathbf{N}^{\max_{b \leq a} h(\phi,0,b)}$.

The way we define $\mathtt{TI}$, and in particular the fact that the output program is only a *pseudo*-program and not a proper equational program, has the consequence of allowing $\mathtt{TI}$ to be defineable by recursion. What $\mathtt{TI}$ produces in output, however, is *not* a type derivation but a *pseudo*-derivation: $\mathcal{E}$ does not give meaning to all function symbols, and in particular not to the symbols occurring in negative position. Getting a proper type derivation, then, requires giving meaning to those symbols. This is the purpose of the algorithm $\mathtt{CTI}$ which, given in input a term M, proceeds as follows:

- It calls $\mathtt{TI}(M, \phi)$, where the variables in ϕ are in bijective correspondence to the negative occurrences of base types in M.
- Once obtained $(\pi, \mathcal{E})$ in output, it complements $\mathcal{E}$ with equations in the form $f_i(\phi) = a_i$ where a_i is the variable corresponding to f_i.
- In the conclusion of π, replace $f_i(\phi)$ by just a_i.

Soundness and Completeness. The way the type-inference algorithm $\mathtt{CTI}$ is defined makes its output correct mostly by definition.

Theorem 2 (Soundness). *If $\mathtt{CTI}(M) = (\pi, \mathcal{E})$, then $\mathcal{E}$ is completely specified and π is a correct type derivation, i.e., all proof obligations in π are true in $\mathcal{E}$.*

Proof. First of all, one can prove, by induction on M, that any completion of the equational program obtained from $\mathrm{TI}(M, \phi)$ turns the obtained pseudo-derivation into a correct type derivation. Then, one can observe that CTI simply completes TI in the obvious way.   □

Since the CTI algorithm, contrarily to what happens traditionally in the context of type-inference, *never* fails when fed with terms which can be linearly typed as from Sect. 2, it means that it is also complete by design:

Theorem 3. (Completeness). *The algorithm* CTI *is total.*

5.1 Termination

We now prove that the equational program $\mathcal{E}$ produced in output by type inference (i.e. $\mathrm{CTI}(M) = (\pi, \mathcal{E})$) is indeed *terminating*. Importantly, this cannot be proved directly, i.e. by induction on M, merely following the way TI is defined. Indeed, a reducibility-like argument is needed, which goes as follows: given an equational program $\mathcal{E}$ and an assignment ρ of natural numbers to some free index variables, we write $\mathcal{E}, \rho \models D$ if for the value of variables as in ρ, $\mathcal{E}$ is *reducible* in D, where *reducible* is a concept defined by induction on D. As an example, if D is just $\mathbf{N}^I$, then I is given a meaning by the equational program $\mathcal{E}$ when the variables occurring free in I are given values according to ρ. Then, as usual, one proves that all equational programs output by TI are reducible, but *for all* assignments ρ.

Theorem 4. (Termination). *If* $\mathrm{CTI}(M) = (\pi, \mathcal{E})$, *then* $\mathcal{E}$ *is terminating.*

Proof. The proof is structured as follows:

- On the one hand, one needs to prove that any equational program $\mathcal{E}$ that $\mathrm{TI}(M, \phi)$ produces in output is indeed reducible for every assignment ρ over ϕ. This property can indeed be proved by induction on the structure of M.
- On the other hand, one also proves that all *reducible* programs, when completed like in CTI, are terminating.

6   Application to Cryptographic Proofs

This section presents an application of dℓT to cryptographic proofs. Typically, such proofs reduce the security of a cryptographic construction to computational assumption(s), and consist of three steps. The first step is the definition of an algorithm $\mathcal{B}$, hereby called the constructed adversary, that breaks the computational assumption(s), using as a subroutine the adversary $\mathcal{A}$ against the cryptographic construction. The second step exhibits and formally justifies upper bounds on the winning probability of the constructed adversary $\mathcal{B}$, as an expression of the winning probability of the adversary $\mathcal{A}$ against the cryptographic construction. This step can be carried out formally using tools such as e.g. CryptoVerif [8] or EasyCrypt [6]. Finally, the third step formally justifies upper bounds for the execution time of the constructed adversary $\mathcal{B}$ as a function of the execution time of the adversary $\mathcal{A}$. We use dℓT for the third step. Specifically, we consider the constructed adversary from the Goldreich-Levin theorem, which shows the existence of hardcore predicates for a class of one-way functions. This example is particularly challenging, because some of the intermediate computations are not polytime w.r.t. the size of their inputs. Another example of application, that of a padding-based encryption (BR93, [7]) is described in [2]. We also believe that we can handle such schemes as RSA-FDH (see [19] Sect. 13.3) but this is left for future work.

Notation. In dℓT we will freely use the combinators map and fold and map$_2$ on lists. Combinators map and fold are defined in the usual way, whereas map$_2$ f $(a_1, \ldots, a_n)$ $(b_1, \ldots, b_m)$ returns the list $(f\ a_1\ b_1, \ldots, f\ a_p\ b_p)$ where $p = \min(n, m)$. Moreover, we let app denote concatenation of lists, and $*^k$ denote the list that repeats k times the constant $*$.

Furthermore, we model bits and bitstrings as booleans and lists of booleans, respectively. In order to increase readability, we often use $\{0, 1\}$ as a synonym for $\mathbf{B}$ and $\{0, 1\}^k$ to denote the set of bitstrings of length k. Moreover, we use standard notations for bitstrings: we let $\oplus$ and $\otimes$ respectively denote the exclusive or operator and multiplication operators (both of type $\{0, 1\} \rightarrow \{0, 1\} \rightarrow \{0, 1\}$), and 0^k denote the 0-bitstring of length k. Using operators on maps, one can define exclusive or on bitstrings, and scalar multiplication of a bitstring by a bit. Moreover, we assume given a probabilistic operator flip : unit $\rightarrow \{0, 1\}$ that samples a bit uniformly at random. Again using standard operators on maps, one can define an operator flip$_k$: unit$^k \rightarrow \{0, 1\}^k$.

Finally, we can define an operator pow$_0$ which takes as input a natural number k and outputs the list of non-empty subsets of $\{1, \ldots, k\}$—we model each subset as a list of bitstrings of length k.

Recall that a one-way function is a function that is easy to compute but hard to invert. Although it seemingly contradicts the definition, one-way functions can also leak information about their inputs. Thus, a natural question is to characterize the amount of information that one-way functions hide from their inputs. This hiding property is captured by the notion of hardcore predicate; informally, a predicate p is a hardcore predicate for a function f if p can be computed efficiently and an efficient adversary with access to f x has a small probability to guess correctly whether p x holds, where the value x is sampled uniformly over the domain of f. The existence of a hardcore predicate for every one-way function is a long-standing open problem in cryptography. However, the celebrated Goldreich-Levin theorem proves that for every one-way function f over bitstrings of length n, there exists a hardcore predicate p for the one-way function g over bitstrings of length $2n$, where g is defined by the clause g(app x y) = app (f x) y, and p is defined by the clause:

$$p(\text{app } x\ y) = \bigoplus_{i=1}^{n} x_i \otimes y_i$$

where x_i denotes the i-th bit of x and we recall that app is the concatenation of strings.

The theorem is proved by showing that for every adversary $\mathcal{A}$ with a non-negligible probability of guessing the value of the hardcore predicate on a randomly chosen value x, there exists a probabilistic polytime inverter $\mathcal{I}$ with a non-negligible probability of guessing the pre-image of f on a randomly sampled value x. Informally, the inverter is given as input a bitstring y of length n, and outputs a bitstring x of length n as follows:

1. it sets ℓ to $\lceil \log(n+1) \rceil$;
2. it defines zerobut as the function that takes as inputs a natural number i and a bitstring w of length n and returns the bitstring z such that $z_j = 0$ for $j \neq i$ and $z_i = w_i$ (note that z also has length n);
3. it samples uniformly at random ℓ bitstrings $z_1 \ldots z_\ell$ of length n, and ℓ bits $r_1 \ldots r_\ell$;
4. for every non-empty subset X of $\{1 \ldots \ell\}$, it computes the bitstrings z^X and the bit r^X, respectively as $\bigoplus_{i \in X} z_i$ and $\oplus_{i \in X} r_i$;
5. for every non-empty subset X of $\{1 \ldots \ell\}$ and for every $i \in \{1 \ldots n\}$, it computes the bit $x_i^X = r^X \oplus \mathcal{A}(\text{app } y \text{ (zerobut } i \; z^X))$, and sets $x_i = \text{majority}(x_i^X)$, where X is drawn from the set of non-empty subsets of $\{1 \ldots \ell\}$.

The formal definition of the inverter $\mathcal{I}$ in $\ell\mathsf{T}$ is given in Fig. 5. It uses two functions, both defined recursively in the expected way: the majority function $\text{majority} : \mathbf{L}(\{0,1\}) \to \{0,1\}$ which returns the most frequent bit from a list, and the function $\text{zerobut} : \mathbf{N} \to \mathbf{L}(\{0,1\}) \to \mathbf{L}(\{0,1\})$ which takes as input a natural number n and a list l and zeroes all elements of l but the nth one.

We refer to e.g. [19, Sect. 6.3] for a proof of the validity of the reduction, and focus on analyzing the complexity of the inverter $\mathcal{I}$. Let us first carry an informal

---

$\lambda y.$	*argument of the inverter*
let $\ell = \lceil \log(n+1) \rceil$ in	*defines ℓ*
let $\mathbf{P} = \text{pow}_0 \; \ell$ in	*enumerates all non-empty subsets of $\{1, \ldots, \ell\}$*
let $R = \text{map (flip) } *^\ell$ in	*samples uniformly at random $(r_1, \ldots, r_\ell)$*
let $Z = \text{map } (\lambda\_. \; \text{map (flip) } *^n) \; *^\ell$ in	*samples uniformly at random $(z_1, \ldots, z_\ell)$*
let $R^P = \text{map } (g_r) \; \mathbf{P}$ in	*computes the list $(r^X)_{X \in \mathbf{P}}$*
let $Z^P = \text{map } (g_z) \; \mathbf{P}$ in	*computes the list $(z^X)_{X \in \mathbf{P}}$*
$\text{map } (G)(1, \ldots, n)$	

    where :
$$\otimes = \lambda x.\text{map } (\otimes \; x)$$
$$\oplus = \text{map}_2 \; (\oplus)$$
$$g_r = \lambda X.\text{fold } (\oplus, 0) \; (\text{map}_2(\otimes) \; X \; R)$$
$$g_z = \lambda X.\text{fold } (\oplus, 0^n) \; (\text{map}_2 \; (\otimes) \; X \; Z)$$
$$G = \lambda i. \; \text{majority } (\text{map}_2 \; (\lambda r \; z. \; \oplus \; r \; (\mathcal{A} \; (\text{app } y \; (\text{zerobut } i \; z)))) \; R^P \; Z^P)$$

Fig. 5. Inverter $\mathcal{I}$ against hardcore predicate, with helper functions

analysis. For each function $\mathsf{zerobut}(i, \cdot)$, the inverter invokes the adversary $2^{\ell} - 1$ times, since the lists R^P and Z^P both have length $2^{\ell} - 1$. So the inverter calls the adversary $n \cdot (2^{\ell} - 1)$ times, i.e. $t_{\mathcal{I}} \sim n^2 \cdot t_{\mathcal{A}}$. Hence $\mathcal{I}$ executes in polytime, assuming that $\mathcal{A}$ does. This example is particularly interesting because it is not hereditarily polytime: the function pow_0 has an output of exponential size (and so is not polytime), but in the program $\mathcal{I}$ it is applied only to a small input (ℓ, of logarithmic size). It does not use references, but it illustrates how higher-order can be used to write concise code.

Now let us sketch how we can type the inverter $\mathcal{I}$. We need for that to extend $\mathcal{IF}$ with two new function symbols $\log$, e with the following equations in $\mathcal{E}$:

$$\log(1) \to 0, \quad \log(2 \cdot a) \to s\log(a), \quad e(0) \to 1, \quad e(sa) \to 2 \cdot e(a).$$

As examples of types for subterms we obtain, where $J = \log(sn)$:

$$\mathsf{pow}_0 : \mathbf{N}^a \multimap \mathbf{L}^{e(a)}(\mathbf{L}^a(\mathbf{B})), \quad P : \mathbf{L}^{e(J)}(\mathbf{L}^J(\mathbf{B})), \quad g_r : \mathbf{L}^J(\mathbf{B}) \multimap \mathbf{B}$$

Finally the inverter $\mathcal{I}$ can be given a type derivation π of conclusion $\mathbf{L}^n(\mathbf{B}) \multimap \mathbf{L}^n(\mathbf{B})$ (see [2]). If we denote as g the index function representing the time complexity of the adversary $\mathcal{A}$, we obtain as weight for the derivation: $\mathbb{W}(\pi) = O(n^2 g(1 + 2n) + n^2 \log(n + 1))$. As we can assume that $\log(n + 1)$ is dominated by $g(1 + 2n)$, we finally obtain $\mathbb{W}(\pi) = O(n^2 g(1 + 2n))$. By Theorem 1 this yields a bound for the running time of $\mathcal{I}$, so this result confirms the informal analysis carried out above.

7   Related Work

There exist many verification techniques for analysing the complexity of programs. What is specific about our proposal is the presence of both higher-order functions and imperative features, which allows a reasonable degree of flexibility, coupled with a nice way to accomodate probabilistic effects and oracles.

Type Systems. To our best knowledge, none of the (many) type systems characterizing polytime from the literature (e.g. [3,16,17,20]) are able to capture non-hereditarily polytime programs. Technically, our type system can be seen as a variation and a simplification of linear dependent types [10,11]. The main novelty is the presence of effects, which allow to deal with imperative features. Duplication of higher-order values is restricted, and this renders the type system simpler. Subrecursivity, in turn, enforces termination of equational programs obtained through type inference. All these aspects were simply missing in previous works on linear dependent types. Other related works are [12,14], which however only deal with linear bounds or with first-order definitions.

Static Analysis. Among the static analysis methodologies for complexity analysis, those based on abstract interpretation [1,15] deserve to be cited. These can be very effective on imperative programs, but are not able to handle higher-order features. It is moreover not clear whether relatively complicated examples like the ones we presented here could be handled. This is even more evident in, e.g., matrix-based calculi for imperative programs [18].

Computer-aided Cryptography. Few tools for computer-aided cryptography support complexity analyses of programs. CryptoVerif [8] ensures that processes are executed in probabilistic polynomial time, but cannot prove that the constructed adversary for the Goldreich-Levin theorem is polytime. CertiCrypt [5] formalizes an instrumented semantics that tracks the execution time of probabilistic program, and allows users to reason about the complexity of programs directly at the level of the instrumented operational semantics. A similar apporach is taken in the Foundational Cryptographic Framework (FCF) [21]. Such an approach is cumbersome. Computational Indistinguishability Logic (CIL) [4] carries an implicit complexity analysis in its judgments but it reasons about mathematical functions rather than programs.

8 Conclusion

We have defined a sound type and effect system for analyzing the complexity of executing higher-order, stateful, programs on a variant of the CEK abstract machine. We have also given a sound and complete type inference algorithm which does not require to check termination of the equational program, which is ensured. There are several interesting avenues for further research. One direction is to implement dℓT and integrate it in a system for computer-aided cryptography. Another direction is to develop automated approaches to reason about expected complexity of programs. Several noteworthy reductions in cryptography are based on constructed adversaries that execute in expected, rather than strict, probabilistic polynomial time; the main challenge here is not only to come up with a type system for expected complexity, but also a definitional one; see [13] for a recent account of the subtleties with existing definitions.

References

1. Albert, E., Arenas, P., Genaim, S., Puebla, G., Zanardini, D.: COSTA: design and implementation of a cost and termination analyzer for java bytecode. In: de Boer, F.S., Bonsangue, M.M., Graf, S., de Roever, W.-P. (eds.) FMCO 2007. LNCS, vol. 5382, pp. 113–132. Springer, Heidelberg (2008)
2. Baillot, P., Barthe, G., Dal Lago, U.: Implicit computational complexity of subrecursive definitions and applications to cryptographic proofs (long version). Technical report, september 2015, HAL archive. http://hal.archives-ouvertes.fr/hal-01197456
3. Baillot, P., Terui, K.: Light types for polynomial time computation in lambda calculus. Inf. Comput. **207**(1), 41–62 (2009)
4. Barthe, G., Daubignard, M., Kapron, B., Lakhnech, Y.: Computational indistinguishability logic. In: Computer and Communications Securitym, CCS 2010, pp. 375–386. ACM, New York (2010)
5. Barthe, G., Grégoire, B., Béguelin, S.Z.: Formal certification of code-based cryptographic proofs. In: POPL, pp. 90–101 (2009)
6. Barthe, G., Grégoire, B., Heraud, S., Béguelin, S.Z.: Computer-aided security proofs for the working cryptographer. In: Rogaway, P. (ed.) CRYPTO 2011. LNCS, vol. 6841, pp. 71–90. Springer, Heidelberg (2011)

7. Bellare, M., Rogaway, P.: Random oracles are practical: a paradigm for designing efficient protocols. In: Computer and Communications Security, pp. 62–73 (1993)
8. Blanchet, B.: A computationally sound mechanized prover for security protocols. In: IEEE Symposium on Security and Privacy, pp. 140–154 (2006)
9. Dal Lago, U.: The geometry of linear higher-order recursion. ACM Trans. Comput. Log. **10**(2), 8:1–8:38 (2009)
10. Dal Lago, U., Gaboardi, M.: Linear dependent types and relative completeness. Logical Methods Comput. Sci. **8**(4), 133–142 (2011)
11. Dal Lago, U., Petit, B.: The geometry of types. In: POPL, pp. 167–178 (2013)
12. Danielsson, N.A.: Lightweight semiformal time complexity analysis for purely functional data structures. In: POPL, pp. 133–144 (2008)
13. Goldreich, O.: On expected probabilistic polynomial-time adversaries: a suggestion for restricted definitions and their benefits. In: Vadhan, S.P. (ed.) TCC 2007. LNCS, vol. 4392, pp. 174–193. Springer, Heidelberg (2007)
14. Grobauer, B.: Cost recurrences for DML programs. In: International Conference on Functional Programming (ICFP 2001), pp. 253–264 (2001)
15. Gulwani, S., Mehra, K.K., Chilimbi, T.M.: Speed: precise and efficient static estimation of program computational complexity. In: POPL, pp. 127–139 (2009)
16. Hoffmann, J., Hofmann, M.: Amortized resource analysis with polynomial potential. In: Gordon, A.D. (ed.) ESOP 2010. LNCS, vol. 6012, pp. 287–306. Springer, Heidelberg (2010)
17. Hofmann, M.: Safe recursion with higher types and BCK-algebra. Ann. Pure Appl. Logic **104**(1–3), 113–166 (2000)
18. Jones, N.D., Kristiansen, L.: A flow calculus of mwp-bounds for complexity analysis. ACM Trans. Comput. Log. 10(4), 28:1–28:41 (2009)
19. Katz, J., Lindell, Y.: Introduction to Modern Cryptography. Chapman & Hall Cryptography and Network Security Series. Chapman & Hall, New York (2007)
20. Leivant, D., Marion, J.: Lambda calculus characterizations of poly-time. Fundam. Inform. **19**(1/2), 167–184 (1993)
21. Petcher, A., Morrisett, G.: The foundational cryptography framework (2015). to appear
22. Xi, H.: Dependent types for program termination verification. High. Order Symb. Comput. **15**(1), 91–131 (2002)

TIP: Tools for Inductive Provers

Dan Rosén[✉] and Nicholas Smallbone[✉]

Department of Computer Science and Engineering,
Chalmers University of Technology, Gothenburg, Sweden
{danr,nicsma}@chalmers.se

Abstract. TIP is a toolbox for users and developers of inductive provers. It consists of a large number of tools which can, for example, simplify an inductive problem, monomorphise it or find counterexamples to it. We are using TIP to help maintain a set of benchmarks for inductive theorem provers, where its main job is to encode aspects of the problem that are not natively supported by the respective provers. TIP makes it easier to write inductive provers, by supplying necessary tools such as lemma discovery which prover authors can simply import into their own prover.

1 Introduction

More and more people are making inductive theorem provers. Besides traditional systems such as ACL2 [14], new provers such as Zeno [18], HipSpec [9], Hipster [13], Pirate [19] and Graphsc [12] have appeared, and some formerly non-inductive provers such as CVC4 [16] and Dafny [15] can now do induction.

To make it easier to scientifically compare these provers, we recently compiled a benchmark suite of 343 inductive problems [10]. We ran into a problem: all of the provers are very different. Some expect the problem to be monomorphic, some expect it to be first-order, some expect it to be expressed as a functional program rather than a logic formula. If we stuck only to features supported by all the provers, we would have very little to work with.

Instead, we designed a rich language which can express a wide variety of problems. The TIP format (short for *Tons of Inductive Problems*) is an extension of SMT-LIB [2] and includes inductive datatypes, built-in integers, higher-order functions, polymorphism, recursive function definitions and first-order logic.

The TIP Tools. In this paper, we demonstrate a set of tools for transforming and processing inductive problems. The tools are based around the TIP format that we used for our benchmark suite, and provide a wide variety of operations that are useful to users and developers of inductive provers. The tools can currently:

- Convert SMT-LIB and Haskell to TIP.
- Convert TIP to SMT-LIB, TPTP TFF, Haskell, WhyML or Isabelle/HOL.
- Remove features from a problem that a prover does not support, such as higher-order functions or polymorphism.

© Springer-Verlag Berlin Heidelberg 2015
M. Davis et al. (Eds.): LPAR-20 2015, LNCS 9450, pp. 219–232, 2015.
DOI: 10.1007/978-3-662-48899-7_16

- Instantiate an induction schema: given a conjecture and a set of variables to do induction over, generate verification conditions for proving the conjecture by induction.
- Model check a problem, to falsify conjectures in it.
- Use theory exploration to invent new conjectures about a theory.

We describe the TIP format itself in Sect. 2, and many of the available transformations in Sect. 3. TIP improves the ecosystem of inductive provers in two ways:

- *Interoperability Between Provers.* Almost all existing inductive theorem provers are incompatible. They all use different input syntax but, more importantly, support entirely different sets of features. This makes it difficult to scientifically compare provers.
  TIP provides conversion tools which allow us to write one problem and try it on several provers. The conversion is not just syntactic but uses tools such as defunctionalisation [17] and monomorphisation to mask the differences between provers. We are using TIP to convert our inductive benchmarks to various provers' input formats.
- *Easier to Make New Provers.* There are many ingredients to a good inductive prover: it must instantiate induction schemas, perform first-order reasoning to discharge the resulting proof obligations, and discover the necessary lemmas to complete the proof. This makes it hard to experiment with new ideas.
  TIP provides many parts of an inductive prover as ready-made components, so that an author who has—say—an idea for a new induction principle can implement just that, leaving the first-order reasoning and lemma discovery to TIP. This is analogous to first-order logic where a tool author might use, for example, an off-the-shelf clausifier instead of writing their own. In Sect. 4 we demonstrate the versatility of the TIP tools by stitching them together to make a simple inductive prover as a shell script!

We are continually adding more tools and input and output formats to TIP. We are working to make TIP a universal format for induction problems, backed by a powerful toolchain which can be used by prover authors and users alike. We describe our plans for improving TIP further in Sect. 6. TIP is publicly available and can be downloaded from https://github.com/tip-org/tools.

2   The TIP Format

The TIP format is a variant of SMT-LIB. The following problem about lists illustrates all of its features. We first declare the polymorphic list datatype (list a), using the widely supported declare-datatypes syntax.

```
(declare-datatypes (a) ((list (nil) (cons (head a) (tail (list a))))))
```

We then define the list **map** function by pattern matching. The **par** construct is used to introduce polymorphism. The **match** expression provides pattern matching and is proposed for inclusion in SMT-LIB 2.6. To support partial functions like **head**, a **match** expression may have missing branches, in which case its value is unspecified. The syntax for higher-order functions is a TIP extension and we discuss it below.

```
(define-fun-rec (par (a b)
  (map ((f (=> a b)) (xs (list a))) (list b)
    (match xs
      (case nil (as nil (list b)))
      (case (cons x xs) (cons (@ f x) (map f xs)))))))
```

Finally, we conjecture that mapping the identity function over a list gives the same list back. As in SMT-LIB we assert the negation of the conjecture and ask the prover to derive **false**. Many inductive provers treat the goal specially, so TIP uses the syntax (assert-not p), which is semantically equivalent to (assert (not p)) but hints that p is a conjecture rather than a negated axiom.

```
(assert-not (par (a) (forall ((xs (list a)))
    (= xs (map (lambda ((x a)) x) xs)))))
(check-sat)
```

To summarise, the TIP format consists of:

- SMT-LIB plus **declare-datatypes** (inductive datatypes), **define-funs-rec** (recursive function definitions), **match** (pattern matching) and **par** (polymorphism), which are all standard or proposed extensions to SMT-LIB.
- Our own TIP-specific extensions: higher-order functions, and **assert-not** for marking the conjecture.

Our tools also understand the SMT-LIB theory of integer arithmetic. We intend TIP to be compatible with the standard theories of SMT-LIB.

First-class Functions. TIP supports higher-order functions, as these often crop up in inductive problems. We chose to make all use of these syntactically explicit: they must be written explicitly as a lambda function and are applied with the operator @. There is no implicit partial application. If **succ** is a function from Int to Int, we cannot write (map succ xs), but instead write (map (lambda ((x Int)) (succ x)) xs). And in the definition of **map**, we use (@ f x) to apply f to the list element. There is a type (=> a b) of first-class functions from a to b; **lambda** introduces values of this type and @ eliminates them. This design allows us to keep the bulk of TIP first-order.

3   Transforming and Translating TIP

TIP is structured as a large number of independent transformations. This is true even for our file format conversions. When TIP and the target prover have different feature sets, our approach is to keep the problem in TIP as long as possible, running many small transformations to reduce the problem to some fragment of TIP which we can translate directly. For example, many formats do not support pattern matching, so we must translate it to if-then-else, or if the format does not support that either, we can transform each function definition into a series of axioms. This happens as a TIP-to-TIP transformation.

This approach makes TIP quite modular. It is quite easy to add a new converter as most of the hard work is taken care of by existing transformations. Furthermore, many of those transformations are useful in their own right. In this section we illustrate many of the available transformations; we will use as a running example the conversion of the map example to SMT-LIB.

Although TIP is a variant of SMT-LIB, the two are quite different. SMT solvers often do not support polymorphism, higher-order functions or pattern-matching so our converter must remove those features. Here is what our tool produces when asked to translate the map example to vanilla SMT-LIB. It has monomorphised the problem, used defunctionalisation to eliminate the lambda and is using is-cons/head/tail instead of pattern matching.

```
(declare-sort sk_a 0)
(declare-sort fun 0)
(declare-datatypes () ((list (nil) (cons (head sk_a) (tail list)))))
(declare-const lam fun)
(declare-fun apply (fun sk_a) sk_a)
(declare-fun map (fun list) list)
(assert (forall ((x sk_a)) (= (apply lam x) x)))
(assert (forall ((f fun) (xs list))
  (= (map f xs)
     (ite (is-cons xs) (cons (apply f (head xs)) (map f (tail xs))) nil))))
(assert (not (forall ((xs list)) (= xs (map lam xs)))))
(check-sat)
```

3.1   Defunctionalisation

To support theorem provers that have no support for first-class functions and lambdas, a TIP problem can be defunctionalised [17]. This replaces all λ-functions in the problem with axiomatised function symbols. Defunctionalisation is sound but incomplete: if the goal existentially quantifies over a function, it may be rendered unprovable. We expect this to be rare for typical inductive problems.

In the example above, defunctionalisation has introduced the new abstract sort `fun` which stands for functions taking one argument. The identity function is replaced by a constant `lam` of sort `fun`. The @ operator has been replaced by the function `apply`, together with an axiom which states that (`apply lam x`) is `x`.

3.2 Monomorphisation

Many functional programs are naturally expressed using polymorphism. However, most provers do not support polymorphism. Though there has been work on supporting polymorphism natively in FO provers and SMT solvers, in particular Alt-Ergo [4], and also initial work for CVC4, it is not yet standard practice. Thus, we provide a monomorphisation transformation that removes polymorphic definitions by cloning them at different ground types.

As calculating the required instances is undecidable [6], our monomorphiser is heuristic. It generates a set of rules, in the form of first-order Horn clauses, which say when we should generate various instances. The minimal model of these Horn clauses then tells us which instances are required. The reason we use rules is that it makes it easy to adjust the behaviour of the monomorphiser: different settings may include or omit instantiation rules.

For a function definition, the principle is that when we instantiate the function, we should also instantiate everything required by the function. For `map`, some of the rules will be:

```
map(a,b) -> cons(a)
map(a,b) -> cons(b)
map(a,b) -> map(a,b)
```

In the snippet above, `a` and `b` are the type arguments to `map`. The first two lines make sure that when we instantiate `map` at types `a` and `b` in the program, we will also instantiate the `cons` constructor at `a` and at `b`. For data types, we have other rules that make sure that if `cons` is needed at some type, we also instantiate `list` at that type. We also generate rules for lemmas.

The last line is present because `map` calls itself. In general, when `f` calls `g`, we add a rule that when we instantiate `f` we must instantiate `g`. The rule makes no difference for this example, but is problematic for *polymorphically recursive functions*, which call themselves at a larger type. This is an obstacle for monomorphisation as the set of instances is infinite. A similar problem can occur when instantiating lemmas. To curb this, our procedure gives up after a predefined number of steps.

To start the procedure, we first Skolemise any type variables in the conjecture, and then add facts to the rule set for the functions called in the conjecture. These seed the procedure, which will either return with a set of ground instances that cover the problem, or give up. The transformation succeeds on all but one of our benchmarks; the failing one has a polymorphically recursive data type.

3.3   Eliminating Pattern matching

TIP provides two passes for eliminating pattern matching. The first one is used in the translated `map` function above, and replaces `match` with if-then-else (`ite`), discriminators (`is-nil` and `is-cons`) and projection functions (`head` and `tail`). For converting SMT-LIB to TIP format, we also provide a reverse transformation which replaces discriminators and projection functions with `match` expressions.

For some theorem provers, using if-then-else is not an option. We can also translate a function definition using `match` into several axioms, one for each case. Using this transformation, the `map` function turns into the following two axioms, which specify its behaviour on `nil` and `cons`:

```
(assert (forall ((f fun)) (= (map f nil) nil)))
(assert (forall ((f fun) (x sk_a) (xs list))
  (= (map f (cons x xs)) (cons (apply f x) (map f xs)))))
```

The transformation works by first lifting all `match` expressions to the outermost level of the function definition. A function with an outermost `match` can easily be split into several axioms.

3.4   Applying Structural induction

We also supply a transformation that applies structural induction to the conjecture. It requires the conjecture to start with a ∀-quantifier, and does induction on the variables quantified there. It splits the problem into several new problems, one for each proof obligation. When using the command line tool, the problems are put in separate files in a directory specified as a command line argument.

The transformation can do induction on several variables and induction of arbitrary depth, depending on what the user chooses. There is some choice about how strong the induction hypothesis should be: we copy HipSpec in assuming the induction hypothesis for all strict syntactic subterms of the conclusion. For example, if p is a binary predicate on natural numbers, proving (p x y) by induction on x and y gives the following proof obligation (among others):

```
(assert-not (forall ((x nat) (y nat))
  (=> (p x y) (p x (succ y)) (p (succ x) y)
      (p (succ x) (succ y)))))
```

This works well in practice: it can for instance prove commutativity of the normal natural number plus without lemmas by doing induction on both variables.

3.5   Other Transformations and External tools

Minor Transformations. TIP also includes simplification passes including inlining, dead code elimination and merging equivalent functions. Another transformation partially axiomatises inductive data types for provers and formats that lack built-in support for them, such as TPTP TFF. This is useful for sending proof obligations to a first-order prover after applying an induction schema.

Theory Exploration. TIP is integrated with the theory exploration system QuickSpec [11]. QuickSpec only accepts Haskell input, so TIP is used to translate the problem to Haskell, and QuickSpec's conjectures are translated back into TIP formulas. This allows theorem provers to easily use theory exploration.

Counterexamples to Non-theorems. TIP properties can also be randomly tested with QuickCheck [8], via the Haskell converter. Furthermore, the Haskell Bounded Model Checker, HBMC, can read TIP files. These tools can be useful to identify non-theorems among conjectures.

4   Rudimentocrates, a Simple Inductive Prover

Rudimentocrates[1] is a rudimentary inductive theorem prover, using the E theorem prover for first-order reasoning and QuickSpec for lemma discovery. It is a rough caricature of HipSpec, but while HipSpec is 6000 lines of Haskell code, Rudimentocrates is a 100-line shell script built on top of TIP.

The source code of Rudimentocrates is found in Appendix A, and an example run in Appendix B. It works as follows:

- Run QuickSpec to find conjectures about the input problem.
- Pick a conjecture, and a variable in that conjecture.
  - Generate proof obligations for proving the conjecture by induction.
  - Translate each obligation to TPTP and send it to E (with a timeout).
  - If all obligations are proved, add the conjecture as an axiom to the problem for use in proving further conjectures.
- Repeat this process until no more conjectures can be proved.

The result is the input problem, but with each proved conjecture (taken either from the input problem or QuickSpec) added as an extra axiom.

---

[1] Named after the lesser-known Ancient Greek philosopher.

Each of the steps—discovering conjectures, generating proof obligations, and translating them to TPTP—is performed by calling TIP. Rudimentocrates is not intended as a serious inductive theorem prover, but it demonstrates how easy it is to experiment with new inductive tools with the help of TIP.

5   Related Work

The system most obviously connected to ours is Why3 [5]. Like us, they have a language for expressing problems and a set of transformations and prover backends. The main difference is that Why3 emphasises imperative program verification with pre- and postconditions. There is a functional language like TIP inside Why3 but it mostly used to write the specifications themselves. By contrast, TIP is specialised to induction and recursive function definitions. This smaller domain allows us to provide more powerful tools, such as theory exploration, random testing and model checking, which would be difficult in a larger language. Another difference is that Why3 manages the entire proof pipeline, taking in a problem and sending it to provers. We intend TIP as a modular collection of tools which can be combined however the user wishes. Nonetheless, on the inside the systems have some similarities and we expect there to be fruitful exchange of ideas between them.

6   Future Work and Discussion

We are experimenting with heuristics for monomorphisation. A particular problem is what to do when the set of instances is infinite. One possibility is to limit the depth of instantiations by using fuel arguments [1], guaranteeing termination and predictability. Function definitions that could not be instantiated because of insufficient fuel would be turned into uninterpreted functions.

Monomorphisation is inherently incomplete. A complete alternative is to encode polymorphic types [3]. These encodings introduce overhead that slows down the provers, but we would like to add them as an alternative. We would also like to extend our monomorphiser so that it can specialise higher-order functions, generating all their first-order instances that are used in the problem [7]. This would be a low-overhead alternative to defunctionalisation.

We want to add more, stronger, kinds of induction, including recursion-induction and well-founded induction. We would also like to extend the format by adding inductive predicates, as well as coinduction.

Inductive theorem proving has seen a new lease of life recently and we believe it has more potential for growth. With TIP we hope to encourage that growth by fostering competition between provers and providing tools.

A   Rudimentocrates Source Code

```
#!/bin/bash

# Run the input file through QuickSpec.
# Discovered lemmas get added as new goals.
echo Dreaming up conjectures...
file=$(tip-spec $1)

# Sends a TIP problem to E, without doing induction.
# Reads the problem from stdin, succeeds if E proves the goal.
# Expects one argument, which is the timeout (in seconds).
e() {
  # Convert the problem to TFF.
  tip --skolemise-conjecture --tff |
  # Use Monotonox to convert the TFF to FOF.
  jukebox fof /dev/stdin 2>/dev/null |
  # Send the FOF problem to E.
  eprover --tstp-in --soft-cpu-limit=$1 --auto --silent >& /dev/null
}

# Sends a whole directory of TIP problems to E, without doing induction.
# Expects two parameters, the directory and the timeout.
dir_e() {
  for i in $1/*; do
    if ! e $2 < $i; then
      return 1
    fi
  done
}

# Attempts to prove a TIP problem by induction with the help of E.
# Uses the TIP tool's induction pass to generate proof obligations,
# and the dir_e command from above to prove them.
# Reads the problem from stdin and expects the timeout as an argument.
inductive_e() {
  local file="$(cat)"
  local n=0   # The position of the variable to do induction on.

  while true; do
    dir=$(mktemp -d)
    # Use TIP to generate proof obligations for doing induction
    # on the nth variable. Fails if n is out of bounds.
    if echo "$file"|tip --induction "[$n]" - $dir >& /dev/null; then
      # Use E to discharge the proof obligations.
      if dir_e $dir $1; then
```

```
      # Success!
      rm -r $dir
      return
    else
      # Failed - try the next variable.
      rm -r $dir
      ((n=$n+1))
    fi
  else
    # Tried all variables unsuccessfully - fail.
    rm -r $dir
    return 1
  fi
  done
}


# Read a problem from stdin and try to prove as many goals as possible.
# Takes a single parameter, which is the timeout to give to E.
prove() {
  file=$(cat)

  progress= # Set to yes if we manage to prove some goal.
  n=0        # The index of the goal we're trying to prove now.

  while true; do
    # Check that n isn't out of bounds.
    if echo "$file"|tip --select-conjecture $n >& /dev/null; then
      # Make a theory where goal n is the only goal.
      goal=$(echo "$file"|tip --select-conjecture $n)
      # Can we prove it without induction?
      if echo "$goal"|e $1; then
        # Proved without induction - delete the goal.
        echo -n ':) ' >&2
        file=$(echo "$file"|tip --delete-conjecture $n)
        progress=yes
      # Can we prove the goal with induction?
      elif echo "$goal"|inductive_e $1; then
        # Proved with induction - change the goal into a lemma.
        echo -n ':D ' >&2
        file=$(echo "$file"|tip --proved-conjecture $n)
        progress=yes
      else
        # Failed to prove the goal - try the next one.
        echo -n ':( ' >&2
        ((n=$n+1))
```

```
        fi
    else
        # We've tried all goals - if we failed to prove any,
        # then stop, otherwise go round again.
        echo >&2
        if [ -z $progress ]; then break; fi
        progress=
        n=0
    fi
done


# Print out the final theory.
echo "$file"
}

# Run the proof loop, gradually increasing the timeout.
echo Trying to prove conjectures...
for i in 0 1 5 30; do
    file=$(echo "$file" | prove $i)
done

# Print the final theory out.
echo
echo ";; Final theory"
echo "$file"
```

B Example Run of Rudimentocrates

Here is an example showing the output of Rudimentocrates on a simple theory of append and reverse. The input file has a single conjecture that reverse (reverse xs) = xs:

```
(declare-datatypes (a)
  ((list (nil) (cons (head a) (tail (list a))))))
(define-fun-rec (par (a)
  (append ((xs (list a)) (ys (list a))) (list a)
    (match xs
      (case nil ys)
      (case (cons z zs) (cons z (append zs ys)))))))
(define-fun-rec (par (a)
  (reverse ((xs (list a))) (list a)
    (match xs
      (case nil (as nil (list a)))
      (case (cons y ys)
        (append (reverse ys) (cons y (as nil (list a)))))))))
(assert-not (par (a)
```

```
(forall ((xs (list a))) (= (reverse (reverse xs)) xs))))
(check-sat)
```

Rudimentocrates first runs QuickSpec to discover likely lemmas about append and reverse:

```
Dreaming up conjectures...
append x Nil = x
append Nil x = x
append (Cons x y) z = Cons x (append y z)
append (append x y) z = append x (append y z)
reverse Nil = Nil
reverse (reverse x) = x
reverse (Cons x Nil) = Cons x Nil
append (reverse y) (reverse x) = reverse (append x y)
```

It then goes into a proof loop, taking one conjecture at a time and trying to prove it. It prints :(when it failed to prove a conjecture, :) when it proved a conjecture without induction, and :D when it proves a conjecture with the help of induction:

```
Trying to prove conjectures...
:( :D :) :) :D :) :( :) :D
:D :)
```

Rudimentocrates prints a newline when it has tried all conjectures, then goes back and retries the failed ones (in case it can now prove them with the help of lemmas). In this case it manages to prove all the discovered conjectures, and prints out the following final theory. Notice that: (a) the property (= xs (reverse (reverse xs))) is now an axiom (assert) rather than a conjecture (assert-not), indicating that it has been proved, and (b) several other proved lemmas have been added to the theory file.

```
(declare-datatypes (a)
  ((list (nil) (cons (head a) (tail (list a)))))))
(define-fun-rec
  (par (a)
    (append
      ((xs (list a)) (ys (list a))) (list a)
      (match xs
        (case nil ys)
        (case (cons z zs) (cons z (append zs ys)))))))
(define-fun-rec
  (par (a)
    (reverse
      ((xs (list a))) (list a)
      (match xs
        (case nil (as nil (list a)))
```

```
          (case (cons y ys)
               (append (reverse ys) (cons y (as nil (list a)))))))))))
(assert
  (par (x)
    (forall ((y (list x))) (= (append y (as nil (list x))) y))))
(assert
  (par (x)
    (forall ((y (list x)) (z (list x)) (x2 (list x)))
      (= (append (append y z) x2) (append y (append z x2)))))))
(assert
  (par (x)
    (forall ((y (list x)) (z (list x)))
      (= (append (reverse z) (reverse y)) (reverse (append y z)))))))
(assert
  (par (a) (forall ((xs (list a))) (= (reverse (reverse xs)) xs))))
(check-sat)
```

References

1. Amin, N., Leino, K.R.M., Rompf, T.: Computing with an SMT solver. In: Seidl, M., Tillmann, N. (eds.) TAP 2014. LNCS, vol. 8570, pp. 20–35. Springer, Heidelberg (2014)
2. Barrett, C., Fontaine, P., Tinelli, C.: The SMT-LIB standard - version 2.5. http://smtlib.cs.uiowa.edu/papers/smt-lib-reference-v2.5-r2015-06-28.pdf
3. Blanchette, J.C., Böhme, S., Popescu, A., Smallbone, N.: Encoding monomorphic and polymorphic types. In: Piterman, N., Smolka, S.A. (eds.) TACAS 2013 (ETAPS 2013). LNCS, vol. 7795, pp. 493–507. Springer, Heidelberg (2013)
4. Bobot, F., Conchon, S., Contejean, E., Lescuyer, S.: Implementing polymorphism in SMT solvers. In: Barrett, C., de Moura, L. (eds.) SMT 2008: 6th International Workshop on Satisfiability Modulo. ACM International Conference Proceedings Series, vol. 367, pp. 1–5 (2008)
5. Bobot, F., Filliâtre, J.C., Marché, C., Paskevich, A.: Why3: Shepherd your herd of provers. In: In Workshop on Intermediate Veri cation Languages, Boogie, August 2011
6. Bobot, F., Paskevich, A.: Expressing polymorphic types in a many-sorted language. In: Tinelli, C., Sofronie-Stokkermans, V. (eds.) FroCoS 2011. LNCS, vol. 6989, pp. 87–102. Springer, Heidelberg (2011)
7. Chin, W.N., Darlington, J.: A higher-order removal method. LISP Symbolic Comput. 9(4), 287–322 (1996)
8. Claessen, K., Hughes, J.: QuickCheck: a lightweight tool for random testing of Haskell programs. In: ICFP 2000 Proceedings of the Fifth ACM SIGPLAN International Conference on Functional Programming, pp. 268–279, ACM, New York (2000)
9. Claessen, K., Johansson, M., Rosén, D., Smallbone, N.: Automating inductive proofs using theory exploration. In: Bonacina, M.P. (ed.) CADE 2013. LNCS, vol. 7898, pp. 392–406. Springer, Heidelberg (2013)
10. Claessen, K., Johansson, M., Rosén, D., Smallbone, N.: TIP: tons of inductive problems. In: Kerber, M., Carette, J., Kaliszyk, C., Rabe, F., Sorge, V. (eds.) CICM 2015. LNCS, vol. 9150, pp. 333–337. Springer, Heidelberg (2015)

11. Claessen, K., Smallbone, N., Hughes, J.: QUICKSPEC: guessing formal specifications using testing. In: Fraser, G., Gargantini, A. (eds.) TAP 2010. LNCS, vol. 6143, pp. 6–21. Springer, Heidelberg (2010)
12. Grechanik, S.A.: Proving properties of functional programs by equality saturation. Program. Comput. Softw. **41**(3), 149–161 (2015)
13. Johansson, M., Rosén, D., Smallbone, N., Claessen, K.: Hipster: integrating theory exploration in a proof assistant. In: Watt, S.M., Davenport, J.H., Sexton, A.P., Sojka, P., Urban, J. (eds.) CICM 2014. LNCS, vol. 8543, pp. 108–122. Springer, Heidelberg (2014)
14. Kaufmann, M., Panagiotis, M., Moore, J.S.: Computer-Aided Reasoning: An Approach. Kluwer Academic Publishers, Norwell (2000)
15. Leino, K.R.M.: Automating induction with an SMT solver. In: Kuncak, V., Rybalchenko, A. (eds.) VMCAI 2012. LNCS, vol. 7148, pp. 315–331. Springer, Heidelberg (2012)
16. Reynolds, A., Kuncak, V.: Induction for SMT solvers. In: D'Souza, D., Lal, A., Larsen, K.G. (eds.) VMCAI 2015. LNCS, vol. 8931, pp. 80–98. Springer, Heidelberg (2015)
17. Reynolds, J.C.: Definitional interpreters for higher-order programming languages. In: The ACM Annual Conference, vol. 2 (1972)
18. Sonnex, W., Drossopoulou, S., Eisenbach, S.: Zeno: an automated prover for properties of recursive data structures. In: Flanagan, C., König, B. (eds.) TACAS 2012. LNCS, vol. 7214, pp. 407–421. Springer, Heidelberg (2012)
19. Wand, D., Weidenbach, C.: Automatic induction inside superposition. https://people.mpi-inf.mpg.de/~dwand/datasup/draft.pdf

Verification of Concurrent Programs Using Trace Abstraction Refinement

Franck Cassez[1](✉) and Frowin Ziegler[2]

[1] Macquarie University, NICTA/UNSW, Sydney, Australia
franck.cassez@mq.edu.au
[2] Augsburg University, Augsburg, Germany

Abstract. Verifying concurrent programs is notoriously hard due to the state explosion problem: (1) the data state space can be very large as the variables can range over very large sets, and (2) the control state space is the Cartesian product of the control state space of the concurrent components and thus grows exponentially in the number of components. On the one hand, the most successful approaches to address the control state explosion problem are based on assume-guarantee reasoning or model-checking coupled with partial order reduction. On the other hand, the most successful techniques to address the data space explosion problem for sequential programs verification are based on the abstraction/refinement paradigm which consists in refining an abstract over-approximation of a program via predicate refinement. In this paper, we show that we can combine partial order reduction techniques with trace abstraction refinement. We apply our approach to standard benchmarks and show that it matches current state-of-the-art analysis techniques.

1 Introduction

Multi-core architectures enable hardware consolidation i.e., less weight and less space which is highly desirable for embedded systems. Multi-threaded (or concurrent) programs are designed to take full advantage of the available computing power of the multi-cores. This is very appealing performance-wise but comes at a price: concurrent programs are a lot more difficult to reason about than sequential programs. They need to *synchronise* or *share* variables and this gives rise to a multitude of subtle bugs, among them deadlocks or data races that are sources of critical defects. At the same time, more and more control tasks are now implemented in software which results in large multi-threaded code bases. The major obstacle to the deployment of multi-threaded software in embedded safety critical systems is the difficulty of ensuring the absence of major critical defects. This calls for scalable automated verification techniques that can analyse multi-threaded software. Unfortunately, as witnessed by the latest *Software Verification Competition (SV-COMP 2015)* [1], there are only a few software verification tools that can analyse concurrent software. Most of them are bug finding tools and fall short of being able to establish the correctness of a program. Their applicability is often limited to rather small programs.

© Springer-Verlag Berlin Heidelberg 2015
M. Davis et al. (Eds.): LPAR-20 2015, LNCS 9450, pp. 233–248, 2015.
DOI: 10.1007/978-3-662-48899-7_17

This is in stark contrast to the state-of-the-art for verification of sequential programs. One of the major breakthrough for verifying sequential programs is probably the *counter-example guided predicate-abstraction refinement* (CEGAR) technique [2]. CEGAR enables one to address the *data state explosion* problem by abstracting away the data into predicates. This has resulted in scalable and practicable techniques to analyse sequential programs, culminating in the design of industrial-strength tools like SLAM [3]. For concurrent programs, the *control state explosion* problem adds up to the data state explosion problem: the state space of a concurrent program is exponential in the size of the program.

Verification of Concurrent Programs. Two main techniques were designed to combat the state explosion problem in concurrent programs: *assume-guarantee* reasoning [4] and *partial order reduction* techniques [5–7]. An assume-guarantee property is a pair of predicates (A, G) (similar to pre and postconditions): a component guarantees to satisfy G if its environment satisfies A. Assume-guarantee reasoning consists in combining the assume-guarantee properties of each component to derive a property of the composition of the components in a modular way. Partial order reduction techniques on the other hand aim at reducing the state space to be explored in concurrent programs by removing *equivalent interleavings*. Both techniques have proved very useful in the context of finite state concurrent programs [8,9]. Combining assume-guarantee reasoning with predicate abstraction refinement for proving properties of multi-threaded C-like programs was first investigated in [10]. However the scope of the approach was limited to *modular* properties and was later extended to more general properties in [11]. The recent work in [12] introduced a combination of predicate abstraction refinement and partial order reduction. In this paper, we propose a method to combine *trace abstraction refinement* and partial order reduction techniques.

Trace Abstraction Refinement. The core principle of *trace abstraction* [13,14] for single-threaded program is to separate the data and the control flows. The abstraction of a program P is a set of *traces* e.g., sequences of *instructions* obtained by viewing the control flow graph of P as an automaton. The instructions are uninterpreted and should be viewed as mere letters in the abstraction. A trace t is *feasible* if there is at least one input of the program the trace of which is t. This is where the data flow comes into play. Some traces of a program abstraction are *error* traces e.g., leading to an error control location in the control flow graph. For instance if the program contains an `assert(cond)` statement, there is an edge in the control flow graph labelled `not(cond)` to the error location. The *language* of the program abstraction, $\mathcal{L}_P$, is composed of these error traces. Proving correctness of the program P amounts to proving that every trace in $\mathcal{L}_P$ is infeasible. This can be done by an iterative refinement algorithm as depicted in Fig. 1. A *refinement* of a program abstraction is also a language $\mathcal{L}_r$ composed exclusively of infeasible traces. One important result in [13] is that a refinement, $\mathcal{L}_r(t)$, can be computed for each infeasible trace t: this refinement contains t and other infeasible traces that are infeasible for the same reason as t is. Moreover, the refinement $\mathcal{L}_r(t)$ is a regular language. For sequential programs, the trace abstraction refinement algorithm refines the program abstraction by computing larger and larger sets of infeasible traces, $\cup_{i=1..k}\mathcal{L}_{r_i}$. As a candidate feasible error trace must be in $\mathcal{L}_P \setminus (\cup_{i=1..k}\mathcal{L}_{r_i})$ a larger set $\cup_{i=1..k}\mathcal{L}_{r_i}$ of infeasible traces narrows down the search at each iteration of the algorithm and in this respect refines the trace abstraction. If at some point all the error traces of the program abstraction are infeasible, the program can be declared error-free. Of course the algorithm is not guaranteed to terminate for C-like programs (with more than two counters) but it is *sound* and relatively *complete* (see [13]).

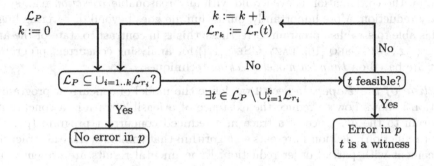

Fig. 1. Trace abstraction refinement algorithm

Trace Abstraction Refinement for Concurrent Programs. The trace abstraction refinement algorithm can be used for concurrent programs, say $P_1 \parallel P_2$, by considering the language $\mathcal{L}_{P_1 \parallel P_2}$. However, the algorithm may need multiple iterations to rule out infeasible traces that are *equivalent* in the sense that some instructions along a trace may be swapped without altering the correctness of the concurrent program, e.g., deadlock freedom.

The solution proposed in [15] is to extend the expressiveness of the trace abstraction refinements: instead of building an automaton that accepts a regular language $\mathcal{L}_r(t)$, the authors define a new refinement device: *Inductive Data Flow Graphs* (iDFGs). One of the nice features of iDFGs is that they can represent infeasibility reasons on sequences of actions while capturing some independence between the ordering of actions. The trace refinement algorithm of Fig. 1 can be adapted to this setting because: (1) iDFGs are closed under union, and (2) language inclusion between regular languages ($\mathcal{L}_P$) and iDFGs is decidable. The approach of [15] is elegant and versatile as it applies to a large spectrum of properties of concurrent programs (Owicki-Gries proof statements which are invariance properties closed under multi-threaded Cartesian abstraction). However the core operation of the algorithm is rather expensive: language inclusion between a parallel composition of n threads and an iDFG is in PSPACE. To the best of our knowledge this technique has not been implemented yet.

Our Contribution. In this work we propose a simple and powerful combination of trace abstraction refinement and partial order reduction. It turns out that combining trace abstraction refinement with partial order (or symmetry) reduction techniques is simplified when instead of proving general Owicki-Gries style statements one restricts to *reachability properties*[1]. This is supported by our main result, Theorem 3. We also argue that combining partial order reduction techniques with refinement techniques is easier and more natural with trace abstraction refinement (trace based) rather than predicate abstraction refinement (state based). The advantages of our combination are manifold. First, the refinement algorithm is simple and builds on two distinct and orthogonal techniques: partial order reduction algorithms and trace abstraction refinement. Second, the combination is even valid with any reasonable *reduction* e.g., symmetry reduction. More importantly, our technique goes beyond discovering bugs and is able to establish program correctness: this is in contrast to state-of-the-art tools (e.g., MU-CSEQ [16], LAZY-CSEQ [17]) for analysing concurrent programs that are based on *bounded model checking* techniques.

Outline of the Paper. In Sect. 2 we define the model of concurrent programs. Section 3 shows how to reduce the existence of a feasible trace in a concurrent program to the existence of a trace in a reduced concurrent program (partial order reduction). Section 4 presents an algorithm that combines trace abstraction refinement with partial order reduction. Experimental results are presented in Sect. 5. Section 6 is devoted to related work.

2   Reachability Checking in Concurrent Programs

In this section we define concurrent programs. For the sake of clarity and following [10], we restrict to 2-threaded programs but all the definitions and proofs carry over to the general setting of n-threaded programs with $n \geq 2$ (see [18]).

2.1   Notations

Let V be a fixed finite set of integer variables. A *valuation* ν is a mapping $\nu : V \to \mathbb{Z}$ and we write $\mathbb{Z}^V$ for the set of valuations. We let Σ be a fixed set of *instructions* with variables in V. Instructions can be either *assignments* with side effects or *conditions* that are side-effect free. Σ^* is the set of finite sequences of instructions and ε is the *empty sequence*. We write $v.w$ for the concatenation of two words $v, w \in \Sigma^*$. We let $|w|$ be the length of $w \in \Sigma^*$ ($|\varepsilon| = 0$). Given $i \in \Sigma$, $\mathcal{R}(i) \subseteq V$ (resp. $\mathcal{W}(i) \subseteq V$) is the set of *read-from* (resp. *written-to*) variables. We let $\mathcal{V}(i) = \mathcal{R}(i) \cup \mathcal{W}(i)$.

The *semantics* of an instruction $i \in \Sigma$ is given by a relation $[\![i]\!] \subseteq \mathbb{Z}^V \times \mathbb{Z}^V$. The post operator is defined for each instruction as follows: given $U \subseteq \mathbb{Z}^V$, $\mathsf{post}(i, U) = \{u' \mid \exists u \in U, (u, u') \in [\![i]\!]\}$. The post operator extends to sequences of instructions: let $v \in \Sigma^*, i \in \Sigma, \mathsf{post}(v.i, U) = \mathsf{post}(i, \mathsf{post}(v, U))$ with $\mathsf{post}(\varepsilon, U) = U$. Given a sequence of instructions $w \in \Sigma^*$, w is *feasible* iff

---

[1] Without loss of generality we focus on reachability of control locations as reachability of a specific data state can easily be encoded in this setting.

$\text{post}(w, \mathbb{Z}^V) \neq \varnothing$. Otherwise w is infeasible. Sets of valuations can be defined by *predicates* e.g., as Boolean combinations of terms in a given logic (e.g., Linear Integer Arithmetic). The predicate *True* denotes the set of all valuations and *False* the empty set of valuations. Feasibility of a trace $w \in \Sigma^*$ thus reduces to $\text{post}(w, True) \not\subseteq False$.

A transition system $\mathcal{S}$ is a tuple (S, S_0, δ) with S a set of states, $S_0 \subseteq S$ the set of *initial* states and $\delta \subseteq S \times \Sigma \times S$ the *transition relation*.

An instruction $i \in \Sigma$ is *enabled* in s if $(s, i, s') \in \delta$ for some s'. A *path* in $\mathcal{S}$ from s_0 to s_n, $n \geq 0$, is a sequence $s_0 \; i_0 \; s_1 \; i_1 \; \cdots \; s_{n-1} \; i_{n-1} \; s_n$ with $\forall 0 \leq k \leq n-1, (s_k, i_k, s_{k+1}) \in \delta$. The trace of a path $s_0 \; i_0 \; s_1 \; i_1 \; \cdots \; s_{n-1} \; i_{n-1} \; s_n$ is $i_0.i_1.\cdots.i_{n-1}$. We write $s_0 \xrightarrow{i_0.i_1.\cdots.i_{n-1}} s_n$ when there is a path from s_0 to s_n with trace $i_0.i_1.\cdots.i_{n-1}$. A state s is reachable if $s_0 \xrightarrow{t} s$ for some $s_0 \in S_0$ and $t \in \Sigma^*$. We let $\text{REACH}(\mathcal{S})$ be the set of reachable states in $\mathcal{S}$.

```
1   shared int x, y, d, m;
2   // thread T1
3   thread T1
4   x = 0;
5   lock(m);
6   if (x == y) {
7     unlock(m);
8     d = 3;
9   } else {
10    unlock(m);
11  }
12  /* end */
13
14  // Thread T2
15  thread T2
16  y = 1;
17  lock(m);
18  if (x <= y) {
19    unlock(m);
20    d = 2;
21  } else {
22    unlock(m);
23  }
24  /* end */
```

Listing 1. Two Simple Threads

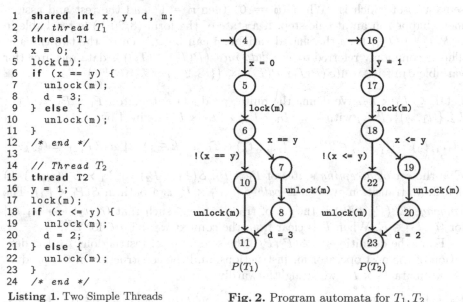

Fig. 2. Program automata for T_1, T_2

2.2 2-Threaded Programs

A *program automaton* P is a tuple (L, ι, T) where: L is a finite set of program *locations*, $\iota \in L$ is the *initial location*, $T \subseteq L \times \Sigma \times L$ is *the control flow graph relation*. The set of *variables* of P is $\mathcal{V}(P) = \bigcup_{(\ell, i, \ell') \in T} \mathcal{V}(i)$.

A *state* of P is a pair $(\ell, \nu) \in L \times \mathbb{Z}^V$. Each program automaton induces a transition system $\mathcal{S}(P) = (L \times \mathbb{Z}^V, \{\iota\} \times \mathbb{Z}^V, \delta(P))$ with $\delta(P)$ defined by: $((\ell, \nu), i, (\ell', \nu')) \in \delta(P) \iff (\ell, i, \ell') \in T, (\nu, \nu') \in [\![i]\!]$.

A *2-threaded program* is a pair (P_1, P_2) with $P_k = (L_k, \iota_k, T_k), k = 1, 2$ two program automata. The *shared variables* of (P_1, P_2) are $\mathcal{V}(P_1) \cap \mathcal{V}(P_2)$ and the other variables $\mathcal{V}(P_k) \backslash (\mathcal{V}(P_1) \cap \mathcal{V}(P_2))$ are the *local* variables for each $P_k, k = 1, 2$.

A 2-threaded program induces a transition system $\mathcal{S}(P_1, P_2) = (L_1 \times L_2 \times \mathbb{Z}^V, \{\iota_1\} \times \{\iota_2\} \times \mathbb{Z}^V, \delta(P_1, P_2))$ where $\delta(P_1, P_2)$ is the *interleaving* of $\delta(P_1)$ and $\delta(P_2)$: $((\ell_1, \ell_2, \nu), i, (\ell_1', \ell_2', \nu')) \in \delta(P_1, P_2)$ iff either $((\ell_1, \nu), i, (\ell_1', \nu')) \in \delta(P_1)$ and $\ell_2 = \ell_2'$ or $((\ell_2, \nu), i, (\ell_2', \nu')) \in \delta(P_2)$ and $\ell_1 = \ell_1'$. A *state* of $\mathcal{S}(P_1, P_2)$ is a triple (ℓ_1, ℓ_2, ν) where $\ell_k \in L_k$ and ν is a valuation for V. Given a set of states $E \subseteq L_1 \times L_2 \times \mathbb{Z}^V$, the *reachability problem* asks whether $\text{REACH}(\mathcal{S}(P_1, P_2)) \cap E \neq \varnothing$ and $\text{REACH}(\mathcal{S}(P_1, P_2))$ may be infinite. For C-like 2-threaded programs this problem is undecidable as the reachability problem for single threaded programs with more than two variables (two-counter machines) is already undecidable. In the sequel, we thus consider semi-algorithms based on abstraction refinement to solve the reachability problem for multi-threaded programs.

Example 1. Listing 1, page 5, shows a 2-threaded C-like program. The program automata $P(T_1)$ and $P(T_2)$ for the threads T1 and T2 are given in Fig. 2. The lock and unlock C-like instructions are interpreted as *guarded* instructions the semantics of which is "When (m == 0) then m = 1" and the test and assignment happen in an atomic step. If a state of the form $(8, 20, \nu)$ is reachable in $\mathcal{S}(P(T_1), P(T_2))$ then the shared variable d can be written by the two threads. This is commonly referred to as a *data race*. $(P(T_1), P(T_2))$ is data race free (for variable d) iff $\text{REACH}(\mathcal{S}(P(T_1), P(T_2))) \cap (\{(8, 20)\} \times \mathbb{Z}^{\{x, y, d, m\}}) = \varnothing$. ∎

Let $E \subseteq L_1 \times L_2$. We define the finite (product) automaton $P_1 \times P_2 = (L_1 \times L_2, \{(\iota_1, \iota_2)\}, T, E)$ with $T \subseteq (L_1 \times L_2) \times (L_1 \times L_2)$ defined by:

$$((\ell_1, \ell_2), i, (\ell_1', \ell_2')) \in T \iff (\ell_k, i, \ell_k') \in T_k \text{ for } k \in \{1, 2\} \text{ and } \ell_{3-k}' = \ell_{3-k}.$$

E is the set of *accepting* states of $P_1 \times P_2$. $\mathcal{S}(P_1 \times P_2) = (L_1 \times L_2, (\iota_1, \iota_2), T)$ is a finite transition system. A *path* ϱ in $P_1 \times P_2$ is a path in $\mathcal{S}(P_1 \times P_2)$. The *language* $\mathcal{L}^E(P_1 \times P_2)$ is the set of traces $t \in \Sigma^*$ such that $(\iota_1, \iota_2) \xrightarrow{t} (\ell_1, \ell_2)$ for $(\ell_1, \ell_2) \in E$. When E is clear from the context we write $\mathcal{L}$ for $\mathcal{L}^E$.

From the definitions of $\mathcal{S}(P_1, P_2)$, the semantics of instructions $[\![\cdot]\!]$, the definition of the post operator for instructions, and the construction of the product of automata $P_1 \times P_2$, we straightforwardly get:

Fact 1. $(\ell_0, \nu_0) i_0 (\ell_1, \nu_1) i_1 \cdots i_{n-1} (\ell_n, \nu_n)$ with $(\nu_k, \nu_{k+1}) \in [\![i_k]\!], 0 \leq k < n$ is a path in $\mathcal{S}(P_1, P_2)$ if and only if $\ell_0 i_0 \ell_1 \cdots i_{n-1} \ell_n$ is a path in $P_1 \times P_2$ and $\text{post}(i_0.i_1. \cdots . i_{n-1}, True) \not\subseteq False$.

Given $E \subseteq L_1 \times L_2$, we use the shorthand $E \times \mathbb{Z}^V$ for $\{(\ell_1, \ell_2, \nu), (\ell_1, \ell_2) \in E, \nu \in \mathbb{Z}^V\}$. The following theorem is a direct consequence of Fact 1:

Theorem 1. *Let* $E \subseteq L_1 \times L_2$. *Then*

$$\text{REACH}(\mathcal{S}(P_1, P_2)) \cap (E \times \mathbb{Z}^V) \neq \varnothing \iff \exists t \in \mathcal{L}^E(P_1 \times P_2), \text{post}(t, True) \not\subseteq False.$$

Remark 1. $\mathcal{S}(P_1, P_2)$ includes the data part of the program and can be infinite whereas $\mathcal{S}(P_1 \times P_2)$ includes only the locations of the CFG and is always finite.

3   Partial-Order Reduction

In this section we show that checking for the existence of a feasible trace in $\mathcal{L}(P_1 \times P_2)$ can be reduced to checking for the existence of a feasible trace in a *reduced* product automaton $(P_1 \times P_2)_R$. The reduced automaton $(P_1 \times P_2)_R$ is obtained by using standard partial order reduction algorithms that preserve properties of interest e.g., reachability of a location in a thread.

3.1   Independent Transitions

Partial order reduction techniques [5–7] were developed to address the state explosion problem in the analysis of concurrent systems.

These reductions rely on the notion of *dependency* and the complementary notion of *independency* between transitions. The intuition is that two *reads* on the same variable are independent whereas two *writes* or a *write* and a *read* to the same variable are dependent. For independent transitions the order of execution is irrelevant for certain properties and one *representative* order can be chosen to represent many interleavings.

Let $i, j \in \Sigma$ be two instructions. According to our definition, the same instruction can appear in two different threads or in the same thread. Instructions within the same sequential component are dependent and thus we have to differentiate these two cases. We assume that $\Sigma = \Sigma_1 \uplus \Sigma_2$, i.e., is partitioned into instructions for thread P_1 and P_2. i and j are *independent*, denoted $i \parallel j$, when $i \in \Sigma_k, j \in \Sigma_{3-k}$ for $k \in \{1, 2\}$ and $\mathcal{W}(i) \cap \mathcal{V}(j) = \varnothing$. By definition of the independency relation the following properties hold [5] for any $i \parallel j$ and any state s of $\mathcal{S}(P_1, P_2)$:

Enabledness if i is enabled in s and $s \xrightarrow{i} s'$, then j is enabled in s iff it is enabled in s' (independent transitions do not enable nor disable each other);

Commutativity if i and j are enabled in s, then $s \xrightarrow{i.j} s'$ and $s \xrightarrow{j.i} s'$, i.e., the order of i and j does not change the final target state (we assume here that the transition relations in P_1, P_2 are deterministic).

The independency relation induces a *trace equivalence* relation $\sim \subseteq \Sigma^* \times \Sigma^*$ which is the least congruence in the free monoid $(\Sigma^*, ., \varepsilon)$ that satisfies: $i \parallel j \implies i.j \sim j.i$. The equivalence classes of $\sim$ are called Mazurkiewicz traces.

Example 2. The instructions x = 0 and y = 1 in the automata of Fig. 2 are independent. Instructions d = 3 and d = 2 are not independent.   ∎

3.2   Selective Search Algorithm

We consider now a generic *selective search* algorithm SelectSearch. The purpose of such an algorithm is to explore a finite graph by avoiding to explore all the interleavings of $\sim$-equivalent sequences of transitions. We do not refer to a specific selective search algorithm but rather consider the minimum requirements needed to fit in our framework. Such a SelectSearch algorithm uses the independency relation $\|$ defined in the previous paragraph to prune out some edges (and states) during the exploration of the set of reachable states of $\mathcal{S}(P_1, P_2)$. If $\mathcal{S}(P_1, P_2)$ is finite, SelectSearch($\mathcal{S}(P_1, P_2)$) generates a finite transition system, called a *trace automaton* in [5]. We only require the SelectSearch algorithm to preserve the reachability of local states[2]. Assume $\mathcal{S}(P_1, P_2)$ is finite.

Theorem 2 (Theorem 6.14, [5]). Let $\ell_1 \in L_1, \ell_2 \in L_2$ and $\nu \in \mathbb{Z}^V$. The state (ℓ_1, ℓ_2, ν) is reachable in $\mathcal{S}(P_1, P_2)$ iff there exists $\ell'_1 \in L_1, \nu' \in \mathbb{Z}^V$ such that state (ℓ'_1, ℓ_2, ν') is reachable in SelectSearch($\mathcal{S}(P_1, P_2)$).

Actual implementations of the SelectSearch algorithms can be based on the selective search algorithm using *persistent sets, sleep sets and proviso* defined in [5, Figure 6.2, Chap. 6] or recent (optimal) algorithms as proposed in [19,20].

Let $\varrho = (\iota_1, \iota_2, \nu_0) \, i_0 \, (\ell_1^1, \ell_1^2, \nu_1) \, i_1 \, (\ell_2^1, \ell_2^2, \nu_2) \, i_2 \cdots i_{n-1} \, (\ell_n^1, \ell_n^2, \nu_n)$ be a path in SelectSearch($\mathcal{S}(P_1, P_2)$). SelectSearch is a *control location based* selective search if the set of transitions selected to be explored after ϱ only depends on the history $(\iota_1, \iota_2)(\ell_1^1, \ell_1^2) \cdots (\ell_n^1, \ell_n^2)$ of control locations of ϱ. Obtaining a location based selective search can be achieved by using a standard dependency relation as defined by $\|$ above. Notice that the selective search algorithm using *persistent sets, sleep sets and proviso* [5, Figure 6.2, Chap. 6] makes use of *conditional dependency relation* $\|_s$ that can vary according to the current state s and may depend on the value of ν in our 2-threaded programs. We disable this feature to obtain a control location based selective search algorithm and use an unconditional dependency relation like $\|$ above. This implies we may miss some pruning as our dependency relation is stronger than the conditional dependency one.

We now assume that the set of reachable states of $\mathcal{S}(P_1, P_2)$ may be infinite and show that Theorem 2 can be extended to infinite systems. Let SelectSearch be a control location based selective search algorithm. Let $P_1 \times P_2 = (L_1 \times L_2, (\iota_1, \iota_2), T, E)$ with $E = L_1 \times \{\ell_2\}$. Define SelectSearch($\mathcal{S}(P_1 \times P_2)$) to be the finite transition system obtained by applying SelectSearch on $\mathcal{S}(P_1 \times P_2)$. We can assume the selective search algorithm is Depth-First Search based and explores each state of $P_1 \times P_2$ at most once. We write $\mathcal{L}_R^E(P_1 \times P_2)$ for the set of traces $t \in \Sigma^*$ such that $(\iota_1, \iota_2) \xrightarrow{t} \ell$ in SelectSearch($\mathcal{S}(P_1 \times P_2)$) with $\ell \in E$. Using Theorem 2 we can prove the following:

Lemma 1. $\exists t \in \mathcal{L}^E(P_1 \times P_2), \mathsf{post}(t, True) \not\subseteq False \iff \exists t' \in \mathcal{L}_R^E(P_1 \times P_2), \mathsf{post}(t', True) \not\subseteq False$.

Proof. The *If* direction is easy as $\mathcal{L}_R^E(P_1 \times P_2) \subseteq \mathcal{L}^E(P_1 \times P_2)$.

To prove the *Only if* direction, let $t \in \mathcal{L}^E(P_1 \times P_2)$ and $\mathsf{post}(t, True) \not\subseteq False$. Let $n = |t|$. As $\mathsf{post}(t, True) \not\subseteq False$, there is some valuation $\nu_0 \in \mathbb{Z}^V$ such that $\mathsf{post}(t, \{\nu_0\}) \neq False$. Using Fact 1 (If direction), this implies that there exists a path of length n in $\mathcal{S}(P_1, P_2)$ that reaches a state (ℓ_1, ℓ_2, ν) from $q_0 = (\iota_1, \iota_2, \nu_0)$.

---

[2] We define it here for local states of P_2 but the property holds for each component of a multi-threaded program.

Let $\mathsf{Dag}_n(q_0)$ (we omit P_1, P_2 in the notation $\mathsf{Dag}_n()$ for clarity) be the Direct Acyclic Graph (DAG), that is obtained by building a depth-first search tree for $\mathcal{S}(P_1, P_2)$, from q_0, up to depth n. As this DAG is a finite transition system, and $E = L_1 \times \{\ell_2\}$, we can apply Theorem 2. This implies that a state (ℓ_1', ℓ_2, ν') is reachable in $\mathsf{SelectSearch}(\mathsf{Dag}_n(q_0))$. Thus there exists a path $q_0 \ i_0 \ q_1 \ \cdots \ i_{m-1} \ q_m$ in $\mathsf{SelectSearch}(\mathsf{Dag}_n(q_0))$ such that $q_m = (\ell_1', \ell_2, \nu')$. This path is in $\mathcal{S}(P_1, P_2)$ and we can apply Fact 1 (Only If direction): there exists $t' = i_0.i_1.\cdots.i_m$ with $\mathsf{post}(t', True) \not\subseteq False$. It remains to prove that $t' \in \mathcal{L}_R^E(P_1 \times P_2)$. As $\mathsf{SelectSearch}$ is control location based, this follows directly from the fact that t' is a path in $\mathsf{SelectSearch}(\mathsf{Dag}_n(q_0))$. $\qquad\square$

Lemma 1 together with Theorem 1 yield the following result:

Theorem 3. Let $E = L_1 \times \{\ell_2\}$. $\mathrm{REACH}(\mathcal{S}(P_1, P_2)) \cap (E \times \mathbb{Z}^V) \neq \varnothing \iff \exists t \in \mathcal{L}_R^E(P_1 \times P_2), \mathsf{post}(t, True) \not\subseteq False$.

This reduces reachability of local states in the infinite system $\mathcal{S}(P_1, P_2)$ to the existence of a feasible trace in a finite reduced product $\mathsf{SelectSearch}(\mathcal{S}(P_1 \times P_2))$.

In the next section, we show how to use *trace refinement* to determine whether a feasible trace exists in $\mathcal{L}_R^E(P_1 \times P_2)$. In the sequel we assume E is fixed and omit it as a superscript.

4   Trace Abstraction Refinement for Concurrent Programs

In this section, we combine the trace refinement algorithm from [13] with partial order reduction. We first recall the trace abstraction refinement method and second present our algorithm that combines trace abstraction refinement and partial order reduction.

4.1   Interpolant Automata

The trace abstraction refinement algorithm from [13] relies on two keys conditions: (a) given a sequence of instructions $t = i_0.i_1.\cdots.i_n \in \Sigma^*$, we can decide whether t is feasible (this can be done using SMT-solvers and decidable theories e.g., Linear Integer Arithmetic) and (b) if t is infeasible there is an explanation in the form of an *inductive interpolant* i.e., a sequence of predicates $I_0, I_1, \cdots, I_{n+1}$ such that (1) $I_0 = True$ and $I_{n+1} = False$, (2) $\forall 0 \leq k \leq n, \mathsf{post}(i_k, I_k) \subseteq I_{k+1}$.

Let $P = (L, \iota, T)$ be a program automaton. Let $\varrho = \ell_0 \ i_0 \ \ell_1 \ i_1 \ \cdots i_{n-1} \ \ell_n$ be a path in P i.e., $\forall 0 \leq k \leq n-1, (\ell_k, i_k, \ell_{k+1}) \in T$. The trace of the path ϱ is $t = i_0.i_1.\cdots i_{n-1}$ and when the trace t is infeasible, the method introduced in [13] consists in building a finite automaton $\mathrm{IA}(t)$, called an *interpolant automaton* that accepts t *and many other traces that are infeasible for the same reason.*

A set of interpolant automata $\mathrm{IA}_1, \mathrm{IA}_2, \cdots, \mathrm{IA}_l$ each of which only accepts infeasible traces is a *refinement*. As regular languages are closed under union, it can actually be collapsed into one automaton that accepts $\cup_{k=1..l} \mathcal{L}(\mathrm{IA}_k)$.

We do not develop the theory of interpolant automata here and refer the reader to [13,14] for a more detailed explanation of the construction of $\mathrm{IA}(t)$.

4.2   Combining Trace Refinement and Partial Order Reduction

Using Theorem 3 we can design an iterative algorithm to check the control location reachability problem in 2-threaded programs. The input of the problem is (P_1, P_2) and a set of local states $E = L_1 \times \{\ell_2\}$. (P_1, P_2) is *safe* if $\text{REACH}(\mathcal{S}(P_1, P_2)) \cap (E \times \mathbb{Z}^V) = \varnothing$, otherwise it is unsafe. In the latter case we want the algorithm to return a witness trace t to reach a state in $E \times \mathbb{Z}^V$.

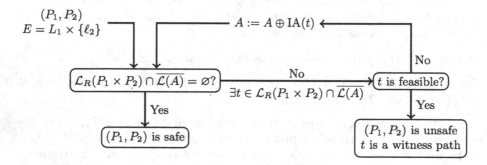

Fig. 3. Trace abstraction refinement algorithm

By Theorem 3, determining whether $\text{REACH}(\mathcal{S}(P_1, P_2)) \cap (E \times \mathbb{Z}^V) \neq \varnothing$ is equivalent to determining whether $\exists t \in \mathcal{L}_R^E(P_1 \times P_2)$ such that t is feasible. This can be done by adapting the generic iterative trace abstraction refinement algorithm of Fig. 1. The new algorithm that combines partial order reduction and trace refinement is given in Fig. 3. As pointed out in the previous paragraph, we can assume that a refinement is composed of one automaton A that accepts infeasible traces. Every time a new interpolant automaton $\text{IA}(t)$ is obtained from an infeasible trace t we combine it with the previous refinement automaton A by computing $A \oplus \text{IA}(t)$ where $A \oplus B$ denotes a finite automaton that accepts $\mathcal{L}(A) \cup \mathcal{L}(B)$. $\mathcal{L}_R(P_1 \times P_2)$ is a finite graph and can be viewed as an automaton with accepting locations in $L_1 \times \{\ell_2\}$. Checking emptiness of $\mathcal{L}_R(P_1 \times P_2) \cap \overline{\mathcal{L}(A)}$ reduces to a standard emptiness check in a synchronised product of automata. Notice that the reduce language $\mathcal{L}_R(P_1 \times P_2)$ should be constant during the iterative refinement. If we choose to generate different representatives of the same $\sim$-equivalent class at different iterations we may need to compute another interpolant automaton to reject the new representative. In our implementation we make sure that the same representative is generated at each refinement step. Ideally, we should compute the *closure* of an interpolant automaton under the equivalence relation $\sim$. This is one direction of future work to use *asynchronous automata* [31] to represent $\sim$-closures.

4.3   Beyond Reachability of Local States

Reachability of local states is general enough to encode reachability of *global* states which is needed to detect data races for instance. It suffices to add an extra component M, a *monitor*, and possibly extra shared variables. M has only one transition to a special location d and the condition to fire the transition is true iff there is a data race. Consider the 3-threaded program (P_1, P_2, M). There is a data race in $\mathcal{S}(P_1, P_2)$ iff a state (ℓ_1, ℓ_2, d, ν) is reachable in $\mathcal{S}(P_1, P_2, M)$ which is a local state reachability problem.

Deadlocks in $\mathcal{S}(P_1, P_2)$ can also be checked for if they are mapped to deadlock states in the product $P_1 \times P_2$ (independent of the data part of the system). This is usually the case, as deadlocks occur on lock/unlock operations or wait/signal that can be explicitly encoded in $\mathcal{S}(P_1 \times P_2)$. A deadlock in $\mathcal{S}(P_1, P_2)$ is then equivalent to the reachability of a global state.

Finally, a general reachability problem depending on data, e.g., specified by a statement of the form `assert(c)` in a multi-threaded program, can be checked using a monitor as well: the monitor has one transition to a location d, and the label of the edge to d is $\neg c$.

5   Implementation and Experiments

Implementation. We have implemented our combined partial order reduction and trace abstraction refinement algorithm in a prototype RAPTOR. The prototype is written is SCALA and is comprised of: (1) a module to perform the partial order reduction implementing an algorithm based on [5, Figure 6.2, Chap. 6]; (2) a module to compute the automata accepting infeasible traces; this module uses a wrapper around SMTINTERPOL [21] to check feasibility of traces and get inductive interpolants when a trace is infeasible. The details of the algorithms and implementation are available in [18].

Our early prototype parses programs in a simple language of our own with integer variables and thread construct. Listing 1, page 5, is an example of such a program. As of now, it does not support C programs, arrays nor pointers yet. However, our language and product construction supports synchronisation and *wait/signal* primitives. We can then model *mutexes* directly as program automata. Another important implementation detail is that we do not compute $\overline{A}$ but rather determinise A *on-the-fly*.

Benchmarks. We used some examples from the Concurrency category [1] from the 4th Competition on Software Verification (SV-COMP 2015). They contain typical concurrent algorithms (Dekker, Lamport, Peterson) some of them coming in two flavours: *safe* and unsafe (column *Safe* in Table 1). Safety amounts to checking the reachability of a local state in one thread. We have translated (for now manually) the C programs of some of the benchmarks into our input language to analyse them. *LOC*, *#T* and *#V* contain respectively the number of lines of code in the source C program, the number of threads and the number of shared variables. Our simple language is very similar to C and the number of lines in the translated version is identical to the C version. *Red* gives the reduction in terms of explored states when partial order reduction is switched on compared to no reduction.

Table 1. RAPTOR results on the SV-COMP benchmarks.

Program	Safe	Steps	States	Red	LOC	#T	#V	RAPTOR	MU-CSEQ	THREADER	IMPARA
stateful01	no	0	22	0 %	34	3	6	1.1s/20	0.9s/1027	0.6s	N/A[5]
stateful01	yes	10	1628	17 %	34	3	6	6.1s	TO	2.6s	N/A[5]
lazy01	no	1	11	0 %	22	3	2	1.3s/9	0.6s/641	4.1s	0.16s
peterson	yes	29	1200	8 %	31	2	4	5.7s	TO	4.6s	0.5s
dekker	yes	9	1276	7 %	46	2	4	6.6s	TO	3.3s	0.7s
szymanski	yes	47	9811	13 %	59	2	3	10s	TO	12s	1.43s
read_write_lock	no	11	2178	16 %	65	4	5	6s/26	0.9s/992	55s	3.9s
read_write_lock	yes	38	10216	24 %	63	4	5	9.5s	TO	57s	15s
time_var_mutex	yes	5	67	38 %	33	2	5	0.69s	TO	4.9s	0.2s
fib_bench_false	no	284	10082	77 %	25	3	2	29s/37	3.58s/949	TO	TO
ext-spin2003	yes	1	203	0 %	44	4	2	3.4s	TO	176s	5.5s

Comparison with Other Tools. We compared our results with one of the leadingtools in the category: MU-CSEQ [16] (silver medal at SV-COMP 2015), THREADER 0.92 (winner of SV-COMP 2013 (winner of SV-COMP 2013), and IMPARA 0.2 [12]. We would have liked to compare with the winner tool LAZY-CSEQ [17] but the competition version is not available any more. We ran the analyses for RAPTOR and MU-CSEQ on an Virtual Linux Machine, running Ubuntu 13.10 64-bit on a MacBook Pro, Intel Core i5, 2.6 GHz, 8 GB of RAM.

Table 1 shows the results of RAPTOR on the selected benchmarks. Column *Steps* gives the number of refinement steps performed by RAPTOR. *States* is the (cumulative) total number of *explored states* in all the selective searches performed at each refinement step. The column RAPTOR contains the analysis time in seconds and, when the program is unsafe, the length of the counterexample (in terms of number of instructions in the program specified using our internal language). The column MU-CSEQ contains similar information for the tool MU-CSEQ [16]. For THREADER and IMPARA we collected only the run times.[3] In Table 1, "TO" stands for *TimeOut* with a time out bound set to 600 s for MU-CSEQ. Notice that both MU-CSEQ and LAZY-CSEQ use a *bounded model checking* back-end (CBMC) and cannot formally establish the correctness of programs in most cases. In the SV-COMP 2015, MU-CSEQ and LAZY-CSEQ applied a strategy [16,17] to interpret the time out as "the program is safe". The result should rather be interpreted as "no bug was found" instead of a formal proof of correctness. In contrast, our method and tool can find bugs or establish program correctness (provided termination) even when programs have loops. This is a key feature of the trace abstraction refinement method that it can discover loop invariants and use them to reject infeasible traces.

On the negative instances (safe column is "no") we incur some overhead compared to MU-CSEQ to discover a counterexample. This can partially be explained by the fact that our SCALA implementation is compiled into an executable JAVA

---

[3] In our experiments, IMPARA 0.2 failed to yield the correct analysis result.

jar file. Every analysis with RAPTOR thus needs to first spawn out the JVM. On the other hand our counterexamples are fairly short and easily mapped to the original programs. For the positive instances (safe column is "yes") we can *prove* all of them within seconds which is a clear advantage.

The rough estimate of the distribution of the execution time for RAPTOR is 30 % in the SMT-solver and the rest in the computation of the refinements and language inclusion check.

6 Related Work

Assume-guarantee reasoning for concurrent programs was first implemented in the CALVIN model checker [22] to check concurrent Java programs. However, program refinement had to be done manually. To the best of our knowledge, the first paper to combine assume-guarantee reasoning with an automated abstraction refinement technique for multi-threaded programs is [10]. The proposed method is *modular* and can prove correctness for programs that admit a modular proof (the predicates on one thread never involve a local variable of another thread). As the authors point out (Sect. 4 in [10]) "[...] the tool ignores thread interleavings [...] and may return false positives". Another limitation of [10] is intrinsic to the modular approach: not all multi-threaded programs admit modular proofs. This means that the algorithm may terminate because no better refinement can be derived and in this case might miss some bugs i.e., generate *false negatives*. This approach was later refined in [23]. Thread modular CEGAR was re-considered in [24] and compared against SPIN. THREADER [11,25] combines predicate abstraction and constraint solving but does not implement any symmetry or reduction techniques that deal with interleavings. THREADER did not participate in the last two editions of SV-COMP 2014 and 2015. Recent work [26] by A. Miné introduced a big-step interference-based thread-modular static analysis as abstract interpretation based on assume-guarantee reasoning.

Partial order reduction techniques have long been recognised as effective for checking concurrent programs and tools implementing the techniques are numerous. The most-well known might be SPIN [8] and VERISOFT [27]. Surprisingly enough, the combination of state-of-the-art predicate abstraction techniques like lazy abstraction (known as the IMPACT algorithm) with partial order reduction techniques has only been achieved recently in [12,28]. It turns out that obtaining a sound algorithm when combining lazy abstractions with partial order techniques is not trivial and it is not clear how other reduction techniques (e.g., symmetry reduction) can be accommodated for in these frameworks. IMPARA implements this technique and according to [12] outperforms all other tools. However, IMPARA did not participate in the SV-COMP 2015 and this is why we have not compared our results against it.

In [29,30], the authors address the verification problem for multi-threaded programs composed of threads executing the *same* procedure. They show how to derive constraints with *shared* and *local* variables, so-called *mixed predicates* but this comes at a rather expensive cost. Indeed, concurrency implies that the abstraction of a program is a concurrent boolean *broadcast* program for which the *image* computation of the *broadcast assignment* is expensive.

Other race checkers tools based on *lock-set* or *type-set* are limited in scope: they check for some conformance to generic patterns at the syntactic level when using mutexes (e.g., if a variable is used within a mutex m in one thread, it should be always used within the same mutex m in all other threads). On the programs we considered, they either report false positives or false negatives (do not detect the bug).

7   Conclusion and Ongoing Work

We have proposed a new method for verifying concurrent programs based on trace abstraction refinement and partial order reduction techniques. The results on some standard benchmarks from the *Software Verification Competition* (SV-COMP 2015) show that our approach compares favourably to existing techniques for finding bugs and is able to establish the correctness of the positive instances.

The combination we have proposed is very natural which is witnessed by the brevity of the correctness proofs (e.g., Lemma 1 and Theorem 3). This is in contrast with the combination of predicate abstraction refinement and partial order reduction [12] which is more involved. It is also clear that our approach extends to other reduction techniques, e.g., symmetry reduction.

Our current work is two-fold: (*i*) on the theoretical side, we aim to compute refinements that are *asynchronous automata* [31] to capture infeasible traces and the all their equivalent traces. A second line of work is to design a modular algorithm (to avoid in-lining of function calls) in the spirit of our recent results [32,33]. (*ii*) on the implementation side, we aim to add more capabilities to our tool, e.g., support for arrays, parsing for C programs and (*iii*) implement recent *optimal* partial order reduction techniques [19,20].

References

1. Beyer, D.: International software verification competition. http://sv-comp. sosy-lab.org/2015/
2. Clarke, E.M., Grumberg, O., Jha, S., Lu, Y., Veith, H.: Counterexample-guided abstraction refinement for symbolic model checking. J. ACM **50**(5), 752–794 (2003)
3. Ball, T., Levin, V., Rajamani, S.K.: A decade of software model checking with SLAM. Commun. ACM **54**(7), 68–76 (2011)
4. Jones, C.B.: Tentative steps toward a development method for interfering programs. ACM Trans. Program. Lang. Syst. **5**(4), 596–619 (1983)
5. Godefroid, P. (ed.): Partial-Order Methods for the Verification of Concurrent Systems: An Approach to the State-Explosion Problem. LNCS, vol. 1032. Springer, Heidelberg (1996)
6. Peled, D.: All from one, one for all: on model checking using representatives. In: Courcoubetis, C. (ed.) CAV 1993. LNCS, vol. 697, pp. 409–423. Springer, Heidelberg (1993)

7. Valmari, A.: Stubborn sets for reduced state space generation. Applications and Theory of Petri Nets. LNCS, vol. 483, pp. 491–515. Springer, Heidelberg (1989)
8. Holzmann, G.J.: Software model checking with spin. Adv. Comput. **65**, 78–109 (2005)
9. Flanagan, C., Qadeer, S., Seshia, S.A.: A modular checker for multithreaded programs. In: Brinksma, E., Larsen, K.G. (eds.) CAV 2002. LNCS, vol. 2404, pp. 180–194. Springer, Heidelberg (2002)
10. Henzinger, T.A., Jhala, R., Majumdar, R., Qadeer, S.: Thread-modular abstraction refinement. In: Hunt Jr., W.A., Somenzi, F. (eds.) CAV 2003. LNCS, vol. 2725, pp. 262–274. Springer, Heidelberg (2003)
11. Gupta, A., Popeea, C., Rybalchenko, A.: Predicate abstraction and refinement for verifying multi-threaded programs. In: POPL, pp. 331–344. ACM (2011)
12. Wachter, B., Kroening, D., Ouaknine, J.: Verifying multi-threaded software with impact. In: FMCAD, pp. 210–217. IEEE (2013)
13. Heizmann, M., Hoenicke, J., Podelski, A.: Refinement of trace abstraction. In: Palsberg, J., Su, Z. (eds.) SAS 2009. LNCS, vol. 5673, pp. 69–85. Springer, Heidelberg (2009)
14. Heizmann, M., Hoenicke, J., Podelski, A.: Software model checking for people who love automata. In: Sharygina, N., Veith, H. (eds.) CAV 2013. LNCS, vol. 8044, pp. 36–52. Springer, Heidelberg (2013)
15. Farzan, A., Kincaid, Z., Podelski, A.: Inductive data flow graphs. In: POPL, pp. 129–142. ACM (2013)
16. Tomasco, E., Inverso, O., Fischer, B., La Torre, S., Parlato, G.: MU-CSeq 0.3: Sequentialization by read-implicit and coarse-grained memory unwindings. In: Baier, C., Tinelli, C. (eds.) TACAS 2015. LNCS, vol. 9035, pp. 436–438. Springer, Heidelberg (2015)
17. Inverso, O. et al.: Lazy-CSeq 0.6c: An improved lazy sequentialization tool for C. In: SV-COMP, (TACAS) 2015
18. Ziegler, F.: Verification of concurrent programs via partial-order reduction and trace refinement. MSc, Institut für Software & Systems Engineering, University of Ausgburg, Germany (2014)
19. Abdulla, P.A., Aronis, S., Jonsson, B., Sagonas, K.F.: Optimal dynamic partial order reduction. In: POPL, pp. 373–384. ACM (2014)
20. Kahlon, V., Wang, C., Gupta, A.: Monotonic partial order reduction: an optimal symbolic partial order reduction technique. In: Bouajjani, A., Maler, O. (eds.) CAV 2009. LNCS, vol. 5643, pp. 398–413. Springer, Heidelberg (2009)
21. Christ, J., Hoenicke, J., Nutz, A.: SMTInterpol: An interpolating SMT solver. In: Donaldson, A., Parker, D. (eds.) SPIN 2012. LNCS, vol. 7385, pp. 248–254. Springer, Heidelberg (2012)
22. Flanagan, C., Qadeer, S.: Thread-modular model checking. In: Ball, T., Rajamani, S.K. (eds.) SPIN 2003. LNCS, vol. 2648, pp. 213–224. Springer, Heidelberg (2003)
23. Henzinger, T.A., Jhala, R., Majumdar, R.: Race checking by context inference. In: PLDI 2004, pp. 1–13. ACM (2004)
24. Malkis, A., Podelski, A., Rybalchenko, A.: Thread-modular counterexample-guided abstraction refinement. In: Cousot, R., Martel, M. (eds.) SAS 2010. LNCS, vol. 6337, pp. 356–372. Springer, Heidelberg (2010)
25. Gupta, A., Popeea, C., Rybalchenko, A.: Threader: A constraint-based verifier for multi-threaded programs. [34] 412–417
26. Miné, A.: Static analysis by abstract interpretation of concurrent programs. Habilitation à Diriger les Recherches, ENS, France (2013)

27. Godefroid, P.: Software model checking: The verisoft approach. Form. Methods Syst. Des. **26**(2), 77–101 (2005)
28. Cimatti, A., Narasamdya, I., Roveri, M.: Boosting lazy abstraction for system C with partial order reduction. In: Abdulla, P.A., Leino, K.R.M. (eds.) TACAS 2011. LNCS, vol. 6605, pp. 341–356. Springer, Heidelberg (2011)
29. Donaldson, A.F., Kaiser, A., Kroening, D., Wahl, T.: Symmetry-aware predicate abstraction for shared-variable concurrent programs. [34] 356–371
30. Donaldson, A.F., Kaiser, A., Kroening, D., Tautschnig, M., Wahl, T.: Counterexample-guided abstraction refinement for symmetric concurrent programs. Form. Methods Syst. Des. **41**(1), 25–44 (2012)
31. Zielonka, W.: Notes on finite asynchronous automata. ITA **21**(2), 99–135 (1987)
32. Cassez, F., Müller, C., Burnett, K.: Summary-based inter-procedural analysis via modular trace refinement. In: FSTTCS 2014, pp. 545–556 (2014)
33. Cassez, F., Matsuoka, T., Pierzchalski, E., Smyth, N.: Perentie: modular trace refinement and selective value tracking. In: Baier, C., Tinelli, C. (eds.) TACAS 2015. LNCS, vol. 9035, pp. 439–442. Springer, Heidelberg (2015)

Synchronized Recursive Timed Automata

Yuya Uezato[1]([⊠]) and Yasuhiko Minamide[2]

[1] University of Tsukuba, Tsukuba, Japan
uezato@score.cs.tsukuba.ac.jp
[2] Tokyo Institute of Technology, Tokyo, Japan
minamide@is.titech.ac.jp

Abstract. We present *synchronized recursive timed automata (SRTA)*
that extend timed automata with a stack. Each frame of a stack is
composed of rational-valued clocks, and SRTA *synchronously* increase
the values of all the clocks within the stack. Our main contribution is
to show that the reachability problem of SRTA is ExpTime-complete.
This decidability contrasts with the undecidability for *recursive timed
automata (RTA)* introduced by Trivedi and Wojtczak, and Benerecetti
et al. Unlike SRTA, the frames below the top are frozen during the computation at the top frame in RTA.

Our construction of the decidability proof is based on the region
abstraction for *dense timed pushdown automata (TPDA)* of Abdulla
et al. to accommodate together diagonal constraints and fractional constraints of SRTA. Since SRTA can be seen as an extension of TPDA with
diagonal and fractional constraints, our result enlarges the decidable class
of pushdown-extensions of timed automata.

1 Introduction

The paper presents a new pushdown-extension of timed automata *synchronized
recursive timed automata (SRTA)*, and we study its expressiveness and the decidability of the reachability problem. Timed automata are a model of real-time systems, and recently several pushdown-extensions of timed automata have been
introduced [1,3,8,12]. Among these pushdown-extensions, our formalization of
SRTA has novel constraints *fractional constraints*—formulae of the form $\{x\} = 0$
and $\{x\} < \{y\}$—for checking fractional parts of clocks. These fractional constraints play important roles. First, fractional constraints enlarge the language
class of (decidable) pushdown-extensions of timed automata *timed pushdown
automata (TPDA)* of Abdulla et al. [1] and TPDA *with diagonal constraints* of
Clemente and Lasota [8]. Indeed, we show that the following SRTA language L_{ex}
cannot be recognized by any TPDA or TPDA with diagonal constraints because
of lack of fractional constraints:

$$L_{ex} \triangleq \{(a, t_1)(a, t_2) \ldots (a, t_n)(b, t'_n) \ldots (b, t'_2)(b, t'_1) : t'_i - t_i \in \mathbb{N}\}.$$

Next, fractional constraints are needed to achieve the theoretical result: For any
SRTA, we can remove *diagonal constraints*—formulae of the form $x - y = k$—

© Springer-Verlag Berlin Heidelberg 2015
M. Davis et al. (Eds.): LPAR-20 2015, LNCS 9450, pp. 249–265, 2015.
DOI: 10.1007/978-3-662-48899-7_18

while preserving the language. Removal of diagonal constraints is one of important results in the theory of timed automata [2,4], and recently Clemente and Lasota showed that in the context of TPDA [8].

Timed automata are a model of real-time systems that includes rational-valued clocks where a configuration $\langle q, \eta \rangle$ is a pair of a control location q and a clock valuation $\eta : X \to \mathbb{Q}^+$ from clocks to the non-negative rationals. In timed automata, *timed transitions* evolve the values of all the clocks at the same rate: $\langle q, \eta \rangle \overset{\delta}{\leadsto} \langle q, \eta + \delta \rangle$. Despite the unboundedness and denseness of rationals, the reachability problem of timed automata was shown decidable by the region abstraction technique in [2].

The two equivalent models, *recursive timed automata (RTA)* and *timed recursive state machines*, were independently introduced by Trivedi and Wojtczak [12] and Benerecetti et al. [3]. A configuration of RTA $\langle q, \langle \gamma_1, \eta_1 \rangle \ldots \langle \gamma_n, \eta_n \rangle \rangle$ is a pair of a location q and a stack where each frame is a pair $\langle \gamma_i, \eta_i \rangle$ of a symbol γ_i and a valuation $\eta_i : X \to \mathbb{Q}^+$. In RTA, timed transitions evolve the values of the clocks only at the top frame: $\langle q, \langle \gamma_1, \eta_1 \rangle \ldots \langle \gamma_n, \eta_n \rangle \rangle \overset{\delta}{\leadsto} \langle q, \langle \gamma_1, \eta_1 \rangle \ldots \langle \gamma_n, \eta_n + \delta \rangle \rangle$. Unfortunately, the reachability problem of RTA is undecidable because RTA can simulate two-counter machines [3,12].

Abdulla et al. introduced *dense timed pushdown automata (TPDA)* [1], and recently Clemente and Lasota extended TPDA to allow diagonal constraints. A configuration of TPDA $\langle q, \eta, \langle \gamma_1, r_1 \rangle \ldots \langle \gamma_n, r_n \rangle \rangle$ is a triple of a location q, a valuation of clocks $\eta : X \to \mathbb{Q}^+$, and a timed stack where each element $\langle \gamma_i, r_i \rangle$ is a pair of a symbol γ_i and its age $r_i \in \mathbb{Q}^+$. TPDA differ from RTA in the following point: In TPDA, timed transitions evolve *synchronously* the values of all the clocks within the stack at the same rate: $\langle q, \eta, \langle \gamma_1, r_1 \rangle \ldots \langle \gamma_n, r_n \rangle \rangle \overset{\delta}{\leadsto} \langle q, \eta + \delta, \langle \gamma_1, r_1 + \delta \rangle \ldots \langle \gamma_n, r_n + \delta \rangle \rangle$. Surprisingly, Abdulla et al. showed the reachability problem of TPDA is decidable and ExpTime-complete [1]. To show this, they designed a region abstraction for pushdown-extensions of timed automata.

Our SRTA are described as *synchronized* RTA; thus a configuration is the same as RTA. But, timed transitions synchronously evolve the values of all the clocks within the stack: $\langle q, \langle \gamma_1, \eta_1 \rangle \ldots \langle \gamma_n, \eta_n \rangle \rangle \overset{\delta}{\leadsto} \langle q, \langle \gamma_1, \eta_1 + \delta \rangle \ldots \langle \gamma_n, \eta_n + \delta \rangle \rangle$. Compared to TPDA, the formalization of SRTA provides both diagonal constraints and fractional constraints. These constraints make SRTA more expressive than TPDA (with diagonal constraints). Even though SRTA extend TPDA, we show that *the reachability problem of SRTA remains ExpTime-complete*. Our decidability proof is separated into two stages.

At the first stage, we translate SRTA into SRTA without diagonal constraints by effectively using fractional constraints. In TPDA, Clemente and Lasota showed that TPDA with diagonal constraints collapse to TPDA with an untimed stack whose configurations are $\langle q, \eta, \gamma_1 \ldots \gamma_n \rangle$ in [8]. This implies that adding diagonal constraints does not enlarge the language class. *However*, we cannot apply their untiming technique to SRTA because the above mentioned language L_{ex} requires unboundedly many clocks, and this contrasts with Clemente's result.

At the second stage, we adapt the region abstraction of Abdulla et al. [1] to show the ExpTime-completeness of the reachability problem of SRTA without diagonal constraints. Interestingly, our fractional constraints are obtained by investigating the region abstraction of Abdulla et al. [1], and thus, our construction is based on their region abstraction. We find out that Abdulla's proof structure is essentially a *backward-forward simulation* of Lynch and Vaandrager [11], and this mixed simulation makes their proof involved. From this insight, we introduce an intermediate semantics to separate the mixed simulation into two simple simulations, and this makes entire proof easy to follow.

Concrete Valuations. The set of non-negative rationals $\mathbb{Q}^+$ is defined by: $\mathbb{Q}^+ \triangleq \{r \in \mathbb{Q} : r \geq 0\}$. For a rational $r \in \mathbb{Q}^+$, we use $\lfloor r \rfloor$ and $\{r\}$ to denote the integral and fractional part of r, respectively: e.g., $\lfloor 1.5 \rfloor = 1$ and $\{1.5\} = 0.5$.

Let X be a clock set. A function $\eta : X \to \mathbb{Q}^+$ is called a *concrete valuation* on X and we write X_V for the set of valuations on X. We define basic operations:

$$\eta[x := r](y) \triangleq \begin{cases} r & \text{if } y = x \\ \eta(y) & \text{otherwise,} \end{cases} \quad \eta[x := y] \triangleq \eta[x := \eta(y)], \quad (\eta + r)(y) \triangleq \eta(y) + r,$$

where $x, y \in X$ and $r \in \mathbb{Q}^+$. The zero valuation on X is defined by: $\mathbf{0}_X(x) \triangleq 0$ for $x \in X$. For $\eta \in X_V$ and $Y \subseteq X$, we write $\eta|Y \in Y_V$ to denote the restriction of η to Y. We define the ordering $\eta \leq \eta'$ on valuations by: $\eta \leq \eta'$ if $\exists r \in \mathbb{Q}^+ . \eta' = \eta + r$.

Pushdown Systems. A pushdown system (PDS) is a triple $(Q, \Gamma, \hookrightarrow)$ where Q is a finite set of control locations, Γ is a (possibly infinite) stack alphabet, and $\hookrightarrow \subseteq (Q \times \Gamma^*) \times (Q \times \Gamma^*)$ is a set of transition rules. A configuration is a pair $\langle q, w \rangle$ of a location $q \in Q$ and a stack $w \in \Gamma^*$. The one-step transition $\langle q, w\,v \rangle \to \langle q', w\,v' \rangle$ is defined if $\langle q, v \rangle \hookrightarrow \langle q', v' \rangle$. We also write $w \to w'$ by omitting locations if the locations are irrelevant. A PDS is called finite-PDS if the set of transition rules is finite. Otherwise, it is called infinite-PDS. The reachability problem from q_{init} to q_{final} decides if $\langle q_{\text{init}}, \epsilon \rangle \to^* \langle q_{\text{final}}, w \rangle$ holds for some stack w, and the reachability problem of finite-PDS is in PTime [5,7,9].

2   Synchronized Recursive Timed Automata

First, we introduce *synchronized recursive timed automata (SRTA)* where the values of all the clocks in the stack are increased *synchronously* at the same rate. Next, we study the expressiveness of SRTA by brief comparisons with recursive timed automata and timed pushdown automata. Finally, we see the overview of our decidability proof.

Clock Constraints. We write $I \in \mathbb{I}$ for an interval: $\mathbb{I} \triangleq \{(i,j), [i,j] : i, j \in \mathbb{N}\}$. Let X be a clock set. Then, the set Φ_X of clock constraints is given by:

$$\varphi ::= x \in I \mid x \bowtie y \mid \{x\} = 0 \mid \{x\} \bowtie \{y\} \mid \varphi \wedge \varphi \mid \neg \varphi$$
$$\text{where } x, y \in X, \, I \in \mathbb{I}, \bowtie \in \{<, =, >\}.$$

For $\varphi \in \Phi_X$ and $\eta \in X_V$, we write $\eta \models \varphi$ if φ holds when clocks are replaced by values of η: e.g., $\eta \models x \in I$ if $\eta(x) \in I$, $\eta \models \{x\} = 0$ if $\{\eta(x)\} = 0$. The fractional constraints $\{x\} = 0$ and $\{x\} \bowtie \{y\}$ are novel and are used to recognize the language L_{ex} and remove diagonal constraints later on.

Definition 1 (Synchronized Recursive Timed Automata). A synchronized recursive timed automaton is a tuple $\mathfrak{S} = (Q, q_{init}, q_{final}, \Sigma, \Gamma, \mathcal{X}, \Delta)$ where Q is a finite set of control locations, q_{init} and q_{final} are the initial and accepting locations respectively, Σ is a finite input alphabet, Γ is a finite set of stack symbols, $\mathcal{X}$ is a finite set of clocks, and $\Delta \subseteq Q \times (\Sigma \cup \{\epsilon\}) \times Op \times Q$ is a finite set of *discrete* transition rules. The operations $\tau \in Op$ are given by:

$$\tau ::= \mathbf{push}(\gamma, X) \mid \mathbf{pop}(\gamma, X) \mid x \leftarrow I \mid \mathbf{check}(\varphi)$$
$$\text{where } \gamma \in \Gamma, X \subseteq \mathcal{X}, x \in \mathcal{X}, I \in \mathbb{I}, \text{ and } \varphi \in \Phi_{\mathcal{X}}.$$

We define the standard semantics **Stnd** of SRTA as a transition system.

Definition 2 (Semantics STND). A configuration is a pair $\langle q, w \rangle$ of a location q and a stack w where each frame $\langle \gamma, \eta \rangle$ consists of a stack symbol γ and a concrete valuation $\eta \in \mathcal{X}_V$. The set of configurations of STND is $Q \times (\Gamma \times \mathcal{X}_V)^*$.

For $\tau \in Op$, we define a discrete transition $w \xrightarrow{\tau} w'$ for $w, w' \in (\Gamma \times \mathcal{X}_V)^*$ by case analysis on τ:

$$\frac{\eta_2 = \mathbf{0}_{\mathcal{X}}[X := \eta_1]}{w \langle \gamma, \eta_1 \rangle \rightarrow w \langle \gamma, \eta_1 \rangle \langle \gamma', \eta_2 \rangle} \mathbf{push}(\gamma', X) \qquad \frac{r \in I \quad \eta' = \eta[x := r]}{w \langle \gamma, \eta \rangle \rightarrow w \langle \gamma, \eta' \rangle} x \leftarrow I$$

$$\frac{\eta_1' = \eta_1[X := \eta_2]}{w \langle \gamma, \eta_1 \rangle \langle \gamma', \eta_2 \rangle \rightarrow w \langle \gamma, \eta_1' \rangle} \mathbf{pop}(\gamma', X) \qquad \frac{\eta \models \varphi}{w \langle \gamma, \eta \rangle \rightarrow w \langle \gamma, \eta \rangle} \mathbf{check}(\varphi)$$

where $\eta[\{x_1, \ldots, x_n\} := \eta'] \triangleq \eta[x_1 := \eta'(x_1), \ldots, x_n := \eta'(x_n)]$.

In addition to discrete transitions, we allow *timed* transitions:

$$\langle \gamma_1, \eta_1 \rangle \langle \gamma_2, \eta_2 \rangle \ldots \langle \gamma_n, \eta_n \rangle \xrightarrow{\delta} \langle \gamma_1, \eta_1 + \delta \rangle \langle \gamma_2, \eta_2 + \delta \rangle \ldots \langle \gamma_n, \eta_n + \delta \rangle$$

where $\delta \in \mathbb{Q}^+$. These transitions for a stack are extended to configurations: $\langle q, w \rangle \xrightarrow{\alpha} \langle q', w' \rangle$ if $w \xrightarrow{\tau} w'$ for some $\langle q, \alpha, \tau, q' \rangle \in \Delta$ and $\langle q, w \rangle \xrightarrow{\delta} \langle q, w' \rangle$ if $w \xrightarrow{\delta} w'$.

Timed Languages. A run π is a finite alternating sequence of timed and discrete transitions. From a run $\pi = c_0 \xrightarrow{\delta_0} c_0' \xrightarrow{\alpha_0} c_1 \xrightarrow{\delta_1} c_1' \xrightarrow{\alpha_1} \cdots \xrightarrow{\delta_n} c_n \xrightarrow{\alpha_n} c_n'$, we define the timed trace $\mathrm{tt}(\pi) \triangleq (\alpha_0, \delta_0)(\alpha_1, \delta_0 + \delta_1) \ldots (\alpha_n, \Sigma_{i=0}^n \delta_i) \in ((\Sigma \cup \{\epsilon\}) \times \mathbb{Q}^+)^*$ and the timed word $\mathrm{tw}(\pi) \in (\Sigma \times \mathbb{Q}^+)^*$ by removing all the (ϵ, t) pairs from $\mathrm{tt}(\pi)$. The timed language of $\mathfrak{S}$ is defined by the runs from q_{init} to q_{final}:

$$\mathcal{L}(\mathfrak{S}) \triangleq \{\mathrm{tw}(\pi) : \pi = \langle q_{init}, \langle \perp, \mathbf{0}_{\mathcal{X}} \rangle \rangle \rightsquigarrow \cdots \rightarrow \langle q_{final}, w \rangle \}.$$

(For the initial configuration $\langle q_{init}, \langle \perp, \mathbf{0}_{\mathcal{X}} \rangle \rangle$, the special stack symbol $\perp \in \Gamma$ is needed.)

Timed Language Example. We consider the following timed language:

$$L_{ex} \triangleq \{(a, t_1)(a, t_2) \ldots (a, t_n)(b, t_n') \ldots (b, t_2')(b, t_1') : t_i' - t_i \in \mathbb{N}\}.$$

Note that if we forget the time stamps from L_{ex} then the language $\{a^n b^n : n \geq 1\}$ is a typical context-free language.

We consider a SRTA $(\{q_0, \ldots, q_4\}, q_0, q_4, \{a, b\}, \{\bot, \natural, \sharp\}, \{x\}, \Delta)$ where Δ is defined as follows:

$$\tau_1 = \mathbf{push}(\natural, \emptyset), \ \tau_1' = \mathbf{push}(\sharp, \emptyset), \ \tau_2 = \mathbf{check}(\{x\} = 0), \ \tau_3 = \mathbf{pop}(\sharp, \emptyset), \ \tau_4 = \mathbf{pop}(\natural, \emptyset).$$

Let us consider the timed word $(a, 0.1)(a, 1.2)(b, 2.2)(b, 3.1) \in L_{\mathrm{ex}}$ and the following run that accepts the word:

$$\langle q_0, \langle \bot, 0 \rangle \rangle \xrightarrow{0.1 \ a} \langle q_1, \langle \bot, 0.1 \rangle \langle \natural, 0 \rangle \rangle \xrightarrow{1.1 \ a} \langle q_1, \langle \bot, 1.2 \rangle \langle \natural, 1.1 \rangle \langle \sharp, 0 \rangle \rangle \xrightarrow{1.0}$$

$$\langle q_1, \langle \bot, 2.2 \rangle \langle \natural, 2.1 \rangle \langle \sharp, 1 \rangle \rangle \xrightarrow[\mathbf{check}(\{x\}=0)]{b} \langle q_2, \langle \bot, 2.2 \rangle \langle \natural, 2.1 \rangle \langle \sharp, 1 \rangle \rangle \xrightarrow{0.5 \ \epsilon}$$

$$\langle q_3, \langle \bot, 2.7 \rangle \langle \natural, 2.6 \rangle \rangle \xrightarrow{0.4 \ b} \langle q_2, \langle \bot, 3.1 \rangle \langle \natural, 3 \rangle \rangle \xrightarrow{0 \ \epsilon} \langle q_4, \langle \bot, 3.1 \rangle \rangle.$$

The action τ_2 (i.e., $\mathbf{check}(\{x\} = 0)$) checks if the fractional part of $t_i' - t_i$ is zero, hence it excludes a run such that $\langle q_0, \langle \bot, 0 \rangle \rangle \xrightarrow{0.1 \ a} \xrightarrow{0.2} \langle q_1, \langle \bot, 0.3 \rangle \langle \natural, 0.2 \rangle \rangle \not\xrightarrow{b} \langle q_2, \langle \bot, 0.3 \rangle \langle \natural, 0.2 \rangle \rangle$.

Simulating Diagonal Constraints $x - y \bowtie k$. In SRTA, every update $x \leftarrow I$ is bounded because I is an interval. This enables us to encode diagonal constraints of the form $x - y \bowtie k$ where $k \in \mathbb{Z}$.

Let us see an idea of encoding the constraint $x - y \bowtie 1$. We prepare an auxiliary clock y_{+1} for denoting $y + 1$ and check $x \bowtie y_{+1}$ instead of $x - y \bowtie 1$. In order to keep $y + 1 = y_{+1}$, when we update $y \leftarrow (i, i+1)$, we also execute $y_{+1} \leftarrow (i+1, i+2)$ and $\mathbf{check}(\{y\} = \{y_{+1}\})$. In the case of $y \leftarrow [i, i]$, we do $y_{+1} \leftarrow [i+1, i+1]$. Since any updates $y \leftarrow I$ can be decomposed into the forms of $y \leftarrow (i, i+1)$ and $y \leftarrow [j, j]$ by nondeterminism of SRTA, our decidability result extends even if we consider general diagonal constraints of the form $x - y \bowtie k$.

Then, this decidability result is analogous to one of Bouyer et al. for timed automata with bounded updates and diagonal constraints [6].

Compare to Recursive Timed Automata. The formulation of recursive timed automata (RTA) [3,12] differs from SRTA in timed transitions: RTA increase only the top of a stack: $\langle q, \langle \gamma_1, \eta_1 \rangle \ldots \langle \gamma_n, \eta_n \rangle \rangle \xrightarrow{\delta} \langle q, \langle \gamma_1, \eta_1 \rangle \ldots \langle \gamma_n, \eta_n + \delta \rangle \rangle$ where $\delta \in \mathbb{Q}^+$. The difference of timed transitions between SRTA and RTA is crucial because RTA can simulate two-counter machines [3,12] by effectively using the timed transitions.

Krishna et al. considered the subset of RTA called RTA$_{\mathrm{RN}}$ in [10] and showed that the reachability problem of RTA$_{\mathrm{RN}}$ is decidable. RTA$_{\mathrm{RN}}$ are subsumed by our SRTA because RTA$_{\mathrm{RN}}$ are SRTA without diagonal and fractional constraints. They adapted Abdulla's construction and proof to RTA$_{\mathrm{RN}}$ by closely following the details. On the other hand, we give a simpler proof by restructuring Abdulla's proof.

Compare to Timed Pushdown Automata. Timed pushdown automata of Abdulla et al. [1] are a pushdown extension of timed automata. Clemente and Lasota [8] equipped TPDA with diagonal constraints and showed that the expressiveness of TPDA with diagonal constraints is equivalent to that of TPDA with respect to languages.

Let us briefly see the formulation of Clemente and Lasota. The constraints $\psi \in \Psi_X$ in their system are given as follows:

$$\psi ::= x \bowtie k \mid x - y \bowtie k \mid \psi \wedge \psi \quad \text{where } x, y \in X \text{ and } k \in \mathbb{Z}.$$

Since there are no fractional constraints ($\{x\} = 0$ or $\{x\} \bowtie \{y\}$), we cannot inspect the fractional parts of clocks. A TPDA is a tuple $(Q, q_{init}, q_{final}, \Sigma, \Gamma, \mathcal{X}, \Delta)$ and a configuration $\langle q, X, \langle \gamma_1, r_1 \rangle \langle \gamma_2, r_2 \rangle \dots \langle \gamma_n, r_n \rangle \rangle$ is a triple of a location q, a (global) valuation X on $\mathcal{X}$, and a stack where $\langle \gamma_i, r_i \rangle \in \Gamma \times \mathbb{Q}^+$. There are four kinds of discrete operations for Δ:

$\mathsf{push}(\gamma) : \langle p, X, w \rangle \rightarrow \langle q, X, w \langle \gamma, 0 \rangle \rangle, \quad \mathsf{reset}(x) : \langle p, X, w \rangle \rightarrow \langle q, X[x := 0], w \rangle,$
$\mathsf{pop}(\gamma, \psi') : \langle p, X, w \langle \gamma, r \rangle \rangle \rightarrow \langle q, X, w \rangle$ if $X \uplus \{z \mapsto r\} \models \psi'$ where $\psi' \in \Psi_{\mathcal{X} \uplus \{z\}}$,
$\mathsf{check}(\psi) : \langle p, X, w \rangle \rightarrow \langle q, X, w \rangle$ if $X \models \psi$ where $\psi \in \Psi_{\mathcal{X}}$.

Since a valuation X of TPDA is simulated by using the value-copying mechanism of $\mathsf{push}(\gamma, \mathcal{X})$ and $\mathsf{pop}(\gamma, \mathcal{X})$ in SRTA, we obtain the following result.

Theorem 1. *For a TPDA $\mathcal{T} = (Q, q_{init}, q_{final}, \Sigma, \Gamma, \mathcal{X}, \Delta)$, we can build a SRTA $\mathfrak{S} = (Q', q'_{init}, q'_{final}, \Sigma, \Gamma \uplus \{\bot\}, \mathcal{X} \uplus \{z, x\}, \Delta')$ such that $\mathcal{L}(\mathcal{T}) = \mathcal{L}(\mathfrak{S})$.*

Proof (Sketch). A push transition $\langle p, X, \epsilon \rangle \xrightarrow{\alpha, \mathsf{push}(\gamma)} \langle q, X, \langle \gamma, 0 \rangle \rangle$ is simulated by $\langle p, \langle \bot, \eta \rangle \rangle \xrightarrow{\alpha, \mathsf{push}(\gamma, \mathcal{X})} \langle q, \langle \bot, \eta \rangle \langle \gamma, \eta' \rangle \rangle$ where $X(x) = \eta(x)$ for all $x \in \mathcal{X}$.

To simulate a pop transition $\langle p, X, \langle \gamma, r \rangle \rangle \xrightarrow{\alpha, \mathsf{pop}(\gamma, \psi')} \langle q, X, \epsilon \rangle$ atomically in $\mathfrak{S}$, we use the extra clock x as follows:

$$\langle p, \langle \bot, \eta \rangle \langle \gamma, \eta' \rangle \rangle \xrightarrow{\epsilon, x \leftarrow [0,0]} \langle p', \langle \bot, \eta \rangle \langle \gamma, \eta'[x := 0] \rangle \rangle \xrightarrow{\delta_1} \xrightarrow{\epsilon, \mathsf{check}(\psi')} \xrightarrow{\delta_2} \xrightarrow{\alpha, \mathsf{pop}(\gamma, \mathcal{X} \uplus \{x\})}$$
$$\langle q', \langle \bot, \eta'' \rangle \rangle \xrightarrow{\delta_3} \xrightarrow{\epsilon, \mathsf{check}(x \in [0,0])} \langle q, \langle \bot, \eta'' \rangle \rangle$$

where $X(x) = \eta'(x)$ for $x \in \mathcal{X}$ and $\eta'(z) = r$. By using the clock x as a stopwatch, we ensure the atomicity of these transitions and $\delta_1 = \delta_2 = \delta_3 = 0.0$. $\square$

Furthermore SRTA have the major advantage over TPDA, namely we can inspect the fractional parts of clocks by fractional constraints. Indeed, the language class of SRTA is strictly larger than TPDA with diagonal constraints.

Theorem 2. *The above timed language L_{ex} cannot be recognized by TPDA with diagonal constraints.*

Intuitively, unboundedly many clocks are needed to keep the exact fractional values to recognize the language L_{ex}. The proof of this theorem can be found in the long version of the paper [13].

This suggests that fractional constraints play a crucial role in pushdown extensions of timed automata. Interestingly, the constraints are obtained by studying Abdulla's proof [1]. Unlike standard regions of timed automata, Abdulla's regions carry the fractional part ordering of clocks even their values are beyond the bound that the maximal constant appears in interval constraints.

As an overview of the rest of the paper, we see the proof of our main theorem.

Main Theorem. *The reachability problem of SRTA, which decides if there is a run from $\langle q_{init}, \langle \bot, \mathbf{0} \rangle \rangle$ to $\langle q_{final}, w \rangle$ for some stack w, is* ExpTime-*complete.*

Proof. The ExpTime-hardness is shown from the result of Abdulla et al. that the reachability problem of TPDA is ExpTime-hard [1] and the above Theorem 1.

Next, to show the reachability problem is decidable and in ExpTime, we build the finite-PDS semantics DIGI through Sects. 3 and 4:

$$\text{SRTA} \xrightleftharpoons{\text{Thm 3}} \text{SRTA without comparisons } x \bowtie y \xrightarrow{\text{Thm 4}} \text{DIGI}$$

where each step preserves the reachability and especially Theorem 3 states that we can safely remove clock comparisons while preserving languages of SRTA.

The obtained finite-PDS DIGI is basically equivalent to the *symbolic pushdown automaton* of Abdulla et al. [1] and they proved the reachability problem of that is in ExpTime by using the PTime algorithm for the reachability problem of finite-PDS [5,7,9]. Hence, the reachability problem of SRTA is in ExpTime. □

3   Language-Preserving Removal of Comparison Constraints

We show that comparison constraints $x \bowtie y$ can be removed from SRTA without losing its expressiveness. Namely, from a given SRTA $\mathfrak{S}$, we construct a SRTA $\mathfrak{S}'$ without comparison constraints such that $\mathcal{L}(\mathfrak{S}) = \mathcal{L}(\mathfrak{S}')$.

We say that a SRTA $\mathfrak{S} = (Q, q_{init}, q_{final}, \Sigma, \Gamma, \mathcal{X}, \Delta)$ is M-bounded if $M \geq j$ holds for any intervals (i, j) and $[i, j]$ in Δ. As a running example of this section, we consider the following run of a 2-bounded SRTA:

$$\eta_1 \xrightarrow{\text{push}(\{u,z\})} \eta_1\,\eta_2 \xrightarrow{y \leftarrow [1,2]} \eta_1\,\eta_2' \xrightsquigarrow{1.3} \eta_1'\,\eta_2'' \xrightarrow{u \leftarrow [0,1]} \eta_1'\,\eta_2''' \xrightarrow{\text{pop}(\{u,y,z\})} \eta_3$$

where

$$\eta_1 = \{x_1 \mapsto 0.1; x_2, u \mapsto 1.2; z \mapsto 2.6\}, \eta_1' = \{x_1 \mapsto 1.4; x_2, u \mapsto 2.5; z \mapsto 3.9\},$$
$$\eta_2 = \{y \mapsto 0.0; u \mapsto 1.2; z \mapsto 2.6\}, \qquad \eta_2' = \{u \mapsto 1.2; y \mapsto 1.4; z \mapsto 2.6\},$$
$$\eta_2'' = \{u \mapsto 2.5; y \mapsto 2.7; z \mapsto 3.9\}, \qquad \eta_2''' = \{u \mapsto 0.3; y \mapsto 2.7; z \mapsto 3.9\}.$$

From the definition, $\eta_3 = \{u \mapsto 0.3; x_1 \mapsto 1.4; x_2 \mapsto 2.5; y \mapsto 2.7; z \mapsto 3.9\}$. For the sake of readability, we only write relevant clocks for an explanation as above. Also, we omit zero timed transitions $\xrightsquigarrow{0.0}$, locations, input alphabet, and stack symbols.

Our basic idea is to encode the liner order between clocks into a stack symbol: e.g., the linear order of η_1 is represented symbolically by $x_1 < \{x_2, u\} < z$ as a stack symbol. Hence, the above run is encoded as follows:

$$\nu_1 \xrightarrow{\mathsf{push}(\{u,z\})} \nu_1\,\nu_2 \xrightarrow{y\leftarrow[1,2]} \nu_1\,\nu_2' \xrightarrow{1.3} \nu_1'\,\nu_2'' \xrightarrow{u\leftarrow[0,1]} \nu_1'\,\nu_2''' \xrightarrow{\mathsf{pop}(\{u,y,z\})} \nu_3$$

where

$$\nu_1 = (\eta_1, x_1 < \{x_2, u\} < z), \quad \nu_2 = (\eta_2, y < u < z), \quad \nu_2' = (\eta_2', u < y < z),$$
$$\nu_1' = (\eta_1', x_1 < \{x_2, u\} < z), \quad \nu_2'' = (\eta_2'', u < y < z), \quad \nu_2''' = (\eta_2''', u < y < z).$$

For this encoding we do the following calculation at each step:

1. At $\mathsf{push}(\{u,z\})$, we extract the order of u and z in ν_1 and pass $u < z$ to ν_2.
2. At update $y \leftarrow [1,2]$, first we actually perform $y \leftarrow [1,2]$ and set $y \mapsto 1.4$, so we obtain $(\eta_2', y < u < z)$. Next, we reconstruct the correct order $u < y$ of y and u in η_2'. *Since our updates $y \leftarrow [i,j]$ or $y \leftarrow (i,j)$ are M-bounded (i.e., $j \leq 2$),* we can calculate the correct order by using M-bounded interval constraints and fractional constraints. After $\mathsf{check}(u \in (1,2))$, $\mathsf{check}(y \in (1,2))$, and $\mathsf{check}(\{u\} < \{y\})$, we find out $u < y$.
3. At time transition $\xrightarrow{1.3}$, we do not need to modify any orderings.
4. At update $u \leftarrow [0,1]$, we also perform $u \leftarrow [0,1]$ first and next we reconstruct the correct ordering of η_2'''.

Finally, we consider the $\mathsf{pop}(\{u,y,z\})$ transition. As above, first we actually perform $\mathsf{pop}(\{u,y,z\})$ and obtain $(\eta_3, \nu_1' : (x_1 < \{x_2, u\} < z)$ & $\nu_2''' : (u < y < z))$. However we have no ways to determine the correct ordering $u < x_1 < x_2 < y < z$ because both $\eta_3(x_2)$ and $\eta_3(y)$ are larger than $M = 2$ and $x_2 < y$ cannot be understood with 2-bounded interval constraints. Of course, if we take $M = 3$ then this matter is solved. But, this ad-hoc solution fails when $\nu_1\,\nu_2' \xrightarrow{2.3} \nu_1'\,\nu_2''$.

To solve this, we introduce *auxiliary clocks* $\overset{\bullet}{\mathsf{C}}_i$ and C_j as follows:

$$\lambda_1 \xrightarrow{\mathsf{push}(\{u,z\})} \lambda_1\,\lambda_2 \xrightarrow{y\leftarrow[1,2]} \lambda_1\,\lambda_2' \xrightarrow{1.3} \lambda_1'\,\lambda_2'' \xrightarrow{u\leftarrow[0,1]} \lambda_1'\,\lambda_2''' \xrightarrow{\mathsf{pop}(\{u,y,z\})} \lambda_3$$

where

$$\lambda_1 = (\eta_1 \cup \{\overset{\bullet}{\mathsf{C}}_0 \mapsto 0.0; \overset{\bullet}{\mathsf{C}}_1 \mapsto 1.0; \overset{\bullet}{\mathsf{C}}_2 \mapsto 2.0\}, \ \overset{\bullet}{\mathsf{C}}_0 < x_1 < \overset{\bullet}{\mathsf{C}}_1 < \{x_2, u\} < \overset{\bullet}{\mathsf{C}}_2 < z),$$
$$\lambda_2 = (\eta_2 \cup \{\mathsf{C}_0 \mapsto 0.0; \mathsf{C}_1 \mapsto 1.0; \mathsf{C}_2 \mapsto 2.0\}, \ \{y, \mathsf{C}_0\} < \mathsf{C}_1 < u < \mathsf{C}_2 < z),$$
$$\lambda_2' = (\eta_2' \cup \{\mathsf{C}_0 \mapsto 0.0; \mathsf{C}_1 \mapsto 1.0; \mathsf{C}_2 \mapsto 2.0\}, \ \mathsf{C}_0 < \mathsf{C}_1 < u < y < \mathsf{C}_2 < z),$$
$$\lambda_1' = (\eta_1' \cup \{\overset{\bullet}{\mathsf{C}}_0 \mapsto 1.3; \overset{\bullet}{\mathsf{C}}_1 \mapsto 2.3; \overset{\bullet}{\mathsf{C}}_2 \mapsto 3.3\}, \ \overset{\bullet}{\mathsf{C}}_0 < x_1 < \overset{\bullet}{\mathsf{C}}_1 < \{x_2, u\} < \overset{\bullet}{\mathsf{C}}_2 < z),$$
$$\lambda_2'' = (\eta_2'' \cup \{\mathsf{C}_0 \mapsto 1.3; \mathsf{C}_1 \mapsto 2.3; \mathsf{C}_2 \mapsto 3.3\}, \ \mathsf{C}_0 < \mathsf{C}_1 < u < y < \mathsf{C}_2 < z),$$
$$\lambda_2''' = (\eta_2''' \cup \{\mathsf{C}_0 \mapsto 1.3; \mathsf{C}_1 \mapsto 2.3; \mathsf{C}_2 \mapsto 3.3\}, \ u < \mathsf{C}_0 < \mathsf{C}_1 < y < \mathsf{C}_2 < z).$$

When taking $\mathsf{push}(\{u,z\})$, we set the clocks $\overset{\bullet}{\mathsf{C}}_i$ by $\overset{\bullet}{\mathsf{C}}_i \leftarrow [i,i]$ in the next frame λ_1 and also set the clocks C_i by $\mathsf{C}_i \leftarrow [i,i]$ in the top frame λ_2. Hence, $\overset{\bullet}{\mathsf{C}}_i$ of λ_1 and C_i of λ_2 have the same values. We require two kinds of the auxiliary clocks $\overset{\bullet}{\mathsf{C}}$ and C because if we push a new frame on top of the current frame λ_2, we also set $\overset{\bullet}{C}_i \leftarrow [i,i]$ in λ_2. To compute the correct ordering in λ_3 at $\mathbf{pop}(\{u,y,z\})$, the auxiliary clocks $\overset{\bullet}{C}$ of λ_1' and $\overset{\bullet}{\complement}$ of λ_2''' behave as *separators* as follows.

Determine $x_2 < y$. With the auxiliary clocks, we determine $x_2 < y$. Performing $\mathbf{pop}(\{u,y,z\})$ makes $(\eta_3 \uplus \{\overset{\bullet}{C}_0 \mapsto 1.3, \overset{\bullet}{C}_1 \mapsto 2.3, \overset{\bullet}{C}_2 \mapsto 3.3\}, \lambda_1' : o_1$ & $\lambda_2''' : o_2)$ where $o_1 = \overset{\bullet}{C}_0 < x_1 < \overset{\bullet}{C}_1 < \lfloor x_2, u \rfloor < \overset{\bullet}{C}_2 < z$ and $o_2 = u < \overset{\bullet}{\complement}_0 < \overset{\bullet}{\complement}_1 < y < \overset{\bullet}{\complement}_2 < z$.

It is easily understood that $\overset{\bullet}{C}_1 < x_2 < \overset{\bullet}{C}_2$ and $\overset{\bullet}{C}_1 < y < \overset{\bullet}{C}_2$ from o_1 and o_2. We also obtain $\{\overset{\bullet}{C}_1\} < \{x_2\} < \{y\}$ by using fractional constraints because of $\{\overset{\bullet}{C}_1\} = 0.3$, $\{x_2\} = 0.5$, and $\{y\} = 0.7$. Then $\overset{\bullet}{C}_1 < x_2 < y < \overset{\bullet}{C}_2$ follows from: 1) the fractional part ordering $\{\overset{\bullet}{C}_1\} < \{x_2\} < \{y\}$, 2) x_2 and y are in between $\overset{\bullet}{C}_1$ and $\overset{\bullet}{C}_2$, and 3) *the fact $\overset{\bullet}{C}_1 + 1.0 = \overset{\bullet}{C}_2$* obtained by the construction.

Treating clocks $< \overset{\bullet}{C}_0$ or $> \overset{\bullet}{C}_M$. From the above argument, in general, we can reconstruct the correct ordering of clocks between $\overset{\bullet}{C}_0$ and $\overset{\bullet}{C}_M$. Here we consider the other clocks: 1) clocks that are smaller than $\overset{\bullet}{C}_0$ and 2) clocks that are larger than $\overset{\bullet}{C}_M$.

(1) We consider $u < \overset{\bullet}{\complement}_0$ in o_2. This implies that u *was updated after* $\mathbf{push}(\{u,z\})$ because the only way to make a clock smaller than $\overset{\bullet}{\complement}_0$ is updating. Hence, we take $x < \overset{\bullet}{C}_0$ in λ_3 if $x < \overset{\bullet}{\complement}_0$ in o_2. And also we take $x \lhd x'$ in λ_3 if $x \lhd x' < \overset{\bullet}{\complement}_0$ in o_2 where $\lhd \in \{<, =\}$. As the result, we obtain $u < \overset{\bullet}{C}_0$ in λ_3.

(2) We consider $\overset{\bullet}{\complement}_M < z$ in o_2. This states that z *was copied by* $\mathbf{push}(\{u,z\})$ *and never updated* because our updates are bounded by $M = 2$ and the bounded updates cannot make a clock larger than $\overset{\bullet}{\complement}_M$. Thus, we take $\overset{\bullet}{C}_M < x$ in λ_3 if $\overset{\bullet}{\complement}_M < x$ in o_2 and $x \lhd x'$ in λ_3 if $\overset{\bullet}{\complement}_M < x \lhd x'$ in o_1. As the result, we obtain $\overset{\bullet}{C}_M < z$ in λ_3. Finally, we find out $u < \overset{\bullet}{C}_0 < x_1 < \overset{\bullet}{C}_1 < x_2 < y < \overset{\bullet}{C}_2 < z$ and it reflects the correct ordering $u < x_1 < x_2 < y < z$ in η_3.

In general, when performing $\mathbf{pop}(X)$ for (η_1, o_1) and (η_2, o_2), we build the ordering o_3 of $\eta_3 (= \eta_1[X := \eta_2])$ in the following steps from 1. to 4.:

We write $\mathcal{X}_{\overset{\bullet}{C}}$ for $\mathcal{X} \cup \{\overset{\bullet}{C}_i, \overset{\bullet}{\complement}_i : i \in [0..M]\}$ and Y for $\{y \in X : y \leq \overset{\bullet}{\complement}_M$ in $o_2\}$.

1. For $x_1, x_2 \in \mathcal{X}_{\overset{\bullet}{C}} \setminus Y$, if $x_1 \bowtie x_2$ in o_1 then add $x_1 \bowtie x_2$ to o_3.
2. For $y \in Y$, if $y \bowtie \overset{\bullet}{\complement}_i$ in o_2, then add $y \bowtie \overset{\bullet}{C}_i$ to o_3.
3. For $z_1, z_2 \in \mathcal{X}_{\overset{\bullet}{C}}$ such that $\overset{\bullet}{C}_i < z_1 < \overset{\bullet}{C}_{i+1}$ and $\overset{\bullet}{C}_i < z_2 < \overset{\bullet}{C}_{i+1}$ in o_3,
   – add $z_1 < z_2$ to o_3 if $\eta_3 \models \{\overset{\bullet}{C}_i\} < \{z_1\} < \{z_2\}$, $\eta_3 \models \{z_2\} < \{\overset{\bullet}{C}_i\} < \{z_1\}$, or $\eta_3 \models \{z_1\} < \{z_2\} < \{\overset{\bullet}{C}_i\}$.
   – add $z_1 = z_2$ to o_3 if $\eta_3 \models \{z_1\} = \{z_2\}$.
4. For $y_1, y_2 \in Y$, if $y_1 \lhd y_2 < \overset{\bullet}{\complement}_0$ in o_2, then add $y_1 \lhd y_2$ in o_3 where $\lhd \in \{<, =\}$.

Note that the computation of o_3 only requires o_1, o_2, and fractional constraints. Then the lemma below holds for well-formed simulating stacks.

A stack $(\eta_1, o_1)(\eta_2, o_2) \ldots (\eta_n, o_n)$ is a well-formed simulating stack if

– For any $i \in [1..n]$, $\eta_i \models x \bowtie y$ iff $x \bowtie y$ in o_i;
– For any $i \in [1..(n-1)]$, $\eta_i(\overset{\bullet}{\complement}_j) = \eta_{i+1}(\overset{\bullet}{\complement}_j)$, $\eta_i(x) = \eta_{i+1}(x)$ if $\overset{\bullet}{\complement}_M < x$ in o_{i+1}, and $\overset{\bullet}{C}_0$ is the smallest in η_i.

Lemma 1. *Let $w\,(\eta_1, o_1)\,(\eta_2, o_2)$ be a well-formed simulating stack. The simulated* **pop**(X) *transition $w\,(\eta_1, o_1)\,(\eta_2, o_2) \xrightarrow{\mathbf{pop}(X)} w\,(\eta_1[X := \eta_2], o_3)$ (where o_3 is obtained by the above steps) preserves well-formedness of the stack.*

Since well-formedness is also preserved under the other transitions, the main result of the present section follows.

Theorem 3. *From a SRTA $\mathfrak{S}$, we can build a SRTA $\mathfrak{S}'$ without comparison constraints such that $\mathcal{L}(\mathfrak{S}) = \mathcal{L}(\mathfrak{S}')$. The size of locations and stack symbols of $\mathfrak{S}'$ are exponential in $|\mathcal{X}|$ and M of $\mathfrak{S}$. However, the size of clocks of $\mathfrak{S}'$ is linear in M of $\mathfrak{S}$.*

Proof (Sketch). In simulated transitions of **pop**, we use the ordering o_2 in the top frame and o_1 in the next frame within a stack at the same time. This operation, however, is not allowed in the formalization of SRTA. Hence we use extended locations q^o with a symbolic ordering o to realize transitions as follows:

a **push** transition: $\langle q_0, w\langle \gamma_1, \eta_1, o_1 \rangle \rangle \xrightarrow{\alpha_1, \mathbf{push}(\gamma_2, X)} \langle q_1, w\langle \gamma_1, \eta_1, o_1 \rangle \langle \gamma_2, \eta_2, o_2 \rangle \rangle$

is realized by

$$\langle q_0^{o_1}, w'\langle (\gamma_1, o), \eta_1 \rangle \rangle \xrightarrow{\alpha_1, \mathbf{push}((\gamma_2, o_1), X)} \langle q_1^{o_2}, w'\langle (\gamma_1, o), \eta_1 \rangle \langle (\gamma_2, o_1), \eta_2 \rangle \rangle.$$

Also, a pop transition

$$\langle q_2, w\langle \gamma_1, \eta_1, o_1 \rangle \langle \gamma_2, \eta_2, o_2 \rangle \rangle \xrightarrow{\alpha_2, \mathbf{pop}(\gamma_2, X)} \langle q_3, w\langle \gamma_1, \eta_1[X := \eta_2], o_3 \rangle \rangle$$

is realized by

$$\langle q_2^{o_2}, w'\langle (\gamma_1, o), \eta_1 \rangle \langle (\gamma_2, o_1), \eta_2 \rangle \rangle \xrightarrow{\alpha_2, \mathbf{pop}((\gamma_2, o_1), X)} \langle q_3^{o_3}, w'\langle (\gamma_1, o), \eta_1[X := \eta_2] \rangle \rangle.$$

To compute o_3 correctly by using fractional constraints, we need multi-step ϵ-transitions that are performed atomically. To ensure this atomicity, we again employ the technique in the proof of Theorem 1. $\qquad\qquad\square$

4   Collapsed and Digital Semantics for Reachability Problem

Based on the result of the previous section, hereafter we consider *SRTA without comparison constraints*. In this section, we consider three techniques and combine them to translate the standard semantics STND into a finite-PDS semantics DIGI via an infinite-PDS semantics COLL. We compare Abdulla's and our proofs of the soundness property that for any transition in the abstract semantics DIGI, there is a corresponding transition in the concrete semantics STND.

The proof of Lemma 4 of Abdulla et al. [1] can be summarized schematically as the left diagram: if $W \to W'$ and $C' \approx W'$, then there exists C such that for all $w \in C$ there exists $w' \in C'$ with $w \to w'$. We find out that this elaborate simulation is called *backward-forward simulations* in Lynch and Vaandrager [11]. It is a source of complications in their proof to simultaneously handle the backward direction (choosing C from C') and the forward direction (finding w' from $w \in C$). In addition, the stack correspondence $\approx$ was defined *indirectly* through a flatten operator, and it is another source of complications in their proof. For example, the operator `flat` flattens a stack of STND $\eta_1 \eta_2 \eta_3$ to a single valuation η where $\eta = \eta_1^{(1)} \uplus \eta_2^{(2)} \uplus \eta_3^{(3)}$ is uniquely obtained by introducing $x^{(i)}$ for x at i-th frame: $\eta_i^{(i)}(x^{(i)}) \triangleq \eta_i(x)$. However, for a stack of the abstract semantics DIGI, `flat` behaves *non*deterministically because as we will see later on we dismiss exact fractional values to obtain a finite-PDS. Then there are many ways to arrange clocks in a linear order.

In contrast, we clearly solve these problems as Lemmas 3 and 6 by considering the intermediate semantics COLL. This allows us to completely separate the above mixed simulation into two simple simulations and *directly* define correspondences $\sim$ and $\models$ in a componentwise manner.

We use the following run of STND as a running example of this section:

$$\eta_1 \, \eta_2 \xrightarrow{\text{push}(\emptyset)} \eta_1 \, \eta_2 \, \mathbf{0}_\chi \xrightarrow{x \leftarrow [1,2]} \eta_1 \, \eta_2 \, \eta_3 \xrightarrow{2.0} \eta_1' \, \eta_2' \, \eta_3' \xrightarrow{\text{pop}(\{x\})} \eta_1' \, \eta_4 \quad \text{where}$$

$\eta_1 = \{x \mapsto 0.5\}$, $\eta_2 = \{x \mapsto 2.0\}$, $\eta_3 = \{x \mapsto 1.5\}$, $\eta_i' = \eta_i + 2$, $\eta_4 = \eta_3' = \{x \mapsto 3.5\}$.

4.1 Collapsed Semantics

Removing the unboundedness. Since we consider SRTA without comparison constraints, we can safely collapse the integral parts of clocks which are larger than M where $\mathsf{M} \geq \max\{j : (i,j) \text{ or } [i,j] \text{ appears in interval constraints}\}$. For example, if $\mathsf{M} = 2$, we cannot distinguish $\{x \mapsto 2.5; y \mapsto 2.6\}$ and $\{x \mapsto 3.5; y \mapsto 4.6\}$ by any constraints. The above run is collapsed as follows (if $\mathsf{M} = 2$):

$$\lambda_1 \, \lambda_2 \xrightarrow{\text{push}(\emptyset)} \lambda_1 \, \lambda_2 \, \mathbf{0}_\chi \xrightarrow{x \leftarrow [1,2]} \lambda_1 \, \lambda_2 \, \lambda_3 \xrightarrow{2.0} \lambda_1' \, \lambda_2' \, \lambda_3' \xrightarrow{\text{pop}(\{x\})} \lambda_1' \, \lambda_4 \quad \text{where}$$

$\lambda_i = \eta_i \, (i = 1, 2, 3)$, $\lambda_1' = \{x \mapsto \infty.5\}$, $\lambda_2' = \{x \mapsto \infty.0\}$, $\lambda_3' = \{x \mapsto \infty.5\}$, $\lambda_4 = \lambda_3'$.

Definition 3. We define the collapse function to formalize the above argument:

$$\mathcal{C} : \mathbb{Q}^+ \to (\{0, 1, \ldots, \mathsf{M}, \infty\}) \times (\mathbb{Q}^+ \cap [0, 1)); \quad \mathcal{C}(r) \triangleq \begin{cases} (\lfloor r \rfloor, \{r\}) & \text{if } r \leq \mathsf{M} \\ (\infty, \{r\}) & \text{otherwise} \end{cases}$$

We write $v.r$ to denote (v, r). Moreover, $\lfloor v.r \rfloor$ and $\{v.r\}$ denote v and r, respectively. For a concrete valuation η on X, we define the *collapsed valuation of* η by $\mathcal{C}(\eta)(x) \triangleq \mathcal{C}(\eta(x))$. We use Greek letters $\lambda, \ldots$ to denote a collapsed valuation.

Proposition 1. *Let η_1 and η_2 be concrete valuations on X. If $\mathcal{C}(\eta_1) = \mathcal{C}(\eta_2)$,*

Validity. $\eta_1 \models \varphi$ *iff* $\eta_2 \models \varphi$ *for any constraint* φ.
Copying. $\mathcal{C}(\eta_1[x := y]) = \mathcal{C}(\eta_2[x := y])$ *for any* $x, y \in X$.
Restriction. $\mathcal{C}(\eta_1|Y) = \mathcal{C}(\eta_2|Y)$ *for any* $Y \subseteq X$.
Updating. $\mathcal{C}(\eta_1[x := r]) = \mathcal{C}(\eta_2[x := r])$ *for any* $x \in X$ *and* $r \in [0, M]$.
Evolve. $\mathcal{C}(\eta_1 + \delta) = \mathcal{C}(\eta_2 + \delta)$ *for any* $\delta \in \mathbb{Q}^+$.

By Proposition 1, we define several notions for collapsed valuations as follows. Let X be a clock set, η and λ be concrete and collapsed valuations on X, respectively, such that $\mathcal{C}(\eta) = \lambda$. For a constraint φ, we write $\lambda \models \varphi$ if $\eta \models \varphi$. Then $\lambda \models \varphi$ is well-defined because Proposition 1 ensures that the result does not depend on the choice of a witness η for λ. We also define copying $\lambda[x := y]$, restriction $\lambda|Y$, updating $\lambda[x := r]$, and evolve $\lambda + \delta$ in the same way.

We define a quasi-ordering for collapsed valuations. Let λ, λ' be collapsed valuations and η be a concrete valuation such that $\mathcal{C}(\eta) = \lambda$. We write $\lambda \preccurlyeq \lambda'$ if there exists η' such that $\eta \leq \eta'$ and $\mathcal{C}(\eta') = \lambda'$.

Removing entire stack modifications. Collapsed valuations are effective to reduce the unboundedness of the nonnegative rational numbers. However, they are ineffective to reduce entire stack modifications of timed transitions in STND and translate STND into an *infinite-PDS* semantics.

To obtain a corresponding infinite-PDS semantics, we adopt the **lazy time elapsing** technique of Abdulla et al. [1]. Then the above collapsed run is simulated as follows:

$$\lambda_1 \xrightarrow{\mathsf{push}(\emptyset)} \lambda_1 \lambda_2 \xrightarrow{x \leftarrow [1,2]} \lambda_1 \lambda_2' \xrightarrow{2.0} \lambda_1 \lambda_2'' \xrightarrow{\mathsf{pop}(\{x\})} \lambda,$$

where $\lambda_1 = \{x \mapsto 0.5; \dot{x} \mapsto 2.0\}$, $\lambda_2 = \{x \mapsto 2.0; \dot{x} \mapsto 0.0\}$, $\lambda_2' = \{x \mapsto 1.5\}$, and $\lambda_2'' = \{x \mapsto \infty.0; \dot{x} \mapsto \infty.5\}$.

Although we do not evolve the frames below the top frame during the timed transition, we *lazily* evolve λ_1 when performing the $\mathsf{pop}(\{x\})$ transition. To correctly evolve λ_1, we use the marked clocks $\dot{x}$ of λ_1 and $\underset{\bullet}{x}$ of λ_2'' and increase $\lambda_1 + \delta$ until they are compatible: $\lambda_1(\dot{x}) + \delta = \lambda_2''(\underset{\bullet}{x})$.

However, there are two possibilities for compatibility:

- $\delta_1 = 1.0$: $\lambda_1 + \delta_1 = \{\underset{\bullet}{x} \mapsto 1.5; \dot{x} \mapsto \infty.0\}$ is compatible with λ_2''.
- $\delta_2 = 2.0$: $\lambda_1 + \delta_2 = \{\underset{\bullet}{x} \mapsto \infty.5; \dot{x} \mapsto \infty.0\}$ is compatible with λ_2''.

The ambiguity happens because we collapse the integral parts of clocks. In order to overcome this problem, we use the reference clock $\mathcal{C}$ and it is inserted as the value 0.0 when a **push** transition is taken as follows:

$$\Lambda_1 \xrightarrow{\mathsf{push}(\emptyset)} \Lambda_1^{\mathsf{reset}} \Lambda_2 \xrightarrow{x \leftarrow [1,2]} \Lambda_1^{\mathsf{reset}} \Lambda_2' \xrightarrow{2.0} \Lambda_1^{\mathsf{reset}} \Lambda_2'' \xrightarrow{\mathsf{pop}(\{x\})} \Lambda,$$
$$\Lambda_1^{\mathsf{reset}} = \{\underset{\bullet}{x} \mapsto 0.5; \ \dot{x} \mapsto 2.0; \ \dot{\mathcal{C}} \mapsto 0.0\}, \ \Lambda_2 = \{x \mapsto 2.0; \ \dot{x} \mapsto 0.0; \ \mathcal{C} \mapsto 0.0\},$$
$$\Lambda_2' = \{\underset{\bullet}{x} \mapsto 2.0; \ \dot{x} \mapsto 1.5; \ \underset{\bullet}{\mathcal{C}} \mapsto 0.0\}, \ \Lambda_2'' = \{x \mapsto \infty.0; \ \dot{x} \mapsto \infty.5; \ \underset{\bullet}{\mathcal{C}} \mapsto 2.0\}.$$

The clock $\mathcal{C}$ enables us to find the correct corresponding valuation Λ_1' of $\Lambda_1^{\mathsf{reset}}$ as $\Lambda_1' = \Lambda_1^{\mathsf{reset}} + 2.0$ (c.f. Lemma 2) and it also appeared in Abdulla's construction.

To formalize the above lazy time elapsing technique, we define the notion of clock marking and extended clock set.

Definition 4. Let X be a clock set. We define the marked clock sets $\dot{X}$ and $\overset{*}{X}$ of X by marking every clock x as $\dot{x}$ and $\overset{*}{x}$, respectively. For a valuation $\eta \in X_V$, the renamed valuation $\dot{\eta} \in \dot{X}_V$ is defined by $\dot{\eta}(\dot{x}) \triangleq \eta(x)$ for all $x \in X$. We also define the renamed valuation $\overset{*}{\eta} \in \overset{*}{X}_V$. Furthermore, for a constraint $\varphi \in \Phi_X$, we define $\dot{\varphi} \in \Phi_{\dot{X}}$ by renaming every clock x in φ to $\dot{x}$.

We extend the clock set $\mathcal{X}$ to $\mathbb{X}$ by $\mathbb{X} \triangleq \mathcal{X} \cup \{\mathbb{C}\}$. We use $\mathbb{C}$ for the set of collapsed valuations on $\overset{*}{\mathbb{X}} \cup \dot{\mathbb{X}}$ and use capital Greek letters $\Lambda, \ldots$ to denote a collapsed valuation in $\mathbb{C}$.

Let Λ_1 and Λ_2 be collapsed valuations on $\overset{*}{\mathbb{X}} \cup \dot{\mathbb{X}}$. Then,

- the two valuations are **compatible** $\Lambda_1 \parallel \Lambda_2$ if $\Lambda_1(\dot{x}) = \Lambda_2(\overset{*}{x})$ for all $x \in \mathbb{X}$.
- If two valuations are compatible, then the **glued** valuation $\Lambda_1 \oplus \Lambda_2 \in \mathbb{C}$ is defined by $(\Lambda_1 \oplus \Lambda_2)(\overset{*}{x}) \triangleq \Lambda_1(\overset{*}{x})$ and $(\Lambda_1 \oplus \Lambda_2)(\dot{x}) \triangleq \Lambda_2(\dot{x})$ for $x \in \mathbb{X}$.

Collapsed valuations lead to the collapsed semantics COLL, which removes the unboundedness of rationals and entire stack modifications of STND.

Definition 5 (Collapsed Semantics). We define the infinite-PDS $(Q, \Gamma \times \mathbb{C}, \hookrightarrow)$ where $\langle q, w \rangle \hookrightarrow \langle q', w' \rangle$ if there is $\langle q, \tau, q' \rangle \in \Delta$ and $w \overset{\tau}{\hookrightarrow} w'$.

For $\tau \in Op$, we define the action $w \overset{\tau}{\hookrightarrow} w'$ by case analysis on τ as follows:

$$\frac{\Lambda_1^{\mathrm{r}} = \Lambda_1[\overset{*}{\mathbb{C}} := 0] \quad \Lambda_1^{\mathrm{r}} \parallel \Lambda_2 \quad \Lambda_2|\overset{*}{\mathbb{X}} = \mathcal{C}(\mathbf{0}_{\overset{*}{\mathbb{X}}})}{\langle \gamma, \Lambda_1 \rangle \hookrightarrow \langle \gamma, \Lambda_1^{\mathrm{r}} \rangle \langle \gamma', \mathcal{U}(X, \Lambda_2) \rangle} \; \mathbf{push}(\gamma', X) \qquad \frac{r \in I \quad \Lambda' = \Lambda[\dot{x} := r]}{\langle \gamma, \Lambda \rangle \hookrightarrow \langle \gamma, \Lambda' \rangle} \; x \leftarrow I$$

$$\frac{\Lambda_1 \preccurlyeq \Lambda_1' \quad \Lambda_1' \parallel \Lambda_2 \quad \Lambda = \Lambda_1' \oplus \mathcal{U}(\mathcal{X} \setminus X, \Lambda_2)}{\langle \gamma, \Lambda_1 \rangle \langle \gamma', \Lambda_2 \rangle \hookrightarrow \langle \gamma, \Lambda \rangle} \; \mathbf{pop}(\gamma', X) \qquad \frac{\Lambda \models \dot{\varphi}}{\langle \gamma, \Lambda \rangle \hookrightarrow \langle \gamma, \Lambda \rangle} \; \mathbf{check}(\varphi)$$

where $\mathcal{U}(\{x_1, \ldots, x_n\}, \Lambda) \triangleq \Lambda[\dot{x}_1 := \overset{*}{x}_1, \ldots, \dot{x}_n := \overset{*}{x}_n]$ and this intuitively means that copying the values of clocks x_i in the next to the top frame into the top frame. Hence, we use $\mathcal{U}(X, \Lambda_2)$ to define $\mathbf{push}(\gamma', X)$. Also, from the fact that $\eta_1 \eta_2 \to \eta_1[X := \eta_2]$ is equal to $\eta_1 \eta_2 \to \eta_2[(\mathcal{X} \setminus X) := \eta_1]$, we employ $\mathcal{U}(\mathcal{X} \setminus X, \Lambda_2)$ to define $\mathbf{pop}(\gamma', X)$ for fitting the definition of gluing $\oplus$.

In addition, the rules $\langle q, \langle \gamma, \Lambda \rangle \rangle \hookrightarrow \langle q, \langle \gamma, \Lambda' \rangle \rangle$ are added for all $q \in Q$, $\gamma \in \Gamma$, and $\Lambda \preccurlyeq \Lambda'$ to reflect timed transitions in STND.

A stack $\langle \gamma_1, \Lambda_1 \rangle \langle \gamma_2, \Lambda_2 \rangle \ldots \langle \gamma_n, \Lambda_n \rangle$ is *well-formed* WF if for all $i \in [1..(n-1)]$

- $\Lambda_i \models \overset{*}{\mathbb{C}} \in [0,0]$ and there exists Λ_i' such that $\Lambda_i \preccurlyeq \Lambda_i'$ and $\Lambda_i' \parallel \Lambda_{i+1}$.

It can be easily shown that transitions preserve well-formedness. As we mentioned above, the condition $\Lambda_i \models \overset{*}{\mathbb{C}} \in [0,0]$ of the well-formedness is key to ensure the following property and the determinacy of **pop** transitions.

Lemma 2 *If* $WF(w\langle \gamma_1, \Lambda_1 \rangle \langle \gamma_2, \Lambda_2 \rangle)$, *then there exists the unique* Λ_1' *such that* $\Lambda \preccurlyeq \Lambda_1'$ *and* $\Lambda_1' \parallel \Lambda_2$.

This defines the stack correspondence $w \sim w$ of STND and COLL with $WF(w)$:

– $\langle \gamma, \eta \rangle \sim \langle \gamma, \Lambda \rangle$ if $\mathcal{C}(\mathring{\eta}) = \Lambda | \mathring{\mathcal{X}}$.
– $w \langle \gamma_1, \eta_1 \rangle \langle \gamma_2, \eta_2 \rangle \sim w \langle \gamma_1, \Lambda_1 \rangle \langle \gamma_2, \Lambda_2 \rangle$ if $\mathcal{C}(\eta_1 \cup \mathring{\eta}_2) = \Lambda_2 | (\mathring{\mathcal{X}} \cup \mathring{\mathcal{X}})$ and $w \langle \gamma_1, \eta_1 \rangle \sim w \langle \gamma_1, \Lambda_1' \rangle$ where Λ_1' is *uniquely* determined from Λ_1 and Λ_2 by Lemma 2.

This correspondence forms a bisimulation of STND and COLL.

Lemma 3. *Let $\langle q, w \rangle$ and $\langle q, \boldsymbol{w} \rangle$ be configurations of STND and COLL, respectively, with $w \sim \boldsymbol{w}$ and $\mathsf{WF}(\boldsymbol{w})$. If $\langle q, w \rangle \twoheadrightarrow \langle q', w' \rangle$, then there exists $\boldsymbol{w}'$ such that $\langle q, \boldsymbol{w} \rangle \rightarrow \langle q', \boldsymbol{w}' \rangle$ and $w' \sim \boldsymbol{w}'$. Conversely, if $\langle q, \boldsymbol{w} \rangle \rightarrow \langle q', \boldsymbol{w}' \rangle$, then there exists $\langle q', w' \rangle$ such that $\langle q, w \rangle \twoheadrightarrow \langle q', w' \rangle$ and $w' \sim \boldsymbol{w}'$. We use $c_1 \twoheadrightarrow c_2$ to denote a timed transition $c_1 \overset{\delta}{\rightsquigarrow} c_2$ or discrete transition $c_1 \overset{\alpha}{\rightarrow} c_2$ in STND.*

4.2   Digital Valuations and Finite-PDS Semantics

The COLL semantics cannot be formalized as finite-PDS for the denseness of rationals. To remove the denseness, we define digital valuations and give the digital semantics DIGI. The definition is based on *regions* of Abdulla et al. in [1].

Definition 6 (Digital Valuations). Let X be a clock set. A sequence of sets $\boldsymbol{d} = d_0 d_1 \ldots d_n$, where $d_i \subseteq X \times \{0, \ldots, \mathsf{M}, \infty\}$, is a *digital valuation* on X if $\boldsymbol{d}$ satisfies the following conditions:

– Every clock in X appears in $\boldsymbol{d}$ exactly once.
– Except d_0, all the sets d_i are not empty: $d_i \neq \emptyset$ for all $i \in [1..n]$.
– The constant M only appears at d_0: if $(x, \mathsf{M}) \in d_i$, then $i = 0$.

Let λ be a collapsed valuations on X. We write $\lambda \models \boldsymbol{d}$ if the following hold:

– $\boldsymbol{d}$ reflects collapsed integrals: for all $x \in X$, $(x, \lfloor \lambda(x) \rfloor) \in d_i$ holds for some i.
– For all $x \in X$, $\{\lambda(x)\} = 0.0$ iff x is in d_0.
– Fractional order: $\{\lambda(x)\} \bowtie \{\lambda(y)\}$ iff x is in d_i and y is in d_j for some $i \bowtie j$.

The realization relation $\models$ is **functional**: for a collapsed valuation λ, there exists the unique digital valuation $\mathcal{D}(\lambda)$ such that $\lambda \models \mathcal{D}(\lambda)$.

Let us see an example with $\mathsf{M} = 1$:

$$\{x \mapsto 0.0; y \mapsto 0.3\} \preccurlyeq \{x \mapsto 0.5; y \mapsto 0.8\} \preccurlyeq \{x \mapsto 0.7; y \mapsto 1.0\} \preccurlyeq \{x \mapsto 0.9; y \mapsto \infty.2\}$$
$$\overset{\mathbb{T}}{} \qquad \overset{\mathbb{T}}{} \qquad \overset{\mathbb{T}}{} \qquad \overset{\mathbb{T}}{}$$
$$\{(x,0)\}\{(y,0)\} \preceq \emptyset\{(x,0)\}\{(y,0)\} \preceq \{(y,1)\}\{(x,0)\} \preceq \emptyset\{(y,\infty)\}\{(x,0)\}$$

The relation $\boldsymbol{d} \preceq \boldsymbol{d}'$ and other operations are defined just as collapsed valuations.

Proposition 2. *Let λ_1 and λ_2 be collapsed valuations on X. If $\mathcal{D}(\lambda_1) = \mathcal{D}(\lambda_2)$,*

Validity. $\lambda_1 \models \varphi$ *iff* $\lambda_2 \models \varphi$ *for any constraint* φ.
Copying. $\mathcal{D}(\lambda_1[x := y]) = \mathcal{D}(\lambda_2[x := y])$ *for any* $x, y \in X$.
Restriction. $\mathcal{D}(\lambda_1|Y) = \mathcal{D}(\lambda_2|Y)$ *for any* $Y \subseteq X$.
Integer Update. $\mathcal{D}(\lambda_1[x := n]) = \mathcal{D}(\lambda_2[x := n])$ *for any* $x \in X$ *and* $n \in [0..\mathsf{M}]$.
Elapse. *If* $\lambda_1 \preccurlyeq \lambda_1'$, *then there exists* λ_2' *such that* $\lambda_2 \preccurlyeq \lambda_2'$ *and* $\mathcal{D}(\lambda_1') = \mathcal{D}(\lambda_2')$.

We define *validity* $\boldsymbol{d} \models \varphi$, *copying* $\boldsymbol{d}[x := y]$, *restriction* $\boldsymbol{d}|Y$, and *quasi-ordering* $\boldsymbol{d} \preceq \boldsymbol{d}'$ similarly as collapsed valuations. Moreover, we define discrete updates $\boldsymbol{d}[x := n]$ for $x \in X$ and $n \in [0..\mathsf{M}]$ by: $\boldsymbol{d}[x := n] \triangleq \mathcal{D}(\lambda[x := n])$ where λ is a witness $\lambda \models \boldsymbol{d}$. These are well-defined by Proposition 2. We define the *update* $\boldsymbol{d}[x \leftarrow I] \triangleq \{\, \mathcal{D}(\,\lambda[x := r]\,) : r \in I, \lambda \models \boldsymbol{d}\,\}$ for a clock x and an interval I.

Lemma 4. *If* $\boldsymbol{d} \preceq \boldsymbol{d}'$ *and* $\lambda' \models \boldsymbol{d}'$, *then there is* λ *such that* $\lambda \preccurlyeq \lambda'$ *and* $\lambda \models \boldsymbol{d}$.

This lemma is crucial for the backward simulation lemma, Lemma 6, and peculiar to collapsed valuations. Indeed, this fails if we consider $\eta \models \boldsymbol{d}$ of concrete and digital valuations. Let us consider $\boldsymbol{d} = \{(y,1)\}\{(x,0)\} \preceq \emptyset\{(y,\infty)\}\{(x,0)\} = \boldsymbol{d}'$ and take $\eta' = \{x \mapsto 0.9; y \mapsto 2.2\}$ for $\eta' \models \boldsymbol{d}'$. There are no concrete valuations η such that $\eta \leq \eta'$ and $\eta \models \boldsymbol{d}$ because $y - x < 1$ in $\boldsymbol{d}$ but $y - x = 1.3$ in η'.

Digital Semantics. We use $\boldsymbol{D}, \ldots$ to denote a digital valuation on $\overset{\bullet}{\mathbb{X}} \cup \overset{\bullet}{\mathbb{X}}$. As the semantics COLL, we define the compatibility and gluing as follows:

- We write $\boldsymbol{D}_1 \parallel \boldsymbol{D}_2$ if $\exists \Lambda_1, \Lambda_2. \ \Lambda_1 \models \boldsymbol{D}_1, \ \Lambda_2 \models \boldsymbol{D}_2$, and $\Lambda_1 \parallel \Lambda_2$;
- The glued valuations are defined by:

$$\boldsymbol{D}_1 \oplus \boldsymbol{D}_2 \triangleq \{\mathcal{D}(\Lambda) : \Lambda_1 \models \boldsymbol{D}_1, \ \Lambda_2 \models \boldsymbol{D}_2, \ \Lambda_1 \parallel \Lambda_2, \ \Lambda \in \Lambda_1 \oplus \Lambda_2\}.$$

Non-determinism Example. We revisit our running example to see the essential non-determinism of the gluing in **pop**.

$$\boldsymbol{D}_1 \xrightarrow{\mathsf{push}(\emptyset)} \boldsymbol{D}_1^{\mathsf{r}} \boldsymbol{D}_2 \xrightarrow{x \leftarrow [1,2]} \boldsymbol{D}_1^{\mathsf{r}} \boldsymbol{D}_2' \overset{2.0}{\leadsto} \boldsymbol{D}_1^{\mathsf{r}} \boldsymbol{D}_2'' \xrightarrow{\mathsf{pop}(\{x\})} \boldsymbol{D},$$

$$\boldsymbol{D}_1^{\mathsf{r}} = \mathcal{D}(\Lambda_1^{\mathsf{reset}}) = \{(\overset{\bullet}{\mathsf{C}}, 0), (\dot{x}, 2)\}\{(x, 0)\}, \quad \boldsymbol{D}_2 = \{(\mathsf{C}, 0), (\dot{x}, 0), (x, 2)\},$$

$$\boldsymbol{D}_2' = \{(\mathsf{C}, 0), (x, 2)\}\{(\dot{x}, 1)\}, \qquad \boldsymbol{D}_2'' = \{(\mathsf{C}, 2), (x, \infty)\}\{(\dot{x}, \infty)\}.$$

To perform **pop**$(\{x\})$, we compute $\boldsymbol{D}_1'$ such that $\boldsymbol{D}_1^{\mathsf{r}} \preceq \boldsymbol{D}_1'$ and $\boldsymbol{D}_1' \parallel \boldsymbol{D}_2''$ and obtain $\boldsymbol{D}_1' = \{(\overset{\bullet}{\mathsf{C}}, 2), (\dot{x}, \infty)\}\{(x, \infty)\}$. Then,

$$\boldsymbol{D}_1' \oplus \mathcal{U}(\emptyset, \boldsymbol{D}_2'') = \big(\{(\overset{\bullet}{\mathsf{C}}, 2), (\dot{x}, \infty)\}\{(x, \infty)\}\big) \oplus \big(\{(\mathsf{C}, 2), (x, \infty)\}\{(\dot{x}, \infty)\}\big)$$
$$= \{\, \emptyset\{(x, \infty), (\dot{x}, \infty)\}, \ \emptyset\{(x, \infty)\}\{(\dot{x}, \infty)\}, \ \emptyset\{(\dot{x}, \infty)\}\{(x, \infty)\} \,\}.$$

Namely there are three choices for $\boldsymbol{D}$ in the order of $\dot{x}$ and x because we dismiss the fractional values from digital valuations to remove the denseness of rationals.

Digital valuations lead to the digital semantics DIGI as *finite-PDS*. Since the definition is given by the same way as the COLL semantics, we give it in the long version [13]. The definition of the well-formedness $\mathsf{WF}(\boldsymbol{W})$ is also omitted.

Lemma 5. *The following properties hold for well-formed stacks.*

- *If* $\mathsf{WF}(\boldsymbol{W})$ *and* $\langle q, \boldsymbol{W} \rangle \to \langle q', \boldsymbol{W}' \rangle$, *then* $\boldsymbol{W}'$ *is also well-formed.*
- *If* $\mathsf{WF}(\boldsymbol{W})$, *then there exists* $\boldsymbol{w}$ *such that* $\mathsf{WF}(\boldsymbol{w})$ *and* $\boldsymbol{w} \models \boldsymbol{W}$.
  The realization $\Lambda_1 \ldots \Lambda_n \models \boldsymbol{D}_1 \ldots \boldsymbol{D}_n$ *holds if* $\Lambda_i \models \boldsymbol{D}_i$ *for all* $i \in [1..n]$.

Let W be a well-formed stack, then there is a well-formed stack $\mathsf{WF}(w)$ such that $w \models W$ by Lemma 5. Since digital valuations are an abstraction of collapsed valuations, if $\langle q, w \rangle \to \langle q', w' \rangle$ then there exists W' such that $\langle q, W \rangle \to \langle q', W' \rangle$ and $w' \models W'$. By contrast, the counterpart does not hold for the nondeterminism of **pop** rule in DIGI (c.f. the above example). However, we can show the following backward-direction simulation by Lemma 4.

Lemma 6. *If $\mathsf{WF}(W)$, $\langle q, W \rangle \to \langle q', W' \rangle$, $w' \models W'$, and $\mathsf{WF}(w')$, then there exists a well-formed stack w such that $\langle q, w \rangle \to \langle q', w' \rangle$ and $w \models W$.*

Finally, Lemmas 3 and 6 imply our main theorem.

Theorem 4. *The following are equivalent:*

(1) In STND, *there is a run from $\langle q_{init}, \langle \bot, \mathbf{0}_\mathcal{X} \rangle \rangle$ to $\langle q_{final}, w \rangle$ for some stack w;*

(2) In DIGI, *there exists W such that $\langle q_{init}, \langle \bot, (\mathcal{D} \circ \mathcal{C})(\mathbf{0}_{\underset{\bullet}{X}} \cup \mathbf{0}_{\underset{\bullet}{X}}) \rangle \rangle \to^* \langle q_{final}, W \rangle$.*

5   Conclusion and Future Works

We have studied synchronized recursive timed automata (SRTA) and shown that the reachability problem of SRTA is EXPTIME-complete. Our SRTA are described from the two perspectives: (1) SRTA are a variant of recursive timed automata (RTA) of Trivedi and Wojtczak, and Benerecetti et al. [3,12] because SRTA are obtained by synchronizing timed transitions of RTA, (2) SRTA extend timed pushdown automata of Abdulla et al. [1] because SRTA are obtained by adding bounded updates ($x \leftarrow [i,j]$ and $x \leftarrow (i,j)$), diagonal constraints, and fractional constraints to their automata. We have also introduced an intermediate semantics to simplify our decidability proof of the reachability problem.

In the formalization of SRTA, we adopt bounded updates. Since our updates are performed within an interval, we can simulate diagonal constraints $x - y \bowtie k$ in Sect. 2 by using comparisons $x \bowtie y$ and fractional constraints $\{x\} \bowtie \{y\}$. As already proved by Bouyer et al. in [6], the presence of both *unbounded* updates $x \leftarrow [i, \infty)$ and diagonal constraints enables timed automata to simulate two-counter machines. However, up to the authors' knowledge, the combination of unbounded updates, comparison constraints, and fractional constraints has not been studied yet. We think that this combination further enlarges the decidable class of pushdown-extensions of timed automata.

Acknowledgement. This work was supported by JSPS KAKENHI Grant Number 15J01843 and 15K00087.

References

1. Abdulla, P., Atig, M., Stenman, J.: Dense-timed pushdown automata. In: LICS 2012, pp. 35–44. IEEE (2012)
2. Alur, R., Dill, D.: A theory of timed automata. TCS **126**(2), 183–235 (1994)

3. Benerecetti, M., Minopoli, S., Peron, A.: Analysis of timed recursive state machines. In: TIME, pp. 61–68. IEEE (2010)
4. Bérard, B., Diekert, V., Gastin, P., Petit, A.: Characterization of the expressive power of silent transitions in timed automata. Fundam. Inf. **36**(2), 145–182 (1998)
5. Bouajjani, A., Esparza, J., Maler, O.: Reachability analysis of pushdown automata: Application to model-checking. In: Mazurkiewicz, A., Winkowski, j (eds.) CONCUR '97: Concurrency Theory. LNCS, vol. 1243, pp. 135–150. Springer, Heidelberg (1997)
6. Bouyer, P., Dufourd, C., Fleury, E., Petit, A.: Updatable timed automata. TCS **321**(2–3), 291–345 (2004)
7. Büchi, J.: Regular canonical systems. Arch. Math. Logik Grundlag **6**, 91–111 (1964)
8. Clemente, L., Lasota, S.: Timed pushdown automata revisited. In: LICS 2015, pp. 738–749. IEEE (2015)
9. Finkel, A., Willems, B., Wolper, P.: A direct symbolic approach to model checking pushdown systems. In: INFINITY 1997, pp. 27–37. Elsevier (1997)
10. Krishna, S., Manasa, L., Trivedi, A.: What's decidable about recursive hybrid automata? In: HSCC 2015, pp. 31–40. ACM (2015)
11. Lynch, N., Vaandrager, F.: Forward and backward simulations. Inf. Comp. **121**(2), 214–233 (1995)
12. Trivedi, A., Wojtczak, D.: Recursive timed automata. In: Bouajjani, A., Chin, W.-N. (eds.) ATVA 2010. LNCS, vol. 6252, pp. 306–324. Springer, Heidelberg (2010)
13. Uezato, Y., Minamide, Y.: Synchronized recursive timed automata (2015). http://score.cs.tsukuba.ac.jp/~uezato/SRTA.pdf

Focused Labeled Proof Systems for Modal Logic

Dale Miller and Marco Volpe$^{(\boxtimes)}$

Inria and LIX, École Polytechnique, Paris, France
marco.volpe@inria.fr, dale.miller@inria.fr

Abstract. Focused proofs are sequent calculus proofs that group inference rules into alternating *positive* and *negative* phases. These phases can then be used to define macro-level inference rules Gentzen's original and tiny introduction and structural rules. We show here that the inference rules of labeled proof systems for modal logics can similarly be described as pairs of such phases within the *LKF* focused proof system for first-order classical logic. We consider the system *G3K* of Negri for the modal logic *K* and define a translation from labeled modal formulas into first-order polarized formulas and show a strict correspondence between derivations in the two systems, i.e., each rule application in *G3K* corresponds to a *bipole*—a pair of a positive and a negative phases—in *LKF*. Since geometric axioms (when properly polarized) induce bipoles, this strong correspondence holds for all modal logics whose Kripke frames are characterized by geometric properties. We extend these results to present a focused labeled proof system for this same class of modal logics and show its soundness and completeness. The resulting proof system allows one to define a rich set of normal forms of modal logic proofs.

1 Introduction

What is an inference rule? If we try to answer this question in the setting of the sequent calculus, then it seems that we should ask that inference rules have duals and that all occurrences of cut rules and non-atomic initial rules can be eliminated. In a two-sided sequent system, dual inference rules are typically pairs of left and right introduction rules for a given connective. In a one-side sequent system, dual inference rules are usually based on introduction rules for de Morgan dual connectives. Such a definition of inference rules has been suggested by Girard in [9, Section F.5] and formalized by Miller and Pimentel in [13].

In recent years, *focused proof systems* have been introduced as a means of building large scale synthetic inference rules from Gentzen's original, small scale introduction rules. In particular, Andreoli introduced a focused proof system for linear logic [1] and described cut-free proofs as alternating phases of inference rules: a *negative* phase is a collection of invertible inference rules and a *positive* phase is a collection of inference rules that are dual to those in negative phases. This same kind of *focused proof system* has also been extended to both intuitionistic and classical logic in the *LJF* and *LKF* proof systems [10]: the *LKF*

© Springer-Verlag Berlin Heidelberg 2015
M. Davis et al. (Eds.): LPAR-20 2015, LNCS 9450, pp. 266–280, 2015.
DOI: 10.1007/978-3-662-48899-7_19

proof system will play a central role in this paper. In all of these focused proof systems, phases can be used to describe synthetic inference rules by identifying them with either an entire positive or negative phase. In all these cases, cuts and non-atomic initial rules can be eliminated *at the level of synthetic inference rules.*

In this paper, we look at focused proof systems and their possible relationship to modal logic proof systems based on labeled sequents. We shall show that it is possible to emulate precisely the $G3K$ proof system [14] using a simple encoding of modal formulas and inference rules into classical first-order logic in such a way that one inference rule of $G3K$ exactly corresponds to one phase in the translated logic. Such tight emulation means that if one does proof search or proof checking on the focused version of the translated formulas, one is modeling nothing more or less than proof search in $G3K$.

One alternation of a positive followed by a negative phase (reading from conclusion to premises) is a natural unit of inference in a focused proof system: such a pair of phases is called a *bipole*. A formula that induces a bipole is a *bipolar formula* and examples of such formulas are *geometric formulas*, when properly polarized. As a result, we are able to show that we can use focused classical proofs to precisely emulate modal proofs whenever Kripke frames are characterized by geometric properties. Since every (infinitary) first-order theory has a geometric conservative extension [6], the limitation to geometric theories is not restrictive. We also present a focused proof system for any classical propositional modal logic whose Kripke frames are described using geometric theories.

2 Background

2.1 Modal Logic

The language of *(propositional) modal formulas* consists of a functionally complete set of classical connectives (here we will use a minimal one, but other connectives, defined as usual, will be sometimes employed in the rest of the paper), a *modal operator* $\Box$ (here we will also use explicitly its dual $\Diamond$) and a denumerable set $\mathcal{P}$ of *propositional symbols*, according to the following grammar:

$$A ::= P \mid \perp \mid A \supset A \mid \Box A \mid \Diamond A,$$

where $P \in \mathcal{P}$. The semantics is usually defined by means of *Kripke frames*, i.e., pairs $\mathcal{F} = (W, R)$ where W is a non empty set of *worlds* and R is a binary relation on W. A *Kripke model* is a triple $\mathcal{M} = (W, R, V)$ where (W, R) is a Kripke frame and $V : W \to 2^{\mathcal{P}}$ is a function that assigns to each world in W a (possibly empty) set of propositional symbols.

Truth of a modal formula at a point w in a Kripke structure $\mathcal{M} = (W, R, V)$ is the smallest relation $\models$ satisfying:

$$
\begin{aligned}
\mathcal{M}, w &\models P & &\text{iff} & &p \in V(w) \\
\mathcal{M}, w &\models A \supset B & &\text{iff} & &\mathcal{M}, w \models A \text{ implies } \mathcal{M}, w \models B \\
\mathcal{M}, w &\models \Box A & &\text{iff} & &\mathcal{M}, w' \models A \text{ for all } w' \text{ s.t. } wRw' \\
\mathcal{M}, w &\models \Diamond A & &\text{iff} & &\text{there exists } w' \text{ s.t. } wRw' \text{ and } \mathcal{M}, w' \models A.
\end{aligned}
$$

By extension, we write $\mathcal{M} \models A$ when $\mathcal{M}, w \models A$ for all $w \in W$ and we write $\models A$ when $\mathcal{M} \models A$ for every Kripke structure $\mathcal{M}$. The former definition characterizes the basic modal logic K. Several further modal logics can be defined as extensions of K by simply restricting the class of frames we consider. Many of the restrictions we are interested in are definable as formulas of first-order logic where the binary predicate $R(x, y)$ refers to the corresponding accessibility relation. Table 1 summarizes some of the most common frame logics, describing the corresponding frame property, together with the modal axiom capturing it [17]. We will refer to the logic satisfying the axioms $F_1, \ldots, F_n$ as $KF_1 \ldots F_n$.

Table 1. Axioms and corresponding first-order conditions on R.

Axiom	Condition	First-order formula
T: $\Box A \supset A$	Reflexivity	$\forall x . R(x, x)$
4: $\Box A \supset \Box \Box A$	Transitivity	$\forall x, y, z . (R(x, y) \wedge R(y, z)) \supset R(x, z)$
5: $\Box A \supset \Box \Diamond A$	Euclideaness	$\forall x, y, z . (R(x, y) \wedge R(x, z)) \supset R(y, z)$
B: $A \supset \Box \Diamond A$	Symmetry	$\forall x, y . R(x, y) \supset R(y, x)$
3: $\Box(\Box A \supset B) \vee \Box(\Box B \supset A)$	Connectedness	$\forall x, y, z . (R(x, y) \wedge R(x, z)) \supset (R(y, z) \vee R(z, y))$
D: $\Box A \supset \Diamond A$	Seriality	$\forall x \exists y . R(x, y)$
2: $\Diamond \Box A \supset \Box \Diamond A$	Directedness	$\forall x, y, z . (R(x, y) \wedge R(x, z)) \supset \exists t (R(y, t) \wedge R(z, t))$

2.2 A Labeled Proof System for Modal Logic

The basic idea behind labeled proof systems for modal logic is to internalize elements of the corresponding Kripke semantics (namely, the worlds of a Kripke structure and the accessibility relation between such worlds) into the syntax. As a concrete example of such a system, here we will consider the system $G3K$ presented in [14]. $G3K$ *formulas* are either *labeled formulas* of the form $x : A$ or *relational atoms* of the form xRy, where x, y range over a set of variables and A is a modal formula (here we consider also $\wedge$ and $\vee$ as primitive connectives). In the following, we will use φ, ψ to denote $G3K$ formulas. $G3K$ *sequents* have the form $\Gamma \vdash \Delta$, where Γ and Δ are multisets containing labeled formulas and relational atoms. In Fig. 1, we present the rules of $G3K$, which is proved to be sound and complete for the basic modal logic K [14]. The system is then extended to cover all modal logics whose Kripke frames are determined by geometric axioms (note that all the logics in Table 1 fall inside this class), i.e., axioms of the form:

$$\forall \overline{z}(P_1 \wedge \ldots \wedge P_m \supset (\exists x_1 (Q_{11} \wedge \ldots \wedge Q_{1k_1}) \vee \ldots \vee \exists x_n (Q_{n1} \wedge \ldots \wedge Q_{nk_n})))$$

where each P_i and Q_{jk} is a relational atom[1]. As described in [14], the following general rule scheme

$$\frac{\overline{Q_1}(y_1/x_1), \overline{P}, \Gamma \vdash \Delta \quad \ldots \quad \overline{Q_n}(y_n/x_n), \overline{P}, \Gamma \vdash \Delta}{\overline{P}, \Gamma \vdash \Delta} \; GRS$$

can be used instead of the geometric axiom above: here $\overline{Q_j}$ and $\overline{P}$ denote the multisets of relational atoms $Q_{j1}, \ldots, Q_{jk_j}$ and $P_1, \ldots, P_m$, respectively, and the eigenvariables

---

[1] Note that, for simplicity, as in [14], we restrict to the case where only a single variable is bound to each existential quantifier.

$y_1, \ldots, y_n$ do not occur free in the conclusion. In Fig. 2, the rules for capturing the frame properties of Table 1 are shown. By modularly adding such rules to the base system $G3K$, we get a system for the corresponding logic. In the following, we will denote by $G3K^*$ any extension of $G3K$ with rules following the geometric rule scheme. We remark that all structural rules (*cut* included) are admissible in $G3K^*$ [14].

INITIAL RULES

$$\overline{x : P, \Gamma \vdash \Delta, x : P} \; init$$

PROPOSITIONAL RULES

$$\frac{x : A, x : B, \Gamma \vdash \Delta}{x : A \wedge B, \Gamma \vdash \Delta} \; L\wedge \qquad \frac{\Gamma \vdash \Delta, x : A \quad \Gamma \vdash \Delta, x : B}{\Gamma \vdash \Delta, x : A \wedge B} \; R\wedge$$

$$\frac{x : A, \Gamma \vdash \Delta \quad x : B, \Gamma \vdash \Delta}{x : A \vee B, \Gamma \vdash \Delta} \; L\vee \qquad \frac{\Gamma \vdash \Delta, x : A, x : B}{\Gamma \vdash \Delta, x : A \vee B} \; R\vee$$

$$\frac{\Gamma \vdash \Delta, x : A \quad x : B, \Gamma \vdash \Delta}{x : A \supset B, \Gamma \vdash \Delta} \; L\supset \qquad \frac{x : A, \Gamma \vdash \Delta, x : B}{\Gamma \vdash \Delta, x : A \supset B} \; R\supset$$

$$\overline{x : \bot, \Gamma \vdash \Delta} \; L\bot$$

MODAL RULES

$$\frac{y : A, x : \Box A, xRy, \Gamma \vdash \Delta}{x : \Box A, xRy, \Gamma \vdash \Delta} \; L\Box \qquad \frac{xRy, \Gamma \vdash \Delta, y : A}{\Gamma \vdash \Delta, x : \Box A} \; R\Box$$

$$\frac{xRy, y : A, \Gamma \vdash \Delta}{x : \Diamond A, \Gamma \vdash \Delta} \; L\Diamond \qquad \frac{xRy, \Gamma \vdash \Delta, x : \Diamond A, y : A}{xRy, \Gamma \vdash \Delta, x : \Diamond A} \; R\Diamond$$

In $R\Box$ and $L\Diamond$, y does not occur in the conclusion.

Fig. 1. $G3K$: a labeled proof system for the modal logic K

$$\frac{xRx, \Gamma \vdash \Delta}{\Gamma \vdash \Delta} \; refl \qquad \frac{xRz, xRy, yRz, \Gamma \vdash \Delta}{xRy, yRz, \Gamma \vdash \Delta} \; trans \qquad \frac{yRx, xRy, \Gamma \vdash \Delta}{xRy, \Gamma \vdash \Delta} \; symm$$

$$\frac{yRz, xRy, xRz, \Gamma \vdash \Delta}{xRy, xRz, \Gamma \vdash \Delta} \; eucl \qquad \frac{xRy, \Gamma \vdash \Delta}{\Gamma \vdash \Delta} \; ser \qquad \frac{yRu, zRu, xRy, xRz, \Gamma \vdash \Delta}{xRy, xRz, \Gamma \vdash \Delta} \; dir$$

$$\frac{xRy, xRz, yRz, \Gamma \vdash \Delta \quad xRy, xRz, zRy, \Gamma \vdash \Delta}{xRy, xRz, \Gamma \vdash \Delta} \; conn$$

In *ser*, $y \notin \Gamma, \Delta$. In *dir*, u does not occur in the conclusion.

Fig. 2. Rules for capturing relational properties.

2.3   The Standard Translation from Modal Logic into Classical Logic

The following *standard translation* (see, e.g., [2]) provides a bridge between propositional modal logic and first-order classical logic:

$$ST_x(P) = P(x) \qquad\qquad ST_x(A \supset B) = ST_x(A) \supset ST_x(B)$$
$$ST_x(\bot) = \bot \qquad\qquad ST_x(\Box A) = \forall y(R(x,y) \supset ST_y(A))$$
$$ST_x(\Diamond A) = \exists y(R(x,y) \wedge ST_y(A))$$

where x is a free variable denoting the world in which the formula is evaluated. The first-order language into which modal formulas are translated is usually referred to as *first-order correspondence language* [2] and consists of a binary predicate symbol R and a unary predicate symbol P for each $P \in \mathcal{P}$. When a modal operator is translated, a new fresh variable[2] is introduced. It is easy to show that for any modal formula A, any model $\mathcal{M}$ and any world w, we have that $\mathcal{M}, w \models A$ if and only if $\mathcal{M} \models ST_x(A)[x \leftarrow w]$.

2.4   A Focused Proof System for First-Order Classical Logic

Figure 3 presents the LKF proof system presented in [10] (where some inference rules have been renamed). This system involves *polarized* formulas, built using atomic formulas, the usual first-order quantifiers $\forall$ and $\exists$, and polarized versions of the logical connectives and constants t^-, t^+, f^-, f^+, $\vee^-$, $\vee^+$, $\wedge^-$, and $\wedge^+$. The positive and negative versions of connectives and constants have identical truth conditions but different inference rules inside the polarized proof system. For example, the introduction rule for $\vee^-$ is invertible while the introduction rule for $\vee^+$ is not. All polarized formulas are (as the name implies) either positive or negative. In particular, if a formula's top-level connective is t^+, f^+, $\vee^+$, $\wedge^+$, or $\exists$, then that formula is positive. Dually, if a formula's top-level connective is t^-, f^-, $\vee^-$, $\wedge^-$, or $\forall$, then it is negative. In this way, every polarized formula is classified except for literals: to polarize them, we are allowed to fix the polarity of atomic formulas in any way we see fit. We may ask that all atomic formulas are positive, that they are all negative, or we can mix polarity assignments. In any case, if A is a positive atomic formula, then it is a positive formula and $\neg A$ is a negative formula: conversely, if A is a negative atomic formula, then it is a negative formula and $\neg A$ is a positive formula.

We shall find it important to break a sequence of negative or positive connectives by inserting *delays*: if B is a polarized formula then we define $\partial^-(B)$ to be (the always negative) $B\wedge^- t^-$ and $\partial^+(B)$ to be (the always positive) $B\wedge^+ t^+$. From such a definition, the following rules can be derived:

$$\frac{\vdash \Theta \Uparrow B, \Gamma}{\vdash \Theta \Uparrow \partial^-(B), \Gamma} \, \partial^- \qquad\qquad \frac{\vdash \Theta \Downarrow B}{\vdash \Theta \Downarrow \partial^+(B)} \, \partial^+$$

Returning to the proof system in Fig. 3, we note that the inference rules there involve two kinds of sequents: $\vdash \Theta \Uparrow \Gamma$ and $\vdash \Theta \Downarrow B$, where Θ is a multiset of polarized formulas, B is a polarized formula, and Γ is a *list* of polarized formulas. (It is possible to relax the list structure of Γ to be a multiset but that relaxation is not useful in this paper). The formula occurrence B in the $\Downarrow$ sequent is called the *focus* of that sequent. The completeness of LKF can be stated as follows [10]: if B is an (unpolarized) classical logic theorem and $\hat{B}$ is any polarization of B, then $\vdash \cdot \Uparrow \hat{B}$ is provable in LKF. Clearly, the choice of polarization does not affect provability but it can have a big impact on the structure of proofs.

To illustrate the use of delays, notice that the sequent $\vdash \Theta \Downarrow \exists x \exists y. B(x, y)$ must be the result of applying (at least) two $\exists$-introduction rules. In contrast, the sequent $\vdash \Theta \Downarrow \exists x \partial^-(\exists y. B(x, y))$ must be the conclusion of only one $\exists$-introduction rule: a separate instantiation of $\exists y$ can take place elsewhere in the proof.

A polarized formula B is a *bipolar formula* if B is a positive formula and no positive subformula occurrence of B is in the scope of a negative connective in B. A *bipole* is

---

[2] In fact, it is possible to show that every modal formula can be translated into a formula in the fragment of first-order logic which uses only two variables [2]. By the decidability of such a fragment, an easy proof of the decidability of propositional modal logic follows.

a pair of a negative phase below a positive phase within LKF: thus, bipoles are macro inference rules in which the conclusion and the premises are ⇑-sequents with no formulas to the right of the up-arrow.

ASYNCHRONOUS INTRODUCTION RULES

$$\frac{}{\vdash \Theta \Uparrow t^-, \Gamma} \; t^- \qquad \frac{\vdash \Theta \Uparrow A, \Gamma \quad \vdash \Theta \Uparrow B, \Gamma}{\vdash \Theta \Uparrow A \wedge^- B, \Gamma} \; \wedge^- \qquad \frac{\vdash \Theta \Uparrow \Gamma}{\vdash \Theta \Uparrow f^-, \Gamma} \; f^- \qquad \frac{\vdash \Theta \Uparrow A, B, \Gamma}{\vdash \Theta \Uparrow A \vee^- B, \Gamma} \; \vee^-$$

$$\frac{\vdash \Theta \Uparrow [y/x]B, \Gamma}{\vdash \Theta \Uparrow \forall x.B, \Gamma} \; \forall \dagger$$

SYNCHRONOUS INTRODUCTION RULES

$$\frac{}{\vdash \Theta \Downarrow t^+} \; t^+ \qquad \frac{\vdash \Theta \Downarrow B_1 \quad \vdash \Theta \Downarrow B_2}{\vdash \Theta \Downarrow B_1 \wedge^+ B_2} \; \wedge^+ \qquad \frac{\vdash \Theta \Downarrow B_i}{\vdash \Theta \Downarrow B_1 \vee^+ B_2} \; \vee^+, i \in \{1,2\} \qquad \frac{\vdash \Theta \Downarrow [t/x]B}{\vdash \Theta \Downarrow \exists x.B} \; \exists$$

IDENTITY RULES

$$\frac{}{\vdash \neg P_a, \Theta \Downarrow P_a} \; init \qquad \frac{\vdash \Theta \Uparrow B \quad \vdash \Theta \Uparrow \neg B}{\vdash \Theta \Uparrow \cdot} \; cut$$

STRUCTURAL RULES

$$\frac{\vdash \Theta, C \Uparrow \Gamma}{\vdash \Theta \Uparrow C, \Gamma} \; store \qquad \frac{\vdash \Theta \Uparrow N}{\vdash \Theta \Downarrow N} \; release \qquad \frac{\vdash P, \Theta \Downarrow P}{\vdash P, \Theta \Uparrow \cdot} \; decide$$

Here, P is a positive formula; N a negative formula; P_a a positive literal; C a positive formula or negative literal; and $\neg B$ is the negation normal form of the negation of B. The proviso marked as $\dagger$ is the usual eigenvariable restriction: y is not free in Θ, in Γ, nor in $\forall x.B$.

Fig. 3. The LKF focused proof systems for classical logic (minor differences from [10]).

3   Labeled Proof Systems and Focused Proof Systems

In this section, we compare derivations in $G3K$ (and its extensions) and LKF. In particular, we show that there is a strict correspondence between rule applications in the former and bipoles in the latter. In order to do that, we will define a translation from labeled modal formulas into first-order polarized formulas.

3.1   From Labeled Modal Formulas to Polarized First-Order Formulas

Note that the set of connectives used in the language of $G3K$ differs from that of LKF, where formulas are assumed to be in negation normal form. Given a modal formula A, we denote with A° its negation normal form. In our translation into polarized formulas, we sometimes put a delay in front of a formula only if it is not a literal. For that purpose, we define A^{∂^+} (when A is a first-order formula in negation normal form) to be A if A is a literal and $\partial^+(A)$ otherwise. We extend such a notion to a multiset Γ of formulas by defining $\Gamma^{\partial^+} = \{A^{\partial^+} | A \in \Gamma\}$.

We are now in a position to present our translation from the language of $G3K$ into the language of LKF. Such a translation is based on the standard translation recalled in Sect. 2. Given a world x, we define the translation $[.]_x$ from modal formulas in negation normal form into polarized first-order formulas as:

$$[P]_x = P(x) \qquad [A° \wedge B°]_x = [A°]_x^{\partial^+} \wedge^- [B°]_x^{\partial^+}$$
$$[\neg P]_x = \neg P(x) \qquad [A° \vee B°]_x = [A°]_x^{\partial^+} \vee^- [B°]_x^{\partial^+}$$
$$[\bot]_x = f^- \qquad [\Diamond A°]_x = \exists y (R(x,y) \wedge^+ \partial^- ([A°]_y^{\partial^+}))$$
$$[\Box A°]_x = \forall y (\neg R(x,y) \vee^- [A°]_y^{\partial^+})$$

Based on this, we define the translation $[.]$ from labeled formulas and relational atoms into polarized first-order formulas as $[x : A] = [A°]_x$ and $[xRy] = R(x,y)$. In the following, we will sometimes use the natural extension of this notion to multisets of labeled formulas, i.e., $[\Gamma] = \{[\varphi] \mid \varphi \in \Gamma\}$. Note that predicates of the form $P(x)$ and $R(x,y)$ are considered as having positive polarity.

Finally, we define a translation from $G3K$ sequents into LKF sequents:

$$[(\varphi_1, \ldots, \varphi_n \vdash \psi_1, \ldots, \psi_m)] = \vdash [\neg\varphi_1]^{\partial^+}, \ldots, [\neg\varphi_n]^{\partial^+}, [\psi_1]^{\partial^+}, \ldots, [\psi_m]^{\partial^+} \Uparrow \cdot$$

where $[\neg\varphi]$ is $[(\neg A)°]_x$ if $\varphi = x : A$ and is $\neg R(x,y)$ if $\varphi = xRy$. We will sometimes write $\neg\Gamma$ to denote $\{\neg A \mid A \in \Gamma\}$.

3.2 From $G3K$ to LKF

Given two multisets of LKF formulas Γ and Γ', we say that Γ' *extends* Γ if Γ' contains Γ and $FV(\Gamma) = FV(\Gamma')$, where $FV(\Delta)$ denotes the set of free variables occurring free in Δ. We say that an LKF sequent $\vdash \Gamma \Uparrow \cdot$ *extends* an LKF sequent $\vdash \Gamma' \Uparrow \cdot$ if Γ extends Γ'.

Lemma 1. *Let* $\dfrac{S_1}{S}$ r $\left(\dfrac{S_1 \quad S_2}{S} r\right)$ *be an application of a rule in G3K. Then for any*

LKF sequent S' that extends $[S]$, there exists a derivation $\begin{array}{c} S_1' \\ \vdots \\ S' \end{array}$ $\left(\begin{array}{cc} S_1' & S_2' \\ \vdots \\ S' \end{array}\right)$ *in LKF,*

which is a bipole, and such that S_1' extends $[S_1]$ (S_1' and S_2' extend $[S_1]$ and $[S_2]$, respectively). Furthermore, if $\dfrac{}{S} r$ is a rule application in G3K, then for any LKF sequent S' that extends $[S]$, there exists a proof of S' that is a bipole.

Proof. The proof proceeds by considering all the rules of $G3K$. For example, the translation of the $R\Box$ from Fig. 1 is given by following derivation in LKF:

$$\cfrac{\cfrac{\cfrac{\cfrac{\cfrac{\cfrac{\vdash \neg\Gamma', \Delta', \partial^+([\Box A°]_x), \neg R(x,y), [A°]_y^{\partial^+} \Uparrow \cdot}{\vdash \neg\Gamma', \Delta', \partial^+([\Box A°]_x), \neg R(x,y) \Uparrow [A°]_y^{\partial^+}} \; store}{\vdash \neg\Gamma', \Delta', \partial^+([\Box A°]_x) \Uparrow \neg R(x,y), [A°]_y^{\partial^+}} \; store}{\vdash \neg\Gamma', \Delta', \partial^+([\Box A°]_x) \Uparrow \neg R(x,y) \vee^- [A°]_y^{\partial^+}} \; \vee^-}{\vdash \neg\Gamma', \Delta', \partial^+([\Box A°]_x) \Uparrow \forall y(\neg R(x,y) \vee^- [A°]_y^{\partial^+})} \; \forall}{\vdash \neg\Gamma', \Delta', \partial^+([\Box A°]_x) \Downarrow \forall y(\neg R(x,y) \vee^- [A°]_y^{\partial^+})} \; release}{\vdash \neg\Gamma', \Delta', \partial^+([\Box A°]_x) \Downarrow \partial^+(\forall y(\neg R(x,y) \vee^- [A°]_y^{\partial^+}))} \; \partial^+}{\vdash \neg\Gamma', \Delta', \partial^+([\Box A°]_x) \Uparrow \cdot} \; decide$$

Here Γ' is any extension of $[\Gamma]^{\partial^+}$ and Δ' is any extension of $[\Delta]^{\partial^+}$. Note that the condition on free variables in the definition of extension ensures that $\forall$ can be applied in the derivation above, as the constraint on eigenvariables is satisfied.

Theorem 2. *Let Π be a G3K derivation of a sequent S from the sequents $S_1, \ldots, S_n$. Then there exists an LKF derivation Π' of $[S]$ from $[S_1], \ldots, [S_n]$ (such that each rule application in Π corresponds to a bipole in Π').*

Proof. We proceed bottom-up by starting from the root of Π and build Π' by repeatedly applying Lemma 1. At each step, we get leaves that are extensions of the ones in Π, so that Lemma 1 can be applied again.

3.3   From *LKF* to *G3K*

Given two multisets of LKF formulas Γ and Γ', we say that Γ' is a *contraction* of Γ if Γ contains Γ' and for each formula A in Γ there is at least one occurrence of A in Γ', i.e., Γ and Γ' contain the same set of formulas but Γ can have more occurrences. We say that an LKF sequent $\vdash \Gamma' \Uparrow \cdot$ is a *contraction* of an LKF sequent $\vdash \Gamma \Uparrow \cdot$ if Γ' is a contraction of Γ.

Lemma 3. *Let S' be an LKF sequent of the form $\vdash \Gamma' \Uparrow \cdot$ such that each formula in S' is the translation $[\varphi]$ of some G3K formula φ. For each derivation of the form*
$$\left(\begin{matrix} S'_1 & S'_2 \\ & \vdots \\ & S' \end{matrix} \right) \text{ in LKF that is a bipole, there exist:}$$

(i) a G3K sequent S, such that S' is a contraction of $[S]$; and

(ii) a rule application $\dfrac{S_1}{S}$ $\left(\dfrac{S_1 \quad S_2}{S} \right)$ in G3K such that $S'_1 = [S_1]$ ($S'_1 = [S_1]$ and $S'_2 = [S_2]$).

Furthermore, for each proof of S' that is a bipole, there exist a G3K sequent S, such that S' is a contraction of $[S]$, and a rule application $\overline{S}^{\ init}$ in G3K.

Proof. We have one case for each possible $G3K$ formula φ on the translation of which a *decide* is applied. Let us consider one representative case.

Let $\varphi = x : \Diamond A$. Then we have the following derivation in LKF:

$$
\cfrac{
  \cfrac{
    \vdash \neg\Gamma', \Delta', \partial^+([\Diamond A^\circ]_x) \Downarrow R(x,y) \quad init \qquad
    \cfrac{
      \cfrac{
        \cfrac{
          \vdash \neg\Gamma', \Delta', \partial^+([\Diamond A^\circ]_x), [A^\circ]_y^{\partial^+} \Uparrow \cdot
        }{
          \vdash \neg\Gamma', \Delta', \partial^+([\Diamond A^\circ]_x) \Uparrow [A^\circ]_y^{\partial^+}
        } \ store
      }{
        \vdash \neg\Gamma', \Delta', \partial^+([\Diamond A^\circ]_x) \Uparrow \partial^-([A^\circ]_y^{\partial^+})
      } \ \partial^-
    }{
      \vdash \neg\Gamma', \Delta', \partial^+([\Diamond A^\circ]_x) \Downarrow \partial^-([A^\circ]_y^{\partial^+})
    } \ release
  }{
    \vdash \neg\Gamma', \Delta', \partial^+([\Diamond A^\circ]_x) \Downarrow R(x,y) \wedge^+ \partial^-([A^\circ]_y^{\partial^+})
  } \ \wedge^+
  \\
  \cfrac{}{
    \vdash \neg\Gamma', \Delta', \partial^+([\Diamond A^\circ]_x) \Downarrow \exists y (R(x,y) \wedge^+ \partial^-([A^\circ]_y^{\partial^+}))
  } \ \exists
  \\
  \cfrac{}{
    \vdash \neg\Gamma', \Delta', \partial^+([\Diamond A^\circ]_x) \Downarrow \partial^+(\exists y (R(x,y) \wedge^+ \partial^-([A^\circ]_y^{\partial^+})))
  } \ \partial^+
  \\
  \vdash \neg\Gamma', \Delta', \partial^+([\Diamond A^\circ]_x) \Uparrow \cdot
}{} \ decide
$$

Note that in order to be able to apply the rule *init*, and thus have indeed a bipole, the multiset $\neg\Gamma'$ must contain the formula $\neg R(x,y)$. But then, in $G3K$, we can have the following corresponding rule application:

$$\frac{xRy, \Gamma \vdash \Delta, x : \Diamond A, y : A}{xRy, \Gamma \vdash \Delta, x : \Diamond A} \, R\Diamond$$

where $\Gamma' = [\Gamma]^{\partial^+}$ and $\Delta' = [\Delta]^{\partial^+}$.

Theorem 4. *Let Π' be a proof of a sequent S' in LKF such that $S' = [S]$ for some G3K-sequent S. Then there exists a proof Π of S in G3K (such that each bipole in Π' corresponds to a single rule application in Π).*

Proof. We proceed top-down starting from the leaves of Π' and build Π by repeatedly applying Lemma 3. At each step, we get as the conclusion of a $G3K$ rule application a sequent S^* such that the one obtained in the corresponding step of Π' is a contraction of $[S^*]$. By observing that the contraction rule is (height-preserving) admissible in $G3K$, we can transform the $G3K$ derivation built so far in order to remove possible undesired multiple occurrences of a formula.

The strong correspondence between labeled rule applications and LKF bipoles can also be used to get an immediate proof of the completeness of $G3K$.

Corollary 5. *The system G3K is complete.*

Proof. Follows from the completeness of LKF, the adequacy of the standard translation from the modal language into the first-order classical language (on which our translation is based) and Theorem 4.

3.4   Extensions of K

Here we show how the results of the previous section can be extended to modal logics whose Kripke frames are characterized by properties expressible by means of geometric axioms.

We recall from Sect. 2 that a geometric axiom has the form:

$$\forall \vec{z}(P_1 \wedge \ldots \wedge P_m \supset (\exists x_1(Q_{11} \wedge \ldots \wedge Q_{1k_1}) \vee \ldots \vee \exists x_n(Q_{n1} \wedge \ldots \wedge Q_{nk_n})))$$

In LKF, we can consider geometric extensions of the logic K by adding the corresponding geometric axioms in the left-side of the sequent to be derived. We propose the following translation, involving polarization of connectives, for axioms G having the form shown above[3]:

$$\exists \vec{z}((P_1 \wedge^+ \ldots \wedge^+ P_m) \wedge^+ (\forall x_1(\neg Q_{11} \vee^- \ldots \vee^- \neg Q_{1k_1}) \wedge^- \ldots \wedge^- \forall x_n(\neg Q_{n1} \vee^- \ldots \vee^- \neg Q_{nk_n})))$$

As recalled in Sect. 2, the system $G3K$ can be extended to capture all the modal logics characterized by geometric axioms, by modularly adding to the base system rules defined according to a proper scheme [14]. Each application of such a rule corresponds to a single bipole in LKF, as shown in Fig. 4. This fact ensures that the statements of Theorems 2 and 4 (as well as Corollary 5) hold also for any geometric extension of K and any system $G3K^*$.

---

[3] Note that in LKF we consider one-sided sequents and the one we propose is in fact a polarization of the negation of the axiom.

$$\cfrac{\cfrac{\cfrac{\cfrac{\cfrac{\cfrac{\vdash \Upsilon, \Delta, \neg\overline{Q_1}(y_1/x_1) \Uparrow \cdot}{\vdash \Upsilon, \Delta \Uparrow \neg\overline{Q_1}(y_1/x_1)}\, store^* \quad \cfrac{\vdash \Upsilon, \Delta, \neg\overline{Q_n}(y_n/x_n) \Uparrow \cdot}{\vdash \Upsilon, \Delta \Uparrow \neg\overline{Q_n}(y_n/x_n)}\, store^*}{\cfrac{\vdash \Upsilon, \Delta \Uparrow \neg Q_1^\vee(y_1/x_1) \quad \vdash \Upsilon, \Delta \Uparrow \neg Q_n^\vee(y_n/x_n)}{\vdash \Upsilon, \Delta \Uparrow \forall x_1(\neg Q_1^\vee(y_1/x_1)) \ldots \vdash \Upsilon, \Delta \Uparrow \forall x_n(\neg Q_n^\vee(y_n/x_n))}\, \vee^*}}{}\, \forall}{}\, }{}}{}}{}$$

$$\cfrac{\cfrac{\cfrac{\vdash \Upsilon, \Delta \Downarrow P_1 \; init \quad \ldots \quad \vdash \Upsilon, \Delta \Downarrow P_m \; init}{\vdash \Upsilon, \Delta \Downarrow P_1 \wedge^+ \ldots \wedge^+ P_m}\, \wedge^{+*} \qquad \cfrac{\cfrac{\vdash \Upsilon, \Delta \Uparrow \forall x_1(\neg Q_1^\vee) \wedge^- \ldots \wedge^- \forall x_n(\neg Q_n^\vee)}{\vdash \Upsilon, \Delta \Downarrow \forall x_1(\neg Q_1^\vee) \wedge^- \ldots \wedge^- \forall x_n(\neg Q_n^\vee)}\, release}{}\, \wedge^+}{\cfrac{\vdash \Upsilon, \Delta \Downarrow (P_1 \wedge^+ \ldots \wedge^+ P_m) \wedge^+ (\forall x_1(\neg Q_1^\vee) \wedge^- \ldots \wedge^- \forall x_n(\neg Q_n^\vee))}{}\, \exists^*}}{\cfrac{\vdash \Upsilon, \Delta \Downarrow G}{\vdash \Upsilon, \Delta \Uparrow \cdot}\, decide}$$

where Υ is an abbreviation for $G, \neg\overline{P}, \neg\Gamma$ and $\neg Q_i^\vee$ stands for $\neg Q_{i1} \vee \ldots \vee \neg Q_{ik_i}$, $\neg\overline{Q_i}$ stands for $\neg Q_{i1}, \ldots, \neg Q_{ik_i}$ and in *, for simplicity, we have applied several instances of the same rule in a single step.

Fig. 4. LKF derivation (bipole) corresponding to a geometric rule application in $G3K^*$.

3.5 Checking $G3K$ Proofs via LKF

The results in this section can be immediately applied to the ProofCert project [4, 11], where a general proof checker, based on LKF (or on its intuitionistic version LJF) and implemented in λProlog [12], is used to check proofs in a wide range of formats. To this aim, LKF is augmented as follows [3]: (*i*) a *proof certificate* term, which describes the proof evidence to be checked, is added to every sequent; (*ii*) every inference rule of LKF has an additional premise using either an *expert* or a *clerk* predicate; and (*iii*) formulas to the left of $\Uparrow$ and $\Downarrow$ are now associated to an *index*, used to regulate the mechanism of storing and deciding.

A *foundational proof certificate* for a given proof format consists in the definition of a translation of formulas from the original language into the language of LKF and in the definition of expert and clerk predicates. Expert predicates are used to drive the checking process during the synchronous phase (e.g., by specifying which term has to be used to instantiate an existential), while clerk predicates are used in the asynchronous phase not to extract information from the certificates but only to do routine computations. (The full augmented system LKF^a is available in the extended version of this paper). To illustrate the idea, we show here the augmented version of the decide rule:

$$\cfrac{\Xi' \vdash \Theta \Downarrow P \quad decide_e(\Xi, \Xi', l) \quad \langle l, P \rangle \in \Theta \quad positive(P)}{\Xi \vdash \Theta \Uparrow \cdot}\, decide^a$$

Here Ξ and Ξ' are certificates, l is the index specifying the formula on which to decide and the expert predicate $decide_e$ extracts Ξ' and l from Ξ.

By using the encoding proposed in this section and by exploiting the shown correspondence between inference rules and bipoles, $G3K$ proof evidence can be described (and then checked in LKF^a) by using very simple proof certificates, basically consisting in the sequence of (translated and polarized) formulas on which to decide. The expert for the decide rule simply decides on the formula on top of the certificate and removes it from the certificate itself. A simple version of it can have the following λ Prolog form:

$$\forall A \forall \Gamma. \; decide_e([A|\Gamma], \Gamma, A).$$

where we use the formula A itself as an index. The other clerk and expert predicates are either empty or only used to "propagate" information.[4]

4 Focused Labeled Proof Systems for Modal Logic

4.1 A Focused System for the Logic K

We have shown how the standard translation from modal logic into classical logic, when enriched with a proper polarization, allows one to define a strong correspondence between labeled modal derivations and focused classical derivations. Here we go further and define a focused labeled system (LMF) for modal logic.

The basic idea is to define a restriction of LKF targeting the formulas arising from the modal language, i.e., such that the quantifier rules are only applied to formulas that represent the translation of modal formulas of the form $\Box A$ or $\Diamond A$. LMF is defined over a labeled modal language: formulas have the form $x : A$, xRy or $\neg xRy$, where A is a polarized modal formula in negation normal form. Note that here, differently from $G3K$, since we consider one-sided sequents, relational atoms can also occur negated. The following LKF derivations show the way we extract the modal rules, from $\forall$ and $\exists$, by restricting the use of the first-order quantifiers to only express (a proper polarization of) the standard translation of formulas having $\Box$ or $\Diamond$ as the main connective:

$$
\cfrac{
\cfrac{
\cfrac{\vdash \Theta, \neg R(x,y) \Uparrow A(y), \Gamma}{\vdash \Theta \Uparrow \neg R(x,y), A(y), \Gamma}\ store
}{\vdash \Theta \Uparrow \neg R(x,y) \vee^- A(y), \Gamma}\ \vee^-
}{\vdash \Theta \Uparrow \forall y(\neg R(x,y) \vee^- A(y)), \Gamma}\ \forall
\qquad
\cfrac{
\cfrac{\vdash \Theta \Downarrow R(x,y) \quad \vdash \Theta \Downarrow A(y)}{\vdash \Theta \Downarrow R(x,y) \wedge^+ A(y)}\ \wedge^+
}{\vdash \Theta \Downarrow \exists y(R(x,y) \wedge^+ A(y))}\ \exists
$$

From such derivations, we get the following rules $\Box_K$ and $\Diamond_K$, respectively:

$$
\cfrac{\vdash \Theta, \neg xRy \Uparrow y : B, \Gamma}{\vdash \Theta \Uparrow x : \Box B, \Gamma}\ \Box_K
\qquad
\cfrac{\vdash \Theta \Downarrow xRy \quad \vdash \Theta \Downarrow y : B}{\vdash \Theta \Downarrow x : \Diamond B}\ \Diamond_K
$$

where, in analogy with the side-condition on the $\forall$ rule, we have that in $\Box_K$, y is not free in Θ nor in Γ. The whole system LMF is presented in Fig. 5.

The notion of polarizing an (unpolarized) propositional modal formula in the LMF setting is essentially the same as it was in the LKF setting. In particular, the polarities of $\Diamond B$ and $\Box B$ are, respectively, positive and negative. The propositional constants and the conjunction and disjunction are ambiguous and can be made either positive or negative. Finally, the atomic formulas that result from translating propositional constants in modal formulas are also ambiguous and can be given any arbitrary but fixed polarization. In the case of LMF, we shall fix the polarity of relational atoms to be positive. This latter choice is important for us in the next section to properly describe the geometric-axioms-as-inference-rules.

Theorem 6. *The system LMF is sound and complete with respect to the logic K, for any polarization of formulas.*

---

[4] We note that in this way, we provide no information on which substitution term to use in case of existential quantifiers, and let such terms be reconstructed by the checker. In order to obtain a completely faithful encoding of the original $G3K$ proof, the label term used for instantiating $\Diamond$-formulas should also be contained in the proof certificate and the expert predicate for the $\exists$ should take that into account.

ASYNCHRONOUS INTRODUCTION RULES

$$\frac{}{\vdash \Theta \Uparrow x : t^-, \Gamma} \; t^-_K \qquad \frac{\vdash \Theta \Uparrow \Gamma}{\vdash \Theta \Uparrow x : f^-, \Gamma} \; f^-_K$$

$$\frac{\vdash \Theta \Uparrow x : A, \Gamma \quad \vdash \Theta \Uparrow x : B, \Gamma}{\vdash \Theta \Uparrow x : A \wedge^- B, \Gamma} \; \wedge^-_K \qquad \frac{\vdash \Theta \Uparrow x : A, x : B, \Gamma}{\vdash \Theta \Uparrow x : A \vee^- B, \Gamma} \; \vee^-_K \qquad \frac{\vdash \Theta, \neg x R y \Uparrow y : B, \Gamma}{\vdash \Theta \Uparrow x : \Box B, \Gamma} \; \Box_K$$

SYNCHRONOUS INTRODUCTION RULES

$$\frac{}{\vdash \Theta \Downarrow x : t^+} \; t^+_K \qquad \frac{\vdash \Theta \Downarrow x : B_1 \quad \vdash \Theta \Downarrow x : B_2}{\vdash \Theta \Downarrow x : B_1 \wedge^+ B_2} \; \wedge^+_K$$

$$\frac{\vdash \Theta \Downarrow x : B_i}{\vdash \Theta \Downarrow x : B_1 \vee^+ B_2} \; \vee^+_K, i \in \{1, 2\} \qquad \frac{\vdash \Theta \Downarrow x R y \quad \vdash \Theta \Downarrow y : B}{\vdash \Theta \Downarrow x : \Diamond B} \; \Diamond_K$$

IDENTITY RULES

$$\frac{}{\vdash x : \neg P_a, \Theta \Downarrow x : P_a} \; init_K \qquad \frac{}{\vdash \neg x R y, \Theta \Downarrow x R y} \; init_{RK} \qquad \frac{\vdash \Theta \Uparrow x : B \quad \vdash \Theta \Uparrow x : \neg B}{\vdash \Theta \Uparrow \cdot} \; cut_K$$

STRUCTURAL RULES

$$\frac{\vdash \Theta, x : C \Uparrow \Gamma}{\vdash \Theta \Uparrow x : C, \Gamma} \; store_K \qquad \frac{\vdash \Theta \Uparrow x : N}{\vdash \Theta \Downarrow x : N} \; release_K \qquad \frac{\vdash x : P, \Theta \Downarrow x : P}{\vdash x : P, \Theta \Uparrow \cdot} \; decide_K$$

Here, $x : P$ is a positive formula; $x : N$ a negative formula; $x : P_a$ and $x R y$ positive literals; $x : C$ a positive formula or negative literal; and $\neg B$ is the negation normal form of the negation of B. In $\Box_K$, y is not free in Θ nor in Γ.

Fig. 5. LMF: a focused labeled proof system for the modal logic K

Proof. If we read a labeled formula $x : A$ as the first-order formula $A(x)$ and a relational atom $x R y$ as $R(x, y)$, we have that LMF is just obtained by LKF by replacing the rules $\forall$ and $\exists$ by $\Box_K$ and $\Diamond_K$, respectively (note that the rule *init* is just split into $init_K$ and $init_{RK}$). We have shown that $\Box_K$ and $\Diamond_K$ are simply restrictions of $\forall$ and $\exists$ to the first-order translation of modalities. Soundness and completeness of LMF then easily follow from soundness and completeness, with respect to any polarization of formulas, of LKF (see Sect. 2) and by the adequacy of the standard translation from propositional modal logic into first-order classical logic.

As it was the case for linear, classical and intuitionistic logic, this focused system allows for obtaining a normal form of cut-free modal derivations. We can illustrate that with a simple example: a proof of the labeled formula $x : \Diamond\Diamond \neg P \vee \Box\Box P$ can have several forms in $G3K$, as we can alternate applications of $R\Box$ and $R\Diamond$, while there is only one cut-free proof of its polarization $x : \Diamond\Diamond \neg P \vee^- \Box\Box P$ in LMF, which first applies (in a single phase) all the $\Box_K$ and then (in another phase) all the $\Diamond_K$.

4.2 Focused Systems for Extensions of K

We can extend LMF to a focused system for any geometric extension of K by replacing the first-order axioms with rules manipulating the relational atoms. Namely, given a geometric axiom of the form $\forall \bar{z}(P_1 \wedge \ldots \wedge P_m \supset (\exists x_1(Q_{11} \wedge \ldots \wedge Q_{1k_1}) \vee \ldots \vee \exists x_n(Q_{n1} \wedge \ldots \wedge Q_{nk_n})))$, we can extract, from an LKF derivation analogous to the one in Fig. 4, the following rule scheme:

$$\frac{\vdash \neg\overline{Q_1}(y_1/x_1), \overline{\neg P}, \Gamma \Uparrow \cdot \quad \ldots \quad \vdash \neg\overline{Q_n}(y_n/x_n), \overline{\neg P}, \Gamma \Uparrow \cdot}{\vdash \overline{\neg P}, \Gamma \Uparrow \cdot} \; GF$$

where $\overline{Q_j}$ and $\overline{P}$ denote the multisets of relational atoms $Q_{j1}, \ldots, Q_{jk_j}$ and $P_1, \ldots, P_m$, respectively, and the eigenvariables $y_1, \ldots, y_n$ do not occur free in the conclusion. Note that in order to build a complete bipole once we focus on the formula representing the geometric axiom (polarized as in Fig. 4), the literals $\overline{P}$ must be present in the context. Given a set of geometric frame properties $F_1, \ldots, F_n$, by adding modularly the corresponding GF-based rules to the base system LMF, we get a focused labeled system for the logic $KF_1, \ldots, F_n$. Soundness and completeness of any such extended system directly follows from the way we have derived the rule.

The rule scheme GF comes along the lines of the one given in [14] (see Sect. 2). We notice that in the more specific case of *universal axioms* (described and treated in the context of sequent systems in [15]), i.e., axioms of the form $\forall \overline{z}(P_1 \wedge \ldots \wedge P_m \supset Q_1 \vee \ldots \vee Q_n)$ the following rule scheme could also be used:

$$\frac{\vdash P_1, \overline{Q}, \Gamma \Uparrow \cdot \quad \ldots \quad \vdash P_m, \overline{Q}, \Gamma \Uparrow \cdot}{\vdash \overline{Q}, \Gamma \Uparrow \cdot} \; UF$$

where $\overline{Q}$ denotes the multiset of relational atoms $Q_1, \ldots, Q_n$. Such a rule scheme is justified by the following LKF derivation, where the formula on the right-side of the root sequent is a proper polarization of (the negation of) a universal axiom:

$$\cfrac{\cfrac{\cfrac{\cfrac{\vdash \overline{Q}, \Gamma, P_1 \Uparrow \cdot}{\vdash \overline{Q}, \Gamma \Uparrow P_1} \; store \quad \ldots \quad \cfrac{\vdash \overline{Q}, \Gamma, P_m \Uparrow \cdot}{\vdash \overline{Q}, \Gamma \Uparrow P_m} \; store}{\vdash \overline{Q}, \Gamma \Uparrow P_1 \wedge^- \ldots \wedge^- P_m} \; \wedge^{-*}}{\vdash \overline{Q}, \Gamma \Downarrow P_1 \wedge^- \ldots \wedge^- P_m} \; release \quad \cfrac{\cfrac{\cfrac{\vdash \overline{Q}, \Gamma \Downarrow \neg Q_1}{} \; init \quad \ldots \quad \cfrac{\vdash \overline{Q}, \Gamma \Downarrow \neg Q_n}{} \; init}{\vdash \overline{Q}, \Gamma \Downarrow \neg Q_1 \wedge^+ \ldots \wedge^+ \neg Q_n} \; \wedge^{+*}}{}}{\cfrac{\vdash \overline{Q}, \Gamma \Downarrow (P_1 \wedge^- \ldots \wedge^- P_m) \wedge^+ (\neg Q_1 \wedge^+ \ldots \wedge^+ \neg Q_n)}{\vdash \overline{Q}, \Gamma \Downarrow \exists \overline{z}((P_1 \wedge^- \ldots \wedge^- P_m) \wedge^+ (\neg Q_1 \wedge^+ \ldots \wedge^+ \neg Q_n))} \; \exists} \; \wedge^+$$

where in *, for simplicity, we have applied several instances of the same rule in a single step. Note that, in this case, relational atoms need to be assigned negative polarity (and small adjustments should be made to the base system LMF in order to deal with this fact).

The rule scheme UF cannot be applied in the general case of geometric axioms. In fact, with regard to the derivation shown above, one can notice that in the presence of a geometric axiom, the conjunction of negated Q_i atoms would occur under the scope of a universal quantification and we would not be able to process the whole formula inside a single bipole.

The different formulation of the GF and UF rule schemes seems to be related to two different approaches present in the literature of labeled (natural deduction) systems for modal logics. As an example, we show here two couples of natural deduction rules for expressing the (universal) property of transitivity and the (non-universal) property of seriality:

$$\frac{xRy \quad yRz \quad w:A}{w:A} \; trans_1 \qquad \frac{\genfrac{}{}{0pt}{}{[xRy]}{\vdots} \atop w:A}{w:A} \; ser_1 \qquad \frac{xRy \quad yRz}{xRz} \; trans_2 \qquad \frac{}{xRf(x)} \; ser_2$$

where y is fresh in ser_1. The rules $trans_1$ and ser_1 (from [18], in the style of GF) follow a pattern that allows capturing all geometric properties and is used in the context of a natural deduction system where no rule has a relational atom in the conclusion. The rules $trans_2$ and ser_2 (from [19], in the style of UF) express relational properties in a more direct fashion (only capturing Horn formulas) where the "freshness" of the variable to be introduced, in the case of a truly geometric axiom, is recovered by using Skolem functions (as in ser_2).

5 Conclusion and Future Work

The approach to describing modal logic proof systems via labeled sequents provides a way to reduce provability in modal logic to provability in first-order logic. This reduction is also modular: different modal logics can be presented using different theories describing the structure of their Kripke frames. When these theories—taken as assumptions—are also geometric, their use can be understood, instead, as inference rules [14]. Our work here using focused proof systems takes this connection one step further: we are able to faithfully encode the inference rules of labeled modal logic as bipoles in focused proofs in first-order logic. We note that in [16], an encoding of the same labeled modal proof system into a framework based on linear logic with subexponentials was proposed, with the aim of checking meta-properties of the system. The kind of encoding that we propose here is useful for the ProofCert project [3,11], where a general proof checker for focused first-order classical (and intuitionistic) logic is used to check proofs in a wide range of different formats: the encoding in Sect. 3 is all that is needed for that general purpose proof checker to check labeled sequent calculus proofs of modal logic formulas. We also believe that the simple foundational proof certificate sketched there for labeled modal sequent systems can be easily adapted and extended to work with prefixed tableaux for modal logic [7]. As a next step, we plan to define and implement, in the context of ProofCert, foundational proof certificates for theorem provers based on such an approach.

Another natural future direction is to consider a version of the focused calculus LMF but for intuitionistic modal logic (as, e.g., the ones considered in [18]) by using as a basis (instead of LKF) the focused proof system LJF for intuitionistic logic [10]. Similarly, this work could be extended to investigate the relationship between focused proof systems and labeled proof systems for other non-classical logics [8,19], such as intermediate logics [5]. Another interesting direction consists in considering non-labeled deduction systems for modal logic (see [7] for a general account), and in particular modal proof systems based on generalizations/extensions of sequents, such as hypersequents or nested sequents. In that setting, more sophisticated focusing mechanisms seem to be necessary in order to get an appropriate correspondence between modal inference rules and bipoles.

Acknowledgments. This work was carried out during the tenure of an ERCIM Alain Bensoussan Fellowship Programme by the second author and was funded by the ERC Advanced Grant ProofCert.

References

1. Andreoli, J.-M.: Logic programming with focusing proofs in linear logic. J. Logic Comput. **2**(3), 297–347 (1992)
2. Blackburn, P., Van Benthem, J.: Modal logic: a semantic perspective. In: Handbook of Modal Logic, pp. 1–82. Elsevier (2007)

3. Chihani, Z., Miller, D., Renaud, F.: Foundational proof certificates in first-order logic. In: Bonacina, M.P. (ed.) CADE 2013. LNCS, vol. 7898, pp. 162–177. Springer, Heidelberg (2013)
4. Chihani, Z., Libal, T., Reis, G.: The Proof Certifier Checkers. To appear in Tableaux, System Description (2015)
5. Dyckhoff, R., Negri, S.: Proof analysis in intermediate logics. Arch. Math. Logic **51**(1–2), 71–92 (2012)
6. Dyckhoff, R., Negri, S.: Geometrisation of first-order logic. Bull. Symbolic Logic **21**, 123–163 (2015)
7. Fitting, M.: Modal proof theory. In: Wolter, F., Blackburn, P., van Benthem, J. (eds.) Handbook of Modal Logic, pp. 85–138. Elsevier, New York (2007)
8. Gabbay, D.M.: Labelled Deductive Systems. Clarendon Press, Oxford (1996)
9. Girard, J.-Y.: On the meaning of logical rules I: syntax vs. semantics. In: Berger, U., Schwichtenberg, H. (eds.) Computational Logic. NATO ASI, pp. 215–272. Springer, Heidelberg (1999)
10. Liang, C., Miller, D.: Focusing and polarization in linear, intuitionistic, and classical logics. Theo. Comput. Sci. **410**(46), 4747–4768 (2009)
11. Miller, D.: A proposal for broad spectrum proof certificates. In: Jouannaud, J.-P., Shao, Z. (eds.) CPP 2011. LNCS, vol. 7086, pp. 54–69. Springer, Heidelberg (2011)
12. Miller, D., Nadathur, G.: Programming with Higher-Order Logic. Cambridge University Press, Cambridge (2012)
13. Miller, D., Pimentel, E.: A formal framework for specifying sequent calculus proof systems. Theo. Comput. Sci. **474**, 98–116 (2013)
14. Negri, S.: Proof analysis in modal logic. J. Philos. Logic **34**(5–6), 507–544 (2005)
15. Negri, S., von Plato, J.: Cut elimination in the presence of axioms. Bull. Symbolic Logic **4**(4), 418–435 (1998)
16. Nigam, V., Pimentel, E., Reis, G.: An extended framework for specifying and reasoning about proof systems. J. Logic Comput. (2014). doi:10.1093/logcom/exu029
17. Sahlqvist, H.: Completeness and correspondence in first and second order semantics for modal logic. In: Kanger, S., (ed.) Proceedings of the Third Scandinavian Logic Symposium, pp. 110–143, North Holland (1975)
18. Simpson, A.K.: The Proof Theory and Semantics of Intuitionistic Modal Logic. Ph.D. thesis, School of Informatics, University of Edinburgh (1994)
19. Viganò, L.: Labelled Non-Classical Logics. Kluwer Academic Publishers, Dordrecht (2000)

On CTL* with Graded Path Modalities

Benjamin Aminof[1], Aniello Murano[2](✉), and Sasha Rubin[2]

[1] Technische Universität Wien, Vienna, Austria
[2] Università degli Studi di Napoli "Federico II", Naples, Italy
murano@na.infn.it

Abstract. Graded path modalities count the number of paths satisfy-ing a property, and generalize the existential (E) and universal (A) path modalities of CTL*. The resulting logic is denoted GCTL*, and is a very powerful logic since (as we show) it is equivalent, over trees, to monadic path logic. We settle the complexity of the satisfiability prob-lem of GCTL*, i.e., 2ExpTime-Complete, and the complexity of the model checking problem of GCTL*, i.e., PSpace-Complete. The lower bounds already hold for CTL*, and so we supply the upper bounds. The significance of this work is two-fold: GCTL* is much more expressive than CTL* as it adds to it a form of quantitative reasoning, and this is done at no extra cost in computational complexity.

1 Introduction

Quantitative Verification and Graded Modalities. Temporal logics are the cornerstone of the field of formal verification. In recent years, much attention has been given to extending these by quantitative measures of function and robust-ness, e.g., [18]. Unfortunately, these extensions often require one to reason about weighted automata for which much is undecidable [1,2,10]. One way to extend classical temporal logics at a lower cost is by counting quantifiers, known as graded modalities. Graded world modalities were introduced in formal verifica-tion as a useful extension of the standard existential and universal quantifiers in branching-time modal logics [7,16,19,23]. These modalities allow one to express properties such as "there exist at least n successors satisfying a formula" or "all but n successors satisfy a formula". A prominent example is the extension of μ-calculus called $G\mu$-calculus [7,19].

Despite its high expressive power, the μ-calculus (which extends modal logic by least and greatest fixpoint operators) is a low-level logic, making it "unfriendly" for users, who usually find it very hard to understand, let alone write, formulas involving even very modest nesting of fixed points. In contrast, CTL and CTL* are much more intuitive and user-friendly. An extension of CTL

Benjamin Aminof is supported by the Austrian National Research Network S11403-N23 (RiSE) of the Austrian Science Fund (FWF) and by the Vienna Science and Technology Fund (WWTF) through grant ICT12-059. Aniello Murano is partially supported by the FP7 EU project 600958-SHERPA. Sasha Rubin is a Marie Curie fellow of the Istituto Nazionale di Alta Matematica.

© Springer-Verlag Berlin Heidelberg 2015
M. Davis et al. (Eds.): LPAR-20 2015, LNCS 9450, pp. 281–296, 2015.
DOI: 10.1007/978-3-662-48899-7_20

with graded *path modalities* called GCTL was defined in [5,6]. Although there are several positive results about GCTL this logic suffers from similar limitations as CTL, i.e., it cannot nest successive temporal operators and so cannot express fairness constraints. This dramatically limits the usefulness of GCTL and so we turn instead to GCTL* in which one can naturally and comprehensibly express complex properties of systems. Although the syntax and semantics of GCTL* were defined and justified in [6], only a rudimentary study of it was made. In particular, the complexity of the satisfiability and model checking problem for this logic was never established, and remained open since its introduction in 2009. Instead, research has focused on the much simpler fragment of GCTL.

Our Results. We establish the exact complexity of the satisfiability and model checking problems for GCTL* to be 2ExpTime-Complete and PSpace-Complete, respectively. Thus, in both cases, the problems for GCTL* are not harder than for CTL*. This is very good news indeed since, as we also show, GCTL* is expressively equivalent, over trees, to monadic path logic, and is thus a powerful, yet relatively friendly logic. Along the way, we prove that GCTL* has the bounded-degree tree-model property, i.e., a satisfiable formula is satisfied in a tree whose branching degree is at most exponential in the size of the formula.

The Importance of Our Results. We obtain that GCTL* has the following desirable combination of attributes:

(a) GCTL* can Naturally Express Properties of Paths as well as Count Them. For example, the formula $E^{\geq 2}G(request \to (request\ U\ granted))$ says: "there are at least two ways to schedule the computation such that every request is eventually granted". This cannot be expressed in CTL* nor in GCTL.

The naive semantics for $E^{\geq n}\psi$ which states that "there are at least n different paths satisfying ψ" while at first glance may seem natural and desirable, when examined more carefully turns out to be undesirable, and less informative. For example, consider a faulty program in which requests are sometimes not granted. In GCTL* (unlike the naive counting) the formula $E^{\geq 2}[F(request \wedge \neg Fgranted)]$ requires at least two *incomparable* sequences of operations, each causing this faulty behaviour. Hence, it indicates whether the faulty behaviour is the result of multiple underlying problems, and is not confused by multiple paths that are extensions of a single faulty prefix. Furthermore, the naive counting very quickly leads to unnatural interpretations, as convincingly argued in [6].

This ability to easily count paths is a natural fit in various application domains. For example, in databases there is a close relationship between model-checking CTL* and XML navigation (see [4]). The logic GCTL* allows one to express quantitative requirements such as" client has at least 5 items in last-month orders". More generally, graded operators are common in description logics, which are prominently used for formal reasoning in AI (e.g., knowledge querying, planning with redundancies).

(b) GCTL* is Extremely Expressive. Not only does GCTL* extend CTL* (and thus, unlike CTL, it can reason about fairness), we prove that it is expressively equivalent, over trees, to Monadic Path Logic (MPL) which is Monadic Second-Order Logic (MSOL) interpreted over trees but with set quantification restricted to branches.

(c) GCTL* has Relatively Low Complexity of Satisfiability. Unfortunately, the complexity of satisfiability of MPL is non-elementary (this is already true for FOL). In sharp contrast, we prove that the complexity of satisfiability of GCTL* is 2ExpTime, and thus is no harder than for CTL*.

Technical Contributions. The upper bounds are obtained by exploiting an automata-theoretic approach for branching-time logics, combined with game theoretic reasoning at a crucial point. The automata-theoretic approach is suitable because GCTL* turns out to have the tree-model property. It is very hard to see how other techniques for deciding questions in logic (e.g. effective quantifier elimination, tableaux, composition) can be used to achieve optimal complexity results for GCTL*. Our proof is not just an easy adaptation of the classical decision procedure. We relate GCTL* to a new model of automata, i.e., *Graded Hesitant Tree Automata* (GHTA). These automata work on finitely-branching trees (not just k-ary trees) and their transition relations can count up to a given number (usual alternating automata only count up to 1).

Related Work. Counting modalities were first introduced by Fine [16] under the name *graded world modalities*. A systematic treatment of the complexity of various graded modal logics followed [9,14,21,23,24]. The extension of μ-calculus by graded world modalities was investigated in [7,19]. Although these articles introduce automata that can count, our GHTA are more complicated since they have to deal with graded path modalities and not just graded world modalities. The extension of CTL* by the ability to say "there exist at least n successors satisfying ψ", called counting-CTL*, was defined in [22], and its connection with Monadic Path Logic studied using the composition method. It is unclear if that method, although elegant, can yield the complexity bounds we achieve (even for counting-CTL*). As shown in [6], $G\mu$-calculus cannot succinctly reason about paths, or even grandchildren of a given node (the same goes for counting-CTL*). The first work to deal with graded path modalities is [5] that introduced GCTL, the extension of CTL by these modalities. Graded path modalities over CTL were also studied in [15], using a different semantics than GCTLwhich is tailored for extending CTL, and it is unclear how one can extend their work to CTL*.

2   The GCTL* Temporal Logic

Let $\mathbb{N}$ denote the positive integers, and $[d] = \{1, 2, \ldots, d\}$ for $d \in \mathbb{N}$. An LTS (Labeled Transition System/Kripke structure) is a tuple $S = \langle \Sigma, S, E, \lambda \rangle$, where Σ is a set of *labels*, S is a countable set of *states*, $E \subseteq S \times S$ is the *transition relation*, and $\lambda : S \mapsto \Sigma$ is the *labeling function*. Typically, $\Sigma = 2^{AP}$ where AP is a finite set of *atomic propositions*. The *degree* of a state s is the cardinality of the set $\{t \in S : (s, t) \in E\}$ of its successors. We assume that E is total, i.e., that every state has a successor. A path in S is a finite or infinite sequence

$\pi_0\pi_1\cdots \in (S^*)\cup(S^\omega)$ such that $(\pi_{i-1},\pi_i) \in E$ for all $1 \le i < |\pi|$ ($|\pi|$ is the *length* of π). The set of (finite and infinite) paths in S is written pth(S), and the set of (finite and infinite) paths in S that start in a given state $q \in S$ is written pth(S, q). Let $\preceq$ be the prefix ordering on paths. If $\pi \preceq \pi'$ say that π' is an *extension* of π. For a set of paths X, denote by min(X) the minimal elements of X according to $\preceq$. A Σ-*labeled tree* T is a pair $\langle T, V \rangle$ where $T \subseteq \mathbb{N}^*$ is a $\prec$-downward closed set of strings over $\mathbb{N}$, and $V : T \to \Sigma$ is a labeling. We implicitly view a tree $T = \langle T, V \rangle$ as the LTS $\langle \Sigma, T, E, V \rangle$ where $(t, s) \in E$ iff s is a son of t. If every node of a tree T has a finite degree then T is *finitely branching*. If every node has at most degree $k \in \mathbb{N}$, then T is *boundedly branching* or *has branching degree k*.

2.1   Syntax and Semantics of GCTL*

GCTL* extends CTL* by *graded path quantifiers* of the form $E^{\ge g}$. We follow the definition of GCTL* from [6], but give a slightly simpler syntax. We assume that the reader is familiar with the logics CTL*, LTL, and CTL (see [20,25]).

The semantics of GCTL* is defined for an LTS S. The GCTL* formula $E^{\ge g}\psi$, for GCTL* path formula ψ, can be read as *"there exist at least g (minimal ψ-conservative) paths"*. Minimality was defined above, and so we now say, informally, what it means for a path to be ψ-conservative. An infinite path of S is ψ-conservative if it satisfies ψ, and a finite path of S is ψ-conservative if all its (finite and infinite) extensions in S satisfy ψ. Note that this notion uses a semantics of GCTL* over finite paths, and thus the semantics of GCTL* needs to be defined for finite paths (as well as infinite paths). As in [6], we use the weak-version of semantics of temporal operators for finite paths (defined in [11]). Intuitively, temporal operators are interpreted pessimistically (with respect to possible extensions of the path), e.g., $(S, \pi) \models X\psi$ iff $|\pi| \ge 2$ and $(S, \pi_{\ge 1}) \models \psi$.

Syntax of GCTL*. Fix a set of atoms AP. The GCTL* *state (φ) and path (ψ) formulas* are built inductively from AP using the following grammar: $\varphi:: = p \mid \neg\varphi \mid \varphi \vee \varphi \mid E^{\ge g}\psi$ and $\psi:: = \varphi \mid \neg\psi \mid \psi \vee \psi \mid X\psi \mid \psi U\psi \mid \psi R\psi$.

In the first part, p varies over AP and g varies over $\mathbb{N}$ (and thus, technically, there are infinitely many rules in this grammar). As usual, X, U and R are called *temporal operators* and $E^{\ge g}$ (for $g \in \mathbb{N}$) are called *path modalities* (also called *path quantifiers*). We write $F\varphi$ instead of **true**$U\varphi$, and $G\varphi$ instead of **false**$R\varphi$. The class of GCTL* *formulas* is the set of state formulas generated by the above grammar. The simpler class of *Graded CTL formulas* (GCTL) is obtained by requiring each temporal operator to be immediately preceded by a path quantifier. The logic LTL is the class of path formulas in which no path quantifier appears. The *degree* of the quantifier $E^{\ge g}$ is the number g. The *degree* $\deg(\varphi)$, of a state formula φ, is the maximum of the degrees of the quantifiers appearing in φ. The *length* $|\varphi|$, of a formula φ, is defined inductively on the structure of φ as usual, and using $|E^{\ge g}\psi|$ equal to $g + 1 + |\psi|$ (i.e., g is coded in unary).

Semantics of GCTL*. Given an LTS S and a state $s \in S$, the definition of $(S, s) \models \varphi$ is done inductively on the structure of φ, exactly as for CTL*, with the only change concerning the new path quantifier $E^{\ge g}$. For $\varphi = E^{\ge g}\psi$, where ψ is a GCTL* path formula, let $(S, s) \models \varphi$ iff the cardinality of the set $\min(Con(S, s, \psi))$ is at least g, where $Con(S, s, \psi) := \{\pi \in \text{pth}(S, s) \mid \forall \pi' \in \text{pth}(S, s) : \pi \preceq \pi'$ implies $(S, \pi') \models \psi\}$. The paths in $Con(S, s, \psi)$ are called ψ-conservative (in S starting at s), and paths in $\min(Con(S, s, \psi))$ are called minimal ψ-conservative. It is not hard to see that, for total LTSs, the classic logic CTL* coincides with the fragment of GCTL* in which the degree g of all quantifiers $\mathsf{E}^{\geq g}$ is 1.

If ψ is an LTL formula, we may write $\pi \models \psi$ instead of $(S, \pi) \models \psi$. This is justifiable since the truth of ψ depends only on the path π independently of the rest of S. Two state formulas ϕ, ϕ' are equivalent if for all S and $s \in S$, we have $(S, s) \models \phi$ iff $(S, s) \models \phi'$. Two path formulas ψ, ψ' are equivalent if for all S and $\pi \in \text{pth}(S)$, we have that $(S, \pi) \models \psi$ if and only if $(S, \pi) \models \psi'$. An LTS S with a designated state $q \in S$ is a model of a GCTL* formula φ, sometimes denoted $S \models \varphi$, if $(S, q) \models \varphi$. For a labeled tree T, the designated node is by default the root, and thus, $T \models \varphi$ means that $(T, \epsilon) \models \varphi$ (recall that ϵ designates the root of T). A GCTL* formula φ is satisfiable iff it has a model.

Example 1. We unpack the meaning of the GCTL* formula from the introduction $\mathsf{E}^{\geq 2}[\mathsf{F}(request \wedge \neg\mathsf{F}granted)]$. Let ψ denote the path formula $\mathsf{F}(request \wedge \neg\mathsf{F}granted)$. First, a finite or infinite path π satisfies ψ if at some point t the atom *request* holds, and at no later point on π does the atom *granted* hold. A finite π is ψ-conservative if and only if it satisfies ψ and the atom *granted* does not hold in any node of the subtree rooted at the end of π; and an infinite path is ψ-conservative if and only if it satisfies ψ. Thus, $\mathsf{E}^{\geq 2}\psi$ holds if and only if there exist two possibly finite paths, say π^1 and π^2, neither one a prefix of the other, both satisfying ψ (i.e., π^i has a request that is never granted on π^i), and such that if π^i is finite then that path has a request that is not granted in any possible extension of π^i.

2.2   Important Properties of GCTL*

Like CTL* (see [20]), one can think of a GCTL* path formula ψ over atoms AP as an LTL formula Ψ over atoms which themselves are GCTL* state formulas, as follows. A formula φ is a *state sub-formula* of ψ if i) φ is a state formula, and ii) φ is a sub-formula of ψ. A formula φ is a *maximal state sub-formula* of ψ if φ is a state sub-formula of ψ, and φ is not a proper sub-formula of any other state sub-formula of ψ. Let $max(\psi) = \{\varphi \mid \varphi$ is a maximal state sub-formula of $\psi\}$, and let $\overline{max(\psi)} = \bigcup_{\varphi \in max(\psi)}\{\varphi, \neg\varphi\}$ be the set of all maximal state sub-formulas of ψ and their negations. Every GCTL* path formula ψ can be viewed as the formula Ψ whose atoms are elements of $max(\psi)$. Note that Ψ is an LTL formula. For example, for $\psi = ((\mathsf{X}p) \ \mathsf{U} \ (\mathsf{E}^{\geq 2}\mathsf{X}q)) \vee p$, the state sub-formulas are $\{p, q, \mathsf{E}^{\geq 2}\mathsf{X}q\}$, and $max(\psi) = \{p, \mathsf{E}^{\geq 2}\mathsf{X}q\}$, and thus Ψ is the LTL formula $(\mathsf{X}\underline{p} \ \mathsf{U} \ \underline{\mathsf{E}^{\geq 2}\mathsf{X}q}) \vee \underline{p}$ over the atoms $\{p, \mathsf{E}^{\geq 2}\mathsf{X}q\}$ (here we underline sub-formulas that are treated as atoms). Given an LTS $S = \langle 2^{AP}, S, E, \lambda \rangle$ and a GCTL* path formula ψ, we define the *relabeling* of the LTS S by the values of the formulas in

$max(\psi)$ as $\mathsf{S}_\psi = \langle max(\psi), S, E, L \rangle$ where $L(s)$ is the union of $\lambda(s)$ and the set of $\varphi \in max(\psi)$ such that $(\mathsf{S}, s) \models \varphi$.

Lemma 1. *For every GCTL* path formula ψ over AP there is an LTL formula Ψ over $max(\psi)$ such that for all S and all paths π in S: $(\mathsf{S}, \pi) \models \psi$ iff $(\mathsf{S}_\psi, \pi) \models \Psi$.*

It is not hard to see that GCTL* is not invariant under bisimulation (cf. [6]), and that it is invariant under unwinding (cf. [6]). The next theorem shows that GCTL* is a powerful logic. Indeed, it is equivalent, over trees, to Monadic Path Logic (MPL) which is MSO with quantification restricted to branches. Note that MPL is only defined over trees, while GCTL* (like CTL*) is defined over arbitrary LTS. This is the reason we compare their expressiveness over trees.

Theorem 1. *GCTL* is equivalent, over trees, to Monadic Path Logic.*

3   Graded Hesitant Tree Automata

In this section we define a new kind of automaton called Graded Hesitant Tree Automata. We also make use of the classical non-deterministic finite word automata (NFW) and non-deterministic Büchi word automata (NBW) (see [25]), alternating parity tree automata (APTA) (see [12]), and alternating hesitant tree automata (AHTA) (see [20]). We write $\langle \Sigma, Q, q_0, \delta, G \rangle$ for NBWs and $\langle \Sigma, Q, q_0, \delta, F \rangle$ for NFWs where Σ is the input alphabet, Q is the set of states, q_0 is the initial state, $\delta \subseteq Q \times \Sigma \times Q$ is the transition relation, $G \subseteq Q$ is the set of accepting states and $F \subseteq Q$ the set of final states. For a set X, let $\mathsf{B}^+(X)$ be the set of positive Boolean formulas over X, including the constants **true** and **false**. A set $Y \subseteq X$ satisfies a formula $\theta \in \mathsf{B}^+(X)$, written $Y \models \theta$, if assigning **true** to elements in Y and **false** to elements in $X \setminus Y$ makes θ true. Graded hesitant tree automata (GHTA) generalise AHTA[1]: (a) they can work on finitely-branching trees (not just k-ary branching trees), and (b) their transition relation allows the automaton to send multiple copies into the successors of the current node in a much more flexible way. Below we formally define AHTA and GHTA.

Definition of AHTA. An *Alternating Hesitant Tree Automaton* (AHTA) is a tuple $\mathsf{A} = \langle \Sigma, D, Q, q_0, \delta, \langle G, B \rangle, \langle \mathsf{part}, \mathsf{type}, \preceq \rangle \rangle$ where Σ is a non-empty finite set of *input letters*; $D \subset \mathbb{N}$ is a finite non-empty set of *directions*, Q is the non-empty finite set of *states*, $q_0 \in Q$ is the *initial state*; the pair $\langle G, B \rangle \in 2^Q \times 2^Q$ is the *acceptance condition*[2] (we sometimes call the states in G *good states*

---

[1] Strictly speaking, GHTA generalise the symmetric variant of AHTA. That is, for every language accepted by an AHTA and that is closed under the operation of permuting siblings, there is a GHTA that accepts the same language.

[2] The combination of a Büchi and a co-Büchi condition that hesitant automata use can be thought of as a special case of the parity condition with 3 colors. Thus, we could have defined Graded Parity Tree Automata instead (using the parity condition, our automata strictly generalise the ones in [5,19]) However, we do not need the full power of the parity condition, and in order to achieve optimal complexity for model checking of GCTL* we need to be able to decide membership of our automata in a space efficient way, which cannot be done with the parity acceptance condition.

and the states in B *bad states*); $\delta : Q \times \Sigma \to \mathsf{B}^+(D \times Q)$ is the *alternating transition function*; part $\subset 2^Q$ is a partition of Q, type : part $\to \{trans, exist, univ\}$ is a function assigning the label *transient, existential* or *universal* to each element of the partition, and $\preceq \subset 2^Q \times 2^Q$ is a partial order on part. Moreover, the transition function δ is required to satisfy the following *hesitancy condition*: for every $\mathbb{Q} \in$ part, every $q \in \mathbb{Q}$, and every $\sigma \in \Sigma$: (i) for every $\mathbb{Q}' \in$ part and $q' \in \mathbb{Q}'$, if q' occurs in $\delta(q, \sigma)$ then $\mathbb{Q}' \preceq \mathbb{Q}$; (ii) if type$(\mathbb{Q}) \in trans$ then no state of $\mathbb{Q}$ occurs in the formula $\delta(q, \sigma)$; (iii) if type$(\mathbb{Q}) \in exist$ (resp., type$(\mathbb{Q}) \in univ$) then there is at most one element of $\mathbb{Q}$ in each disjunct of the DNF (resp., conjunct of CNF) of $\delta(q, \sigma)$.

An *input tree (for AHTA)* is a Σ-labeled tree $\mathsf{T} = \langle T, V \rangle$ with $T \subseteq D^*$. Since D is finite, such trees have fixed finite branching degree. A *run (or run tree)* of an alternating tree automaton A on input tree $\mathsf{T} = \langle T, V \rangle$ is a $(T \times Q)$-labeled tree $\langle T_r, r \rangle$, such that *(a)* $r(\varepsilon) = (\varepsilon, q_0)$ and *(b)* for all $y \in T_r$, with $r(y) = (x, q)$, there exists a *minimal* set $\mathsf{S} \subseteq D \times Q$, such that $\mathsf{S} \models \delta(q, V(x))$, and for every $(d, q') \in \mathsf{S}$, it is the case that $x \cdot d$ is a son of x, and there exists a son y' of y, such that $r(y') = (x \cdot d, q')$.

Note that if $\delta(q, V(x)) = \mathbf{true}$ then $S = \emptyset$ and the node y has no children; and if there is no S as required (for example if x does not have the required sons) then there is no run-tree with $r(y) = (x, q)$. Observe that disjunctions in the transition relation are resolved into different run trees, while conjunctions give rise to different sons of a node in a run tree. If v is a node of the run tree, and $r(v) = (u, q)$, call u the *location associated with* v, denoted $loc(v)$, and call q the *state associated with* v, denoted $state(v)$.

We now discuss the acceptance condition. Fix a run tree $\langle T_r, r \rangle$ and an infinite path π in it. Say that the path *visits* a state q at time i if $state(\pi_i) = q$. The hesitancy restriction (i) guarantees that the path π eventually gets trapped and visits only states in some element of the partition, i.e., there exists $\mathbb{Q} \in$ part such that from a certain time i on, $state(\pi_j) \in \mathbb{Q}$ for all $j \geq i$. The condition (ii) ensures that this set is either existential or universal, i.e., type$(\mathbb{Q}) \in \{exist, univ\}$. Thus, we say that the path π *gets trapped in an existential set* if type$(\mathbb{Q}) = exist$, and otherwise we say that it *gets trapped in a universal set*. We can now define what it means for a path in a run tree to be *accepting*. A path that gets trapped in an existential set is *accepting* iff it visits some state of G infinitely often, and a path that gets trapped in a universal set is *accepting* iff it visits every state of B finitely often. A run $\langle T_r, r \rangle$ of an AHTA is *accepting* iff all its infinite paths are accepting. An automaton A accepts an input tree $\langle T, V \rangle$ iff there is an accepting run of A on $\langle T, V \rangle$. The *language* of A, denoted $\mathcal{L}(\mathsf{A})$, is the set of Σ-labeled D-trees accepted by A. We say that A is nonempty iff $\mathcal{L}(\mathsf{A}) \neq \emptyset$.

The *membership problem* of AHTA is the following decision problem: given an AHTA A with direction set D, and a finite LTS S in which the degree of each node is at most $|D|$, decide whether or not A accepts S. The *depth* of the AHTA is the size of the longest chain in $\prec$. The *size* $||\delta||$ of the transition function is the sum of the lengths of the formulas it contains. The *size* $||\mathsf{A}||$ of the AHTA is

$|D| + |Q| + ||\delta||$. The partition, partial order and type function are not counted in the size of the automaton. The following is implicit in [20]:

Theorem 2. *The membership problem for AHTA can be solved in $O(\partial \log^2(|S| \cdot ||A||))$ space where ∂ is the depth of A and S is the state set of S.*

Definition of GHTA. We now introduce *Graded Hesitant Tree Automata* (GHTA). These can run on finitely-branching trees (not just trees of a fixed finite degree), and the transition function is graded, i.e., instead of a Boolean combination of direction-state pairs, it specifies a Boolean combination of distribution operations. There are two distribution operations: $\Diamond(q_1,...,q_k)$ and its dual $\Box(q_1,...,q_k)$. Intuitively, $\Diamond(q_1,...,q_k)$ specifies that the automaton picks k *different* sons $s_1,...,s_k$ of the current node and, for each $i \leq k$, sends a copy in state q_i to son s_i. Note that the states $q_1,...,q_k$ are not necessarily all different.

A GHTA A is a tuple $\langle \Sigma, Q, q_0, \delta, \langle G, B \rangle, \langle \mathsf{part}, \mathsf{type}, \preceq \rangle \rangle$ where all elements but δ are defined as for AHTA, and $\delta : Q \times \Sigma \to \mathsf{B}^+(\Diamond_Q \cup \Box_Q)$ is a transition function that maps a state and an input letter to a positive Boolean combination of elements in $\Diamond_Q = \{\Diamond(q_1,...,q_k) \mid (q_1,...,q_k) \in Q^k, k \in \mathbb{N}\}$ and $\Box_Q = \{\Box(q_1,...,q_k) \mid (q_1,...,q_k) \in Q^k, k \in \mathbb{N}\}$.

We show how to define the run of a GHTA A on a Σ-labeled finitely-branching tree $\mathsf{T} = \langle T, V \rangle$ by (locally) unfolding every $\Diamond_Q$ and $\Box_Q$ in $\delta(q, V(t))$ into a formula in $\mathsf{B}^+([d] \times Q)$ where d is the branching-degree of node t. For $k, d \in \mathbb{N}$, let $S(k, d)$ be the set of all ordered different k elements in $[d]$, i.e., $(s_1,...,s_k) \in S(k, d)$ iff for every $i \in [k]$ we have that $s_i \in [d]$, and that if $i \neq j$ then $s_i \neq s_j$. Observe that if $k > d$ then $S(k, d) = \emptyset$. For every $d \in \mathbb{N}$, define the function $expand_d : \mathsf{B}^+(\Diamond_Q \cup \Box_Q) \to \mathsf{B}^+([d] \times Q)$ that maps formula ϕ to the formula formed from ϕ by replacing every occurrence of a sub-formula of the form $\Diamond(q_1,...,q_k)$ by the formula $\bigvee_{(s_1,...,s_k) \in S(k,d)}(\bigwedge(s_i, q_i))$, and every occurrence of a sub-formula of the form $\Box(q_1,...,q_k)$ by the formula $\bigwedge_{(s_1,...,s_k) \in S(k,d)}(\bigvee(s_i, q_i))$. Observe that if $k > d$ then $\Diamond(q_1,...,q_k)$ becomes the constant formula **false**, and $\Box(q_1,...,q_k)$ becomes the constant formula **true**. The *run of a GHTA* A is defined as for an alternating tree automaton, except that one uses $expand_n(\delta(q, V(x)))$ instead of $\delta(q, V(x))$ for nodes x of T of degree n. Finally, the *hesitancy condition* defined above for AHTA is required to apply to the expanded transition function, i.e., insert the phrase "every $n \in \mathbb{N}$," before the phrase "and every $\sigma \in \Sigma$", and in items (i)-(iii) replace $\delta(q, \sigma)$ by $expand_n(\delta(q, \sigma))$. Acceptance is as for AHTA.

Lemma 2. *The emptiness problem for GHTA A over trees of branching degree at most d is decidable in time $2^{O(d \cdot |Q|^3)}$, where Q is the state set of A.*

Proof. Given a GHTA A with state set Q, convert it into an AHTA A′ with the same state space by using the function $expand_d$ defined above to transform its transition relation into a non-graded one. This is possible since we assumed a bound d on the branching degree of the input trees, and thus the transformation $expand_d$ can be used in advance. This construction takes time that is $2^{O(|Q| \log d)}$. Recall that AHTA are a special case of alternating parity tree automata (APTA) with 3 priorities. Now apply the fact that the emptiness problem for APTA with p priorities over d-ary trees can be solved in time $2^{O(d \cdot |Q|^p)}$ [12].

4   From GCTL* to Graded Hesitant Automata

Elegant and optimal algorithms for solving the satisfiability and model-checking problems of CTL* were given using the automata-theoretic approach for branching-time temporal logics [20]. Using this approach, one reduces satisfiability to the non-emptiness problem of a suitable tree automaton accepting all tree-models of a given temporal logic formula. We follow the same approach here, by reducing the satisfiability problem of GCTL* to the non-emptiness problem of GHTA. By Theorem 1, a GCTL* formula is satisfiable (in some, possibly infinite, labeled transition system) iff it has a finitely branching (though possibly unboundedly branching) tree model, which exactly falls within the abilities of GHTA. Our main technical result states that every GCTL* formula can be compiled into an exponentially larger GHTA (the rest of this section provides the proof):

Theorem 3. *Given a* GCTL* *formula ϑ, one can build a GHTA A_ϑ that accepts all the finitely-branching tree-models of ϑ. Moreover, A_ϑ has $2^{O(|\vartheta| \cdot \deg(\vartheta))}$ states, depth $O(|\vartheta|)$, and transition function of size $2^{O(|\vartheta| \cdot \deg(\vartheta))}$.*

An important observation that allows us to achieve an optimal construction is the following. Suppose that the formula $E^{\geq g}\psi$ holds at some node w of a tree. Then, by definition, there are at least g different paths $\rho'^1, ..., \rho'^g \in \min(Con(S, w, \psi))$. Look at any g infinite extensions $\rho^1, ..., \rho^g$ of these paths in the tree, and note that by the definition of ψ-conservativeness all these extensions must satisfy ψ. Also observe that for every $i \neq j$, the fact that ρ'^i, ρ'^j are different and minimal implies that the longest common prefix ρ'^{ij} of ρ^i and ρ^j is not ψ-conservative. As it turns out, the other direction is also true, i.e., if there are g infinite paths $\rho^1, ..., \rho^g$ satisfying ψ, such that for every $i \neq j$ the common prefix ρ'^{ij} is not ψ-conservative, then there are g prefixes $\rho'^1, ..., \rho'^g$ of $\rho^1, ..., \rho^g$ respectively, such that $\rho'^1, ..., \rho'^g \in \min(Con(S, w, \psi))$. Note that this allows us to reason about the cardinality of the set $\min(Con(S, w, \psi))$, by considering only the infinite paths $\rho^1, ..., \rho^g$ and their common prefixes, without actually looking at the minimal ψ-conservative paths $\rho'^1, ..., \rho'^g$. In reality, we do not even have to directly consider the common prefixes ρ'^{ij}. Indeed, since the property of being ψ-conservative is upward closed (with respect to the prefix ordering $\preceq$ of paths), showing that ρ'^{ij} is not ψ-conservative can be done by finding any extension of ρ'^{ij} that is not ψ-conservative. The following proposition formally captures this.

Proposition 1. *Given a* GCTL* *path formula ψ and a 2^{AP}-labeled tree $T = (T, V)$, then $T \models E^{\geq g}\psi$ iff there are g distinct nodes $y_1, ..., y_g \in T$ (called breakpoints) such that for every $1 \leq i, j \leq g$ we have: (i) if $i \neq j$ then y_i is not a descendant of y_j; (ii) the path from the root to the father x_i of y_i is not ψ-conservative; (iii) there is an infinite path ρ^i in T, starting at the root and going through y_i, such that $\rho^i \models \psi$.*

We are in a position to describe our construction of a GHTA accepting all finitely-branching tree-models of a given GCTL* formula. Naturally, the main difficulty lies in handling the graded modalities. The basic intuition behind the way our construction handles formulas of the form $\varphi = \mathsf{E}^{\geq g}\psi$ is the following. Given an input tree, the automaton A_φ for this formula has to find at least g minimal ψ-conservative paths. At its core, A_φ runs g pairs of copies of itself in parallel. The reason these copies are not run independently is to ensure that the two members of each pair are kept coordinated, and that different pairs do not end up making the same guesses (and thus overcounting the number of minimal ψ-conservative paths). The task of each of the g pairs is to detect some minimal ψ-conservative path that contributes 1 to the count towards g. This is done indirectly by using the characterization given by Proposition 1. Since this proposition requires checking if certain paths satisfy ψ, the automaton A_φ will access certain classic NBWs. We begin by establishing the existence of these:

Theorem 4. *Given an LTL formula ζ, there is an NBW A_ζ (resp. NFW $\mathbb{B}_\zeta$), both of size $2^{O(\zeta)}$, accepting exactly all infinite (resp. finite) words that satisfy ζ.*

Lemma 3. *Given an LTL formula ζ, there is an NBW A^ζ (of size $2^{O(\psi)}$) such that A^ζ accepts a word w iff $w \models \zeta$, or $u \models \zeta$ for a prefix u of w. Moreover, A^ζ has an accepting sink $\top$, such that if $r_0, r_1, \ldots$ is an accepting run of A^ζ on w, and $i \geq 0$ satisfies $r_i \neq \top$, then a (finite or infinite) prefix u of w, of length $|u| > i$, satisfies ζ, and vice-versa (i.e., if a prefix u of w satisfies ζ, then there is an accepting run on w with $r_i \neq \top$ for all $i < |u|$).*

We can now finish the intuitive description of the construction of the automaton A_φ associated with a formula $\varphi = \mathsf{E}^{\geq g}\psi$. Let Ψ be the LTL formula resulting from applying Lemma 1 to ψ. In essence, A_φ guesses the g descendants $y_1, \ldots, y_g$ of the root of the input tree as given in Proposition 1. For every $1 \leq i \leq g$, the automaton uses one copy of $\mathsf{A}^{\neg\Psi}$ to verify that the path π, from the root to the father of y_i, is not ψ-conservative (by guessing some finite or infinite extension $\pi \preccurlyeq \pi'$ of it such that $\pi' \models \neg\Psi$), and one copy of A_Ψ to guess an infinite path π'' from the root through y_i such that $\pi'' \models \Psi$ (and is thus ψ-conservative).

4.1   The Construction of GHTA A_ϑ for a GCTL* Formula ϑ

We induct on the structure of ϑ. Given a state sub-formula ϕ of ϑ (possibly including ϑ), for every formula $\theta \in \overline{\max \phi}$, let $\mathsf{A}_\theta = \langle \Sigma, Q^\theta, q_0^\theta, \delta^\theta, \langle G^\theta, B^\theta \rangle, \langle \mathsf{part}^\theta, type^\theta, \preceq^\theta \rangle \rangle$ be a GHTA accepting the finitely-branching tree-models of θ. The proof of correctness plus the definition of the hesitancy structure, i.e., of $\langle \mathsf{part}^\theta, type^\theta, \preceq^\theta \rangle$, is in the full version (recall that the hesitancy structure is only used to decide in a space-efficient way membership, which is needed for our result that model-checking of GCTL* is in PSPACE). We build the GHTA A_ϕ accepting all finitely-branching tree-models of ϕ by suitably composing the automata of its maximal sub-formulas and their negations. Note that when composing these automata, we assume w.l.o.g. that the states of any occurrence of a constituent automaton of a sub-formula are disjoint from the states of any other occurrence of a constituent automaton (of the same or of a different sub-formula), as well as from any newly introduced states[3]. Formally:

1. If $\phi = p \in AP$, then $\mathsf{A}_\phi = \langle \Sigma, \{q\}, q, \delta, \langle \emptyset, \emptyset \rangle, \langle \mathsf{part}, \mathsf{type}, \preceq \rangle \rangle$ where $\delta(q, \sigma) =$ **true** if $p \in \sigma$ and **false** otherwise.

2. If $\phi = \varphi_0 \vee \varphi_1$ then A_ϕ is obtained by nondeterministically invoking either A_{φ_0} or A_{φ_1}. Thus, $\mathsf{A}_\phi = \langle \Sigma, \bigcup_{i=0,1} Q^{\varphi_i} \cup \{q_0\}, q_0, \delta, \langle \bigcup_{i=0,1} G^{\varphi_i}, \bigcup_{i=0,1} B^{\varphi_i} \rangle, \beta \rangle$, where $\beta = \langle \mathsf{part}, \mathsf{type}, \preceq \rangle$, and for every $i \in \{0,1\}$, every $\sigma \in \Sigma$, and every $q \in Q^{\varphi_i}$ we have that: $\delta(q, \sigma) = \delta^{\varphi_i}(q, \sigma)$, and $\delta(q_0, \sigma) = \delta^{\varphi_0}(q_0^{\varphi_0}, \sigma) \vee \delta^{\varphi_1}(q_0^{\varphi_1}, \sigma)$.

3. If $\phi = \neg \varphi$, then A_ϕ is obtained by dualizing the automaton A_φ. Formally, the *dual of a GHTA* A is the GHTA obtained by dualizing the transition function of A (i.e., switch $\vee$ and $\wedge$, switch $\top$ and $\bot$, and switch $\square$ and $\Diamond$), replacing the acceptance condition $\langle G, B \rangle$ with $\langle B, G \rangle$ (and toggling types).

Finally we deal with the case that $\phi = \mathsf{E}^{\geq g} \psi$. Observe that ψ is a path formula and, by Lemma 1, reasoning about ψ can be reduced to reasoning about the LTL formula Ψ whose atoms are elements of $\max \psi$. Let $\Sigma' = 2^{max(\psi)}$. By Theorem 4, there is an NBW $\mathbb{A}_\Psi = \langle \Sigma', Q^+, q_0^+, \delta^+, G^+ \rangle$ accepting all infinite words in Σ'^ω satisfying Ψ. By Lemma 3, there is an NBW $\mathsf{A}^{\neg \Psi} = \langle \Sigma', Q^-, q_0^-, \delta^-, G^- \rangle$ accepting all infinite words in Σ'^ω that either satisfy $\neg \Psi$ or have a prefix that does. Note that the states of these automata are denoted Q^+ and Q^-. We let A_ϕ be $\langle \Sigma, Q, q_0, \delta, \langle G, B \rangle, \langle \mathsf{part}, \mathsf{type}, \preceq \rangle \rangle$, whose structure we now define.

The Set of States. $Q = Q_1 \cup Q_2$, where $Q_1 = (Q^+ \cup \{\bot\})^g \times (Q^- \cup \{\bot\})^g \setminus \{\bot\}^{2g}$, and $Q_2 = \bigcup_{\theta \in \max \psi} Q^\theta$. The Q_1 states are used to run g copies of $\mathsf{A}^{\neg \Psi}$ and g copies of A_Ψ in parallel. Every state in Q_1 is a vector of $2g$ coordinates where coordinates $1, \ldots, g$ (called Ψ *coordinates*) contain states of A_Ψ, and coordinates $g+1, \ldots, 2g$ (called $\neg \Psi$ *coordinates*) contain states of $\mathsf{A}^{\neg \Psi}$. In addition, each coordinate may contain the special symbol $\bot$ indicating that it is *disabled*, as opposed to *active*. We disallow the vector $\{\bot\}^{2g}$ with all coordinates disabled. States in Q_2 are all those from the automata A_θ for every maximal state subformula of ψ, or its negation. These are used to run A_θ whenever A_ϕ guesses that θ holds at a node. Also, for every $1 \leq i \leq g$, we denote by $Q^i_{single} = \{(q_1, \ldots, q_{2g}) \in Q_1 \mid q_i \neq \bot$, and for all $j \leq g$, if $j \neq i$ then $q_j = \bot\}$ the set of all states in Q_1 in which the only active Ψ coordinate is i.

The Initial State. $q_0 = (q_1, \ldots, q_{2g})$ where for every $1 \leq i \leq g$ we have that $q_i = q_0^+$ and for every $g+1 \leq i \leq 2g$ we have that $q_i = q_0^-$.

The Acceptance Condition. $B = \bigcup_{\theta \in \max \psi} B^\theta$ and $G = G' \cup G'' \cup (\bigcup_{\theta \in \max \psi} G^\theta)$, where $G' = \{(q_1, \ldots, q_{2g}) \in Q^i_{single} \mid q_i \in G^+\}$ is the set of all states in Q_1 in which the only active Ψ coordinate contains a good state, and $G'' =$

---

[3] For example, when building an automaton for $\phi = \varphi_0 \vee \varphi_1$, in the degenerate case that $\varphi_0 = \varphi_1$ then A_{φ_1} is taken to be a copy of A_{φ_0} with its states renamed to be disjoint from those of A_{φ_0}. Also, the new state q_0 may be renamed to avoid a collision with any of the other states.

$\{(q_1, \ldots, q_{2g}) \in Q_1 \mid \forall i.1 \leq i \leq g \rightarrow q_i = \bot,$ and $\exists j.g+1 \leq j \leq 2g \wedge q_j \in G^\neg\}$ is the set of all states in Q_1 in which all the Ψ coordinates are inactive, and some $\neg\Psi$ coordinate contains a good state.

The Transition Function. δ is defined, for every $\sigma \in \Sigma$, as follows:

- For every $q \in Q_2$, let $\theta \in \overline{max(\psi)}$ be such that $q \in Q^\theta$, and define $\delta(q, \sigma) = \delta^\theta(q, \sigma)$. I.e., for states in Q_2, follow the rules of their respective automata.
- For every $q \in Q_1$, we define $\delta(q, \sigma) := \bigvee_{\sigma' \in \Sigma'} (J \wedge K \wedge L)$ where $J = \bigvee_{X \in Legal(q, \sigma')} \Diamond(X)$, $K = \bigwedge_{\theta \in \sigma'} \delta^\theta(q_0^\theta, \sigma)$, $L = \bigwedge_{\theta \notin \sigma'} \delta^{\neg\theta}(q_0^{\neg\theta}, \sigma)$, where $Legal(q, \sigma')$ is the set of all *legal distributions* of (q, σ'), and is defined later.

Informally, the disjunction $\bigvee_{\sigma' \in \Sigma'}$ corresponds to all possible guesses of the set of maximal subformulas of ψ that currently hold. Once a guess σ' is made, the copies of $\mathbb{A}^{\neg\Psi}$ and $\mathbb{A}_\Psi$ simulated by the states appearing in $Legal(q, \sigma')$ proceed as if the input node was labeled by the letter σ'. The conjunction $(\wedge_{\theta \in \sigma'} \delta^\theta(q_0^\theta, \sigma)) \wedge (\wedge_{\theta \notin \sigma'} \delta^{\neg\theta}(q_0^{\neg\theta}, \sigma))$ ensures that a guess is correct by launching a copy of $\mathbb{A}_\theta$ for every subformula $\theta \in \sigma'$ that was guessed to hold, and a copy of $\mathbb{A}_{\neg\theta}$ for every subformula θ guessed not to hold.

We define *legal distribution*. Intuitively, a legal distribution of (q, σ') is a sequence $q^1, \ldots, q^m$ of different states from Q_1 that "distribute" among them, without duplication, the coordinates active in q, while making sure that for every $1 \leq i \leq g$ coordinate i (which simulates a copy of $\mathbb{A}_\Psi$) does not get separated from the coordinate $i + g$ (which simulates its partner copy of $\mathbb{A}^{\neg\Psi}$) for as long as i is not the only active Ψ coordinate. As expected, every active coordinate j, in any of the states $q^1, \ldots, q^m$, follows from q_j by using the transitions available in the automaton it simulates: $\mathbb{A}_\Psi$ if $j \leq g$, or $\mathbb{A}^{\neg\Psi}$ if $j > g$.

More formally, given a letter $\sigma' \in \Sigma'$, and a state $q = (q_1, \ldots q_{2g}) \in Q_1$ in which the active coordinates are $\{i_1, \ldots, i_k\}$, we say that a sequence $X = q^1, \ldots, q^m$ (for some $m \geq 1$) of distinct states in Q_1 is a *legal distribution* of (q, σ') if the following conditions hold: *(i)* the coordinates active in the states $q^1, \ldots, q^m$ are exactly $i_1, \ldots, i_k$, i.e., $\{i_1, \ldots, i_k\} = \cup\{i \in \{1, \ldots, 2g\} \mid \exists 1 \leq l \leq m \text{ s.t. } q_i^l \neq \bot\}$. *(ii)* if a coordinate i_j is active in some $q' \in X$ then it is not active in any other $q'' \in X$; *(iii)* if $1 \leq i_j < i_l \leq g$ are two active Ψ coordinates in some $q' \in X$, then $q'_{i_j+g}, q'_{i_l+g} \in Q^\neg \setminus \{\top\}$, i.e., the coordinates $i_j + g, i_l + g$ are also active in q' and do not contain the accepting sink of $\mathbb{A}^{\neg\Psi}$; *(iv)* if i_j is active in some $q' \in X$ then $(q_{i_j}, \sigma', q'_{i_j}) \in \delta^+$ if $i_j \leq g$, and $(q_{i_j}, \sigma', q'_{i_j}) \in \delta^\neg$ if $i_j > g$. I.e., active Ψ coordinates evolve according to the transitions of $\mathbb{A}_\Psi$, and active $\neg\Psi$ coordinates according to the those of $\mathbb{A}^{\neg\Psi}$.

Remark 1. We make two observations. First, the $2g$ copies of $\mathbb{A}^{\neg\Psi}$ and $\mathbb{A}_\Psi$ can not simply be launched from the root of the tree using a conjunction in the transition relation. The reason is that if this is done then there is no way to enforce property (i) of Proposition 1. Second, a cursory look may suggest that different copies of $\mathbb{A}^{\neg\Psi}$ and $\mathbb{A}_\Psi$ that are active in the current vector may be merged. Unfortunately, this cannot be done since $\mathbb{A}^{\neg\Psi}$ and $\mathbb{A}_\Psi$ are nondeterministic, and thus, different copies of these automata must be able to make independent guesses in the present in order to accept different paths in the future.

Proposition 2. *The automaton* A_ϑ *is a GHTA with depth* $O(|\vartheta|)$ *and* $2^{O(|\vartheta| \cdot \deg(\vartheta))}$ *many states, and the size of its transition function is* $2^{O(|\vartheta| \cdot \deg(\vartheta))}$.

5   Complexity of Satisfiability and MC of GCTL*

Theorem 5. *A satisfiable* GCTL* *formula* ϑ *has a tree model of branching degree at most* $2^{O(|\vartheta| \cdot \deg(\vartheta))}$.

Proof. Suppose ϑ is satisfiable. By Theorem 1, ϑ has a finitely-branching tree model. Observe, by Theorem 3, that $|Q| = 2^{O(|\vartheta| \cdot \deg(\vartheta))}$, where Q is the state set of the automaton A_ϑ defined in that proof. Hence, it is enough to prove that every tree model of ϑ has a subtree of branching degree $|Q|^2$ that also models ϑ.

To prove this claim, we use the membership game G_{T,A_ϑ} of the input tree T and the automaton A_ϑ. There are two players, *automaton* and *pathfinder*. Player automaton moves by resolving disjunctions in the transition relation of A_ϑ, and is trying to show that T is accepted by A_ϑ. Player pathfinder moves by resolving conjunctions, and is trying to show that T is not accepted by A_ϑ. The game uses auxiliary tree structured arenas to resolve each transition of the automaton. This is a simple case of a *hierarchical parity game* [3]. As usual, player automaton has a winning strategy if and only if $T \models A_\vartheta$. By memoryless determinacy of parity games on infinite arenas, player automaton has a winning strategy if and only if he has a memoryless winning strategy. For a fixed memoryless strategy str, one can prove, by looking at the transition function of A_ϑ, that every play consistent with str, and every node t of the input tree T, only visits at most $|Q|^2$ sons of t, thus inducing a subtree which is the required boundedly-branching tree model.

Theorem 6. *The satisfiability problem for* GCTL* *over LTSs is* 2EXPTIME-COMPLETE, *and model checking* GCTL* *for finite LTSs is* PSPACE-COMPLETE.

Proof. The lower-bounds already hold for CTL*. Theorems 3 and 5 and Lemma 2 give the upper-bound for satisfiability. For the upper-bound for model checking, given an LTS S (with largest degree d), and a GCTL* formula ϑ, using Theorem 3 construct the GHTA $A_{\neg\vartheta}$, which has $2^{O(|\vartheta| \cdot \deg(\vartheta))}$ states, transition function of size $2^{O(|\vartheta| \cdot \deg(\vartheta))}$, and depth $O(|\vartheta|)$. As in the proof of Lemma 2, build an equivalent AHTA A' of size $d + (2^{O(|\vartheta| \cdot \deg(\vartheta))} \cdot |Q|^d) + 2^{O(|\vartheta| \cdot \deg(\vartheta))} = 2^{O(|\vartheta| \cdot \deg(\vartheta) + d \cdot |\vartheta| \cdot \deg(\vartheta))}$, and of depth $\partial = O(|\vartheta|)$. By Theorem 2, the membership problem of the AHTA A' on S can be solved in space $O(\partial \log^2(|S| \cdot ||A'||))$ which is polynomial in $|\vartheta|$ and $|S|$ (using $\deg(\vartheta) \leq |\vartheta|$ and $d \leq |S|$).

6   Discussion

This work shows that GCTL* is an expressive logic (it is equivalent, over trees, to MPL and can express fairness and counting over paths) whose satisfiability and model-checking problems have the same complexity as that of CTL*.

GCTL* was defined in [5]. However, only the fragment GCTL was studied. As the authors note in the conference version of that paper, their techniques, that worked for GCTL, do not work for GCTL*. Moreover, they also suggested a line of attack that does not seem to work; indeed, it was left out of the journal version of their paper [6]. Instead, our method is a careful combination of the automata-theoretic approach to branching-time logics [20], a characterization of the graded path modality (Proposition 1), and a boundedly-branching tree model property whose proof uses game-theoretic arguments (Theorem 5). Moreover, our technique immediately recovers the main results about GCTL from [5], i.e., satisfiability for GCTL is EXPTIME-COMPLETE and the model checking problem for GCTL is in PTIME (Indeed, consider the construction in Theorem 3 of A_ϑ when ϑ it taken from the fragment GCTL of GCTL*, and in particular where it comes to a subformula ϕ of the form $\phi = E^{\geq g}\psi$. Since ψ is either of the form pBq or Xp, the number of new states added at this stage is a constant. Thus, the number of states of A_ϑ is linear in the size of ϑ). In other words, our technique suggests a powerful new way to deal with graded path modalities.

When investigating the complexity of a logic with a form of counting quantifiers, one must decide how the numbers in these quantifiers contribute to the length of a formula, i.e., to the input of a decision procedure. In this paper we assume that these numbers are coded in unary, rather than binary. There are a few reasons for this. First, the unary coding naturally appears in description and predicate logics [8]. As pointed out in [19], this reflects the way in which many decision procedures for these logics work: they explicitly generate n individuals for $\exists^{\geq n}$. Second, although the complexity of the binary case is sometimes the same as that of the unary case, the constructions are significantly more complicated, and are thus much harder to implement [6,7]. At any rate, as the binary case is useful in some circumstances we plan to investigate this in the future.

Comparison with (Some) Other Approaches. Although showing that satisfiability of GCTL* is decidable is not hard (for example, by reducing to MSOL), identifying the exact complexity is much harder. Indeed, there is no known satisfiability-preserving translation of GCTL* to another logic that would yield the optimal 2EXPTIME upper bound. We discuss two such candidate translations. First, in this article we show a translation from GCTL* to MPL. Unfortunately, the complexity of satisfiability of MPL is non-elementary. Second, there is no reason to be optimistic that a translation from GCTL* to $G\mu$-calculus (whose satisfiability is EXPTIME-COMPLETE) would yield the optimal complexity since (a) already the usual translation from CTL* to μ-calculus does not yield optimal complexity [13], and (b) the translation given in [6] from GCTL to $G\mu$-calculus does not yield optimal complexity. Moreover, the usual translation from CTL* to μ-calculus uses automata, and thus automata for GCTL* (from which we get our results directly) have to be developed anyway.

Future Work. Recall that the graded μ-calculus was used to solve questions (such as satisfiability) for the description logic $\mu ALCQ$ [7]. Similarly, our techniques for GCTL* might be useful for solving questions in $ALCQ$ combined with temporal logic, such as for the graded extension of CTL*$_{ALC}$ [17]. Second, the GCTL model checking algorithm from [6] has been implemented in the NuSMV model-checker to provide more than one counter-example when a GCTL formula is not satisfied. We are thus optimistic that existing CTL* model-checkers can be fruitfully extended to handle GCTL*.

References

1. Almagor, S., Boker, U., Kupferman, O.: What's decidable about weighted automata? In: Bultan, T., Hsiung, P.-A. (eds.) ATVA 2011. LNCS, vol. 6996, pp. 482–491. Springer, Heidelberg (2011)
2. Aminof, B., Kupferman, O., Lampert, R.: Rigorous approximated determinization of weighted automata. In: Symposium on Logic in Computer Science, pp. 345–354, IEEE (2011)
3. Aminof, B., Kupferman, O., Murano, A.: Improved model checking of hierarchical systems. Inf. Comput. **210**, 68–86 (2012)
4. Arenas, M., Barceló, P., Libkin, L.: Combining temporal logics for querying XML documents. In: Schwentick, T., Suciu, D. (eds.) ICDT 2007. LNCS, vol. 4353, pp. 359–373. Springer, Heidelberg (2006)
5. Bianco, A., Mogavero, F., Murano, A.: Graded computation tree logic. In: Symposium on Logic in Computer Science, pp. 342–351, IEEE (2009)
6. Bianco, A., Mogavero, F., Murano, A.: Graded computation tree logic. ACM Trans. Comput. Log. **13**(3), 25 (2012)
7. Bonatti, P.A., Lutz, C., Murano, A., Vardi, M.Y.: The complexity of enriched Mu-Calculi. Log. Methods Comput. Sci. **4**(3), 1–27 (2008)
8. Calvanese, D., De Giacomo, G., Lenzerini, M.: Reasoning in expressive description logics with fixpoints based on automata on infinite trees. In: International Joint Conference on Artificial Intelligence, pp. 84–89 (1999)
9. de Rijke, M.: A note on graded modal logic. Studia Logica **64**(2), 271–283 (2000)
10. Droste, M., Kuich, W., Vogler, H.: Handbook of Weighted Automata. Monographs in Theoretical Computer Science. An EATCS Series. Springer, Heidelberg (2009)
11. Eisner, C., Fisman, D., Havlicek, J., Lustig, Y., McIsaac, A., Van Campenhout, D.: Reasoning with temporal logic on truncated paths. In: Hunt, Jr., W.A., Somenzi, F. (eds.) CAV 2003. LNCS, vol. 2725, pp. 27–39. Springer, Heidelberg (2003)
12. Emerson, E.A., Jutla, C.S.: The complexity of tree automata and logics of programs. SIAM J. Comput. **29**(1), 132–158 (1999)
13. Emerson, E.A., Sistla, A.P.: Deciding branching time logic, pp. 14–24. In: Symposium on Theory of Computing (1984)
14. Ferrante, A., Murano, A., Parente, M.: Enriched μ-calculi module checking. Log. Methods Comput. Sci. **4**(3), 1–21 (2008)
15. Ferrante, A., Napoli, M., Parente, M.: Model checking for graded CTL. Fundamenta Informaticae **96**(3), 323–339 (2009)
16. Fine, K.: In so many possible worlds. Notre Dame J. Formal Log. **13**, 516–520 (1972)
17. Gutiérrez-Basulto, V., Jung, J.C., Lutz, C.: Complexity of branching temporal description logics. In: European Conference on Artificial Intelligence, pp. 390–395 (2012)
18. Henzinger, T.A.: Quantitative reactive modeling and verification. Comput. Sci. **28**(4), 331–344 (2013)
19. Kupferman, O., Sattler, U., Vardi, M.Y.: The complexity of the graded μ-calculus. In: Voronkov, A. (ed.) CADE 2002. LNCS (LNAI), vol. 2392, pp. 423–437. Springer, Heidelberg (2002)

20. Kupferman, O., Vardi, M.Y., Wolper, P.: An automata theoretic approach to branching-time model checking. J. ACM **47**(2), 312–360 (2000)
21. Malvone, V., Mogavero, F., Murano, A., Sorrentino, L.: On the counting of strategies. In: International Symposium on Temporal Representation and Reasoning, IEEE (2015, to appear)
22. Moller, F., Rabinovich, A.: Counting on CTL*: on the expressive power of monadic path logic. Inf. Comput. **184**(1), 147–159 (2003)
23. Tobies, S.: PSPACE reasoning for graded modal logics. J. Log. Comput. **11**(1), 85–106 (2001)
24. van der Hoek, W., Meyer, JJ.Ch.: Graded modalities in epistemic logic. In: Symposium on Logical Foundations of Computer Science, pp. 503–514 (1992)
25. Vardi, M.Y., Wolper, P.: Reasoning about infinite computations. Inf. Comput. **115**(1), 1–37 (1994)

On Subexponentials, Synthetic Connectives, and Multi-level Delimited Control

Chuck Liang[1] and Dale Miller[2(✉)]

[1] Department of Computer Science, Hofstra University, Hempstead, NY, USA
chuck.liang@hofstra.edu
[2] Inria & LIX/Ecole Polytechnique, Palaiseau, France
dale.miller@inria.fr

Abstract. We construct a partially-ordered hierarchy of delimited control operators similar to those of the CPS hierarchy of Danvy and Filinski [5]. However, instead of relying on nested CPS translations, these operators are directly interpreted in linear logic extended with subexponentials (i.e., multiple pairs of ! and ?). We construct an independent proof theory for a fragment of this logic based on the principle of focusing. It is then shown that the new constraints placed on the permutation of cuts correspond to multiple levels of delimited control.

1 Introduction

This paper formulates a system, motivated by linear logic with multiple pairs of exponentials, with the intent of giving a Curry-Howard style basis for multiple levels of delimited control operators similar to those of Danvy and Filinski [5]. The computational interpretation of classical logic that began with Griffin [8] and Parigot [17] can already explain *undelimited* control operators such as *call/cc*. However, there is nothing in classical logic that can explain directly why the capturing of a continuation should be stopped by a delimiter. Continuation capture is reflected in classical proof theory by the phenomenon of contraction and scope extrusion, which are restricted in intuitionistic logic. The fine-grained control over the capture of continuations suggests a *combination* of classical logic with intuitionistic logic. In [9], delimitation is explained by a *transition from an intuitionistic to a non-intuitionistic mode of derivation,* which necessitates a cut-elimination strategy to deal with these transitions. However, it is known that multiple levels of delimitation can be used to block control operators from crossing programming boundaries and interfering with control operators in different modules (see [10]). We may even wish to have a partially ordered hierarchy of operators. For example, in the term $(f \ \sharp_i(g \ \sharp_j[control^j \ c. \ldots control^k c.s]))$ we can require that $control^j$ is not delimited by $\sharp_j$ but is delimited by $\sharp_i$ if i is stronger or unrelated to j. Suppose also that an external procedure is then called that contains a $control^k$ construct. We may wish to specify what, if any, part of the continuation of the calling program can be captured by this operator by designating the relationship of i and j to k.

© Springer-Verlag Berlin Heidelberg 2015
M. Davis et al. (Eds.): LPAR-20 2015, LNCS 9450, pp. 297–312, 2015.
DOI: 10.1007/978-3-662-48899-7_21

At the proof-theoretic level, subexponential linear logic alone is not enough. Simply adding more pairs of ? and ! does not fundamentally change the cut-elimination algorithm of linear logic. We construct a stand-alone fragment of linear logic by using the principle of focusing (focalisation) in formulating *synthetic connectives*. The existing definitions of focusing [1,15] in linear logic are inadequate for fully exploiting the power of exponentials. Thus a new proof theory is needed.

Previous studies of Curry-Howard interpretations of classical logic using linear logic are exemplified by the systems LKT and LKQ [3]. These systems represent different focusing strategies for eliminating non-determinism in reduction (call-by-value for LKQ, by name for LKT). These uses of focusing are by now well understood and we shall not reconstruct them. What we emphasize in this paper is a different effect of subexponentials on reduction that can operate orthogonally to the elimination of nondeterminism with focusing. The use of focusing in this paper is at a deeper level.

To motivate the need for subexponentials, a naive attempt at combining classical and intuitionistic logics can easily result in a collapse into the former even within the context of linear logic. The single-conclusion characterization of intuitionistic logic was inherited by linear logic. Unfortunately, this characterization leaves little *in between* intuitionistic and classical logic. The representation of intuitionistic implication as $!A \multimap B$ is not modular. Since $\multimap$ is equivalent to a disjunction ($\invamp$), its intuitionistic strength evaporates in the in the presence of multiple conclusions. However, multiple conclusions represent saved continuations in classical computation. Fortunately, there are also multiple conclusion characterizations of intuitionistic logic:

$$\frac{\Gamma \vdash A, A, \Delta}{\Gamma \vdash A, \Delta} \ C \qquad \frac{\Gamma \vdash \Delta}{\Gamma \vdash A, \Delta} \ W \qquad \frac{A, \Gamma \vdash B}{\Gamma \vdash A \to B, \Delta} \ IL \qquad \frac{A, \Gamma \vdash B, \Delta}{\Gamma \vdash A \to B, \Delta} \ CL$$

Structural rules are allowed and the distinction between classical and intuitionistic logics rests on the $\to$ introduction rule: the "IL" rule prevents scope extrusion since it enforces the scope of A to include only B and not also the formulas in Δ. This perspective offers a new opportunity for combining classical and intuitionistic logics. Informally, we can hope for something of the form

$$\frac{A, \Gamma \vdash B, \Delta_2}{\Gamma \vdash A \overset{2}{\to} B, \Delta_1 \Delta_2}$$

Here, the indices 1 and 2 represent different levels of *modality*. Introducing an implication at level 2 can require forgetting level 1 conclusions while keeping those at level 2 or higher. This is the kind of system that we can build with subexponentials.

2   Subexponential Linear Logic

Subexponential, or *multi-colored* linear logic was suggested by Girard and first described in [4]. Given a preordered set of indices, there is a $!_i$ for each index i

with $?_i$ as it's dual: $?_i A = (!_i A^\perp)^\perp$. A $?_i$ does not need to admit contraction or weakening. However, the availability of these structural rules must respect the ordering relation: if $j \geq i$ then $?_j$ must admit all the structural rules admitted by $?_i$. This restriction is required to preserve the cut elimination procedure of linear logic. For all indices k, the usual dereliction rule is allowed for $?_k$ on the right and $!_k$ on the left. The promotion rule is generalized as follows, which we display in two forms:

$$\frac{\vdash ?_{n_1}A^1, \ldots ?_{n_k}A^k, B}{\vdash ?_{n_1}A^1, \ldots ?_{n_k}A^k, !_j B} \; j \leq n_1, \ldots n_k \qquad \frac{!_{n_1}A^1, \ldots !_{n_k}A^k \vdash B}{!_{n_1}A^1, \ldots !_{n_k}A^k \vdash !_j B} \; j \leq n_1, \ldots n_k$$

The single sided rule is equivalent to the two-sided version with a single conclusion. The second form is closer to what we use. The promotion rule applies dually on the left-hand side since $!_j A$ on one side is equivalent to $?_j A^\perp$ on the other side.

The term *subexponential* was introduced in [15] along with a focused proof system for them. Semantically, subexponentials can be characterized as restrictions to subspaces. In phase semantics it is easily seen that $!_k$ restricts a fact to a submonoid that corresponds to k, with the ordering of submonoids determined by inclusion.

Subexponentials appear to be a simple generalization of linear logic save for one significant fact. In most proof systems for ordinary linear logic, and for classical and intuitionistic logics, weakening can be pushed to the initial rules. There is never a need to force weakening at other points in a proof and, therefore, it can be ignored. With indexed exponentials, however, *weakening cannot be pushed to the initial rules*. The sequent $!_1 A, !_2 B \vdash !_2 C$ may only be provable if $!_1 A$ is weakened away. If a proof of $!_1 A \multimap !_2 B \multimap !_2 C$ is represented by $\lambda x \lambda y.t$, then x cannot appear free in t. This represents a form of resource control: not how many times but *where* a resource can appear.

3   Extending the Focusing Principle

A central goal of this paper is to derive a refinement of classical logic from subexponential linear logic that is well-behaved and self-contained with respect to cut-elimination. In this regard, the principle of focusing remains important even though our target here is not a focused sequent calculus for cut-free proofs but a natural deduction system for writing programs with possibly many cuts. We wish to synthesize new connectives by combining linear logic connectives, but not every combination can be used. An important test for the integrity of synthetic introduction rules is *initial elimination*: that $A \vdash A$ is provable (in sequent calculus). Attempts to create synthetic connectives that ignore the focusing principle generally end in failure. For example, we may naively wish to consider $(A \otimes B) \& C$ as a ternary connective with the following introduction rules:

$$\frac{\Gamma_1 \vdash A \quad \Gamma_2 \vdash B \quad \Gamma_1 \Gamma_2 \vdash C}{\Gamma_1 \Gamma_2 \vdash (A \otimes B) \& C} \&R$$

$$\frac{A, B, \Gamma \vdash \mathcal{D}}{(A \otimes B) \,\&\, C, \Gamma \vdash \mathcal{D}} \,\&L_1 \qquad \frac{C, \Gamma \vdash \mathcal{D}}{(A \otimes B) \,\&\, C, \Gamma \vdash \mathcal{D}} \,\&L_2$$

Here, $\otimes$ is positive but $\&$ is negative. But it is easily seen that

$$(A \otimes B) \,\&\, C \vdash (A \otimes B) \,\&\, C$$

is not provable with *these* introduction rules. In contrast, connectives of the same polarity can be combined to form synthetic connectives (e.g. $(A \otimes B) \oplus C$). While this principle is clear with regard to the binary connectives, with exponentials there is more flexibility. In terms of focusing, ? builds a negative formula and ! builds a positive formula because they have the following properties (with implied duals for !) with respect to the negative (dually positive) binary connectives:

$$?(?A \,\mathbin{\rotatebox[origin=c]{180}{\&}}\, ?B) \equiv ?A \,\mathbin{\rotatebox[origin=c]{180}{\&}}\, ?B \qquad ?(?A \,\&\, ?B) \equiv ?A \,\&\, ?B$$

These properties are not ordinary logical equivalences: they express an important property in the structure of proofs, e.g., *a contraction on* $?(?A \,\mathbin{\rotatebox[origin=c]{180}{\&}}\, ?B)$ *can be recursively replaced by contraction on its immediate subformulas.* This is the basis of focusing in classical logic. To explain focusing in intuitionistic logic in terms of linear logic [12], we also have the following property: $!(!A \multimap B) \equiv\ !(!A \multimap\, !B)$. Intuitionistic implication is usually translated as $!A \multimap B$, but it is better to regard it as $!(!A \multimap B)$: the outer ! is excluded because promotion on the right is always possible in simulations of LJ sequents. With subexponentials, however, this promotion may not always be possible. One can regard focusing proof systems as the application of these properties in one direction: removing as many exponentials as possible. Our usage of them is rather in the other direction: *adding more exponentials harmlessly.* A contraction-enabled ? must be present for a programmer to use *call/cc* or similar control operations.

In our system it is of crucial importance to identify the conditions under which the following properties are preserved in the presence of subexponentials:

- $?_{i'}(?_k A \,\mathbin{\rotatebox[origin=c]{180}{\&}}\, ?_{j'} B) \equiv\ ?_k A \,\mathbin{\rotatebox[origin=c]{180}{\&}}\, ?_{j'} B$ if and only if $i' \le k$ and $i' \le j'$
- $!_i(!_k A \multimap\, !_j B) \equiv\ !_i(!_k A \multimap B)$ if and only if $j \le k$ and $j \le i$.

The index names are chosen to correspond to formulas in Sect. 4. A consideration of the cut-free proofs of these properties shows that the restrictions on indices are *necessary and sufficient.* Although our use of subexponentials will be effusive, we only admit formulas that satisfy these restrictions.

Proof theoretically, the core of this paper is a rather bold proposition: *a formula of the form* $!_i?_{i'}(!_k?_{k'} A \multimap\, !_j?_{j'} B)$, *provided that* $i' \le k, j'$ *and* $j \le i, k$, *forms a valid synthetic connective.* Clearly it cannot be seen as such according to the current definitions of focusing and the polarities of ! and ?. The consequence of this boldness is that we can no longer rely on the proof theory of (subexponential) linear logic. Although we use linear logic formulas, cut-elimination within our system cannot inherit the cut-elimination procedure of linear logic (the cut-free proofs will not stay within the fragment). What's needed is a new, unique proof theory that is suitable to this new sense of synthetic connective, with its own procedure for cut-elimination that is sensitive to the index restrictions on formulas. The proof theory, presented in a longer version of this paper [13], allows our system to stand independently of linear logic.

4 The Fragment MC: Multi-colored Classical Logic

For our purpose, all subexponentials $?_i$ admit both weakening and contraction (on the right). The aspect of linear logic that prevents resources from being reused is an orthogonal issue. For clarity, we assume that subexponential indices form a partial order, although some of our examples will simply use natural numbers as indices. We also assume the existence of finite joins and meets and that there is a maximum index mx and a minimum 0. We write $min(a, b)$ for meets and $max(a, b)$ for joins.

With a single pair of exponentials there are seven equivalence classes of exponential prefixes or *modalities*: $?, !, ?!, !?, ?!?, !?!$ and the empty prefix. This property extends to any pair of subexponentials $!_i$ and $?_k$. For any prefix ν, $\nu\nu \equiv \nu$. For example, $!_i?_k!_i?_kA \equiv !_i?_kA$. Most studies of linear logic consider only a few of these modalities. The LC fragment of linear logic [7], for example, uses only ! and ? although ?! and !? may appear applied to atoms.

Since our main connective is implication and we wish to capture (at least) classical computations, let us review how classical implication can be represented in linear logic. The most straightforward translation is $!A \multimap ?B$ (equivalently $?A^\perp \parr ?B$). This representation is sufficient for cut-free proofs, but for proofs with cuts it is clearly inadequate: one cannot form a cut with a right-side $?B$ and a left-side $!B$. In the terminology of [3], we require an *adequate inductive decoration*. Two well-known ones are the T-translation: $!?A \multimap ?B$, and the Q-translation $!A \multimap ?!B$. In each case one modality is a suffix of the other. With subexponentials however, we need a more flexible way to switch between left and right modalities because a promotion of $?_kB$ to $!_i?_kB$ may not always be possible.

The modalities we use will be $!_i?_k$ and $?_k!_i?_k$ (for every pair of i and k). Note that since $!_i?_k!_i?_kA \equiv !_i?_kA$, *each modality can be seen as a suffix of the other*. Promotion and dereliction will be restricted to forms that render them *inverse operations*:

$$\frac{\dfrac{!_i?_kA}{?_k!_i?_kA}\ derelict}{!_i?_kA}\ promote$$

Adding a $!_i$ or $?_k$ before $!_i?_k$ or $?_k!_i?_k$ will still result in something equivalent to one of the two forms. We only use equivalence classes of modalities and never write $!_i?_k!_i?_k$.

The T and Q translations gave rise to LKT and LKQ respectively, which are semi-focused sequent calculi, and cut-elimination for these systems distinguish between a call-by-name (T) and call-by-value (Q) strategies. On the surface, our system does not have such properties because we rely on *logical equivalences*, such as between $!_i?_kA$ and $!_i?_k!_i?_kA$, and between $?A\mathbin{\invamp}?B$ and $?(?A\mathbin{\invamp}?B)$. The correspondence between our system and (subexponential) linear logic exists only at the level of provability, but not in the structure of cut-elimination and cut-free proofs. However, our "fragment" of linear logic in fact forms a logical system in its own right, with its own notion of what "cut free proof" means. As we show in the longer version of this paper [13], cut-elimination within this fragment requires a more delicate procedure than for unrestricted subexponential linear logic. The non-determinism eliminated by polarization and focusing can also be achieved here, but that is not the purpose of this paper. Rather it is to demonstrate the effect on cut permutation of something quite different from polarity information.

Only the form $!_i?_k$ may appear on the left side of $\multimap$ (left-side of sequents), thus we effectively use three modalities for each pair of indices i and k ($?_i!_k$ as well).

As already indicated, our "arrow" appears as follows:

$$!_i?_{i'}(!_k?_{k'}A\multimap!_j?_{j'}B) \quad \text{or} \quad ?_{i'}!_i?_{i'}(!_k?_{k'}A\multimap!_j?_{j'}B) \quad \textbf{such that } i' \le k, j' \textbf{ and } j \le k, i$$

The index restrictions are not ad-hoc: they are motivated by focusing. Under these restrictions, we can show that the above formula is equivalent to several other forms:

$$!_i?_{i'}(!_k?_{k'}A\multimap!_j?_{j'}B) \;\equiv\; !_i(!_k?_{k'}A\multimap!_j?_{j'}B) \;\equiv\; !_i(!_k?_{k'}A\multimap?_{j'}B)$$

The first condition, $i' \le k, j'$, makes $?_{i'}$ gratuitous and allows us to write a synthetic introduction rule as long as the rule does not break apart $!_k?_{k'}$ in the premise. The second condition, $j \le k, i$, means that a conclusion $?_{j'}!_j?_{j'}B$ *can always be promoted* to $!_j?_{j'}B$ (thus it does not matter if we write $!_j?_{j'}B$ or $?_{j'}!_j?_{j'}B$ on the right of $\multimap$). All of these conditions are required for cut elimination.

The following also hold: $!_j?_{j'}(!_k?_{k'}A\multimap!_m?_{m'}B) \;\multimap\; (!_k?_{k'}A\multimap!_m?_{m'}B)$ (to construct a proof bottom-up, first promote $!_m$, then derelict $!_j$, then promote $?_{j'}$). This will allow us to form an adequate $\rightarrow$-elimination rule.

For this presentation we restrict to the adequately decorated arrow as our only connective, although other connectives can be added along similar lines[1]. It is also possible to interpret sequents as formulas: a (two-sided) sequent such as $\Gamma, !_k?_{k'}A \vdash !_j?_{j'}B$ can be interpreted recursively as $\Gamma \vdash !_{mx}?_{min(k,j')}(!_k?_{k'}A\multimap!_j?_{j'}B)$. This being overly cumbersome, we simplify the interpretation of sequents by also using the empty modality and the connective $\mathbin{\invamp}$, but only for sequents. To formally define the language of MC, we use the following grammar:

---

[1] Adding second-order quantifiers will, however, encounter problems similar to those found in polarized settings: how can one enforce the index restrictions on the bound variable when they are instantiated. First-order $\forall$ can be represented by $!_i?_{i'}\forall x.!_k?_{k'}A$ where $i' \le k'$ and $k \le i$. These restrictions guarantee $?_{i'}\forall x.?_{k'}A \;\equiv\; \forall x.?_{k'}A$ and $!_i\forall x.!_kA \;\equiv\; !_i\forall x.A$.

$$S \longrightarrow F \mid F_1^{\perp} \mid F_1^{\perp} \otimes S \mid F_2 \otimes S$$
$$F \longrightarrow F_1 \mid F_2$$
$$F_1 \longrightarrow !_i?_{i'}C. \qquad F_2 \longrightarrow ?_{i'}!_i?_{i'}C$$
$$C \longrightarrow (!_k?_{k'}C \multimap !_j?_{j'}C) \mid p$$

The syntactic variable p ranges over atomic formulas; S ranges over formulas that represent sequents; F ranges over formulas preceded by the modalities $!_i?_{i'}$ or $?_{i'}!_i?_{i'}$ for any i, i'; and C ranges over formulas that are not preceded by these modalities. It is also required that the restrictions on implication $i' \le k, j'$ and $j \le k, i$ are imposed recursively on $!_i?_{i'}C$ and on all $?_{i'}!_i?_{i'}C$. Furthermore, *all end-sequents are of the form* $\vdash F$. When we speak of a *formula of the MC fragment,* we are referring to a F-generated formula of the above grammar, since such formulas form end-sequents. Notice that the grammar generates at most one F_1 formula in a sequent, which means there is at most one $!_i?_{i'}C$ on the right-hand side (left side occurrences are represented by $F_1^{\perp}$). This is the only kind of sequent that will appear in proofs starting from valid end-sequents.

Informally speaking, the index of an exponential operator indicates a *resource class*. A proof of $!_kA$ can only contain resources (free variables) of class k or higher. One useful analogy is that ? represents a *producer* and ! represents a *consumer*. A formula prefixed by $!_i?_kA$ or $?_k!_i?_kA$ has both a *consumer level i* and a *producer level k*. The special forms of promotion and dereliction switch the formula between the producer and consumer modes. For example, a level-2 consumer will not consume level-1 products. As long as $?_k$ hides behind $!_i$, it does not affect what can be consumed. But once revealed, it produces a resource, which can only be used by consumers at level k or below, i.e., appear in subproofs outside of the context of a promotion to a level higher than k. A producer has the ability to replicate itself (contraction). On the left hand side of $\multimap$, $!_i?_k$ becomes a level i producer.

For example, the equivalence between $!_i(!_kA \multimap !_jB)$ and $!_i(!_kA \multimap B)$ when $j \le k, i$ can be understood using this analogy as follows. In a term $\lambda x.t$ representing the proof of a formula such as $!_3(!_4A \multimap !_2B)$, the outer $!_3$ states that no products lower than level-3 will be consumed by $\lambda x.t$. The only new product in t is the variable x, which is at level 4. So of course stating that t does not use products lower than level 2 is redundant.

5   Natural Deduction and Proof Terms in MC

In the following we adopt the convenient notations $!_{ij} = !_{i,j} = !_i?_j$ and $?_{jij} = ?_{j,i,j} = ?_j!_i?_j$. So $?_{jij}A$ promotes to $!_{ij}A$, for example. We revert to the unabbreviated forms for clarity when needed.

Single sided sequents suffice for classical linear logic. However, since our principal connective is an arrow, using one-sided sequents will appear awkward. Thus we shall make a small concession to Gentzen style systems and use two sided sequents with at most one formula on the right. This means that instead of $\Gamma \vdash ?_{iki}A, ?_{jmj}B$ we write $!_j?_m!_jB^{\perp}, \Gamma \vdash ?_{iki}A$. This concession is superficial since negation in linear logic is involutive. The interpretation of a sequent $A_1, A_2, \ldots, A_n \vdash B$ is the formula $A_1^{\perp} \otimes A_2^{\perp}, \ldots, \otimes A_n^{\perp} \otimes B$, or just

$A_1^\perp \otimes A_2^\perp, \ldots, \otimes A_n^\perp$ if the right side is empty. The concession is only one of *notation*. In this two-sided scenario the modalities that can appear to the right of $\vdash$ are $!_i?_k$ and $?_k!_i?_k$ while those that can appear on the left are $!_i?_k$ and $!_k?_i!_k$. We store multiple conclusions on the left. Since contractions are allowed, the left-hand side of a sequent can be considered a set. The notation B, Γ does not preclude the possibility that $B \in \Gamma$. Certain rules, such as explicit weakening and the renaming of variable indices are excluded from the system because they can be shown to be admissible. The set Γ consists of formulas $!_{n_1} A_1, \ldots !_{n_m} A_m$. We write $\Gamma^{(k)}$ to indicate that k is the smallest n_i. In other words, a promotion (on the right) to $!_m$ is allowed by $\Gamma^{(k)}$ if $m \leq k$. We write $\Gamma^{(n_1, \ldots, n_k)}$ to mean $\Gamma^{(min(n_1, \ldots, n_k))}$. We refer to n and m as the *maximum promotion level* of their contexts. The empty context has maximum promotion level mx. The natural deduction style proof system for MC, along with their term annotations, appear in Fig. 1.

$$\frac{u : \Gamma \vdash !_i?_k A}{[d]u : (!_k?_i!_k A^\perp)^d, \Gamma \vdash} \; Name \qquad \frac{t : (!_k?_i!_k A^\perp)^d, \Gamma \vdash}{\mu^k d.t : \Gamma \vdash ?_k!_i?_k A} \; Unname$$

$$\frac{f : \Gamma_1^{(n)} \vdash !_i?_{i'}(!_k?_{k'} A \multimap !_j?_{j'} B) \qquad t : \Gamma_2^{(m)} \vdash !_k?_{k'} A}{(f \;\sharp_{n'} t) : \Gamma_1^{(n)} \Gamma_2^{(m)} \vdash !_j?_{j'} B} \; App, \; n' \leq min(n, j')$$

$$\frac{t : !_k?_{k'} A^x, \Gamma^{(n)} \vdash !_j?_{j'} B}{\lambda x.t : \Gamma' \Gamma^{(n)} \vdash !_i?_{i'}(!_k?_{k'} A \multimap !_j?_{j'} B)} \; Abs, \; i \leq n$$

$$\frac{t : \Gamma^{(n)} \vdash ?_i!_k?_i A}{t : \Gamma' \Gamma^{(n)} \vdash !_k?_i A} \; Produce \; (k \leq n) \qquad \frac{t : \Gamma \vdash !_j?_i A}{t \; (\equiv \mu^i d.[d]t) : \; \Gamma \vdash ?_i!_j?_i A} \; Consume$$

$$\frac{}{x : !_i?_j C^x, \Gamma \vdash !_i?_j C} \; Id \qquad \frac{t : \Gamma \vdash !_a?_b q}{t : \Gamma \vdash !_c?_d q} \; !DR \; (a \geq c, \; b \leq d, \; q \; \text{atomic})$$

Fig. 1. Natural deduction in MC

We prefer natural deduction to present delimited controls operators in direct style. We refer to the implication introduction and elimination rules as *Abs* and *App*. Because of the index restrictions already imposed on formulas, no further conditions are required in *App*. In addition to the *Produce* rule, promotion has been folded into *App* and, implicitly, the *Id* rule. *Produce* does not cross $!_i?_k$ but switches the formula from consumer to producer mode going upward. In each rule that requires promotion, implicit or otherwise, weakening is also folded in. The dereliction rule *Consume* can also be simulated by *Name* followed immediately by *Unname*. However, we have included it as a separate rule for convenience. The *!DR* rule is only needed for atoms. The restrictions on implication means that the $?_{i'}$ in $!_i?_{i'}(!_k?_{k'} A \multimap !_j?_{j'} B)$ does not interfere with its introduction rule (i.e., it does not destroy focus, despite appearance). However, $!_a?_b q$ when q is an atom posses a slight problem. This is the only rule that violates focusing boundaries, but it is required for completeness, by which we mean the following (see [13] for proof):

Theorem 1. *A formula of the MC fragment is provable by natural deduction in MC if and only if it is provable in subexponential linear logic.*

The correctness of MC depends on not just this theorem but on proof theoretic results for its sequent calculus, with the most important difference being the restriction of Id to atoms C, plus the replacement of App with a left introduction rule:

$$\frac{\Gamma^{(n)} \vdash !_k?_{k'}A \qquad !_j?_{j'}B, \Gamma^{(n)} \vdash C}{!_i?_{i'}(!_k?_{k'}A \multimap !_j?_{j'}B), \Gamma^{(n)} \vdash C}$$

Cut elimination in this system requires all the index restrictions on formulas to succeed. Furthermore, one can check that instances of this rule can be *stacked*, i.e., focused (consider B to be another implication), by verifying the initial elimination test for synthetic connectives. These results are presented in detail in [13].

Despite the index restrictions on implication formulas, it is possible to have Γ contain formulas preceded by any $!_i$. For example, $!_4?_0(!_5?_1A \multimap !_3?_2(!_8?_6B \multimap !_2?_2C))$ is a legal formula. Observe that in the sequent

$$\vdash !_i?_{i'}(!_k?_{k'}A \multimap !_j?_{j'}(!_m?_{m'}C \multimap !_r?_{r'}D)),$$

the restriction $j \leq k, i$ means that the second, inner $\multimap$ can be introduced immediately above the introduction of the first, because the addition of $!_k?_{k'}A$ to the left-side context will not prevent the promotion of $!_j$. Thus instances of Abs can always be stacked, i.e., focused as well. Thus focusing is possible should one pursue the extension of the proof system in that direction.

The proof terms here are referred to as *bounded $\lambda\mu$-terms* because we have adopted several aspects of the original $\lambda\mu$ calculus as presented in [17]. First, we prefer to associate the proof term with the entire subproof, and not just the single formula on the right of a sequent. Secondly, Parigot referred to $[d]t$ as a *named term*, which is then unnamed, or bound, by μ. If one wishes to make sense of $\lambda\mu$ calculus in terms of intuitionistic logic, then μ must be considered a non-logical constant of type $((A \to \bot) \to \bot) \to A$, which would of course require a double negation/CPS translation to become intuitionistically admissible. Under this interpretation, $[d]t$ is just $(d\ t)$ where d is of type $A \to \bot$. This means that the answer type of a captured continuation can only be $\bot$, which is a problem if the continuation is to be used as a procedure. In a logic with involutive negation, such an interpretation becomes unnecessary. The only meaningful operation that $Name$ embeds is a dereliction[2]. We have adopted the strategy that neither promotion nor dereliction are reflected in proof terms: they do not appear to serve any purpose. The only extra notation we add are the *bounded μ^k binder,* superscripted by the producer class/level of its type, and the *bounded reset indicator* $\natural_n$, which is used to decorate every application term, with its subscript index indicating whether this continuation may be captured by some μ^k. Unlike in other formulations of delimited control operators, $\natural_n$ is not an independent operator but a form of type annotation.

---

[2] When restricted to the modalities $!_i?_{i'}$ and $?_{i'}!_i?_{i'}$, dereliction can be expressed by the axiom $!A \to A$: this is an intuitionistic implication, which surely has proof $\lambda x.x$.

To illustrate the system we show a generalized proof of a Peirce-like formula:

$$
\cfrac{
\cfrac{
\cfrac{
\cfrac{
\cfrac{
\cfrac{
\cfrac{
\cfrac{!_{b'}?_{b}!_{b'}Q^{\perp},!_{aa'}P \vdash !_{aa'}P}{!_{b'}?_{b}!_{b'}Q^{\perp},!_{a'}?_{a}!_{a'}P^{\perp},!_{aa'}P \vdash}\ Name
}{!_{a'}?_{a}!_{a'}P^{\perp},!_{aa'}P \vdash ?_{b'}!_{b}?_{b'}Q}\ Unname
}{!_{a'}?_{a}!_{a'}P^{\perp},!_{aa'}P \vdash !_{bb'}Q}\ Produce,\ b \le a, a'
}{\ \ldots \vdash !_{jj'}(!_{kk'}(!_{aa'}P \multimap !_{bb'}Q) \multimap !_{aa'}P) \quad !_{a'}?_{a}!_{a'}P^{\perp} \vdash !_{kk'}(!_{aa'}P \multimap !_{bb'}Q)}\ \substack{Abs,\ k \le a' \\[2pt] App}
}{!_{a'}?_{a}!_{a'}P^{\perp},!_{jj'}(!_{kk'}(!_{aa'}P \multimap !_{bb'}Q) \multimap !_{aa'}P) \vdash !_{aa'}P}\ Name-Unname
}{!_{jj'}(!_{kk'}(!_{aa'}P \multimap !_{bb'}Q) \multimap !_{aa'}P) \vdash ?_{a',a,a'}P}\ Produce,\ a \le j\ (automatic)
}{!_{jj'}(!_{kk'}(!_{aa'}P \multimap !_{bb'}Q) \multimap !_{aa'}P) \vdash !_{aa'}P}\ Abs,\ i \le max
}{\vdash !_{ii'}(!_{jj'}(!_{kk'}(!_{aa'}P \multimap !_{bb'}Q) \multimap !_{aa'}P) \multimap !_{aa'}P)}
$$

There are only a few restrictions in addition to those already imposed on formulas ($k \le a'$ and $b \le a'$). One can easily choose indices that would make this proof valid, including using the same index everywhere. The proof term is $\lambda x.\mu^{a'}d.[d](x\ \natural_m(\lambda y.\mu^{b'}e.[d]y))$ where $m \le min(j,a')$. As we shall show, the $\mu^{a'}$ term is guaranteed to be able to catch continuations up to the nearest $\natural_n$ with $n \not\ge a'$. In a linear ordering, if $n = k - 1$, for example, then capturing the continuation beyond $\natural_n$ would mean that the promotion to $!_k$ (as part of the upper *Produce* rule) cannot be duplicated in the proof.

6   Intuitionistic Logic in MC

The resource control aspect of MC generalizes intuitionistic logic. Restrict all formulas to use only the modalities $!_2?_1$ and $?_1!_2?_1$. Then any copies of $?_1!_2?_1$ must be weakened away before an implication can be introduced with the *Abs* rule. This corresponds to the multiple-conclusion version of intuitionistic sequent calculus, at least when restricted to the $\rightarrow$ fragment. Indeed that proof system shares the rare property with subexponential linear logic that weakening is forced beneath initial rules. Peirce's formula, $((P \rightarrow Q) \rightarrow P) \rightarrow P$, cannot be proved using only $!_{ik}$ and $?_{kik}$ with $i \not\le k$:

$$!_{21}(!_{21}(!_{21}(!_{21}P \multimap !_{21}Q) \multimap !_{21}P) \multimap !_{21}P)$$

Although promotion is applicable (backwards) on $!_{21}P$, any copy of P created by contraction, which will appear as $?_1!_2?_1P$ (or $!_1?_2!_1P^{\perp}$ on the left), must be weakened away upon introduction of $!_{21}(!_{21}P \multimap !_{21}Q)$. The only producers that do not labor in vain are those on the left side of (an odd number of occurrences of) $\multimap$. In terms of the generalized proof of Peirce's formula shown earlier, the condition $k \le a'$ would fail. Contracting the entire formula first will similarly fail.

It is simple to verify that any formula where the maximum producer level is lower than the minimum consumer level can only have an intuitionistic proof. From this perspective, classical and intuitionistic logics are at opposite ends of a spectrum. Intuitionistic logic allows no scope extrusion, whereas classical logic make no such restrictions. With the appropriate indexing scheme in MC, we can choose to extrude into the scope of some $\rightarrow$ while keeping others intact. MC represents a new way to combine these logics without one collapsing into the other.

7   Reductions for Bounded $\lambda\mu$

When proofs are combined by cut, the potential danger of merging two contexts $\Gamma_1^{(n)}$ and $\Gamma_2^{(m)}$ into $\Gamma_1\Gamma_2^{(n,m)}$ is that the lowering of the maximum promotion level will mean that some promotions can no longer be duplicated. To determine what remains as valid reduction strategies, first we note the following, which is easily proved:

Lemma 2. *If* $\Gamma^{(n)} \vdash !_i?_k A$ *is provable without weakening (all formulas in* Γ *appear as free variables in the proof term), then* $i \leq n$.

Using this property, first we verify that β-reduction is still a valid strategy:

$$\cfrac{\cfrac{s: \, !_{uu'}A^x, \Gamma_1^{(n,u)} \vdash !_{rr'}B}{\lambda x.s: \Gamma_1^{(n)} \vdash !_{vv'}(!_{uu'}A \multimap !_{rr'}B)} \, v \leq n \qquad t: \Gamma_2^{(m)} \vdash !_{uu'}A}{s[t/x]: \Gamma_1\Gamma_2^{(n,m)} \vdash !_{rr'}B}$$

We are only concerned with those branches of the left subproof where $!_{uu'}A$ persists (has not been weakened away). Clearly in these branches there cannot be any promotion higher than to $!_u$. But by Lemma 2, the right subproof either ends in weakening, which permutes easily with cut, or it holds that $u \leq m$, and thus $min(n, m)$ is not lower than $min(n, u)$, which means these promotions can still occur after $\Gamma_2^{(m)}$ has been added to the left subproof. Thus β-**reduction is still a valid strategy**.

The restriction $n' \leq min(n, j')$ on the *App* rule can be strengthened to $n' \leq min(i, j')$ since $i \leq n$ by Lemma 2.

Next, we examine the possibility of capturing the continuation in the style of the original $\lambda\mu$ calculus. In order to not clash with β-reduction, the original $\lambda\mu$ calculus only allowed the continuation to the right of μ to be captured, by which we mean the following scenario:

$$\cfrac{\cfrac{\cfrac{\cfrac{\cfrac{w: \Gamma' \vdash !_{vv'}(!_{uu'}A \multimap !_{rr'}B)}{[d]w: \, (!_{v'vv'}(!_{uu'}A \multimap !_{rr'}B)^\perp)^d, \Gamma' \vdash}}{\vdots}}{s: \, (!_{v'vv'}(!_{uu'}A \multimap !_{rr'}B)^\perp)^d, \Gamma_1^{(n)} \vdash}}{\mu^{v'}d.s: \Gamma_1^{(n)} \vdash ?_{v'vv'}(!_{uu'}A \multimap !_{rr'}B)}}{\Gamma_1^{(n)} \vdash !_{vv'}(!_{uu'}A \multimap !_{rr'}B)} \, v \leq n \qquad t: \Gamma_2^{(m)} \vdash !_{uu'}A}{\mu^{v'}d.s\{[d]wt/[d]w\}: \Gamma_1\Gamma_2^{(n,m)} \vdash !_{rr'}B}$$

Again relevant are the branches of the left subproof that contains $!_{v'vv'}(!_{uu'}A \multimap !_{rr'}B)^\perp$, which means that there can only be promotions up to level $!_{v'}$. But $v' \le u$ is required of well-formed formulas and by Lemma 2, $u \le m$. So once again substituting $\Gamma_2^{(m)}$ into the left subproof will not prevent any promotions from being duplicated. **This type of continuation capture is also valid.**

However, it was soon recognized (e.g., [16]) that continuation capture need not clash with β-reduction as long as we define a (call-by-value) reduction strategy carefully. The resulting form of continuation capture can be generalized to the capture of an entire evaluation context:

$$
\cfrac{f : \Gamma_1^{(n)} \vdash !_{vv'}(!_{uu'}A \multimap !_{rr'}B) \qquad \cfrac{
\cfrac{
\cfrac{t : \Gamma' \vdash !_{uu'}A}{[d]t : (!_{u'uu'}A^\perp)^d, \Gamma' \vdash}
\\ \vdots \\
\cfrac{s : (!_{u'uu'}A^\perp)^d, \Gamma_2^{(m)} \vdash}{\cfrac{\mu^{u'}d.s : \Gamma_2^{(m)} \vdash ?_{u'uu'}A}{\mu^{u'}d.s : \Gamma_2^{(m)} \vdash !_{uu'}A}}
}{\ } \ u \le m
}{(f \ \natural_k \ \mu^{u'}d.s) : \Gamma_1\Gamma_2^{(n,m)} \vdash !_{rr'}B}
$$

In order to permute the cut with f into the right subproof, we need to be able to retain promotions up to level $!_{u'}$. Unlike the two previous cases, however, now it would possible for this condition to be violated if n or r' is smaller than u' (see the proof of Peirce's formula). Thus here we mark the redex with $\natural_k$ where $k \le min(n, r')$ (or $k \le min(v, r')$). The continuation f can be captured by $\mu^{u'}$ only if $min(n, r') \ge u'$. We allow k to be less than $min(n, r')$ because we may decide to force β-reduction anyway. We can reserve the minimum index 0 for this purpose, and require $k > 0$ in all terms $\mu^k d.t$. Then $(f \ \natural_0 s)$ will always force β-reduction: we can just write $(f \ s)$ in that case. If capturing f is legal, then the resulting proof can have the following form:

$$
\cfrac{
\cfrac{
\cfrac{(f \ \natural_k t) : \Gamma_1^{(n)}\Gamma' \vdash !_{rr'}B}{!_{r'rr'}B^\perp, \Gamma_1^{(n)}\Gamma' \vdash} \ Consume
\\ \vdots \\
\cfrac{!_{r'rr'}B^\perp, \Gamma_1\Gamma_2^{(n,m)} \vdash}{\Gamma_1\Gamma_2^{(n,m)} \vdash ?_{r'rr'}B} \ null
}{\ }
}{s\{(f \ \natural_k t)/[d]t\} : \Gamma_1\Gamma_2^{(n,m)} \vdash !_{rr'}B} \ r \le m, n
$$

Recall that merely moving a formula from one side of the sequent to the other is a null operation in linear logic due to involutive negation. It is important to note that the final promotion from $?_{r'}!_r?_{r'}B$ to $!_r?_{r'}B$ is always valid because it is required of legal formulas that $r \le u, v$ in $!_{vv'}(!_{uu'}A \multimap !_{rr'}B)$. But by Lemma 2,

$v \leq n$ and $u \leq m$, and thus $r \leq n, m$ which makes the promotion valid. This is a consequence of the focusing-related property $!(!A \multimap !B) \equiv !(!A \multimap B)$ when generalized to subexponentials.

8   A Call-by-Value Reduction Strategy

In a term such as $(f \; \sharp_2 (g \; \sharp_5 (h \; \sharp_4 \mu^3 d.s)))$, μ^3 should be able to capture both h and g but not f. To formalize an evaluation strategy, we define the following.

Terms and Values:

λ-variables $x, \ldots$ and μ-variables $d, \ldots$
Values $V \longrightarrow x \mid \lambda x.T$
Terms $T \longrightarrow V \mid (T_1 \; \sharp_i T_2) \mid \mu^k d.T \mid [d]T$

Evaluation Contexts:

$$F^k \longrightarrow [] \mid (F^k \; \sharp_n T) \mid (V \; \sharp_j F^k) \; (j \geq k)$$
$$E \; \longrightarrow [] \mid (V \; \sharp_m E) \mid (E \; \sharp_n T)$$

E is an evaluation context while F^k is a *level-k* context that represents a continuation that be captured by $\mu^k d.t$ in the "hole" of the context. Note that in the definition of F^k there is no restriction on the index n, because *forward* capture is always allowed. The rules for F^k implies that terms such as $(\mu^m d.s) \; \sharp_i (\mu^k d.t)$ will have the form $F^m[\mu^m d.s]$ where $F^m = [\;] \sharp_i (\mu^k d.t)$ since μ-terms are not values: the μ^k term will be part of the context captured by μ^m regardless of whether $i \geq k$.

Evaluation Rules:

$$E[(\lambda x.t) \; \sharp_n V)] \quad \longrightarrow \quad E[t\{V/x\}]$$
$$E[V \; \sharp_i F^k[\mu^k d.t]] \quad \longrightarrow \quad E[V \; \sharp_i \; t\{F^k[u]/[d]u\}] \quad (i \not\geq k)$$

A term of the form $(\lambda x.u) \; \sharp_n V$ or $(V \; \sharp_i F^k[\mu^k d.r])$ with $i \not\geq k$ is called a *redex*.

There is no evaluation rule for when $i \geq k$, which forces F^k to represent the maximum context that can be captured. If no μ^k appears in a term, then the second evaluation rule will never be used, the $\sharp_k$ labels are universally ignored and standard call-by-value reduction takes place.

All application terms include a $\sharp_i$, which can act as a delimiter, stopping the capture of continuations by μ^k with $i \not\geq k$. Instead of a null evaluation rule $\sharp_i(V) \longrightarrow V$, which is found in most other systems, in our system β-reduction simply ignores the symbol.

We are missing an evaluation rule for when the entire term is of the form $F^n[\mu^n d.t]$. However, a $\lambda x.x$ can always be added in front of such a term. We can require that the minimum index 0, or some reserved index unrelated to any k that may appear in $\mu^k d.t$, is reserved for the purpose of forcing β-reduction. For example, $(\lambda x.x) \; \sharp_0 \; \mu^n d.t$, with $n > 0$, reduces to $(\lambda x.x) \; \sharp_0 \; t\{u/[d]u\}$ (because here $F^n = [\;]$). In other words it simply deletes the annotations placed on t.

The following key lemma illustrates the workings of the contexts and evaluation rules. A proof term is closed if all variables are bound by some λ or μ. Our results are for closed terms (which are the only proofs possible for end-sequents of the form $\vdash F$), but they can also be generalized.

Lemma 3. *Decomposition. For all non-value, closed terms T, either T is of the form $F^k[\mu^k d.s]$ or of the form $E[r]$ where r is a redex. Furthermore, E or F^k is uniquely determined.*

The proof is by induction on the structure of T. It follows easily from the property established by the lemma that if we placed an extra $\lambda x.x$ before a term t then all non-value, closed terms have uniquely determined redexes. If t has type $!_k?_{k'}A$, then $(\lambda x.x) \natural_n t$ is well-typed for all $n \leq k'$. The lemma also implies the following:

Corollary 4. *Progress. If $s = (\lambda x.x) \natural_0 t$ is a closed proof term, then $s = E[r]$ where r is a redex. Furthermore, r is unique.*

Thus *evaluation is deterministic*. The following lemma shows that evaluation is type-safe, and forms part of the Subject Reduction proof.

Lemma 5. *Let C represent either a context E or F^k,*

1. *if $s : \Gamma \vdash A$, $s' : \Gamma \vdash A$ and $C[s] : \Gamma' \vdash A'$ are provable, then $C[s'] : \Gamma' \vdash A'$ is also provable.*
2. *if $F^k[\mu^k d.s] : \Gamma \vdash A$ is provable, then $s\{F^k[w]/[d]w\} : \Gamma \vdash A$ is also provable.*

Each part is proved by induction on the context. The difference between sequents $\Gamma \vdash A$ and $A^\perp, \Gamma \vdash$ is merely notational in classical linear logic. The central argument is similar to the reductions at the end of Sect. 7. Type soundness then follows:

Theorem 6. *Subject Reduction. If $s : \Gamma \vdash A$ is provable and $s \longrightarrow t$ using the evaluation rules, then $t : \Gamma \vdash A$ is also provable.*

In terms of the existing literature on delimited control operators, the behavior of our operators is dynamic as opposed to static: they are closer to the *control/prompt* of [6]. Since we do not interpret $\natural_k$ as an independent operator, we cannot use it to guarantee a static behavior. How μ-terms in the body of the substitution term $F^k[u]$ is to be delimited would depend on its surrounding context, which is not statically known. It is known that such dynamic, delimited control operators can have non-terminating behavior, even in a typed setting (see [2,11]). The following term, adopted from [11], confirms this:

$$(\lambda x.x)\natural_0((\lambda z.\mu^i d.(\lambda y.[d]t)\natural_i[d]t)\natural_i(\mu^i d.(\lambda y.[d]t)\natural_i[d]t))$$

Here, t can be any value of type $!_j?_iA$ while y and z are vacuous. Let V represent the value $\lambda z.(\mu^i d.(\lambda y.[d]t) \natural_i[d]t)$, then $F^i = V\natural_i[\ ]$ and the term reduces to

$$(\lambda x.x) \natural_0 ((\lambda y.V\natural_i t) \natural_i(\mu^i d.(\lambda y.[d]t) \natural_i[d]t))$$

leading to an infinite sequence of reductions. However, the term is well-typed. Also, it does have a normal form, namely t, but this is not reachable using the call-by-value strategy. This phenomenon does not contradict cut-elimination. The reduction steps still correspond to valid proof transformations. The possibility of non-termination is hardly cause for alarm from a programming perspective, and it is entirely consistent with what we already know to be possible with delimited control operators. A static behavior can be simulated using $(\lambda x.x)\natural_0[\,]$, changing the continuation capture rule to:

$$E[V \; \natural_i F^k[\mu^k d.t]] \quad \longrightarrow \quad E[V \; \natural_i \; t\{(\lambda x.x)\natural_0 F^k[u]/[d]u\}] \quad (i \ngeq k)$$

A call-by-name strategy can likewise avoid non-termination but then we can only capture continuations in the form of the original $\lambda\mu$-calculus, which is very limited for direct style programs. Call-by-value offers a much more general way to capture continuations. Forcing a particular evaluation strategy proof theoretically can be accomplished through focusing and this is well known. What we have shown here is that, however a continuation capturing strategy was chosen, *the presence of subexponentials in MC forces it to be delimited.*

9 Conclusion

The casual reader who opens this article to an arbitrary page may become dismayed by the large numbers of $?_i!_k?_i$ and $!_j?_{j'}$ that appear in formulas. Beneath this apparent chaos, however, are the fundamental proof-theoretic principles of adequate inductive decoration, cut-elimination, and focusing. We have extended these principles to a fragment of subexponential linear logic that enhances classical logic. In the MC fragment intuitionistic logic is found not as a restriction on proofs but as a restriction on formulas. This represents a new way to combine classical with intuitionistic logic which is quite different from the polarization approach of other systems. Although MC is defined using the formulas of subexponential linear logic, and is consistent with it in terms of provability, it is self-contained as a logical system, with its own, rather unique proof theoretic properties. The hierarchy of subexponentials naturally leads to a hierarchy of delimited control operators.

Acknowledgments. The authors wish to thank the reviewers of this paper for their comments, and to Danko Ilik for valuable discussion. This work was funded by the ERC Advanced Grant ProofCert.

References

1. Andreoli, J.-M.: Logic programming with focusing proofs in linear logic. J. Logic Comput. **2**(3), 297–347 (1992)
2. Ariola, Z.M., Herbelin, H., Sabry, A.: A type-theoretic foundation of delimited continuations. High. Order Symbolic Comput. **22**(3), 233–273 (2009)

3. Danos, V., Joinet, J.-B., Schellinx, H.: LKT and LKQ: sequent calculi for second order logic based upon dual linear decompositions of classical implication. In: Girard, J.-Y., Lafont, Y., Regnier, L. (eds.) Advances in Linear Logic. London Mathematical Society Lecture Note Series, vol. 222, pp. 211–224. Cambridge University Press, Cambridge (1995)

4. Danos, V., Joinet, J.-B., Schellinx, H.: The structure of exponentials: uncovering the dynamics of linear logic proofs. In: Gottlob, G., Leitsch, A., Mundici, D. (eds.) Kurt Gödel Colloquium. LNCS, vol. 713, pp. 159–171. Springer, Heidelberg (1993)

5. Danvy, O., Filinski, A.: Abstracting control. In: LISP and Functional Programming, pp. 151–160 (1990)

6. Felleisen, M.: The theory and practice of first-class prompts. In: 15th ACM Symposium on Principles of Programming Languages, pp. 180–190. ACM, New York (1988)

7. Girard, J.-Y.: A new constructive logic: classical logic. Math. Struct. Comput. Sci. 1, 255–296 (1991)

8. Griffin, T.: The formulae-as-types notion of control. In: 17th Annual ACM Symposium on Principles of Programming Languages, pp. 47–57 (1990)

9. Ilik, D.: Delimited control operators prove double-negation shift. Ann. Pure Appl. Logic 163(11), 1549–1559 (2012)

10. Kameyama, Y.: Axioms for delimited continuations in the CPS hierarchy. In: Marcinkowski, J., Tarlecki, A. (eds.) CSL 2004. LNCS, vol. 3210, pp. 442–457. Springer, Heidelberg (2004)

11. Kameyama, Y., Yonezawa, T.: Typed dynamic control operators for delimited continuations. In: Garrigue, J., Hermenegildo, M.V. (eds.) FLOPS 2008. LNCS, vol. 4989, pp. 239–254. Springer, Heidelberg (2008)

12. Liang, C., Miller, D.: Focusing and polarization in linear, intuitionistic, and classical logics. Theor. Comput. Sci. 410(46), 4747–4768 (2009)

13. Liang, C., Miller, D.: On subexponentials, synthetic connectives, and multi-level delimited control - long version (2015). Unpublished manuscript available online at http://www.lix.polytechnique.fr/Labo/Dale.Miller/papers/subdelim-long.pdf

14. Materzok, M., Biernacki, D.: A dynamic interpretation of the CPS hierarchy. In: Jhala, R., Igarashi, A. (eds.) APLAS 2012. LNCS, vol. 7705, pp. 296–311. Springer, Heidelberg (2012)

15. Nigam, V., Miller, D.: Algorithmic specifications in linear logic with subexponentials. In: ACM SIGPLAN Conference on Principles and Practice of Declarative Programming (PPDP), pp. 129–140 (2009)

16. Ong, C.H.L., Stewart, C.: A Curry-Howard foundation for functional computation with control. In: Symposium on Principles of Programming Languages, pp. 215–227 (1997)

17. Parigot, M.: λμ-calculus: an algorithmic interpretation of classical natural deduction. In: Voronkov, A. (ed.) LPAR 1992. LNCS, vol. 624, pp. 190–201. Springer, Heidelberg (1992)

18. Saurin, A.: A hierarchy for delimited continuations in call-by-name. In: Ong, L. (ed.) FOSSACS 2010. LNCS, vol. 6014, pp. 374–388. Springer, Heidelberg (2010)

On the Expressive Power of Communication Primitives in Parameterised Systems

Benjamin Aminof[1], Sasha Rubin[2], and Florian Zuleger[1]([✉])

[1] Technische Universität Wien, Vienna, Austria
zuleger@forsyte.at
[2] Università Degli Studi di Napoli "Federico II", Naples, Italy

Abstract. We study foundational problems regarding the expressive power of parameterised systems. These (infinite-state) systems are composed of arbitrarily many finite-state processes that synchronise using a given communication primitive, i.e., broadcast, asynchronous rendezvous, broadcast with message loss, pairwise rendezvous, or disjunctive guards. With each communication primitive we associate the class of parameterised systems that use it. We study the relative expressive power of these classes (can systems in one class be simulated by systems in another?) and provide a complete picture with only a single question left open. Motivated by the question of separating these classes, we also study the absolute expressive power (e.g., is the set of traces of every parameterised system of a given class ω-regular?). Our work gives insight into the verification and synthesis of parameterised systems, including new decidability and undecidability results for model checking parameterised systems using broadcast with message loss and asynchronous rendezvous.

1 Introduction

Parameterised systems are composed of arbitrarily many copies of the same finite-state process. The processes in a system run independently, but are given a mechanism by which they can synchronise, e.g., in broadcast systems one process can send a message to all the other processes, while in a rendezvous system the message is received by a single process [12,17]. Examples of such systems abound in theoretical computer science (e.g., distributed algorithms [18]) and biology (e.g., cellular processes [15]).

Problem Statement. Different synchronisation mechanisms, or *communication primitives* as we call them here, yield systems with different capabilities. For instance, broadcast is at least as expressive as rendezvous since in two steps broadcast may simulate a rendezvous (I broadcast "I want to rendezvous", and someone broadcasts the reply "I will rendezvous with you", illustrated in Fig. 5).

Benjamin Aminof and Florian Zuleger are supported by the Austrian National Research Network S11403-N23 (RiSE) of the Austrian Science Fund (FWF) and by the Vienna Science and Technology Fund (WWTF) through grant ICT12-059. Sasha Rubin is a Marie Curie fellow of the Istituto Nazionale di Alta Matematica.

© Springer-Verlag Berlin Heidelberg 2015
M. Davis et al. (Eds.): LPAR-20 2015, LNCS 9450, pp. 313–328, 2015.
DOI: 10.1007/978-3-662-48899-7_22

On the other hand, intuitively, broadcast is more expressive than rendezvous (since to simulate a broadcast a process would have to rendezvous with all other processes before anyone made a different move). The motivation of this paper is to formalise such reasoning and make such intuitions precise.

Communication Primitives. This paper focuses on representative primitives from the literature on formal methods for parameterised systems: Broadcast (BC), like CBP message passing can model ethernet-like broadcast, GSM's cell-broadcast, or the notifyAll method in Concurrent Java [5,12,20]; Asynchronous Rendezvous (AR) can model the notify method in Concurrent Java [5]; Broadcast with Message Loss (BCML) can model mobile ad hoc networks (MANETS) and systems that use selective broadcast with nodes that can be activated or deactivated at any time [6–8]; and Pairwise Rendezvous (PR), like CSP message passing, can model population protocols [4,17]. For comparison we also consider a primitive that admits cutoffs, i.e., disjunctive guards (DG) [10], a property not shared by the previous primitives.[1]

Executions of Parameterized Systems. We systematically compare communication primitives using the standard notion of executions from the point of view of single processes. Indeed, many papers (e.g. [2,3,5–7,9,11–13,17]) consider specifications from the point of view of single processes — important examples of such specifications are safety specifications like coverability and liveness specifications like repeated coverability and termination. Given a process P, and a communication primitive CP, let P_{CP}^n be the finite-state system composed of n copies of P that synchronise using CP (note that there is no special "controller" process). An *execution* is a (finite or infinite) sequence of labels[2] of states of a single process in P_{CP}^n. In many applications (e.g., in parameterised verification), one needs to consider systems of all sizes. Thus, we let P_{CP}^∞ denote the infinite-state system consisting of the (disjoint) union of the systems P_{CP}^n for each $n \in \mathbb{N}$.

Relative Expressive Power. We define the natural comparison CP $\leq_{\text{IE}}$ CP' as follows: for every process P that uses CP there is a process Q that uses CP', such that P_{CP}^∞ and $Q_{\text{CP}'}^\infty$ have the same set of infinite executions. Similarly, we write $\leq_{\text{FE}}$ if considering only finite executions. The informal meaning of these comparisons $\leq$ is that CP' can simulate CP, with respect to linear-time specifications. All of our simulations (except of AR by PR) have the added properties that they also hold for systems of a fixed finite size, and that they are efficiently computable. This latter fact is useful for example for model checking (MC) classes of parameterised systems with respect to linear-time specifications (over a single process), i.e., if CP $\leq$ CP' and the translation from P to Q is efficient, then MC CP-systems is (immediately) reduced to MC CP'-systems. We remark that most decidability results for MC parameterised systems are for linear-time specifications, whereas for branching-time specifications it is typically undecidable [2,3,11,17].

---

[1] A cutoff is a maximal number of processes that needs to be model checked in order to guarantee correct behaviour of any number of processes. Our results show that, indeed, having a cutoff lowers the expressive power.

[2] Typically, each label is a set of atomic propositions.

Absolute Expressive Power. Motivated by the problem of comparing communication primitives, we also study their absolute expressive power. That is, a communication primitive CP determines a class of languages $\mathcal{L}_{CP}$, i.e., the sets of executions of such systems. How does the class $\mathcal{L}_{CP}$ relate to canonical classes of languages, such as regular, context-free, ω-regular, etc.? Answers to such questions allow one to deduce that certain communication primitives *cannot be simulated* by certain others, as well as directing one's choice of communication primitive for modeling and synthesis of distributed systems.

Our contributions.[3]

Relative Expressive Power. We provide a full picture of the relative expressive power of these communication primitives, see Figs. 1 and 2 — an arrow from CP to CP′ means CP′ ≤ CP,[4] and a mark across an arrow means that CP < CP′.

Section 3 establishes all but three of the arrows in Figs. 1 and 2: we get PR $\leq_{IE}$ BCML from Theorems 6 and 4, PR $\leq_{FE}$ DG from Theorem 2 and Proposition 5, and AR $\leq_{FE}$ PR from Proposition 5 and Theorem 3.

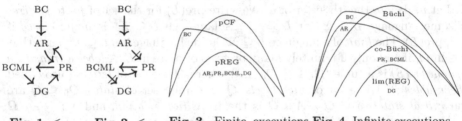

Fig. 1. $\leq_{FE}$ **Fig. 2.** $\leq_{IE}$ **Fig. 3.** Finite executions **Fig. 4.** Infinite executions
of P_{CP}^{∞} of P_{CP}^{∞}

Absolute Expressive Power. The classes of languages of finite executions generated by the different primitives are illustrated in Fig. 3. BC can generate languages that are not context free, whereas DG, PR, BCML, AR generate exactly the prefix-closed regular languages (pREG). However, no communication primitive can generate all prefix-closed context-free languages (pCF). The case of infinite executions is illustrated in Fig. 4. We show that DG can generate exactly limits of regular languages, BCML, PR can generate exactly co-Büchi languages, AR, BC can generate non ω-regular languages, whereas no communication primitive can generate all ω-regular languages. We present our results on absolute expressive power in Sect. 5. The strictness of the arrows in Figs. 1 and 2 follow from our results on absolute expressive power. To get DG $<_{IE}$ PR (and thus also deduce DG $<_{IE}$ BCML) use Theorems 4 and 7 (and the fact that there are co-Büchi languages that are not the limit of any regular language, e.g., all words over $\{a, b\}$

---

[3] For lack of space, some proofs are missing or only sketched and can be found in the full version of this paper.

[4] We note that the transitivity of the relations $\leq$ gives rise to additional simulations that, for clarity, are not drawn in the figures.

with finitely many as). To get PR $<_{IE}$ AR use Proposition 9 and Theorem 6. To get AR $<_{FE}$ BC use Proposition 6 and Theorem 3. To get AR $<_{IE}$ BC use Proposition 8 and Theorem 5.

Model Checking Linear-Time Specifications. Our techniques yield new results about model checking (MC) AR and BCML parameterised systems for liveness properties.[5] In particular, even the simplest liveness property (i.e., does there exist an infinite run) is undecidable for AR systems (Sect. 4). Also, liveness properties are decidable in PTIME for systems using BCML (a problem that was not even known to be decidable); this follows because BCML can be efficiently simulated by PR (Proposition 2), and the fact that MC of PR-systems can be done in PTIME (which itself follows from [17, Section 4]).

2 Definitions and Preliminaries

Tuples f over a set X may be written $(x_1, \cdots, x_k)$ or in functional notation $f \in X^{[k]}$, i.e., $f(i) = x_i$. Given a set Σ, we denote by Σ^*, Σ^+, Σ^ω the sets of all finite strings, all non-empty finite string, and all infinite strings, respectively, over Σ. Let u_i denote the ith letter of u. We write $pre(L)$ for the set of *finite prefixes* of some language $L \subseteq \Sigma^*$ or $L \subseteq \Sigma^\omega$. A language $L \subseteq \Sigma^*$ is *prefix closed* if $L = pre(L)$. The *limit* of a language $L \subseteq \Sigma^*$ is the language $\lim L \subseteq \Sigma^\omega$ such that $\alpha \in \lim L$ if and only if infinitely many prefixes of α are in L. A *labeled transition system (LTS)* is a tuple $\langle \Omega, A, Q, Q_0, \delta, \lambda \rangle$ where Ω is a set of *letters* (also called *observables*),[6] A is a set of *edge labels*, Q is a finite set of *states*, $Q_0 \subseteq Q$ are the *initial states*, $\delta \subseteq Q \times A \times Q$ is the *transition relation*, and $\lambda : Q \to \Omega$ is the *labeling function*. For $\tau = (q, a, q')$ we write $src(\tau) = q$, $des(\tau) = q'$ and $edglab(\tau) = a$, and we also write $q \xrightarrow{a} q'$. A *path* of an LTS is a (finite or infinite) string of transitions $\pi := \pi_1 \pi_2 \ldots$ of δ such that $src(\pi_{i+1}) = des(\pi_i)$ for every i. We write $src(\pi) := src(\pi_1)$, and if π is finite we write $des(\pi) := des(\pi_{|\pi|})$. A *run* is a path π where $src(\pi) \in Q_0$. We write $edglab(\pi)$ for the sequence $edglab(\pi_1)edglab(\pi_2)\ldots$. Typically the edge-labels will carry information, i.e., an action (e.g., send message m), and whether or not the edge is visible. See [22] for basic notions about automata. In particular, we use the following acronyms: NFW, NBW and NCW where N stands for "nondeterministic", F for "finite", B for "Büchi", C for "co-Büchi", and W for "word automata". Counter machines CM are standard variations of Minsky Machines, i.e., they have a fixed number of counters that can be incremented, decremented if not zero, and tested for zero. In the rest of this paper, the word "simulation" is used as in ordinary natural language, and not as part of the technical term "(bi)simulation relation".

A note about simulations and visibility. In order to reason about simulations we have to be able to hide some of the inner steps involved. Consider the following motivating example. All the x86 family of processes support the same basic

---

[5] As in [9,12] we formalise safety properties as regular sets (of finite words) and liveness properties as ω-regular sets (of infinite words).

[6] In applications one typically takes $\Omega := 2^{AP}$ where AP is a set of atomic predicates.

instruction set, but they implement each instruction using their own sequences of microcode instructions. This is fine since to the running software these sequences of microcode are invisible and it can only see their effect on the observables, i.e., the values of the registers. In order to capture this basic trait of simulations, our definition of local process labels each transition with a Boolean flag indicating whether it is visible or not, with the added condition that invisible transitions do not change the observables[7]. To demonstrate, in the introduction we illustrated that BC (effectively) simulates PR by replacing every PR transition by two (successive) BC transitions. Thus, in order to preserve the set of executions, we have to hide one of these two transitions (see Fig. 5).

System Model. For a set Σ, let $\Sigma_{\mathsf{sync}} = \{\mathtt{m!}, \mathtt{m?} \mid \mathtt{m} \in \Sigma\}$ be the *synchronisation-actions*. Let Π be a set of *internal-actions*, disjoint from Σ. A *local process* is a finite LTS $P = \langle \Omega, A, S, S_0, \delta, \lambda \rangle$ where $A := (\Sigma_{\mathsf{sync}} \cup \Pi) \times \mathbf{B}$ and for every $(q, (\sigma, b), q') \in \delta$, if $b = \mathbf{false}$ then we must have that $\lambda(q) = \lambda(q')$. A transition $\tau = (q, (\sigma, b), q')$ is called *visible* if $b = \mathbf{true}$ and *invisible* if $b = \mathbf{false}$. Thus, an invisible transition may change the state but not what is observed.

Define functions $\mathsf{act}, \mathsf{vis}$ such that $\mathsf{act}(\tau) = \sigma$ and $\mathsf{vis}(\tau) = b$. A state $s \in S$ is *able to receive* (resp. *able to send*) message $\mathtt{m} \in \Sigma$ if there is a transition $\tau \in \delta$ with $\mathsf{src}(\tau) = s$ and $\mathsf{act}(\tau) = \mathtt{m?}$ (resp. $\mathsf{act}(\tau) = \mathtt{m!}$). States and transitions of P are called *local states* and *local transitions*. Informally, local transitions with $\sigma \in \Pi$ are transitions that a single process must take alone, and are called *local internal transitions*, whereas local transitions with $\sigma \in \Sigma_{\mathsf{sync}}$ may involve synchronising with other processes, and are called *local synchronising transitions*.

For a local process P we now define the *global system*, i.e., the composition P_{CP}^n of n-many copies of P that communicate using CP. A *global state* of P_{CP}^n is an n-tuple of elements of S, collectively S^n. For $f = (s_1, \cdots, s_n), f' = (s_1', \cdots, s_n') \in S^n$ a *global transition* $\tau = (f, \nu, f') \in S^n \times (\Sigma \cup \Pi) \times S^n$ satisfies:

1. If $\nu \in \Pi$ then there exists i and $b \in \mathbf{B}$ such that $s_i \xrightarrow{\nu, b} s_i'$, and $s_\ell = s_\ell'$ for $\ell \neq i$ *(internal transition)*.
2. If $\nu = \mathtt{m} \in \Sigma$:
   - If CP = BC: there exist i and $b_i \in \mathbf{B}$ such that $s_i \xrightarrow{\mathtt{m!}, b_i} s_i'$ and letting R be the set of processes $j \neq i$ that are able to receive $\mathtt{m}$, we must have that R is non-empty and $s_j \xrightarrow{\mathtt{m?}, b_j} s_j'$ for all $j \in R$ (and some $b_j \in \mathbf{B}$), and $s_\ell = s_\ell'$ for $\ell \notin R \cup \{i\}$ *(broadcast transition)*.[8]
   - If CP = AR: there exist i and $b_i \in \mathbf{B}$ such that $s_i \xrightarrow{\mathtt{m!}, b_i} s_i'$ and either: there exists $j \neq i$ such that $s_j \xrightarrow{\mathtt{m?}, b_j} s_j'$ and $s_\ell = s_\ell'$ for $\ell \neq i, j$; or there is no

---

[7] It is common to allow specifications (e.g., the LTL formula G_p) to be satisfied by computations that loop forever in the same state. Thus, we *don't* consider every transition in which the observables don't change to be invisible. In particular, we can have both visible and invisible self loops. Using the CPU analogy, the former corresponds to a NOP in the instruction set, and the latter to a NOP in microcode.

[8] A slightly different version of BC, in which R is also allowed to be empty, also appears in the literature [12]. Our results also hold for this version.

$j \neq i$ such that j is able to receive m, and $s_\ell = s'_\ell$ for $\ell \neq i$ *(asynchronous rendezvous transition)*.

- If CP = PR: there exist $i \neq j$ and $b_i, b_j \in \mathbf{B}$ such that $s_i \xrightarrow{\text{m!},b_i} s'_i$ and $s_j \xrightarrow{\text{m?},b_j} s'_j$, and $s_\ell = s'_\ell$ for $\ell \neq i, j$ *(rendezvous transition)*.

- If CP = BCML: there exist i and $b_i \in \mathbf{B}$ such that $s_i \xrightarrow{\text{m!},b_i} s'_i$ and there is some, possibly empty, set R of processes (not containing i) such that $s_j \xrightarrow{\text{m?},b_j} s'_j$ for all $j \in R$ (and some $b_j \in \mathbf{B}$), and $s_\ell = s'_\ell$ for $\ell \notin R \cup \{i\}$ *(broadcast with message loss transition)*.

- If CP = DG: there exist $j \neq i$ and $b \in \mathbf{B}$ such that $s_i \xrightarrow{s_j?,b} s'_i$ and $s_j \xrightarrow{s_j!,\textbf{false}} s_j$, and $s_\ell = s'_\ell$ for $\ell \neq i, j$ *(guarded transition)*. [9]

A process k is said to be *involved* in a global transition τ if it takes a local transition γ from s_k to s'_k (e.g., in all cases above process i is involved in τ). Moreover, it is *visibly involved* if $\mathsf{vis}(\gamma) = \textbf{true}$.

Finally, P^n_{CP} is the LTS $\langle \Omega^n, \Sigma \cup \Pi, S^n, S^n_0, \Delta, \Lambda \rangle$ where Δ consists of the global transitions (just defined), and $\Lambda(f)(i) := \lambda(f(i))$ for every $i \in [n]$. The infinite state LTS P^∞_{CP} is the disjoint union of P^n_{CP} for $n \in \mathbb{N}$, and it is called a *parameterised system*, or just a *system*.

Executions. Let π be a path of P^n_{CP}. We will relate π to paths in P corresponding to a single process. Fix a process index $k \in [n]$. Let $i_1 < i_2 < \dots$ be the set of indices such that process k is visibly involved in the global transition π_{i_j}, and define $s_j := \Lambda(\mathsf{src}(\pi_{i_j}))(k) \in \Omega$ (for all j). If there are only finitely many indices $i_1 < i_2 < \dots < i_l$, we let $vislet_k(\pi)$ be the concatenation of $s_1 s_2 \dots s_l$ with the additional letter $\Lambda(\mathsf{des}(\pi_{i_l}))(k)$ at the end. Otherwise, we set $vislet_k(\pi) := s_1 s_2 \dots$. We define the *set of 1-executions of* P^n_{CP} by

$$\text{EXEC}(P^n_{\text{CP}}) := \{vislet_k(\pi) : k \in [n], \pi \text{ is a run of } P^n_{\text{CP}}\} \subseteq \Omega^\omega \cup \Omega^*$$

and the *set of 1-executions of* P^∞_{CP} as $\text{EXEC}(P^\infty_{\text{CP}}) := \cup_{n \in \mathbb{N}^+} \text{EXEC}(P^n_{\text{CP}})$. We denote the infinite (resp. finite) elements of $\text{EXEC}(\cdot)$ by $\text{INFEXEC}(\cdot)$ (resp. $\text{FINEXEC}(\cdot)$). It is worth noting that if a run π is infinite, but $vislet_k(\pi)$ is finite, then process k was only doing finitely many meaningful moves in π (which is akin, in a system with only visible transitions, to it being scheduled only finitely many times) which is why we do not include such traces in INFEXEC.

3   Relative Expressive Power

For communication primitives CP, CP', write CP $\leq_{\text{IE}}$ CP' if for every local process P there is a local process Q (computable from P) such that $\text{INFEXEC}(P^\infty_{\text{CP}}) =$

---

[9] If CP = DG then we also assume $\Sigma = S$ (i.e., the synchronization alphabet is the set of local states), and for every local state $s \in S$ there is a transition $s \xrightarrow{t!,a} r$ if and only if $s = r = t$ and $a = \textbf{false}$ (i.e., the only transition τ with $\mathsf{act}(\tau) = s!$ is an invisible self-loop on state s).

INFEXEC($Q_{CP'}^\infty$). Similarly, define $\leq_{FE}$ with FINEXEC replacing INFEXEC. For $x \in \{IE, FE\}$, if CP $\leq_x$ CP' $\leq_x$ CP then write CP $\equiv_x$ CP'. If CP $\leq_x$ CP' and CP $\not\equiv_x$ CP' then write CP $<_x$ CP' (and define $<_x$ similarly). Informally, if CP $\leq_x$ CP' we say that CP' *simulates* CP. Note that, in the definition of $\leq_x$, if there is a PTIME algorithm that given P produces the corresponding Q then we say that CP' *efficiently simulates* CP. All the simulation results CP $\leq_x$ CP' in this paper (except for AR $\leq_{FE}$ PR) are efficient simulations.

Relationship with Verification. Every regular language of finite words is called a *safety* property, and every ω-regular language of infinite words is called a *liveness* property, cf. [12]. The model checking problem for parameterised systems using CP for a given safety (resp. liveness) property L over Ω is the following: given P, decide whether or not FINEXEC(P_{CP}^∞) $\subseteq L$ (resp. INFEXEC(P_{CP}^∞) $\subseteq L$). This model checking problem is sometimes called the "parameterised model checking problem" or "parameterised verification", e.g., [11]. If CP' effectively simulates CP then the parameterised verification problem for systems using CP is reducible to the parameterised verification problem for systems using CP'.

3.1 Simulations

The simulations DG $\leq_x$ PR $\leq_x$ BC, with $x \in \{FE, IE\}$, have already been discovered in the literature [9]; we illustrate PR $\leq_x$ BC in Fig. 5. These results are the starting point for our fine-grained analysis. In this section we establish the simulations DG $\leq_x$ BCML $\leq_x$ PR $\leq_x$ AR $\leq_x$ BC for $x \in \{IE, FE\}$. All these simulations were not previously known. In all the proofs we efficiently construct, given a local process P, a local process Q such that EXEC(P_{CP}^n) = EXEC($Q_{CP'}^n$).

$$q \xrightarrow{(m!,a)} q' \qquad\qquad q \xrightarrow{(m_s!,a)} \cdot \xrightarrow{(ack_m?,false)} q'$$

$$r \xrightarrow{(m?,b)} r' \qquad\qquad r \xrightarrow{(m_s?,false)} \cdot \xrightarrow{(ack_m!,b)} r'$$

$$\xleftarrow{\quad\quad} (ack_m?,false)$$

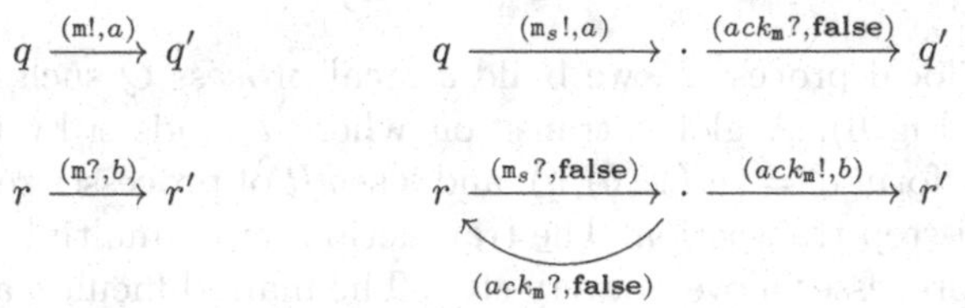

Fig. 5. Simulation of PR (left) by BC (right)

Proposition 1. AR $\leq_x$ BC, *for* $x \in \{FE, IE\}$.

Proof. Recall that the difference between PR and AR is only that in AR a process can send a message m even if there is no other process to receive it (but if there is, then one such process must receive m). We divide the global transitions of an AR system into three types: internal transitions, synchronous transitions involving two processes, and those involving only one process. Given local process P, we build local process Q such that Q_{BC}^n simulates P_{PR}^n (for every $n > 2$), by using a sequence (called a *transaction*) of 1 or 2 global transitions. Simulating the internal transitions is done directly, the synchronous transitions involving two processes are simulated by a 2-step transaction as in the simulation of PR by BC, and the synchronous transitions in which there is only a sender are simulated by a single-step transaction as follows: let $e = (p, (\mathtt{m}!, b), q)$ be a local transition in P; in Q, a process can take the local transition $(p, (\mathtt{m}_{solo}!, b), q)$ broadcasting the message that it is simulating a send of $\mathtt{m}$ that should have no receivers, and every process that is in a state that is able to receive $\mathtt{m}$ in P, receives $\mathtt{m}_{solo}$ and invisibly moves to a new special "disabled" copy of its current state from which it can no longer do anything; all other processes simply receive $\mathtt{m}_{solo}$ and invisibly self-loop. The intuition is that by sending $\mathtt{m}_{solo}$ process i guessed that there is no process able to receive $\mathtt{m}$ in the simulated system, and thus we disable the processes that witness the fact that the guess is wrong — effectively making it right. Note that if we do not disable them then one of these processes will be in the wrong state (since in the AR system one of them must receive $\mathtt{m}$ and move, but in the simulating system none moved) and will be able to later allow moves in the simulating system that are not possible in the simulated one.   □

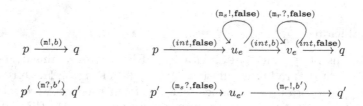

Fig. 6. Simulation of BCML (left) by PR (right)

Proposition 2. BCML $\leq_x$ PR, *for* $x \in \{\mathrm{FE}, \mathrm{IE}\}$.

Proof. Given a local process P, we build a local process Q such that Q_{AR}^n simulates P_{PR}^n (see Fig. 6). A global transition where i sends $\mathtt{m}$ by taking a local transition of the form $e := (p, (\mathtt{m}!, b), q)$, and a set R of processes receive, is simulated by a multi-step transaction. The transaction needs multiple steps because in PR only two processes move in every step. The main difficulty, and the reason the transaction is complicated, is that we must be careful not to introduce new executions that are not possible in the BCML system.

The simulation of sending the lossy broadcast message $\mathtt{m}$ is done in three stages: (a) process i internally and invisibly moves from state p to the new intermediate state u_e; state u_e has an invisible self-loop that sends message $\mathtt{m}_s$ (indicating it is trying to simulate sending $\mathtt{m}$); the self-loop enables the message to be sent to an arbitrary number of processes; (b) process i internally moves from state u_e to the new intermediate state v_e with visibility b; state v_e has an invisible self-loop that receives message $\mathtt{m}_r$; the self-loop allows to acknowledge that an arbitrary number of processes have received the message; (c) process i internally and invisibly moves from state v_e to state q.

The simulation of receiving message $\mathtt{m}$, by taking a local transition of the form $e' := (p', (\mathtt{m}?, b'), q')$, is in two stages: (a) process j invisibly moves from state p' to the new intermediate state $u_{e'}$ receiving message m_s. (b) process j moves from state $u_{e'}$ to state q' with visibility b' sending message m_r.

Unfortunately, we can not guarantee that this transaction is atomic, i.e., that no other global transitions intertwine with the simulation of a single lossy broadcast. We can not even guarantee that if a process j has received a message m_s from process k, then it is going to send m_r to process k, and not to another process. The solution is to consider the processes that performed the second stage with some process k as the ones which received the lossy broadcast message m from k. This works since, for each process j, the first stage of receiving a lossy broadcast message is invisible, and after that it can not do anything but participate in a second stage of receiving a message.   □

Proposition 3. PR $\leq_x$ AR, *for* $x \in \{\text{FE}, \text{IE}\}$.

Proposition 4. DG $\leq_x$ BCML, *for* $x \in \{\text{FE}, \text{IE}\}$.

Remark: There is a version of broadcast, lets call it ABC, where a process can broadcast a message even when no other process is able to receive it. All our results about BC hold also for ABC since BC $\equiv_x$ ABC, for $x \in \{\text{FE}, \text{IE}\}$.

4   Model Checking Asynchronous-Rendezvous Systems

The theorem below states that model checking even the most basic liveness properties of AR systems is undecidable. The proof of the theorem is an adaptation of the one used in [12] to prove a similar result for BC. Unfortunately, there is a serious complication: [12] makes central use of the fact that BC systems can elect a controller, but AR systems are not powerful enough to do that.

Fortunately, we can make do with a temporary controller, which AR can elect: from the initial state a process can send the message "I am now the controller" and enter the initial state of the "controller" component of the process template. If later on another process sends this message then it becomes the new controller, and the current controller, who receives this message, enters a special state D, from which it can do nothing. Thus, there are never two controllers at the same time, and at most n controller switches in a system with n processes.

The ability of AR to elect a temporary controller allows us not only to prove the theorem below, it also allows us to later show (see Fig. 4) that AR systems have an expressive power that is in between PR (which cannot elect even a temporary controller) and BC (which can elect a permanent controller). However, interestingly enough, this is only true for infinite traces. For finite traces, having a temporary controller, in contrast to a permanent one, provides no extra expressive power (see Fig. 3).

Theorem 1. *(i) Model checking liveness properties of parameterised systems communicating via* AR *is undecidable. (ii) In particular, the following problem is undecidable: given local process* P, *decide if* $\text{INFEXEC}(P_{\text{AR}}^{\infty})$ *is empty or not.*

Proof. For the first item, it is enough to reduce the halting problem for input-free deterministic counter machines CM (which is undecidable [19]) to the existence of a run in an AR system P_{AR}^∞ that visits a halting state infinitely often. It is convenient to assume that when (and if) the halting location is reached then the CM resets itself, i.e., it decrements all its counters until they become zero and then loops back to the initial state. The basic encoding for the simulation is from [12]. It uses one process called the *controller* to orchestrate the simulation and store the line of the CM, and many *memory* processes. Each memory process stores one bit for each counter, and the value of a counter is the number of processes having a non-zero bit for it. Each process has a special dead state D, which once entered cannot be exited.

A process may, from the initial state, nondeterministically become either the temporary controller or a memory process. The transitions in a memory process are, for each counter $c \in C$: if the stored c-bit is 0, then it can send the message "inc(c)" and set the c-bit to 1; if the stored c-bit is 1, then it can send the message "notzero(c)" and leave c unchanged, or send the message "dec(c)" and set c to 0, or *receive* the message "iszero(c)" and go to state D. From every state of the controller there is a complementary send/receive transition as specified by the CM line that this state represents. Thus, for example, an "increment c" is simulated by the controller receiving an "inc(c)" and moving to the next line of the CM (or to the state D, if the current command to simulate is not "increment c"), and an "if $c = 0$ goto l_1 else goto l_2" command is simulated by the controller either receiving "notzero(c)" and moving to state l_2; or moving to state l_1 and sending an "iszero(c)" which, if counter c is zero, is not received, and otherwise is received by a memory process with a 1 c-bit which then enters state D.

It is not hard to show that P_{AR}^n can faithfully simulate the CM as long as the counters stay below $n - 1$. Thus, if the CM reaches the halting location h then there is an infinite run of P_{AR}^n, for a large enough n, in which the process playing the controller is in h infinitely often. For the reverse direction, the key point is that whenever the simulation makes an error (such as replacing the temporary controller in mid simulation, or having the controller guess a counter is zero when it is not, or when a memory process simulates a command that is not what the controller wants to simulate) one process dies (i.e., enters state D). Thus, since there are only finitely many processes participating in any execution of P_{AR}^∞, in every infinite run of P_{AR}^∞, from some point on, no more processes die, and thus from that point on the simulation is correct. It follows that if there is a run of P_{AR}^∞ in which a process is in state h infinitely often then the run of the CM reaches the halting location. This completes the sketch of the proof of the first item. The second item uses a standard trick (see e.g. [12]) of adding an extra counter that increases in every step, and gets reset only when the halting state is reached. Thus, the system will run out of its finite number of memory processes and hang unless the CM reaches h.   □

5   Absolute Expressive Power

Finite Executions. First note that, since every prefix of a finite run is a run, for every CP and P we have that $\text{FINEXEC}(P_{\text{CP}}^{\infty})$ is prefix-closed.[10]

Proposition 5. *For every* CP *and prefix-closed regular language L there exists P such that $\text{FINEXEC}(P_{\text{CP}}^{\infty}) = L$.*

Proof. Transform an automaton for L into P by pushing letters into states (i.e., by changing L so that it remembers the last read input-letter in its state, labeling each state by this letter, and adjusting the initial states), and making all local transitions of P internal (i.e., not synchronisation transitions) and visible.   □

Proposition 6 (cf. [16]). *(i) There is a P s.t. $\text{FINEXEC}(P_{\text{BC}}^{\infty}) = pre(\{a^n b^n \mid n \geq 1\})$. Moreover,* BC *can generate non-context free languages; (ii) None of our communication primitives can generate all prefix-closed context-free languages.*

Theorem 2 ([17]). *For every P, the language $\text{FINEXEC}(P_{\text{PR}}^{\infty})$ is regular.*

Theorem 3. *For every P, the language $\text{FINEXEC}(P_{\text{AR}}^{\infty})$ is regular.*

Proof. Let $P = \langle \Omega, A, S, S_0, \delta, \lambda \rangle$ be some local process. We will construct a finite automaton (NFW) $\mathcal{A}$ that accepts exactly the traces in $\text{FINEXEC}(P_{\text{AR}}^{\infty})$. We call a local state $s \in S$ *unbounded* if for every $k \in \mathbb{N}$ there is an $n \in \mathbb{N}$, and a reachable global state f in P_{AR}^n, such that $|f^{-1}(s)| \geq k$. We denote by $U \subseteq S$ the set of *unbounded states* of P and by $B = S \setminus U$ the set of *bounded states*. Observe that $S_0 \cap B = \emptyset$, and that there is a $K \in \mathbb{N}$ such that $|f^{-1}(s)| \leq K$ for every $s \in B$, and every global state f in P_{AR}^{∞}.

We now define an automaton $\mathcal{A}$. States of $\mathcal{A}$ are pairs $\langle s, f \rangle$, where $s \in S$ is the state of the process whose execution we are observing, and $f \in S \to \{0, 1, \dots, K\} \cup \{\infty\}$, is such that $f(u) = \infty$ for every $u \in U$. Intuitively, for each state in B, f keeps track of the number the other processes in that state. A state $\langle s, f \rangle$ of $\mathcal{A}$ is initial iff: $s \in S_0$ and $f(u) = 0$ for all $u \in B$. $\mathcal{A}$ has a transition from $\langle s, f \rangle$ to $\langle s', f' \rangle$ if there is a local transition $\tau \in \delta$ where the counter values of f change to f' according to τ (and any possible matching transition if τ is a synchronising transition), and if s is involved in τ then s changes to s'. Such a transition is labeled by $\lambda(s)$ if s was involved in the transition and $\text{vis}(\tau) = \textbf{true}$, and otherwise by ϵ. For example, if $\tau = (p, (\text{m}?, \textbf{true}), p')$ then, together with the any transition of the form $(q, (\text{m}!, b), q')$ in δ, it induces the following transitions in $\mathcal{A}$: (i) a transition $\langle p, f \rangle \xrightarrow{\lambda(p)} \langle p', f' \rangle$ for every f, f' such that $f(q) \neq 0$, and f' is obtained from f by decrementing the value assigned to q and incrementing the value assigned to q'; (ii) a transition $\langle s, f \rangle \xrightarrow{\epsilon} \langle s, f' \rangle$ for every s and every f, f' such that $f(p) \neq 0, f(q) \neq 0$, and f' is obtained from f by decrementing the values assigned to p, q and incrementing the values assigned to p', q' (as usual, $\infty - 1 = \infty = \infty + 1$).

---

[10] Although distributed systems are routinely studied this way, one may also introduce final states to the local process and restrict to runs that end in final states [16].

Clearly, $\mathcal{A}$ is a finite automaton. We show that $\mathcal{A}$ (with all states accepting) accepts exactly the traces in $\text{FINEXEC}(P_{\text{AR}}^\infty)$. For every $n \in \mathbb{N}$, every execution obtained from some path of $\text{FINEXEC}(P_{\text{AR}}^n)$ is accepted by a run of $\mathcal{A}$ that "simulates" this execution by correctly updating the components s, f of its states.

It remains to prove that every word accepted by $\mathcal{A}$ is in $\text{FINEXEC}(P_{\text{AR}}^\infty)$. We claim (*): for every k there exists $n_k \in \mathbb{N}$ and a path π_k of $\text{FINEXEC}(P_{\text{AR}}^{n_k})$ reaching a global state such that there are at least k processes in every local state $s \in U$. To see that (*) yields $L(\mathcal{A}) \subseteq \text{FINEXEC}(P_{\text{AR}}^\infty)$, let π be some run of $\mathcal{A}$, and take $k \geq 2|\pi|$. Observe that in such a run at most k processes are involved. We build a corresponding run in $P_{\text{AR}}^{n_k}$. First, (†): using (*) we take a path that results in at least k processes in every local state $s \in U$. Recall that $S_0 \cap B = \emptyset$ and thus, in particular, there is at least one process in each of the initial states. Then, (‡): the process we want to observe starts from the relevant initial state and we imitate the run π of $\mathcal{A}$ step by step. This is indeed possible since whenever a step of ‡ requires a process with a state in U then such a process is available, and the same for processes in B. The former is guaranteed by ‡, and the latter since (by induction on the step number) the number of processes with states in B is at least as specified by the function f of the mimicked point in π.

We now prove (*). Let $u_1, ..., u_m$ be the states in U. Inducting on $0 \leq i \leq m$, we construct paths π^i in systems $\text{FINEXEC}(P_{\text{AR}}^{n_i})$ such that load at least k processes in states $u_1, ..., u_i$. We start with the empty run π^0 in $\text{FINEXEC}(P_{\text{AR}}^1)$. Clearly, π^0 satisfies the inductive claim. Given π^i, we construct π^{i+1} as follows: Let l_i be the length of π^i. By the definition of U, there is a path π in some system $\text{FINEXEC}(P_{\text{AR}}^n)$ that ends with at least $l_i + k$ processes in state u_{i+1} and at least one process in each of the initial states (thus, executing π in a larger system does not force any of the additional processes out of the initial states). We set $n_{i+1} = n + n_i$ and define π^{i+1} to be the concatenation of π and π^i in the system $\text{FINEXEC}(P_{\text{AR}}^{n_{i+1}})$. Clearly, π^{i+1} loads at least k processes in states $u_1, ..., u_{i+1}$ (since π^i can remove at most l_i states from u_{i+1}). $\square$

It is open if there is a constructive proof of Theorem 3.

Infinite Executions.

Theorem 4. *For every co-Büchi language L, and for* $\text{CP} \in \{\text{PR}, \text{BCML}, \text{AR}, \text{BC}\}$, *there is a local process P s.t.* $\text{INFEXEC}(P_{\text{CP}}^\infty) = L$.

Proof. Given an NCW $\mathcal{A}$ recognizing L we build a local process P, in which all transitions are visible, such that $\text{INFEXEC}(P_{\text{CP}}^\infty) = L$. The local process P has exactly the same structure, when viewed as a graph, as $\mathcal{A}$, with an added special sink state. In order to take a transition to a co-Büchi state (i.e., a state that an accepting run of $\mathcal{A}$ can only visit finitely many times) the process has to receive a message. A process that sends a message enters the sink state, and can not send again. Thus, in a system with n processes a process can visit a co-Büchi state up to $n - 1$ times. Transitions to other states are internal transitions of the process, and can always be taken. $\square$

We now show that not all ω-regular languages can be generated by our parameterised systems. In fact, the proof is general enough to apply to any reasonable notion of communication primitive (not only those defined in this paper), unless some additional fairness conditions are imposed. The proof employs a standard pumping argument to derive a contradiction by showing that if $ab^1ab^2a\ldots$ is in $\text{EXEC}(P_{\text{CP}}^n)$ then so is $ab^1ab^2\ldots ab^cab^\omega$, where c is the number of states in P_{CP}^n.

Proposition 7. *For every local process P, primitive CP, and $n \in \mathbb{N} \cup \{\infty\}$, the set $\text{INFEXEC}(P_{\text{CP}}^n)$ is not equal to the ω-regular language $L \subseteq \{a,b\}^\omega$ consisting of all infinite sequences that contain infinitely many occurrences of a.*

The following is not hard to see:

Proposition 8. *There is a BC-system that can generate the non co-Büchi language $\{a^l b^m c^\omega \mid l \geq m \geq 1\}$).*

We use a variation of the proof of Theorem 1 to show that AR-systems can generate languages that are not ω-regular:

Proposition 9. *There is an AR-system that can generate a language $L \subset \{a,b\}^\omega$ that has the property that*

1. *every string $\alpha \in L$ has a suffix $(a^n b^n)^\omega$ for some integer $n \in \mathbb{N}$, and*
2. *every string $(a^n b^n)^\omega$ is the suffix of some string in L.*

In particular, the language L is not co-Büchi.

Proof. Standard fooling arguments show that any L with the properties described is not Büchi (and thus not co-Büchi). We now describe an AR-system that can generate a language L with the properties stated in the lemma. The idea follows that in the proof of Theorem 1: a controller starts in mode a; in mode a it repeatedly increments a counter c; at some point it checks if all memory processes are 1 by issuing an "allone(c)" message (which can be implemented symmetric to the "iszero(c)" message), and moves to mode b; in mode b it repeatedly decrements the counter c; at some point it checks if all memory processes are 0 by issuing a "iszero(c)" message, and moves back to mode a to repeat the computation. Build the local process P based on M and note that a process that becomes a controller forever in P_{AR}^l does not err from some point on, and thus traces a path whose suffix is $(a^n b^n)^\omega$ with $n \leq l$. Note that an abdicating controller does not trace an infinite path (since the dead state is a dead-end). $\square$

The following is proved in almost the same way as Theorem 3:

Theorem 5. *For every P, the language $pre(\text{INFEXEC}(P_{\text{AR}}^\infty))$ is regular.*

Model checking safety and liveness properties (given as automata) of parameterised systems communicating via PR is decidable in PTIME [17]. Actually:

Theorem 6 (Implicit in [17]). *For every local process P, one can compute, in PTIME, a non-deterministic co-Büchi automaton for the set $\text{INFEXEC}(P_{\text{PR}}^\infty)$.*

Theorem 7. *Every* $\text{INFEXEC}(P_{\text{DG}}^{\infty})$ *is the limit of a regular language.*

Proof. By [10] there exists $N \in \mathbb{N}$ such that $\text{INFEXEC}(P_{\text{DG}}^{\infty}) = \text{INFEXEC}(P_{\text{DG}}^{N})$ (the idea is to pick N large enough such that every reachable state can be reached and adding one extra process; this choice of N ensures that every reachable self-loop $(s, (s!, \text{false}), s)$ can always be fired; the extra process can therefore move unrestrained). The language $L := \text{FINEXEC}(P_{\text{DG}}^{N})$ is regular (because it is the projection of the finite-state machine P_{DG}^{N}). It is sufficient to prove that $\text{INFEXEC}(P_{\text{DG}}^{N}) = \lim L$. Clearly $\text{INFEXEC}(P_{\text{DG}}^{N}) \subseteq \lim L$. To see the converse let $\alpha \in \lim L$. So there exists $k \in [N]$ and an infinite set $I \subseteq \mathbb{N}$ such that for every $i \in I$ there exists a run ρ_i of P_{DG}^{N} such that the prefix of α of length i is equal to $vislet_k(\rho_i)$. The set $\text{pre}\{\rho_i : i \in I\}$ is an infinite tree (under the prefix-ordering) that is finitely-branching (this is where we use the fact that the ρ_is are in P_{DG}^{N} and not P_{DG}^{∞}), and thus by Kőnig's Lemma, it has an infinite branch ρ. Clearly ρ is an infinite run of P_{DG}^{N} and $vislet_k(\rho) = \alpha$. Thus $\alpha \in \text{INFEXEC}(P_{\text{DG}}^{N})$. □

6   Related Work and Conclusion

Related Work. The absolute and relative expressive power of Petri nets and their extensions were studied for finite and infinite executions, e.g., [1,14,16]. They show a strict hierarchy of relative expressive power: Petri nets (PN) are less expressive than Petri nets with non-blocking arcs (PN+NBA), which are less expressive than Petri nets with transfer arcs (PN+T). Translating these results into the language of parameterised systems, one finds that these extensions roughly correspond to a very powerful model of parameterised systems with a controller and in which processes can be created and destroyed at any time. By this translation, PNs correspond to communication by PR, PN+NBA to communication by AR, and PN+T to communication by BC. In contrast, we focus on the setting with no controller and with no process creation or destruction. Thus, neither their simulation nor separation results are directly applicable to our more restricted setting.

The paper [9] organises communication primitives by whether or not model checking (MC) is decidable. Although they do have a notion of simulation, that notion is based on reducing the MC problem of systems using one primitive to systems using another primitive. In particular, their reduction transforms, while ours preserves, the set of behaviours. For instance, despite their result that MC safety properties of DG- and PR-systems are inter-reducible, we prove that there is a set of traces of a PR system that can't be generated by any DG system.

It was previously known that MC safety properties for systems using each of the primitives in this paper is decidable, liveness for BC is undecidable, and liveness for PR and DG is decidable [6,9,10,12,17]. We complete the picture, and prove, in particular, that for AR systems liveness is undecidable. The result in [9] on the undecidability of liveness for AR systems makes the additional assumption that there exists a unique "leader" process. The presence of a leader usually dramatically increases the expressive power, cf. [11,17], and makes it easier to establish undecidability than in our fully symmetric case. A number of papers focus on supplying the exact complexity of MC various parameterised systems, e.g., [2, 6–8, 11, 17, 21].

Conclusion. Comparing the expressive power of various models of computation is a central theme in theoretical computer science. In our case, such comparisons can be used to transfer results from one model to another. For instance, we prove that AR can be effectively simulated by BC, and thus the fact that safety is decidable for BC (cf. [12]) implies that safety is decidable for AR [9]. We also deduced the new result, using [17] and the fact that BCML can be efficiently simulated by PR, that liveness for BCML is decidable in PTIME.

The results about absolute expressive power are useful not only to show, e.g., that PR can not simulate AR, but also to point to the inherent limitations of each communication primitive. Such results can be used in synthesis to show that certain specifications are not realisable. As a concrete example, a minor variation of our proof that no system can generate the language "infinitely many a's" (Proposition 7) yields that there is no parameterised system (and thus no point in trying to synthesise one without adding external fairness conditions) that satisfies the conjunction of the properties "every run has infinitely many grants" and "some run has arbitrarily large gaps between successive grants".

References

1. Abdulla, P.A., Delzanno, G., Begin, L.V.: A classification of the expressive power of well-structured transition systems. Inf. Comput. **209**(3), 248–279 (2011)
2. Aminof, B., Kotek, T., Rubin, S., Spegni, F., Veith, H.: Parameterized model checking of rendezvous systems. In: Baldan, P., Gorla, D. (eds.) CONCUR 2014. LNCS, vol. 8704, pp. 109–124. Springer, Heidelberg (2014)
3. Aminof, B., Rubin, S., Zuleger, F., Spegni, F.: Liveness of parameterized timed networks. In: Halldórsson, M.M., Iwama, K., Kobayashi, N., Speckmann, B. (eds.) ICALP 2015. LNCS, vol. 9135, pp. 375–387. Springer, Heidelberg (2015)
4. Aspnes, J., Ruppert, E.: An introduction to population protocols. In: Garbinato, B., Miranda, H., Rodrigues, L. (eds.) Middleware for Network Eccentric and Mobile Applications, pp. 97–120. Springer, Heidelberg (2009)
5. Delzanno, G., Raskin, J.-F., Van Begin, L.: Towards the automated verification of multithreaded java programs. In: Katoen, J.-P., Stevens, P. (eds.) TACAS 2002. LNCS, vol. 2280, pp. 173–187. Springer, Heidelberg (2002)
6. Delzanno, G., Sangnier, A., Traverso, R., Zavattaro, G.: The cost of parameterized reachability in mobile ad hoc networks. CoRR abs/1202.5850 (2012)
7. Delzanno, G., Sangnier, A., Zavattaro, G.: Parameterized verification of ad hoc networks. In: Gastin, P., Laroussinie, F. (eds.) CONCUR 2010. LNCS, vol. 6269, pp. 313–327. Springer, Heidelberg (2010)
8. Delzanno, G., Sangnier, A., Zavattaro, G.: Verification of ad hoc networks with node and communication failures. In: Giese, H., Rosu, G. (eds.) FORTE 2012 and FMOODS 2012. LNCS, vol. 7273, pp. 235–250. Springer, Heidelberg (2012)
9. Emerson, E., Kahlon, V.: Model checking guarded protocols. In: LICS, pp. 361–370. IEEE (2003)

10. Emerson, E., Kahlon, V.: Reducing model checking of the many to the few. In: McAllester, D. (ed.) CADE 2000. LNCS, vol. 1831, pp. 236–254. Springer, Heidelberg (2000)
11. Esparza, J.: Keeping a crowd safe: on the complexity of parameterized verification. In: STACS (2014)
12. Esparza, J., Finkel, A., Mayr, R.: On the verification of broadcast protocols. In: LICS, p. 352. IEEE (1999)
13. Esparza, J., Ganty, P., Majumdar, R.: Parameterized verification of asynchronous shared-memory systems. In: Sharygina, N., Veith, H. (eds.) CAV 2013. LNCS, vol. 8044, pp. 124–140. Springer, Heidelberg (2013)
14. Finkel, A., Geeraerts, G., Raskin, J., Begin, L.V.: On the omega-language expressive power of extended petri nets. Theor. Comput. Sci. **356**(3), 374–386 (2006)
15. Fisher, J., Henzinger, T.A.: Executable cell biology. Nat. Biotechnol. **25**(11), 1239–1249 (2007)
16. Geeraerts, G., Raskin, J., Begin, L.V.: Well-structured languages. Acta Inf. **44** (3–4), 249–288 (2007)
17. German, S.M., Sistla, A.P.: Reasoning about systems with many processes. J. ACM **39**(3), 675–735 (1992)
18. Lynch, N.: Distributed Algorithms. Morgan Kaufman, San Francisco (1996)
19. Minsky, M.L.: Computation: Finite and Infinite Machines. Prentice-Hall, Upper Saddle River (1967)
20. Prasad, K.V.S.: A calculus of broadcasting systems. Sci. Comput. Program. **25** (2–3), 285–327 (1995)
21. Schmitz, S., Schnoebelen, P.: The power of well-structured systems. In: D'Argenio, P.R., Melgratti, H. (eds.) CONCUR 2013. LNCS, vol. 8052, pp. 5–24. Springer, Heidelberg (2013)
22. Vardi, M.Y.: An automata-theoretic approach to linear temporal logic. In: Banff Higher Order Workshop, pp. 238–266 (1995)

There Is No Best β-Normalization Strategy for Higher-Order Reasoners

Alexander Steen[✉] and Christoph Benzmüller

Institute of Computer Science, Freie Universität Berlin, Berlin, Germany
{a.steen,c.benzmueller}@fu-berlin.de

Abstract. The choice of data structures for the internal representation of terms in logical frameworks and higher-order theorem provers is a crucial low-level factor for their performance. We propose a representation of terms based on a polymorphically typed nameless spine data structure in conjunction with perfect term sharing and explicit substitutions.

In related systems the choice of a β-normalization method is usually statically fixed and cannot be adjusted to the input problem at runtime. The predominant strategies are hereby implementation specific adaptions of leftmost-outermost normalization. We introduce several different β-normalization strategies and empirically evaluate their performance by reduction step measurement on about 7000 heterogeneous problems from different (TPTP) domains.

Our study shows that there is no generally best β-normalization strategy and that for different problem domains, different best strategies can be identified. The evaluation results suggest a problem-dependent choice of a preferred β-normalization strategy for higher-order reasoning systems.

1 Introduction

Higher-order (HO) automated theorem proving (ATP) is, in many ways, more complex and involved than ATP in first-order or propositional logic. This additional complexity can be found on the proof search layer as well as on the layer of terms respectively formulas. However, one advantage is that the increased practical expressiveness of higher-order logic often enables more intuitive and concise problem representations and solutions. Many interactive and automated theorem provers for higher-order logic are based on Church's simple type theory [7] – also called classical higher-order logic (HOL) – or extensions of it.

In automated reasoning systems, terms are the most general and common pieces of information that are accessed, manipulated and created by most routines of the reasoning system. It is therefore not surprising, that the internal representation of terms is a crucial detail which has direct consequences on the efficiency of the whole system.

This work has been supported by the German National Research Foundation (DFG) under grant BE 2501/11-1 (Leo-III).

© Springer-Verlag Berlin Heidelberg 2015
M. Davis et al. (Eds.): LPAR-20 2015, LNCS 9450, pp. 329–339, 2015.
DOI: 10.1007/978-3-662-48899-7_23

We present a combination of term representation techniques for HO ATP systems that is based on locally nameless spine terms [4] and explicit treatment of substitutions [1]. These base choices are appropriately adjusted to meet the requirements of HO ATP systems. In particular, our representation natively admits an expressive typing system, efficient term operations and reasonable memory consumption through term sharing in a combination that is novel to HO reasoners.

The support for efficient term operations hereby not only covers those adopted from the first-order universe, but also the essential operation of β-normalization. To this end, we differ from prominent other reasoning systems in proposing several new (modified) β-normalization strategies that allow a problem-dependent handling of β-reduction. Thus, we do not hard-wire a single, preferred β-normalization strategy that we anticipate to perform best over all possible problem inputs. We think that this approach can in fact increase the overall performance of HO ATP systems in which β-(re-)normalization has to be repeatedly carried out during proof search.

This research is motivated by previous observations [18] that suggest that there is no single best normalization strategy. The here proposed strategies have been empirically evaluated using a representative set of benchmark problems for theorem proving. This evaluation confirms that there are problem classes at which the de-facto standard leftmost-outermost strategy is outperformed by our rather simple alternative strategies. The evaluation has been conducted within the LEOPARD [21] system platform for HOL reasoners.[1]

2   HOL Term Representation

HOL is an elegant and expressive formal system that extends first-order logic with quantification over arbitrary sets and functions. We consider Alonzo Church's *simple type theory* [7] which is a formulation of HOL that is built on top of the simply typed λ-calculus [5,6].

The simply typed λ-calculus, denoted $\lambda_\rightarrow$, augments the untyped λ-calculus with *simple types*, which are freely generated from a set of base types and the function type constructor $\rightarrow$. In HOL, the set of base types is usually taken as a superset of $\{\iota, o\}$ with ι and o for individuals and truth values, respectively.

The work presented here focuses on an extended variant of $\lambda_\rightarrow$ that natively supports *parametric polymorphism* and incorporates a locally nameless representation using de-Bruijn indices for bound variables [3]. The notion of de-Bruijn indices is extended for nameless type variables to keep up the guarantee of syntactical uniqueness of α-equivalent terms. Types (denoted by τ or ν) are thus given by

$$\tau, \nu ::= s \in T \mid \underline{i} \in \mathbb{N} \mid \tau \rightarrow \nu \mid \forall.\, \tau$$

where T is a non-empty set of base type symbols and $\underline{i}$ is a nameless type variable.

---

[1] The LEOPARD framework is freely available under BSD license and can be downloaded at https://github.com/cbenzmueller/LeoPARD.

The term data structure presented next adopts, combines and extends techniques that are employed in state-of-the-art HO reasoning systems, such as *Teyjus* λProlog [12] (which is based on explicit substitutions of the *Suspension Calculus* [11]), the logical frameworks *TWELF* [13] and *Beluga* [14], and the interactive *Abella* prover [8]. In particular, the combination of techniques for term data structures presented here is, up to our knowledge, novel in the context of HO ATP and not employed in any modern system.

On the basis of nameless terms, spine notation [4] in conjunction with explicit substitutions [1] is employed. The first technique allows quick head access and a left-to-right traversal method that is more efficient than in classical curried representation. The latter method's explicit treatment of substitutions enables the combination of substitution runs which in turn permits a more efficient β-normalization procedure.

More specifically, the internal representation of polymorphic HOL syntax is given by (types are partially omitted for simplicity):

$$s ::= (h \cdot S) \mid (s \cdot S) \mid (\lambda_\tau.\ s) \mid (\Lambda.\ s) \mid s[\sigma]$$
$$h ::= i_\tau \mid c_\tau \mid h[\sigma]$$
$$S ::= \text{NIL} \mid s_\tau; S \mid \tau; S \mid S[\sigma]$$
$$\sigma_{term} ::= \uparrow^i \mid s_\tau \cdot \sigma_{term} \qquad \sigma_{type} :: = \uparrow^i \mid \tau \cdot \sigma_{type}$$

where the terms s are either *roots*, redexes, term and type abstraction, or closures (respectively) with *heads* h (that are bound indices i, constants $c_\tau \in \Sigma$ from the signature Σ or itself closures) and *spines* S. We support defined constants c_τ and their expansion using directed equation axioms ($c_\tau := d_\tau$). The spines collect arguments in a linear sequence, concatenated by the ; constructor. A substitution $\sigma = (\sigma_{term}, \sigma_{type})$ is internally represented by a pair of a term- and a type substitution, for which each individual substitution exclusively contains substitutes for the corresponding de-Bruijn indices. In the current version, closures cannot occur within types. This is because the number of type variables within current common ATP problems is typically very low (often zero), and, hence, merging of substitution runs in types is not crucial.

We extend the notion of β-normalization to substitutions $\sigma = (\sigma_{term}, \sigma_{type})$ by $\sigma\!\downarrow_\beta = (\sigma_{term}\!\downarrow_\beta, \sigma_{type})$ where $\sigma_{term}\!\downarrow_\beta$ denotes the substitution ρ for which it holds that $\rho(i) = \sigma_{term}(i)\!\downarrow_\beta$, i.e. all components of the substitution are β-normalized individually.

The type abstraction mechanism $(\Lambda.\ s)$ is due to Girard and Reynolds, who independently developed a polymorphically typed λ-calculus today widely known as System F [9,16]. We use a *Church-style* λ-calculus in which each type is considered a part of the term's name and thus intrinsic to it. This has several advantages over the extrinsic, or *Curry-style*, interpretation, but comes with some downsides, e.g., wrt. typing flexibility.

3   Normalization Strategies

We now introduce corresponding strategies, two of them novel (wrt. earlier experiments in [18]), and present them along with a brief discussion of possible benefits (and downsides). Subsequently, these strategies are empirically evaluated using an extensive benchmark set. The strategies are:

1. **DEFAULT** *(Leftmost-outermost)*: This normalization method corresponds to the standard *normal-order* strategy, that is, the leftmost-outermost redex is processed first at each step during β-normalization. We use **DEFAULT** as starting point for the presentation and explanation of further strategies below. The complete rules for **DEFAULT** can be found in Fig. 1. Here, $s\downarrow_\beta^\sigma$ denotes β-normalization relative to substitution σ. The computation of the β-normal form of term s is initiated by $s\downarrow_\beta := s\downarrow_\beta^{(id,id)}$, where id is the identity substitution $id := \uparrow^0$.

2. **HSUBSTn** *($n > 0$, Heuristic application of substitution in RxApp)*: If the size of the term to be prepended onto the substitution is smaller than n, it is normalized strictly. Otherwise, the substitution is postponed using closures as before. The rule RxApp from Fig. 1 is thus replaced by the two rules

$$\frac{(s \cdot t; S_{tail})\downarrow_\beta^{\sigma,\sigma'} \qquad s = \lambda_\tau.\, s' \qquad |t| \geq n}{(s' \cdot S_{tail})\downarrow_\beta^{(t[\sigma]\cdot\sigma_{term},\sigma_{type}),\sigma'}} \text{ RxApp}_\geq$$

$$\frac{(s \cdot t; S_{tail})\downarrow_\beta^{\sigma,\sigma'} \qquad s = \lambda_\tau.\, s' \qquad |t| < n}{(s' \cdot S_{tail})\downarrow_\beta^{(t\downarrow_\beta^\sigma\cdot\sigma_{term},\sigma_{type}),\sigma'}} \text{ RxApp}_<$$

where $|t|$ denotes the *size of term* t (i.e. the number of term nodes in internal representation).

3. **WHNF** *(Normalize substitution once WHNF is obtained)*: When arrived at weak head normal form $c \cdot S$ of the current (sub-)term during β-normalization, the substitution σ is normalized and then used to further β-normalize the spine S. Thus, the rule RAtom (cf. Fig. 1) is replaced by

$$\frac{(c \cdot S)\downarrow_\beta^\sigma \qquad c \in \Sigma \qquad \sigma' = \sigma\downarrow_\beta}{c \cdot S\downarrow_\beta^{\sigma'}} \text{ RAtom}'$$

4. **STRCOMP** *(Strict composition of term-substitutions)*: The standard (meta-operation) of term-substitution composition with closures is given by

$$(s_\tau \cdot \sigma_{term}) \circ \rho_{term} \longrightarrow s_\tau[\rho_{term}] \cdot (\sigma_{term} \circ \rho_{term}) \tag{1}$$

In **STRCOMP** it is instead calculated strictly:

$$(s_\tau \cdot \sigma_{term}) \circ \rho_{term} \longrightarrow s_\tau\downarrow_\beta^{(\rho_{term},id)} \cdot (\sigma_{term} \circ \rho_{term}) \tag{2}$$

In contrast to (1), the application of substitution ρ_{term} in (2) is not postponed using closures but applied immediately by β-normalization.

Root rules

$$\frac{(c \cdot S) \Downarrow_\beta^\sigma \qquad c \in \Sigma}{c \cdot S \Downarrow_\beta^\sigma} \text{ RAtom}$$

$$\frac{(i_\tau \cdot S) \Downarrow_\beta^\sigma \qquad \sigma_{term}(i) = j}{j_{\tau[\sigma_{type}]} \cdot S \Downarrow_\beta^\sigma} \text{ RBndSub} \qquad \frac{(i \cdot S) \Downarrow_\beta^\sigma \qquad \sigma_{term}(i) = s}{(s \cdot S) \Downarrow_\beta^{(id, \sigma_{type}), \sigma}} \text{ RTermSub}$$

$$\frac{(h[\rho'][\rho] \cdot S) \Downarrow_\beta^\sigma}{(h[\rho' \circ \rho] \cdot S) \Downarrow_\beta^\sigma} \text{ RClosClos} \qquad \frac{(c[\rho] \cdot S) \Downarrow_\beta^\sigma \qquad c \in \Sigma}{c \cdot S \Downarrow_\beta^\sigma} \text{ RAtomClos}$$

$$\frac{(i_\tau[\rho] \cdot S) \Downarrow_\beta^\sigma \qquad (\rho_{term} \circ \sigma_{term})(i) = j}{j_{\tau[\rho_{type} \circ \sigma_{type}]} \cdot S \Downarrow_\beta^\sigma} \text{ RBndClos}$$

$$\frac{(i[\rho] \cdot S) \Downarrow_\beta^\sigma \qquad (\rho_{term} \circ \sigma_{term})(i) = s}{(s \cdot S) \Downarrow_\beta^{(id, \rho_{type} \circ \sigma_{type}), \sigma}} \text{ RTermClos}$$

Abstraction/Closure rule

$$\frac{(\lambda_\tau. s) \Downarrow_\beta^\sigma}{\lambda_{\tau[\sigma_{type}]}. s \Downarrow_\beta^{(1 \cdot \sigma_{term} \circ \uparrow, \sigma_{type})}} \text{ ABS} \qquad \frac{(\Lambda. s) \Downarrow_\beta^\sigma}{\Lambda. s \Downarrow_\beta^{(\sigma_{term}, 1 \cdot \sigma_{type} \circ \uparrow)}} \text{ TyAbs} \qquad \frac{(s[\sigma']) \Downarrow_\beta^\sigma}{s \Downarrow_\beta^{\sigma' \circ \sigma}} \text{ Clos}$$

Redex rules

$$\frac{(s \cdot \text{Nil}) \Downarrow_\beta^{\sigma, \sigma'}}{s \Downarrow_\beta^\sigma} \text{ RxSpNil} \qquad \frac{(s \cdot S[\rho]) \Downarrow_\beta^{\sigma, \sigma'}}{(s \cdot S) \Downarrow_\beta^{\sigma, \rho \circ \sigma'}} \text{ RxSpClos}$$

$$\frac{(s \cdot t; S_{tail}) \Downarrow_\beta^{\sigma, \sigma'} \qquad s = \lambda_\tau. s'}{(s' \cdot S_{tail}) \Downarrow_\beta^{(t[\sigma] \cdot \sigma_{term}, \sigma_{type}), \sigma'}} \text{ RxApp} \qquad \frac{(s \cdot \tau; S_{tail}) \Downarrow_\beta^{\sigma, \sigma'} \qquad s = \Lambda. t}{(t \cdot S_{tail}) \Downarrow_\beta^{(\sigma_{term}, \tau[\sigma'_{type}] \cdot \sigma_{type}), \sigma'}} \text{ RxTyApp}$$

$$\frac{(s \cdot S) \Downarrow_\beta^{\sigma, \sigma'} \qquad s = h \cdot S'}{(h[\sigma] \cdot S'[\sigma] + S[\sigma']) \Downarrow_\beta^{(id, id)}} \text{ RxRMrg} \qquad \frac{(s \cdot S) \Downarrow_\beta^{\sigma, \sigma'} \qquad s = t \cdot S'}{(t \cdot S'[\sigma] + S[\sigma']) \Downarrow_\beta^{\sigma, (id, id)}} \text{ RxRxMrg}$$

$$\frac{(s \cdot S) \Downarrow_\beta^{\sigma, \sigma'} \qquad s = t[\rho]}{(t \cdot S) \Downarrow_\beta^{\rho \circ \sigma, \sigma'}} \text{ RxClos}$$

Spine rules

$$\frac{}{\text{Nil} \Downarrow_\beta^\sigma} \text{ SpNil} \qquad \frac{(S[\rho]) \Downarrow_\beta^\sigma}{S \Downarrow_\beta^{\rho \circ \sigma}} \text{ SpClos} \qquad \frac{(s_0; S_{tail}) \Downarrow_\beta^\sigma}{(s_0 \Downarrow_\beta^\sigma); S_{tail} \Downarrow_\beta^\sigma} \text{ SpApp} \qquad \frac{(\tau; S_{tail}) \Downarrow_\beta^\sigma}{(\tau[\sigma_{type}]); S_{tail} \Downarrow_\beta^{\rho \circ \sigma}} \text{ SpTyApp}$$

Fig. 1. β-normalization strategy **DEFAULT**

5. **WEAK** *(Weakly normalize substitutions on demand)*: Before application of RTERMSUB or RTERMCLOS, β-normalize the term before substituting, and update σ accordingly. This means that each time a term is supposed to be substituted, its β-normal form is substituted instead. Also, in order to avoid re-computations, the original term is replaced by its β-normal form in the substitution σ, too. Thus, rule RTERMSUB from Fig. 1 is replaced by

$$\frac{(i \cdot S) \downarrow_\beta^\sigma \qquad \sigma_{term}(i) = s \qquad s' = s\downarrow_\beta}{(s' \cdot S) \downarrow_\beta^{(id,\sigma_{type}),(\sigma_{term}[i \leftarrow t\downarrow_\beta],\sigma_{type})}} \text{ RTERMSUB}'$$

and RTERMCLOS is replaced analogously. Here, when term t is substituted for de-Bruijn index i, the substitution σ is updated to hold the normalized t at position i, i.e. $\sigma'(j) = t\downarrow_\beta$ iff $j = i$ and $\sigma'(j) = \sigma(j)$ otherwise.

4 Evaluation and Further Work

In order to estimate the expected effects of using different β-normalization strategies in practical scenarios of automated reasoning, a worst-case analysis seems inappropriate and is therefore omitted. In lieu thereof, a representative set of problems for (HO) theorem proving has been chosen for which the number of β-normalization reduction steps has been compared empirically between all strategies. Since the proposed strategies do not include costly heuristics (e.g. based on structural properties of terms), a decrease in reduction counts can directly be translated to a speed-up with respect to actual time consumption. The evaluation has been conducted with the LEOPARD system platform, in which the term data structures from Sect. 2 and the strategies from Sect. 3 have been implemented.

The Benchmarks. The benchmark problems were chosen from a relatively broad field of diversity: The first three benchmark domains are the sets denoted CHURCH I, CHURCH II and CHURCH III that contain reducible arithmetic terms (of the form $mult(i, i)$, $power(i, 3)$, $power(3, i)$ respectively) in polymorphic Church numerals encoding [17]. The domains S4E and S4F contain a total of 3480 HO problems, converted from propositional and first-order modal logic problems from the QMLTP library [15]. Both domains differ wrt. to the details of the employed semantic embedding of logic S4 in HOL [2].[2]

The remaining benchmarks (a total of 3246 problems) are (typed) first-order and HO problems from the TPTP problem library [19,20]. These benchmark domains are denoted according to their problem domain name as given by the TPTP library. Generally, first-order CNF problems, as well as TPTP domains that only contain them, were not considered for the evaluation, since the contained formulae are already given in clause normal form which results in likewise β-normalized internal clause representations in LEOPARD.

---

[2] The archive of semantically embedded S4-formulae from QMLTP can be found at http://page.mi.fu-berlin.de/cbenzmueller/papers/THF-S4-ALL.zip.

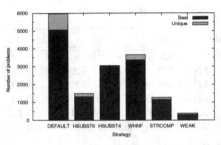

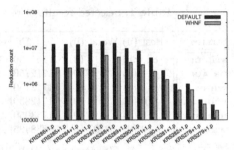

(a) Distribution of best performance over all benchmark problems

(b) Highest reduction count differences in problem domain KRS

Fig. 2. Evaluation results

The benchmark problem selection embodies, in its sum, a representative set of nearly 7000 practical inputs for reasoning systems and a heterogeneous set of (syntactic and semantic) term characteristics is covered.

Results and Discussion. Figure 2a shows the number of benchmark problems (throughout all domains) that were β-normalized (uniquely) best using the given strategy. It can be seen that, in our benchmark set, the **DEFAULT** strategy has the higher number of problems normalized with minimal reduction count (compared to the other strategies). Nevertheless, **HSUBST4** and **WHNF** are competitive alternatives, and there are even problems that are uniquely normalized best in the remaining strategies. It should be pointed out again that the competing strategies are relatively simple, since they do not use sophisticated term structure heuristics and yet already admit a fair effectiveness in certain domains.

In order to give a brief idea of the amount of potential reduction count savings, a quantitative comparison of 14 problems from KRS with highest reduction count differences between default leftmost-outermost and the alternative **WHNF** strategy is shown in Fig. 2b. These difference are, in the most striking cases, up to factor 4.5 which is considerable in magnitudes of 10^6 reduction steps and above.

More detailed results that underline our observations can be found in Table 1. Here, for selected problem domains[3], and each relevant β-normalization strategy, the number of problems that performed best and worst are displayed (i.e. the number of problems that had the lowest respectively highest overall reduction count for this strategy). Additionally, the number of unique problems – denoted (u) – which normalized strictly faster in this strategy than in any other strategy within the domain is given. The sum of all reduction steps, denoted Σr_i, throughout the whole problem domain, as well as the maximal number of reduction steps (for a single problem) are given. The remaining three values, $\widetilde{r_i}$, $\overline{r_i}$ and

---

[3] The complete evaluation results can be found at http://inf.fu-berlin.de/~lex/files/betaresults.pdf.

Table 1. Selected results of reduction count measurements

Strategy	Best (u)	Worst (u)	Σr_i	$\min r_i$	$\max r_i$	$\overline{r_i}$	$\widetilde{r_i}$	σ
STRCOMP	88 (88)	3 (3)	1151350	79	32650	$11 \cdot 10^3$	9014.5	$9 \cdot 10^3$
DEFAULT	12 (0)	0 (0)	1712750	17	50408	17127.5	12962.5	$15 \cdot 10^3$
WHNF	12 (0)	0 (0)	1712750	17	50408	17127.5	12962.5	$15 \cdot 10^3$
HSUBST4	0 (0)	0 (0)	1712850	18	50409	17128.5	12963.5	$15 \cdot 10^3$
HSUBST6	0 (0)	0 (0)	1733050	22	50809	17330.5	13165.5	$15 \cdot 10^3$
WEAK	0 (0)	97 (0)	39838425	33	1546215	398384.2	205336.5	$445 \cdot 10^3$

(a) Domain CHURCH1 (100 problems)

Strategy	Best (u)	Worst (u)	Σr_i	$\min r_i$	$\max r_i$	$\overline{r_i}$	$\widetilde{r_i}$	σ
STRCOMP	17 (17)	0 (0)	147516	150	25782	7764.0	4704.0	$7 \cdot 10^3$
DEFAULT	2 (0)	0 (0)	236075	80	42110	12425.0	7325.0	$12 \cdot 10^3$
WHNF	2 (0)	0 (0)	236075	80	42110	12425.0	7325.0	$12 \cdot 10^3$
HSUBST6	0 (0)	0 (0)	1262759	107	271331	66461.0	27665.0	$80 \cdot 10^3$
HSUBST4	0 (0)	0 (0)	1262759	107	271331	66461.0	27665.0	$80 \cdot 10^3$
WEAK	0 (0)	1 (0)	1359621	171	289215	71559.0	30483.0	$86 \cdot 10^3$

(b) Domain CHURCH2 (19 problems)

Strategy	Best (u)	Worst (u)	Σr_i	$\min r_i$	$\max r_i$	$\overline{r_i}$	$\widetilde{r_i}$	σ
WHNF	14 (0)	0 (0)	704503	511	14846	5636.0	5378.0	$3 \cdot 10^3$
HSUBST6	0 (0)	0 (0)	834604	513	22883	6676.8	5475.0	$5 \cdot 10^3$
DEFAULT	80 (16)	0 (0)	848536	511	23663	6788.3	5472.0	$5 \cdot 10^3$
HSUBST4	50 (0)	0 (0)	848599	513	23663	6788.8	5472.0	$5 \cdot 10^3$
STRCOMP	14 (0)	3 (0)	8443020	511	419068	67544.2	13622.0	$106 \cdot 10^3$
WEAK	0 (0)	14 (0)	23354287	913	1069897	186834.3	89193.0	$252 \cdot 10^3$

(c) Domain GRA (125 problems)

Strategy	Best (u)	Worst (u)	Σr_i	$\min r_i$	$\max r_i$	$\overline{r_i}$	$\widetilde{r_i}$	σ
WHNF	173 (14)	95 (0)	35695447	0	6106161	129801.6	689.0	$67 \cdot 10^4$
HSUBST6	96 (0)	85 (0)	106292434	0	15011396	386517.9	835.0	$206 \cdot 10^4$
DEFAULT	254 (12)	95 (0)	106316948	0	15028663	386607.1	689.0	$206 \cdot 10^4$
HSUBST4	239 (0)	109 (14)	106317316	0	15028665	386608.4	689.0	$206 \cdot 10^4$
STRCOMP					*Unfeasible*			
WEAK					*Unfeasible*			

(d) Domain KRS (275 problems)

σ, denote the arithmetic mean, the median value and the standard derivation of the measurement results (respectively).

As an example, in benchmark domain CHURCH I (cf. Table 1a) **STRCOMP** performs drastically better than in any other domain: Although **DEFAULT** and **WHNF** have the lowest minimum value, **STRCOMP** is by far the best strategy (in problem count and overall reduction sum) with 88 of 100 problems (uniquely) normalized best. In terms of reduction steps per problem, **STRCOMP** takes only roughly 70 % of the number of steps required by **DEFAULT** (in both average and mean). Similar results also apply for the remaining CHURCH domains. Also, in the GRA domain (cf. Table 1c), the mean normalization step count $\overline{r_i}$ is more than 100 steps lower in the **WHNF** strategy than when using **DEFAULT**. These results demonstrate that the alternative normalization strategies can in fact perform better (wrt. reduction count per problem) than default leftmost-outermost in certain problem domains.

Further Work. While the present evaluation grouped problems by a (given, practically motivated) semantic classification, further investigations need to identify syntactic criteria in order to group problems with similar properties (with respect to β-normalization performance) for a specific strategy.

Based on observation and some preliminary experiments, we are positive that methods based on syntactic criteria such as the following can be employed for choosing an appropriate normalization strategy at runtime:

- Recognition of regular patterns in terms
- The term's size and depth
- The number of abstractions not occurring at top-level
- The number of bound indices

For future work, not only concrete (syntactical) heuristics but also machine learning techniques could be employed to study representative sets of problems.

5   Conclusion

A sophisticated internal representation mechanism for (second-order) polymorphically typed HO terms, including a locally nameless spine notation combined with explicit substitutions and perfect term sharing, has been presented.

Using the above representation, several new β-normalization strategies have been introduced. These strategies vary in their extent of laziness and strictness in certain normalization rules, e.g. during composition of substitutions. They have subsequently been implemented and evaluated within the LEOPARD framework. The conducted evaluation was based on a representative benchmark set.

For logical frameworks and meta languages, the representation of objects such as programs and proofs in λProlog has previously been studied [10]. However, a fine-grained evaluation of normalization strategies in context of HO ATP as reported here has not been carried out before. Extending previous studies in a rather orthogonal manner (wrt. application domain, granularity, and system of explicit substitutions), our benchmarks reveal that there is no single best β-normalization strategy for a relevant set of problem classes. In particular, our findings show that the performance of a strategy rather depends on some (syntactic) characteristics of the input problem. The reduction count difference between the default leftmost-outermost strategy and the leading strategy can, in fact, be as high as factor four.

References

1. Abadi, M., Cardelli, L., Curien, P.L., Levy, J.J.: Explicit substitutions. In: Proceedings of the 17th Symposium on Principles of Programming Languages, POPL 1990, pp. 31–46. ACM, New York, NY, USA (1990)
2. Benzmüller, C., Raths, T.: HOL based first-order modal logic provers. In: McMillan, K., Middeldorp, A., Voronkov, A. (eds.) LPAR-19 2013. LNCS, vol. 8312, pp. 127–136. Springer, Heidelberg (2013)
3. Bruijn, N.G.D.: Lambda calculus notation with nameless dummies, a tool for automatic formula manipulation, with application to the church-rosser theorem. INDAG. MATH **34**, 381–392 (1972)
4. Cervesato, I., Pfenning, F.: A linear spine calculus. J. Logic Comput. **13**(5), 639–688 (2003)
5. Church, A.: A set of postulates for the foundation of logic. Ann. Math. **33**(2), 346–366 (1932)
6. Church, A.: A set of postulates for the foundation of logic. Second Paper. Ann. Math. **34**(4), 839–864 (1933)
7. Church, A.: A formulation of the simple theory of types. J. Symb. Log. **5**(2), 56–68 (1940)
8. Gacek, A.: The abella interactive theorem prover (system description). In: Armando, A., Baumgartner, P., Dowek, G. (eds.) IJCAR 2008. LNCS (LNAI), vol. 5195, pp. 154–161. Springer, Heidelberg (2008)
9. Girard, J.: Interprétation fonctionnelle et élimination des coupures de l'arithmétique d'ordre supérieur. Ph.D. thesis, Université Paris VII (1972)
10. Liang, C., Nadathur, G., Qi, X.: Choices in representation and reduction strategies for lambda terms in intensional contexts. J. Autom. Reasoning **33**(2), 89–132 (2004)
11. Nadathur, G.: A fine-grained notation for lambda terms and its use in intensional operations. J. Funct. Logic Program. **1999**(2), 1–62 (1999)
12. Nadathur, G., Mitchell, D.J.: System description: teyjus - a compiler and abstract machine based implementation of λprolog. In: Ganzinger, H. (ed.) CADE 1999. LNCS (LNAI), vol. 1632, pp. 287–291. Springer, Heidelberg (1999)
13. Pfenning, F., Schürmann, C.: System description: Twelf - a meta-logical framework for deductive systems. In: Ganzinger, H. (ed.) CADE 1999. LNCS (LNAI), vol. 1632, pp. 202–206. Springer, Heidelberg (1999)
14. Pientka, B., Dunfield, J.: Beluga: a framework for programming and reasoning with deductive systems (system description). In: Giesl, J., Hähnle, R. (eds.) IJCAR 2010. LNCS, vol. 6173, pp. 15–21. Springer, Heidelberg (2010)
15. Raths, T., Otten, J.: The QMLTP problem library for first-order modal logics. In: Gramlich, B., Miller, D., Sattler, U. (eds.) IJCAR 2012. LNCS, vol. 7364, pp. 454–461. Springer, Heidelberg (2012)
16. Reynolds, J.C.: Towards a theory of type structure. In: Robinet, B. (ed.) Symposium on Programming. LNCS, vol. 19, pp. 408–423. Springer, Heidelberg (1974)
17. Reynolds, J.C.: An introduction to polymorphic lambda calculus. In: Logical Foundations of Functional Programming, pp. 77–86. Addison-Wesley (1994)
18. Steen, A.: Efficient Data Structures for Automated Theorem Proving in Expressive Higher-Order Logics. Master's thesis, Freie Universität Berlin, Berlin (2014)

19. Sutcliffe, G.: The TPTP problem library and associated infrastructure: The FOF and CNF parts, v3.5.0. J. Autom. Reasoning **43**(4), 337–362 (2009)
20. Sutcliffe, G., Benzmüller, C.: Automated reasoning in higher-order logic using the TPTP THF infrastructure. J. Formalized Reasoning **3**(1), 1–27 (2010)
21. Wisniewski, M., Steen, A., Benzmüller, C.: LeoPARD — A generic platform for the implementation of higher-order reasoners. In: Kerber, M., Carette, J., Kaliszyk, C., Rabe, F., Sorge, V. (eds.) CICM 2015. LNCS, vol. 9150, pp. 325–330. Springer, Heidelberg (2015)

Fine Grained SMT Proofs for the Theory of Fixed-Width Bit-Vectors

Liana Hadarean[1]([⊠]), Clark Barrett[2], Andrew Reynolds[3],
Cesare Tinelli[4], and Morgan Deters[2]

[1] Oxford University, Oxford, England
liana.hadarean@cs.ox.ac.uk
[2] New York University, New York, USA
[3] EPFL, Lausanne, Switzerland
[4] The University of Iowa, Iowa City, USA

Abstract. Many high-level verification tools rely on SMT solvers to efficiently discharge complex verification conditions. Some applications require more than just a yes/no answer from the solver. For satisfiable quantifier-free problems, a satisfying assignment is a natural artifact. In the unsatisfiable case, an externally checkable proof can serve as a certificate of correctness and can be mined to gain additional insight into the problem. We present a method of encoding and checking SMT-generated proofs for the quantifier-free theory of fixed-width bit-vectors. Proof generation and checking for this theory poses several challenges, especially for proofs based on reductions to propositional logic. Such reductions can result in large resolution subproofs in addition to requiring a proof that the reduction itself is correct. We describe a fine-grained proof system formalized in the LFSC framework that addresses some of these challenges with the use of computational side-conditions. We report results using a proof-producing version of the CVC4 SMT solver on unsatisfiable quantifier-free bit-vector benchmarks from the SMT-LIB benchmark library.

1 Introduction

SMT solvers are often used to reason in theories whose satisfiability problem ranges in complexity from NP-complete to undecidable. To be able to do this, they implement complex algorithms combining efficient SAT solving with theory-specific reasoning, requiring many lines of highly optimized code.[1] Because the solvers' code base changes frequently to keep up with the state of the art, bugs are still found in mature tools: during the 2014 SMT competition, five SMT solvers returned incorrect results. In a field where correctness is paramount, this is particularly problematic. While great progress has been made in verifying

---

Work partially supported by DARPA award FA8750-13-2-0241 and ERC project 280053 (CPROVER).

[1] For example, the CVC4 code base consists of over 250 K lines of C++ code.

© Springer-Verlag Berlin Heidelberg 2015
M. Davis et al. (Eds.): LPAR-20 2015, LNCS 9450, pp. 340–355, 2015.
DOI: 10.1007/978-3-662-48899-7_24

complex software systems [18,19], the verification of SAT and SMT solvers still remains a challenge [20].

One approach for addressing this concern is to instrument an SMT solver to emit a certificate of correctness. If the input formula is satisfiable and quantifier-free, a natural certificate is a satisfying assignment to its variables. Correctness can be checked by evaluating the input formula under that assignment. In the unsatisfiable case, the solver could emit an externally-checkable proof of unsatisfiability. Proof checkers usually consist of a small trusted core that implements a set of simple rules. These can be composed to prove complex goals, while maintaining trustworthiness.

Proof-producing SMT solvers have been successfully used to improve the performance of sceptical proof assistants, as shown in several recent papers [1,5,6, 8,9,14]. The proof assistant can discharge complex sub-goals to the SMT solver. It can then check or reconstruct the proof returned by the solver without having to trust the result. In some applications, such as interpolant generation [26] and certified compilation [11], the proof object itself is used for more than just establishing correctness.

Proofs for the theory of fixed-width bit-vectors are of particular practical importance, with applications in both hardware and software verification. Previous work [7] shows how to reconstruct proofs from the Z3 SMT solver in HOL4 and Isabelle/HOL. However, due to the lack of detail in the Z3 bit-vector proofs, proof reconstruction is not always successful. In this paper, we seek to address this limitation by presenting a method of encoding and checking fine-grained SMT-generated proofs for the theory $\mathcal{T}_{bv}$ of bit-vectors as formalized in the SMT-LIB 2 standard [3]. Proof generation and checking for the bit-vector theory poses several unique challenges. Algebraic reasoning is typically not sufficient by itself to decide most bit-vector formulas of practical interest, so often bitvector (sub)-problems are solved by reduction to SAT. However, such reductions usually result in very large propositional proofs. In addition, the reduction itself must be proven correct. LFSC is a meta-logic that was specifically designed to serve as a unified proof format for SMT solvers. Encoding the $\mathcal{T}_{bv}$ proof rules in LFSC helps address some of these challenges.

We make the following contributions: (i) we develop an LFSC proof system for the quantifier-free theory of fixed-width bit-vectors that includes proof rules for bit-blasting and allows for a two-tiered DPLL($\mathcal{T}$) proof structure; (ii) we instrument the CVC4 SMT solver to output proofs in this proof system; and (iii) we report experimental results on an extensive set of unsatisfiable SMT-LIB benchmarks in the QF_BV logic.

We start with a discussion of related work in Sect. 2. Section 3 explains the structure of SMT-generated proofs, while Sect. 4 introduces the LFSC proof language and illustrates how to use it to encode the kinds of inferences routinely done by SMT solvers. We discuss how bit-vector constraints are decided in CVC4 and how to generate proofs for them in Sect. 5. Section 6 introduces the LFSC proof rules that are specific to the bit-vector theory. We show experimental results in Sect. 7 and conclude with future work in Sect. 8.

2 Related Work

Early approaches to proof-checking for SMT relied on using interactive theorem provers to certify proofs produced by SMT solvers. One effort [21] used HOL Light to certify proofs generated by the CVC Lite SMT solver. Another [13] generated proofs for quantifier-free problems in the logic of equality with uninterpreted symbols using the haRVey SMT solver and translated these into Isabelle/HOL. A contrasting approach [22] traded off assurance for speed by using a special-purpose external checker to check proofs generated by the Fx7 solver. Our approach aims to balance trust and efficiency by using LFSC. Using a logical framework with a generic proof checker provides both trust and flexibility, while LFSC's computational side-conditions increase performance.

None of the work mentioned above supports proofs for the theory of bit-vectors. The work in [15] targets SMT-generated proofs for the theory of bit-vectors for the purpose of generating interpolants. It is similar to ours in that it uses a lazy bit-vector solver, integrated into a DPLL($\mathcal{T}$) framework and in that if algebraic reasoning fails, it falls back on a resolution proof generated by the SAT solver. However, the work is different in that its focus is on producing interpolants rather than proof-checking. They do not address the correctness of bit-blasting, for instance.

The work whose scope is most similar to ours is an effort that was undertaken to reconstruct bit-vector proofs produced by Z3 within Isabelle/Hol [7]. The main difference in that work is that Z3 does not produce full proofs, but rather "proof sketches." Specifically, Z3 provides some "large-step" inferences, lemmas that are valid in the theory of bit-vectors, without proof. As the authors remark, the coarse granularity of Z3's proofs makes proof reconstruction particularly challenging. A significant part of the proof checking time is spent re-proving large-step inferences that Z3 does not provide details for. In contrast, our approach is more fine-grained as it provides full details for every step. As we show below, this enables our approach to check more proofs.

The LFSC meta-framework has been successfully used for encoding proofs generated by SMT solvers for other theories in [24,25,28]. The current paper extends this line of work to support LFSC proofs for the bit-vector theory. In [26] the authors show how to use LFSC to compute interpolants from unsatisfiability proofs in the theory of equality and uninterpreted function symbols. We believe this approach can be extended to generate bit-vector interpolants from LFSC bit-vector proofs.

3 Proofs in SMT

In the rest of the paper, we assume some familiarity with automated reasoning, many-sorted first-order logic, and the syntax of simply-typed lambda calculus. Let $\_^P$ be an *abstraction* operator that replaces each atom (a predicate symbol applied to one or more terms) in a formula with a unique propositional variable. Most SMT solvers are based on some variant of the DPLL($\mathcal{T}$) architecture [23], which combines Boolean reasoning on the abstraction φ^P of a quantifier-free input formula φ with theory-specific reasoning in order to determine the satisfiability of φ with respect to a background theory $\mathcal{T}$.[2] Boolean reasoning on φ^P is performed by a SAT solver, while theory-specific reasoning is delegated to a *theory solver* for $\mathcal{T}$ (or $\mathcal{T}$-solver). The SAT solver enumerates satisfying assignments A^P for φ^P. The $\mathcal{T}$-solver checks whether the corresponding set of $\mathcal{T}$-literals A is $\mathcal{T}$-satisfiable. If A is not $\mathcal{T}$-satisfiable, a $\mathcal{T}$-valid clause is added that blocks the assignment A^P, and the process continues until either a satisfying assignment is found or a contradiction can be derived purely at the propositional level. From a proof-theoretic perspective, one can think of the $\mathcal{T}$-solver as refining the propositional abstraction φ^P with the addition of selected *theory lemmas* (clauses valid in $\mathcal{T}$) until a propositionally unsatisfiable formula is obtained [4].

The *resolution* calculus is refutationally complete for propositional clause logic [27] and has been successfully used as the basis for a common proof format for SAT solvers [30]. However, as we describe below, SMT proofs are significantly more sophisticated than SAT proofs (see, e.g., [2] for more details). First, SMT solvers convert their input to CNF; thus, a proof object produced by an SMT solver must incorporate a proof establishing that the CNF clauses used internally by the solver follow from the input formula. Second, the Boolean abstraction of the input formula is obtained by replacing $\mathcal{T}$-atoms with propositional variables. Hence, SMT proof generation must also rely on a mechanism that maintains a connection between input atoms and the propositional variables representing them in the SAT solver. Finally, each theory lemma generated by the theory solver must have a proof expressed in terms of $\mathcal{T}$-specific proof rules.

As a consequence, SMT proofs typically have a three-tiered structure: (*i*) a derivation of the internal CNF formula ψ from the input formula φ;[3] (*ii*) a

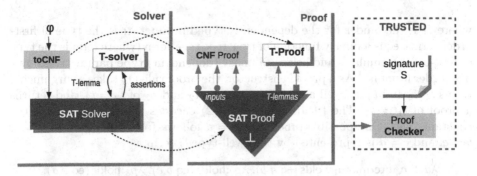

Fig. 1. DPLL($\mathcal{T}$) architecture, SMT proof structure, and proof checker.

---

[2] For simplicity, we will ignore here the issue of whether the background theory is the combination of several more basic theories or not.

[3] This step typically also includes the application of simplifying rewrite rules, which we ignore in this paper. Extending the approach here to include the many pre-processing rewrite rules used in real solvers is tedious but straightforward.

resolution refutation of ψ in the form of a resolution tree whose root is the empty clause and whose leaves are either clauses from ψ or theory lemmas; and (*iii*) theory proofs of all the theory lemmas occurring in the resolution tree.

Figure 1 depicts the DPLL($\mathcal{T}$) architecture and how it relates to the structure of SMT proofs. In this paper, we consider proofs with this structure expressed as terms in the LFSC framework, which we discuss next.

4   LFSC

LFSC is an extension of the Edinburgh Logical Framework (LF) [17], a meta-framework based on a extension of simply-typed lambda calculus with dependent types. LF has been used extensively to encode various kinds of deductive systems. In general, a specific proof system P can be defined in LF by representing its proof rules as LF constants and encoding their premises and conclusions as a type. In this setting, a formal proof in the encoded proof system is represented as an LF term whose constants (in the sense of higher-order logic) are proof-rule names. A collection of type and term constant declarations is called a *signature* in LF. Checking the correctness of a proof then reduces to type checking: an LF proof checker takes as input both a signature S defining a proof system P and a proof term t encoding a proof in P. It verifies the correctness of the proof by checking that t is well-typed with respect to S. For example, the equality transitivity proof rule:

$$\frac{t_1 = t_2 \quad t_2 = t_3}{t_1 = t_3} \; \text{trans} \tag{1}$$

in (unsorted) first-order logic can be encoded in LF as a constant with type:

$$\text{trans} : \Pi t_1, t_2, t_3 : \text{tr.} \; \Pi p_1 : \text{holds} \, (\text{eq} \, t_1 \, t_2). \, \Pi p_2 : \text{holds} \, (\text{eq} \, t_2 \, t_3). \, \text{holds} \, (\text{eq} \, t_1 \, t_3) \tag{2}$$

where Π is the binder for the dependently typed product, tr is the type of first-order terms, eq is a binary function of type $\text{tr} \times \text{tr} \rightarrow \text{form}$ (where form is the type of first-order formulas), and holds is a unary (dependent) type parametrized by a first-order formula.[4] As a proof constructor, the proof rule (1) takes as arguments terms t_1, t_2 and t_3, as well as proofs p_1 of $t_1 = t_2$ and p_2 of $t_2 = t_3$, and returns a proof of $t_1 = t_3$. The LF declaration in (2) encodes this in the type of the constant trans. One possible proof that $a = d$ follows from the premises $a = b$, $b = c$, and $c = d$ is represented by the (well-typed) term:

$$\lambda a, b, c, d : \text{term.} \; \lambda p_1 : \text{holds} \, (\text{eq} \, a \, b). \, \lambda p_2 : \text{holds} \, (\text{eq} \, b \, c). \, \lambda p_3 : \text{holds} \, (\text{eq} \, c \, d).$$
$$(\text{trans} \, a \, c \, d \, (\text{trans} \, a \, b \, c \, p_1 \, p_2) \, p_3)$$

Using the wild-card symbol _, the body of the innermost lambda term can be simplified to $(\text{trans} \, \_ \, \_ \, \_ \, (\text{trans} \, \_ \, \_ \, \_ \, p_1 \, p_2) \, p_3)$, since the omitted arguments can be inferred automatically during type-checking.

---

[4]   Intuitively, an LF expression of dependent type $\Pi \varphi : \text{form.} \, \text{holds}(\varphi)$ represents a proof that the formula φ holds.

Purely declarative proof systems like those defined in LF cannot always efficiently model the kind of complex reasoning usually employed by SMT solvers. LFSC addresses this issue by extending LF types with computational *side conditions*, explicit computational checks defined as programs in a small but expressive functional first-order programming language. The language has built-in types for arbitrary precision integers and rationals, ML-style pattern matching over LFSC type constructors, recursion, limited support for exceptions, and a very restricted set of imperative features. A proof rule in LFSC may optionally include a side condition written in this language. When checking the application of such a proof rule, an LFSC checker computes actual parameters for the side condition and executes its code. If the side condition fails, the LFSC checker rejects the rule application.

As shown in Fig. 1, when using LFSC, the trusted core includes both the (generic) LFSC checker and the specific LFSC signature which consists of a set of proof rules, each of which may have side conditions.

We refer the reader to [28] for a detailed description of the LFSC language and its formal semantics. Here we introduce LFSC syntax via examples to illustrate the main features of the framework.

Example 1. An inference rule at the heart of SAT and SMT solvers is the propositional resolution rule:

$$\frac{l_1 \vee \ldots l_n \vee l \quad \neg l \vee l'_1 \vee \ldots l'_m}{l_1 \vee \ldots l_n \vee l'_1 \vee \ldots \vee l'_m} \text{ Res}$$

where l's are literals. This rule alone is actually not enough to express resolution derivations as formal objects, since one also has to account for the associativity, commutativity and idempotency of the $\vee$ operator. In LF, this problem can be addressed only by adding additional proof rules for those properties. Doing so makes it possible to move literals around in a clause and remove duplicate literals, but at the cost of requiring many proof rules for each resolution step, resulting in the generation of very large proofs. Alternative solutions [31] eschew the generic, declarative approach provided by meta-frameworks like LF and instead hard-code the clause data structure in the proof checker, requiring a proof-checker with higher complexity and lower generality.

In contrast, an LFSC proof rule for resolution can use a side condition to encode that the resulting clause is computed by removing the complementary

---

unit, var, lit, clause : type   holds : clause $\rightarrow$ type   cln : clause

ok : unit   pos, neg : var $\rightarrow$ lit   clc : lit $\rightarrow$ clause $\rightarrow$ clause

resolve $(c_1, c_2$:clause, v:var):clause $=$ let p (pos v) in let n (neg v) in
    let _ (occurs p c_1) in let _ (occurs n c_2) in merge (remove p c_1) (remove n c_2)

Res : $\Pi c, c_1, c_2$:clause. holds c_1 $\rightarrow$ holds c_2 $\rightarrow$ Πv:var $\{$(resolve c_1 c_2 v) $\downarrow$ $c\}$. holds c

Fig. 2. LFSC declarations encoding propositional resolution.

literals in the two input clauses and then merging the remaining literals. One encoding of the rule and its side condition, together with all the necessary types and constants, is shown in Fig. 2. In the figure and in the remainder of the paper, we write $\tau_1 \to \tau_2$ to abbreviate as usual a type of the form $\Pi x{:}\tau_1.\ \tau_2$ where τ_2 contains no occurrences of x. Clauses are encoded essentially as nil-terminated lists of literals. They are built with the constructors cln, for the empty clause, and clc, for non-empty clauses. Literals are built from propositional variables using the constructors pos and neg, for positive and negative literals. Variables do not have constructors because LFSC variables can be used directly.

The resolution rule Res takes as input the clauses c_1, c_2, and c, together with a proof of c_1 of type holds c_1, one of c_2 of type holds c_2, and a variable v to be used as the resolved atom. The resolve side condition function computes the resolvent of clause c_1 with c_2, provided that c_1 contains at least one occurrence of the positive literal (pos v) and c_2 contains at least one occurrence of the negative literal (neg v). The side condition $\{(\text{resolve } c_1\ c_2\ v) \downarrow c\}$ succeeds if c is the result of resolving c_1 and c_2 on v. In that case, the proof rule returns a proof of c. The definitions of the auxiliary functions occurs, remove, and merge are omitted from Fig. 2 due to space constraints. (occurs l c) does nothing if the literal l is in the clause c; otherwise, it raises a failure exception; (remove l c) returns the result of removing the literal l from the clause c; (merge c_1 c_2) returns the clause with no repeated literals resulting from merging clauses c_1 and c_2.   □

LFSC has previously been successfully used to encode the constructs necessary for Boolean resolution, CNF conversion, and propositional abstraction of theory lemmas [28]. In this paper, we will not cover these constructs, but instead focus on how to encode bit-vector specific reasoning in LFSC.

5   Bit-Vector Proof Generation in CVC4

Decision procedures for the theory $\mathcal{T}_{bv}$ of bit-vectors almost always involve a reduction to propositional logic. One approach for encoding a bit-vector formula φ into an equisatisfiable propositional formula φ^{BB} is known as *bit-blasting*. For each variable v denoting a bit-vector of size n, bit-blasting introduces n fresh propositional variables, $v_0, \ldots v_{n-1}$, to represent each bit in the vector. To be able to encode this mapping in $\mathcal{T}_{bv}$, we extend the $\mathcal{T}_{bv}$ signature with a family of interpreted predicate symbols $(\text{bitOf}_i : BV_n \mapsto \text{bool})_{0 \le i < n}$, where bitOf_i takes a bit-vector x of width n and returns *true* iff the ith bit of x is 1. Let φ be a bit-vector formula. For each atom a appearing in φ, let $bbAtom(a)$ denote a propositional formula consisting of the circuit representation of a. Let C^{BB} denote the conjunction of bit-blasting clauses obtained from converting to CNF the atom definitions:

$$C^{BB} \equiv CNF \left(\bigwedge_{a \in Atoms(\varphi)} a^{BB} \Leftrightarrow bbAtom(a) \right),$$

where a^{BB} is a fresh propositional variable representing atom a and CNF represents conversion to CNF. The formula $\varphi^{BB} := \varphi[a \mapsto a^{BB}]_{a \in Atoms(\varphi)} \wedge C^{BB}$ is a propositional formula equisatisfiable with φ. Most state-of-the-art solvers for $\mathcal{T}_{bv}$ generate a formula like φ^{BB} and then rely on a single query to a SAT solver to check its satisfiability. Thus, a proof of unsatisfiability for φ could consist of: (i) a proof that φ is equisatisfiable with φ^{BB} in $\mathcal{T}_{bv}$, (ii) a propositional proof that φ^{BB} is equisatisfiable with $CNF(\varphi^{BB})$, and (iii) a monolithic, potentially very large, resolution-based refutation of $CNF(\varphi^{BB})$.

CVC4 incorporates an *eager* bit-vector decision procedure (cvcE) based on the approach sketched above. It also provides, as an alternative, a lazy DPLL($\mathcal{T}$)-style bit-vector solver (cvcLz) that maintains the word-level structure of the input terms and separates reasoning over the propositional structure of the input formula φ from bit-vector term reasoning [16]. In cvcLz, the bit-vector theory is treated like any other theory: the main DPLL($\mathcal{T}$) SAT engine SAT_{main} reasons on the propositional abstraction φ^P whereas a $\mathcal{T}_{bv}$-solver BV decides conjunctions A of $\mathcal{T}_{bv}$-literals. Essentially, BV corresponds to the $\mathcal{T}$-solver box in the DPLL($\mathcal{T}$) diagram in Fig. 1.

Recall from Sect. 3 that the $\mathcal{T}_{bv}$ solver BV must *repeatedly* decide the satisfiability of the $\mathcal{T}_{bv}$-literals A and return a $\mathcal{T}_{bv}$-valid clause over the atoms of A if A is $\mathcal{T}_{bv}$-unsatisfiable. We achieve this by relying on a second SAT solver, SAT_{bb}, to decide the satisfiability of each assignment A. It does this by checking the propositional formula $A^{BB} \wedge C^{BB}$, where $A^{BB} = A[a \mapsto a^{BB}]_{a \in Atoms(A)}$. Note that this may be significantly smaller than the formula $\varphi[a \mapsto a^{BB}]_{a \in Atoms(\varphi)} \wedge C^{BB}$ checked in the eager approach.

If $A^{BB} \wedge C^{BB}$ is unsatisfiable, SAT_{bb} returns a set of literals $L^{BB} \subseteq A^{BB}$ that is inconsistent with C^{BB}. The clause $\neg L$ is a $\mathcal{T}_{bv}$-valid lemma, and the $\neg L^P$ clause is added to SAT_{main}. We can efficiently use SAT_{bb} to check the satisfiability of C^{BB} with different assumptions A^{BB} by using the *solve with assumptions* feature of SAT solvers [12].

The lazy solver cvcLz in CVC4 also has several algebraic word-level sub-solvers. However, we do not yet support proof production for these sub-solvers, so in this paper, we focus on the $\mathcal{T}_{bv}$-lemmas generated by SAT_{bb}.

6   LFSC Bit-Vector Signature

In this section, we discuss proof generation for the lazy bit-vector solver cvcLz described in Sect. 5. Figure 3 shows the overall structure of the $\mathcal{T}_{bv}$ proof by zooming in on the $\mathcal{T}_{bv}$-lemmas that occur as leaves in the resolution SAT proof in Fig. 1. We start with the bit-blasting proofs that each atom a is equivalent to its bit-blasted formula: $a \Leftrightarrow bbAtom(a)$. These proofs require no assumptions as $a \Leftrightarrow bbAtom(a)$ is $\mathcal{T}_{bv}$-valid.[5] Next, the CNF proof establishes that the bit-blasting clauses C^{BB} follow from the atom definitions.[6] Note that this step also

---

[5] Recall that $bbAtom(a)$ is a propositional formula encoding the semantics of atom a, and contains $bitOf_i$ applications on the bit-vector variables in a.

[6] For details on how to use LFSC to encode proofs for CNF conversion, see [28].

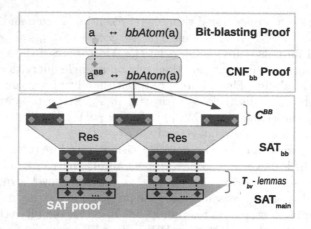

Fig. 3. Bit-vector proof structure.

establishes the mapping from the $\mathcal{T}_{bv}$-atom a to the abstract Boolean variable a^{BB} used in the SAT_{bb} SAT solver.

Each $\mathcal{T}_{bv}$-lemma has a corresponding resolution proof in SAT_{bb} with C^{BB} as leaves. The resolution proof constructs a clause over the a^{BB} SAT variables. To use this in SAT_{main}, we need to map the lemma to $\mathcal{T}_{bv}$ atoms, and then to the SAT variables a^{P} in SAT_{main}. In the figure, circles denote $\mathcal{T}_{bv}$-atoms and diamonds the propositional variables that abstract them (either in SAT_{bb} or in SAT_{main}).

6.1   Encoding Bit-Vector Formulas

Figure 4 shows the LFSC constructs needed to represent formulas in the theory of bit-vectors. Note that the encoding distinguishes between formulas and terms: formulas are represented by the simple type form and terms by the dependent type term, parametrized by the sort of the term: Πs:sort. term s. Formulas are constructed with the usual logical operators and with an equality operator over terms which is parametric in the terms' sort. The int type is LFSC's own built-in infinite precision integer type. Bit-vector sorts are represented by the dependent

sort : type	term : sort → type	BV : int → sort
form : type	true, false : form	and, or, impl, iff : form → form → form
	not : form → form	= : Πs:sort. term s → term s → form
varBV : type	var2BV : Πn:int. varBV → term (BV n)	
bit : type	b0, b1 : bit	const2BV : Πn:int. constBV → term (BV n)
constBV : type	bvn : constBV	bvc : bit → constBV → constBV

Fig. 4. Partial LFSC signature for the theory $\mathcal{T}_{bv}$ of bit-vectors.

type Πn:int. BV n where n is the width of the bit-vector. Bit-vector constants are represented as lists of bits using the constBV type with the two constructors bvn and bvc, for the empty sequence and the list cons operator respectively. The constBV bit-vector constants are converted to bit-vector terms with the const2BV function. Bit-vector variables are represented as LFSC variables of type varBV and converted to terms with var2BV.

Example 2. The bit-wise conjunction operator is encoded in LFSC as:

$$\text{bvand} : \Pi n\text{:int. term (BV } n) \rightarrow \text{term (BV } n) \rightarrow \text{term (BV } n)$$

Similarly, the unsigned comparison operator $<$ is encoded as:

$$\text{bvult} : \Pi n\text{:int. term (BV } n) \rightarrow \text{term (BV } n) \rightarrow \text{form}$$

The $\mathcal{T}_{bv}$ formula $(t_1 = t_2 \ \& \ t_3) \lor (t_1 < 0_{[3]})$ where $\&$ is bvand, $0_{[3]}$ is the zero bit-vector of size 3, and t_1, t_2, t_3 have type (term (BV 3)) can be encoded in LFSC as

```
(or (= _ t₁ (bvand _ t₂ t₃))
    (bvult _ t₁ (const2BV 3 (bvc b0 (bvc b0 (bvc b0 bvn)))))),
```

with b0 representing the zero bit.   □

6.2   Bit-Blasting

Recall that a bit-blasting proof (see Fig. 3) makes the connection between a bit-vector formula and its propositional logic encoding by proving for each bit-blasted atom a in the input formula, the following formula:

$$a \Leftrightarrow bbAtom(a).$$

We represent a bit-blasted bit-vector term of width n as a sequence of n formulas, with the ith formula in the sequence corresponding to the ith bit. The bbt type encodes bit-blasted terms and has two type constructors bbtn and bbtc as shown in Fig. 5. We introduce the dependent type constructor bbTerm to encode the fact that the bit-vector term x:BV n. corresponds to a bit-blasted term y:bbt. For example, the following term encodes that $15_{[4]}$ is bit-blasted as [*true, true, true, true*]:

```
(bbTerm _ (const2BV 4 (bvc b1 (bvc b1 (bvc b1 (bvc b1 bvn))))))
         (bbtc true (bbtc true (bbtc true (bbtc true bbtn)))))
```

We can define proof rules for each piece of syntax in bit-vector terms and compose them in order to build up arbitrary bit-blasted terms. Figure 5 shows several such bit-blasting rules. The bbVar rule takes a bit-vector variable v, its width n, and a sequence of bit-blasted terms vb, and checks that the sequence computed by the side condition code in bb-var matches vb. The side condition code just builds a

bbt : type   bbtn : bbt   bbtc : formula → bbt → bbt

bitOf : varBV → int → form   bbTerm : Πn:int. term (BV n) → bbt → type

bb-var (v : varBV, n : int) : bbt =
      if $n < 0$ *then* bbtn *else* (bbtc (bitOf v n) (bb-var v ($n-1$)))

bbVar : Πn:int. Πv:varBV.
             Πvb:bbt $\{$(bb-var v ($n-1$)) ↓ $vb\}$. (bbTerm n (var2BV n v) vb)

bbAnd : Πn:int. $\Pi x, y$:term (BV n). $\Pi xb, yb, rb$:bbt.
             Πxbb:bbTerm n x xb.
             Πybb:bbTerm n y xb $\{$(bb-bvand xb yb) ↓ $rb\}$. bbTerm n (bvand n x y) rb

bbEq : Πn:int. $\Pi x, y$:term (BV n). $\Pi bx, by$:bbt. Πf:form.
             Πbbx:bbTerm n x bx.
             Πbby:bbTerm n y by $\{$(bb-eq bx by) ↓ $f\}$. thHolds (iff (= (BV n) x y) f)

Fig. 5. Partial list of the LFSC bit-blasting rules for $\mathcal{T}_{bv}$.

sequence of applications of the bitOf operator to v—with (bitOf v i) representing the $\mathcal{T}_{bv}$ predicate $bitOf_i$ introduced at the beginning of Sect. 5. Similarly, the rule that establishes how to bit-blast bit-wise conjunction (&) takes a proof xbb that xb is the bit-blasted term corresponding to x as well as a proof ybb for yb corresponding to y and returns a proof that $x \& y$ is bit-blasted to rb. The rb term is constructed by the side condition code bb-bvand (not shown) which works similarly to bb-var. The bbEq rule for equality $\mathcal{T}_{bv}$-atoms follows a similar pattern, but returns a formula instead of a bbTerm. Note that bit-blasting proof rules do not take any $\mathcal{T}_{bv}$-assertions as assumptions: their conclusions are $\mathcal{T}_{bv}$-valid.

Example 3. Encoding in LFSC the bit-blasting proof for the formula $a_{[8]} = x_{[8]} \& y_{[8]}$ requires the following proof rule applications:

(bbEq _ _ _ _ _ _ (bbVar 8 a _) (bbAnd _ _ _ _ _ _ (bbVar 8 x _) (bbVar 8 y _)))

Assuming previously defined variables $a, x,$ and y, the above term has type thHolds(φ) where φ is:

$$(a_{[8]} = x_{[8]} \& y_{[8]}) \Leftrightarrow \bigwedge_{0 \le i < 8} (a_i \Leftrightarrow (\text{bitOf } v\, i) \wedge (\text{bitOf } v\, i)).$$

The bit-blasting LFSC proof rules rely on the side-condition code to build up the bit-blasted terms. This side-condition code thus becomes part of the trusted core and offers an efficient way to encode bit-blasting proofs.

6.3   Resolution in SAT$_{bb}$

A resolution refutation can be obtained from a SAT solver by instrumenting it to store resolution proofs of all the clauses learned during search. The empty clause is then derived by resolving input clauses and learned clauses. Recall that SAT_{bb} uses "solve with assumptions" to identify a subset $L^{BB} \subseteq A^{BB}$ that is inconsistent with C^{BB} and thereby produce the theory lemma $\neg L$. Because the assumption literals are implemented as decisions in SAT_{bb}, all clauses learned in SAT_{bb} follow from the bit-blasting clauses alone and can thus be reused in subsequent checks by SAT_{bb}. In particular, we can retrieve a resolution proof of the $\neg L^{BB}$ clause from SAT_{bb} starting from the bit-blasting clauses C^{BB} and using the stored resolutions of the learned clauses. We are careful to reuse the resolution proofs of learned clauses in multiple $\mathcal{T}_{bv}$ lemmas.

Stepping back and examining the overall $\mathcal{T}_{bv}$ proof structure, it looks like we could obtain one big resolution proof if we could plug the SAT_{bb} resolution trees into the SAT_{main} resolution tree. However, this cannot be done directly as the SAT variable a^{BB} abstracting $\mathcal{T}_{bv}$-atom a in the resolution proof in SAT_{bb} is not the same as the a^P variable used to abstract the same atom in SAT_{main}. Therefore, we need a proof construct to map the proof of a clause c^{BB} to c^P (the dashed lines between SAT_{main} and SAT_{bb} in Fig. 3).

In previous work on encoding SMT proofs in LFSC [28], we developed a specialized proof rule assump used to transform a $\mathcal{T}$-proof of $\bigwedge_{i=0}^{n} \neg l_i \models_{\mathcal{T}} \bot$ to a proof of the clause $c^P = [l_1^P, \ldots, l_n^P]$ where we use the square brackets as a shorthand for the LFSC syntax for clauses. Chaining assump rules turns a term of type $thHolds(\neg l_1) \rightarrow \ldots \rightarrow thHolds(\neg l_n).holds$ cln into a term of type holds $[l_1^P \ldots l_n^P]$. Our goal here is to build a proof that takes as assumptions the negation of each literal l_i as well as a proof of the clause $c^{BB} = [l_1^{BB}, \ldots, l_n^{BB}]$ and returns a term of type holds cln. We will do this using the introUnit rule:[7]

introUnit : Πf:form. Πv:var. Πc:clause.
$\quad\quad$ thHolds $f \rightarrow$ atom v $f \rightarrow$ (holds $[v] \rightarrow$ holds $c) \rightarrow$ holds c

This natural deduction style rule states that if formula f holds (thHolds f) and is abstracted by propositional variable v (atom v f), and if we can derive clause c from the unit clause corresponding to f (holds $[v] \rightarrow$ holds c), then we can derive clause c.

Example 4. We show how to put these rules together to lift a proof of a clause in SAT_{bb} to a proof of the corresponding clause in SAT_{main}. In the sub-expression below, assume c has type holds $[\neg a_1^{BB}, \neg a_2^{BB}]$ and that at_1 and at_2 have types atom(a_1^{BB}, a_1) and atom(a_2^{BB}, a_2), respectively. The two resolution steps between the assumption unit clauses u_1 and u_2 derive the empty clause from c. Therefore, the computed type of the following term is thHolds(not a_1) $\rightarrow$ thHolds(not a_2) $\rightarrow$ holds cln, which is exactly what the assump rule requires:

λh_1 : thHolds(not a_1). λh_2 : thHolds(not a_2).
$\quad$ (introUnit $\_\_\_$ h_1 at_1 (λu_1 : (holds$[a_1^{BB}]$).
$\quad\quad$ (introUnit $\_\_\_$ h_2 at_2 (λu_2 : (holds$[a_2^{BB}]$).
$\quad\quad\quad$ (Res $\_\_$ (Res $\_\_$ c u_1 v_1) u_2 v_2)))))

---

[7] For simplicity, introUnit only introduces literals in positive polarity. In reality, we also use a dual version that introduces literals in negative polarity.

7   Experimental Results

All the experiments in this section were run on the StarExec [29] cluster infrastructure with a timeout of 600 seconds and a memory limit of 200 GB.[8] We selected all of the 17,172 unsatisfiable QF_BV benchmarks used in the 2015 SMT-COMP competition and evaluated the overhead of proof generation for both the lazy cvcLz and the eager cvcE configurations of CVC4. CVC4 is a competitive bit-vector solver that placed second in the QF_BV division of the 2015 SMTCOMP by running cvcLz and cvcE in parallel.[9] The proof generated by cvcE uses the same proof signature as cvcLz but has a single monolithic resolution proof as opposed to the modular two-tiered structure of cvcLz proofs.

Table 1 shows the results for both solvers. We ran the following configurations: solving with proof generation disabled (default); solving with proofs enabled (i.e., the solver logs the information needed to produce the proof) but without actually producing proofs (+log); solving with proof generation including writing the proof object to disk (+log + proof); and solving with proof generation as well as proof checking (+log + proof + check). For the lazy solver cvcLz, the overhead of proof logging results in 2 fewer problems solved while adding an 11 % overhead to solving time.[10] The additional overhead of stitching the proof together and outputting it to a file is only 3 % of the solving time. For the eager solver cvcE, proof logging adds a higher overhead of 19 % and solves 18 fewer problems than the default configuration of cvcE. The overhead of proof generation is higher for the eager solver than for the lazy one.

Table 1. Overhead of proof generation and its impact on the number of problems solved.

	default		+log			+log+proof			+log+proof+check		
	solved	time (s)	solved	time (s)	%	solved	time (s)	%	solved	time (s)	%
cvcLz	16665	38575	16663	43684	11	16662	43729	14	14063	118544	973
cvcE	16601	65009	16583	78187	19	16582	78256	22	13734	137931	737

To ensure the correctness of the proofs we generated, we checked them using our LFSC proof checker. Within the 600 s time limit, we were able to succesfully check 84 % of the problems we could solve with cvcLz and 82 % of the ones solved with cvcE. Proof checking failed due to unsupported proof steps in our generated proof for 33 problems attempted by cvcLz, and for 92 attempted by cvcE. The other failures in proof checking were due to timeouts: proof checking is an order

---

[8] Experiments were run on the queue all.q consisting of Intel(R) Xeon(R) CPU E5-2609 0 @ 2.40 GHz machines with 268 GB of memory.

[9] CVC4 solved 26001 problems in that division compared to 26260 problems solved by the winning solver, Boolector [10].

[10] Overhead in each column is measured by comparing the time taken to solve only those problems solved by *both* the default and the column configuration.

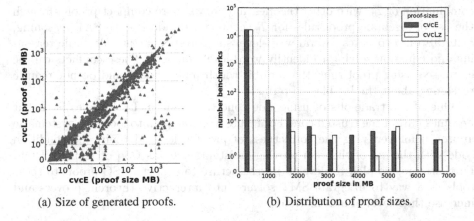

(a) Size of generated proofs.   (b) Distribution of proof sizes.

Fig. 6. Proof sizes both cvcLz and cvcE

of magnitude slower than solving. We believe that with additional work on the
LFSC proof checker, this can be improved.

Despite the slow checking times, we achieve higher proof checking rates for
QF_BV than the proof reconstruction approach in Böhme et al. [7]. In that work,
proofs could be produced for 735 of the 1377 QF_BV benchmarks available at
the time. Out of these, the produced proofs were successfully checked only for
38.5 % of the total; 48.4 % timed out and 13.1 % produced errors. The authors
attribute the timeouts to the long time taken to reprove large-step Z3 inferences.
Our experimental results indicate that fine-granularity bit-vector proofs enable
proof checking for a significantly larger number of problems.

Finally, we compared the sizes of the proof files generated. Figure 6(a) is
a log-scale scatter plot comparing the sizes of the proofs generated by the two
solvers. Overall, the proofs generated by the two-tiered lazy approach are smaller:
adding the sizes of all the lazy generated proofs results in 276 GB while for the
eager solver it is 328 GB. Figure 6(b) shows, with the y-axis in log-scale, the
distribution of the proof sizes over the benchmark selection. The majority of the
benchmarks have relatively small proofs, well under 1 GB.

8   Conclusion and Future Work

We have discussed a fine-grained LFSC proof system for the quantifier-free theory of bit-vectors. Our proof system takes advantage of LFSC's support for side
conditions to efficiently check large resolution proofs and proofs of bit-blasting-
based encodings to SAT. Used in the context of a lazy bit-vector solver, this
proof system allows for modular two-tiered proofs that are smaller and more
efficiently checked than a monolithic resolution proof, as shown by our experimental evaluation on a large set of QF_BV benchmarks.

The two-tiered proofs have several additional advantages we plan to investigate further in future work. For instance, it simplifies proof generation in the

combination of $\mathcal{T}_{bv}$ with other theories and allows more compact proofs through the use of algebraic proof rules for $\mathcal{T}_{bv}$ conflicts. In addition to SAT reasoning, cvcLz also incorporates several word-level sub-solvers that use algebraic reasoning and equation solving to identify word-level conflicts. These conflicts can be expressed using proof rules that are bit-width independent and do not require reasoning about the bit-blasted terms.

One of the trade-offs of using side condition code in LFSC rules is that it becomes part of the trusted core. For future work we plan to look at a systematic approach for verifying the correctness of proof rules and their side condition code with the aid of theorem proving assistants such as Coq or Isabelle/HOL. Furthermore, we plan to develop infrastructure to export LFSC proofs to these tools as a way to integrate SMT solvers into interactive theorem provers and increase their level of automation.

References

1. Armand, M., Faure, G., Grégoire, B., Keller, C., Théry, L., Werner, B.: A modular integration of SAT/SMT solvers to Coq through proof witnesses. In: Jouannaud, J.-P., Shao, Z. (eds.) CPP 2011. LNCS, vol. 7086, pp. 135–150. Springer, Heidelberg (2011)
2. Barrett, C., de Moura, L., Fontaine, P.: Proofs in satisfiability modulo theories. In: All about Proofs, Proofs for All, pp. 23–44 (2015)
3. Barrett, C., Fontaine, P., Tinelli, C.: The Satisfiability Modulo Theories Library (SMT-LIB) (2015). www.SMT-LIB.org
4. Barrett, C.W., Dill, D.L., Stump, A.: Checking satisfiability of first-order formulas by incremental translation to SAT. In: Conference on Computer Aided Verification (2002)
5. Besson, F., Cornilleau, P.-E., Pichardie, D.: Modular SMT proofs for fast reflexive checking inside Coq. In: Jouannaud, J.-P., Shao, Z. (eds.) CPP 2011. LNCS, vol. 7086, pp. 151–166. Springer, Heidelberg (2011)
6. Blanchette, J.C., Böhme, S., Paulson, L.C.: Extending sledgehammer with SMT solvers. J. Autom. Reason. 51(1), 109–128 (2013)
7. Böhme, S., Fox, A.C.J., Sewell, T., Weber, T.: Reconstruction of Z3's bit-vector proofs in HOL4 and Isabelle/HOL. In: Jouannaud, J.-P., Shao, Z. (eds.) CPP 2011. LNCS, vol. 7086, pp. 183–198. Springer, Heidelberg (2011)
8. Böhme, S., Weber, T.: Fast LCF-style proof reconstruction for Z3. In: Kaufmann, M., Paulson, L.C. (eds.) ITP 2010. LNCS, vol. 6172, pp. 179–194. Springer, Heidelberg (2010)
9. Bouton, T., Caminha, D., De Oliveira, B., Déharbe, D., Fontaine, P.: veriT: an open, trustable and efficient SMT-solver. In: Conference on Automated Deduction (2009)
10. Brummayer, R., Biere, A.: Boolector: an efficient SMT solver for bit-vectors and arrays. In: Kowalewski, S., Philippou, A. (eds.) TACAS 2009. LNCS, vol. 5505, pp. 174–177. Springer, Heidelberg (2009)
11. Chen, J., Chugh, R., Swamy, N.: Type-preserving compilation of end-to-end verification of security enforcement. In: Programming Language Design and Implementation (2010)

12. Eén, N., Sörensson, N.: An extensible SAT-solver. In: Giunchiglia, E., Tacchella, A. (eds.) SAT 2003. LNCS, vol. 2919, pp. 502–518. Springer, Heidelberg (2004)
13. Fontaine, P., Marion, J.-Y., Merz, S., Nieto, L.P., Tiu, A.F.: Expressiveness + automation + soundness: towards combining SMT solvers and interactive proof assistants. In: Hermanns, H., Palsberg, J. (eds.) TACAS 2006. LNCS, vol. 3920, pp. 167–181. Springer, Heidelberg (2006)
14. Ge, Y., Barrett, C.: Proof translation and SMT-LIB benchmark certification: a preliminary report. In: Workshop on Satisfiability Modulo Theories (2008)
15. Griggio, A.: Effective word-level interpolation for software verification. In: Formal Methods in Computer-Aided Design (2011)
16. Hadarean, L., Bansal, K., Jovanović, D., Barrett, C., Tinelli, C.: A tale of two solvers: eager and lazy approaches to bit-vectors. In: Biere, A., Bloem, R. (eds.) CAV 2014. LNCS, vol. 8559, pp. 680–695. Springer, Heidelberg (2014)
17. Harper, R., Honsell, F., Plotkin, G.: A framework for defining logics. J. Assoc. Comput. Mach. 40(1), 143–184 (1993)
18. Klein, G., Elphinstone, K., Heiser, G., Andronick, J., Cock, D., Derrin, P., Elkaduwe, D., Engelhardt, K., Kolanski, R., Norrish, M., Sewell, T., Tuch, H., Winwood, S.: SeL4: formal verification of an OS kernel. In: Symposium on Operating Systems Principles (2009)
19. Leroy, X.: Formal certification of a compiler back-end, or: programming a compiler with a proof assistant. In: Principles of Programming Languages (2006)
20. S. Lescuyer and S. Conchon. A Reflexive Formalization of a SAT Solver in Coq. In Theorem Proving in Higher Order Logics, 2008
21. McLaughlin, S., Barrett, C., Ge, Y.: Cooperating theorem provers: a case study combining HOL-Light and CVC lite. In: Pragmatics of Decision Procedures in Automated Reasoning (PDPAR 2005) (2006)
22. Moskal, M.: Rocket-fast proof checking for SMT solvers. In: Ramakrishnan, C.R., Rehof, J. (eds.) TACAS 2008. LNCS, vol. 4963, pp. 486–500. Springer, Heidelberg (2008)
23. Nieuwenhuis, R., Oliveras, A., Tinelli, C.: Solving SAT and SAT modulo theories: from an abstract davis-putnam-logemann-loveland procedure to DPLL(T). J. ACM 53(6), 937–977 (2006)
24. Oe, D., Reynolds, A., Stump, A.: Fast and flexible proof checking for SMT. In: Workshop on Satisfiability Modulo Theories (2009)
25. Reynolds, A., Hadarean, L., Tinelli, C., Ge, Y., Stump, A., Barrett, C.: Comparing proof systems for linear real arithmetic with LFSC. In: Workshop on Satisfiability Modulo Theories (2010)
26. Reynolds, A., Tinelli, C., Hadarean, L.: Certified interpolant generation for EUF. In: Workshop on Satisfiability Modulo Theories (2011)
27. Robinson, J.A.: Logic: Form and Function: The Mechanization of Deductive Reasoning. Elsevier, New York (1980)
28. Stump, A., Oe, D., Reynolds, A., Hadarean, L., Tinelli, C.: SMT proof checking using a logical framework. Formal Methods Syst. Des. 42(1), 91–118 (2013)
29. Stump, A., Sutcliffe, G., Tinelli, C.: StarExec: a cross-community infrastructure for logic solving. In: Demri, S., Kapur, D., Weidenbach, C. (eds.) IJCAR 2014. LNCS, vol. 8562, pp. 367–373. Springer, Heidelberg (2014)
30. Van, A.: Gelder. http://users.soe.ucsc.edu/avg/ProofChecker/ProofChecker-file format.txt
31. Wetzler, N., Heule, M.J.H., Hunt, Jr., W.A.: DRAT-trim: efficient checking and trimming using expressive clausal proofs. In: Sinz, C., Egly, U. (eds.) SAT 2014. LNCS, vol. 8561, pp. 422–429. Springer, Heidelberg (2014)

Abstract Domains and Solvers
for Sets Reasoning

Arlen Cox[1]([✉]), Bor-Yuh Evan Chang[1], Huisong Li[2], and Xavier Rival[2]

[1] University of Colorado Boulder, Boulder, USA
arlencox@gmail.com in
[2] Inria/CNRS/ENS Paris/PSL, Paris, France

Abstract. When constructing complex program analyses, it is often useful to reason about not just individual values, but collections of values. Symbolic set abstractions provide building blocks that can be used to partition elements, relate partitions to other partitions, and determine the provenance of multiple values, all without knowing any concrete values. To address the simultaneous challenges of scalability and precision, we formalize and implement an interface for symbolic set abstractions and construct multiple abstract domains relying on both specialized data structures and off-the-shelf theorem provers. We develop techniques for lifting existing domains to improve performance and precision. We evaluate these domains on real-world data structure analysis problems.

1 Introduction

The verification of program properties that involve data structures is a challenging problem [2,9,10,12,13,16,19]. One key reason for this is that if a data structure is unbounded, there is a potentially unbounded number of constraints on its elements. Since these constraints often affect important properties such as memory safety [16], functional correctness [19], or basic program behavior [9], it is vital to develop techniques for efficiently reasoning about relationships between unbounded numbers of elements.

This paper focuses on the use of set constraints to reason about unbounded collections of elements. Set constraints can be used to dynamically partition data structures, correlate collections of elements with one another, or determine analysis case splits. They are useful for representing data and pointer relationships in structures such as maps, graphs, lists, sets, and arrays. They can be combined with other techniques such as separation logic [9,16] and numerical analyses [8] to enhance those analyses.

For example, consider the program in Fig. 1 that copies one map on top of another. Within the loop, there is a complex relationship between the sets of keys of src and dst. At the specified point, the keys of src can be partitioned into three parts. The keys already visited X_v by the loop, the element currently being visited {x} by the loop, and the keys not visited X_n by the loop. The keys of dst can be partitioned into those $keys(dst)_0$ originally in dst that have not been overwritten,

© Springer-Verlag Berlin Heidelberg 2015
M. Davis et al. (Eds.): LPAR-20 2015, LNCS 9450, pp. 356–371, 2015.
DOI: 10.1007/978-3-662-48899-7_25

```
def extend(dst, src):
    for x in src:
```
$$(\exists X_v, X_n.\, keys(\texttt{src}) = X_v \uplus \{\texttt{x}\} \uplus X_n \wedge keys(\texttt{dst}) = (keys(\texttt{dst})_0 \setminus X_v) \uplus X_v)$$
```
        dst[x] = src[x]
```

Fig. 1. Set constraints can relate portions of data structures

and those X_v that have been overwritten or added from src. This set reasoning allows precise symbolic tracking of the provenance of map partitions.

This paper focuses on abstractions for states described by the logic for *symbolic sets*. The logic consists of a Boolean algebra over the set variables with singleton sets. We find that this subset is sufficiently large to be useful and we believe that it serves as a good starting point for extensions to the logic, such as reasoning about explicit set contents or more precise cardinality.

However, despite the fact that we are not reasoning about the values contained in sets or complex cardinalities, Boolean algebras, by themselves, are challenging for invariant generation. Naive approaches such as saturation and pattern matching rarely work without complex heuristics [10,19]. It is unavoidable that the worst-case time for precise invariant generation will be exponential because of the Boolean algebra. However, it is desirable that invariant generation should be efficient in the common cases, and unlike systems that involve complex heuristics, lose precision only in understandable and predictable ways.

In this paper we aim to design scalable, precise, and predictable abstractions for symbolic sets by combining new abstract domains with performance/precision-enhancing functors that lift existing set abstractions to new set abstractions. Specifically, we make the following contributions:

- We define a common interface for symbolic set abstractions that is designed to meet the needs of static analyzers (Sect. 3).
- Using specialized data structures, we construct a battery of symbolic set abstract domains and performance-/precision-enhancing functors designed to target real-world data structure verification problems (Sect. 4).
- We adapt an off-the-shelf satisfiability-modulo-theories solver to the set abstraction interface (Sect. 5).
- We compare abstractions for symbolic sets, finding that, while specialized abstractions are preferable, binary decision diagrams lifted with dynamic packing is a good compromise in scalability, performance, and predictability (Sect. 6).

2   Overview

In this section, we present two static analyses that make use of set reasoning in order to compute high-level semantic properties of programs. These analyses rely on abstract interpretation [6] and on an abstraction of program states that describes data structures and their contents. An abstract domain defines a set of predicates that an analysis may use, as well as operators to over-approximate the effect of program behaviors on these predicates, and their implementation.

Inference of properties of open objects. Dynamic programming languages such as JavaScript feature *open objects* that support dynamic addition and deletion of attributes and iteration over them. The analysis presented in [9] verifies open-object-/map-manipulating programs such as the one in Fig. 1, by inferring relations between the sets of attributes of distinct objects. Since objects may have an unbounded number of attributes, the analysis must abstract the attributes and their contents. Figure 2 represents a simplified state at the indicated point in Fig. 1 after two iterations (thus two fields were copied). We focus on the set of attributes of each object and ignore their contents (which could be described using similar techniques). To precisely abstract the relations between the attributes of both objects (e.g. copied attributes are common to both objects), we partition the attributes into a series of attribute sets and express relations among these sets. The purpose of the set abstract domain is to represent such set relations. Figure 2b depicts such an abstract state, where X_n, X_r, X_v stand for sets of attributes, which are made explicit in Fig. 2a, the concrete state.

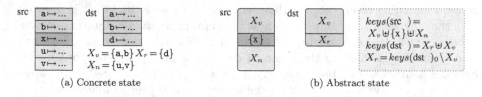

(a) Concrete state   (b) Abstract state

Fig. 2. Open objects and their abstraction

Moreover, to infer these invariants, the analysis needs to reason about both object structures and attribute sets. Initially it assumes no set relations, and the fields of each object should be associated to an arbitrary set of attributes. When the analysis enters the body of the loop, it needs to *single out* attribute x, i.e. to replace set X_v by $X_v \uplus \{x\}$, which produces the equalities of Fig. 2. When it exits the loop, the analysis should *generalize* both the object and set constraints abstractions, which requires *eliminating* the singleton $\{x\}$ from the equations (it is visible only in the loop body) and synthesizing a new, more general collection of constraints. To allow these steps, the set abstraction should provide basic operations over set predicates, including (1) the addition of a set constraint, (2) the proving of a set constraint, (3) the removal of a set variable, and (4) the generalization of two set abstract states.

Shape Analysis in Presence of Unstructured Sharing. The shape analysis for data-structures with unbounded sharing presented in [16] relies on separation logic [20] to describe memory states and on inductive definitions to summarize unbounded structures such as lists. Unstructured sharing is very challenging as it cannot be described using conventional inductive definitions. Figure 3a displays the representation of a three nodes graph using an adjacency list data-structure. To summarize such a structure using inductive predicates in separation logic,

[16] augments the list inductive predicates with set information, which express where edges may point to. Figure 3b shows this representation in a form where the first node is kept materialized. It asserts that the edges of that node and other nodes point to the address of a valid node, namely an element of $\{n_0\} \uplus \mathcal{E}$. The analysis of [16] introduces a summary predicate $\mathbf{graph}(n_0, \mathcal{N})$ where n_0 is the address of the first node and $\mathcal{N}$ the set of all node addresses. This predicate is defined by induction over the "backbone" of the structure, and fully takes into account the property that all edges point to a valid node address in $\mathcal{N}$. Henceforth, abstract states comprise both a *memory* part (which consists of a formula in separation logic with inductive predicates) and a *set abstraction*.

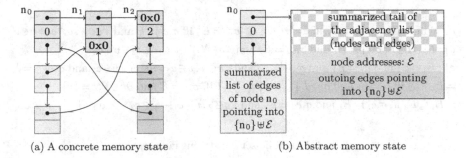

(a) A concrete memory state   (b) Abstract memory state

Fig. 3. Summarization of an adjacency list-based graph representation

To compute such summaries, the analysis needs to perform similar operations as the analysis for open objects, in order to add set constraints to the set abstract state, prove set constraints, remove set variables, and generalize abstract states.

3   Logic and Set Abstraction

We now define the elements and operators of a set abstract domain that meets the needs of all the analyses shown in Sect. 2.

Concrete States. In this paper, we use symbols W, X, Y, and Z as set variables and let $\mathbb{X}_s$ represent the set of all such variables. We are interested in purely symbolic set relations, and do not make any assumption on the type of the set elements (in practice these are pointers or scalars). We let $\mathbb{V}$ denote the set of all these elements. A concrete state is a function $\sigma : \mathbb{X}_s \to \mathcal{P}(\mathbb{V})$. We write $\mathbb{S}$ for the set of such elements.

Symbolic Sets. Before we set up the signature of abstract domains, we fix a language of set predicates, that will be used as a basis for abstract elements, and for the communication with the set abstract domain.

Definition 1 (Symbolic Sets). Symbolic sets *are defined by the grammar:*

$$L(\in \mathbb{C}) ::= L \wedge L \mid E \subseteq E \mid |X| = 1 \mid \top \mid \bot \qquad E ::= \emptyset \mid X \mid E^c \mid E \cup E \mid E \uplus E$$

The meaning of these constraints is straightforward, but we give a formal definition in Fig. 4 for clarity. A model of a set expression E is a concrete state σ and a set of concrete values c. A model of a logical expression L is a concrete state σ. The concretization is $\gamma(L) = \{ \sigma \mid \sigma \models L \}$ and we use $(\!| L |\!)$ for abstract states with the same concretization. We shall also use the following derived logical forms for simplicity:

$$E_1 \cap E_2 \stackrel{\text{def}}{=} (E_1{}^c \cup E_2{}^c)^c \qquad E_1 = E_2 \stackrel{\text{def}}{=} E_1 \subseteq E_2 \wedge E_2 \subseteq E_1 \qquad E_1 \setminus E_2 \stackrel{\text{def}}{=} E_1 \cap E_2{}^c$$

$\sigma,c \models \emptyset$ iff $c = \emptyset$ $\quad \sigma,c \models X$ iff $c = \sigma(X)$ $\quad \sigma,c \models E^c$ iff $\sigma,c' \models E$ and $\forall v \in \mathbb{V}. v \in c \Leftrightarrow v \notin c'$

$\sigma,c \models E_1 \cup E_2$ iff $\sigma,c_1 \models E_1$ and $\sigma,c_2 \models E_2$ and $\forall v \in \mathbb{V}. v \in c \Leftrightarrow v \in c_1 \vee v \in c_2$

$\sigma,c \models E_1 \uplus E_2$ iff $\sigma,c_1 \models E_1$ and $\sigma,c_2 \models E_2$ and $\forall v \in \mathbb{V}. v \in c \Leftrightarrow v \in c_1 \vee v \in c_2$ and $c_1 \cap c_2 = \emptyset$

$\sigma \models L_1 \wedge L_2$ iff $\sigma \models L_1$ and $\sigma \models L_2$ $\qquad \sigma \models |E| = 1$ iff $\sigma,c \models E$ and $\exists v \in \mathbb{V}. c = \{v\}$

$\sigma \models E_1 \subseteq E_2$ iff $\sigma,c_1 \models E_1$ and $\sigma,c_2 \models E_2$ and $\forall v \in \mathbb{V}. v \in c_1 \rightarrow v \in c_2$ $\qquad \sigma \models \top$ $\qquad \sigma \not\models \bot$

Fig. 4. Symbolic set constraint language

Set Abstraction. A *set abstract domain* is defined by a set of *abstract elements* $\mathbb{D}^\sharp$ which describe the family of logical properties it can express and a concretization function $\gamma : \mathbb{D}^\sharp \rightarrow \mathcal{P}(\mathbb{S})$ that maps each element of $\mathbb{D}^\sharp$ into the set of concrete states that satisfy it. Abstract elements are characterized by (1) the symbolic sets they describe and (2) their machine representation. The latter is usually very different from the formulas, and will be discussed in Sect. 4.

Example 1 ((Non-)Emptiness set domain). A very basic example of such a domain is the *(non-)emptiness* domain that comprises the following elements:

- $\bot$, which denotes the unsatisfiable abstract constraint (i.e., $\gamma(\bot) = \emptyset$));
- the functions from $\mathbb{X}_\mathbf{s}$ into $\{[= \emptyset], [\neq \emptyset], \top\}$, which map each set variable into its emptiness value.

For instance, $\{X \mapsto \top; Y \mapsto [= \emptyset]\}$ stands for $(\!| Y \subseteq \emptyset |\!)$ and concretizes into $\gamma(Y \subseteq \emptyset)$.

Operations over Set Abstractions. We now formalize the main operations and logical elements needed so that we can use a set abstract $\mathbb{D}^\sharp$ domain for either of the static analyses shown in Sect. 2.

– *Basic logical elements.* Static analyses typically start with an unconstrained state. This is indicated by a $\top_{\mathbb{D}^\sharp} \in \mathbb{D}^\sharp$ element with full concretization, i.e., $\gamma(\top_{\mathbb{D}^\sharp}) = \mathbb{S}$. Similarly, the abstract element $\bot_{\mathbb{D}^\sharp} \in \mathbb{D}^\sharp$ should describe the unsatisfiable abstract constraint (i.e., $\gamma(\bot_{\mathbb{D}^\sharp}) = \emptyset$). In Example 1, $\bot_{\mathbb{D}^\sharp}$ is $\bot$ and $\top_{\mathbb{D}^\sharp}$

is $\lambda(x \in \mathbb{X}_s) \cdot \top$. Moreover, a static analysis often has to determine if an abstract state describes unsatisfiable constraints. Thus, $\mathbb{D}^\sharp$ should provide an operator $\mathbf{isbot}_{\mathbb{D}^\sharp} : \mathbb{D}^\sharp \to \{\mathbf{true}, \mathbf{false}\}$ such that $\mathbf{isbot}_{\mathbb{D}^\sharp}(\sigma^\sharp) = \mathbf{true} \Longrightarrow \gamma(\sigma^\sharp) = \emptyset$.

– *Forgetting a set variable.* Static analysis tools drop set variables that become redundant. In the open object example of Sect. 2, this occurs when the singleton symbol is eliminated at the end of the loop. To do this, we require the set abstract domain $\mathbb{D}^\sharp$ to provide an operator $\mathbf{forget}_{\mathbb{D}^\sharp} : \mathbb{D}^\sharp \times \mathbb{X}_s \to \mathbb{D}^\sharp$ that discards a symbol from the abstract state.

– *Assuming set constraints.* As noted in Sect. 2, an important set reasoning step *restricts an abstract state with set constraints*, thus set domain $\mathbb{D}^\sharp$ should provide an operator $\mathbf{assume}_{\mathbb{D}^\sharp} : \mathbb{D}^\sharp \times \mathbb{C} \to \mathbb{D}^\sharp$, which conservatively represents a constraint into an abstract state, i.e. ensures that, for all $\sigma^\sharp, L$, $\gamma(\sigma^\sharp) \cap \gamma(L) \subseteq \gamma(\mathbf{assume}_{\mathbb{D}^\sharp}(\sigma^\sharp, L))$. Note that this operator also makes use of the symbolic set language of Definition 1 in order to describe constraints communicated to the domain.

– *Verifying set constraints.* Similarly, set reasoning should allow *verifying set constraints*, thus the set domain $\mathbb{D}^\sharp$ should provide an operator $\mathbf{prove}_{\mathbb{D}^\sharp} : \mathbb{D}^\sharp \times \mathbb{C} \to \{\mathbf{true}, \mathbf{false}\}$, which conservatively attempts to verify that a symbolic set constraint holds under some abstract states, i.e. ensures that, for all $\sigma^\sharp, L$, $\mathbf{prove}_{\mathbb{D}^\sharp}(\sigma^\sharp, L) = \mathbf{true}$ implies that $\gamma(\sigma^\sharp) \subseteq \gamma(L)$.

– *Generalizing set abstractions.* The analysis of loops is commonly based on the computation of abstract post-fixpoints [6], thus $\mathbb{D}^\sharp$ should provide sound over-approximation of the union of sets concrete states. In the logical point of view, this amounts to computing a common weakening for two abstract constraints. This is performed by an operator $\mathbf{join}_{\mathbb{D}^\sharp} : \mathbb{D}^\sharp \times \mathbb{D}^\sharp \to \mathbb{D}^\sharp$ such that, for all $\sigma_0^\sharp, \sigma_1^\sharp$, $\gamma(\sigma_0^\sharp) \cup \gamma(\sigma_1^\sharp) \subseteq \gamma(\mathbf{join}_{\mathbb{D}^\sharp}(\sigma_0^\sharp, \sigma_1^\sharp))$. Widening operator $\mathbf{widen}_{\mathbb{D}^\sharp}$ should satisfy the same property and ensure termination of any sequence of abstract iterates.

– *Deciding entailment over set abstractions.* Finally, the operator $\mathbf{is\_le}_{\mathbb{D}^\sharp} : \mathbb{D}^\sharp \times \mathbb{D}^\sharp \to \{\mathbf{true}, \mathbf{false}\}$ conservatively decides implication among abstract set constraints (by ensuring that $\mathbf{is\_le}_{\mathbb{D}^\sharp}(\sigma_0^\sharp, \sigma_1^\sharp) = \mathbf{true} \Longrightarrow \gamma(\sigma_0^\sharp) \subseteq \gamma(\sigma_1^\sharp)$), and allows verifying the convergence of abstract iterates.

4   Constructed Set Abstractions

An abstract domain is defined by a class of set constraints, their machine representation, and the abstract operations following the signatures given in Sect. 3. In this section, we introduce three basic set abstract domains (respectively based on linear constraints, QUIC graphs, and BDDs) and two set abstract domain functors, that lift a set domain into another, more expressive or efficient one.

4.1   Linear Set Constraints

Abstract elements and their concretization. Our first set abstract domain relies on *linear* set equality constraints, of the form $(\!| X = \{y_0, \ldots, y_k\} \uplus Z_0 \uplus \ldots \uplus Z_l |\!)$.

The advantage of such constraints is to provide a rather straightforward normalization of the representation of constraints. Note they also include emptiness constraints. Our implementation of abstract domain $\mathbb{D}_\ell^\sharp$ describes three kinds of constraints:

- acyclic *linear* constraints of the form $(\!|X = Y_0 \uplus \ldots \uplus Y_k \uplus Z_0 \uplus \ldots \uplus Z_l|\!)$, where $Y_0, \ldots, Y_k$ are singletons (containing $y_0, \ldots, y_k$ respectively). In the implementation, each variable may appear at most *once* as the left-hand side of such a constraint, to enable normalization;
- inclusion constraints of the form $(\!|Y \subseteq X|\!)$;
- equality constraints of the form $(\!|Y = X|\!)$.

Thus, an element of $\mathbb{D}_\ell^\sharp$ is either $\bot$ or a conjunction of such constraints. The associated concretization $\gamma_\ell : \mathbb{D}_\ell^\sharp \to \mathcal{P}(\mathbb{S})$ is of the same form as that of the symbolic sets language of Definition 1 (thus, we do not formalize it in full details). The machine representation utilizes persistent dictionaries, that stand for functions over a finite domain. This reduces basic queries for facts (such as, "does abstract state $\sigma^\sharp$ entail that $X \subseteq Y \uplus Z$?") to dictionary searches.

Abstract operators. The core algorithm of $\mathbb{D}_\ell^\sharp$ normalizes abstract values by expanding nested linear constraints. For instance, $(\!|X_0 = X_1 \uplus X_2 \wedge X_1 = X_3 \uplus X_4|\!)$ is rewritten into $(\!|X_0 = X_2 \uplus X_3 \uplus X_4 \wedge X_1 = X_3 \uplus X_4|\!)$ at the machine representation level. This process terminates as constraints represented in $\mathbb{D}_\ell^\sharp$ do not contain cycles. It is performed incrementally by all abstract operations.

Abstract operations $\mathbf{isbot}_{\mathbb{D}^\sharp}$, $\mathbf{assume}_{\mathbb{D}^\sharp}$, $\mathbf{prove}_{\mathbb{D}^\sharp}$ are all made very fast by this normalization. Operation $\mathbf{forget}_{\mathbb{D}^\sharp}$ simply drops all constraints that involve a given set variable. Finally, $\mathbf{join}_{\mathbb{D}^\sharp}$ and $\mathbf{widen}_{\mathbb{D}^\sharp}$ need to *generalize* constraints.

Example 2. Let us assume that $\sigma_0^\sharp$ (resp., $\sigma_1^\sharp$) stands for the set of constraints $(\!|X_0 = X_1 \uplus X_2 \wedge X_3 = \emptyset|\!)$ (resp., $(\!|X_0 = X_1 \uplus X_2 \uplus X_3|\!)$). Then $\mathbf{join}_{\mathbb{D}^\sharp}(\sigma_0^\sharp, \sigma_1^\sharp)$ returns an element that represents the constraint $(\!|X_0 = X_1 \uplus X_2 \uplus X_3|\!)$.

MemCAD [16] relies on $\mathbb{D}_\ell^\sharp$ to represent set constraints since it mainly needs to express constraints over set partitions. On the other hand, $\mathbb{D}_\ell^\sharp$ is not adapted to the precise description of non disjoint unions.

4.2   QUIC Graphs

A QUIC graph [10] is a directed hypergraph data structure used to represent relational set constraints. Each edge in the hypergraph corresponds to a subset constraint and each hypergraph is a conjunction of subset constraints where each constraint is of the form $(\!|X_1 \cap \ldots \cap X_n \subseteq Y_1 \cup \ldots \cup Y_m|\!)$. Each variable can also be constrained to be a singleton, with constraints such as $(\!|\,\|X\| = 1|\!)$. The concretization $\gamma_q : \mathbb{D}_q^\sharp \to \mathcal{P}(\mathbb{S})$ is of the same form as that of the symbolic sets language of Definition 1.

QUIC graphs are designed for efficiently performing two operations: (1) $\mathbf{forget}_{\mathbb{D}^\sharp}$, which matches edges containing the symbol to be forgotten with each other to produce new edges without that symbol; and (2) content reasoning, which is not a design goal for symbolic sets. The $\mathbf{join}_{\mathbb{D}^\sharp}$ and $\mathbf{widen}_{\mathbb{D}^\sharp}$ operations are primarily based on saturation heuristics. They keep common conjunctions from both arguments. To aid this process, they use a form of saturation that produces new conjuncts based on pattern matches. A sufficiently large set of patterns must be provided to attain precision, but additional patterns increase the cost of joins.

Example 3 (QUIC graph join). Consider the following join operation:

$$\sigma_0^\sharp = (\!| W \subseteq X \wedge X \subseteq Z |\!) \quad \sigma_1^\sharp = (\!| W \subseteq Y \wedge Y \subseteq Z |\!) \quad \mathbf{join}_{\mathbb{D}^\sharp}(\sigma_0^\sharp, \sigma_1^\sharp)$$

There is an obvious result: $(\!| W \subseteq Z |\!)$. Whether or not QUIC graphs derive this result or $(\!| \top |\!)$ is determined by the pattern matches that are installed. If the pattern that takes $(\!| X \subseteq Y \wedge Y \subseteq Z |\!)$ and generates $(\!| X \subseteq Z |\!)$ is used, the pattern will be applied to both sides and then common conjuncts kept, getting the desired result. Without that pattern or a similar substitute, QUIC graphs derive $(\!| \top |\!)$.

4.3 BDD-based Set Constraints

Binary decision diagrams (BDDs) [21] are a canonical representation of Boolean algebraic functions. There are three basic syntactic elements of a BDD. The TRUE and FALSE elements represent the obvious constants, but $\text{ITE}(X, B_t, B_e)$ is an if-then-else structure. If the variable X is **true**, the result of evaluating B_t is returned, otherwise the result of evaluating B_e is returned.

$$B ::= \text{TRUE} \mid \text{FALSE} \mid \text{ITE}(X, B_t, B_e)$$

What makes BDDs canonical is that we only consider reduced, ordered BDDs, where it is assumed that there is a total order $\prec$ on the variables. An $\text{ITE}(X, B_t, B_e)$ can only be constructed if $X \prec X'$ for all variables X' in B_t or B_e. Additionally, structural sharing is mandated, so the reuse of the same syntax is referentially identical to any other use of that syntax.

The encoding of constraints maps operators from their constraint form (as in Definition 1) to their Boolean algebraic form: $\cup \mapsto \vee$, $\cap \mapsto \wedge$, $^c \mapsto \neg$, $\subseteq \mapsto \to$, $= \mapsto \leftrightarrow$. All but singleton set constraints are directly and exactly represented by the BDD. Singleton constraints are not currently used by the BDD-based abstraction.

Domain operations are straightforward: $\mathbf{join}_{\mathbb{D}^\sharp}$ and $\mathbf{widen}_{\mathbb{D}^\sharp}$ are implemented with the $\vee$ operation, which is precise and does not need any rules or heuristics; $\mathbf{forget}_{\mathbb{D}^\sharp}$ takes advantage of reasonably efficient quantifier elimination provided by BDDs and uses existential quantifier elimination to drop variables. Queries such as $\mathbf{is\_le}_{\mathbb{D}^\sharp}$ are easily implemented using validity checking functionality provided by BDDs. Critically, because BDDs are a canonical form, many operations such as $\mathbf{forget}_{\mathbb{D}^\sharp}$ and $\mathbf{assume}_{\mathbb{D}^\sharp}$ become much more efficient, whereas the operation $\mathbf{isbot}_{\mathbb{D}^\sharp}$ becomes an $O(1)$ check.

Example 4 (BDD-based join). Consider the same inputs as Example 3. Encoding them to BDDs (and using some Boolean-algebraic notation as shorthand) yields the following results:

$$\sigma_0^\sharp = (\!|W \subseteq Y \wedge Y \subseteq X|\!) = \text{ITE}(W, X \wedge Y, \text{ITE}(X, \text{TRUE}, \neg Y))$$
$$\sigma_1^\sharp = (\!|W \subseteq Z \wedge Z \subseteq X|\!) = \text{ITE}(W, X \wedge Z, \text{ITE}(X, \text{TRUE}, \neg Z))$$
$$\textbf{join}_{\mathbb{D}^\sharp}(\sigma_0^\sharp, \sigma_1^\sharp) = \text{ITE}(W, X \wedge \text{ITE}(Y, \text{TRUE}, Z),$$
$$\text{ITE}(X, \text{TRUE}, \text{ITE}(Y, \neg Z, \text{TRUE})))$$

The result of this join is equivalent to the set constraints $(\!|W \subseteq X|\!)$, $(\!|W \subseteq Y \cup Z|\!)$, and $(\!|Y \cap Z \subseteq X|\!)$, which includes not only the obvious result of $(\!|W \subseteq X|\!)$, but also other, possibly useful results. It is a precise join.

We implement the BDD abstraction on top of the CU decision diagrams package [22], which is high performance and offers the ability to extract prime implicants (as in [5]). The prime implicants of the negation of the Boolean function are easily converted to conjuncts of the form used by QUIC graphs.

4.4   The Equalities Domain Functor: Compact Equality Constraints

When analyzing real programs, in addition to complex set constraints, there are often many very simple equality constraints of the form $(\!|X = Y|\!)$. These can be a problem in several ways. For example, equalities are normalized and handled precisely in BDDs, but they can grow the size of the representation significantly. This results in significantly increased memory usage and decreased efficiency since many BDD operations rebuild the BDD. In QUIC graphs, equalities grow the size of the graph, and place significantly more load on the pattern matching system, potentially causing an explosion in the number of constraints. This is because QUIC graphs can represent each variant of an expression rewritten using all available equalities. In linear set abstractions, there are similar potential problems.

As a result, abstractions like QUIC graphs and the linear set abstraction have special handling for equality. This improves performance and precision at the cost of complexity. Instead, much of this complexity can be moved outside the abstraction and handled by lifting the abstraction to one that keeps track of equalities separately from other kinds of constraints.

The equality functor serves as an intermediary between the domain interface and the abstract domain that is being lifted. It intercepts equality constraints and handles them externally, preventing them from being seen by the underlying abstract domain. This saves the domain from the cost and complexity of handling the equalities.

The equality functor defines a set of equivalence classes Q. The set of equivalence classes is a map $\mathbb{X}_s \to \mathbb{X}_s$ that maps each variable to the chosen representative for the equivalence class. The functor then lifts an abstract state $\mathbb{D}^\sharp$ into a tuple $(\mathbb{D}^\sharp, Q)$. In the lifting, $\mathbb{D}^\sharp$ is restricted to only have symbols that are representatives for the equivalence class. Therefore, when an equality is added that merges two equivalence classes, the resulting representative replaces the two previous representatives in $\mathbb{D}^\sharp$.

The concretization ensures that all symbols in the same equivalence class map to the same concrete set:

$$\gamma((Q, \mathbb{D}^\sharp)) = \{\, \sigma \mid \sigma \in \gamma(\mathbb{D}^\sharp) \wedge \forall X, Y \in \mathbb{X}_s^2.\, Q(X) = Q(Y) \to \sigma(X) = \sigma(Y)\,\}$$

Domain operations $\mathbf{join}_{\mathbb{D}^\sharp}$, $\mathbf{widen}_{\mathbb{D}^\sharp}$, and $\mathbf{is\_le}_{\mathbb{D}^\sharp}$ unify their corresponding Qs, pushing any non-common equalities into the underlying domain. This ensures that the underlying domain determines the precision, but it is not required to handle most of the load of the equalities. The $\mathbf{assume}_{\mathbb{D}^\sharp}$ operation rewrites the constraint, extracting the equalities and rewriting remaining variables to their representatives before passing the constraint to the underlying domain.

Example 5 (Equality functor join). Consider the following two abstract states, where the underlying domain is just shown as symbolic set constraints:

$$\sigma_0^\sharp = ([W \mapsto W, X \mapsto W, Y \mapsto W], (\!| W \subseteq Z |\!)) \quad \sigma_1^\sharp = ([X \mapsto X, Y \mapsto X], (\!| W \subseteq X \wedge X \subseteq Z |\!))$$

In the join, the equivalence classes are unified, producing the resulting Q: $[X \mapsto X, Y \mapsto X]$. The equality $(\!| W = X |\!)$ from $\sigma_0^\sharp$ is not represented in the unification, so it is added back to the underlying domain in $\sigma_0^\sharp$. The result is therefore

$$([X \mapsto X, Y \mapsto X], \mathbf{join}_{\mathbb{D}^\sharp}((\!| W = X \wedge W \subseteq Z |\!), (\!| W \subseteq X \wedge X \subseteq Z |\!)))$$

4.5   The Packing Domain Functor: Sparse Constraints

Most relational domains have a complexity that is related to the number of variables constrained by the abstract state. For example, BDDs, in the worst case, are exponential in the number of variables. However, in many programs, there are relatively small clusters of variables that are related. Therefore it is possible to increase the efficiency of an analysis by representing each cluster of variables by a separate abstract state [1].

If each of m clusters of n variables is represented by a separate abstract state, rather than operations having a complexity of, for example, $O(2^{m \cdot n})$, they can have complexity $O(m \cdot 2^n)$. To do this, all variables are initially assumed to be in their own cluster. Clusters are merged whenever variables from each cluster occur in the same constraint. In this way the clusters are dynamically determined, which is required when an abstract domain is used as a library and thus a pre-analysis cannot be performed.

An abstract state in the packing functor consists of one of three values: $\top$, $\bot$, or a map $M : \#_M \to \mathbb{D}^\sharp$ that maps cluster ids in $\#_M$ to abstract states from the domain being lifted. The $\top$ and $\bot$ values concretize as they do in Fig. 4. The map concretizes as follows:

$$\gamma(M) = \{\sigma \mid \forall \sigma^\sharp \in \mathrm{Range}(M).\, \sigma \in \gamma(\sigma^\sharp)\}$$

Example 6 (Constraining a packed abstract state). Consider the following abstract state represented by the logic from Definition 1, lifted into two packs with ids 0 and 1: $\sigma_0^\sharp = [0 \mapsto (\!|X_0 \subseteq X_1|\!); 1 \mapsto (\!|Y_0 \subseteq Y_1|\!)]$. The operation $\textbf{assume}_{\mathbb{D}^\sharp}(\sigma_0^\sharp, Y_1 \subseteq Y_2)$ operates only on pack id 1. It does not have to involve any computation on pack 0. The resulting pack 1 is: $1 \mapsto \textbf{assume}_{\mathbb{D}^\sharp}((\!|Y_0 \subseteq Y_1|\!), Y_1 \subseteq Y_2)$.

5 Solver-Based Abstractions

Because one of the core components of set abstraction is the Boolean algebra, it is possible to construct abstract domains from off-the-shelf satisfiability solvers. The construction relies upon the fact that the standard Boolean algebra is a finite height lattice ordered by implication. This means that no specific invariant generation procedure is required.

The syntax of the abstraction is the standard Boolean algebra with existential quantification. There are two reasons this is a good logic to use. First, it is a fairly well-supported logic for which there are efficient solvers. Second, it remains finite height and thus needs no specialized invariant generation procedure as would be required with a set logic such as BAPA [14]. Since cardinality is not a key requirement for symbolic sets, the analysis can often be sufficient without it.

Domain operations are translated into Boolean algebra formulas: $\textbf{join}_{\mathbb{D}^\sharp}(\sigma_1^\sharp, \sigma_2^\sharp)$ translates into $\sigma_1^\sharp \vee \sigma_2^\sharp$; $\textbf{assume}_{\mathbb{D}^\sharp}(\sigma^\sharp, L)$ translates into $\sigma^\sharp \wedge \text{conv}(L)$, assuming that $\text{conv}(L)$ converts the constraint L into its Boolean algebra equivalent as in Sect. 4.3; $\textbf{forget}_{\mathbb{D}^\sharp}(\sigma^\sharp, X)$ translates into $\exists X. \sigma^\sharp$. These are accumulated across the whole analysis and thus may grow arbitrarily deep. It is possible that on-the-fly simplification could be used, but we elect to use whatever internal functionality is provided by the solver (in this case Z3 [11]).

Query operations are translated into solver queries. The implication test $\textbf{is\_le}_{\mathbb{D}^\sharp}(\sigma_1^\sharp, \sigma_2^\sharp)$ translates to $\text{VALID}(\sigma_1^\sharp \to \sigma_2^\sharp)$. This is implemented incrementally by conditionally adding constraints for each query and checking satisfiability under assumptions. The $\textbf{isbot}_{\mathbb{D}^\sharp}(\sigma^\sharp)$ query translates into $\text{VALID}(\neg\sigma^\sharp)$.

Example 7 (Solver-based abstraction operations). Domain operations accumulate constraints, so simplification is performed by the solver when a query happens. In the following sequence, there are no queries, so constraints only accumulate.

$$\sigma_0^\sharp = \top \qquad\qquad\qquad\qquad\qquad\qquad = \text{TRUE}$$
$$\sigma_1^\sharp = \textbf{assume}_{\mathbb{D}^\sharp}(\sigma_0^\sharp, X \subseteq Y \wedge Y \subseteq Z) \qquad = \text{TRUE} \wedge X \to Y \wedge Y \to Z$$
$$\sigma_2^\sharp = \textbf{forget}_{\mathbb{D}^\sharp}(\sigma_1^\sharp, Y) \qquad\qquad\qquad = \exists Y. \text{TRUE} \wedge X \to Y \wedge Y \to Z$$

If the query $\textbf{prove}_{\mathbb{D}^\sharp}(\sigma_2^\sharp, X \subseteq Z)$ is performed, the following check is made: $\text{VALID}((\exists Y. \text{TRUE} \wedge X \to Y \wedge Y \to Z) \to (X \to Z))$. This holds trivially.

6 Evaluation

In this section, we evaluate the set abstractions. We aim to answer the following questions about set abstractions. Can set abstractions be sufficiently precise to be useful? Can precision be made available while providing scalability? What trade-offs are necessary to achieve scalability? To evaluate these questions we implemented all of the aforementioned abstractions as an OCaml library and then evaluated the abstractions using three different sets of problems: (1) traces of set domain operations as used in Memcad to perform shape analysis in the presence of unstructured sharing (from [16]), totaling 4521 domain operations; (2) traces of set domain operations as used in JSAna to verify functions in selected JavaScript libraries (from [7,9]), totaling 23086 domain operations; and (3) the expressible subset of tests of the Python set data structure (as used for QUIC graphs [10]), totaling 207 lines of code. Results are shown in Table 1.

Table 1. Number of proved properties ($\mathbf{prove}_{D\sharp}$), average aggregate run time for non-timed-out benchmarks (Time), and number of timed-out benchmarks (TO) for 24 Memcad benchmarks, 5 JSAna benchmarks, and 24 Python benchmarks.

Config	Memcad(24)		JSAna(5)		Python(24)	
	$\mathbf{prove}_{D\sharp}$	Time(TO)	$\mathbf{prove}_{D\sharp}$	Time(TO)	$\mathbf{prove}_{D\sharp}$	Time(TO)
lin	612/1366	0.036(0)	0/525	0.435(0)	4/42	0.004(0)
eq	608/1366	0.035(0)	0/525	0.235(0)	4/42	0.007(0)
pack	612/1366	0.049(0)	0/525	0.652(0)	4/42	0.006(0)
eq+pack	609/1366	0.045(0)	0/525	0.785(0)	4/42	0.011(0)
pack+eq	608/1366	0.067(0)	0/525	0.393(0)	4/42	0.011(0)
bdd	612/1366	0.021(0)	176/525	21.793(0)	34/42	0.105(0)
eq	612/1366	0.041(0)	176/525	1.206(0)	34/42	0.112(0)
pack	612/1366	0.052(0)	176/525	0.262(0)	34/42	0.109(0)
eq+pack	612/1366	0.055(0)	176/525	1.692(0)	34/42	0.116(0)
pack+eq	612/1366	0.086(0)	176/525	1.796(0)	34/42	0.119(0)
quic	596/1366	4.299(1)	155/525	54.616(0)	20/39	0.412(2)
eq	549/1366	2.289(0)	116/525	4.633(0)	18/39	0.416(2)
pack	605/1366	5.556(0)	155/525	48.517(0)	20/39	0.454(2)
eq+pack	549/1366	2.307(0)	121/525	8.201(0)	18/39	0.456(2)
pack+eq	55/58	0.080(10)	121/525	9.307(0)	17/38	0.362(3)
smt	177/315	44.995(4)	12/23	0.0389(4)	34/41	0.296(1)
eq	416/927	35.798(1)	62/152	5.753(2)	31/41	0.294(1)
pack	177/315	16.329(4)	12/23	0.787(4)	34/41	5.553(1)
eq+pack	438/927	40.621(1)	27/73	9.355(3)	31/41	10.884(1)
pack+eq	231/458	12.027(3)	12/23	0.609(4)	31/41	10.838(1)

Because the definition of necessary precision depends on the use of a domain, we measure precision by comparing against a standard for precision. For Memcad, the linear set abstraction (**lin**) was designed to be as precise as is needed for the Memcad benchmarks. This means that any abstraction that achieves the same number of proofs without timeout is sufficiently precise. It is important to note that many of these proofs are not intended to succeed. They are used as queries internally with the analysis, so it is not possible to achieve 100 %. From the results, we see that all of the BDD-based abstractions (**bdd**) achieve this. We can also see that the equality (eq) and packing (pack) functors, regardless of the order in which they are applied, do not change precision when applied to the BDD. However, when applied to the linear set abstraction, they sometimes change precision. This is because they affect internal representation and may affect the heuristics used within the abstract domain. QUIC graphs (**quic**) and SMT (**smt**) do not perform as well under any configuration. The reason is that QUIC graphs do not employ appropriate heuristics for all of the cases needed by Memcad and both have performance problems that cause them to time out before completing some benchmarks.

For the JSAna benchmarks, the BDD abstraction was designed to meet its precision needs and adding the equality or packing functor does not affect precision in any way. It only affects performance. However, the linear sets abstraction is not able to cope with the non-disjoint-union constraints that arise frequently in the JSAna benchmarks and thus loses all precision rapidly. By comparison, QUIC graphs perform well. They are unable to prove as many properties as is needed by JSAna, but they are still able to prove many properties. Once again, tuning the heuristics could improve this precision, but possibly at the cost of performance. SMT, once again, does not perform well because of efficiency problems. On the benchmarks where it completes, it is identical in precision to BDDs.

The Python benchmarks are slightly different because they are an analysis of programs rather than traces of domain operations. Each program contains a couple of properties to verify, so the target is 100 %. Here we see that none of the abstractions are able to achieve 100 %. The linear set abstraction cannot achieve this because it is unable to represent the non-disjoint-union constructs. The BDD and SMT abstractions cannot achieve 100 % because they do not support full cardinality reasoning. Once again, QUIC graphs are insufficient because of the limited heuristics they employ as well as some performance problems.

The scalability of the abstractions can be seen in Table 1 in the total analysis time, which measures the time to run the full benchmark suite, on average. The times are only directly comparable if there are no time outs, which happens after 60 seconds per benchmark. We first see that the linear domain is reliably fast. Applying the equality and packing functors generally does not affect performance significantly. By comparison, BDDs are less reliable. While they perform well in the Memcad benchmarks, nearly matching the linear domain, we see significant variability in the JSAna benchmarks. In fact, without any of the functors as in [10], performance can be unacceptably slow at almost 22 s to analyze five functions. However, the addition of the packing functor, in particular, makes a significant difference. It lowers the cost of the analysis to a fraction of a second without losing any precision. However, the variability here indicates that, depending on the particular benchmark (or, in fact, the BDD implementation), the optimum combination of functors may vary. Regardless, selecting the packing functor seems to be a benefit without significant risk. The QUIC graphs performance is unreliable. Due to the expensive pattern matching machinery, it does not compare in terms of performance, though it is helped significantly by the equality functor, at the cost of precision. The SMT domain fails to perform, timing out on at least one test in each benchmark suite. This is because the SMT solver is failing to operate incrementally. In essence, it has the same workload as the BDD, but it discharges its proofs lazily. This laziness is not necessarily a problem if work can be reused from one proof to the next, but it appears that this is not the case right now. We suspect that the combination of doing validity proofs (instead of satisfiability queries) with quantifiers is preventing this reuse.

The results make four things clear. First, if it is possible to design a targeted abstraction as the linear abstraction is for Memcad, it is worth it. The performance is reliable and the precision is predictable. Second, if it is not clear what the constraints may be, BDDs provide a good alternative that gives excellent (if not perfect due to the insufficient cardinality reasoning) precision with the risk of less reliable performance. Third, much of the risk can be eliminated through the use of functors. For equality heavy loads, the equality functor provides a significant benefit. The packing functor seems to reliably improve performance by simply lowering the cost of each BDD operation without any measurable impact on precision. Lastly, unless the content-centric reasoning of QUIC graphs is necessary, it does not make sense to use it due to both unreliable performance and precision. Similarly, with the current state of SMT, this is not an appropriate use. It may be possible to fix this, but today it remains impractical for performance reasons.

7   Conclusions and Related Work

The problem of creating scalable, precise, and predictable abstractions for sets remains challenging. This paper introduced several ways of approaching this problem and showed that for symbolic set abstractions, binary decision diagrams offer good performance, precision, and predictability trade-offs. However, it is preferable to craft a custom abstraction such as the linear abstraction. This offers more predictable performance by only having the necessary precision.

There are other set abstractions available. They all offer different functionality at different costs. The QUIC graphs abstraction [8,10] focuses on combining reasoning about contents with symbolic set reasoning. This comes at the cost of performance, precision, and predictability when it comes to purely symbolic set reasoning. The FixBag abstraction [19] attacks the problems of multisets or bags offering cardinality reasoning as well as symbolic set reasoning. Similar to QUIC graphs, it exchanges performance, precision, and predictability for this functionality. The linear and the BDD-based abstractions we present here are designed to be scalable, precise, and predictable rather than complex.

There are several decision procedures for sets. Bradley et al. [3] introduced a decision procedure for set contents and relationships (without cardinality). BAPA [13,14] is a decision procedure for sets with cardinality. Z3 [11] also includes a decision procedure for sets with contents. None of these decision procedures are designed for invariant generation. It is possible that interpolation procedures [18] could be designed based upon these procedures, but to our knowledge this has not been done. Regardless, without invariant generation that is compatible with static analysis, it is difficult to use this work as a component of an existing analysis.

Due to the prevalence of Boolean algebra in the algorithms presented here, there is a natural correspondence to hardware model checking [4] and predicate abstraction [15]. However, one significant difference is the composability of the abstractions presented here. The equality and packing functors alter the underlying abstractions, making problems that were previously intractable, tractable. Additionally, because these are abstract domains, there is no conflation of control flow with data flow and as a result, many of the analysis problems are changed.

Additionally, the use of BDDs is similar to [17], where BDDs are extended to be possibly-cyclic graphs. These are used to represent tree structures.

As a result, we find that for now, abstractions that construct normal forms, such as the linear abstraction and binary decision diagrams, offer the best way of handling sets in static analysis. We have shown that depending on the application, both of these techniques offer sufficient performance and precision, especially when combined with functors for performing packing and managing equalities. The end result is that these abstractions are scalable, precise, and predictable in their behavior.

Acknowledgements. This material is based upon work supported in part by a Chateaubri and Fellowship, by the National Science Foundation under Grant Numbers CCF-1055066 and CCF-1218208, and by the European Research Council under the FP7 grant agreement 278673 (Project MemCAD).

References

1. Blanchet, B., Cousot, P., Cousot, R., Feret, J., Mauborgne, L., Miné, A., Monniaux, D., Rival, X.: A static analyzer for large safety-critical software. In: PLDI (2003)
2. Bouajjani, A., Drăgoi, C., Enea, C., Sighireanu, M.: Abstract domains for automated reasoning about list-manipulating programs with infinite data. In: Kuncak, V., Rybalchenko, A. (eds.) VMCAI 2012. LNCS, vol. 7148, pp. 1–22. Springer, Heidelberg (2012)
3. Bradley, A.R., Manna, Z., Sipma, H.B.: What's decidable about arrays? In: Emerson, E.A., Namjoshi, K.S. (eds.) VMCAI 2006. LNCS, vol. 3855, pp. 427–442. Springer, Heidelberg (2006)
4. Clarke, E.M., Emerson, E.A., Sistla, A.P.: Automatic verification of finite-state concurrent systems using temporal logic specifications. TOPLAS 8(2), 244–263 (1986)
5. Coudert, O., Madre, J.C.: A new method to compute prime and essential prime implicants of boolean functions. In: Advanced research in VLSI and Parallel Systems. MIT (1992)

6. Cousot, P., Cousot, R.: Abstract interpretation: a unified lattice model for static analysis of programs by construction or approximation of fixpoints. In: POPL (1977)
7. Cox, A., Chang, B.-Y.E., Rival, X.: Desynchronized multi-state abstractions for open programs in dynamic languages. In: Vitek, J. (ed.) ESOP 2015. LNCS, vol. 9032, pp. 483–509. Springer, Heidelberg (2015)
8. Cox, A., Chang, B.-Y.E., Sankaranarayanan, S.: QUICr: a reusable library for parametric abstraction of sets and numbers. In: Biere, A., Bloem, R. (eds.) CAV 2014. LNCS, vol. 8559, pp. 866–873. Springer, Heidelberg (2014)
9. Cox, A., Chang, B.-Y.E., Rival, X.: Automatic analysis of open objects in dynamic language programs. In: Müller-Olm, M., Seidl, H. (eds.) Static Analysis. LNCS, vol. 8723, pp. 134–150. Springer, Heidelberg (2014)
10. Cox, A., Chang, B.-Y.E., Sankaranarayanan, S.: QUIC graphs: relational invariant generation for containers. In: Castagna, G. (ed.) ECOOP 2013. LNCS, vol. 7920, pp. 401–425. Springer, Heidelberg (2013)
11. de Moura, L., Bjørner, N.S.: Z3: an efficient SMT solver. In: Ramakrishnan, C.R., Rehof, J. (eds.) TACAS 2008. LNCS, vol. 4963, pp. 337–340. Springer, Heidelberg (2008)
12. Dillig, I., Dillig, T., Aiken, A.: Precise reasoning for programs using containers. In: POPL (2011)
13. Kuncak, V.: Modular Data Structure Verification. Ph.D. thesis, EECS Department, Massachusetts Institute of Technology (2007)
14. Kuncak, V., Nguyen, H.H., Rinard, M.C.: Deciding boolean algebra with presburger arithmetic. J. Autom. Reason. 36(3), 213–239 (2006)
15. Lahiri, S.K., Bryant, R.E., Cook, B.: A symbolic approach to predicate abstraction. In: Hunt, Jr., W.A., Somenzi, F. (eds.) CAV 2003. LNCS, vol. 2725, pp. 141–153. Springer, Heidelberg (2003)
16. Li, H., Rival, X., Chang, B.-Y.E.: Shape analysis for unstructured sharing. In: Blazy, S., Jensen, T. (eds.) SAS 2015. LNCS, vol. 9291, pp. 90–108. Springer, Heidelberg (2015)
17. Mauborgne, L.: Representation of Sets of Trees for Abstract Interpretation. Ph.D. thesis, École Polytechnique (1999)
18. McMillan, K.L.: Interpolation and SAT-based model checking. In: Hunt, Jr., W.A., Somenzi, F. (eds.) CAV 2003. LNCS, vol. 2725, pp. 1–13. Springer, Heidelberg (2003)
19. Pham, T.-H., Trinh, M.-T., Truong, A.-H., Chin, W.-N.: FixBag: a fixpoint calculator for quantified bag constraints. In: Gopalakrishnan, G., Qadeer, S. (eds.) CAV 2011. LNCS, vol. 6806, pp. 656–662. Springer, Heidelberg (2011)
20. Reynolds, J.: Separation logic: a logic for shared mutable data structures. In: LICS. IEEE (2002)
21. Somenzi, F.: Binary decision diagrams. In: Calculational System Design. IOS Press (1999)
22. Somenzi, F.: CUDD: CU decision diagram package, version 2.5.0 (2012). http://vlsi.colorado.edu/~fabio/CUDD/

Sharing HOL4 and HOL Light Proof Knowledge

Thibault Gauthier$^{(\boxtimes)}$ and Cezary Kaliszyk

University of Innsbruck, Innsbruck, Austria
{thibault.gauthier,cezary.kaliszyk}@uibk.ac.at

Abstract. New proof assistant developments often involve concepts similar to already formalized ones. When proving their properties, a human can often take inspiration from the existing formalized proofs available in other provers or libraries. In this paper we propose and evaluate a number of methods, which strengthen proof automation by learning from proof libraries of different provers. Certain conjectures can be proved directly from the dependencies induced by similar proofs in the other library. Even if exact correspondences are not found, learning-reasoning systems can make use of the association between proved theorems and their characteristics to predict the relevant premises. Such external help can be further combined with internal advice. We evaluate the proposed knowledge-sharing methods by reproving the HOL Light and HOL4 standard libraries. The learning-reasoning system HOL(y)Hammer, whose single best strategy could automatically find proofs for 30 % of the HOL Light problems, can prove 40 % with the knowledge from HOL4.

1 Introduction

As *Interactive Theorem Prover* (ITP) libraries were developed for decades, today their size can often be measured in tens of thousands of facts [4,19]. The theorem provers typically differ in their logical foundations, interfaces, functionality, and the available formalized knowledge. Even if the logic and the interface of the chosen prover are convenient for a user's purpose, its library often lacks some formalizations already present in other provers' libraries. Her only option is then to manually repeat the proofs inside her prover. She will then take ideas from the previous proofs and adapt them to the specifics of her prover. This means that in order to formalize the desired theory, the user needs to combine the knowledge already present in the library of her prover, with the knowledge present in the other formalization.

We propose an approach to automate this time-consuming process: It consists of overlaying the two libraries using concept matching and using learning-assisted automated reasoning methods [15], modified to learn from multiple libraries and able to predict advice based on multiple libraries. In this research we will focus on sharing proof knowledge between libraries of proof assistants based on higher-order logic, in particular HOL4 [23] and HOL Light [9]. Extending the approach to learning from developments in provers that do not share the same logic lies beyond the scope of this paper.

© Springer-Verlag Berlin Heidelberg 2015
M. Davis et al. (Eds.): LPAR-20 2015, LNCS 9450, pp. 372–386, 2015.
DOI: 10.1007/978-3-662-48899-7_26

Once a sufficient number of matching concepts is discovered, theorems and proofs about these concepts can be found in both libraries, and we can start to implement methods for using the combined knowledge in future proofs. To this end, we will use the AI-ATP system HOL(y)Hammer [15]. We will propose various scenarios augmenting the learning and prediction phases of HOL(y)Hammer to make use of the combined proof library. In order to evaluate the approach, we will simulate incrementally reproving a prover's library given the knowledge of the library of the other prover. The use of the combined knowledge significantly improves the proof advice quality provided by HOL(y)Hammer. Our description of the approach focuses on HOL Light and HOL4, but the method can be applied to any pair of provers for which a mapping between the logics is known.

1.1 Related Work

As reuse of mathematical knowledge formalizations is an important problem, it has already been tackled in a number of ways. In the context of higher-order logic, OpenTheory [12] provides cross-prover packages, which allow theory sharing and simplify development. These packages provide a high-quality standard library, but need to be developed manually. The *Common HOL Platform* [1] provides a way to re-use the proof infrastructure across HOL provers.

Theory morphisms provide a versatile way to prove properties of objects of the same structure. The idea has been tried across Isabelle formalizations in the AWE framework by Bortin et al. [5]. It also serves as a basis for the MMT (Module system for Mathematical Theories) framework [22].

With our method, this principle was developed in both directions. We first search for similar properties of structures to find possible morphism between different fields. We then use these conjectured morphisms to translate the properties between the two fields. Our main idea is that we don't prove the isomorphism which is often a complex problem but we learn from the knowledge gained from the derived properties. Moreover, even when the two fields are not completely isomorphic, the method often gives good advice. Indeed, suppose the set of reals in one library were incorrectly matched to the set of rationals in the other, we can still rely on properties of rationals that are also true for reals.

A direct approach is to create translations between formal libraries. This can only be applied when the defined concepts have the same or equivalent definitions. The HOL/Import translation from HOL4 and HOL Light to Isabelle/HOL implemented by Obua and Skalberg [20] already mapped a number of concepts. This was further extended by the second author [13] to map 70 concepts, including differently defined real numbers. HOL Light has also been translated into Coq by Keller and Werner [18]. It is the first translation between systems based on significantly different logics. In each of these imports, the mapping of the concepts has been done manually.

Compared with manually defined translations, our approach can find the mappings and the knowledge that is shared automatically. It can also be used to prove statements that are slightly different and in some cases even more general. Additionally, the proof can use preexisting theorems in the target library. On the other hand, when a correct translation is found by hand, it is guaranteed to succeed, while our approach relies on AI-ATP methods which fail for some goals. The possibility of combining the two approaches is left open.

Overview. The rest of this paper is organized as follows. In Sect. 2, we introduce the AI-ATP system HOL(y)Hammer and describe automatic recognition of similar concepts in different formal proof developments. In Sect. 3, we propose a number of scenarios for combining the knowledge of multiple provers. In Sect. 4, we evaluate the ability to reprove the HOL4 and HOL Light libraries using the combined knowledge. In Sect. 5 we conclude and present an outlook on the future work.

2   Preliminaries

2.1   HOL(y)Hammer

HOL(y)Hammer [16] is an AI-ATP proof advice system for HOL Light and HOL4. Given a user conjecture, it uses machine learning to select a subset of the accessible facts in the library, that are likely to prove the conjecture. It then translates the conjecture together with the selected facts to the input language of one of the available ATP systems to find the exact dependencies necessary to prove the theorem in higher-order logic. This method is also followed by the system Sledgehammer [21].

In this section we shortly describe how HOL(y)Hammer processes conjectures, as we will augment some of these steps in Sect. 3. First, we describe how libraries are exported. Then, we explain how the exported objects and dependencies are processed to find suitable lemmas. Finally, we briefly show how the conjecture can be proven from these lemmas. More detailed descriptions of these steps are presented in [7,15].

Export. We will associate each ITP library with the set of constants and theorems that it contains. In particular, the type constructors will also be regarded as constants in this paper. As a first step, we define a format for representing formulas in type theory, as we aim to support formulas from various provers. A subset of this format is chosen to represent the higher-order logic statements in HOL Light and HOL4. Each object is exported in this format with additional information about the theory where it was created. The theory information will let us export incompatible developments (i.e. ones that can not be loaded into the same ITP session or even originate from different ITPs) into HOL(y)Hammer [14]. Additionally, we can fully preserve the names of the original constants in the export. Finally, the dependencies of each theorem (i.e. the set of theorems which were directly used to proved it) are extracted. This last step is achieved by patching the kernels of HOL4 and HOL Light.

Premise Selection. The premise selection algorithm takes as input an (often large) set of accessible theorems, a conjecture, and the information about previous successful proofs. It returns a subset of the theorems that is likely to prove the conjecture. It involves three phases: feature extraction, learning, and prediction.

The features of a formula are a set of characteristics of the theorem, which we represent by strings. Depending on the choice of characterization, it can simply be the list of the constants and types present in the formula, or the string representation of the normalized sub-terms of the formula, or even features based on formula semantics [17]. The *feature extraction* algorithm takes a formula as input and computes this set.

A relation between the features of conjectures and their dependencies is inferred from the features of all proved theorems and their dependencies by the *learning* algorithm. This step effectively finds a function that given conjecture characteristics finds the premises that are likely to be useful to prove this conjecture. *Prediction* refers to the evaluation of this function on a given conjecture.

These phases will be influenced by the concept matching (see Sect. 2.2) and differentiated in each of the scenarios (see Sect. 3).

Translation and Reconstruction. A fixed number of most relevant predicted lemmas (all the experiments in this paper fix this number to 128, as it has given best results for HOL in combination with E-prover [7]) are translated together with the conjecture to an ATP problem. If an ATP prover is able to find a proof, various reconstruction methods are attempted. The most basic reconstruction method is to inspect the ATP proof for the premises that were necessary to prove the conjecture. This set is usually sufficiently small, so that certified ITP proof methods (such as MESON [8] or Metis [11]) can prove the higher-order counterpart of the statement and obtain an ITP theorem.

2.2 Concept Matching

Concept matching [6] allows the automatic discovery of concepts from one proof library or proof assistant in another. An AI-ATP method can benefit from the library combination only when some of the concepts in the two libraries are related: Without such mappings the sets of features of the theorems in each library are disjoint and premise selection can only return lemmas from the library the conjecture was stated in. As more similar concepts are matched (for example we conjecture that the type of integers in HOL4 h4/int and the type of integers in HOL Light hl/int describe the same type), the feature extraction mechanism will characterize theorems talking about the matched concepts by the same features. As a consequence, we will also get predicted lemmas from the other library. We will discuss how such theorems from a different library can be used without sacrificing soundness in Sect. 3.

For a step by step of the concept matching algorithm, we will refer to our previous work [6] and only present here a short summary and the changes that improve the matching for the scenarios proposed in this paper. Our algorithm is implemented for HOL4 and HOL Light, but we believe the procedure can work for any pair of provers based on similar logics such as Coq [10] and Matita [2].

Summary. Our matching algorithm is based on the properties (such as associativity, commutativity, nilpotence, ...) of the objects of our logic (constants and types). If two objects from two libraries share a large enough number of relevant properties, they will eventually be matched, even though they may have been defined or represented differently. In the description of the procedure, we will consider every type as a constant. Initially, the set of matched constants contains only logical constants. First, we give a highest weight for rare properties with a lot of already matched constants. Second, we look at all possible pairs of constants and find their shared properties. The final score for a pair of constant is the sum of their weights amortised by the total number of properties of each constant. The two constants with the highest similarity score are matched. The previous two steps are repeated until there are no more shared properties between unmatched constants.

Improvements and Limitations. The similarity scoring heuristic can be evaluated more efficiently than the ones presented in [6] and is able to map more constants correctly: Thanks to a better representation of the data the time taken to run our implementation of the matching algorithm on the standard library of HOL Light (including complex and multivariate) and the standard library of HOL4 was decreased from 1 h to 5 min. By computing only the initial property frequencies and using them together with the proportion of matched constants to influence the weight of each property in the iterative part the time can be further decreased to 2 min. The algorithm now returns 220 correct matches instead of the 178 previously obtained and 15 false positives (pairs that are matched but do not represent the same concept) instead of 32. The better results are a consequence of the inclusion of types in the properties and the updated scoring function.

The proposed approach can only match objects that have the same structure. In the case of the two proof assistants we focus on, it can successfully match the types of natural numbers, integers or real number, however it is not able to match the dedicated HOL Light type `hl/complex` to the complex numbers of HOL4 represented by pairs of real numbers `h4/pair(h4/real,h4/real)`. This issue could be partially solved by the introduction of a matching between subterms combined with a directed matching. The type `hl/complex` could then be considered as pair of reals in HOL4. For the reverse direction, we would need to know if the pair of reals was intended to represent a pair of reals or a complex. One idea to solve this problem could be to create a matching substitution that also depends on the theorems. These general ideas could form a basis for a future extension of the matching algorithm.

3   Scenarios

In this section we propose four ways an AI-ATP system can benefit from the knowledge contained in a library of a different prover. We will call these methods "scenarios" and we will call the library of a different prover "external". All four scenarios require the base libraries to already be matched. This means, that we have already computed a matching substitution from the theorems of both libraries and in all the already available facts in the libraries, the matched constants are replaced by their common representatives.

Throughout our scenarios, we will rely on the notion of equivalent theorems to map lemmas from one library to the other. This notion is defined below, as well as some useful notations.

Definition 1 (Equivalent Theorems). *Two theorems are considered equivalent if their conjunctive normal forms are equal modulo the order of conjuncts, disjuncts, and symmetry of equality. Given a theorem t, the set of the theorems equivalent to it in the library lib will be noted $E(lib, t)$.*

Remark 1. This definition only makes sense if the two libraries can be represented in the same logic. This is straightforward if the two share the same logic.

Definition 2 (Notations).
Given a library, we define the following notations:

- *$Dep(t)$ stands for the set of lemmas from which a theorem t was proved. We call them the dependencies of t. This definition is not recursive, i.e. the set does not include theorems used to prove these lemmas.*
- *The function $Learn()$ infers a relation between conjectures and sets of relevant lemmas from the relation between theorems and their dependencies.*
- *$Pred(c, L)$ is the set of lemmas related to a conjecture c predicted by the relation L.*

In each scenario, each library plays an asymmetric role. In the following, the library where we want to prove the conjecture, is called the internal or the initial library. In contrast, the library from which we get extra advice from, is called the external library. In this context, using HOL(y)Hammer alone without any knowledge sharing is our default scenario, naturally named "internal predictions". We illustrate each selection method by giving an example of a theorem that could only be reproved by its strategy. These examples are extracted from our experiments described in Sect. 4.

Scenario 1: External Dependencies. The first scenario assumes that the proof libraries are almost identical. We compute the set of theorems equivalent to the conjecture in the external library. For all of their dependencies, we return the lemmas in the library equivalent to these dependencies. The scenario is presented in Fig. 1. This scenario would work very well, if the corresponding theorem is present in the external library and a sufficient corresponding subset of its dependencies is already present in the initial library. As this is often not the case (see Sect. 4), we will use an AI-ATP method next.

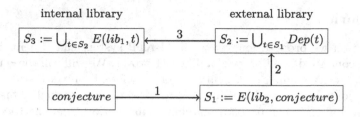

Fig. 1. Finding lemmas from dependencies in the external library.

Example 1. The theorem REAL_SUP_UBOUND in HOL4 asserts that each element of a bounded subset of reals is less than its supremum. The equivalent theorem in HOL Light has 3 dependencies: the relation between $<$ and $\leq$ REAL_NOT_LT, the antisymmetry of $<$ REAL_LT_REFL and the definition of supremum REAL_SUP. Each of them have one equivalent in HOL4. The resulting problem was translated and solved by an ATP and the 3 lemmas appeared in the proof.

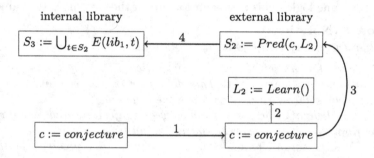

Fig. 2. Learning and predicting lemmas in the external library

Scenario 2: External Predictions. The next scenario is depicted in Fig. 2. The steps are as follows: We translate the conjecture to the external library (step 1). We predict the relevant lemmas in the external library (steps 2 and 3). We map the predicted lemmas back to the initial library using their equivalents (step 4). To sum up, this scenario proposes an automatic way of proving a conjecture providing that the external library contains relevant lemmas that have equivalents in the internal library. One advantage of this scenario over the standard "internal predictions" is that the relation between features and dependencies is fully developed in the external library, yielding better predictions.

In our experiments, the translation step is not needed because the matching is already applied and the logic of our provers are the same.

Example 2. The theorem LENGTH_FRONT from the HOL4 theory rich_list states that the length of a non-empty list without its last element is equal to its length

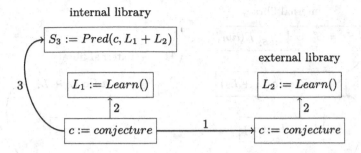

Fig. 3. Learning in both libraries and predicting lemmas in the internal library.

minus one. The subset of predicted lemmas used by the ATP were 6 theorems about natural numbers and 6 theorems about list. These theorems are HOL4 equivalents of selected HOL Light lemmas.

Scenario 3: Combined Learning. In this and the next scenario we will combine the knowledge from the external library with the information already present in the internal library. The scenario is presented in Fig. 3. First, the conjecture is translated to the external prover. Second, the features suitable for proving the conjecture are learned from the dependencies between the theorems in both systems. Third, lemmas from the original library containing these features are predicted. In a nutshell, this scenario defines an automatic method, that enhances the standard "internal predictions" by including advice from the external library about the relevance of each feature.

Example 3. This example and the next one are using advice from HOL4 in HOL Light which means that the roles of the two provers are reversed compared to the first two examples. The HOL Light theorem SQRT_DIV asserts that the square root of the quotient of two non-negative reals is equal to the quotient of their square roots. In this scenario no external theorems are translated but learning form the HOL4 proofs still improved the predictions directly made in HOL Light. The proof found for this theorem is based on the dual theorems for multiplication SQRT_MUL and inversion SQRT_INV and basic properties of division real_div, multiplication REAL_MUL_SYM, inversion REAL_LE_INV_EQ and absolute value REAL_ABS_REFL.

Scenario 4: Combined Predictions. The last and most developed scenario, shown in Fig. 4, associate the strategies from the two preceding scenarios, effectively learning and predicting lemmas from both libraries. The first and second steps are the same as in "combined learning". The third step predicts lemmas in both libraries from the whole learned data. Finally, we map back the external predictions and return them together with the internal predictions.

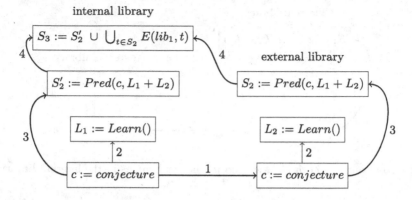

Fig. 4. Learning and predicting lemmas from both libraries.

Example 4. Let n, m, p be natural numbers.
The HOL Light theorem HAS_SIZE_DIFF declares that if a set A has n elements and B is a subset of A that has m elements then the difference $B \setminus A$ has $n - m$ elements. The first two lemmas necessary for the proof were directly found in HOL Light. One is the definition of the constant HAS_SIZE which asserts that a set has size p if and only if it is finite and has cardinality p. The other CARD_DIFF is almost the same as the theorem to be proved but stated for the cardinality of finite sets. The missing piece FINITE_DIFF is predicted inside the HOL4 library. Its equivalent in HOL Light declares that the difference of two finite sets is a finite set, which allows the ATP to conclude.

3.1   Unchecked Scenarios

In each of the previous scenarios, the final predicted lemmas come from the initial library. This means that our approach is sound with respect to the internal prover. The application of the matching substitution on one library renames the constants in all theorems injectively because no non-trivial matching is performed between two constants of the same library.

We will now consider the possibility of returning matched lemmas from the external library even if they do not have an equivalent in the internal one. This means giving advice to the user in the form: "your conjecture can be proved using the theorems th_1 and th_2 that you already have and an additional hypothesis with the given statement which you should be able to prove." To verify that these scenarios are well-founded, a user would need to prove the proposed hypotheses. That could be achieved by either importing the theorems or applying the approach recursively. If a constant contained in these lemmas is matched inconsistently then each method would fail to reprove the lemmas, preserving the coherence of the internal library. We do not yet have an import mechanism from HOL4 to HOL Light (and conversely) or a recursive mechanism for our scenarios. In this recursive approaches, the predicted facts in the external library should be restricted to those proved before the conjecture when it has an equivalent in the external library. Otherwise, a loop in the recursive algorithm may be created.

We will still evaluate the "unchecked" scenarios to see what is the maximum added value such mechanisms could generate.

4   Evaluation

We perform all the experiments on a subset of the standard libraries of HOL Light and HOL4. The HOL4 dataset includes 15 type constructors, 509 constants, and 3935 theorems. The HOL Light dataset contains 21 type constructors, 359 constants and 4213 theorems. The subsets were chosen to include a variety of fields ranging from list to real analysis. The most similar pairs of theories are listed by their number of common equivalent classes of theorems in Table 1. The number of theorems in each theory is indicated in parenthesis.

Table 1. The seven most similar pairs of theories by their number of common equivalent classes of theorems according to our matching

HOL4 theory	HOL Light theory	Common theorems
pred_set(434)	sets(490)	128
real(469)	real(291)	81
poly(87)	poly(142)	72
bool(177)	theorems(90)	61
transc(229)	transc(355)	58
arithmetic(385)	arith(245)	57
integral(83)	transc(355)	48

The matching, predictions, and the preparation of the ATP problems have been done on a laptop with 4 Intel Core i5-3230M 2.60 GHz processors and 3.6 GB RAM. All ATP problems are evaluated on a server with 48 AMD Opteron 6174 2.2 GHz CPUs, 320 GB RAM and 0.5 MB L2 cache per CPU. A single core is assigned to each ATP problem. The ATP used is E-prover version 1.8 running in the automatic mode with a time limit of 30 s.

Simulation. We will try to prove each theorem in an environment, where information is restricted to the one that was available when this theorem was proved. This amounts to:

- forgetting that it is a theorem and the knowledge of its dependencies,
- finding the subset of facts in the library that are accessible from this theorem,
- computing the matching with the other library based on this subset only,
- predicting lemmas from this subset (plus the other library in the "unchecked" scenarios).

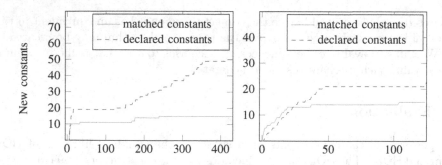

Fig. 5. Evolution of the number of matched constants in the HOL4 theory list and in the HOL Light theory lists

For the purpose of our simulation, the external library is always completely known, as we suppose that it was created previously. In reality, the two libraries were developed in parallel, with many HOL4 theories available before similar formalizations in HOL Light have been performed.

In Fig. 5, we show the evolution of the number of matched constants and compare it to the number of declared constants in the theory during the incremental reproving of two theories. The first graph shows that the number of matched constants stagnate whereas the declared constants continue to increase in the second half of the theory. This suggests that theories formalizing the same concepts may be developed in different directions for each prover. The second graph indicates a better coverage of the HOL Light theory lists. In the beginning, the number of matched constants grows even more rapidly than the number of declared constants because new matches are found for constants defined in previous theories.

Table 2. Percentage of reproved theorems in the HOL4 library (internal) with the knowledge from the HOL Light library (external).

Scenario	checked(%)	unchecked(%)
empty	4.19	
external dependencies	5.06 (23.50)	10.75 (49.94)
external predictions	17.49	34.42
external any	18.07	34.74
internal predictions	**43.57**	
combined learning	44.03	
combined predictions	44.59	53.46
any	**50.06**	55.73
any checked or unchecked	62.80	

Table 3. Percentage of reproved theorems in the HOL Light library (internal) with the knowledge from the HOL4 library (external).

Scenario	checked(%)	unchecked(%)
empty	3.14	
external dependencies	6.08 (29.22)	10.11 (48.63)
external predictions	12.74	33.94
external any	13.55	34.32
internal predictions	**30.92**	
combined learning	35.13	
combined predictions	35.56	44.06
any	**40.19**	47.07
any checked or unchecked	54.71	

In the first column, scenarios are listed based on their predicted lemmas.
empty: no lemmas.
external dependencies: dependencies of equivalent external theorems.
external predictions: external lemmas from external advice.
external any: problems solved by any of the two previous scenarios.
internal predictions: internal lemmas from internal advice.
combined learning: internal lemmas from external and internal advice.
combined predictions: external and internal lemmas from external and internal advice.
any: problems solved by at least one scenario of the same column.
In the second column, we restrict ourself from using external theorems that do not have an internal equivalent, where as we allow it in the third column. The last line combines all the problems solved by at least one checked or unchecked scenario.

Results. The success rates for each scenario and each proof assistant are compiled in Tables 2 and 3. The scenario "empty" gives the number of facts provable without lemmas and is fully subsumed by the other methods.

The external dependencies scenario is the only one that is not directly comparable to the others, as it was performed only on the theorems that have an equivalent in the other library (876 in HOL Light and 847 in HOL4). The percentage of theorems proved by this strategy relative to its experimental subset is shown in parentheses. This strategy is quite efficient on its subset but contributes weakly to the overall improvement. These results are combined with the "external predictions" scenario to evaluate what can be reproved with external help only. In HOL4, the combined learning and predictions increases the number of problems solved over the initial "internal predictions" approach only by one percent. The improvement is sharper in HOL Light. It suggests that HOL4 provides a better set for the learning algorithm. The improvement provided by all scenarios can be combined to yield a significant gain compared to the performance of HOL(y)Hammer alone, namely additional 6.5 % of all HOL4 and 9.3 % of all HOL Light theorems. Another 10–15 % could be added by the "unchecked" scenarios.

Results by Theory. In Table 4, we investigate the performance of the "external dependencies" scenario on the largest theories in our dataset. Some theories only minimally benefit from the external help. This is the case for rich_list and iterate, where only few correct mappings could be found. We can see asymmetric results in pairs of similar theories. For example, the real theory in HOL Light can be 72.16 % reproved from HOL4 theories whereas the similar theory in HOL4 does not benefit as much. This suggest that the real theory HOL4 is more dense than its counterpart. A similar effect is observed for the transc formalization. The theories pred_set and sets seem to be comparably dense.

Table 4. Reproving success rate in the six largest theories in HOL4 using HOL Light and the "checked external dependencies" scenario, as well as in the six largest HOL Light theories using HOL4.

Scenario	real	pred_set	list	arithmetic	rich_list	transc
external dependencies	30.91	24.65	10.23	18.18	1.52	5.24

Scenario	sets	analysis	transc	int	iterate	real
external dependencies	25.51	27.1	25.91	52.61	5.47	72.16

5   Conclusion

We proposed several methods for combining the knowledge of two ITP systems in order to prove more theorems automatically. The methods adapt the premise selection and proof advice components of the HOL(y)Hammer system to include the knowledge of an external prover. In order to do it, the concepts defined in both libraries are related through an improved matching algorithm. As the constants in two libraries become related, so are the statements of the theorems. Machine learning algorithms can combine the information about the dependencies in each library to predict useful dependencies more accurately.

We evaluated the influence of an external library on the quality of advice, by reproving all the theorems in a large subset of the HOL4 and HOL Light standard libraries. External knowledge can improve the success from 43 % to 50 % in HOL4 and from 30 % to 40 % in the number of HOL Light solved goals. This number could reach 54 % for HOL4 and 62 % for HOL Light if we include the "unchecked" scenarios, where the user is not only suggested known theorems, but also hypotheses left to prove. Proving such proposed lemmas, either with the help of a translation or by calling an AI-ATP method with shared knowledge is left as future work.

The proposed approach evaluated the influence of an external proof assistant library for the quality of learning and prediction. An extension of the approach could be used inside a single library: mappings of concepts inside a single library, such as those the work of Autexier and Hutter [3], could provide additional knowledge for a learning-reasoning system.

Acknowledgments. This work has been supported by the Austrian Science Fund (FWF): P26201.

References

1. Adams, M.: The common HOL platform. In: Kaliszyk, C., Paskevich, A., (eds.) Fourth International Workshop on Proof Exchange for Theorem Proving, PxTP 2015, Berlin, Germany, 2–3 August 2015. to appear in EPTCS (2015)
2. Asperti, A., Ricciotti, W., Coen, C.S.: Matita tutorial. J. Formaliz. Reason. **7**(2), 91–199 (2014)
3. Autexier, S., Hutter, D.: Structure formation in large theories. In: Kerber, M., Carette, J., Kaliszyk, C., Rabe, F., Sorge, V. (eds.) CICM 2015. LNCS, vol. 9150, pp. 155–170. Springer, Heidelberg (2015)
4. Blanchette, J.C., Haslbeck, M., Matichuk, D., Nipkow, T.: Mining the archive of formal proofs. In: Kerber, M., Carette, J., Kaliszyk, C., Rabe, F., Sorge, V. (eds.) CICM 2015. LNCS, vol. 9150, pp. 3–17. Springer, Heidelberg (2015)
5. Bortin, M., Johnsen, E.B., Lüth, C.: Structured formal development in Isabelle. Nordic J. Comput. **13**, 1–20 (2006)
6. Gauthier, T., Kaliszyk, C.: Matching concepts across HOL libraries. In: Watt, S.M., Davenport, J.H., Sexton, A.P., Sojka, P., Urban, J. (eds.) CICM 2014. LNCS, vol. 8543, pp. 267–281. Springer, Heidelberg (2014)
7. Gauthier, T., Kaliszyk, C.: Premise selection and external provers for HOL4. In: Leroy, X., Tiu, A., (eds.) Proceedings of the 4th ACM-SIGPLAN Conference on Certified Programs and Proofs, pp. 49–57 (2015)
8. Harrison, J.: Optimizing proof search in model elimination. In: McRobbie, M.A., Slaney, J.K. (eds.) CADE 1996. LNCS, vol. 1104. Springer, Heidelberg (1996)
9. Harrison, J.: HOL Light: an overview. In: Berghofer, S., Nipkow, T., Urban, C., Wenzel, M. (eds.) TPHOLs 2009. LNCS, vol. 5674, pp. 60–66. Springer, Heidelberg (2009)
10. Huet, G., Herbelin, H.: 30 years of research and development around Coq. In: Jagannathan, S., Sewell, P., (eds.) The 41st Annual ACM SIGPLAN-SIGACT Symposium on Principles of Programming Languages, POPL 2014, San Diego, CA, USA, 20–21 January 2014, pp. 249–250. ACM (2014)
11. Hurd, J.: First-order proof tactics in higher-order logic theorem provers. In: Archer, M., Di Vito, B., Muñoz, C., (eds.) Design and Application of Strategies/Tactics in Higher Order Logics (STRATA 2003), number NASA/CP-2003-212448 in NASA Technical reports, pp. 56–68, September 2003

12. Hurd, J.: The OpenTheory standard theory library. In: Bobaru, M., Havelund, K., Holzmann, G.J., Joshi, R. (eds.) NFM 2011. LNCS, vol. 6617, pp. 177–191. Springer, Heidelberg (2011)

13. Kaliszyk, C., Krauss, A.: Scalable LCF-Style proof translation. In: Blazy, S., Paulin-Mohring, C., Pichardie, D. (eds.) ITP 2013. LNCS, vol. 7998, pp. 51–66. Springer, Heidelberg (2013)

14. Kaliszyk, C., Rabe, F.: Towards knowledge management for HOL Light. In: Watt, S.M., Davenport, J.H., Sexton, A.P., Sojka, P., Urban, J. (eds.) CICM 2014. LNCS, vol. 8543, pp. 357–372. Springer, Heidelberg (2014)

15. Kaliszyk, C., Urban, J.: Learning-assisted automated reasoning with Flyspeck. J. Autom. Reason. **53**(2), 173–213 (2014)

16. Kaliszyk, C., Urban, J.: HOL(y)Hammer: online ATP service for HOL Light. Math. Comput. Sci. **9**(1), 5–22 (2015)

17. Kaliszyk, C., Urban, J., Vyskočil, J.: Efficient semantic features for automated reasoning over large theories. In: Proceedings of the 24th International Joint Conference on Artificial Intelligence, IJCAI 2015 (2015). (to appear)

18. Keller, C., Werner, B.: Importing HOL Light into Coq. In: Kaufmann, M., Paulson, L.C. (eds.) ITP 2010. LNCS, vol. 6172, pp. 307–322. Springer, Heidelberg (2010)

19. The Mizar Mathematical Library. http://mizar.org/

20. Obua, S., Skalberg, S.: Importing HOL into Isabelle/HOL. In: Furbach, U., Shankar, N. (eds.) IJCAR 2006. LNCS (LNAI), vol. 4130, pp. 298–302. Springer, Heidelberg (2006)

21. Paulson, L.C., Blanchette, J.C.: Three years of experience with Sledgehammer, a practical link between automated and interactive theorem provers. In: 8th IWIL (2010). Invited talk

22. Rabe, F.: The MMT API: a generic MKM system. In: Carette, J., Aspinall, D., Lange, C., Sojka, P., Windsteiger, W. (eds.) CICM 2013. LNCS, vol. 7961, pp. 339–343. Springer, Heidelberg (2013)

23. Slind, K., Norrish, M.: A brief overview of HOL4. In: Mohamed, O.A., Muñoz, C., Tahar, S. (eds.) TPHOLs 2008. LNCS, vol. 5170, pp. 28–32. Springer, Heidelberg (2008)

Relational Reasoning via Probabilistic Coupling

Gilles Barthe[1], Thomas Espitau[1,2], Benjamin Grégoire[3], Justin Hsu[4(✉)],
Léo Stefanesco[1,5], and Pierre-Yves Strub[1]

[1] IMDEA Software, Madrid, Spain
[2] ENS Cachan, Cachan, France
[3] Inria, Sophia Antipolis, France
[4] University of Pennsylvania, Philadelphia, USA
email@justinh.su
[5] ENS Lyon, Lyon, France

Abstract. Probabilistic coupling is a powerful tool for analyzing pairs of probabilistic processes. Roughly, coupling two processes requires finding an appropriate witness process that models both processes in the same probability space. Couplings are powerful tools proving properties about the relation between two processes, include reasoning about convergence of distributions and *stochastic dominance*—a probabilistic version of a monotonicity property.

While the mathematical definition of coupling looks rather complex and cumbersome to manipulate, we show that the relational program logic pRHL—the logic underlying the EasyCrypt cryptographic proof assistant—already internalizes a generalization of probabilistic coupling. With this insight, constructing couplings is no harder than constructing logical proofs. We demonstrate how to express and verify classic examples of couplings in pRHL, and we mechanically verify several couplings in EasyCrypt.

1 Introduction

Probabilistic couplings [7,9,10] are a powerful mathematical tool for reasoning about pairs of *probabilistic processes*: streams of values that evolve randomly according to some rule. While the two processes may be difficult to analyze independently, a probabilistic coupling arranges processes $\{u_i\}$, $\{v_i\}$ in the same space—typically, by viewing the pair of processes as randomly evolving *pairs* of values $\{(u_i, v_i)\}$, coordinating the samples so that each pair of values are related. In this way, couplings can reason about the relation between the two processes.

From the point of view of program verification, a coupling is a *relational* program property, since it describes the relation between two programs (perhaps one program run on two different inputs, or two completely different programs). However, couplings are particularly interesting for several reasons.

Useful Consequences. Couplings imply many other relational properties, and are a powerful tool in mathematical proofs.

© Springer-Verlag Berlin Heidelberg 2015
M. Davis et al. (Eds.): LPAR-20 2015, LNCS 9450, pp. 387–401, 2015.
DOI: 10.1007/978-3-662-48899-7_27

A classic use of coupling is showing that the distribution of the value of two random processes started in different locations eventually converges to the same distribution if we run the processes long enough. This property is a kind of *memorylessness*—or *Markovian*—property: The long-term behavior of the process is independent of its starting point. To prove memorylessness, the typical strategy is to couple the two processes so that their values move closer together; once the values meet, the two processes move together, yielding the same distribution.

A different use of couplings is showing that one (numeric-valued) process is, in some sense, bigger than the other. This statement has to be interpreted carefully—since both processes evolve independently, we can't guarantee that one process is always larger than the other on all traces. *Stochastic domination* turns out to be the right definition: for any k, we require $\Pr[u \geq k] > \Pr[v \geq k]$. This property follows if we can demonstrate a coupling of a particular form.

Relational from Non-relational. Often, the behavior of the second coupled process is completely specified by the behavior of the first; for instance, the second process may mirror the first process. In such cases, the coupling allows us to reason just about the first process. In other words, a coupling allows us to prove certain relational properties by proving properties of a single program.

Compositional Proofs. Typically, couplings are proved by coordinating corresponding samples of the two processes, step by step; paper proofs call this process "building a coupling", reflecting the piecewise construction of the coupled distribution. As a result, couplings can be proved locally by considering small pieces of the programs in isolation, enabling convenient mechanical verification of couplings.

Contributions

In this paper, we apply relational program verification to probabilistic couplings. While the mathematical definition of coupling is seemingly far from program verification technology, our primary insight is that the logic pRHL from Barthe, Grégoire, and Zanella-Béguelin [1] already internalizes coupling in disguise. More precisely, pRHL is built around a *lifting* construction, which turns a relation R on two sets A and B into a relation $R^\dagger$ over the set of sub-distributions over A and the set of sub-distributions over B. Two programs are related by $R^\dagger$ precisely when there exists a coupling of their output sub-distributions whose support only contains pairs of values (u, v) which satisfy R.

This observation has three immediate consequences. First, by selecting the relation R appropriately, we can express a wide variety of coupling properties, like distribution equivalence and stochastic domination. Second, by utilizing the proof system of pRHL, we can constructing and manipulate couplings while abstracting away the mathematical details. Finally, we can leverage EasyCrypt, a proof assistant implementing pRHL, to mechanically verify couplings.

2 Preliminaries

Probabilistic Coupling. We begin by giving an overview of probabilistic coupling. As we described before, a coupling places two probabilistic processes (viewed as probability distributions) in the same probabilistic space.

We will work with sub-distributions over discrete (finite or countable) sets. A sub-distribution μ over a discrete set A is a function $A \to [0,1]$ such that $\sum_{a \in A} \mu(a) \leq 1$, and its support $\mathsf{supp}(\mu)$ is the pre-image of $(0,1]$. We let $\mathbf{Distr}(A)$ denote the set of sub-distributions over A. Every sub-distribution can be given a monadic structure; the unit operator maps every element a in the underlying set to its Dirac distribution δ_a and the monadic composition $\mathsf{Mlet}(\mu, F) \in \mathbf{Distr}(B)$ of $\mu \in \mathbf{Distr}(A)$ and $F : A \to \mathbf{Distr}(B)$ is $\mathsf{Mlet}(\mu, F)(b) = \sum_{a \in A} \mu(a) \times F(a)(b)$.

When working with sub-distributions over tuples, the probabilistic versions of the usual projections on tuples are called *marginals*. The first and second marginals $\pi_1(\mu)$ and $\pi_2(\mu)$ of a distribution μ over $A \times B$ are defined by $\pi_1(\mu)(a) = \sum_{b \in B} \mu(a, b)$ and $\pi_2(\mu)(b) = \sum_{a \in A} \mu(a, b)$. We can now formally define coupling.

Definition 1. *The* Frechet class $\mathfrak{F}(\mu_1, \mu_2)$ *of two sub-distributions μ_1 and μ_2 over A and B respectively is the set of sub-distributions μ over $A \times B$ such that $\pi_1(\mu) = \mu_1$ and $\pi_2(\mu) = \mu_2$. Two sub-distributions μ_1, μ_2 are said to be* coupled *with witness μ if $\mu \in \mathfrak{F}(\mu_1, \mu_2)$, i.e. μ is in the Frechet class of μ_1, μ_2.*

Lifting Relations. Before introducing pRHL, we describe the *lifting* construction. This operation allows pRHL to make statements about pairs of (sub-) distributions, and is a generalized form of probabilistic coupling.

The idea is to define a family of couplings based on the support of the witness distribution. Given a relation $R \subseteq A \times B$ and two distributions μ_1 and μ_2 over A and B respectively, we let $\mathfrak{L}_R(\mu_1, \mu_2)$ denote the subset of sub-distributions $\mu \in \mathfrak{F}(\mu_1, \mu_2)$ such that $\mathsf{supp}(\mu) \subseteq R$. Given a ground relation R, we view distributions in $\mathfrak{L}_R$ as witnesses for a *lifted* relation on distributions.

Definition 2. *The* lifting *of a relation $R \subseteq A \times B$ is the relation $R^\dagger \subseteq \mathbf{Distr}(A) \times \mathbf{Distr}(B)$ with $\mu_1 \, R^\dagger \, \mu_2$ iff $\mathfrak{L}_R(\mu_1, \mu_2) \neq \emptyset$.*

Before turning to the definition of pRHL, we give some intuition for why lifting is useful. Roughly, if we know two distributions are related by a lifted relation $R^\dagger$, we can treat two samples from the distribution as if they were related by R. In other words, the lifting machinery gives a powerful way to translate between information about distributions and information about samples. Deng and Du [6] provide an excellent introductory exposition to lifting, and give several equivalent characterizations of lifting.

2.1 A pRHL Primer

We are now ready to present pRHL, a relational program logic for probabilistic computations. In its original form [1], implemented in the EasyCrypt proof assistant [4], pRHL reasons about programs written in an imperative language extended with random assignments with the following syntax of commands:

$$c ::= x \leftarrow e \mid x \xleftarrow{\$} d \mid \text{if } e \text{ then } c \text{ else } c \mid \text{while } e \text{ do } c \mid \text{skip} \mid c;\ c$$

where e ranges over expressions, d ranges over distribution expressions, and $x \xleftarrow{\$} d$ stores a sample from d into x. Commands are interpreted as functions from memories to distributions over memories; using the fixed point theorem for Banach spaces, one can define for each command c a function $[\![c]\!] : \text{Mem} \rightarrow \textbf{Distr}(\text{Mem})$, where Mem is the set of well-typed maps from program variables to values.

Assertions in the language are first-order formulae over generalized expressions. The latter are built from tagged variables x_1 and x_2, which correspond to the interpretation of the program variable x in the first and second memories. Assertions in pRHL are deterministic and do not refer to probabilities.

Definition 3. *A pRHL judgment is a quadruple of the form* $\vDash c_1 \sim c_2 : \Psi \Rightarrow \Phi$, *where Ψ and Φ are assertions, and c_1 and c_2 are separable statements, i.e. they do not have any variable in common. A judgment is* valid *iff for all memories m_1 and m_2, we have $(m_1, m_2) \vDash \Psi \Rightarrow ([\![c_1]\!](m_1), [\![c_2]\!](m_2)) \vDash \Phi^{\dagger}$* .

Judgments can be proved valid with a variety of rules.

Two-sided and One-sided Rules. The pRHL logic features two-sided rules (Fig. 1) and one-sided rules (Fig. 2). Roughly speaking, two-sided rules relate two commands with the same structure and control flow, while one-sided rules relate two commands with possibly different structure or control flow; the latter rules allow pRHL to express *asynchronous* couplings between programs that may exhibit different control flow.

We point out two rules that will be especially important for our purposes. The rule [SAMPLE] is used for relating two sampling commands. Note that it requires an injective function $f : T_1 \rightarrow T_2$ from the domain of the first sampling command to the domain of the second sampling command. When the two sampling commands have the same domain—as will be the case in our examples—f is simply a bijection on $T = T_1 = T_2$. This bijection gives us the freedom to specify the relation between the two samples when we couple the samples.

The rule [WHILE] is the standard while rule adapted to pRHL. Note that we require the guard of the two commands to be equal—so in particular the two loops must make the same number of iterations—and Φ plays the role of the while loop invariant as usual.

Structural and Program Transformation Rules. pRHL also features structural rules that are very similar to those of Hoare logic, including the rule of consequence and the case rule. In addition, it features a rule for program transformations, based on an equivalence relation $\simeq$ that provides a sound approximation of semantical equivalence. For our examples, it is sufficient that the relation $\simeq$ models loop range splitting and biased coin splitting, as given by the following clauses:

$$\text{SAMPLE} \;\; \frac{f \in T_1 \xrightarrow{1-1} T_2 \qquad \forall v \in T_1.\; d_1(v) = d_2(f\,v)}{\vDash x_1 \xleftarrow{\$} d_1 \sim x_2 \xleftarrow{\$} d_2 : \forall v, \Phi[v/x_1, f(v)/x_2] \Rightarrow \Phi}$$

$$\text{IF} \;\; \frac{\Psi \Rightarrow e_1 = e_2 \qquad \vDash c_1 \sim c_2 : \Psi \wedge e_1 \Rightarrow \Phi \qquad \vDash c_1' \sim c_2' : \Psi \wedge \neg e_1 \Rightarrow \Phi}{\vDash \text{if } e_1 \text{ then } c_1 \text{ else } c_1' \sim \text{if } e_2 \text{ then } c_2 \text{ else } c_2' : \Psi \Rightarrow \Phi}$$

$$\text{WHILE} \;\; \frac{\Phi \Rightarrow e_1 = e_2 \qquad \vDash c_1 \sim c_2 : \Phi \wedge e_1 \Rightarrow \Phi}{\vDash \text{while } e_1 \text{ do } c_1 \sim \text{while } e_2 \text{ do } c_2 : \Phi \Rightarrow \Phi \wedge \neg e_1}$$

Fig. 1. Two-sided proof rules (selection)

$$\text{SAMPLEL} \;\; \frac{\vDash \text{skip} \sim c : \forall v, \Psi[v/x_1] \Rightarrow \Phi}{\vDash x_1 \xleftarrow{\$} d_1 \sim c : \Psi \Rightarrow \Phi}$$

$$\text{IFL} \;\; \frac{\vDash c_1 \sim c : \Psi \wedge e_1 \Rightarrow \Phi \qquad \vDash c_1' \sim c : \Psi \wedge \neg e_1 \Rightarrow \Phi}{\vDash \text{if } e_1 \text{ then } c_1 \text{ else } c_1' \sim c : \Psi \Rightarrow \Phi}$$

$$\text{WHILEL} \;\; \frac{\vDash c_1 \sim \text{skip} : \Phi \wedge e_1 \Rightarrow \Phi \qquad \text{while } e_1 \text{ do } c_1 \text{ lossless}}{\vDash \text{while } e_1 \text{ do } c_1 \sim \text{skip} : \Phi \Rightarrow \Phi}$$

Fig. 2. One-sided proof rules (selection)

$$\text{while } e \text{ do } c \simeq \text{while } e \wedge e' \text{ do } c; \text{while } e \text{ do } c$$
$$x \xleftarrow{\$} \mathbf{Bern}(p_1 \cdot p_2) \simeq x_1 \xleftarrow{\$} \mathbf{Bern}(p_1); x_2 \xleftarrow{\$} \mathbf{Bern}(p_2); x \leftarrow x_1 \wedge x_2$$

Figure 3 provides a selection of structural and program transformation rules.

$$\text{CONSEQ} \;\; \frac{\vDash c_1 \sim c_2 : \Psi' \Rightarrow \Phi' \qquad \Psi \Rightarrow \Psi' \qquad \Phi' \Rightarrow \Phi}{\vDash c_1 \sim c_2 : \Psi \Rightarrow \Phi}$$

$$\text{CASE} \;\; \frac{\vDash c_1 \sim c_2 : \Psi \wedge \Psi' \Rightarrow \Phi \qquad \vDash c_1 \sim c_2 : \Psi \wedge \neg \Psi' \Rightarrow \Phi}{\vDash c_1 \sim c_2 : \Psi \Rightarrow \Phi}$$

$$\text{EQUIV} \;\; \frac{\vDash c_1' \sim c_2' : \Psi \Rightarrow \Phi \qquad c_1 \simeq c_1' \qquad c_2 \simeq c_2'}{\vDash c_1 \sim c_2 : \Psi \Rightarrow \Phi}$$

Fig. 3. Structural and program transformation rules (selection)

2.2 From pRHL Judgments to Probability Judgments

We will derive two kinds of program properties from the existence of an appropriate probabilistic coupling. We will first discuss the mathematical theorems, where the notation is lighter and the core idea more apparent, and then demonstrate how the mathematical version can be expressed in terms of pRHL judgments.

Total Variation and Coupling. The first principle bounds the distance between two distributions in terms of a probabilistic coupling. We first define the total variation distance, also known as statistical distance, on distributions.

Definition 4. *Let X and X' be distributions over a countable set A. The* total variation (TV) distance *between X and X' is defined by*
$$\|X - X'\|_{tv} \triangleq \tfrac{1}{2} \textstyle\sum_{a \in A} |X(a) - X'(a)| \ .$$

To bound the distance between two distributions, it is enough to find a coupling and bound the probability that the two coupled variables differ.

Theorem 1 (Total Variation, See [7]). *Let X and X' be distributions over a countable set. Then for any coupling $Y = (\hat{X}, \hat{X}')$, we have*
$$\|X - X'\|_{tv} \leq \Pr_{(x,x') \sim Y}[x \neq x'].$$

This theorem is useful for reasoning about convergence of distributions.

To describe a pRHL analog of this theorem, we first introduce some useful notation. For all memories m and expressions e, we write $m(e)$ for the interpretation of e in memory m. For all expressions e of type T and distribution μ over memories, let $[\![e]\!]_\mu$ be defined as Mlet $m = \mu$ in unit $m(e)$; note that $[\![e]\!]_\mu$ denotes a *distribution* over T. Similarly, for all events E (modeled as a boolean expression encoding a predicate over memories) and distribution μ over memories, let $[\![E]\!]_\mu$ be defined as Mlet $m = \mu$ in unit $E(m)$. Thus, $[\![E]\!]_\mu$ is the probability of event E holding in the distribution μ. Then, Theorem 1 can be written in terms of pRHL.

Proposition 1. *If $\vDash c_1 \sim c_2 : \Psi \Rightarrow \Phi \Rightarrow v_1 = v_2$, where Φ exclusively refers to variables in c_1, then for all initial memories m_1 and m_2 that satisfy the precondition, the total variation distance between $[\![v_1]\!]_{[\![c]\!](m_1)}$ and $[\![v_2]\!]_{[\![c]\!](m_2)}$ is at most $[\![\neg\Phi]\!]_{[\![c]\!](m_1)}$, i.e. $\|[\![v_1]\!]_{[\![c_1]\!](m_1)} - [\![v_2]\!]_{[\![c_2]\!](m_2)}\|_{tv} \leq [\![\neg\Phi]\!]_{[\![c]\!](m_1)}$.*

This proposition underlies the "up-to-bad" reasoning in EasyCrypt.

Stochastic Domination and Coupling. A second relational property of distributions is *stochastic domination*.

Definition 5. *Let X and X' be distributions over set A with an order relation $\geq$. We say X* stochastically dominates *X', written $X \geq_{sd} X'$, if for all $a \in A$,*
$$\Pr_{x \sim X}[x \geq a] \geq \Pr_{x' \sim X'}[x' \geq a].$$

Intuitively, stochastic domination defines a partial order on distributions over A given an order over A. Strassen's theorem shows that stochastic dominance is intimately related to coupling.

Theorem 2 (Strassen's Theorem, See [7]). *Let X and X' be distributions over a countable ordered set A. Then $X \geq_{sd} X'$ if and only if there is a coupling $Y = (\hat{X}, \hat{X}')$ with $Y \in \mathfrak{L}_\geq(X, X')$.*

The forward direction is usually the more useful direction; we can express it in the following pRHL form.

Proposition 2. *If $\vDash c_1 \sim c_2 : \Psi \Rightarrow v_1 \geq v_2$, then for all initial memories m_1 and m_2 that satisfy the precondition, $[\![v_1]\!]_{[\![c]\!](m_1)} \geq_{sd} [\![v_2]\!]_{[\![c]\!](m_2)}$.*

```
pos ← start; H ← []; i ← 0;
while i < k do
  b ←$ {0,1};
  H ← b :: H;
  if b then pos++ else pos-- fi;
  i ← i + 1;
end
return pos
```

```
pos ← start; H ← []; i ← 0;
while i < k do
  mov ←$ {0,1};
  dir ←$ {0,1};
  crd ←$ [1,d];
  H ← (mov, dir, crd) :: H;
  if mov then
    pos ← pos + (dir ? 1 : -1 ) * u(crd)
  fi;
  i   ← i + 1;
end
return pos
```

(a) Random walk on $\mathbb{Z}$ | (b) Random walk on $(\mathbb{Z}/k\mathbb{Z})^d$

Fig. 4. Two random walks

3   Warming Up: Random Walks

We warm up with couplings for random walks. These numeric processes model the evolution of a token over a discrete space: at each time step the token will choose its next movement randomly. We will show that if the two initial positions satisfy some property, the distributions of the two positions converge.

3.1   The Basic Random Walk

Our first example is a random walk on the integers. Starting at an initial position, at each step we flip a fair coin. If heads, we move one step to the right. Otherwise, we move one step to the left. The code for running process k steps is presented in the left side of Fig. 4. The variable H stores the history of coin flips. While this history isn't needed for computation of the result (it is *ghost code*), we will state invariants in terms of this history.

We consider two walks that start at locations start_1 and start_2 that are an even distance apart: $\text{start}_2 - \text{start}_1 = 2n \geq 0$. We want to show that the distribution on end positions in the two walks converges as k increases. From Theorem 1, it suffices to find a coupling of the two walks, i.e., a way to coordinate their random samplings.

The basic idea is to *mirror* the two walks. When the first process moves towards the second process, we have the second process also move closer; when the first process moves away, we have the second process move away too. When the two processes meet, we have the two processes make identical moves.

To carry out this plan, we define $\Sigma(\text{H})$ to be the number of true in H minus the number of false; in terms of the random walk, $\Sigma(\text{H})$ measures the net change in position of a process with history H. Then, we define a predicate such that $P(\text{H})$ holds when H contains a prefix H' such that $\Sigma(\text{H}') = n$.

Accordingly, $P(\text{H}_1)$ holds when the first process has moved at least n spots to the right. Under the coupling, this means that the second process must have moved at least n spots to the left since the two particles are mirrored. Since the first process starts out exactly $2n$ to the left of the second process, $P(\mathrm{H}_1)$ is true exactly when the coupled processes have already met. If the processes start out an *odd* distance apart, then they will *never* meet under this coupling—the coupling preserves the parity of the distance between the two positions.

To formalize this coupling in pRHL, we aim to couple two copies of the program above, which we denote c_1 and c_2. We relate the two while loops with rule [WHILE] using the following invariant:

$$(\mathrm{pos}_1 \neq \mathrm{pos}_2 \Rightarrow \mathrm{pos}_1 = \mathrm{i}_1 + \Sigma(\mathrm{H}_1) \wedge \mathrm{pos}_2 = \mathrm{i}_2 - \Sigma(\mathrm{H}_1)) \wedge (P(\mathrm{H}_1) \Rightarrow \mathrm{pos}_1 = \mathrm{pos}_2).$$

The loop invariant states that before the two particles meet, their trajectories are mirrored, and that once they have met, they coincide forever.

To prove that this is an invariant, we need to relate the loop bodies. The key step is relating the two sampling operations using the rule [SAMPLE]; note that we must provide a bijection f from booleans to booleans. We choose the bijection based on whether the two coupled walks have met or not.

More precisely, we perform a case analysis on $\mathrm{pos}_1 = \mathrm{pos}_2$ with rule [CASE]. If they are equal then the walks move together, so we use the identity map for f; this has the effect of forcing both processes to see the same sample. If the walks are at different positions, we use the negation map ($\neg$) for f, so as to force the two processes to take opposite steps.

Putting everything together, we can prove the following judgment in pRHL:

$$\vDash c_1 \sim c_2 : \mathrm{start}_1 + 2n = \mathrm{start}_2 \Rightarrow (P(\mathrm{H}_1) \Rightarrow \mathrm{pos}_1 = \mathrm{pos}_2).$$

By Theorem 1, we can bound the TV distance between the final positions. If two memories m_1, m_2 satisfy $m_1(\mathrm{start}) + 2n = m_2(\mathrm{start})$, we have

$$\| [\![\mathrm{pos}_1]\!]_{[\![c_1]\!]}(m_1) - [\![\mathrm{pos}_2]\!]_{[\![c_2]\!]}(m_2) \|_{tv} \leq [\![\neg P(\mathrm{H}_1)]\!]_{[\![c_1]\!]}(m_1).$$

Note that the right hand side depends only on the first program. In other words, proving this quantitative bound on two programs is reduced to proving a quantitative property on a *single* program—this is the power of coupling.

3.2   Lazy Random Walk on a Torus

For a more interesting example of a random walk, we can consider a walk on a torus. Concretely, the position is now a d-tuple of integers in $[0, k-1]$. The walk first flips a fair coin; if heads it stays put, otherwise it moves. If it moves, the walk chooses uniformly in $[1, d]$ to choose the coordinate to move, and a second fair coin to determine the direction (positive, or negative). The positions are cyclic: increasing from $k-1$ leads to 0, and decreasing from 0 leads to $k-1$.

We can simulate this walk with the program in the right side of Fig. 4, where $\mathrm{u}(i)$ is the i-th canonical base vector in $(\mathbb{Z}/k\mathbb{Z})^d$. As before, we store the trace of the random walk in the list H. All arithmetic is done modulo k.

Like the simple random walk, we start this process at two locations start_1 and start_2 on the torus and run for k iterations. We aim to prove that the distributions of the two walks converge as k increases by coupling the two walks, iteration by iteration. Each iteration, we first choose the same coordinate crd and the same direction dir in both walks. If the two positions coincide in coordinate crd, we arrange both walks to select the same movement flag mov, so that the walks either move together, or both stay put. If the two positions differ in crd, we arrange the walks to select opposite samples in mov so that exactly one walk moves.

As in the basic random walk, we can view our coupling as letting the first process evolve as usual, then coordinating the samples of the second process to perform the coupling. In other words, given a history H_1 of samples for the first process, the behavior of the second coupled process is completely specified.

Thus, we can define operators to extract the movements of each walk from the trace H_1 of the samplings of the first process: $\Sigma_1(i, H_1)$ is the drift of the ith coordinate of the first process, and $\Sigma_2(i, H_1)$ is the drift of the second process. Essentially, these operators encode the coupling by describing how the second process moves as a function of the first process's samples.

In pRHL, we will use the rule [WHILE] with the following invariant:

$$\forall i \in [1, d]. \ (\Sigma_1(i, H_1) - \Sigma_2(i, H_1) = \Delta[i] \Rightarrow \text{pos}_1[i] = \text{pos}_2[i])$$

$$\wedge \ (\text{pos}_1[i] \neq \text{pos}_2[i] \Rightarrow \text{pos}_1[i] = \text{start}_1[i] + \Sigma_1(i, H_1) \wedge \text{pos}_2[i] = \text{start}_2[i] + \Sigma_2(i, H_1)),$$

where Δ is the vector $\text{start}_2 - \text{start}_1$. The first conjunct states that the walks move together in coordinate i once they couple in coordinate i, while the second conjunct describes the positions in terms of the history H_1.

To prove that the invariant is preserved, we encode the coupling described above into pRHL, via three uses of the rule [SAMPLE]. The first two samples—for crd and dir—are coupled with f being identity bijections (on $[1, d]$ and on booleans), ensuring that the processes make identical choices. When sampling mov, we inspect the history H_1 to see whether the two walks agree in position crd. If so, we choose the identity bijection for mov; if not, we choose negation. This coupling is sufficient to verify the loop invariant.

To conclude our proof, the first conjunct in the invariant implies that we can prove the pRHL judgment $\vDash c_1 \sim c_2 : \text{start}_2 - \text{start}_1 = \Delta \Rightarrow \Phi$, where

$$\Phi \triangleq (\forall i \in [1, d]. \ \Sigma_1(i, H_1) - \Sigma_2(i, H_1) = \Delta[i]) \Rightarrow \forall i \in [1, d]. \ \text{pos}_1[i] = \text{pos}_2[i].$$

Finally, Theorem 1 implies that for any two initial memories m_1, m_2 with $m_2(\text{start}) - m_1(\text{start}) = \Delta$, we have

$$\| [\![\text{pos}_1]\!]_{[\![c_1]\!](m_1)} - [\![\text{pos}_2]\!]_{[\![c_2]\!](m_2)} \|_{tv} \leq [\![\exists i \in [1, d]. \ \Sigma_1(i, H_1) - \Sigma_2(i, H_1) \neq \Delta[i]]\!]_{[\![c_1]\!](m_1)}.$$

Again, proving a quantitative bound on the convergence of two distributions is reduced to proving a quantitative bound on a single program.

4   Combining Coupling with Program Transformation

So far, we have seen examples where the coupling is proved directly on the two original programs c_1 and c_2. Often, it is convenient to introduce a third program c^* that is equivalent to c_1, and then couple c^* to c_2. Applying transitivity (rule [EQUIV]), this gives a coupling between c_1 and c_2. Let's consider two examples.

4.1   Two Biased Coins

Consider a coin flipping process that flips a coin k times, and returns the number of heads observed. We consider this process run on two different biased coins: The first coin has probability q_1 of coming up heads, while the second coin has probability q_2 of coming up heads with $q_1 \geq q_2$. Let the distribution on the number of heads be μ_1 and μ_2 respectively.

Intuitively, it is clear that the first process is somehow bigger than the second process: it is more likely to see more heads, since the first coin is biased with a higher probability. Stochastic dominance turns out to be the proper way to formalize our intuition. To prove it, Proposition 2 implies that we just need to find an appropriate coupling of the two processes.

While it is possible to define a coupling directly by carefully coordinating the corresponding coin flips, we will give a simpler coupling that proceeds in two stages. First, we will couple a program c_1 computing μ_1 to an intermediate program c^*. Then, we will show that c^* is equivalent to a program c_2 computing μ_2, thus exhibiting a coupling between μ_1 and μ_2. Letting $r = q_2/q_1$ and denoting the coin flip distribution with probability p of sampling true by $\mathbf{Bern}(p)$, we give the programs in Fig. 5.

For the first step, we want to couple c_1 and c^*. For a rough sketch, we want to use rule [WHILE] with an appropriate loop invariant; here, $n_1 \geq n^*$. To show that the invariant is preserved, we need to relate the loop bodies. We use the two-sided rule [SAMPLE] when sampling x and y (taking the bijection f to be the identity), the one-sided rule [SAMPLE-L] to relate sampling nothing (skip) in c_1 with sampling z in c^*, and the one-sided rule [IFL] to relate the two conditionals. (The one-sided rule is needed, since the two conditionals may take different branches.) Thus, we can prove the judgment $\vDash c_1 \sim c^* : q_1 \geq q_2 \wedge r = q_2/q_1 \Rightarrow n_1 \geq n^*$.

For the second step, we need to prove that c^* is equivalent to c_2. Here, we use a sound approximation $\simeq$ to semantic equivalence as described in the preliminaries. Specifically, we have x $\xleftarrow{\$}$ $\mathbf{Bern}(q_1 \cdot r) \simeq$ y $\xleftarrow{\$}$ $\mathbf{Bern}(q_1)$; r $\xleftarrow{\$}$ $\mathbf{Bern}(r)$; x $\leftarrow$ y $\wedge$ z for the loop bodies; showing equivalence of c^* and c_2 is then straightforward. Thus, we can show $\vDash c^* \sim c_2 : q_1 \geq q_2 \wedge r = q_2/q_1 \Rightarrow n^* = n_2$. Applying rule [EQUIV] gives the final judgment $\vDash c_1 \sim c_2 : q_1 \geq q_2 \wedge r = q_2/q_1 \Rightarrow n_1 \geq n_2$, showing stochastic domination by Proposition 2.

4.2   Balls into Bins: Asynchronous Coupling

The examples we have seen so far are all *synchronous* couplings: they relate the iterations of the while loop in lock-step. For some applications, we may want to reason asynchronously, perhaps allowing one side to progress while holding the other side fixed. One example of an asynchronous coupling is analyzing the *balls into bins* process. We have two bins, and a set of n balls. At each step, we throw a ball into a random bin, returning the count of both bins when we have thrown all the balls. The code is on the left side in Fig. 6.

```
n ← 0; i ← 0;
whil i < k do:

    x ←$ Bern(q₁);



    if x then
        n ← n + 1;
    fi
    i ← i + 1;
end
return n
```

(a) Program c_1

```
n ← 0; i ← 0;
while i < k do:

    y ←$ Bern(q₁);
    z ←$ Bern(r);
    x ← y ∧ z;
    if x then
        n ← n + 1;
    fi;
    i ← i + 1;
end
return n
```

(b) Program c^*

```
n ← 0; i ← 0;
while i < k do:

    x ←$ Bern(q₂);



    if x then
        n ← n + 1
    fi;
    i ← i + 1
end
return n
```

(c) Program c_2

Fig. 5. Coupling for biased coin flips

```
i, binA, binB ← 0;
while i < n do
    i ← i + 1;

    b ←$ {0,1};
    if b then binA++ else binB++ fi
end






    return (binA, binB)
```

(a) Original programs c_1, c_2

```
i, binA, binB ← 0;
while i < n ∧ i < m do

    b ←$ {0,1};
    if b then binA++ else binB++ fi;
    i ← i + 1;
end
while i < n do
    b ←$ {0,1};
    if b then binA++ else binB++ fi;
    i ← i + 1;
end
return (binA, binB)
```

(b) Intermediate program c^*

Fig. 6. Coupling balls into bins

Now, we would like to consider what happens when we run two processes with different numbers of balls. Intuitively, it is clear that if the first process throws more balls than the second process, it should result in a higher load in the bins; we aim to prove that the first process stochastically dominates the second with the following coupling. Assume that the first process has more balls ($n_1 \geq n_2$). For the first n_2 balls, we have the two process do the same thing—they choose the same bucket for their tosses. For the last $n_1 - n_2$ steps, the first process throws the rest of the balls. Evidently, this coupling forces the bins in the first run to have higher load than the bins in the second run.

To formalize this example, we again introduce a program c^*, proving equivalence with c_1 and showing a coupling with c_2. The code for c^* is on the right side in Fig. 6; we require the dummy input m to be equal to n_2.

Proving equivalence with program c_1 is direct, using the loop range splitting transformation in EasyCrypt: while e do $c \simeq$ while $e \wedge e'$ do c; while e do c. Once this is done, we simply need to provide a coupling between c^* and c_2. By our choice of m, we can trivially couple the first loop in c^* to the (single) loop in c_2, ensuring that $\Phi \triangleq \text{binA}^* \geq \text{binA}_2 \wedge \text{binB}^* \geq \text{binB}_2$ after the first loop.

Then, we can apply the one-sided rules to couple the second loop in c^* with a skip statement in c_2. It is straightforward to show that Φ is an invariant in rule [WHILEL], from which we can conclude $\vDash c^* \sim c_2 : n_1 \geq n_2 \wedge m = n_2 \Rightarrow$ $\text{binA}^* \geq \text{binA}_2 \wedge \text{binB}^* \geq \text{binB}_2$, and by equivalence of c_1 and c^* we have $\vDash c_1 \sim$ $c_2 : n_1 \geq n_2 \Rightarrow \text{binA}_1 \geq \text{binA}_2 \wedge \text{binB}_1 \geq \text{binB}_2$, enough for stochastic domination by Proposition 2.

5 Non-deterministic Couplings: Birth and Death

So far, we have seen *deterministic* couplings, which reuse randomness from the coupled processes in the coupling; this can be seen in the [SAMPLE] rule, when we always choose a deterministic bijection. In this section, we will see a more sophisticated coupling that injects new randomness.

For our example, we consider a classic Markov process. Roughly speaking, a Markov process moves within a set of states each transition depending only on the current state and a fresh random sample. The random walks we saw before are classic examples of Markov processes.

A more complex Markov process is the *birth and death chain*. The state space is $\mathbb{Z}$, and the process starts at some integer x. At every time step, if the process is at state i, the process has some probability b_i of increasing by one, and some probability a_i of decreasing by one. Note that a_i and b_i may add up to less than 1: there can be some positive probability $1 - a_i - b_i$ where the process stays fixed.

To model this process, we define a sum type Move with three elements (Left, Right and Still) which correspond to the possible moves a process can make. Then, the chains are modeled by the code in the left of Fig. 7, where the distribution bd(state) is the distribution of moves from state.

Just like the biased coin and balls into bins processes, we want to prove stochastic domination for two processes started at states $\text{start}_1 \geq \text{start}_2$ via coupling. The difficulty is that if the processes become adjacent and they both move, the two processes may swap positions, losing stochastic domination.

The solution is to use a special coupling when the two processes are on two adjacent states as in Mufa [8]. Unlike the previous examples, the coupling is not deterministic: the behavior of one process is not fully determined by the randomness of the other. Our loop invariant is the usual one for stochastic domination: $\text{state}_1 \geq \text{state}_2$. To show that this invariant is preserved, we perform a case analysis on whether $\text{state}_1 = \text{state}_2$, $\text{state}_1 = \text{state}_2 + 1$ or $\text{state}_1 > \text{state}_2 + 1$.

We focus on the interesting middle case, when the states are adjacent. Here, we perform a trick: we switch c_1, c_2 for two equivalent intermediate programs c_1^*, c_2^*, and prove a coupling on the two intermediate programs. The two intermediate programs each sample from dcouple, a distribution on pairs of moves, and project out the first or second component as dir; in other words, we explicitly code c_1^*, c_2^* as sampling from the two marginals of a common distribution dcouple. By proving that the marginals are indeed distributed as bd(state_1) and bd(state_2), we can prove equivalences $c_1 \simeq c_1^*$ and $c_2 \simeq c_2^*$. The code is in the right side of Fig. 7, where proj [1—2] is the first and second projections in c_1 and c_2, respectively.

All that remains is to prove a coupling between c_1^* and c_2^* satisfying the loop invariant $\text{state}_1 \geq \text{state}_2$. With adjacent states, dcouple is given by the following function from pairs of moves to probabilities:

```
op distr-adjacent aᵢ aᵢ₊₁ bᵢ bᵢ₊₁ (x : Move * Move) =
    if x = (Right , Left ) then min(bᵢ₊₁,aᵢ)              else
    if x = (Still , Left ) then (bᵢ₊₁ - aᵢ)⁺              else
    if x = (Right , Still) then (aᵢ - bᵢ₊₁)⁺              else
    if x = (Still , Right) then aᵢ₊₁                      else
    if x = (Left  , Still) then bᵢ                        else
    if x = (Still , Still) then
        1 - min(bᵢ₊₁,aᵢ) - aᵢ₊₁ - bᵢ - |bᵢ₊₁ - aᵢ| else
    if x = (`     ,     ) then 0.
```

where x^+ denotes the *positive part* of x: simply x if $x \geq 0$, and 0 otherwise. Note that the case (Left, Right) has probability 0: this forbids the first process from skipping past the second process.

Now the coupling is easy: we simply require both samples from dcouple to be the same. Since $\text{state}_1 = \text{state}_2 + 1$ and the distribution never returns (Left, Right), the loop invariant is trivially preserved. This shows the desired coupling, and stochastic domination by Proposition 2.

```
H ← []; state ← start; i ← 0;
while i < k do
    dir ←$ bd(state);


    if dir = Left then
        state ← state - 1;
    else if dir = Right then
        state ← state + 1;
    fi
    H ← state :: H;
    i ← i + 1;
end
return state
```

(a) Original programs c_1, c_2

```
H ← []; state ← start; i ← 0;
while i < steps do
    d ←$ dcouple;
    dir ← proj [1|2] d;
    if dir = Left then
        state ← state - 1;
    else if dir = Right then
        state ← state + 1;
    fi
    H ← state :: H;
    i ← i + 1;
end
return state
```

(b) Intermediate programs c_1^*, c_2^*

Fig. 7. Coupling the birth and death chain

6   Conclusion and Future Work

We have established the connection between relational verification of probabilistic programs using pRHL, and probabilistic couplings. Furthermore, we have used the connection by using pRHL to verify several well-known examples of couplings from the literature on randomized algorithms. More broadly, our work is a blend between the two main approaches to relational verification: (i) reasoning about a single program combining the two programs (e.g. cross-products [12], self-composition [3], and product programs [2]); and (ii) using a program logic to reason directly about two programs (e.g. relational Hoare logic [5], relational separation logic [11], and pRHL [1]). We have only scratched the surface in verifying couplings; we see three natural directions for future work.

A more General Verification Framework. When we construct a coupling, the core data is encoded by the bijection f for the rule [SAMPLE], which specifies how the two samples are to be coupled. A careful look at the rule reveals that the coupling is a *deterministic* coupling, as defined by Villani [10]. While such couplings are already quite powerful, there are many examples of couplings that cannot be verified using deterministic couplings. We have worked around this difficulty by using program transformation rules, but an alternative approach could be interesting: allow more general binary relations when relating samples, rather than just bijections. This generalization could enable a more general class of couplings and yield cleaner proofs.

Moreover, it would be interesting to extend EasyCrypt with mechanisms for handling the non-relational reasoning in couplings. To prove quantitative bounds on total variation in the random walk example, we need to bound the time it takes for a single random walk to reach a certain position. Proving such bounds requires more complex, non-relational reasoning. We are currently developing a program logic for this purpose, but it has not yet been integrated into EasyCrypt.

Extending to Shift and Path Coupling. The couplings realized in the random walks are instances of exact couplings, where we reason about synchronized samples: we relate the first samples, the second samples, etc. A more general notion of coupling is *shift-coupling*, where we are allowed to first shift one process by a random number of samples, then couple. The general theory of path couplings provides similar-shaped inequalities as the ones in exact coupling, allowing powerful mathematical-based reasoning inside the logic with the [CONSEQ] rule. These coupling notions are complex, and it is not yet clear how they can be verified.

Other Examples. There are many other examples of couplings, in particular the proof of the constructive Lovasz Local Lemma, a fundamental tool used in the *probabilistic method*, a powerful proof technique for showing existence in combinatorics.

Acknowledgments. We thank Arthur Azevedo de Amorim and the anonymous reviewers for their close reading and useful suggestions. This work was partially supported by a grant from the Simons Foundation (#360368 to Justin Hsu), NSF grant CNS-1065060, Madrid regional project S2009TIC-1465 PROMETIDOS, Spanish national projects TIN2009-14599 DESAFIOS 10 and TIN2012-39391-C04-01 Strongsoft, and a grant from the Cofund Action AMAROUT II (#291803).

References

1. Barthe, G., Grégoire, B., Zanella-Béguelin, S.: Formal certification of code-based cryptographic proofs. In: ACM SIGPLAN-SIGACT Symposium on Principles of Programming Languages (POPL), Savannah, Georgia, pp. 90–101, New York (2009)
2. Barthe, G., Crespo, J.M., Kunz, C.: Relational verification using product programs. In: International Symposium on Formal Methods (FM), Limerick, Ireland, pp. 200–214 (2011a)
3. Barthe, G., D'Argenio, P.R., Rezk, T.: Secure information flow by self-composition. Math. Struct. Comput. Sci. **21**(06), 1207–1252 (2011b)
4. Barthe, G., Grégoire, B., Heraud, S., Béguelin, S.Z.: Computer-aided security proofs for the working cryptographer. In: Rogaway, P. (ed.) CRYPTO 2011. LNCS, vol. 6841, pp. 71–90. Springer, Heidelberg (2011)
5. Benton, N.: Simple relational correctness proofs for static analyses and program transformations. In: ACM SIGPLAN-SIGACT Symposium on Principles of Programming Languages (POPL), Venice, Italy, pp. 14–25 (2004)
6. Deng, Y., Du, W.: Logical, metric, and algorithmic characterisations of probabilistic bisimulation. Technical report CMU-CS-11-110, Carnegie Mellon University, March 2011
7. Lindvall, T.: Lectures on the coupling method. Courier Corporation, Mineola (2002)
8. Mufa, C.: Optimal markovian couplings and applications. Acta Mathematica Sinica **10**(3), 260–275 (1994)
9. Thorisson, H.: Coupling, Stationarity, and Regeneration. Springer, New York (2000)
10. Villani, C.: Optimal Transport: Old and New. Springer Science, Heidelberg (2008)
11. Yang, H.: Relational separation logic. Theor. Comput. Sci. **375**(1–3), 308–334 (2007)
12. Zaks, A., Pnueli, A.: CoVaC: compiler validation by program analysis of the cross-product. In: Cuellar, J., Sere, K. (eds.) FM 2008. LNCS, vol. 5014, pp. 35–51. Springer, Heidelberg (2008)

A Contextual Logical Framework

Peter Brottveit Bock$^{(\boxtimes)}$ and Carsten Schürmann

IT University of Copenhagen, Copenhagen, Denmark
{pbrb,carsten}@itu.dk

Abstract. A new logical framework with explicit linear contexts and names is presented with the purpose of enabling direct and flexible manipulation of contexts, both for representing systems and meta-properties. The framework is a conservative extension of the logical framework LF, and builds on linear logic and contextual modal type theory. We prove that the framework admits canonical forms, and that it possesses all desirable meta-theoretic properties, in particular hereditary substitutions.

As proof of concept, we give an encoding of the one-sided sequent calculus for classical linear logic and the corresponding cut-admissibility proof, as well as an encoding of parallel reduction of lambda terms with the corresponding value-soundness proof.

1 Introduction

The Logical Framework (LF) [3] has successfully served as a meta-language for representing languages with binders, in particular programming languages and logics, type systems, and operational semantics. It forms the basis of several proof assistants, such as Twelf [6], Delphin [10] and Beluga [8], all of which support reasoning about LF representations.

However, representing and reasoning about systems which are resource aware and require linearity is challenging in LF. In this paper we describe XLF, an extension of LF with explicit linear conteXts, which supports elegant higher-order representation of such systems and their meta-theory. Linear logics and the corresponding linear type theories are known to support representations of state, communication, processes, and multi-set rewriting. Having a framework which can deliver both, representation of such systems and their meta-theory, is therefore useful and one of the main contributions of this paper.

As a motivating example, consider the simply typed linear λ-calculus with intrinsic typing. The syntax for terms is $t, s ::= x^\tau \mid \lambda x^\tau.s \mid s\,t$, where terms use their variables linearly, i.e. exactly once. Borrowing notation from Twelf (except λ-abstraction, which we write as \x.) we represent this language in XLF as:

```
tp: type. arrow : tp -> tp -> tp. tm : tp -> type.
lam: (n [G, n : tm T] tm S) -> [G] tm (arrow T S).
app: [G]tm (arrow T S) -> [D]tm T -> [G, D]tm S.
```

While we are getting a bit ahead of ourselves, the central idea underlying this work is that we can control the linear context explicitly, using a modal box

M. Davis et al. (Eds.): LPAR-20 2015, LNCS 9450, pp. 402–417, 2015.
DOI: 10.1007/978-3-662-48899-7_28

type that is inspired by that of Contextual Modal Type Theory (CMTT) [4]. Observe that [D]tm T and [G, D]tm S are both instances of this box type. The occurrences of G and D are *context variables*, that are here implicitly universally bound. The variable n is a *name variable* that ranges over names of linear variables and should not be confused with a variable bound by λ-abstraction. n is bound by an explicit name abstraction operator {n} that occurs in a negative position in the type of lam. As an example, the identity function is represented in XLF as lam \n. box n, where box is the introduction form for the box type.

Since we want to support *adequate* representations, we will design XLF in such a way that the box type is agnostic to re-orderings of its linear context. We only consider linear contexts up to exchange. In particular, this means that in XLF the type [m : tm S, n : tm (arrow S T)] tm T is equivalent to the type [n : tm (arrow S T), m : tm S] tm T. Furthermore, we would like to point out that by having exchange, we can always reorder the context in such a way that any particular assumption that we wish to work on can be permuted to the right of the context. See, for example, n : tm T in the declaration of lam. Also, there is no need to explicitly interleave contexts, as a standard union suffices. An instance of this is G, D in the app rule. The downside of having exchange in the linear context is that it forces us to talk about names, which renders the system more complicated.

The contributions of this paper are: A logical framework XLF with hereditary substitutions (see Sect. 2) and canonical forms (see Sect. 3) that we apply in two examples in Sect. 4: Cut elimination for a one-sided sequent calculus for Multiplicative-Additive Linear Logic (MALL) and value soundness for the parallel λ-calculus.

2   The Logical Framework XLF

In this section we define the syntax and semantics of the logical framework XLF. We assume some familiarity with the with the original logical framework LF [3], as well as linear logic [2].

We begin our exposition with the two most important type constructors of LF: $A, B ::= \Pi x : B. A \mid a \cdot S$. Here, a refers to a type family, and S to a spine, the list of arguments of the type family. We have chosen to disregard the type level λ-abstraction as it is mostly of theoretical interest.

Next, we add a the box type, a modal operator that is indexed by a linear context Δ.

$$A, B ::= \ldots \mid [\Delta]A \qquad \Delta ::= \cdot \mid \Delta, n : A$$

In this definition, n is a name variable or simply a name. This is necessary, as we will need to quantify over names, as we have already discussed in the introduction. We can think of the context Δ as a record type, as found in functional programming languages, for example, Haskell or SML.

Next, we will increase the expressiveness of XLF by quantifying over linear contexts. We add variables for linear contexts, and denote them by φ, and a suitable "context variable" quantifier. Let us try to define a quantifier that resembles that of [7]. Returning to our intuition of records, we may think of this as a form of *row polymorphism*.

$$A, B ::= \ldots \mid \Pi\varphi{:}\mathtt{lctx}.\,A \qquad\qquad \Delta ::= \cdot \mid \Delta, \varphi \mid \Delta, n : A$$

If we had such a quantifier, we could make the type of app from the motivating example from the introduction more precise. Note that for better readability, we continue to use G and D as context variables.

$$\Pi\ \mathtt{G{:}lctx}.\ \Pi\ \mathtt{D{:}lctx}.\ [\mathtt{G}]\mathtt{tm}\ (\mathtt{arrow\ T\ S}) \to [\mathtt{D}]\mathtt{tm}\ \mathtt{T} \to [\mathtt{G,D}]\mathtt{tm}\ \mathtt{S}$$

However, there is a problem. Consider, for a moment, that if both context variables G and D are instantiated with the same context, say for example, n : tm T, then the resulting type is ill formed, as G, D becomes n : tm T, n : tm T, declaring n twice! Just quantifying over context variables is therefore too naive. In order to solve this apparent problem, we introduce a new quantifier over names, and restrict the context variable quantifiers in a clever way.

$$A, B ::= \ldots \mid \Pi\varphi{:}\mathtt{lctx}(\delta).\,A \mid \Pi n{:}\mathtt{lvar}(\delta).\,A$$
$$\delta ::= \emptyset \mid \delta_0 \cup \delta_1 \mid \{n\} \mid \mathtt{dom}(\varphi)$$

The purpose of δ is to denote a set of names from which a context ought to be disjoint. Therefore δ can be empty, the union of two of those sets, singleton names, or even the domain of a context variable. Both, the newly introduced quantification over names and the quantification over context variables, are restricted by δ: One may only eliminate such a quantifier in the case that the names used in the linear context (resp. linear variable name) is disjoint from (resp. not in) δ. Drawing intuition from nominal logic, the quantifier over contexts can be thought of as $\forall\varphi : \mathtt{lctx}.\,\varphi\#\delta \to A$, and similar for quantifying over names. Notice that in XLF, there are no name *constants*, only name *variables*.

Syntactic Categories. We summarize now the syntactic categories of XLF. Since we are really only interested in canonical terms, we will — as is now standard — give a *canonical* presentation of XLF, where all well-typed terms are forced to be β-normal and η-long. Consequently, there will be no β-redexes. The typing system will enforce η-long forms. The syntactic categories are depicted in Fig. 1. φ range over *context variables*, and n range over *name variables*. We let a range over type family constants, c range over object level constants, and x range over object level variables, which is common in LF.

The term language is a variant of the λ-calculus, denoted by M. In our presentation, we use *spines* [11] to represent iterated applications, corresponding to a sequence of eliminations. This means that an atomic term H, called a head, applied to a list of arguments S, called a spine, is written $H \cdot S$. We proceed as follows. For each new type, we will add an introduction form to M and an elimination form to S.

$$K ::= \Pi x{:}A.\,K \mid \Pi \varphi{:}\mathtt{lctx}(\delta).\,K \mid \Pi n{:}\mathtt{lvar}(\delta).\,K \mid \mathtt{type}$$
$$A,B ::= \Pi x{:}B.\,A \mid \Pi \varphi{:}\mathtt{lctx}(\delta).\,A \mid \Pi n{:}\mathtt{lvar}(\delta).\,A \mid [\Delta]A \mid a \cdot S$$
$$M,N ::= \lambda x.M \mid \lambda \varphi.M \mid \lambda n.M \mid \mathtt{box}(M) \mid H \cdot S$$
$$H ::= c \mid x \mid n \qquad\qquad S ::= \epsilon \mid M :: S \mid \Delta :: S \mid n :: S \mid \sigma :: S$$
$$\sigma ::= \cdot \mid \sigma_0, \sigma_1 \mid \mathtt{id}(\varphi) \mid M/n \qquad \Delta ::= \cdot \mid \Delta_0, \Delta_1 \mid n : A \mid \varphi$$
$$\delta ::= \emptyset \mid \delta_0 \cup \delta_1 \mid \{n\} \mid \mathtt{dom}(\varphi)$$

Fig. 1. Syntax.

We have atomic types $a \cdot S$, with the corresponding term $H \cdot S$, i.e. a variable, constant or linear variable applied to a spine, and we have the dependent function space from A to B, $\Pi x : A.\,B$, with $\lambda x.M$ as its introduction form, and $M :: S$ as the elimination form.

The first new type for the framework is $\Pi n : \mathtt{lvar}(\delta).\,A$, which we can see from the choice of syntax, is a kind of dependent function space. It ranges over names that do not occur in δ (where δ is a set of names, described below). It is best thought of as quantification over names. The introduction form is $\lambda n.M$, and the elimination form is $n :: S$, which replaces the name in the type with n.

In a similar fashion, the new type $\Pi \varphi : \mathtt{lctx}(\delta).\,A$, is also a dependent function space, where the domain is linear contexts with domain disjoint from δ. The introduction form is $\lambda \varphi.M$, and the elimination form is $\Delta :: S$, which replaces the context variable with Δ.

Finally, we add the contextual modal type operator $[\Delta]A$. The introduction form is $\mathtt{box}(M)$, and it means that the term M is of type A and valid Δ (using each variable from Δ exactly once). The elimination form is $\sigma :: S$, where σ is a substitution for the variables in Δ. It is important to note that the term $\mathtt{box}(M)$ doesn't contain and binders, although the type would suggest this. The reason for this is that we are presenting a canonical presentation of XLF, where the omitted context Δ can always be inferred, as the box introduction occurs in the checking phase.

A linear context Δ is defined to be either empty, $\cdot$, the union of two contexts, Δ_0, Δ_1, a linear assumption, $n : A$ where A is not a box type[1], or a linear context variable, φ. A linear substitution σ is either the empty substitution, $\cdot$, the combination of two substitutions, σ_0, σ_1, a single substitution M/n, or the identity substitution $\mathtt{id}(\varphi)$. Finally, the set of names δ that we discussed earlier, is either empty set $\emptyset$, the union of two sets $\delta_0 \cup \delta_1$, the singleton set of a name $\{n\}$, or the domain of a context variable, $\mathtt{dom}(\varphi)$.

The definitions of Δ, σ, and δ, follow a similar pattern, which makes it easy to define equalities modulo exchange, assuming (in the interest of brevity) that

---

[1] This is the same restriction as in traditional CMTT for LF, since it would lead to commuting conversions.

for $\langle X; \iota; \circ \rangle \in \{\langle \Delta; \cdot; , \rangle, \langle \sigma; \cdot; , \rangle, \langle \delta; \emptyset; \cup \rangle\}$, the following equalities hold:

$$X = X \circ \iota \qquad X_0 \circ X_1 = X_1 \circ X_0 \qquad (X_0 \circ X_1) \circ X_2 = X_0 \circ (X_1 \circ X_2)$$

Furthermore, we assume the that $\delta \cup \delta = \delta$, which guarantees that δ always denotes a set.

$\Gamma \vdash n \text{ NOM}(\delta)$

$$\frac{n : \text{lvar}(\delta') \in \Gamma \quad \Gamma \vdash \{n\} \perp \delta}{\Gamma \vdash n \text{ NOM}(\delta)}$$

- -

$\Gamma \vdash \delta \text{ NOM-SET}$

$$\frac{}{\Gamma \vdash \emptyset \text{ NOM-SET}} \qquad \frac{\Gamma \vdash \delta_0 \text{ NOM-SET} \quad \Gamma \vdash \delta_1 \text{ NOM-SET}}{\Gamma \vdash \delta_0 \cup \delta_1 \text{ NOM-SET}}$$

$$\frac{\varphi : \text{lctx}(\delta) \in \Gamma}{\Gamma \vdash \text{dom}(\varphi) \text{ NOM-SET}} \qquad \frac{\Gamma \vdash n \text{ NOM}(\emptyset)}{\Gamma \vdash \{n\} \text{ NOM-SET}}$$

- -

$\Gamma \vdash \delta_0 \perp \delta_1$. The conclusion is symmetric. Let $p ::= \{n\} \mid \text{dom}(\varphi)$.

$$\frac{}{\Gamma \vdash \emptyset \perp \delta} \qquad \frac{\Gamma \vdash \delta_0 \perp \delta \quad \Gamma \vdash \delta_1 \perp \delta}{\Gamma \vdash \delta_0 \cup \delta_1 \perp \delta}$$

$$\frac{n : \text{lvar}(\delta \cup p) \in \Gamma}{\Gamma \vdash \{n\} \perp p} \qquad \frac{\varphi : \text{lctx}(\delta \cup p) \in \Gamma}{\Gamma \vdash \text{dom}(\varphi) \perp p}$$

Fig. 2. Judgments related to names.

Typing Rules. Next we turn to the static semantics of XLF. The typing judgments are defined relative to a signature (which contains the declaration of all type level and object level constants), and an intuitionistic, ordered LF context:

$$\Sigma ::= \cdot \mid \Sigma, a : K \mid \Sigma, c : A \qquad \qquad \vdash \Sigma \text{ SIG}$$
$$\Gamma ::= \cdot \mid \Gamma, x : A \mid \Gamma, \varphi : \text{lctx}(\delta) \mid \Gamma, n : \text{lvar}(\delta) \qquad \vdash \Gamma \text{ CTX}$$

The two judgments to the right check that the signature and context, respectively, are well formed. In the interest of space, we omit the defining rules; they can be inferred from the typing rules that we give below. We implicitly assume that both Σ and Γ are always valid, which means that we will omit $\vdash \Sigma$ SIG and $\vdash \Gamma$ SIG from XLF's axioms that we introduce next.

Types and Kinds. The complete set of typing rules for types and kinds is given in Fig. 2. But first, we introduce some auxiliary judgments. Names are always variables, they must be bound in Γ. This is expressed by the judgment $\Gamma \vdash n$ NOM(δ). This judgment will also check that n does not occur in δ. For a set of names to be well formed, it simply needs to check that all the variables are bound, which is captured by the judgment $\Gamma \vdash \delta$ NOM-SET.

The judgment $\Gamma \vdash \delta_0 \perp \delta_1$ captures the fact that the sets δ_0 and δ_1 are *disjoint*. The conclusion is symmetric, i.e. if $\Gamma \vdash \delta_0 \perp \delta_1$, then $\Gamma \vdash \delta_1 \perp \delta_0$. The axiom rules state that the empty set is disjoint from any set, and that a set assumed to be disjoint from a set δ, is also disjoint from subsets of δ. Finally, union preserves disjointness. Note that this judgment does not provide proof terms and can therefore be regarded as *external* to the definition of XLF.

Next, we discuss the individual judgments depicted in Fig. 3 in turn, commenting only on the most important rules.

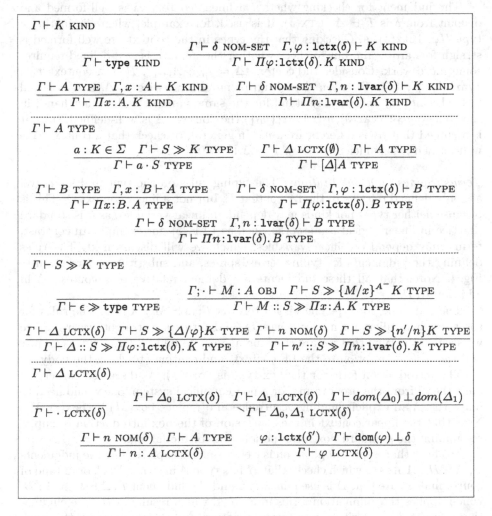

Fig. 3. Type checking kinds and types.

The judgment $\Gamma \vdash A$ TYPE checks that a type is well formed. The most interesting rule is the formation rule for the box type requiring that the type A must not depend on any linear assumptions (by requiring the linear context to be empty). Furthermore, note that this rule forces Δ to be well formed, but it need not be disjoint from any other names.

The judgment $\Gamma \vdash S \gg K$ TYPE checks the well-formedness of the eliminations described by the spine S. When applied to any type family of kind K the result must be of kind type. We remark that the two new rules for quantifying names and contexts are straightforward.

The judgment $\Gamma \vdash K$ KIND checks that a kind is well formed, and should not need any explanation, given the description of $\Gamma \vdash A$ TYPE.

The judgment for checking whether a linear context Δ is well-formed and disjoint from δ is $\Gamma \vdash \Delta$ LCTX(δ). It is used, for example, when eliminating a type $\Pi\varphi$:lctx(δ). A. Checking that the types in the context are well formed is straightforward again, but to check whether the *domain* is well-defined requires some more work. Consider the context $\Delta = n_0 : A, n_1 : B$ in a context $n_0 :$ lvar$(\emptyset), n_1 :$ lvar$(\emptyset)$. Even though no name occurs twice in Δ, it is not well formed, since n_0 and n_1 may stand for the same name. On the other hand, in the context $n_0 :$ lvar$(\emptyset), n_1 :$ lvar$(\{n_0\})$ the context Δ is well-defined, since it is assumed that n_1 is different from n_0. In general, to check that a context Δ is well-formed it is sufficient to show $\Gamma \vdash \Delta$ LCTX$(\emptyset)$.

Terms, Spines, and Substitutions. The typing rules on the type and kind level are only defined relative to the LF context Γ, but not a linear context Δ. This is because neither types nor kinds may depend on linear variables, as it is standard practice in linear logical frameworks, such as LLF [5], for example. In contrast, terms may depend on linear variables, which we will discuss next. The rules defining the judgments for typing terms, spines, and substitutions are given in Fig. 4. Note, that all these judgments are defined relative to a context Δ in addition to Γ.

The judgment for type checking a term is $\Gamma; \Delta \vdash M : A$ OBJ. The rules for the three quantifiers for names, contexts, and terms are straightforward. Since we assume the type that we are checking against to be well-formed, we can just add the new assumption to the LF context, and continue to check the body.

The introduction form for the box type is box(M). As discussed earlier, we omit the Δ from the proof term. For a non-canonical system, one would need to make the Δ an explicit binding occurrence and replace box(M) by box$(\Delta; M)$. Note that the linear context in the conclusion of the box introduction is empty, resembling the standard box introduction rule for modal logic.

To check that a spine application is well formed is expressed by the judgments $\Gamma; \Delta \vdash H : A$ HEAD, which checks that H has type A in either Σ, Γ, or Δ (and of course makes sure that Δ is used linearly), and the judgment $\Gamma; \Delta \vdash S \gg A : B$, which applies the elimination forms in S to A, which results in B. The elimination rules for the quantifiers over names, contexts, and spines are straightforward. In the case of the box type, the spine must provide substitution as argument.

Both substitution, and remaining spine are may consume different sets of variables, which explains the use of context splitting in the conclusion of the rule.

A substitution σ translates one linear context into another, captured by the judgment $\Gamma; \Delta_0 \vdash \sigma : \Delta_1$ SUB. We give the rules for all four constructors of substitutions: The empty substitution satisfies the empty context; to combine to substitutions requires us to distribute the linear resources accordingly. Contexts that consist only of one context variable can only be instantiated by the identity substitution, which must have the same context variable in its codomain, because of linearity. XLF provides three kinds of substitutions: substitutions for names, contexts, and terms.

$$\Gamma; \Delta \vdash M : A \text{ OBJ}$$

$$\frac{\Gamma; \Delta \vdash M : A \text{ OBJ}}{\Gamma; \cdot \vdash \mathbf{box}(M) : [\Delta]A \text{ OBJ}}$$

$$\frac{\Gamma, \varphi : \mathtt{lctx}(\delta); \Delta \vdash M : A \text{ OBJ}}{\Gamma; \Delta \vdash \lambda\varphi.M : \Pi\varphi{:}\mathtt{lctx}(\delta).\, A \text{ OBJ}} \qquad \frac{\Gamma, n : \mathtt{lvar}(\delta); \Delta \vdash M : A \text{ OBJ}}{\Gamma; \Delta \vdash \lambda n.M : \Pi n{:}\mathtt{lvar}(\delta).\, A \text{ OBJ}}$$

$$\frac{\Gamma; \Delta_0 \vdash H : A \text{ HEAD} \quad \Gamma; \Delta_1 \vdash S \gg A : a \cdot S'}{\Gamma; \Delta_0, \Delta_1 \vdash H \cdot S : a \cdot S' \text{ OBJ}} \qquad \frac{\Gamma, x : B; \Delta \vdash M : A \text{ OBJ}}{\Gamma; \Delta \vdash \lambda x.M : \Pi x{:}B.\, A \text{ OBJ}}$$

$$\Gamma; \Delta \vdash H : A \text{ HEAD}$$

$$\frac{}{\Gamma; n : A \vdash n : A \text{ HEAD}} \qquad \frac{x : A \in \Gamma}{\Gamma; \cdot \vdash x : A \text{ HEAD}} \qquad \frac{c : A \in \Sigma}{\Gamma; \cdot \vdash c : A \text{ HEAD}}$$

$$\Gamma; \Delta \vdash S \gg A : B$$

$$\frac{}{\Gamma; \cdot \vdash \epsilon \gg A : A} \qquad \frac{\Gamma; \epsilon \vdash M : A \text{ OBJ} \quad \Gamma; \Delta \vdash S \gg \{M/x\}^{A^-} B : C}{\Gamma; \Delta \vdash M :: S \gg \Pi x{:}A.\, B : C}$$

$$\frac{\Gamma \vdash \Delta \text{ LCTX}(\delta) \quad \Gamma; \Delta \vdash S \gg \{\Delta'/\varphi\}A : C}{\Gamma; \Delta \vdash \Delta' :: S \gg \Pi\varphi{:}\mathtt{lctx}(\delta).\, A : C}$$

$$\frac{\Gamma \vdash n \text{ NOM}(\delta) \quad \Gamma; \Delta \vdash S \gg \{n/n'\}A : C}{\Gamma; \Delta \vdash n :: S \gg \Pi n'{:}\mathtt{lvar}(\delta).\, A : C} \qquad \frac{\Gamma; \Delta_0 \vdash \sigma : \Delta \text{ SUB} \quad \Gamma; \Delta_1 \vdash S \gg A : B}{\Gamma; \Delta_0, \Delta_1 \vdash \sigma :: S \gg [\Delta]A : B}$$

$$\Gamma; \Delta_0 \vdash \sigma : \Delta_1 \text{ SUB}$$

$$\frac{}{\Gamma; \cdot \vdash \cdot : \cdot \text{ SUB}} \qquad \frac{\Gamma; \Delta_0 \vdash \sigma_0 : \Delta_0' \text{ SUB} \quad \Gamma; \Delta_1 \vdash \sigma_1 : \Delta_1' \text{ SUB}}{\Gamma; \Delta_0, \Delta_1 \vdash \sigma_0, \sigma_1 : \Delta_0', \Delta_1' \text{ SUB}}$$

$$\frac{\Gamma; \Delta \vdash M : A \text{ OBJ}}{\Gamma; \Delta \vdash M/n : (n : A) \text{ SUB}} \qquad \frac{}{\Gamma; \varphi \vdash \mathbf{id}(\varphi) : \varphi \text{ SUB}}$$

Fig. 4. Type checking canonical objects.

Substitution of Names. We write $\{n/n'\}X$ for the substitution of a name n for a name n' in the term X. The substitution is naive, capture avoiding, and terminating.

Substitution of Contexts. We write $\{\Delta/\varphi\}X$ for the substitution of a context Δ for a context variable φ in X. Substitutions for contexts variables are defined in a straightforward, capture-avoiding way, with two notable exceptions (note the different fonts),

$$\{\Delta/\varphi\}(\mathtt{id}(\varphi')) = id(\{\Delta/\varphi\}\varphi') \qquad \{\Delta/\varphi\}(\mathtt{dom}(\varphi')) = dom(\{\Delta/\varphi\}\varphi')$$

where the functions $id(\Delta)$ [4] and $dom(\Delta)$ constructs the identity substitution and domain. They are defined as:

$$
\begin{aligned}
dom(\cdot) &= \emptyset & id(\cdot) &= \cdot \\
dom(\Delta_0, \Delta_1) &= dom(\Delta_0) \cup dom(\Delta_1) & id(\Delta_0, \Delta_1) &= id(\Delta_0), id(\Delta_1) \\
dom(n : A) &= \{n\} & id(n : A) &= \eta(n : A)/n \\
dom(\varphi) &= \mathtt{dom}(\varphi) & id(\varphi) &= \mathtt{id}(\varphi)
\end{aligned}
$$

Substitution of Terms and Application of Substitutions. We present here the canonical version of XLF, which means that we need to define a hereditary substitutions for terms, to remain within the canonical fragment. Otherwise, substitution application may create redexes that are not part of any of our syntactic categories. Since we eventually wish to argue that any application of such a hereditary substitution is terminating, we define *erased types* $\tau ::= \bullet \mid \tau \to \tau \mid [\theta]\tau$ and *erased contexts* $\theta ::= \cdot \mid \theta, \theta \mid \bullet \mid n : \tau$. Type erasure is defined as follows:

$$
\begin{aligned}
(a \cdot S)^- &= \bullet & (\cdot)^- &= \cdot \\
(\Pi x : A.\, B)^- &= A^- \to B^- & (\Delta_0, \Delta_1)^- &= \Delta_0^-, \Delta_1^- \\
(\Pi \varphi : \mathtt{lctx}(\delta).\, A)^- &= \bullet \to A^- & (\varphi)^- &= \bullet \\
(\Pi n : \mathtt{lvar}(\delta).\, A)^- &= \bullet \to A^- & (n : A)^- &= n : A^- \\
([\Delta]A)^- &= [\Delta^-]A^-
\end{aligned}
$$

In XLF, substitution application is defined similarly to a standard hereditary substitution application on terms and spines. When the substitution reaches an application of a head to a spine, it will check if the head will be substituted, and if so, it will start reducing the head until it is atomic again. We need to define both substitution application to terms and substitutions simultaneously, since both are mutually recursive. As usual for hereditary substitution, the erased type will either decrease, or remain unchanged and the term decreases (this is easy to see; the only difficult case is if we transition from substitution to head reduction, but after one reduction step, we can see that it really holds).

$$
\begin{aligned}
\{M/x\}^\tau (x \cdot S) &= M@^\tau \{M/x\}^\tau S \\
\{M/x\}^\tau (H \cdot S) &= H \cdot \{M/x\}^\tau S \\
\{M/n, \sigma\}^{n : \tau, \theta} (n \cdot S) &= M@^\tau \{\sigma\}^\theta S \\
\{\sigma\}^\theta (H \cdot S) &= H \cdot \{\sigma\}^\theta S
\end{aligned}
$$

$$
\begin{aligned}
M@^\bullet \epsilon &= M \\
(\lambda x.M)@^{\tau_0 \to \tau_1} (N :: S) &= (\{N/x\}^{\tau_0})@^{\tau_1} S \\
(\lambda \varphi.M)@^{\bullet \to \tau} (\Delta :: S) &= (\{\Delta/\varphi\}M)@^\tau S \\
(\lambda n.M)@^{\bullet \to \tau} (n' :: S) &= (\{n'/n\}M)@^\tau S \\
\mathtt{box}(M)@^{[\theta]\tau} (\sigma :: S) &= (\{\sigma\}^\theta M)@^\tau S
\end{aligned}
$$

3 Meta Theory

XLF has canonical forms and conservatively extends LF. In the previous section we introduced hereditary substitutions for name, context, term, and linear substitutions variables. Here we show that when we substitute one entity for another that all types will be preserved. In the interest of brevity, let $\mathcal{J}$ be an intuitionistic judgment and $\mathcal{L}$ a linear judgment. All the theorems follow from standard induction proofs.

Theorem 1 (Substitution, Names). *Assume $\Gamma_0 \vdash n_0$ NOM(δ), then:*

1. *If $\Gamma_0, n_1 : lvar(\delta), \Gamma_1 \vdash \mathcal{J}$, then $\Gamma_0, \{n_0/n_1\}\Gamma_1 \vdash \{n_0/n_1\}\mathcal{J}$; and*
2. *If $\Gamma_0, n_1 : lvar(\delta), \Gamma_1; \Delta \vdash \mathcal{L}$, then $\Gamma_0, \{n_0/n_1\}\Gamma_1; \{n_0/n_1\}\Delta \vdash \{n_0/n_1\}\mathcal{L}$.*

Theorem 2 (Substitution, Context). *Assume $\Gamma_0 \vdash \Delta$ LCTX(δ), then:*

1. *If $\Gamma_0, \varphi : lvar(\delta), \Gamma_1 \vdash \mathcal{J}$, then $\Gamma_0, \{\Delta/\varphi\}\Gamma_1 \vdash \{\Delta/\varphi\}\mathcal{J}$; and*
2. *If $\Gamma_0, \varphi : lvar(\delta), \Gamma_1; \Delta' \vdash \mathcal{L}$, then $\Gamma_0, \{\Delta/\varphi\}\Gamma_1; \{\Delta/\varphi\}\Delta' \vdash \{\Delta/\varphi\}\mathcal{L}$.*

Theorem 3 (Substitution, Term). *Assume $\Gamma_0; \cdot \vdash M : A$ OBJ, then:*

1. *If $\Gamma_0, x : A, \Gamma_1 \vdash \mathcal{J}$, then $\Gamma_0, \{M/x\}^{A^-}\Gamma_1 \vdash \{M/x\}^{A^-}\mathcal{J}$; and*
2. *If $\Gamma_0, x : A, \Gamma_1; \Delta \vdash \mathcal{L}$, then $\Gamma_0, \{M/x\}^{A^-}\Gamma_1; \{M/x\}^{A^-}\Delta \vdash \{M/x\}^{A^-}\mathcal{L}$.*

Theorem 4 (Substitution, Linear Substitution). *Assume $\Gamma; \Delta_0 \vdash \sigma : \Delta_1$* SUB, *and $\Gamma; \Delta_1, \Delta \vdash \mathcal{L}$, then $\Gamma; \Delta_0, \Delta \vdash \{\sigma\}^{\Delta_1}\mathcal{L}$.*

It follows implicitly that XLF satisfies the weak normalization property, which means, that there exists a particular reduction order to reduce XLF terms to canonical form. Conversely, we have shown that is that for each type A inhabited by M, the form of M is uniquely determined.

Theorem 5 (Inversion). *We have:*

1. *If $\Gamma; \Delta \vdash M : a \cdot S$ OBJ, then $M = H \cdot S$ for some H and S.*
2. *If $\Gamma; \Delta \vdash M : \Pi x : A. B$ OBJ, then $M = \lambda x.M'$ for some x and M'.*
3. *If $\Gamma; \Delta \vdash M : \Pi\varphi : lctx(\delta). A$ OBJ, then $M = \lambda\varphi.M'$ for some φ and M'.*
4. *If $\Gamma; \Delta \vdash M : \Pi n : lvar(\delta). A$ OBJ, then $M = \lambda n.M'$ for some n and M'.*
5. *If $\Gamma; \Delta \vdash M : [\Delta']A$ OBJ, then $M = box(M')$ for some M'.*

4 Examples

In this section, we give some illustrative examples, on how to use XLF to encode languages, meta-theorems, and their proofs. As we assume that the reader may be familiar with Twelf, we will employ the same syntactic conventions. For example, we write {x : A} B for the dependent type $\Pi x : A. B$, and we will use the same syntax for the other dependent types for names and contexts. We will abbreviate this type with {x} B if the type A is inferable. Furthermore, in order not to get over-whelmed by syntax, all uppercase variables are assumed implicitly bound and their type can always be inferred. We only support the standard notation for application that will be internally translated into spine notation as follows: (H M1 M2) stands for $H \cdot (M_1 :: M_2 :: nil)$.

We want to remark, even though neither a computational interpretation of LF signatures as logic programs nor and algorithm for determining if such signatures correspond to real meta-theorems was given in this paper, it is still meaningful to represent meta-theorems as relations, and logic programs as their proofs. The totality proof has to be carried out on paper.

4.1 Multiplicative Additive Linear Logic

Our first example is classical Multiplicative-Additive Linear Logic (MALL) [2]. We give an adequate representation of MALL in XLF and encode the meta-proof that cut is admissible. The formulas, F, G, of MALL are atoms and negation of atoms (a and $a^\perp$), binary connectives "tensor" ($\otimes$), "par" ($\invamp$), "plus" ($\oplus$), and "and" ($\&$), with the units 1, $\perp$, 0, 1, and $\top$ respectively. An adequate encoding can be defined as follows. We declare a type for atoms: atom:type and a type prop:type for propositions. With a slight abuse of notation we declare multiple constants (separated by commas) of the same type.

```
at, ~at                   : atom -> prop.
tensor, plus, par, with : prop -> prop -> prop.
one, zero, bot, top       : prop.
```

We work with a one-sided sequent calculus, defined by the judgment $\vdash F_0, \ldots, F_n$. MALL does neither admit weakening nor contraction. In XLF, we represent this judgment as [h0 : conc F0, ..., h1 : conc Fn]pf, where conc : prop -> type and pf : type. Next, we give a selection of the MALL rules together with their representations.

$$\overline{\vdash a, a^\perp}$$

```
pf/ax : {h} {h'}
    [h : conc (at A), h' : conc (~at A)]pf.
```

$$\frac{\vdash \Gamma, F \quad \vdash \Delta, G}{\vdash \Gamma, \Delta, F \otimes G}$$

```
pf/tensor : {h}
    [G, h: conc F]pf -> [D, h: conc G]pf
    -> [G, Delta, h: conc (tensor F G)]pf.
```

$$\frac{\vdash \Gamma, F \quad \vdash \Gamma, G}{\vdash \Gamma, F \& G}$$

```
pf/with : {h}
    [G, h: conc F]pf -> [G, h: conc G]pf
    -> [G, h: conc (with F G)]pf.
```

$$\frac{\vdash \Gamma, F, G}{\vdash \Gamma, F \invamp G}$$

```
pf/par : {Gamma}{h}{h'}
    [G, h: conc F, h' : conc G]pf
    [G, h: conc (par F G)]pf.
```

$$\overline{\vdash \Gamma, \top}$$

```
pf/top : {h}
    [G, h: conc top]pf.
```

These rules illustrate important aspects of the representation. The first rule shows that we can force the context to have exactly two assumptions. The second rule requires that we split a context. Recall, that there is no need to merge contexts and that we can always assume the principal formula to be rightmost. The third rule illustrates how to duplicate a context. Finally, the fourth rule shows how to quantify over an arbitrary context.

The way the final rule is stated, it is not necessary adequate unless we are sure what form G has. This could be achieved by extending XLF with regular worlds, which would allow us to express that G must be in the world ($\exists N$: prop.conc N)*. Proposing such an extension, however, is beyond the scope of this paper.

We now show that cut is an admissible rule. The formulation of cut in MALL and the corresponding lemma is defined as,

$$\frac{\vdash \Gamma, F \quad \vdash \Delta, F^{\perp}}{\vdash \Gamma, \Delta}$$

```
cut : {h} dual F FDual
      -> [G, h: conc F] pf
      -> [D, h: conc FDual] pf
      -> [G, D]pf -> type.
```

where $F^{\perp}$ is the dual formula of F. Duality can be easily captured as a binary relation (and hence an XLF type family) relating two MALL formulas. We omitted some cases, because of space limitations.

```
dual : prop -> prop -> type.
dual/at : dual (at A) (~at A).     dual/~at : dual (~at A) (at A).
dual/tensor: dual F G -> dual H R -> dual (tensor F H) (par G R).
```

We can now start inhabiting the cut family with constants, where each constant represents one case of the proof. There are a total of 26 cases and each case takes about 2–3 lines (omitting several implicit quantifiers). Since the cut-rule is symmetric, each case appears twice. Here are a few selected cases.

```
- : cut H dual/at (pf/ax H H') D box(D {id(Delta), H'/H}).
- : cut H (dual/tensor P0 P1) (pf/tensor H D0 D1) (pf/par H E) Res
      <- ({h'} cut H P0 D0 (E H h') (R h'))
      <- cut H P1 D1 (R H) Res.
- : cut H P (pf/with H D0 D1) E (pf/with H R0 R1)
      <- cut H P D0 E R0
      <- cut H P D1 E R1.
```

The first is the axiom case with an atomic cut-formula. The second declaration depicts the an essential case with tensor as a cut-formula. And finally, the third declaration describes a commuting conversion.

On paper, we proved that under a suitable logic programming interpretation of XLF that the type family cut is total, since either the evidence for duality (or equivalently, the cut formula) decreases, or, it remain unchanged and one of the derivations decrease and the other remains unchanged.

4.2   Parallel λ-calculus

The final example is a parallel operational semantics for the λ-calculus. In order not to clutter the presentation too much, we present the calculus in its untyped form. Types can be easily added, for example through extrinsic typing. Proof terms are formed from variables, λ-abstractions, and application. When we evaluate, we always evaluate a closed term. To express the operational semantics, we use destinations that denote a location where an expression is executed, and from where the result can be recovered. We define the following judgments:

$$\frac{\text{eval } (e_1 \ e_2) @ d}{\exists d_1.\exists d_2.\text{eval } e_1 @ d_1 \otimes \text{eval } e_2 @ d_2 \otimes \text{fr } d \, d_1 \, d_2} evapp$$

$$\frac{\text{eval } (\lambda x.e) @ d}{\text{ret } (\lambda x.e) @ d} evlam \qquad \frac{\text{ret } (\lambda x.e) @ d_1 \otimes \text{ret } v @ d_2 \otimes \text{fr } d \, d_1 \, d_2}{\text{eval } [v/x]e @ d} evframe$$

The encoding of these rules in XLF is as follows where we declare # : type as the type of valid traces. We represent judgements as types, for example, "eval $e @ d$" is represented by ev E D (where E and D are the respective representations of e and v).

```
evapp :   {D} {h} {E1:exp} {E2:exp} {d:dest}
     ({d1 d2:dest} {h0 h1}
          [D, h0: ev E1 d1, h1: ev E2 d2, h: fr d d1 d2] #)
     -> [D, h: ev (app E1 E2) d] #.
evlam :   {D} {h} {E:exp -> exp} {d:dest}
     [D, h : ret (lam \x.E x) d] #
     -> [D, h : ev (lam \x. E x) d] #.
evframe: {D} {h h0 h1} {E:exp -> exp} {V: exp} {d1 d2 d:dest}
     [D, h: ev (E V) d] # ->
     [D, h0: ret (lam \x. E x) d1, h1: ret V d2, h: fr d d1 d2] #.
```

Note, that compared to the rules above, their representation appears to be up-side-down. It is easy to see that the representation is adequate.

Here is an example for a forward chaining evaluation of $(\lambda x.x) \ (\lambda x.x)$ using the rules, which we express using multi-set rewriting notation, disregarding the declaration of new destinations.

$$\begin{array}{ll}
\text{eval } (\lambda x.x) \ (\lambda x.x) @ d & \text{given} \\
\to \text{eval } \lambda x.x @ d_1, \text{eval } \lambda x.x @ d_2, \text{fr } d \, d_1 \, d_2 & \text{by evapp} \\
\to \text{ret } \lambda x.x @ d_1, \text{eval } \lambda x.x @ d_2, \text{fr } d \, d_1 \, d_2 & \text{by evlam} \\
\to \text{ret } \lambda x.x @ d_1, \text{ret } \lambda x.x @ d_2, \text{fr } d \, d_1 \, d_2 & \text{by evlam} \\
\to \text{eval } \lambda x.x @ d & \text{by evframe} \\
\to \text{ret } \lambda x.x @ d & \text{by evlam}
\end{array}$$

When we express this derivation formally, assuming that the context provides a destination d : dest, we obtain

```
\n.\u. evapp (\d1. \d2. (evlam (evlam (evframe (evlam u))))) :
{n}[n:ret (lam \x.x) d]# -> [n:ev (app (lam \x.x) (lam \x.x)) d]#
```

Next, we look at a simple meta-theorem that we wish to establish: Any expression that is returned from the evaluation is a λ-abstraction.

We begin the discussion with defining an invariant for the linear contexts. This invariant simply states that each return declaration provides a value. In XLF, this invariant is represented as inv:type, and the different cases as constructors.

```
inv/empty : [] inv.
inv/ret   : {d:dest} [D] inv -> [D, H: ret (lam \x. E x) d] inv.
inv/eval  : {d:dest} [D] inv -> [D, H: ev E d] inv.
inv/frame : {d}{d1}{d2} [D] inv -> [D, H: fr d d1 d2] inv.
```

Using this invariant, we can now formally state the value soundness theorem: If e evaluates to v (at destination d), then v is a value (also at destination d).

```
vs : {D0} {D1} ([D1] # -> [D0] #) -> [D0] inv -> [D1] inv -> type.
```

The two first arguments to vs should be read as input, and the third as output. To apply this theorem, simply instantiate D1 to n:ret v d and D0 to n:ev e d and provide an encoding of the trace and a proof that the invariant is satisfied.

To prove the theorem, we will need to prove three lemmas to establish that if the invariant holds for a context, it also holds for any sub-context. We only state the lemma in the case of ev assumptions, noting that the formulation and proofs of the other cases of fr and ret are similar.

```
inv-drop-ev : {d} {D} {H} [D, H : ev E d]inv -> [D]inv -> type.
```

Here, the first three arguments are inputs, while the last is an output. The proof goes by induction on the third argument (i.e. the proof of the invariant).

Returning to our main theorem, it is done by induction over the argument [D1]# -> [D0]# and consists of four cases. We give two representative cases.

```
vs/base : vs D D (\h. h) I I.
vs/evlam : {d:dest}
    vs (D0, H : ev (lam E) d) D1 (\t. evlam (TR t)) I0 I1
    <- inv-drop-ev d D0 H I0 I0'
    <- vs (D0, H : re (lam E) d) D1 TR (inv/ret I0') I1.
```

The vs/base case is straightforward. vs/evlam covers the case when we apply the theorem to an evaluation ending in evlam. We have that invariant I0 holds for the context D0, H : ev (lam E) D1. Before making the inductive call, we use lemma inv-drop-ev to establish the invariant I0' for the sub-context D0.

5   Conclusion and Further Work

In this paper, we develop the logical framework XLF, a conservative extension of LF with explicit linear contexts. We prove that XLF has all the desired meta-properties, and we give several examples that show how such a system can be used to represent and reason about linear systems. In future work, we plan to develop a proof assistant based on XLF.

Extending LF with linearity is not new. The Linear Logical Framework (LLF) [5] and its extension the Concurrent Logical Framework (CLF) [12] provide linear types. While they have been successfully used as representation languages, it has been difficult to design meta-logics for these frameworks. We hope to have alleviated this problem with the design of XLF. We leave a more detailed analysis to future work. XLF differs from LLF in that LLF works with one implicit ambient linear context whereas XLF supports explicit context quantification. In the case of CLF, it is worth noting that is also supports true concurrency. CLF provides a concurrency monad where terms are considered equivalent modulo interleavings. It appears that XLF can also be used to represent concurrent systems, however, a detailed study of concurrent equality in XLF is left to future work.

Another direction of research is the Hybrid Logical Framework (HLF) [11], which can represent linear systems, interesting properties of such systems, and prove these properties, all implemented as an extension of Twelf. Different from XLF, HLF is built on hybrid logic, not linear logic, and the linear connectives are defined in terms of hybrid logic.

While our modal type operator is inspired by that of traditional CMTT, it differs in that the context no longer needs to be ordered. Instead, we consider linear contexts up to exchange using names. In traditional CMTT, one cannot have exchange for contexts occurring in types, since the introduction form for box-types is a binder, and uses the position in the context to associate each variable in the context with the local variable used in the term. Further research about the connections to other systems with names and nominals, such as Abella [1] and Nominal Logic [9] is needed.

Acknowledgments. We would like to thank Daniel Gustafsson for invaluable feedback. This work is funded by the DemTech grant 10-092309 of the Danish Council for Strategic Research on Democratic Technologies.

References

1. Gacek, A.: The abella interactive theorem prover (system description). In: Armando, A., Baumgartner, P., Dowek, G. (eds.) IJCAR 2008. LNCS (LNAI), vol. 5195, pp. 154–161. Springer, Heidelberg (2008)
2. Girard, J.-Y.: Linear Logic: Its Syntax and Semantics. London Mathematical Society Lecture Note Series, pp. 1–42. Cambridge University Press, New York (1995)
3. Harper, R., Honsell, F., Plotkin, G.: A framework for defining logics. J. ACM (JACM) **40**(1), 143–184 (1993)

4. Nanevski, A., Pfenning, F., Pientka, B.: Contextual modal type theory. ACM Trans. Comput. Logic (TOCL) **9**(3), 23 (2008)
5. Pfenning, F., Cervesato, I.: A linear logical framework. In: Clarke, E. (ed.) 11th Annual Symposium on Logic in Computer Science – LICS 1996, pp. 264–275. IEEE Computer Society Press, New Brunswick, 27–30 July 1996. This work appeared as Preprint 1834 of the Department of Mathematics of Technical University of Darmstadt, Germany
6. Pfenning, F., Schürmann, C.: System description: twelf - a meta-logical framework for deductive systems. In: Ganzinger, H. (ed.) CADE 1999. LNCS (LNAI), vol. 1632, pp. 202–206. Springer, Heidelberg (1999)
7. Pientka, B.: A type-theoretic foundation for programming with higher-order abstract syntax and first-class substitutions. In: 35th Annual ACM Symposium on Principles of Programming Languages (POPL 2008), pp. 371–382. ACM (2008)
8. Pientka, B., Dunfield, J.: Beluga: a framework for programming and reasoning with deductive systems (system description). In: Giesl, J., Hähnle, R. (eds.) IJCAR 2010. LNCS, vol. 6173, pp. 15–21. Springer, Heidelberg (2010)
9. Pitts, A.M.: Nominal logic, a first order theory of names and binding. Inf. Comput. **186**(2), 165–193 (2003)
10. Poswolsky, A.: Functional Programming with Logical Frameworks: The Delphin Project. Ph.D. thesis, Yale University (2008)
11. Reed, J.: A hybrid logical framework. Ph.D. thesis, School of Computer Science, Carnegie Mellon University (2009)
12. Watkins, K., Cervesato, I., Pfenning, F., Walker, D.: A concurrent logical framework i: Judgments and properties. Technical report CMU-CS-02-101, Department of Computer Science, Carnegie Mellon University (2002)

Enhancing Search-Based QBF Solving by Dynamic Blocked Clause Elimination

Florian Lonsing[1]([⊠]), Fahiem Bacchus[2], Armin Biere[3], Uwe Egly[1], and Martina Seidl[3]

[1] Knowledge-Based Systems Group,
Vienna University of Technology, Vienna, Austria
florian.lonsing@tuwien.ac.at

[2] Department of Computer Science, University of Toronto, Toronto, Canada

[3] Institute for Formal Models and Verification, JKU Linz, Linz, Austria

Abstract. Among preprocessing techniques for quantified Boolean formula (QBF) solving, quantified blocked clause elimination (QBCE) has been found to be extremely effective. We investigate the power of dynamically applying QBCE in search-based QBF solving with clause and cube learning (QCDCL). This dynamic application of QBCE is in sharp contrast to its typical use as a mere preprocessing technique. In our dynamic approach, QBCE is applied eagerly to the formula interpreted under the assignments that have been enumerated in QCDCL. The tight integration of QBCE in QCDCL results in a variant of cube learning which is exponentially stronger than the traditional method. We implemented our approach in the QBF solver DepQBF and ran experiments on instances from the QBF Gallery 2014. On application benchmarks, QCDCL with dynamic QBCE substantially outperforms traditional QCDCL. Moreover, our approach is compatible with incremental solving and can be combined with preprocessing techniques other than QBCE.

1 Introduction

Quantified Boolean formulas (QBF) extend propositional logic with universal and existential quantifiers over propositional variables. QBFs potentially allow for exponentially more succinct encodings compared to plain propositional logic and provide a natural representation of applications which can be seen as two-player games [22] as found, e.g., in program synthesis or formal verification [2].

A typical representation of QBFs is *prenex conjunctive normal form (PCNF)*, consisting of a quantifier prefix and a propositional CNF. In the game-based QBF semantics a universal and an existential player play against each other. The players assign truth values to the respective variables in the order enforced by the quantifier prefix. The universal player aims to falsify the formula while the existential player aims to satisfy it. PCNF allows to detect more easily when

---

Supported by the Austrian Science Fund (FWF) under grants S11408-N23 and S11409-N23.

M. Davis et al. (Eds.): LPAR-20 2015, LNCS 9450, pp. 418–433, 2015.
DOI: 10.1007/978-3-662-48899-7_29

the universal player has won. Once the literals of one clause are all set to false, a conflict is detected and the universal player wins the current round of the game. In contrast, all clauses must be satisfied before we can detect a win for the existential player. This bias is reflected in the sizes of clauses (small) and cubes (large) derived by search-based QBF solvers with clause and cube learning (QCDCL) [8,16,28].

While the uniformity of a CNF representation simplifies reasoning [6], it also blurs information essential for solving [1]. As a remedy, structural solvers directly operate on non-CNF formulas [5,9,15]. Dual propagation approaches combine structural and CNF-based reasoning and consider both a CNF and a DNF representation at the same time. This can be done explicitly so that a DNF and a CNF encoding of a problem are solved independently in parallel [25] or it can be directly integrated in a solver [10,15,27]. However, these approaches require a structural formulation of the problem that is often not available.

Another option is preprocessing, e.g., [3,7,11,21,26] which uses alternative techniques to recover structural information from a CNF ϕ. The goal is to rewrite ϕ into a new CNF that is easier to solve. For most QBF solvers preprocessing is vital and has been integrated in most QBF-based solving tool chains. Modern SAT solvers go even further and interleave preprocessing and standard search. In this approach called *inprocessing* [13], preprocessing is applied in bounded fashion to the formula simplified by unit clauses derived during the search. Until this work inprocessing had not found its way into modern QBF solvers.

The QBF solver StruQS heuristically combines search-based solving and variable elimination [17]. The latter is a complete decision procedure potentially exponential in space. Its bounded variant is a powerful preprocessing technique [11]. Preprocessing, however, can only recover structural information before search. Structural solvers, on the other hand, can exploit such information during search. Hence in this work we investigate a tighter integration of *blocked clause elimination (QBCE)* [11] in QCDCL-based QBF solvers. While QBCE originally is a preprocessing technique applied to QBFs in CNF, here we apply it *dynamically* during the search process of QCDCL. This way, we leverage the power of QBCE as a technique to simulate structural reasoning on CNFs in QCDCL. In our dynamic approach, QBCE is applied to the CNF interpreted under the assignment that has currently been enumerated in QCDCL. We show that this tight integration of QBCE in QCDCL results in cube learning that is exponentially stronger than its traditional variant. Dynamic QBCE also influences clause learning in that clauses identified as redundant by QBCE are not used to produce learned clauses in the current search context. In addition to dynamic QBCE we also investigate inprocessing in a QBF solver using QBCE.

We implemented inprocessing based on QBCE and dynamic QBCE in the QCDCL-based QBF solver DepQBF. On application benchmarks from the QBF Gallery 2014, QCDCL with dynamic QBCE *substantially* outperforms traditional QCDCL in terms of solved instances, run time and backtracks. We also observed a performance gain with inprocessing. We report on the details of our implementation of dynamic QBCE. Since QBCE is applied frequently during the search in QCDCL, sophisticated data structures are necessary to limit the computational costs. Dynamic QBCE is compatible with incremental solving and is extensible in that it can be combined with preprocessing techniques other than QBCE.

2   Preliminaries

We consider QBFs in *prenex conjunctive normal form* (PCNF). A QBF $\Pi.\psi$ in PCNF consists of a prefix Π and a matrix ψ. The prefix Π has the form $Q_1 X_1 Q_2 X_2 \ldots Q_n X_n$ with disjoint variable sets X_i and $Q_i \in \{\forall, \exists\}$. Furthermore, $Q_i \neq Q_{i+1}$ and $\mathsf{var}(\Pi) = X_1 \cup \ldots \cup X_n$. We consider only closed QBFs: the matrix ψ of a QBF $\Pi.\psi$ contains only variables that occur in Π. The matrix ψ is a propositional formula in conjunctive normal form, i.e., a conjunction of clauses. A *clause* (*cube*) is a disjunction (conjunction) of literals. A *literal* is either a variable x or a negated variable $\bar{x}$. The negation of a literal l is denoted by $\bar{l}$. If convenient, we consider clauses and cubes as sets of literals. The variable of a literal is denoted by $\mathsf{var}(l)$ where $\mathsf{var}(l) = x$ if $l = x$ or $l = \bar{x}$. The quantifier $\mathsf{Q}(\Pi, l)$ of a literal l is Q_i if $\mathsf{var}(l) \in X_i$. Let $\mathsf{Q}(\Pi, l) = Q_i$ and $\mathsf{Q}(\Pi, k) = Q_j$, then $l \leq_\Pi k$ iff $i \leq j$.

A set of literals $A = \{l_1, \ldots, l_n\}$ is called *assignment* of the QBF $\Pi.\psi$ if $\{\mathsf{var}(l_i) \mid l_i \in A\} \subseteq \mathsf{var}(\Pi)$ and for any $l_i, l_j \in A$ with $l_i \neq l_j$, $\mathsf{var}(l_i) \neq \mathsf{var}(l_j)$. By $\phi[A]$ we denote the QBF ϕ *under assignment* A, i.e., for $l \in A$, all clauses containing l are removed, all occurrences of $\bar{l}$ are deleted, and $\mathsf{var}(l)$ is removed from the prefix. The empty matrix is satisfiable, the matrix containing the empty clause is unsatisfiable. If the matrix of $\phi[A]$ is empty, then A is a *satisfying assignment* (written as $\phi[A] = \mathsf{T}$). If the matrix of $\phi[A]$ contains the empty clause, then A is a *falsifying assignment* (written as $\phi[A] = \mathsf{F}$). For a cube $C = (l_1 \wedge \ldots \wedge l_n)$, the set $\{l_1, \ldots, l_n\}$ is the assignment defined by C. We write $\phi[C]$ to denote ϕ under the assignment defined by C. A closed QBF $\Pi.\psi$ with $Q_1 = \exists$ (resp. $Q_1 = \forall$) is satisfiable iff $\Pi.\psi[\{x\}]$ or (resp. and) $\Pi.\psi[\{\bar{x}\}]$ is satisfiable where $x \in X_1$. Two PCNFs ϕ and ϕ' are *satisfiability-equivalent*, written as $\phi \equiv_{sat} \phi'$, if and only if ϕ is satisfiable whenever ϕ' is satisfiable.

We introduce the *Q-resolution calculus* as a proof system which underlies search-based QBF solving with clause and cube learning [8,14,16,28].

Definition 1 (Q-Resolution Calculus). *Let* $\phi = \Pi.\psi$ *be a PCNF. The rules of the* Q-resolution calculus (QRES) *are as follows.*

$$\frac{C_1 \cup \{p\} \qquad C_2 \cup \{\bar{p}\}}{C_1 \cup C_2} \quad \begin{array}{l} \text{if } \{x, \bar{x}\} \not\subseteq (C_1 \cup C_2),\ \bar{p} \notin C_1,\ p \notin C_2 \\ \text{and either} \\ (1)\ C_1, C_2 \text{ are clauses and } \mathsf{Q}(\Pi, p) = \exists \text{ or} \\ (2)\ C_1, C_2 \text{ are cubes and } \mathsf{Q}(\Pi, p) = \forall \end{array} \quad (res)$$

$$\frac{C \cup \{l\}}{C} \quad \begin{array}{l} \text{if } \{x, \bar{x}\} \not\subseteq (C \cup \{l\}) \text{ and either} \\ (1)\ C \text{ is a clause, } \mathsf{Q}(\Pi, l) = \forall, \\ \quad l' <_\Pi l \text{ for all } l' \in C \text{ with } \mathsf{Q}(\Pi, l') = \exists \text{ or} \\ (2)\ C \text{ is a cube, } \mathsf{Q}(\Pi, l) = \exists, \\ \quad l' <_\Pi l \text{ for all } l' \in C \text{ with } \mathsf{Q}(\Pi, l') = \forall \end{array} \quad (red)$$

$$\frac{}{C} \quad \begin{array}{l} \text{if } \{x, \bar{x}\} \not\subseteq C \text{ and either} \\ (1) \ C \text{ is a clause and } C \in \psi \text{ or} \\ (2) \ C \text{ is a cube and } \phi[C] = \emptyset \end{array} \qquad (init)$$

Note that $\phi[C] = \emptyset$ in case (2) of rule *init* means that the matrix of $\phi[C]$ is empty. We write $\Pi.\psi \vdash C$ to denote that a clause or cube C is derivable from the PCNF $\Pi.\psi$ by rules *init*, *red*, and *res*. In a derivation of a clause (cube), the rules *init*, *red*, and *res* operate only on clauses (cubes). Q-resolution of clauses [14] is a generalization of propositional resolution, which is given by rules *init* and *res* when applied to clauses. Q-resolution of cubes was introduced in the context of solving satisfiable PCNFs [8,16,28]. Applications of rule *red* to clauses (cubes) are called *universal (existential) reduction*. We write $UR(C)$ ($ER(C)$) to denote the clause (cube) resulting from universal (existential) reduction of C. The PCNF $UR(\phi)$ is obtained by universal reduction of all clauses in the PCNF ϕ.

QRES is sound and refutationally complete for PCNFs [8,14,16,28]. The empty clause (cube) $C = \emptyset$ is derivable from a PCNF ϕ if and only if ϕ is unsatisfiable (satisfiable). A derivation of the empty clause (cube) from ϕ is a *clause (cube) resolution proof* of ϕ. The clausal variant of rule *res* is the basis for the definition of blocked clauses which is as follows.

Definition 2 (Blocked Clause). *A literal l with $Q(\Pi, l) = \exists$ in a clause $C \in \psi$ of a QBF $\phi = \Pi.\psi$ is a blocking literal if for all $C' \in \psi$ with $\bar{l} \in C'$, a literal l' with $l' \leq_\Pi l$ exists such that $l', \bar{l}' \in C \cup (C' \setminus \{\bar{l}\})$. A clause is blocked if it contains a blocking literal.*

Note that blocking literal l in Definition 2 must be existential whereas literals $l', \bar{l}'$ can be existential or universal. *Blocked clause elimination (QBCE)* [11] removes blocked clauses from a PCNF ϕ until completion and takes time polynomial in the size of ϕ. The resulting PCNF is satisfiability-equivalent to ϕ.

3 Search-Based QBF Solving with Learning

In order to present our approach of dynamically applying QBCE in search-based QBF solvers, which results in a powerful variant of cube learning, we review the basic concepts of search-based QBF solving with learning.

Search-based QBF solving is based on a QBF-specific variant of the DPLL algorithm [4]. Similar to conflict-driven clause learning (CDCL) in SAT solving [23], search-based QBF solving has been equipped with clause and cube learning [8,16,28], called QCDCL. We briefly describe QCDCL based on the pseudo code shown in Fig. 1.

In QCDCL, assignments to the variables in a given input PCNF $\phi = \Pi.\psi$ are successively generated. Initially, the current assignment A is empty. During a run, ϕ is interpreted under A and $\phi[A]$ is simplified in a QBF-specific variant of *Boolean constraint propagation (QBCP)* in function qbcp. Additionally, in QBCP universal reduction according to rule *red* is applied to all clauses $C \in \phi[A]$, resulting in the PCNF $UR(\phi[A])$ with potentially shortened clauses $UR(C) \subseteq C$.

```
Result qcdcl (PCNF φ)
  Result R = UNDEF;
  Assignment A = ∅;
  while (true)
    /* Simplify under A. */
    (R,A) = qbcp(φ,A);
    if (R == UNDET)
      /* Decision making. */
      A = assign_dec_var(φ,A);
    else
      /* Backtracking. */
      /* R == UNSAT/SAT */
      B = analyze(R,A);
      if (B == INVALID)
        return R;
      else
        A = backtrack(B);
```

Fig. 1. Pseudo code of QCDCL.

Assignment A is extended based on the detection of *unit* and *pure literals* in $UR(\phi[A])$. A clause $UR(C[A]) = (l)$, with $UR(C[A]) \in UR(\phi[A])$ containing the single literal l and $Q(\Pi, l) = \exists$, is *unit* in $UR(\phi[A])$. Given such a unit clause, A is extended to $A := A \cup \{l\}$ and C is recorded as the *antecedent clause* of the assignment $\{l\}$. A literal l is *pure* in $UR(\phi[A])$ if $\bar{l}$ does not occur in $UR(\phi[A])$. Given a pure literal l, A is extended to $A := A \cup \{l\}$ if $Q(\Pi, l) = \exists$ and to $A := A \cup \{\bar{l}\}$ if $Q(\Pi, l) = \forall$. Simplifications of $\phi[A]$ and unit and pure literal detection are always applied until completion in QBCP. Assignments l_i in $A = \{l_1, \ldots, l_n\}$ are ordered chronologically.

If $\phi[A] \neq F$ and $\phi[A] \neq T$, then the satisfiability of $\phi[A]$ is still undetermined (R == UNDET). Some variable from the leftmost quantifier block of $\phi[A]$ is selected and tentatively assigned a value, thus extending A. Making tentative assignments is also called *decision making*.

If $\phi[A] = F$ then $\phi[A]$ contains a clause C so that $UR(C[A]) = \emptyset$ is empty. If $\phi[A] = T$, then $\phi[A]$ reduces to the empty matrix under A. In either case, the satisfiability of $\phi[A]$ has been determined (R == UNSAT or R == SAT). Assignment A is analyzed based on whether $\phi[A] = F$ or $\phi[A] = T$. A subset $B \subseteq A$ of assignment A is identified and retracted during backtracking. The run proceeds with the new, current assignment A obtained by backtracking. QCDCL generates assignments which have the following properties.

Definition 3 (QCDCL Assignment). *Given a QBF $\phi = \Pi.\psi$. Let assignment $A = A' \cup A''$ where A' are variables assigned in decision making and A'' are variables assigned by unit/pure literal detection. A is a QCDCL assignment if (1) for a maximal $l \in A'$ with $\forall l' \in A' : l' \leq_\Pi l$ it holds that $\forall x <_\Pi l : x \in \text{var}(A)$ and (2) all $l \in A''$ are unit/pure in $\phi[A']$ after applying QBCP until completion.*

Clause and cube learning is carried out in function **analyze**. If $\phi[A] = F$ then by rules *init*, *red*, and *res* the clause C where $UR(C[A]) = \emptyset$ is resolved with antecedent clauses to derive a learned clause C'.

If $\phi[A] = T$, then a new learned cube is derived similarly to clause learning. However, rule *init* is special for cube learning in that cubes to be resolved later must be first derived from satisfying assignments. In contrast to that, clauses present in the input PCNF ϕ can be simply selected by rule *init*. QBCP is also applied to learned clauses and cubes. Related to unit clauses, a cube $ER(C[A]) = (l)$ containing the single literal l with $Q(\Pi, l) = \forall$ is *unit* under A and existential reduction. Existential reduction is also applied in QBCP. Given a unit cube

$ER(C[A]) = (l)$, A is extended to $A := A \cup \{\bar{l}\}$ and C is recorded as the *antecedent cube* of the assignment $\{l\}$. In cube learning, resolution by rule *res* is applied to cubes derived by rule *init* and to antecedent cubes.

Learned clauses (cubes) C' are constructed so that $UR(C'[A])$ $(ER(C'[A]))$ is unit after backtracking. QCDCL terminates if the empty learned clause (cube) $C' = \emptyset$ is derived (B == INVALID). The derivations of learned clauses (cubes) up to $C' = \emptyset$ are a clause (cube) resolution proof of ϕ. The application of the rules of QRES is driven by the assignments generated in QCDCL.

In practice, the set θ of learned clauses is added conjunctively to $\phi = \Pi.\psi$ and we have $\phi \equiv_{sat} \Pi.(\psi \wedge \bigwedge_{C \in \theta} C)$. The set γ of learned cubes is added disjunctively to $\phi = \Pi.\psi$ and we have $\phi \equiv_{sat} \Pi.(\psi \vee (\bigvee_{C \in \gamma} C))$. These equivalence are due to the soundness of QRES. In general, a formula $\phi' = \Pi'.\psi'$ with $\psi' = \bigvee_{C \in \gamma} C$ in *prenex disjunctive normal form* can be derived by rule *init* so that $\phi \equiv_{sat} \phi'$ [8].

Preprocessing [3,7,11,21,26] aims at transforming the input PCNF ϕ into a simplified PCNF ϕ' with $\phi \equiv_{sat} \phi'$ so that ϕ' is solved faster than ϕ. In QCDCL, preprocessing can be applied once to ϕ before entering the while-loop (Fig. 1).

Inprocessing [13] combines preprocessing techniques and formula simplification under assignments which were fixed during a run of QCDCL. An assignment to a variable x is fixed if a unit clause (cube) $C = (l)$ with $var(l) = x$ is learned. Inprocessing can be applied after QBCP each time a unit clause (cube) is learned.

4 Improved Cube Learning by Dynamic QBCE

We take a closer look at cube learning by QRES. It is well known that in the worst case an exponential number of cubes must be derived by rule *init* even on PCNFs with a simple syntactic structure. The PCNFs in the following example are hard for QCDCL based on QRES. We develop a generalization of QRES which allows to solve these PCNFs easily by tightly integrating QBCE in QCDCL.

Example 1. Let $\Phi(n) = \exists z_1, z_1' \forall u_1 \exists y_1, \ldots, \exists z_n, z_n' \forall u_n \exists y_n. \bigwedge_{i=1}^{n} [C_0(i) \wedge C_1(i) \wedge C_2(i)]$, where $C_0(i) = (u_i \vee \bar{y}_i) \wedge (\bar{u}_i \vee y_i)$, $C_1(i) = (z_i \vee u_i \vee \bar{y}_i) \wedge (z_i' \vee \bar{u}_i \vee y_i)$, and $C_2(i) = (\bar{z}_i \vee \bar{u}_i \vee \bar{y}_i) \wedge (\bar{z}_i' \vee u_i \vee y_i)$ be a family of satisfiable PCNFs.

Clauses in $C_0(i)$ encode the equivalence of u_i and y_i. In general, PCNFs of the form $\Psi(n) = \forall u_1 \exists y_1, \ldots, \forall u_n \exists y_n. \bigwedge_{i=1}^{n} C_0(i)$ are typical examples where every cube resolution proof requires an exponential number of applications of rule *init* [12,16,18]. Since $\Psi(n)$ is a subformula of $\Phi(n)$, this also holds for every cube resolution proof of $\Phi(n)$. No clause is blocked in $\Phi(n)$, hence QBCE alone cannot solve $\Phi(n)$, in contrast to $\Psi(n)$ [12].

Consider $n = 1$ and $\Phi(n) = \exists z_1, z_1' \forall u_1 \exists y_1.(u_1 \vee \bar{y}_1) \wedge (\bar{u}_1 \vee y_1) \wedge (z_1 \vee u_1 \vee \bar{y}_1) \wedge (z_1' \vee \bar{u}_1 \vee y_1) \wedge (\bar{z}_1 \vee \bar{u}_1 \vee \bar{y}_1) \wedge (\bar{z}_1' \vee u_1 \vee y_1)$. By rule *init*, we derive $C_0 = (\bar{z}_1 \wedge \bar{z}_1' \wedge \bar{u}_1 \wedge \bar{y}_1)$ and $C_1 = (\bar{z}_1 \wedge \bar{z}_1' \wedge u_1 \wedge y_1)$. By existential reduction we get $C_2 = ER(C_0) = (\bar{z}_1 \wedge \bar{z}_1' \wedge \bar{u}_1)$ and $C_3 = ER(C_1) = (\bar{z}_1 \wedge \bar{z}_1' \wedge u_1)$. By resolving C_2 and C_3 we get $C_4 = (\bar{z}_1 \wedge \bar{z}_1')$ and finally $C_5 = ER(C_4) = \emptyset$.

The PCNFs $\Phi(n)$ in Example 1 can be solved by preprocessing by eliminating subsumed clauses and QBCE. In practice, however, preprocessing might not be fully applicable to QBF-based workflows involving advanced techniques such as, e.g., incremental QBF solving. Hence we aim at improving QCDCL with clause and cube learning also in the absence of preprocessing.

The application of rule *init* to derive cubes from satisfying assignments is also called *model generation* [8]. Model generation derives cubes C from a PCNF $\phi = \Pi.\psi$ such that $\phi[C] = \emptyset$. The PCNFs $\Phi(n)$ in Example 1 only have cube resolution proofs in QRES whose size is exponential in n since an exponential number of cubes must be derived by rule *init* [12,16,18]. Hence the run time of QCDCL with cube learning by QRES scales exponentially in n.

In the following, we generalize model generation by rule *init* by relaxing the condition $\phi[C] = \emptyset$. This way, we obtain a variant of QRES for cube learning which is exponentially stronger than the traditional variant from Definition 1. The stronger calculus allows for cube resolution proofs of the PCNFs $\Phi(n)$ in Example 1 whose size is polynomial in n.

To show the soundness of generalized model generation, we first show that a cube C which contains only variables assigned in decision making in QCDCL is derivable by QRES if $\phi[C]$ is satisfiable. To this end, we introduce the notion of cubes obtained from assignments generated in QCDCL.

Definition 4 (QCDCL Cube). *Given a QBF $\phi = \Pi.\psi$. The QCDCL cube C of QCDCL assignment A is defined by $C = (\bigwedge_{l \in A} l)$. Then $C = C' \cup C''$ where C' is the maximal subset of C such that $X_1 \cup \ldots \cup X_{i-1} \subset \text{var}(C')$ and $C' \cap X_i \neq \emptyset$. The literals in C' are the first $|C'|$ consecutive variables of Π which are assigned, i.e., C' contains all the variables in C assigned in decision making.[1] The literals in C'' are assigned due to pure and unit literal detection and may occur anywhere in Π starting from X_{i+1}. For QCDCL cube C we further define $\text{dec}(C) = C'$ and $\text{der}(C) = C''$.*

Lemma 1. *Given the satisfiable PCNF $\phi = \Pi.\psi$ with $|\text{var}(\Pi)| = n$ and a QCDCL cube C with $\text{dec}(C) = C$. If $\phi[C]$ is satisfiable, then $\phi \vdash C$.*

Proof. We argue that $\phi \vdash C$ by induction over $k = n - m$ where $m = |C|$ and the rules of QRES shown in Definition 1.

If $k = 0$, then $\phi \vdash C$ by rule *init*. Consider $k > 0$. Let $l \in C$ with $\text{var}(l) \in X_i$ be maximal in C w.r.t. $<_\Pi$. Let $h, \bar{h} \notin C$ and $\text{var}(h) \in X_i$ if $X_i \backslash \text{var}(C) \neq \emptyset$ and $\text{var}(h) \in X_{i+1}$ otherwise.

Suppose that $\phi[C]$ is satisfiable. If $\mathsf{Q}(\Pi, h) = \forall$ then both $\phi[C \cup \{h\}]$ and $\phi[C \cup \{\bar{h}\}]$ are satisfiable. By induction hypothesis it holds that $\phi \vdash C \cup \{h\}$ and $\phi \vdash C \cup \{\bar{h}\}$, so $\phi \vdash C$ by the application of rule *res* (cf. Theorem 1 in [20]).

If $\mathsf{Q}(\Pi, h) = \exists$ then at least one of $\phi[C \cup \{h\}]$ and $\phi[C \cup \{\bar{h}\}]$ is satisfiable. W.l.o.g. assume that $\phi[C \cup \{h\}]$ is satisfiable. Then by induction hypothesis it holds that $\phi \vdash C \cup \{h\}$, so $\phi \vdash C$ by the application of rule *red*. $\square$

---

[1] C' can also contain literals assigned by pure/unit literal detection, but as they are left to the maximal decision variable in the prefix, we treat them like decision variables.

Definition 5 (Generalized Model Generation). *Given a PCNF ϕ and a QCDCL assignment A according to Definition 3. If $\phi[A]$ is satisfiable, then the QCDCL cube $C = (\bigwedge_{l \in A} l)$ is obtained by* generalized model generation.

Condition $\phi[C] = \emptyset$ in case (2) of rule *init* is a special case of the condition in Definition 5 that $\phi[A]$ is satisfiable to obtain C. In general $\phi \nvdash C$ in QRES.

Example 2. Given a satisfiable PCNF $\phi = \exists x_1, x_2 \forall u_1 \exists x_3.(x_1 \vee u_1 \vee \bar{x}_3) \wedge (x_1 \vee u_1 \vee x_3) \wedge (\bar{x}_1 \vee \bar{x}_2 \vee \bar{u}_1 \wedge x_3) \wedge (x_2 \vee \bar{x}_3)$, where no variable is pure initially. Let $A = \{x_1\}$ by decision making. Then u_1 becomes pure and $\phi[A] = \exists x_2, x_3.(\bar{x}_2 \vee x_3) \wedge (x_2 \vee \bar{x}_3)$ is satisfiable under $A = \{x_1, u_1\}$, so $C = (\bigwedge_{l \in A} l) = (x_1 \wedge u_1)$ is obtained by generalized model generation. However, $\phi \nvdash C$ since rule *res* is not applicable as this would eliminate u_1. Further, any cube $C' \supset C$ derived by rule *init* contains also a literal of x_2 which cannot be reduced by rule *red*.

Theorem 1. *Given PCNF $\phi = \Pi.\psi$ and a QCDCL cube C obtained from ϕ by generalized model generation. Then it holds that $\Pi.\psi \equiv_{sat} \Pi.(\psi \vee C)$.*

Proof (Sketch). Let $C = C' \cup C''$ as defined in Definition 4 with $C' = \mathsf{dec}(C)$ and $C'' = \mathsf{der}(C)$. Recall that $\phi[C]$ is satisfiable, because C is obtained by generalized model generation.

First, assume that $\phi[C']$ is unsatisfiable. The literals in C'' are assigned according to pure and unit literal detection in $\phi[C']$ which is sound. Therefore, these assignments do not change the satisfiability status of the formula. Hence, $\phi[C']$ has to be satisfiable.

According to Lemma 1, it holds that $\Pi.\psi \vdash C'$ and due to the soundness of QRES it holds that $\Pi.\psi \equiv_{sat} \Pi.(\psi \vee C')$. Because of subsumption, it holds that $\Pi.\psi \equiv_{sat} \Pi.(\psi \vee (C' \wedge C''))$. $\qquad\square$

Corollary 1. *By Theorem 1, a cube C obtained from PCNF $\Pi.\psi$ by generalized model generation can be used as a learned cube in QCDCL.*

Definition 6. *Let $\phi = \Pi.\psi$ be a PCNF. The* Q-resolution calculus with generalized model generation (QRES-GMG) *is obtained by replacing condition $\phi[C] = \emptyset$ in case (2) of rule* init *in Definition 1 by the condition that $\phi[C]$ is satisfiable.*

QRES-GMG can be used as a proof system underlying QCDCL to derive learned clauses and cubes. For generalized model generation as part of rule *init*, it is necessary to check whether $\phi[A]$ is satisfiable based on the current assignment A enumerated in QCDCL. Since $\phi[A]$ is a PCNF in general, such check is as hard as solving the original PCNF ϕ (i.e., PSPACE-complete).

In order to combine QRES-GMG and QCDCL in practice, we apply QBCE *dynamically* to $\phi[A]$, i.e., with respect to the current assignment A. If all clauses in $\phi[A]$ are blocked then QBCE reduces $\phi[A]$ to the empty matrix, thus showing that $\phi[A]$ is satisfiable in time which is *polynomial* in the size of $\phi[A]$. This way, we apply QBCE as an incomplete decision procedure inside QCDCL to efficiently check if $\phi[A]$ is satisfiable. To this end, in general any sound decision procedure can be applied. However, QBCE is appealing since it only removes clauses and can be implemented using data structures which fit in the QCDCL framework.

Generalized model generation in QRES-GMG is related to *sign abstraction* (Proposition 7 in [16]). Based on a previously derived learned cube C', sign abstraction allows to detect whether $\phi[A]$ is satisfiable in polynomial time based on the sets of clauses satisfied by C' and by A. However, our approach to checking $\phi[A]$ based on dynamic QBCE is independent from previously learned cubes.

In contrast to QRES, the PCNFs $\Phi(n)$ in Example 1 have short cube resolution proofs in QRES-GMG. Hence QCDCL with QRES-GMG and dynamic QBCE allows for more powerful cube learning than with QRES.

Example 3 (Continues Example 1). For $n = 2$ consider $\Phi(n) = \exists z_1, z_1' \forall u_1 \exists y_1, \exists z_2,$ $\exists z_2' \forall u_2 \exists y_2 . \mathcal{C}_0(1) \wedge \mathcal{C}_1(1) \wedge \mathcal{C}_2(1) \wedge \mathcal{C}_0(2) \wedge \mathcal{C}_1(2) \wedge \mathcal{C}_2(2)$. We solve $\Phi(n)$ by QCDCL with QRES-GMG and dynamic QBCE. We start with the empty assignment $A = \emptyset$. No clause is blocked in the PCNF $\Phi(n)[A]$ and hence rule *init* is not applicable. By decision making we assign variables from left to right in prefix ordering and extend A to $A = A \cup \{\bar{z}_1, \bar{z}_1'\}$. The clauses in the subformula $(\mathcal{C}_0(1) \wedge \mathcal{C}_1(1))[A] = (u_1 \vee \bar{y}_1) \wedge (\bar{u}_1 \vee y_1)$ of $\Phi(n)[A]$ are blocked since all clauses in $\mathcal{C}_2(1)[A]$ are satisfied under A.

Before making further assignments, the PCNF $\Phi(n)$ is simplified to $\Phi(n)' = \exists z_2, z_2' \forall u_2 \exists y_2 . \mathcal{C}_0(2) \wedge \mathcal{C}_1(2) \wedge \mathcal{C}_2(2)$ under A and QBCE. No clause is blocked in $\Phi(n)'[A]$ and A is extended to $A \cup \{\bar{z}_1, \bar{z}_1', \bar{z}_2, \bar{z}_2'\}$. Like before, clauses in the subformula $(\mathcal{C}_0(2) \wedge \mathcal{C}_1(2))[A] = (u_2 \vee \bar{y}_2) \wedge (\bar{u}_2 \vee y_2)$ of $\Phi(n)'[A]$ are blocked since all clauses in $\mathcal{C}_2(2)[A]$ are satisfied under A. We have $\Phi(n)[A] = \emptyset$ under $A = \{\bar{z}_1, \bar{z}_1', \bar{z}_2, \bar{z}_2'\}$ and QBCE. By rule *init* of QRES-GMG, we derive the learned cube $C = (\bar{z}_1 \wedge \bar{z}_1' \wedge \bar{z}_2 \wedge \bar{z}_2')$ and finally the empty cube $C' = ER(C) = \emptyset$ by existential reduction, after which QCDCL terminates.

Note that on the PCNFs $\Phi(n)$ from Example 1, for *any* value of n QCDCL with QRES-GMG based on dynamic QBCE learns *exactly* one cube by rule *init* which is reduced to the empty cube immediately. Hence in this special case the actual run time of QCDCL depends on how efficiently QBCE is applied to $\Phi(n)$.

5 Integrating Dynamic QBCE in QCDCL

We implemented QCDCL with clause and cube learning based on QRES-GMG in our solver DepQBF.[2] DepQBF is a QCDCL-based solver which originally relies on QRES [8,16,28]. For efficient generalized model generation in QRES-GMG, we apply QBCE dynamically as illustrated by Example 3.

QBCE is carried out eagerly as part of QBCP (function qbcp in Fig. 1). After the current assignment A has been extended in QBCP by unit and pure literal detection, QBCE is applied to $\phi[A]$ until completion. If all clauses in $\phi[A]$ are blocked, then a cube is learned by rule *init* in QRES-GMG. Otherwise, A is further extended by decision making and again QBCP including QBCE is applied. All clauses containing a literal of a variable x may be blocked in $\phi[A]$ and x may be removed from the prefix of $\phi[A]$. Hence in decision making variables are selected from the left end of the prefix of $\phi[A]$ simplified under A and QBCE.

---

[2] http://lonsing.github.io/depqbf/.

Clause learning works as in traditional QCDCL based on QRES. Clauses currently blocked with respect to A are ignored when it comes to the detection of unit clauses and empty clauses in QBCP. Consequently, such blocked clauses are not used to derive learned clauses. However, since QBCE preserves unsatisfiability, QCDCL will eventually find a clause resolution proof of ϕ if ϕ is unsatisfiable even if dynamic QBCE effectively removes blocked clauses. Hence we apply QBCE in a fully dynamic way where QCDCL with clause and cube learning operates on the PCNF $\phi[A]$ simplified under A and QBCE. QBCE is applied only to clauses in the input PCNF ϕ, not to learned ones.

5.1   Witness Clauses for Efficient Dynamic QBCE

Dynamic QBCE is part of QBCP and hence is applied frequently in QCDCL. Our implementation of dynamic QBCE relies on watched data structures like QBCP [6]. In the following, let A be the current assignment in QCDCL.

Dynamic QBCE is carried out based on a *working set* of pairs (C, l) of a clause C and a literal $l \in C$ to be checked whether l is a blocking literal in C. The working set is fully processed as part of QBCP. Variable assignments made in QBCP might trigger further applications of QBCE, which causes the working set to be filled based on watched data structures as described in the following.

For each clause C in the input PCNF ϕ a *notification list* is maintained. The notification list of C contains pairs (C', l') of clauses C' and an existential literal $l' \in C'$ such that $\bar{l}' \in C$ and C is a witness that $l' \in C'$ is not a blocking literal by Definition 2 in C' under A. The witness C is neither blocked nor satisfied under A. If C becomes either blocked or satisfied, then the pair (C', l') is put in the working set to be checked whether $l' \in C'$ is a blocking literal in C'.

Each variable v has two lists L_v and $L_{\bar{v}}$ containing clauses $C \in \phi$ with a positive and negative literal of v, respectively. Each clause C in L_v or $L_{\bar{v}}$ is a witness that some other clause $C' \in \phi$ is not blocked with a blocking literal $l \in C'$, $\bar{l} \in C$, and $\mathsf{var}(l) = v$. If v is assigned true (false), then previously non-satisfied witness clauses $C \in L_v$ ($C \in L_{\bar{v}}$) are satisfied. All pairs (C', l') in the notification list of the now satisfied witness C are put in the working set.

Watched data structures based on witness clauses allow to carry out dynamic QBCE precisely when a witness clause becomes blocked or satisfied under A. Superfluous checks of Definition 2 are entirely avoided.

5.2   Dynamic QBCE Limits

The input PCNF ϕ may contain clauses with a large number of literals or variables whose literals appear in a large number of clauses (called *occurrences*). In these cases, the performance of dynamic QBCE may deteriorate with respect to run time and memory footprint since the working set and the notification lists become prohibitively large. To control the computational costs of dynamic QBCE, we implemented a limit max_lits on the size $|C|$ (i.e. number of literals) of a clause and a limit max_occs on the number of occurrences of variables.

For all pairs (C, l) ever put in the working set it holds that $|C| \leq max\_lits$. Clauses C whose size $|C|$ exceeds max_lits are permanently ignored in dynamic QBCE. Additionally, the size $|C'|$ of each occurrence C' with $\bar{l} \in C'$ of variable var(l) must not exceed max_lits. This way, literals of variables with occurrences larger than max_lits are never checked as potential blocking literals. Limit max_lits allows to avoid inspecting large clauses when checking Definition 2.

For all pairs (C, l) ever put in the QBCE working set the number of occurrences of literal $\bar{l}$ does not exceed max_occs. This way, no more than max_occs occurrences of var$(\bar{l})$ have to be inspected when checking whether $l \in C$ is a blocking literal in C by Definition 2.

QCDCL based on QRES-GMG is sound in the presence of limits max_lits and max_occs. For generalized model generation, clauses ignored in dynamic QBCE due to the limits must be satisfied under the current assignment A.

In our implementation of dynamic QBCE we used limits of $max\_lits = 50$ and $max\_occs = 50$ which we determined empirically.

6   Experiments

We evaluated our implementation of QCDCL with QRES-GMG based on dynamic QBCE in the solver DepQBF. To this end, we compared three variants of DepQBF. The plain version of DepQBF (no-qbce) is based on traditional QCDCL with QRES. As a first step towards dynamic QBCE, we implemented QBCE as inprocessing in DepQBF (qbce-inp) where the input PCNF ϕ is simplified by QBCE only with respect to fixed assignment due to learned *unit clauses* and *unit cubes*. This variant of DepQBF is still based on QRES. Finally, we implemented QCDCL with QRES-GMG based on fully dynamic QBCE (qbce-dyn) as presented in Sect. 5. To focus on dynamic QBCE, we used the linear quantifier ordering given by the prefix of the input PCNF ϕ and hence disabled advanced analysis of variable dependencies [19] in all variants of DepQBF.

Further, we consider the solvers GhostQ (ghostq) and RAReQS (rareqs) which were both among the winning solvers of the QBF Gallery 2014 and which are publicly available. All experiments reported in the following were run on an AMD Opteron 6238 at 2.6 GHz under 64-bit Linux with time and memory limits of 1800 s and 7 GB. We use the benchmarks in the applications set of the QBF Gallery consisting of 735 formulas.[3] We do not consider structural solvers because the benchmarks are not available in a structural, non-CNF format.

First, we consider the original applications set without preprocessing. The results are shown in Table 1 and Fig. 2. The combinations of QBCE and QCDCL in qbce-inp and qbce-dyn considerably outperform DepQBF (no-qbce) by solved instances and run time. Moreover, qbce-dyn performs best among the variants of DepQBF and outperforms RAReQS, an expansion-based solver. Whereas the variants of DepQBF did not run out of memory, RAReQS did on 115 instances.

In order to evaluate the impact of preprocessing on solver performance, we applied the preprocessor Bloqqer [11] prior to solving. The results are shown in

---

[3] http://qbf.satisfiability.org/gallery.

Table 1. Total solved instances, solved unsatisfiable, and solved satisfiable ones of the original applications set of the QBF Gallery 2014 without preprocessing. Reported times are total run times including time outs. Running out of memory is counted as a time out.

Solver	Solved	Unsat	Sat	Time
qbce-dyn	441	222	219	573,142
rareqs	414	272	142	611,742
qbce-inp	360	161	199	735,073
ghostq	347	166	181	752,950
no-qbce	278	128	150	880,485

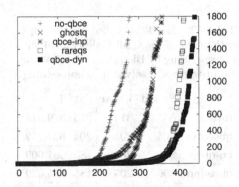

Fig. 2. Sorted run times (y-axis) of instances (x-axis) related to Table 1.

Table 2 and Fig. 4. RAReQS and DepQBF (no-qbce) benefit from preprocessing. RAReQS ran out of memory on 34 instances. DepQBF (no-qbce) solves as many formulas as qbce-inp. Among the variants of DepQBF, qbce-dyn still solves the largest number of instances. However, preprocessing has an overall negative effect on qbce-dyn as only 405 instances are solved with preprocessing compared to 441 instances without preprocessing (Tables 1 and 2 are comparable since no instance was solved by preprocessing).

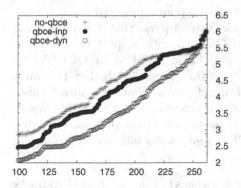

Fig. 3. Related to Table 1: sorted numbers of backtracks (log_{10} scale y-axis) by DepQBF, qbce-inp, and qbce-dyn on 262 instances solved by all three (x-axis).

Preprocessing by Bloqqer, which includes QBCE among other techniques, changes the formula structure such that dynamic QBCE (qbce-dyn) does not pay off any more. Although RAReQS solves 142 instances more, DepQBF with dynamic QBCE solves 25 instances not solved by RAReQS.

In additional experiments, we found out that the actual selection of techniques applied for preprocessing by Bloqqer has a considerable impact on the number of instances solved by RAReQS and DepQBF with dynamic QBCE (qbce-dyn). Limited preprocessing is beneficial for qbce-dyn whereas it has a negative impact on RAReQS compared to full preprocessing (Table 2). We preprocessed the applications set by Bloqqer using only QBCE and expansion of universal variables [3]. On this preprocessed set, RAReQS solves only 471 instances compared to 547 with full preprocessing (Table 2). In contrast to that, qbce-dyn solves 463 instances compared to 405 with full preprocessing. Hence limited preprocessing reduces the gap between

Table 2. Like Table 1, but on the applications set of the QBF Gallery 2014 with preprocessing by Bloqqer prior to solving. No instance was solved in preprocessing.

Solver	Solved	Unsat	Sat	Time
rareqs	547	314	233	379,916
qbce-dyn	405	201	204	624,719
no-qbce	390	205	185	651,909
qbce-inp	390	205	185	655,329
ghostq	350	176	174	739,294

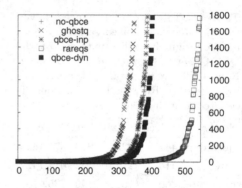

Fig. 4. Sorted run times (y-axis) of instances (x-axis) related to Table 2.

RAReQS and qbce-dyn from 142 (Table 2) to eight solved instances. This is due to the fact that RAReQS performs worse with limited preprocessing than with full preprocessing.

In addition to solved instances, the benefits of dynamic QBCE are also reflected by backtracks in QCDCL. DepQBF with dynamic QBCE backtracks less frequently than the other variants of DepQBF. Figure 3 illustrates the numbers of backtracks on those 262 instances which were solved by all three variants of DepQBF. The average (median) number of backtracks is 160,597 (3,119) by no-qbce, 133,919 (1,793) by qbce-inp, and 66,372 (350) by qbce-dyn. We made similar observations when comparing only qbce-inp and qbce-dyn.

A comparison of no-qbce and qbce-dyn in Table 3 shows that dynamic QBCE results in fewer *redundant* backtracks in QCDCL with respect to resolution proofs. For example, when solving an unsatisfiable PCNF ϕ by QCDCL, we consider backtracks from satisfiable subcases (i.e., R == SAT in Fig. 1) redundant because these backtracks result in learned cubes. However, learned cubes are irrelevant to the clause resolution proof of ϕ produced by QCDCL. On unsatisfiable instances, the numbers of redundant backtracks by no-qbce and qbce-dyn differ by a factor of 24 (54,078 vs. 2,199). These results indicate the potential

Table 3. Related to Table 1: average run time in seconds (T) and number of backtracks resulting from satisfiable (SB) and unsatisfiable (UB) subcases in QCDCL (i.e. R == UNSAT/SAT in Fig. 1) on instances solved by both DepQBF without QBCE (no-qbce) and DepQBF with dynamic QBCE (qbce-dyn). Statistics are shown based on all solved instances (265) and separately for solved satisfiable (141) and unsatisfiable (124) ones.

	ALL (265)			SAT (141)			UNSAT (124)		
	T	SB	UB	T	SB	UB	T	SB	UB
no-qbce	181	59,044	103,080	81	63,412	17,356	295	54,078	200,557
qbce-dyn	80	22,805	42,969	51	40,927	15,979	114	2,199	73,660

benefits of generalized model generation in QRES-GMG for deriving learned cubes to prune the search space tackled by QCDCL. On satisfiable instances, the difference in redundant backtracks is less pronounced (17,356 vs. 15,979).

We also ran experiments on the preprocessing and QBFLIB tracks of the QBF Gallery 2014. Dynamic QBCE (qbce-dyn) does not pay off on the massively preprocessed instances in the preprocessing track. There, RAReQS solves the largest number of instances (107) and qbce-dyn solves 95 compared to 101 solved by no-qbce and qbce-inp. On the QBFLIB track, both qbce-inp (108 solved) and qbce-dyn (104) clearly outperform no-qbce (83) and RAReQS (80), where GhostQ solves 139 instances. On the QBFLIB track with full preprocessing by Bloqqer, the performance of qbce-dyn (131 solved), no-qbce (130), and qbce-inp (129) is close to each other, where RAReQS solves 134 instances.

7 Conclusion

We presented dynamic blocked clause elimination (QBCE) in QCDCL-based QBF solvers as an approach to overcome the bias towards unsatisfiability in solving that is due to the CNF structure of QBFs. Thereby, QBCE is applied eagerly to the QBF interpreted under the assignments generated in QCDCL. Dynamic QBCE results in a variant of cube learning by QRES-GMG in QCDCL which is exponentially stronger than the traditional variant.

On application instances, we observed a considerable performance boost with dynamic QBCE—despite its computational overhead—in terms of solved instances, run time, and backtracks. Without preprocessing, our approach outperforms expansion-based QBF solving. Depending on the selection of techniques, preprocessing may have a negative impact on the performance of dynamic QBCE since formula structure is blurred. However, dynamic QBCE may improve the performance of QCDCL solvers in workflows involving incremental solving, which cannot yet be combined with full-scale preprocessing. Dynamic QBCE is compatible with incremental solving, in contrast to expansion-based solving.

Our approach is extensible in that techniques other than QBCE like bounded variable elimination or expansion can be applied dynamically for generalized model generation. Further, dynamic QBCE can be readily combined with any variant of Q-resolution like QU-resolution [24] and long-distance resolution [28] as part of rule *res* in QRES-GMG. We also aim at combining our approach with full generation of proofs and certificates.

References

1. Ansótegui, C., Gomes, C.P., Selman, B.: The achilles' heel of QBF. In: AAAI/IAAI, pp. 275–281. AAAI Press/The MIT Press (2005)
2. Benedetti, M., Mangassarian, H.: QBF-based formal verification: experience and perspectives. JSAT **5**(1–4), 133–191 (2008)
3. Bubeck, U., Kleine Büning, H.: Bounded universal expansion for preprocessing QBF. In: Marques-Silva, J., Sakallah, K.A. (eds.) SAT 2007. LNCS, vol. 4501, pp. 244–257. Springer, Heidelberg (2007)

4. Davis, M., Logemann, G., Loveland, D.W.: A machine program for theorem-proving. Commun. ACM **5**(7), 394–397 (1962)
5. Egly, U., Seidl, M., Woltran, S.: A solver for QBFs in negation normal form. Constraints **14**(1), 38–79 (2009)
6. Gent, I.P., Giunchiglia, E., Narizzano, M., Rowley, A.G.D., Tacchella, A.: Watched data structures for QBF solvers. In: Giunchiglia, E., Tacchella, A. (eds.) SAT 2003. LNCS, vol. 2919, pp. 25–36. Springer, Heidelberg (2004)
7. Giunchiglia, E., Marin, P., Narizzano, M.: sQueezeBF: an effective preprocessor for QBFs based on equivalence reasoning. In: Strichman, O., Szeider, S. (eds.) SAT 2010. LNCS, vol. 6175, pp. 85–98. Springer, Heidelberg (2010)
8. Giunchiglia, E., Narizzano, M., Tacchella, A.: Clause/term resolution and learning in the evaluation of quantified boolean formulas. JAIR **26**, 371–416 (2006)
9. Goultiaeva, A., Bacchus, F.: Exploiting circuit representations in QBF solving. In: Strichman, O., Szeider, S. (eds.) SAT 2010. LNCS, vol. 6175, pp. 333–339. Springer, Heidelberg (2010)
10. Goultiaeva, A., Seidl, M., Biere, A.: Bridging the gap between dual propagation and CNF-based QBF solving. In: Järvisalo, M., Van Gelder, A. (ed.) DATE, pp. 811–814. ACM (2013)
11. Heule, M., Järvisalo, M., Lonsing, F., Seidl, M., Biere, A.: Clause elimination for SAT and QSAT. JAIR **53**, 127–168 (2015)
12. Janota, M., Grigore, R., Marques-Silva, J.: On QBF proofs and preprocessing. In: McMillan, K., Middeldorp, A., Voronkov, A. (eds.) LPAR-19 2013. LNCS, vol. 8312, pp. 473–489. Springer, Heidelberg (2013)
13. Järvisalo, M., Heule, M.J.H., Biere, A.: Inprocessing rules. In: Gramlich, B., Miller, D., Sattler, U. (eds.) IJCAR 2012. LNCS, vol. 7364, pp. 355–370. Springer, Heidelberg (2012)
14. Kleine Büning, H., Karpinski, M., Flögel, A.: Resolution for quantified boolean formulas. Inf. Comput. **117**(1), 12–18 (1995)
15. Klieber, W., Sapra, S., Gao, S., Clarke, E.: A non-prenex, non-clausal QBF solver with game-state learning. In: Strichman, O., Szeider, S. (eds.) SAT 2010. LNCS, vol. 6175, pp. 128–142. Springer, Heidelberg (2010)
16. Letz, R.: Lemma and model caching in decision procedures for quantified boolean formulas. In: Egly, U., Fermüller, C. (eds.) TABLEAUX 2002. LNCS (LNAI), vol. 2381, pp. 160–175. Springer, Heidelberg (2002)
17. Pulina, L., Tacchella, A.: A structural approach to reasoning with quantified boolean formulas. In: IJCAI, pp. 596–602 (2009)
18. Ramesh, A., Becker, G., Murray, N.V.: CNF and DNF considered harmful for computing prime implicants/implicates. JAIR **18**(3), 337–356 (1997)
19. Samer, M., Szeider, S.: Backdoor sets of quantified boolean formulas. JAR **42**(1), 77–97 (2009)
20. Samulowitz, H., Bacchus, F.: Dynamically partitioning for solving QBF. In: Marques-Silva, J., Sakallah, K.A. (eds.) SAT 2007. LNCS, vol. 4501, pp. 215–229. Springer, Heidelberg (2007)
21. Samulowitz, H., Davies, J., Bacchus, F.: Preprocessing QBF. In: Benhamou, F. (ed.) CP 2006. LNCS, vol. 4204, pp. 514–529. Springer, Heidelberg (2006)
22. Schaefer, T.J.: On the complexity of some two-person perfect-information games. J. Comput. Syst. Sci. **16**(2), 185–225 (1978)
23. Silva, J.P.M., Sakallah, K.A.: GRASP: a search algorithm for propositional satisfiability. IEEE Trans. Comput. **48**(5), 506–521 (1999)

24. Van Gelder, A.: Contributions to the theory of practical quantified boolean formula solving. In: Milano, M. (ed.) CP 2012. LNCS, vol. 7514, pp. 647–663. Springer, Heidelberg (2012)
25. Van Gelder, A.: Primal and dual encoding from applications into quantified boolean formulas. In: Schulte, C. (ed.) CP 2013. LNCS, vol. 8124, pp. 694–707. Springer, Heidelberg (2013)
26. Van Gelder, A., Wood, S.B., Lonsing, F.: Extended failed-literal preprocessing for quantified boolean formulas. In: Cimatti, A., Sebastiani, R. (eds.) SAT 2012. LNCS, vol. 7317, pp. 86–99. Springer, Heidelberg (2012)
27. Zhang, L.: Solving QBF by combining conjunctive and disjunctive normal forms. In: Dustdar, S., Schall, D., Skopik, F., Juszczyk, L., Psaier, H. (eds.) AAAI/IAAI, pp. 143–150. AAAI Press (2006)
28. Zhang, L., Malik, S.: Conflict driven learning in a quantified boolean satisfiability solver. In: ICCAD, pp. 442–449. ACM/IEEE Computer Society (2002)

Reasoning About Loops Using Vampire in KeY

Wolfgang Ahrendt, Laura Kovács, and Simon Robillard[✉]

Chalmers University of Technology, Gothenburg, Sweden
simon.robillard@chalmers.se

Abstract. We describe symbol elimination and consequence finding in the first-order theorem prover Vampire for automatic generation of quantified invariants, possibly with quantifier alternations, of loops with arrays. Unlike the previous implementation of symbol elimination in Vampire, our work is not limited to a specific programming language but provides a generic framework by relying on a simple guarded command representation of the input loop. We also improve the loop analysis part in Vampire by generating loop properties more easily handled by the saturation engine of Vampire. Our experiments show that, with our changes, the number of generated invariants is decreased, in some cases, by a factor of 20. We also provide a framework to use our approach to invariant generation in conjunction with pre- and post-conditions of program loops. We use the program specification to find relevant invariants as well as to verify the partial correctness of the loop. As a case study, we demonstrate how symbol elimination in Vampire can be used as an interface for realistic imperative languages, by integrating our tool in the KeY verification system, thus allowing reasoning about loops in Java programs in a fully automated way, without any user guidance.

1 Introduction

Reasoning about the (partial) correctness of programs with loops requires loop invariants. Typically, loop invariants are provided by the user as annotations to the program, see e.g. [2,5,14]. Providing such annotations requires a considerable amount of work by highly qualified personnel and often makes program analysis prohibitively expensive. Therefore, automation of invariant generation is invaluable in making program analysis scale to large, realistic examples.

In [11], the symbol elimination method for generating invariants was introduced. The approach uses first-order theorem proving, in particular the Vampire prover [12]. Symbol elimination allows the generation of quantified invariants, possibly with quantifier alternations, for programs with unbounded data structures, such as arrays. While experiments of invariant generation in Vampire show that symbol elimination generates non-trivial invariants, the initial implementation [7] of program analysis and invariant generation in Vampire has various disadvantages: it can only be used with programs written in C, the number of

This work was partially supported by the Wallenberg Academy Fellowship 2014, the Swedish VR grant D0497701 and the Austrian research project FWF S11409-N23.

© Springer-Verlag Berlin Heidelberg 2015
M. Davis et al. (Eds.): LPAR-20 2015, LNCS 9450, pp. 434–443, 2015.
DOI: 10.1007/978-3-662-48899-7_30

generated invariants is too large, and generating relevant invariants did not take into account the program specification. Moreover, the process of invariant generation was not integrated, nor evaluated in a verification framework, making it hard to assess the quality and practical impact of invariant generation by symbol elimination. In this paper we address these limitations, as follows.

We provide a new and fully automated tool for invariant generation, by using symbol elimination in Vampire (Sect. 2). To this end, we re-implemented program analysis and invariant generation in Vampire. Our implementation is fully compatible with the most recent development changes in Vampire. It is designed to be independent of any particular programming language: inputs to our tool are program loops written in a simple guarded command language. We also improved program analysis in Vampire by generating loop properties that are more easily handled by the saturation engine of Vampire. We also show that symbol elimination can be used not only to produce invariants, but also as a (incomplete) direct method to prove the correctness of the loop. Our work provides an alternative approach to Hoare-style loop verification and cancels the need for explicitly stated invariants as program annotations.

Reasoning about real programming languages poses several challenges, e.g. using machine integers instead of mathematical ones or reasoning about out-of-bound array accesses. In order to showcase the relevance of our implementation in real applications, we integrated our approach to loop reasoning in Vampire into the KeY verification system [2], thus allowing automatic reasoning about loops in Java programs (Sect. 3). We experimentally evaluate invariant generation in Vampire on realistic examples (Sect. 4).

The main advantage of our tool comes with its full automation for generating invariants, possibly with quantifier alternations. Unlike [8,9], where user-given invariant templates are used, we require no user guidance and infer first-order invariants with arbitrary quantifiers. Contrary to [4], we do not use specialized abstract domains, but use saturation theorem proving to generate quantified invariants. Theorem proving, in the form of SMT solving, is also used in [13] to automatically compute loop invariants, however only with universal quantifiers.

Our implementation of invariant generation in Vampire[1] required 3000 lines of C++ code. The integration of Vampire with KeY required about 1000 lines of Java code.

2   Invariant Generation in Vampire

In this section, we describe our tool to generate quantified loop invariants in a fully automatic manner. Our work uses symbol elimination and consequence finding in Vampire and extends Vampire with a new framework for reasoning about loops. Compared to the earlier implementation [7] of invariant generation in Vampire, our tool is independent of the language in which the loops are expressed, simplifies symbol elimination in saturation theorem proving,

---

[1] available at www.cse.chalmers.se/~simrob.

and provides various ways to generate a relevant set of loop invariants. The overall workflow of our tool is given in Fig. 1 and detailed below.

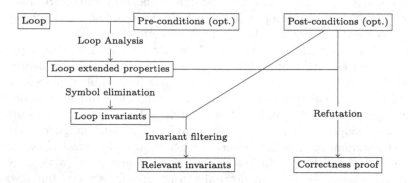

Fig. 1. Loop reasoning in Vampire.

Input. Inputs to our tool are loops with nested conditionals, written in a simple guarded command language. Optionally, pre- and post-conditions can also be specified. We use standard arithmetical function symbols $+, -, \cdot, \div$ and predicate symbols $\leq, \geq$.

Loops may contain scalar variables and arrays ranging over Boolean values and (unbounded) integers. We write $A[p]$ to mean (an access to) the array element at position p in the array A. We describe loops by a *loop condition* and an ordered collection of *guarded assignments*; the loop condition is a quantifier-free Boolean formula over program variables. A guarded assignment is a pair of a *guard* (also a Boolean formula) and a collection of assignments. In our setting, a guarded assignment cannot contain two assignments to the same scalar variable v. If two array assignments $A[i] := e$ and $A[j] := e'$ occur in a guarded assignment, the condition $i \neq j$ is added to the guard. Figure 2 gives an example of a loop using the syntax supported by our tool.

Loop Semantics. We assume basic knowledge about program states and transition relations. We use n to denote the upper bound on the number of loop iterations and write σ_0 and σ_n to respectively speak about the initial and final state of the loop. For any loop iteration i we have $0 \leq i \leq n$. Given a program state σ_i describing the value of each program variable after a loop iteration i, the semantics of the loop is as follows. If the loop condition is valid in σ_i, the first guarded assignment whose guard is valid is executed: its assignments are applied simultaneously to σ_i. This way the state σ_{i+1} corresponding to the loop iteration $i+1$ is obtained from σ_i. For example, executing the guarded assignment `true -> x = 0; y = x;` in a state where $x = 1$ holds, yields a state in which $y = 1$. If the loop condition is not valid, or if none of the guards hold, σ_i becomes the final state of the loop σ_n.

Loop Assertions and Invariants. For each loop variable v, we denote by v_{init} the value of v at the initial state σ_0 of the loop. Those symbols belong to the language of *loop assertions* denoted by $\mathcal{L}_{asrt}$. An invariant is a formula that uses symbols from $\mathcal{L}_{asrt}$ and is valid for any state σ_i. The pre- and post-conditions of the loops are formulas in $\mathcal{L}_{asrt}$ that are required to hold at σ_0 and σ_n, respectively. Note that assertions, including invariants, may be universally and existentially quantified.

Extended Loop Properties. For every (scalar and array) variable v, we introduce a function $v^{(i)}$ denoting the values of v at states σ_i corresponding to loop iterations i. Note that $v^{(0)}$ is v_{init}. We call $v^{(i)}$ an *extended expression* and denote the language of loop properties with extended expressions by $\mathcal{L}_{extd}$. Formulas in $\mathcal{L}_{extd}$ that are valid at any loop iteration are called *extended loop properties*. Compared to [7], we simplified $\mathcal{L}_{extd}$ as we do not use extended expressions describing loop iteration properties or update predicates over arrays. This simplification brought a significant performance increase to using symbol elimination for invariant generation (see Sect. 4).

```
requires (k == 0);
ensures forall int p,  (0 <= p & p < n)
                    ==> (A[p] >= B[p]
                     & A[p] >= C[p]
                     & (A[p] == B[p] | A[p] == C[p]));
while (k < n) do
  :: B[k] >= C[k] -> A[k] = B[k]; k = k + 1;
  :: true         -> A[k] = C[k]; k = k + 1;
od
```

Fig. 2. Example of an input to our tool. This example loop is composed of two guarded assignments, computes the maximum of elements in arrays B and C at every position and writes it in the corresponding position in the array A. The program specification is given by the pre- (**requires**) and post-conditions (**ensures**).

Loop Analysis. In the first step of our invariant generation procedure, we perform simple static analysis to generate extended loop properties. These formulas express (i) monotonicity properties of scalars; (ii) the transition relation of the loop by translating the guarded assignments into logical formulas; (iii) update properties of the array, and (iv) the validity of the loop condition at arbitrary loop iterations. For the loop in Fig. 2, the following formula describing a monotonically increasing behavior of k is one of the generated properties: $(\forall i)(0 \leq i < n \implies k^{(i+1)} = k^{(i)} + 1)$.

Compared to [7], we simplified and improved loop analysis in Vampire. In particular, array update properties expressing last updates to array positions and extended properties using loop conditions are now formulated in a way that makes them easier to handle by a first-order theorem prover, for example by introducing fewer Skolem functions. With these improvements, we generate a significantly smaller number of invariants, without loss of interesting properties (see Sect. 4).

Symbol Elimination. While the properties in $\mathcal{L}_{extd}$ are valid at arbitrary loop iterations, they are not yet invariants as they use symbols that are not in $\mathcal{L}_{asrt}$ (they use extended expressions). The next step in our invariant generation process is to eliminate the symbols that are not in $\mathcal{L}_{asrt}$, by generating formulas that only use symbols from $\mathcal{L}_{asrt}$ and are logical consequences of the properties in $\mathcal{L}_{extd}$. To this end we use the prover to perform symbol elimination and generate invariants in $\mathcal{L}_{asrt}$. For more details on symbol elimination we refer to [11].

Invariant Filtering. As a result of symbol elimination, a set of loop invariants is computed. While [7] returned all invariants discovered during symbol elimination, we note that not all generated invariants are relevant to the user when proving the partial correctness of the loop. In our work, we provide additional options to control the process of invariant generation, as follows. If the user provides a loop post-condition ϕ, we add an invariant filtering step to symbol elimination by proving $\neg\psi \wedge I_1 \wedge \ldots \wedge I_k \implies \phi$, where ψ is the loop condition and $I_1, \ldots, I_k$ are the invariants generated so far by symbol elimination. If proving this implication succeeds, the invariants that were effectively used in the proof are reported to the user.

Recall that invariants are logical consequences of extended loop properties, hence the loop post-condition can be proved directly from the extended loop properties. We therefore also extended loop analysis in Vampire by proving partial correctness of loops using extended loop properties, without the need for generating loop invariants by symbol elimination.

Output. We provide three options regarding the output of our tool. It can consist of (i) the set of all invariants generated by symbol elimination, (ii) the set of relevant invariants after filtering using the loop specification, or (iii) a partial correctness proof of the loop.

3   Integration with the KeY System

In this section we describe the integration of our invariant generation method to the KeY verification system. We discuss the modularity afforded by our tool and its applicability to realistic examples.

Dynamic Logic. KeY [2] is a deductive verifier for functional correctness properties of Java source code. It uses dynamic logic (DL), a modal logic for reasoning about programs. DL extends first-order logic with the modality $[p]\phi$, where p is a program and ϕ is another DL formula; $[p]\phi$ is true in a state from which running the program p, in case of termination, results in a state where ϕ is true.

Symbolic Execution. KeY uses symbolic execution. For that, DL is extended by "explicit substitutions", called updates. During the symbolic execution of a program p, the effects of p are *gradually*, from the front, turned into updates, and applied to each other. After some proof steps, an intermediate proof node may look like $\Gamma \vdash \mathcal{U}[p']\phi$, where a certain prefix of p has turned into update

$\mathcal{U}$, representing the effects so far, while a "remaining" program p' is yet to be executed. Note that most proofs branch over case distinctions, usually triggered by Boolean expressions in the source code. The semantics of the $\Gamma \vdash \mathcal{U} \dots$ part of a sequent is in many ways close to those of a guarded assignment in Vampire's programming model. Γ can be understood in the same way as Vampire's guards, while updates and Vampire's assignments share the same semantics of simultaneous application. We therefore use symbolic execution to perform the translation of Java programs to Vampire's guarded command language, as follows. Given a program p containing a loop, we apply symbolic execution to all instructions preceding the loop, leading to a sequent:

$$\Gamma \vdash \mathcal{U}[\texttt{while (se) }\{b\};p']\phi$$

where se is a *side effect-free* Java expression[2]. As a step towards employing Vampire, we launch a separate KeY proof at this point, starting from the sequent: $\Gamma, se' \vdash \mathcal{U}\mathcal{V}[b]\psi$. Here, se' is the result of applying $\mathcal{U}$ to se, $\mathcal{V}$ is an anonymizing update [3] meant to remove information on variables modified by the loop body b, and ψ is an uninterpreted predicate. This side proof is not meant to prove anything, but only to carry out symbolic execution of *any* iteration (hence $\mathcal{V}$) of the loop body b. Since ψ is uninterpreted, the side proof started with this sequent cannot be completed; however, assuming that they do not themselves contain an unannotated loop, instructions of b can be symbolically executed. We are then left with a proof tree containing one or more open nodes, all of which have the form: $\Gamma' \vdash \{v_1 := e_1; \dots; v_k := e_k\}[]\psi$. Each of these nodes corresponds to a possible path of symbolic execution, which is transformed into a guarded assignment:

```
Gamma' -> v1 = e1; ... ; vk = ek;
```

The translation of Java programs to Vampire's model has limitations however. It is for example not yet possible to fully express heap-related properties in Vampire. Another limitation is the lack of support for unannotated loops within b.

Integration. If the user is satisfied with delegating the proof of correctness of the loop to Vampire, when the Vampire proof succeeds, it is possible to simply complete the main KeY proof by applying a dedicated axiomatic rule. If more transparency is desired, it is of course possible to import the invariants produced by Vampire (with or without invariant filtering) into KeY and use these invariants in the KeY inference rule normally used with user-annotated invariants. KeY will however need to prove that the invariants generated by Vampire are indeed invariants.

4   Experimental Results

We evaluated our tool on 19 challenging array benchmarks taken from academic papers [6,7] and the C standard library. Our benchmarks are listed in Table 1.

---

[2] More complex Boolean expressions are transformed away by KeY rules.

The program `absolute` computes the absolute value of every element in an array, whereas `copy`, `copyOdd` and `copyPositive` copy (some) elements of an array to another. The example `find` searches for the position of a certain value in an array, returning -1 if the value is absent. The program `findMax` locates the maximum in an unsorted array. The examples `init`, `initEven`, and `initPartial` initialize (some) array elements with a constant, whereas `initNonConstant` sets the value of array elements to a value depending on array positions. `inPlaceMax` replaces every negative value in an array by 0, and `max` computes the maximum of two arrays at every position. `mergeInterleave` interleaves the content of two arrays, whereas `partition` copies negative and non-negative values from a source array into two different destination arrays. `reverse` copies an array in reverse order, and `swap` exchanges the content of two arrays. Finally, `strcpy` and `strlen` are taken from the standard C library. Each benchmark contains a loop together with its specification. Our benchmarks are available at the URL of our tool.

We carried out two sets of experiments: (i) invariant generation, by using a guarded command representation of the benchmarks as inputs to our tool; (ii) loop analysis of realistic Java programs, by specifying the examples as Java

Table 1. Experimental results on loop reasoning using Vampire.

Name	Cond	Δ_{direct}	Δ_{filter}	N_5	N_{filter}
absolute	yes	0.271	2.358	19	3
copy	no	0.043	2.194	9 (37)	1
copyOdd	no	0.122	2.090	9 (214)	1
copyPartial	no	0.042	3.145	9	1
copyPositive	yes			9	
find	yes			123	
findMax	yes			3	
init	no	0.035	2.059	9 (35)	1
initEven	no			10	
initNonConstant	no	0.114	2.054	9 (104)	1
initPartial	no	0.042	3.129	9	1
inPlaceMax	yes			39	
max	yes	0.696	3.535	20	2
mergeInterleave	no			20	
partition	yes			164 (647)	
partitionInit	yes			98 (169)	
reverse	no	0.038		9 (42)	
strcpy	no	0.036	2.126	9	1
strlen	no	0.018	2.023	2 (26)	1
swap	no			26	

methods with JML contracts as inputs to our tool and using our integration of invariant generation in KeY. All experiments were performed on a computer with a 2.1 GHz quad-core processor and 8 GB of RAM.

Table 1 summarizes our results. The second column indicates whether the benchmark loops contain conditionals. Column Δ_{direct} shows the time required to prove the partial correctness of the benchmarks, by proving the loop specification from the extended properties generated by program analysis in Vampire. On the other hand, column Δ_{filter} gives the time needed by our tool to generate the relevant invariants from which the loop post-condition can be proved. The time results are given in seconds. Where no time is given, a correctness proof/filtering of relevant invariants was not successful. Column N_5 shows the number of all invariants generated by our tool with a time limit of 5 s (before filtering of relevant invariants). The figure listed in parentheses gives the number of invariants produced by a previous implementation [7] of invariant generation in Vampire. Finally, column N_{filter} reports the number of invariants selected as relevant invariants; the conjunction of these invariants is the relevant invariant from which the loop specification can be derived.

Invariant Generation. Note that for all examples, our tool successfully generated quantified loop invariants. Moreover, when compared to the previous implementation [7] of invariant generation in Vampire, our tool brings a significant performance increase: in all examples where the implementation of [7] succeeded to generate invariants, the number of invariants generated by our tool is much less than in [7]. For example, in the case of the program copyOdd, the number of invariants generated by our tool has decreased by a factor of 24 when compared to [7]. This increase in performance is due to our improved program analysis for generating extended loop properties. For the examples where the number of invariants generated by [7] is missing, the approach of [7] failed to generate quantified loop invariants over arrays. We also note that invariants generated by [7] are logical consequences of the invariants generated by our tool.

Invariant Filtering. When evaluating our tool for proving correctness of the examples, we succeeded for 11 examples out of 19, as shown in column Δ_{direct} of Table 1. For these 11 examples, the partial correctness of the loop was proved by Vampire by using the extended loop properties generated by our tool. Further, for 10 out of these 11 examples, our tool successfully selected the relevant invariants from which the loop specification could be proved. For the example reverse the relevant invariants could not be selected within a 5 s time, even though the partial correctness of the loop was established using the extended properties of the loop. The reason why the relevant invariants were not generated lies in the translation of the Java method into our guarded command representation: due to the limited representation of heap-related properties, the post-condition given to Vampire is weaker than the original proof obligation in KeY. This causes the invariant relevance filter to miss properties required to carry out the proof within KeY, even though the relevant invariants were generated by our tool.

When analyzing the 8 examples for which our tool failed to generate relevant invariants and to prove partial correctness, we noted that these examples involve non-trivial arithmetic and array reasoning. We believe that improving reasoning with full first-order theories in Vampire would allow us to select the relevant invariants from those generated by our tool.

5   Conclusion

We provide a new and fully automated tool for invariant generation, by re-implementing and improving program analysis and symbol elimination in Vampire. We also extend symbol elimination to prove partial correctness of loops. We integrated our tool with the KeY verification system, allowing automatic reasoning about realistic Java programs using first-order proving. We experimentally evaluated our tool on a number of examples coming from KeY. For future work, we intend to improve theory reasoning in Vampire. We believe that our examples coming from invariant filtering are challenging benchmarks for reasoning with quantifiers and theories, and intend to add these examples to the CASC theorem proving competition. We are also interested in analyzing more complex programs and support the translation of the full semantics of a programming language such as Java into our program analysis framework. For doing so, new features and extensions of the TPTP language supported by first-order theorem provers are needed, for example the use of a first class Boolean sort as described in [10]. Finally, in order to target a greater number of programming languages, it would be useful to provide a front-end to an intermediate verification language, e.g. Boogie [1].

Acknowledgments. We wish to thank Martin Hentschel for his help with KeY.

References

1. Barnett, M., Chang, B.-Y.E., DeLine, R., Jacobs, B., M. Leino, K.R.: Boogie: a modular reusable verifier for object-oriented programs. In: de Boer, F.S., Bonsangue, M.M., Graf, S., de Roever, W.-P. (eds.) FMCO 2005. LNCS, vol. 4111, pp. 364–387. Springer, Heidelberg (2006)
2. Beckert, B., Hähnle, R., Schmitt, P.H.: Verification of Object-Oriented Software: The KeY Approach. Springer, Heidelberg (2007)
3. Beckert, B., Schlager, S., Schmitt, P.H.: An improved rule for while loops in deductive program verification. In: Lau, K.-K., Banach, R. (eds.) ICFEM 2005. LNCS, vol. 3785, pp. 315–329. Springer, Heidelberg (2005)
4. Cousot, P., Cousot, R., Logozzo, F.: A parametric segmentation functor for fully automatic and scalable array content analysis. In: Symposium on Principles of Programming Languages, pp. 105–118. ACM (2011)
5. Cuoq, P., Kirchner, F., Kosmatov, N., Prevosto, V., Signoles, J., Yakobowski, B.: Frama-C. In: Eleftherakis, G., Hinchey, M., Holcombe, M. (eds.) SEFM 2012. LNCS, vol. 7504, pp. 233–247. Springer, Heidelberg (2012)
6. Dillig, I., Dillig, T., Aiken, A.: Fluid updates: beyond strong vs. weak updates. In: Gordon, A.D. (ed.) ESOP 2010. LNCS, vol. 6012, pp. 246–266. Springer, Heidelberg (2010)

7. Dragan, I., Kovács, L.: Lingva: generating and proving program properties using symbol elimination. In: Voronkov, A., Virbitskaite, I. (eds.) PSI 2014. LNCS, vol. 8974, pp. 67–75. Springer, Heidelberg (2015)
8. Galeotti, J.P., Furia, C.A., May, E., Fraser, G., Zeller, A.: DynaMate: dynamically inferring loop invariants for automatic full functional verification. In: Yahav, E. (ed.) HVC 2014. LNCS, vol. 8855, pp. 48–53. Springer, Heidelberg (2014)
9. Gupta, A., Rybalchenko, A.: InvGen: an efficient invariant generator. In: Bouajjani, A., Maler, O. (eds.) CAV 2009. LNCS, vol. 5643, pp. 634–640. Springer, Heidelberg (2009)
10. Kotelnikov, E., Kovács, L., Voronkov, A.: A first class boolean sort in first-order theorem proving and TPTP. In: Kerber, M., Carette, J., Kaliszyk, C., Rabe, F., Sorge, V. (eds.) CICM 2015. LNCS, vol. 9150, pp. 71–86. Springer, Heidelberg (2015)
11. Kovács, L., Voronkov, A.: Finding loop invariants for programs over arrays using a theorem prover. In: Chechik, M., Wirsing, M. (eds.) FASE 2009. LNCS, vol. 5503, pp. 470–485. Springer, Heidelberg (2009)
12. Kovács, L., Voronkov, A.: First-order theorem proving and VAMPIRE. In: Sharygina, N., Veith, H. (eds.) CAV 2013. LNCS, vol. 8044, pp. 1–35. Springer, Heidelberg (2013)
13. Larraz, D., Rodríguez-Carbonell, E., Rubio, A.: SMT-based array invariant generation. In: Giacobazzi, R., Berdine, J., Mastroeni, I. (eds.) VMCAI 2013. LNCS, vol. 7737, pp. 169–188. Springer, Heidelberg (2013)
14. Leino, K.R.M.: Dafny: an automatic program verifier for functional correctness. In: Clarke, E.M., Voronkov, A. (eds.) LPAR-16 2010. LNCS, vol. 6355, pp. 348–370. Springer, Heidelberg (2010)

Compositional Propositional Proofs

Marijn J.H. Heule[1]([✉]) and Armin Biere[2]

[1] Department of Computer Science, The University of Texas, Austin, USA
marijn@cs.utexas.edu
[2] Institute for Formal Models and Verification, JKU, Linz, Austria
biere@jku.at

Abstract. Many hard-combinatorial problems have only be solved by SAT solvers in a massively parallel setting. This reduces the trust one has in the final result as errors might occur during parallel SAT solving or during partitioning of the original problem. We present a new framework to produce clausal proofs for cube-and-conquer, arguably the most effective parallel SAT solving paradigm for hard-combinatorial problems. The framework also provides an elegant approach to parallelize the validation of clausal proofs efficiently, both in terms of run time and memory usage. We evaluate the presented approach on some hard-combinatorial problems and validate constructed clausal proofs in parallel.

1 Introduction

Several long-standing open problems have recently been solved with SAT solvers, including the Erdős discrepancy conjecture [1], van der Waerden numbers [2,3], and optimal sorting networks [4]. These problems have been open for decades and only SAT techniques were able to make progress. Ever since the four-color theorem was solved using heavy computer assistance [5], there have been doubts about the correctness of such results as it is impossible for humans to verify the proof [6]. For most impressive applications of SAT technology, proofs are not provided, since their size would be enormous and due to the absence of validation tools. We present a method and tools to generate and validate *compositional propositional proofs* to increase confidence in the results for such problems.

Unsatisfiability proofs (or refutations) are traditionally expressed as either *resolution proofs* [7] or *clausal proofs* [8]. A proof is a sequence of *lemmas*, i.e., redundant clauses, which when added to the formula preserve satisfiability. Resolution proofs explicitly state which clauses should be resolved to derive a lemma, making them too verbose for hard problems. This detailed information is absent in clausal proofs, leaving it up to the clausal proof checker to determine why a lemma is redundant. Practically all top-tier SAT solvers support clausal proof logging in the DRAT format [9], which was used to check the SAT Competition 2014 results. This paper focuses on how to make compositional DRAT proofs.

This work was supported by the Austrian Science Fund (FWF) through the national research network RiSE (S11408-N23), DARPA contract number N66001-10-2-4087, and the National Science Foundation under grant number CCF-1526760.

© Springer-Verlag Berlin Heidelberg 2015
M. Davis et al. (Eds.): LPAR-20 2015, LNCS 9450, pp. 444–459, 2015.
DOI: 10.1007/978-3-662-48899-7_31

Classical propositional proof systems, such as resolution, are of course compositional, in the sense that concatenating two proofs derives the union of the conclusions of both proofs. However, clausal proofs also support clause deletion to realize efficient validation [10] and expressing techniques that do not preserve logical equivalence — in contrast to resolution proofs. Thus, we must come up with a compositional proof system for clausal proofs that *includes deletion information* and operations that do not preserve logical equivalence.

One of the major obstacles for checking proofs obtained from parallel solvers, such as the proofs from portfolio solvers [11], is the huge gap between the time to solve a problem and time to validate the corresponding proof — even with deletion information. One reason for this gap is that the solver runs on all cores of a machine, while a checker uses only one. We address this problem by partitioning proofs in such a way that the validation can be performed in parallel.

The recent SAT result on the Erdős discrepancy conjecture [1] produced a 13 gigabyte clausal proof —comparable to the compressed size of all English text on Wikipedia— and validated it using the DRATtrim checker [9]. The ability to verify that result significantly increased the confidence with regards to its correctness. However, for most hard-combinatorial problems that have been solved with SAT solvers no such proof exists: e.g., van der Waerden number $W(2,6)$ [2] and the optimality result of sorting networks with nine wires [4]. These problems require enormous SAT solving time resulting in proofs that are terabytes in size.

One of the leading parallel SAT solving paradigms is *cube-and-conquer* [12], which uses a lookahead solver to generate millions of *cubes* for a conflict-driven clause learning (CDCL) solver. Cube-and-conquer is particularly effective on hard-combinatorial problems where it can heavily outperform both lookahead and CDCL solvers, even on a single core machine. We present a method which allows to produce proofs for problems solved by parallel cube-and-conquer.

Our paper proceeds by presenting some preliminaries in Sect. 2. Section 3 introduces rules regarding compositional propositional proofs. We provide in Sect. 4 a method to validate clausal proofs in parallel. In Sect. 5, we show how to log proofs in parallel for cube-and-conquer solvers. Our tools are presented in Sect. 6. We give an evaluation in Sect. 7, and we conclude in Sect. 8.

2   Preliminaries

CNF Satisfiability. For a Boolean variable x, there are two *literals*, the positive literal x and the negative literal $\bar{x}$. A *clause* is a disjunction of literals and a CNF formula a conjunction of clauses. A clause can be seen as a finite set of literals and a CNF formula as a finite set of clauses. A truth assignment is a function τ that maps literals to $\{\mathbf{f}, \mathbf{t}\}$ under the assumption $\tau(x) = v$ if and only if $\tau(\bar{x}) = \neg v$. A clause C is satisfied by τ if $\tau(l) = \mathbf{t}$ for some literal $l \in C$. An assignment τ satisfies F if it satisfies every clause in F. Two formulas are *logically-equivalent* if they are satisfied by exactly the same set of assignments, and *satisfiability-equivalent* if both formulas are satisfiable or both unsatisfiable.

Resolution and Extended Resolution. The resolution rule states that, given two clauses $C_1 = (x \vee a_1 \vee \ldots \vee a_n)$ and $C_2 = (\bar{x} \vee b_1 \vee \ldots \vee b_m)$, the clause $C = (a_1 \vee \ldots \vee a_n \vee b_1 \vee \ldots \vee b_m)$, can be inferred by resolving on variable x. We say C is the *resolvent* of C_1 and C_2. C is logically implied by any formula containing C_1 and C_2. For a given CNF formula F, the *extension rule* [13] allows one to iteratively add definitions of the form $x := a \wedge b$ by adding the *extended resolution clauses* $(x \vee \bar{a} \vee \bar{b}) \wedge (\bar{x} \vee a) \wedge (\bar{x} \vee b)$ to F, where x is a new variable and a and b are literals in the current formula.

Unit Propagation. For a CNF formula F, *unit propagation* simplifies F based on unit clauses ; that is, it repeats the following until fixpoint: if there is a unit clause $(l) \in F$, remove all clauses that contain the literal l from the set $F \setminus \{(l)\}$ and remove the literal $\bar{l}$ from all clauses in F. If unit propagation on formula F produces complementary units (l) and $(\bar{l})$, we say that unit propagation *derives a conflict* and write $F \vdash_1 \epsilon$ with ϵ referring to the (unsatisfiable) empty clause.

Example 1. Consider the formula $F = (a) \wedge (\bar{a} \vee b) \wedge (\bar{b} \vee c) \wedge (\bar{b} \vee \bar{c})$. We have $(a) \in F$, so unit propagation removes literal $\bar{a}$, resulting in the new unit clause (b). After removal of the literals $\bar{b}$, two complementary unit clauses (c) and $(\bar{c})$ are created. From these two units the empty clause can be derived: $F \vdash_1 \epsilon$.

Clause Redundancy. A clause C is called *redundant* with respect to a formula F if $F \wedge \{C\}$ is satisfiability equivalent to F. A *tautology* is a redundant clause that contains literals x and $\bar{x}$ for some variable x. A clause $C \in F$ is also redundant if there exists a clause $D \in F$ such that $D \subseteq C$, i.e., D *subsumes* C.

Asymmetric tautologies, also known as *reverse unit propagation* (RUP) clauses, are the most common redundant (learned) clauses in CDCL SAT solvers. Let $\overline{C}$ denote the conjunction of unit clauses that falsify all literals in C. A clause C is an asymmetric tautology with respect to a CNF formula F if $F \wedge \overline{C} \vdash_1 \epsilon$. *Resolution asymmetric tautologies* (or RAT clauses) [14] are a generalization of both asymmetric tautologies and extended resolution clauses. A clause C has RAT on $l \in C$ (referred to as the *pivot* literal) with respect to a formula F if for all $D \in F$ with $\bar{l} \in D$, it holds that $F \wedge \overline{C} \wedge (\overline{D} \setminus \{(l)\}) \vdash_1 \epsilon$.

Not only can RAT be computed in polynomial time, but all preprocessing, inprocessing, and solving techniques in state-of-the-art SAT solvers can be expressed in terms of addition and removal of RAT clauses [14].

Clausal Proofs. A *proof of unsatisfiability* (also called a *refutation*) is a sequence of redundant clauses, called *lemmas*, containing the empty clause. There are two prevalent types of unsatisfiability proofs: *resolution proofs* and *clausal proofs*. Several formats have been designed for resolution proofs [7,15,16], but they all share the same disadvantages. Resolution proofs are often huge, and it is hard to express important techniques, such as conflict clause minimization, with resolution steps. Other techniques, such as bounded variable addition [17], cannot be polynomially-simulated by resolution. Clausal proof formats [9,18,19] are syntactically similar; they involve a sequence of clauses that are claimed to be redundant with respect to a given formula. It is important that the redundancy property of clauses can be checked in polynomial time.

A *DRUP proof*, short for *Deletion Reverse Unit Propagation*, is a sequence of addition and deletion steps of RUP clauses. A *DRAT proof*, short for *Deletion Resolution Asymmetric Tautology*, is a sequence of addition and deletion steps of RAT clauses. A DRAT *refutation* is a DRAT proof that contains the empty clause. Figure 1 shows an example DRAT refutation.

CNF formula	DRAT proof
p cnf 4 8	
1 2 -3 0	-1 0
-1 -2 3 0	d -1 2 4 0
2 3 -4 0	2 0
-2 -3 4 0	0
-1 -3 -4 0	
1 3 4 0	
-1 2 4 0	
1 -2 -4 0	

Fig. 1. Left, a formula in DIMACS CNF format, the conventional input for SAT solvers which starts with `p cnf` to denote the format, followed by the number of variables and the number of clauses. Right, a DRAT proof for that formula. Each line in the proof is either an addition step (no prefix) or a deletion step identified by the prefix "d". Spacing in both examples is used to improve readability. Each clause in the proof should be an asymmetric tautology or a RAT clause using the first literal as the pivot.

Example 2. Consider the CNF formula $F = (a \vee b \vee \bar{c}) \wedge (\bar{a} \vee \bar{b} \vee c) \wedge (b \vee c \vee \bar{d}) \wedge (\bar{b} \vee \bar{c} \vee d) \wedge (a \vee c \vee d) \wedge (\bar{a} \vee \bar{c} \vee \bar{d}) \wedge (\bar{a} \vee b \vee d) \wedge (a \vee \bar{b} \vee \bar{d})$, shown in DIMACS format in Fig. 1 (left), where 1 represents a, 2 is b, 3 is c, 4 is d, and negative numbers represent negation. The first clause in the proof, $(\bar{a})$, is a RAT clause with respect to F because all possible resolvents are asymmetric tautologies:

$$F \wedge (a) \wedge (\bar{b}) \wedge (c) \vdash_1 \epsilon \quad \text{using} \quad (a \vee b \vee \bar{c})$$
$$F \wedge (a) \wedge (\bar{c}) \wedge (\bar{d}) \vdash_1 \epsilon \quad \text{using} \quad (a \vee c \vee d)$$
$$F \wedge (a) \wedge (b) \wedge (d) \vdash_1 \epsilon \quad \text{using} \quad (a \vee \bar{b} \vee \bar{d})$$

3 Rules

In this section, we introduce rules for composing propositional proofs. We first establish a notation to describe operations, or *derivations* on formulas and proofs, and then continue with basic rules for addition or deletion of a clause/lemma. Finally, we propose compositional rules that address merging proofs produced in parallel and validating proofs that have been produced in parallel.

Throughout this section, we will use $\bigcirc$ to express a CNF formula and $\triangle$ to express a proof composed of a sequence of proof steps. Note that a formula is a multi-set of clauses as elements may be duplicated by some of the operations below. Furthermore, a formula may be treated as a part of a proof by treating each clause as an added lemma. Concatenation of proofs is simply the concatenation of the sequences of their proof steps. The union of two formulas is interpreted as multi-set union. Both operations are denoted by juxtaposition.

3.1   The Base Rules

Each element of a derivation is either the addition of a clause C, denoted by $a(C)$ or the deletion of a clause C, denoted by $d(C)$. Given a formula $\bigcirc_i$, a clause C and a modification $m \in \{a, d\}$, a proof step is denoted as

$$\bigcirc_i \xrightarrow{m(C)} \bigcirc_{i+1}$$

We introduce two base rules ADD and DEL which produce atomic proof steps.

$$\text{ADD:} \quad \frac{}{\bigcirc \xrightarrow{a(C)} \bigcirc C} \quad \text{where } C \text{ has RAT on } l \in C \text{ w.r.t. } \bigcirc$$

$$\text{DEL:} \quad \frac{}{\bigcirc C \xrightarrow{d(C)} \bigcirc} \quad \text{(no side condition)}$$

The ADD rule has the precondition that there exists a literal $l \in C$ such that C had RAT on l with respect to the formula $\bigcirc$. The correctness of the ADD rule follows from the observation that the addition of RAT clauses preserves satisfiability. Practically all techniques used in modern CDCL SAT solvers can be simulated by these rules bas they can be expressed as a RAT derivation[1] [14].

The DEL rule has no precondition, and the removal of clauses from a formula is always allowed. We are only interested in proofs of unsatisfiability and deletion of a clause trivially preserves satisfiability. For proofs of satisfiability, the situation is reversed: the (same) precondition is required for the DEL rule, while the ADD rule has no precondition. The most important function of the DEL rule is to facilitate fast validation of proofs. Without clause deletion, validation costs can be two orders of magnitude larger on reasonable-sized proofs. The achievable speed-up factor increases for larger proofs.

A *DRAT derivation* is a sequence of proof steps that consists for each step i of a clause C_i and a modification $m_i \in \{a, d\}$. Applying a DRAT derivation of n steps to a CNF formula $\bigcirc_0$ results in $\bigcirc_n$ by applying each step in the order in which they occur in the derivation. A DRAT derivation of n steps is *valid* for a given formula $\bigcirc_0$ if for all steps $i \in \{1..n\}$ holds that C_i has RAT on a $l \in C_i$ w.r.t. $\bigcirc_{i-1}$ if $m_i = a$ and C_i occurs in $\bigcirc_{i-1}$ if $m_i = d$. Consider the proof:

$$\bigcirc_0 \xrightarrow{m_1(C_1)} \bigcirc_1 \xrightarrow{m_2(C_2)} \bigcirc_2 \dots \bigcirc_{n-1} \xrightarrow{m_n(C_n)} \bigcirc_n$$

---

[1] All solver techniques can be expressed as a RAT derivation. For some techniques, such as symmetry-breaking, the construction of a RAT derivation is complex [20].

We say, the proof $\triangle = m_1(C_1)m_2(C_2)\cdots m_n(C_n)$ gives a *derivation* from $\bigcirc_0$ to $\bigcirc_n$, or in symbols

$$\bigcirc_0 \xrightarrow{\overbrace{m_1(C_1)m_2(C_2)\dots m_n(C_n)}^{\triangle}} \bigcirc_n \quad \text{or} \quad \bigcirc_0 \xrightarrow{\triangle} \bigcirc_n$$

We also represent rules as a triple containing: a *pre-CNF* $\bigcirc_{\text{pre}}$, a proof $\triangle$, and a *post-CNF* $\bigcirc_{\text{post}}$, denoting that proof $\triangle$ is a derivation from $\bigcirc_{\text{pre}}$ to $\bigcirc_{\text{post}}$.

Definition 1. $(\bigcirc_{\text{pre}}, \triangle, \bigcirc_{\text{post}})$ *is* valid *iff* $\bigcirc_{\text{pre}} \xrightarrow{\triangle} \bigcirc_{\text{post}}$ *is a derivation.*

The addition of RAT clauses preserves satisfiability [14], as does the deletion of any clause. Thus, we get the following soundness result for valid compositional triples and derivations respectively.

Proposition 1. *Given a valid composition triple* $(\bigcirc_{\text{pre}}, \triangle, \bigcirc_{\text{post}})$, *if* $\bigcirc_{\text{pre}}$ *is satisfiable then* $\bigcirc_{\text{post}}$ *is satisfiable as well.*

In practice, we focus on the contrapositive, e.g., if $\bigcirc_{\text{post}}$ contains the empty clause then $\bigcirc_{\text{pre}}$ is unsatisfiable, and we consider $\triangle$ to be a proof (refutation) for the unsatisfiability of $\bigcirc_{\text{pre}}$.

3.2   The Composition Rules

In this section, the notion of a satisfiability-preserving derivation, as defined in the previous section, will be lifted to the compositional case.

In addition to the two base rules ADD and DEL, we propose two composition rules which combine two compositional triples into one. The first rule SEQ, short for "sequential", combines two compositional triples for which the post-CNF of one triple equals the pre-CNF of the other triple. The second rule PAR, short for "parallel", combines two compositional triples for which the two pre-CNFs are equal. Visualizations of the SEQ rule PAR rule can be found in Fig. 2.

The SEQ rule has no preconditions and can be used for any two valid compositional triples for which one pre-CNF is equal to the other post-CNF. We will use this rule to develop a method to validate DRAT derivations in parallel. The soundness result for SEQ follows directly from the definition of how proofs are concatenated and formulas are joined.

Proposition 2. *Given two valid compositional triples as antecedents, then the* SEQ *rule produces a valid compositional triple as consequent.*

Note that validity of a compositional triple is still defined in terms of basic derivations which are sequences of addition and deletion steps. Thus these compositional rules allow one to generate a basic derivation from a "compositional proof", which in turn is sound.

The PAR rule expresses how to merge DRUP (*not* DRAT) derivations which are obtained by running multiple solvers running on the same pre-CNF in parallel. Notice that the merged derivation by the PAR rule start with a copy of

SEQ: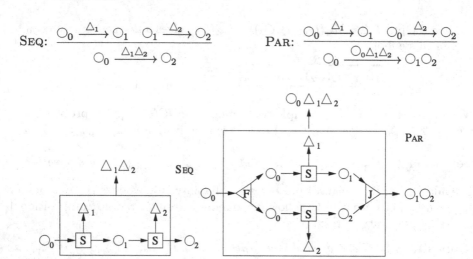

Fig. 2. Visualization of SEQ and PAR rules (S = Solve, F = Fork, J = Join). A solver (S) takes a formula as input and produces a modified formula as well as a derivation that describes the modifications. Forking (F) can be used to let two solvers work on the same formula. Internally this means that the formula is duplicated. If all added clauses preserve logical equivalence (DRUP), the resulting formulas can be joined (J).

the pre-CNF. The pre-CNF is included because both derivations may delete the same clause from the original formula.

Notice that the DRUP proof $\bigcirc_0 \, \triangle_1 \, \triangle_2$ in the conclusion of the PAR rule cannot be replaced by $\triangle_1 \, \bigcirc_0 \, \triangle_2$, because $\triangle_1$ may have eliminated clauses from $\bigcirc_0$ in such a way that a clause $C \in \bigcirc_0$ no longer has DRUP w.r.t. $\bigcirc_1$. For example consider an unsatisfiable formula $\bigcirc_0$, let $\bigcirc_1$ be the empty formula, and let $\triangle_1$ simply remove all clauses from $\bigcirc_0$ (without adding anything). Clearly, $\triangle_1 \bigcirc_1$ is a valid DRUP proof for $\bigcirc_0$ as it contains only deletion information. However, it is not possible to create a valid DRUP proof by appending $\bigcirc_0$ to $\triangle_1 \bigcirc_1$ because $\bigcirc_1$ is satisfiable and $\bigcirc_0$ unsatisfiable.

Proposition 3. *Given two valid compositional triples as antecedents with DRUP proofs, then the* PAR *rule produces a valid compositional triple with DRUP proof as consequent.*

Proof. (sketch) All the added $\bigcirc_0$ clauses in the combined proof are valid DRUP clauses (since they occur in the pre-CNF $\bigcirc_0$ and are even subsumed). Further note, that DRUP is monotonic, in the sense, that if a clause has the DRUP property w.r.t. $\bigcirc$ it will also have DRUP w.r.t. all $\bigcirc'$ with $\bigcirc \subseteq \bigcirc'$ (as multi-sets). Thus adding $\bigcirc_0$ in front of $\triangle_1$ does not destroy the property of $\triangle_1$ to be a derivation. Because we use a multi-set interpretation for formulas all the clauses in $\triangle_1$ are still in the intermediate formula reached after the sub-proof $\bigcirc_0 \triangle_1$ and $\triangle_2$ just works as before, also keeping all the derived $\bigcirc_1$ clauses in the post-CNF in addition to deriving all its own $\bigcirc_2$ clauses. $\square$

The above argument does not hold for DRAT proofs (instead of DRUP), because DRAT is not monotonic: A clause C can have RAT w.r.t. a formula F, but not with respect to $F \wedge G$ for some formula G. Hence, $\triangle_1$ may add a clause which breaks the RAT property of a clause addition step in $\triangle_2$.

As an optimization, to avoid the duplication of the original clauses in the PAR rule, one can consider a modified rule, which has a side condition that neither $\triangle_1$ nor $\triangle_2$ eliminate clauses from $\bigcirc_0$.

4 Parallel Proof Checking

Existing tools to validate clausal proofs, such as DRATtrim [9] and our new proof checker DRABT, can check proofs of reasonable size (dozens of gigabytes) efficiently (within in a day). Yet existing tools are not well-equipped to deal with huge proofs because they keep the full proof in memory and validation is done on a single core. In this section, we present a method to validate DRAT proofs in parallel effectively with only a few changes to existing proof-checking tools.

4.1 Proofs Checking Optimizations

There are several optimizations that make the efficient, serial validation of clausal proofs possible. The most significant gains can be realized by exploiting deletion information in proofs. Ignoring deletion information can increase the validation costs by two orders of magnitude on reasonable-sized proofs of say several giga-bytes [10,21]. We will provide an example of the impact of deletion information on the validation costs in the introduction of Sect. 7.

One, so far unpublished, optimization in DRATtrim and DRABT is ignoring deletion information of unit clauses or *pseudo-unit clauses*, i.e., clauses that have become unit under the top-level assignment. For example, (a) is a unit clause in formula $F := (a) \wedge (\bar{a} \vee b)$, while $(\bar{a} \vee b)$ is a pseudo-unit clause. Deleting (pseudo-)unit clauses during proof checking can be very costly as the checker has to unassign all variables and compute a new top-level assignment. When a proof claims to show unsatisfiability, the deletion of unit clauses is not useful.

Enhancing a clausal proof with deletion information can be somewhat tricky. While working on this paper, we discovered that there is a bug in the proof logging of several CDCL SAT solvers. The bug is caused by deleting pseudo-unit clauses without first adding the corresponding unit clauses to the proof. Due to this bug, many clausal proofs produced by these solvers are invalid, which would have been reported by the checker if it did not ignore the deletion of (pseudo-)unit clauses. We even observed cases where the intermediate formula becomes satisfiable after the invalid deletion of a pseudo-unit clause. Appendix A offers details and a fix for this bug for the SAT solver Glucose.

4.2 Backward Checking of Derivations

The validation of a clausal proof for a given formula requires checking the validity of each clause addition step, i.e., the precondition of the ADD rule. This can be implemented using *forward checking*: go over the proof from the start to end, modify the formula at each step, and check the validity of addition steps.

A refutation can also be validated using *backward checking* [8]: First, mark the empty clause as a *core* lemma, i.e., a lemma that needs to be validated. Second, process the proof in reverse order and only validate the addition of core lemmas, assuming that all added lemmas occurring earlier in the proof — and that are not deleted prior to the checked core lemma — can be validated. Checking a core lemma may mark other lemmas occurring earlier in the proof as core. Successful backward checking does not imply that the original proof was valid, but that a new valid proof was obtained that consists of the sequence of added and deleted core lemmas. The order of the lemmas in the new proof will match the order of the lemmas in the original proof. Backward checking enables optimizating deletion information, i.e., the clause deletion steps in the proof [21].

Backward checking can be generalized for arbitrary derivations to check the validness of compositional triples efficiently. Instead of marking the empty clause as core, initially all lemmas occurring in the derivation that are not deleted will be marked as core. Furthermore, it is allowed to unmark a marked lemma if it is subsumed by another marked lemma or by a clause in the pre-CNF which will not be deleted. This can be computed efficiently using backward subsumption [22]. Notice that when this restriction is applied, backward checking for refutations is unaffected, because the empty clause subsumes all other lemmas. Recall, successful backward checking does not guarantee that the original derivation is valid, but only that a new valid derivation was obtained.

4.3   Parallel Proof Checking via SEQ Rule

The SEQ rule provides an elegant method for validating DRAT proofs in parallel: given a CNF formula $\bigcirc_0$ and DRAT refutation $\triangle$, partition $\triangle$ into k derivations such that $\triangle_1 \triangle_2 \ldots \triangle_k = \triangle$. Second, compute the pre- and post-CNFs $\bigcirc_i$, where $\bigcirc_i$ denotes the result of applying derivation $\triangle_i$ to formula $\bigcirc_{i-1}$. Notice that this cannot be done in parallel because the computation of $\bigcirc_{i+1}$ depends on the existence of $\bigcirc_i$. Finally, check that all $(\bigcirc_{i-1}, \triangle_i, \bigcirc_i)$ with $i \in \{1..k\}$ are valid compositional triples and that $\epsilon \in \bigcirc_k$. When all checks are successful, the SEQ rule states that $\triangle$ is a valid refutation for $\bigcirc_0$. Below it is shown in symbols how to deduce the validness of refutation $\triangle$ by applying the SEQ rule $k-1$ times:

$$\frac{\bigcirc_0 \xrightarrow{\triangle_1} \bigcirc_1 \quad \bigcirc_1 \xrightarrow{\triangle_2} \bigcirc_2 \quad \cdots \quad \bigcirc_{k-1} \xrightarrow{\triangle_k} \epsilon}{\bigcirc_0 \xrightarrow{\triangle_1 \triangle_2 \ldots \triangle_k} \epsilon}$$

4.4   Validating the Post-CNF

One method to check that $(\bigcirc_{\text{pre}}, \triangle, \bigcirc_{\text{post}})$ is a valid compositional triple is to check that $\triangle$ is a valid derivation for $\bigcirc_{\text{pre}}$ and assumes that the computation of the $\bigcirc_{\text{post}}$ was done correctly. As partitioning problems can easily result in errors, confidence in the correctness of the complete proof checking chain can be improved by fully validating compositional triples. One can explicitly check that $\bigcirc_{\text{post}}$ is derived from $\bigcirc_{\text{pre}}$ by applying $\triangle$. This is implemented in our checker DRABT by hashing, which requires $\bigcirc_{\text{post}}$ to be provided as a third input file.

Alternatively, one can increase confidence in the tool chain by checking that $\triangle\bigcirc_{\text{post}}$ is a valid derivation for $\bigcirc_{\text{pre}}$. This validates that there exists a valid compositional triple $(\bigcirc_{\text{pre}}, \triangle', \bigcirc_{\text{post}})$ and the checker should able to produce $\triangle'$. In practice, appending $\triangle$ with $\bigcirc_{\text{post}}$ can significantly increase the costs of validating proofs as many clauses in post-CNF $\bigcirc_{\text{post}}$ occur also in pre-CNF $\bigcirc_{\text{pre}}$. Validating such clauses will mark the equivalent clauses in the pre-CNF as core, which will obstruct the core-first optimization of proof checking [21]. If the computation of the post-CNFs was done correctly, all clauses in the post-CNFs will be unmarked and hence not be validated.

5 Parallel Proof Generation

Traditionally, proof generation has only been supported by non-parallel SAT solvers. A recent study [11] presented an approach to construct clausal proofs from clause-sharing portfolio parallel SAT solvers. The proofs constructed with that method were very costly to validate. In this section, we present a method to construct clausal proofs from parallel SAT solvers based on the cube-and-conquer paradigm, such as march_cc+iLingeling. The experimental evaluation shows that these proofs can be validated in parallel efficiently.

In short, cube-and-conquer solvers consist of two parts: a lookahead (or cube) solver and a CDCL (or conquer) solver. First, the cube solver partitions the problem into many subproblems, frequently millions. Each of the subproblems is represented by a cube, i.e., a conjunction of literals. In the second phase, one or more CDCL solvers will use these cubes to guide their search. Clauses learned while solving a cube are typically not useful for solving other cubes. One can solve cubes massively in parallel and obtain almost a linear time speed-up with the number of solvers — assuming that there are as many cores as solvers.

We now show how to construct a DRUP refutation for cube-and-conquer solvers. First, the cube solver computes cubes for the input formula. guide the conquer solvers. Assume that we have k conquer solvers S_i with $i \in \{1..k\}$. Each solver S_i gets a set of cubes $\overline{\bigcirc}_i$. After solver S_i refutes all of its cubes, it generates a DRUP proof $\triangle_i$ that expresses how to produce all clauses $\bigcirc_i$ from the original formula $\bigcirc_0$ and deletes all the other learned and original clauses. Then, a refutation is computed for the conjunction of all cubes $\bigcirc_1 \bigcirc_2 \cdots \bigcirc_k$, the conquer proof $\triangle_c$.

The composition rules explain how to merge these derivations in a refutation for the input formula. First, all $\triangle_i$ derivations are merged using the PAR rule, by starting with the $k-1$ copies of the input formula and adding the concatenation of the derivations. Second, the merged derivation is combined with the conquer proof using the SEQ rule.

$$\frac{\bigcirc_0 \xrightarrow{\triangle_1} \bigcirc_1 \quad \bigcirc_0 \xrightarrow{\triangle_2} \bigcirc_2 \quad \cdots \quad \bigcirc_0 \xrightarrow{\triangle_k} \bigcirc_k}{\bigcirc_0 \xrightarrow{\bigcirc_0 \cdots \bigcirc_0 \triangle_1 \triangle_2 \cdots \triangle_k} \bigcirc_1 \bigcirc_2 \cdots \bigcirc_k \qquad \bigcirc_1 \bigcirc_2 \cdots \bigcirc_k \xrightarrow{\triangle_c} \epsilon}$$
$$\bigcirc_0 \xrightarrow{\bigcirc_0 \cdots \bigcirc_0 \triangle_1 \triangle_2 \cdots \triangle_k \triangle_c} \epsilon$$

6   Tools

We have implemented several tools to support compositional proof generation and validation, which are available at www.cs.utexas.edu/~marijn/cpp and at http://fmv.jku.at/drabt. The DRATtrim proof checking tool [9] was enhanced to support backward checking [8] for arbitrary DRAT derivations. The previous version only supported backward checking of refutations. We improved the speed of validating DRAT derivations by unmarking all lemmas that are subsumed by other marked lemmas or undeleted clauses in the pre-CNF, see Sect. 4.2.

We also added a new feature, called *proof application*, to DRATtrim: Given an input formula (the pre-CNF) and a DRAT proof , the tool computes the post-CNF formula that would be the result of applying the proof to pre-CNF. In other words, the post-CNF contains all clauses in pre-CNF that are not deleted in the proof together with all lemmas in proof that are added (and not deleted). Proof application facilitates parallel proof checking via the SEQ rule, see Sect. 4.3.

To further increase confidence in the results, the second author independently implemented a new clausal proof checker, called DRABT. The current version of DRABT supports forward checking of DRUP proofs and implements checking validity of compositional triples natively in contrast to DRATtrim which checks it implicitly by appending the post-CNF to the proof. The DRABT tool puts also much more focus on proper error messages as well as improved diagnostic capabilities if an error occurs. It is, however, missing core generating features.

The SAT solver march_cc [12] can be used in a cube-and-conquer setting to produce cubes to guide a conquer solver. We had to slightly change march_cc in order to use it for compositional propositional proofs. The change consists of extending the cube output with all the branches that march_cc was able to refute using lookahead techniques. Without those cubes, the cube output does not cover the entire search space — which would cause the proof checker to fail. We observed that the cubes which can be refuted by lookahead techniques are also easy for a CDCL solver to refute. Consequently, adding these cubes to the cube output hardly increases the overall performance.

The CDCL solver iLingeling [12] is a parallel SAT solver that solves benchmarks in the iCNF format[2], which combines a CNF formula with a sequence of cubes that guide the solver. We extended iLingeling with DRUP proof logging support. The iLingeling solver runs multiple Lingeling solvers in parallel and guides them using the cubes. Each of these Lingeling solvers emits its own DRUP proof. Additionally, a separate Lingeling solver computes a proof for the cube file, the so-called conquer proof.

---

[2] see http://www.siert.nl/icnf/ for details.

7   Evaluation

In this section, we evaluate parallel proof generation based on the PAR rule and parallel proof validation based on the SEQ rule. All experiments were performed on the Stampede cluster of the Texas Advanced Computing Center (TACC) which has two 8-core Xeon E5 processors and 32 GB of memory per node.

Before describing the experiments, we want to reiterate the importance of deletion information in clausal proofs: on the smaller proofs discussed in this section, ignoring the deletion information would increase the validation costs by a factor of 20. For the large proofs, this increases to two orders of magnitude.

7.1   Parallel Compositional Proof Checking

We evaluated our parallel proof checking method on some existing DRAT proofs focusing on the speed-up in wall-clock time. Our method consists of multiple phases, some of which can be parallelized while other cannot. The first phase is partitioning a given proof $\triangle$ into k derivations: $\triangle_1, \ldots, \triangle_k$. This can simply be realized by the Unix utility split, the computational costs of which are practically ignorable. In the second phase, we need to compute the pre- and post-CNFs for proof checking, which is performed by DRATtrim using the new "proof application" mode. As described in Sect. 4.3, this part cannot be done in parallel. However, one could preprocess the derivations in parallel by removing all lemmas that are added and deleted within the same partial proof, because these lemmas will not influence the creation of the pre- and post-CNFs. Since most lemmas are added and deleted in the same proof, such preprocessing could significantly reduce the cost of this phase. This is not yet implemented. The third phase consists of checking that all $(\bigcirc_{i-1}, \triangle_i, \bigcirc_i)$ are valid compositional triples. We checked all proofs running $k = 16$ DRATtrim executables in parallel in the default mode, which validates a partial proof using backward checking and checks the post-CNFs implicitly via subsumption.

Table 1 shows the usefulness of parallel proof checking of proofs expressing symmetry-breaking techniques[3]. There are several interesting observations. First, the speed-up of checking derivations in parallel (on a 16-core machine) compared to checking them in serial is about a factor of nine on all instances when ignoring the initialization cost of splitting the proof and computing the pre- and post CNF. Taking these costs into account clearly reduces the speed-up on the smaller proofs. However, parallel proof checking is only interesting for large proofs. Second, checking derivations sequentially is more costly than checking the original refutation if the proofs are small. However, for the larger proofs the opposite happens. Third, computing the pre- and post-CNFs is quite costly for small proofs, but becomes relatively cheaper for larger proofs.

---

[3] available on http://www.cs.utexas.edu/~marijn/sbp/.

Table 1. Sequential versus parallel proof checking of DRAT proofs expressing symmetry-breaking techniques. The first column shows the benchmark name. The second and third column shows size of the original proof (in MB) and the DRATtrim checking time (in seconds). The fourth and fifth column show the time to split the proofs and to compute the pre- and post-CNFs, respectively. The last four columns show the costs to validate the derivations, sequentially, in parallel, and the speed-up with and without initialization costs on a 16-core machine.

benchmark	size	DRATtrim	split	CNFs	seq-chk	par-chk	$\frac{\text{seq+init}}{\text{par+init}}$	$\frac{\text{seq}}{\text{par}}$
EDP2_1161	2,180.98	3331.73	2.91	85.70	3288.78	455.93	6.20	7.21
R_4_4_18	20.01	2.55	0.04	1.91	4.19	0.43	2.58	9.74
tph6	2.78	0.61	0.01	1.25	2.03	0.22	2.22	9.23
tph7	5.09	1.30	0.02	1.39	2.70	0.29	2.41	9.31
tph8	10.68	2.98	0.03	1.61	4.29	0.46	2.82	9.32
tph9	34.18	6.17	0.04	1.98	7.33	0.83	3.28	8.83
tph10	19.86	11.78	0.06	2.51	12.67	1.32	3.92	9.60
tph11	56.49	22.96	0.09	3.39	22.64	2.85	4.13	7.94
tph12	92.29	39.42	0.15	4.73	39.07	3.89	5.01	10.04

7.2 Parallel Proof Generation

For the evaluation of parallel proof generation based on the PAR rule, we used the cube-and-conquer solver march_cc+iLingeling. We picked a notoriously hard benchmark eq.atree.braun.12.unsat.cnf which has been used in several SAT competitions. This formula is a miter (a circuit equivalence-checking benchmark) which cannot be solved by sequential SAT solvers in hours and by very few parallel SAT solvers.

Figure 3 shows the results of the experiments, which were performed on a 16-core cluster node using 1, 2, 4, 8, or 16 cores. The solving process time is very stable, close to 6,000 seconds. The wall-clock solving time of the conquer phase by iLingeling almost scales linearly in the number of cores. iLingeling emits a separate proof for each used Lingeling solver (one per core). For the experiment with k cores, each core validated one compositional triple consisting of the original formula (as pre-CNF), one of the proof files, and the precomputed post-CNF based on the pre-CNF and the proof. The size of the full proof is the concatenation of all these proofs together with the duplication of the original clauses due to the PAR rule.

We validated the proofs with both DRABT and DRATtrim. Figure 3 reports the DRATtrim times. The Drabt times, both process and wall-clock, were about twice as long. Notice that both the process and wall-clock time significantly drop when increasing the number of cores. The process time decreases by about a factor of 1.5 when doubling the number of cores. For the wall-clock time, the speed-up is close to a factor of 3 when doubling the number of cores. This indicates a super-linear speed-up to validate proofs. Apparently, DRATtrim slows down when

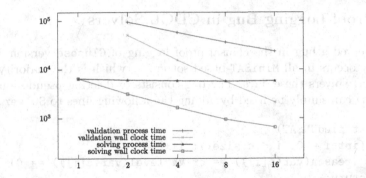

Fig. 3. A log-log plot of the effect of the number of cores (x-axis) on the wall-clock and process time (y-axis in seconds) to solve `eq.atree.braun.12.unsat.cnf` using `march_cc+iLingeling` and validate the emitted proof in parallel using `DRATtrim`. All experiments were performed on a single 16-core cluster node.

dealing with larger and larger proofs. This may be caused by an increase in the number of cache misses. Studying the reasons for the super-linear speed-up will be focus of future research.

8   Conclusion

SAT solvers have recently been used to tackle long-standing open problems. These problems are frequently solved in a massively parallel setting without emitting proofs to validate these results. Clausal proofs with deletion information are easy to emit from state-of-the-art, non-parallel SAT solvers, they are relatively compact, and they can be checked in a reasonable amount of time. However, for long-standing open problems, we need to construct clausal proofs of solvers based on arguably the most effective parallel SAT solving paradigm: cube-and-conquer. Additionally, we need tools to validate these proofs in parallel and bridge the gap between the solving and validation costs.

We presented the concept of compositional clausal proofs with deletion information. Following this concept, we developed and implemented an algorithm to validate clausal proofs in parallel effectively. Moreover, we show how to obtain clausal proofs from cube-and-conquer solvers and demonstrate how to validate those proofs in parallel. The experiments show that the speed-up can be super-linear in the number of cores.

Acknowledgements. The authors thank Nathan Wetzler for his helpful comments to improve the paper and acknowledge the Texas Advanced Computing Center (TACC) at The University of Texas at Austin for providing grid resources that have contributed to the research results reported within this paper.

A   Proof-Logging Bug in CDCL Solvers

We observed a bug in the clausal proof logging of `Glucose` version 3.0, which actually occurs in all `MiniSAT`-based solvers — which is the majority of state-of-the-art solvers these days. The bug consists of deleting pseudo-unit clauses. This bug can simply be fixed by adding the following lines to `Solver.cc`:

```
if (certifiedUNSAT)
  for (int i = 0; i < c.size(); i++)
    if (reason(var(c[i])) == cr && level(var(c[i])) == 0)
    ' return;
```

just below the beginning of the removeClause procedure

```
void Solver::removeClause(CRef cr) {
  Clause& c = ca[cr];
```

References

1. Konev, B., Lisitsa, A.: Computer-aided proof of Erdős discrepancy properties. Artif. Intell. **224**, 103–118 (2015)
2. Kouril, M., Paul, J.L.: The van der waerden number W(2, 6) is 1132. Exp. Math. **17**(1), 53–61 (2008)
3. Kouril, M.: Computing the van der Waerden number $w(3, 4) = 293$. Integers 12 (2011) Paper A46, 13 p., electronic only
4. Codish, M., Cruz-Filipe, L., Frank, M., Schneider-Kamp, P.: Twenty-five comparators is optimal when sorting nine inputs (and twenty-nine for ten). In: ICTAI 2014, pp. 186–193. IEEE Computer Society (2014)
5. Appel, K., Haken, W.: The solution of the four-color-map problem. Sci. Am. **237**(4), 108–121 (1977)
6. Aron, J.: Wikipedia-size maths proof too big for humans to check. New Sci. **221**(2957), 11 (2014)
7. Zhang, L., Malik, S.: Validating SAT solvers using an independent resolution-based checker: Practical implementations and other applications. In: DATE 2003, pp. 10880–10885 (2003)
8. Goldberg, E.I., Novikov, Y.: Verification of proofs of unsatisfiability for CNF formulas. In: DATE, pp. 10886–10891 (2003)
9. Wetzler, N., Heule, M.J.H., Hunt, W.A., Jr.: DRAT-trim: efficient checking and trimming using expressive clausal proofs. In: Sinz, C., Egly, U. (eds.) SAT 2014. LNCS, vol. 8561, pp. 422–429. Springer, Heidelberg (2014)
10. Heule, M.J.H., Hunt, W.A., Jr., Wetzler, N.: Bridging the gap between easy generation and efficient verification of unsatisfiability proofs. Softw. Test. Verification Reliab. (STVR) 24(8), 593–607 (2014)
11. Heule, M.J.H., Manthey, N., Philipp, T.: Validating unsatisfiability results of clause sharing parallel SAT solvers. In: Pragmatics of SAT, pp. 12–25 (2014)
12. Heule, M.J.H., Kullmann, O., Wieringa, S., Biere, A.: Cube and conquer: guiding CDCL SAT solvers by lookaheads. In: Eder, K., Lourenço, J., Shehory, O. (eds.) HVC 2011. LNCS, vol. 7261, pp. 50–65. Springer, Heidelberg (2012)

13. Tseitin, G.S.: On the complexity of derivation in propositional calculus. In: Siekmann, J.H., Wrightson, G. (eds.) Automation of Reasoning 2, pp. 466–483. Springer, Heidelberg (1983)
14. Järvisalo, M., Heule, M.J.H., Biere, A.: Inprocessing rules. In: Gramlich, B., Miller, D., Sattler, U. (eds.) IJCAR 2012. LNCS, vol. 7364, pp. 355–370. Springer, Heidelberg (2012)
15. Eén, N., Sörensson, N.: An extensible SAT-solver. In: Giunchiglia, E., Tacchella, A. (eds.) SAT 2003. LNCS, vol. 2919, pp. 502–518. Springer, Heidelberg (2004)
16. Biere, A.: Picosat essentials. JSAT 4(2–4), 75–97 (2008)
17. Manthey, N., Heule, M.J.H., Biere, A.: Automated reencoding of boolean formulas. In: Biere, A., Nahir, A., Vos, T. (eds.) HVC. LNCS, vol. 7857, pp. 102–117. Springer, Heidelberg (2013)
18. Van Gelder, A.: Verifying RUP proofs of propositional unsatisfiability. In: ISAIM (2008)
19. Heule, M.J.H., Hunt, W.A., Jr., Wetzler, N.: Verifying refutations with extended resolution. In: Bonacina, M.P. (ed.) CADE 2013. LNCS, vol. 7898, pp. 345–359. Springer, Heidelberg (2013)
20. Heule, M.J.H., Hunt, W.A., Jr., Wetzler, N.: Expressing symmetry breaking in DRAT proofs. In: Felty, A.P., Middeldorp, A. (eds.) Automated Deduction - CADE-25. LNCS, vol. 9195, pp. 591–606. Springer, Heidelberg (2015)
21. Heule, M.J.H., Hunt, W.A., Jr., Wetzler, N.: Trimming while checking clausal proofs. In: Formal Methods in Computer-Aided Design, pp. 181–188. IEEE (2013)
22. Eén, N., Biere, A.: Effective preprocessing in SAT through variable and clause elimination. In: Bacchus, F., Walsh, T. (eds.) SAT 2005. LNCS, vol. 3569, pp. 61–75. Springer, Heidelberg (2005)

ELPI: Fast, Embeddable, λProlog Interpreter

Cvetan Dunchev[1]([⊠]), Ferruccio Guidi[1], Claudio Sacerdoti Coen[1],
and Enrico Tassi[2]

[1] Department of Computer Science, University of Bologna, Bologna, Italy
{Tsvetan.Dunchev,Ferruccio.Guidi,Claudio.SacerdotiCoen}@unibo.it
[2] Inria Sophia-Antipolis, Valbonne, France
Enrico.Tassi@inria.fr

Abstract. We present a new interpreter for λProlog that runs consistently faster than the byte code compiled by Teyjus, that is considered the best available implementation of λProlog. The key insight is the identification of a fragment of the language, which we call reduction-free fragment $(\mathcal{L}_\lambda^\beta)$, that occurs quite naturally in λProlog programs and that admits constant time reduction and unification rules.

1 Introduction

λProlog is a logic programming language based on an intuitionistic fragment of Church's Simple Theory of Types. An extensive introduction to the language with examples can be found in [9]. Teyjus [7,10] is a compiler for λProlog that is considered to be the fastest implementation of the language. The main difference with respect to Prolog is that λProlog manipulates λ-tree expressions, i.e. syntax containing binders. Therefore, the natural application of λProlog is meta-programming (see [11] for an interesting discussion), including: automatic generation of programs from specifications; animation of operational semantics; program transformations and implementation of type checking algorithms.

Via the Curry-Howard isomorphism a type-checker is a proof-checker, the main component of an interactive theorem prover (ITP). The motivation of our interest in λProlog is that we are looking for the best language to implement the so called *elaborator* component of an ITP. The elaborator is used to type check the terms input by the user. Such data, for conciseness reasons, is typically incomplete and the elaborator is expected to infer what is missing. The possibility to extend Coq's built-in elaborator with user provided "logic programs" (in the form of Canonical Structures [1,4] or Type Classes [12]) to help it infer the missing data, turned out to be a key ingredient in successful formalizations like [3]. Embedding a λProlog interpreter in an ITP would enable the elaborator and its extensions to be expressed in the same, high level, language. A crucial requisite for this plan to be realistic is the efficiency of the λProlog interpreter.

In this paper we introduce ELPI, a fast λProlog interpreter written in OCaml that can be easily embedded in OCaml softwares, like Coq. In particular we focus on the insight that makes ELPI fast when dealing with binders by identifying a reduction-free fragment $(\mathcal{L}_\lambda^\beta)$ of λProlog that, if implemented correctly, admits

M. Davis et al. (Eds.): LPAR-20 2015, LNCS 9450, pp. 460–468, 2015.
DOI: 10.1007/978-3-662-48899-7_32

constant-time unification and reduction operations. We analyze the role of β-reduction in Sect. 2 and higher order unification in Sect. 3; we discuss bound names representations in Sect. 4; we define $\mathcal{L}_\lambda^\beta$ in Sect. 5 and we assess the results in Sect. 6.

2   The Two Roles of β-reduction in λProlog

Example 1 implements type-checking and reduction for λ-terms represented in λ-tree syntax. For instance, the object-level encoding of $(\lambda x.xx)$ is the term (lam (x\ app x x)) of type T. The syntax (x\ F) denotes the λ-abstraction of λProlog, that binds x in F; lam is the constructor for object-level abstraction, that builds a term of type T from a function of type $T \to T$; app takes two terms of type T and builds their object-level application of type T. Following the tradition of Prolog, capitals letters denote unification variables.

The second clause for the of predicate shows a recurrent pattern in λProlog: in order to analyze an higher order term, one needs to recurse under a binder. This is achieved combining the forall quantifier, written pi x\ G, with logical implication H => I. The operational semantics implements the standard introduction rules of implication and the universal quantifier: the forall quantifier declares a new local constant x, meant to be fresh in the entire program; logical implication temporarily augments the program with the new axiom H about x.

In Example 1, line 4, the functional (sub-)term F is applied to the fresh constant x. Since F is a function, the β-redex (F x), once reduced, denotes the body of our object-level function where the bound variable is replaced by the fresh constant x. The implication is used to assume A to be the type of x, in order to prove that the body of the abstraction has type B and therefore the whole abstraction has type (arr A B) (i.e. $A \to B$). Note that, unlike in the standard presentation of the typing rules, we do not need to manipulate an explicit context Γ to type the free variables. Instead the assumptions of the form (of x A) are just added to the program's set of clauses, and λProlog takes care of dropping them when x goes out of scope. Example: if the initial goal is (of (lam (w\ app w w)) T) by applying the second clause we assign (arr A B) to T and generate a new goal (of (app c c) B) (where c is the fresh constant substituted for w) to be solved with the extra clause (of c A) at disposal.

In the type-checking example, the meta-level β-reduction is only employed to inspect a term under a binder by replacing the bound name with a fresh constant. The reduction example in line 6 shows instead a radically different

```
1  of (app M N) B :-                    5  cbn (lam F) (lam F).
2     of M (arr A B), of N A.           6  cbn (app (lam F) N) M :- cbn (F N) M.
3  of (lam F) (arr A B) :-              7  cbn (app M N) R :-
4     pi x\ of x A => of (F x) B.       8     cbn M (lam F), cbn (app (lam F) N) R.
```

Example 1: Type checker and Weak CBN for simply typed λ-calculus.

pattern: in order to implement object-level substitution — and thus object-level β-reduction — we use the meta-level β-reduction. E.g. if F is (w\ app w w) then (F N) reduces to (app N N). Note that in this case β-reduction is fully general, because it replaces a name with a general term, not constrained to be a fresh constant. This distinction is crucial in the definition of $\mathcal{L}_\lambda^\beta$ in Sect. 5.

3   Higher Order Unification

Higher order (HO) unification admits no most general unifiers (MGUs), forcing implementations to enumerate all solutions or delay the flexible-rigid and the flexible-flexible problems. Moreover, the presence of binders requires a way to avoid captures, i.e. to check that unification variables are instantiated with terms containing only bound variables in their scope.

To cope with the absence of MGUs, Dale Miller identified in [8] a well-behaved fragment $(\mathcal{L}_\lambda)$ of higher-order unification that admits MGUs and that is stable under λProlog resolution. The restriction defining $\mathcal{L}_\lambda$ is that unification variables can only be applied to (distinct) variables (i.e. not arbitrary terms) that are not already in the scope of the variable. Such fragment can effectively serve as a primitive for a programming language and indeed Teyjus 2.0 is built around this fragment: no attempt to enumerate all possible unifiers is performed, and unification problems falling outside $\mathcal{L}_\lambda$ are just delayed. Many interesting λProlog programs can be rewritten to fall in the fragment. For example, we can make cbn of Example 1 stay in $\mathcal{L}_\lambda$ by replacing line 6 (that contains the offending (F N) term) with the following code:

```
1 cbn (app (lam F) N) M :- subst F N B, cbn B M.
2 subst F N B :- pi x\ copy x N => copy (F x) B.
3 copy (lam F1) (lam F2) :- pi x\ copy x x => copy (F1 x) (F2 x).
4 copy (app M1 N1) (app M2 N2) :- copy M1 M2, copy N1 N2.
```

The idea of subst is that the term F is recursively copied in the following way: each bound variable is copied in itself but for the top one that is replaced by N. The interested reader can find a longer discussion about copy in [9, page 199]. The of program falls naturally in $\mathcal{L}_\lambda$, since F is only applied to the fresh variable x (all unification variables in a λProlog program are implicitly existentially bound in front of the clause, so F does not see x). The same holds for copy.

In λProlog unification takes place under a mixed prefix of $\forall$ and $\exists$ quantifiers. Their order determines if a unification variable (an existential) can be assigned to a term that contain a universally quantified variable. E.g. $\forall x, \exists Y, Y = x$ is provable while $\exists Y, \forall x, Y = x$ is not. An implementation can keep track of the scoping constraints using *levels*. When a clause's head is unified with the goal in a context of length n, the universally quantified variables of the clause are instantiated to unification variables X^n where the level n records that X has only visibility of the initial prefix of length n of the context. If later a fresh constant is added by the pi rule, the constant occupies position $n+1$ (its level is $n+1$) and it will not be allowed to occur in instances of the variable X^n. From now on we will write levels in superscript.

If we run the program `(of (lam f\lam w\app f w) T⁰)`, after two steps the goal becomes `(of (app c¹ d²) B⁰)`. Concretely, Teyjus replaces the bound names `f` and `w` with the level-annotated fresh constants c^1 and d^2 performing the β-reductions. As a crucial optimization [7] Teyjus implements reductions in a lazy way using an explicit substitution calculus. The reader can find this example developed in full details at page 6, where we demonstrate how substitutions of bound names by fresh level-annotated constants can be avoided in $\mathcal{L}_\lambda^\beta$.

4 Bound Variables

The last missing ingredient to define $\mathcal{L}_\lambda^\beta$ and explain why it can be implemented efficiently is to see how systems that manipulate λ-terms accommodate α-equivalence. Bound variables are not represented by using real names, but canonical "names" (hence α-equivalence becomes syntactic equality). De Bruijn introduced two, dual, naming schemes for λ-terms in [2]: depth indexes (DBI) and levels (DBL). In the former, that is the most widely adopted one, a variable is named n if its binder is found by crossing n binders going in the direction of the root. In the latter a variable named n is bound by the n-th binder one encounters in the path from the root to the variable. Below we write the term $\lambda x.(\lambda y.\lambda z.f\ x\ y\ z)\ x$ and its reduct in the two notations:

$$\text{Indexes: } \lambda x.(\lambda y.\lambda z.f\ x_2\ y_1\ z_0)\ x_0 \to_\beta \lambda x.\lambda z.f\ x_1\ x_1\ z_0$$
$$\text{Levels: } \lambda x.(\lambda y.\lambda z.f\ x_0\ y_1\ z_2)\ x_0 \to_\beta \lambda x.\lambda z.f\ x_0\ x_0\ z_1$$

In both notations when a binder is removed and the corresponding variable substituted some "renaming" (called lifting) is performed. Teyjus follows a third approach that mixes the two, using indexes for variables bound in the terms, and levels for variables bound in the context. The advantage is that no lifting is required when moving a term under additional binders. However, an expensive substitution of a level for an index is required to push a binder to the context.

In ELPI we crucially chose DBL because of the following three properties:

DBL1 x_i in Γ keeps the same name x_i in any extended context Γ, Δ
DBL2 the variables bound by Γ in a β-redex keep their name in the reduct
DBL3 when a binder is pushed to the context, the bound occurrences keep their name: no lifting is required to move from $\Gamma \vdash \forall x_i, p(x_i)$ to $\Gamma, x_i \vdash p(x_i)$

Another way to put it is that variables already pushed in the context are treated *exactly as constants*, and that the two notions of level — De Bruijn's and the position in the context introduced in Sect. 3 — coincide.

5 The Reduction-Free Fragment $\mathcal{L}_\lambda^\beta$

λProlog is a truly higher order language: even clauses can be passed around, unified, etc. Nevertheless this plays no role here, so we exclude formulas from the syntax of terms. Therefore, our terms are defined just by:

$$t ::= x_i \mid X^j \mid \lambda x_i.t \mid t\ t$$

Since variables follow the DBL representation, we do not have a case for constants like app or lam, that are represented as x_i for some negative i. Since the level of a variable completely identifies it, when we write $x_i \ldots x_{i+k}$ we mean k distinct bound (i.e. $i \geq 0$) variables. The superscript j annotates unification variables with their visibility range ($0 \leq j$, since all global constants are in range). A variable X^j has visibility of all names strictly smaller than j. E.g. X^1 has visibility only of $\{\ldots, x_{-1}, x_0\}$, and X^3 has visibility of $\{\ldots, x_{-1}, x_0, x_1, x_2\}$. Technically, when following the De Bruijn convention, we could just write $\lambda x_i.t$ as $\lambda.t$. We keep writing the name x_i to ease reading.

Definition 1 ($\mathcal{L}_\lambda^\beta$). *A term is in the reduction-free fragment $\mathcal{L}_\lambda^\beta$ iff every occurrence of a unification variable X^j is applied to $x_j \ldots x_{j+k-1}$ for $k \geq 0$.*

We allow $k = 0$ to accept variables that are not applied. A consequence of the definition is that if a term is in $\mathcal{L}_\lambda^\beta$ then all occurrences of applications of unification variables can be instantiated with a term closed in an initial segment of the λProlog context seen as a ordered list. Examples: $X^2 \, x_2 \, x_3$ and X^2 are in the fragment; $X^2 \, x_3$ and $X^2 \, x_3 \, x_2$ are not; $X^2 \, x_2 \, x_3$ can be instantiated with any term closed in $\{\ldots, x_0, x_1, x_2, x_3\}$.

Observe that the programs in Example 1 (when cbn is rewritten to be in the pattern fragment as in Sect. 3) are in $\mathcal{L}_\lambda^\beta$. Also, every Prolog program is in $\mathcal{L}_\lambda^\beta$. As we will see in Sect. 6, a type-checker for a dependently typed language and evaluator based on a reduction machine are also naturally in $\mathcal{L}_\lambda^\beta$. Thus, in practice, the fragment is quite expressive and is expressive enough to specify a realistic verifier, a first step towards the specification of a full-fledged elaborator.

Property 1 (Decidability of HO Unification). *Being $\mathcal{L}_\lambda^\beta$ included in the pattern-fragment $\mathcal{L}_\lambda$, higher order unification is decidable for $\mathcal{L}_\lambda^\beta$.*

The most interesting property of $\mathcal{L}_\lambda^\beta$, which also justifies its name, is:

Property 2 (Constant Time Head β-Reduction). *Let σ be a valid substitution for existentially quantified variables. Then the first $k - 1$ head reductions of $(X^j \, x_j \ldots x_{j+k-1})\sigma$ can be computed in constant time.*

A valid substitution assigns to X^j a term t of the right type (as in simply typed λ-calculus) and such that the free variables of t are all visible by X^j (all x_i are such that $i < j$). Therefore $X^j\sigma = \lambda x_j.\ldots.\lambda x_{j+n}.t$ for some n. Then

$$(X^j \, x_j \ldots x_{j+k-1})\sigma = \begin{cases} t \, x_{j+n+1} \ldots x_{j+k-1} & \text{if } n + 1 < k \\ \lambda x_{j+k}.\ldots.\lambda x_{j+n}.t & \text{otherwise} \end{cases} \tag{1}$$

Thanks to property **DBL2**, Eq. 1 is *syntactical*: no lifting of t is required. Hence the β-reductions triggered by the substitution of X^j take constant time.

Property 3 (Constant Time Unification). *A unification problem of the form $X^j \, x_j \ldots x_{j+k-1} \equiv t$ can be solved in constant time when no occur-check is needed for X.*

The unification problem $X^j\ x_j \ldots x_{j+k-1} \equiv t$ can always be rewritten as two simpler problems: $X^j \equiv \lambda x_j. \ldots . \lambda x_{j+k-1}.Y^{j+k}$ and $Y^{j+k} \equiv t$ for a fresh Y. The former is a trivial assignment that requires no check. The latter can be implemented in constant time iff no occur-check is needed for X and if the level of the highest free variable in t can be recovered in $O(1)$ and is smaller than $j+k$. The recovery can be economically implemented caching the maximum level in the term, that is something often pre-computed on the input term in linear time. Avoiding useless occur-check is a typical optimization of the Warren Abstract Machine (WAM), e.g. when X occurs linearly in the head of a clause. These properties enable us to implement the operational semantics of `pi` in constant time for terms in $\mathcal{L}_\lambda^\beta$.

We detail an example. The first column gathers the fresh constants and extra clauses. The second one shows the current goal(s) and the program clause that is used to back chain.

Test	ELPI		Teyjus		ELPI/Teyjus	
	time (s)	space (Kb)	time (s)	space (Kb)	time	space
crypto-mult	3.48	27,632	6.59	18,048	0.52	1.53
μ-puzzle	1.82	5,684	3.62	50,076	0.50	0.11
queens	1.41	108,324	2.02	69,968	0.69	1.54
zebra	0.85	7,008	1.89	8,412	0.44	0.83
typeof	0.27	8,872	5.64	239,892	0.04	0.03
reduce_cbv	0.15	7,248	11.11	57,404	0.01	0.12
reduce_cbn	0.33	8,968	0.81	102,896	0.40	0.08
SKI	1.32	15,472	2.68	8,896	0.49	2.73

After the first step we obtain F^0 := `x`$_0$ `\lam x`$_1$`\app x`$_0$ `x`$_1$; T^0 := `arr` $A^0\ B^0$; the extra clause about `x`$_0$ in the context and a new subgoal. Thanks to property **DBL3**, `x`$_0$ has been pushed to the context in constant time. Note that the redex (F^0 `x`$_0$) is in $\mathcal{L}_\lambda^\beta$ and thanks to Eq. 1 head normalizes in constant time to (`lam x`$_1$`\app x`$_0$ `x`$_1$). The same phenomenon arises in the second step, where we obtain G^1 := `x`$_1$ `\app x`$_0$ `x`$_1$ and we generate the redex (G^1 `x`$_1$). Unification variables are refreshed in the context under with the clause is used, e.g. `C` is placed at level 1 initially, but in consequence to a unification step they may be *pruned* when occurring in a term assigned to a lower level unification variable. Example: unifying B^0 with (`arr C`^{1} D^1) prunes `C` and `D` to level 0.

The choice of using DBL for bound variables is both an advantage and a complication here. Clauses containing no bound variables, like (`of x`$_0$ A^0), require no processing thanks to **DBL1**: they can be indexed as they are, since the name `x`$_0$ is stable. The drawback is that clauses with bound variables, like the one used in the first two back chains, need to be lifted: the first time the bound variable is named `x`$_0$, while the second time `x`$_1$. Luckily, this renaming, because of property **DBL1**, can be performed in constant time using the very same machinery one uses to refresh the unification variables. E.g. when the WAM unifies the head of a clauses it assigns fresh stack cells: the clause is not really refreshed and the stack pointer is simply incremented. One can represent the locally bound variable as an extra unification variable, and initialize, when `pi` is crossed, the corresponding stack cell to the first x_i free in the context.

Stability of $\mathcal{L}_\lambda^\beta$. Unlike $\mathcal{L}_\lambda$, $\mathcal{L}_\lambda^\beta$ is not stable under λProlog resolution: a clause that contains only terms in $\mathcal{L}_\lambda^\beta$ may generate terms outside the fragment. Therefore an implementation must handle both terms in $\mathcal{L}_\lambda^\beta$, with their efficient computation rules, and terms outside the fragment. Our limited experience so far, however, is that several programs initially written in the fragment remains in the fragment during computation, or they can be slightly modified to achieve that property.

6   Assessment and Conclusions

We assess ELPI on a set of synthetic benchmarks and a real application. Synthetic benchmarks are divided into three groups: first order programs from the Aquarius test suite (crypto-multiplication, μ-puzzle, generalized eight queens problem and the Einstein's zebra puzzle); higher order programs falling in $\mathcal{L}_\lambda^\beta$; and an higher order program falling outside $\mathcal{L}_\lambda^\beta$ taken from the test suite of Teyjus normalizing expressions in the SKI calculus.

The programs in $\mathcal{L}_\lambda^\beta$ are respectively type checking lambda terms using the `of` program of Example 1 and reducing expressions like 5^5 in the syntax of Church numerals using a call by value/name (CBV/CBN) strategy. The typeof test was specifically conceived to measure the cost of moving under binders: the type checked terms, projections, are mainly made of `lam` nodes.

Test	ELPI		Teyjus		ELPI/Teyjus	
	time (s)	space (Kb)	time (s)	space (Kb)	time	space
crypto-mult	3.48	27,632	6.59	18,048	0.52	1.53
μ-puzzle	1.82	5,684	3.62	50,076	0.50	0.11
queens	1.41	108,324	2.02	69,968	0.69	1.54
zebra	0.85	7,008	1.89	8,412	0.44	0.83
typeof	0.27	8,872	5.64	239,892	0.04	0.03
reduce_cbv	0.15	7,248	11.11	57,404	0.01	0.12
reduce_cbn	0.33	8,968	0.81	102,896	0.40	0.08
SKI	1.32	15,472	2.68	8,896	0.49	2.73

The data in the table shows that ELPI shines on programs in $\mathcal{L}_\lambda^\beta$, and compares well outside it. The alternating performance Teyjus on the reduction tests has to be attributed to the explicit substitutions (ES) machinery [7] when employed to cross binders: by its very nature ES fit well a lazy reduction strategy like CBN (even if some space overhead is visible). On the contrary ES are counterproductive in the CBV case since the program, by fully traversing the redex argument, systematically pushes the suspended substitution to the leaves of the term, completely defeating the purpose of the entire machinery (i.e. if the substitution has to be performed, there is no gain in delaying it). If one makes Teyjus artificially push explicit substitutions in the CBN case too, it halves memory consumption but degrades the performances by 10 seconds, confirming the time we see in the CBV case is dominated by the overhead of ES. By avoiding substitution when crossing binders ELPI is not only faster, but also more predictable performance wise: as one expects CBV is faster than CBN in computing the normal form of 5^5 since it avoids duplicating non-normal terms.

The real application we present is a checker for the formal system $\lambda\delta$ [5,6]. Such checker is able to validate the proof terms of the formalization of Landau's "Grundlagen" [13] done in Automath. The reference checker for $\lambda\delta$, named Helena, has been implemented in OCaml. Our λProlog implementation follows it closely, and naturally falls in $\mathcal{L}_\lambda^\beta$. Nevertheless, the λProlog code is much simpler than the corresponding OCaml code and consists of just 50 clauses.

The "Grundlagen" is a theory comprising definitions and proofs for a total of 6911 items (circa 8MB of data). Teyjus seems to have a fixed maximum heap size of 256MB that in turn limits it to the verification of the first 2615 items. In the table we compare pre-processing (Pre) time like parsing, compilation or elaboration, and verification (Ver). We compare ELPI with Helena, Teyjus, and Coq. The Coq system implements a type checker for a λ-calculus strictly more expressive than $\lambda\delta$, hence can check the proof terms directly but surely incurs in some overhead. We use its timings as a reference for the order of magnitude between the performance of ELPI and the ones of a state-of-the-art ITP. We compare native code against interpreted code where applicable.

Time (s) for 2615 items only			
	ELPI	Teyjus	ELPI/Teyjus
Pre	2.55	49.57	0.05
Ver	3.06	203.36	0.02
RAM (Mb)	91,628	1,072,092	0.09

Time (s) for all 6911 items					
Task	Helena		ELPI	Coq	
	interp.	comp.	interp.	interp.	comp.
Pre	2.42	0.41	9.04	49.28	8.83
Ver	4.40	0.33	13.90	7.21	1.19

Our conclusion is that $\mathcal{L}_\lambda^\beta$ admits a very efficient implementation and is large enough to express realistic programs like a type checker for a dependently typed λ-calculus. ELPI is under active development at http://lpcic.gforge.inria.fr.

References

1. Asperti, A., Ricciotti, W., Sacerdoti Coen, C., Tassi, E.: Hints in unification. In: Berghofer, S., Nipkow, T., Urban, C., Wenzel, M. (eds.) TPHOLs 2009. LNCS, vol. 5674, pp. 84–98. Springer, Heidelberg (2009)
2. de Bruijn, N.G.: Lambda calculus notation with nameless dummies, a tool for automatic formula manipulation, with application to the Church-Rosser theorem. In: Nederpelt, R.P., Geuvers, J.H., de Vrijer, R.C. (eds.) Selected Papers on Automath, pp. 375–388. North-Holland, Amsterdam (1994)
3. Gonthier, G., Asperti, A., Avigad, J., Bertot, Y., Cohen, C., Garillot, F., Le Roux, S., Mahboubi, A., O'Connor, R., Ould Biha, S., Pasca, I., Rideau, L., Solovyev, A., Tassi, E., Théry, L.: A machine-checked proof of the odd order theorem. In: Blazy, Sandrine, Paulin-Mohring, Christine, Pichardie, David (eds.) ITP 2013. LNCS, vol. 7998, pp. 163–179. Springer, Heidelberg (2013)
4. Gonthier, G., Ziliani, B., Nanevski, A., Dreyer, D.: How to make ad hoc proof automation less ad hoc. J. Funct. Program. **23**(4), 357–401 (2013)

5. Guidi, F.: The formal system $\lambda\delta$. In: ToCL, vol. 11(1), pp. 1–37, November 2009
6. Guidi, F.: Verified representations of Landau's "Grundlagen" in $\lambda\delta$ and in the calculus of constructions (2015). http://lambdadelta.info/, Submitted to JFR
7. Liang, C., Nadathur, G., Qi, X.: Choices in representation and reduction strategies for lambda terms in intensional contexts. JAR **33**(2), 89–132 (2004)
8. Miller, D.: A logic programming language with lambda-abstraction, function variables, and simple unification. J. Logic Comput. **1**, 253–281 (1991)
9. Miller, D., Nadathur, G.: Programming with Higher-Order Logic. Cambridge University Press, Cambridge (2012)
10. Nadathur, G., Mitchell, D.J.: System description: Teyjus - a compiler and abstract machine based implementation of λ prolog. In: Ganzinger, Harald (ed.) CADE 1999. LNCS (LNAI), vol. 1632, pp. 287–291. Springer, Heidelberg (1999)
11. Ridoux, O.: λ-Prolog de A a Z... ou presque. Habilitation à diriger des recherches, Université de Rennes 1 (1998)
12. Sozeau, M., Oury, N.: First-class type classes. In: Mohamed, O.A., Muñoz, C., Tahar, S. (eds.) TPHOLs 2008. LNCS, vol. 5170, pp. 278–293. Springer, Heidelberg (2008)
13. van Benthem Jutting, L.S.: Checking Landau's "Grundlagen" in the Automath system. In: Mathematical Centre Tracts, vol. 83. Mathematisch Centrum (1979)

Normalisation by Completeness
with Heyting Algebras

Gaëtan Gilbert[1,2](✉) and Olivier Hermant[3,4]

[1] ENS Lyon, Lyon, France
gaetan.gilbert@ens-lyon.fr
[2] Inria Paris, Paris, France
[3] MINES ParisTech, PSL Research University, Paris, France
[4] Wesleyan University, Middletown, CT, USA
olivier.hermant@mines-paristech.fr

Abstract. Usual normalization by evaluation techniques have a strong relationship with completeness with respect to Kripke structures. But Kripke structures is not the only semantics that fits intuitionistic logic: Heyting algebras are a more algebraic alternative.

In this paper, we focus on this less investigated area: how completeness with respect to Heyting algebras generate a normalization algorithm for a natural deduction calculus, in the propositional fragment. Our main contributions is that we prove in a direct way completeness of natural deduction with respect to Heyting algebras, that the underlying algorithm natively deals with disjunction, that we formalized those proofs in Coq, and give an extracted algorithm.

1 Introduction

In logic, a restriction to cut-free proofs makes analysis of a theory and proof-search significantly simpler. Evaluating programs boils down to finding efficient ways to reach a normal form, in order to produce a result.

Through the proof-as-programs paradigms, those two processes can be reduced to a single one: reduction steps of lambda-terms, such as β reduction, can be seen as a way to remove cuts from proofs expressed in natural deduction. Under this correspondence, a proof is cut-free when the associated proof-term is in normal form.

But there exist other, semantic, ways to eliminate cuts from proofs [15], through a completeness theorem that produces cut-free proofs, hereafter strong completeness, in combination with soundness. When those proofs can be made constructive [3,10,17], a natural question arises: what is the computational content of such proofs?

A link has already been exhibited. A line of research in program normalization, dubbed normalisation by evaluation, aims at evaluating a program in a type-directed fashion, by reusing the reduction mechanisms at hand at the meta

© Springer-Verlag Berlin Heidelberg 2015
M. Davis et al. (Eds.): LPAR-20 2015, LNCS 9450, pp. 469–482, 2015.
DOI: 10.1007/978-3-662-48899-7_33

level[1] through a pair of reflection/reification functions [2]. Soon after, Coquand noticed a strong similarity with completeness proofs [4].

This seminal work has been extended to more complex types [1,5], and also studied from the point of view of the completeness theorem for intuitionistic natural deduction with respect to Kripke-like structures [6,8,9]. But when it comes to incorporating disjunction, one must be very careful, in particular because Kripke structures require worlds to *decide* between both members of the conjunction - from a pure normalization by evaluation point of view, dealing with sum types also requires special care.

In this paper, we follow this line, relating constructive completeness proofs and normalization procedures. But, instead of considering Kripke semantics, as has been done in the works described above, we consider *Heyting algebras*:

- completeness theorems for the cut-free system (strong completeness), and therefore cut elimination [7,11] can be proved constructively;
- handling disjunction is straightforward, and hence we get cut elimination for sum types.

An adaptation of existing completeness proofs with respect to Heyting algebras is required, since all the known proofs, starting from Okada's contribution to linear logic [12], use sequent calculus.

To support these claims, we have formalized the proofs of this paper in Coq, and used extraction to get an executable interpreter. To keep the complexity of the formalization reasonable, we remained in the propositional fragment. The Coq sources are available at https://github.com/SkySkimmer/NormalisationByCompleteness.

The organization of this paper is the following: in Sect. 2 we recall natural deduction, in particular the notion of cut, and show basic lemmas. In Sect. 3, we develop the strong completeness proof, and discuss its Coq formalization in the next Sect. 4.1, where we also devise the behavior of the extracted algorithm on examples. Section 5 concludes the paper.

2   Natural Deduction

Definition 1 (Terms and formulas). *Let $\mathcal{V}$ be an infinite set of variables, $\mathcal{S}$ be a set of function symbols along with an arity and $\mathcal{P}$ be a set of predicate symbols along with an arity. The set of terms $\mathcal{T}$ is defined by:*

$$t ::= x \mid f(t_1, ..., t_n)$$

where $x \in \mathcal{V}$ and $f \in \mathcal{S}$ has arity n. The set of formulas $\mathcal{F}$ is defined by:

$$A, B ::= P(t_1, ..., t_n) \mid A \wedge B \mid A \vee B \mid A \Rightarrow B \mid \top \mid \bot \mid \forall x.A \mid \exists x.A$$

where $P \in \mathcal{P}$ has arity n.

---

[1] namely, the programming language in which the evaluation function is written.

Definition 2 (Substitutions). *A substitution σ is a partial function from variables to terms, with finite domain.*
We expand it inductively to a function from terms to terms and formulas to formulas, letting $\sigma(x) = x$ for $x \notin dom(\sigma)$.

Notably for $\mathcal{Q} \in \{\forall, \exists\}, \sigma(\mathcal{Q}\ x.A) := \mathcal{Q}x.\sigma(A)$, assuming x fresh w.r.t. the image of σ by α-conversion. This is always possible since $dom(\sigma)$ is finite, and so the image of σ is also finite.

Definition 3 (Updated Substitution). *Let σ be a substitution, $x \in \mathcal{V}$ and $t \in \mathcal{T}$, $\sigma[x \mapsto t]$ is the substitution with domain $dom(\sigma) \cup \{x\}$ such that for all $y \neq x$, $\sigma[x \mapsto t](y) = \sigma(y)$ and $\sigma[x \mapsto t](x) = t$.*

The substitution with the empty set as domain is denoted $\emptyset$. For t a term (resp. A a formula), x a variable and u a term, we abbreviate $\emptyset[x \mapsto u](t)$ (resp. $\emptyset[x \mapsto u](A)$) as $t[u/x]$ (resp. $A[t/x]$).

Definition 4 (Contexts). *A context Γ is a list of formulas $[A_1, ..., A_n]$. We let Γ, A be the concatenation of A and Γ. Membership is denoted $B \in \Gamma$. Inclusion, denoted $\Gamma \subseteq \Sigma$, holds when any $B \in \Gamma$ is also in Σ.*

Remark 1. The relation $\subseteq$ is a preorder, but not an order. Indeed, it strictly subsumes contraction ($\Gamma, A, A \subseteq \Gamma, A$) as well as reordering of premises.

Definition 5 (Cut-Free Proofs). *Figure 1 defines the relations $\vdash_{ne}$ (neutral proof) and $\vdash^*$ (cut-free proof) by mutual induction.*

In Fig. 1, rules on the left are introduction rules and produce cut-free proofs, while rules on the right are elimination rules and produce neutral proofs. FV denotes the set of free variables. The usual natural deduction calculus NJ is a merge of both relations. For two contexts Γ, Σ and any relation $\vdash'$, $\Sigma \vdash' \Gamma$ denotes $\Sigma \vdash' A$ for all $A \in \Gamma$.

Definition 6 (Natural Deduction). *The judgment $\Gamma \vdash A$ has the same rules as both $\Gamma \vdash^* A$ and $\Gamma \vdash_{ne} A$.*

Therefore, if $\Gamma \vdash^* A$ or $\Gamma \vdash_{ne} A$, then $\Gamma \vdash A$.

Lemma 1 (Weakening). *Let Γ, Σ be contexts such that $\Gamma \subseteq \Sigma$. Let A be a formula. The three following rules are admissible:*

$$\frac{\Gamma \vdash^* A}{\Sigma \vdash^* A} \qquad \frac{\Gamma \vdash_{ne} A}{\Sigma \vdash_{ne} A} \qquad \frac{\Gamma \vdash A}{\Sigma \vdash A}$$

Proof. By mutual induction on $\Gamma \vdash^* A$ and $\Gamma \vdash_{ne} A$, and by induction on $\Gamma \vdash A$. $\qquad\square$

Corollary 1 (Contraction). *For any context Γ and any formula B, if $\Gamma, A, A \vdash B$ then $\Gamma, A \vdash B$.*

$$\frac{\Gamma \vdash_{ne} A}{\Gamma \vdash^* A} \; coerce \qquad\qquad \frac{A \in \Gamma}{\Gamma \vdash_{ne} A} \; ax$$

$$\frac{\Gamma \vdash^* A \quad \Gamma \vdash^* B}{\Gamma \vdash^* A \wedge B} \wedge_I \qquad \frac{\Gamma \vdash_{ne} A \wedge B}{\Gamma \vdash_{ne} A} \wedge_{E_l} \qquad \frac{\Gamma \vdash_{ne} A \wedge B}{\Gamma \vdash_{ne} B} \wedge_{E_r}$$

$$\frac{\Gamma \vdash^* A}{\Gamma \vdash^* A \vee B} \vee_{I_l} \frac{\Gamma \vdash^* B}{\Gamma \vdash^* A \vee B} \vee_{I_r} \qquad \frac{\Gamma \vdash_{ne} A \vee B \quad A, \Gamma \vdash^* C \quad B, \Gamma \vdash^* C}{\Gamma \vdash_{ne} C} \vee_E$$

$$\frac{\Gamma, A \vdash^* B}{\Gamma \vdash^* A \Rightarrow B} \Rightarrow_I \qquad\qquad \frac{\Gamma \vdash_{ne} A \Rightarrow B \quad \Gamma \vdash^* A}{\Gamma \vdash_{ne} B} \Rightarrow_E$$

$$\frac{}{\Gamma \vdash^* \top} \top_I \qquad\qquad \frac{\Gamma \vdash_{ne} \bot}{\Gamma \vdash_{ne} A} \bot_E$$

$$\frac{\Gamma \vdash^* A \quad x \notin FV(\Gamma)}{\Gamma \vdash^* \forall x.A} \forall_I \qquad\qquad \frac{\Gamma \vdash_{ne} \forall x.A}{\Gamma \vdash_{ne} A[t/x]} \forall_E$$

$$\frac{\Gamma \vdash^* A[t/x]}{\Gamma \vdash^* \exists x.A} \exists_I \qquad \frac{\Gamma \vdash_{ne} \exists x.A \quad A, \Gamma \vdash^* C \quad x \notin FV(C, \Gamma)}{\Gamma \vdash_{ne} C} \exists_E$$

Fig. 1. Rules of natural deduction

Neutral proofs are such that they can replace axioms in cut-free proofs without introducing any cut.

Lemma 2 (Axiom Replacement). *Let Γ, Σ be contexts and A be a formula. The three following rules are admissible:*

$$\frac{\Sigma \vdash_{ne} \Gamma \quad \Gamma \vdash^* A}{\Sigma \vdash^* A} \qquad \frac{\Sigma \vdash_{ne} \Gamma \quad \Gamma \vdash_{ne} A}{\Sigma \vdash_{ne} A} \qquad \frac{\Sigma \vdash \Gamma \quad \Gamma \vdash A}{\Sigma \vdash A}$$

Proof. By mutual induction on $\Gamma \vdash^* A$ and $\Gamma \vdash_{ne} A$, and by induction on $\Gamma \vdash A$. Note that we need the weakening lemma (Lemma 1) when the context is modified in a premise of a rule.

Consider for instance the $\Rightarrow_I$ case of Fig. 1. $\Gamma, A \vdash^* B$ is derivable. $\Sigma, A \vdash_{ne} \Gamma, A$ holds, by weakening for Γ and by ax for A. By induction hypothesis, $\Sigma, A \vdash^* B$ and by $\Rightarrow_I$ we conclude $\Sigma \vdash^* A \Rightarrow B$. □

Lemma 3 (Kleene's Inversion Lemma). *Let Γ be a context, A and B be formulas.*
If $\Gamma \vdash_{ne} A \Rightarrow B$ (resp. $\Gamma \vdash^* A \Rightarrow B$) then $\Gamma, A \vdash_{ne} B$ (resp. $\Gamma, A \vdash^* B$).

Proof. If $\Gamma \vdash_{ne} A \Rightarrow B$, then by weakening $\Gamma, A \vdash_{ne} A \Rightarrow B$. By ax and $coerce$ we have $\Gamma, A \vdash^* A$. Then by $\Rightarrow_E$, $\Gamma, A \vdash_{ne} B$.

If $\Gamma \vdash^* A \Rightarrow B$, we analyze the last rule of the derivation:

- it is *coerce*: the premiss is $\Gamma \vdash_{ne} A \Rightarrow B$, then $\Gamma, A \vdash_{ne} B$ and by *coerce*, $\Gamma, A \vdash^* B$.
- otherwise it is $\Rightarrow_I$: the premiss is $\Gamma, A \vdash^* B$. □

3   Strong Completeness by Heyting Algebras

3.1   Heyting Algebras

Definition 7 (Complete Lattice). *A complete lattice is a tuple*

$$\mathcal{A} = (A, \leq, \bigwedge, \bigvee)$$

such that $(A, \leq)$ *is a partial order with arbitrary meet* $\bigwedge$ *and join* $\bigvee$.

In the sequel, we distinguish the binary meet $\wedge$, join $\vee$ and the global maximum $\top$ (empty meet) and minimum $\bot$ (empty join).

Definition 8 (Complete Heyting Algebra). *A Heyting algebra is a structure* $\mathcal{H} = (H, \leq, \wedge, \vee, \Rightarrow, \top, \bot, \bigwedge, \bigvee)$ *such that* $(H, \leq, \bigwedge, \bigvee)$ *is a complete lattice and verifies the implication property*

$$\forall a\, b\, c, a \leq b \Rightarrow c \text{ if and only if } a \wedge b \leq c$$

Lemma 4. *In a Heyting algebra, binary meet and join distribute over each other.*

Proof. Let $a, b, c \in H$

- $a \wedge (b \vee c) \leq (a \wedge b) \vee (a \wedge c)$: we have $a \wedge b \leq (a \wedge b) \vee (a \wedge c)$ and $a \wedge c \leq (a \wedge b) \vee (a \wedge c)$. By the implication property,

$$b \leq a \Rightarrow ((a \wedge b) \vee (a \wedge c)) \text{ and } c \leq a \Rightarrow ((a \wedge b) \vee (a \wedge c))$$

Then $b \vee c \leq a \Rightarrow ((a \wedge b) \vee (a \wedge c))$ and we conclude by the implication property.
- $(a \wedge b) \vee (a \wedge c) \leq a \wedge (b \vee c)$: holds in all lattices
- $a \vee (b \wedge c) \leq (a \vee b) \wedge (a \vee c)$: holds in all lattices
- $(a \vee b) \wedge (a \vee c) \leq a \vee (b \wedge c)$: By the implication property, this is equivalent to $a \vee b \leq (a \vee c) \Rightarrow (a \vee (b \wedge c))$
  $\Longleftrightarrow a \leq (a \vee c) \Rightarrow (a \vee (b \wedge c))$ and $b \leq (a \vee c) \Rightarrow (a \vee (b \wedge c))$
  $\Longleftrightarrow a \wedge (a \vee c) \leq a \vee (b \wedge c)$ (trivial) and $b \wedge (a \vee c) \leq a \vee (b \wedge c)$
  $\Longleftrightarrow a \vee c \leq b \Rightarrow (a \vee (b \wedge c))$
  $\Longleftrightarrow a \leq b \Rightarrow (a \vee (b \wedge c))$ and $c \leq b \Rightarrow (a \vee (b \wedge c))$
  $\Longleftrightarrow a \wedge b \leq a \vee (b \wedge c)$ (trivial) and $c \wedge b \leq a \vee (b \wedge c)$ (trivial)   □

Definition 9 (Interpretation). *A valuation on a set* $\mathcal{D}$, *called the domain, is a partial function* $\varphi : \mathcal{V} \to \mathcal{D}$ *with finite support. The syntax for updating valuations is the same as in Definition 3.*

A model on a Heyting algebra $\mathcal{H}$ *is given by a domain* $\mathcal{D}$, *and for each function symbol* $f \in \mathcal{S}$ *(resp. predicate symbol* $P \in \mathcal{P}$*) of arity* n *a function* $[\![f]\!] : \mathcal{D}^n \to \mathcal{D}$ *(resp. a function* $[\![P]\!] : \mathcal{D}^n \to H$*).*

Let φ *be a valuation,* t *a term and* A *a formula, such that* $FV(t) \cup FV(A) \subseteq dom(\varphi)$. *The interpretations* $[\![t]\!]_\varphi \in \mathcal{D}$ *and* $[\![A]\!]_\varphi \in \mathcal{H}$ *are defined in the usual inductive way.*

We define interpretation for contexts to be $[\![\Gamma]\!]_\varphi ::= \bigwedge_{C \in \Gamma} [\![C]\!]_\varphi$.

Notably:

$$[\![P(t_1, ..., t_k)]\!]_\varphi := [\![P]\!]([\![t_1]\!]_\varphi, ..., [\![t_k]\!]_\varphi)$$
$$[\![\forall x.A]\!]_\varphi := \bigwedge_{v \in \mathcal{D}}\{[\![A]\!]_{\varphi[x \mapsto v]}\}$$
$$[\![\exists x.A]\!]_\varphi := \bigvee_{v \in \mathcal{D}}\{[\![A]\!]_{\varphi[x \mapsto v]}\}$$

Theorem 1 (Soundness). *Let Γ be a context and A be a formula. If $\Gamma \vdash A$ is derivable, then for any Heyting algebra $\mathcal{H}$, for any model on $\mathcal{H}$ and valuation φ, $[\![\Gamma]\!]_\varphi \leq [\![A]\!]_\varphi$*

Proof. Standard induction [14].   □

3.2   Completeness

We now proceed to the construction of a universal Heyting algebra, that is suitable for *cut-free*, or *strong*, completeness, that is to say, that produces cut-free proofs [13]. This contrasts with more usual Lindenbaum algebras [14], formed with (provability-)equivalence classes of formulas.

Definition 10 (Extraction). *Let A be a formula. We define $\lfloor A \rfloor$ (the extraction of A) to be $\{\Gamma, \Gamma \vdash^* A\}$.*

$\lfloor A \rfloor$ is the set of contexts that prove A without cut, and will represent an upper bound for the interpretation of A, and as well the basis of our Heyting algebra below.

Definition 11 (Universal Heyting Algebra). *The underlying set of the universal Heyting algebra (aka the context algebra) is:*

$$\Omega ::= \{\bigcap \lfloor A_i \rfloor, (A_i)_{i \in I} \text{ family of formulas}\}$$

That is to say, the closure by arbitrary intersections of formula extractions. The partial order is inclusion and the operations are:

$$a \leq b := a \subseteq b$$
$$a \wedge b := a \cap b$$
$$\bigwedge A := \bigcap A$$
$$a \vee b := \bigcap\{\omega \in \Omega, a \cup b \leq \omega\}$$
$$\bigvee A := \bigcap\{\omega \in \Omega, \bigcup A \leq \omega\}$$
$$a \Rightarrow b := \bigvee\{c \in \Omega, a \wedge c \leq b\}$$
$$\top := \{\Gamma, \Gamma \text{ context}\} = \lfloor \top \rfloor$$
$$\bot := \{\Gamma, \forall A, \Gamma \vdash A\} = \lfloor \bot \rfloor$$

By abuse of notation, we also denote this algebra as Ω. $\bigwedge$ and $\bigvee$ are clearly greatest lower and lowest upper bounds, respectively. We can also simplify a bit lowest upper bounds, thanks to the following lemma:

Lemma 5. *The following identities are verified:*

$$a \vee b = \bigcap\{\lfloor D \rfloor, a \cup b \leq \lfloor D \rfloor, D \in \mathcal{F}\}$$
$$\bigvee A = \bigcap\{\lfloor D \rfloor, \bigcup A \leq \lfloor D \rfloor, D \in \mathcal{F}\}$$
$$a \Rightarrow b = \bigcap\{\lfloor D \rfloor, \bigcup\{c \in \Omega, a \wedge c \leq b\} \leq \lfloor D \rfloor, D \in \mathcal{F}\}$$

Proof. We focus on the first identity. The two other have a similar proof, as $a \vee b$, $\bigvee A$ and $a \Rightarrow b$ are all defined as lowest upper bound.

By definition of $\vee$, $a \vee b \leq \bigcap\{\lfloor D \rfloor, a \cup b \leq \lfloor D \rfloor, D \in \mathcal{F}\}$. Conversely, let ω such that $a \cup b \leq \omega$. Since $\omega \in \Omega$, $\omega = \bigcap_{i \in I} \lfloor C_i \rfloor$ for some $(C_i)_{i \in I}$. For all $i \in I$, $a \vee b \leq \lfloor C_i \rfloor$, and therefore $\omega \leq \bigcap\{\lfloor D \rfloor, a \cup b \leq \lfloor D \rfloor\}$.

Lemma 6. *Let $\omega \in \Omega$, and $\Gamma \in \omega$. Then, for any context Δ, $\Delta, \Gamma \in \omega$.*

Proof. By applying Lemma 1 to Definitions 10 and 11. $\qquad\qquad\square$

Lemma 7. *Ω forms a Heyting algebra.*

Proof. Ω is closed by arbitrary intersection and for all A, $\lfloor A \rfloor \in \Omega$, so the operations produce values in Ω. As already said, $\leq$ is an order for which $\wedge$ and $\bigwedge$ are greatest lower bounds, and $\vee$ and $\bigvee$ are lowest upper bounds. $\top$ and $\bot$ are trivially is the greatest and least element, respectively. It remains to check the implication property:

- Assume $a \leq b \Rightarrow c$, with $c = \bigcap_{k \in K} \lfloor C_k \rfloor$. Let $\Gamma \in a \wedge b$ and $k \in K$, we want to show $\Gamma \in \lfloor C_k \rfloor$, that is to say $\Gamma \vdash^* C_k$.
  $\Gamma \in a$ so $\Gamma \in b \Rightarrow c$ and we have for any D, if $\bigcup\{e \in \Omega, b \wedge e \leq c\} \leq \lfloor D \rfloor$ then $\Gamma \in \lfloor D \rfloor$.
  Let us show that $D ::= \Gamma \Rightarrow C_k$ verifies this hypothesis, where $\Gamma \Rightarrow B ::= A_1 \Rightarrow ... \Rightarrow A_n \Rightarrow B$ (with $\Gamma = A_1, ..., A_n$ and B formula).
  Let $e \in \Omega$ with $b \wedge e \leq c$. Let $\Delta \in e$, $\{\Delta, \Gamma\} \in b \wedge e$ by Lemma 1, then $\Delta, \Gamma \in c$, and $\Delta, \Gamma \vdash^* C_k$.
  By $\Rightarrow_I$, $\Delta \vdash^* \Gamma \Rightarrow C_k$, that is to say $\Delta \vdash^* D$. This holds for any such Δ, so $e \leq \lfloor D \rfloor$, and D verifies the desired hypothesis.
  Therefore $\Gamma \vdash^* \Gamma \Rightarrow C_k$ and by repeated application of Lemmas 1 and 3 $\Gamma \vdash^* C_k$.
  Finally, $\Gamma \in c$.
- Conversely, assume $a \wedge b \leq c$, then $a \leq \bigvee\{e, e \wedge b \leq c\} = b \Rightarrow c$. $\qquad\square$

Definition 12 (Interpretation in the Context Algebra). *The domain $\mathcal{D}$ of the model on Ω is defined as the set of terms. If f is a function symbol of arity n, P is a predicate symbol of arity n, we let:*

$$\llbracket f \rrbracket := (t_1, ..., t_n) \mapsto f(t_1, ..., t_n)$$
$$\llbracket P \rrbracket := (t_1, ..., t_n) \mapsto \lfloor P(t_1, ..., t_n) \rfloor$$

A consequence of this lemma is the following, where we implicitly coerce valuations with their underlying substitution.

Lemma 8. *For any t and valuation φ, $\llbracket t \rrbracket_\varphi = \varphi(t)$.*

Proof. By induction. $\qquad\qquad\square$

Definition 13 (Closure). *Let A be a formula. We define the closure of A to be*

$$cl(A) ::= \bigcap\{d \in \Omega, \lfloor A \rfloor \in d\}$$

Remind that $[A]$ is the one-formula context, containing only A (Definition 4).

Lemma 9. *For any A, $cl(A) \in \Omega$.*

Proof. Ω is stable by arbitrary intersection.   □

Lemma 10. $[A] \in cl(A)$

Proof. $cl(A)$ is the greatest lower bound of all d containing $[A]$.   □

Lemma 11. *For any A, $cl(A) = \bigcap\{\lfloor D \rfloor, [A] \in \lfloor D \rfloor\}$.*

Proof. Similar to the proof of Lemma 5.   □

Then $\Gamma \in cl(A)$ means for all formulas D, if $[A] \vdash^* D$ then $\Gamma \vdash^* D$. In a sense, the members of $cl(A)$ verify the axiom replacement lemma, except that this new operation does not necessarily preserve the structure of the derivation. $\Gamma \in cl(A)$ is a weaker statement than $\Gamma \vdash_{ne} A$:

Lemma 12. *For Γ context and A formula, if $\Gamma \vdash_{ne} A$ then $\Gamma \in cl(A)$.*

Proof. By Lemma 2, considering the previous Lemma 11.   □

Theorem 2 (Key Theorem). *For any formula A and valuation σ into Ω, σ is also a substitution and*

$$cl(\sigma(A)) \leq [\![A]\!]_\sigma \leq \lfloor \sigma(A) \rfloor$$

Proof. For clarity, we omit the valuation/substitution σ when it plays no role. The proof is done by induction on A:

- A is atomic: $[\![A]\!] = \lfloor A \rfloor$, so we only need to check $cl(A) \leq \lfloor A \rfloor$. Let $\Gamma \in cl(A)$. as we have $A \vdash^* A$, by definition of $cl(A)$, we have $\Gamma \vdash^* A$ and therefore $\Gamma \in \lfloor A \rfloor$.
- $cl(A \wedge B) \leq [\![A \wedge B]\!]$: by induction hypothesis we only need to show $cl(A \wedge B) \leq cl(A) \cap cl(B)$.
  Let $\Gamma \in cl(A \wedge B)$ and D such that $A \vdash^* D$ (resp. $B \vdash^* D$). Since $A \wedge B \vdash_{ne} A$ (resp. $A \wedge B \vdash_{ne} B$), by Lemma 2 we have $\Gamma \vdash^* D$ and $\Gamma \in cl(A)$ (resp. $\Gamma \in cl(B)$).

  $[\![A \wedge B]\!] \leq \lfloor A \wedge B \rfloor$: by the induction hypothesis we have $[\![A \wedge B]\!] \leq \lfloor A \rfloor \cap \lfloor B \rfloor$. The $\wedge_I$ rule concludes the proof.
- $cl(A \vee B) \leq [\![A \vee B]\!]$: consider C such that $[\![A]\!] \cup [\![B]\!] \leq \lfloor C \rfloor$. We have to show $[A \vee B] \in \lfloor C \rfloor$.
  Since, by Lemma 10 and induction hypothesis, $[A] \in cl(A) \leq \lfloor C \rfloor$ (resp. $[B] \in cl(B) \leq \lfloor C \rfloor$), we have $A \vdash^* C$ (resp. $B \vdash^* C$). Then by $\vee_E$ and *coerce* we have $A \vee B \vdash^* C$.

  $[\![A \vee B]\!] \leq \lfloor A \vee B \rfloor$: by definition of $[\![A]\!] \vee [\![B]\!]$, we need to show that $[\![A]\!] \cup [\![B]\!] \leq \lfloor A \vee B \rfloor$.
  By induction hypothesis, $[\![A]\!] \cup [\![B]\!] \leq \lfloor A \rfloor \cup \lfloor B \rfloor$, then the $\vee_I$ rule concludes.

– $cl(A \Rightarrow B) \leq [\![A \Rightarrow B]\!]$: by the implication rule we need $cl(A \Rightarrow B) \wedge [\![A]\!] \leq$ $[\![B]\!]$, and by induction hypothesis, it is sufficient to show $cl(A \Rightarrow B) \wedge \lfloor A \rfloor \leq$ $cl(B)$.

Let $\Gamma \in cl(A \Rightarrow B) \wedge \lfloor A \rfloor$, that is to say:

$$\Gamma \vdash^* A \text{ and for any } C, \text{ if } A \Rightarrow B \vdash^* C \text{ then } \Gamma \vdash^* C$$

Let D such that $B \vdash^* D$. To show $\Gamma \vdash^* D$, we first show that $\Gamma \vdash^* \Gamma \Rightarrow D$. We have, by hypothesis and Lemma 1, the following proof:

$$\frac{A \Rightarrow B, \Gamma \vdash_{ne} A \Rightarrow B \qquad A \Rightarrow B, \Gamma \vdash^* A}{A \Rightarrow B, \Gamma \vdash_{ne} B}$$

So, by Lemma 2, $A \Rightarrow B, \Gamma \vdash^* D$, and by repeated $\Rightarrow_I$, $A \Rightarrow B \vdash^* \Gamma \Rightarrow D$. By hypothesis on Γ, $\Gamma \vdash^* \Gamma \Rightarrow D$. By a repeated application of Lemmas 1 and 3, we get $\Gamma \vdash^* D$.

$[\![A \Rightarrow B]\!] \leq \lfloor A \Rightarrow B \rfloor$: by induction hypothesis, $[\![B]\!] \leq \lfloor B \rfloor$, so $[\![A]\!] \Rightarrow [\![B]\!] \leq$ $[\![A]\!] \Rightarrow \lfloor B \rfloor$ by the intersection (with $[\![A]\!]$) and the implication properties. By induction hypothesis also, $cl(A) \leq [\![A]\!]$, and therefore $cl(A) \wedge ([\![A]\!] \Rightarrow \lfloor B \rfloor) \leq$ $[\![A]\!] \wedge ([\![A]\!] \Rightarrow \lfloor B \rfloor) \leq \lfloor B \rfloor$, that is to say $[\![A]\!] \Rightarrow \lfloor B \rfloor \leq cl(A) \Rightarrow \lfloor B \rfloor$.
All in all, $[\![A \Rightarrow B]\!] \leq cl(A) \Rightarrow \lfloor B \rfloor$, and showing $cl(A) \Rightarrow \lfloor B \rfloor \leq \lfloor A \Rightarrow B \rfloor$ suffices.
Let c such that $cl(A) \wedge c \leq \lfloor B \rfloor$, we show that $\lfloor A \Rightarrow B \rfloor$ is an upper bound for c, so let $\Gamma \in c$. By Lemma 1 $A, \Gamma \in cl(A) \wedge c$, and $A, \Gamma \vdash^* B$, so by $\Rightarrow_I$, $\Gamma \vdash^* A \Rightarrow B$. This holds for any c, so $cl(A) \Rightarrow \lfloor B \rfloor \leq \lfloor A \Rightarrow B \rfloor$.

– $\top$ and $\bot$ are trivial cases.
– $cl(\sigma(\forall x.A)) \leq [\![\forall x.A]\!]_\sigma$:
Without loss of generality, we assume $\sigma(\forall x.A) = \forall x.\sigma(A)$ (see Definition 2).
Let $\Gamma \in cl(\sigma(\forall x.A))$.
We need to prove that for any term d, $\Gamma \in [\![A]\!]_{\sigma[x \mapsto d]}$. Let d a term, showing $\Gamma \in cl(\sigma[x \mapsto d](A))$ suffices by induction hypothesis.
Let D such that $\sigma[x \mapsto d](A) \vdash^* D$. As x does not appear in the image of σ, $\sigma[x \mapsto d](A) = (\sigma(A))[d/x]$, and we have:

$$\frac{\dfrac{}{[\forall x.\sigma(A)] \vdash_{ne} \forall x.\sigma(A)} \; ax}{[\forall x.\sigma(A)] \vdash_{ne} \sigma[x \mapsto d](A)} \; \forall_E$$

Then by Lemma 2, $[\forall x.\sigma(A)] \vdash^* D$. As we assumed $\Gamma \in cl(\forall x.\sigma(A))$, the claim follows.

$[\![\forall x.A]\!]_\sigma \leq \lfloor \sigma(\forall x.A) \rfloor$:
Let $\Gamma \in [\![\forall x.A]\!]_\sigma$, where by α-conversion we assume x fresh.
By Definition 9, $\Gamma \in [\![A]\!]_{\sigma[x \mapsto x]}$. By induction hypothesis we conclude $\Gamma \in$ $\lfloor \sigma[x \mapsto x](A) \rfloor$.
Finally, by the $\forall_I$ rule $\Gamma \vdash^* \forall x.\sigma[x \mapsto x](A)$, and by freshness of x, $\Gamma \vdash^*$ $\sigma(\forall x.A)$.

– $cl(\sigma(\exists x.A)) \le [\![\exists x.A]\!]_\sigma$:

Let $\Gamma \in cl(\sigma(\exists x.A))$, assuming x fresh. By Lemma 5, $\Gamma \in [\![\exists x.A]\!]_\sigma$ if and only if for any D, such that for each term d $[\![A]\!]_{\sigma[x \mapsto d]} \le \lfloor D \rfloor$, then $\Gamma \vdash^* D$. Let such a D, we give a derivation of $[\exists x.\sigma(A)] \vdash^* D$, which allows to conclude by assumption on Γ.

By induction hypothesis, $[\sigma(A)] \in cl(\sigma(A)) \le [\![A]\!]_\sigma$, and by hypothesis on D, $[\sigma(A)] \in \lfloor D \rfloor$. With Lemma 1, we get a derivation of the sequent $\exists x.\sigma(A), \sigma(A) \vdash^* D$. As $\exists x.\sigma(A) \vdash_{ne} \exists x.\sigma(A)$ has a neutral proof, we can build the desired derivation:

$$\frac{\exists x.\sigma(A), \sigma(A) \vdash^* D \qquad \exists x.\sigma(A) \vdash_{ne} \exists x.\sigma'(A)}{\exists x.\sigma(A) \vdash_{ne} D} \exists_E$$

$[\![\exists x.A]\!]_\sigma \le \lfloor \sigma(\exists x.A) \rfloor$, assuming x fresh in the image of σ:

We show that $\lfloor \sigma(\exists x.A) \rfloor$ is an upper bound for all $[\![A]\!]_{\sigma[x \mapsto d]}$, where d is any term. This allows to conclude.

Let d, Γ, such that $\Gamma \in [\![A]\!]_{\sigma[x \mapsto d]}$. By induction hypothesis $\Gamma \in \lfloor \sigma[x \mapsto d](A) \rfloor$.

$\sigma[x \mapsto d](A) = (\sigma(A))[d/x]$, so $\Gamma \vdash^* (\sigma(A))[d/x]$ and by the $\Rightarrow_I$ rule, $\Gamma \vdash^* \exists x.\sigma(A)$, i.e. $\Gamma \vdash^* \sigma(\exists x.A)$. $\qquad\qquad \square$

Theorem 3 (Strong Completeness). *Let Γ be a context and A a formula. If for any Heyting algebra, any model and any valuation φ, $[\![\Gamma]\!]_\varphi \le [\![A]\!]_\varphi$, then $\Gamma \vdash^* A$.*

Proof. We apply the hypothesis on the universal algebra of Definition 11, the interpretation of Definition 12 and the empty valuation/substitution.

Consider $C \in \Gamma$. $C \in cl(C)$ by Lemma 10. By Lemma 6 and Theorem 2, $\Gamma \in cl(C) \le [\![C]\!]$. So $\Gamma \in [\![\Gamma]\!] \le [\![A]\!]$. By Theorem 2, $[\![A]\!] \le \lfloor A \rfloor$. Finally $\Gamma \vdash^* A$.

Theorem 4 (Cut Elimination). *Let Γ be a context and A a formula. If $\Gamma \vdash A$, then $\Gamma \vdash^* A$.*

Proof. By soundness (Theorem 1) and strong completeness (Theorem 3).

4 The Algorithm in Practice

This work has been formalized in Coq for the propositional fragment, so as to focus on the core of the algorithm, without dealing with binders.

4.1 Formalization: The Algorithm

Ω contains *arbitrary intersections* of extractions. To define it, we need to range over index predicates for the formulas A_i, that have type form $\to Prop$ and let Ω be $\{\{\Gamma : \text{context}, \forall A, \mathcal{P}(A) \to \Gamma \vdash^* A\} \mid \mathcal{P} : \text{form} \to Prop\}$. We cannot range over predicates of type form $\to Type$, because of the need for impredicativity.

As a consequence, the predicate $\Gamma \vdash^* A$ lives in *Prop*, which prevents us to extract a program due to proof irrelevance. Nevertheless, we can apply the theorem to a derivation and use *Eval compute* to observe the behavior of the algorithm. However, since formulas are processed by Theorem 2 which performs case analysis, computation stalls if the derivation involves formula variables.

To have both impredicativity and extraction, we considered using an impredicative *Set* type, but we were not able to extract a program due to internal limitations. As a last resort, we relaxed the universe constraint, deliberately making the system inconsistent, but gaining an impredicative *Type* type and a (possibly unsound) algorithm.

Three difficulties obfuscate the investigation of the algorithm (see the proofs of Theorems 3 and 4):

- the $\Gamma \in cl(\Gamma)$ step involves a conjunction of formula closures, and calls technical lemmas. This step can be avoided by considering empty contexts, i.e. $\Gamma = []$ and $[\![\Gamma]\!] = \top$.
- the $[\![A]\!] \subseteq \lfloor A \rfloor$ and $cl(\Gamma) \subseteq [\![\Gamma]\!]$ steps, i.e. calling Theorem 2, the key theorem, that in many cases makes a very indirect use of the NJ rules, potentially appealing to inversion results (Lemma 3).
- the $[\![\Gamma]\!] \subseteq [\![A]\!]$ step, i.e. soundness of NJ with respect to Ω. It involves in particular the proof that Ω is a Heyting algebra, which is non-trivial especially for the $\Rightarrow$ operator, and then composes these properties somehow.

Simplifying those steps is necessary for a further analysis. For the time being, we are only able to investigate the behavior of the algorithm by observational means, applying it to specific derivations, as shown below.

4.2 Examples

Implication cut. When applied to a simple implication cut, the algorithm does what expected.

Initial proof		Reduct
$\dfrac{\dfrac{\overline{A, A \vdash A}\ ax}{A \vdash A \Rightarrow A}\Rightarrow_I \quad \dfrac{}{A \vdash A}\ ax}{A \vdash A}\Rightarrow_E$		$\dfrac{}{A \vdash A}\ ax$

Disjunction cut. A disjunction cut is also properly reduced:

Initial proof			Reduct
$\dfrac{\dfrac{\dfrac{\overline{A \vdash A}\ ax}{A \vdash A \vee A}\vee_{I_l} \quad \dfrac{\overline{A, A \vdash A}\ ax}{A, A \vdash A \vee A}\vee_{I_r} \quad \dfrac{\overline{A, A \vdash A}\ ax}{A, A \vdash A \vee A}\vee_{I_l}}{A \vdash A \vee A}\vee_E}{}$			$\dfrac{\dfrac{}{A \vdash A}\ ax}{A \vdash A \vee A}\vee_{I_r}$

Eta expansion. As the algorithm is type-directed, it is not neutral on elementary proofs, when formulas are not atomic:

Initial proof	Reduct
$$\cfrac{}{A \Rightarrow B \vdash A \Rightarrow B} \, ax$$	$$\cfrac{\cfrac{\cfrac{}{A \Rightarrow B, A \vdash A \Rightarrow B} \, ax \qquad \cfrac{}{A \Rightarrow B, A \vdash A} \, ax}{A \Rightarrow B, A \vdash B} \Rightarrow_E}{A \Rightarrow B \vdash A \Rightarrow B} \Rightarrow_I$$
$$\cfrac{}{A \wedge B \vdash A \wedge B} \, ax$$	$$\cfrac{\cfrac{}{A \wedge B \vdash A \wedge B} \, ax}{A \wedge B \vdash A} \wedge_{E_l} \qquad \cfrac{\cfrac{}{A \wedge B \vdash A \wedge B} \, ax}{A \wedge B \vdash B} \wedge_{E_r} \atop \cfrac{}{A \wedge B \vdash A \wedge B} \wedge_I$$
$$\cfrac{}{A \vee B \vdash A \vee B} \, ax$$	$$\cfrac{\cfrac{}{A \vee B \vdash A \vee B} \, ax \qquad \cfrac{\cfrac{}{A \vee B, A \vdash A} \, ax}{A \vee B, A \vdash A \vee B} \vee_{I_l} \qquad \cfrac{\cfrac{}{A \vee B, B \vdash B} \, ax}{A \vee B, B \vdash A \vee B} \vee_{I_r}}{A \vee B \vdash A \vee B} \vee_E$$

When applying iteratively the theorem once again to those proofs, one can notice that we already have reached a fixed point in the $\Rightarrow$ and $\wedge$ cases, while we continue reducing in the disjunction case, where we can notice that the context is abstracted via a $\Rightarrow_I$ rule, that introduces a commutative cut:

$$\cfrac{}{A \vee B \vdash A \vee B} \, ax \qquad \cfrac{\cfrac{\cfrac{\cfrac{}{A \vee B, A, A \vee B \vdash A} \, ax}{A \vee B, A, A \vee B \vdash A \vee B} \vee_{I_l}}{A \vee B, A \vdash (A \vee B) \Rightarrow (A \vee B)} \Rightarrow_I \qquad \cfrac{\cfrac{\cfrac{}{A \vee B, B, A \vee B \vdash B} \, ax}{A \vee B, B, A \vee B \vdash A \vee B} \vee_{I_r}}{A \vee B, B \vdash (A \vee B) \Rightarrow (A \vee B)} \Rightarrow_I}{A \vee B \vdash (A \vee B) \Rightarrow (A \vee B)} \vee_E \qquad \cfrac{}{A \vee B \vdash A \vee B} \, ax \atop \cfrac{}{A \vee B \vdash A \vee B} \Rightarrow_E$$

5   Conclusion

Strong completeness with respect to Heyting algebras has a constructive proof. In this paper, we have applied this result to natural deduction, and formalized it in Coq, so as to produce an algorithm for proof normalization. This argument can also be lifted to classical logic, using Boolean algebras instead, although we would have to carefully choose a classical natural deduction calculus. Obviously, this also applies to sequent calculus, in an even more straightforward way.

Our algorithm can be studied by evaluating it on specific derivations and by *Print*ing the Coq function to review the generated code. However, simplifying Coq proofs, via more general inversion (Kleene) or weakening lemmas for instance, is still necessary for a more in-depth understanding. Moreover, we still have to show that the normal proof obtained is really a reduct of the original proof. This could be done by carrying the original proof along soundness and completeness, as a for of proof-relevant version of those theorems.

It would also be interesting to compare the algorithm that we obtain with the ones that come from completeness with respect to Kripke structure [6,8,9], and in particular the produced normal proofs. One of the interests of our methodology is that we deal with disjunction (sum types) without requiring any modification of the semantics.

Semantic transformations could help in the study of the relationship between both algorithms. In particular, turning a Heyting algebra into a Kripke structure is not purely constructive [16]. Applied to the particular universal Heyting algebra/Kripke structure, translations may also be more informative and constructive [8].

As for disjunction, we did not focus on commutative cuts, and more work is required in this direction. It theoretically possible, as we can always eliminate those cuts by translating back and forth natural deduction into sequent calculus, semantically normalizing there. But a direct study is much more preferable.

Strong completeness for higher-order logic is also within reach, which, besides giving a normalization algorithm for a powerful logic, would give another way of studying disjunction, through their higher-order encoding.

Acknowledgments. The authors would like to thanks the reviewers for their insightful and constructive comments and pointers. Unfortunately we lacked time to include them all.

References

1. Altenkirch, T., Dybjer, P., Hofmann, M., Scott, P.: Normalization by evaluation for typed lambda calculus with coproducts. In: 16th Annual IEEE Symposium on Logic in Computer Science, pp. 303–310 (2001)
2. Berger, U., Schwichtenberg, H.: An inverse of the evaluation functional for typed λ-calculus. In: Vemuri, R. (ed.) Proceedings of the Sixth Annual IEEE Symposium on Logic in Computer Science, pp. 203–211. IEEE Computer Society Press, Los Alamitos (1991)
3. Bonichon, R., Hermant, O.: On constructive cut admissibility in deduction modulo. In: Altenkirch, T., McBride, C. (eds.) TYPES 2006. LNCS, vol. 4502, pp. 33–47. Springer, Heidelberg (2007)
4. Coquand, C.: From semantics to rules: a machine assisted analysis. In: Meinke, K., Börger, E., Gurevich, Y. (eds.) CSL 1993. LNCS, vol. 832, pp. 91–105. Springer, Heidelberg (1994)
5. Danvy, O.: Type-directed partial evaluation. In: Hatcliff, J., Thiemann, P. (eds.) Practice and Theory DIKU 1998. LNCS, vol. 1706, pp. 367–411. Springer, Heidelberg (1999)
6. Herbelin, H., Lee, G.: Formalizing logical metatheory: semantic cut-elimination using kripke models for first-order predicate logic, 2014. http://formal.hknu.ac.kr/Kripke/, Accessed on 06–11–2014
7. Hermant, O., Lipton, J.: A constructive semantic approach to cut elimination in type theories with axioms. In: Kaminski, M., Martini, S. (eds.) CSL 2008. LNCS, vol. 5213, pp. 169–183. Springer, Heidelberg (2008)
8. Ilik, D.: Continuation-passing style models complete for intuitionistic logic. Ann. Pure Appl. Logic **164**(6), 651–662 (2012)
9. Ilik, D., Lee, G., Herbelin, H.: Kripke models for classical logic. Ann. Pure Appl. Logic **161**(11), 1367–1378 (2010)
10. Krivine, J.-L.: Une preuve formelle et intuitionniste du théorème de complétude de la logique classique. Bull. Symbolic Logic **2**, 405–421 (1996)
11. Maehara, S.: Lattice-valued representation of the cut-elimination theorem. Tsukuba J. Math. **15**(2), 509–521 (1991)

12. Okada, M.: An introduction to linear logic: expressiveness and phasesemantics. In: Takahashi, M., Okada, M., Dezani-Ciancaglini, M., (eds.) Theories of Types and Proofs, MSJ Memoirs, vol. 2, pp. 255–295. The Mathematical Society of Japan, Tokyo, Japan (1998)
13. Okada, M.: Phase semantic cut-elimination and normalization proofs of first- and higher-order linear logic. Theoret. Comput. Sci. **227**, 333–396 (1999)
14. Rasiowa, H., Sikorski, R.: The Mathematics of Metamathematics. Polish Scientific Publishers PWN, Warszawa (1963)
15. Tait, W.W.: A non constructive proof of gentzen's hauptsatz for second order logic. Bull. AMS **72**, 980–983 (1966)
16. Troelstra, A.S., van Dalen, D.: Constructivism in Mathematics. North-Holland, Amsterdam (1988)
17. Veldman, W.: An intuitionistic completeness theorem for intuitionistic predicate logic. J. Symbolic Logic **41**, 159–166 (1976)

Using Program Synthesis for Program Analysis

Cristina David[1]([✉]), Daniel Kroening[1], and Matt Lewis[1,2]

[1] University of Oxford, Oxford, UK
{cristina.david,daniel.kroening}@cs.ox.ac.uk
[2] Improbable Worlds Ltd., London, UK
matt@improbable.io

Abstract. In this paper, we propose a *unified* framework for designing static analysers based on *program synthesis*. For this purpose, we identify a fragment of second-order logic with restricted quantification that is expressive enough to capture numerous static analysis problems (e.g. safety proving, bug finding, termination and non-termination proving, superoptimisation). We call this fragment the *synthesis fragment*. We build a decision procedure for the synthesis fragment over finite domains in the form of a program synthesiser. Given our initial motivation to solve static analysis problems, this synthesiser is specialised for such analyses. Our experimental results show that, on benchmarks capturing static analysis problems, our program synthesiser compares positively with other general purpose synthesisers.

1 Introduction

Fundamentally, every static program analysis is searching for a *program proof*. For safety analysers this proof takes the form of a program invariant [1], for bug finders it is a counter-model [2], for termination analysis it can be a ranking function [3], whereas for non-termination it is a recurrence set [4]. Finding each of these proofs was subject to extensive research resulting in a multitude of *specialised* techniques.

In this paper, we propose a *unified* framework for designing static analysers. This framework allows implementing new analyses easily by only providing a description of the corresponding program proofs. This essentially enables a declarative way of designing static analyses, where we specify what we want to achieve rather than the details of how to achieve it.

The theoretical basis for this framework is a fragment of second-order logic with restricted quantification that is expressive enough to capture numerous static analysis problems (e.g. safety proving, bug finding, termination and non-termination proving, superoptimisation). This fragment is decidable over finite domains and we build a decision procedure for it based on *program synthesis*. Accordingly, we call this fragment *the synthesis fragment*.

This research was supported by ERC project 280053 (CPROVER).

M. Davis et al. (Eds.): LPAR-20 2015, LNCS 9450, pp. 483–498, 2015.
DOI: 10.1007/978-3-662-48899-7_34

In our framework, finding a program proof for some static analysis problem amounts to finding a satisfying model for a synthesis formula, where the second-order entities denote the program proofs. If the synthesis formula is satisfiable, a solution consists of a satisfying assignment from the second order variables to *functions over finite domains*. Every function over finite domains is computed by some *program* that can be synthesised.

Our program synthesiser is specialised for program analysis in the following three dimensions (identified as the three key dimensions in program synthesis [5]):

1. Expression of User Intent: Our specification language is a fragment of C, which results in *concise specifications* of static analyses. Using our tool to build a program analyser only requires providing a generic specification of the problem to solve. The programs to be analysed do not need to be modified, symbolically executed or compiled to an intermediate language. Our experiments show that this results in specifications that are an order of magnitude smaller than the equivalent specifications with other general purpose program synthesisers.

2. Space of Programs Over Which to Search: The language in which we synthesise our programs is universal, i.e. every finite function is computed by at least one program in our language. Our solution language also has first-class support for *programs computing multiple outputs*, as well as *constants*. The former allows the direct encoding of lexicographic ranking functions of unbounded dimension, whereas the latter improves the efficiency when synthesising programs with non-trivial constants (as shown by our experimental results).

3. The Search Technique: An important aspect of our synthesis algorithm is how we search the space of candidate programs. We parameterise the solution language, which induces a lattice of progressively more expressive languages. As well as giving us an automatic search procedure, this parametrisation greatly increases the efficiency of our system since languages low down the lattice are very easy to decide safety for. Consequently, our solver's runtime is heavily influenced by the *length of the shortest proof*, i.e. the Kolmogorov complexity of the problem. If a short proof exists, then the solver will find it quickly. This is particularly useful for program analysis problems, where, if a proof exists, then most of the time many proofs exist and some are short ([6] relies on a similar remark about loop invariants).

Our Contributions.

- We define the synthesis fragment and show that its decision problem over finite domains is NEXPTIME-complete (Sect. 2).
- By using program synthesis, we design a decision procedure for the synthesis fragment. The resulting program synthesiser uses a combination of bounded model checking, explicit-state model checking and genetic programming (Sect. 5).
- We propose the use of second-order tautologies for avoiding unsatisfiable instances when solving program analysis problems with program synthesis (Sect. 8).

– We implemented the program synthesiser and tried it on a set of static analysis problems. Our experimental results show that, on benchmarks generated from static analysis, our program synthesiser compares positively with other general purpose synthesisers (Sect. 9).

Related Work. A recent successful approach to program synthesis is Syntax Guided Synthesis (SyGuS) [7]. The SyGuS synthesisers supplement the logical specification with a syntactic template that constrains the space of allowed implementations. Thus, each semantic specification is accompanied by a syntactic specification in the form of a grammar. In contrast to SyGuS, our program synthesiser is optimised for program analysis according to the three aforementioned key dimensions.

Other second-order solvers are introduced in [8,9]. As opposed to ours, these are specialised for Horn clauses and the logic they handle is undecidable. Wintersteiger et al. present in [10] a decision procedure for a logic related to the synthesis fragment, the Quantified bit-vector logic, which is a many sorted first-order logic formula where the sort of every variable is a bit-vector sort. It is possible to reduce formulae in the synthesis fragment over finite domains to Effectively Propositional Logic [11], but the reduction would require additional axiomatization and would increase the search space, thus defeating the efficiency we are aiming to achieve.

2   The Synthesis Fragment

In this section, we identify a fragment of second-order logic with a constrained use of quantification that is expressive enough to encode numerous static analysis problems. We will suggestively refer to the fragment as the *synthesis fragment*:

Definition 1 (Synthesis Fragment (SF)). *A formula is in the synthesis fragment iff it is of the form*

$$\exists P_1 \ldots P_m.Q_1 x_1 \ldots Q_n x_n.\sigma(P_1, \ldots, P_m, x_1, \ldots, x_n)$$

where the P_i range over functions, the Q_i are either $\exists$ or $\forall$, the x_i range over ground terms and σ is a quantifier-free formula.

If a pair $(\vec{P}, \vec{x})$ is a satisfying model for the synthesis formula, then we write $(\vec{P}, \vec{x}) \models \sigma$. For the remainder of the presentation, we drop the vector notation and write x for $\vec{x}$, with the understanding that all quantified variables range over vectors.

3   Program Analysis Specifications in the Synthesis Fragment

Program analysis problems can be reduced to the problem of finding solutions to a second-order constraint [8,12,13]. The goal of this section is to show that the synthesis fragment is expressive enough to capture many interesting such problems. For brevity reasons, we will only express safety, termination and non-termination. When we describe analyses involving loops, we will characterise each loop as having initial state I, guard G and transition relation B.

Safety Invariants. Given a safety assertion A, a safety invariant is a set of states S which is inductive with respect to the program's transition relation, and which excludes an error state. A predicate S is a safety invariant iff it satisfies the following criteria:

$$\exists S. \forall x, x'. I(x) \to S(x) \land \tag{1}$$
$$S(x) \land G(x) \land B(x, x') \to S(x') \land \tag{2}$$
$$S(x) \land \neg G(x) \to A(x) \tag{3}$$

(1) says that each state reachable on entry to the loop is in the set S, and in combination with (2) shows that every state that can be reached by the loop is in S. The final criterion (3) says that if the loop exits while in an S-state, the assertion A is not violated.

Termination and Non-termination. As shown in [13], termination of a loop can be encoded as the following formula, where W is an inductive invariant of the loop that is established by the initial states I if the loop guard G is met, and R is a ranking function as restricted by W:

$$\exists R, W. \forall x, x'. I(x) \land G(x) \to W(x) \land$$
$$G(x) \land W(x) \land B(x, x') \to W(x') \land R(x){>}0 \land R(x){>}R(x')$$

Similarly, non-termination can be expressed in the synthesis fragment as follows:

$$\exists N, C, x_0. \forall x. N(x_0) \land N(x) \to G(x) \land N(x) \to B(x, C(x)) \land N(C(x))$$

Here, N denotes a recurrence set, i.e. a nonempty set of states such that for each $s \in N$ there exists a transition to some $s' \in N$, and C is a Skolem function that chooses the successor x'. More details on the formulations for termination and non-termination can be found in [13].

4   The Synthesis Fragment over Finite Domains

When interpreting the ground terms over a finite domain $\mathcal{D}$, the synthesis fragment is decidable and its decision problem is NEXPTIME-complete. We use the notation $SF_{\mathcal{D}}$ to denote the synthesis fragment over a finite domain $\mathcal{D}$.

Theorem 1 ($SF_{\mathcal{D}}$ is NEXPTIME-Complete).   *For an instance of Definition 1 with n first-order variables, where the ground terms are interpreted over $\mathcal{D}$, checking the truth of the formula is NEXPTIME-complete.*

Proof. In the extended version [14].

Next, we are concerned with building a solver for $SF_{\mathcal{D}}$. A satisfying model for a formula in $SF_{\mathcal{D}}$ is an assignment mapping each of the second-order variables to some function of the appropriate type and arity. When deciding whether a particular $SF_{\mathcal{D}}$ instance is satisfiable, we should think about how solutions are encoded and in particular how a function is to be encoded. The functions all have a finite domain and co-domain, so their canonical representation would be a finite set of ordered pairs. Such a set is exponentially large in the size of the domain, so we would prefer to work with a more compact representation if possible.

We will generate *finite state programs* that compute the functions and represent these programs as finite lists of instructions in SSA form. This representation has the following properties, proofs for which can be found in the extended version [14].

Theorem 2. *Every total, finite function is computed by at least one finite state program.*

Theorem 3. *Furthermore, this representation as finite lists of instructions in SSA form is optimally concise – there is no encoding that gives a shorter representation to every function.*

Finite State Program Synthesis. To formally define the finite state synthesis problem, we need to fix some notation. We will say that a program P is a finite list of instructions in SSA form, where no instruction can cause a back jump, i.e. our programs are loop free and non-recursive. Inputs x to the program are drawn from some finite domain $\mathcal{D}$. The synthesis problem is given to us in the form of a specification σ which is a function taking a program P and input x as parameters and returning a boolean telling us whether P did "the right thing" on input x. Basically, the finite state synthesis problem checks the truth of Definition 2.

Definition 2 (Finite Synthesis Formula).

$$\exists P.\forall x \in \mathcal{D}.\sigma(P, x)$$

To express the specification σ, we introduce a function $\texttt{exec}(P, x)$ that returns the result of running program P with input x. Since P cannot contain loops or recursion, $\texttt{exec}$ is a total function.

Example 1. The following finite state synthesis problem is satisfiable:

$$\exists P.\forall x \in \mathbb{N}_8.\texttt{exec}(P, x) \geq x$$

One such program P satisfying the specification is **return 8**, which just returns 8 for any input.

We now present our main theorem, which says that satisfiability of $SF_{\mathcal{D}}$ can be reduced to finite state program synthesis. The proof of this theorem can be found in the extended version [14].

Theorem 4 ($SF_\mathcal{D}$ **is Polynomial Time Reducible to Finite Synthesis).**
Every instance of Definition 1, where the ground terms are interpreted over $\mathcal{D}$ is polynomial time reducible to a finite synthesis formula (i.e. an instance of Definition 2).

Corollary 1. *Finite-State Program Synthesis is NEXPTIME-Complete.*

We are now in a position to sketch the design of a decision procedure for $SF_\mathcal{D}$: we will convert the $SF_\mathcal{D}$ satisfiability problem to an equisatisfiable finite synthesis problem, which we will then solve with a finite state program synthesiser. This design will be elaborated in Sect. 5.

5   Deciding $SF_\mathcal{D}$ via Finite-State Program Synthesis

In this section we will present a sound and complete algorithm for finite-state synthesis that we use to decide the satisfiability of formulae in $SF_\mathcal{D}$. We begin by describing a general purpose synthesis procedure (Sect. 5.1), then detail how this general purpose procedure is instantiated for synthesising finite-state programs. We then describe the algorithm we use to search the space of possible programs (Sects. 5.3 and 6).

5.1   General Purpose Synthesis Algorithm

Algorithm 1. Abstract refinement algorithm

```
 1: function SYNTH(inputs)              16: function REFINEMENT LOOP
 2:     (i₁,...,iₙ) ← inputs           17:     inputs ← ∅
 3:     query ← ∃P.σ(i₁,P)∧...∧σ(iₙ,P) 18:     loop
 4:     result ← decide(query)         19:         candidate ← SYNTH(inputs)
 5:     if result.satisfiable then     20:         if candidate = UNSAT then
 6:         return result.model        21:             return UNSAT
 7:     else                           22:         res ← VERIF(candidate)
 8:         return UNSAT               23:         if res = valid then
                                       24:             return candidate
 9: function VERIF(P)                  25:         else
10:     query ← ∃x.¬σ(x,P)             26:             inputs ← inputs ∪ res
11:     result ← decide(query)
12:     if result.satisfiable then
13:         return result.model
14:     else
15:         return valid
```

We use Counterexample Guided Inductive Synthesis (CEGIS) [15,16] to find a program satisfying our specification. Algorithm 1 is divided into two procedures: SYNTH and VERIF, which interact via a finite set of test vectors INPUTS.

The SYNTH procedure tries to find an existential witness P that satisfies the partial specification: $\exists P.\forall x \in$ INPUTS$.\sigma(x, P)$

If SYNTH succeeds in finding a witness P, this witness is a candidate solution to the full synthesis formula. We pass this candidate solution to VERIF which determines whether it does satisfy the specification on all inputs by checking satisfiability of the verification formula: $\exists x.\neg\sigma(x, P)$

If this formula is unsatisfiable, the candidate solution is in fact a solution to the synthesis formula and so the algorithm terminates. Otherwise, the witness x is an input on which the candidate solution fails to meet the specification. This witness x is added to the INPUTS set and the loop iterates again. It is worth noting that each iteration of the loop adds a new input to the set of inputs being used for synthesis. If the full set of inputs is finite, this means that the refinement loop can only iterate a finite number of times.

5.2 Finite-State Synthesis

We will now show how the generic construction of Sect. 5.1 can be instantiated to produce a finite-state program synthesiser. A natural choice for such a synthesiser would be to work in the logic of quantifier-free propositional formulae and to use a propositional SAT or SMT-$\mathcal{BV}$ solver as the decision procedure. However we propose a slightly different tack, which is to use a decidable fragment of C as a "high level" logic. We call this fragment C^-.

The characteristic property of a C^- program is that safety can be decided for it using a single query to a Bounded Model Checker. A C^- program is just a C program with the following syntactic restrictions:

(i) all loops in the program must have a constant bound;
(ii) all recursion in the program must be limited to a constant depth;
(iii) all arrays must be statically allocated (i.e. not using `malloc`), and be of constant size.

C^- programs may use nondeterministic values, assumptions and arbitrary-width types.

Since each loop is bounded by a constant, and each recursive function call is limited to a constant depth, a C^- program necessarily terminates and in fact does so in $O(1)$ time. If we call the largest loop bound k, then a Bounded Model Checker with an unrolling bound of k will be a complete decision procedure for the safety of the program. For a C^- program of size l and with largest loop bound k, a Bounded Model Checker will create a SAT problem of size $O(lk)$. Conversely, a SAT problem of size s can be converted trivially into a loop-free C^- program of size $O(s)$. The safety problem for C^- is therefore NP-complete, which means it can be decided fairly efficiently for many practical instances.

5.3 Candidate Generation Strategies

A candidate solution P is written in a simple RISC-like language $\mathcal{L}$, whose syntax is given in the extended version [14]. We supply an interpreter for $\mathcal{L}$ which is written in C^-. The specification function σ will include calls to this interpreter, by which means it will examine the behaviour of a candidate $\mathcal{L}$ program.

For the SYNTH portion of the CEGIS loop, we construct a C^- program SYNTH.C which takes as parameters a candidate program P and test inputs. The program contains an assertion which fails iff P meets the specification for each of the inputs. Finding a new candidate program is then equivalent to checking the safety of SYNTH.C. There are many possible strategies for finding these candidates; we employ the following strategies in parallel:

(i) Explicit Proof Search. The simplest strategy for finding candidates is to just exhaustively enumerate them all, starting with the shortest and progressively increasing the number of instructions.

(ii) Symbolic Bounded Model Checking. Another complete method for generating candidates is to simply use BMC on the SYNTH.C program.

(iii) Genetic Programming and Incremental Evolution. Our final strategy is genetic programming (GP) [17,18]. GP provides an adaptive way of searching through the space of $\mathcal{L}$-programs for an individual that is "fit" in some sense. We measure the fitness of an individual by counting the number of tests in INPUTS for which it satisfies the specification.

To bootstrap GP in the first iteration of the CEGIS loop, we generate a population of random $\mathcal{L}$-programs. We then iteratively evolve this population by applying the genetic operators CROSSOVER and MUTATE. CROSSOVER combines selected existing programs into new programs, whereas MUTATE randomly changes parts of a single program. Fitter programs are more likely to be selected.

Rather than generating a random population at the beginning of each subsequent iteration of the CEGIS loop, we start with the population we had at the end of the previous iteration. The intuition here is that this population contained many individuals that performed well on the k inputs we had before, so they will probably continue to perform well on the $k + 1$ inputs we have now. In the parlance of evolutionary programming, this is known as incremental evolution [19].

6   Searching the Space of Possible Solutions

An important aspect of our synthesis algorithm is the manner in which we search the space of candidate programs. The key component is parametrising the language $\mathcal{L}$, which induces a lattice of progressively more expressive languages. We start by attempting to synthesise a program at the lowest point on this lattice and increase the parameters of $\mathcal{L}$ until we reach a point at which the synthesis succeeds. Note that this parametrisation applies to all three strategies in the previous section.

As well as giving us an automatic search procedure, this parametrisation greatly increases the efficiency of our system since languages low down the lattice are very easy to decide safety for. If a program can be synthesised in a low-complexity language, the whole procedure finishes much faster than if synthesis had been attempted in a high-complexity language.

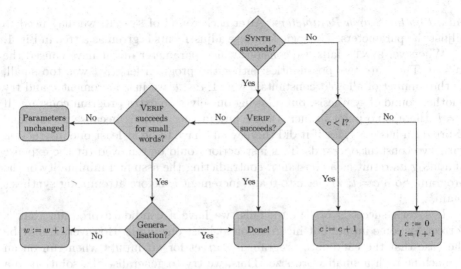

Fig. 1. Decision tree for increasing parameters of $\mathcal{L}$.

6.1   Parameters of Language $\mathcal{L}$

Program Length: l. The first parameter we introduce is program length, denoted by l. At each iteration we synthesise programs of length exactly l. We start with $l = 1$ and increment l whenever we determine that no program of length l can satisfy the specification. When we do successfully synthesise a program, we are *guaranteed that it is of minimal length* since we have previously established that no shorter program is correct.

Word Width: w. An $\mathcal{L}$-program runs on a virtual machine (the $\mathcal{L}$-machine) that is parametrised by the *word width*, that is, the number of bits in each internal register and immediate constant.

Number of Constants: c. Instructions in $\mathcal{L}$ take up to three operands. Since any instruction whose operands are all constants can always be eliminated (since its result is a constant), we know that a loop-free program of minimal length will not contain any instructions with two constant operands. Therefore the number of constants that can appear in a minimal program of length l is at most l. By minimising the number of constants appearing in a program, we are able to use a particularly efficient program encoding that speeds up the synthesis procedure substantially.

6.2   Searching the Program Space

The key to our automation approach is to come up with a sensible way in which to adjust the $\mathcal{L}$-parameters in order to cover all possible programs. Two important components in this search are the adjustment of parameters and the generalisation of candidate solutions. We discuss them both next.

Adjusting the Search Parameters. After each round of SYNTH, we may need to adjust the parameters. The logic for these adjustments is given as a tree in Fig. 1.

Whenever SYNTH fails, we consider which parameter might have caused the failure. There are two possibilities: either the program length l was too small, or the number of allowed constants c was. If $c < l$, we just increment c and try another round of synthesis, but allowing ourselves an extra program constant. If $c = l$, there is no point in increasing c any further. This is because no minimal $\mathcal{L}$-program has $c > l$, for if it did there would have to be at least one instruction with two constant operands. This instruction could be removed (at the expense of adding its result as a constant), contradicting the assumed minimality of the program. So if $c = l$, we set c to 0 and increment l, before attempting synthesis again.

If SYNTH succeeds but VERIF fails, we have a candidate program that is correct for some inputs but incorrect on at least one input. However, it may be the case that the candidate program is correct for *all* inputs when run on an $\mathcal{L}$-machine with a small word size. Thus, we try to generalise the solution to a bigger word size, as explained in the next paragraph. If the generalisation is able to find a correct program, we are done. Otherwise, we need to increase the word width of the $\mathcal{L}$-machine we are currently synthesising for.

Generalisation of Candidate Solutions. It is often the case that a program which satisfies the specification on an $\mathcal{L}$-machine with $w = k$ will continue to satisfy the specification when run on a machine with $w > k$. For example, the program in Fig. 2 isolates the least-significant bit of a word. This is true irrespective of the word size of the machine it is run on – it will isolate the least-significant bit of an 8-bit word just as well as it will a 32-bit word. An often successful strategy is to synthesise a program for an $\mathcal{L}$-machine with a small word size and then to check whether the same program is correct when run on an $\mathcal{L}$-machine with a full-sized word.

The only wrinkle here is that we will sometimes synthesise a program containing constants. If we have synthesised a program with $w = k$, the constants in the program will be k-bits wide. To extend the program to an n-bit machine (with $n > k$), we need some way of deriving n-bit-wide numbers from k-bit ones. We have several strategies for this and just try each in turn. Our strategies are shown in Fig. 3. $\mathcal{BV}(v, n)$ denotes an n-bit wide bitvector holding the value v and $b \cdot c$ means the concatenation of bitvectors b and c. For example, the first rule says that if we have the 8-bit number with value 8, and we want to extend it to some 32-bit number, we'd try the 32-bit number with value 32. These six rules are all heuristics that we have found to be fairly effective in practice.

```
int isolate_lsb(int x) {
    return x & -x;
}
```

Example:

x	$= 1\ 0\ 1\ 1\ 1\ 0\ 1\ 0$
-x	$= 0\ 1\ 0\ 0\ 0\ 1\ 1\ 0$
x & -x	$= 0\ 0\ 0\ 0\ 0\ 0\ 1\ 0$

Fig. 2. A tricky bitvector program

$$\mathcal{BV}(m,m) \to \mathcal{BV}(n,n) \qquad\qquad \mathcal{BV}(x,m) \to \mathcal{BV}(x,n)$$

$$\mathcal{BV}(m-1,m) \to \mathcal{BV}(n-1,n) \qquad \mathcal{BV}(x,m) \to \mathcal{BV}(x,m) \cdot \mathcal{BV}(0, n-m)$$

$$\mathcal{BV}(m+1,m) \to \mathcal{BV}(n+1,n) \qquad \mathcal{BV}(x,m) \to \underbrace{\mathcal{BV}(x,m) \cdot \ldots \cdot \mathcal{BV}(x,m)}_{\frac{n}{m}\ \text{times}}$$

Fig. 3. Rules for extending an m-bit wide number to an n-bit wide one.

6.3 Stopping Condition for Unsatisfiable Specifications

If a specification is unsatisfiable, we would still like our algorithm to terminate with an "unsatisfiable" verdict. To do this, we can observe that any total function taking n bits of input is computed by some program of at most 2^n instructions (a consequence of Theorems 2 and 3). Therefore every satisfiable specification has a solution with at most 2^n instructions. This means that if we ever need to increase the length of the candidate program we search for beyond 2^n, we can terminate, safe in the knowledge that the specification is unsatisfiable.

Although this gives us a theoretical termination condition for unsatisfiable instances, in practice the program synthesiser may not terminate. In order to avoid such cases, we use the approach described in Sect. 8.

7 Soundness, Completeness and Efficiency

We will now state soundness and completeness results for the $SF_\mathcal{D}$ solver. Proofs for each of these theorems can be found in the extended version [14].

Theorem 5. *Algorithm 1 is sound – if it terminates with witness P, then $P \models \sigma$.*

Theorem 6. *Algorithm 1 with the stopping condition described in Sect. 6.3 is complete when instantiated with C^- as a background theory – it will terminate for all specifications σ.*

Since safety of C^- programs is decidable, Algorithm 1 is sound and complete when instantiated with C^- as a background theory and using the stopping condition of Sect. 6.3. This construction therefore gives as a decision procedure for $SF_\mathcal{D}$.

Runtime as a Function of Solution Size. We note that the runtime of our solver is heavily influenced by the length of the shortest program satisfying the specification, since we begin searching for short programs. We will now show that the number of iterations of the CEGIS loop is a function of the Kolmogorov complexity of the synthesised program. Let us first recall the definition of the Kolmogorov complexity of a function f:

Definition 3 (Kolmogorov Complexity). *The Kolmogorov complexity $K(f)$ is the length of the shortest program that computes f.*

We can extend this definition slightly to talk about the Kolmogorov complexity of a synthesis problem in terms of its specification:

Definition 4 (Kolmogorov Complexity of a Synthesis Problem). *The Kolmogorov complexity of a program specification $K(\sigma)$ is the length of the shortest program P such that P is a witness to the satisfiability of σ.*

Let us consider the number of iterations of the CEGIS loop n required for a specification σ. Since we enumerate candidate programs in order of length, we are always synthesising programs with length no greater than $K(\sigma)$ (since when we enumerate the first correct program, we will terminate). So the space of solutions we search over is the space of functions computed by $\mathcal{L}$-programs of length no greater than $K(\sigma)$. Let's denote this set $\mathcal{L}(K(\sigma))$. Since there are $O(2^{K(\sigma)})$ *programs* of length $K(\sigma)$ and some functions will be computed by more than one program, we have $|\mathcal{L}(K(\sigma))| \leq O(2^{K(\sigma)})$.

Each iteration of the CEGIS loop distinguishes at least one incorrect function from the set of correct functions, so the loop will iterate no more than $|\mathcal{L}(K(\sigma))|$ times. Therefore another bound on our runtime is $NTIME\left(2^{K(\sigma)}\right)$.

8   Avoiding Unsatisfiable Instances

As described in the previous section, our program synthesiser is efficient at finding satisfying assignments, when such assignments have low Kolmogorov complexity. However, if a formula is unsatisfiable, the procedure may not terminate in practice. This illustrates one of the current shortcomings of our program synthesis based decision procedure: we can only conclude that a formula is unsatisfiable once we have examined candidate solutions up to a very high length bound.

However, we note that many interesting properties of programs can be expressed as tautologies. For illustration, let us consider that we are trying to prove that a loop L terminates. Thus, as shown in Sect. 3, we can construct two formulae: one that is satisfiable iff L is terminating and another that is satisfiable iff L is non-terminating. We will call these formulae ϕ and ψ, respectively, and we denote by P_N and P_T the proofs of non-termination and termination, respectively: $\exists P_T.\forall x, x'.\phi(P_T, x, x')$ and $\exists P_N.\forall x.\psi(P_N, x)$.

We can combine these: $(\exists P_T.\forall x, x'.\phi(P_T, x, x')) \vee (\exists P_N.\forall x.\psi(P_N, x))$.

Which simplifies to: $\exists P_T, P_N.\forall x, x', y.\phi(P_T, x, x') \vee \psi(P_N, y)$.

Since L either terminates or does not terminate, this formula is a tautology in the synthesis fragment. Thus, either P_N or P_T must exist. Similarly, when proving safety, a program is either safe of has a bug. In this manner we avoid the bad case where we try to synthesise a solution for an unsatisfiable specification.

9   Experiments

We implemented our decision procedure for SF_D as the KALASHNIKOV tool. We used KALASHNIKOV to solve formulae generated from a variety of problems taken from superoptimisation, code deobfuscation, floating point verification, ranking function and recurrent set synthesis, safety proving, and bug finding. The superoptimisation and code deobfuscation benchmarks were taken from the experiments of [20]; the termination benchmarks were taken from SVCOMP'15 [21]

Table 1. Experimental results.

Category	#Benchmarks	#Solved	Avg. solution size	Avg. iterations	Avg. time (s)	Total time (s)
Superoptimisation	29	22	4.1	2.7	7.9	166.1
Termination	47	35	5.7	14.4	11.2	392.9
Safety	20	18	8.3	7.1	11.3	203.9
Total	96	75	5.9	9.2	10.3	762.9

Table 2. Statistics about the experimental results.

CBMC	Explicit	GP
21%	46%	31%

(a) How often each solver "wins".

SYNTH	VERIF	GENERALIZE
86%	14%	7%

(b) Where the time is spent.

and they include the experiments of [13]; the safety benchmarks are taken from the experiments of [22].

We ran our experiments on a 4-core, 3.30 GHz Core i5 with 8 GB of RAM. Each benchmark was run with a timeout of 180 s. The results are shown in Table 1. For each category of benchmarks, we report the total number of benchmarks in that category, the number we were able to solve within the time limit, the average solution size (in instructions), the average number of iterations of the CEGIS loop, the average time and total time taken. The deobfuscation and floating point benchmarks are considered together with the superoptimisation ones.

For the termination benchmarks, KALASHNIKOV must prove that the input program is either terminating or non-terminating, i.e. it must synthesise either ranking functions and supporting invariants, or recurrence sets. For the safety benchmarks, KALASHNIKOV must prove that the program is either safe or unsafe. For this purpose, it synthesises either a safety invariant or a compact representations of an error trace.

Discussion of the Experimental Results. The timings show that for the instances where we can find a satisfying assignment, we tend to do so quite quickly (on the order of a few seconds). Furthermore the programs we synthesise are often short, even when the problem domain is very complex, such as for liveness and safety.

To help understand the role of the different solvers involved in the synthesis process, we provide a breakdown of how often each solver "won", i.e. was the first to return an answer. This breakdown is given in Table 2a. We see that GP and explicit account for the great majority of the responses, with the load spread fairly evenly between them. This distribution illustrates the different strengths of each solver: GP is very good at generating candidates, explicit is very good at finding counterexamples and CBMC is very good at proving that candidates are correct. The GP and explicit numbers are similar because they are approximately "number of candidates found" and "number of candidates refuted" respectively. The CBMC column is approximately "number of candidates proved correct". The spread of winners here shows that each of the search strategies is contributing something to the overall search and that the strategies are able to co-operate with each other.

To help understand where the time is spent in our solver, Table 2b how much time is spent in SYNTH, VERIF and constant generalization. Note that generalization counts towards VERIF's time. We can see that synthesising candidates takes much longer than verifying them, which suggests that improved procedures for candidate synthesis will lead to good overall performance improvements. However, the times considered for this table include all the runs that timed out, as well as those that succeeded. We have observed that runs which time out spend more time in synthesis than runs which succeed, so the distribution here is biased by the cost of timeouts.

9.1   Comparison to SyGuS

In order to compare KALASHNIKOV to other program synthesisers, we translated the 20 safety benchmarks into the SyGuS format [7] (for the bitvector theory) and ran the enumerative CEGIS solver ESOLVER, winner of the SyGuS 2014 competition (taken from the SyGuS Github repository on 5/7/2015), as well as the program synthesiser in CVC4 [23] (the version for the SyGuS 2015 competition on the StarExec platform [24]), winner of the SyGuS 2015 competition. We could not compare against ICE-DT [25], the winner of the invariant generation category in the SyGuS 2015 competition, as it does not seem to offer support for bitvectors. Our comparison only uses 20 of the 96 benchmarks as we had to manually convert from our specification format (a subset of C) into the SyGuS format. Moreover, our choice of benchmarks was also restricted by the fact that we could not express lexicographic ranking functions of unbounded dimension in the SyGuS format, which we require for our termination benchmarks.

The results of these experiments are given in Table 3, which contains the number of benchmarks solved correctly, the number of timeouts, the number of crashes (exceptions thrown by the solver), the mean time to successfully solve and the total number of lines in the 20 specifications.

Since the ESOLVER tool crashed on many of the instances we tried, we reran the experiments on the StarExec platform to check that we had not made mistakes setting up our environment, however the same instances also caused exceptions on StarExec.

An important point to notice in Table 3 is that KALASHNIKOV specifications are significantly more concise than SyGuS specifications, as witnessed by the total size of the specifications: the KALASHNIKOV specifications are around 11 % of the size of the SyGuS ones. Overall, we can see that KALASHNIKOV performs better on these benchmarks than ESOLVER and CVC4, which validates our claim that KALASHNIKOV is suitable for program analysis problems.

Table 3. Comparison of KALASHNIKOV, ESOLVER and CVC4 on the safety benchmarks.

	#Solved	#TO	#Crashes	Avg. time (s)	Spec. size
KALASHNIKOV	18	2	0	11.3	341
ESOLVER	7	5	8	13.6	3140
CVC4	5	13	2	61.7	3140

We noticed that for a lot of the cases in which ESOLVER and CVC4 timed out, KALASHNIKOV found a solution that involved non-trivial constants. Since the SyGuS format represents constants in unary (as chains of additions), finding programs containing constants, or finding existentially quantified first order variables is expensive. KALASHNIKOV's strategies for finding and generalising constants make it much more efficient at this subtask.

10 Conclusions

We have shown that the synthesis fragment is well-suited for program verification by using it to directly encode safety, liveness and superoptimisation properties.

We built a decision procedure for SF_D via a reduction to finite state program synthesis. The synthesis algorithm is optimised for program analysis and uses a combination of symbolic model checking, explicit state model checking and stochastic search. An important strategy is generalisation – we find simple solutions that solve a restricted case of the specification, then try to generalise to a full solution. We evaluated the program synthesiser on several static analysis problems, showing the tractability of the approach.

References

1. Cousot, P., Cousot, R.: Abstract interpretation: a unified lattice model for static analysis of programs by construction or approximation of fixpoints. In: POPL (1977)
2. Clarke, E.M., Kroening, D., Yorav, K.: Behavioral consistency of C and verilog programs using bounded model checking. In: DAC, pp. 368–371 (2003)
3. Floyd, R.W.: Assigning meanings to programs (1967)
4. Gupta, A., et al.: Proving non-termination. In: POPL (2008)
5. Gulwani, S.: Dimensions in program synthesis. In: Formal Methods in Computer-Aided Design, FMCAD, p. 1 (2010)
6. Kong, S., Jung, Y., David, C., Wang, B.-Y., Yi, K.: Automatically inferring quantified loop invariants by algorithmic learning from simple templates. In: Ueda, K. (ed.) APLAS 2010. LNCS, vol. 6461, pp. 328–343. Springer, Heidelberg (2010)
7. Alur, R., et al.: Syntax-guided synthesis. In: FMCAD (2013)
8. Grebenshchikov, S., Lopes, N.P., Popeea, C., Rybalchenko, A.: Synthesizing software verifiers from proof rules. In: PLDI, pp. 405–416 (2012)
9. Beyene, T.A., Popeea, C., Rybalchenko, A.: Solving existentially quantified horn clauses. In: Sharygina, N., Veith, H. (eds.) CAV 2013. LNCS, vol. 8044, pp. 869–882. Springer, Heidelberg (2013)

10. Wintersteiger, C.M., Hamadi, Y., de Moura, L.M.: Efficiently solving quantified bit-vector formulas. In: FMCAD (2010)
11. Piskac, R., de Moura, L.M., Bjørner, N.: Deciding effectively propositional logic using DPLL and substitution sets. J. Autom. Reasoning **44**(4), 401–424 (2010)
12. Gulwani, S., Srivastava, S., Venkatesan, R.: Program analysis as constraint solving. In: PLDI, pp. 281–292 (2008)
13. David, C., Kroening, D., Lewis, M.: Unrestricted termination and non-termination arguments for bit-vector programs. In: Vitek, J. (ed.) ESOP 2015. LNCS, vol. 9032, pp. 183–204. Springer, Heidelberg (2015)
14. David, C., Kroening, D., Lewis, M.: Using program synthesis for program analysis. CoRR abs/1508.07829 (2015)
15. Solar-Lezama, A.: Program sketching. STTT **15**(5–6), 475–495 (2013)
16. Brain, M., Crick, T., De Vos, M., Fitch, J.: TOAST: applying answer set programming to superoptimisation. In: Etalle, S., Truszczyński, M. (eds.) ICLP 2006. LNCS, vol. 4079, pp. 270–284. Springer, Heidelberg (2006)
17. Langdon, W.B., Poli, R.: Foundations of Genetic Programming. Springer, Heidelberg (2002)
18. Brameier, M., Banzhaf, W.: Linear Genetic Programming. Springer, Heidelberg (2007)
19. Gomez, F., Miikkulainen, R.: Incremental evolution of complex general behavior. Adapt. Behav. **5**, 317–342 (1997)
20. Gulwani, S., Jha, S., Tiwari, A., Venkatesan, R.: Synthesis of loop-free programs. In: PLDI, pp. 62–73 (2011)
21. SV-COMP. http://sv-comp.sosy-lab.org/2015/
22. David, C., Kroening, D., Lewis, M.: Danger invariants. CoRR (2015)
23. Reynolds, A., Deters, M., Kuncak, V., Tinelli, C., Barrett, C.: Counterexample-guided quantifier instantiation for synthesis in SMT. In: Kroening, D., Păsăreanu, C.S. (eds.) CAV 2015. LNCS, vol. 9207, pp. 198–216. Springer, Heidelberg (2015)
24. StarExec. https://www.starexec.org
25. Garg, P., Löding, C., Madhusudan, P., Neider, D.: ICE: a robust framework for learning invariants. In: Biere, A., Bloem, R. (eds.) CAV 2014. LNCS, vol. 8559, pp. 69–87. Springer, Heidelberg (2014)

Finding Inconsistencies in Programs with Loops

Temesghen Kahsai[1], Jorge A. Navas[2], Dejan Jovanović[3], and Martin Schäf[3]([✉])

[1] Carnegie Mellon University, Pittsburgh, USA
temesghen.kahsaiazene@nasa.gov
[2] NASA Ames Research Center/SGT, Mountain View, USA
jorge.a.navaslaserna@nasa.gov
[3] SRI International, Menlo Park, USA
{dejan.jovanovic,martin.schaef}@sri.com

Abstract. Inconsistent code is an important class of program abnormalities that appears in real-world code bases and often reveals serious bugs. A piece of code is inconsistent if it is not part of any safely terminating execution. Existing approaches to inconsistent code detection scale to programs with millions of lines of code, and have lead to patches in applications like the web-server Tomcat or the Linux kernel. However, the ability of existing tools to detect inconsistencies is limited by gross over-approximation of looping control-flow. We present a novel approach to inconsistent code detection that can reason about programs with loops without compromising precision. To that end, by leveraging recent advances in software model checking and Horn clause solving, we demonstrate how to encode the problem as a sequence of Horn clauses queries enabling us to detect inconsistencies that were previously unattainable.

1 Introduction

Static analysis techniques can be insufficient to eliminate all false alarms in large-code bases. In an effort to build static analyzers that report close to zero false alarms, we have seen an increasing interest in inconsistent code detection. Broadly speaking, inconsistent code comprises code where two program locations make contradicting assumptions about the execution of the program. This includes, for example, checking if a chunk of memory is properly allocated only after it has already been dereferenced, or accessing an array at an index that is guaranteed to be out of bounds.

Formally, inconsistent code is defined as a program location that only occurs on executions that must reach an error state. In other words, a code fragment is said to be inconsistent if it is never part of a "normal" execution of the program. For example, unreachable code is inconsistent because it has no execution. Previous techniques have demonstrated that inconsistent code is a very practical methodology to find likely bugs in a scalable fashion. For example, in [11] inconsistent code is used to reveal bugs in the Linux kernel, and in [27] the authors

This material is based upon work supported by the National Science Foundation under Grant No. 1422705, AFRL contract No. FA8750-15-C-0010, and NASA contract NNX14AI05A.

© Springer-Verlag Berlin Heidelberg 2015
M. Davis et al. (Eds.): LPAR-20 2015, LNCS 9450, pp. 499–514, 2015.
DOI: 10.1007/978-3-662-48899-7_35

found inconsistent code in the web-server Tomcat and the project management Maven.

Inconsistent code detection algorithms (e.g., [11,18,22,27,34]) share the same basic architecture. They analyze a program one procedure at a time. For each procedure, they over-approximate the feasible executions and try to enumerate the feasible control-flow paths. Everything that cannot be covered is provably inconsistent code.

So far, all implementations that detect inconsistent code or subsets of it use very coarse abstractions to handle looping control-flow which limits their ability to detect inconsistencies significantly. All of these approaches over-approximate the effect of loops, by simply replacing them with non-deterministic assignments to the variables modified inside the loop body. Some of the approaches additionally add an unwinding of the last loop iteration (to detect typical off-by-one errors).

In this paper, we present a novel algorithm to detect inconsistent code that is able to reason more effectively about looping control-flow. To that end, we follow the recent trend and reformulate the problem of detecting inconsistencies as a problem of solving a system of constrained Horn clauses (CHC). Instead of unwinding looping control-flow, we allow for recursive Horn clause definitions. As in previous approaches that detect inconsistencies, we encode programs into logic such that a model for this Horn clause system can be mapped to a feasible control-flow path in the program, but, unlike existing approaches, our encoding does not require loop elimination.

Each time we find such a feasible path, we block it and check for the existence of another model that exercises a different control-flow path. However, since our Horn clause definitions may be recursive, enumerating all feasible path may not be possible as there may be infinitely many. For this case, we make use of the recent developments in software model checking for solving Horn clause systems which may be able to prove unsatisfiability by inferring local invariants using, for example, property-directed reachability (PDR)/IC3 [7]. For cases where such a proof exists, our analysis can find inconsistencies that existing tools could not find. For cases where such a proof does not exist, we can still fall back to previous approaches by abstracting the looping control-flow.

As a side effect, the invariants produced by our Horn clause solver can be used to implement existing fault localization techniques for inconsistent code [32].

We evaluate our approach on a set of handcrafted problems which we made available on-line. In our experiments, our approach only times out in a single case and finds several inconsistencies that cannot be detected with current tools that checks for inconsistency.

2   Related Work

The idea that code inconsistencies represent an interesting class of possible defects goes back to Engler et al. [11]. Their technique to detect inconsistencies was mostly based on syntactic comparison but it is already able to find bugs in the Linux kernel and other major pieces of software. The work by

Dillig et al. [10] uses the term *semantic inconsistencies* to refer to contradicting assumptions on control-flow paths. While their work also detects inconsistencies as defined by Engler et al., they also include inconsistencies on individual paths (even though each statement on these paths might have a feasible execution). That is, they scan for a larger class of errors but introduce possible false alarms as they cannot guarantee that the inconsistent paths they report are in fact feasible in a larger context.

The idea of using deductive verification to prove inconsistencies has been presented in [18, 22, 34]. Janota et al. [22] use a variation of the Boogie tool [2] to verify that code is unreachable in an annotated program. This is only a subset of inconsistent code, but the detection algorithm could easily be extended to detect inconsistent code. Hoenicke et al. [18] prove the existence of inconsistent code but use the term *doomed program points*. Tomb et al. [34] use a very similar approach and also give a definition of inconsistent code that we are going to reuse in this paper. In our earlier work, we have developed a tool to detect inconsistent code [27] and demonstrated that it finds relevant bugs in popular open-source Java applications.

In [6], the authors use inconsistency detection to prioritize error messages produced by a static analyzer. Their approach post-processes static analysis warnings and gives them a high priority if the warning contains an *abstract semantic inconsistency bug*, which is inconsistent code on an abstract model of the code.

An approach that is similar in spirit but not immediately related is the work by Wang et al. [35] where the authors try to identify local invariants to detect undefined behavior of C programs. While the class of errors that we want to detect are not immediately comparable, we share the idea of searching for invariants to prove the presence of errors while accepting false negatives in return for a low false positive rate.

The local invariants computed by our approach when proving code to be inconsistent can be seen as *error invariants* [12] which can be used for fault localization. The approach presented in [32] shows how these invariants can be used to explain inconsistent code.

Constraint Horn clauses have been used as the basis for software model checking [9, 13] of concurrent systems and its use in software verification tools is rapidly growing. For example, they have been adopted in Threader [29], UFO [1], SeaHorn [16], HSF [14], VeriMAP [8], Eldarica [31], and TRACER [21]. Our tool has many similarities with some of these tools and in fact, our current implementation is built on the top of SeaHorn. However, ours is the first available implementation based on Horn clauses that detects inconsistent code.

3   Running Example

We illustrate the different steps of our approach along the running code example in Fig. 1. The procedure foo takes an integer x as input and computes the sum of 10/i, for all i between -x and x. That is, for any x less or equal to

```
1   int foo(int x) {
2       int ret = 0;
3       for (int i=-x; i<x; i++) {
4           ret += 10/i;
5       }
6       return ret;
7   }
```

Fig. 1. Illustrative example. The procedure foo takes an integer x as input and sums up the integer divisions $10/i$ for all i between $-x$ and x. For any $x > 0$, the division in line 4 must raise an exception once the iterator i becomes zero. For any $x \leq 0$, line 4 cannot be reached.

zero, the procedure skips the loop and returns 0 immediately. For any x greater zero, however, the procedure will perform a division by zero once the iterator i becomes zero resulting in undefined behavior. Executing this undefined behavior causes the program to terminate with an exception (when compiled with gcc). Since the loop is iterating from -x to x, any execution that enters the loop must raise this exception. Hence, line 4 is *inconsistent code*. We acknowledge that this is a fairly artificial example but it is designed so that its Horn clause representation and the invariants used to prove the inconsistency are succinct for presentation reasons.

Let us quickly discuss the concepts of reachability, feasibility, and inconsistency using this example. Every line in this procedure is (forward) *reachable*, meaning that, for each statement of the procedure, we can find a sequence of statements that reaches it from the entry of the procedure and is *feasible*. That is, assuming that x can take arbitrary values, there exist a concrete value for x that triggers an execution ending in the statement. If, on the other hand, we would assume that x ≤ 0, then the body of the for-loop would not have any feasible executions and would thus be *unreachable*. However, every feasible execution of line 4 must terminate exceptionally later due to unavoidable division by 0. Hence, we declare line 4 as *inconsistent* because any feasible execution containing this line must terminate exceptionally.

Now, we want to use formal techniques to prove the inconsistency in line 4. In the literature one finds several algorithms that (among other things) prove the existence of inconsistencies (e.g., [10,18,22,34]). However, none of the existing algorithms would be able to detect the inconsistency because of their inability to handle looping control-flow. Unwinding the loop is not an option either in this example because the bounds are unknown at compile time. Even though each unwinding would reveal the error, this is not sufficient to prove the inconsistency (because, for the statement to be inconsistent, the error has to occur on every iteration). Hence, we need an approach that is able to infer an inductive invariant that allows us to prove that every feasible execution containing line 4 must terminate exceptionally.

In the following sections, we first describe how we encode the running example from Fig. 1 as a system of constrained Horn clauses and then we present an algorithm to prove that line 4 is in fact inconsistent.

4   Horn Clause Encoding

In this section, we describe how we encode the example from Fig. 1, as a system of constrained Horn clauses. First, we describe the syntax and semantics of Horn clauses.

Given a set $\mathcal{F}$ of function symbols (e.g., $+$, $=$, etc.), a set $\mathcal{P}$ of predicate symbols, and a set $\mathcal{V}$ of variables, a *Constrained Horn Clause (CHC)* is a formula:

$$\forall \mathcal{V}.(p[X] \leftarrow \phi \wedge p_1[X_1] \wedge \ldots \wedge p_k[X_k])$$

for $k \geq 0$, where ϕ is a constraint over $\mathcal{F}$ and $\mathcal{V}$. Each $p_i[X_i]$ is the application of a predicate $p_i \in \mathcal{P}$ for first-order terms constructed from $\mathcal{F}$ and $\mathcal{V}$. We refer to the left-hand side of the implication as *head* and to the right-hand side as the *body* of the Horn clause. A clause is called a *query* if its head is $\mathcal{P}$-free, and otherwise, it is called a *rule*. We say a clause is *linear* if its body contains at most one predicate symbol $\mathcal{P}$, otherwise, it is called *non-linear*. For scalability reasons, our algorithm, described in Sect. 6, for detecting inconsistencies is intra-procedural. As a result, all of our CHCs will be linear[1]. Finally, we will follow the CLP convention of writing Horn clauses as $h[X] \leftarrow \phi, p_1[X_1], \ldots, p_k[X_k]$.

A system of CHCs is satisfiable if there exists an interpretation $\mathcal{J}$ of the predicate symbols $\mathcal{P}$ such that each constraint ϕ is true under $\mathcal{J}$. If satisfiable, we assume that the CHC solver (e.g., GPDR [17], Eldarica [31], or Spacer [25]) also returns a *model*: assignments of values to variables.

We assume that the reader is familiar with the basic concepts of how to encode programs using Horn clauses (see e.g., [5,16,30] for details). For simplicity, we use in this presentation an encoding based on small-step operational semantics [28] and describe informally how to translate programs to CHCs. Note that our approach is not limited to a particular encoding and we can also use other encodings, for instance, large-step [4,15] (*a.k.a.* Large Block Encoding, or LBE).

Thinking in terms of programs and basic blocks (sequence of statements without branching), the predicates $p_1 \ldots p_k$ encode the control-location where a program could have been before reaching the current basic block. The constraint ϕ encodes the transition relation of the statements in this basic block, and the predicate p in the head of the Horn clause indicates where control flows if the transition relation ϕ allows for a feasible execution of the basic block.

Figure 2 shows a CHC encoding of our running example from Fig. 1. Each predicate $p_0, \ldots, p_4$ corresponds to a control location in our program. The predicate p_0 in the first line is the procedure entry encoding that the entry of the

---

[1] In presence of function calls, a CHC will have at least two predicate symbols in its body: one that represents the callee and the other modelling the successor. If callsites are ignored then CHCs will have only one predicate symbol modelling the successor.

$$p_0(x, ret, i) \leftarrow \; true.$$
$$p_1(x, ret', i') \leftarrow \; ret' = 0 \land i' = -x \land p_0(x, i, ret). \hspace{2cm} procedure\ entry$$
$$p_2(x, ret, i) \leftarrow \; i < x \land p_1(x, ret, i). \hspace{2.6cm} loop\ conditional$$
$$p_3(x, ret, i) \leftarrow \; i \geq x \land p_1(x, ret, i).$$
$$p_1(x, ret', i') \leftarrow \; i \neq 0 \land ret' = 10/i \land i' = i + 1 \land p_2(x, ret, i). \hspace{0.8cm} loop\ body$$
$$p_4(x, ret, i) \leftarrow \; p_3(x, ret, i). \hspace{3.7cm} procedure\ return$$

Fig. 2. Constrained Horn clause representation of the example from Fig. 1. The $i \neq 0$ colored in red is the implicit runtime assertion introduced by the division in line 4 of our running example (Color figure online).

function is always reachable. The second line states that if we are at the procedure entry p_0 and $ret' = 0$ and $i' = -x$ can be established, we are allowed to proceed to the loop head p_1. The next two lines state that, if we are at the loop head and the loop condition $i < x$ holds, we proceed into the loop body p_2, or otherwise, we go to the loop exit p_3. The next line represents the loop body. Note the $i \neq 0$ colored in red. This is the implicit run-time assertion that needs to hold when executing the division in the loop body of our running example in Fig. 1. We assume that these assertions have been introduced during the translation. If the loop body is executed successfully, control moves back to the loop head p_1. The last line is the loop exit. For brevity, we do not model the return statement and just assume that ret is visible to the outside.

Once obtained the system of constrained Horn clauses representing a program, we can add a query. A typical query for our example from Fig. 2 would be:

$$p_4(x, ret, i) \hspace{6cm} (1)$$

which checks if the control location associated p_4 at the end of the procedure is reachable. If this query is satisfiable, the CHC solver produces a *model*. For our encoding, a model also encodes a program state, and the existence of this state witnesses that there is a *feasible path* reaching the associated control-location. For short: if a model for p_4 exists then foo has a feasible complete path.

If no such model exists, the CHC solver provides a proof that the program has no feasible execution (that reaches the end of foo). For our example, we can find a model that sets x to a value less or equal to zero. For this input, the execution of the procedure skips the loop and terminates normally.

The challenge now is, how do we check if there is another model that executes a different path? Let us assume that our previous query provided us with a path through p_0, p_1, p_3, and p_4. Now we want to check if there is also a path through p_2. It would be tempting to build the following query

$$p_4(x, ret, i) \land p_2(x, ret, i). \hspace{5cm} (2)$$

Unfortunately, this query does not ask for a path that passes through p_2 and p_4. Instead, it asks whether p_2 and p_4 are reachable (not necessarily on the same execution) with the same values for x, ret, and i. Even if we rename the variables of p_2 and p_4 to disjoint sets of variables the same problem remains. The reason is that our Horn clause encoding allows only for checking forward reachability. However, our aim is to check if a particular location can be passed during an execution that reaches the end of a procedure. Hence, we have to extend our encoding to capture which locations have been visited on a path.

$$p_0(x, ret, i, \top, \bot, \bot, \bot, \bot) \leftarrow true.$$

$$p_1(x, ret', i', r_0, \top, r_2, r_3, r_4) \leftarrow ret' = 0 \wedge i' = -x \wedge p_0(x, i, ret, r_0, r_1, r_2, r_3, r_4).$$

$$p_2(x, ret, i, r_0, r_1, \top, r_3, r_4) \leftarrow i < x \wedge p_1(x, ret, i, r_0, r_1, r_2, r_3, r_4).$$

$$p_3(x, ret, i, r_0, r_1, r_2, \top, r_4) \leftarrow i \geq x \wedge p_1(x, ret, i, r_0, r_1, r_2, r_3, r_4).$$

$$p_1(x, ret', i', r_0, \top, r_2, r_3, r_4) \leftarrow i \neq 0 \wedge ret' = 10/i \wedge i' = i + 1$$
$$\wedge\, p_2(x, ret, i, r_0, r_1, r_2, r_3, r_4).$$

$$p_4(x, ret, i, r_0, r_1, r_2, r_3, \top) \leftarrow p_3(x, ret, i, r_0, r_1, r_2, r_3, r_4).$$

Fig. 3. Constrained Horn clause representation of the example from Fig. 1 with crumb variables. Each crumb variable r_i corresponds the a program location associated with the predicate p_i. In the head of each clause, we can see that the crumb variable for that predicate is set to true ($\top$) which corresponds to updating the variable to $\top$ when the location is reached. For p_0 all the crumb variables are set to false ($\bot$) except the one that corresponds to the entry of the procedure (r_0).

5   Crumb Variables

To extend our encoding in a way that allows us to extract a feasible path directly from the model returned by the Horn clause solver while blocking paths that we have already covered, we add auxiliary Boolean variables to our encoding. Our approach is inspired by a similar approach using Integer variables that has been presented in [3]. Thinking in terms of programs and executions, the idea is to add one Boolean variable r_i per control location (i.e., per predicate p_i in the Horn clause system). All these variables are initially set to false. If a control location is reached, the corresponding Boolean variable is set to true. Now, we can obtain a path from a model by looking at the values of these Boolean variables at the last program location. Throughout the rest of this paper, we refer to these variables as *crumb variables* because we disperse them in the encoding so that the Horn clause solver can find a path while constructing a model.

Figure 3 shows how we encode the procedure foo from our running example into another system of Horn clauses. For each predicate $p_0 \ldots p_4$ we introduced a crumb variable $r_0, \ldots r_4$. In the head of each Horn clause, we enforce that the crumb variable r_i is set to true when transferring control to pi (alternatively, we could update r_i in the body of the Horn clause like a proper assignment, but this representation is shorter).

Note that, in practice, we do not need one crumb variable per location. It is sufficient to add crumb variables for the minimal subset of locations that need to be covered to ensure that all locations can be covered (in our example this would be p_2 and p_3). The definition of this minimal set is given in [3].

For example, using crumb variables, the incorrect query from (2) in previous section, is encoded correctly as follows:

$$p_4(x, ret, i, \top, r_1, \top, r_3, \top) \tag{3}$$

That is we are asking if it is possible to reach the end of the procedure (by enforcing that p_4 has to hold) in a state where r_0, r_2, and r_4 have been set to true. Thus, we only allow models representing executions of complete paths that visit p_2 at least once.

Lemma 1. *Given a system of CHCs for a program P with a set of predicates $p_0 \ldots p_n$ and a set of crumb variables $r_0 \ldots r_n$, and $p_i(\overrightarrow{v}, r_0, \ldots, r_n)$, where $\overrightarrow{v}$ is a vector of program variables. A query $p_i(\overrightarrow{v}, r_0, \ldots, r_n)$ has a model m if and only if there exists a feasible path in P that reaches the control location associated with p_i. Further $m(r_i)$ is* true *for all r_i associated with control-locations on this path.*

From Lemma 1 follows that querying the predicate that represents the exit of a program allows us to check for the existence of a feasible path. Further, by adding additional conjuncts to the query that certain crumb variables have to be true, we can check if a feasible path through certain locations exists.

Also note that, unlike in encodings that eliminate loops, a model m encodes paths with loops (that is a path rather than a walk in terms of graph theory). Hence, if $m(r_i)$ is true we know that there exists a feasible path through p_i, but we do not know how often p_i is visited when executing this path.

A proof of Lemma 1 in the context of programs and control-flow graphs is given in [3]. Assuming that our Horn clause representation captures the semantics of this control-flow graph as described in [16], this proof also holds for our Horn clause representation of programs.

Fault Localization. In query (3), we checked for the existence of a feasible path that passes through the loop body (represented by p_2). Since no such path exists, the query is unsatisfiable and a Horn clause solver will give us an *invariant* for each predicate. Such invariants can be used to apply static fault localization techniques such as [32] or [23].

For our running example, a Horn clause solver would provide us the following invariants[2]:

$$p_0(x, ret, i) \leftarrow \text{true}, \quad p_1(x, ret, i) \leftarrow i < 0, \quad p_2(x, ret, i) \leftarrow i < 0,$$
$$p_3(x, ret, i) \leftarrow \text{false}, \quad p_4(x, ret, i) \leftarrow \text{false}$$

The first statement proofs that the program location p_0 is valid. Once we enter the loop at p_1, the invariant $i < 0$ holds and takes us into the loop body

---

[2] For clarity, we have eliminated from the invariants all crumb variables.

at p_2 where the invariant still holds. Further, for p_3 and p_4 the invariant is false meaning that the execution of the program must end once the invariant $i < 0$ does not hold anymore. This exactly describes the error. If we enter the loop, we must have a negative i. We can iterate the loop until i becomes zero and then we crash.

One can think of different ways of presenting this information to a programmer. For example, using automaton based representation as described in [32], or a compressed trace with annotations. In summary, using a Horn clause solver to detect inconsistent code provides us a fault localization for free. This is a significant improvement over previous approaches where the fault localization had to be computed manually.

6   Inconsistency Detection Through Horn Clause Coverage

Using our Horn clause encoding with the crumb variables from the previous section, we are able to ask for any location in a program whether it is inconsistent or not. However, in practice, we want to know if a procedure contains *any* inconsistencies. Checking each location individually would not be very efficient (see [3]). Instead, we propose an algorithm that repeatedly asks the solver for a feasible path and then blocks this path to ensure that, in the next query, the solver will exercise a different path that visits at least one control location that has not been visited previously. In a nutshell, we want to compute a *path coverage* for the generated system of Horn clauses.

Algorithm 1. Horn clause coverage algorithm.

Input: $\mathcal{HC}$: constrained Horn clause encoding of a program with crumb variables.

Output: *feasible*   : Crumb that can occur on a feasible path.

```
1  begin
2      crumbs ← getCrumbs(HC) ;
3      p_sink ← getSink(HC) ;
4      feasible ← ∅;
5      blocking ← true ;
6      while query(p_sink ∧ blocking) do
7          model ← getModel(p_sink) ;
8          blocking ← blocking ∧ getBlockingClause(model);
9          feasible ← feasible ∪ {r|r ∈ crumbs ∧ model(r)};
10     end while
11     return feasible;
12 end
```

Algorithm 1 shows our covering algorithm for Horn clause systems. The algorithm takes a program encoded as system of constrained Horn clauses $\mathcal{HC}$ augmented with crumb variables as input and returns the set of crumb variables *feasible* that occurred on feasible paths. To that end, the algorithm first uses the helper function `getCrumbs` to collect all crumb variables from the input Horn clauses. Then, the algorithm calls `getSink` to get the predicate associated with the last control location p_{sink} in the program encoded by $\mathcal{HC}$. This location is needed later on to query if there exists a feasible complete path (that is a path reaching p_{sink}). Further, the algorithm uses the helper variable *blocking*, which is initially true to exclude all models representing program paths that have already been visited.

The main loop of Algorithm 1 repeatedly checks if p_{sink} in conjunction with the blocking clause *blocking* has a model. It uses the helper function `query` which either returns true or false (or runs forever). If `query` returns false, we have a proof from the solver that no feasible path exists and we return the set *feasible*. If `query` returns true, we use the helper function `getModel` to obtain a *model* from the solver that assigns each variable in p_{sink} to a value. In particular, *model* contains an assignment for each crumb variable r such that set of crumb variables assigned to true represent a feasible path.

Using the *model* obtained from the solver, we now extend our blocking clause *blocking* to exclude the feasible path represented by *model*. To that end, we use the function `getBlockingClause` which constructs a conjunction of all crumb variables where the variables that are assigned to false in `model` occur in negated form, and the ones assigned to true in positive form:

$$\texttt{getBlockingClause}(model) = \neg \left(\bigwedge_{r \in \texttt{getCrumbs}(\mathcal{HC})} \begin{cases} r & \text{if} \quad model(r) = \text{true} \\ \neg r & \text{if} \quad model(r) = \text{false} \end{cases} \right)$$

One important difference between computing such a blocking clause for Horn clause systems with loops compared to Horn clause systems without loops is that our blocking clause also *must* include conjunctions for the crumb variables that are assigned to false in the *model*. If we would only include those crumb variables set to true by the *model*, we would also block all paths that visit a superset of the locations visited on this path. Think, for example, of a program containing a single loop with one conditional choice in its body. Let us further assume the then-branch must be visited in the first iteration of the loop, and the else-branch must be visited in all other iterations. If our Horn clause solver gives us a *model* in which the then-branch is visited but not the else-branch, and we would add a blocking clauses containing only the crumb variables that are true in *model*, we would also block all feasible paths through the else-branch. This is because any path through the else-branch must go through the then-branch in the first iteration of the loop. Hence it must set all crumb variables to true that are true in *model* and, in addition to that, the crumb variable for the else-branch.

After updating our blocking clause, Algorithm 1 adds all crumb variables assigned to true by *model* to the set *feasible*. This loop is iterated until no new model can be found. Then, the algorithm returns the set *feasible* of all crumb variables which correspond to feasible control locations in the program. All other control locations in the program are inconsistent.

Note that Algorithm 1 is guaranteed to terminate if `query` terminates: each iteration of the loop extends the blocking clause in a way that the next iteration has to visit at least one new control location. Since the number of control locations is finite (even if the number of paths is not), the loop must reach a point where all control locations that occur on feasible paths have been visited. Then it is up to `query` to prove that there is no more feasible path (this, however, is undecidable).

Remarks on soundness and completeness. Since finding inconsistent code is not safety checking, let us briefly clarify what *soundness* means in the context of inconsistent code detection: An inconsistent code detection algorithm is *sound*, if every inconsistency reported in $\mathcal{HC}$ is in fact an inconsistency in the program it encodes (i.e., a proof that no feasible paths through a control location exists in the Horn clause encoding also is a proof that no such path exists in the original program). So, to be sound, our Horn clause encoding must over-approximate the feasible executions of the original program (which is usually easier than over-approximating the failing executions which is needed to prove safety). Our implementation for C is not sound as we will discuss later. Further, our algorithm is only sound if our Horn clause solver is sound. That is, Algorithm 1 does not introduce unsoundness, but our implementation used in the evaluation is unsound.

Completeness in the context of inconsistent code detection means that an algorithm detects all inconsistencies. Our algorithm is complete if the employed Horn clause solver is complete - which is not the case since the problem is undecidable. Further, we lose completeness during the translation into Horn because we cannot guarantee that the translation preserves all feasible executions of the original program which we will discuss later.

7   Experimental Evaluation

We have implemented our technique on top of the SeaHorn framework [16]. Our tool uses SeaHorn capabilities for translating LLVM-based programs into a set of recursive Horn clauses. This saved us a huge amount of work since SeaHorn deals with the translation from C to LLVM bitecode, performs LLVM optimizations and runs some useful transformations (e.g. mixed-semantics transformation) as well as a pointer analysis. This also allowed us to support programs with pointers and arrays without extra effort. We implemented a variant of the small-step encoding in order to accommodate the crumb variables. We leave for future work the extension to more efficient encoding such as Large-Block Encoding (LBE).

We have implemented the algorithm described in Sect. 6 in Python. The code that is publicly available at [33]. The algorithm is applied on each function separately rather than the whole program. Although our prototype analyzes several functions concurrently one important limitation is that it generates the Horn clauses for the whole program. This has limited us significantly with real applications. For future work, we will instead generate Horn clauses for each function.

Table 1. Results of applying our inconsistent code detection on a set of benchmarks. The benchmarks are handcrafted in the spirit of SV-COMP benchmarks challenge the algorithm with different categories of loops. We check for each benchmark if the inconsistency can be detected by our approach (with loops) and by an approach where loops are abstracted (with abstraction). We further record the number of iterations of our algorithm (i.e., number of feasible paths) and the computation time.

Benchmark	Inconsistency detected				# iterations
	with loops	time (sec)	with abstraction	time (sec)	
example 1	✓	0.09	✗	0.045	1
example 2	✓	0.065	✓	0.06	2
example 3	✓	5.78	✓	5.78	33
example 4	✗	TIMEOUT	✗	0.22	?
example 5	✓	0.33	✗	0.03	3
example 6	✓	0.04	✓	0.085	1
example 7	✓	0.12	✗	0.09	3
example 8	✓	2.956	✓	0.085	5
example 9	✓	0.01	✓	0.02	1
example 10	✓	3.66	✗	1.15	4
example 11	✓	7.91	✗	0.08	2
example 12	✓	44.64	✗	0.14	2
example 13	✗	0.33	✗	0.03	2

For this purpose we will still need a scalable and precise pointer analysis that can analyze the whole program in presence of pointers and arrays. Fortunately, SeaHorn relies on a heap analysis called *Data Structure Analysis (DSA)* which has been very effective for real applications [26].

Experimental setup. To evaluate our approach we handcraft a set of benchmark problems. The idea is to create a set of small but hard benchmarks in the spirit of what is being used in the software verification competition that will allow us to compare different Horn clause solving strategies in the future. All our benchmarks are available online[3] and contain different kinds of inconsistencies which we will describe below in more detail.

For the experiments we used SeaHorn running Spacer [24] in the backend to solve the generated CHCs. All experiments are run on a Macbook Pro with 2.4 Ghz and 8 GB or memory.

Discussion. Table 1 shows the results of running our tool on the set of hand-crafted benchmarks. The first column shows the name of our benchmark, the second column shows a ✓ if our tool detects the inconsistency in the benchmark, and a ✗ if it fails to do so.

All examples contain inconsistent code. Example 1 is our running example. The other examples represent different challenging problems for Horn clause solvers. The examples 2 and 3 do not contain loops, and hence can be solved by

---

[3] https://github.com/seahorn/seahorn/tree/inconsistency/play/inconsistency.

approaches that abstract loops. The examples 6, 8, 9, and 10 are taken from [20], a Wikipedia list of common loop errors, and [27]. They represent cases where inconsistencies in code can be found even with abstraction. Example 6 is an inconsistency that must happen in the first iteration of the loop. For 8 and 9, the inconsistency is local to the loop body and thus can be detected without considering the loop. Example 10 is a typical off-by-one error that can still be detected using, e.g., the loop abstraction in [19] or [34].

Our approach fails on the examples 4, and 13. Example 4 is a faulty implementation of binary search that sets the mid point in a way that leads to an endless loop. Our Horn clause solver is not able to infer a suitable invariant to prove this and infinitely unwinds the loop. Example 13 contains two loops. The first loop allocates a two dimensional matrix but erroneously iterates over the wrong variable which results in unallocated fields in the matrix. The second loop assigns all fields leading to an inevitable segmentation fault. SeaHorn currently does not check if memory is allocated, hence we cannot find this inconsistency.

For all other examples, our approach is able to find inductive invariants that are sufficient to prove the existence of the inconsistency. That is, our approach only times out on a single example and is able to identify six instances of inconsistent code that went undetected before. Hence, we believe that our approach of using CHCs to detect inconsistencies is viable in practice (in particular because we can always fall back to abstraction-based approaches in case of a timeout).

Comparing the computation time of our approach with inconsistent code detection that abstracts loops shows that our approach is not significantly slower on examples that can be solved by both, and sometimes even faster. On examples that can only be solved by our approach, the overhead is sometimes significant (e.g., 8, 11, and 12) but we believe that there is still room for improvement.

Threats to Validity. We report on several threats to validity. Our internal validity is affected by choosing SeaHorn as a frontend to translate C into CHCs, and by using Spacer as a backend to solve those CHCs. Using different frontends or backends may give completely different results. However, we do not claim that our setup is more effective than others. In fact, we encourage readers to try other setups that outperform our approach. The other obvious internal threat to validity is selection bias. We cannot guarantee that our handcrafted benchmarks resemble real inconsistencies. However, we believe that, as a first step, these experiments are sufficient to motivate that inconsistent code detection in the presence loops is an interesting problem, and that our benchmark programs can serve as a baseline for researchers.

A threat to external validity (i.e., generalizibility of the results) for any inconsistent code detection algorithm is that we cannot quantify the number of false negatives (because it is undecidable). Hence, we cannot quantify how much better our approach performs at finding inconsistencies than previous approaches. However, by design, we can say that it finds at least the same inconsistencies as previous approaches and maybe more. A suitable way to evaluate this would be by injecting inconsistencies into real code. However, there is no related empirical work on how *realistic* inconsistencies can be injected into code. Another way to reduce the threat to external validity is to run our tool on industrial benchmarks.

8   Conclusion

In this paper, we have presented a novel approach to detect inconsistent code in the presence of looping control-flow. Our approach encodes the problem of detecting inconsistent code into the problem of solving a system of constrained Horn clauses. Unlike existing approaches, we do not need to abstract looping control-flow in a preprocessing step. Hence, our ability to detect inconsistencies is only limited by the employed Horn clause solver. This allows us to detect a larger class of inconsistencies than any existing techniques. Moreover, this represents an interesting novel application of Horn clause solving.

We propose a set of benchmark programs containing inconsistent code that we made available online. Our experiments show that our implementation is able to detect several inconsistencies in these programs that could not be detected by other tools at a reasonable overhead. In particular, we can always fall back to abstraction-based approaches if our technique does not converge. In fact, to achieve better scalability we envision a technique that integrates our method with abstraction-based approaches. In the future we also plan to validate our approach to industrial scale code base.

References

1. Albarghouthi, A., Li, Y., Gurfinkel, A., Chechik, M.: UFO: a framework for abstraction- and interpolation-based software verification. In: Madhusudan, P., Seshia, S.A. (eds.) CAV 2012. LNCS, vol. 7358, pp. 672–678. Springer, Heidelberg (2012)
2. Barnett, M., Chang, B.-Y.E., DeLine, R., Jacobs, B., M. Leino, K.R.: Boogie: a modular reusable verifier for object-oriented programs. In: de Boer, F.S., Bonsangue, M.M., Graf, S., de Roever, W.-P. (eds.) FMCO 2005. LNCS, vol. 4111, pp. 364–387. Springer, Heidelberg (2006)
3. Bertolini, C., Schäf, M., Schweitzer, P.: Infeasible code detection. In: Joshi, R., Müller, P., Podelski, A. (eds.) VSTTE 2012. LNCS, vol. 7152, pp. 310–325. Springer, Heidelberg (2012)
4. Beyer, D., Cimatti, A., Griggio, A., Keremoglu, M.E., Sebastiani, R.: Software model checking via large-block encoding. In: FMCAD, pp. 25–32 (2009)
5. Bjørner, N., Gurfinkel, A., McMillan, K., Rybalchenko, A.: Horn clause solvers for program verification. In: Beklemishev, L.D., Blass, A., Dershowitz, N., Finkbeiner, B., Schulte, W. (eds.) Gurevich Festschrift II 2015. LNCS, vol. 9300, pp. 24–51. Springer, Heidelberg (2015)
6. Blackshear, S., Lahiri, S.K.: Almost-correct specifications: a modular semantic framework for assigning confidence to warnings. In: PLDI, pp. 209–218 (2013)
7. Bradley, A.R.: IC3 and beyond: incremental, inductive verification. In: Madhusudan, P., Seshia, S.A. (eds.) CAV 2012. LNCS, vol. 7358, pp. 4–4. Springer, Heidelberg (2012)
8. De Angelis, E., Fioravanti, F., Pettorossi, A., Proietti, M.: VeriMAP: a tool for verifying programs through transformations. In: Ábrahám, E., Havelund, K. (eds.) TACAS 2014 (ETAPS). LNCS, vol. 8413, pp. 568–574. Springer, Heidelberg (2014)
9. Delzanno, G., Podelski, A.: Model checking in CLP. In: Cleaveland, W.R. (ed.) TACAS 1999. LNCS, vol. 1579, pp. 223–239. Springer, Heidelberg (1999)

10. Dillig, I., Dillig, T., Aiken, A.: Static error detection using semantic inconsistency inference. In: PLDI, pp. 435–445 (2007)
11. Engler, D., Chen, D.Y., Hallem, S., Chou, A., Chelf, B.: Bugs as deviant behavior: a general approach to inferring errors in systems code. In: SOSP (2001)
12. Ermis, E., Schäf, M., Wies, T.: Error invariants. In: Giannakopoulou, D., Méry, D. (eds.) FM 2012. LNCS, vol. 7436, pp. 187–201. Springer, Heidelberg (2012)
13. Flanagan, C.: Automatic software model checking via constraint logic. Sci. Comput. Program. **50**(1–3), 253–270 (2004)
14. Grebenshchikov, S., Lopes, N.P., Popeea, C., Rybalchenko, A.: Synthesizing software verifiers from proof rules. In: PLDI, pp. 405–416 (2012)
15. Gurfinkel, A., Chaki, S., Sapra, S.: Efficient predicate abstraction of program summaries. In: Bobaru, M., Havelund, K., Holzmann, G.J., Joshi, R. (eds.) NFM 2011. LNCS, vol. 6617, pp. 131–145. Springer, Heidelberg (2011)
16. Gurfinkel, A., Kahsai, T., Komuravelli, A., Navas, J.A.: The seahorn verification framework. In: Kroening, D., Păsăreanu, C.S. (eds.) CAV 2015. LNCS, vol. 9206, pp. 343–361. Springer, Heidelberg (2015)
17. Hoder, K., Bjørner, N.: Generalized property directed reachability. In: Cimatti, A., Sebastiani, R. (eds.) SAT 2012. LNCS, vol. 7317, pp. 157–171. Springer, Heidelberg (2012)
18. Hoenicke, J., Leino, K.R.M., Podelski, A., Schäf, M., Wies, T.: It's doomed; we can prove it. In: Cavalcanti, A., Dams, D.R. (eds.) FM 2009. LNCS, vol. 5850, pp. 338–353. Springer, Heidelberg (2009)
19. Hoenicke, J., Leino, K.R.M., Podelski, A., Schäf, M., Wies, T.: Doomed program points. In: FMSD, pp. 171–199 (2010)
20. Hovemeyer, D., Pugh, W.: Finding more null pointer bugs, but not too many. In: PASTE, pp. 9–14 (2007)
21. Jaffar, J., Murali, V., Navas, J.A., Santosa, A.E.: TRACER: a symbolic execution tool for verification. In: Madhusudan, P., Seshia, S.A. (eds.) CAV 2012. LNCS, vol. 7358, pp. 758–766. Springer, Heidelberg (2012)
22. Janota, M., Grigore, R., Moskal, M.: Reachability analysis for annotated code. In: SAVCBS, pp. 23–30 (2007)
23. Jose, M., Majumdar, R.: Bug-assist: assisting fault localization in ANSI-C programs. In: Gopalakrishnan, G., Qadeer, S. (eds.) CAV 2011. LNCS, vol. 6806, pp. 504–509. Springer, Heidelberg (2011)
24. Komuravelli, A., Gurfinkel, A., Chaki, S.: SMT-based model checking for recursive programs. In: Biere, A., Bloem, R. (eds.) CAV 2014. LNCS, vol. 8559, pp. 17–34. Springer, Heidelberg (2014)
25. Komuravelli, A., Gurfinkel, A., Chaki, S., Clarke, E.M.: Automatic abstraction in SMT-based unbounded software model checking. In: Sharygina, N., Veith, H. (eds.) CAV 2013. LNCS, vol. 8044, pp. 846–862. Springer, Heidelberg (2013)
26. Lattner, C., Adve, V.S.: Automatic pool allocation: improving performance by controlling data structure layout in the heap. In: PLDI, pp. 129–142 (2005)
27. McCarthy, T., Rümmer, P., Schäf, M.: Bixie: finding and understanding inconsistent code. In: ICSE, pp. 645–648 (2015)
28. Peralta, J.C., Gallagher, J.P., Saglam, H.: Analysis of imperative programs through analysis of constraint logic programs. In: Levi, G. (ed.) SAS 1998. LNCS, vol. 1503, pp. 246–261. Springer, Heidelberg (1998)
29. Popeea, C., Rybalchenko, A.: Threader: a verifier for multi-threaded programs. In: Piterman, N., Smolka, S.A. (eds.) TACAS 2013 (ETAPS 2013). LNCS, vol. 7795, pp. 633–636. Springer, Heidelberg (2013)

30. Rümmer, P., Hojjat, H., Kuncak, V.: Classifying and solving horn clauses for veri-
    fication. In: Cohen, E., Rybalchenko, A. (eds.) VSTTE 2013. LNCS, vol. 8164, pp.
    1–21. Springer, Heidelberg (2014)
31. Rümmer, P., Hojjat, H., Kuncak, V.: Disjunctive interpolants for horn-clause verifi-
    cation. In: Sharygina, N., Veith, H. (eds.) CAV 2013. LNCS, vol. 8044, pp. 347–363.
    Springer, Heidelberg (2013)
32. Schäf, M., Schwartz-Narbonne, D., Wies, T.: Explaining inconsistent code. In:
    ESEC/FSE, pp. 521–531 (2013)
33. SeaHorn Inconsistency Checker. https://github.com/seahorn/seahorn/tree/
    inconsistency
34. Tomb, A., Flanagan, C.: Detecting inconsistencies via universal reachability analy-
    sis. In: ISSTA, pp. 287–297 (2012)
35. Wang, X., Zeldovich, N., Kaashoek, M.F., Solar-Lezama, A.: A differential app-
    roach to undefined behavior detection. TOCS **33**(1), 1–29 (2015)

Modular Multiset Rewriting

Iliano Cervesato$^{(\boxtimes)}$ and Edmund S.L. Lam

Carnegie Mellon University, Pittsburgh, PA, USA
iliano@cmu.edu, sllam@andrew.cmu.edu

Abstract. Rule-based languages are being used for ever more ambitious applications. As program size grows however, so does the overhead of team-based development, reusing components, and just keeping a large flat collection of rules from interfering. In this paper, we propose a module system for a small logically-motivated rule-based language. The resulting modules are nothing more than rewrite rules of a specific form, which are themselves just logic formulas. Yet, they provide some of the same features found in advanced module systems such as that of Standard ML, in particular name space separation, support for abstract data types, and parametrization (functors in ML). Our modules also offer essential features for concurrent programming such as facilities for sharing private names. This approach is directly applicable to other rule-based languages, including most forward-chaining logic programming languages and many process algebras.

1 Introduction

Rule-based programming, a model of computation by which rules modify a global state by concurrently rewriting disjoint portions of it, is having a renaissance as a number of domains are finding a use for its declarative and concise specifications, natural support for concurrency, and relative ease of reasoning [2,8,12,14,15]. Furthermore, the asynchronous state transformation model it embodies has been shown to subsume various models of concurrency [6], in particular multiset rewriting, Petri nets and process algebra [20], and several general-purpose languages based on it have been proposed [3,10].

As languages gain popularity, the need for modularity emerges, since the overhead associated with writing code grows with program size. Modularity tames complexity. In traditional programming languages, it addresses the challenges of breaking a large program into a hierarchy of components with clear interfaces, swappable implementations, team-based development, dependency management, code reuse, and separate compilation. Yet, even rule-based languages used for sizable applications [10,15] provide no support for modular programming.

Programming-in-the-large in a rule-based languages brings about additional challenges not typically found in imperative or functional languages. First, languages such as Datalog [12] and CHR [10] have a flat name space which gives no protections against accidentally reusing a name. Moreover, each rule in them adds to the definition of the names it contains rather than overriding them.

© Springer-Verlag Berlin Heidelberg 2015
M. Davis et al. (Eds.): LPAR-20 2015, LNCS 9450, pp. 515–531, 2015.
DOI: 10.1007/978-3-662-48899-7_36

Second, these languages tend to have an open scope, meaning that there is no support for local definitions or private names. Finally, a rule can apply as soon as its prerequisites enter the global state, as opposed to when a procedure is called in a conventional language. This, together with the pitfalls of concurrency, makes writing correct code of even moderate size difficult. These challenges make enriching rule-based languages with a powerful module system all the more urgent if we want them to be used for large applications.

In this paper, we develop a module system for a small rule-based programming language. This language, $\mathcal{L}^1$, subsumes many languages founded on multiset rewriting, forward-chaining proof search and process algebra [6]. Moreover, $\mathcal{L}^1$ is also a syntactic fragment of intuitionistic linear logic in that state transitions map to derivable sequents. In fact, the transition rules for each operator of $\mathcal{L}^1$ correspond exactly to the left sequent rules of this logic, and furthermore the notion of a whole-rule rewriting step originates in a focused presentation of proof search for it [21].

We engineer a module system for $\mathcal{L}^1$ by observing that certain programming patterns capture characteristic features of modularity such as hiding implementation details, providing functionalities to client code through a strictly defined interface, parametricity and the controlled sharing of names. We package these patterns into a handful of constructs that we provide to the programmer as a syntactic extension of $\mathcal{L}^1$ we call $\mathcal{L}^M$. The module system of $\mathcal{L}^M$ supports many of the facilities for modular programming found in Standard ML [19], still considered by many an aspirational gold standard, in particular fine-grained name management and module parametricity (functors). Furthermore, $\mathcal{L}^M$ naturally supports idioms such as higher-order functors and recursive modules, which are not found in [19]. Yet, because the modular constructs of $\mathcal{L}^M$ are just programming templates in $\mathcal{L}^1$, programs in $\mathcal{L}^M$ can be faithfully compiled into $\mathcal{L}^1$. Moreover, since $\mathcal{L}^1$ subsumes the model of computation of a variety of rule-based languages (including those founded on forward-chaining, multiset rewriting and process algebra), it provides a blueprint for enriching these languages with a powerful, yet lightweight and declarative, module system.

With a few exceptions such as [17], research on modularity for rule-based languages has largely targeted backward-chaining logic programming [4]. Popular open-source and commercial implementations of Prolog (e.g., SWI Prolog and SICStus Prolog) do provide facilities for modular programming although not in a declarative fashion. The present work is inspired by several attempts at understanding modularity in richer backward-chaining languages. In particular [18] defines a module system for λProlog on the basis of this language's support for embedded implication, while [1] achieves a form of modularization via a mild form of second-order quantification [11].

The main contributions of this paper are threefold. First, we define a language, $\mathcal{L}^1$, that resides in an operational sweet spot between the stricture of traditional rule-based languages and the freedom of the rewriting reading of intuitionistic linear logic [6]. Second, we engineer a powerful module system on top of this core language with support for name space separation, parametricity, and controlled name sharing. Third, we show that this module infrastructure is little more than syntactic sugar over the core language, and can therefore be compiled away. In fact, this work provides a logical foundation of modularity in rule-based languages in general.

The remainder of this paper is organized as follows: Sect. 2 defines the language $\mathcal{L}^1$, Sect. 3 introduces our modular infrastructure through examples, Sect. 4 collects the resulting language $\mathcal{L}^M$ and elaborates it back into $\mathcal{L}^1$, and Sect. 5 outlines future developments. Further details can be found in the companion technical report [5].

2   Core Language

This section develops a small, logically-motivated, rule-based language that will act as the core language in which we write (non-modular) programs. It is also the language our modular infrastructure will compile into.

2.1   Multiset Rewriting with Existentials and Nested Rules

Our core formalism, which we call $\mathcal{L}^1$, is a first-order multiset rewriting language extended with dynamic name generation and support for nested rewrite rules. As such, it is a fragment of the logically-derived language of ω-multisets studied in [6]. Because we are interested in writing actual programs, we consider a simply-typed variant.

The syntax of $\mathcal{L}^1$ is specified by the following grammar (the productions on the far right — in blue — will be discussed in Sect. 2.3):

$$
\begin{array}{rlll}
\textit{Types} & \tau ::= \iota \mid o \mid \tau \to \tau \mid \tau \times \tau \mid \top \\
\textit{Terms} & t ::= x \mid f\,t \mid (t,t) \mid () & \mid X \mid p \\
\textit{Atoms} & A ::= p\,t & \mid X\,t \\
\textit{LHS} & l ::= \cdot \mid A,l \\
\textit{Rules} & R ::= l \multimap P \mid \forall x : \iota.\,R & \mid \forall X : \tau \to o.\,R \\
\textit{Programs} & P ::= \cdot \mid P,P \mid A \mid R \mid !R \mid \exists x : \tau \to \iota.\,P & \mid \exists X : \tau \to o.\,P
\end{array}
$$

Terms, written t, are built from other terms by pairing and by applying function symbols, f. The starting point is either the unit term $()$ or a term variable, generically written x. In examples, we abbreviate $f\,()$ to just f. We classify terms by means of simple types, denoted τ. We consider two base types, the type of terms themselves, denoted ι, and the type of formulas, denoted o. Type constructors match term constructors, with the type of $()$ written $\top$. This minimal typing infrastructure can be considerably enriched with additional type and term constructors, as done in some examples of Sect. 3.

Programs are built out of rules, left-hand sides, and ultimately atoms. An *atom* A is a predicate symbol p applied to a term. A *rule*, R, is the universal closure of a rewrite directive of the form $l \multimap P$. The *left-hand side* l is a multiset of atoms, where we write "$\cdot$" for the empty multiset and "A, l" for the extension of l with atom A. We consider "$,$" commutative and associative with unit "$\cdot$".

The right-hand side P of a rewrite directive is a multiset of either atoms A, single-use rules R or reusable rules $!R$. A right-hand side can also have the form $\exists x : \tau \rightarrow \iota. P$, which, when executed, will have the effect of creating a new function symbol for x of type $\tau \rightarrow \iota$ for use in P. As rules consist of a rewrite directive embedded within a layer of universal quantifiers, generically $\forall x_1 : \tau_1. \ldots \forall x_n : \tau_n. (l \multimap P)$ with τ_i equal to ι for the time being, we will occasionally use the notation $\forall \vec{x} : \vec{\tau}. (l \rightarrow P)$ where $\vec{x}$ stands for $x_1, \ldots, x_n$ and $\vec{\tau}$ for $\tau_1, \ldots, \tau_n$. A *program* is what we just referred to as a right-hand side. A program is therefore a collection of atoms, single-use and reusable rules, and existentially quantified programs.

The quantifiers $\forall x : \tau. R$ and $\exists x : \tau. P$ are binders in $\mathcal{L}^1$. We adopt the standard definitions of free and bound variables, closed expressions (called ground in the case of terms and atoms), and α-renaming. Given a syntactic entity O possibly containing a free variable x, we write $[t/x]O$ for the capture-avoiding substitution of term t of the same type for every free occurrence of x in O. Given sequences $\vec{x}$ and $\vec{t}$ of variables and terms of the same length, we denote the simultaneous substitution of every term t_i in $\vec{t}$ for the corresponding variable x_i in $\vec{x}$ in O as $[\vec{t}/\vec{x}]O$. We write θ for a generic substitution $\vec{t}/\vec{x}$ and $O\theta$ for its application.

Function and predicate symbols have types of the form $\tau \rightarrow \iota$ and $\tau \rightarrow o$ respectively. The symbols in use during execution together with their type are collected in a *signature*, denoted Σ. We treat free existential variables as symbols and account for them in the signature. The type of free universal variables are collected in a *context* Γ. Signatures and contexts are defined as follows (again, ignore the rightmost production):

$$
\begin{array}{rll}
\textit{Signatures} & \Sigma ::= \cdot \mid \Sigma, f : \tau \rightarrow \iota \mid \Sigma, p : \tau \rightarrow o & \\
\textit{Contexts} & \Gamma ::= \cdot \mid \Gamma, x : \iota & \mid \Gamma, X : \tau \rightarrow o
\end{array}
$$

We write $\Gamma \vdash_\Sigma t : \tau$ to mean that term t has type τ in Γ and Σ. The routine typing rules for this judgment can be found in [5], together with the straightforward definition of validity for the other entities of the language. Valid rewrite directives $l \multimap P$ are also subject to the *safety requirement* that the free variables in P shall occur in l or in the left-hand side of an enclosing rule.

Computation in $\mathcal{L}^1$ takes the form of state transitions. A *state* is a pair $\Sigma. \Pi$ consisting of a closed program Π and a signature Σ that accounts for all the function and predicate symbols in Π. We emphasize that the program must be closed by writing it as Π rather than P. Since rules R in Π are closed, we further abbreviate $\forall \vec{x} : \vec{\tau}. (l \multimap P)$ as $\forall (l \multimap P)$. Observe that a state contains both atoms, which carry data, and rules, which perform computation on such data.

We give two characterizations of the rewriting semantics of $\mathcal{L}^1$, each rooted in the proof theory of linear logic as discussed in Sect. 2.2. The *unfocused rewriting semantics* interprets each operator in $\mathcal{L}^1$ as an independent state transformation directive. It is expressed by means of a step judgment of the form

$$\Sigma. \Pi \mapsto \Sigma'. \Pi' \qquad \textit{State } \Sigma. \Pi \textit{ transitions to state } \Sigma'. \Pi' \textit{ in one step}$$

In this semantics, each operator in the language is understood as a directive to carry out one step of computation in the current state. Therefore, each operator yields one transition rule, given in the following table (please, ignore the starred entries in blue):

$$\Sigma. (\Pi, l, l \multimap P) \mapsto \Sigma. (\Pi, P)$$
$$\Sigma. (\Pi, \forall x : \iota. R) \mapsto \Sigma. (\Pi, [t/x]R) \qquad \text{if } \cdot \vdash_\Sigma t : \iota$$
$$\Sigma. (\Pi, \forall X : \tau \to o. R) \mapsto \Sigma. [p/X]R \qquad \text{if } p : \tau \to o \text{ in } \Sigma \quad (*)$$
$$\Sigma. (\Pi, !R) \mapsto \Sigma. (\Pi, !R, R)$$
$$\Sigma. (\Pi, \exists x : \tau \to \iota. P) \mapsto (\Sigma, x : \tau \to \iota). (\Pi, P)$$
$$\Sigma. (\Pi, \exists X : \tau \to o. P) \mapsto (\Sigma, X : \tau \to o). \Pi, P \qquad (*)$$

In words, $\multimap$ is a rewrite directive which has the effect of identifying its left-hand side atoms in the surrounding state and replacing them with the program in its right-hand side. The operator $\forall$ is an instantiation directive: it picks a term of the appropriate type and replaces the bound variable with it. Instead, ! is a replication directive, enabling a reusable rule to be applied while keeping the master copy around. Finally, $\exists$ is a name generation directive which installs a new symbol of the appropriate type in the signature.

The rules of this semantics are pleasantly simple as they tease out the specific behavior of each individual language construct. However, by considering each operator in isolation, this semantics falls short of the expected rewriting behavior. Consider the state $\Sigma. \Pi = (p : \iota \to o, q : \iota \to o, a : \iota, b : \iota). (p\,a, \forall x : \iota. p\,x \multimap q\,x)$. From it, the one transition sequence of interest is $\Pi \mapsto p\,a, (p\,a \multimap q\,a) \mapsto q\,a$, where we have omitted the signature Σ for succinctness. However, nothing prevents picking the "wrong" instance of x and taking the step $\Pi \mapsto p\,a, (p\,b \multimap q\,b)$ from where we cannot proceed further. This second possibility is unsatisfactory as it does not apply the rule fully.

The *focused rewriting semantics* makes sure that rules are either fully applied, or not applied at all. It corresponds to the standard operational semantics of most languages based on multiset rewriting, forward chaining and process transformation. It also leverages the observation that some of the state transformations associated with individual operators, here the existential quantifier, never preempt other transitions from taking place, while others do (here both the universal instantiation and the rewrite directive).

A closed program without top-level existential quantifiers is called *stable*. We write $\underline{\Pi}$ for a state program Π that is stable. A stable state has the form $\Sigma. \underline{\Pi}$. The focused operational semantics is expressed by two judgments:

$$\Sigma. \Pi \Rrightarrow \Sigma'. \Pi' \quad \text{Non-stable state } \Sigma. \Pi \text{ transitions to state } \Sigma'. \Pi' \text{ in one step}$$
$$\Sigma. \underline{\Pi} \Rrightarrow \Sigma'. \Pi' \quad \text{Stable state } \Sigma. \underline{\Pi} \text{ transitions to state } \Sigma'. \Pi' \text{ in one step}$$

The first judgment is realized by selecting an existential program component in Π and eliminating the quantifier by creating a new symbol. A finite iteration yields a stable state. At this point, the second judgment kicks in. It selects a rule and fully applies it. To fully apply a rule $\forall(l \multimap P)$, the surrounding state must contain an instance $l\theta$ of the left-hand side l. The focused semantics replaces it with the corresponding instance $P\theta$ of the right-hand side P. The resulting state may not be stable as $P\theta$ could contain existential components. The following (non-starred) transitions formalize this insight.

$$\Sigma. (\Pi, \exists x : \tau \rightarrow \iota. P) \mapsto (\Sigma, x : \tau \rightarrow \iota). (\Pi, P)$$
$$\Sigma. (\Pi, \exists X : \tau \rightarrow o. P) \mapsto (\Sigma, X : \tau \rightarrow o). (\Pi, P) \qquad (*)$$

$$\Sigma. \Pi. l\theta. \forall (l \multimap P) \Rrightarrow \Sigma. (\Pi, P\theta)$$
$$\Sigma. \Pi. l\theta. !\forall (l \multimap P) \Rrightarrow \Sigma. (\Pi, !\forall (l \multimap P), P\theta)$$

Both the focused and unfocused semantics transform valid states into valid states [5]. Furthermore, any transition step achievable in the focused semantics is also achievable in the unfocused semantics, although possibly in more than one step in the case of rules.

Theorem 1.

1. *If* $\Sigma. \Pi \Rrightarrow \Sigma'. \Pi'$, *then* $\Sigma. \Pi \mapsto \Sigma'. \Pi'$.
2. *If* $\Sigma. \Pi \Rrightarrow \Sigma'. \Pi'$, *then* $\Sigma. \Pi \mapsto^* \Sigma'. \Pi'$.

where $\mapsto^*$ is the reflexive and transitive closure of $\mapsto$. This property is proved in [5]. The reverse does not hold, as we saw earlier.

The language $\mathcal{L}^1$ is a syntactic fragment of the formalism of ω-multisets examined in [6] as a logical reconstruction of multiset rewriting and some forms of process algebra. The main restriction concerns the left-hand side of rules, which in $\mathcal{L}^1$ is a multiset of atoms, while in an ω-multiset it can be any formula in the language. This restriction makes implementing rule application in $\mathcal{L}^1$ much easier than in the general language, is in line with all rule-based languages we are aware of, and is endorsed by a focusing view of proof search. Therefore, $\mathcal{L}^1$ occupies a sweet spot between the freewheeling generality of ω-multiset rewriting and the implementation simplicity of many rule-based languages. $\mathcal{L}^1$ also limits the usage of the ! operator to just rules. This avoids expressions that are of little use in programming practice (for example doubly reusable rules $!!R$ or left-hand side atoms of the form $!A$). This is relaxed somewhat in [5] where we allow reusable atoms in the right-hand side of a rule. We also left out the choice operator of ω-multisets (written &) because we did not need it in any of the examples in this paper. Adding it back is straightforward.

Syntactic fragments of $\mathcal{L}^1$ correspond to various rule-based formalisms. First-order multiset rewriting, as found for example in CHR [10], relies on reusable rules whose right-hand side is a multiset of atoms, and therefore corresponds to $\mathcal{L}^1$ rules of the form $!\forall \vec{x}. (l_1 \multimap l_2)$. Languages such as MSR additionally permit the creation of new symbols in the right-hand side of a rule, which is supported by $\mathcal{L}^1$ rules of the form $!\forall \vec{x}. (l_1 \multimap \exists \vec{y}. l_2)$.

As shown in [6], ω-multiset rewriting, and therefore $\mathcal{L}^1$, also subsumes many formalisms based on process algebra. Key to doing so is the possibility to nest rules (thereby directly supporting the ability to sequentialize actions), a facility to create new symbols (which matches channel restriction), and the fact that multisets are commutative monoids (like processes under parallel composition). For example, the asynchronous π-calculus [20] is the fragment of $\mathcal{L}^1$ where rule left-hand sides consist of exactly one atom (corresponding to a receive action — send actions correspond to atoms on the right-hand side of a rule).

Our language, like ω-multiset rewriting itself, contains fragments that correspond to both the state transition approach to specifying concurrent computations (as multiset rewriting for example) and specifications in the process-algebraic style. It in fact supports hybrid specifications as well, as found in the Join calculus [9] and in CLF [22].

2.2 Logical Foundations

The language $\mathcal{L}^1$, like ω-multisets [6], corresponds exactly to a fragment of intuitionistic linear logic [13]. In fact, not only can we recognize the constructs of our language among the operators of this logic, but $\mathcal{L}^1$'s rewriting semantics stem directly from its proof theory.

The operators "," and "$\cdot$", $\multimap$, !, $\forall$ and $\exists$ of $\mathcal{L}^1$ correspond to the logical constructs $\otimes$, 1, $\multimap$, !, $\forall$ and $\exists$, respectively, of multiplicative-exponential intuitionistic linear logic (MEILL). We write the derivability judgment of MEILL as $\Gamma; \Delta \longrightarrow_\Sigma \varphi$, where φ is a formula, the linear context Δ is a multiset of formulas that can be used exactly once in a proof of φ, while the formulas in the persistent context Γ can be used arbitrarily many times, and Σ is a signature defined as for $\mathcal{L}^1$.

The transitions of the unfocused rewriting semantics of $\mathcal{L}^1$ can be read off directly from the left sequent rules of the above connectives. Consider for example the transition for an existential $\mathcal{L}^1$ program and the left sequent rule $\exists L$ for the existential quantifier:

$$\Sigma. (\Pi, \exists x : \tau \to \iota. P) \mapsto (\Sigma, x : \tau \to \iota). (\Pi, P) \quad\rightsquigarrow\quad \frac{\Gamma; \Delta, \varphi \longrightarrow_{\Sigma, x : \tau \to \iota} \psi}{\Gamma; \Delta, \exists x : \tau \to \iota. \varphi \longrightarrow_\Sigma \psi} \exists L$$

The antecedent $\Pi, \exists x : \tau \to \iota. P$ of the transition corresponds to the linear context $\Delta, \exists x : \tau \to \iota. \varphi$ of the rule conclusion, while its consequent (Π, P) matches the linear context of the premise (Δ, φ) and the signatures have been updated in the same way. A similar correspondence applies in all cases, once we account for shared structural properties of states and sequents. In particular, multiplicative conjunction $\otimes$ and its unit 1 are the materialization of the formation operators for the linear context of a sequent, context union and the empty context. This means that linear contexts can be interpreted as the multiplicative conjunction of their formulas. There is a similar interplay between persistent formulas $!\varphi$ and the persistent context Γ [6]. Altogether, this correspondence is captured by the following property, proved in [5,6], where $\ulcorner \Pi \urcorner$ is the MEILL formula corresponding to state Π and $\exists \Sigma'. \ulcorner \Pi' \urcorner$ is obtained by prefixing $\ulcorner \Pi' \urcorner$ with an existential quantification for each declaration in the signature Σ'.

Theorem 2. *If $\Sigma. \Pi$ is valid and $\Sigma. \Pi \mapsto \Sigma'. \Pi'$, then $\cdot; \ulcorner \Pi \urcorner \longrightarrow_\Sigma \exists \Sigma'. \ulcorner \Pi' \urcorner$.*

The transitions of the focused rewriting semantics of $\mathcal{L}^1$ originate from the focused presentation of linear logic [16], and specifically of MEILL. Focusing is a proof search strategy that alternates two phases: an inversion phase where invertible sequent rules are applied exhaustively and a chaining phase where it selects a formula (the focus) and decomposes it maximally using non-invertible rules. Focusing is complete for many logics of interest, in particular for traditional intuitionistic logic [21] and for linear logic [16], and specifically for MEILL [5]. Transitions of the form $\Sigma.\Pi \Mapsto \Sigma'.\Pi'$ correspond to invertible rules and are handled as in the unfocused case. Instead, transitions of the form $\Sigma.\Pi \Rightarrow \Sigma'.\Pi'$ correspond to the selection of a focus formula and the consequent chaining phase. Consider for example the transition for a single-use rule $\forall(l \multimap P)$. The derivation snippet below selects a context formula $\forall(\varphi_l \multimap \varphi_P)$ of the corresponding form from a sequent where no invertible rule is applicable (generically written $\Gamma; \Delta \Longrightarrow_\Sigma \psi$), puts it into focus (indicated as a red box), and then applies non-invertible rules to it exhaustively. In the transcription of $\mathcal{L}^1$ into MEILL, the formula $\varphi_l\theta$ is a conjunction of atomic formulas matching $l\theta$, which allows continuing the chaining phase in the left premise of $\multimap L$ into a complete derivation when Δ_2 consists of those exact atoms. The translation φ_P of the program P re-enables an invertible rule and therefore the derivation loses focus in the rightmost open premise.

$$
\Sigma.\Pi, l\theta, \forall(l \multimap P) \;\Rightarrow\; \Sigma.(\Pi, P\theta) \qquad \rightsquigarrow \qquad
\frac{
\dfrac{
\dfrac{\cdots\; \overline{\Gamma; A\theta \Longrightarrow_\Sigma \boxed{A\theta}} \;\cdots}{\Gamma; \Delta_2 \Longrightarrow_\Sigma \boxed{\varphi_l\theta}} \quad
\dfrac{\Gamma; \Delta_1, \varphi_P\theta \Longrightarrow_\Sigma \psi}{\Gamma; \Delta_1, \boxed{\varphi_P\theta} \Longrightarrow_\Sigma \psi}\;{\scriptstyle\text{blurL}}
}{
\dfrac{\Gamma; \Delta_1, \Delta_2, \boxed{\varphi_l\theta \multimap \varphi_P\theta} \Longrightarrow_\Sigma \psi}{\dfrac{\Gamma; \Delta_1, \Delta_2, \boxed{\forall(\varphi_l \multimap \varphi_P)} \Longrightarrow_\Sigma \psi}{\Gamma; \Delta_1, \Delta_2, \forall(\varphi_l \multimap \varphi_P) \Longrightarrow_\Sigma \psi}\;{\scriptstyle\text{focusL}}}\;{\scriptstyle\forall\text{L(repeated)}}
}\;{\scriptstyle\multimap L}
$$

Reusable $\mathcal{L}^1$ rules $!\forall(l \multimap P)$ are treated similarly. The correspondence is formalized in the following theorem, proved in [5].

Theorem 3. *Let $\Sigma.\Pi$ state be a valid state.*

1. *If Π is stable and $\Sigma.\Pi \Rightarrow \Sigma'.\Pi'$, then $\cdot;\ulcorner\Pi\urcorner \Longrightarrow_\Sigma \exists\Sigma'.\ulcorner\Pi'\urcorner$.*
2. *If Π is not stable and $\Sigma.\Pi \Mapsto \Sigma'.\Pi'$, then $\cdot;\ulcorner\Pi\urcorner \Longrightarrow_\Sigma \exists\Sigma'.\ulcorner\Pi'\urcorner$.*

In focused logics, the formula patterns involved in a chaining phase can be viewed as *synthetic connectives* and are characterized by well-behaved derived rules. The generic single-use rules $\forall(l \multimap P)$ and reusable rules $!\forall(l \multimap P)$ define such synthetic connectives, and their transitions match exactly the derived left sequent rule in the focused presentation of MEILL.

2.3   Mild Higher-Order Quantification

As we prepare to modularize $\mathcal{L}^1$ programs, it is convenient to give this language a minor second-order flavor. Doing so significantly improves code readability with only cosmetic changes to the underlying formalism and its logical interpretation. In fact, programs in this extended language, that we call $\mathcal{L}^{1.5}$, are readily transformed into $\mathcal{L}^1$ programs, as shown in [5].

The language $\mathcal{L}^{1.5}$ is obtained by taking into account the snippets written in blue throughout the earlier definitions. It extends $\mathcal{L}^1$ with second-order variables and a very weak form of quantification over them. Second-order variables, written X, allow us to define atoms of the form $X t$ that are parametric in their predicate. However, we permit these variables to be replaced only with predicate names, which are now legal ingredients in terms. The second-order universal quantifier $\forall X$ carries out this substitution by drawing an appropriate predicate name from the signature. The second-order existential quantifier $\exists X$ extends the signature with new predicate names. This use of second-order entities is closely related to Gabbay and Mathijssen's "one-and-a-halfth-order logic" [11]. It comes short of the expressiveness (and complexity) of a traditional second-order infrastructure (which in our case would permit instantiating a variable X with a parametric program rather than just a predicate name).

The notions of free and bound variables, ground atoms, closed rules and programs, and substitution carry over from the first-order case, and so does the safety requirement. Second-order universal variables are subject to an additional requirement: if a parametric atom $X t$ with X universally quantified occurs in the left-hand side of a rule, then X must occur in a term position either in the same left-hand side or in an outer left-hand side. This additional constraint is motivated by the need to avoid rules such as

$$!\forall X : \tau \rightarrow o. \forall x : \tau. \ X\, x \multimap \cdot$$

which would blindly delete any atom $p t$ for all p of type $\tau \rightarrow o$. Instead, we want a rule to be applicable only to atoms it "knows" something about, by requiring that their predicate name be passed to it in a "known" atom. The following rule is instead acceptable

$$!\forall X : \tau \rightarrow o. \forall x : \tau. \ \mathsf{delete\_all}(X), X\, x \multimap \cdot$$

as only the predicate names marked to be deleted through the predicate $\mathsf{delete\_all}$ can trigger this rule. A type system that enforces this restriction is given in [5].

Both the focused and unfocused rewriting semantics of $\mathcal{L}^1$ are extended to process the second-order quantifiers. The notion of state remains unchanged. The properties seen for $\mathcal{L}^1$, in particular the preservation of state validity, also hold for $\mathcal{L}^{1.5}$.

3 Adding Modularity

In this section, we synthesize a module system for $\mathcal{L}^{1.5}$ by examining a number of examples. In each case, we will write rules in a way as to emulate characteristics of modularity, and then develop syntax to abstract the resulting linguistic pattern.

For readability, types will be grayed out throughout this section. In most cases, they can be automatically inferred from the way the variables they annotate are used.

Name Space Separation. Consider the problem of adding two unary numbers — we write z and $s(n)$ for zero and the successor of n, respectively, and refer to the type of such numerals as nat. Addition is then completely defined by the single rule

$$!\forall x\colon \text{nat}.\, \forall y\colon \text{nat}.\quad \text{add}(\text{s}(x), y) \multimap \text{add}(x, \text{s}(y))$$

For any concrete values m and n, inserting the atom $\text{add}(m, n)$ in the state triggers a sequence of applications of this rule that will end in an atom of the form $\text{add}(\text{z}, r)$, with r the result of adding m and n. The way this adding functionality will typically be used is by having one rule generate the request in its right-hand side and another retrieve the result in its left-hand side, as in the following client code snippet:

$$\forall m\colon \text{nat}.\, \forall n\colon \text{nat}.\qquad \cdots \qquad \multimap \cdots , \text{add}(n, m)$$
$$\forall r\colon \text{nat}.\, \text{add}(\text{z}, r), \cdots \multimap \cdots$$

This code is however incorrect whenever there is the possibility of two clients performing an addition at the same time. In fact, any concurrent use of add will cause an interference as the clients have no way to sort out which result (r in $\text{add}(\text{z}, r)$) is who's.

We obviate to this problem by using a second-order existential quantifier to generate the predicate used to carry out the addition, as in the following code snippet where we nested the rule that uses the result inside the rule that requests the addition so that they share the name *add*.

$$\forall m\colon \text{nat}.\, \forall n\colon \text{nat}.\, \cdots \multimap \exists add\colon \text{nat} \times \text{nat} \to o.$$
$$\begin{bmatrix} !\forall x\colon \text{nat}.\, \forall y\colon \text{nat}.\quad add(\text{s}(x), y) \multimap add(x, \text{s}(y)), \\ \cdots , add(n, m), \\ \forall r\colon \text{nat}.\, add(\text{z}, r), \cdots \multimap \cdots \end{bmatrix}$$

The safety constraint on second-order variables prevents a rogue programmer from intercepting the freshly generated predicate out of thin air. In fact, the rule

$$\forall X\colon \text{nat} \times \text{nat} \to o.\, \forall m\colon \text{nat}.\, \forall n\colon \text{nat}.\quad X(m, n) \multimap X(\text{z}, \text{s}(\text{z}))$$

is invalid as X does not appear in a term position in the left-hand side.

While the above approach eliminates the possibility of interferences, it forces every rule that relies on addition to embed its definition. This goes against the spirit of modularity as it prevents code reuse, reduces maintainability, and diminishes readability.

We address this issue by providing a public name for the addition functionality, for example through the predicate adder, but pass to it the name of the private predicate used by the client code (*add*). Each client can then generate a fresh name for it. The definition of addition, triggered by a call to adder, can then be factored out from the client code. The resulting rules are as follows:

$$!\forall add: \text{nat} \times \text{nat} \rightarrow o. \; \text{adder}(add) \multimap \big[\, !\forall x: \text{nat}. \forall y: \text{nat}. \; add(\mathsf{s}(x), y) \multimap add(x, \mathsf{s}(y)) \,\big]$$

$$\forall m: \text{nat}. \forall n: \text{nat}. \cdots \multimap \exists add: \text{nat} \times \text{nat} \rightarrow o. \begin{bmatrix} \text{adder}(add), \\ \cdots, add(n, m), \\ \forall r: \text{nat}. \; add(\mathsf{z}, r), \cdots \multimap \cdots \end{bmatrix}$$

Observe that, as before, the client generates a fresh name for its private adding predicate ($\exists add: \text{nat} \times \text{nat} \rightarrow o.$). It now passes it to adder, which has the effect of instantiating the rule for addition with the private name *add*. The client can then retrieve the result by having $add(\mathsf{z}, r)$ in the left-hand side of an embedded rule like before.

This idea will be the cornerstone of our approach to adding modules to $\mathcal{L}^{1.5}$. We isolate it in the following derived syntax for the exported module (first rule above):

$$\begin{array}{l} \textbf{module adder} \\ \quad \textbf{provide} \quad add : \text{nat} \times \text{nat} \rightarrow o \\ \qquad !\forall m: \text{nat}. \forall n: \text{nat}. \; add(\mathsf{s}(m), n) \multimap add(m, \mathsf{s}(n)) \\ \quad \textbf{end} \end{array}$$

Here, the public name adder is used as the name of the module. The names of the exported operations, the module's interface, are introduced by the keyword **provide**. By isolating the public predicate name adder in a special position (after the keyword **module**), we can statically preempt one newly-introduced problem with the above definition: that a rogue client learn the private name through the atom adder(X). We shall disallow predicates used as module names (here adder) from appearing in the left-hand side of other rules.

We also provide derived syntax for the client code to avoid the tedium of creating a fresh predicate name and using it properly. Our client is re-expressed as:

$$\forall m: \text{nat}. \forall n: \text{nat}. \cdots \multimap A \textbf{ as adder}. \begin{bmatrix} \cdots, A.add(n, m), \\ \forall r: \text{nat}. \; A.add(\mathsf{z}, r), \cdots \multimap \cdots \end{bmatrix}$$

Here, A is a *module reference name* introduced by the line "A **as** adder.". This syntactic artifact binds A in the right-hand side of the rule. The name A allows constructing *compound predicate names*, here $A.add$, which permits using the exact same names exported by the **provide** stanza of a module. Uses of compound names and the "**as**" construct are elaborated into our original code, as described in Sect. 4.

Modes. In the face of it, our adder module is peculiar in that it requires client code to use an atom of the form $add(\mathsf{z}, r)$ to retrieve the result r of an addition. A better approach is to split *add* into a predicate *add_req* for issuing an addition request and a predicate *add_res* for retrieving the result. However, uses of *add_req* in the left-hand side of client rules would intercept requests, while occurrences of *add_res* on their right-hand side could inject forged results. We prevent such misuses by augmenting the syntax of modules with *modes* that describe how exported predicates are to be used. The mode **in** in the **provide** stanza forces a (compound) predicate to be used only on the left-hand side of a client rule, while the mode **out** enables it on the right-hand side only. A declaration without either, for example *add* earlier, can be used freely. The updated adder module is written as follows in the concrete syntax:

$$
\boxed{
\begin{array}{l}
\textbf{module adder}' \\
\quad \textbf{provide out } add\_req : \mathsf{nat} \times \mathsf{nat} \to o \quad \textbf{in } add\_res : \mathsf{nat} \to o \\
\quad !\forall x : \mathsf{nat}.\, \forall y : \mathsf{nat}.\ add\_req(\mathsf{s}(x), y) \multimap add\_req(x, \mathsf{s}(y)) \\
\qquad\qquad \forall z : \mathsf{nat}.\quad add\_req(\mathsf{z}, z) \quad \multimap add\_res(z) \\
\quad \textbf{end}
\end{array}
}
$$

and the client code assumes the following concrete form:

$$
\boxed{
\forall m : \mathsf{nat}.\, \forall n : \mathsf{nat}.\ \cdots \multimap A \textbf{ as adder}'.\ \begin{bmatrix} \cdots, A.add\_req(n, m), \\ \forall r : \mathsf{nat}.\ A.add\_res(r), \cdots \multimap \cdots \end{bmatrix}
}
$$

Abstract Data Types. The infrastructure we developed so far already allows us to write modules that implement abstract data types. Our next module defines a queue with two operations: enqueuing a data item (for us a nat) and dequeuing an item, which we implement as a pair of request and result predicates. An empty queue is created when a queue module is first invoked. We give a name, here QUEUE, to the exported declarations as follows

$$
\boxed{
\begin{array}{l}
\textbf{interface QUEUE} \\
\quad \textbf{out} \quad enq : \mathsf{nat} \to o \\
\quad \textbf{out } deq\_req : o \qquad \textbf{in } deq : \mathsf{nat} \to o \\
\quad \textbf{end}
\end{array}
}
$$

The module queue uses linked lists built from the local predicates $head(d'')$, $tail(d')$ and $data(n, d', d'')$, where the terms d' and d'' identify the predecessor and the successor element, respectively. Such a list will start with atom $head(d_0)$, continue as series of atoms $data(n_i, d_i, d_{i+1})$ and end with the atom $tail(d_n)$.

$$
\boxed{
\begin{array}{l}
\textbf{module queue} \\
\quad \textbf{provide QUEUE} \\
\quad \textbf{local} \quad head : \iota \to o \quad tail : \iota \to o \quad data : \mathsf{nat} \times \iota \times \iota \to o \\
\qquad\qquad\qquad\qquad\qquad\qquad \multimap \exists d : \iota.\, head(d), tail(d) \\
\quad !\forall e : \mathsf{nat}.\, \forall d : \iota. \qquad\quad enq(e), head(d) \qquad \multimap \exists d' : \iota.\, data(e, d', d), head(d') \\
\quad !\forall e : \mathsf{nat}.\, \forall d : \iota.\, \forall d' : \iota.\ deq\_req, tail(d'), data(e, d, d') \multimap deq(e), tail(d) \\
\quad \textbf{end}
\end{array}
}
$$

A second implementation based on a term representation of lists can be found in [5].

Sharing Private Names. As our next example, we define a module that provides the functionalities of a reference cell in a stateful language. The initial value of the cell will be a parameter v to the module itself, which will be an actual value when the module is instantiated. This corresponds to a functor that takes a value as an argument in Standard ML. This form of parametricity is achieved in $\mathcal{L}^{1.5}$ by simply passing v as an argument to the public predicate used to call the module, in addition to the normal interface predicates [5]. In the concrete syntax, we simply supply v as an argument to the module declaration, as in the following code snippet:

$$
\begin{array}{l}
\textbf{module cell } (v\text{: nat}) \\
\quad \textbf{provide out } get : o \qquad\qquad \textbf{in } got : \text{nat} \to o \\
\qquad\qquad \textbf{out } set : \text{nat} \to o \\
\quad \textbf{local } \; content : \text{nat} \to o \\
\qquad\qquad\qquad\qquad\qquad\qquad\quad \multimap content(v) \\
\qquad\qquad \forall v\text{: nat. } \; get, content(v) \; \multimap got(v), content(v) \\
\qquad \forall v\text{: nat. } \forall v'\text{: nat. } set(v'), content(v) \multimap content(v') \\
\quad \textbf{end}
\end{array}
$$

Reference cells are often shared by various subcomputations. One way to do so is to pass the exported predicates to the subcomputations, after instantiation. In the following example, the client code (first rule) creates a cell C initialized with the value $s(z)$. It then passes the setter to the second rule through the predicate p and passes the getters to the third rule through the predicate q. The second rule can only write to the cell. The third rule can only read the content of the cell (here, it then outputs it through predicate s).

$$
\begin{array}{l}
\qquad\qquad\qquad\qquad\qquad \multimap C \textbf{ as cell}(s(z)). \left[\begin{array}{l} p(C.set), \\ q(C.get, C.got) \end{array}\right] \\[2ex]
\forall write\text{: nat} \to o. \qquad p(write) \qquad \multimap write(z) \\[1ex]
\left[\begin{array}{l} \forall read\_req\text{: } o. \\ \forall read\text{: nat} \to o. \end{array}\right] q(read\_req, read) \multimap \left[\begin{array}{l} read\_req, \\ \forall r\text{: nat. } read(r) \multimap s(r) \end{array}\right]
\end{array}
$$

This example shows how the private names obtained through a module invocation can be shared with other rules. Furthermore this sharing can be selective.

Reference cells can be implemented in a much simpler way by exporting just the predicate *content* that holds the content of the cell [5]. By doing so, however, we prevent the client code from passing distinct capabilities to its subcomputations.

Parametric Modules. As our last example, we define a producer-consumer module. We rely on a queue, as defined earlier, to act as the buffer where the producer deposits data and the consumer retrieves them from.

Now, rather than selecting a priori which implementation of queues to use, we make the producer-consumer module parametric with respect to the implementation of queues. This corresponds a functor parametrized by a structure in Standard ML.

$$
\begin{array}{l}
\textbf{module prodcons}(Q\colon \text{QUEUE}) \\
\quad \textbf{provide } \textbf{in} \qquad \textit{produce} : \text{nat} \to o \\
\qquad\qquad \textbf{in } \textit{consume\_req} : o \qquad\qquad \textbf{out } \textit{consume} : \text{nat} \to o \\
\quad \cdot \multimap B \textbf{ as } Q.\ \left[\begin{array}{l}
!\forall e\colon \text{nat}.\ \ \textit{produce}(e) \quad \multimap B.\textit{enq}(e) \\[2mm]
\ !\ \textit{consume\_req} \ \multimap \left[\begin{array}{l} B.\textit{deq\_req}, \\ \forall e\colon \text{nat}.\ B.\textit{deq}(e) \multimap \textit{consume}(e) \end{array}\right]
\end{array}\right] \\
\quad \textbf{end}
\end{array}
$$

The argument Q of prodcons is the name of a module with interface QUEUE. The following code uses queue defined earlier, and triggers two producers and one consumer by passing them the appropriate interface predicates exported by the module.

$$
\cdot \multimap B \textbf{ as } \text{prodcons}(\text{queue}).\ \left[\begin{array}{l} p_1(B.\textit{produce}), p_2(B.\textit{produce}), \\ c_1(B.\textit{consume\_req}, B.\textit{consume}) \end{array}\right]
$$

Modules in our language can do a lot more than taking other modules as arguments. For example, a networking module may itself make use of the functionalities of our producer-consumer module. We may therefore make the networking module parametric with respect to the specific implementation of the producer-consumer module. In ML parlance, this would be a functor that takes another functor as a parameter — a higher-order functor (something that is available in some extensions of Standard ML, but not in the official definition [19]). By the same token, nothing prevents us from defining a module that uses an instance of itself in some of its rules — a recursive module.

4   Multiset Rewriting with Modules

The module infrastructure we developed in the previous section had two parts:

1. We introduced convenience syntax for the programming patterns of $\mathcal{L}^{1.5}$ that realized module definitions (**module** ... **end**), module instantiations (N **as** $p\,t.\ \ldots$), and the use of exported names (e.g., $N.add$).
2. We imposed a series of restrictions on where and how predicates can be used (through the **in** and **out** markers), as well as a correspondence between the names exported by a module and the compound names used in client code.

We call the extension of $\mathcal{L}^{1.5}$ with both aspects $\mathcal{L}^{M}$. In this section, we describe how the added syntax (1) can be compiled away, thereby showing that $\mathcal{L}^{M}$ is just syntactic sugar for $\mathcal{L}^{1.5}$ — $\mathcal{L}^{1.5}$ has already all the ingredients to write modular code. We call this process *elaboration*. We handle the restrictions (2) by typechecking $\mathcal{L}^{M}$ code directly, as a user could violate them even if her code elaborates to a valid $\mathcal{L}^{1.5}$ program. In [5] we describe an extension of the typing infrastructure of $\mathcal{L}^{1.5}$ that checks that these restrictions as satisfied at the level of $\mathcal{L}^{M}$. Our module language is actually more flexible than what we saw in the examples of Sect. 3.

Once an $\mathcal{L}^M$ program has been typechecked, it is elaborated into an $\mathcal{L}^{1.5}$ program by compiling the module-specific constructs into native syntax. We then execute this $\mathcal{L}^{1.5}$ program.

The general syntax of a module definition has the form

module $p\,(\Sigma_{par})$	Module name and parameters
provide Σ_{export}	Exported names
local Σ_{local}	Local predicates and constructors
P	Module definition
end	

The module interface is Σ_{export}. The modes of the exported predicate names (**in** and **out** in Sect. 3) are irrelevant after type checking — we ignore them. Let Σ^* denote the tuple of the names declared in signature Σ. Then this construct is elaborated into the $\mathcal{L}^{1.5}$ rule

$$\forall\Sigma_{par}.\,\forall\Sigma_{export}.\,p\,(\Sigma^*_{par}, \Sigma^*_{export}) \multimap \exists\Sigma_{local}.\,P$$

where the notation $\forall\Sigma.\,R$ prefixes the rule R with one universal quantification for each declaration in Σ, and similarly for $\exists\Sigma.\,P$.

Let Σ_{export} be the interface exported by the module p, defined as in the previous paragraph. For convenience, we express Σ_{export} as $\vec{X} : \vec{\tau}$, where the i-th declaration in Σ_{export} is $X_i : \tau_i$. Then, we elaborate the derived syntax for module instantiation,

$$N \text{ as } p\,t.\,P \qquad \text{into} \qquad \exists\Sigma_{export}.\,p(t, \vec{X}), [\vec{X}/N.\vec{X}]P$$

where $[\vec{X}/N.\vec{X}]P$ replaces each occurrence of $N.X_i$ in P with X_i. We implicitly assume that variables are renamed as to avoid capture.

Elaboration transforms a valid $\mathcal{L}^M$ program into a valid $\mathcal{L}^{1.5}$ program, ready to be executed. In particular, it removes all compound names of the form $N.X$.

5   Future Work and Conclusions

In this paper, we developed an advanced module system for $\mathcal{L}^1$, a small rule-based programming language. $\mathcal{L}^1$ corresponds to a large fragment of polarized intuitionistic linear logic under a derivation strategy based on focusing. Modules are rewrite rules of a specific form and can therefore be compiled away. Yet, they share many of the features of the module system of Standard ML, and provide several more. $\mathcal{L}^1$ incorporates key features of languages based on multiset rewriting [10,22], forward-chaining logic programming [2,7,8,12,14], and many process algebras [9,20]. Therefore, the module infrastructure developed in this paper can be applied directly to any of these formalisms.

Our immediate next step will be to implement our module system in the CoMingle system [15]. CoMingle is a rule-based framework aimed at simplifying the development of applications distributed over multiple Android devices.

CoMingle programs are compiled, and one of the most interesting challenges of extending it with modules will be to support separate compilation, one of the key feature of advanced module systems à la Standard ML. We also intend to further study the languages defined in this paper. In particular, we want to investigate uses of second-order quantification to support reflection and runtime rule construction without sacrificing performance. We are also keen on adapting reasoning techniques commonly used in process calculi, for example bi-simulation [20], to our language as $\mathcal{L}^1$ supports many of their features.

Acknowledgments. This paper was made possible by grants NPRP 09-667-1-100 (*Effective Programming for Large Distributed Ensembles*) and NPRP 4-341-1-059 (*Usable automated data inference for end-users*) from the Qatar National Research Fund (a member of the Qatar Foundation). The statements made herein are solely the responsibility of the authors.

References

1. Abdallah, M.N.: Procedures in horn-clause programming. In: Shapiro, E. (ed.) ICLP 1986. LNCS, vol. 225, pp. 433–447. Springer, Heidelberg (1986)
2. Ashley-Rollman, M.P., Lee, P., Goldstein, S.C., Pillai, P., Campbell, J.D.: A language for large ensembles of independently executing nodes. In: Hill, P.M., Warren, D.S. (eds.) ICLP 2009. LNCS, vol. 5649, pp. 265–280. Springer, Heidelberg (2009)
3. Banâtre, J.-P., Le Métayer, D.: Programming by multiset transformation. Commun. ACM **36**(1), 98–111 (1993)
4. Bugliesi, M., Lamma, E., Mello, P.: Modularity in logic programming. J. Logic Program. **19–20**(1), 443–502 (1994)
5. Cervesato, I., Lam, E.S.: Modular multiset rewriting in focused linear logic. In: Technical ReportCMU-CS-15-117, Carnegie Mellon University, Pittsburgh, PA (2015)
6. Cervesato, I., Scedrov, A.: Relating state-based and process-based concurrency through linear logic. Inf. Comput. **207**(10), 1044–1077 (2009)
7. Cruz, F., Ashley-Rollman, M., Goldstein, S., Rocha, R., Pfenning, F.: Bottom-up logic programming for multicores. In: DAMP 2012 (2012)
8. Cruz, F., Rocha, R., Goldstein, S., Pfenning, F.: A linear logic programming language for concurrent programming over graph structures. In: ICLP 2014, Vienna, Austria (2014)
9. Fournet, C.: The join-calculus: a calculus for distributed mobile programming. Ph.D thesis, École Polytechnique, Palaiseau (1998)
10. Frühwirth, T.: Constraint Handling Rules. Cambridge University Press, Cambridge (2009)
11. Gabbay, M.J., Mathijssen, A.: One-and-a-halfth-order Logic. J. Logic Comput. **18**(4), 521–562 (2008)
12. Gallaire, H., Minker, J., Nicolas, J.M.: Logic and databases: a deductive approach. ACM Comput. Surv. **16**(2), 153–185 (1984)
13. Girard, J.-Y.: Linear logic. Theor. Comput. Sci. **50**, 1–102 (1987)
14. Grumbach, S., Wang, F.: Netlog, a rule-based language for distributed programming. In: Carro, M., Peña, R. (eds.) PADL 2010. LNCS, vol. 5937, pp. 88–103. Springer, Heidelberg (2010)

15. Lam, E.S.L., Cervesato, I., Fatima, N.: Comingle: distributed logic programming for decentralized mobile ensembles. In: Holvoet, T., Viroli, M. (eds.) Coordination Models and Languages. LNCS, vol. 9037, pp. 51–66. Springer, Heidelberg (2015)
16. Laurent, O., Quatrini, M., Tortora de Falco, L.: Polarized and focalized linear and classical proofs. Ann.Pure Appl. Logic 134(2–3), 217–264 (2005)
17. Meseguer, J., Braga, C.O.: Modular rewriting semantics of programming languages. In: Rattray, C., Maharaj, S., Shankland, C. (eds.) AMAST 2004. LNCS, vol. 3116, pp. 364–378. Springer, Heidelberg (2004)
18. Miller, D.: A proposal for modules in λprolog. In: Dyckhoff, R. (ed.) ELP 1993. LNCS, vol. 798, pp. 206–221. Springer, Heidelberg (1994)
19. Milner, R., Harper, R., MacQueen, D., Tofte, M.: The Definition of Standard ML - Revised. MIT Press, Cambridge (1997)
20. Sangiorgi, D., Walker, D.: The Pi-Calculus - a Theory of Mobile Processes. Cambridge University Press, Cambridge (2001)
21. Simmons, R.J.: Structural focalization. ACM Trans. Comput. Logic 15(3), 1–33 (2014)
22. Watkins, K., Pfenning, F., Walker, D., Cervesato, I.: Specifying properties of concurrent computations in CLF. In: LFM 2004, pp. 67–87. ENTCS 199, Cork, Ireland (2007)

Modelling Moral Reasoning and Ethical Responsibility with Logic Programming

Fiona Berreby[✉], Gauvain Bourgne, and Jean-Gabriel Ganascia

LIP6, University Pierre and Marie Curie, 4 Place Jussieu, 75005 Paris, France
{fiona.berreby,gauvain.bourgne,jean-gabriel.ganascia}@lip6.fr

Abstract. In this paper, we investigate the use of high-level action languages for representing and reasoning about ethical responsibility in goal specification domains. First, we present a simplified Event Calculus formulated as a logic program under the stable model semantics in order to represent situations within Answer Set Programming. Second, we introduce a model of causality that allows us to use an answer set solver to perform reasoning over the agent's ethical responsibility. We then extend and test this framework against the Trolley Problem and the Doctrine of Double Effect. The overarching aim of the paper is to propose a general and adaptable formal language that may be employed over a variety of ethical scenarios in which the agent's responsibility must be examined and their choices determined. Our fundamental ambition is to displace the burden of moral reasoning from the programmer to the program itself, moving away from current computational ethics that too easily embed moral reasoning within computational engines, thereby feeding atomic answers that fail to truly represent underlying dynamics.

1 Introduction

The study of morality from a computational point of view has attracted a growing interest from researchers in artificial intelligence; as reviewed in [1]. This endeavour can help us better understand morality, and reason more clearly about ethical concepts that are employed throughout philosophical, legal and even technological domains. Confronting ethical theories and philosophical works with the systematicity and logical constraints of programming languages indeed forces us to think about, and make explicit, the underlying mechanisms that characterize those works. It also sheds light on the possible inconsistencies or ambiguities that they may contain. In addition, as the autonomy of artificial agents grows and as an increasing amount of tasks are delegated to them, it becomes vital to equip them with the capacity to process moral restrictions and goals, be it within their own reasoning scheme or for interaction with human users.

The challenge therefore is to shift the burden of moral reasoning from the user or programmer to the program itself. Current works in computational ethics too often tend to embed moral factors within their computational engine, without generating moral reasoning to speak of. The moral worth and causal implications of actions are atomically afforded, rather than extracted and 'understood'

© Springer-Verlag Berlin Heidelberg 2015
M. Davis et al. (Eds.): LPAR-20 2015, LNCS 9450, pp. 532–548, 2015.
DOI: 10.1007/978-3-662-48899-7_37

from facts and rules. In contrast, our aim is to provide a general and adaptable framework that enables the artificial agent to both understand the situation in which the dilemma arises and the ethical rules that constrain its actions, so as to determine from these only the correct course of action. To achieve this, we combine an entirely ethics-free model of the world with an ethical over-layer that the agent can understand and apply back onto its knowledge of the world. What is particularly important to note here is that at the centre of this process lies the notion of causality, for only when the agent can reason about causes and consequences can he begin to reason about moral choice and responsibility. Therefore, our model of moral reasoning and responsibility pivots around our discussion of causal models, which we implement in Event Calculus.

Formally, we chose the use of nonmonotonic logic as its study has been put forward by A.I. researchers as a way to handle the kind of defeasible generalisations that pervade much of our commonsense reasoning, and that are poorly captured by classical logic systems [11]. The term covers a family of formal frameworks devised to apprehend the kind of inference in which conclusions stay open to modification in the light of new information. On a regular basis it seems we draw conclusions from bodies of data that can be dropped when faced with new data. For example, we will hold that a certain bird can fly, until we learn that it is a penguin. This kind of default based reasoning is significantly present in ethical reasoning: we may determine the moral value of an action, for example theft, differently depending on surrounding information. Such factors as the presence of alternative options, indirect consequences, or extenuating circumstances might overthrow our ethical judgement. Accordingly, nonmonotonic goal specification languages are particularly well suited to modelling ethical reasoning.

The Doctrine of Double Effect (DDE) introduces fundamentally nonmonotonic precepts. It is a set of ethical criteria that was put forward most prominently by Philippa Foot for evaluating the ethical permissibility of an action that has both good and bad consequences [5]. It allows that while actions with negative consequences are morally prohibited a priori, there may be instances in which they are morally permissible. We therefore chose the DDE as the basis for moral recommendation, and applied it onto the dilemma of Trolley. Moreover, the DDE has been the focus of research in cognitive science, and was shown to be consistently corroborated by demographically different groups [21]; we aim to computationally explain but also test these intuitions. We begin by introducing the DDE and related current works in computational ethics, then lay out the basic tenets of ASP and the Event Calculus [Sects. 2 and 3]. Next, we expose our extension of the Event Calculus that enables us to handle issues pertaining to causal paths, and introduce our representation of the planning domain and problem [Sects. 4 and 5]. We then discuss the definitions and models of the notions of responsibility and prevention [Sect. 6], and describe the ethical motor and implementation of the Doctrine of Double Effect [Sect. 7], before concluding [Sect. 8].

2   Motivation

2.1   The Doctrine of Double Effect and the Trolley Problem

The DDE specifies four conditions that must be satisfied in order to render morally permissible an action that has both a good and a bad effect:

1. *Nature-of-the-act.* The action itself must either be morally good or indifferent.
2. *Means-end.* The good effect must not be reached by means of the bad effect.
3. *Right-intention.* Only the good effect must be intended, while the bad effect may only be an unintended side effect.
4. *Proportionality.* The good effect must be at least equivalent to the bad effect.

The DDE draws a distinction between intending harm and merely foreseeing harm, and can justify departures from purely consequentialist thinking in which only the proportionality condition operates. Significantly, it provides a reading of the Trolley Problem, an ethical dilemma formulated in Foot's 1967 paper. Consider the following scenario:

> (*switch*) A train is running towards five workmen repairing train tracks. If the agent does nothing, the train will run over and kill them. However, the agent has the option of actioning a switch that will deviate the train off the tracks and onto side tracks along which one person is walking. This will kill that person.

Intuitively, respondents tend to agree that this action (actioning the switch), is ethically admissible [29]. This fits with the utilitarian notion that killing one person to save five is the better option (the other option being no action at all). Now take another case,

> (*push*) There is no switch button, instead there is a bridge above the tracks on which stands an onlooker. Here, the agent knows that if they push the onlooker onto the tracks, the train will hit and kill the onlooker, stop as a result of the crash, and spare the five workmen.

Respondents have significantly deemed this action ethically impermissible [29], and are motivated by something other than utilitarian reasoning, since they choose the death of five over the death of one. The DDE successfully interprets this dilemma by justifying these seemingly inconsistent intuitions. Indeed, in the second case (*push*), while the nature-of-the-act and proportionality conditions are met, the means-end and right-intention conditions are violated: the death of the onlooker is used as a means to preventing the death of the five workmen, and as such is not just a foreseen side-effect but an intended act. About the nature-of-the-act condition it is important to note that only the intrinsic nature of the act itself is considered: even though *pushing someone off a bridge* is morally wrong, the act of *pushing* alone is not, unlike, for instance, stealing or lying. Looking back at the first case (*switch*), the death of the person walking on the other track plays no upstream causal role in the saving of the five: they are saved whether or not that one person dies, as long as the train leaves its original tracks.

2.2   Existing Works

In order to make clear the contribution of the present paper, it is necessary to first look at existing approaches in computational ethics before discussing our own. Pereira and Saptawijaya, in particular, also modelled the Trolley Problem and the DDE using prospective logic [26].
They represent the situation in which the agent throws the switch as follows:

> *turnSide ← consider(throwingSwitch).*
> *kill(1) ← human(X), onSide(X), turnSide.*
> *end(saveMen, niKill(N)) ← turnSide, kill(N).*
> *observedEnd ← end(X, Y).*

In parallel, the case in which the agent pushes a person on the tracks is modelled as follows:

> *onTrack(X) ← consider(shove(X)).*
> *stopTrain(X) ← onTrack(X), heavy(X).*
> *kill(1) ← human(X), onTrack(X).*
> *kill(0) ← inanimateObject(X), onTrack(X).*
> *end(saveMen,iKill(N)) ← human(X), stopTrain(X), kill(N).*

In order to ascribe ethical criteria, they employ a priori constraints which rule out impermissible actions according to a particular ethical rule (corresponding to the means-end condition of the DDE) and a posteriori preferences that eliminate those solutions with worse consequences (the proportionality condition). The means end condition, importantly, is obtained via the two rules *'falsum ← intentionalKilling.'* and *'intentionalKilling ← end(saveMen,iKill(Y)).'*
   The difficulty with this kind of formalization is that it directly embeds the moral requirement into the model of the situation by indicating whether the killing is intentional (*'iKill(N)'*), or not (*'niKill(N)'*). The program is 'told' whether the outcome of the action fits with the ethical rules in place, through atomic statements of the form *'end(saveMen,iKill(N)) ← human(X), stopTrain (X), kill(N)'*. This is problematic for a number of reasons. First, it fails to represent the actual reasoning that underpins moral decision making, in particular concerning what constitutes intentionality. Second, because it atomically specifies the ethical character of the situation's outcome, it requires the creation of a different program for each new case. Therefore, even situations that share common features must be modelled independently, as is the case with trolley variations. This is redundant and can also lead to inconsistencies. Because rules lack expressive power, two identical expressions might refer to diverging stories, for example there is nothing in *'human(X), stopTrain(X), kill(N)'* that indicates whether the killing is intentional or not, and as such could be employed in either case (here it is used for the push case). Moreover, there is no account of causality, such that the action and its consequences are not dynamically linked; the relationship between them is stated rather than inferred. Therefore, no account of ethical responsibility can be discussed on its basis. Finally, the model cannot logically confront ethical theories so as to make explicit their assumptions

and give insight into them, nor can it enable us to explore and generate new ethical dilemmas for further testing. Even though it successfully points to the expressive power of nonmonotonic logic for ethical reasoning, it seems that this account fails to "provide a general framework to model morality computationally" [26]. These remarks also apply to other current works in computational ethics, including models concerned with the Belief Desire Intention framework [15,27]. Instead, establishing an unchanging and ethics-free account of the world atop which can fit changeable ethical restrictions allows for generalisation, flexibility and automation. Separating the ethical constraints from the facts of the world is imperative if we are to model general ethical rules instead of performing case by case discrimination that resembles ethical judgement more than it does ethical theory.

3   Preliminaries

3.1   ASP

Answer Set Programming is a form of declarative logic programming suited for representing different Artificial Intelligence problems, particularly those that relate to knowledge representation and automated reasoning with incomplete information. Problems are encoded as *extended disjunctive programs*, finite logic theories from which are extracted stable models (answer sets) that declaratively identify the solutions to these problems [6].

We give here a very succinct overview of the answer set semantics for a program defined over a set of literals Lit (see [7] for more details). An *extended disjunctive program* (EDP) is a set of *rules* of the form: $L_1; \cdots;$ $L_l \leftarrow L_{l+1}, \ldots, L_m, not\, L_{m+1}, \ldots, not\, L_n$ $(n \geq m \geq l \geq 0)$ where each $L_i \in Lit$ is a positive/negative literal, namely, A or $\neg A$ for an atom A. not is *negation as failure* (NAF), and $not\, L$ is called an *NAF-literal*. The symbol ";" represents disjunction. For each rule r of the above form, $head(r)$, $body^+(r)$, $body^-(r)$, and $not\_body^-(r)$ denote the sets of (NAF-)literals $\{L_1, \ldots, L_l\}$, $\{L_{l+1}, \ldots, L_m\}$, $\{L_{m+1}, \ldots, L_n\}$, and $\{not\, L_{m+1}, \ldots, not\, L_n\}$, respectively. A rule r is an *integrity constraint* if $head(r) = \emptyset$; and r is a *fact* if $body(r) = \emptyset$. A program P with variables is semantically identified with its ground instantiation. The semantics of EDPs is given by the *answer set semantics* [7]. A set $S \subseteq Lit$ satisfies a rule r if $body^+(r) \subseteq S$ and $body^-(r) \cap S = \emptyset$ imply $head(r) \cap S \neq \emptyset$. S satisfies a ground program P if S satisfies every rule in P. Let P be a program such that $\forall r \in P, body^-(r) = \emptyset$. Then, a set $S \subset Lit$ is a (consistent) *answer set* of P if S is a minimal set such that (i) S satisfies every rule from the ground instantiation of P, and (ii) S does not contain a pair of complementary literals L and $\neg L$. Next, let P be any EDP and $S \subseteq Lit$. For every rule r in the ground instantiation of P, the rule r^S : $head(r) \leftarrow body^+(r)$ is included in the *reduct* P^S if $body^-(r) \cap S = \emptyset$. Then, S is an *answer set* of P if S is an answer set of P^S.

3.2   The Event Calculus

The "Event Calculus" was first introduced in a 1986 paper by Bob Kowalski and Marek Sergot [16] as a logic programming framework used to represent and reason about the effects of events or actions [23]. First employed in database applications, it has since then been integrated into other forms of logic programming, classical logic and modal logic, and used in wider contexts such as planning, abductive reasoning or cognitive robotics [17,18,22].

The Event Calculus typically states that fluents (which are time-varying properties of the world) are true or false depending on whether they have been initiated or terminated by action occurrences. For the purpose of simplicity and to make the study of causality clearer, discrete time is employed, and is represented by integers. To fit the requirements of modeling ethical dilemmas pertaining to complex and realistic scenarios, one of our contributions has been to introduce automatic events in addition to actions. These automatic events occur when all their preconditions, in the form of fluents, hold, without direct input from the agent. Actions additionally require that the agent carries them out. As such, there are two types of events: actions and automatic events. We have made a further distinction between what we have called inertial fluents and non inertial fluents [22]. Once initiated by an event occurrence (or if initially true), inertial fluents remain true until they are terminated by another event occurrence. Non inertial fluents are only true at the point in time at which they have been initiated by an event occurrence, or at time T0 if they were true initially. An action is performed by the agent when the course of events begins, at time T0. A maximum of one automatic event can occur at each time point.

4   Adapted Event Calculus

Domain dependent axioms describe which events initiate and terminate which fluents, and which fluents are preconditions to which events. The dynamic domain given here is composed as follows: $\mathcal{T}$ is a set of time points (as integers, variables T1, T2, T3...), $\mathcal{P}$]is a set of positive fluents (variables P1, P2, P3...), $\mathcal{F}$]is a set of fluents, composed of the items in the set P and of their negation (variables F1, F2, F3...), $\mathcal{E}$]is a set of events (variables E1, E2, E3...). Our calculus is based on eight primary predicates. *Holds(F, T)* indicates that F is true at T; *Initially(F)* means that F is true at T0; *NonInertial(F)* points out the special kinds of fluents that are non inertial. *Occurs(E, T)* indicates that E occurs at T; *Automatic(E)* points out the special kinds of events that occur without direct agent input - all events that are not automatic are actions by default and require the agent's volition in addition to fluent preconditions. *Priority(E1, E2)* allows for prioritisation among automatic events but also among goals, i.e. between actions undertaken by the agent in cases where it is required to act more than once. *Effect(E, F)* expresses that F is an effect of E and *Precondition(F, E)* expresses that F is a precondition for E.

Fluents. In order to capture the behaviour of fluents relative to the occurrence of events, we define auxiliary predicates in terms of primary predicates. *Initiates*

(E, P, T) indicates that E occurs and initiates P at T; *Terminates(E, P, T)* indicates that E occurs and terminates P at T; *Clipped(P, T)* indicates that a fluent which has been terminated by an occurrence of an event at T is clipped at T.

> *Initiates(E, P, T) ← Effect(E, P), Occurs(E, T).*
> *Terminates(E, P, T) ← Effect(E, neg(P)), Occurs(E, T).*
> *Clipped(P, T) ← Terminates(E, P, T).*

We can now axiomatize the principles that govern fluents. A fluent which has been initiated by an occurrence of an event at T, or was initially true, continues to hold until the occurrence of another event which terminates it. However, if it is non inertial, it holds at T only (or T0 if it was true initially). If it is not stated that a fluent holds, then its negation is true.

> *Holds(P, T+1) ← Initiates(E, P, T).*
> *Holds(P, T0) ← Initially(P).*
> *Holds(P, T+1) ← Holds(P, T), not Clipped(P, T), not NonInertial(P).*
> *Holds(neg(S), T) ← not Holds(S, T).*

Events. In order to capture the behaviour of events relative to the truth values of fluents (their preconditions), we first define a number of auxiliary predicates that constrain this mechanism. *MissingPrecondition(F, E, T)* means that there exists a precondition fluent F for E that does not hold at T; *Incomplete(E, T)* expresses that E is incomplete at T if it is missing one or more preconditions; *Possible(E, T)* expresses that E is possible at T if it is not missing any preconditions. *Overtaken(E, T)* expresses the fact that an event E has been overtaken by another event at T. This axiom must ensure that only one automatic event occurs at each time point, while an infinite number of events might be possible at any given time.

> *MissingPrecondition(F, E, T) ← Precondition(F, E), not Holds(F, T).*
> *Incomplete(E, T) ← MissingPrecondition(F, E, T).*
> *Possible(E, T) ← not Incomplete(E, T).*
> *Overtaken(E1, T) ← Possible(E1, T), Possible(E2, T), Priority(E2, E1), E1!=E2.*

We can now axiomatize the principles that govern the occurrence of events. *Occurs(E, T)* denotes that E occurs at T if all its preconditions are true at T and no other event that has priority over it is also possible at T. We also specify that an event can only occur if it is possible.

> *Occurs(E, T) ← Possible(E, T), not Overtaken(E, T), Automatic(E).*
> *← Occurs(E, T), not Possible(E, T).*

5   Representing the Planning Domain and Problem

Defining the Domain and Problem. In order to represent the situation onto which ethical constraints are to be applied, we must hierarchize and specify a number of facts about the world we are aiming to represent. Within the present model, the simulation of a situation is characterised by **(a)** An initial situation that is composed by the truth values of all fluents at time T0; **(b)** A specification of the actions available to the agent, and of their causal powers over fluents; **(c)** A specification of automatic events, and of their causal powers over fluent; **(d)** A specification of the precondition fluents for events.

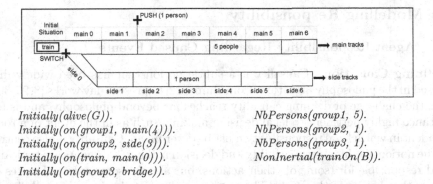

Initially(alive(G)).   NbPersons(group1, 5).
Initially(on(group1, main(4))).   NbPersons(group2, 1).
Initially(on(group2, side(3))).   NbPersons(group3, 1).
Initially(on(train, main(0))).   NonInertial(trainOn(B)).
Initially(on(group3, bridge)).

Fig. 1. The Trolley Problem

Representing the Trolley Problem. *Initial Situation.* Because our model aims at handling a general account of the world, it allows for the fact that both *switch* and *push* are actions that the agent can carry out in a single situational environment, rather than in two separate ones. As such, the initial situation states that all persons are alive, that there are 5 people on the 4th section of the main tracks and one person on the 3rd section of the side tracks (the sections of the tracks on which the people are stationed were chosen arbitrarily), and that the train is stationed on section 0 of the main tracks (see Fig. 1). There is a consequentialist specification in the DDE's proportionality condition, namely that the good effect must be at least equivalent to the bad effect. Therefore, people who are involved in the dilemma are organised in numbered groups. Moreover, *on(train, B)* is *NonInertial* since the train only stays on a section of the tracks for one time point.

Event Preconditions and Effects. We determine the actions *push* and *switch*, and the automatic events *run* and *crash*. *Crash* has priority over *Run*; therefore the train stops as its preconditions for running are no longer fulfilled. In the following statements, $\mathcal{N}$ refers to numbers, $\mathcal{G}$ denotes groups of people, $\mathcal{M}$ denotes sections of the main tracks, $\mathcal{L}$ denotes sections of the side tracks, $\mathcal{B}$ denotes both tracks $(\mathcal{B} = \mathcal{K} \cup \mathcal{L})$.

Precondition(on(train, B), run(train, B)).   Precondition(on(G, bridge), push(G, B))
Precondition(on(G, B), crash(G, B)).   Precondition(on(train, main(0), switch))
 Precondition(on(train, B), crash(G, B))
Effect(push(G, B), on(G, B)).   Effect(crash(G, B), neg(on(train, B)))
Effect(switch, neg(on(train, main(0)))).   Effect(crash(G, B), neg(alive(G)))
Effect(switch, on(train, side(0))).   Priority(crash(G, B), run(B))
Effect(run(train, main(N)), on(train, main(N+1)))
Effect(run(train, side(N)), on(train, side(N+1))).

6   Modelling Responsibility

6.1   Agent Responsibility Regarding Caused Events

Defining Causation. Causality is a subtle notion that has been widely discussed in the philosophy literature, from Hume [12] to present day works [8,25,30]. But the challenge of defining causality reaches far beyond philosophy, and is for instance highly pertinent to legal decision making, such as in the event of a road accident in which legal responsibility must be determined. Causality is also central to the notion of ethical responsibility and decision making [3]. Agents are typically held responsible for (some of) their actions, but also for some external states of affairs that belong in the world. The question, when attributing responsibility, is therefore to determine what these states of affairs are and why. As far as the causal powers of an agent's actions seem to constitute the only links between them and the world, it is natural to suggest that agents are responsible for those states of affairs *which they have caused* [4]. But there are also cases in which an agent can be held responsible for something *they didn't cause*, say by failing to rescue a drowning child. Here, the fact that they may be in a position to interact with the world and prevent a certain outcome still involves the notion of *causality*. As such, this notion must be investigated and defined.

Going back to Hume, we may be tempted to suggest a definition of causality in terms of counter-factual dependence: α *is a cause of* β, *if, had* α *not happened, then* β *would not have happened.* However, this naive definition fails to capture a number of subtleties present in causality, as it cannot deal with cases of preemption and over determination (when one cause may be replaced by another or when there are more causes than are necessary to produce the effect). Consider the following: *Suzy throws a rock at a bottle (s-throws), and shatters it (shatters). Billy was standing by with a second rock. Had Suzy not thrown her rock, Billy would have shattered the bottle by throwing his rock (b-throws)* [14]. Here, it is not the case that if (s-throws) had not happened, then (shatters) would not have happened, since (b-throws) would have made (shatters) happen. This definition therefore fails to capture the fact that something might have a cause while not being counter-factually dependent on it. This is particularly problematic when we want to address questions of responsibility: surely Suzy is responsible for shattering the bottle regardless of Billy's volitions.

Another branch of research has focused on structural causal models [9,24,25]. These have been particularly effective in assessing causal relationships between variables. However, while they handle well issues of counter-factual dependency, they fail to capture some of the intricacies emanating from the fact that causal relations hold in dynamically changing situations [10]. In particular, they cannot distinguish between conditions and transitions, or between actions and omissions [9], yet these distinctions are central to the study of responsibility (for instance, causal weight is not equally divided between acting and omitting to act). Reversely, as argued by Hopkins and Pearl in [10], the formal semantics of Situation Calculus succeed in handling these issues. This is also true of Event Calculus, and further motivates our choice of this particular formalism. The fluent/event distinction in

Event Calculus allows us to model the condition/transition divide, and the facts that *events occur* and *fluents hold or fail to hold* provide the adequate tools for addressing the action/omission distinction. These formal objects that correspond in natural ways to the situations at hand. For more, see [10]. In the next section, we present our corresponding account of causation.

Modelling Causation. We consider a fluent P to be a consequence of an event E1 if E1 initiates P (or terminates neg(P)), regardless of whether another event E2 would have initiated P in the absence of E1. Likewise, an event E1 is a consequence of a fluent P if P is a precondition to E1, and both are true. This accommodates for the possibility that there may be more than one precondition for the occurrence of E1, and that P be not considered a cause of E1 if E1 does not occur (say because the other preconditions were not fulfilled). Our model considers the causal links that hold between events and fluents (i.e. the consequences that these would have on the world were they to obtain), separately from whether they actually obtain. This, and our choice to define causality in terms of consequences, affords us with a useable trace of causal paths and allows us to dynamically assess causal relationships.

We first define a domain $\mathcal{D}$ such that $\mathcal{D} \equiv \mathcal{F} \cup \mathcal{E}$. *Consequence(D1, D2)* indicates that D2 is a consequence of D1. The reflexivity of consequences is necessary to simplify the definitions of predicates that contain the *Consequence* predicate. For the sake of simplifying rules that pertain to causal chains, all fluents and events that hold or occur are also considered consequences of themselves. As such:

> *Consequence(E, F)* ← *Effect(E, F), Occurs(E, T), Holds(F, T+1).*
> *Consequence(F, E)* ← *Precondition(F, E), Holds(F, T), Occurs(E, T).*
> *Consequence(D1, D3)* ← *Consequence(D1, D2), Consequence(D2, D3).*
> *Consequence(D, D)* ← *Holds(D, T).*
> *Consequence(D, D)* ← *Occurs(D, T).*

Now that we have established a model of causality, we can see that formulating the bottle example in terms of an Event Calculus model, rather than via counter-factual dependence, is unproblematic: If Suzy throws and hits the bottle, then she is considered responsible for its shattering. If she doesn't throw, and it is specified that 'b-throw ← not s-throw', then Billy will throw and be considered responsible.

6.2   Agent Responsibility Regarding Prevented Events

Defining Prevention. Ethical responsibility is most often associated with the occurrence of events, for example pertaining to the number of deaths caused by an air strike or the amount of aid given to a relief centre. Yet agent responsibility is equally a question of avoided or prevented harms; think of lives saved by a particular military strategy or medical investment, or of people rescued from falling beneath the poverty threshold. Works in the computational ethics

literature often fail to even address this fact, or consider prevention uniformly
with causation [15,26]. However, these two concepts rely on severely different
mechanisms, and make different computational demands. In particular, unlike
causality which is concerned with the actual state of affairs of the world, prevention requires that we be able to represent possible, but untrue worlds: we must
account for what *could* have happened - but didn't. We must be able to say *why*
it didn't happen, and whether the agent is truly responsible for this. Thus, to
model the fact that an agent prevents an event from occurring by performing
an action A, we must be in a position to compare the actual chain of events
with the hypothetical chain of events in which the agent does not perform A.
Within ASP, one way to achieve this is to simulate both cases and compare
the results, however, this solution requires post processing the individual answer
sets. The action theory architecture that specifies preconditions for events and
fluents allows us to avoid this procedure, and provides us with the traceable
account of causal paths needed to model ethical responsibility.

An event E1 prevents an event E2 if all three of the following are true:
(a) E1 terminates a fluent F that is a precondition to an event E3 of which
E2 is a consequence (note that it is possible that E2 ≡ E3); **(b)** all other preconditions of E2 hold; **(c)** E2 does not occur. (a) ensures that the E1 may
break the causal chain between E1 and E2 at any point. For example E1 may
impede a precondition to E2, or impede the precondition to a precondition to E2.
(b) ensures that E2 would have happened had E1 not happened: it guarantees
the counter-factual dependency of E2 on ¬E1. (c) ensures that if E2 occurs as
a result of being caused by another event through another causal path, then E1
cannot be said to succeed in preventing E2.

Modelling Prevention. We model the *Prevents* predicate, which accounts for
the causal relations that exist but that have not been executed. We define the
predicate *HypConsequence (D1, D2)*, which denotes that a fluent and an event
are causally linked, but says nothing about the actual state of the world, i.e.,
about whether this causal link has been instantiated. Hypothetical consequences,
like consequences, are transitive (and reflexive).

HypConsequence(E, F) ← Effect(E, F).
HypConsequence(F, E) ← Precondition(F, E).
HypConsequence(D1,D3) ← HypConsequence(D1,D2), HypConsequence(D2,D3).
HypConsequence(D,D).

Next, we define a number of prior predicates: *TransTerminates(E1, F2)*
denotes that an event E transterminates a fluent F2 if it terminates a fluent
F1 that is causally linked, and causally anterior to F2. This definition allows for
indirect cases where E affects a non contiguous fluent further down the causal
chain. *NotPrevents(E1, E2)* identifies the cases in which an event E1 causes
the termination of a precondition fluent to an event E2, but where at least one
other precondition for E2 is missing (i.e., one that has not been transterminated
by E1). Finally, in order to preclude the possibility that the event occurs via

another causal path, it is necessary to define the *Happens(E)* predicate that characterises any event that has occurred at some point in time.

> *TransTerminates(E, F2) ← Terminates(E, F1, T), HypConsequence(F1, F2).*
> *NotPrevents(E1, E2) ← TransTerminates(E1, F1), Precondition(F1, E2), MissingPrecondition(F2, E2, T1), not TransTerminates(E1, F2), F1!=F2.*
> *Happens(E) ← Occurs(E, T).*

We can now define the pivot predicate *Prevents(E1, E2)*, which states that an event E1 prevents and event E2 if E1 transterminates a precondition for E2, all other preconditions for E2 hold and E2 does not happen.

> *Prevents(E1, E2) ← Occurs(E1, T), TransTerminates(E1, F), Precondition(F, E2), not NotPrevents(E1, E2), not Happens(E2).*

7   Ethical Implementation

7.1   Determining the Desirability of Events

In order to implement the DDE, which places additional ethical valuation on actions with already determined desirable and undesirable effects, we must first have an account of which events are desirable and which are not. One way of doing this is by simply stating that, for instance, a train crash is undesirable and that people staying alive is desirable. Within our semantics, however, it is fitting to evaluate the desirability of events in terms of the effect they have on ethically relevant fluents. Indeed, an event can only be measured relative to the effect it has on the world. For instance, a collision is significant only in so far as it changes the state or condition of the parties involved in it. We therefore are interested in the moment at which events, atomically and independently of surrounding factors, become desirable or undesirable.

Rights-based ethical theories are particularly well suited to this task, as they make moral claims over the permissibility of actions depending on whether these respect certain rights, which can be likened to states of affairs, such as, for example, the right *to property* or the right *to safety* [20,28]. We base ourselves on Beauchamp and Childress's account of a right which they define as a *"justified claim that individuals and groups can make upon other individuals or upon society; to have a right is to be in a position to determine by one's choices, what others should do or need not do"* [2]. This definition captures well the fact that a right denotes both a state of affairs for the person concerned (the exercise of the right) and a constraint on others (which they can respect or violate through their actions). We therefore chose to define an undesirable event as one that clips (violates) a right, which is here a special kind of fluent. We specify the corresponding situational domain $\mathcal{R}$ as a set of rights, and the definitional axioms:

> *Undesirable(E) ← Effect(E, neg(R)).*
> *Desirable(E) ← Effect(E, R).*
> *Indifferent(E) ← not Desirable(E), not Undesirable(E).*

7.2 The Doctrine of Double Effect

The Nature-of-the-act Condition. The first axiom of the DDE is modelled as such: *Impermissible(A) ← not Desirable(A), not Indifferent(A).*

The Means-end and the Right-intention Conditions. These two axioms are collapsed into one rule within our model, for we consider that using an event as a means to an end (i.e. for the occurrence or prevention of another event), is equivalent to intending that event. Correspondingly, unintended side effects cannot be means to ends. It follows that the two axioms are analogous computationally, unless intentions are explicitly modelled. A good effect may be reached in one of two ways, either by causing a desirable event or by preventing an undesirable one. The reverse is true for bad effects, therefore, four rules must be specified.

> *Impermissible(A, T) ← Occurs(A, T), Consequence(A, E1), Consequence(E1, E2), Undesirable(E1), Desirable(E2).*
> *Impermissible(A, T) ← Occurs(A, T), Consequence(A, E1), Prevents(E1, E2), Undesirable(E1), Undesirable(E2).*
> *Impermissible(A, T) ← Occurs(A, T), Prevents(A, E1), Prevents(E1, E2), Desirable(E1), Undesirable(E2).*
> *Impermissible(A, T) ← Occurs(A, T), Prevents(A, E1), Consequence(E1, E2), Desirable(E1), Desirable(E2).*

The Proportionality Condition. The fourth axiom of the DDE introduces a consequentialist requirement, as it demands the weighing against each other of the action's good and bad effects. There are numerous ways in which effects can be measured, both quantitatively and qualitatively. We chose to gauge events in terms of the number of people involved in them and define the predicate *Weight* $\subseteq \mathcal{E} \times \mathcal{N}$, determined for each event by rules of the type "*Weight(crash(G, B), N) ← NbPersons(G, N)*". As such, performing an action A at T is not permissible if it causes two automatic events E1 and E2, which respectively involve N1 and N2 numbers of people, and where E1 is undesirable and E2 is desirable, if N1 is greater than N2.

> *Impermissible(A, T) ← Occurs(A, T), Consequence(A, E1), Consequence(A, E2), Undesirable(E1), Desirable(E2), Weight(E1, N1), Weight(E2, N2), N1>N2.*

Because of the combination of causation and prevention, as with the means-end condition, three other axioms are also necessary to represent every possible situation that might result from an action with both a good and bad effect, corresponding to the Consequence x Prevents matrix (as with the previous condition). In the model, if we reverse the number of people on the side and main tracks, the switch action becomes impermissible, since more people will die if the agent pushes the switch. The modular nature of the model allows us to play around with the characteristics of the dilemma and explore the DDE.

7.3   Ethical Choice

The agent selects one and only one action (here either *push* or *switch*) to carry out in separate scenarios, resulting in different answer sets, then only chooses to perform the actions that are not impermissible.

$1\{Occurs(push(group3, main(2)), T), Occurs(switch, T)\}1 \leftarrow T=0.$
$\leftarrow Occurs(A, T), Impermissible(A, T).$

We are then left with no, one or a number of stable models that each represent an action that is permissible in regards to the specified situation and the ethical rules that regulate the agent's behaviour. In our model of the Trolley Problem and consistently with experimental findings [21], the unique stable model represents the choice of the *switch* action (see Appendix A). Note that for now, this is a mostly non disjunctive stratified problem that could be programmed with logic programming tools other than ASP. However, the extensions we envisage for the model will make full use of the properties of ASP, in particular regarding ethical plans.

8   Conclusion

Computing ethical theories allows us to reach a greater understanding of the concepts at play, both formally in relation to the predicates and formalisms employed, and in relation to notions used by philosophers and law-makers. Using ASP to model the DDE has shed light on the importance and difficulty of handling causal paths in order to justify claims of ethical responsibility. In particular, it has exposed the necessity to tackle both caused and prevented events. Moreover, in the case of prevention, it has made clear the requirement of adequately handling situational circumstances: an agent can only prevent an event that would have occurred had he not acted. This underlines the fact that responsibility concerns not just the effect of actions, but is to be apprehended from the state of the world itself. While these remarks belong in the realm of common sense for human agents, they are remarkably heavy in repercussion for the modelling of autonomous agents faced with ethical challenges.

The model we have presented here adapts the Event Calculus to facilitate the examination and resolving of ethical dilemmas within a nonmonotonic logic domain. While its present focus is on the Trolley Problem and the DDE, its scope is extensive and adaptable. In order to develop our model, we therefore envision a number of future avenues. First, we believe that we need to further explore ways of expressing intentionality so as to enable artificial agents to evaluate their own moral choices as well as those of others. This will enable the study of other ethical theories that are concerned with agent intention, such as the Doctrine of Triple Effect, put forward by Kamm as a response to dilemmas that the DDE fails to properly handle [13,19]. Staying within the Trolley Problem, we are also currently working on the generation of ethical dilemmas based on the situational domain. The aim of this is to test the DDE on numerous and novel variations of the problem, with the possible adjunction of new empirical data. Creating new dilemmas opens avenues for testing ethical theories and refining them. Finally, we intend to model different ethical criteria such as Kant's categorical imperative or value-based ethics, thereby extending our framework to other ethical traditions and applicative domains. This might also include the formulation of ethical plans of action, working up towards a true planning domain.

A   Appendix

The rules '1{occurs(push(group3, main(2)), T), occurs(switch, T)}1:- T=0.' and ':- occurs(A, T), impermissible(A, T).' generate one stable model that corresponds to the *permissible* switch action.

    initiates(switch, on(train, side(0)), 0).
    initiates(run(train, main(0)), on(train, main(1)), 0).
    initiates(run(train, side(0)), on(train, side(1)), 1).
    initiates(run(train, side(1)), on(train, side(2)), 2).
    initiates(run(train, side(2)), on(train, side(3)), 3).
    occurs(switch, 0).
    occurs(run(train, main(0)), 0).
    occurs(run(train, side(0)), 1).
    occurs(run(train, side(1)), 2).
    occurs(run(train, side(2)), 3).
    occurs(crash(group2, side(3)), 4).
    overtaken(run(train, main(1)), 1).
    overtaken(run(train, side(3)), 4).
    prevents(switch, crash(group1, main(4))).
    terminates(switch, on(train, main(0)), 0).
    terminates(crash(group2, side(3)), alive(group2), 4).
    terminates(crash(group2, side(3)), on(train, side(3)), 4).
    permissible(switch, 0).

Disabling the second rule (':- occurs(A, T), impermissible(A, T).') allows us to look at the stable model for the *impermissible* push action:

    initiates(push(group3, main(2)), on(group3, main(2)), 0).
    initiates(run(train, main(0)), on(train, main(1)), 0).
    initiates(run(train, main(1)), on(train, main(2)), 1).
    occurs(run(train, main(0)), 0).
    occurs(push(group3, main(2)), 0).
    occurs(run(train, main(1)), 1).
    occurs(crash(group3, main(2)), 2).
    overtaken(run(train, main(2)), 2).
    prevents(crash(group3, main(2)), crash(group1, main(4))).
    terminates(crash(group3, main(2)), alive(group3), 2).
    terminates(crash(group3, main(2)), on(train, main(2)), 2).
    impermissible(push(group3, main(2)), 0).

References

1. Anderson, M., Anderson, S.: Machine Ethics. Cambridge University Press, Cambridge (2011)
2. Beauchamp, T., Childress, J.: Principles of Biomedical Ethics. Oxford University Press, New York (2001)
3. Beebee, H., Hitchcock, C., Menzies, P.: The Oxford Handbook of Causation. Oxford University Press, New York (2009)
4. Feinberg, J.: Doing & Deserving Essays in The Theory of Responsibility. Princeton University Press, Princeton (1970)
5. Foot, P.: The problem of abortion and the doctrine of the double effect. In: Applied Ethics: Critical Concepts in Philosophy, vol. 2, p. 187 (2002)
6. Gelfond, M.: Answer sets. Found. Artif. Intell. **3**, 285–316 (2008)
7. Gelfond, M., Lifschitz, V.: Classical negation in logic programs and disjunctive databases. New Gener. Comput. **9**, 365–385 (1991)
8. Halpern, J., Hitchcock, C.: Actual causation and the art of modelling. In: Dechter, R., Geffner, H., Halpern, J. (eds.) Heuristics, Probability, and Causality (2010)
9. Halpern, J., Pearl, J.: Causes and explanations: a structural-model approach. Part I: causes. Br. J. Philos. Sci. **56**(4), 843–887 (2005)
10. Hopkins, M., Pearl, J.: Causality and counterfactuals in the situation calculus. J. Logic Comput. **17**(5), 939–953 (2007)
11. Horty, J.: Defeasible deontic logic. In: Nute, D. (ed.) Nonmonotonic Foundations for Deontic Logic. Springer, The Netherlands (1997)
12. Hume, D.: A Treatise of Human Nature. Courier Corporation, Mineola (2012)
13. Kamm, F.M.: The doctrine of triple effect and why a rational agent need not intend the means to his end: Frances M. Kamm. Aristotelian Soc. Suppl. **74**, 21–39 (2000)
14. Kment, B.: Modality and Explanatory Reasoning. Oxford University Press, Oxford (2014)
15. Kowalski, R.: Computational Logic and Human Thinking: How To Be Artificially Intelligent. Cambridge University Press, Cambridge (2011)
16. Kowalski, R., Sergot, M.: A logic-based calculus of events. In: Schmidt, J.W., Thanos, C. (eds.) Foundations of Knowledge Base Management, pp. 23–55. Springer, Heidelberg (1989)
17. Lee, J., Palla, R.: Reformulating the situation calculus and the event calculus in the general theory of stable models and in answer set programming. J. Artif. Intell. Res. **43**(1), 571–620 (2012)
18. Lévy, F., Quantz, J.: Representing beliefs in a situated event calculus. In: Proceedings of the 13th European Conference on Artificial Intelligence. Citeseer (1997)
19. Liao, S.M.: The loop case and Kamm's doctrine of triple effect. Philos. Stud. **146**(2), 223–231 (2009)
20. Locke, J.: Two Treatises of Government. C. and J. Rivington, London (1824)
21. Mikhail, J.: Universal moral grammar: theory, evidence and the future. Trends Cogn. Sci. **11**(4), 143–152 (2007)
22. Miller, R., Shanahan, M.: Some alternative formulations of the event calculus. In: Kakas, A.C., Sadri, F. (eds.) computational logic: logic programming and beyond. LNCS (LNAI), vol. 2408, p. 452. Springer, Heidelberg (2002)
23. Mueller, E.T.: Commonsense Reasoning: An Event Calculus Based Approach. Elsevier Science, Amsterdam (2014)
24. Pearl, J.: Causal diagrams for empirical research. Biometrika **82**(4), 669–688 (1995)

25. Pearl, J.: Causality: models, reasoning, and inference. Econometric Theo. **19**, 675–685 (2003)
26. Pereira, L.M., Saptawijaya, A.: Modelling morality with prospective logic. In: Neves, J., Santos, M.F., Machado, J.M. (eds.) EPIA 2007. LNCS (LNAI), vol. 4874, pp. 99–111. Springer, Heidelberg (2007)
27. Pereira, L.M., Saptawijaya, A.: Moral decision making with ACORDA. In: Short Paper LPAR, vol. 7 (2007)
28. Ridley, A.: Beginning Bioethics: A Text with Integrated Readings. Bedford, New York (1998)
29. Singer, P.: Ethics and intuitions. J. Ethics **9**(3–4), 331–352 (2005)
30. Sosa, E., Tooley, M.: Causation, vol. 27. Oxford University Press, Oxford (1993)

Constrained Term Rewriting tooL

Cynthia Kop[1]([✉]) and Naoki Nishida[2]

[1] Institute of Computer Science, University of Innsbruck, Innsbruck, Austria
cynthia.kop@uibk.ac.at
[2] Graduate School of Information Science, Nagoya University, Nagoya, Japan
nishida@is.nagoya-u.ac.jp

Abstract. This paper discusses Ctrl, a tool to analyse – both automatically and manually – term rewriting with logical constraints. Ctrl
can be used with TRSs on arbitrary underlying logics, and automatically analyse various properties such as termination, confluence and
quasi-reductivity. Ctrl also offers both a manual and automatic mode
for equivalence tests using inductive theorem proving, giving support for
and verification of "hand-written" term equivalence proofs.

1 Introduction

Given the prevalence of computer programs in modern society, an important
role is reserved for program analysis. Such analysis could take the form of for
instance *termination* ("will every program run end eventually, regardless of user
input?"), *productivity* ("will this program stay responsive during its run?") and
equivalence ("will this optimised code return the same result as the original?").

In recent years, there have been several results which transform a real-world
program analysis problem into a query about term rewriting systems (TRSs).
Such transformations are used to analyse termination of small, constructed languages (e.g. [2]), but also real code, like Java Bytecode [13], Haskell [7] or
LLVM [4]. Similar transformations are used to analyse code equivalence in [3,5].

In these works, *constraints* arise naturally. Where traditional term rewriting systems generally consider well-founded sets like the natural numbers, more
dedicated techniques are necessary when dealing with for instance integers or
floating point numbers. This is why, typically, *extensions* of basic term rewriting
are considered, adding a (usually infinite) number of predefined symbols and
rules – for instance including all integers as constant symbols, and rules such as
$1 + 0 \rightarrow 1$, $1 + 1 \rightarrow 2$, ... – along with some way of specifying constraints. The
Logically Constrained Term Rewriting Systems (LCTRSs) from [10] take this a
step further, by not limiting interest to a fixed theory (such as the integers with
standard functions and relations), but rather allowing an *arbitrary* underlying
theory. This makes it possible to define systems corresponding to (and immediately obtain theoretical results for), e.g., imperative programs with arrays,

This research is supported by the Austrian Science Fund (FWF) international project
I963 and the Graduate Program for RWDC Leaders of Nagoya University.

© Springer-Verlag Berlin Heidelberg 2015
M. Davis et al. (Eds.): LPAR-20 2015, LNCS 9450, pp. 549–557, 2015.
DOI: 10.1007/978-3-662-48899-7_38

or to functional programs with advanced data structures. As observed in [10], LCTRSs conservatively extend many typical forms of constrained rewriting.

To analyse LCTRSs automatically, we have created the tool Ctrl. Like the general LCTRS framework, Ctrl can be equipped with an arbitrary underlying theory, provided an SMT-solver is given to solve its satisfiability and validity problems. The tool has the functionality to test confluence and quasi-reductivity, extensive capability to verify termination, and both automatic and manual support for inductive theorem proving, by which one may prove equivalence of two different functions. Ctrl participated in the *Integer Transition Systems* and *Integer TRS* categories of the 2014 termination competition (no corresponding categories for other theories were present). Ctrl is open-source, and available at:

http://cl-informatik.uibk.ac.at/software/ctrl/

Contribution. Compared to other tools on forms of constrained rewriting (e.g. AProVE [6]), Ctrl is unique in supporting *arbitrary* theories. Of the tool's many features, only automatic equivalence proving has been presented before [11].

Structure. In this paper, we will consider the various aspects of Ctrl. In Sect. 2, we start by recalling the definition of LCTRSs. In Sect. 3, we show how these notions translate to Ctrl, and in Sect. 4 we discuss the problems Ctrl can solve. The next sections treat the two most sophisticated options: termination (Sect. 5) and term equivalence (Sect. 6). Experiments and practical usage, where relevant, are explained in the corresponding sections. Finally, we conclude in Sect. 7.

2   Logically Constrained Term Rewriting Systems

The full definition of LCTRSs is given in [10,11]. We will here explain by example.

In LCTRSs, many-sorted term rewriting is combined with pre-defined *functions* and *values* over arbitrary sets, along with *constraints* to limit reduction. For example, we might define an LCTRS to calculate the Fibonacci numbers:

$$\mathtt{fib}(n) \to 1 \; [n \le 1] \quad \mathtt{fib}(n) \to \mathtt{fib}(n-1) + \mathtt{fib}(n-2) \; [n > 1]$$

Here, the *integers* are added to term rewriting, along with functions for addition, subtraction and comparison. To be precise, we have the following symbols:

values	theory functions	TRS functions
$\mathtt{true, false : Bool}$	$+, - : [\mathtt{Int} \times \mathtt{Int}] \Rightarrow \mathtt{Int}$	$\mathtt{fib} : [\mathtt{Int}] \Rightarrow \mathtt{Int}$
$0, 1, -1, 2, \dots : \mathtt{Int}$	$\le, > : [\mathtt{Int} \times \mathtt{Int}] \Rightarrow \mathtt{Bool}$	

The values and theory functions each have a pre-defined *meaning* in the underlying theory of the booleans and integers. The TRS functions are used to define custom functions, like in a functional programming language (although at the moment, higher-order functions such as map are not permitted), but also for constructors, which make it possible to define inductive types.

Rewriting is constrained as follows: a rule may only be applied if the variables in its constraint are all instantiated by values, and the constraint evaluates to true in the theory. In addition, theory functions occurring inside terms are evaluated step by step. For example, $\mathtt{fib}(2+(0+1))$ cannot be reduced with the second rule, as $2+(0+1)$ is not a value. Instead, $\mathtt{fib}(2+(0+1)) \to \mathtt{fib}(2+1) \to \mathtt{fib}(3)$ by two calculation steps, and $\mathtt{fib}(3) \to \mathtt{fib}(3-1)+\mathtt{fib}(3-2)$.

A key feature of LCTRSs is that we do not fix the underlying sets, theory functions or values, nor their meanings. Predicates, too, are merely functions mapping to booleans, which could be anything according to need. For instance, to model an implementation of the $\mathtt{strlen}$ function in C, we might use

$$\mathtt{slen}(s) \to \mathtt{u}(s,0) \quad \mathtt{u}(s,i) \to \mathtt{err} \qquad [i < 0 \lor \mathtt{size}(s) \leq i]$$
$$\mathtt{u}(s,i) \to \mathtt{ret}(i) \qquad [0 \leq i < \mathtt{size}(s) \land \mathtt{get}(s,i) = \mathtt{c0}]$$
$$\mathtt{u}(s,i) \to \mathtt{u}(s,i+1) \; [0 \leq i < \mathtt{size}(s) \land \mathtt{get}(s,i) \neq \mathtt{c0}]$$

and the following signature, where $\mathtt{Carr}$ is interpreted as the set $\{0,\ldots,255\}^*$ and $\mathtt{Int}$ as the set $\{-2^{15},\ldots,2^{15}-1\}$, with addition subject to overflow:

values	TRS functions
$\mathtt{true},\mathtt{false} : \mathtt{Bool}$	$\mathtt{slen} : [\mathtt{Carr}] \Rightarrow \mathtt{X}$
$-32768,\ldots,32767 : \mathtt{Int}$	$\mathtt{u} : [\mathtt{Carr} \times \mathtt{Int}] \Rightarrow \mathtt{X}$
$\mathtt{c0},\mathtt{c1},\ldots,\mathtt{c255} : \mathtt{Char}$	$\mathtt{err} : \mathtt{X}$
$\{\},\{0\},\{1,0\},\ldots : \mathtt{Carr}$	$\mathtt{ret} : [\mathtt{Int}] \quad \mathtt{X}$

theory functions
$+ : [\mathtt{Int} \times \mathtt{Int}] \Rightarrow \mathtt{Int}$
$\leq,<,=,\neq : [\mathtt{Int} \times \mathtt{Int}] \Rightarrow \mathtt{Bool}$
$\lor,\land : [\mathtt{Bool} \times \mathtt{Bool}] \Rightarrow \mathtt{Bool}$
$\mathtt{not} : [\mathtt{Bool}] \Rightarrow \mathtt{Bool}$
$\mathtt{size} : [\mathtt{Carr}] \Rightarrow \mathtt{Int}$
$\mathtt{get} : [\mathtt{Carr} \times \mathtt{Int}] \Rightarrow \mathtt{Char}$

It is common to assume that at least all the usual boolean operators $(\land, \lor, \mathtt{not})$ are present in Σ_{logic} and have the standard interpretation.

Quantifiers are *not* supported directly, but can typically be replaced by a theory function; e.g., turning $\forall x \in \{0, \mathtt{size}(a)\}[\mathtt{select}(a,x) > 0]$ into $\mathtt{positive}(a)$, with $\mathtt{positive} : [\mathtt{IntArray}] \Rightarrow \mathtt{Bool}$ a new theory function with the meaning "all elements of the argument are greater than 0".

3 Fundamentals

Ctrl is invoked with an input file defining an LCTRS and a query, using the format in Fig. 1. Each of the fields (e.g. SOLVER *solver*) can be omitted.

```
THEORY theory
LOGIC logic
SOLVER solver
SIGNATURE
    signature
RULES
    rules
QUERY query
```

Fig. 1. Input file

Ctrl follows the core idea of LCTRSs by not using a pre-defined theory; instead, theory functions and values are defined in a theory file, which is included using the THEORY field. The underlying logic is handled by an external SMT-solver (as given by the SOLVER field), which uses the input and output format of SMT-LIB (see http://smtlib.cs.uiowa.edu/). The LOGIC field provides the name of an SMT-LIB logic following http://smtlib.cs.uiowa.edu/logics.shtml or any other logic supported by the SMT-solver. For the $\mathtt{fib}$ example of Sect. 2, we would for instance use QF_LIA.

The signature is given by listing TRS function symbols, along with their type declaration and separated by commas or semi-colons, e.g., `err : X ; u : Carr * Int => X`. Type declarations may be omitted (writing, e.g., `err, u`), in which case types are derived automatically; if this fails, Ctrl aborts. Rules have the form `term₁->term₂ [constraint]` where both `term₁` and `term₂` are well-typed terms on variables and declared symbols (values, theory functions or TRS functions), and `constraint` is a term of sort `Bool`, not containing TRS functions. Rules must be separated by semi-colons, and constraints may be omitted. For example: `slen(s) -> u(s,0) ; u(s,i) -> err [i < 0 or size(s) <= i]`.

Finally, *query* determines the action Ctrl should take, as detailed in Sect. 4. The shape of a theory file is given in Fig. 2. Theory files, in order to be used, are expected to be in the `theories/` subdirectory in the program folder. A theory can extend another theory (effectively including all its symbols) using the INCLUDE field, e.g. `INCLUDE ints`; it is recommended to include at least `core`, which contains symbols like `true, false, and, or` and `not`. The DECLARE field corresponds to SIGNATURE in an input file; here, all theory functions and values must be listed, along with their type declaration. The symbols listed after WELLFOUNDED should all be well-founded relations, i.e. symbols $R : [\iota \times \iota] \Rightarrow$ Bool such that no infinite sequence $s_1 R s_2 R \ldots$ exists; this is used for termination analysis. CHAIN is used to define syntactic sugar, allowing, e.g., `x > y > z` to be shorthand for `x > y and y > z`. Finally, SMT-TRANSLATIONS allows users to assign a meaning to custom symbols. That is, if a theory symbol was declared which is not typically supported by SMT-solvers for this theory – such as `positive(a)` from the previous section – we may instead express its meaning as an SMT-term (e.g. `(forall ((x Int)) (or (< x 0) (>= x (size a)) (> (select a x) 0)))`); of course, in this case the LOGIC must support quantifiers).

```
INCLUDE theories
DECLARE
    signature
WELLFOUNDED names
CHAIN chainings
SMT-TRANSLATIONS
    translations
```

Fig. 2. Theory file

Note that Ctrl itself does not know much theory: aside from basic properties on the core theory (i.e. symbols like `and` and `or`) and minor reasoning on integers, all calculations and validity questions which arise during a program run are passed to the given SMT-solver (which must be present in the folder from which Ctrl is invoked), along with the given LOGIC field. This makes it possible to handle arbitrary theories. If no solver is given, the default SMT-solver called smtsolver in the program directory is automatically used; this is currently Z3 [1].

To support realistic systems, Ctrl provides three constructions to declare infinitely many values at once. A declaration `!INTEGER : sort` causes all integer symbols to be read as values with sort *sort*. Similarly, `!ARRAY!α`, with α the name of a sort, includes all sequences of the form $\{a_1:\ldots:a_n\}$ where each a_i is a value sort α. `!MIXED!o!c`, with o and c strings, includes all strings of the form $o\langle string \rangle c$[1]. The string values are passed to the SMT-solver *without* the

---

[1] However, to avoid ambiguity in the input parser, the brackets and individual strings in the input file may not use the protected symbols [, , and ;, or spaces.

"bracketing" o, c. As it is not needed that each integer/array/string represents a value, these constructions allow you to support arbitrary types; for instance:

- `!INTEGER` : `Byte` (but users should make sure the input file only includes integers in $\{0, \dots, 255\}$, and the SMT-solver only returns such numbers);
- `!ARRAY!ARRAY!Int` : `Matrix` (values would be, e.g., `{{1,3}:{2:1}}`);
- `!MIXED!"!"` : `Real` (values would be, e.g., `"3.14"`, and passed to the SMT-solver as `3.14`; Ctrl does not assume all values can be represented).

To demonstrate how the various fields and constructions are used, the Ctrl download at http://cl-informatik.uibk.ac.at/software/ctrl/ contains both example input files (in the `examples/` folder) and theories (in `theories/`).

Comment: Instead of an external SMT-solver, users might set the SOLVER to `manual`, which indicates that they will manually perform calculations and satisfiability or validity checks; or to `internal`, which causes Ctrl to attempt simplifying formulas with booleans, integers and integer arrays itself before passing any remaining problems to smtsolver. This gives a speedup by avoiding external calls in many cases. The internal solver is consistent with the core and ints theories in http://smtlib.cs.uiowa.edu/theories.shtml.

4   Queries

Ctrl is a generic tool for constrained rewriting, designed to solve a variety of problems (as requested by the QUERY field). We consider the possibilities. Note that example uses of all queries are available in the Ctrl download.

Simplifying. The literature offers several translations from restricted imperative programs to constrained rewriting (see e.g. [2,12]), enabling the analysis of imperative languages with rewriting techniques. Initially, this often gives large and somewhat impractical systems. Ctrl's simplification module (invoked using `simplification` $[f_1 \dots f_n]$) simplifies such LCTRSs, chaining together rules and removing unused arguments, but leaving the symbols f_i untouched. For instance, $\{f(x, y) \rightarrow g(x, 0) \ [\varphi], \ g(x, y) \rightarrow h(x + y, x, x * y), \ h(x, 0, y) \rightarrow f(x, x) \ [x < 0]\}$ becomes $\{f(x, y) \rightarrow h(x + 0, x) \ [\varphi], \ h(x, 0) \rightarrow f(x, x) \ [x < 0]\}$.

Reducing. Ctrl can reduce both terms (using the SMT-solver to test whether constraints are satisfied and to do calculations), and *constrained terms*, which intuitively indicates how *groups* of terms are reduced, following [11, Sec. 2.1]. For example, `fib(n)` $[n > 3] \rightarrow$ `fib(n - 1) + fib(n - 2)` $[n > 3]$ proves that *all* terms `fib(`s`)` with s a value > 3 can be reduced as given. Ctrl reduces (constrained) terms using an innermost strategy to normal form, or until the SMT-solver simply fails to verify that any specific rule can be applied[2]. In a non-terminating LCTRS, it is possible that evaluation never ends.

---

[2] This failure is not unlikely, as constrained reduction following [11] requires validity of quantified formulas $\exists x [\varphi(x)]$, which is hard for most solvers. To improve performance, Ctrl uses default choices for x; this method is omitted here for space reasons.

Boolean Properties. Ctrl tests three properties which apply to the full LCTRS:

- Confluence: $\forall s, u, v[(s \rightarrow^* u \wedge s \rightarrow^* v) \Rightarrow \exists w[u \rightarrow^* w \wedge v \rightarrow^* w]]$; put differently, *how* we reduce a term does not affect the results we can obtain.
- Quasi-reductivity: all irreducible ground terms are built entirely of *constructor symbols*: values and TRS functions f where no rule $f(\boldsymbol{\ell}) \rightarrow r\ [\varphi]$ exists.
- Termination: there is no infinite reduction $s_1 \rightarrow s_2 \rightarrow s_3 \rightarrow \dots$.

All three are undecidable yet commonly studied properties in the world of (unconstrained) TRSs. Techniques to verify them often extend naturally to LCTRS.

For confluence, Ctrl tests the sufficient condition of *orthogonality* [10]. This property is straightforward to check – testing satisfiability of formulas which are little more complicated than the rule constraints – yet captures a large and natural collection of LCTRS, as typical functional programs are orthogonal. LCTRSs obtained from imperative programs and simplified are usually orthogonal as well, provided variables are obviously instantiated before they are used.

For quasi-reductivity, Ctrl uses the nameless but powerful algorithm described in [12]. Termination uses a combination of techniques, described in Sect. 5.

Equivalence. Finally, Ctrl has a module on *inductive theorem proving*, which can help a user prove reducibility between two groups of terms, either automatically or in an interactive mode. This is explained in more detail in Sect. 6.

5   Termination

Termination is the property that, regardless of the order and position in which rules are applied, evaluation of every term ends eventually. Many termination methods for unconstrained TRSs rely on the *dependency pair framework* [8], a powerful approach which enables modular use of many sub-techniques.

While this framework extends naturally to constrained rewriting [9], the ordering methods which form a core part unfortunately do not – or rather, they are useful in theory, but automation fails in the presence of infinitely many values. Consider for example a TRS with a rule f(x,y) → f(x - 1, y + 2) [x > 0]. To see that it terminates, we must know that there is no infinite sequence $x_1, x_2, \dots$ where each $x_i > x_{i+1}$ and $x_i > 0$. This we cannot express as a constraint over integer arithmetic: rather, it requires domain-specific knowledge.

Here, the WELLFOUNDED declaration comes in. Ctrl will test whether arguments decrease with respect to any given well-founded relation. To handle the example above, we may introduce a custom symbol >! : [Int × Int] ⇒ Bool, and translate $x >! y$ to $x > y \wedge x \geq 0$. Currently, the stronger *polynomial interpretations* are limited to the integers, but we intend to generalise this in the near future.

Practical Results. There is no database of LCTRS termination problems, but there *are* large collections of integer TRSs (ITRSs) and transition systems (ITSs) in the *termination problem database* (see http://termination-portal.org/wiki/TPDB), both of which can be translated to LCTRSs[3]. Figure 3 shows Ctrl's

---

[3] The translation for integer transition systems uses a variation of Marc Brockschmidt's SMT-Pushdown tool at https://github.com/mmjb/SMTPushdown.

power on these benchmarks, evaluated with a 1-minute timeout. Here, *Time* indicates the average runtime in seconds, disregarding timeouts. Ctrl currently has no non-termination functionality.

Ctrl's apparent weakness on ITSs is partly caused by the greater size of many benchmarks, and partly due to non-termination: many of them only terminate if you fix a given start symbol. Ctrl proves the stronger property of termination for *all* terms. Consequently, it performs somewhat worse than dedicated tools for ITSs like T2 (http://research.microsoft.com/en-us/projects/t2/). In addition, neither integer rewriting nor termination are the main focus of Ctrl: the primary goal is generality. In the future, we hope to add further termination techniques; both general and theory-specific ones.

	ITRSs	ITSs
Yes	85	371
Maybe	29	455
Timeout	3	396
Time	0.85	6.88

Fig. 3. Results on the TPDB

6 Equivalence

Finally, *equivalence* studies the question whether two groups of terms are reducible to each other; this is done in the form of *equations* $s \approx t \; [\varphi]$. For instance $f(x, y) \approx g(x, z) \; [x > y \wedge x > z]$ is an inductive theorem if for all values x, y, z such that $x > y \wedge x > z$ holds in the underlying theory, $f(x, y) \leftrightarrow_{\mathcal{R}}^* g(x, z)$. In a confluent, terminating system, this exactly means that they reduce to the same normal form. If $f(x_1, \dots, x_n) \approx g(x_1, \dots, x_n) \; [\varphi]$ is an inductive theorem, then f and g define the same function (under the conditions dictated by φ), which could be used in practice to replace (parts of) functions by optimised variations.

Unfortunately, this is a hard problem to solve automatically, even for quite simple systems. Ctrl uses *rewriting induction* [11], a method introduced in [14] which relies on termination of $\to_{\mathcal{R}}$ for the induction principle. There are a number of inference rules to simplify equations, but the key to successful rewriting induction is guessing suitable *lemma equations*, for which no single obvious method exists (although many techniques exist to capture certain kinds of systems).

Ctrl offers two ways of testing equivalence: automatic and interactive. In interactive mode, the user manually chooses inference rules to apply, using Ctrl to guard applicability of these steps and allowing "auto" steps to do obvious simplifications. Beside the basic steps, a lemma generation method is included: generalise, which is especially useful for the LCTRSs obtained from imperative programs, by focusing on loop counters. Figure 4 shows an example LCTRS comparing a recursive and iterative calculation of the factorial function. The Ctrl solution is: auto, swap, expand, auto, auto, expand, auto, generalise, expand, auto, auto. To see these commands in action, download the tool and run it on examples/ft.ctrs.

$$\mathtt{ft1}(x) \to 1 \qquad\qquad [x \le 0]$$
$$\mathtt{ft1}(x) \to x * \mathtt{ft1}(x - 1) \quad [x > 0]$$
$$\mathtt{ft2}(x) \to \mathtt{u}(x, 1, 1)$$
$$\mathtt{u}(x, i, z) \to \mathtt{u}(x, i + 1, z * i) \; [i \le x]$$
$$\mathtt{u}(x, i, z) \to z \qquad\qquad\quad [i > x]$$

Goal: $\mathtt{ft1}(x) \approx \mathtt{ft2}(x)$ [true]

Fig. 4. Example LCTRS problem.

The automatic mode requires no user interaction (although lemma equations can be added in the input file), but combines some heuristics with backtracking to obtain a proof. Ctrl can automatically handle quite complicated examples, as evidenced by the results in [11] (http://cl-informatik.uibk.ac.at/software/ctrl/aplas14/): on 7 groups of manually translated student homework programs, Ctrl could automatically prove correctness of two thirds. This includes array / string functions such as strcpy or summing array elements. To our knowledge, there are no other provers which can handle systems like Fig. 4.

7   Conclusions

We have discussed Ctrl, a versatile tool for constrained rewriting. A key focus of Ctrl is *generality*: the functionality is not limited to, e.g., linear integer arithmetic, but supports almost any theory, provided an SMT-solver is available for it. This makes it possible to use Ctrl in many different settings; once support is available, we could for instance use it to analyse confluence of oriented mathematical equations over the real number field, termination of functional programs with mappings as core objects, or equivalence of imperative string functions.

What is more, the techniques themselves are designed with extension in mind, allowing for more sophisticated techniques to be added in the future. Another obvious future work (which is already in progress) is to translate reasonable subsets of certain imperative languages into LCTRSs automatically.

The version of Ctrl used in this work, and evaluation pages for the experimental results on termination and equivalence, are available at:

http://cl-informatik.uibk.ac.at/software/ctrl/lpar15/

References

1. de Moura, L., Bjørner, N.S.: Z3: an efficient SMT solver. In: Ramakrishnan, C.R., Rehof, J. (eds.) TACAS 2008. LNCS, vol. 4963, pp. 337–340. Springer, Heidelberg (2008)
2. Falke, S., Kapur, D.: A term rewriting approach to the automated termination analysis of imperative programs. In: Schmidt, R.A. (ed.) CADE-22. LNCS, vol. 5663, pp. 277–293. Springer, Heidelberg (2009)
3. Falke, S., Kapur, D.: Rewriting Induction + Linear arithmetic = Decision procedure. In: Gramlich, B., Miller, D., Sattler, U. (eds.) IJCAR 2012. LNCS, vol. 7364, pp. 241–255. Springer, Heidelberg (2012)
4. Falke, S., Kapur, D., Sinz, C.: Termination analysis of C programs using compiler intermediate languages. In: Schmidt-Schauß, M. (ed.) Proc. RTA 2011. LIPIcs, vol. 10, pp. 41–50. Dagstuhl (2011)
5. Furuichi, Y., Nishida, N., Sakai, M., Kusakari, K., Sakabe, T.: Approach to procedural-program verification based on implicit induction of constrained term rewriting systems. IPSJ Trans. Program. 1(2), 100–121 (2008). In Japanese

6. Giesl, J., Brockschmidt, M., Emmes, F., Frohn, F., Fuhs, C., Otto, C., Plücker, M., Schneider-Kamp, P., Ströder, T., Swiderski, S., Thiemann, R.: Proving Termination of Programs Automatically with AProVE. In: Kapur, D., Weidenbach, C., Demri, S. (eds.) IJCAR 2014. LNCS, vol. 8562, pp. 184–191. Springer, Heidelberg (2014)

7. Giesl, J., Raffelsieper, M., Schneider-Kamp, P., Swiderski, S., Thiemann, R.: Automated termination proofs for Haskell by term rewriting. ACM Trans. Program. Lang. Syst. (TOPLAS) 33(2), 71–739 (2011)

8. Giesl, J., Thiemann, R., Schneider-Kamp, P., Falke, S.: Mechanizing and improving dependency pairs. J. Autom. Reason. 37(3), 155–203 (2006)

9. Kop, C.: Termination of LCTRSs. In: Waldmann, J. (ed.) Proceedings of WST, pp. 59–63 (2013)

10. Kop, C., Nishida, N.: Term Rewriting with Logical Constraints. In: Fontaine, P., Ringeissen, C., Schmidt, R.A. (eds.) FroCoS 2013. LNCS, vol. 8152, pp. 343–358. Springer, Heidelberg (2013)

11. Kop, C., Nishida, N.: Automatic constrained rewriting induction towards verifying procedural programs. In: Garrigue, J. (ed.) APLAS 2014. LNCS, vol. 8858, pp. 334–353. Springer, Heidelberg (2014)

12. Kop, C., Nishida, N.: Towards verifying procedural programs using constrained rewriting induction. Technical report (2014). http://arxiv.org/abs/1409.0166

13. Otto, C., Brockschmidt, M., von Essen, C., Giesl, J.: Automated termination analysis of Java Bytecode by term rewriting. In: Lynch, C. (ed.) Proc. RTA 2010. LIPIcs, vol. 6, pp. 259–276. Dagstuhl (2010)

14. Reddy, U.S: Term rewriting induction. In: Stickel, M. (ed.) Proc. CADE 1990. LNCS, vol. 449, pp. 162–177. Springer, Heidelberg (1990)

Proof Search in Nested Sequent Calculi

Björn Lellmann[1](✉) and Elaine Pimentel[2]

[1] Institute of Computer Languages, TU Wien, Vienna, Austria
lellmann@logic.at
[2] Departamento de Matemática, UFRN, Natal, Brazil
elaine.pimentel@gmail.com

Abstract. We propose a notion of focusing for nested sequent calculi for modal logics which brings down the complexity of proof search to that of the corresponding sequent calculi. The resulting systems are amenable to specifications in linear logic. Examples include modal logic K, a simply dependent bimodal logic and the standard non-normal modal logics. As byproduct we obtain the first nested sequent calculi for the considered non-normal modal logics.

1 Introduction

A main concern in proof theory for modal logics is the development of philo-sophically and, at the same time, computationally satisfying frameworks to cap-ture large classes of logics in a uniform and systematic way. Unfortunately the standard sequent framework satisfies these desiderata only partly. Undoubtedly, there are sequent calculi for a number of modal logics exhibiting many good properties (such as analyticity), which can be used in complexity-optimal deci-sion procedures. However, their construction often seems ad-hoc, they are usually not modular, and they mostly lack philosophically relevant properties such as separate left and right introduction rules for the modalities. These problems are often connected to the fact that the modal rules in such calculi usually introduce more than one connective at a time. For example, in the rule

$$\frac{\Gamma \vdash A}{\Gamma', \Box\Gamma \vdash \Box A, \Delta} \ \mathsf{k}$$

for modal logic K [4], the context Γ could contain an arbitrary finite number of formulae. Hence this rule can also be seen as an infinite set of rules

$$\left\{ \frac{B_1, \ldots, B_n \vdash A}{\Gamma', \Box B_1, \ldots, \Box B_n \vdash \Box A, \Delta} \ \mathsf{k}_n \mid n \geq 0 \right\}$$

each with a fixed number of principal formulae. Both of these perspectives are somewhat dissatisfying: the first since it requires modifying the context, and the

B. Lellmann—Funded by the EU under Marie Skłodowska-Curie grant agreement No. 660047.

E. Pimentel—Funded by CNPq.

M. Davis et al. (Eds.): LPAR-20 2015, LNCS 9450, pp. 558–574, 2015.
DOI: 10.1007/978-3-662-48899-7_39

second since it explicitly discards the distinction between left and right rules for the modal connective.

One way of solving this problem is to consider extensions of the sequent framework that are expressive enough for capturing these modalities using separate left and right introduction rules. This is possible e.g. in the frameworks of *labelled sequents* [14] or in that of *nested sequents* or *tree-hypersequents* [2,17,18]. Intuitively, in the latter framework a single sequent is replaced with a tree of sequents, where successors of a sequent are interpreted under a modality. The modal rules of these calculi govern the transfer of (modal) formulae between the different sequents, and it can be shown that it is sufficient to transfer only one formula at a time. However, the price to pay for this added expressivity is that the obvious proof search procedure is of suboptimal complexity since it constructs potentially exponentially large nested sequents [2].

In this work, we reconcile the added superior expressiveness and modularity of nested sequents with the computational behaviour of the standard sequent framework by proposing a *focusing discipline* for *linear nested sequents* [9], a restricted form of nested sequents where the tree-structure is restricted to that of a line. The result is a notion of normal derivations in the linear nested setting, which directly correspond to derivations in the standard sequent setting. Moreover, the resulting calculi lend themselves to specification and implementation in linear logic following the approach in [13]. Since we are interested in the connections to the standard sequent framework, we concentrate on logics which have a standard sequent calculus, with examples including normal modal logic K and simple extensions, the exemplary *simply dependent bimodal logic* $\mathsf{KT} \oplus_{\subseteq} \mathsf{S4}$ [5], but also several non-normal modal logics, i.e., standard extensions of *classical modal logic* [4]. As a side effect we obtain, to the best of our knowledge, the first nested sequent calculi for all the considered non-normal modal logics.

2   Linear Nested Sequent Systems

We briefly recall the basic notions of the linear nested sequent framework [9], essentially a reformulation of Masini's 2-sequents [11] in the nested sequent framework (also compare the $\mathsf{G\text{-}CK}_n$ sequents of [12]). In the following, we consider a *sequent* to be a pair $\Gamma \vdash \Delta$ of multisets and adopt the standard conventions and notations (see e.g. [14]). In the linear nested sequent framework, the tree structure of nested sequents is restricted to a line, i.e., a linear nested sequent is simply a finite list of sequents. This data structure matches exactly the *history* in a backwards proof search in an ordinary sequent calculus, a fact we will heavily use in what follows.

Definition 1. *The set* LNS *of linear nested sequents is given recursively by:*

1. *if* $\Gamma \vdash \Delta$ *is a sequent then* $\Gamma \vdash \Delta \in$ LNS
2. *if* $\Gamma \vdash \Delta$ *is a sequent and* $\mathcal{G} \in$ LNS *then* $\Gamma \vdash \Delta /\!/ \mathcal{G} \in$ LNS.

$$\frac{}{S\{\Gamma, p \vdash p, \Delta\}} \text{ init} \qquad \frac{S\{\Gamma, A, B \vdash \Delta\}}{S\{\Gamma, A \wedge B \vdash \Delta\}} \wedge_L \qquad \frac{S\{\Gamma \vdash A, \Delta\} \quad S\{\Gamma \vdash B, \Delta\}}{S\{\Gamma \vdash A \wedge B, \Delta\}} \wedge_R$$

$$\frac{}{S\{\Gamma, \bot \vdash \Delta\}} \bot_L \qquad \frac{S\{\Gamma, B \vdash \Delta\} \quad S\{\Gamma \vdash A, \Delta\}}{S\{\Gamma, A \supset B \vdash \Delta\}} \supset_L \qquad \frac{S\{\Gamma, A \vdash B, \Delta\}}{S\{\Gamma \vdash A \supset B, \Delta\}} \supset_R$$

Fig. 1. System $\mathsf{LNS_G}$ for classical propositional logic. In the init rule, p is atomic.

$$\frac{S\{\Gamma \vdash \Delta /\!/ \Sigma, A \vdash \Pi\}}{S\{\Gamma, \Box A \vdash \Delta /\!/ \Sigma \vdash \Pi\}} \Box_L \qquad \frac{\mathcal{G} /\!/ \Gamma \vdash \Delta /\!/ \vdash A}{\mathcal{G} /\!/ \Gamma \vdash \Delta, \Box A} \Box_R$$

Fig. 2. The modal rules of the linear nested sequent calculus $\mathsf{LNS_K}$ for K.

We will write $S\{\Gamma \vdash \Delta\}$ for denoting a context $\mathcal{G} /\!/ \Gamma \vdash \Delta /\!/ \mathcal{H}$ where $\mathcal{G}, \mathcal{H} \in \mathsf{LNS}$ or $\mathcal{G}, \mathcal{H} = \emptyset$. We call each sequent in a linear nested sequent a component and slightly abuse notation and abbreviate "linear nested sequent" to LNS.

In this work we consider only modal logics based on classical propositional logic, and we take the system $\mathsf{LNS_G}$ (Fig. 1) as our base calculus. Note that the initial sequents are atomic, contraction, weakening and cut are admissible and all rules are invertible.

Figure 2 presents the modal rules for the linear nested sequent calculus $\mathsf{LNS_K}$ for K, essentially a linear version of the standard nested sequent calculus from [2,17]. Conceptually, the main point is that the sequent rule k is split into the two rules $\Box_L$ and $\Box_R$, which permit to simulate the sequent rule treating one formula at a time. This piecewise treatment could be seen as one of the main features of nested sequent calculi and deep inference in general [7]. In particular, it is the key to modularity for nested and linear nested sequent calculi [9,18]. Completeness of $\mathsf{LNS_K}$ w.r.t. modal logic K is shown by simulating a sequent derivation bottom-up in the last two components of the linear nested sequents, marking applications of transitional rules by the nesting $/\!/$ and simulating the k-rule by a block of $\Box_L$ and $\Box_R$ rules [9]. E.g., an application of k on a branch with history captured by the LNS $\mathcal{G}$ is simulated by:

$$\frac{\Gamma \vdash A}{\substack{\Gamma', \Box\Gamma \vdash \Box A, \Delta \\ \vdots \ \mathcal{G}}} \text{ k} \qquad \rightsquigarrow \qquad \frac{\dfrac{\mathcal{G} /\!/ \Gamma' \vdash \Delta /\!/ \Gamma \vdash A}{\mathcal{G} /\!/ \Gamma', \Box\Gamma \vdash \Delta /\!/ \vdash A} \Box_L}{\mathcal{G} /\!/ \Gamma', \Box\Gamma \vdash \Box A, \Delta} \Box_R$$

where the double line indicates multiple rule applications. Observe that this method relies on the view of linear nested sequents as histories in proof search. It also simulates the propositional sequent rules in the *rightmost* component of the linear nested sequents. This gives a different way of looking at system K, where formulas in the context can be handled separately. However, the modal rules do not need to occur in a block corresponding to one application of the sequent rule anymore. For instance, one way of deriving the instance $\Box(p \supset q) \supset (\Box p \supset \Box q)$ of the normality axiom for modal logic K is as follows.

$$\cfrac{\cfrac{}{\Box p \vdash \mathop{/\!/} q \vdash q}\ \text{init} \quad \cfrac{\cfrac{\cfrac{}{\vdash \mathop{/\!/} p \vdash p, q}\ \text{init}}{\Box p \vdash \mathop{/\!/} \ \vdash p, q}\ \Box_L}{\Box p \vdash \mathop{/\!/} p \supset q \vdash q}\ \supset_L}{\cfrac{\cfrac{\Box p \vdash \mathop{/\!/} p \supset q \vdash q}{\Box(p \supset q), \Box p \vdash \Box q}\ \Box_R, \Box_L}{\vdash \Box(p \supset q) \supset (\Box p \supset \Box q)}\ \supset_R}$$

Note that the propositional rule $\supset_L$ is applied between two modal rules. Hence there are many derivations in $\mathsf{LNS_K}$ which are not the result of simulating a derivation of the sequent calculus for K. Thus, while the linear nested sequent calculus $\mathsf{LNS_K}$ has conceptual advantages over the standard sequent calculus for K, its behaviour in terms of proof search is worse: there are many more possible derivations with the same conclusion, when compared to the sequent calculus. We will address this issue by proposing a *focusing discipline* [1] similar to that of [3] to restrict proof search to a smaller class of derivations, while retaining the conceptual advantages of the framework.

3 Labelled Line Sequent Systems

For simplifying the notation of the focused systems and also for encoding linear nested sequent calculi in linear logic (see Sect. 6), we follow the correspondence between nested sequents and labelled tree sequents given in [6], and consider the *labelled sequents* [14] corresponding to linear nested sequents. Intuitively, the components of a LNS are labelled with variables and their order is encoded in a relation.

Formally, a (possibly empty) set of relation terms (*i.e.* terms of the form xRy) is called a *relation set*. For a relation set $\mathcal{R}$, the *frame* $Fr(\mathcal{R})$ *defined by* $\mathcal{R}$ is given by $(|\mathcal{R}|, \mathcal{R})$ where $|\mathcal{R}| = \{x \mid xRv \in \mathcal{R} \text{ or } vRx \in \mathcal{R} \text{ for some state } v\}$. We say that a relation set $\mathcal{R}$ is *treelike* if the frame defined by $\mathcal{R}$ is a tree or $\mathcal{R}$ is empty. A treelike relation set $\mathcal{R}$ is called *linelike* if each node in $\mathcal{R}$ has at most one child.

Definition 2. *A* labelled line sequent LLS *is a labelled sequent* $\mathcal{R}, X \vdash Y$ *where*

1. $\mathcal{R}$ *is linelike;*
2. *if* $\mathcal{R} = \emptyset$ *then* X *has the form* $x : A_1, \ldots, x : A_n$ *and* Y *has the form* $x : B_1, \ldots, x : B_m$ *for some state variable* x;
3. *if* $\mathcal{R} \neq \emptyset$ *then every state variable* x *that occurs in either* X *or* Y *also occurs in* $\mathcal{R}$.

Observe that, in LLS, if $xRy \in \mathcal{R}$ then $uRy \notin \mathcal{R}$ and $xRv \notin \mathcal{R}$ for any $u \neq x$ and $v \neq y$.

Definition 3. *A* labelled line sequent calculus *is a labelled sequent calculus whose initial sequents and inference rules are constructed from* LLS.

$$\frac{}{\mathcal{R}, X, x{:}p \vdash x{:}p, Y} \text{ init} \qquad \frac{\mathcal{R}, X, x{:}A, x{:}B \vdash Y}{\mathcal{R}, X, x{:}A \wedge B \vdash Y} \wedge_L \qquad \frac{\mathcal{R}, X \vdash x{:}A, Y \quad \mathcal{R}, X \vdash x{:}B, Y}{\mathcal{R}, X \vdash x{:}A \wedge B, Y} \wedge_R$$

$$\frac{}{\mathcal{R}, X, x{:}\bot \vdash Y} \bot_L \qquad \frac{\mathcal{R}, X \vdash Y, x{:}A \quad \mathcal{R}, X, x{:}B \vdash Y}{\mathcal{R}, X, x{:}A \supset B \vdash Y} \supset_L \qquad \frac{\mathcal{R}, X, x{:}A \vdash Y, x{:}B}{\mathcal{R}, X \vdash Y, x{:}A \supset B} \supset_R$$

Fig. 3. Labelled line sequent calculus $\mathsf{LLS_G}$.

In Fig. 3 we present the rules for the labelled line classical calculus $\mathsf{LLS_G}$.

Since linear nested sequents form a particular case of nested sequents, the algorithm given in [6] can be used for generating LLS from LNS, and vice versa. However, one has to keep the linearity property invariant through inference rules. For example, the following rule (here considered more generally as a *labelled sequent rule*)

$$\frac{\mathcal{R}, xRy, X \vdash Y, y{:}A}{\mathcal{R}, X, \vdash Y, x{:}\Box A} \Box'_R$$

where y is fresh, is not adequate w.r.t. the system $\mathsf{LNS_K}$, since there may exist $z \in |\mathcal{R}|$ such that $xRz \in \mathcal{R}$. That is, for labelled sequents in general, freshness alone is not enough for guaranteeing unicity of x in $\mathcal{R}$. And it does not seem to be trivial to assure this unicity by using logical rules without side conditions. To avoid this problem, we slightly modify the framework by restricting $\mathcal{R}$ to singletons, that is, $\mathcal{R} = \{xRy\}$ will record only the two last components, in this case labelled by x and y, and by adding a base case $\mathcal{R} = \{y_0 R x_0\}$ for x_0, y_0 different state variables when there are no nested components. The rule for introducing $\Box_R$ then is

$$\frac{xRy, X \vdash Y, y{:}A}{zRx, X, \vdash Y, x{:}\Box A} \Box_R$$

with y fresh. Note that this solution corresponds to recording the history of the proof search up to the last two steps. We adopt the following terminology for calculi where this restriction is possible.

Definition 4. *A LNS calculus is* end-active *if in all its rules the rightmost components of the premisses are active and the only active components (in premisses and conclusion) are the two rightmost ones. An* end-active LLS *is a singleton relation set $\mathcal{R}$ together with a sequent $X \vdash Y$ of labelled formulae, written $\mathcal{R}, X \vdash Y$. The rules of an end-active LLS calculus are constructed from end-active labelled line sequents such that the active formulae in a premiss $xRy, X \vdash Y$ are labelled with y and the labels of all active formulae in the conclusion are in its relation set.*

Observe that the completeness proof for $\mathsf{LNS_K}$ via simulating a sequent derivation in the last component actually shows that the end-active version of the calculus $\mathsf{LNS_K}$ is complete for K [9]. From now on, we will use the end-active version of the propositional rules (see Fig. 4). Note that, in an end-active LLS, state variables might occur in the sequent and not in the relation set. Such formulae

$$\frac{}{zRx, X, x:p \vdash x:p, Y} \text{ init} \qquad \frac{zRx, X, x:A, x:B \vdash Y}{zRx, X, x:A \wedge B \vdash Y} \wedge_L \qquad \frac{zRx, X \vdash x:A, Y \quad zRx, X \vdash x:B, Y}{zRx, X \vdash x:A \wedge B, Y} \wedge_R$$

$$\frac{}{zRx, X, x:\bot \vdash Y} \bot_L \qquad \frac{zRx, X \vdash Y, x:A \quad zRx, X, x:B \vdash Y}{zRx, X, x:A \supset B \vdash Y} \supset_L \qquad \frac{zRx, X, x:A \vdash Y, x:B}{zRx, X \vdash Y, x:A \supset B} \supset_R$$

Fig. 4. The end-active version of LLS_G. In rule init, p is atomic.

will remain inactive towards the leaves of the derivation. In fact, a key property of end-active LNS calculi is that rules can only move formulas "forward", that is, either an active formula produces other formulae in the same component or in the next one. Hence one can automatically generate LLS from LNS. In the following we write $x:\Gamma$ if the label of every labelled formula in Γ is x.

Definition 5. *For a state variable x, define the mapping $\mathbb{TL}_x$ from LNS to end-active LLS as follows*

$$\mathbb{TL}_{x_0}(\Gamma_0 \vdash \Delta_0) \qquad\qquad = y_0 Rx_0, x_0:\Gamma_0 \vdash x_0:\Delta_0$$
$$\mathbb{TL}_{x_n}(\Gamma_0 \vdash \Delta_0 /\!/ \ldots /\!/ \Gamma_n \vdash \Delta_n) = x_{n-1} Rx_n, x_0:\Gamma_0, \ldots, x_n:\Gamma_n \vdash x_0:\Delta_0, \ldots, x_n:\Delta_n \quad n > 0$$

with all state variables pairwise distinct.

It is straightforward to use $\mathbb{TL}_x$ in order to construct a LLS inference rule from an inference rule of an end-active LNS calculus. The procedure, that can be automatised, is the same as the one presented in [6], as we shall illustrate it here.

Example 6. Consider the following application of the rule $\Box_R$ of Fig. 2:

$$\frac{\Gamma_0 \vdash \Delta_0 /\!/ \ldots /\!/ \Gamma_{n-1} \vdash \Delta_{n-1} /\!/ \Gamma_n \vdash \Delta_n /\!/ \vdash A}{\Gamma_0 \vdash \Delta_0 /\!/ \ldots /\!/ \Gamma_{n-1} \vdash \Delta_{n-1} /\!/ \Gamma_n \vdash \Delta_n, \Box A} \Box_R$$

Applying $\mathbb{TL}_x$ to the conclusion we obtain $x_{n-1} Rx_n, X \vdash Y, x_n : \Box A$, where $X = x_1:\Gamma_1, \ldots, x_n:\Gamma_n$ and $Y = x_1:\Delta_1, \ldots, x_n:\Delta_n$. Applying $\mathbb{TL}_x$ to the premise we obtain $x_n Rx_{n+1}, X \vdash Y, x_{n+1}:A$. We thus obtain an application of the LLS rule

$$\frac{x_n Rx_{n+1}, X \vdash Y, x_{n+1}:A}{x_{n-1} Rx_n, X \vdash Y, x_n:\Box A} \mathbb{TL}_x(\Box_R)$$

which is the rule $\Box_R$ presented in Fig. 5.

The following result follows readily by transforming derivations bottom-up.

$$\frac{xRy, X, y:A \vdash Y}{xRy, X, x:\Box A \vdash Y} \Box_L \qquad\qquad \frac{xRy, X \vdash Y, y:A}{zRx, X \vdash Y, x:\Box A} \Box_R \quad (y \text{ is a fresh variable})$$

Fig. 5. The modal rules of LLS_K.

Theorem 7. $\Gamma \vdash \Delta$ *is provable in a certain end-active* LNS *calculus if and only if* $\mathbb{TL}_{x_0}(\Gamma \vdash \Delta)$ *is provable in the corresponding end-active* LLS *calculus.*

The end-active labelled line sequent calculus $\mathsf{LLS_K}$ for K is given in Fig. 5. The following is immediate from completeness of the end-active version of $\mathsf{LNS_K}$.

Corollary 8. *A sequent* $\Gamma \vdash \Delta$ *has a proof in* $\mathsf{LNS_K}$ *if and only if* $yRx, x : \Gamma \vdash x : \Delta$ *has a proof in* $\mathsf{LLS_K}$ *for some different state variables* x, y.

4   Focused Labelled Line Sequent Systems

Although adding labels and restricting systems to their end-active form enhance proof search a little, this is still not enough for guaranteeing that modal rules occur in a block.

In [1], Andreoli introduced a notion of normal form for cut-free proofs in linear logic. This normal form is given by a *focused* proof system organised around two "phases" of proof construction: the *negative* phase for invertible inference rules and the *positive* phase for non-necessarily-invertible inference rules. Observe that a similar organisation is adopted when moving from $\mathsf{LNS_K}$ to $\mathsf{LLS_K}$: invertible rules are done eagerly while the non invertible ones $(\Box_R + \Box_L)$ are done only in the last two components.

We will now define $\mathsf{FLLS_K}$, a focused system for $\mathsf{LLS_K}$. Sequents in $\mathsf{FLLS_K}$ have one of the following shapes:

1. $zRx \Uparrow \Gamma; X \vdash Y; \Delta$ is an unfocused sequent, where Γ contains only modal formulae and Δ contains only modal or atomic formulae.
2. $zR[x] \Downarrow \Gamma; X \vdash \cdot; \Delta$ is a sequent focused on a right boxed or atomic formula.
3. $[x]Ry \Downarrow \Gamma; X \vdash Y; \Delta$ is a sequent focused on a left boxed formula.

In the *negative phase* sequents have the shape (1) above and all invertible propositional or modal rules are applied eagerly on formulae labelled with the variable x until there are only atomic or boxed formulae left. Some of those are moved to special contexts Γ, Δ using `store` rules. These contexts store the formulae that can be chosen for focusing. When this process terminates, the *positive phase* starts by deciding on one of the formulae in Δ, indicated by a sequent of the form (2). If this formula is an atom, then the proof should terminate. Otherwise, the focusing is over a modal formula, and the rule $\Box_R$ creates a fresh label y and moves the unboxed part of the formula to this new label, resulting in a sequent of the form (3). The positive phase then continues by possibly moving boxed formulae in Γ, labelled with x, to the label y. Finally, focusing is lost and we come back to the negative phase, now inside the component labelled by y. Note that this procedure gives a forward-chaining flavor to the system.

The rules for $\mathsf{FLLS_K}$ are presented in Fig. 6. Note that the rule store_R systematically moves all atomic and boxed formulae from Y to Δ, and hence Y will be eventually empty. This is the trigger for switching from the negative to the positive phase. Note also that the contexts may carry some "garbage", i.e., formulae which will never be principal. In fact, since the calculus is end-active, only formulae in one of the two last components can be principal. Similar to standard systems where weakening is admissible, these formulae are then absorbed by the initial sequents init. Since the focusing procedure described above is just a

$$\dfrac{}{zRx \Uparrow \Gamma;X,x{:}\bot \vdash Y;\varDelta}\,\bot_L \qquad \dfrac{zRx \Uparrow \Gamma;X,x{:}A,x{:}B \vdash Y;\varDelta}{zRx \Uparrow \Gamma;X,x{:}A \wedge B \vdash Y;\varDelta}\,\wedge_L \qquad \dfrac{zRx \Uparrow \Gamma;X,x{:}A \vdash Y,x{:}B;\varDelta}{zRx \Uparrow \Gamma;X \vdash Y,x{:}A \supset B;\varDelta}\,\supset_R$$

$$\dfrac{zRx \Uparrow \Gamma;X \vdash x{:}A,Y;\varDelta \quad zRx \Uparrow \Gamma;X \vdash x{:}B,Y;\varDelta}{zRx \Uparrow \Gamma;X \vdash x{:}A \wedge B,Y;\varDelta}\,\wedge_R \qquad \dfrac{zRx \Uparrow \Gamma;X \vdash Y,x{:}A;\varDelta \quad zRx \Uparrow \Gamma;X,x{:}B \vdash Y;\varDelta}{zRx \Uparrow \Gamma;X,x{:}A \supset B \vdash Y;\varDelta}\,\supset_L$$

$$\dfrac{zRx \Uparrow \Gamma,x{:}B_b;X \vdash Y;\varDelta}{zRx \Uparrow \Gamma;X,x{:}B_b \vdash Y;\varDelta}\,\text{store}_L \qquad \dfrac{zRx \Uparrow \Gamma;X \vdash Y;\varDelta,x{:}A_b}{zRx \Uparrow \Gamma;X \vdash Y,x{:}A_b;\varDelta}\,\text{store}_R$$

$$\dfrac{}{zR[x] \Downarrow \Gamma;X,x{:}A \vdash \cdot;\varDelta,x{:}A}\,\text{init} \qquad \dfrac{zR[x] \Downarrow \Gamma;X \vdash \cdot;\varDelta}{zRx \Uparrow \Gamma;X \vdash \cdot;\varDelta}\,D \qquad \dfrac{xRy \Uparrow \cdot;X \vdash Y;\varDelta}{[x]Ry \Downarrow \cdot;X \vdash Y;\varDelta}\,R$$

$$\dfrac{[x]Ry \Downarrow \Gamma;X \vdash y{:}A;\varDelta}{zR[x] \Downarrow \Gamma;X \vdash \cdot;\varDelta,x{:}\Box A}\,\Box_R \qquad \dfrac{[x]Ry \Downarrow \Gamma;X,y{:}A \vdash Y;\varDelta}{[x]Ry \Downarrow \Gamma,x{:}\Box A;X \vdash Y;\varDelta}\,\Box_L$$

Fig. 6. Focused labelled line sequent calculus FLLS$_K$ for K. A_b is atomic or a boxed formula, B_b is a boxed formula. As usual, the negative phase is marked by $\Uparrow$, the positive by $\Downarrow$.

systematic organisation of proofs, soundness and completeness proofs are often straightforward permutation-of-rules arguments.

Theorem 9. *The system* FLLS$_K$ *is sound and complete w.r.t. modal logic* K, *i.e., a formula A is a theorem of* K *iff the sequent* $zRx \Uparrow \cdot; \cdot \vdash x{:}A; \cdot$ *is derivable in* FLLS$_K$.

Proof. Observe that propositional rules permute up over the $\Box_L$ rule. Hence all the applications of $\Box_L$ can be done in sequence, just after the $\Box_R$ rule. □

Example 10. The normality axiom is derived as shown in Fig. 7. Note that the modal rules occur in a block corresponding to an application of the sequent rule k. That is, focusing effectively blocks derivations where propositional rules are applied between modal ones.

$$\dfrac{\dfrac{\dfrac{\dfrac{\dfrac{\dfrac{\dfrac{xR[y] \Downarrow \cdot;y{:}q,y{:}p \vdash \cdot;y{:}q}{xRy \Uparrow \cdot;y{:}q,y{:}p \vdash y{:}q;\cdot}\,\text{init}\ \text{store}_R, D \qquad \dfrac{xR[y] \Downarrow \cdot;y{:}p \vdash y{:}q;y{:}p}{xRy \Uparrow \cdot;y{:}p \vdash y{:}p,y{:}q;\cdot}\,\text{init}\ \text{store}_R, D}{xRy \Uparrow \cdot;y{:}p \supset q,y{:}p \vdash y{:}q;\cdot}\,\supset_L}{[x]Ry \Downarrow \cdot;y{:}p \supset q,y{:}p \vdash y{:}q;\cdot}\,R}{[x]Ry \Downarrow x{:}\Box(p \supset q),x{:}\Box p;\cdot \vdash y{:}q;\cdot}\,\Box_L}{zR[x] \Downarrow x{:}\Box(p \supset q),x{:}\Box p;\cdot \vdash \cdot;x{:}\Box q}\,\Box_R}{zRx \Uparrow x{:}\Box(p \supset q),x{:}\Box p;\cdot \vdash \cdot;x{:}\Box q}\,D}{\dfrac{zRx \Uparrow \cdot;x{:}\Box(p \supset q),x{:}\Box p \vdash x{:}\Box q;\cdot}{zRx \Uparrow \cdot;\cdot \vdash x{:}\Box(p \supset q) \supset (\Box p \supset \Box q);\cdot}\,\supset_R}\,\text{store}_L,\text{store}_R$$

Fig. 7. The derivation of the normality axiom in FLLS$_K$

5   Some More Involved Examples

It is straightforward to see that the method described above apply to any sequent calculus which can be written as an end-variant linear nested sequent calculus, in particular to extensions of K with combinations of the axioms D, T, 4 or to the multi-succedent calculus for intuitionistic logic [9]. We now consider some less trivial examples.

5.1   Simply Dependent Bimodal Logics

As a first example, we consider a bimodal logic with a simple interaction between the modalities. While we only treat one example, our method is readily adapted to other such logics. The language of *simply dependent bimodal logic* $\mathsf{KT} \oplus_{\subseteq} \mathsf{S4}$ from [5] contains two modalities $\square$ and $\heartsuit$, and the axioms are the KT axioms for $\square$ together with the $\mathsf{S4}$ axioms for $\heartsuit$ and the *interaction* axiom $\heartsuit A \supset \square A$ (Fig. 8). Using the methods in [10], these axioms are easily converted into the sequent system $\mathsf{G}_{\mathsf{KT} \oplus_{\subseteq} \mathsf{S4}}$ extending the standard propositional rules with the modal rules of Fig. 9. It is straightforward to check that these rules satisfy the criteria for cut elimination from [10], and hence $\mathsf{G}_{\mathsf{KT} \oplus_{\subseteq} \mathsf{S4}}$ is cut-free.

$$\heartsuit A \supset \square A \qquad \mathsf{k}_\square\ \square(A \supset B) \supset (\square A \supset \square B) \qquad \mathsf{t}_\square\ \square A \supset A \qquad \frac{\vdash A}{\vdash \square A}\ \mathsf{nec}_\square$$

$$\mathsf{k}_\heartsuit\ \heartsuit(A \supset B) \supset (\heartsuit A \supset \heartsuit B) \qquad \mathsf{t}_\heartsuit\ \heartsuit A \supset A \qquad \mathsf{4}_\heartsuit\ \heartsuit A \supset \heartsuit\heartsuit A \qquad \frac{\vdash A}{\vdash \heartsuit A}\ \mathsf{nec}_\heartsuit$$

Fig. 8. The modal axioms for logic $\mathsf{KT} \oplus_{\subseteq} \mathsf{S4}$.

$$\frac{\Gamma, \heartsuit\Sigma, \Sigma, \square\Theta, \Theta \vdash \Delta}{\Gamma, \heartsuit\Sigma, \square\Theta \vdash \Delta}\ \mathsf{T} \qquad \frac{\heartsuit\Gamma, \heartsuit\Sigma, \Sigma, \Theta \vdash A}{\Omega, \heartsuit\Gamma, \heartsuit\Sigma, \square\Theta \vdash \square A, \Xi}\ \square_R \qquad \frac{\heartsuit\Gamma \vdash A}{\Omega, \heartsuit\Gamma \vdash \heartsuit A, \Xi}\ \heartsuit_R$$

Fig. 9. The modal rules of the sequent calculus $\mathsf{G}_{\mathsf{KT} \oplus_{\subseteq} \mathsf{S4}}$ for $\mathsf{KT} \oplus_{\subseteq} \mathsf{S4}$

To obtain a focused system, we again convert the sequent calculus into a LNS calculus. However, since now we have two different non-invertible right rules ($\square_R$ and $\heartsuit_R$), we need to modify the linear nested setting slightly, introducing the two different nesting operators $/\!/^\square$ and $/\!/^\heartsuit$ for the rules $\square_R$ resp. $\heartsuit_R$. The intended interpretation is

$$\iota(\Gamma \vdash \Delta) := \bigwedge \Gamma \supset \bigvee \Delta$$

$$\iota(\Gamma \vdash \Delta /\!/^\square \mathcal{H}) := \bigwedge \Gamma \supset \bigvee \Delta \vee \square \iota(\mathcal{H})$$

$$\iota(\Gamma \vdash \Delta /\!/^\heartsuit \mathcal{H}) := \bigwedge \Gamma \supset \bigvee \Delta \vee \heartsuit \iota(\mathcal{H})$$

The modal sequent rules are then converted into the rules of Fig. 10. The propositional rules are those of LNS$_G$ (Fig. 1). Cut-free completeness of (the end-active variant of) this calculus again follows from simulating sequent derivations in the rightmost two components.

$$\frac{\mathcal{G}/\!/^*\Gamma \vdash \Delta/\!/^\square \vdash A}{\mathcal{G}/\!/^*\Gamma \vdash \Delta, \square A}\,\square_{R\square} \qquad \frac{S\{\Gamma \vdash \Delta/\!/^\square\Sigma, A \vdash \Pi\}}{S\{\Gamma, \square A \vdash \Delta/\!/^\square\Sigma \vdash \Pi\}}\,\square_L \qquad \frac{S\{\Gamma \vdash \Delta/\!/^\square\Sigma, \heartsuit A \vdash \Pi\}}{S\{\Gamma, \heartsuit A \vdash \Delta/\!/^\square\Sigma \vdash \Pi\}}\,\heartsuit_{L\square}$$

$$\frac{\mathcal{G}/\!/^*\Gamma \vdash \Delta/\!/^\heartsuit \vdash A}{\mathcal{G}/\!/^*\Gamma \vdash \Delta, \heartsuit A}\,\heartsuit_{R\heartsuit} \qquad \frac{S\{\Gamma \vdash \Delta/\!/^\heartsuit\Sigma, \heartsuit A \vdash \Pi\}}{S\{\Gamma, \heartsuit A \vdash \Delta/\!/^\heartsuit\Sigma \vdash \Pi\}}\,\heartsuit_{L\heartsuit} \qquad \frac{S\{\Gamma, \square A, A \vdash \Delta\}}{S\{\Gamma, \square A \vdash \Delta\}}\,t_\square \qquad \frac{S\{\Gamma, \heartsuit A, A \vdash \Delta\}}{S\{\Gamma, \heartsuit A \vdash \Delta\}}\,t_\heartsuit$$

Fig. 10. The modal linear nested sequent rules for KT $\oplus_\subseteq$ S4. Here $* \in \{\square, \heartsuit\}$.

Lemma 11 (Soundness). *The rules of* LNS$_{\mathsf{KT}\oplus_\subseteq\mathsf{S4}}$ *preserve validity of the formula interpretation of the sequents with respect to* KT $\oplus_\subseteq$ S4 *frames.*

Proof. By showing that if the negation of the interpretation of the conclusion of a rule is satisfiable in a KT $\oplus_\subseteq$ S4 frame, then so is its conclusion, using that in such frames the accessibility relation $R_\square$ for $\square$ is contained in the accessibility relation $R_\heartsuit$ for $\heartsuit$. $\square$

Note that this also shows that the obvious adaption of this calculus to the full nested sequent setting is sound and cut-free complete for KT $\oplus_\subseteq$ S4. For proposing a focused version for the linear nested sequent rules we essentially follow the method given in Sect. 4, adapting the framework slightly to the multimodal setting by introducing two different kinds of relation terms $xR_\square y$ and $xR_\heartsuit y$ corresponding to the accessibility relations of the modalities $\square$ and $\heartsuit$ respectively. The frame $Fr(\mathcal{R})$ is defined as $(|R_\square \cup R_\heartsuit|, R_\square \cup R_\heartsuit)$ and linelike relation sets are defined using this definition. The FLLS rules then are defined straightforwardly (Fig. 11). Soundness and completeness of the resulting system FLLS$_{\mathsf{KT}\oplus_\subseteq\mathsf{S4}}$ follow as above. Summing up we have:

Theorem 12. LNS$_{\mathsf{KT}\oplus_\subseteq\mathsf{S4}}$ *and* FLLS$_{\mathsf{KT}\oplus_\subseteq\mathsf{S4}}$ *are sound and complete for* KT $\oplus_\subseteq$ S4.

5.2   Non-normal Modal Logics

The same ideas also yield LNS calculi and their focused versions for some *non-normal* modal logics, i.e., modal logics that are not extensions of modal logic K (see [4] for an introduction). The calculi themselves are of independent interest since, to the best of our knowledge, nested sequent calculi for the logics below have not been considered before in the literature. The most basic non-normal logic, *classical modal logic* E, is given Hilbert-style by stipulating only the rule (E) (or *congruence rule*) for the connective $\Box$

$$\frac{A \supset B \quad B \supset A}{\Box A \supset \Box B} \ (E)$$

which allows exchanging logically equivalent formulae under the modality. Some of the better known extensions of this logic are formulated by the addition of axioms from

M $\Box(A \land B) \supset (\Box A \land \Box B)$ C $(\Box A \land \Box B) \supset \Box(A \land B)$ N $\Box\top$

Figure 12 shows the modal rules of the standard cut-free sequent calculi for these logics [8], where in addition weakening is embedded in the conclusion. Extensions of E are written by concatenating the names of the axioms, and in presence of the monotonicity axiom M, the initial E is dropped. E.g., the logic MC is the extension of E with axioms M and C. Its sequent calculus G_{MC} is given by the standard propositional and structural rules together with the rule (E) as well as the rules (Mn) for $n \geq 1$.

We first consider *monotone logics*, i.e., extensions of M. To simulate the rules from Fig. 12 in the linear nested setting, we introduce an auxiliary nesting operator $/\!/^m$ to capture a state where a sequent rule has been partly processed. In contrast, the intuition for the original nesting $/\!/$ is that the simulation of a rule is finished. In view of end-active systems, we restrict the occurrences of $/\!/^m$

$$\frac{[x]R_\Box y \ \Downarrow \ \Gamma; X \vdash y{:}A; \Delta}{zR_*[x] \ \Downarrow \ \Gamma; X \vdash \cdot; \Delta, x{:}\Box A} \ \Box_{R\Box} \qquad \frac{[x]R_\heartsuit y \ \Downarrow \ \Gamma; X \vdash y{:}A; \Delta}{zR_*[x] \ \Downarrow \ \Gamma; X \vdash \cdot; \Delta, x{:}\heartsuit A} \ \heartsuit_{R\heartsuit}$$

$$\frac{[x]R_\Box y \ \Downarrow \ \Gamma, y{:}\heartsuit A; X \vdash Y; \Delta}{[x]R_\Box y \ \Downarrow \ \Gamma, x{:}\heartsuit A; X \vdash Y; \Delta} \ \heartsuit_{L\Box} \qquad \frac{[x]R_\Box y \ \Downarrow \ \Gamma, X, y{:}A \vdash Y; \Delta}{[x]R_\Box y \ \Downarrow \ \Gamma, x{:}\Box A; X \vdash Y; \Delta} \ \Box_L$$

$$\frac{[x]R_\heartsuit y \ \Downarrow \ \Gamma, y{:}\heartsuit A; X \vdash Y; \Delta}{[x]R_\heartsuit y \ \Downarrow \ \Gamma, x{:}\heartsuit A; X \vdash Y; \Delta} \ \heartsuit_{L\heartsuit} \qquad \frac{zR_*x \ \Uparrow \ \Gamma, x{:}\Box A; X, x{:}A \vdash Y; \Delta}{zR_*x \ \Uparrow \ \Gamma, X, x{:}\Box A \vdash Y; \Delta} \ t_\Box$$

Fig. 11. The modal rules of $FLLS_{KT\oplus_{\subseteq}S4}$. Here $* \in \{\Box, \heartsuit\}$ and y is fresh in rules $\Box_{R\Box}$ and $\Box_{R\heartsuit}$. Rule $t_\heartsuit$ is analogous to $t_\Box$ and is omitted. The propositional rules are as in Fig. 4 with R_* instead of R.

$$\frac{A \vdash B \quad B \vdash A}{\Gamma, \Box A \vdash \Box B, \Delta} \ (E) \qquad \frac{A \vdash B}{\Gamma, \Box A \vdash \Box B, \Delta} \ (M) \qquad \frac{\vdash A}{\Gamma \vdash \Box A, \Delta} \ (N)$$

$$\frac{A_1, \ldots, A_n \vdash B \quad B \vdash A_1 \quad \cdots \quad B \vdash A_n}{\Gamma, \Box A_1, \ldots, \Box A_n \vdash \Box B, \Delta} \ (En) \qquad \frac{A_1, \ldots, A_n \vdash B}{\Gamma, \Box A_1, \ldots, \Box A_n \vdash \Box B, \Delta} \ (Mn)$$

G_E $\{(E)\}$	G_{EC} $\{(En) : n \geq 1\}$	G_{MN} $\{(M),(N)\}$
G_M $\{(M)\}$	G_{MC} $\{(Mn) : n \geq 1\}$	G_{MCN} $\{(Mn) : n \geq 0\}$

Fig. 12. Sequent rules and calculi for some non-normal modal logics

to the end of the structures. Linear nested sequents for monotonic non-normal modal logics then are given by:

$$\mathsf{LNS_m} ::= \Gamma \vdash \Delta \mid \Gamma \vdash \Delta /\!/^m \Sigma \vdash \Pi \mid \Gamma \vdash \Delta /\!/ \mathsf{LNS_m}$$

The modal linear nested sequent rules are given in Fig. 13. The propositional rules are those of the end-active version of $\mathsf{LNS_G}$ (Fig. 1) with the restriction that they cannot be applied inside $/\!/^m$. The sequent rule $(\mathsf{M}n)$ is then simulated by the following derivation

$$\frac{\mathcal{G} /\!/ \Gamma \vdash \Delta /\!/^m \vdash B}{\mathcal{G} /\!/ \Gamma \vdash \Box B, \Delta} \; \Box_R^m \qquad \frac{\mathcal{G} /\!/ \Gamma \vdash \Delta /\!/ \Sigma, A \vdash \Pi}{\mathcal{G} /\!/ \Gamma, \Box A \vdash \Delta /\!/^m \Sigma \vdash \Pi} \; \Box_L^m$$

$$\frac{\mathcal{G} /\!/ \Gamma \vdash \Delta /\!/^m \Sigma, A \vdash \Pi}{\mathcal{G} /\!/ \Gamma, \Box A \vdash \Delta /\!/^m \Sigma \vdash \Pi} \; \Box_L^c \qquad \frac{\mathcal{G} /\!/ \Gamma \vdash \Delta /\!/ \vdash B}{\mathcal{G} /\!/ \Gamma \vdash \Box B, \Delta} \; \Box_R^n$$

$\mathsf{LNS_M} \; \{ \Box_R^m, \Box_L^m \} \quad \mathsf{LNS_{MC}} \; \{ \Box_R^m, \Box_L^m, \Box_L^c \} \quad \mathsf{LNS_{MN}} \; \{ \Box_R^m, \Box_L^m, \Box_R^n \} \quad \mathsf{LNS_{MCN}} \; \{ \Box_R^m, \Box_L^m, \Box_L^c, \Box_R^n \}$

Fig. 13. Modal linear nested sequent rules for some monotone non-normal modal logics.

$$\frac{\mathcal{G} /\!/ \Gamma \vdash \Delta /\!/^e (\vdash B; B \vdash)}{\mathcal{G} /\!/ \Gamma \vdash \Box B, \Delta} \; \Box_R^e \qquad \frac{\mathcal{G} /\!/ \Gamma \vdash \Delta /\!/ \Sigma, A \vdash \Pi \quad \mathcal{G} /\!/ \Gamma \vdash \Delta /\!/ \Omega \vdash A, \Theta}{\mathcal{G} /\!/ \Gamma, \Box A \vdash \Delta /\!/^e (\Sigma \vdash \Pi; \Omega \vdash \Theta)} \; \Box_L^e$$

$$\frac{\mathcal{G} /\!/ \Gamma \vdash \Delta /\!/^e (\Sigma, A \vdash \Pi; \Omega \vdash \Theta) \quad \mathcal{G} /\!/ \Gamma \vdash \Delta /\!/ \Omega \vdash A, \Theta}{\mathcal{G} /\!/ \Gamma, \Box A \vdash \Delta /\!/^e (\Sigma \vdash \Pi; \Omega \vdash \Theta)} \; \Box_L^{ec}$$

$\mathsf{LNS_E} \; \{ \Box_R^e, \Box_L^e \} \qquad \mathsf{LNS_{EC}} \; \{ \Box_R^e, \Box_L^e, \Box_L^{ec} \}$

Fig. 14. Modal linear nested sequent rules for some non-monotone non-normal modal logics

$$\frac{A_1, \ldots, A_n \vdash B}{\Box A_1, \ldots, \Box A_n \vdash \Box B} \; (\mathsf{M}n) \qquad \rightsquigarrow \qquad \frac{\dfrac{\dfrac{\mathcal{G} /\!/ \vdash /\!/ A_1, \ldots, A_{n-1}, A_n \vdash B}{\mathcal{G} /\!/ \vdash /\!/^m A_1, \ldots, A_{n-1} \vdash B} \; \Box_L^m}{\dfrac{\mathcal{G} /\!/ \Box A_1, \ldots, \Box A_n \vdash /\!/^m \vdash B}{\mathcal{G} /\!/ \Box A_1, \ldots, \Box A_n \vdash \Box B} \; \Box_R^m} \; \Box_L^c}{}$$
$$\vdots \; \mathcal{G}$$

For extensions of classical modal logic E not containing the monotonicity axiom M we need to store more information about the unfinished premisses. Thus instead of $/\!/^m$ we introduce a *binary* nesting operator $/\!/^e(.;.)$. Linear nested sequents then are given by

$$\mathsf{LNS_e} ::= \Gamma \vdash \Delta \mid \Gamma \vdash \Delta /\!/^e (\Sigma \vdash \Pi; \Omega \vdash \Theta) \mid \Gamma \vdash \Delta /\!/ \mathsf{LNS_e}$$

Figure 14 shows the modal rules for these logics, where again the propositional rules are those of end-active $\mathsf{LNS_G}$ (Fig. 1) with the restriction that they are not applied inside the nesting $/\!/^e$. The derivation simulating the rule (En) then is

$$
\cfrac{\mathcal{G}/\!/\,\Gamma \vdash \Delta /\!/ A_1, \ldots, A_n \vdash B \quad \mathcal{G}/\!/\,\Gamma \vdash \Delta /\!/ B \vdash A_n}{\mathcal{G}/\!/\,\Gamma, \Box A_n \vdash \Delta /\!/^e (A_1, \ldots, A_{n-1} \vdash B; B \vdash)}\ \Box_L^e
$$

$$
\vdots
$$

$$
\cfrac{\cfrac{\mathcal{G}/\!/\,\Gamma, \Box A_2, \ldots, \Box A_n \vdash \Delta /\!/^e (A_1 \vdash B; B \vdash) \qquad \mathcal{G}/\!/\,\Gamma, \Box A_2, \ldots, \Box A_n \vdash \Delta /\!/ B \vdash A_1}{\mathcal{G}/\!/\,\Gamma, \Box A_1, \ldots, \Box A_n \vdash \Delta /\!/^e (\vdash B; B \vdash)}\ \Box_L^{ec}}{\mathcal{G}/\!/\,\Gamma, \Box A_1, \ldots, \Box A_n \vdash \Box B, \Delta}\ \Box_R^e
$$

Theorem 13 (Completeness). *The linear nested sequent calculi of Figs. 13 and 14 are complete w.r.t. the corresponding logics.*

For showing soundness of such calculi we need a different method, though. This is due to the fact that, unlike for normal modal logics, there is no clear formula interpretation for linear nested sequents for non-normal modal logics. However, since the propositional rules cannot be applied inside the auxiliary nestings $/\!/^m$ resp. $/\!/^e$, the modal rules can only occur in blocks. Together with the fact that the (end-variant) propositional rules can only be applied in the last component, this means that we can straightforwardly translate LNS derivations back into sequent derivations.

Theorem 14 (Soundness). *If a sequent $\Gamma \vdash \Delta$ is derivable in $\mathsf{LNS}_{\mathcal{L}}$ for $\mathcal{L}$ one of the logics presented in this section, then it is derivable in the corresponding sequent calculus.*

Proof. By translating a $\mathsf{LNS}_{\mathcal{L}}$ derivation into a $\mathsf{G}_{\mathcal{L}}$ derivation, discarding everything apart from the last component of the linear nested sequents, and translating blocks of modal rules into the corresponding modal sequent rules. E.g., a block consisting of an application of $\Box_L^m$ followed by n applications of $\Box_L^c$ and an application of $\Box_R^m$ is translated into an application of the rule (Mn). The propositional rules only work on the last component and never inside the nesting $/\!/^m$ resp. $/\!/^e$ and are translated easily by the corresponding sequent rules. $\Box$

Remark 15. It is possible to consider linear nested sequent calculi for these non-normal modal logics in which the propositional rules are not restricted to their end-active versions. In this case, soundness can be shown by a permutation-of-rules argument, similar to the argument for *levelled derivations* in [11], using "levelling-preserving" invertibility of the propositional rules.

The modal FLLS rules for the non-monotone non-normal modal logics are given in Fig. 15, writing R_e for the relation corresponding to $/\!/^e$. The propositional rules are those of FLLS_K (Fig. 6). The systems for monotone logics are constructed similarly.

$$\dfrac{yR_m[z,w] \Downarrow \Gamma; X, w{:}A \vdash z{:}A; \Delta}{xR[y] \Downarrow \Gamma; X \vdash \cdot; \Delta, y{:}\Box A} \; \Box_R^e \qquad \dfrac{yRz \Uparrow \Gamma; X, z{:}A \vdash Y; \Delta \quad yRw \Uparrow \Gamma; X \vdash Y, w{:}A; \Delta}{yR_m[z,w] \Downarrow \Gamma, y{:}\Box A; X \vdash Y; \Delta} \; \Box_L^e$$

$$\dfrac{yR_m[z,w] \Downarrow \Gamma; X, z{:}A \vdash Y; \Delta \quad yRw \Uparrow \Gamma; X \vdash Y, w{:}A; \Delta}{yR_m[z,w] \Downarrow \Gamma, y{:}\Box A; X \vdash Y; \Delta} \; \Box_L^{ec}$$

$$\mathsf{FLLS_E} \quad \{\Box_R^e, \Box_L^e\} \qquad \mathsf{FLLS_{EC}} \quad \{\Box_R^e, \Box_L^e, \Box_L^{ec}\}$$

Fig. 15. The modal FLLS rules for non-monotone non-normal modal logics

6   Automatic Proof Search in Linear Nested Sequents

The method for constructing focused systems from Sect. 4 generates *optimal* systems, in the sense that proof search complexity matches exactly that of the original sequent calculi. We will now go one step further and exploit the fact that these calculi sport separate left and right introduction rules for the modalities to present a systematic way of encoding labelled line nested sequents in linear logic. This enables us to both: (i) use the rich linear logic meta-level theory in order to reason about the specified systems; and (ii) use a linear logic prover in order to do automatic proof search in those systems.

Observe that, while the goal in (ii) is also achieved by implementing the focused versions of the various systems case by case, using a meta-level framework like linear logic allows the use of *a single* prover for various logics: all one has to do is to change the theory, *i.e.*, the specified introduction clauses. The implementation of a number of specified systems is available online at http:// subsell.logic.at/nestLL/.

6.1   From Sequent Rules to Linear Logic Clauses

We now consider *focused linear logic* (LLF) as a "meta-logic" and the formulae of a labelled modal logic as the "object-logic" and then illustrate how sets of bipoles in linear logic can be used to specify sequent calculi for the object-logic. Since we follow mostly the procedure of [13], here we only give a general idea.

Specifying Sequents. Let *obj* be the type of object-level formulae and let $\lfloor \cdot \rfloor$ and $\lceil \cdot \rceil$ be two meta-level predicates on these, i.e., both of type $obj \to o$. Object-level sequents of the form $B_1, \ldots, B_n \vdash C_1, \ldots, C_m$ (where $n, m \geq 0$) are specified as the multiset $\lfloor B_1 \rfloor, \ldots, \lfloor B_n \rfloor, \lceil C_1 \rceil, \ldots, \lceil C_m \rceil$ within the LLF proof system. The $\lfloor \cdot \rfloor$ and $\lceil \cdot \rceil$ predicates identify which object-level formulas appear on which side of the sequent – brackets down for left (useful mnemonic: $\lfloor$ for "left") and brackets up for right. Finally, binary relations R are specified by a meta-level atomic formula of the form $R(\cdot, \cdot)$.

Specifying Inference Rules. Inference rules are specified by a re-writing clause that replaces the active formulae in the conclusion by the active formulae in the premises. The linear logic connectives indicate how these object level formulae are connected: contexts are copied (&) or split ($\otimes$), in different inference rules ($\oplus$) or in the same sequent ($\mathbin{⅋}$). For example, the specification of (a representative sample of) the rules of $\mathsf{LLS_K}$ are

$$
\begin{aligned}
&(\text{init}) && \exists A, x. \lfloor x{:}A \rfloor^{\perp} \otimes \lceil x{:}A \rceil^{\perp} \otimes \texttt{atomic}(A) \\
&(\wedge_l) && \exists A, B, x. \lfloor x{:}A \wedge B \rfloor^{\perp} \otimes \lfloor x{:}A \rfloor \mathbin{⅋} \lfloor x{:}B \rfloor \\
&(\wedge_r) && \exists A, B, x. \lceil x{:}A \wedge B \rceil^{\perp} \otimes \lceil x{:}A \rceil \mathbin{\&} \lceil x{:}B \rceil \\
&(\square_R) && \exists A, B, x. \lceil x{:}\square A \rceil^{\perp} \otimes \forall y. (\lceil y{:}A \rceil \mathbin{⅋} R(x,y)) \otimes \exists z. R(z,x)^{\perp} \\
&(\square_L) && \exists A, B, x. \lfloor x{:}\square A \rfloor^{\perp} \otimes \exists y. (\lfloor y{:}A \rfloor \mathbin{⅋} R(x,y)) \otimes R(x,y)^{\perp}
\end{aligned}
$$

The correspondence between focusing on a formula and an induced big-step inference rule is particularly interesting when the focused formula is a *bipole*. Roughly speaking, bipoles are positive formulae in which no positive connective can be in the scope of a negative one (see [13, Definition 3]). Focusing on such a formula will produce a single positive and a single negative phase. This two-phase decomposition enables the adequate capturing of the application of an object-level inference rule by the meta-level logic. For example, focusing on the bipole clause ($\square_R$) will produce the derivation

$$
\cfrac{
\pi_1 \qquad
\cfrac{
\cfrac{\Psi; \Delta', \lceil y{:}A \rceil, R(x,y)) \Uparrow}
{\Psi; \Delta' \Downarrow \forall y. (\lceil y{:}A \rceil \mathbin{⅋} R(x,y))} \; [R \Downarrow, \forall, \mathbin{⅋}, R \Uparrow]
\qquad \pi_2
}
{\Psi; \Delta \Downarrow \exists A, B. \lceil x{:}\square A \rceil^{\perp} \otimes \forall y. (\lceil y{:}A \rceil \mathbin{⅋} R(x,y)) \otimes \exists z. R(z,x)^{\perp}}
} {} \; [\exists, \otimes]
$$

where $\Delta = \lceil x{:}\square A \rceil \cup R(z,x) \cup \Delta'$, and π_1 and π_2 are, respectively,

$$
\cfrac{}{\Psi; \lceil x{:}\square A \rceil \Downarrow \lceil x{:}\square A \rceil^{\perp}} \; I_1
\qquad\qquad
\cfrac{}{\Psi; R(z,x) \Downarrow \exists z. R(z,x)^{\perp}} \; [\exists, I_1]
$$

This one-step focused derivation will: (a) consume $\lceil x : \square A \rceil$ and $R(z,x)$; (b) create a fresh label y; and (c) add $\lceil y : A \rceil$ and $R(x,y)$ to the context. Observe that this matches *exactly* the application of the object-level rule $\square_R$.

When specifying a system (logical, computational, etc.) into a meta level framework, it is desirable and often mandatory that the specification is *faithful*, that is, one step of computation on the object level should correspond to one step of logical reasoning in the meta level. This is what is called *adequacy* [15].

$$
\begin{aligned}
&(\square_R^{\mathsf{e}}) && \lceil x : \square B \rceil^{\perp} \otimes \forall y \forall z. (\lceil y : B \rceil \mathbin{⅋} \lfloor z : B \rfloor \mathbin{⅋} R_{\mathsf{e}}(x,y,z)) \otimes \exists z. R(z,x)^{\perp} \\
&(\square_L^{\mathsf{e}}) && \lfloor x : \square A \rfloor^{\perp} \otimes \exists y \exists z. ((\lfloor y : \square A \rfloor \mathbin{⅋} R(x,y)) \otimes (\lceil z : \square A \rceil \mathbin{⅋} R(x,z)) \otimes R_{\mathsf{e}}(x,y,z)^{\perp}) \\
&(\square_L^{\mathsf{ec}}) && \lfloor x : \square A \rfloor^{\perp} \otimes \exists y \exists z. ((\lfloor y : \square A \rfloor \mathbin{⅋} R_{\mathsf{e}}(x,y,z)) \otimes (\lceil z : \square A \rceil \mathbin{⅋} R(x,z)) \otimes R_{\mathsf{e}}(x,y,z)^{\perp})
\end{aligned}
$$

Fig. 16. The LLF specification of the modal rules of $\mathsf{LLS_{EC}}$ for the logic EC from Sect. 5.2.

Definition 16. *A specification of an object sequent system is* adequate *if provability is preserved for (open) derivations, such as inference rules themselves.*

Figure 16 shows adequate specifications in LLF of the labelled systems for the logic EC. These specifications can be used for automatic proof search as illustrated by the following theorem which is shown readily using the methods in [13].

Theorem 17. *Let L be a* LLS *system and let L be the theory given by the clauses of an adequate specification of the inference rules of L. A sequent* $\mathcal{R}, \Gamma \vdash \Delta$ *is provable in L if and only if* $\mathcal{L}; \mathcal{R} \Uparrow \lfloor \Gamma \rfloor, \lceil \Delta \rceil$ *is provable in LLF.*

It is an easy task to show that all the specifications shown in this paper are adequate.

Specifying Modalities. The reason why the specifications in LLF and the construction of focused systems for LLS systems work rather well is the fact that the LNS modal rules only manipulate a fixed number of principal formulae, i.e., one can choose some formulae and replace them with some other formulae. If there are no principal formulae, or if the object rule is context dependent, then proposing such encodings or a neat notion of focusing becomes tricky, as it is often the case with sequent systems for modal logics. In [16] linear logic with *subexponentials* (SELL) was used as a framework for specifying a number of modal logics. Unfortunately, the encodings are far from natural, and cannot be automated. Thus, in our opinion, the use of linear nested systems constitutes a significant step towards defining efficient methods for proof search, but also the construction of automatic provers for modal logics.

7 Concluding Remarks and Future Work

In this work we used the correspondence between linear nested sequents and labelled line sequents to (a) propose focused nested sequent systems for a number of modal logics (including a non-trivial bimodal logic and non-normal logics) which match the complexity of existing sequent calculi; and (b) specify the labelled systems in linear logic, thereby obtaining automatic provers for all of them. This not only constitues a significant step towards a better understanding of proof theory for modal logics in general, but also opens an avenue for research in proof search for a broad set of systems (not only modal).

One natural line of investigation concerns the applicability of this approach to logics based on non-classical propositional logic such as constructive modal logics. Moreover, we would like to understand whether our methods work for "proper" nested sequent calculi, i.e., calculi for logics which are not based on a cut-free sequent calculus, such as the calculi for K5 or KB [2]. Finally, it might be possible to automatically extract focused systems from LLF specifications. It would be rather interesting to compare these systems with ours.

References

1. Andreoli, J.M.: Logic programming with focusing proofs in linear logic. J. Logic Comput. **2**(3), 297–347 (1992)

2. Brünnler, K.: Deep sequent systems for modal logic. Arch. Math. Log. **48**, 551–577 (2009)
3. Chaudhuri, K., Guenot, N., Straßburger, L.: The focused calculus of structures. In: Bezem, M. (ed.) CSL 2011, pp. 159–173. Leibniz International Proceedings in Informatics (2011)
4. Chellas, B.F.: Modal Logic. Cambridge University Press, Cambridge (1980)
5. Demri, S.: Complexity of simple dependent bimodal logics. In: Dyckhoff, R. (ed.) TABLEAUX 2000. LNCS, vol. 1847, pp. 190–204. Springer, Heidelberg (2000)
6. Goré, R., Ramanayake, R.: Labelled tree sequents, tree hypersequents and nested (deep) sequents. In: AiML, vol. 9, pp. 279–299 (2012)
7. Guglielmi, A., Straßburger, L.: Non-commutativity and MELL in the calculus of structures. In: Fribourg, L. (ed.) CSL 2001. LNCS, vol. 2142, pp. 54–68. Springer, Heidelberg (2001)
8. Lavendhomme, R., Lucas, T.: Sequent calculi and decision procedures for weak modal systems. Studia Logica **65**, 121–145 (2000)
9. Lellmann, B.: Linear nested sequents, 2-sequents and hypersequents. In: De Nivelle, H. (ed.) TABLEAUX 2015. LNCS (LNAI), vol. 9323, pp. 135–150. Springer, Heidelberg (2015)
10. Lellmann, B., Pattinson, D.: Constructing cut free sequent systems with context restrictions based on classical or intuitionistic logic. In: Lodaya, K. (ed.) ICLA 2013. LNCS (LNAI), vol. 7750, pp. 148–160. Springer, Heidelberg (2013)
11. Masini, A.: 2-sequent calculus: a proof theory of modalities. Ann. Pure Appl. Logic **58**, 229–246 (1992)
12. Mendler, M., Scheele, S.: Cut-free Gentzen calculus for multimodal CK. Inf. Comput. (IANDC) **209**, 1465–1490 (2011)
13. Miller, D., Pimentel, E.: A formal framework for specifying sequent calculus proof systems. Theor. Comput. Sci. **474**, 98–116 (2013)
14. Negri, S., van Plato, J.: Proof Analysis: A Contribution to Hilbert's Last Problem. Cambridge University Press, Cambridge (2011)
15. Nigam, V., Miller, D.: A framework for proof systems. J. Autom. Reasoning **45**(2), 157–188 (2010)
16. Nigam, V., Pimentel, E., Reis, G.: An extended framework for specifying and reasoning about proof systems. J. Logic Comput. (2014). doi:10.1093/logcom/exu029, http://logcom.oxfordjournals.org/content/early/2014/06/06/logcom.exu029.abstract
17. Poggiolesi, F.: The method of tree-hypersequents for modal propositional logic. In: Makinson, D., Malinowski, J., Wansing, H. (eds.) Towards Mathematical Philosophy. Trends in Logic, vol. 28, pp. 31–51. Springer, Heidelberg (2009)
18. Straßburger, L.: Cut elimination in nested sequents for intuitionistic modal logics. In: Pfenning, F. (ed.) FOSSACS 2013. LNCS, vol. 7794, pp. 209–224. Springer, Heidelberg (2013)

Tableau-Based Revision over $\mathcal{SHIQ}$ TBoxes

Thinh Dong$^{(\boxtimes)}$, Chan Le Duc, Philippe Bonnot, and Myriam Lamolle

LIASD - IUT of Montreuil, University of Paris 8, Saint-Denis, France
{dong,leduc,bonnot,lamolle}@iut.univ-paris8.fr

Abstract. Semantics-based applications encapsulate commonly a set of ontologies which represent knowledge formalized from different data sources. Some of these ontologies may change over time since, not only data would be updated but also our understanding on application domain would evolve. To ensure that ontologies remain usable, it is needed to revise ontologies in such a way that takes into account new knowledge and guarantees the principle of minimal change. In this paper, we propose an ontology revision approach which uses finite structures equipped with a total pre-order to characterize a set of models of an ontology. This allows us to introduce a revision operation that satisfies all revision postulates. Moreover, we propose a procedure for revising an ontology expressed in an expressive description logic, namely $\mathcal{SHIQ}$, and show that the resulting ontology remains expressible in $\mathcal{SHIQ}$.

1 Introduction

Formalisms based on Description Logics (DLs) such as OWL are widely used to represent ontologies encapsulated in semantics-based applications. An interesting feature of ontologies expressed in DLs (called DL ontologies) is to support automated inference services which allow designers to detect possible errors and allow users to entail new knowledge from ontologies. However, ontologies are not static but evolve over time. If we consider an ontology as a set of statements that describe our understanding about an application domain, it is needed to revise ontology to take into account new knowledge about the domain.

The problem of revising a DL ontology is closely related to the problem of belief revision which has been widely discussed in the literature. Among early works on belief revision, Alchourrón, Gärdenfors and Makinson (AGM) [1] introduced intuitive and plausible constraints (namely AGM postulates) which should be satisfied by any rational belief revision operator. These classical belief revision approaches can be classified into *syntax-based* and *model-based (semantic)* approaches [5].

Syntax-based approaches manipulate directly syntactical entities such as formulas of a knowledge base. To take into account a new formula in preserving consistency, these approaches try to identify other formulas which should be removed. The main issues are that (i) the procedures resulting from these approaches heavily depend on the syntax of knowledge bases, and (ii) the principle of minimal change is not guaranteed since it refers to logical consequences of a

© Springer-Verlag Berlin Heidelberg 2015
M. Davis et al. (Eds.): LPAR-20 2015, LNCS 9450, pp. 575–590, 2015.
DOI: 10.1007/978-3-662-48899-7_40

knowledge base. Despite these issues, there are some syntax-based belief revision operators which have been adapted to revise DL ontologies. Qi and colleagues [10] reformulated the AGM postulates for DL ontologies and they proposed two revision operators by *weakening* assertion axioms and GCIs. However, none of their operators satisfies all the AGM postulates. Ribeiro and Wassermann [11] investigated ontology contraction with Levy identity (i.e. removing an axiom). The absence of axiom negation in DLs has leaded the authors to study ontology *semi-revision* with two different constructions for revising a knowledge base K by an axiom α. The first one ensures that the resulting revised KB is always consistent but α is not necessarily entailed from the resulting revised KB, i.e., success of the revision does not hold. In the second construction, success always holds but consistency of the resulting revised KB is not guaranteed. Thus, the postulates about success and consistency are not simultaneously guaranteed.

Contrary to syntax-based approaches, semantic approaches investigate and manipulate models of ontologies rather than their syntactical entities. The main issues in adapting semantic approaches to DL ontologies are how to define a distance between models and how to compute a revision ontology from the models selected according to the defined distance. In addition, other problems may arise from dealing with models of DL ontologies. First, DL ontologies may have infinitely many models which make impossible to construct a revision ontology from models. Second, models of a DL ontology have usually (possibly infinite) complex structures, which may require a complex definition of distance between two models. Third, there may not exist a unique ontology that admits exactly a given set of models. Despite these problems, there have been many attempts to adapt classical model-based revision approaches to DL ontologies. Qi and Du [9] adapted the well-known Dalal's revision operator [2] for revising terminologies in DL. Their operators that do not depend on a specific DL are defined by using sets of models of KBs. They also showed that their operators satisfy the AGM postulates. However, the authors have not proposed any procedure for computing a revision ontology. Wang and colleagues [13] adapted Satoh's revision operator [12] for revision over DL-Lite ontologies. The authors have introduced a finite structure, namely *feature*, for representing a possibly infinite model.

We will present in this paper a new model-based approach for revision of ontologies in $\mathcal{SHIQ}$, which is an expressive DL. To address the mentioned issues, we use a finite set of finite structures, namely *completion tree*, to represent a possibly infinite set of models of a $\mathcal{SHIQ}$ ontology. These finite structures equipped with a total pre-order allow one to determine semantic difference between two ontologies represented as two sets of models. Indeed, revising an ontology $\mathcal{O}$ by another ontology $\mathcal{O}'$ can be reduced to selecting "appropriate" models from a set of all models admitted by $\mathcal{O}'$ such that the selected models are as close as possible to models of $\mathcal{O}$. The selected models are employed to build a revision ontology of $\mathcal{O}$ by $\mathcal{O}'$. To illustrate the idea behind the construction, we consider the following running example.

Example 1. *Let $\mathcal{O}$ be an ontology that contains a unique axiom:*

$$\top \sqsubseteq \mathsf{Train} \sqcap \mathsf{Carriage} \sqcap \exists \mathsf{isPartOf}.\mathsf{Train} \tag{1}$$

This axiom says that "everything is a train and also a carriage which is a part of a train". A better understanding about the railway domain may lead us to add the following axioms from another ontology $\mathcal{O}'$:

$$\neg\mathsf{Carriage} \sqsubseteq \forall\mathsf{isPartOf}.(\neg\mathsf{Train}) \tag{2}$$

$$\mathsf{Train} \sqsubseteq \mathsf{Carriage} \sqcap \forall\mathsf{isPartOf}.(\neg\mathsf{Train}) \tag{3}$$

The new axioms stipulate that "something that is not a carriage is not a part of any train", and "a train is a carriage which is not a part of any train". The ontology $\mathcal{O} \cup \mathcal{O}'$ is inconsistent since (3) contradicts (1). The goal is to build a new ontology $\mathcal{O}^*$ which is "compatible" with the axioms from $\mathcal{O}'$ such that $\mathcal{O}^*$ is semantically as close as possible to $\mathcal{O}$, that means minimal change. We can check that the following completion tree T_1 yields a model of $\mathcal{O}$.

$$T_1: \quad \textcircled{a}\ \{\mathsf{Train, Carriage}, \exists\mathsf{isPartOf}.\mathsf{Train}\}$$
$$\mathsf{isPartOf} \downarrow$$
$$\textcircled{b}\ \{\mathsf{Train, Carriage}, \exists\mathsf{isPartOf}.\mathsf{Train}\}$$

Similarly, we can check that the two following completion trees yield models of $\mathcal{O}'$.

$$T_1': \quad \textcircled{a}\ \{\neg\mathsf{Train, Carriage}, \exists\mathsf{isPartOf}.\mathsf{Train}\}$$
$$\mathsf{isPartOf} \downarrow$$
$$\textcircled{b}\ \{\mathsf{Train, Carriage}, \forall\mathsf{isPartOf}.(\neg\mathsf{Train})\}$$

$$T_2': \quad \textcircled{a}\ \{\mathsf{Train, Carriage}, \forall\mathsf{isPartOf}.(\neg\mathsf{Train})\}$$

If we define a distance between completion trees based on structural similarity, it would be plausible to say that T_1' is closer to T_1 than T_2'. Therefore, a resulting revision ontology $\mathcal{O}^*$ should admit T_1' rather than T_2'.

Another issue our approach has to deal with is that there may not exist a revision ontology such that (i) it is expressible in the logic that is used for expressing initial ontologies $\mathcal{O}, \mathcal{O}'$, and (ii) it admits *exactly* a set of completion trees as models. For this reason, we borrow from De Giacomo and colleagues the notion of *maximal approximation* [4] which enables us to generate a *semantically minimal* revision ontology such that it admits a precise set of models built from $\mathcal{O}$ and $\mathcal{O}'$.

The present paper is organized as follows. Section 2 describes the DL $\mathcal{SHIQ}$. In Sect. 3 we present a novel tableau algorithm for building a set of completion trees which represents all models of a $\mathcal{SHIQ}$ ontology. Section 4 introduces a distance over a set of completion trees. This distance provides a means to equip a set of completion trees with a total pre-order. This is a crucial point allowing for defining a revision operation which satisfies all revision postulates reformulated for DL ontologies. Based on the defined revision operation, we introduce in Sect. 5 the notion of maximal approximation which allows us to propose a procedure for computing a revision ontology from a set of completion trees. Section 6 describes some techniques for optimizing our procedure. Finally, Sect. 7 consists of a discussion on how to extend our approach to deal with individuals.

2   Preliminaries

In this section, we begin by presenting the syntax and the semantics of $\mathcal{SHIQ}$. Next, we describe some notations which will be useful for constructing a new version of tableau algorithm in the next section.

Definition 1 (Role Hierarchy). *Let* $\mathbf{R}$ *be a non-empty set of* role names *and* $\mathbf{R}_+ \subseteq \mathbf{R}$ *be a set of transitive role names. We use* $\mathbf{R}_1 = \{R^- \mid R \in \mathbf{R}\}$ *to denote a set of inverse roles. Each element of* $\mathbf{R} \cup \mathbf{R}_1$ *is called a* $\mathcal{SHIQ}$-role. *To simplify notations for nested inverse roles, we define a function* $\mathsf{Inv}(S) = R^-$ *if* $S = R$; *and* $\mathsf{Inv}(S) = R$ *if* $S = R^-$ *where* $R \in \mathbf{R}$.

- *A* role inclusion axiom *is of the form* $R \sqsubseteq S$ *for two (possibly inverse)* $\mathcal{SHIQ}$-*roles* R *and* S. *A* role hierarchy $\mathcal{R}$ *is a finite set of role inclusion axioms. A sub-role relation* $\underline{\underline{\sqsubseteq}}$ *is defined as the transitive-reflexive closure of* $\sqsubseteq$ *on* $\mathcal{R}^+ = \mathcal{R} \cup \{\mathsf{Inv}(R) \sqsubseteq \mathsf{Inv}(S) \mid R \sqsubseteq S \in \mathcal{R}\}$. *We define a function* $\mathsf{Trans}(R)$ *which returns* true *iff* R *is a transitive role. More precisely,* $\mathsf{Trans}(R) = true$ *iff* $R \in \mathbf{R}_+$ *or* $\mathsf{Inv}(R) \in \mathbf{R}_+$. *A role* R *is called* simple *w.r.t.* $\mathcal{R}$ *if* $\mathsf{Trans}(R) = \mathsf{false}$.
- *An interpretation* $\mathcal{I} = (\Delta^{\mathcal{I}}, \cdot^{\mathcal{I}})$ *consists of a non-empty set* $\Delta^{\mathcal{I}}$ *(domain) and a function* $\cdot^{\mathcal{I}}$ *which maps each role name to a subset of* $\Delta^{\mathcal{I}} \times \Delta^{\mathcal{I}}$ *such that* $R^{-\mathcal{I}} = \{\langle x, y \rangle \in \Delta^{\mathcal{I}} \times \Delta^{\mathcal{I}} \mid \langle y, x \rangle \in R^{\mathcal{I}}\}$ *for all* $R \in \mathbf{R}$, *and* $\langle x, z \rangle \in S^{\mathcal{I}}, \langle z, y \rangle \in S^{\mathcal{I}}$ *implies* $\langle x, y \rangle \in S^{\mathcal{I}}$ *for each* $S \in \mathbf{R}_+$. *An interpretation* $\mathcal{I}$ *satisfies a role hierarchy* $\mathcal{R}$ *if* $R^{\mathcal{I}} \subseteq S^{\mathcal{I}}$ *for each* $R \sqsubseteq S \in \mathcal{R}$. *Such an interpretation is called a model of* $\mathcal{R}$, *denoted by* $\mathcal{I} \models \mathcal{R}$.   ◁

Definition 2 (Ontology). *Let* $\mathbf{C}$ *be a non-empty set of* concept names. *The set of* $\mathcal{SHIQ}$-concepts *is inductively defined as the smallest set containing all* C *in* $\mathbf{C}$, $\top$, $C \sqcap D$, $C \sqcup D$, $\neg C$, $\exists R.C$, $\forall R.C$, $(\leq n\, S.C)$ *and* $(\geq n\, S.C)$ *where* n *is a positive integer,* C *and* D *are* $\mathcal{SHIQ}$-*concepts,* R *is a* $\mathcal{SHIQ}$-*role and* S *is a simple role w.r.t. a role hierarchy. We write* $\bot$ *for* $\neg\top$. *The interpretation function* $\cdot^{\mathcal{I}}$ *of an interpretation* $\mathcal{I} = (\Delta^{\mathcal{I}}, \cdot^{\mathcal{I}})$ *maps each concept name to a subset of* $\Delta^{\mathcal{I}}$ *such that* $\top^{\mathcal{I}} = \Delta^{\mathcal{I}}$, $(C \sqcap D)^{\mathcal{I}} = C^{\mathcal{I}} \cap D^{\mathcal{I}}$, $(C \sqcup D)^{\mathcal{I}} = C^{\mathcal{I}} \cup D^{\mathcal{I}}$, $(\neg C)^{\mathcal{I}} = \Delta^{\mathcal{I}} \backslash C^{\mathcal{I}}$, $(\exists R.C)^{\mathcal{I}} = \{x \in \Delta^{\mathcal{I}} \mid \exists y \in \Delta^{\mathcal{I}}, \langle x, y \rangle \in R^{\mathcal{I}} \text{ and } y \in C^{\mathcal{I}}\}$, $(\forall R.C)^{\mathcal{I}} = \{x \in \Delta^{\mathcal{I}} \mid \forall y \in \Delta^{\mathcal{I}}, \langle x, y \rangle \in R^{\mathcal{I}} \Rightarrow y \in C^{\mathcal{I}}\}$, $(\geq n\, S.C)^{\mathcal{I}} = \{x \in \Delta^{\mathcal{I}} \mid |\{y \in C^{\mathcal{I}} \mid \langle x, y \rangle \in S^{\mathcal{I}}\}| \geq n\}$, $(\leq n\, S.C)^{\mathcal{I}} = \{x \in \Delta^{\mathcal{I}} \mid |\{y \in C^{\mathcal{I}} \mid \langle x, y \rangle \in S^{\mathcal{I}}\}| \leq n\}$ *where* $|S|$ *stands for the cardinality of a set* S. *An axiom* $C \sqsubseteq D$ *is called a* general concept inclusion (GCI) *where* C, D *are (possibly complex)* $\mathcal{SHIQ}$-*concepts, and a finite set of GCIs is called a* terminology $\mathcal{T}$. *An interpretation* $\mathcal{I}$ *satisfies a GCI* $C \sqsubseteq D$, *denoted* $\mathcal{I} \models (C \sqsubseteq D)$, *if* $C^{\mathcal{I}} \subseteq D^{\mathcal{I}}$ *and* $\mathcal{I}$ *satisfies a terminology* $\mathcal{T}$ *if* $\mathcal{I}$ *satisfies each GCI in* $\mathcal{T}$. *Such an interpretation is called a model of* $\mathcal{T}$, *denoted by* $\mathcal{I} \models \mathcal{T}$.

A pair $(\mathcal{T}, \mathcal{R})$ *is called a* $\mathcal{SHIQ}$ ontology, *denoted* $\mathcal{O} = (\mathcal{T}, \mathcal{R})$ *if* $\mathcal{R}$ *is a* $\mathcal{SHIQ}$ *role hierarchy and* $\mathcal{T}$ *is a* $\mathcal{SHIQ}$ *terminology. An ontology* $\mathcal{O} = (\mathcal{T}, \mathcal{R})$ *is said to be* consistent *if there is a model* $\mathcal{I}$ *of both* $\mathcal{T}$ *and* $\mathcal{R}$, *i.e.,* $\mathcal{I} \models \mathcal{T}$ *and* $\mathcal{I} \models \mathcal{R}$. *Additionally, we use* $\mathsf{Mod}(\mathcal{O})$ *to denote all the models of an ontology* $\mathcal{O}$, *and* $\mathcal{S}(\mathcal{O}) = \mathbf{R} \cup \mathbf{C}$ *to denote the* signature *of an ontology* $\mathcal{O}$ *where* $\mathbf{R}$ *is the set of role names occurring in* $\mathcal{O}$, *and* $\mathbf{C}$ *is the set of concept names occurring in* $\mathcal{T}$.   ◁

For the ease of construction, we assume all concepts to be in *negation normal form* (NNF), i.e., negation occurs only in front of concept names. Any $\mathcal{SHIQ}$-concept can be transformed to an equivalent one in NNF by using De Morgan's laws and some equivalences [6]. For a concept C, we denote the nnf of C by $\mathrm{nnf}(C)$ and the nnf of $\neg C$ by $\dot{\neg} C$. In the remaining of this section, we introduce some notations which will be useful for the next sections.

Definition 3 (Sub-concepts). *Let* $\mathcal{O} = (\mathcal{T}, \mathcal{R})$ *be a* $\mathcal{SHIQ}$ *ontology with* $\mathcal{S}(\mathcal{O}) = \mathbf{R} \cup \mathbf{C}$. *A set* $\mathrm{sub}(\mathcal{O})$ *is inductively defined as follows:*

$\mathrm{sub}(\mathcal{O}) = \mathrm{sub}(\mathcal{T}) \cup \{\dot{\neg} C \mid C \in \mathrm{sub}(\mathcal{T})\};$

$\mathrm{sub}(\mathcal{T}) = \bigcup\limits_{C \sqsubseteq D \in \mathcal{T}} \mathrm{sub}(\mathrm{nnf}(\neg C \sqcup D));$

$\mathrm{sub}(C) = \{C\} \; \textit{if} \; C \in \mathbf{C}; \; \mathrm{sub}(\neg C) = \mathrm{sub}(\dot{\neg} C);$

$\mathrm{sub}(C) = \mathrm{sub}(E) \cup \mathrm{sub}(F) \; \textit{if} \; C \in \{E \sqcap F, E \sqcup F\};$

$\mathrm{sub}(C) = \{C\} \cup \{\exists R'.E \mid R \trianglelefteq R'\} \cup \mathrm{sub}(E) \; \textit{if} \; C = \exists R.E;$

$\mathrm{sub}(C) = \{C\} \cup \{\forall R'.E \mid R \trianglelefteq R'\} \cup \mathrm{sub}(E) \; \textit{if} \; C = \forall R.E;$

$\mathrm{sub}(C) = \{C\} \cup \{\geq n R'.E \mid R \trianglelefteq R'\} \cup \mathrm{sub}(E) \; \textit{if} \; C = (\geq n R.E);$

$\mathrm{sub}(C) = \{C\} \cup \mathrm{sub}(E) \; \textit{if} \; C = (\leq n R.E).$ ◁

Note that all concepts in the form of disjunctions and of conjunctions are replaced with their disjuncts and conjuncts. Additionally, $\mathrm{sub}(\mathcal{O})$ includes (i) all sub-concepts occurring in $\mathcal{O}$, (ii) concepts of the form $\exists R'.C$, (resp. $\forall R'.C$ and $(\geq nR'.E)$) if $\exists R.C$ (resp. $\forall R.C$, $(\geq nR.E)$) occurs in $\mathcal{O}$ with $R \trianglelefteq R'$, and (iii) the negation of each concept added to $\mathrm{sub}(\mathcal{O})$.

To avoid processing conjunctions and disjunctions at top-level of a concept C (i.e. those that do not appear in the filler of a universal, existential, numbering restrictions occurring in C) when constructing a completion tree for an ontology, we need a function $\mathrm{Flat}(C)$ which returns a set of subsets of $\mathrm{sub}(C)$.

Definition 4 (Flattening). *Let* C *be a* $\mathcal{SHIQ}$ *concept. We define a function* $\mathrm{Flat}(C)$ *which returns a set of subsets of* $\mathrm{sub}(C)$ *as follows:*

1. *If* C *is a concept name or* C *is neither any conjunction nor any disjunction, i.e.,* $C = \exists R.D$, *or* $C = \forall R.D$, *or* $C = (\leq nR.D)$, *or* $C = (\geq nR.D)$, *we define* $\mathrm{Flat}(C) = \{\{C\}\};$
2. *If* $C = E \sqcap F$ *such that* E *and* F *are not a disjunction, we define* $\mathrm{Flat}(C) = \{\mathrm{Ser}(\mathrm{Flat}(E)) \cup \mathrm{Ser}(\mathrm{Flat}(F))\}$ *where* $\mathrm{Ser}(\mathrm{Flat}(F)) = \bigcup_{W \in \mathrm{Flat}(F)} W;$
3. *If* $C = E \sqcup F$, *we define* $\mathrm{Flat}(C) = \mathrm{Flat}(E) \cup \mathrm{Flat}(F);$
4. *If* $C = E \sqcap F$ *such that* $X = E' \sqcup E''$ *and* Y *is not a disjunction with* $X, Y \in \{E, F\}$ *and* $X \neq Y$, *we define* $\mathrm{Flat}(C) = \mathrm{Flat}(Y \sqcap E') \cup \mathrm{Flat}(Y \sqcap E'');$
5. *Otherwise, i.e.,* $C = E \sqcap F$ *such that* $E = E' \sqcup E''$ *and* $F = F' \sqcup F''$, *we define* $\mathrm{Flat}(C) = \mathrm{Flat}(F' \sqcap E') \cup \mathrm{Flat}(F'' \sqcap E') \cup \mathrm{Flat}(F' \sqcap E'') \cup \mathrm{Flat}(F'' \sqcap E'').$

◁

We can check that (i) each element $X \in \mathrm{Flat}(C)$ is a subset of $\mathrm{sub}(C)$ and does not contain any conjunction and disjunction at top-level; (ii) if C does not contain any conjunction and disjunction at top-level, $\mathrm{Flat}(C) = \{\{C\}\}$; (iii) if C

does not contain any disjunction at top-level, $\mathsf{Flat}(C)$ contains a unique subset of $\mathsf{sub}(C)$ that includes all conjuncts of C at top-level; (iv) if C does not contain any conjunction at top-level and C is a disjunction, all disjuncts of C must appear in distinct elements of $\mathsf{Flat}(C)$.

3 A New Tableau Algorithm for $\mathcal{SHIQ}$

Horrocks, Sattler and Tobies [6] have proposed a tableau algorithm for checking consistency of a $\mathcal{SHIQ}$ ontology $\mathcal{O}$. This algorithm attempts to construct a finite labeled graph, namely completion tree, from which one can devise a model for $\mathcal{O}$. The algorithm returns "YES" if such a completion tree is built, and returns "NO" if it fails to build such a completion tree after considering all possibly non-deterministic cases. In this section, we present an algorithm with new rules which allow for constructing a set of all completion trees from each of which one can devise a model for $\mathcal{O}$.

Definition 5 (Completion Tree). *Let* $\mathcal{O} = (\mathcal{T}, \mathcal{R})$ *be a* $\mathcal{SHIQ}$ *ontology. A completion tree for* $\mathcal{O}$ *is a tree* $T = \langle V, E, L, \hat{x} \rangle$ *where*

- V *is a set of nodes containing a root node* $\hat{x} \in V$. *Each node* $x \in V$ *is labeled with a function* L *such that* $L(x) \subseteq \mathsf{sub}(\mathcal{O})$. *In addition,* $\neq$ *is a symmetric binary relation over* V. E *is a set of edges. Each edge* $\langle x, y \rangle \in E$ *is labeled with a set* $L(\langle x, y \rangle)$ *which contains (possibly inverse)* $\mathcal{SHIQ}$ *roles occurring in* $\mathcal{O}$.
- *If two nodes* x *and* y *are connected by an edge* $\langle x, y \rangle$, *then* y *is called a* successor *of* x, *denoted* $y \in \mathsf{succ}(x)$, *and* x *is called a* predecessor *of* y, *denoted* $x \in \mathsf{pred}(x)$; *ancestor is the transitive closure of* predecessor. *A node* y *is called an* R-successor *of* x, *denoted* $y \in \mathsf{succ}_R(x)$ *if, for some role* R' *with* $R' \sqsubseteq R$, $R' \in L(\langle x, y \rangle)$; x *is called an* R-predecessor *of* y, *denoted* $x = \mathsf{pred}_R(y)$, *if* y *is an* R-successor *of* x. *A node* y *is called an* R-neighbor *of* x *if* y *is an* R-successor *or* x *is an* $\mathsf{Inv}(R)$-successor *of* y. *For a node* x *and a role* S, *we define the set* $S^T(x, C)$ *of* x*'s* S-neighbors *as follows:* $S^T(x, C) = \{y \in V \mid y$ *is an* S-neighbor *of* x *and* $X \subseteq L(y)$ *for some* $X \in \mathsf{Flat}(C)\}$.
- *A node* x *is called* blocked *by* y *if it has ancestors* x', y *and* y' *such that (i)* x *is a successor of* x' *and* y *is a successor of* y', *(ii)* $L(x) = L(y)$, $L(x') = L(y')$, *and (iii)* $L(\langle x', x \rangle) = L(\langle y', y \rangle)$.
- T *is said to contain a* clash *if (i) there is some node* $x \in V$ *such that either* $\{A, \neg A\} \subseteq L(x)$ *for some concept name* $A \in \mathbf{C}$, *or (ii)* $(\leq nS.C) \in L(x)$ *and there are* $(n+1)$ S-neighbors $y_1, \cdots, y_{n+1}$ *of* x *with* $y_i \neq y_j$ *and* $X \subseteq L(y_i)$ *for some* $X \in \mathsf{Flat}(C)$ *and all* $1 \leq i < j \leq (n+1)$. $\lhd$

New Tableau Algorithm. Based on the work of Horrocks, Sattler and Tobies [6], we design a new tableau algorithm by using the expansion rules in Fig. 1. This algorithm starts by creating a root node and applies the sat-rule to the root node (sat stands for *saturate*). Applications of generating rules ($\exists$- and $\geq$-rules) can create fresh nodes whose label is entirely filled by an application of the sat-rule to each one, or partially filled by one of the $\forall$-, $\forall_+$-rules. The algorithm applies the sat-rule to a node x by choosing a set $S \subseteq \mathsf{sub}(\mathcal{O})$ and

∃-**rule:** if 1. $\exists S.C \in L(x)$, x is not blocked, and
   2. x has no S-neighbor y s.t. $X \subseteq L(y)$ for some $X \in \mathsf{Flat}(C)$
  then create a new node y with $L(\langle x, y \rangle) := \{S\}$ and $L(y) := X$ for some $X \in \mathsf{Flat}(C)$.

∀-**rule:** if 1. $\forall S.C \in L(x)$, and
   2. there is an S-neighbor y of x s.t. $X \not\subseteq L(y)$ for all $X \in \mathsf{Flat}(C)$
  then $L(y) := L(y) \cup X$ for some $X \in \mathsf{Flat}(C)$.

∀₊-**rule:** if 1. $\forall S.C \in L(x)$,
   2. there is an R with $\mathsf{Trans}(R)$ s.t. $R \sqsubseteq S$, and
   3. there is an R-neighbor y of x s.t. $\forall R.C \notin L(y)$
  then $L(y) := L(y) \cup \{\forall R.C\}$.

≥-**rule:** if 1. $(\geq nS.C) \in L(x)$, x is not blocked, and
   2. x has no n S-neighbors $y_1, \cdots, y_n$ such that $X \subseteq L(y_i)$ for some $X \in \mathsf{Flat}(C)$
   and $y_i \neq y_j$ for $0 \leq i < j \leq n$
  then create n new nodes $y_1, \cdots, y_n$ with $L(\langle x, y_i \rangle) := \{S\}$,
   $L(y_i) := X$ for some $X \in \mathsf{Flat}(C)$ and $y_i \neq y_j$ for $1 \leq i < j \leq n$.

≤-**rule:** if 1. $(\leq nS.C) \in L(x)$,
   2. x has $n + 1$ S-neighbors $y_0, \ldots, y_n$ s.t. $X \subseteq L(y_i)$ for some $X \in \mathsf{Flat}(C)$,
   3. there are two S-neighbors y, z of x with $X_1 \subseteq L(y)$, $X_2 \subseteq L(z)$
   for some $X_1, X_2 \in \mathsf{Flat}(C)$, y is not an ancestor of z, and not $y \neq z$
  then (i) $L(z) := L(z) \cup L(y)$ and $L(\langle x, y \rangle) := \emptyset$
   (ii) if z is an ancestor of x
    then $L(\langle z, x \rangle) := L(\langle z, x \rangle) \cup \{\mathsf{Inv}(R) \mid R \in L(\langle x, y \rangle)\}$;
    else $L(\langle x, z \rangle) := L(\langle x, z \rangle) \cup L(\langle x, y \rangle)$, and
   (iii) add $u \neq z$ for all u such that $u \neq y$.

sat-**rule:** if sat-rule has never been applied to x
  then choose a subset $S \subseteq \mathsf{sub}(\mathcal{O})$ s.t. $L(x) \cup \displaystyle\bigcup_{X \in \mathsf{Flat}(\mathsf{nnf}(\neg C \sqcup D)), C \sqsubseteq D \in \mathcal{T}} X \subseteq S$, and
  set $L(x) := S \cup \bar{S}$ where $\bar{S} = \{\neg C \mid C \in \mathsf{sub}(\mathcal{O}) \setminus S\}$

Fig. 1. Expansion rules for $\mathcal{SHIQ}$

adding S to $L(x)$ such that S covers the existing $L(x)$ and a subset of concepts being flattened from $\neg C \sqcup D$ for each axiom $C \sqsubseteq D$ in $\mathcal{O}$. After applying the sat-rule to a node, its label is no longer changed. This explains why usual rules in a standard tableau algorithm such as $\sqsubseteq$- and ch-rules become useless when allowing for the sat-rule. In addition, the procedure Flat makes the usual $\sqcap$- and $\sqcup$-rules unnecessary since the behavior of these rules is straightforwardly integrated into Flat which is non-deterministic as well. A completion tree is *clash-free* if none of its nodes contains a clash, and it is *complete* if no rule from Fig. 1 is applicable. Note that the sat-rule in Fig. 1 can be extended in such a way that it chooses a subset S from an arbitrary set sub including $\mathsf{sub}(\mathcal{O})$. This flexibility is applied for building completion trees of an ontology $\mathcal{O}$ with importing sub-concepts from another ontology $\mathcal{O}'$, or inversely. This importing is needed for revising $\mathcal{O}$ by $\mathcal{O}'$ in a case where $\mathcal{O}'$ contains symbols not included in $\mathcal{O}$, or where the information of $\mathcal{O}$ needs to be kept as much as possible in revision ontology. As a direct consequence of the sat-rule's definition, its behavior is very non-deterministic since the number of possibilities for choosing a subset from sub is bounded by an exponential function in the cardinality of sub. Moreover, completion trees constructed by the new tableau algorithm with the rules in Fig. 1 allow us to efficiently define a distance between them since node labels are optimized by removing unnecessary concepts (in the form of conjunction or disjunction at top-level) from the procedure Flat.

Lemma 1 (Correctness and Completeness). *Let $\mathcal{O}$ be a $\mathcal{SHIQ}$ ontology.*

1. *The tableau algorithm with the expansion rules in Fig. 1 terminates.*
2. *If the tableau algorithm with the expansion rules in Fig. 1 can be applied to $\mathcal{O}$ such that it yields a complete and clash-free completion tree, then $\mathcal{O}$ is consistent;*
3. *If $\mathcal{O}$ is consistent then the tableau algorithm with the expansion rules in Fig. 1 can be applied to $\mathcal{O}$ such that it yields a complete and clash-free completion tree.*

Proof Sketch. We use the same technique by Horrock, Sattler and Tobies [6] to show termination, soundness and completeness of the algorithm. First, we define a tableau for a $\mathcal{SHIQ}$ ontology $\mathcal{O}$. Next, we show that $\mathcal{O}$ has a tableau iff $\mathcal{O}$ is consistent. Termination of the algorithm is ensured by the blocking condition and monotonicity of the construction of a completion tree T (i.e. we never remove something from T). From the blocking condition, it can be shown that the size of T is bounded by a doubly exponential function in the size of $\mathcal{O}$. To prove soundness, one can devise a tableau from a completion tree T by unraveling. This process generates descendants of blocked nodes by replicating descendants of blocking nodes. The obtained tableau is of the tree-like structure that may be infinite. To prove completeness, we use a tableau for $\mathcal{O}$ to guide non-deterministic expansion rules to choose right concepts (or right successors) for building a complete and clash-free completion tree T.   □

The following theorem is a consequence of Lemma 1.

Theorem 1. *Let $\mathcal{O}$ be a $\mathcal{SHIQ}$ ontology. The tableau algorithm with the expansion rules in Fig. 1 can decide consistency of $\mathcal{O}$ in doubly exponential time in the size of $\mathcal{O}$.*

Notation 1 (Tree-Like Model). *Let $\mathcal{O}$ be a $\mathcal{SHIQ}$ ontology. A complete and clash-free completion tree T that is built by applying the tableau algorithm with the expansion rules in Fig. 1 to $\mathcal{O}$ is called a* tree-like model. *According to Lemma 1, for each complete and clash-free completion tree T it is possible to obtain a model, denoted $\mathcal{I}(T)$, by unraveling. In this case, a node of T may be replicated for an infinite number of individuals of the model. Given an axiom $C \sqsubseteq D$, define $\mathcal{I}(T) \models (C \sqsubseteq D)$ if $C^{\mathcal{I}(T)} \subseteq D^{\mathcal{I}(T)}$.*

Sets of Tree-Like Models. Contrary to standard tableau algorithms which terminate when a tree-like model is found, the new tableau algorithm has to consider all non-deterministic cases and build all tree-like models for $\mathcal{O}$. We use $\mathsf{MT}(\mathcal{O})$ to denote a set of all tree-like models for a $\mathcal{SHIQ}$ ontology $\mathcal{O}$. We can straightforwardly extend $\mathsf{MT}(\mathcal{O})$ to $\mathsf{MT}(\mathcal{O}, \mathsf{sub}(\mathcal{O}'))$ as follows. The set $\mathsf{MT}(\mathcal{O}, \mathsf{sub}(\mathcal{O}'))$ is built by the new tableau algorithm for $\mathcal{O}$ with an extra set of concepts $\mathsf{sub}(\mathcal{O}')$ that is imported into $\mathsf{sub}(\mathcal{O})$ when applying the sat-rule. This enables one to import additional concepts into node labels of a completion tree for $\mathcal{O}$ while respecting the axioms of $\mathcal{O}$. Note that we do not import any semantic constraint from $\mathcal{O}'$ to completion trees in $\mathsf{MT}(\mathcal{O})$ when building $\mathsf{MT}(\mathcal{O}, \mathsf{sub}(\mathcal{O}'))$. What we really carry out in this construction is to import into $\mathcal{O}$ the signature of $\mathcal{O}'$ with formulas written in that signature. This importation may change $\mathsf{MT}(\mathcal{O})$ but does never change consistency of $\mathcal{O}$.

The following corollary is a direct consequence of Theorem 1.

Corollary 1. *Let $\mathcal{O}$ and $\mathcal{O}'$ be two consistent $\mathcal{SHIQ}$ ontologies. It holds that*

1. $\mathsf{MT}(\mathcal{O}) \neq \emptyset$ *iff* $\mathsf{Mod}(\mathcal{O}) \neq \emptyset$.
2. $\mathsf{MT}(\mathcal{O} \cup \mathcal{O}') = \mathsf{MT}(\mathcal{O}, \mathsf{sub}(\mathcal{O}')) \cap \mathsf{MT}(\mathcal{O}', \mathsf{sub}(\mathcal{O}))$.

Corollary 1 affirms semantic equivalence between $\mathsf{Mod}(\mathcal{O})$ and $\mathsf{MT}(\mathcal{O})$. This result allows us to replace a possibly infinite set $\mathsf{Mod}(\mathcal{O})$ with a finite set $\mathsf{MT}(\mathcal{O})$ in constructions presented in the following sections.

4 Revision Operation

We begin this section by introducing a distance between two completion trees which allows one to talk about similarity between two ontologies. This distance is defined for two completion trees which are isomorphic.

Definition 6 (Isomorphism). *Let $T = \langle V, L, E, \widehat{x} \rangle$ and $T' = \langle V', L', E', \widehat{x}' \rangle$ be two completion trees.*

- *T and T' are isomorphic if there is a bijection π from V to V' such that $\pi(\widehat{x}) = \widehat{x}'$; and for each $x \in V$ with $\pi(x) = y$, we have $\pi(\mathsf{succ}(x)) = \mathsf{succ}(y)$. In this case, we say that π is an isomorphism between T and T'.*
- *T and T' are equivalent if there is an isomorphism π between T and T' s.t. $L(x) = L'(\pi(x))$ for each $x \in V$, and $L(\langle x, y \rangle) = L'(\langle \pi(x), \pi(y) \rangle)$ for each $\langle x, y \rangle \in E$.* ◁

Note that we can always obtain such an isomorphism between two completion trees by adding empty nodes and edges to completion trees since node and edge labels are ignored in the definition of isomorphisms. In the following, a distance between two isomorphic completion trees can be computed by extending the definition of symmetric difference $\triangle$. Recall that $S \triangle S' = (S \cup S') \setminus (S \cap S')$ for any two sets S and S'.

Definition 7 (Distance). *Let $T = \langle V, L, E, \widehat{x} \rangle$ and $T' = \langle V', L', E', \widehat{x}' \rangle$ be two completion trees. Let $\Pi(T, T')$ be the set of all isomorphisms between T and T'. A distance between T and T', denoted $T \triangle T'$, is defined as follows:*

$$T \triangle T' = \min_{\pi \in \Pi(T, T')} \{ \max_{x \in V} (|L(x) \triangle L'(\pi(x))|) \quad +$$
$$\max_{\langle x, y \rangle \in E} (|L(\langle x, y \rangle) \triangle L'(\langle \pi(x), \pi(y) \rangle)|) \} \qquad ◁$$

The function max in Definition 7 returns the greatest difference of node labels (or edge labels) from all pairs of nodes $x, \pi(x)$ with $x \in V$ (or pairs of edges $\langle x, y \rangle, \langle \pi(x), \pi(y) \rangle$ with $\langle x, y \rangle \in E$) for some isomorphism π between two trees. If max is removed from Definition 7, a null distance does not imply identity of two trees in question. We can check that $\triangle$ is a distance over a set of isomorphic trees. Indeed, (**symmetry**) $T \triangle T' = T' \triangle T$ is due to commutativity of the operator $S \triangle S'$; (**identity**) $T \triangle T' = 0$ iff $T = T'$ is a consequence of the fact that $S \triangle S' = \emptyset$ iff $S = S'$ for all sets S, S'; (**triangle inequality**) $T \triangle T'' \leq (T \triangle T') + (T' \triangle T'')$ is a consequence of the fact that $S \triangle S'' \subseteq (S \triangle S') \cup (S' \triangle S'')$ for all sets S, S', S''. In addition, we can show that this distance yields a total pre-order over a set of isomorphic completion trees. To do this, we define a relation "$T \leq T'$" over a set of isomorphic completion trees, which includes a tree T_0 containing only empty labels, as follows: $T \leq T'$ if $T_0 \triangle T \leq T_0 \triangle T'$. The relation "$\leq$" is a total pre-order over a set of isomorphic completion trees since it is transitive, total and reflexive.

All of the above notions provide sufficiently elements to define a revision operation for a $\mathcal{SHIQ}$ ontology $\mathcal{O}$ by another ontology $\mathcal{O}'$. This operation determines a set of models a revision ontology should admit. Under the hypothesis which says that the semantics of an ontology $\mathcal{O}$ is characterized by $\mathsf{Mod}(\mathcal{O})$, Corollary 1 allows us to represent the semantics of $\mathcal{O}$ by using a finite set $\mathsf{MT}(\mathcal{O})$ instead of a possibly infinite set $\mathsf{Mod}(\mathcal{O})$.

Definition 8 (Revision Operation). *Let $\mathcal{O}$ and $\mathcal{O}'$ be two consistent ontologies in $\mathcal{SHIQ}$. A set of tree-like models of the revision of $\mathcal{O}$ by $\mathcal{O}'$, denoted $\mathsf{MT}(\mathcal{O}, \mathcal{O}')$, is defined as follows:*

$$\mathsf{MT}(\mathcal{O}, \mathcal{O}') = \{T \in \mathsf{MT}(\mathcal{O}', \mathsf{sub}(\mathcal{O})) \mid \exists T_0 \in \mathsf{MT}(\mathcal{O}, \mathsf{sub}(\mathcal{O}')),$$
$$\forall T' \in \mathsf{MT}(\mathcal{O}', \mathsf{sub}(\mathcal{O})), T'' \in \mathsf{MT}(\mathcal{O}, \mathsf{sub}(\mathcal{O}')) : T \triangle T_0 \leq T' \triangle T''\} \quad \triangleleft$$

Intuitively, among the tree-like models in $\mathsf{MT}(\mathcal{O}', \mathsf{sub}(\mathcal{O}))$, $\mathsf{MT}(\mathcal{O}, \mathcal{O}')$ retains only those which are closest to tree-like models from $\mathsf{MT}(\mathcal{O}, \mathsf{sub}(\mathcal{O}'))$ thanks to the operator $T_1 \triangle T_2$ that characterizes the difference between T_1 and T_2.

Example 2. *Reconsider Example 1. By applying the new tableau algorithm for $\mathcal{O}$, the set $\mathsf{MT}(\mathcal{O}, \mathsf{sub}(\mathcal{O}'))$ contains a unique tree-like model T_1 as described in Example 1. Similarly, the set $\mathsf{MT}(\mathcal{O}', \mathsf{sub}(\mathcal{O}))$ contains 4 tree-like models two of which are T_1' and T_2' described in Example 1, and two others T_3' and T_4' have a unique root node $\{a'\}$ whose label is (T_3'): $L_3(a') = \{\neg\mathsf{Train}, \mathsf{Carriage}, \forall\mathsf{isPartOf}.(\neg\mathsf{Train})\}$, and (T_4'): $L_4(a') = \{\neg\mathsf{Train}, \neg\mathsf{Carriage}, \forall\mathsf{isPartOf}.(\neg\mathsf{Train})\}$. According to Definition 7 (distance), we have $T_1' \triangle T_1 = 2$ that is minimal. Thus, $\mathsf{MT}(\mathcal{O}, \mathcal{O}')$ contains a unique tree-like model T_1'.*

As mentioned in Sect. 1, our goal is to propose a revision operation that ensures the principle of minimal change introduced by Alchourrón, Gärdenfors and Makinson [1] as postulates in belief revision framework. Katsuno and Mendelzon [7] have rephrased these postulates for propositional knowledge bases, namely

(R1)–(R6), and shown that the existence of a total pre-order over models of a propositional knowledge base is equivalent to (R1)–(R6). The argument of the proof has not required any specific structure of models of a propositional knowledge base.

The revision operation according to Definition 8 that is based on the total pre-order "$\leq$" over tree-like models provides directly satisfaction of the principle of minimal change. Indeed, $\mathsf{MT}(\mathcal{O}, \mathcal{O}')$ retains only tree-like models in $\mathsf{MT}(\mathcal{O}', \mathsf{sub}(\mathcal{O}))$ which are closest to tree-like models in $\mathsf{MT}(\mathcal{O}, \mathsf{sub}(\mathcal{O}'))$ according to the distance "$\triangle$" yielding the total pre-order "$\leq$". This observation allows us to get straightforwardly the result saying that revision postulates imply a total pre-order "$\leq$" over tree-like models, since we consider only models such as tree-like models over which a total pre-order exists already. What remains to be proved is that the revision operation in Definition 8 satisfies revision postulates. To do this, we use the revision postulates (G1)–(G6) that were formulated by Qi, Liu and Bell [9] for DL ontologies with sets of ontology models $\mathsf{Mod}(\mathcal{O})$ and $\mathsf{Mod}(\mathcal{O}')$. To provide a precise idea about how the postulates (G1)–(G6) are translated into those in our setting, the following postulate (G2) is taken from the Qi, Liu and Bell's paper [9]:

(G2) If $\mathsf{Mod}(\mathcal{O}) \cap \mathsf{Mod}(\mathcal{O}') \neq \emptyset$, then $\mathsf{Mod}(\mathcal{O} \circ \mathcal{O}') = \mathsf{Mod}(\mathcal{O}) \cap \mathsf{Mod}(\mathcal{O}')$
where revision ontology of $\mathcal{O}$ by $\mathcal{O}'$ is denoted by $\mathcal{O} \circ \mathcal{O}'$. According to Corollary 1 and Definition 8, we can replace $\mathsf{Mod}(\mathcal{O})$ and $\mathsf{Mod}(\mathcal{O} \circ \mathcal{O}')$ with $\mathsf{MT}(\mathcal{O}, \mathsf{sub}(\mathcal{O}'))$ and $\mathsf{MT}(\mathcal{O}, \mathcal{O}')$, respectively, to obtain revision postulates that refer only to computable structures. Indeed, the postulates (G1)–(G6) by Qi, Liu and Bell can be rephrased in our setting as follows.

(P1) $\mathcal{I}(T) \models \alpha$ for each tree-like model $T \in \mathsf{MT}(\mathcal{O}, \mathcal{O}')$ and each axiom $\alpha \in \mathcal{O}'$
(P2) If $\mathsf{MT}(\mathcal{O}, \mathsf{sub}(\mathcal{O}')) \cap \mathsf{MT}(\mathcal{O}', \mathsf{sub}(\mathcal{O})) \neq \emptyset$,
   then $\mathsf{MT}(\mathcal{O}, \mathcal{O}') = \mathsf{MT}(\mathcal{O}, \mathsf{sub}(\mathcal{O}')) \cap \mathsf{MT}(\mathcal{O}', \mathsf{sub}(\mathcal{O}))$
(P3) If $\mathcal{O}'$ is consistent then $\mathsf{MT}(\mathcal{O}, \mathcal{O}') \neq \emptyset$
(P4) If $\mathsf{MT}(\mathcal{O}_1, \mathsf{sub}(\mathcal{O}_1')) = \mathsf{MT}(\mathcal{O}_2, \mathsf{sub}(\mathcal{O}_2'))$ and
   $\mathsf{MT}(\mathcal{O}_1', \mathsf{sub}(\mathcal{O}_1)) = \mathsf{MT}(\mathcal{O}_2', \mathsf{sub}(\mathcal{O}_2))$, then $\mathsf{MT}(\mathcal{O}_1, \mathcal{O}_1') = \mathsf{MT}(\mathcal{O}_2, \mathcal{O}_2')$
(P5) $\mathsf{MT}(\mathcal{O}, \mathcal{O}') \cap \mathsf{MT}(\mathcal{O}'', \mathsf{sub}(\mathcal{O}) \cup \mathsf{sub}(\mathcal{O}')) \subseteq \mathsf{MT}(\mathcal{O}, \mathcal{O}' \cup \mathcal{O}'')$
(P6) If $\mathsf{MT}(\mathcal{O}, \mathcal{O}') \cap \mathsf{MT}(\mathcal{O}'', \mathsf{sub}(\mathcal{O}) \cup \mathsf{sub}(\mathcal{O}')) \neq \emptyset$,
   then $\mathsf{MT}(\mathcal{O}, \mathcal{O}' \cup \mathcal{O}'') \subseteq \mathsf{MT}(\mathcal{O}, \mathcal{O}') \cap \mathsf{MT}(\mathcal{O}'', \mathsf{sub}(\mathcal{O}) \cup \mathsf{sub}(\mathcal{O}'))$

Intuitively, (P1) guarantees that all axioms in the new ontology $\mathcal{O}'$ can be inferred from the result of revision. (P2) says that the initial ontology $\mathcal{O}$ does not be changed if there is no conflict. (P3) is a condition preventing a revision from introducing unwarranted inconsistency. (P4) says that the revision operation should be independent of the syntax of ontologies. The principle of minimal change is ensured by (P5) and (P6) since they allow one to devise a total pre-order over tree-like models [7]. We are able to prove that all postulates always hold in our setting.

Theorem 2. *The revision operation* $\mathsf{MT}(\mathcal{O}, \mathcal{O}')$ *described in Definition 8 satisfies the postulates (P1)–(P6).*

Proof Sketch. **(P1)**: it can be proved from Definition 8 that says that $\mathsf{MT}(\mathcal{O}, \mathcal{O}') \subseteq \mathsf{MT}(\mathcal{O}', \mathsf{sub}(\mathcal{O}))$. **(P2)**: By Definition 8, if $\mathsf{MT}(\mathcal{O}, \mathsf{sub}(\mathcal{O}')) \cap \mathsf{MT}(\mathcal{O}', \mathsf{sub}(\mathcal{O})) \neq \emptyset$, $\mathsf{MT}(\mathcal{O}, \mathcal{O}')$ retains uniquely the tree-like models which belongs to the intersection of $\mathsf{MT}(\mathcal{O}, \mathsf{sub}(\mathcal{O}'))$ and $\mathsf{MT}(\mathcal{O}', \mathsf{sub}(\mathcal{O}))$ since $T' \triangle T' = 0$ for each T' belonging to this intersection. **(P3)**: By Definition 8, $\mathsf{MT}(\mathcal{O}, \mathcal{O}')$ is never empty if $\mathsf{MT}(\mathcal{O}', \mathsf{sub}(\mathcal{O}))$ is not empty. **(P4)**: a direct consequence of Definition 8. **(P5)**: Let $T' \in \mathsf{MT}(\mathcal{O}, \mathcal{O}') \cap \mathsf{MT}(\mathcal{O}'', \mathsf{sub}(\mathcal{O}) \cup \mathsf{sub}(\mathcal{O}'))$. By Definition 8, $T' \in \mathsf{MT}(\mathcal{O}' \cup \mathcal{O}'', \mathsf{sub}(\mathcal{O}) \cup \mathsf{sub}(\mathcal{O}') \cup \mathsf{sub}(\mathcal{O}'')) \subseteq \mathsf{MT}(\mathcal{O}', \mathsf{sub}(\mathcal{O}) \cup \mathsf{sub}(\mathcal{O}') \cup \mathsf{sub}(\mathcal{O}''))$, and there is a $T \in \mathsf{MT}(\mathcal{O}, \mathsf{sub}(\mathcal{O}'))$ which is closest to T' since $T' \in \mathsf{MT}(\mathcal{O}, \mathcal{O}')$. **(P6)**: Let $T \in \mathsf{MT}(\mathcal{O}, \mathcal{O}' \cup \mathcal{O}'')$. By Definition 8, we have $T \in \mathsf{MT}(\mathcal{O}'', \mathsf{sub}(\mathcal{O}') \cup \mathsf{sub}(\mathcal{O}'))$. To show that $T \in \mathsf{MT}(\mathcal{O}, \mathcal{O}')$, we use $T_0 \in \mathsf{MT}(\mathcal{O}, \mathcal{O}') \cap \mathsf{MT}(\mathcal{O}'', \mathsf{sub}(\mathcal{O}) \cup \mathsf{sub}(\mathcal{O}'))$ and the total pre-order over tree-like models. □

5 Computing Revision Ontology

In this section, we present a procedure for constructing a $\mathcal{SHIQ}$ ontology $\mathcal{O}^*$ that admits at least tree-like models in $\mathsf{MT}(\mathcal{O}, \mathcal{O}')$. It has turned out [3] that there may not exist a DL-lite ontology which admits exactly a given set of models. By the following example, we show that it is also the case for $\mathcal{SHIQ}$ ontologies.

Example 3.
Reconsider Example 2 with $\mathsf{MT}(\mathcal{O}, \mathcal{O}') = \{T_1'\}$. *Assume that there exists* $\widehat{\mathcal{O}}$ *with* $\mathsf{sub}(\widehat{\mathcal{O}}) = \{\mathsf{Carriage}, \neg\mathsf{Carriage}, \exists\mathsf{isPartOf}.\mathsf{Train}, \forall\mathsf{isPartOf}.(\neg\mathsf{Train}), \mathsf{Train}, \neg\mathsf{Train}\}$ *which admits the unique* T_1' *as tree-like model. By applying the new tableau algorithm for* $\widehat{\mathcal{O}}$, $\mathsf{MT}(\widehat{\mathcal{O}})$ *must contain* T_1' *and another* T_2' *having one node* $\{x\}$ *with* $L(x) = \{\mathsf{Train}, \mathsf{Carriage}, \forall\mathsf{isPartOf}.(\neg\mathsf{Train})\}$, *which is a contradiction.*

To address this issue, we are borrowing the notion of *maximal approximation* from the work of De Giacomo and colleagues [4]. This notion can be reformulated in our setting as follows.

Definition 9 (Maximal Approximation). *Let* $\mathcal{O}$ *and* $\mathcal{O}'$ *be two consistent* $\mathcal{SHIQ}$ *ontologies with revision operation* $\mathsf{MT}(\mathcal{O}, \mathcal{O}')$. *We use* $\mathcal{S}(\mathcal{O}'')$ *to denote the signature of an ontology* $\mathcal{O}''$. *An ontology* $\mathcal{O}^*$ *is a* maximal approximation *from* $\mathsf{MT}(\mathcal{O}, \mathcal{O}')$ *if*

1. $\mathcal{S}(\mathcal{O}^*) \subseteq \mathcal{S}(\mathcal{O}) \cup \mathcal{S}(\mathcal{O}')$;
2. $\mathsf{MT}(\mathcal{O}, \mathcal{O}') \subseteq \mathsf{MT}(\mathcal{O}^*)$;
3. *There does not exist any ontology* $\mathcal{O}''$ *s.t.* $\mathsf{MT}(\mathcal{O}, \mathcal{O}') \subseteq \mathsf{MT}(\mathcal{O}'') \subset \mathsf{MT}(\mathcal{O}^*)$. ◁

Definition 9 provides a best approximation of $\mathcal{SHIQ}$ ontologies we should build such that it admits all models in $\mathsf{MT}(\mathcal{O}, \mathcal{O}')$. An interesting point is that if such a maximal approximation exists it is unique up to semantic equivalence. In fact, assume that there exists a maximal approximation $\mathcal{O}''$ such that $\mathsf{MT}(\mathcal{O}'', \mathsf{sub}(\mathcal{O}^*)) \neq \mathsf{MT}(\mathcal{O}^*, \mathsf{sub}(\mathcal{O}''))$. We can show that $\mathsf{sub}(\mathcal{O}^*) = \mathsf{sub}(\mathcal{O}'') = \mathsf{sub}(\mathcal{O} \cup \mathcal{O}')$. Then, by Lemma 1, $\mathsf{MT}(\mathcal{O}'' \cup \mathcal{O}^*) = \mathsf{MT}(\mathcal{O}'', \mathsf{sub}(\mathcal{O}^*)) \cap \mathsf{MT}(\mathcal{O}^*, \mathsf{sub}(\mathcal{O}''))$, it follows $\mathsf{MT}(\mathcal{O}'' \cup \mathcal{O}^*) = \mathsf{MT}(\mathcal{O}'') \cap \mathsf{MT}(\mathcal{O}^*) \subset \mathsf{MT}(\mathcal{O}^*)$ or $\mathsf{MT}(\mathcal{O}'' \cup \mathcal{O}^*) \subset \mathsf{MT}(\mathcal{O}'')$, which contradicts Condition 3 in Definition 9. Moreover, the existence of $\mathcal{O}''$ in Condition 3 implies Condition 1, i.e., $\mathcal{S}(\mathcal{O}'') \subseteq \mathcal{S}(\mathcal{O}) \cup \mathcal{S}(\mathcal{O}')$. In the sequel, we show that such a maximal approximation actually exists and propose a procedure to build it.

Definition 10 (Revision Ontology). *Let* $\mathcal{O} = (\mathcal{T}, \mathcal{R})$ *and* $\mathcal{O}' = (\mathcal{T}', \mathcal{R}')$ *be two consistent* $\mathcal{SHIQ}$ *ontologies with* $\mathsf{MT}(\mathcal{O}, \mathcal{O}') = \{T_1, \cdots, T_n\}$ *where* $T_i = \langle V_i, L_i, E_i, \widehat{x}_i \rangle$ *for* $1 \leq i \leq n$. *A revision ontology* $\mathcal{O}^* = (\widehat{\mathcal{T}}, \widehat{\mathcal{R}})$ *of* $\mathcal{O}$ *by* $\mathcal{O}'$ *is defined as follows:*

- $\widehat{\mathcal{R}} := \mathcal{R}'$
- $\widehat{\mathcal{T}} := \mathcal{T}' \cup \{\top \sqsubseteq \bigsqcup_{\langle V_i, L_i, E_i, \widehat{x}_i \rangle \in \mathsf{MT}(\mathcal{O}, \mathcal{O}')} (\bigsqcup_{x \in V_i} (\bigsqcap_{C \in L_i(x)} C))\}$ ◁

The only difference between $\mathcal{O}'$ and $\mathcal{O}^*$ is the new axiom built from $\mathsf{MT}(\mathcal{O}, \mathcal{O}')$. This axiom allows for selecting from $\mathsf{MT}(\mathcal{O}', \mathsf{sub}(\mathcal{O}))$ tree-like models that are closest to $\mathsf{MT}(\mathcal{O}, \mathsf{sub}(\mathcal{O}'))$. The subsumer of the axiom contains all concepts appearing in each node of each tree-like model $T_i = \langle V_i, L_i, E_i, \widehat{x}_i \rangle \in \mathsf{MT}(\mathcal{O}, \mathcal{O}')$.

Example 4. *To continue Example 2, we construct from* $\mathsf{MT}(\mathcal{O}, \mathcal{O}')$ *an ontology* $\mathcal{O}^*$ *which admits a unique tree-like model* T_1' *according to Definition 10. Thus,* $\mathcal{O}^*$ *contains the following axioms:*

¬Carriage $\sqsubseteq$ ∀isPartOf.(¬Train),   Train $\sqsubseteq$ Carriage $\sqcap$ ∀isPartOf.(¬Train) *(from* $\mathcal{O}'$*), and* $\top$ $\sqsubseteq$ (Carriage $\sqcap$ ∃isPartOf.Train $\sqcap$ ¬Train)$\sqcup$ (Train $\sqcap$ Carriage $\sqcap$ ∀isPartOf.¬Train).

We formulate and show the most important result which affirms that the revision ontology $\mathcal{O}^*$ in Definition 10 satisfies the conditions of a maximal approximation. Our argument relies heavily on the specific behavior of the sat-rule. In fact, this rule allows one to know about a tree-like model built by the new tableau algorithm without indicating a precise sequence of applications of expansion rules.

Theorem 3. *Let* $\mathcal{O}$ *and* $\mathcal{O}'$ *be two consistent* $\mathcal{SHIQ}$ *ontologies. The revision ontology* $\mathcal{O}^*$ *of* $\mathcal{O}$ *by* $\mathcal{O}'$ *is a maximal approximation from* $\mathsf{MT}(\mathcal{O}, \mathcal{O}')$. *Additionally, the size of* $\mathcal{O}^*$ *is bounded by a doubly exponential function in the size of* $\mathcal{O}$ *and* $\mathcal{O}'$.

Proof Sketch. By construction, $\mathcal{S}(\mathcal{O}^*) \subseteq \mathcal{S}(\mathcal{O}) \cup \mathcal{S}(\mathcal{O}')$ and $\mathsf{sub}(\mathcal{O}) \cup \mathsf{sub}(\mathcal{O}') = \mathsf{sub}(\mathcal{O}^*)$. Let $T \in \mathsf{MT}(\mathcal{O}, \mathcal{O}')$. Due to $\mathsf{MT}(\mathcal{O}, \mathcal{O}') \subseteq \mathsf{MT}(\mathcal{O}', \mathsf{sub}(\mathcal{O}))$ there exists a sequence Seq_T of rule applications executed by the new tableau algorithm for $\mathcal{O}'$ with $\mathsf{sub}(\mathcal{O})$ such that Seq_T allows for constructing T. We use Seq_T to guide the construction of a sequence $Seq_{T'}$ of rule applications executed by the new tableau algorithm for $\mathcal{O}^*$ such that $Seq_{T'}$ allows for constructing a tree-like model $T' = T$. Thus, $\mathsf{MT}(\mathcal{O}, \mathcal{O}') \subseteq \mathsf{MT}(\mathcal{O}^*)$. To prove Condition 3, we show that if there exists an ontology $\mathcal{O}''$ with $\mathsf{MT}(\mathcal{O},\mathcal{O}') \subseteq \mathsf{MT}(\mathcal{O}'') \subseteq \mathsf{MT}(\mathcal{O}^*)$ then $\mathsf{MT}(\mathcal{O}'') = \mathsf{MT}(\mathcal{O}^*)$. Firstly, we show that $\mathsf{sub}(\mathcal{O}'') = \mathsf{sub}(\mathcal{O}^*)$. The remainder can be done by using the same argument over sequences of rule applications executed by the new tableau algorithm for $\mathcal{O}''$ and $\mathcal{O}^*$. The point is that when we know Seq_T with the specific behavior of the sat-rule (for building a tree-like model T for $\mathcal{O}''$) and $\mathsf{sub}(\mathcal{O}'') = \mathsf{sub}(\mathcal{O}^*)$, it is possible to replicate that Seq_T to build the same tree-like model $T' = T$ for $\mathcal{O}^*$, and inversely. In addition, there is at most a doubly exponential number of tree-like models in $\mathsf{MT}(\mathcal{O},\mathcal{O}')$, and the size of each tree-like model is bounded by a doubly exponential function. □

Algorithm 1. Algorithm for computing the revision ontology $\mathcal{O}^*$ of $\mathcal{O}$ by $\mathcal{O}'$

Input : $\mathcal{O} = (\mathcal{T},\mathcal{R})$, $\mathcal{O}' = (\mathcal{T}',\mathcal{R}')$: two consistent $\mathcal{SHIQ}$ ontologies
Output: $\mathcal{O}^* = (\widehat{\mathcal{T}},\widehat{\mathcal{R}})$: revision ontology of $\mathcal{O}$ by $\mathcal{O}'$

1 Apply the new tableau algorithm to $\mathcal{O}$ and $\mathcal{O}'$ for building $\mathsf{MT}(\mathcal{O},\mathsf{sub}(\mathcal{O}'))$ and $\mathsf{MT}(\mathcal{O}',\mathsf{sub}(\mathcal{O}))$;
2 Compute $\mathsf{MT}(\mathcal{O},\mathcal{O}')$ from $\mathsf{MT}(\mathcal{O},\mathsf{sub}(\mathcal{O}'))$ and $\mathsf{MT}(\mathcal{O}',\mathsf{sub}(\mathcal{O}))$ according to Definition 8;
3 **foreach** $\alpha \in \mathcal{R}'$ **do**
4 $\quad\lfloor$ Add α to $\widehat{\mathcal{R}}$;
5 **foreach** $\alpha \in \mathcal{T}'$ **do**
6 $\quad\lfloor$ Add α to $\widehat{\mathcal{T}}$;
7 Add to $\widehat{\mathcal{T}}$ the concept axiom $\top \sqsubseteq \bigsqcup_{\langle V_i,L_i,E_i,\widehat{x}_i\rangle \in \mathsf{MT}(\mathcal{O},\mathcal{O}')} (\bigsqcup_{x\in V_i}(\bigsqcap_{C\in L_i(x)} C))$;
8 **return** $\mathcal{O}^*$;

Based on Definition 10, one can devise a procedure (Algorithm 1) for computing the revision ontology $\mathcal{O}^*$ of $\mathcal{O}$ by $\mathcal{O}'$. The construction of the axiom by Line 7 is performed by traversing each completion tree $T_i \in \mathsf{MT}(\mathcal{O},\mathcal{O}')$ to get node labels from T_i. Each disjunct at top-level of the subsumer of this axiom corresponds to the label of each node $x \in V_i$ with $T_i = (V_I, L_i, E_i, \widehat{x}_i)$.

6   Optimizing the Algorithm

Algorithm 1 for constructing a revision ontology $\mathcal{O}^*$ of $\mathcal{O}$ by $\mathcal{O}'$ requires to compute in the worst case all tree-like models in $\mathsf{MT}(\mathcal{O},\mathsf{sub}(\mathcal{O}'))$ and $\mathsf{MT}(\mathcal{O}',\mathsf{sub}(\mathcal{O}))$ whose cardinality is bounded by a doubly exponential function in the size of $\mathcal{O}$ and $\mathcal{O}'$.

A first idea which can help to reduce the number of tree-like models to be computed for building $\mathsf{MT}(\mathcal{O},\mathcal{O}')$ comes from an observation of Definition 8. For each tree-like model $T' \in \mathsf{MT}(\mathcal{O}',\mathsf{sub}(\mathcal{O}))$, if we get a "good" candidate T from $\mathsf{MT}(\mathcal{O},\mathsf{sub}(\mathcal{O}'))$ such that $T \vartriangle T'$ is small enough, we could avoid computing all $T_x \in \mathsf{MT}(\mathcal{O},\mathsf{sub}(\mathcal{O}'))$ such that $T_x \vartriangle T' \geq T \vartriangle T'$. Note that it is not needed to obtain the whole T_x for deciding whether $T_x \vartriangle T' \geq T \vartriangle T'$ since the construction of T_x is monotonic. If we use $\mathfrak{T}(T') \subseteq \mathsf{MT}(\mathcal{O}, \mathsf{sub}(\mathcal{O}'))$ to denote a set of such completion trees T_x for each $T' \in \mathsf{MT}(\mathcal{O}', \mathsf{sub}(\mathcal{O}))$, it suffices to compute just one T_x in $\mathfrak{T}(T')$. Figure 2 depicts how $\mathsf{MT}(\mathcal{O}, \mathsf{sub}(\mathcal{O}'))$ is partitioned into subsets $\mathfrak{T}(T_i')$ for each $T_i' \in \mathsf{MT}(\mathcal{O}', \mathsf{sub}(\mathcal{O}))$.

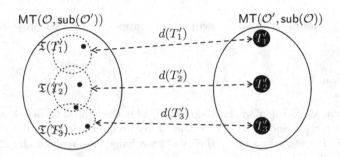

Fig. 2. Optimizing the computation of $\mathsf{MT}(\mathcal{O}, \mathcal{O}')$

In addition, the computation of $\mathfrak{T}(T')$ is independent from $\mathfrak{T}(T'')$ with $T' \neq T''$. This allows us to parallelize the computation of all $\mathfrak{T}(T')$ with $T' \in \mathsf{MT}(\mathcal{O}', \mathsf{sub}(\mathcal{O}))$.

A second optimization is related to the size of completion trees. It has turned out that the size of each completion tree is bounded by a doubly exponential function in the size of ontology. A method presented by Le Duc, Lamolle and Curé [8] allows one to build a structure, namely a *frame*, which compresses similar nodes of a completion tree instead of building whole completion tree. It could be shown that the size of a frame is bounded by a (simply) exponential function in the size of ontology. An advantage of this method is that almost all optimization techniques designed for standard tableau algorithms remain usable.

7 Conclusion and Future Work

We have presented in this paper an approach for revising a $\mathcal{SHIQ}$ ontology. This revision operation guarantees minimal change and the revised ontology remains expressible in the logic of initial ontologies. An interesting feature of our approach is to introduce finite structures, namely *completion trees*, for characterizing a set of models of a $\mathcal{SHIQ}$ ontology. These structures are built by a tableau algorithm with a new expansion rule, namely sat-rule. Although non-deterministic behavior of this rule betrays good characteristics of standard tableau algorithms, this disadvantage is justified by obtaining a revision operation that guarantees all revision postulates (thus, the principle of minimal change), and a revision ontology expressible in the logic of initial ontologies.

The main limitation of our approach in this paper is to omit individuals in ontologies. However, our approach can be extended in a straightforward way in order to deal with individuals. This extension would be performed by extending the distance given in Definition 7 to graphs. For this purpose, we plan to extend our approach to the logic $\mathcal{SHOIQ}$ that includes individuals. In addition to this limitation, we have not provided in this paper complexity result on the $\mathcal{SHIQ}$ ontology revision problem. This would lead us to investigate complexity of distance computation between completion trees.

Acknowledgements. This work was partially supported by FUI project "Learning Café".

References

1. Alchourrón, C., Gärdenfors, P., Makinson, D.: On the logic of theory change: partial meet contraction and revision functions. J. Symbolic Logic **50**, 510–530 (1985)
2. Dalal, M.: Investigations into a theory of knowledge base revision. In: Proceedings of AAAI, pp. 475–479 (1988)
3. De Giacomo, G., Lenzerini, M., Poggi, A., Rosati, R.: On the update of description logic ontologies at the instance level. In: Proceedings of AAAI (2006)
4. De Giacomo, G., Lenzerini, M., Poggi, A., Rosati, R.: On the approximation of instance level update and erasure in description logics. In: Proceedings of AAAI, pp. 403–408 (2007)
5. Eiter, T., Gottlob, G.: On the complexity of propositional knowledge base revision, updates, and counterfactuals. Artif. Intell. **57**, 227–270 (1992)
6. Horrocks, I., Sattler, U., Tobies, S.: Practical reasoning for expressive description logics. In: Ganzinger, H., McAllester, D., Voronkov, A. (eds.) LPAR 1999. LNCS, vol. 1705, pp. 161–180. Springer, Heidelberg (1999)
7. Katsuno, H., Mendelzon, A.O.: Propositional knowledge base revision and minimal change. Artif. Intell. **53**(3), 263–294 (1991)
8. Le Duc, C., Lamolle, M., Curé, O.: A decision procedure for $\mathcal{SHIQ}$ with transitive closure of roles. In: Alani, H., Kagal, L., Fokoue, A., Groth, P., Biemann, C., Parreira, J.X., Aroyo, L., Noy, N., Welty, C., Janowicz, K. (eds.) ISWC 2013, Part I. LNCS, vol. 8218, pp. 264–279. Springer, Heidelberg (2013)
9. Qi, G., Du, J.: Model-based revision operators for terminologies in description logics. In: IJCAI (2009)
10. Qi, G., Liu, W., Bell, D.A.: Knowledge base revision in description logics. In: Fisher, M., van der Hoek, W., Konev, B., Lisitsa, A. (eds.) JELIA 2006. LNCS, vol. 4160, pp. 386–398. Springer, Heidelberg (2006)
11. Ribeiro, M.M., Wassermann, R.: Base revision in description logics - preliminary results. In: Proceedings of IWOD, pp. 69–82 (2007)
12. Satoh, K.: Nonmonotonic reasoning by minimal belief revision. In: Proceedings of the International Conference on Fifth Generation Computer Systems, pp. 455–462 (1988)
13. Wang, Z., Wang, K., Topor, R.: A new approach to knowledge base revision in dl-lite. In: Proceedings of 24th AAAI, pp. 369–374 (2010)

Gamifying Program Analysis

Daniel Fava[1], Julien Signoles[2], Matthieu Lemerre[2],
Martin Schäf[3]([⊠]), and Ashish Tiwari[3]

[1] University of California, Santa Cruz, USA
[2] CEA, LIST, Software Reliability and Security Laboratory,
P.C. 174, 91191 Gif-sur-Yvette, France
[3] SRI International, Menlo Park, USA
martin.schaef@sri.com

Abstract. Abstract interpretation is a powerful tool in program verification. Several commercial or industrial scale implementations of abstract interpretation have demonstrated that this approach can verify safety properties of real-world code. However, using abstract interpretation tools is not always simple. If no user-provided hints are available, the abstract interpretation engine may lose precision during widening and produce an overwhelming number of false alarms. However, manually providing these hints is time consuming and often frustrating when re-running the analysis takes a lot of time.

We present an algorithm for program verification that combines abstract interpretation, symbolic execution and crowdsourcing. If verification fails, our procedure suggests likely invariants, or program patches, that provide helpful information to the verification engineer and makes it easier to find the correct specification. By complementing machine learning with well-designed games, we enable program analysis to incorporate human insights that help improve their scalability and usability.

1 Introduction

Abstract interpretation [1] is a powerful technique for program verification. Tools like Astrée [2] and Frama-C [11] have successfully demonstrated not only that abstract interpretation is able to prove the absence of run-time errors in real-world C programs, but also that it is commercially viable to do so.

To verify a given program P, abstract interpretation approximates the semantics of P based on monotonic functions. The analysis symbolically executes P keeping a set of possible states at each program point. If an error is not reachable in this abstraction, we have a proof that this error is also not reachable in the original program.

Unfortunately, even if these tools are fully automated, it does not mean that using them is simple. Sometimes, in particular when analyzing looping control-flow, abstract interpretation loses precision and the set representing the possible states of the analyzed program becomes too imprecise. This can result in a large number of false alarms, up to a point where the only option is to abort the analysis. In these cases, to help the analysis regain precision, a verification engineer

© Springer-Verlag Berlin Heidelberg 2015
M. Davis et al. (Eds.): LPAR-20 2015, LNCS 9450, pp. 591–605, 2015.
DOI: 10.1007/978-3-662-48899-7_41

has to step in and provide hints in the form of code annotations or custom parameterizations. In the case of large programs, writing these annotations can be a painful experience. The process tends to be incremental because an annotation that was used to drive the analysis forward may be insufficient a few statements later. In other words, previous annotations which were considered sufficient may have to be revised because they were either too weak or too strong to continue the analysis at a later point in the program. This leads to a labor intensive process that is also costly because, in order to provide useful annotations, the analyst not only has to understand the analyzed code, but also the details of the abstraction used by the verification engine.

In an effort to lower the cost of applying abstract interpretation, we have seen a new trend of using machine learning to identify likely invariants. The idea is to collect two sets of concrete program states that are either part of a successful execution (*good states*) or failing executions (*bad states*), and use machine learning to find a classifier that separates those sets. Approaches such as Daikon [5], ICE [8], and work by Sharma et al. [15–17], have successfully demonstrated that machine learning can be used to learn likely invariants. Unlike widening, which is commonly used in abstract interpretation to generalize program behavior, machine learning can also provide generalization guarantees.

However, there are limitations to using machine learning for finding likely invariants. First, collecting good states and bad states is expensive (if it were easy to enumerate them, we would not need abstraction) and thus the machine learner has to operate on a small data set. This increases the risk of over-fitting. Second, learners have a tendency to produce large invariants that are not fit for "human consumption." And third, machine learners operate on a hypothesis space which allows them to express certain kinds of knowledge and empowers them with the ability to generalize. However, there can be mismatches in the type of representation strength of a classifier and the domain of the program under analysis.

We present an approach that combines abstract interpretation, machine learning, and crowdsourcing to learn likely invariants. We have developed a system called Chekofv that maintains three values at each program point:

1. a set of states, which represents our current estimate of the likely invariant at that program point,
2. a set of good states, which are concrete states such that executions starting from those states do not cause any assertion violations, and
3. a set of bad states, which are concrete states such that executions starting from those states cause an assertion violation.

None of these sets is necessarily a strict over- or under-approximation of the reachable set at that program point. We use abstract interpretation to initialize the first set, but later update it with likely invariants learnt using machine learning or crowdsourcing. The set of good and bad states are collected using testing and symbolic execution, and they form the inputs for the machine learning and crowdsourced games. In particular, Chekofv complements machine learning procedures by using two games, Xylem [14] and Binary Fission[1]. These games enable

---

[1] http://chekofv.net/.

the non-expert crowd to solve the problem of finding likely invariants. The first game, Xylem, resembles Daikon: for a given set of states, the player has to find a predicate that describes all states. The second game, Binary Fission, gamifies a decision tree learning procedure: the player is presented with a set of good states and bad states, and she has to generate a classifier to separate these sets.

The intuition is that crowdsourcing has three major benefits over machine learning: (1) invariants are not limited by a particular kernel function or hypothesis space; instead, we can obtain a very diverse set of solutions from different players; (2) humans tend to produce invariants that are readable (unlike the machine, which can produce illegible predicates); (3) given our natural limitations handling large amounts of data, we believe that humans are less likely to produce a solution that overfits. The crowdsourced experiment has to run long enough for a reasonable set of solutions to be available. However, compared to the several man-months of effort of verifying a real system, this may still be a cheap preprocessing step. Another potential problem is that human intuition breaks at high dimensions, and the dimensionality of the data to be classified depends on the number of variables in scope at a particular program point. This is why, when designing a verification game, the choices of visualization and data representation are important.

Our tool Chekofv shares several similarities with machine learning based approaches such as [16]. We perform an abstract interpretation of a given C program using the plug-in Value of Frama-C. Each time when we reach a program location where Value loses precision (e.g., due to widening or unspecified inputs), we use dynamic or symbolic execution to collect good and bad states. Unlike previous approaches, we use these sets as input to the two games described above. The games produce likely invariants which are then inserted as assertions into the program. This process is iterated until we cannot find any bad state that satisfies our current invariant and we cannot find a good state that violates this invariant. Unlike [16] where the focus is on verification, we use the approach to also generate preconditions and checks as suggestive program patches for the developer.

In the following, we discuss our infrastructure, provide a motivating example and an overview of our crowdsourcing game. Our main contribution is the program analysis and patching procedure that combines abstraction interpretation with machine learning and crowdsourcing via gamification. A secondary goal is to increase the visibility of our games and get feedback from the community. We hope to collect enough data this way to perform a statistically significant study that compares the quality of crowdsourced invariants with the quality of machine learned ones.

2   Related Work

The idea of learning likely invariants from program states goes back to Daikon [5]. Daikon learns likely invariants from a given set of (good) program states by working with a fixed set of grammar patterns. Numerous approaches have used

Daikon; for example, iDiscovery [18] uses symbolic execution to improve on Daikon's invariants. Similar to our approach, it inserts the learned invariants back in the code under analysis and then uses symbolic execution to confirm or break these candidate invariants. This process generates new states that can be fed to Daikon and can be iterated until either an inductive invariant is found, or symbolic execution fails to generate new states.

Sharma et al. [16] formulate the problem of extrapolation in static analysis as a classification problem in machine learning. They also use *good* and *bad* states and a greedy set cover algorithm to obtain loop invariants. In a follow up work, a similar algorithm to detect likely invariants using randomized search is described [15]. While our approach is similar in the sense that we learn invariants from good and bad examples, our application is different. Rather than finding accurate loop invariants, we are interested in finding human-readable annotations using crowdsourcing that prevent abstract interpretation from losing precision.

The architecture of our approach strongly resembles the decision tree learning based approach of DTInv [12]. In fact, the authors of that paper kindly provided their implementation which we use to test our approach. The key difference between the two techniques is that we use gamification instead of machine learning to find invariants.

Another popular approach for learning likely invariants is the ICE-learning framework [8]. Similar to Daikon, ICE-based algorithms search for invariants by iterating through a set of templates. Unlike Daikon, ICE does not discard likely invariants that are inductive. Instead, it checks a set of implications to decide if the counterexample is a new good or bad state.

Predicate abstraction [9] based on abstract interpretation has also been used to learn universally-quantified loop invariants [7] and was implemented in ESC/-Java [6]. This approach may require manual annotations to infer smart invariants. It is a 100 % correct technique but at the price of precision. Counterexample driven refinement has been used to automatically refine predicate abstractions and reduce false errors [10]. Fixpoint-based approaches have also been studied [3]; however they do not explicitly generate bad states, unlike the work we describe here.

An approach to gamify type checking has been presented by Dietl et al. [4].

3   Motivating Example

We explain how Chekofv works by dissecting the famous Heartbleed bug in OpenSSL.[2] The code snippet that caused the bug is sketched in Fig. 1. For space reasons, we omit a few lines from the original code which are not relevant to understanding the bug.

---

[2] http://blog.cryptographyengineering.com/2014/04/attack-of-week-openssl-heart bleed.html.

```
1   int dtls1_process_heartbeat(SSL *s)
2   {
3     unsigned char *p = &s->s3->rrec.data[0], *pl;
4     unsigned short hbtype;
5     unsigned int payload; // message size
6     unsigned int padding = 16;
7
8     hbtype = *p++;
9     n2s(p, payload); // read message size from input
10    pl = p;
11
12    if (hbtype == TLS1_HB_REQUEST)
13    {
14      unsigned char *buffer, *bp;
15      buffer = OPENSSL_malloc(1 + 2 + payload +
            padding);
16      bp = buffer;
17
18      *bp++ = TLS1_HB_RESPONSE;
19      s2n(payload, bp);
20
21      memcpy(bp, pl, payload);
```

Fig. 1. Heartbleed bug in OpenSSL. The problem in this snippet is that, when calling memcpy in line 21, we cannot guarantee that pl is actually of size payload. That is, by providing a wrong payload, an attacker is able to read a few bytes of arbitrary memory.

The bug is a missing bounds check in the heartbeat extension inside the transport layer security protocol implementation. A heartbeat essentially establishes whether another machine is still alive by sending a message containing a string (called payload) and expecting to receive that exact same message in response. The bug is that, although the message also contains the size of this payload, the receiver does not check if this size is correct. Therefore, an attacker can read arbitrary memory by sending a message that declares a payload size that is greater than the actual message.

Figure 1 shows the part of the code that processes a heartbeat message. On line 3, the pointer p is set to point to the beginning of the message. Then, on line 8, the message type is read, and on line 9, the size of the payload is read through the macro n2s which reads two bytes from p and put them into payload. However, since the whole incoming message might be controlled by an attacker, there is no guarantee that this payload really correspond to its actual length and there is no check in the code. Indeed payload might be as much as $2^{16} - 1 = 65535$. Line 10 then puts the heartbeat data into pl.

In line 15, a buffer is allocated and its size is actually as much as $1 + 2 + 65535 + 16 = 65554$. Then lines 18 and 19 fill the first bytes of the buffer with the type and the size of the response message. Finally, line 21 attempts to copy the heartbeat data from the incoming message to the response through a call to memcpy. Since the payload can be longer than the actual size of pl, close-by data in the memory (included potential confidential user data) may be inadvertently copied.

Frama-C can detect this bug. It adds an implicit assertion just before the memcpy that enforces bp and pl to be at least of size payload. Since it cannot prove this property, it warns about a potential bug. However, since this is not the only warning emitted by Frama-C, chances are it will go unnoticed.

Let us now see how our approach can make it easier for a human analyst who is employing Frama-C to notice this bug. First, even if it does not appear in Fig. 1, the length of &s->s3->rrec.data[0] is fixed and equal to SSL3_RT_HEADER_LENGTH. Starting with the abstract state computed by value analysis at line 10, the abstract state looks roughly as follows:

$$\text{hbtype} \in [0, 255] \qquad \textit{(a one-byte positive integer)}$$
$$\text{payload} \in [0, 2^{16} - 1] \qquad \textit{(a two-byte positive integer)}$$
$$size_p = \text{SSL3\_RT\_HEADER\_LENGTH} - 3$$
$$\text{padding} = 16$$

For readability, we use this abbreviated version of the abstract state computed by Frama-C. The actual abstract state would contain a lot more information about the input parameter s, about the value of p, pl, and about other global variables. The important thing to note in this abstract state is that payload can be an arbitrary two-byte unsigned integer, while the size of the allocated memory for pointer p is fixed and equal to SSL3_RT_HEADER_LENGTH − 3.

Since none of the variables in the abstract state depicted above is modified by any statement until line 21, these variables will have the same intervals. Hence, the implicit assertion that $\text{payload} \leq size_p$ which is required by memcpy does not hold.

Now, we use symbolic execution to refine our abstract state just before line 10. We pick this program point because it assigns a value from an unknown source to a variable. Chekofv refines all states where we receive unknown inputs (user input, files, network, etc.), or we lost information due to widening (e.g., after loops).

First, we collect bad states that lead to assertion violations. To that end, we construct a precondition that ensures that the symbolic execution may only pick initial values that are in our current abstract state. The symbolic execution will then search for concrete states from which the assertion can be violated. Next, we need to collect good states from which the assertion is not violated. We can either use the same symbolic execution approach that we used to collect bad states or fall back on data from previously recorded test cases, if available.

Figure 2 shows the distribution of the collected data points for payload and $size_p$. As discussed above, all good states (depicted by a plus sign) are states

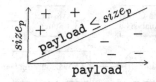

Fig. 2. Data points collected by our symbolic execution for `payload` and $size_p$. A plus indicates a good state and a minus indicates a bad state.

where $size_p$ is greater or equal to `payload`. All bad states (shown as a minus sign) are states where `payload` is greater than $size_p$. Using these data points, we can now employ our crowdsourcing games (or a machine learner) to find a classifier (that is a likely invariant) that separates the good states from the bad states. The ideal classifier would be `payload` $\leq size_p$. However, let us assume that our symbolic execution picked extreme values and we get an over-fitted invariant $2 * $ `payload` $\leq size_p$.

We merge the invariant $2 * $ `payload` $\leq size_p$ into the program at line 10 and re-run our Value analysis. The invariant refines the abstract state at line 10 such that `payload` is in the interval $[0, size_p/2]$. Hence, the assertion violation in line 21 is now gone and we know that we cannot find new bad states that violate this assertion. However, we still have to ensure that the inserted invariant did not throw away too many good states. Thus, we start our symbolic execution again, this time with the precondition that the invariant does not hold (i.e., $2 * $ `payload` $> size_p$ and thus the abstract value of `payload` is $[size\_p/2 + 1, 2^{16} - 1]$). This will reveal new good states that ensure that we cannot find the same invariant again. This loop is repeated until we cannot find new good or bad states. We mark likely invariants where this is the case as potential solutions. However, we do not stop the crowdsourcing immediately because there might be several invariants that have this property.

Eventually, Chekofv finds the invariant `payload` $\leq size_p$ for line 10 which is sufficient to prove the assertion in line 21. Note that we cannot actually prove that this is an invariant (in fact it is not an invariant because there is a bug). It is a likely invariant that shall help the verification engineer when verifying the program. In the remainder of this paper, we show the architecture of Chekofv and how it finds likely invariants using crowdsourcing.

4   Overview of the Chekofv System

Our approach to learn likely invariants to assist abstract interpretation is implemented as part of the Chekofv system outlined in Fig. 3. The system takes a given terminating C program as input and returns either a proof of correctness or a copy of the input program annotated with the learned invariants and a set of assertions that could not be verified.

Our procedure for program analysis is as follows:

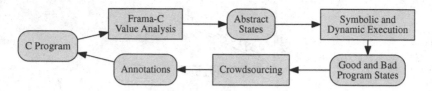

Fig. 3. Overview of our Chekofv system. Chekofv takes a C program as input and performs an abstract interpretation. If abstract interpretation fails to verify the program, the computed abstract states are passed to a symbolic execution engine to sample concrete good and bad states. These sets are then passed to our crowdsourcing games to compute likely invariants which are inserted back into the program. This loop terminates if either the program is verified or the invariants cannot be improved further.

1. *Initialize:* At every program point, initialize the likely invariant to *true*, good states to ∅ and bad states to ∅.
2. *Update1:* Update the likely invariant at each program point using abstract interpretation. Terminate with success if all assertions are verified. If the likely invariants are left unchanged, goto *Terminate*.
3. *Update2:* Find new good states that lie outside the current likely invariant, and new bad states that lie inside the current likely invariant. If such states are found, *add* them to the set of good and bad states at each program point. Otherwise, goto *Terminate*.
4. *Update3:* Use the current set of good and bad states to learn an invariant, using either machine learning or crowdsourcing, and use it to update the likely invariant at each program point. If we fail to separate good and bad states, then goto *Terminate*, else goto *Update1*.
5. *Terminate:* Terminate with the likely invariants as hints for the verification engineer.

We now describe the different pieces of the procedure above as implemented in Chekofv.

Abstract Interpreter. Chekofv uses the Frama-C plug-in Value to perform abstract interpretation, which computes, at each program point, an abstract state that over-approximates the set of all possible states the program may be at that point. The abstract state is a mapping from every memory location to the set of possible values that this location may have at the current program point. If the value is an integer, possible values are represented using an interval and a modulo as soon as the number of such values becomes too large (small sets are represented in an exact way). If the value is a floating point, only an interval is used. Pointers are represented using an interval per memory region where the pointer may point. Frama-C emits a warning if it cannot prove that the execution of an (implicit) assertion always succeeds from the current abstract state. If Frama-C does not emit any warning, we have a proof that the program is safe and our analysis terminates.

If we fail to prove that the given program is safe, the program either has a genuine error, or some of our abstract states were too imprecise to prove the program's safety. To refine this result, we try to learn likely invariants for each program point.

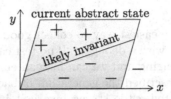

Fig. 4. Example of abstract states, concrete states, and likely invariants. Assuming a program over two variable x and y, the possible values of these variables form a two-dimensional space. The parallelogram describes a possible abstract state. Plus and minus refer to known concrete good and bad states. A likely invariant is a plane that cuts the parallelogram in two parts, one containing only good states, one containing only bad states.

Good and Bad States. For a given program point in our input program, Frama-C gives us the corresponding abstract state. This abstract state, as depicted in Fig. 4, contains a subset of *good states* and *bad states*. Good states are program states from which the program terminates normally. Bad states are (possibly unreachable) program states which lead to an assertion violation. Further, the abstract state may contain states that are not reachable but also do not violate any assertion and states that are reachable but lead to non-termination (we do not handle non-termination). Our goal is to learn an invariant for this program point that excludes all bad states and preserves all good states.

Note that, if the program is actually unsafe, such an invariant cannot be established because there exists a reachable bad state starting from this program point. That is, these invariants (when violated) can help the verification engineer to trace a safety property violation back to its origin.

Unfortunately, we cannot compute the set of good and bad states automatically (otherwise we would not need abstract states), so we can only approximate the invariant that we are looking for. To that end, we use symbolic execution to sample good and bad states. As sampling the good and bad states is only an under-approximation, the likely invariants that we learn may be too strong or too weak. Hence, we may need several passes through the program until we find a suitable likely invariant.

Sampling Bad States. To find a state which results in an assertion violation, we employ a symbolic execution tool to check if an error state is reachable from any state in the abstract domain of the current program point. That is, we turn the current abstract state into a precondition (or an assume statement) for the symbolic execution. For each variable v with an abstract domain $v \in [min, max]$, we add a conjunct $min \leq v \leq max$ to the precondition. If symbolic execution finds a reachable error state under this precondition, we add it to the set of bad states. If the program point we are analyzing is the program entry, or if we know that our precondition only describes reachable states, we have found a genuine error.

Sampling Good States. The easiest way to collect good states is to run the program and monitor its state with a debugger. If no test cases are available, finding good states is more challenging and we can instead employ symbolic execution (similar to how we have described the generation of bad state above). However, since we might have inserted a too strong invariant in a previous iteration of a loop, symbolic execution may fail because the set of possible states to start from is, for example, empty. To avoid this problem, we also check if there exists a state outside the current abstract domain from which an execution terminates normally. Here, we proceed in a similar way as for the bad states but we compute a precondition for the complement of the current abstract state. This step is important to prevent the machine learning from producing overly strong likely invariants.

Once we have collected the sets of good and bad states, we can start looking for a likely invariant. Finding this likely invariant can be seen as a binary classification problem in machine learning. We are looking for an approximation of a function that labels all good states as good and all bad states as bad. The connection between invariant generation and classification has been explored in many recent works [8,12,15–17]. Instead of using machine learning, we propose a crowdsourcing solution to perform this classification.

Gamification of Machine Learning. The main contribution of this paper is the use of crowdsourcing as an alternative to machine learning. The motivation is to avoid two problems that are inevitable when using machine learning: over-fitting, and limited expressiveness of the kernel function. Over-fitting is an inherent problem to machine learning when operating on small data sets. If only a small number of points is available, the machine learner may find a formula that describes exactly this set, resulting in a large formula with no predictive power. This is in particular relevant because we cannot collect arbitrary large sets of good and bad states. Gamification reduces this risk because different players may come up with different solutions, and humans are usually good at finding the *easiest* solution.

The second issue that we are trying to tackle by gamifying machine learning is the limitation of using a fixed kernel function in machine learning. Fixing a kernel function (e.g., conjunctions of linear inequalities) is vital for a machine learner to find a good solution, but it is not clear a priori which kernel function to pick. By gamifying machine learning, we do not have to fix a kernel function and can allow players to come up with arbitrary invariants.

We have developed two games, Xylem and Binary Fission, that crowdsource the machine learning aspect of Chekofv. Xylem is a gamification of Daikon while Binary Fission is a gamification of decision tree learning. These games are discussed in detail in Sect. 5. Both games interface with Chekofv in the same way as a machine learner would. They receive sets of good and bad states and return likely invariants. We merge the learned (likely) invariants into the program and start over with the first step of our analysis by recomputing the abstract states with value analysis.

Termination. Chekofv terminates if either the system is verified, or one of following situation occurs:

- *Failure to find new good and bad states:* Symbolic execution can fail to find new states. This may happen because the problem of finding good and bad states is undecidable in general and very expensive in practice. In this case, we terminate with the last learned invariants as a hint for the verification engineer.
- *Failure to classify good and bad states:* For crowdsourcing this may happen because the games do not have enough players, or the needed invariant is not expressible with the tools offered by the game. The latter case is equivalent to the case where a machine learner fails due to the choice of the kernel functions. Assuming that the language of the game or the kernel function of the machine learner are strictly more expressive than the abstract domain of Frama-C, we can terminate reporting the last learned invariants.
- *Failure to improve abstract domain with the learned invariants:* This may happen because the language of the likely invariants is more expressive than what can be expressed in the abstract domain. In this case, we know that there are bad states that cannot be excluded in the current abstract domain and we can report a warning that the current abstract domain is not sufficient to verify the program.

5   Crowdsourcing Games

To crowdsource the problem of finding likely invariants, we have developed two games, Xylem [14] and Binary Fission. Both games are available online at chekofv.net.

Xylem. The goal of Xylem is to generate new predicates that can be used for invariant construction. Players are presented with a sequence of (good or bad) program states and are asked to find a non-linear inequality that is satisfied by these states. In that sense, Xylem can be seen as a crowdsourced version of Daikon. To cap the cognitive load on players, Xylem splits the predicate construction problem into several game levels, with each level being composed of a limited number of states and a subset of variables. To ensure that we obtain a diverse set of solutions, Xylem gives different subsets of states and variables to different players.

Figure 5 shows a scene of the game. Players takes on the role of a botanist exploring new forms of plant life on a mysterious island. Program states are presented as growth phases of a plant in the top half of the screen. Each variable in the state is presented as a blossom of distinct color. The number of petals per blossom represents a variable value in the current state. At each level, players are presented between four and ten states and are asked to create a predicate that holds on all of the states. The

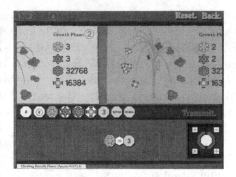

Fig. 5. Screenshot from Xylem

bottom half of the screen contains a toolbox that is used to assemble the predicate; the toolbox contains variables (i.e., blossoms), numbers, operators, and helper functions such as array length. This toolbox was a challenging part of the game design and remains an open area of research. The major difficulty is in striking a balance between user interface simplicity at the same time as providing sufficiently expressive constructs with which players can generate predicates. As players assemble predicates from the elements in the toolbox, the growth phases that satisfy the current predicate turn green while others turn red. Players can submit a predicate once all growth phases are green. That is, the game guarantees that the resulting predicate is a valid invariant for the given subset of states and variables (note that the predicate does not have to be an invariant on the data as a whole).

Binary Fission. In Binary Fission, players construct likely invariants from a fixed set of predicates. To that end, players are presented with good and bad states represented by blue and brown dots as shown in Fig. 6. The objective is to separate the two sets by building a decision tree. All states are initially mixed together in a single root node. The player can then choose a predicate from the given set and apply it to the root. Applying a predicate to a node generates two child nodes, one containing all states that satisfy the applied predicate and another containing all states that falsify it. The player grows this decision tree until each leaf becomes pure (i.e., contains only good or only bad states), or until a depth limit is reached. Loosely speaking, Binary Fission is the gamification version of DTInv, a decision tree based invariant learner [12]. Once a tree is built, we can trace down from the root to a pure good node (a node composed of good states only) taking the conjunction of predicates along the way. A conjunction of predicates from the root of the tree to a leaf containing only good states is a likely invariant for our program. Note that there may be several leaf nodes containing only good states. We combine them into one likely invariant by forming a disjunction.

The set of predicates available to player can be obtained from different sources. Ideally, they are generated by Xylem as discussed previously. Currently we seed this set using Daikon.

If the available predicates are not sufficient to separate the good from the bad states within a given tree-depth, some leaf nodes will contain both good and bad states. These states are then taken aside and re-entered as input into Xylem and/or Daikon. Since these sets are smaller than the initial set, Xylem and Daikon are allowed to search for more complex likely invariants (which

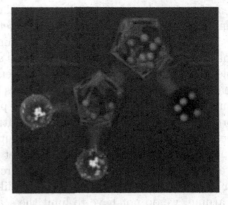

Fig. 6. Screenshot from Binary Fission

would otherwise be computationally expensive and lead to many useless candidates).

Implementation Notes. The Chekofv system provides both games with sets of states and collects the predicates and candidate invariants provided by the players. Chekofv uses Frama-C for abstract interpretation and extends it by several plugins to extract the abstract state at particular program points, and to insert likely invariants. This implements the steps *Initialize* and *Update1* from our abstract algorithm in Sect. 4. Note that Chekofv only samples states at entry points of procedures and before procedure calls that precede Frama-C warnings. As shown in Sect. 3 this is sufficient to find real bugs.

For practical reasons, we use the bounded model checker CBMC [13] instead of symbolic execution to implement step *Update2* from Sect. 4. We perform minor program transformations (e.g., insert assumptions and non-determinism) to make the result resemble a symbolic execution. The collected good and bad states are stored in a database and serve as input to both games.

For testing, we also seed or database the sets of good and bad states from the experiments in [12,18] to our database. The sets of good and bad states differ greatly between the benchmarks. For example, the TCAS benchmark in [18] comes with hundreds of states collected from dynamic execution, while other benchmarks come with less than a dozen states obtained by symbolic execution.

Step *Update3* from Sect. 4 is realized by the two games; each game has its own web server that pulls program states from the database and presents them to the game client. Predicates produced by the players are sent back to the server and stored in a database. Likely invariants generated from game play are post-processed and then used by Frama-C, thus closing the loop in Fig. 3.

6   Conclusion

We have presented an approach that uses crowdsourcing to learn likely invariants that assist abstract interpretation. Our approach extends previous machine learning based techniques by reformulating the machine learning problem of finding a classifier that separates two sets as puzzle games.

Crowdsourcing the invariant learning has several potential benefits over machine learning: finding good and bad states is expensive and often only possible to a limited extend. Hence, these sets are small which often causes machine learning to over-fit and find correlations that may be true on the observed data, but irrelevant (or even wrong) in the program. Crowdsourcing can avoid this problem. First, given our natural limitations handling large amounts of data, we believe that humans prefer shorter solutions that are less likely to overfit. Second, crowdsourcing returns a diverse set of different likely invariants from which we can choose. Beyond that, crowdsourcing is not limited by a set of templates or kernel functions when constructing likely invariants. That is, unlike machine learning, we do not have to limit the search space for likely invariants a priori. This may lead to a more diverse set of invariants and allow us to discover invariants and requires less interaction through the verification engineer, like trying different kernel functions.

The games are now open to the public. We hope that the interested reader will enjoy playing them and help us to collect valuable data along the way.

Acknowledgement. This work was supported in part by the National Science Foundation under grant contracts CCF 1423296 and CNS 1423298, and DARPA under agreement number FA8750-12-C-0225.

We gratefully acknowledge the contributions of our collaborators at UCSC especially Kate Compton, Heather Logas, Joseph Osborn, Zhongpeng Lin, Dylan Lederle-Ensign, Joe Mazeika, Afshin Mobrabraein, Chandranil Chakrabortii, Johnathan Pagnutti, Kelsey Coffman, Richard Vallejos, Lauren Scott, John Thomas Murray, Orlando Salvatore, Huascar Sanchez, Michael Shavlovsky, Daniel Cetina, Shayne Clementi, Chris Lewis, Dan Shapiro, Michael Mateas, E. James Whitehead Jr., at SRI John Murray, Min Yin, Natarajan Shankar, Sam Owre, and at CEA Florent Kirchner, Boris Yakobowski.

References

1. Cousot, P., Cousot, R.: Abstract interpretation: a unified lattice model for static analysis of programs by construction or approximation of fixpoints. In: POPL (1977)
2. Cousot, P., Cousot, R., Feret, J., Mauborgne, L., Miné, A., Monniaux, D., Rival, X.: The astrée analyzer. In: PLS (2005)
3. Cousot, P., Ganty, P., Raskin, J.-F.: Fixpoint-guided abstraction refinements. In: Riis Nielson, H., Filé, G. (eds.) SAS 2007. LNCS, vol. 4634, pp. 333–348. Springer, Heidelberg (2007)
4. Dietl, W., Dietzel, S., Ernst, M.D., Mote, N., Walker, B., Cooper, S., Pavlik, T., Popović, Z.: Verification games: making verification fun. In: Proceedings of the 14th Workshop on Formal Techniques for Java-like Programs, pp. 42–49. ACM (2012)
5. Ernst, M.D., Perkins, J.H., Guo, P.J., McCamant, S., Pacheco, C., Tschantz, M.S., Xiao, C.: The daikon system for dynamic detection of likely invariants. Sci. Comput. Program **69**(1–3), 35–45 (2007)

6. Flanagan, C., Leino, K.R.M., Lillibridge, M., Nelson, G., Saxe, J.B., Stata, R.: Extended static checking for java. In: PLDI (2002)
7. Flanagan, C., Qadeer, S.: Predicate abstraction for software verification. In: POPL (2002)
8. Garg, P., Löding, C., Madhusudan, P., Neider, D.: ICE: a robust framework for learning invariants. In: Biere, A., Bloem, R. (eds.) CAV 2014. LNCS, vol. 8559, pp. 69–87. Springer, Heidelberg (2014)
9. Graf, S., Saidi, H.: Construction of abstract state graphs with PVS. In: Grumberg, O. (ed.) CAV 1997, vol. 1254, pp. 72–83. Springer, Heidelberg (1997)
10. Gulavani, B.S., Chakraborty, S., Nori, A.V., Rajamani, S.K.: Automatically refining abstract interpretations. In: Ramakrishnan, C.R., Rehof, J. (eds.) TACAS 2008. LNCS, vol. 4963, pp. 443–458. Springer, Heidelberg (2008)
11. Kirchner, F., Kosmatov, N., Prevosto, V., Signoles, J., Yakobowski, B.: Frama-C: a software analysis perspective. Formal Aspects Comput. **27**(3), 1–37 (2015)
12. Krishna, S., Puhrsch, C., Wies, T.: Learning invariants using decision trees. CoRR (2015)
13. Kroening, D., Tautschnig, M.: CBMC – C bounded model checker. In: Ábrahám, E., Havelund, K. (eds.) TACAS 2014 (ETAPS). LNCS, vol. 8413, pp. 389–391. Springer, Heidelberg (2014)
14. Logas, H., Whitehead, J., Mateas, M., Vallejos, R., Scott, L., Shapiro, D., Murray, J., Compton, K., Osborn, J., Salvatore, O., et al.: Software verification games: Designing xylem, the code of plants (2014)
15. Sharma, R., Aiken, A.: From invariant checking to invariant inference using randomized search. In: Biere, A., Bloem, R. (eds.) CAV 2014. LNCS, vol. 8559, pp. 88–105. Springer, Heidelberg (2014)
16. Sharma, R., Gupta, S., Hariharan, B., Aiken, A., Nori, A.V.: Verification as learning geometric concepts. In: Logozzo, F., Fähndrich, M. (eds.) Static Analysis. LNCS, vol. 7935, pp. 388–411. Springer, Heidelberg (2013)
17. Sharma, R., Nori, A.V., Aiken, A.: Interpolants as classifiers. In: Madhusudan, P., Seshia, S.A. (eds.) CAV 2012. LNCS, vol. 7358, pp. 71–87. Springer, Heidelberg (2012)
18. Zhang, L., Yang, G., Rungta, N., Person, S., Khurshid, S.: Feedback-driven dynamic invariant discovery. In: ISSTA (2014)

Automated Discovery of Simulation Between Programs

Grigory Fedyukovich[1]([✉]), Arie Gurfinkel[2], and Natasha Sharygina[1]

[1] USI, Lugano, Switzerland
{grigory.fedyukovich,natasha.sharygina}@usi.ch
[2] SEI, CMU, Pittsburgh, USA
arie@cmu.com

Abstract. The paper presents SimAbs, the first fully automated SMT-based approach to synthesize an abstraction of one program (called target) that simulates another program (called source). SimAbs iteratively traverses the search space of existential abstractions of the target and choses the strongest abstraction among them that simulates the source. Deciding whether a given relation is a simulation relation is reduced to solving validity of $\forall\exists$-formulas iteratively. We present a novel algorithm for dealing with such formulas using an incremental SMT solver. In addition to deciding validity, our algorithm extracts witnessing Skolem relations which further drive simulation synthesis in SimAbs. Our evaluation confirms that SimAbs is able to efficiently discover both, simulations and abstractions, for C programs from the Software Verification Competition.

1 Introduction

Simulation is one of the oldest logical concepts behind program analysis. Introduced by Milner in his seminal paper [15], a simulation relation is used to represent a condition under which the complete set of behaviors of one program (called *source* and denoted by S) is included into the set of behaviors of another program (called *target* and denoted by T). The programs can, however, be substantially different, thus making the task of finding an appropriate simulation relation difficult.

A lesson learnt from Milner suggests to abstract some irrelevant details from the target program and thus to improve the chances of the simulation relation to be found. In this paper, we propose a solution to the problem known for the past half century, and in particular: (1) the challenge of constructing automatically a total simulation relation between two programs, and (2) whenever the target

This material is based upon work funded and supported by the Department of Defense under Contract No. FA8721-05-C-0003 with Carnegie Mellon University for the operation of the Software Engineering Institute, a federally funded research and development center. Any opinions, findings and conclusions or recommendations expressed in this material are those of the author(s) and do not necessarily reflect the views of the United States Department of Defense. This material has been approved for public release and unlimited distribution. DM-0001771.

M. Davis et al. (Eds.): LPAR-20 2015, LNCS 9450, pp. 606–621, 2015.
DOI: 10.1007/978-3-662-48899-7_42

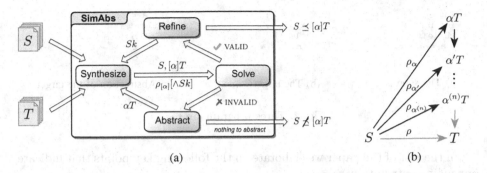

Fig. 1. (a) SIMABS and (b) its search space.

T does not simulate the source S, the challenge of finding an abstraction of the target T that simulates the source S.

We present SIMABS, a novel iterative abstraction-refinement algorithm to find an abstraction of the target T that simulates the source S. The flow of the algorithm is illustrated in Fig. 1(a). Initially, in the ⟨Synthesize⟩ step, SIMABS guesses a relation ρ between S and T. Then, in the ⟨Solve⟩ step, SIMABS checks whether T simulates S via ρ. If the check fails, SIMABS iteratively performs the ⟨Abstract⟩ step to find an abstraction αT of T and a simulation relation ρ_α between S and αT. Finally, in the ⟨Refine⟩ step, SIMABS refines both αT and ρ_α. The algorithm terminates when either no refinement or no abstraction is possible. The search space of the algorithm is shown in Fig. 1(b): SIMABS explores the space of abstractions of T, starting with the most general abstraction αT that simulates S via ρ_α, and iteratively refines it to $\alpha^{(n)}T$ that simulates S via $\rho_{\alpha^{(n)}}$.

In contrast to existing algorithms for checking whether T simulates S via a relation ρ (e.g., [11,15,18]), we reduce the problem to deciding validity of $\forall\exists$-formulas. Intuitively, the formulas say "for each behavior of S there exists a corresponding behavior of T". We present a novel decision procedure, AE-VAL, for deciding validity of $\forall\exists$-formulas over Linear Real Arithmetic. Our procedure is similar to [16,19]. However, in addition to deciding validity, it extracts a Skolem relation to witness the existentially-quantified variables of the formula. This Skolem relation (represented by Sk in Fig. 1) is the key to the ⟨Refine⟩ and the ⟨Synthesize⟩ steps of SIMABS.

We implemented SIMABS and AE-VAL on the top of the UFO framework [1,12] and the SMT solver Z3 [4], respectively. We evaluated SIMABS by discovering total simulation relations between programs and their LLVM optimizations. Our results show that SIMABS is able to efficiently synthesize abstractions and simulations between original and optimal programs in both directions. The application of SIMABS, however, is not limited to optimizations. It is able to deal with any program transformations preserving the program loop structures. In addition to checking optimizations, we also applied it to mutation testing.

```
int a = *;              int a = *;              int a = *;
int b = *;              int b = *;              while(*){
while(*){               while(*){                  int b = *;
   a = a + b;              int c = a - b;           int c = a - b;
}                          a = c;                   a = c;
                        }                        }

(a) The source          (b) The target          (c) Abstraction of the target
```

Fig. 2. Three programs in C.

In the rest of the paper we elaborate on the following key points that indicate our main contributions:

- A formulation of the simulation-relation-discovery problem as deciding validity of ∀∃-formulas and extracting Skolem relations (presented in Sect. 3).
- The first, to the best of our knowledge, SMT-based decision procedure AE-VAL for ∀∃-formulas that extracts Skolem relations (presented in Sect. 4).
- The algorithm SimAbs, driven by AE-VAL, to automatically synthesize abstractions and simulations between S and T (presented in Sect. 5)
- A prototype implementation of SimAbs which deals with LLVM-preprocessed programs and several LLVM optimizations (presented in Sect. 6).

2 Background and Notation

Our approach inductively iterates over individual loop-free program fragments. Without loss of generality, in Sects. 2 and 3, we describe simulation relations for loop-free programs, but in Sect. 5, we extend this to the case of programs sharing the same loop structure. Throughout the paper (but except Sect. 4), we use the same three example programs shown in Fig. 2. For demonstration purposes, we focus on their loop bodies in an arbitrary iteration.

We use vector notation to denote sets of *real and boolean* variables (and set-theoretic operations of *subset* $\vec{u} \subseteq \vec{x}$, *complement* $\vec{x}_{\vec{u}} = \vec{x} \setminus \vec{u}$, *union* $\vec{x} = \vec{u} \cup \vec{x}_{\vec{u}}$). For the first-order formulas $\varphi(\vec{x}) \in Expr$ in the paper, we assume that all free variables $\vec{x}$ are implicitly universally quantified. For simplicity, we omit the arguments and simply write φ when the arguments are clear from the context. Furthermore, for a model m of $\varphi \in Expr$ we write $m \models \varphi$, and for an implication between $\varphi, \psi \in Expr$ we write $\varphi \implies \psi$.

Definition 1. A *program* P is a tuple $\langle Var, Init, Tr \rangle$, where $Var \equiv V \cup L \cup V'$ is a set of *input, local* and *output variables*; $Init \in Expr$ encodes the *initial states* over V; and $Tr \in Expr$ encodes the *transition relation* over Var.

A state $\vec{s} \in S$ is a valuation to all variables in V. While Tr encodes an entire computation between initial and final states, the values of variables in L explicitly capture all intermediate states along the computation. If for states $\vec{s}, \vec{s'}$ there exists a valuation $\vec{l}$ to the local variables in L, such that $(\vec{s} \cup \vec{l} \cup \vec{s'}) \models Tr$, we call the pair $(\vec{s}, \vec{s'})$ *computable*. V' is used to denote the values of variables in V at the end of the computation. We write $\vec{s'}$ for $\vec{s}(x')$ and S' for $\{\vec{s'} \mid \vec{s} \in S\}$.

Definition 2. Given a program $P = \langle Var, Init, Tr \rangle$, a *transition system* $T(P) = \langle \mathcal{S}, \mathcal{I}, \mathcal{R} \rangle$, where $\mathcal{I} = \{\vec{s} \in \mathcal{S} \mid \vec{s} \models Init\}$ is the set of *initial states*, $\mathcal{R} = \{(\vec{s}, \vec{s'}) \mid \vec{s} \in \mathcal{S}, \vec{s'} \in \mathcal{S'} . (\vec{s}, \vec{s'})$ is computable$\}$ is a *transition relation*.

Throughout, we use programs and their transition systems interchangeably.

Definition 3. Program $P_1 = \langle V_1 \cup L_1 \cup V', Init_1, Tr_1 \rangle$ is an *abstraction* of program $P_2 = \langle V_2 \cup L_2 \cup V_2', Init_2, Tr_2 \rangle$ iff *(1)* $V_1 \subseteq V_2$, *(2)* $Init_2 \implies Init_1$, *(3)* each $(\vec{s}, \vec{s'})$ that is computable in Tr_2, is also computable in Tr_1.

Consider an example in Fig. 2(b)–(c). The loop bodies of the concrete and abstract programs differ in the sets of input variables: for the abstract one $V_1 = \{a, b\}$, for the concrete one: $V_2 = \{a\}$; and the sets of local variables: $L_1 = \{c\}$, $L_2 = \{b, c\}$, respectively. The difference in the initial states and the transition relations of both programs can be seen in Examples 1, 2.

Definition 4. Given transition systems S and T, a *left-total* relation $\rho \subseteq \mathcal{S}_S \times \mathcal{S}_T$ is a *simulation relation* if *(1)* every state in $\mathcal{I}_S$ is related by ρ to some state in $\mathcal{I}_T$, and *(2)* for all states $\vec{s}$, $\vec{s'}$ and $\vec{t}$, such that $(\vec{s}, \vec{t}) \in \rho$ and $(\vec{s}, \vec{s'}) \in \mathcal{R}_S$ there is some state $\vec{t'}$, such that $(\vec{t}, \vec{t'}) \in \mathcal{R}_T$ and $(\vec{s'}, \vec{t'}) \in \rho$.

We write $S \preceq_\rho T$ to denote that the source S is simulated by the target T via a simulation relation ρ. We write $S \preceq T$ to indicate existence of a simulation between S and T. The identity relation id, i.e., pairwise-equivalence of values of common variables, is an example of ρ. Each program S is simulated by a *universal abstraction* $\mathbb{U}$ of any other program T (which is in fact the only common abstraction to all possible programs). Since such cases do not provide any practical significance, in our approach they are algorithmically disqualified. Note that the programs in scope of the paper are not required to have an *error* location. Thus, the approach proposed in the following sections is not limited to dealing only with safe programs.

3   From Simulation to Validity

In this section we show that deciding whether a given relation ρ is a simulation relation is reducible to deciding validity of $\forall\exists$-formulas. We then show how Skolem functions witnessing the existential quantifiers are used to refine ρ.

3.1   Deciding Simulation Symbolically

Let $S(\vec{s}, \vec{x}, \vec{s'})$, $T(\vec{t}, \vec{y}, \vec{t'}) \in Expr$ encode transition relations of programs, where $\vec{s}$ and $\vec{t}$, $\vec{s'}$ and $\vec{t'}$, $\vec{x}$ and $\vec{y}$ are input, output, and local variables, respectively. Let $Init_S(\vec{s})$, $Init_T(\vec{t}) \in Expr$ encode the initial states in S and T, respectively. Let $\rho(\vec{s}, \vec{t}) \in Expr$ encode a left-total relation between variables in S and T.

Lemma 1. *T simulates S via relation ρ iff*

$$Init_S(\vec{s}) \implies \exists \vec{t}.\, \rho(\vec{s}, \vec{t}) \wedge Init_T(\vec{t}) \tag{1}$$

$$\rho(\vec{s}, \vec{t}) \wedge \exists \vec{x}.\, S(\vec{s}, \vec{x}, \vec{s'}) \implies \exists \vec{t'}, \vec{y}.\, T(\vec{t}, \vec{y}, \vec{t'}) \wedge \rho(\vec{s'}, \vec{t'}) \tag{2}$$

Implication (1) reflects the matching of initial states in S and T via ρ. The left-hand-side of implication (2) reflects the set of all behaviors in S and the set of all input conditions matched via ρ. The right-hand-side of (2) reflects the existence of a behavior in T and an output condition matched via ρ.

Example 1. Consider two programs in Fig. 2(a) and (b). Assume that constants X, Y are assigned to the input variables as in (3), so the computation starts at the identical states. The fragments of the transition relation corresponding to the single loop body are encoded into (4):

$$Init_S \equiv (a_S = X) \wedge (b_S = Y) \qquad Init_T \equiv (a_T = X) \wedge (b_T = Y) \tag{3}$$

$$S \equiv (a'_S = a_S + b_S) \qquad T \equiv (c_T = a_T - b_T) \wedge (a'_T = c_T) \tag{4}$$

where the subscript indicates in which program the variables are defined.

Let ρ be a relation between variables in S and T:

$$\rho \equiv (a_S = a_T) \wedge (b_S = b_T) \qquad \rho' \equiv (a'_S = a'_T) \wedge (b_S = b_T) \tag{5}$$

ρ is a simulation relation iff the two formulas are valid:

$$Init_S \implies \exists a_T, b_T.\, Init_T \wedge \rho \qquad \rho \wedge S \implies \exists c_T, a'_T.\, T \wedge \rho' \tag{6}$$

Note that since T is deterministic, the existential quantifiers in (6) are eliminated trivially by substitution. In our example, the left implication of (6) is valid, but the second implication of (6) simplifies to $0 = 1$. Hence, $S \not\preceq_\rho T$.   □

3.2   Abstract Simulation

If the complete simulation relation between S and T is not found, we can proceed with checking whether S is simulated by an abstraction αT of T via relation ρ_α. As a key result, we show that such abstract-simulation checking can be done without constructing an abstraction explicitly. We focus on an existential abstraction $\alpha_{\vec{u}}^{\exists} T$ of T that abstracts away a subset of variables $\vec{u} \subseteq \vec{t}$ of T [2].

Definition 5. $Init_{\alpha_{\vec{u}}^{\exists}T} \equiv \exists \vec{u}.\, Init_T(\vec{t})$, and $\alpha_{\vec{u}}^{\exists}T \equiv \exists \vec{u}, \vec{u}'.\, T(\vec{t}, \vec{y}, \vec{t'})$.

Deciding whether $\alpha_{\vec{u}}^{\exists}T$ simulates S via $\rho_\alpha(\vec{s}, \vec{t}_{\vec{u}})$ (where $\vec{t}_{\vec{u}}$ is the complement of $\vec{u}$ in $\vec{t}$) can be done if the variables $\vec{u}$ are treated as locals in T.

Lemma 2. $\alpha_{\vec{u}}^{\exists}T$ *simulates S via relation ρ_α iff*

$$Init_S(\vec{s}) \implies \exists \vec{t}_{\vec{u}}, \vec{u}.\, \rho_\alpha(\vec{s}, \vec{t}_{\vec{u}}) \wedge Init_T(\vec{t}) \tag{7}$$

$$\rho_\alpha(\vec{s}, \vec{t}_{\vec{u}}) \wedge \exists \vec{x}.\, S(\vec{s}, \vec{x}, \vec{s'}) \implies \exists \vec{u}, \vec{y}, \vec{t'}_{\vec{u}'}, \vec{u}'.\, T(\vec{t}, \vec{y}, \vec{t'}) \wedge \rho_\alpha(\vec{s'}, \vec{t'}_{\vec{u}'}) \tag{8}$$

Recall that in Example 1, the loop body T was shown to not simulate the loop body S via identity relation. Interestingly, this result is still useful to obtain a simulation relation between S and T by creating an implicit abstraction of T and further refining it. We demonstrate this 2-steps procedure in Example 2.

Example 2. As the first (*abstraction*) step, we create an abstraction of T by choosing a variable (say b) to be existentially quantified. Note that the produced abstraction is equivalent to the program in Fig. 2(c). Instead of encoding initial states $Init_{\alpha T}$ and a transition relation of αT from scratch (similarly to (3) and (4)), we let $Init_{\alpha T} \equiv \exists b_T . Init_T$ and $\alpha T \equiv \exists b_T . T$. Relation (5) (disproven to be a simulation between S and T) is weakened in correspondence with αT:

$$\rho_\alpha \equiv (a_S = a_T) \qquad\qquad \rho'_\alpha \equiv (a'_S = a'_T) \qquad\qquad (9)$$

ρ_α is a simulation relation between S and αT iff the following formulas are valid:

$$Init_S \implies \exists a_T, b_T . Init_T \wedge \rho_\alpha \qquad \rho_\alpha \wedge S \implies \exists c_T, a'_T, b_T . T \wedge \rho'_\alpha \qquad (10)$$

Clearly, (10) are valid iff there is a Skolem function for the existentially quantified variable b_T. Note that $sk_{b_T}(b_S) = -b_S$ is such function, and (11) are valid.

$$Init_S \implies (b_T = -b_S) \implies \exists a_T . Init_T \wedge \rho_\alpha$$
$$\rho_\alpha \wedge S \implies (b_T = -b_S) \implies \exists c_T, a'_T . T \wedge \rho'_\alpha \qquad (11)$$

As the second (*refinement*) step, sk_{b_T} is used to strengthen the simulation relation (9) between S and αT to become (12).

$$\rho_\alpha^{ext} \equiv (a_S = a_T) \wedge (b_S = -b_T) \qquad \rho_\alpha'^{ext} \equiv (a'_S = a'_T) \wedge (b_S = -b_T) \qquad (12)$$

Note that ρ_α^{ext} is a simulation relation between S and T. □

3.3   Refining Simulation by Skolem Relations

Definition 6. Given a formula $\exists y . f(x, y)$, a relation $Sk_y(x, y)$ is a *Skolem relation* for y iff (1) $Sk_y(x, y) \implies f(x, y)$, (2) $\exists y . Sk_y(x, y) \iff \exists y . f(x, y)$.

In Definition 6, we allow Sk_y to be a relation between x and y such that (1) Sk_y maps each x to a value of y that makes f true, (2.1) if for a given x, Sk_y maps x to some value of y then there is a value of y that makes f valid for this value of x, (2.2) if for a given x, there is a value of y such that f holds, then Sk_y is not empty. A Skolem relation Sk_y is *functional* iff it is of the form $Sk_y(x, y) \equiv y = f_y(x)$ (also known as *Skolem function*, as in [20]). $Sk_{\vec{y}}$ is *Cartesian* iff it is a Cartesian product of Skolem relations of individual variables from $\vec{y}$. $Sk_{\vec{y}}$ is *guarded* iff it is a guarded disjunction of Cartesian Skolem relations.

In other words, validity of a $\forall\exists$-formula is equivalent to existence of an appropriate total Skolem relation. As sketched in Example 2, our use of a Skolem relation Sk witnessing the validity of the formulas (7, 8) is to refine an abstract

Algorithm 1:
AE-VAL $\left(S(\vec{x}), \exists \vec{y}. T(\vec{x}, \vec{y}) \right)$

Input: $S(\vec{x}), \exists \vec{y}. T(\vec{x}, \vec{y})$
Output: return value $\in \{\text{VALID, INVALID}\}$ of
   $S(\vec{x}) \implies \exists \vec{y}. T(\vec{x}, \vec{y})$
Data: SMTSOLVER, counter i, models $\{m_i\}$,
   MBPs $\{T_i(\vec{x})\}$, conditions $\{\phi_i(\vec{x}, \vec{y})\}$

1 SMTADD($S(\vec{x})$);
2 $i \leftarrow 0$;
3 **forever do**
4 | $i{+}{+}$;
5 | **if** (ISUNSAT(SMTSOLVE())) **then**
6 | | **return** VALID;
7 | SMTPUSH();
8 | SMTADD($T(\vec{x}, \vec{y})$);
9 | **if** (ISUNSAT(SMTSOLVE())) **then**
10 | | **return** INVALID;
11 | $m_i \leftarrow$ SMTGETMODEL();
12 | $(T_i, \phi_i(\vec{x}, \vec{y})) \leftarrow$ GETMBP($\vec{y}, m_i, T(\vec{x}, \vec{y})$);
13 | SMTPOP();
14 | SMTADD($\neg T_i$);

$S \equiv (a = b + 2)$
$T \equiv (a' > a) \wedge (b = 1 \implies b' = b) \wedge$
$\qquad (b = 2 \implies b' > b) \wedge$
$\qquad (b = 3 \implies b' < b)$
$m_1 \equiv \{a = 0, b = -2, a' = {}^1/_2, b' = -{}^5/_2\}$
$m_2 \equiv \{a = 4, b = 2, a' = {}^9/_2, b' = {}^5/_2\}$
$m_3 \equiv \{a = 3, b = 1, a' = {}^7/_2, b' = 1\}$

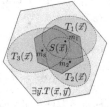

Fig. 3. (a) S and T for $\vec{x} \equiv \{a, b\}$, $\vec{y} \equiv \{a', b'\}$, models of $S \wedge T$ and (b) the correspondent Venn diagram.

simulation relation ρ_α to $\rho_\alpha^{ext} = \rho_\alpha \wedge Sk$. However, ρ_α^{ext} is guaranteed to be a simulation relation only in case if the corresponding formulas (7, 8) are valid, thus requiring an extra simulation-check.

In Sect. 5, we continue building the iterative algorithm for discovering simulation relations based on the abstraction-refinement reasoning, described here. However, in the next section, we restrict our attention on the main solving routine that makes the simulation discovery possible.

4   Validity and Skolem Extraction

We present AE-VAL, a novel algorithm for deciding validity of $\forall\exists$-formulas and constructing witnessing Skolem relations. Without loss of generality, we restrict the input formula to have the form $S(\vec{x}) \implies \exists \vec{y}. T(\vec{x}, \vec{y})$, where S has no universal quantifiers, and T is quantifier-free.

4.1   Deciding Validity of $\forall\exists$-formulas

Our algorithm is based on a notion of Model-Based Projection (MBP), introduced in [12], that under-approximates existential quantification. An $MBP_{\vec{y}}$ is a function from models of $T(\vec{x}, \vec{y})$ to $\vec{y}$-free formulas iff:

$$\text{if } m \models T(\vec{x}, \vec{y}) \text{ then } m \models MBP_{\vec{y}}(m, T) \tag{13}$$

$$MBP_{\vec{y}}(m, T) \implies \exists \vec{y}. T(\vec{x}, \vec{y}) \tag{14}$$

There are finitely many MBPs for fixed $\vec{y}$ and T and different models $m_1, \ldots, m_n$ (for some n): $T_1(\vec{x}), \ldots, T_n(\vec{x})$, such that $\exists \vec{y} . T(\vec{x}, \vec{y}) = \bigvee_{i=1}^{n} T_i(\vec{x})$. In our implementation, we are using an MBP-algorithm from [12] for Linear Rational Arithmetic (LRA) based on Loos-Weispfenning [14] quantifier elimination.

Additionally, we assume that for each projection T_i, the MBP-algorithm gives a condition ϕ_i under which T is equisatisfiable with T_i:

$$\phi_i(\vec{x}, \vec{y}) \implies (T_i(\vec{x}) \iff T(\vec{x}, \vec{y})) \tag{15}$$

Such a relation ϕ_i is a natural by-product of the MBP-algorithm in [12]. Intuitively, each ϕ_i captures the substitutions made in T to produce T_i. We assume that each ϕ_i is in the Cartesian form, i.e., a conjunction of terms, in which each $y \in \vec{y}$ appears at most once. That is, for $y \in \vec{y}$ and $\sim \in \{<, \leq, =, \geq, >\}$,

$$\phi_i(\vec{x}, \vec{y}) = \bigwedge_{y \in \vec{y}} (y \sim f_y(\vec{x})) \tag{16}$$

We write $(T_i, \phi_i) \leftarrow \text{GETMBP}(\vec{y}, m_i, T(\vec{x}, \vec{y}))$ for the invocation of the MBP-algorithm that takes a formula T, a model m_i of T and a vector of variables $\vec{y}$, and returns a projection T_i of T based on m_i and the corresponding relation ϕ_i.

AE-VAL is shown in Algorithm 1. Given formulas $S(\vec{x})$ and $\exists \vec{y} . T(\vec{x}, \vec{y})$, it decides validity of $S(\vec{x}) \implies \exists \vec{y} . T(\vec{x}, \vec{y})$. AE-VAL enumerates the models of $S \wedge T$ and blocks them from S. In each iteration i, it first checks whether S is non-empty (line 3) and then looks for a model m_i of $S \wedge T$ (line 11). If m_i is found, AE-VAL gets a projection T_i of T based on m_i (line 12) and blocks all models contained in T_i from S (line 14). The algorithm iterates until either it finds a model of S that can not be extended to a model of T (line 9), or all models of S are blocked (line 5). In the first case, the input formula is invalid. In the second case, every model of S has been extended to some model of T, and the formula is valid.

Three possible iterations of AE-VAL are depicted graphically in Fig. 3. In the first iteration, AE-VAL selects a model m_1 and generalizes it to a projection $MBP_{\vec{y}}(m_1, T) = T_1$. Then, it picks a model m_2 that is not contained in T_1 and generalizes it to $MBP_{\vec{y}}(m_2, T) = T_2$. Finally, it picks a model m_3 that is contained neither in T_1 nor in T_2, and generalizes it to $MBP_{\vec{y}}(m_3, T) = T_3$. At this point, all models of S are covered by $\vec{y}$-free implicants of $\exists \vec{y} . T(\vec{x}, \vec{y})$, and the algorithm terminates. We demonstrate this further in the following example.

Example 3. Let S and T be as defined in Fig. 3. We use Φ_i to denote the formula in the SMT context at the beginning of iteration i of AE-VAL. Initially, $\Phi_1 = S$. The first model is m_1, and $\text{GETMBP}(\vec{y}, m_1, T)$ returns:

$$T_1 \equiv (b \neq 1) \wedge (b \neq 2) \qquad \phi_1 \equiv (a' > a) \wedge (b' < b)$$

In the iteration 2, $\Phi_2 = \Phi_1 \wedge \neg T_1$, $\text{GETMBP}(\vec{y}, m_2, T)$ returns:

$$T_2 \equiv (b \neq 1) \wedge (b \neq 3) \qquad \phi_2 \equiv (a' > a) \wedge (b' > b)$$

In the iteration 3, $\Phi_3 = \Phi_2 \wedge \neg T_2$, GETMBP$(\vec{y}, m_3, T)$ returns:

$$T_3 \equiv (b \neq 2) \wedge (b \neq 3) \qquad\qquad \phi_3 \equiv (a' > a) \wedge (b' = b)$$

In the iteration 4, $\Phi_4 = \Phi_3 \wedge \neg T_3$ is unsatisfiable, and consequently AE-VAL returns VALID and terminates. □

4.2   Extracting Skolem Relation

AE-VAL is designed to construct a Skolem relation $Sk_{\vec{y}}(\vec{x}, \vec{y})$, that maps each model of $S(\vec{x})$ to a corresponding model of $T(\vec{x}, \vec{y})$. We use a set of projections $\{T_i(\vec{x})\}$ for $T(\vec{x}, \vec{y})$ and a set of conditions $\{\phi_i(\vec{x}, \vec{y})\}$ that make the corresponding projections equisatisfiable with $T(\vec{x}, \vec{y})$.

Lemma 3. *For each i, the relation $\phi_i(\vec{x}, \vec{y})$ is a Skolem relation for $\vec{y}$ in formula $S(\vec{x}) \wedge T_i(\vec{x}) \implies \exists \vec{y}. T(\vec{x}, \vec{y})$.*

Intuitively, ϕ_i maps each model of $S \wedge T_i$ to a model of T. However, $\{T_i\}$ are not disjoint (e.g., see Fig. 3), and each conjunction $S \wedge T_i$ could be simplified and minimized. Thus, to define the Skolem relation Sk, we need to find a partitioning $\{I_i\}_{i=1}^n$ of S, such that each partition I_i must be associated with an appropriate ϕ_i. The constraints on the partitions I_i are as follows. First, a partition I_i must cover all models of T_i that are not already covered by $I_1 \ldots I_{i-1}$. Second, it should not include any models that are not contained in T_i. Writing these requirements formally, we get the system of constraints (17).

$$\begin{cases} S(\vec{x}) \wedge T_1(\vec{x}) \implies I_1(\vec{x}) \\ S(\vec{x}) \wedge T_2(\vec{x}) \wedge \neg T_1(\vec{x}) \implies I_2(\vec{x}) \\ \cdots \\ S(\vec{x}) \wedge T_n(\vec{x}) \wedge \neg T_1(\vec{x}) \wedge \ldots \\ \qquad \ldots \wedge \neg T_{n-1}(\vec{x}) \implies I_n(\vec{x}) \\ S(\vec{x}) \wedge I_1(\vec{x}) \wedge \neg T_1(\vec{x}) \implies \bot \\ \cdots \\ S(\vec{x}) \wedge I_n(\vec{x}) \wedge \neg T_n(\vec{x}) \implies \bot \end{cases} \qquad Sk_{\vec{y}}(\vec{x}, \vec{y}) \equiv \begin{cases} \phi_1(\vec{x}, \vec{y}) & \text{if } I_1(\vec{x}) \\ \phi_2(\vec{x}, \vec{y}) & \text{else if } I_2(\vec{x}) \\ \cdots & \text{else } \cdots \\ \phi_n(\vec{x}, \vec{y}) & \text{else } I_n(\vec{x}) \end{cases}$$

$$(17) \qquad\qquad\qquad\qquad (18)$$

Note that in (17), S and $\{T_i\}$ are the first-order formulas, and $\{I_i\}$ are the uninterpreted predicates. The set of constrains corresponds to a system of second-order recursion-free Horn clauses. Thus, we can find an interpretation of the predicates $\{I_i\}$ using a Horn-clause solver. In our implementation, we use the solver of Z3, but other solutions, for example, based on interpolation, are also possible. The guarded Skolem relation $Sk_{\vec{y}}(\vec{x}, \vec{y})$ is defined in (18).

Algorithm 2: SimAbs(S, T)

Input: programs S and T, abstraction quality
     metric $Q : \alpha \rightarrow \{\top, \bot\}$
Output: abstraction $\alpha^{ext}T$, simulation relation ρ_α^{ext},
     such that $S \preceq_{\rho_\alpha^{ext}} \alpha^{ext}T$

1 $\alpha^{ext}T \leftarrow T$;
2 **forever do**
3     $\alpha_{pre}T \leftarrow \alpha^{ext}T$;
4     $\alpha T, \rho_\alpha \leftarrow$ Abstract(S, T);
5   **if** $(\alpha T \neq U)$ **then return** $U, \varnothing$;
6     $\alpha^{ext}T, \rho_\alpha^{ext} \leftarrow$ Refine$(S, \alpha T, \rho_\alpha)$;
7   **if** $(Q(\alpha^{ext}T) \vee (\alpha_{pre}T = \alpha^{ext}T))$ **then**
8   **return** $\alpha^{ext}T, \rho_\alpha^{ext}$;

Algorithm 3: Abstract(S, T)

Input: programs S and T
Output: abstraction αT, simulation relation ρ_α,
     such that $S \preceq_{\rho_\alpha} \alpha T$

1 **for each** $(u, v) \in E$ **do**
2     $\rho(v) \leftarrow$ Synthesize$(\tau_S(u, v), \tau_T(u, v))$;
3   **if** $(\tau_S(u, v) \npreceq_\rho \tau_T(u, v))$ **then**
4       $\alpha T \leftarrow$ Weaken$(T, Var(u) \cup Var(v))$;
5   **if** $(\alpha T \neq U)$ **then**
6   **return** Abstract$(S, \alpha T)$;
7   **else**
8   **return** $U, \varnothing$;
9 **return** T, ρ;

Algorithm 4: Refine$(S, \alpha T, \rho_\alpha)$

Input: program S, abstraction αT, simulation relation ρ_α
Output: abstraction $\alpha^{ext}T$, simulation relation ρ_α^{ext}

1 $\rho_\alpha^{ext} \leftarrow \rho_\alpha$; $\alpha^{ext}T \leftarrow \alpha T$; $WL \leftarrow E$;
2 **while** $(WL \neq \varnothing)$ **do**
3     $(u, v) \leftarrow$ GetEdge (WL);
4     $WL \leftarrow WL \setminus \{(u, v)\}$;
5   **if** $(\tau_S(u, v) \preceq_{\rho_\alpha^{ext}} \tau_{\alpha^{ext}(T)}(u, v))$ **then**
6       $\rho_\alpha^{ext}(u) \leftarrow \rho_\alpha^{ext}(u) \wedge$ Skolem$(u, v, \rho_\alpha^{ext})$;
7       $\alpha^{ext}T \leftarrow$ Strengthen$(\alpha T, Sk)$;
8       $WL \leftarrow WL \cup \{(u, x) \in E \mid x \in CP\}$
                 $\cup \{(y, u) \in E \mid y \in CP\}$;
9   **else return** $\alpha T, \rho_\alpha$;
10 **return** $\alpha^{ext}T, \rho_\alpha^{ext}$;

Algorithm 5: Synthesize(S, T)

Input: loop-free programs S, T
Output: candidate relation ρ

1 **return** $\bigwedge_{a'_S \in V'_S, a'_T \in V'_T} (a'_S = a'_T)$;

Algorithm 6: Weaken(T, U)

Input: program T, $U \subseteq Var_T$
Output: abstraction αT

1 **guess** $U' \subseteq U$; **return** $\alpha_{U'}^{\exists}(T)$;

Algorithm 7: Strengthen$(\alpha T, Sk)$

Input: abstraction αT, relation Sk
Output: abstraction $\alpha^{ext}T$

1 $U^{ext} \leftarrow Var(Sk)$; **return** $\alpha_{U^{ext}}^{\exists}(T)$;

The following theorem states that $Sk_{\vec{y}}(\vec{x}, \vec{y})$ satisfies Definition 6 for the chosen model of $\vec{x}$, and $Sk_{\vec{y}}(\vec{x}, \vec{y})$ is defined for all models of $\vec{x}$. It follows immediately from the constraints of (17) and Lemma 3 that in turn follows from (14, 15, 16).

Theorem 1. (Soundness and Completeness). *If the set $\{I_i(\vec{x})\}$ is a solution to (17), and $Sk_{\vec{y}}(\vec{x}, \vec{y})$ is as in (18) then:* (1) $Sk_{\vec{y}}(\vec{x}, \vec{y})$ *is a Skolem relation for* $\vec{y}$ *in formula* $S(\vec{x}) \implies \exists \vec{y} . T(\vec{x}, \vec{y})$, (2) $S(\vec{x}) \implies \bigvee_i^n I_i(\vec{x})$.

Example 4. A partitioning I_1, I_2, I_3 that determines a Skolem relation for Example 3 is: $I_1 \equiv (b \neq 1) \wedge (b \neq 2)$, $I_2 \equiv b \geq 2$, and $I_3 \equiv b = 1$.   □

Any solution to (17) creates a Skolem relation. But not all Skolem relations are equal. In practice, we often like a Skolem relation that minimizes the number of variables on which each partition depends. For example, in Example 4, we have chosen a partition that only depends on the variable b alone. A simple way to find a minimal solution is to iteratively restrict the number of variables in each partition in (17) until no smaller solution can be found. We leave the problem of finding the minimum partitioning for future work.

5 Simulation-Abstraction-Refinement Loop

This section generalizes the approach of the symbolic simulation discovery to programs with non-trivial Control Flow Graphs. Assuming that programs S and

T are loop-free, αT is an abstraction of T and ρ_α encodes a relation between S and αT (as in Sect. 3), the check $S \preceq_{\rho_\alpha} \alpha T$ is done by constructing two $\forall\exists$-formulas of the form (7) and (8), and by applying the AE-VAL algorithm to decide validity (as in Sect. 4.1). Furthermore, ρ_α and αT might be refined by means of a Skolem relation (whose extraction is shown in Sect. 4.2).

In contrast to the programs with simplified structure considered in Sect. 3, realistic programs involve communication of two or more components with independent transition relations. Simulation relations should be discovered independently for each pair of the matched components and then inductively checked for the compatibility with the pairs of the remaining components. We propose an algorithm SIMABS that implements a complete *Simulation-Abstraction-Refinement Loop* and enables such inductive reasoning.

We use the Cut Point Graph (CPG) representation of a program and treat each program as a graph $\langle CP, E \rangle$. Here CP is the set of locations which represent heads of the loops (called cutpoints), and $E \subseteq CP \times CP$ is the set of longest loop-free program fragments. For example, CPGs of programs in Fig. 2(a)–(b) are shown in Fig. 4(a)–(b) respectively. We assume that the considered programs S and T share the graph $\langle CP, E \rangle$, but might have different labeling of the edges by first-order formulas $\tau_S, \tau_T : E \to Expr$ encoding the transition relations of S and T respectively: $\tau_S \neq \tau_T$.

SIMABS (outlined in Algorithm 2) gets as input programs S and T, and delivers an abstraction αT. If $\alpha T \neq \mathbb{U}$ and αT satisfies some quality metric $\mathcal{Q}$ (e.g., if it preserves some safety property of T), SIMABS also returns a simulation relation ρ_α^{ext}, such that $S \preceq_{\rho_\alpha^{ext}} \alpha T$. SIMABS uses ABSTRACT (which in turn uses SYNTHESIZE) to guess an initial relation ρ. The initial guess can be an arbitrary total relation between the CPGs of S and T. In our implementation (line 2 of ABSTRACT), for every cutpoint v, we take $\rho(v)$ to be a conjunction of equalities between the *live* variables of S and T at v that have identical names.

ABSTRACT (outlined in Algorithm 3) iteratively checks for each edge $(u, v) \in E$ (line 3), whether the labeling of (u, v) in T, $\tau_T(u, v)$, simulates the labeling of (u, v) in S, $\tau_S(u, v)$, via the guessed relation ρ. If the check succeeds for all edges, ρ is returned to the main loop of SIMABS to be further refined. Otherwise, ABSTRACT chooses an abstraction αT of T using the method WEAKEN (line 4), and repeats the check for S and αT (line 6). WEAKEN introduces nondeterminism to τ_T, and in our implementation (shown in Algorithm 6), it existentially abstracts away a subset of input variables of the edge (u, v) for which the simulation check has failed. Note that in the next iteration of ABSTRACT, ρ will be weakened correspondingly, since SYNTHESIZE in that iteration is given S and αT.

REFINE (outlined in Algorithm 4) constructs a refinement ρ_α^{ext} of simulation relation ρ_α, and the corresponding strengthening $\alpha^{ext} T$ of abstraction αT. REFINE maintains a work-list WL of the CPG-edges to be processed. Initially, WL is populated with E (line 1). In each iteration, while processing the edge (u, v), REFINE adds a Skolem relation Sk to $\rho_\alpha(u)$ (line 6). Sk is produced for the existentially abstracted input variables in (u, v) and furthermore is used to

(a)   (b)

Fig. 4. CPGs of programs in Fig. 2(a)–(b).

strengthen $\alpha^{ext}T$ (line 7). Finally, REFINE updates WL with the outgoing edges from u and other incoming edges to u (line 8) and iterates until WL is empty (line 10). If in some iteration a strengthening is impossible, REFINE returns the last successful values for ρ_α^{ext} and $\alpha^{ext}T$ (line 9).

It is worth reminding that for every iteration of ABSTRACT, as well as for every iteration of REFINE, there is a need to decide validity of simulation-abstraction-checking formulas (7) and (8). For this goal, SIMABS invokes AE-VAL (Algorithm 1). Algorithm SKOLEM, used as a subroutine of REFINE, is an essential extension of AE-VAL that produces a Skolem relation as in (18). Notably, it does not extract a Skolem relation for local variables, but does it only for existentially abstracted input variables in the current CPG-edge (in particular, it constrains the sets of variables over which the partitions $\{I_i\}$ are expressed).

For the progress of the algorithm, it is enough to note that in each iteration of SIMABS, ABSTRACT is given a concrete program T, and always constructs a new abstraction from scratch. Thus, if the space of possible abstractions is finite (which is the case for existential abstraction) the algorithm always terminates.

Theorem 2. *Given the implementation of* WEAKEN *(Algorithm 6),* SIMABS *always terminates.*

Recall the source and the target programs from Fig. 2(a)–(b). In Example 2, we found simulation relation between their loop bodies. In the following, we show how SIMABS is used to discover a simulation relation between whole programs.

Example 5. The programs share the set of cutpoints $CP = \{en, CP_0\}$, and the set of CPG-edges $E = \{(en, CP_0), (CP_0, CP_0)\}$. First, ABSTRACT considers the CPG-edge (en, CP_0), and synthesizes an identity relation $\rho \equiv (a_S = a_T) \wedge (b_S = b_T)$ which is then proven to be a simulation relation for the current edge. Then ABSTRACT considers the CPG-edge (CP_0, CP_0) and checks whether ρ (and its variant ρ') is an inductive simulation relation for the current edge. Since this check does not succeed (recall Example 1), WEAKEN produces an implicit abstraction of the target, by eliminating a subset of variables (e.g., $\{b\} \subset \{a,b\}$), and ABSTRACT recursively calls itself.

In the second iteration of ABSTRACT, E is traversed again, and relation $\rho_\alpha \equiv (a_S = a_T)$ is checked w.r.t. the source and the abstraction of the target. Since the check succeeds for all edges, REFINE extracts a Skolem relation and creates $\rho_\alpha^{ext} \equiv (a_S = a_T) \wedge (b_S = -b_T)$. Finally, the abstraction of the target is strengthened and becomes the target itself. SIMABS successfully terminates. $\square$

6 Evaluating SimAbs and AE-VAL

We implemented SimAbs and AE-VAL in the UFO framework. As an SMT and Horn solver AE-VAL uses Z3. We evaluated them on the Software Verification Competition (SVCOMP) benchmarks and constprop, globalopt, instcombine, simplifycfg, adce, and mem2reg optimizations of LLVM. The constprop performs constant propagation, the globalopt transforms global variables, the instcombine simplifies local arithmetic operations, the simplifycfg performs dead code elimination and basic block merging, the adce performs aggressive dead code elimination, and mem2reg promotes memory references to be register references. Notably, combinations of the optimizations provide more aggressive optimizations than each individual optimization, thus increasing a *semantic gap* between the original and the optimized programs. In our evaluation, we aim at synthesizing concrete or abstract simulation relations for programs with a bigger semantic gap and empirically demonstrate the power of AE-VAL (that is expected to have a higher number of AE-VAL iterations in such cases).

For each of the 228 considered source programs S (300 - 5000 lines of source code), we created an optimized program[1] T, and applied SimAbs to discover abstractions and simulations in two directions: $S \preceq [\alpha]T$ and $T \preceq [\alpha]S$. We present the results[2] in two diagrams in Fig. 5. Each diagram is a pie chart and a collection of SimAbs execution times for each benchmark in the spherical coordinate system. The pie chart in Fig. 5(a) represents a *proportion* of four main classes of SimAbs results:

◐ : T simulates S via identity relation;
◑ : T simulates S via some Skolem-relation-based ρ;
◒ : some abstraction αT simulates S;
◓ : we did not find an abstraction αT that simulates S.

Each dot represents a runtime of SimAbs on a single benchmark. It is placed in one of the circular sectors, ◐, ◑, ◒ or ◓, with respect to the outcome, and is assigned the radial distance to represent time in seconds. For example, a benchmark on which $S \preceq_{id} T$ solved in 20 s is placed in the sector ◐ in a distance 20 from the center. Being closer to the center means being faster. Runs that took longer than 60 s are placed on the boundary. Figure 5(b) is structured similarly, but with inverse order of S and T.

The experiment shows that SimAbs is able to effectively discover abstractions and simulations between S and T in both directions. While in many cases (101 in Fig. 5(a), and 65 in Fig. 5(b)) it proved simulation by identity, in the remaining cases SimAbs goes deeper into the abstraction-refinement loop and delivers either a concrete or abstract simulation in 124 and 160 cases respectively. SimAbs terminates with a positive result in all, but 3 pairs of programs. The 3 negative cases can be exaplained by the fact that T happened to have some CPG-edge (u, v) with the inconsistent labeling $\tau_T(u, v)$.

---

[1] We combined the optimizations in the following order to create each T: -constprop -globalopt -instcombine -simplifycfg -mem2reg -adce -instcombine -simplifycfg.

[2] Full results are available at http://www.inf.usi.ch/phd/fedyukovich/niagara.

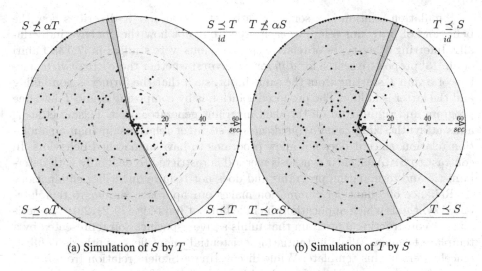

(a) Simulation of S by T (b) Simulation of T by S

Fig. 5. Pie chart and running times in the spherical coordinate system.

The core solving engine, AE-VAL, invoked on the low level of SIMABS was shown to be effective while eliminating quantifiers. Overall, it solved 84587 formulas (each formula contains up to 1055 existentially quantified variables, and requires up to 617 iterations to terminate), and extracted 3503 Skolem relations.

7 Related Work

The first symbolic automatic construction of simulation relations was proposed by Dill et al. in [5]. However, that work was based on BDDs, so quantifiers are eliminated directly. We target to solve this problem by exploiting recent advancements in SMT and thus allowing synthesis of non-trivial simulation relations.

The classical approach to check simulation relations is *game-theoretic*: the state space of the source and the target programs is traversed by the evader and the pursuer players. For instance, Henzinger et al. [11] apply it to prove validity of a simulation relation between infinite graphs. In our setting, this result can be used to extend SIMABS to deal with programs with different CPGs.

The problem of constructing and checking simulation relations arises when there is a need to prove equivalence between two programs. Necula [18] proposes to check correctness of compiler optimizations by constructing simulation relations heuristically. Namjoshi et al. in [10,17] propose a more precise way to construct simulation relations, which requires augmenting a particular optimizer. Ciobâcă et al. [3] develop a parametric proof system for proving mutual simulation between programs written in different programming languages. These approaches do not deal with cases when programs are not equivalent (i.e., there exists only an abstract simulation or when there is some other form of simulation relation rather than identity). SIMABS goes beyond these limitations.

Simulation relation is a sort of relative specifications: it describes how the behaviors of programs relate to each other, but not how they behave individually. Inferring other types of relative specifications were studied in [7,13]. Lahiri et al. [13] propose to search for *differential errors*: whether there exist two behaviors of S and T starting from the same input, such that the former is non-failing and the latter is failing. The proposed solution is by composing S and T into one program and running an off-the-shelf invariant generator on it. Felsing et.al [7] aims at synthesizing *coupling predicates*, a stronger relationship than a simulation relation, since it does not allow programs to have unmatched behaviors. In contrast to SIMABS, their synthesis method is restricted to deal only with deterministic and terminating programs and does not require quantifier elimination.

Reliance on quantifier elimination makes our approach similar to template-based synthesis which applications include but not limited to [9,21,22]. Synthesis aims at constructing a program that fulfils a given specification represented by a template formula. While instantiating existential quantifiers, synthesis is filling placeholders in this template. While discovering a Skolem relation from a valid simulation-relation-checking formula, AE-VAL also performs synthesis, but does not require any template for it.

8   Conclusion and Future Work

We proposed a solution to the problem of automated discovery of simulations between programs. Our main contribution is SIMABS, a novel algorithm to automatically synthesize both, abstractions and simulations, between the source and the target programs. If the target does not simulate the source, SIMABS iteratively performs abstraction-refinement reasoning to detect an abstraction of the target that simulates the source. In contrast to existing techniques, SIMABS operates by deciding validity of $\forall\exists$-formulas iteratively. The second contribution of the paper is AE-VAL, a novel decision procedure that extracts Skolem relations from valid $\forall\exists$-formulas in Linear Rational Arithmetic. The third contribution is our implementation of SIMABS and AE-VAL that supports (and not limited by) different LLVM optimizer and mutator passes.

In future, we plan to use simulation relations produced by SIMABS to migrate the safe inductive invariants across program transformations, thus achieving a *property-directed equivalence* between programs [6]. AE-VAL can be used as a stand-alone solver. We believe, it has a great potential, and in future we plan to apply it for other tasks (e.g., [8]) of realizability and synthesis.

References

1. Albarghouthi, A., Li, Y., Gurfinkel, A., Chechik, M.: UFO: a framework for abstraction- and interpolation-based software verification. In: Madhusudan, P., Seshia, S.A. (eds.) CAV 2012. LNCS, vol. 7358, pp. 672–678. Springer, Heidelberg (2012)
2. Clarke, E.M., Grumberg, O., Long, D.E.: Model checking and abstraction. ACM Trans. Program. Lang. Syst. **16**(5), 1512–1542 (1994)

3. Ciobâcă, Ş., Lucanu, D., Rusu, V., Roşu, G.: A language-independent proof system for mutual program equivalence. In: Merz, S., Pang, J. (eds.) ICFEM 2014. LNCS, vol. 8829, pp. 75–90. Springer, Heidelberg (2014)

4. de Moura, L., Bjørner, N.S.: Z3: an efficient SMT solver. In: Ramakrishnan, C.R., Rehof, J. (eds.) TACAS 2008. LNCS, vol. 4963, pp. 337–340. Springer, Heidelberg (2008)

5. Dill, D.L., Hu, A.J., Wong-Toi, H.: Checking for language inclusion using simulation preorders. In: Larsen, K.G., Skou, A. (eds.) CAV 1991. LNCS, vol. 575. Springer, Heidelberg (1992)

6. Fedyukovich, G., Gurfinkel, A., Sharygina, N.: Incremental verification of compiler optimizations. In: Badger, J.M., Rozier, K.Y. (eds.) NFM 2014. LNCS, vol. 8430, pp. 300–306. Springer, Heidelberg (2014)

7. Felsing, D., Grebing, S., Klebanov, V., Rümmer, P., Ulbrich, M.: Automating regression verification. In: ASE, pp. 349–360. ACM (2014)

8. Gacek, A., Katis, A., Whalen, M.W., Backes, J., Cofer, D.: Towards realizability checking of contracts using theories. In: Havelund, K., Holzmann, G., Joshi, R. (eds.) NFM 2015. LNCS, vol. 9058, pp. 173–187. Springer, Heidelberg (2015)

9. Gascón, A., Subramanyan, P., Dutertre, B., Tiwari, A., Jovanovic, D., Malik, S.: Template-based circuit understanding. In: FMCAD, pp. 83–90. IEEE (2014)

10. Gjomemo, R., Namjoshi, K.S., Phung, P.H., Venkatakrishnan, V.N., Zuck, L.D.: From verification to optimizations. In: D'Souza, D., Lal, A., Larsen, K.G. (eds.) VMCAI 2015. LNCS, vol. 8931, pp. 300–317. Springer, Heidelberg (2015)

11. Henzinger, M.R., Henzinger, T.A., Kopke, P.: Computing simulations on finite and infinite graphs. In: FOCS, pp. 453–462 (1995)

12. Komuravelli, A., Gurfinkel, A., Chaki, S.: SMT-based model checking for recursive programs. In: Biere, A., Bloem, R. (eds.) CAV 2014. LNCS, vol. 8559, pp. 17–34. Springer, Heidelberg (2014)

13. Lahiri, S.K., McMillan, K.L., Sharma, R., Hawblitzel, C.: Differential assertion checking. In: FSE, pp. 345–355. ACM (2013)

14. Loos, R., Weispfenning, V.: Applying linear quantifier elimination. Comput. J. **36**(5), 450–462 (1993)

15. Milner, R.: An algebraic definition of simulation between programs. In: IJCAI, pp. 481–489 (1971)

16. Monniaux, D.: A quantifier elimination algorithm for linear real arithmetic. In: Cervesato, I., Veith, H., Voronkov, A. (eds.) LPAR 2008. LNCS (LNAI), vol. 5330, pp. 243–257. Springer, Heidelberg (2008)

17. Namjoshi, K.S., Zuck, L.D.: Witnessing program transformations. In: Logozzo, F., Fähndrich, M. (eds.) Static Analysis. LNCS, vol. 7935, pp. 304–323. Springer, Heidelberg (2013)

18. Necula, G.C.: Translation validation for an optimizing compiler. In: PLDI, pp. 83–94. ACM (2000)

19. Phan, A.-D., Bjørner, N., Monniaux, D.: Anatomy of alternating quantifier satisfiability (work in progress). In: SMT, EPiC Series, vol. 20, pp. 120–130. EasyChair (2012)

20. Skolem, T.: Über die mathematische logik. Norsk Matematisk Tidsskrift **10**, 125–142 (1928)

21. Solar-Lezama, A., Tancau, L., Bodík, R., Seshia, S.A., Saraswat, V.A.: Combinatorial sketching for finite programs. In: ASPLOS, pp. 404–415. ACM (2006)

22. Srivastava, S., Gulwani, S., Foster, J.S.: From program verification to program synthesis. In: POPL, pp. 313–326. ACM (2010)

SAT Modulo Intuitionistic Implications

Koen Claessen$^{(\boxtimes)}$ and Dan Rosén$^{(\boxtimes)}$

Chalmers University of Technology, Gothenburg, Sweden
{koen,danr}@chalmers.se

Abstract. We present a new method for solving problems in intuitionistic propositional logic, which involves the use of an incremental SAT-solver. The method scales to very large problems, and fits well into an SMT-based framework for interaction with other theories.

1 Introduction

Let us take a look at *intuitionistic propositional logic*. Its syntax looks just like classical propositional logic:

$$
\begin{aligned}
A ::= &\; a \mid b \mid c \mid .. \mid q & &\text{-- atoms} \\
      &\mid A_1 \wedge A_2 & &\text{-- conjunction} \\
      &\mid A_1 \vee A_2 & &\text{-- disjunction} \\
      &\mid A_1 \to A_2 & &\text{-- implication} \\
      &\mid \bot \mid \top & &\text{-- false/true}
\end{aligned}
$$

However, its definition of truth is considerably weaker than for classical logic. In Fig. 1, we show a Hilbert-style proof system for intuitionistic propositional logic. In the figure, we use $A_1, .., A_n \vdash B$ as a short-hand for $A_1 \to ..(A_n \to B)$. Only "computationally valid" derivations can be made in intuitionistic logic. For example, the classical law of the excluded middle $a \vee \neg\, a$ does not hold. Here, we use $\neg\, a$ as a short-hand for $a \to \bot$.

In this paper, we are interested in building a modern, scalable, automated method for proving formulas in intuitionistic propositional logic. By modern, we mean that we would like to make use of the enormous recent advances in automated theorem proving in the form of SAT and SMT techniques. We do not want to reinvent the wheel, rather we would like to investigate if there exists an SMT-like way of building an intuitionistic theorem prover *on top of* an existing SAT-solver. The hope is that this also results in a scalable method.

It is perhaps surprising that we ask this question, because at first sight it does not seem natural to embed intuitionistic logic into classical logic; after all, we can derive much more in classical logic than intuitionistic logic.

The key insight we make use of comes from Barr [1]. Given a set S of propositional clauses of the shape:

$$
(a_1 \wedge .. \wedge a_n) \to (b_1 \vee .. \vee b_m)
$$

© Springer-Verlag Berlin Heidelberg 2015
M. Davis et al. (Eds.): LPAR-20 2015, LNCS 9450, pp. 622–637, 2015.
DOI: 10.1007/978-3-662-48899-7_43

$$\frac{A \quad A \to B}{B} \ (MP)$$

$$
\begin{array}{rl}
A, B \ \vdash A & (K) \\
A \to B \to C, A \to B \vdash A \to C & (S) \\
A \land B \ \vdash A & (FST) \\
A \land B \ \vdash B & (SND) \\
A, B \ \vdash A \land B & (PAIR) \\
A \quad \vdash A \lor B & (INL) \\
B \quad \vdash A \lor B & (INR) \\
A \to C, B \to C \vdash (A \lor B) \to C & (CASE) \\
\bot \quad \vdash A & (BOT) \\
A \quad \vdash \top & (TOP)
\end{array}
$$

Fig. 1. A Hilbert-style proof system for intuitionistic propositional logic

Here, a_i and b_j are propositional atoms. Now, the remarkable insight is this: The question of whether or not a given other clause of that same shape is derivable from the set S is oblivious to which logic we are in: classical or intuitionistic. The derivation power of these two logics on this subset is *equivalent*!

In other words, if we have an intuitionistic logic problem that we are interested in solving, we would like to "distill" this problem into two parts: The first, and hopefully largest, part would be expressible using clauses of the above shape, and the second, hopefully tiny, part would consist of the part of the problem not expressible using clauses of the above shape. We can then use a standard SAT-solver to solve the first part, and an extra theory on the side to deal with the second part.

Indeed, it turns out that clauses of the above shape are not quite enough to represent all intuitionistic formulas. We also need clauses of the following shape:

$$(a \to b) \to c$$

Here, a, b, c are propositional atoms. We call these clauses *implication clauses*, and clauses of the first kind are called *flat clauses*.

Finally, we need one more rule that tells us how flat clauses interact with implication clauses:

$$\frac{(p_1 \land .. \land p_n \land a) \to b \qquad (a \to b) \to c}{(p_1 \land .. \land p_n) \to c} \ (IMPL)$$

From one implication clause and one flat clause, we can generate a new flat clause. This rule, together with any complete proof system for classical logic applied to flat clauses, turns out to be a complete proof system for intuitionistic logic. The fact that no new implication clauses are generated during a proof is an extra bonus that alleviates automated proof search even more: Rule ($IMPL$) can be implemented as an SMT-style theory on top of a SAT-solver.

Thus, we ended up constructing a simple, scalable, automated theorem prover for intuitionistic propositional logic based on a SAT-solver.

To our knowledge, this is the first paper to take an SMT-based approach on top of a SAT-solver to intuitionistic logic. As we shall see, the implementation of the theory of intuitionistic implications turns out to be rather unconventional, because it has a recursive structure (calling the theorem prover itself!). But the overall design of the prover is quite simple; only one SAT-solver is needed to do all the reasoning, and no extra quantification is necessary. The result is a robust prover that performs very well on existing as well as new benchmarks.

2   The Procedure

In this section, we describe our procedure for proving (and disproving) formulas in intuitionistic propositional logic.

2.1   Canonical Form

The first thing we do when trying to prove a formula A, is to transform it into canonical form, by a process called *clausification*. A problem in canonical form is characterized by two sets of different kinds of clauses R and X, plus an atom q:

$$(\bigwedge R \wedge \bigwedge X) \to q$$

Here, the set R only contains so-called *flat clauses* r, which are of the following shape:

$$r ::= (a_1 \wedge .. \wedge a_n) \to (b_1 \vee .. \vee b_m)$$

In the above, a_i and b_j denote atoms. When $n = 0$, the left-hand side is $\top$; when $m=0$, the right-hand side is $\bot$. The set X only contains *implication clauses* i, which have the following shape:

$$i ::= (a \to b) \to c$$

Here, a, b, c are atoms or the constants $\bot$ or $\top$.

Any formula A can be rewritten into a provability-equivalent formula in canonical form. As an example, consider the formula $a \vee\neg a$. Its canonical form is:

$$((a \rightarrow q) \wedge ((a \rightarrow \bot) \rightarrow q)) \rightarrow q$$

We can see that the canonical form consists of one flat clause $a \rightarrow q$ and one implication clause $(a \rightarrow \bot) \rightarrow q$, and a final goal q.

The procedure we use to rewrite any formula into canonical form is very similar to the Tseitin method for clausification of formulas in classical propositional logic [6], but adapted to be sound for intuitionistic logic.

We start by assuming that A is of the shape $B \rightarrow q$, for some atom q. If it is not, we can make it so by introducing a new atom q and using $(A \rightarrow q) \rightarrow q$ (where B would thus be $A \rightarrow q$) instead[1].

Next, we transform B into the two sets of clauses R and X. We can do this using a number of transformation steps of the shape $A \twoheadrightarrow B_1, .., B_n$, which transform an assumption A into an equivalent set of assumptions B_i. Most of these transformations assume that the formulas they work on are implications. However, the first transformation step can be used when a formula is not already an implication:

$$A \quad \twoheadrightarrow \quad \top \rightarrow A$$

The next 3 transformations can be used when the left-hand or right-hand side of an implication does not have the right shape, as dictated by the clause being a flat clause or an implication clause:

$$(A \vee B) \rightarrow a \quad \twoheadrightarrow \quad A \rightarrow a, \quad B \rightarrow a$$
$$a \rightarrow (A \wedge B) \quad \twoheadrightarrow \quad a \rightarrow A, \quad a \rightarrow B$$
$$A \rightarrow (B \rightarrow C) \quad \twoheadrightarrow \quad (A \wedge B) \rightarrow C$$

In the above, a stands for either a regular atom, or one of the constants $\bot$ or $\top$. In order to have atoms appear at the right places, we can use the following 5 transformation steps:

$$A \rightarrow (.. \vee B \vee ..) \quad \twoheadrightarrow \quad A \rightarrow (.. \vee b \vee ..), b \rightarrow B$$
$$(.. \wedge A \wedge ..) \rightarrow B \quad \twoheadrightarrow \quad (.. \wedge a \wedge ..) \rightarrow B, A \rightarrow a$$
$$(A \rightarrow B) \rightarrow C \quad \twoheadrightarrow \quad (a \rightarrow B) \rightarrow C, \quad a \rightarrow A$$
$$(A \rightarrow B) \rightarrow C \quad \twoheadrightarrow \quad (A \rightarrow b) \rightarrow C, \quad B \rightarrow b$$
$$(A \rightarrow B) \rightarrow C \quad \twoheadrightarrow \quad (A \rightarrow B) \rightarrow c, \quad c \rightarrow C$$

In the above rules, a, b and c appearing on the right-hand side of a rule denotes a fresh atom not appearing anywhere else.

The above rules are a complete set of rules to turn any formula B into a set of flat clauses R and implication clauses X. The combined size of the clauses in R and X can be kept to at most twice the size of the size of the original formula B, because we never copy whole formulas, and we only need to introduce a fresh atom b for any subformula at most once.

---

[1] provability-equivalent to A because (1) A implies the formula, and (2) if we take $q:=A$, the formula implies A.

```
                 -- flat clauses R
                 -- implication clauses X
                 -- proof goal q
              procedure prove (R, X, q)
                 s = newSolver ();
                 for r ∈ R :
                    addClause (s, r);
                 for i ∈ X :
                    let (a → b) → c = i
                    addClause (s, b → c);
                 return intuitProve (s, X, ∅, q);
```

Fig. 2. Top-level procedure for intuitionistic proving

2.2 The SAT-Solver

The proving procedure makes use of a standard off-the-shelf (classical) SAT-solver s, that supports the following operations:

$$\textbf{procedure } newSolver\ ();$$
$$\textbf{procedure } addClause\ (s, r);$$
$$\textbf{procedure } satProve\ (s, A, q);$$

The procedure *newSolver* creates a new, unconstrained SAT-solver. The procedure *addClause* takes a SAT-solver s and a flat clause r, and adds the clause r as a constraint to s.

The procedure *satProve* takes a SAT-solver s, a set of assumptions A, and a goal q. The assumptions A as well as the goal q are atoms. The procedure *satProve* tries to prove the goal q, from the assumptions A and all flat clauses that have been added so far. It produces one of two results:

- *No (M)*, if no proof could be found. Here, M is a model that is found by the SAT-solver represented as a set of true atoms. The model M is guaranteed to satisfy all added clauses, all assumptions, but it makes the goal q false. So, we know $A \subset M$ and $q \notin M$.
- *Yes (A′)*, if a proof could be found. Here, A' is the subset of the assumptions that were actually used in the proof of q from the clauses. So, we know that $A' \subset A$.

The set A' in the *Yes* answer can be produced by most modern SAT-solvers. Some solvers (such as MiniSAT [2] which we use in our implementation) support this operation directly in their API. Other solvers support the construction of an unsatisfiable core, which can be used to get the same information.

```
-- SAT-solver s
-- implication clauses X
-- assumptions A
-- proof goal q
procedure intuitProve (s, X, A, q)
    loop
        switch satProve (s, A, q)
            case Yes (A') :
                return Yes (A');
            case No (M) :
                if intuitCheck (s, X, M) then
                    return No (M);
```

Fig. 3. Standard CEGAR-loop for intuitionistic proving

2.3 Proving Procedure

The complete proving procedure (after transformation to canonical form) is pictured in ≈ 25 lines of code in Figs. 2–4.

The top-level procedure *prove* is shown in Fig. 2. Its arguments are a set of flat clauses R, a set of implication clauses X, and a goal q. It first creates a SAT-solver s, and adds all flat clauses r to it. Furthermore, for each implication clause $(a \to b) \to c$ from X, it adds the flat clause $b \to c$ (which is implied by the implication clause). Finally, it calls the main proving procedure *intuitProve*.

The main proving procedure *intuitProve* is shown in Fig. 3. Its arguments are a SAT-solver, a set of implication clauses X, a set of assumptions A, and a goal q. The procedure has the standard shape of a CEGAR-loop. First, it tries to find a classical proof, using the SAT-solver only on the flat clauses. If this succeeds, we are done. If not, there is a classical model M which is going to be checked by the procedure *intuitCheck*, explained in the next subsection.

If *intuitCheck* determines that the found model indeed corresponds to an intuitionistic model, it returns *True*, and we return the model as the answer. If *intuit Check* finds the model inadequate, it will have generated an *extra* flat clause in the SAT-solver, and it returns *False*. In this case, we simply loop and try again.

2.4 Checking Procedure

When we find a classical model M, which is guaranteed to satisfy all flat clauses, we have to check whether or not it corresponds to an intuitionistic model. This means that, for each implication clause $(a \to b) \to c$ in X, we have to check that if $a \to b$ is true under M, then c should also be true under M.

In order to help us decide which implication clauses should be investigated, let us take a look at the following table, where we consider an implication clause

	a	b	c	$(a \rightarrow b) \rightarrow c$
(1)	-	-	1	Yes
(2)	-	1	0	No
(3)	1	0	0	Yes
(4)	0	0	0	?

$(a \rightarrow b) \rightarrow c$, and we have partitioned the 2^3 possibilities for valuations of a, b, c into 4 separate cases.

In case (1), the implication clause is fulfilled, since c is true, and so the whole implication is also true. Case (2) is definitely something that contradicts the implication clause; b is true and therefore also $a \rightarrow b$, but c is not true. Fortunately, for each implication clause $(a \rightarrow b) \rightarrow c$, we have already added the flat clause $b \rightarrow c$ (see Fig. 2) which excludes this case. In case (3), $a \rightarrow b$ is definitely not true, and so c does not have to be true either.

The only case that is left that we have to check is case (4). Here, $a \rightarrow b$ is classically true, but intuitionistically, we do not know whether or not it is true, and therefore we do not know whether or not c should be true.

Thus, what we have to do is check whether or not we can prove $a \rightarrow b$ using the true atoms from the current model M. If we can, then surely the current model was wrong since c was not true. If we cannot not, the current model fulfills the implication clause also.

As we can see in Fig. 4, the way we check whether or not $a \rightarrow b$ is provable under the current model, is to call *intuitProve* recursively, using $M \cup \{a\}$ as assumptions, and b as the proof goal. If the answer is No $(-)$, everything is fine. If the answer is Yes (A'), we generate a new flat clause, using the following proof rule ($IMPL$):

```
            -- SAT-solver s
            -- implication clauses X
            -- model M
        procedure intuitCheck (s, X, M)
          for i ∈ X :
            let (a → b) → c = i
            if a, b, c ∉ M then
              switch intuitProve (s, X − {i}, M ∪ {a}, b)
              case Yes (A') :
                addClause (s, (⋀ A' − {a}) → c)
                return False;
          return True;
```

Fig. 4. Checking whether or not a SAT-model is also an intuitionistic model

$$\frac{(p_1 \wedge \ldots \wedge p_n \wedge a) \rightarrow b \qquad (a \rightarrow b) \rightarrow c}{(p_1 \wedge \ldots \wedge p_n) \rightarrow c} \quad (IMPL)$$

When the answer is $Yes\ (A')$, it means that we have proved that $\bigwedge A' \rightarrow b$ (left-hand premise) and using the implication clause (right-hand premise), we can conclude $\bigwedge A' - \{a\} \rightarrow c$ (conclusion), which is the flat clause we then add to the SAT-solver.

We would like to note here that the efficiency of our algorithm is mainly brought by reducing the assumptions $M \cup \{a\}$ from the question to the assumptions A' in the answer. It is the actually needed assumptions A' that are used when constructing the new flat clause, not the originally given assumptions $M \cup \{a\}$!

Rule $(IMPL)$ allows us to create a new flat clause from an existing flat clause and an implication clause. It is the only extra proof rule we use (apart from classical resolution on flat clauses), and thus the total number of implication clauses during proof search remains constant. It is easy to see that $(IMPL)$ is sound once one realizes that the left-hand side premise is equivalent to $(p_1 \wedge \ldots \wedge p_n) \rightarrow (a \rightarrow b)$; then $(IMPL)$ is simply an instance of the cut rule:

$$\frac{A \rightarrow B \qquad B \rightarrow C}{A \rightarrow C} \quad (CUT)$$

The three procedures $prove, intuitProve, intuitCheck$ together completely make up the proving algorithm.

2.5   Correctness

Correctness of the algorithm consists of three parts: Termination (the algorithm terminates on all inputs), soundness (when the algorithm claims to have proven a formula, there indeed is a proof), and completeness (when the algorithm claims the unprovability of a formula, it indeed is not provable).

Termination. There are two possible causes of non-termination: The loop in $intuitProve$, and the mutual recursion between $intuitProve$ and $intuitCheck$.

The loop in $intuitProve$ terminates, because in each loop iteration, a clause is added to the SAT-solver that is false in the model M that made all previously added clauses true. Thus, each loop iteration strictly reduces the number of models that satisfy all clauses in the SAT-solver. Eventually, the loop must terminate.

The mutual recursion between $intuitProve$ and $intuitCheck$ terminates because in each recursive call to $intuitProve$, the set X shrinks by one element i.

Soundness. If the algorithm terminates with a Yes (–) answer, the SAT-solver will have proved the goal from the flat clauses and the assumptions. Soundness is thus argued based on two arguments: (1) classical inference may be used to intuitionistically conclude flat clauses from sets of flat clauses, and (2) all flat clauses in the SAT-solver are implied by the original clauses R and X.

As to (1), this observation was already made by Barr [1], but we briefly restate the argument here. Any classical inference of a flat clause from a set of flat clauses can be simulated by the resolution rule:

$$\frac{A \to (C \vee a) \qquad (a \wedge B) \to D}{(A \wedge B) \to (C \vee D)} \quad (RES)$$

The resolution rule (RES) as stated above also holds intuitionistically. Thus, any classical proof deriving a flat clause from a set of flat clauses also admits an intuitionistic proof.

As to (2), all flat clauses in the SAT-solver either directly come from the set R, or they are derived using the rule $(IMPL)$, which we have already argued is sound.

Completeness. We show that when the algorithm terminates with a *No* (M) answer, there exists an intuitionistic Kripke model with a "starting world" w_0 that satisfies all flat clauses, all implication clauses, and in which the proof goal q is false. We construct this Kripke model below.

Consider the last top-level call to *intuitCheck*, the call that validated the last model that was found. It executed many (recursive) calls to *intuitCheck*, each of them returning *True*. Now, let each of these calls be a unique world w in the set of worlds W. The valuation $M(w)$ associated with each world w is the model M with which the corresponding call of *intuitCheck* was given. The world w_0 is associated with the top-level call to *intuitCheck*.

Define the call-relation C as follows: $w_1 \ C \ w_2$ if and only if the call w_1 made the call w_2. The accessibility relation $\leqslant$ on W is defined to be the *reflexive, transitive* closure of C. The relation $\leqslant$ satisfies the *persistency condition*: each call to *intuitCheck* makes the set of true atoms larger by adding the atom a to M in the calls to *intuitProve*.

All flat clauses in R are satisfied by the valuations of all w, because all of these are models of the SAT-solver s, which guarantees that all flat clauses are made true by all models. This also means that all flat clauses are true in all w.

The proof goal q is false in w_0, because the top-level call to *intuitProve* generated a counter-model to q.

All implication clauses in X are true in w_0. To see this, consider an implication clause $i = (a \to b) \to c$ from X and a world w in which $a \to b$ is true, but c is false. If c is false in w, then so is b, because we have the flat clause $b \to c$ that we added to s. If b is false in w, then so is a, because $a \to b$ is true in w by our assumption. Every world is reachable by C-steps from w_0, and thus so is w. By persistency, a, b, c must be false in *every* world on the C-path from w_0 to w. This means that the implication clause i is still part of the set of implication clauses that belonged to the *intuitCheck*-call represented by w. This means that a call to *intuitProve* will be made from w in which a will be added to the assumptions, and with b as the goal, and which furthermore returns with *No* $(-)$. This contradicts our assumption that $a \to b$ is true in w. So, all original implication clauses are true in w_0.

3 Optimizations

In this section, we discuss a number of possible optimizations that can be made to the basic algorithm, and their perceived effect on efficiency.

Keep Checking After Finding an Offending Implication Clause. The procedure *intuitCheck* only generates one new clause when something is wrong with a found model. Typically, a CEGAR-loop may benefit from generating multiple clauses that indicate what is wrong with a proposed model. The reason is that if we find k unrelated reasons for why a found model is wrong, we may save time by not having to find k different models, each triggering that reason.

```
                 -- SAT-solver s
                 -- implication clauses X
                 -- model M
             procedure intuitCheck2 (s, X, M)
                okay = True;
                for i ∈ X :
                   let (a → b) → c = i
                   if a, b, c ∉ M then
                      switch intuitProve (s, X − {i}, M ∪ {a}, b)
                      case Yes (A'):
                         satAddClause (s, (⋀ A' − {a}) → c)
                         okay = False;
                return okay;
```

Fig. 5. Checking whether or not a SAT-model is also an intuitionistic model

In Fig. 5, we present a slightly adapted version of *intuitCheck* that checks for all implication clauses whether or not they are content with the currently found model, instead of aborting after finding the first offending implication clause.

We implemented this adapted method, and compared it experimentally against the simple first version. The change made some running times of the benchmarks worse, others better. All running times remained in the same order of magnitude. There were slightly more cases in which the running time was improved, so we decided to keep this variant.

Conclusion: The balance in favor of this optimization was not completely convincing, and it may change with more different benchmarks.

Minimize the Number of Offending Implication Clauses. It is obvious that the running time of the algorithm is affected mostly by the number of implication clauses that need to be checked. So, instead of just finding any model M, we considered adding an optimization phase that tried to minimize the number of implication clauses that needed to be investigated (i.e. the number of implication clauses where $a = b = c = 0$).

The experimental results showed that this method was worse in every case where a difference could be observed. The reason was that the minimization methods we tried were slowing things down very much, and the final effect on the number of implications that had to be checked was not as great as we hoped for. We tried global minimization methods (minimizing the number of offending implication clauses) as well as local optimization methods (using subset-minimization).

Conclusion: We are still interested in minimization, but we need to (1) find better suited minimization methods, and (2) more suitable benchmarks where this would make an actual difference.

Reuse of Already Found Models. From the correctness proof, it becomes clear that a Kripke model can be constructed from a run of the algorithm that results in a *No* (−) answer. Currently, this Kripke model always has a tree-shape. Some trees can be compacted into directed acyclic graphs (DAGs), enabling a possible exponential speed-up.

The algorithm can be adapted to keep a table of already found and checked models, which grows during calls of *intuitCheck*. Whenever we call *intuitProve*, we can consult the table of models to see if we can immediately see that the answer is going to be *No* (−).

We have implemented this optimization, but have not thoroughly evaluated it. This remains future work.

4　Related Work and Experimental Results

In this section, we compare our method against other, existing methods for automated proving of intuitionistic propositional formulas.

Competing Tools. The main competitors for automated proof for intuitionistic propositional logic are IntHistGC [4] and fCube [3]. Both are provers that perform a backtracking search directly on a proof calculus, and are therefore rather different from the approach taken here. IntHistGC implements clever backtracking optimizations that avoid recomputations in many cases. fCube implements several pruning techniques on a tableau-based calculus.

Benchmarks. We have used three different benchmark suites to compare the provers experimentally.

– ILTP [5], these are 12 problems parametrized by a size. Being from 2006, this is a quite old set of benchmarks now. We used the extended version that was used in the evaluation of IntHistGC. In this version, two problems were generated up to size 38 and all other problems up to size 100, leading up to a total of 555 problem instances.

- IntHistGC benchmarks, these are 6 problems parametrized by a natural number. These benchmarks are newer. They are carefully constructed sequences of formulas that separate classical and intuitionistic logic. The total number of instances here is 610.
- API solving, these are 10 problems where a rather large API (set of functions with types) is given, and the problem is to construct a new function of a given type. Each problem has variants with API sizes that vary in size from a dozen to a few thousand functions. These problems were constructed by the authors in an attempt to create practically useful problems. The total number of instances here is 35.

The total number of benchmark problems we used is 1200. We did not have access to these benchmarks when we developed our tool.

Experimental Set-up. The experiments were run on a 2013 laptop computer with an Intel Xeon E3-1200 v2 processor and the processes were allowed 7 GB of RAM. IntHistGC was run with its best flags (-b -c -c3). We used the latest versions of the tools: fCube version 11.1 and IntHistGC 1.29. We used a 300 s timeout.

Results. All three tools eventually solve a good portion of the benchmarks: our tool intuit solved all but 37 benchmarks, fCube solved all but 38 benchmarks, and IntHistGC all but 39. More interesting is to compare the running times. We compare our tool intuit against IntHistGC and fCube for provable problems (Valid) and unprovable problems (CoSat) in Fig. 6. All time axes are logarithmic.

We can see that intuit outperforms both IntHistGC and fCube significantly on virtually all provable problems. The comparison for unprovable problems is in favor of intuit as well, although there are a few outliers demanding further scrutiny. We show a table of "interesting" problems (problems that were out of reach for at least one tool but not for all tools) in Fig. 7.

The problems cross2x – mapf3x are all instances of the API benchmark suite. They contain relatively large sets of axioms, of which typically only a few are needed for a proof, which is representative for automatically generated verification problems in general. Our tool intuit does well on these.

The problems SYJ202 are pigeon-hole problems. In fact, after generating clauses in the fashion described in this paper, there were no implication clauses generated, and thus the problems became purely classical! No surprise that intuit does well on these, given that it uses a state-of-the-art SAT-solver internally.

The problems that intuit struggled with (and which are the outliers in the scatterplots in Fig. 6) are all instances of SYJ212. These are problems that are all counter-satisfiable, and consist of long chains of nested equivalences. Interestingly, on these problems, the running time of intuit was not increasing as a function of the size of the problem. Hence there are some gaps in the figure: only the instances where intuit times out are shown. The reason for this is not

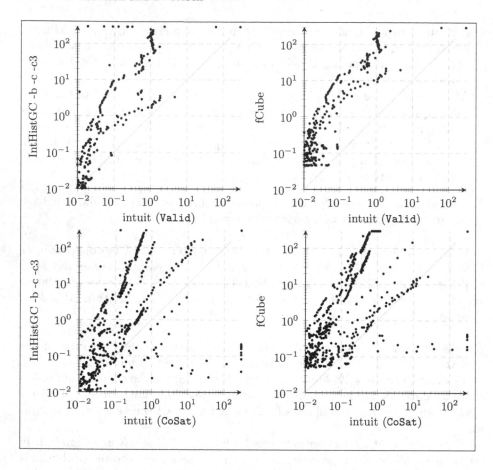

Fig. 6. Comparison. Runtimes in seconds, timeout was 300 s.

completely obvious to us; it seems that `intuit` seems particularly sensitive to exactly what models are found by the SAT-solver on these problems. Sometimes, the models indicate just the right implications to check, leading to intuitionistic models quickly, and other times, the models lead the prover astray, and it takes a long time.

5   Future Work

The main reason for initiating the work described in this paper was to understand how to build a scalable prover for a logic like intuitionistic propositional logic. However, the number of practical applications of intuitionistic propositional logic is limited. We believe that our insights can benefit two other kinds of logic that have more applications: classical modal logics and intuitionistic first-order logic.

Benchmark	Our Tool	IntHistGC	fCube	Status
cross2x	0.05	–	0.69	Valid
cross3x	0.13	–	4.39	Valid
jm_cross3x	0.13	–	6.84	CoSat
jm_lift2x	0.31	–	9.38	Valid
lift2x	0.23	–	9.50	Valid
mapf3x	0.69	–	–	CoSat
SYJ202+1.006	0.01	–	0.67	Valid
SYJ202+1.007	0.09	–	3.61	Valid
SYJ202+1.008	0.22	–	27.47	Valid
SYJ202+1.009	2.43	–	241.06	Valid
SYJ202+1.010	62.79	–	–	Valid
SYJ208+1.031	0.70	38.22	–	CoSat
SYJ208+1.032	0.75	47.12	–	CoSat
SYJ208+1.033	0.83	49.82	–	CoSat
SYJ208+1.034	0.88	69.35	–	CoSat
SYJ208+1.035	0.95	76.12	–	CoSat
SYJ208+1.036	1.02	96.03	–	CoSat
SYJ208+1.037	1.07	119.56	–	CoSat
SYJ208+1.038	1.17	140.49	–	CoSat
SYJ212+1.030	–	0.03	0.19	CoSat
SYJ212+1.038	–	0.08	0.15	CoSat
SYJ212+1.041	–	0.10	0.37	CoSat
SYJ212+1.043	–	0.12	0.30	CoSat
SYJ212+1.046	–	0.15	0.36	CoSat
SYJ212+1.047	–	0.17	0.41	CoSat
SYJ212+1.048	–	0.18	0.35	CoSat
SYJ212+1.049	–	0.19	0.41	CoSat
SYJ212+1.050	–	0.21	0.37	CoSat

Fig. 7. Interesting problems (where one tool failed but not all). Runtimes are in seconds. A hyphen indicates that the time limit of 300 s was exceeded.

Generalization to Modal Logic. We are currently building a theorem prover for classical modal logic based on the same ideas as presented in this paper. When we want to prove a formula A, we generate a fresh literal q, and generate constraints that represent the formula $\Box (A \to q)$. The insight is that, in order to do so, it is enough to consider constraints of one of the following three shapes:

1. $\Box p$, for a propositional logic formula p,
2. $\Box (a \to \Box b)$, for propositional logic literals a and b, and
3. $\Box (a \to \Diamond b)$, for propositional logic literals a and b.

Just like the prover we have described in this paper, the theorem prover for modal logic uses one SAT-solver that stores all constraints that hold in all worlds, which are the formulas p above. If q can be proven from these, the proof is done. Otherwise, we get a counter-model which satisfies all p but not q, and we have to investigate whether or not constraints of type 2. and 3. are fulfilled. If the answer is yes, we have found a counter model to A, otherwise, more constraints of type 1. will be generated and we start over.

Generalization to Intuitionistic First-Order Logic. We also have started to look at building an automated prover for intuitionistic first-order logic. There are two strands of work here. The first basically augments a standard SMT-solver with implication clauses. Most SMT-solvers have a heuristic for instantiating universal quantifiers. After that, the implication clauses are dealt with in the same way as in this paper.

However, this can only deal with a fragment of first-order logic. To cope with the full logic, we analyze intuitionistic first-order logic and come to the conclusion that we only have to support "clauses" of the following three shapes:

1. $\forall\, \boldsymbol{x}.(A_1 \wedge .. \wedge A_n) \to (B_1 \vee .. \vee B_m)$, also called flat clauses,
2. $\forall\, \boldsymbol{x}.(A \to B) \to C$, also called implication clauses, and
3. $\forall\, \boldsymbol{x}.(\forall\, \boldsymbol{y}.A) \to B$, called quantification clauses.

The idea is to let a model-generating first-order prover (SMT-solver) take care of the flat clauses. Every so often, we investigate the (partial) models that are generated, and use the implication clauses and the quantification clauses to generate more flat clauses, and we continue.

The main difficulties here are: (1) first-order logic is only semi-decidable, so we cannot expect to get either a model or a proof from the set of flat clauses, which means that we have to settle for a heuristic method based on partial models, and (2) most representations of partial models use some kind of ground model which makes it hard to deal with the universally quantified variables x in the implication clauses and quantification clauses.

6   Conclusions

We presented a new method for automated proving and disproving of formulas in intuitionistic propositional logic. The method makes use of a single instance of an incremental SAT-solver, and implements an SMT-style theory of intuitionistic implication clauses on top of it. The result is a robust theorem prover that can easily tackle most existing benchmarks.

Intuitionistic propositional logic seems to have limited practical applications, as indicated by the (un)availability of standard benchmark sets. Our hope is that the method described in this paper can give rise to scalable and robust methods for related logics with more clear practical applications, such as various modal logics and intuitionistic first-order logic.

Acknowledgments. We thank Thierry Coquand and Rajeev Gore for feedback on earlier versions of this work.

References

1. Barr, M.: Toposes without points. J. Pure Appl. Algebra **5**(3), 265–280 (1974)
2. Eén, N., Sörensson, N.: An extensible SAT-solver. In: Giunchiglia, E., Tacchella, A. (eds.) SAT 2003. LNCS, vol. 2919, pp. 502–518. Springer, Heidelberg (2004)

3. Ferrari, M., Fiorentini, C., Fiorino, G.: FCUBE: an efficient prover for intuitionistic propositional logic. In: Fermüller, C.G., Voronkov, A. (eds.) LPAR-17. LNCS, vol. 6397, pp. 294–301. Springer, Heidelberg (2010)
4. Goré, R., Thomson, J., Wu, J.: A history-based theorem prover for intuitionistic propositional logic using global caching: IntHistGC system description. In: Demri, S., Kapur, D., Weidenbach, C. (eds.) IJCAR 2014. LNCS, vol. 8562, pp. 262–268. Springer, Heidelberg (2014)
5. Raths, T., Otten, J., Kreitz, C.: The ILTP problem library for intuitionistic logic - release v1.1. J. Autom. Reasoning (2006)
6. Tseitin, G.S.: On the complexity of derivation in propositional calculus. In: Siekmann, J.H., Wrightson, G. (eds.) Automation of Reasoning. Symbolic Computation, pp. 466–483. Springer, Heidelberg (1983)

Author Index

Printed in the United States
By Bookmasters